A WORLD BIBLIOGRAPHY
OF BIBLIOGRAPHIES

A WORLD BIBLIOGRAPHY OF BIBLIOGRAPHIES

1964-1974

A LIST OF WORKS REPRESENTED BY
LIBRARY OF CONGRESS PRINTED CATALOG CARDS
A DECENNIAL SUPPLEMENT TO THEODORE BESTERMAN,
A WORLD BIBLIOGRAPHY OF BIBLIOGRAPHIES

VOLUME I
A–J

COMPILED BY
ALICE F. TOOMEY

WITH A FOREWORD BY
FRANCESCO CORDASCO

Rowman and Littlefield
Totowa, New Jersey

Published 1977 by
Rowman and Littlefield

Library of Congress Cataloging in Publication Data

Toomey, Alice F
   A world bibliography of bibliographies, 1964-1974.

   Includes bibliographical references.
   1. Bibliography--Bibliography. I. Besterman,
Theodore, 1904-1976. A world bibliography of
bibliographies. II. Title.
Z1002.T67   016.011   77-6719
ISBN 0-87471-999-2

Printed in the United States of America

In Memoriam
THEODORE BESTERMAN (1904-1976)

FOREWORD

It is generally acknowledged that Theodore Besterman (1904-1976) was one of the great bibliographers of modern times: in a strict sense, he was out of place in our century, and more correctly belonged to the great age of 19th century bibliography when giant works, largely planned and carried through by single individuals, established the bibliographical watershed from which our century has continuously drawn.

In the annals of English systematic bibliography (the enumeration and classification of books as distinguished from historical and comparative bibliography which is critical) there is an unbroken continuity extending from John Bale's *Illustrium Maioris Britanniae Scriptorum . . .* (1548-1549) to the prodigious labors of Theodore Besterman's *A World Bibliography of Bibliographies.*[1] That a single bibliographer could plan, and carry through to completion, a work so massive and authoritative, remained cause for continuing wonder and amazement; it is this wonder which explains Louise-Noëlle Malclès's captiously phrased encomium: "L'auteur ne peut, humainement parlant, connaitre tous. Aussi, peut-on regretter que T. Besterman ne se soit pas attribué pour son oeuvre monumentale, le role d'animateur et de coordonnateur, et qu'une fois en possession de son impressionnant materiel il n'en ait pas confié la distribution, sous les grosses rubriques, à des spécialistes très avertis."[2]

There is no question but that Theodore Besterman's *A World Bibliography of Bibliographies* is an "oeuvre monumentale:" a recent research guide characterizes it as "the authoritative source for bibliographies of bibliographies covering all countries and all centuries;"[3] and Robert L. Collison wistfully observes: *"Pace* Mr. Theodore Besterman and his admirable compilations, the day of the one-man bibliographer seems almost over: witness the case of Paetow whose bibliographical work was deemed too great to be continued by less than a large and learned committee."[4] It is in these perspectives that the continuing importance of Theodore Besterman's *A World Bibliography of Bibliographies* is to be understood, and the clear need for this Decennial Supplement to be perceived.

---

[1] For systematic bibliography, see Louise-Noëlle Malclès, *Manuel de Bibliographie* (Paris: Presse Universitaires de France, 1963); and Theodore Besterman, *The Beginnings of Systematic Bibliography* (Oxford University Press, 1935).

[2] Louise-Noëlle Malclès, *Les Sources du Travail Bibliographique* (3 vols. in 4 vols. Genève: E. Droz; Lille: Girard, 1950-1958), I, p. 29.

[3] Margaret C. Patterson, *Literary Research Guide* (Detroit: Gale Research Co., 1976), p. 23.

[4] Robert L. Collison, *Bibliographies: Subject and National* 3rd ed. (London: Crosby Lockwood, 1968), p. xv.

The first edition of Theodore Besterman's *A World Bibliography of Bibliographies* appeared in 1939-40; the second in 1947-49; the third in 1955-56; and the fourth and final edition in 1965-66.[5] In the preface to the last edition, Besterman wrote:

When I published the third edition of this bibliography ten years ago I was firmly resolved that it should be the last. It seemed impossible to face once again the vast labour of bringing it up-to-date, to say nothing of the necessary revision, and in any case it was likely that another task would last out my time. However, that task has been completed, and the demand for a new edition of the present work has become insistent. So here is the fourth edition, this time really the last, of a work first undertaken thirty years ago.

This edition has been brought down to 1963, inclusive, and a good many bibliographies of later date are being recorded as the work passes through the press. Large parts of the field have been surveyed anew, the text has been minutely revised throughout, and very many changes and improvements have been made. In particular, the scientific, political and other developments of the post-war years have made necessary many additions to the subject-headings, and many changes. The number of cross-references has been increased. Most important, however, are the additional entries of new bibliographies (the output of the last ten years has been prodigious), and even of a few older ones. The number of volumes recorded and separately collated is now over 117,000, arranged under about 16,000 headings and subheadings. The exact figures, classified by language, will be given in the preface to the fourth volume.

In this edition many entries are followed by an asterisk; this space-saving device is explained below, near the top of columns 37-38.

---

[5]Theodore Besterman, *A World Bibliography of Bibliographies and of Bibliographical Catalogues, Calendars, Abstracts, Digests, Indexes and the Like*. 4th ed., rev. and greatly enlarged. 5 vols. (Lausanne: Societas Bibliographica, 1965-1966; Totowa, N.J.: Rowman and Littlefield, 1971). A series of volumes which gathered together all the titles in some of the major fields found throughout the 6664 columns of the 4th edition were published in 1971 (Totowa, N.J.: Rowman and Littlefield) under the collective title, *The Besterman World Bibliographies*, i.e., *Academic Writings; Agriculture; Art and Architecture* (including *Archaeology*); *Bibliography; Biological Sciences; Commerce, Manufactures, Labour; Education* (including *Vocational Education*); *Family History* (including *Genealogy and Heraldry*); *History and Geography; Law* (including *International Law*); *Literature: English and American, Medicine; Music and Drama; Periodical Publications* (Including *Almanacs and Directories*); *Physical Sciences; Printing; Technology* (including *Inventions*).

Some readers may be interested to know that about 2050 sorts (separate and different monotype printing characters) have been used in the setting of this work in its fourth edition.

For some thirty years, Theodore Besterman had continuously nurtured and expanded a prodigious reference corpus which had assumed a gargantuan form, firmly disciplined by the carefully defined and articulated matrix into which it had been set. It is Besterman's plan of arrangement (deriving from his unrivaled knowledge of systematic bibliography) which explains the success of his *A World Bibliography of Bibliographies.* He acknowledged the merits of Julius Petzholdt's *Bibliotheca Bibliographica* (1866), perceptively recorded the deficiencies of Léon Vallée's *Bibliographie des Bibliographies* (1883/1887), and Henri Stein's *Manuel de Bibliographie* (1897): and out of these cogently evaluative analyses, he enunciated clear methodologies:

My bibliography is limited to separately published bibliographies, as are in effect the three we have considered. This rule I have not only established, but, unlike my predecessors, I have adhered to it rather strictly. Let me make quite clear what I mean by a separately published work. For our present purpose I define such a work as one having separate pagination. Exception has been made for a few bibliographies not separately paginated, where there is definite evidence that they were published in that form, as, for instance, in the case of separate works which also form part of series. From this definition it is clear that no bibliography in a book is included unless it forms the bulk, or at least the principal purpose, of that book.

It is, of course, somewhat illogical to limit ourselves in this way, since valuable bibliographies are occasionally published in periodicals and appended to general works. This procedure is, however, quite unavoidable. It would now be impossible, as much for a committee as for an individual, to prepare a list of all bibliographies. Even if the undertaking were possible it would be singularly unprofitable, since the vast majority of the resulting millions of entries would be without value. Nor do I think it at all a useful plan to restrict oneself in the main to separately published bibliographies, but to include as well a selection of others, as some of my predecessors have done. Whence and how could such a selection be made? A selection can be profitably made, as I shall have occasion to say again, only from full resources. As these resources are not available the resulting selection would merely tantalize the user of the bibliography, misleading him far more often than it helped him; this conclusion will be confirmed by any one who has used even Petzholdt. The only sensible course is to make the necessary rule and stick to it; then we know where we are.

It must be remembered that in some of the chief publishing countries the printing of a monograph in a learned journal is often merely a formal preliminary to its reissue as a separate work. A large proportion of, for instance, French learned and scientific work is published in this way, and it would be narrowly pedantic to treat such bibliographies as offprints. Nor have I done so, with the result that 'separate publication' is by no means so great a limitation in these pages as might appear at first sight.

My bilbliography is definitely one of bilbliographies, and of bibliographies only. I have elsewhere written as follows: 'I define . . . a bibliography as a "list of books arranged according to some permanent principle". It is, of course, understood that by a book is meant any sort of written matter or any printed from type, directly or indirectly. The real danger may possibly lie in the interpretation of the words "permanent principle". Here common sense must come to the rescue. Common sense will tell us without fail that, whereas Madan's *Oxford books* is arranged according to a permanent principle, any one issue even of the Oxford university press's catalogue, in this context, is not, since it merely lists the books, published by one firm, which happen to be in print at a given moment. Similarly the catalogue even of the British museum is not a bibliography (however many bibliographies it may contain), since it lists only the books that happen to be in the possession of a particular general library. On the other hand, the catalogue of a special library, or of a special section of a general library, may be said to be arranged according to a permanent principle: such a catalogue is in effect the more or less complete bibliography of a particular subject.

I do not claim that this is a perfect definition, for far too little thought has been given by systematic bibliographers to these theoretical considerations. Still, it at least enables us to clarify the position a little. In accordance with this definition I have included bibliographies of books, pamphlets, broadsides, periodicals, and, indeed, of every kind of type-set and 'near-print' matter, together, by an extension, with systematic lists of music, maps, plans, and the like.[6]

---

[6]*A World Bibliography of Bibliographies*, I, cols. 23-27.

The *Decennial Supplement* is based on the principles laid down by Besterman, and has been compiled from copies of catalog entries produced by the Library of Congress. During the period which the *Supplement* covers (1964-1974), the Library of Congress was engaged in a world-wide cataloging program. In the field of research tools, particularly bibliographies, the Library of Congress's coverage is considered to be quite exhaustive, and the *Decennial Supplement* is, therefore, congruent with the principles of inclusion which Besterman had defined. In all, the *Supplement* records some 18,000 titles, arranged under some 6000 subject headings and sub-headings.

It is singularly appropriate that the Library of Congress provided the resources out of which the *Decennial Supplement* has been compiled; it was to the great national libraries that Theodore Besterman expressed his chief indebtedness: "I am conscious that this whole enterprise will appear over-ambitious for one man to have undertaken entirely single-handed, without any kind of subsidy, in his own time and at his own risk. I therefore think it well to make it clear that if the project has been carried through successfully this is due above all to the exceptional facilities given to me over the years by the British Museum Library and the Library of Congress."

FRANCESCO CORDASCO
Montclair State College

NOTE ON ARRANGEMENT

This bibliography has been compiled to serve as a decennial supplement to the fourth and final edition of Theodore Besterman's *A World Bibliography of Bibliographies* (1965-1966); the fourth edition includes bibliographies issued to 1963, inclusive, but also contains some later imprints. The present cumulation (**i.e.,** a decennial supplement) covers the years 1964 through 1974, in so far as Library of Congress catalog entries were available. In addition, it includes post-1963 reprints or later editions of titles listed in the Besterman bibliography, as well as entries for such works for which supplements or later volumes have been issued.

The present compilation follows in general the principles set forth by Besterman. It is limited to separately published bibliographies, including, however, some offprints of bibliographies which originally appeared as part of a larger work. Its coverage includes bibliographical catalogs, abstracts, indexes, inventories, registers, sales catalogs of special collections, and private libraries of subject interest. Bibliographies of discographies are entered but not lists of sound recordings, except for recordings for the blind. Among other exclusions are lists of works of art, stamp collections, film catalogs and indexes of individual periodical publications.

Within these guidelines this publication contains all available entries regardless of country of origin or language of text. Approximately 18,000 titles are recorded, arranged under some 6,000 subject headings and sub-headings.

Form of Entries

The bibliographical entries reproduced in these volumes are copies of Library of Congress catalog cards down to and including collation and series statement if any. However, additional information is given for many works: for example, reprint statements, references to earlier editions or related publications, authorship, etc.

The variations in choice or form of entry, typography, format, etc., reflect the changes in cataloging rules and Library of Congress practice during the period covered. References have been made between varying forms of many personal and corporate headings.

Arrangement

This is a subject bibliography. The entries are arranged alphabetically by author or title main entry under appropriate subject headings or sub-headings. Successive editions of a title are listed in chronological order. The subject headings are based on, but not without modifications, the *Library of Congress Subject Headings* (8th edition). In many cases, headings used by Besterman have been chosen and references made from those of the Library of Congress. Sub-headings and special arrangements of entries have been used only when the number of entries or the type of material listed indicated it to be useful.

Attention is called to two major special arrangements. Bibliographies of academic theses, dissertations, reports, etc., have been brought together under the heading DISSERTATIONS, ACADEMIC. Under this form heading the entries have been grouped as follows: (1) general bibliographies not restricted to a single subject or institution; (2) by subject, if the dissertations are limited to one subject; or (3) by country or state (of the United States) if limited to an individual institution. **See also** references to this special subject compilation have generally been made from pertinent subject headings throughout these volumes.

General bibliographies, catalogs and indexes of periodical publications — newspapers, journals, etc. — have been brought together under PERIODICAL PUBLICATIONS. Those identified as library catalogs or union catalogs have been subarranged accordingly. Lists of publications issued in individual countries or regions have been entered under geographical sub-headings. Bibliographies of periodicals limited to a given subject are entered throughout this work under the appropriate heading, usually with the sub-heading **Periodicals.** A list of those subjects is given at the end of the PERIODICAL PUBLICATIONS section.

Cross References and Notes

Approximately 1400 subject references have been provided. These include **see** references from synonymous terms or alternative forms, especially variations in the spelling of personal or place names. References have been made from variants used by Besterman whenever considered necessary or helpful to the user. **See also** references are used to indicate closely related subject headings. In the case of bibliographies which cover two or more distinct subjects **see under** or **see also under** references direct the user to the chosen heading.

Explanatory notes are supplied under certain general headings or sub-headings to define the type of bibliographies listed there. These scope notes also indicate other or more specific headings under which similar material may be found.

Many members of the staff of the Library of Congress have been helpful in providing encouragement and guidance in the preparation of this publication. I am particularly indebted to the Library's Photoduplication Service and the Bibliography Section, General Reference and Bibliography Division, for their cooperation.

A.F.T.

A

AACHEN. TECHNISCHE HOCHSCHULE

Schuwirth, Georg.
 Bibliographie zur Geschichte der Rheinisch-Westfälischen Technischen Hochschule Aachen. 1870–1970. Aachen (Rheinisch-Westfälische Technische Hochschule), Hochschulbibliothek, 1970.

   v, 125 p. 21 cm.

AALST see Alost

AARGAU

Aargauische Bibliographien und **Repertorien.** 1–
 Aarau, Switzerland, 1964–

   v. 21 cm.

   Issued by the Kantonsbibliothek and the Staatsarchiv of Aargau.

AAVIK, JUHAN

Juhan Aavik: helitööde nimestik. Catalogue of works. Stokholm, 1968.

   26 l. 24 cm.

   Some captions also in English.

ABBAYE d'AYWIERES see under Sainte Gertrude

ABBAYE DE LA RAMÉE

Belgium. Archives générales du Royaume.
 Inventaire des archives de l'abbaye de La Ramée à Jauchelette, par Georges Despy [et] André Uyttebrouck. Bruxelles, 1970–

   v. 30 cm. (Its Inventaire analytique des archives ecclésiastiques du Brabant. 1. sér.: Abbayes et chapitres, t. 4, fasc. 1

ABBOT, GEORGE, ABP. OF CANTERBURY

Christophers, Richard A
 George Abbot, Archbishop of Canterbury, 1562–1633; a bibliography [by] Richard A. Christophers. Charlottesville, Published for the Bibliographical Society of the University of Virginia [by] University Press of Virginia [1966]

   xxiv, 211 p. 24 cm.

ABDIJ VAN DRONGEN

Buntinx, J
 Inventaris van het archief der abdij van Drongen. Door

J. Buntinx. Brussel, Algemeen Rijksarchief, Ruisbroekstr., 2–6, 1971.

   iv, 63 p. 29 cm.

ABEL, KARL FRIEDRICH

Knape, Walter.
 Bibliographisch-thematisches Verzeichnis der Kompositionen von Karl Friedrich Abel (1723–1787) Cuxhaven, W. Knape [1972?]

   200 p. illus. 30 cm.

ABERCROMBIE, LASCELLES

Cooper, Jeffrey.
 A bibliography and notes on the works of Lascelles Abercrombie. [Hamden, Conn.] Archon Books, 1969.

   166 p. illus., facsims., port. 23 cm.

Cooper, Jeffrey.
 A bibliography and notes on the works of Lascelles Abercrombie. London, Kaye & Ward, 1969.

   166 p. 5 plates, 1 illus., 8 facsims., port. 23 cm.

ABORTION

Dollen, Charles.
 Abortion in context: a select bibliography. Metuchen, N. J., Scarecrow Press, 1970.

   150 p. 22 cm.

Floyd, Mary K
 Abortion bibliography. 1970–
 Troy, N. Y., Winston Pub. Co.

   v. 24 cm. annual.

Geijerstam. Gunnar af, 1915–
 An annotated bibliography of induced abortion, edited by Gunnar K. af Geijerstam. Ann Arbor, Center for Population Planning, University of Michigan [1969]

   vi, 359 p. 23 cm.

Karkal, Malini, 1927–
 A bibliography of abortion studies in India. Bombay, International Institute for Population Studies [1970]

   10 p. 28 cm.

ABRAMOWITZ, SHALOM JACOB

Jerusalem. Hebrew University. Jewish National and University Library.
 תערוכת מנדלי מוכר ספרים (שלום יעקב אברמוביץ) במלאת

המישים שנה לפטירתו; קטלוג. –ָנערכו על־ידי שמואל ורסם
יחיאל שיינטוֹך ירושלים ‏1968‏‏ ו

17, 66, viii p. illus., facsims. port. 24 cm.
Added t. p. in English; pref. in Hebrew, Yiddish, and English.
At head of title: בית הספרים הלאומי והאוניברסיטאי. המכון למדעי
היהדות, מפעל מנדלי.
Held at the Jewish National and University Library, Berman
Hall, during 1968.

Jerusalem. Hebrew University. *Mendele Project.*
מנדלי מוכר ספרים; רשימת כתביו ואגרותיו להתקנת מהדורתם
האקדימית. ירושלים. הוצאת ספרים ע״ש י״ל מאגנס, האוני־
ברסיטה העברית, תשכ״ח ‏1965‏‏

60 p. 28 cm.
Added t. p.: Mendele Mokher Sepharim; bibliography of his
works and letters for the academic edition; added t. p. also in
Yiddish.

ABRUZZI, ITALY

Aurini, Raffaele.
Bibliografia di preistoria e protostoria abruzzese. (1867–
1970). ‏n. p.‏, A cura del Centro ricerche storiche Abruzzo
teramano, 1972.

140 p. 24 cm. (Centro di ricerche storiche Abruzzo teramano.
‏Pubblicazioni‏, 4)

ABŪ TAMMĀN HABĪB IBN IBN AWS AL-ṬĀ'Ī

'Awwād, Kūrkīs.
(Abū Tammām al-Ṭā'ī)
أبو تمام الطائي: حياته وشعره في المراجع العربية والاجنبية.
تأليف كوركيس عواد ‏و‏ ميخائيـــل عواد. بغداد، مطبعـة
الارشاد ، 1971.

96 p. 24 cm. (مطبوعات وزارة الاعلام)

ABUTALYBOV, MUZAFAR GEÏDAROVICH

Kostina, D   D
М. Г. Абуталыбов. Библиография. ‏Вступит. статья
канд. биол. наук А. А. Марданова‏. Баку, Изд. АН
АзССР, 1968.
76 p. 16 cm. (Деятели науки и культуры Азербайджана)

ABYSSINIA   see   Ethiopia

ACADEMIA NACIONAL DE SAN CARLOS, MEXICO

Fernández, Justino, 1904–
Guía del archivo de la antigua Academia de San Carlos.
‏1. ed.‏ México ‏Universidad Nacional Autónoma de Méx-
ico‏ 1968–

v. illus. 24 cm. (v. 2– : Instituto de Investigaciones Estéticas. Estudios y fuentes del arte in México, 31.

Vol. 2 by E. Báez Macías.
‏Vol. 1, "Suplemento 3 del núm. 37 de los Anales del Instituto de
Investigaciones Estéticas."
CONTENTS: ‏1‏ 1781–1800.—‏2‏ 1801–1843.

——————Indice de nombres. 1781–1800. Formado por
Danilo Ongay Muza. ‏1. ed.‏ México ‏Universidad Nacional Autónoma de México‏ 1971.

23 p. 23 cm.
"Suplemento 2 del núm. 40 de los Anales del Instituto de Investigaciones Estéticas."

ACADEMIA SINICA   see   Chung yang yen chiu yuan

ACADEMIC DISSERTATIONS   see   Disserta-tions, Academic

ACADÉMIE FRANÇAISE, PARIS

Kerviler, René Pocard du Cosquer de, 1842–1907.
Essai d'une bibliographie raisonnée de l'Académie française ‏par‏ René Kerviler. Genève, Slatkine Reprints, 1968.

109 p. 23 cm.

On spine: Bibliographie de l'Académie.
"Réimpression de l'édition de Paris, 1877."

ACCELERATION

Smith, Janice L.
The effect of accelerations on the vestibular analyzer;
bibliography ‏by‏ Janice L. Smith. Washington‏ Aerospace
Technology Division, Library of Congress, 1966.

iii, 21 l. 28 cm. (ATD report 66–62)

"Compiled from Soviet open sources published 1955–1966 together
with 5 Western sources."

ACCIDENT PREVENTION   see   Safety education

ACCOUNTING

Bentley, Harry Clark, 1877–1967.
Bibliography of works on accounting by American au-
thors, by Harry C. Bentley and Ruth S. Leonard. New
York, A. M. Kelley, 1970.

2 v. in 1. 23 cm. (Reprints of economic classics)

Reprint of the 1934 ed.

Chūō Keizaisha, *Tokyo.*
中央経済社
会計学文献目録大集
東京 昭和44‏1969‏
415p 22cm

Commerce Clearing House.
Accounting articles, describing accounting articles published in accounting and business periodicals, books, pamphlets. Chicago ‏1965–

1 v. (loose-leaf) 26 cm. (Topical law reports)

Commerce Clearing House.
Accounting articles, 1963–1966; describing and indexing
accounting articles published in accounting and business
periodicals, books, and pamphlets for the years, 1963–1966.
New York, 1967.

1 v. (loose-leaf) 25 cm. (*Its* Topical law reports)

Commerce Clearing House.
Accounting articles, 1967–1970; describing and indexing accounting articles published in accounting and business periodicals, books, and pamphlets for the years 1967–1970. New York [1971]

1 v. (various pagings) 25 cm. (Its Topical law reports)

Demarest, Rosemary R
Accounting: information sources [by] Rosemary R. Demarest. Detroit, Gale Research Co. [1970]

420 p. 22 cm. (Management information guide, 18)

"An annotated guide to the literature, associations and federal agencies concerned with accounting."

Institute of Chartered Accountants in England and Wales, London. Library.
Current accounting literature 1971; a catalogue of books, pamphlets, and periodicals of current interest in the members' library of the Institute of Chartered Accountants in England and Wales at 31 August 1971. Edited by M. G. J. Harvey. London, Mansell [c1971]

xii, 586 p. 29 cm.

Institute of Chartered Accountants of Scotland. Library.
Catalogue of printed books and pamphlets on accounting and allied subjects dated 1494–1897, forming a collection of antiquarian interest in the Institute's Edinburgh Library. 2d ed. Edinburgh, 1968.

49, vii p. 25 cm.

Mueller, Gerhard G
A bibliography of international accounting [by] Gerhard G. Mueller. Rev. ed. [Seattle, International Accounting Studies Institute, University of Washington] 1968.

iii, 66 l. 29 cm.

Pryce-Jones, Janet E
Accounting in Scotland : a historical bibliography / compiled by Janet E. Pryce-Jones ; annotated by R. H. Parker. — Edinburgh : Accountants' Publishing Co. for the Institute of Chartered Accountants of Scotland and the Scottish Committee on Accounting History, 1974.

[4], x, 96 p., [8] p. of plates : facsims., ports. ; 30 cm.

Rice, John Wade.
Recordkeeping systems, small store and service trade. Rev. by J. Wade Rice. Washington, Small Business Administration, 1964.

12 p. 27 cm. (Small business bibliography no. 15, revision)

Rice, John Wade.
Recordkeeping systems, small store and service trade. Rev. by J. Wade Rice. Washington, Small Business Administration, 1965.

12 p. 26 cm. (Small business bibliography no. 15)

Rice, John Wade.
Recordkeeping systems: small store and service trade. Rev. by Nathan H. Olshan. Washington, Small Business Administration, 1966.

10 p. 26 cm. (Small business bibliography no. 15)

Caption title.

Russia (*1923–   U. S. S. R.*) *Glavnoe upravlenie vychisli-tel'nykh rabot.*
Библиографический аннотированный указатель литературы по механизации учета и вычислительных работ, за 1954–1963 гг. [Составлен О. И. Коростелевой и С. В. Пясковским] Москва [Статистика] 1965.

271 p. 23 cm.
At head of title: ЦСУ СССР.

Russia (*1923–   U. S. S. R.*). *Glavnoe upravlenie vychis-litel'nykh rabot.*
Библиографический аннотированный указатель литературы по механизации учета и вычислительных работ, за 1964–1967 гг. [Сост. С. В. Пясковский]. Москва, "Статистика," 1969.

244 p. 22 cm.

Thomson, Hugh W
Foreign books on bookkeeping and accounts 1494 to 1750: a bibliography [by] H. W. Thomson and B. S. Yamey. [London, Institute of Chartered Accountants in England & Wales], 1968.

34 p. 21 cm.

"The present bibliography supplements the 'Bibliography: Books on Accounting in English, 1543–1800' which is included in Accounting in England and Scotland: 1543–1800, by B. S. Yamey, H. C. Edey and H. W. Thomson."

Vaisto, Erkki.
Laskentatoimen kirjallisuus Suomessa vuosilta 1945–1971. Bibliography of accountancy in Finland 1945–1971. Helsinki, Kauppakorkeakoulu; jakelu: Kyriiri, 1973.

244 p. 21 cm. (Kauppakorkeakoulun julkaisuja, Sarja C: II: 15)

English and Finnish.

Zur Geschichte der Rechnungslegung im engeren deutsch-sprachigen Raum. [Zusammenstellung und Katalogbearbeitung der Ausstellung: Rosa-Elisabeth Gassmann. Düsseldorf, 1971?]

40 p. facsims. 20 cm.

Catalog of an exhibition sponsored by the Institut der Wirtschaftsprüfer in Deutschland, held at Wirtschaftsprüfer-Haus, Düsseldorf, June 21–July 2, 1971.

ACCRA

Brand, Richard R
A selected bibliography on Accra, Ghana, a West African colonial city (1877 to 1960) [by] Richard R. Brand. [Monticello, Ill., Council of Planning Librarians] 1971.

27 p. 29 cm. (Council of Planning Librarians. Exchange bibliography, 242)

ACETAMINOPHEN

Atco Chemical-Industrial Products, inc.
General bibliography of acetaminophen N. F. Parsippany, N. J., ATCO Chemical-Industrial Products, Fine Chemicals Division, Technical Information Service, 1964.

[8] l. 30 cm.

ACEVEDO DÍAZ, EDUARDO

Rela, Walter.
Eduardo Acevedo Díaz. Montevideo, Editorial Ulises [1967]

83 p. facsims. 20 cm. (His Guía bibliográfica)

ACHTERBERG, GERRIT

Achterberg in kaart. Den Haag, Bakker/Daamen, 1971.
113 p., 13 p. of photos. 22 x 22 cm.

ACKERMAN, CARL WILLIAM

United States. Library of Congress. Manuscript Division.
Carl William Ackerman: a register of his papers in the Library of Congress. Washington, Library of Congress, 1973.
iii, 78 p. 27 cm.

ACOSTA SAIGNES, MIGUEL

Rodulfo Cortés, Santos, 1924–
Miguel Acosta Saignes. 2. ed. Caracas, Escuela de Biblioteconomía y Archivos, Universidad Central de Venezuela, 1970.
44 p. 16 cm. (Serie bibliográfica, 1)

ACOUSTICS see Architectural acoustics

ACQUISITIONS (LIBRARIES) see Library science - Processing

ACUPUNCTURE

Acupuncture; a selected bibliography. v. 1–
1800/1972–
Los Angeles, National Acupuncture Association.
v. 28 cm.

Chung i yen chiu yüan, Peking. T'u shu kuan.
[Chung-kuo chen chiu t'u shu lien ho mu lu]
中国針灸图书联合目録 （初稿） 中医研究院图書館 北京图書館合編 [北京] 北京图書館 1959. [1972]
ii, 34, viii l. 28 cm.
全国中医圖書联合目録單行本
Xerox copy.

Tam, Billy K   S
Acupuncture: an international bibliography, by Billy K. S. Tam and Miriam S. L. Tam. Metuchen, N. J., Scarecrow Press, 1973.
137 p. 22 cm.

ADAMIC, LOUIS

Christian, Henry Arthur, 1931–
Louis Adamic; a checklist, by Henry A. Christian. [1st ed. Kent, Ohio] Kent State University Press [1971]
xlvii, 104 p. 23 cm. (The Serif series: bibliographies and checklists, no. 20)

ADAMS, HAMPTON

Disciples of Christ Historical Society.
Hampton Adams; a register of his papers in the Disciples of Christ Historical Society. Nashville, 1969.
26 l. 28 cm. (Its Register no. 3)

ADAPTABILITY

Coping and adaptation; a behavioral sciences bibliography. Edited by George V. Coelho [and others] Chevy Chase, Md., National Institute of Mental Health; [for sale by the Supt. of Docs., U. S. Govt. Print. Off., Washington, 1970]
vii, 231 p. 26 cm. (Public Health Service publication no. 2087)

ADENYLIC ACID

Semenuk, Nick S   1937–
Cyclic AMP, 1957–1969; a classified bibliography of publications. Compiled by Nick S. Semenuk and Helen Zimmerberg. New Brunswick, N. J., E. R. Squibb [1970]
ix, 384 p. (p. 384 blank) 28 cm.

ADHESIVES

Currier, Raymond A   1925–
Selected bibliography on glues and gluing for 1964, 1965, and 1966, compiled by Raymond A. Currier. Corvallis Forest Research Laboratory, Oregon State University, 1968.
28 p. 23 cm. ([Oregon. State University, Corvallis. Forest Research Laboratory] Bibliography 7)

Laszkiewicz, Olga T   M
Industrial adhesives, compiled by O. T. M. Laszkiewicz. Adelaide, State Library of South Australia, 1969.
97 p. 27 cm. (Research Service bibliographies. Series 4, no. 123)

Laszkiewicz, Olga T   M
Select list of patents on the preparation of adhesives. Compiled by O. T. M. Laszkiewicz. Adelaide, State Library of South Australia, 1968.
38 p. 26 cm. (State Library of South Australia. Research Service. Bibliographies, ser. 4, no. 117)

Murphy, Janet.
Adhesive bonding: a selected bibliography. Hatfield (Herts.), Hertis, 1968.
[2], 25, 11p. 21 cm.

Weiner, Jack, 1910–
Adhesives [by] Jack Weiner and Lillian Roth. [Appleton, Wis., Institute of Paper Chemistry] 1963–64.
4 v. 28 cm. (Appleton, Wis. Institute of Paper Chemistry. Bibliography series, no. 205)
CONTENTS: 1. General applications, theory, and testing.—2. Paper.—3. Board, plastics, and textiles.—4. Tapes and machinery.
——— ——— Supplement I–   [by] Jack Weiner and Lillian Roth. Appleton, Wis., Institute of Paper Chemistry, 1968–   .
v. in   28 cm. (Appleton, Wis. Institute of Paper Chemistry. Bibliography series, nr. 205)
Each supplement consists of 4 v. corresponding to original work.

ADLER, MAX

Schroth, Hans.
Max Adler ⟨1873–1937⟩. Eine Bibliographie. Zsgest v. Hans Schroth unter Mitarb. v. Herbert Exenberger. Mit einem Geleitw. v. Hertha Firnberg. Bundesmin. f. Wissenschaft u. Forschung. (Wien) Europaverl. (1973).
63 p. 21 cm. (Schriftenreihe des Ludwig-Boltzmann-Instituts für Geschichte der Arbeiterbewegung, 2)

ADMINISTRATION see Management; Political science

ADMINISTRATIVE LAW

McDermott, Beatrice S.

Government regulation of business including antitrust information sources; a comprehensive annotated bibliography of works pertaining to the Antitrust Division, Department of Justice, and to the major regulatory agencies of the Federal Government [by] Beatrice S. McDermott [and] Freada A. Coleman. Detroit, Mich., Gale Research Co. [1967]

229 p. 23 cm. (Management information guide, 11)

Ochodnický, Pavel, *comp.*

Bibliografia československého socialistického správneho právo za roky 1963–1966. Zostavil Pavel Ochodnický. V Bratislave, Univerzitní knižnica, 1967.

29 l. 29 cm.

ADOLESCENCE

Boorer, David R

Adolescence: a select bibliography, [by] D. R. Boorer and S. J. Murgatroyd. Caerphilly, MTM Publishing House, 1972.

[5], 121 p. 21 cm.

ADOPTION

Jacka, Alan A

Adoption in brief: research and other literature in the United States, Canada and Great Britain, 1966–72: an annotated bibliography, [by] Alan A. Jacka. Windsor, National Foundation for Educational Research, 1973.

71 p. 22 cm. (National children's Bureau. Report)

Pringle, Mia Lilly (Kellmer)

Adoption facts and fallacies: a review of research in the United States, Canada and Great Britain between 1948 and 1965, by M. L. Kellmer Pringle, with the assistance of Micheline Dewdney, Eileen Crellin, Rosemary Dinnage. London, Longmans in association with the National Bureau for Co-operation in Child Care, 1967.

x, 251 p. table. 22½ cm. (Studies in child development)

Sansó, Benito.

La adopción: Estudio comparativo del proyecto de ley venezolana con otras leyes recientes [por] Benito Sansó guía bibliográfica [por] Hanna Binstock. Caracas, Universidad Central de Venezuela, Facultad de Derecho, Instituto de Derecho Privado, 1967.

vii, 97 p. 22 cm. (Series "Guías bibliográficas y legislativas," 1)

ADULT EDUCATION see Education of adults

ADVENTURE

Allinson, A   A

Adventure [by] A. A. Allinson and F. E. Hotchin. Melbourne, Canberra [etc.] Cheshire [1969]

23 p. illus. 20 cm. (14–16: a reading guide)

ADVERTISING
see also Public relations

Kästing, Friederike.

Bibliographie der Werbeliteratur. Verz. deutschsprachiger Werbeliteratur ab 1945, einschl. ausgew. Literatur über Markterkundg u. Absatz. Unter Mitarb. v. Rüdiger Schiller. Stuttgart, Poeschel, 1972.

206 p. 23 cm.

"Werbewissenschaftliches Referatenblatt. Sonderheft."

Millican, Richard Donald, 1907–

Advertising; volume and expenditures, by Richard D. Millican. Revision. Washington, Small Business Administration, 1965.

4 p. 26 cm. (Small business bibliography no. 7)

Mrázová, Viera.

Pramene o firemnej literatúre. Sprac. Viera Mrázová. Bratislava, Slov. techn. knižnica, rozmn., 1972.

26, [2] p. 21 cm. (Bratislava. Slovenská technická knižnica. Edícia: Metodické pomôcky SITK. Séria D: Bibliografie, č. 13)

Summary also in Russian, German, and English.

Rice, John Wade.

Advertising, retail store. Rev. by J. Wade Rice. Washington, Small Business Administration, 1966.

7 p. 26 cm. (Small business bibliography no. 20)

Caption title.
1963 edition by Leland L. Howell.

Rice, John Wade.

Advertising-retail store. Rev. by J. Wade Rice. Washington, Small Business Administration [1970]

7 p. 26 cm. (Small business bibliography no. 20)

Caption title.
1963 ed. by Leland L. Howell.

Thompson (J. Walter) Company.

Advertising; an annotated bibliography 1972, selected by the J. Walter Thompson Co. Ltd. With an introduction by J. A. P. Treasure. London, National Book League [1972]

35 p. 21 cm.

At head of title: National Book League with the J. Walter Thompson Co. Ltd.

ADVISORY OPINIONS

Kisch, Guido, 1889–

Consilia. Eine Bibliographie der juristischen Konsiliensammlungen. Basel, Stuttgart, Helbing und Lichtenhahn, 1970.

86 p. 23 cm.

ADY, ENDRE

Vitályos, László.

Ady-bibliográfia 1896–1970; Ady Endre önállóan megjelent művei és az Ady-irodalom [írta] Vitályos László [és] Orosz László. Budapest [Magyar Tudományos Akadémia Könyvtára] 1972.

xxiv, 425 p. illus. 25 cm. (A Magyar Tudományos Akadémia Könyvtárának kiadványai, 67)

Table of contents also in German and Russian.

AERIAL PHOTOGRAPHY

Grossová, Ivana.

Lesnícka fotogrametria. Výberový zoznam odb. knižnej

a čas. lit. z fondov ŠVK Zvolen. Zost. Ivana Grossová. Zvolen, ŠVK, cyklostyl, 1969.

[2], 31, [2] l. 20 cm.

Hildebrandt, Gerd.
Bibliographie des Schrifttums auf dem Gebiet der forstlichen Luftbildauswertung 1887–1968. Bearb. und hrsg. von G[erd] Hildebrandt. Freiburg i. Br., Institut für Forsteinrichtung u. Forstliche Betriebswirtschaft d. Universität, 1969.

307 p. 25 cm.

Mel'nikov, E S
Аэрометоды в инженерной геологии и гидрогеологии; краткий обзор и библиографический указатель литературы, опубликованной с 1892 по 1963 г. Москва, Недра, 1964.

34 p. 22 cm.
At head of title: Государственный геологический комитет СССР. Всесоюзный научно-исследовательский институт экономики, минерального сырья и геологоразведочных работ. Е. С. Мельников, А. В. Садов.

Selected bibliography of the terrain sciences. 1967–
Alexandria, Va., Raytheon Co., Space and Information Systems Division, Autometric Operation.

v. 28 cm. annual.

Vols. for 1967– prepared by R. F. Holmes and J. J. Footen.

U. S. *Geological Survey.*
A descriptive catalog of selected aerial photographs of geologic features in areas outside the United States, assembled by Charles R. Warren [and others] Washington, U. S. Govt. Print. Off., 1969.

23 p. illus., fold. col. map (in pocket) 29 cm. (*Its* Professional paper 591)

United States. National Archives.
Aerial photographs in the National Archives. Compiled by Charles E. Taylor and Richard E. Spurr. Washington, 1971.

vii, 106 p. 27 cm. (**Its Special list no. 25**)

United States. National Archives.
Aerial photographs in the National Archives. Compiled by Charles E. Taylor and Richard E. Spurr. Washington, National Archives and Records Service, 1973.

vii, 106 p. 27 cm. (**Its Special list no. 25**)

"Revision of the list first published in 1971."

AERODYNAMICS

Göttingen. Aerodynamische Versuchsanstalt.
Bibliographie der Veröffentlichungen über Hydro- und Aerodynamik der Aerodynamischen Versuchsanstalt und des Max-Planck-Instituts für Strömungsforschung, 1960–1970, mit einem Nachtrag zu Bibliographie der Veröffentlichungen 1907–1959. [Göttingen, Selbstverlag Max-Planck-Institut für Strömungsforschung und Aerodynamische Versuchsanstalt, 1971]
118 p. 21 cm. (Mitteilungen aus dem Max-Planck-Institut für Strömungsforschung und der Aerodynamischen Versuchsanstalt, Nr. 50)

Harting, A
Selective bibliography on air cushion vehicles. By A. Harting. Amsterdam [National Aerospace Laboratory NLR] 1967.

115 p. 30 cm.

Industrial aerodynamics abstracts. v. 1–
Jan./Feb. 1970–
[Cranfield, Eng., British Hydromechanics Research Association]

v. 30 cm. bimonthly.

Newman, Perry A
An annotated bibliography on transonic flow theory, by Perry A. Newman and Dennis O. Allison. Washington, National Aeronautics and Space Administration; [for sale by the National Technical Information Service, Springfield, Va.] 1971.
v, 131 p. 27 cm. (NASA technical memorandum, NASA TM X-2363)

Schwantes, Eckart.
Übersicht über den Bodeneffekt bei strahlgestützten V/STOL-Flugzeugen. Literaturbericht von E. Schwantes. (München, Zentralstelle für Luftfahrtdokumentation und -information <ZLDI>) 1968.

38 p. illus. 30 cm. (Deutsche Luft- und Raumfahrt. Mitteilung 68–28)

Summary in English.

AERONAUTICAL CHARTS

International Civil Aviation Organization.
Aeronautical chart catalogue. Catalogue des cartes aéronautiques. Catalogo de cartas aeronauticas. [9th ed. Montreal, 1970]

1 v. (various pagings) maps (part fold., 1 col.) 27 cm. (Its Document] 7101-MAP/565/9)

U. S. *Aeronautical Chart and Information Center, St. Louis.*
DOD catalog of aeronautical charts and flight information publications. St. Louis [1968–

1 v. (loose-leaf) illus., charts, maps (all part col.) 30 cm.

AERONAUTICS
see also Airplanes; Astronautics; Rockets; and under Dissertations, Academic

American Institute of Aeronautics and Astronautics.
Journals of the AIAA: 1970 subject and author indexes; AIAA journal, Journal of spacecraft and rockets, Journal of aircraft, Journal of hydronautics. [New York, 1970]

48 p. (p. [44]–48 advertisements) 29 cm.

Brockett, Paul, 1872–1946.
Bibliography of aeronautics. Washington, Smithsonian Institution, 1910; Detroit, Gale Research Co., 1966.

xiv, 940 p. 23 cm. (Smithsonian miscellaneous collections, v. 55)
[Smithsonian Institution] Publication 1920.
At head of title: Hodgkins Fund.

France. *Service de documentation scientifique et technique de l'armement.*
Bulletin signalétique. no. 1–296; mai 1945–déc. 1964. [Paris]

296 no. in 69 v. illus. 21–25 cm.

Monthly, 1945–59; semimonthly, 1960–64.
Title varies: 1945–June 1949, Bulletin mensuel de documentation.—July 1949–1959, Bulletin mensuel signalétique.
Other slight variations in title.
Issues for 1945–Sept. 1963 published by the Service de documentation et d'information technique de l'aéronautique.
Superseded by a publication with the same title issued by the Service de documentation scientifique et technique de l'armement.

Hanniball, August, 1922–
Aircraft, engines and airmen: a selective review of the periodical literature, 1930–1969. Metuchen, N. J., Scarecrow Press, 1972.

xxiv, 825 p. 22 cm.

Lermer, Lowisa.
Polskie skrzydła; poradnik bibliograficzny. Warszawa, Biblioteka Narodowa, 1970.

80 p. 21 cm.

At head of title: Biblioteka Narodowa. Instytut Bibliograficzny. Lowisa Lermer, Bronisław Lermer.

Marienfeld, Horst.
GRS-Dokumentation. Bibliographien 1960–1968. (Darmstadt-Arheilgen) Gesellschaft für Regelungstechnik und Simulationstechnik GmbH (1969–
5 v. 21 cm.
English or German.
Contents.—Bd. 1. Luftfahrttechnik, Raumfahrttechnik, Weltraumforschung.—Bd. 2. Biowissenschaften, Biotechnik.—Bd. 3. Elektronik, Nachrichtentechnik, Rechenanlagen, Regelungstechnik, Messtechnik.—Bd. 4. Maschinenbau, Mechanik, Thermodynamik, Verbrennung, Kerntechnik.—Bd. 5. Physik, Geowissenschaften, Meteorologie, Chemie. Mathematik.

Marshall, Jane N
Aviation education bibliography: a compilation of books, references, periodicals, films, filmstrips, and other teaching aids related to aviation and flight in the atmosphere [by] Jane N. Marshall. 4th ed. Washington, National Aerospace Education Council, 1964.

ii, 64 p. illus. 28 cm.

NASA Scientific and Technical Information Facility.
Aeronautical engineering; a special bibliography with indexes. Washington, Scientific and Technical Information Office, National Aeronautics and Space Administration, 1970.

vii, 611 p. 27 cm. (NASA SP-7037)

New York (City). Public Library.
History of aeronautics; a selected list of references to material in the New York Public Library. Compiled by William B. Gamble. New York [1971]

325 p. 24 cm.

Reprint of the 1938 ed.
First published in the Bulletin of the New York Public Library, Jan. 1936–Sept. 1937.

Potocko, Richard J
Bibliography related to human factors system program, July 1962–February 1964, by Richard J. Potocko. Washington, Scientific and Technical Information Division, National Aeronautics and Space Administration; [for sale by the Office of Technical Services, Dept. of Commerce] 1964.

v, 237 p. 27 cm. (NASA SP-7014)

Proceedings in print. v. 1–
Oct. 1964–
[n. p.] Aerospace Section, Science-Technology Division, Special Libraries Association.

v. 28 cm. bimonthly.

Sokoll, Alfred Hermann.
Deutschsprachiges Schrifttum zur Aero- und Astronautik. Bibliographie 1945–1964. Hrsg. von Alfred H. Sokoll. 2., verb. und erw. Aufl. München, Alkos-Verlag (1967).

viii, 376 p. 21 cm. (Bibliothek der Aero-und Astronautik, Bd. 4)

First ed. published in 1962 under title: Bibliographie zur Aero- und Astronautik.

Šteinerová, Svatava, comp.
Bibliografie dějin čsl. letectví. Excerpováno z knih a časopisů v Knihovně Národního technického muzea. Sest. Svatava Šteinerová s kolektivem. Praha, 1964.

131 p. 21 cm. (Rozpravy Národního technického muzea v Praze. Populárně-vědecká řada, 12)

Tissandier, Gaston, 1843–1899.
Bibliographie aéronautique. [Unchanged reprint of the ed. Paris, 1887]. Amsterdam, B. M. Israël, 1971.

63 p. illus. 22 cm.

U. S. Aeronautical Center, Oklahoma City. Library Branch.
Bibliographic list. no. 1–
Oklahoma City, 1964–

no. 27 cm.

U. S. Air Force Academy. Library.
A survey of aeronautics. [Colorado Springs] 1967.

42 p. 20 cm. (Its Special bibliography series, no. 87)

U. S. Civil Aeronautics Board.
Research and reference directory. [Washington] 1969.

ii, 22, [21] p. 27 cm.

Cover title.

U. S. Federal Aviation Agency. Library Services Division. Information Retrieval Branch.
Title listing of CAA publications. Washington, 1964.

85 p. 26 cm. ([U. S.] Federal Aviation Agency. Library Services Division. Information retrieval list no. 2)

U. S. National Aeronautics and Space Administration. Scientific and Technical Information Division.
Bibliographies on aerospace science; a continuing bibliography. 1962/64–
Washington [Available from the Office of Technical Services, Dept. of Commerce]

v. 27 cm. (NASA SP)

BIBLIOGRAPHIES

Dickson, Katherine Murphy.
History of aeronautics and astronautics; a preliminary bibliography. Washington, National Aeronautics and Space Administration, 1967.

vi, 117 l. 27 cm.

Wayne State University, Detroit. Center for Application of Sciences and Technology.
Bibliography of aerospace bibliographies; a keyword-in-context index (KWIC) Compiled by Robert E. Booth [and others] Detroit [1965]

iv, 57, 126 p. 28 cm.

LAW

McGill University, Montreal. Law Library.
Catalogue of air and space law materials. Montreal [1965]

103 l. 28 cm.

Cover title.

Catalogue date October covered by label: July 1, 1965.

"A revision and up-dating of the first catalogue of air and space law materials prepared by Professor Peter Sand and issued in July 1963."

At head of title: Institute of Air and Space Law, McGill University.

SAFETY MEASURES

Bulford, Dorothy E

Collision avoidance; a bibliography, 1955–April 1967, compiled by Dorothy E. Bulford. [Atlantic City, NAFEC Library, National Aviation Facilities Experimental Center, 1967]

iii, 66 p. 27 cm.

Bulford, Dorothy E

Collision avoidance: an annotated bibliography, September 1968–April 1972. Dorothy E. Bulford, comp. Washington, Dept. of Transportation; for sale [by] National Technical Information Service, Springfield, Va., 1972.

vii, 262 p. 27 cm. ([United States. National Aviation Facilities Experimental Center, Atlantic City] Report no. FAA–NA–72–41)

Cover title.

Prepared by the National Aviation Facilities Experimental Center, Atlantic City, N. J., for the Federal Aviation Administration Systems Research and Development Service.

Pierson, William R

Biomedical references for aviation safety / William R. Pierson. — Arlington, Va. : Flight Safety Foundation, [1974]

v. 90 leaves ; 28 cm.

U. S. Aeronautical Center, Oklahoma City. Library Branch.

Aircraft accidents; investigation and prevention; selected references. Oklahoma City, 1971.

ix, 180 p. 27 cm. (Its Bibliographic list no. 4)

Cover title.

"Updates the Library's Bibliographic list no. 1 of aircraft accident references dated January, 1964."

U. S. *Aeronautical Center, Oklahoma City. Library Branch.*

Whatdunnit: aircraft accidents, their prevention and prevention practices; selected references. Oklahoma City, Aeronautical Center, 1964.

76 p. 27 cm. (*Its* Bibliographic list no. 1)

AERONAUTICS, MILITARY

Köhler, Karl.

Bibliographie zur Luftkriegsgeschichte. Bearb. im Militärgeschichtlichen Forschungsamt von Karl Köhler. Frankfurt a. M., Bernard & Graefe, 1966–

v. 21 cm. (Schriften der Bibliothek für Zeitgeschichte, Weltkriegsbücherei, Stuttgart: n. F. der Bibliographien der Weltkriegsbücherei, Heft 5.)

CONTENTS.—T. 1. Literatur bis 1960.

AEROSOLS

Davies, Charles Norman, 1910–

Recent advances in aerosol research, a bibliographical review, by C. N. Davies. New York, Macmillan, 1964.

ix, 80 p. 23 cm.

"A Pergamon Press book."

Moscow. TSentral'naĭa nauchno-tekhnicheskaĭa biblioteka pishchevoĭ promyshlennosti. *Nauchno-bibliograficheskiĭ otdel.*

Аэрозольная упаковка и ее применение в пищевой и родственных отраслях промышленности. (Аннот. библиогр. указатель рус. и иностр. литературы за 1963–1967, 1968 (I кв.) гг.) Москва, 1968.

31 p. 26 cm.

Naletova, N B

Применение аэрозолей в сельском хозяйстве. Библиогр. указатель литературы за 1966–1968 гг.—отечественной и иностранной. [Сост. Н. Б. Налетова]. Москва, 1968.

35 p. 20 cm.

AESOP

Keidel, George Charles, 1868–1942.

A manual of Aesopic fable literature; a first book of reference for the period ending A. D. 1500. First fascicle. With three facsims. New York, B. Franklin [1972]

xxiv, 76 p. 22 cm. (Burt Franklin research and source works series) (Selected essays and texts in literature and criticism 176)

Reprint of the 1896 ed. published by Friedenwald Co., Baltimore, which was the only part published, issued as no. 2 of Romance and other studies.

AESTHETICS
see also   Art

Baxandall, Lee.

Marxism and aesthetics: a selective annotated bibliography; books and articles in the English language. New York, Humanities Press, 1968.

xxii, 261 p. 28 cm.

Bibliographische Zeitschrift für Ästhetik. Bd. 1– Mai 1966–

Lindenberg [Ger., Semester-Vertrieb]

v. 30 cm. 4 no. a year.

Vol. for 1966 covers material issued 1963–66.

Draper, John William, 1893–

Eighteenth century English aesthetics; a bibliography, by John W. Draper. New York, Octagon Books, 1968.

140 p. 24 cm.

Reprint of the 1931 ed.

Formigari, Lia, 1931–

Studi sull'estetica dell'empirismo inglese, 1931–1965. Roma, Edizioni dell'Ateneo, 1971.

200 p. 21 cm. (Collana del Centro di ricerche di storia della storiografia filosofica)

Hammond, William Alexander, 1861–1938.

A bibliography of aesthetics and of the philosophy of the fine arts from 1900–1932, compiled and edited by William A. Hammond. Rev. and enl. ed. New York, Russell & Russell [1967]

x, 205 p. 22 cm.

Mexico (City) Universidad Nacional. *Instituto de Investigaciones Estéticas.*

Bibliografía del Instituto de Investigaciones Estéticas, 1935–1965, por Danilo Ongay Muza. [1. ed.] México, Universidad Nacional Autónoma de México, 1966.

140 p. facsims. 23 cm.

Miladinova, Milka.
(Marksistko-leninska estetika)
Марксистко-ленинска естетика. Библиогр. ⟨В помощ на лектори, пропагандисти и слушатели⟩. София, Инст. за пропаганда на марксизма-ленинизма, 1969.

119 p. 19 cm.

At head of title: Софийска градска библиотека.
By M. Miladinova and D. Danailova.

Petrova, Galina Aleksandrovna.
(Kommunisticheskaia partiia Sovetskogo Soiuza i voprosy literatury i iskusstva)
Коммунистическая партия Советского Союза и вопросы литературы и искусства. Произведения В. И. Ленина. Докум. материалы. Труды сов. ученых и творч. работников о партийности литературы и искусства. (Изд. 1966 1971 гг. на рус. яз.) ⟨Библиогр. список⟩. Москва, 1971.

55 p. 20 cm.

At head of title: Государственная библиотека СССР имени В. И. Ленина. Информационно-библиографический отдел.

Turich, Irina Mikhaĭlovna.
Эстетическое воспитание детей; рекомендательный указатель литературы. Под ред. В. К. Скатерщикова. Москва, Просвещение, 1966.

102 p. 20 cm.

At head of title: Академия педагогических наук РСФСР. Государственная библиотека по народному образованию им. К. Д. Ушинского. И. М. Турич.

AFFERDEN, PIETER VAN

Graaf, Bob de.
Petrus Apherdianus, ludimagister ca. 1510–1580. ⟨Translation M. Hollander⟩ Nieuwkoop B. de Graaf, 1968 ⟨1969⟩

96 p. with illus. 22 cm. (Bibliographies of Dutch humanists, no. 1)

AL-AFGHĀNĪ, JAMĀL AL-DĪN

Kudsi-Zadeh, A   Albert.
Sayyid Jamāl al-Dīn al-Afghānī; an annotated bibliography, by A. Albert Kudsi-Zadeh. Leiden, Brill, 1970.

xxii, 118 p. 25 cm.

AFGHANISTAN

Bibliographie der Afghanistan-Literatur 1945–1967 ⟨von⟩ Arbeitsgemeinschaft Afghanistan und Deutsches Orient-Institut (Deutsche Orient-Stiftung) in Zusammenarbeit mit der Dokumentationsleitstelle für den Modernen Orient beim Deutschen Orient-Institut Hamburg und dem Institut für Entwicklungsforschung und Entwicklungspolitik der Ruhr-Universität Bochum. Hamburg, 1968–69.

2 v. 25 cm.
CONTENTS: T. 1. Literatur in europäischen Sprachen.—T. 2. Literatur in orientalischen Sprachen und Ergänzungen in europäischen Sprachen.

Kukhtina, Tat'iana Ivanovna, comp.
Библиография Афганистана; литература на русском языке. Составитель Т. И. Кухтина. Москва, Наука; Глав. ред. восточной лит-ры, 1965.

271 p. 22 cm.

At head of title: Академия наук СССР. Институт народов Азии.

Wilber, Donald Newton.
Annotated bibliography of Afghanistan, by Donald N.

Wilber. 3d ed. New Haven, Human Relations Area Files Press, 1968.

ix, 252 p. 23 cm. (Behavior science bibliographies)

AFRICA
see also under Asia; Middle East; and Dissertations, Academic

African Bibliographic Center.
African affairs for the general reader; a selected and introductory bibliographical guide, 1960–1967, compiled by the African Bibliographic Center for the Council of the African-American Institute. New York, Council of the African-American Institute ⟨1967⟩

III, 210 p. 29 cm. (Its Special bibliographic series, v. 5, no. 4)

African Bibliographic Center.
The new Afro-Asian states in perspective, 1960–1963; a select bibliography. Washington, 1965.

20 p. (incl. cover) 28 cm. (Its Special bibliographic series, v. 3, no. 1)

Cover title.

African Bibliographic Center.
News. v. 1–
June 1972–
⟨Washington⟩

v. illus. 28 cm. bimonthly.

African Bibliographic Center.
Rural development in Africa. ⟨Compiled by Anita Rhett⟩ Washington, 1972.

vii, 120 p. 28 cm. (Current reading list series, v. 9, no. 2)

Africana bulletin. 1–
1964–
⟨Warsaw⟩

no. maps. 24 cm. (Wydawnictwa Uniwersytetu Warszawskiego)

English or French.
Issued by the Center of African Studies, University of Warsaw.

Africana catalogue. 1–
New York, International University Booksellers, inc., Africana Center.

v. 26 cm. quarterly.

First catalogue covers Jan. 1967/Oct. 1968.

Africana library journal. v. 1
spring 1970–
⟨New York, Africana Pub. Corp.⟩

v. 28 cm. quarterly.

Akademiia nauk SSSR. *Institut Afriki.*
Библиография Африки; дореволюционная и советская литература на русском языке, оригинальная и переводная. ⟨Составители: С. Л. Милявская и И. Е. Синицына⟩ Москва, Наука, 1964–

v. 22 cm.

On leaf preceding t. p., v. 1– : Академия наук СССР. Институт Африки. Фундаментальная библиотека общественных наук.

Baltimore Co., Md. Public Library.
Africa; a selected, annotated bibliography. Prepared for the Board of Education of Baltimore County, Adult Education Dept. ⟨Towson, Md.⟩ 1964.

44 l. 29 cm.

Bederman, Sanford Harold, 1932–
A bibliographic aid to the study of the geography of Africa: a selected listing of recent literature published in the English language [by] Sanford H. Bederman. [Atlanta] Bureau of Business and Economic Research, Georgia State University, 1970.

ix, 212 p. 28 cm.

Bederman, Sanford Harold, 1932–
A bibliographic aid to the study of the geography of Africa: a selected listing of recent literature published in the English language [by] Sanford H. Bederman. 2d ed. [Atlanta] Bureau of Business and Economic Research, Georgia State University, 1972.

xi, 287 p. 28 cm.

Bloomfield, Barry Cambray.
Africa in the contemporary world; compiled in the Library of the School of Oriental & African Studies by B. C. Bloomfield and Malcolm McKee. London, Published for National Library Week by the National Book League, 1967.

30 p. 22 cm.

Boston University. *African Studies Program.*
Selected African bibliographies: Cameroun, Gabon, Ivory Coast, Morocco, Rwanda and Burundi [and] Tunisia. Prepared for the Agency for International Development [by] Édouard Bustin, Elaine Hagopian, and John Sommer. Boston, 1964.

1 v. (various pagings) 28 cm.

Bridgman, Jon.
German Africa: a select annotated bibliography, by Jon Bridgman and David E. Clarke. [Stanford, Calif.] Hoover Institution on War, Revolution, and Peace, Stanford University, 1965.

ix, 120 p. 26 cm. (Hoover Institution bibliographical series, 19)

Cercle français du livre.
L'Afrique. Nouv. éd. Paris [1965]

237 l. 13 x 21 cm.

Chiang, Lu-yü, 1915–

(Kuan yü Fei-chou chi ch'i hsin hsing kuo chia) 關於非洲及其新興國家書籍的評介　江赦煜著 [臺中] 東海大學圖書館 [1964]

18 p. 27 cm.

Cover title.
Summary in English, with title: An annotated bibliography on Africa and its emergent nations.

Dargitz, Robert E
A selected bibliography of books and articles in the Disciples of Christ Research Library in Mbandaka, Democratic Republic of the Congo and the Department of Africa and Jamaica of the United Christian Missionary Society in Indianapolis, Indiana. Une bibliographie choisie des livres et des articles dans la Bibliotheque de Recherche des Disciples du Christ a Mbandaka dans la Republique democratique du Congo, et au Departement d'Afrique et de Jamaique de l'United Christian Missionary Society a Indianapolis, Indiana. Compiled by Robert E. Dargitz. Indianapolis, Dept. of Africa and Jamaica, United Christian Missionary Society [1967?]

431 p. 29 cm.
English and French.

Davis, Lenwood G
Pan-Africanism; a selected bibliography. Compiled by Lenwood G. Davis. Portland, Or. [1972]

ii, 49 l. 28 cm.

French & European Publications, inc.
Afro writers: bibliography of recent works in French. New York [1971]

35 p. 22 cm.

Georgetown, Guyana. Public Library.
Africa: catalogue of a book exhibition. November 6–11, 1967. [Georgetown] Guyana Group for Social Studies, 1967.

74 p. 28 cm.

Gutkind, Peter Claus Wolfgang.
A select bibliography on traditional and modern Africa. Compiled by Peter C. W. Gutkind and John B. Webster. Syracuse. N. Y., Bibliographic Section, Program of Eastern African Studies. Syracuse University, 1968.

xiv, 323 l. 28 cm. (Program of Eastern African Studies. Occasional bibliography no. 8)

Harvey, Joan M
Statistics Africa: sources for market research [by] Joan M. Harvey. Beckenham (Kent), C. B. D. Research Ltd, 1970.

iii–xii, 175 p. 30 cm.

Leyden. Rijksuniversiteit. *Afrika-Studiecentrum.*
Documentatieblad. 1.–
jaarg.; [jan.] 1968–
Leiden.

v. 30 cm. monthly.

Liniger-Goumaz, Max.
Eurafrique: bibliographie générale. Genève, Éditions du Temps, 1970.

160 p. 24 cm.

London. Commonwealth Institute.
The Commonwealth in Africa: an annotated list. London, National Book League, 1969.

[2], 59 p. 22 cm.

Meulen, J　　　　van der.
Literatuurlijst over Afrika. Door J. van der Meulen en S. M. S. Philipse. [Voorburg, Prisma-Lectuurvoorlichting (Parkweg 20A), 1970].

48 p. 26 cm.

Osomor, Tibor.
Afrika; bibliográfia. Budapest, Fővárosi Szabó Ervin Könyvtár, 1968.

391 p. 19 cm.

Polski Instytut Spraw Międzynarodowych, *Warsaw. Zakład Krajów Afryki.*
Bibliografia polskich publikacji na temat Afryki. Opracowali Maciej Koźmiński i Jan Milewski. Warszawa, 1965.
3 v. 29 cm.
At head of title: Polski Instytut Spraw Międzynarodowych. Zakład Krajów Afryki. Zakład Informacji Naukowej i Dokumentacji.
"Na prawach rękopisu."
———— Index. Warszawa, 1965.
55 p. 29 cm.

Quarterly bulletin of African materials. v. 1–
Mar. 1972–
[Boston, Mass.] African Studies Center, Development Pro-

gram, Boston University.

v. 28 cm.

Rosenblum, Paul.
Checklist of paperbound books on Africa. Compiled under the auspices of the University of the State of New York, State Education Dept. ₁New York₎ Reproduced by African Studies Association ₁1964–65₎

2 v. 28 cm.

CONTENTS.—₁1₎ In print February 1964.—₁2₎ In print September 1965.

Rosenblum, Paul.
Checklist of paperbound books on Africa (in print September 1965) Compiled under the auspices of the University of the State of New York, State Education Dept. Albany, Distributed in cooperation with African Studies Association ₁1966?₎

34 p. 28 cm.

Cover title.
"Based largely on the June 1965 edition of Paperbound books in print."

Sommer, John W.
Bibliography of African geography, 1940–1964, by John W. Sommer. ₁Hanover, N. H., Dartmouth College, Dept. of Geography₎ 1965.

viii, 139 p. 28 cm. (Geography publications at Dartmouth, no. 3)

Spohr, Otto H
Recent indexes to Africana books, compiled by O. H. Spohr for South African Library Association, Bibliographical Committee. ₁Cape Town₎ O. H. Spohr, "Hillrise", Cecil Road, Rosebank, 1967.

9 p. 24 cm.

United States. Dept. of the Army. Army Library.
Africa : a bibliographic survey of literature. — ₁Washington₎ : Headquarters, Dept. of the Army, 1973.

xiv, 545 p. : maps (1 fold. col. in pocket) ; 27 cm.

"DA pamphlet 550–17."
Cover title.
Published in 1962 under title: Africa: its problems and prospects and in 1967 under title: Africa: problems & prospects.

U. S. *Dept. of the Army. Army Library.*
Africa: problems & prospects; a bibliographic survey. ₁Washington₎ 1967.

x, 226 p. col. maps (1 fold. in pocket) 26 cm.

"DA pam 550–5."
Cover title.
"Supersedes DA pam 20–62, 27 September 1962."

U. S. *Library of Congress. European Affairs Division.*
Introduction to Africa; a selective guide to background reading. ₁Prepared by Helen F. Conover₎ New York, Negro Universities Press ₁1969₎

ix, 230 p. map. 27 cm.

Reprint of the 1952 ed.

Venys, Ladislav.
A select bibliography of Soviet publications on Africa in general and Eastern Africa in particular, 1962–1966. Syracuse, N. Y., Bibliographic Section, Program of Eastern African Studies, Syracuse University, 1968.

iv, 125 l. 28 cm. (Program of Eastern African Studies. Occasional bibliography no. ₁11₎)

——— ———— Supplement 1 (1967)-
Syracuse, N. Y., Bibliographic Section, Program of East-

ern African Studies, Syracuse University, 1968–
v. 28 cm. (Program of Eastern African Studies. Occasional bibliography, no. 14, 16,   20

Supplement 1 (1967) compiled by Vlastimila Venys.

Wallenius, Anna-Britta, 1918–
Africana Scandinavica, 1960–1968. Books on Africa published in Denmark, Finland, Norway and Sweden. A selected bibliography compiled by Anna-Britta Wallenius. ₁Publ. by₎ the Scandinavian institute of Africa studies. Uppsala, Afrika Institutet. ₁Solna, Seelig₎, 1971.

(8), 104 p. 21 cm.

English or Swedish.

Wisconsin. University—Madison. Land Tenure Center. Library.
Rural development in Africa: a bibliography. Madison, 19– 17.

v. 28 cm. (Training & methods series, no.   –17)
CONTENTS :
—pt. 2. North, South, West.

——————— Supplement 1–   Madison, 1973–
v. in   28 cm. (Training & methods series, no. 16–17, suppl. 1–)

Žižiūnaitė, V
Afrikos šalys. Rekomenduojamosios literatūros rodyklė. Vilnius, 1969.

138 p. with illus. 21 cm. (Pažinkime užsienio šalis)

At head of title: Lietuvos TSR Valystybine respublikne biblioteka. V. Zizlunaite.

BIBLIOGRAPHIES

Brasseur, Paule.
Les sources bibliographiques de l'Afrique de l'ouest et de l'Afrique équatoriale d'expression française ₁par₎ Paule Brasseur ₁et₎ Jean-François Maurel. ₁Dakar, Bibliothèque de l'Université de Dakar, 1970₎

87 p. 21 cm.

Garling, Anthea.
Bibliography of African bibliographies. Cambridge, African Studies Centre, ₁1968₎.

1 v. ₁4₎, 138 p. on publication. 28 cm. (African Studies Centre. Occasional papers, no. 1)

Loose-leaf.

BIOGRAPHY

Oslo. Norske Nobelinstitutt. *Biblioteket.*
Biografier i Nobelinstituttets bibliotek. En bibliografi. Afrikanere. Oslo, 1966.

4 l. 30 cm.

DIRECTORIES

Anderson, Ian Gibson.
Current African directories, incorporating "African companies—a guide to sources of information": a guide to directories published in or relating to Africa, and to sources of information on business enterprises in Africa ₁by₎ I. G. Anderson. Beckenham, CBD Research Ltd, 1972.

iii–xii, 187 p. 31 cm.

GOVERNMENT PUBLICATIONS

Boston University. *Libraries.*
Catalog of African government documents and African area index. Compiled by Mary Darrah Herrick. 2d ed., rev. and enl. Boston, G. K. Hall, 1964.

471 p. 27 cm.

Staatsbibliothek der Stiftung Preussischer Kulturbesitz.
Catalogue of African official publications available in European libraries as of 1 May 1971, compiled by the Staatsbibliothek Preussischer Kulturbesitz. Berlin, International Federation of Library Associations, Committee for Official Publications, 1971.

vii, 251 p. 30 cm.

HISTORY

Guide to the sources of the history of the nations. B. Africa. Guide des sources de l'histoire des nations. B. Afrique. Zug, Inter Documentation [c1970–

v. 21 cm.

At head of title: International Council on Archives.

Matthews, Daniel G
Current themes in African historical studies; a selected bibliographical guide to resources for research in African history. Daniel G. Matthews, editor. Westport, Conn., Negro Universities Press [°1970]

vi, 389 p. 26 cm. (African Bibliographic Center. Special bibliographic series, v. 7, no. 2)

Nersesov, G   A
Soviet literature on the history of the African countries for the period 1965–1969 [by] G. A. Nersesov. Moscow, "Nauka" Pub. House, Central Dept. of Oriental Literature, 1970.

18 p. 21 cm. (Studies by Soviet historians for the period 1965–1969)

"XIII International Congress of Historical Sciences, Moscow, 16–23 August, 1970."
Includes bibliographical references in Russian and English.

Oxford. University. *Rhodes House Library.*
Manuscript collections of Africana in Rhodes House Library, Oxford; compiled by Louis B. Frewer, Superintendent of the Library. Oxford, Bodleian Library, 1968.

100 p. 25 cm.

JUVENILE LITERATURE

Africa; an annotated list of printed materials suitable for children, selected and annotated by a Joint Committee of the American Library Association, Children's Services Division, and the African-American Institute. [New York] Information Center on Children's Cultures, 1968.

iv, 76 p. 23 cm.

Johnson, James Peter, 1929–
Africana for children and young people; a current guide for teachers and librarians, compiled by James P. Johnson. Westport, Conn., Greenwood Periodicals Co. [c1971]

172 p. 26 cm. (African Bibliographic Center. Special bibliographic series, v. 8, no. 1)

Sewitz, Maureen Beatrice.
Children's books in English in an African setting, 1914–1964; a bibliography. Johannesburg, University of Witwatersrand, Dept. of Bibliography, Librarianship, and

Typography, 1965.

vi, 89 l. 30 cm.

Tigers' in the classroom; an annotated bibliography of books about Africa available for Canadian school children. Edited by J. Bilesky [and others] With foreword by P. Bartle. [Vancouver, B. C. Teachers' Federation] 1970.

iii, 99 p. 28 cm.

Prepared by "Anthropology 200" students at the University of British Columbia in 1969–70.

LAW   see   Law - Africa

LIBRARY CATALOGS

Ghana. University, Legon. Library.
Early Africana (1556–1900) in the Balme Library. Legon, 1972.

70 p. 34 cm.

Harvard University. *Library.*
Africa: classification schedule, classified listing by call number, alphabetical listing by author or title, chronological listing. Cambridge, Published by the Harvard University Library; distributed by the Harvard University Press, 1965.

302, 204, 196 p. 29 cm. (*Its* Widener Library shelflist, no. 2)

Harvard University. Library.
African history and literatures: classification schedule, classified listing by call number, chronological listing, author and title listing. Cambridge, Mass.; distributed by Harvard University Press, 1971.

600 p. 29 cm. (Harvard University. Library. Widener Library shelflist, 34)

Ibadan, Nigeria. University. Library.
Africana catalogue of the Ibadan University Library, Ibadan, Nigeria. Boston, Mass., G. K. Hall, 1973.

2 v. (v, 1605 p.) 37 cm.

International African Institute. Library.
Cumulative bibliography of African studies; author catalogue. Boston, Mass., G. K. Hall, 1973.

2 v. 37 cm.

International African Institute. Library.
Cumulative bibliography of African studies; classified catalogue. Boston, Mass., G. K. Hall, 1973.

3 v. 37 cm.

Melville J. Herskovits Library of African Studies.
Catalog of the Melville J. Herskovits Library of African Studies, Northwestern University Library (Evanston, Illinois) and Africana in selected libraries. Boston, G. K. Hall, 1972.

8 v. 36 cm.

Edition of 1962 (2 v.) by the Northwestern University Library, published under title: Catalog of the African collection.

Paris. Bibliothèque nationale. Département des imprimés.
Catalogue de l'histoire de l'Afrique. Paris, Bibliothèque nationale, 1969.

iv, 312 p. 28 cm.

"Reproduction de l'édition de 1895."—Bibl. de la Fr.

Paris. Bibliothèque nationale. Département des imprimés.
Catalogue de l'histoire de l'Afrique. New York, B. Franklin [1971]

308 p. 32 cm. (Burt Franklin bibliography and reference series, 412. Sources of Negro history and culture, 5)

Reprint of the 1895 ed.

Paris. Musée de l'homme. *Bibliothèque.*
Catalogue systématique de la section Afrique. Boston, G. K. Hall, 1970.

2 v. 37 cm.

Added t. p. in English: Classified catalog of the Africa section.

CONTENTS.—v. 1. Afrique en général—Mozambique.—v. 2. Isles de l'océan Indien en général—Afrique préhistorique.

MAPS

Kašparová, Marta.
Soupis map a atlasů afrických zemí uložených v ČSSR. Sest. M. Kašparová—J. Mojdl. Předml.: Ctibor Votrubec. Brno, Geografický ústav ČSAV, 1968.

97, [1] l. 28 cm. (Rozvojové země, sv. 10)

At head of title: Československá akademie věd. Geografický ústav v Brně. Výzkumný ústav geodetický, topografický a kartografický.
Introduction also in English.

Tooley, Ronald Vere, 1898–
Collectors' guide to maps of the African continent and southern Africa, by R. V. Tooley. London, Carta P., 1969.

xvi, 132 p. 100 plates, illus., maps (part col.), ports. 26 cm.

Tooley, Ronald Vere, 1898–
Maps of Africa, a selection of printed maps from the sixteenth to the nineteenth centuries, by R. V. Tooley. London, Map Collectors' Circle, 1968.

2 v. maps. 25 cm. (Map Collectors' Circle. Map collectors' series, no. 47, 48)

Tooley, Ronald Vere, 1898–
The printed maps of the continent of Africa and regional maps south of the Tropic of Cancer, 1500–1900, by R. V. Tooley. London, Map Collectors' Circle, 1966–

v. maps. 25 cm. (Map collectors' series, no. 29–

CONTENTS. — pt. 1. 1500–1600. — pt. 2. 1500–1600. Regional maps south of the Tropic of Cancer.

PERIODICALS

Michigan. State University, *East Lansing. Library.*
Research sources for African studies; a checklist of relevant serial publications based on library collections at Michigan State University, by Eugene de Benko [and] Patricia L. Butts. [East Lansing] African Studies Center, Michigan State University, 1969.

vii, 384 p. 23 cm.

Nordiska Afrikainstitutet. *Biblioteket.*
Periodica i Nordiska Afrikainstitutets bibliotek. Sammanställd av Anna-Britta Wallenius. Uppsala, Nordiska Afrikainstitutet, 1966.

21 l. 30 cm.

Nordiska Afrikainstitutet. *Biblioteket.*
Periodica i Nordiska Afrikainstitutets bibliotek. Periodicals in the library of the Scandinavian institute of African studies. Périodiques dans la bibliotheque de l'Institut scandinave des études africaines. [Ny uppl.] 1.1.1968.

Uppsala, Institutet, 1968.

(5), 86 p. 30 cm.

POLITICS AND GOVERNMENT

Africa Research Group.
Radical study group. [Cambridge, Mass., 1969?]

38 p. illus. 28 cm.

Alderfer, Harold Freed, 1903–
A bibliography of African government, 1950–1964, prepared by Harold F. Alderfer. [Lincoln University, Pa., 1964?]

119 l. 28 cm.

At head of title: Lincoln University, Dept. of Political Science, Lincoln University, Pa.

Alderfer, Harold Freed, 1903–
A bibliography of African government, 1950–1966, by Harold F. Alderfer. [2d rev. ed.] Lincoln University, Pa., Lincoln University Press; [distributed by Livingston Pub. Co., Narberth, Pa., 1967]

163 p. 23 cm.

Alman, Miriam.
Debates of African legislatures; edited by Miriam Alman. Cambridge, Heffer [for] the Standing Conference on Library Materials on Africa, 1972.

xi, 79 p. 25 cm.

Boston University. *African Studies Program.*
Bibliographie sélective des livres, articles, et documentations traitant le sujet des problèmes administratifs africains. A selective bibliography of books, articles, and documents on the subject of African administrative problems. [Prepared by Wilbert J. Le Melle. Boston, 1964]

iii, 51 l. 28 cm.
On cover: Boston University. African Studies Program. Development Research Center.
"The present publication includes ... books in both English and French. ... Special emphasis has been placed on the states of former French Africa."
"Prepared under contract for the Agency for International Development."

Chiang, Lu-yü, 1915–
(Chieh shao Fei-chou hsin hsing kuo chia) 介紹非洲新興國家政府與政治的書籍 江祿煜著 [臺中] 東海大學圖書館 [1969]

14 p. 26 cm.

Cover title.

圖書館學報第 10 期抽印本

Gt. Brit. *Commonwealth Office. Library.*
African military coups. Compiled in the Library of the Commonwealth Office. London [1966]

[5] l. 34 cm.

McGowan, Patrick J
African politics; a guide to research resources, methods, and literature, by Patrick J. McGowan. [Syracuse, Program of Eastern African Studies, Syracuse University, 1970.

85, A45 l. 28 cm. (Syracuse University. Program of Eastern African Studies. Occasional paper no. 55)

Shaw, Robert Baldwin, 1945–
A bibliography for the study of African politics, by Robert B. Shaw and Richard L. Sklar. Los Angeles, African Studies Center, University of California, 1973.

x, 206 p. 28 cm. (University of California. African Studies Center. Occasional paper no. 9)

Africa index: Selected articles on socio-economic development. Catalogue Afrique: Articles choisis sur le développement économique et social. no. 1–
Apr. 1971–
[New York]
    v. 28 cm. quarterly. (United Nations. [Document] E/CN.14/LIB/ser. E/1)
    Issued by the Library of the United Nations Economic Commission for Africa.

アフリカの経済開発 [東京] アジア経済研究所
昭和39 [1964]

    iv, 221 p. 21 cm. (文献解題シリーズ 第6集)
    アジア経済研究所出版物 通巻第841号

Bouhdiba, Abdelwahab.
    La sociologie du développement africain; tendances actuelles de la recherche et bibliographie. Établi pour l'Association internationale de sociologie sous les auspices du Comité international pour la documentation des sciences sociales. La Haye, Mouton, 1971.
    102 p. 23 cm. (La Sociologie contemporaine, v. 18, no. 2)
    Includes summary in English.

Irvine, S   H
    Human behaviour in Africa: a bibliography of psychological & related writings, edited by S. H. Irvine, J. T. Sanders and E. L. Klingelhofer. [London, Ont., 1970?]
    vii, 174 p. 28 cm.

Irvine, S   H
    Human behavior in Africa: a bibliography of psychological and related writings. Compiled by S. H. Irvine, J. T. Sanders [and] E. L. Klingelhofer. Westport, Conn., Greenwood Press [1973]
    xxvi, 344 p. 26 cm. (African Bibliographic Center. Special bibliographic series, v. 8, no. 2)

Mortimer, Delores M
    Economic cooperation and regional integration in Africa. [Compiled by Delores M. Mortimer, Gita Rao, and Sandra Ann Howell] Washington, African Bibliographic Center [1973]
    vi, 49 p. 28 cm. (Current reading list series, v. 10, no. 6)

Mortimer, Delores M
    Implementation & administration of development activities in Africa. [Compiled by Delores M. Mortimer (project researcher), and research assistants: Gita Rao and Anita M. Rhett] Washington, African Bibliographic Center, 1973.
    vi, 68 p. 28 cm. (Current reading list series, v. 10, no. 8)

Mortimer, Delores M
    Population problems in Africa. [Compiled by Delores M. Mortimer and research assistants: Gita Rao and Anita M. Rhett] Washington, African Bibliographic Center, 1973.
    vi, 71 p. 28 cm. (Current reading list series, v. 10, no. 7)
    Cover title.
    Verso of cover has title: Population studies on Africa: social, cultural, and attitudinal factors.

Tamuno, Olufunmilayo G
    A bibliography of economic integration in Africa, compiled by Olufunmilayo G. Tamuno. Ibadan, Nigerian Institute of Social and Economic Research, 1968.
    vii, 23 p. 26 cm.
    Photocopy of type-script.

Tamuno, Olufunmilayo G
    Co-operation for development; a bibliography on inter-state relations in economic, technical, and cultural fields in Africa, 1950–1968, compiled by Olufunmilayo G. Tamuno. Ibadan, Nigerian Institute of Social and Economic Research, 1969.
    xx, 113 p. 25 cm.

United Nations. Economic Commission for Africa.
    Bibliography: economic and social development plans of African countries. Bibliographie: plans de développement économique et social des pays africains. [New York] 1968.
    ii, 40 p. 28 cm. ([United Nations. Document] E/CN.14/LIB/ser.C/4)
    Cover title.

AFRICA, EAST

Baumhögger, Goswin.
    Grundzüge der Geschichte und politischen Entwicklung Ostafrikas: Eine Einf. an Hand d. neueren Literatur./ Von Goswin Baumhögger. Ifo-Inst. f. Wirtschaftsforschung, München. — München: Weltforum-Verlag 1971.
    156 p.; 30 cm.
    Enlarged and rev. version of the author's article "Die Geschichte Ostafrikas im Spiegel der neueren Literatur" originally published in "Wissenschaft und Unterricht," Heft 11–12, 1971.

Kasfir, Nelson.
    Bibliography on administration in East Africa, by Nelson Kasfir and Timothy M. Shaw. Kampala, Uganda, Dept. of Political Science and Public Administration, Makerere University College, 1968.
    26 l. 34 cm.

Mezger, Dorothea.
    Wirtschaftswissenschaftliche Veröffentlichungen über Ostafrika in englischer Sprache; eine Bibliographie des neueren englisch-sprachigen Schrifttums mit Inhaltsangaben, von Dorothea Mezger [und] Eleonore Littich. München, 1967.
    3 v. (357, xxvi l.) 30 cm.
    At head of title: IFO-Institut für Wirtschaftforschung, München. Afrika-Studienstelle.

Molnos, Angela.
    Development in Africa: planning and implementation: a bibliography (1946–1969) and outline with some emphasis on Kenya, Tanzania, and Uganda. [Nairobi] East African Academy, Research Information Centre, 1970.
    vi, 120 p. 33 cm. (East African Academy. Research Information Centre. Information circular no. 8)

Molnos, Angela.
    Die sozialwissenschaftliche Erforschung Ostafrikas 1954–1963 (Kenya, Tanganyika/Sansibar, Uganda) Berlin, New York, Springer-Verlag, 1965.
    xv, 304 p. 2 fold. maps. 24 cm. (Afrika-Studien, Nr. 5)
    At head of title: IFO-Institut für Wirtschaftsforschung. Afrika-Studienstelle.

Rogers, M   H
    Report on a tour of East Africa, July–August, 1966, by M. H. Rogers. [Brighton, Library, University of Sussex, 1967]
    i, 97 l. 28 cm.
    Sponsored by the School of African and Asian Studies, University of Sussex.

BIBLIOGRAPHIES

Molnos, Angela.
    Sources for the study of East African cultures and de-

velopment; a bibliography of social scientific bibliographies, abstracts, reference works, catalogues, directories, writings on archieves, bibliographies, book production, libraries, and museums. With special reference to Kenya, Tanzania, and Uganda. 1946–1966 (1967–1968) ₍Nairobi₎ East African Research Information Centre, 1968.

iv, 54 p. 34 cm. (EARIC information circular no. 1)

———————Area, ethnic, and subject indices. ₍Nairobi?₎ 1969.

26 p. 33 cm.

AFRICA, EASTERN

Morton, Rodger F
Microfilms relating to Eastern Africa; a guide to recent acquisitions of Syracuse University ₍by₎ Rodger F. Morton ₍and₎ Harvey Soff. ₍Syracuse, N. Y.₎ Program of Eastern African Studies, Syracuse University, 1971–

v. 28 cm. (₍Syracuse University. Program of Eastern African Studies. Bibliographic Section₎ Occasional bibliography no. 19, 21

CONTENTS: pt. 1. Morton, R. F. and Soff, H. Kenya, miscellaneous.—pt. 2. Leigh, D. and Morton, R. F. Kenya, Asian, and miscellaneous.

U. S. *Library of Congress. Library of Congress Office, Nairobi.*
Accessions list, Eastern Africa. v. 1–
Jan. 1968–
Nairobi.

v. 28 cm. quarterly.

At head of title, 1968–   : The Library of Congress National Program for Acquisitions and Cataloging.

AFRICA, FRENCH-SPEAKING EQUATORIAL

France. *Institut national de la statistique et des études économiques. Service de coopération.*
Bibliographie démographique (1945–1964). Travaux publiés par l'I. N. S. E. E. (Service de coopération), les services de statistique des États africains d'expression française ou de Madagascar et le Ministère de la coopération. Paris, l'Institut, 1965.

36 l. 27 cm.

U. S. *Library of Congress. African Section.*
Official publications of French Equatorial Africa, French Cameroons, and Togo, 1946–1958; ₍a guide₎ compiled by Julian W. Witherell, African Section. Washington, General Reference and Bibliography Division, Reference Dept., Library of Congress; ₍for sale by the Superintendent of Documents, U. S. Govt. Print. Off.₎ 1964.

xi, 78 p. 27 cm.

Witherell, Julian W
French-speaking central Africa; a guide to official publications in American libraries, compiled by Julian W. Witherell, African Section. Washington, General Reference and Bibliography Division, Library of Congress; ₍for sale by the Supt. of Docs., U. S. Govt. Print. Off.₎ 1973.
xiv, 314 p. 26 cm.

AFRICA, FRENCH-SPEAKING WEST

France. *Institut national de la statistique et des études économiques. Service de coopération.*
Bibliographie demographique 1945–1967. Travaux publiés par l'I. N. S. E. E. (Service de la coopération), les services de statistique des États africains d'expression française ou de Madagascar, et le Ministère de la Coopération. Paris, 1967.

67 p. 27 cm.

Witherell, Julian W
French-speaking West Africa; a guide to official publications. compiled by Julian W. Witherell, African Section. Washington, General Reference and Bibliography Division, Library of Congress; ₍for sale by the Supt. of Docs., U. S. Govt. Print. Off.₎ 1967.

xii, 201 p. 26 cm.

AFRICA, NORTH

Inventario delle fonti manoscritte relative alla storia dell'Africa del Nord esistenti in Italia. Sotto la direzione di Carlo Giglio. Istituto di storia ed istituzioni dei paesi afro-asiatici della Università di Pavia. Leiden, Brill, 1971–

v. 25 cm.

CONTENTS: v. 1. Gli archivi storici del soppresso Ministero dell'Africa italiana e del Ministero degli affari esteri dalle origini al 1922.—v. 2. Gli archivi storici del Ministero della difesa (Esercito, Marina, Aeronautica).

Tangier. African Training and Research Centre in Administration for Development. Documentation Centre.
Bibliography on Maghreb. Bibliographie sur le Maghreb. Tanger, 1971.

24 l. 27 cm.

U. S. *Library of Congress. General Reference and Bibliography Division.*
North and Northeast Africa; a selected, annotated list of writings, 1951–1957. Compiled by Helen F. Conover. New York, Greenwood Press ₍1968₎
v, 182 p. 27 cm.
Reprint of the 1957 ed.
"Bibliography on North and Northeast Africa completes the survey of writings on that continent during the past six years, of which the first part, Africa South of the Sahara, was published in June 1957. The two lists are supplementary to the … publication of 1952, Introduction to Africa."

AFRICA, PORTUGUESE   see   Portugal - Colonies

AFRICA, SOUTH

Africa Bureau, *London.*
A bibliography of recent pamphlets on South Africa and Rhodesia. London ₍1967₎
7 l. 33 cm.

Both, Ellen Lisa Marianne.
Catalogue of books and pamphlets published in German relating to South Africa and South West Africa, as found in the South African Public Library published between 1950–1964. Cape Town, University of Cape Town Libraries, 1969.

₍x₎, 132 p. 23 cm. (University of Cape Town. School of Librarianship. Bibliographical series)

Cape Town. University of Cape Town. *Library.*
Handlist of manuscripts in the University of Cape Town Libraries, comp. by Gerald D. Quinn and Otto H. Spohr; ed. by R. F. M. Immelman. Cape Town, University of Cape Town Libraries, 1968–

v. illus. 23 cm. (*Its* Varia series, no. 10)

Cape Town. University of Capetown. *School of Librarianship.*
Bibliographical series: consolidated list, 1941–1900. Cape Town, Univ. of Cape Town Libraries, 1966.

88 p. 23 cm.

Cox, Katheleen Mae.
Immigration into South Africa 1940–1967; a bibliography. Cape Town, University of Cape Town Libraries, 1970.

[x] 26 p. 24 cm. (University of Cape Town. School of Librarianship. Bibliographical series).

"Presented in partial fulfilment of the requirements for the Higher Certificate in Librarianship, 1968."

Grivainis, Ilze.
Material published after 1925 on the Great Trek until 1854; a bibliography. Cape Town, University of Cape Town, School of Librarianship, 1967.

vii, 63 p. 23 cm.

Hodge, Gillian M   M
South African politics, 1933–1939; a select bibliography, compiled by Gillian M. M. Hodge. [Cape Town] School of Librarianship, University of Cape Town, 1965.

94 p. 23 cm. ([Cape Town] University of Cape Town. School of Librarianship. Bibliographical series)

Muller, C   F   J   ed.
A select bibliography of South African history; a guide for historical research, edited by C. F. J. Muller, F. A. van Jaarsveld and Theo van Wijk. Pretoria, University of South Africa, 1966.

xii, 215 p. 25 cm. (Communications of the University of South Africa, D. 3)

Musiker, Reuben.
Guide to South African reference books. 4th rev. ed. Cape Town, A. A. Balkema, 1965.

x, 110 p. 25 cm. (Balkema academic and technical publications)
Errata and addenda slips inserted.

Musiker, Reuben.
Guide to South African reference books. 5th rev. ed. Cape Town, A. A. Balkema, 1971, [c1965]

viii, 136 p. 23 cm. (Balkema academic and technical publications)

Pretoria. State Library.
Bibliografie van buitelandse publikasies oor Suid-Afrika; insluitende publikasies van Suid-Afrikaners en vertalings van Suid-Afrikaanse werke in die buiteland uitgegee, 1969–1971. Pretoria, 1973.

ix, 39 p. 26 cm.

Title also in English: Bibliography of overseas publications about South Africa.

Raper, P   E
Naamkunde-Bronnegids, 1970 / [saamgestel deur] P. E. Raper. — Kapstad : Tafelberg-uitgewers vir die S. A. Naamkundesentrum van die Raad vir Geesteswetenskaplike Navorsing, 1972–
v. ; 23 cm. — (Naamkundereeks ; nr. 2   )
Title also in English: Onomastics source guide, 1970.
Afrikaans and English.
Previous ed. by P. J. Nienaber published in 1947–   under title: Bronnegids by die studie van die Afrikaanse taal en letterkunde.

South Africa. Dept. of Cultural Affairs. Division of Library Services.
Africana; select bibliography of the Frederick Wagener and E. G. Jansen collections. Pretoria, the Department, 1970.

[v] 35 l. 30 cm.

English and Afrikaans.

Spohr, Otto H   comp.
German Africana; German publications on South- and South West Africa, compiled and indexed by Otto H. Spohr, assisted by Manfred R. Poller. Pretoria, State Library, 1968.

xiv, 332 p. 24 cm. (Pretoria. State Library. Bibliografieë, No. 14)

Tötemeyer, Gerhard.
Südafrika, Südwestafrika; eine Bibliographie. 1945–1963. South Africa, South West Africa; a bibliography. Freiburg i. Br. [Rota Druck J. Krause] 1964.

284 p. 21 cm. (Materiallen des Arnold-Bergstraesser-Instituts für Kulturwissenschaftliche Forschung)

BIBLIOGRAPHIES

Musiker, Reuben.
South African bibliography; a survey of bibliographies and bibliographical work. Hamden, Conn., Archon Books [1970]

105 p. 23 cm.

Musiker, Reuben.
South African bibliography: a survey of bibliographies & bibliographical work. London, Lockwood, 1970.

[1], 105 p. 23 cm. index. (New librarianship series)

IMPRINTS

Books South Africa: a selection from the books issued during the first ten years of the Republic of South Africa. Boeke Suid-Afrika: 'n Keur uit die boeke wat gedurende die eerste tien jaar van die Republiek van Suid-Afrika uitgegee is, [by the] Festival Book Committee. Cape Town: the Festival Book Committee, 1971.

[vii] 70 p. illus. 30 cm.

Cover title: 1961–1971: Books South Africa.
Afrikaans and English.

Johannesburg. Public Library.
South African printing, 1800–1968; an exhibition of a publication of each year. Suid-afrikaanse drukwerk, 1800–1968; 'n uitstalling van 'n uitgawe van elke jaar. Johannesburg, the Library, 1968.

vi, 64, 8 l. 26 cm.

Exhibition September 16–October 5, 1968.
English and Afrikaans.

RACE QUESTION

Kaplan, Beverley Berkah.
Race relations in South Africa, as illustrated by the writings of A. W. Hoernlé, R. F. A. Hoernlé and J. D. Rheinallt Jones; a bibliography. Johannesburg, University of the Witwatersrand, Dept. of Bibliography, Librarianship and Typography, 1971.

vii. 59 p. 29 cm.

Lurie, Angela Shulmith.
Urban Africans in the Republic of South Africa, 1950–1966; a bibliography. Johannesburg, University of the Witwatersrand, Department of Bibliography, Librarianship and Typography, 1969.

[x] 55 p. 29 cm.

Compiled in part fulfilment for the requirements of the Diploma in Librarianship, University of the Witwatersrand.

South African Institute of Race Relations.
Classification of publications issued by the S. A. Institute of Race Relations. Johannesburg, S. A. Institute of Race Relations, 1971.

107 p. 26 cm.

United Nations. Secretariat.
Apartheid; a selective bibliography on the racial policies of the Government of the Republic of South Africa. ₍New York₎ 1970.

57 p. 28 cm. (₍United Nations. Document₎ ST/LIB/22/rev.1)

AFRICA, SOUTHERN

Anderson, Irene.
Rock paintings and petroglyphs of South and Central Africa, 1959–1970; a bibliography. Johannesburg, University of the Witwatersrand, Department of Bibliography, Librarianship and Typography, 1971.

₍vii₎ 25 p. 30 cm.

Abridgement of author's thesis.

Ansari, S
Liberation struggle in Southern Africa; a bibliography of source material, by S. Ansari. Foreword by Basil Davidson. Gurgaon, Indian Documentation Service ₍1972₎

118 p. 22 cm.

Holm, S   Erik.
Bibliography of South African pre- and proto-historic archaeology, by S. E. Holm. Pretoria, Van Schaik, 1966.

xxv, 144 p. 24 cm. (National Council for Social Research. Publication series, no. 16)

Thompson, Leonard Monteath.
Southern African history before 1900: a select bibliography of articles, by Leonard Thompson, Richard Elphick and Inez Jarrick. Stanford, Calif., Hoover Institution Press ₍1971₎

xii, 102 p. 29 cm. (Hoover Institution bibliographical series, 49)

Tooley, Ronald Vere, 1898–
Printed maps of Southern Africa and its parts; catalogue of a collection, described by R. V. Tooley. London, Map Collectors' Circle, 1970.

39 p. maps. 25 cm. (Map collectors' series, no. 61)

AFRICA, SOUTHWEST
    see also under Africa, South

Decalo, Samuel.
South-West Africa, 1960–1968: an introductory bibliography. ₍Kingston, University of Rhode Island, 1968₎

20 l. 28 cm. (Occasional papers in political science no. 5)

De Jager, Theo.
South West Africa. Suidwes-Afrika. Compiled by Theo De Jager. Edited by Brigitte Klaas. Pretoria, State Library, 1964.

216 p. 26 cm. (Pretoria. State Library. Bibliographies, no. 7)

Johanson, K   Peter.
Dokumentation ₍über afrikakundliche Lehrveranstaltungen in Zürich und Bibliographie Südwestafrika 1971, von₎ Johanson, Schlettwein ₍und₎ Vogt. ₍Schwäbisch Gmünd, Afrika-Verlag Der Kreis bei Lempp, 1972₎

76 p. 21 cm. (Mitteilungen der Basler Afrika Bibliographien, Heft 2/3)

Loening, Louise Susanne Ernestine.
A bibliography of the status of South-West Africa up to June 30th, 1951. ₍Cape Town₎ University of Cape Town Libraries, 1969.

iv, 27 p. 23 cm. (University of Cape Town. School of Librarianship. Bibliographical series)

"Presented in partial fulfilment of the requirements for the Higher Certificate in Librarianship, 1951."

Logan, Richard F
Bibliography of South West Africa; geography and related fields, ₍by₎ Richard F. Logan. Windhoek, S. W. A. Scientific Society, 1969.

152 p. 24 cm. (Scientific research in South West Africa, ser. 8)

South West African Scientific Society. Bibliothek.
Vorläufiges Verzeichnis der in der Bibliothek der S. W. A. Wissenschaftlichen Gesellschaft enthaltenen Literatur ueber Sued- und Suedwestafrika. Bearb.: A. Benseler und U. Scholz. Windhoek, 1969.

71 p. 33 cm.

Voigts, Barbara.
South West African imprints, a bibliography. ₍Cape Town₎ University of Capetown, School of Librarianship, 1963 ₍cover 1964₎

iii, 58 p. 23 cm. (University of Cape Town. School of Librarianship. Bibliographical series)

Welch, Florette Jean.
South West Africa: a bibliography. Cape Town, University of Cape Town, School of Librarianship, 1967.

iv, 41 p. 23 cm. (University of Cape Town. School of Librarianship. Bibliographical series)

AFRICA, SUB-SAHARAN

Afrika-Schrifttum. Bibliographie deutschsprachiger wissenschaftlicher Veröffentlichungen über Afrika südlich der Sahara. Literature on Africa. Études sur l'Afrique. (Mitarbeiter: H. Becker ₍u. a.₎ Generalredaktion: Geo T. Mary.) Wiesbaden, Steiner in Kommission (1966–71.)

2 v. 22 cm.

Vol. 2: Index.
Text in English, French and German.

Bogaert, Jozef.
Sciences humaines en Afrique noire. Guide bibliographique. 1945–1965. Bruxelles, Centre de documentation économique et sociale africaine, CEDESA, 1966.

226 p. 22 cm. (Enquêtes bibliographiques, 15)

Botha, Carol, *comp.*
A catalogue of manuscripts and papers in the Killie Campbell Africana collection relating to the African peoples, compiled by Carol Botha. Johannesburg, University of the Witwatersrand, Department of Bibliography, Librarianship and Typography, 1967.

₍viii₎, 85 p. 29 cm.

Cartry, Michel.
L'Afrique au sud du Sahara; guide de recherches par Michel Cartry, avec la collaboration de Bernard Charles. Paris, Fondation nationale des sciences politiques, 1962.

85 l. 27 cm. (Centre d'étude des relations internationales. ₍Publications₎ Série D: Textes et documents, no 3)

Centre d'analyse et de recherche documentaires pour l'Afrique noire, *Paris.*
Afrique noire d'expression française: sciences sociales et

humaines; guide de lecture ₁par le₁ Centre d'analyse et de recherche documentaires pour l'Afrique noire ₁et le₁ Club des lecteurs d'expression française. ₁Paris, 1969?₁

vi, 301 p. maps. 25 cm.

"Bibliographie ... rédigée par Mme M. C. Jacquey ... et par Mlle F. Niellon."

Deregowska, Eva Loft.
Some aspects of social change in Africa south of the Sahara, 1959–66; a bibliography. ₁Lusaka? Zambia, 1967₁

x, 93 p. 25 cm. (University of Zambia. Institute for Social Research. Communication no. 3)

"Originally submitted in part requirement for the University of London Postgraduate Diploma in Librarianship."

Glazier, Kenneth M
Africa south of the Sahara; a select and annotated bibliography, 1958–1963, by Kenneth M. Glazier. ₁Stanford, Calif.₁ Hoover Institution on War, Revolution, and Peace, Stanford University, 1964.

iv, 65 p. 26 cm. (Hoover Institution bibliographical series, 16)

Glazier, Kenneth M
Africa south of the Sahara; a select and annotated bibliography, 1964–1968, by Kenneth M. Glazier. Stanford, Calif., Hoover Institution Press ₁°1969₁

vii, 139 p. 23 cm. (Hoover Institution bibliographical series, 42)

Hanna, William John, 1931–
Politics in black Africa ₁by₁ William John Hanna & Judith Lynne Hanna. ₁East Lansing, Mich., Published by the African Studies Center in cooperation with the Office of International Programs, Michigan State University, 1964₁

vii, 139 p. 23 cm.

International Council on Archives.
España, guía de fuentes para la historia de Africa subsahariana. Zug. Switzerland, Inter Documentation ₁1971₁

x, 210 p. 21 cm. (Guide to the sources of the history of the nations. B: Africa, 2)

Introduction in English, French, and Spanish.
Errata slip inserted.

International Council on Archives.
Quellen zur Geschichte Afrikas südlich der Sahara in den Archiven der Bundesrepublik Deutschland. Zug, Inter Documentation ₁c1970₁

xiv, 126 p. 21 cm. (Guide to the sources of the history of the nations. B: Africa, 1)

This volume comprises "the contributions of the Federal Republic of Germany".
Preface in French; introduction in English, French, and German.

International Council on Archives.
Sources de l'histoire de l'Afrique au sud du Sahara dans les archives et bibliothèques françaises. Zug, Inter Documentation Co. ₁1971–

v. 21 cm. (Guide des sources de l'histoire de l'Afrique, 3

CONTENTS: 1. Archives.

Malengreau, Guy.
Problèmes politiques de l'Afrique; bibliographie sommaire ₁par₁ G. Malengreau, avec la collaboration de P. Demunter. ₁Louvain₁ Institut d'étude des pays en développement ₁1967?₁
58 l. 28 cm.

—— Supplément à la bibliographie sur les problèmes politiques de l'Afrique ₁par₁ G. Malengreau, avec la collabora-

tion de P. Demunter. ₁Louvain₁, Institut d'étude des pays en développement, ₁1968?₁
8 l. 28 cm.

Matthews, Noel.
A guide to manuscripts and documents in the British Isles relating to Africa, compiled by Noel Matthews and M. Doreen Wainwright; edited by J. D. Pearson. London, Oxford University Press, 1971.

xvi, 321 p. 26 cm.

Tervuren, Belgium. Musée royal de l'Afrique centrale.
Catalogus der uitgaven van het Koninklijk Museum voor Midden-Afrika. Catalogue des publications du Musée royal de l'Afrique centrale. ₁Bruxelles₁ 1967.

44 p. 24 cm.

Cover title.

U. S. *Foreign Service Institute. Center for Area and Country Studies.*
Africa, sub-Sahara; a selected functional bibliography. ₁Washington, 1967₁

27 p. 27 cm.

Caption title.

U. S. *Library of Congress. African Section.*
Africa south of the Sahara; a selected, annotated list of writings, compiled by Helen F. Conover, African Section. Washington, General Reference and Bibliography Division, Reference Dept., Library of Congress ₁for sale by the Superintendent of Documents, U. S. Govt. Print. Off.₁ 1963 ₁i. e. 1964₁

vi, 354 p. 26 cm.

Replaces Introduction to Africa; Africa south of the Sahara, 1951–1956.

BIBLIOGRAPHIES

Bogaert, Jozef.
Les sciences humaines et l'Afrique noire au sud du Sahara. Guide bibliographique. Compilé par J. Bogaert. Léopoldville, Éditions de l'Université, 1964.

79 p. 23 cm.

Cover title.
"Extrait de 'Les sciences humaines et l'Afrique à l'Université Lovanium,'₁sic₁ 2. éd. publiée par les soins de Willy Bal, Léopoldville, 1964."

Duignan, Peter.
Guide to research and reference works on Sub-Saharan Africa. Edited by Peter Duignan. Compiled by Helen F. Conover and Peter Duignan. With the assistance of Evelyn Boyce, Liselotte Hofmann ₁and₁ Karen Fung. Stanford, Calif., Hoover Institution Press, Stanford University ₁1971 or 2₁

xiii, 1102 p. 29 cm. (Hoover Institution bibliographical series, 46)

Wepsiec, Jan, 1909–
A checklist of bibliographies and serial publications for studies of Africa south-of-the-Sahara. Chicago ₁University of Chicago₁ 1966.

60 p. 28 cm.

At head of title: The University of Chicago Committee on African Studies.
"Includes publications in the University of Chicago libraries."

PERIODICALS

Maison des sciences de l'homme, Paris. *Service d'échange d'informations scientifiques.*

United States. Library of Congress. African Section.
Africa south of the Sahara; index to periodical literature, 1900–1970. Boston, G. K. Hall, 1971.

4 v. 37 cm.
"Covers primarily material published in the 20th century."
CONTENTS: v. 1. Africa-General-Central Africa.—v. 2. Central African Republic-Ivory Coast.—v. 3. Kenya-Somalia.—v. 4. South Africa-Zambia. Literary index.
———— First supplement. Boston, G. K. Hall, 1973.
lxxvii, 521 p. 37 cm.

U. S. *Library of Congress. African Section.*
Sub-Saharan Africa: a guide to serials. Washington, Library of Congress; ₍for sale by the Supt. of Docs., U. S. Govt. Print. Off.₎ 1970.

xx, 409 p. 27 cm.

Wepsiec, Jan, 1909–
Serial publications on the foreign trade of the countries of Africa south-of-the-Sahara. ₍Waltham, Mass.₎ Research Liaison Committee, African Studies Association ₍1972₎

AFRICA, WEST

Banque centrale des États de l'Afrique de l'Ouest. *Direction des études.*
Une Communauté économique Ouest africaine? ... ₍Paris, Banque centrale des États de l'Afrique de l'Ouest,₎ 1968.

200 p. 21 cm. (Bibliographie B. C. E. A. O. nº 1)

Illustrated cover.
"Références bibliographiques recueillies par la Direction des études de la Banque centrale des États de l'Afrique de l'Ouest."

Carson, Patricia.
Materials for West African history in French archives. London, Athlone P.; distributed by Constable, 1968.

viii, 170 p. 21 cm. (Guide to Materials for West African history in European archives, 4)

Gray, Richard, 1929–
Materials for west African history in Italian archives, by Richard Gray and David Chambers. ₍London₎ University of London, Athlone Press, 1965.

viii, 164 p. 20 cm. (Guides to materials for west African history in European archives, 3)

Selected reading lists for advanced study: Ghana, Sierra Leone, the Gambia.
₍London₎ Commonwealth Institute.

v. 22 cm. annual.
Began in 1967. Cf. Brit. union cat., 1967.

AFRICAN LANGUAGES

Der-Houssikian, Haig.
A bibliography of African linguistics. Edmonton ₍Alta.₎ Champaign ₍Ill.₎ Linguistic Research, Inc. ₍c1972₎

xxx, 96 p. 23 cm. (Current inquiry into language & linguistics. 7)

(I︠A︡zyki Afriki)
Языки Африки. Аннот. библиогр. Москва, "Наука," 1974.

125 p. 21 cm.

At head of title: Академия наук СССР. Институт этнографии имени Н. Н. Миклухо-Маклая.
By D. A. Ol'derogge and others.

Molnos, Angela.
Language problems in Africa: a bibliography (1946–

1967) and summary of the present situation, with special reference to Kenya, Tanzania, and Uganda. ₍Nairobi₎ East African Research Information Centre, 1969.

62 p. 34 cm. (EARIC information circular no. 2)

Murphy, John D 1921–
A bibliography of African languages and linguistics, compiled by John D. Murphy and Harry Goff. Washington, Catholic University of America Press, 1969.

vii, 147 p. 27 cm.

University of Rhodesia. Library.
Catalogue of the C. M. Doke Collection on African Languages in the Library of the University of Rhodesia. Boston, G. K. Hall, 1972.

xxxii, 546 p. front 27 cm. (Its Bibliographical series, no. 2)

AFRICAN LITERATURE
see also under Oriental languages and literature

Abrash, Barbara.
Black African literature in English since 1952; works and criticism. With an introd. by John F. Povey. New York, Johnson Reprint Corp., 1967.

xiv, 92 p. 23 cm.

Africa Centre.
Contemporary African writing, 1967. London, African Centre ₍and₎ the National Book League, 1967.

iv, 48 p. 21 cm.

Baratte-Eno Belinga, Thérèse.
Bibliographie: auteurs africains et malgaches de langue française. Paris, Office de coopération radiophonique, 1965.

50 p. 24 cm.

Baratte-Eno Belinga, Thérèse.
Bibliographie, auteurs africains et malgaches de langue française ₍par₎ Thérèse Baratte-Eno Belinga; avec la collaboration du Service Études et documentation, O. R. T. F.–D. A. E. C., ₍Office de radiodiffusion télévision française -Direction des affaires extérieures et de la coopération₎. 3ᵉ éd. revue et mise à jour. Paris, O. R. T. F.; Paris (38, rue Saint-Sulpice, 75006) 1972.

vi, 124 p. 23 cm.

France. *Office de coopération radiophonique.*
Bibliographie, auteurs africains et malgaches de langue française. Paris, Office de coopération radiophonique, 1965.

52 p. 23 cm.

Herdeck, Donald E 1924–
African authors; a companion to Black African writing, by Donald E. Herdeck. ₍1st ed.₎ Washington, Black Orpheus Press, 1973–

v. illus. 23 cm.

Includes bibliographies.
CONTENTS: v. 1. 1300–1973.

Jahn, Janheinz.
Bibliography of creative African writing ₍by₎ Janheinz Jahn and Claus Peter Dressler. Nendeln, ₍Liechtenstein₎ Kraus-Thomson Organization Ltd., 1971.

xi, 446 p. maps. 23 cm.

English, French, and German.

Jahn, Janheinz.
Bibliography of creative African writing [by] Janheinz Jahn and Claus Peter Dressler. Millwood, N. Y., Kraus-Thomson Organization, 1973.

xl, 446 p. maps. 23 cm.

English, French, and German.

Jahn, Janheinz.
Die neoafrikanische Literatur; Gesamtbibliographie von den Anfängen bis zur Gegenwart. [1. Aufl. Düsseldorf] E. Diederichs [1965]

xxxv, 359 p. map. 22 cm.

Pref. in German, English, and French.

Художественная литература стран Африки на европейских языках (книги); библиография. [Составители: Ф. Брескина и др.] Москва, 1967.

52 p. 22 cm.

At head of title: Академия наук СССР. Институт Африки.

Moser, Gerald M 1915–
A tentative Portuguese-African bibliography: Portuguese literature in Africa and African literature in the Portuguese language, by Gerald M. Moser. University Park, Pennsylvania State University Libraries, 1970.

x, 148, 2 p. illus., ports. 28 cm. (Pennsylvania. State University. Libraries. Bibliographical series no. 3)

National Book League, London.
Creative writing from Black Africa (Sub-Sahara): checklist. London, National Book League, 1971.

[4], 2, 30 p. 26 cm.

Páricsy, Pál.
A new bibliography of African literature. Budapest, Center for Afro-Asian Research of the Hungarian Academy of Sciences, 1969.

xi, 108 p. 24 cm. (Studies on developing countries, no. 24)

CONTENTS: An additional bibliography to J. Jahn's A bibliography of Neo-African literature from Africa, America, and the Caribbean. [1965].—A preliminary bibliography of African writing (from 1965 to the present).

Ramsaran, John A.
New approaches to African literature; a guide to Negro-African writing and related studies [by] J. A. Ramsaran. [Ibadan, Nigeria] Ibadan University Press, 1965.

v, 177 p. 19 cm.

Ramsaran, John A.
New approaches to African literature; a guide to Negro-African writing and related studies, by J. A. Ramsaran. 2d ed. [Ibadan, Nigeria] Ibadan University Press, 1970.

xi, 168 p. 22 cm.

University of Ife Bookshop.
Contemporary African literature; catalogue of books and periodicals displayed during an exhibition. Ile-Ife [1971]

xviii, 84 p. 22 cm.

Co-sponsored by the British Council and the Institute of African Studies, University of Ife and held at various sites in Ibadan, Ile-Ife, and Lagos, Nov. 25-Dec. 21, 1971.

Zand, Ninella Moiseevna.
Художественная литература стран Африки в советской печати; библиография русских переводов и критической литературы на русском языке, 1958–1964. Москва, Книга, 1967.

175 p. 23 cm.

At head of title: Всесоюзная государственная библиотека иностранной литературы. Н. М. Занд и В. А. Эльвова.

Zell, Hans M
A reader's guide to African literature, compiled and edited by Hans M. Zell and Helene Silver. With contributions by Barbara Abrash and Gideon-Cyrus M. Mutiso. New York, Africana Pub. Corp. [1971]

xxi, 218 p. illus. 23 cm.

Zell, Hans M
A reader's guide to African literature; compiled and edited by Hans M. Zell and Helene Silver; with contributions by Barbara Abrash and Gideon-Cyrus M. Mutiso. London, Heinemann Educational, 1972.

xxi, 218 p. ports. 23 cm. (Studies in African literature)

Zell, Hans M
Writings by West Africans, in print at December 1967. Compiled & edited by Hans M. Zell. New & rev. ed. Freetown, Sierra Leone University Press [1968]

ii, 31 p. 25 cm.

"Originally published as a guide to an exhibition held in Freetown, Sierra Leone in April 1967."

AFRICAN, SOUTH, LITERATURE

Beinash, Judith.
Books and pamphlets by South African Jewish writers, 1940–1962; a bibliography. Johannesburg, University of the Witwatersrand, Dept. of Bibliography, Librarianship and Typography, 1965.

v, 44 l. 30 cm.

Thesis (diploma in librarianship)—University of the Witwatersrand.

Davidson, Elizabeth.
Some English writings by non-European South Africans (1928–1971); a bibliography compiled by Elizabeth A. Davidson. Johannesburg, University of the Witwatersrand, Dept. of Bibliography, Librarianship and Typography, 1972.

24 p. 30 cm.

"Compiled in part fulfilment for the requirements of the Diploma in Librarianship, University of the Witwatersrand."

Priebe, Richard.
Letters and manuscripts from southern Africa; a survey of the holdings of the Humanities Research Center, the University of Texas at Austin. Austin, African and Afro-American Research Institute, University of Texas at Austin, 1972.

24 p. 23 cm. (Occasional publication of the African and Afro-American Research Institute, the University of Texas at Austin, 6)

AFRICAN STUDIES
see also under Asian studies

Bal, Willy, 1916– *comp.*
Les sciences humaines et l'Afrique à l'Université Lovanium. 2. éd. publiée es soins de Willy Bal. Léopoldville, Éditions de l'Université, 1964.

232 p. illus. 24 cm. (Publications de l'Université Lovanium de Lépoldville)

PARTIAL CONTENTS.—Bibliothèque centrale de Lovanium; réalisations et problèmes en matièr· de sciences humaines, par P. Gorissen. Guide bibliographique, par J. Bogaert (p. 35–113)—Service des publications de l'Université Lovanium de Léopoldville, par J. Gengoux.

Current Africanist research. La recherche africaniste en cours. no. 1– Nov. 1971–
London, Research Information Liaison Unit, International African Institute.

no. 30 cm.

English and French.

Dakar. Université. *Faculté des lettres et sciences humaines.* Enseignements et recherches africanistes propres à la Faculté des lettres et sciences humaines de Dakar (Sénégal) Dakar [1965]

25 l. illus. 27 cm.

AFRICANS

Andor, L   E
Aptitudes and abilities of the black man in Sub-Saharan Africa, 1784–1963; an annotated bibliography, compiled by L. E. Andor, with an introd. by W. Hudson. Johannesburg, National Institute for Personnel Research, South African Council for Scientific and Industrial Research, 1966.

vii, 174 p. 22 cm.

Descloitres, Claudine.
La Psychologie appliquée en Afrique, bibliographie ... Aix-en-Provence, Centre africain des sciences humaines appliquées, 46, avenue Paul-Cézanne, 1968.

iii, 34 l. 27 cm. (Collection des travaux du C. A. S. H. A., 4)

Hoorweg, J   C
Psychology in Africa; a bibliography [by] J. C. Hoorweg [and] H. C. Marais. Leyden, Afrika-Studiecentrum, 1969.

139 p. 24 cm.

Klingelhofer, Edwin L   1920–
A bibliography of psychological research and writings on Africa [by] E. L. Klingelhofer. Dar es Salaam, Tanzania, University College, University of East Africa, 1967.

31 p. 33 cm.

Klingelhofer, Edwin L   1920–
A bibliography of psychological research and writings on Africa. [By] E. L. Klingelhofer. Uppsala, Scandinavian institute of African studies [1967].

(4), v, 33 l. 30 cm.

AFRIKAANS LANGUAGE AND LITERATURE

Davies, Merle.
Literêre polemieke 1919–1959. 'n Lys saamgestel deur Merle Davies. Johannesburg, Universiteit van die Witwatersrand, 1966.

v, 31 l. 30 cm.

"Saamgestel ter vervulling van 'n deel van die vereistes vir die Diploma in Bibliotheekwese."

Suid-Afrikaanse Akademie vir Wetenskap en Kuns.
Gekeurde lys van Afrikaanse boeke, 1861–1970. [3. druk.] Pretoria, 1971.

80 p. 18 cm.

Cover title: Die Afrikaanse taal en letterkunde.

Van Erdelen, Marianne Nicoline.
A bibliography of some Sestigers: Chris Barnard, Breyten Breytenbach, Abraham de Vries, Jan Rabie, Bartho Smit, Dolf van Niekerk. Johannesburg, University of

Witwatersrand, Dept. of Bibliography, Librarianship and Typography, 1970.

v, 57 p. 30 cm.

"Compiled in part fulfilment for the requirements of the Diploma in Librarianship, University of the Witwatersrand, Johannesburg."

AFRO-AMERICAN STUDIES

Johnson, Harry Alleyn.
Multimedia materials for Afro-American studies; a curriculum orientation and annotated bibliography of resources. New York, R. R. Bowker Co., 1971.

353 p. 27 cm.

AFRO-AMERICANS   see   Negroes

AFRO-ASIAN POLITICS

Potsdam. Deutsche Akademie für Staats- und Rechtswissenschaft "Walter Ulbricht." Abteilung Aussenpolitik der Staaten Asiens und Afrikas.
Die Politik der Nichtpaktgebundenheit in Asien und Afrika. Auswahlbibliographie. (Redaktion: Diethelm Weidemann.) Potsdam-Babelsberg (Deutsche Akademie für Staats- und Rechtswissenschaft "Walter Ulbricht," Zentralstelle für staats- und rechtswissenschaftliche Information und Dokumentation) 1968.

96 p. 21 cm. (Spezialbibliographien zu Fragen des Staates und des Rechts, Heft 8)

AFZELIUS, NILS

Andersson, Eva, 1935–
Nils Afzelius. Tryckta skrifter 1917–1969. Bibliografi utg. till 75-årsdagen, 21 januari 1969. Stockholm, Kungl. biblioteket, 1969.

xiii, 29 p. 25 cm. (Acta Bibliothecae regiae Stockholmiensis, 7)

AGED
see also   Gerontology

Balkema, John B
The aged in minority groups: a bibliography. Compiled by John B. Balkema. Washington, National Council on the Aging, 1973.

19 p. 28 cm.

Balkema, John B
Housing and living arrangements for older people; a bibliography. Compiled by John B. Balkema. Washington, National Council on the Aging, 1972.

20 p. 28 cm.

Bergman, Shim'on.
הקשישים בישראל; תדריך ביבליוגרפי [מאת] ש. ברגמן. תל-אביב. האגודה הישראלית לגרונטולוגיה, תשכ"ז [1966]

4, 69, ix p. 24 cm.

Added t. p.: Aged in Israel; a selected bibliography.

Central Mortgage and Housing Corporation. Library.
Housing for the aged; bibliography. Ottawa, 1968.

17 l. 28 cm.

CONTENTS: Canada. Great Britain. United States. Architecture. Miscellaneous.

Jones, Rennie C

Housing for the elderly; selected references, compiled by Rennie C. Jones. Melbourne, State Library of Victoria, 1966.

38 p. 26 cm. (Victoria. State Library. Research service bibliographies, 1966, no. 9)

Koncelik, Joseph A

Considerate design and the aging: review article with a selected and annotated bibliography ₍by₎ Joseph A. Koncelik. ₍Monticello, Ill.; Council of Planning Librarians₎ 1972.

12 p. 29 cm. (Council of Planning Librarians. Exchange bibliography 253)

Kramer, Mollie W

A selected bibliography on the aging, and the role of the library in serving them, by Mollie W. Kramer. ₍Champaign, University of Illinois, Graduate School of Library Science₎ 1973.

39 p. 28 cm. (University of Illinois. Graduate School of Library Science. Occasional papers, no. 107)

Caption title.

Library Association. *County Libraries Group.*

Readers' guide to books on care of the elderly. London, Library Association (County Libraries Group), 1967.

18 p. 18½ cm. (*Its* Readers' guide, new series, no. 95)

Cover title: Care of the elderly.

Oslo. Norges byggforskningsinstitutt.

Litteratur om eldre og uføre. ₍Oslo₎ 1970.

₍3₎, 17 l. 30 cm.

Peth, Peter R

Older worker resources; a selective annotated bibliography of work and aging ₍by₎ Peter R. Peth. ₍Minneapolis? 1971₎

iii, 35 l. 29 cm.

Simko, Margaret D

Nutrition and aging; a selected annotated bibliography, 1964-1972, compiled by Margaret D. Simko and Karen Colitz. ₍Washington, U.S. Administration on Aging; for sale by the Supt. of Docs., U.S. Govt. Print. Off., 1973₎

v, 41 p. 28 cm. (DHEW publication no. (SRS) 73-20237)

Snyder, Lorraine Hiatt.

The environmental challenge and the aging individual. ₍Monticello, Ill., Council of Planning Librarians₎ 1972.

43 p. 29 cm. (Council of Planning Librarians. Exchange bibliography 254)

United States. Congress. Senate. Special Committee on Aging.

Publications list: 87th to 91st Congresses, 1961-1970. Washington, U.S. Govt. Print. Off., 1971.

ii, 8 p. 23 cm.

U. S. Dept. of Housing and Urban Development. Library and Information Division.

The built environment for the elderly and the handicapped; a bibliography. Washington; For sale by the Supt. of Docs., U. S. Govt. Print. Off., 1971.

46 p. 27 cm.

Young, Olive Mary.

Care of the aged in South Africa, 1822-1963; a select bibliography. ₍Cape Town₎ University of Cape Town, School of Librarianship, 1964.

xii, 92 p. 23 cm. (University of Cape Town. School of Librarianship. Bibliographical series)

AGENCE HAVAS

France. Archives nationales.

Les archives de l'Agence Havas, branche information, conservées aux Archives nationales (5 AR). Inventaire par Isabelle Brot, conservateur. Paris, S. E. V. P. E. N., 1969.

xxxvi, 270 p. plates, ports. 24 cm. (Its Inventaires et documents)

AGGREY, JAMES EMMAN KWEGYIR

Livingstone College, *Salisbury, N. C. Carnegie Library.*

An annotated bibliography on James Emman Kwegyir Aggrey, 1875-1927. Compiled at Livingstone College, by Louise M. Rountree, assistant librarian. Salisbury, 1964.

1 v. (unpaged) 28 cm.

AGING see Gerontology

AGNON, SAMUEL JOSEPH

Arnon, Johanan.

ש"י עגנון; ביבליוגרפיה על שמואל יוסף עגנון ויצירתו ₍מאת₎ יוחנן ארנון. תל אביב. עתיקות, 731 ₍1971₎

97 p. 27 cm.

Added t. p.: S. J. Agnon; bibliography on Samuel Josef Agnon and his work.

David, Yona.

₍Sefarim u-ma'amarim 'al Shai 'Agnon₎

ספרים ומאמרים על ש"י עגנון ויצירותיו; ביבליוגראפיה ₍מאת₎ יונה דוד. ירושלים, הוצאת תמיר ₍1972₎

100 p. 22 cm.

On verso of t. p.: Books and essays on S. J. Agnon and his works; bibliography, ₍by₎ Yonah David.

Jerusalem. Hebrew University. *Jewish National and University Library.*

תערוכת ש"י עגנון, חתן פרס נובל לספרות 1966; קטלוג. בית הספרים הלאומי והאוניברסיטאי. אולם ברמן, ירושלים, תשכ"ז ₍ערך: מלאכי בית-אריה. נוסח אנגלי: מירה פרנקל. ירושלים, 1967₎

50, 52 p. facsims., mounted port. 25 cm.
Added t. p.: Exhibition in honour of S. J. Agnon, recipient of Nobel Prize for literature 1966; catalogue.
Hebrew and English.

Kefar Ata. Sifriyah tsiburit.

חוברת הדרכה וביבליוגרפיה ל-"תערוכת עגנון" תשכ"ז ב-"קרית אתא". ערוך בידי יהושע אייבשיץ. ₍כפר אתא. ספריה ציבורית, 727 ₍1966₎

3, 19 l. 33 cm.

At head of title: המועצה המקומית קריר-אתא. המחלקה לחנוך. תרבות ונוער, משרד החינוך והתרבות. המדור לספריות.

AGRARIAN REFORM see Land

AGRICOLA, GEORG

Michaëlis, Rudolf, 1901-1964.

Agricola-Bibliographie 1520-1963. Von Rudolf Michaëlis u. Hans Prescher. Bestandsaufnahme der Werke des Dr. Georgius Agricola mit bibliographischen Forschungsergebnissen. Von Ulrich Horst. Berlin, Deutscher Verl. d. Wissenschaften, 1971.

935 p., 32 p. of illus. 25 cm. (Georgius Agricola. Ausgewählte Werke. Bd. 10)

AGRICULTURAL CHEMISTRY

(Agronomicheskaîa khimiîa v Gruzii)
Агрономическая химия в Грузии. Библиогр. указ. ₍за 1858–1968 гг.₎ Под ред. и с вводной статьей проф. И. Ф. Саришвили. Тбилиси, Груз. с.-х. ин-т, 1971.

xvi, 294 p. 22 cm.

At head of title: Министерство сельского хозяйства СССР.
Added t. p. in Georgian.
By L. L. Gelovani and others.
Russian and Georgian; prefatory matter in Russian only.

Guseĭnov, Dzhebrail Mukhtarovich.
Библиография по вопросу изучения и применения нефтяного ростового вещества (НРВ), комплексного органо-минерального микроудобрения (МУ) и других отходов нефтяной промышленности в сельском хозяйстве и медицине. ₍Составитель Д. М. Гусейнов₎ Баку, Изд-во Академии наук Азербайджанской ССР, 1966.

83 p. 22 cm.

At head of title: Академия наук Азербайджанской ССР.

Leningrad. Publichnaîa biblioteka.
Химия в сельском хозяйстве; рекомендательный указатель литературы в помощь агрохимическому всеобучу. ₍Составитель А. Н. Ермолаева₎ Ленинград, 1964.

51 p. 21 cm.

At head of title: Министерство культуры РСФСР. Государственная публичная библиотека имени М. Е. Салтыкова-Щедрина.

Mieserova, S   I
Микроэлементы. Библиогр. указатель книг и статей. 1961–1965 гг. Вып. 1–   Ростов н/Д, 1968–

v. 20 cm.

At head of title, v. 1–   : Ростовский-на-Дону государственный университет. Научная библиотека. С. И. Миесерова, В. А. Ткачева.

Moscow. TSentral'naîa nauchnaîa sel'skokhozîaĭstvennaîa biblioteka. *Spravochno-bibliograficheskiĭ otdel.*
Химия в сельском хозяйстве; выборочный библиографический список отечественных книг за 1960–1965 гг. в количестве 1124 названий. Москва, 1966.

135 p. 20 cm.

At head of title: Всесоюзная академия сельскохозяйственных наук имени В. И. Ленина. Центральная научная сельскохозяйственная библиотека. Справочно-библиографический отдел.

Moscow. Vsesoîuznaîa gosudarstvennaîa biblioteka inostrannoĭ literatury.
Химикаты для сельского хозяйства; библиографический указатель иностранной литературы. Москва, 1966.

187 p. 21 cm.

At head of title: Всесоюзная государственная библиотека иностранной литературы. Центральная научная сельскохозяйственная библиотека ВАСХНИЛ.

U. S. *Library of Congress. Aerospace Technology Division.*
CBE factors; annotated bibliography. no. 1–3. ₍Washington₎ 1965.

3 no. 28 cm. (*Its* ATD report)

Covers available Soviet open-source literature on or related to chemical factors, biological factors, and environmental factors.
No. 1 is compiled from sources published prior to Dec. 31, 1962; no. 2–3 from sources published 1963–64.
Superseded by the Division's CBE factors; monthly survey.

AGRICULTURAL EDUCATION

Brown, Mary Ruth, 1925–
Agricultural education in a technical society; an annotated bibliography of resources ₍by₎ Mary Ruth Brown, Eugenie Lair Moss, and Karin Drudge Bright. Foreword by Howard Sidney. Chicago, American Library Association, 1973.

xii, 228 p. 25 cm.

Horňák, Kamil.
Zemědělské školství; výběr literatury. Připravil Kamil Horňák. Brno, 1967.

14 l. 21 cm. (Státní pedagogická knihovna v Brne. Bibliografický leták, čis. 182) (Státní pedagogická knihovna v Brne. Publikace, čis. 277)

At head of title: Státní pedagogická knihovna v Brne.

AGRICULTURAL ENGINEERING

Food and Agriculture Organization of the United Nations. Documentation Center.
Agricultural engineering. Machinisme agricole. Maquinaria agricola. Annotated bibliography. Author and subject index. FAO publications and documents (1945–May 1971). ₍Rome, 1971₎

1v. (various pagings) 28 cm.

"DC/Sp. 22"
Introductory material in English, French and Spanish.

Hall, Carl W
Agricultural engineering index. Reynoldsburg, Ohio, Agricultural Consulting Associates; order from Edwards Brothers, Ann Arbor, 1961–72.

2 v. 29 cm.

Vol. 2, by G. E. Hall and C. W. Hall; order from American Society of Agricultural Engineers, St. Joseph, Mich.
Includes bibliographies.
CONTENTS: ₍1₎ 1907–1960.—₍2₎ 1961–1970.

Willis, Albert Henry.
Annotated bibliography of publications in agricultural engineering in Australia, 1950–1965 ₍by₎ A. H. Willis. ₍Kensington, N. S. W., Institute of Rural Technology, University of New South Wales, 1971₎

131 p. 26 cm.

AGRICULTURAL EXTENSION WORK

Estación Experimental Agropecuaria Pergamino.
Bibliografía sobre extensión agrícola. Dirigió: Eduardo Ferreira Sobral. ₍Pergamino, 1966₎

225 p. 26 cm. (*Its* Serie bibliográfica, t. 5)

Added t. p.: Extension bibliography.
Introd. in Spanish and English.

Thomas, Ulrich, 1917–
Bibliography on agricultural extension; working paper ₍by₎ U. Thomas. Rome, Food and Agriculture Organization of the United Nations, 1964.

A27, B27, C27, 871 p. 27 cm.

Title and introductory matter also in French, Spanish, and German.

Vries, C   A   de
Agricultural extension in the developing countries; a bibliography, compiled by C. A. de Vries. Wageningen, International Institute for Land Reclamation and Improvement, 1968.

125 p. 24 cm. (International Institute for Land Reclamation and Improvement. Bibliography 7)

AGRICULTURAL MACHINERY

Donskai͡a, Galina Kupri͡anovna.
В помощь молодому механизатору сельского хозяйства; рекомендательные списки литературы. [Составители: Г. К. Донская и И. П. Черемисинова. Редактор Ф. М. Тютчева] Москва, 1963.

50 p. 17 cm.

At head of title: Министерство культуры РСФСР. Государственная ордена Ленина библиотека СССР имени В. И. Ленина.

Gorbatov, A   L
Экономика и организация использования сельскохозяйственной техники. Библиогр. указатель отечеств. литературы за 1966–1969 гг. и иностр. литературы за 1966–1968 гг. [Сост. А. Л. Горбатов] Москва, 1969.

94 p. 20 cm.

At head of title: Всесоюзная ордена Ленина академия сельскохозяйственных наук имени В. И. Ленина. Центральная научная сельскохозяйственная библиотека.

I͡Akovleva, O   I
(Ochistka traktorov, avtomobileĭ, sel'skokhozi͡aĭstvennykh mashin i ikh detaleĭ pri remonte)
Очистка тракторов, автомобилей, сельскохозяйственных машин и их деталей при ремонте. Библиогр. указатель за 1967–1969 гг. [Сост. Яковлева О. И.] Москва, 1971.

52 p. 20 cm.

At head of title: Государственный всесоюзный научно-исследовательский технологический институт ремонта и эксплуатации машинно-тракторного парка.

Italy. Centro nazionale meccanico agricolo.
Relazione sull'attività svolta nel quadriennio 1964–1967 ed elenco completo delle pubblicazioni. Torino, Tipo-offset Ernani [1967?]

37 l. 29 cm.

Moscow. Vsesoi͡uznyĭ nauchno-issledovatel'skiĭ institut sel'skokhozi͡aĭstvennogo mashinostroenii͡a. Nauchno-tekhnicheskai͡a biblioteka.
(Sel'skokhozi͡aĭstvennye mashiny)
Сельскохозяйственные машины. Библиогр. указатель. Разд. 1–   Москва, 1969–   [v. 1, pt. 1, 1970]

v. 21 cm.

At head of title, v. 1–   : Всесоюзный научно-исследовательский институт сельскохозяйственного машиностроения имени В. П. Горячкина. Научно-техническая библиотека.—
"Составитель ... И. И. Левина."

Vinogradova, O   N
Испытания сельскохозяйственных машин и тракторов. Библиогр. указатель литературы ... отечеств. и иностр. Москва, 1968.

116 p. 20 cm.

At head of title: Всесоюзная ордена Ленина академия с.-х. наук имени В. И. Ленина. Центральная научная сельскохозяйственная библиотека. Справочно-библиографический отдел.

Vinogradova, O   N
Механизация уборки зерновых культур. Библиогр. указатель отечеств. и иностр. литературы ... за 1967–1969 гг. [Сост. О. Н. Виноградова]. Москва, 1970.

123 p. 20 cm.

At head of title: Всесоюзная академия сельскохозяйственных наук имени В. И. Ленина. Центральная научная сельскохозяйственная библиотека. Справочно-библиографический отдел.
Edited by M. N. Al͡shamovskai͡a.

Vinogradova, O   N
Механизация возделывания и уборки овощных культур. Библиогр. указатель отечеств. литературы за 1965–1968 гг. и иностр. за 1966–1968 гг. [Сост.: О. Н. Вино-

градова]. Москва, 1968.

76 p. 20 cm.

At head of title: Всесоюзная ордена Ленина академия сельскохозяйственных наук имени В. И. Ленина. Центральная научная сельскохозяйственная библиотека.

Vinogradova, O   N
Повышенные скорости и широкозахватная техника в сельском хозяйстве; библиографический список отечественной литературы в количестве 380 названий и иностранной в количестве 56 названий за 1963–1965 гг. [Составитель О. Н. Виноградова] Москва, 1966.

50 p. 21 cm.

At head of title: Всесоюзная академия с.-х. наук имени В. И. Ленина. Центральная научная сельскохозяйственная библиотека. Справочно-библиографический отдел.

Vinogradova, O   N
Повышенные скорости и широкозахватная техника в сельском хозяйстве. Библиогр. указатель отечеств. и иностр. литературы за 1966–1969 гг. Москва, 1970.

70 p. 20 cm.

At head of title: Всесоюзная ордена Ленина Академия сельскохозяйственных наук имени В. И. Ленина. Центральная научная сельскохозяйственная библиотека. Справочно-библиографический отдел.
"Составитель: О. Н. Виноградова."

AGRICULTURE
see also under   Dissertations, Academic

Arboleda-Sepúlveda, Orlando.
2000 [i. e. Dos mil] libros en ciencias agrícolas en castellano, 1958–1969. Turrialba, Costa Rica, Instituto Interamericano de Ciencias Agrícolas, Biblioteca y Servicio de Documentación, 1969.

viii, 169 p. 28 cm. (IICA. Bibliotecología y documentación, no. 17)

Bjørlykke, Borghild.
Litteraturliste. Meldinger om forsøks- og forskningsarbeider, småskrifter og andre opplysningsskrifter for landbruket. 1962–1966. [Utg. av] Kontoret for landbruksforskning. Oslo, 1968.

172 p. 21 cm.

Brünn. Universita. Knihovna.
Soupis rešerší z oboru zemědělství a přírodních věd za léta 1962–1964. Sest. Dušan Štěpánek. V Brně, 1965.

9 p. 21 cm. (Its Výberový seznam, 107)

Büscher, K
Verzeichnis der Lehr- und Arbeitsmittel für landwirtschaftliche Fachschulen. Abteilung Landwirtschaft und Hauswirtschaft sowie für landwirtschaftliche Beratung. Zusammengestellt im Auftrage des Lehrmittelausschusses für landwirtschaftliche Fachschulen und Beratung. Besorgt von K. Büscher. (Bonn-Bad Godesberg, AID, Land- u. Hauswirtschaftl. Auswertungs- u. Informationsdienst e. V.; Frankfurt am Main, Verlag Kommentator, 1970.)

215 p. 24 cm. (Schriftenreihe des AID)

Chernova, L   V
Борьба с засухой. Библиогр. указатель отечеств. литературы и иностр. литературы за 1960–1967 гг. Москва, 1968.

79 p. 20 cm.

At head of title: Всесоюзная ордена Ленина академия сельскохозяйственных наук имени В. И. Ленина. Центральная научная сельскохозяйственная библиотека.

Chernova, L   V
Борьба с засухой. Библиогр. указ. отечественной литературы за 1968–1970 гг. и иностранной литературы за 1968–1969 гг. [Сост. Л. В. Чернова]. Москва, 1971.

36 p. 21 cm.

At head of title: Всесоюзная академия сельскохозяйственных наук имени В. И. Ленина. Центральная научная сельскохозяйственная библиотека.

Davis, John Henry, 1901–
Selected bibliography for agriculture for tropical and warm temperate regions. John H. Davis, editor. [Gainesville, University of Florida [Dept. of Botany] 1965.

72 l. 28 cm.

Caption title.

Estación Experimental Agropecuaria Anguil.
Catálogo de publicaciones editadas por la Estación Experimental Agropecuaria Anguil, La Pampa. [Anguil, Argentina, 1968]

12 l. 35 cm.

Estación Experimental Agropecuaria Pergamino.
Serie bibliográfica. t. 1–
[Pergamino] 1964–

no. 26 cm.

Added title   : Bibliographical series (varies slightly).
Supplements accompany some numbers.

Fachliteraturkunde Landwirtschaft. Als Manuskript gedruckt. Leipzig, Fachschule für Bibliothekare "Erich Weinert" (1966).

2 v. 30 cm. (Lehrbriefe für das Fachschulfernstudium. Reihe D: Fachrichtungsausbildung, Nr. 4)

"Das Manuskript dieses Lehrbriefes schrieb Dr. Gunther Helbig."

(FAO dokyumentēshon refarensu)
FAO ドキュメンテーションレファレンス 1–
1968–

[東京] FAO受託図書館

no. 26 cm.

Food and Agriculture Organization of the United Nations. Documentation Centre.
FAO/UNDP(SF) projects—reports and documents; index. Projets FAO/PNUD(FS)—rapports et documents; indice. Proyectos FAO/PNUD(FE)—informes y documentos. [Rome, 1969–
v. 28 cm.
Introductory material in English, French and Spanish.
"DC/Sp. 13 May 1969," "15 February 1970," "16 April 1970," "18 December 1970."

Food and Agriculture Organization of the United Nations. Documentation Center.
Index. Indice. 1963–1966. FAO/UNDP (SF) project reports. Rapports de projets FAO/PNUD(FS). Informes de proyectos FAO/PNUD (FE). [Rome] 1967.

1 v. (various pagings) 28 cm.

"PU: DC/Sp. 3, May-Mai-Mayo 1967"
English, French, and Spanish.

Idaho. *Division of Agricultural Education.*
Reference list for vocational agriculture. Rev. with the cooperation of the Dept. of Agricultural Education, University of Idaho. [Boise] 1964.

5–9, ii–v, 27 l. 28 cm. (Vo-ed no. 82)

Institut za poljoprivredna istraživanja. Zavod za fiziologiju bilja.
Bibliography of publications. Novi Sad, 1966–69.

2 v. 24 cm.

Cover title.
At head of title: Dept. of Plant Physiology. Institute of Agricultural Research.
Vol. constituting v. 1 called "First edition."

Janowska, Zofia.
Bibliografia publikacji pracowników naukowych SGGW za lata 1961–1965. Warszawa, Dział Wydawnictw SGGW, 1968.

430 p. 25 cm. (Szkoła Główna Gospodarstwa Wiejskiego w Warszawie. Prace Biblioteki Głównej, nr. 4)

At head of title: Zofia Janowska, Grażyna Czyżewicz.

Japan. Nōrinshō. Toshokan.

(Nōrinshō Toshokan sankō tosho mokuroku)
農林省図書館参考図書目録 辞典・事典・便覧・ハンドブック類 [東京] 農林省図書館 昭和41 [1966]

70 p. 25 cm.

Library Association. *County Libraries Group.*
Readers' guide to books on agriculture. 4th ed. London, Library Association (County Libraries Group), 1968.

58 p. 19 cm. (*Its* Readers' guide, new series, no. 102)

Maryland. Agricultural Experiment Station, College Park.
Maryland Agricultural Experiment Station publications: 1965–1970. [College Park] 1972.

54 p. 24 cm. (Its Bulletin, A–178)

Matthews, *Mrs.* James D
An author and subject index to the publications of the Georgia Agricultural Experiment Station and the Georgia Coastal Plain Experiment Station, 1888–1946. Edited by Jane Oliver. [Athens] University of Georgia, University Libraries, 1948.

138 l. 28 cm.

———— Supplement ... for the years 1947–June 1954. Compiled by Virginia Michaelis. [Athens] University of Georgia, University Libraries, 1956.

77 l. 28 cm.

Max-Planck-Institut für Landarbeit und Landtechnik.
Verzeichnis der Veröffentlichungen seit der Gründung im Jahre 1940. Max-Planck-Institut für Landarbeit und Landtechnik. (Bearbeiter: W[alter] Glasow und P. Czepluch.) Bad Kreuznach (Max-Planck-Institut für Landarbeit und Landtechnik) 1965.

23–123 p. 21 cm.

Mikheev, Nikolaĭ Mikhaĭlovich.
Из истории русской сельскохозяйственной литературы. Москва, 1964.

87 p. 21 cm. (Центральная научная сельскохозяйственная библиотека ВАСХНИЛ. Методические материалы)

New Brunswick. *Dept. of Agriculture and Rural Development.*
List of publications, 1968/69. [Fredericton, 1968]

11 p. 23 cm.

Cover title.

Ontario. *Dept. of Agriculture and Food. Farm Economics, Co-operatives and Statistics Branch.*

A selective list of available publications of the Farm Economics, Co-operatives and Statistics Branch. Toronto, 1968.

6 l. 28 cm.

Prague. Ústřední zemědělská a lesnická knihovna.

Světové zemědělství; v cestovních zprávách ze studijních cest do zahraniči. ₁Odpovedny redaktor František Lazecký₁ Praha, Ústav vědeckotechnických informací MZLH; Ústřední zemědělská a lesnická knihovna, 1966–

v. 20 cm.

CONTENTS: 1. 1955–1965.

Tarr, Raissa.

L'Alimentation et l'agriculture dans les pays de développement. Food and agriculture in developing countries. Paris, Organisation de coopération et de développement économiques, 1967.

2 v. 27 cm. (O. E. C. D. Library. Bibliographie spéciale analytique. Special annotated bibliography, 12–13)

"This bibliography has been compiled and annotated by Mrs. R. Tarr."

Указатель книг, журнальных и газетных статей по сельскому хозяйству за 1914 год. (По материалам А. Д. Педашенко). ₁В 15-ти т.₁ Т. 1– Москва-Ленинград, 1970–

v. 19 cm.

At head of title, v. 1– : Всесоюзная ордена Ленина академия сельскохозяйственных наук имени В. И. Ленина. Центральная научная сельскохозяйственная библиотека.

Velásquez Gallardo, Pablo.

Obras de consulta agrícolas en español ₁por₁ Pablo Velásquez G. ₁y₁ Ramón Nadurille T. México, Instituto Nacional de Investigaciones Agrícolas, 1967.

xv, 263 p. 24 cm.

Vilna. Lietuvos TSR Valstybinė respublikinė biblioteka.

Naujoji žemės ūkio literatūra; bibliografinis sąrašas. ₁Sudarė: S. Vėlavičienė ir E. Grineckaitė₁ Vilnius, 1965.

24 p. 21 cm.

Warsaw. Szkoła Główna Gospodarstwa Wiejskiego.

Bibliografia prac magisterskich, kandydackich, doktorskich i habilitacyjnych, przyjętych w Szkole Głównej Gospodarstwa Wiejskiego w Warszawie w latach 1918–1963. Wyd. 2., uzup. i popr. Warszawa, Dział Wydawn. SGGW, 1966.

2 v. 24 cm. (Szkoła Główna Gospodarstwa Wiejskiego w Warszawie. Prace Biblioteki Głównej, nr. 3

At head of title: Amalia Kurlandzka i Bolesław Tuhan-Taurogiński.

First ed. published in 1959–60 under title: Bibliografia prac dyplomowych, kandydackich, doktorskich i habilitacyjnych, złożonych w Szkole Głównej Gospodarstwa Wiejskiego do roku 1958.

BIBLIOGRAPHIES

Besterman, Theodore, 1904–

Agriculture; a bibliography of bibliographies. Totowa, N. J., Rowman and Littlefield, 1971.

302 p. 20 cm. (The Besterman world bibliographies)

Compiled by the publisher from the 4th ed. of the author's A world bibliography of bibliographies and of bibliographical catalogues, calendars, abstracts, digests, indexes, and the like.

Cáceres Ramos, Hugo.

Bibliografía de bibliografías agrícolas de América La-

tina. ₁Turrialba₁ Instituto Interamericano de Ciencias Agrícolas. Centro de Enseñanza e Investigación, 1967.

ii, 45 l. 28 cm. (Instituto Interamericano de Ciencias Agrícolas. Centro de Enseñanza e Investigación. Bibliotecología y documentación, no. 10)

Cardozo Gonzáles, Armando.

Bibliografía de bibliografías agrícolas bolivianas ₁por₁ Armando Cardozo. ₁La Paz, Empresa Editora "Universo"₁ 1969.

8 p. 19 cm.

Cover title.

Estación Experimental Agropecuaria Pergamino.

Bibliografía de bibliografías argentinas en ciencias agrícolas y naturales. ₁Pergamino₁ 1969.

56 p. 27 cm. (*Its* Serie bibliográfica, t. 53, apéndice)

Frauendorfer, Sigmund von.

Survey of abstracting services and current bibliographical tools in agriculture, forestry, fisheries, nutrition, veterinary medicine and related subjects. München, Basel, Wien, BLV Verlagsgesellschaft (1969).

192 p. 21 cm.

Mikheev, Nikolaĭ Mikhaĭlovich.

Библиографические указатели сельскохозяйственной литературы. 1783–1966. ₁Изд. 2-е, переработ.₁ Москва, "Колос," 1968.

282 p. 21 cm.

At head of title: Центральная научная сельскохозяйственная библиотека ВАСХНИЛ.

DICTIONARIES

Chmelař, František.

Zemědělské odborné jazykové slovníky. Pomůcky pro vědeckotechn. informace zeměd. Sest. František Chmelař. Brno, Univ. knihovna, t. G 03, Vyškov, 1969–

v. 21 cm. (Výběrový seznam, 188

ECONOMIC ASPECTS

American bibliography of agricultural economics. v. 1–

July 1971–
₁Washington?₁ American Agricultural Economics Association₁

v. 26 cm. 6 no. a year.

Prepared by American Agricultural Economics Documentation Center.

Brünn. Universita. *Knihovna.*

Lineární programování a matematické metody v ekonomice zemědělství. ₁Sest. František Chmelař a Dušan Štěpánek₁ V Brně, 1965.

20 l. 21 cm. (*Its* Výběrový seznam, 104)

Addendum slip inserted.

Commonwealth Bureau of Agricultural Economics.

Agribusiness: an annotated bibliography prepared by Commonwealth Bureau of Agricultural Economic, Oxford. Farnham Royal, Commonwealth Agricultural Bureaux, 1971.

₁1₁, ii, 8 leaves 30 cm. (*Its* Annotated bibliography no. 10)

Dillon, John L

An Australasian bibliography of agricultural economics,

AGRICULTURE

1788–1960, compiled by John L. Dillon and G. C. Mc-Farlane. Sydney, Govt. Pr., 1967.

433 p. 25 cm.

At head of title: Department of Agriculture, New South Wales.

Florida. University, *Gainesville.* *Agricultural Economics Dept.*
15, fifteen years of publications, July 1, 1950–June 30, 1965. Gainesville, 1966.

103 l. 28 cm. (Agricultural economics mimeo report EC 66–12)

Food and Agriculture Organization of the United Nations. Documentation Center.
Micro-economics of agriculture: production economics and farm management; annotated bibliography, author and subject index, FAO publications and documents (1945–May 1971). Micro-économie de l'agriculture: économie de la production et gestion des exploitations; bibliographie annotée, index par auteurs et par sujets, publications et documents de la FAO (1945–mai 1971) Micro-economía de la agricultura, economía de la producción y administración rural, bibliografía anotada, índice por autores y temas, publicaciones y documentos de la FAO (1945–mayo 1971). ₁Rome₁, 1971.

1 v. (various pagings) 28 cm.

"DC/Sp. 23"
English, French and Spanish.

Food and Agriculture Organization of the United Nations. Documentation Centre.
Rural institutions. Institutions rurales. Instituciones rurales. Index. Indice, 1945–1966. ₁Rome₁ 1968.

1 v. (various pagings) 28 cm.

"DC/Sp. 9."
English, French, and Spanish.

Gorbatov, A   L
(Agrarno-promyshlennye kompleksy o ob″edineniﬁa)
Аграрно-промышленные комплексы и объединения. Библиогр. указ. отеч. литературы за 1960–1973 гг. и иностр. за 1962–1973 гг. (2-е изд., перераб. и доп.) Москва, 1973.

190 p. 20 cm.
At head of title: Всесоюзная академия сельскохозяйственных наук имени В. И. Ленина. Центральная научная сельскохозяйственная библиотека.

Institut Pertanian Bogor. Departemen Agronomi.
Ringkasan agronomi; kompilasi laporan-laporan praktikum, survey dan thesis mahasiswa. Bogor, 1971–

v. 29 cm.

Cover title.

Istituto nazionale di economia agraria.
Documentazione di economia e politica agraria. Roma, 1968.

265 p. 24 cm.

"Ha coordinato il lavoro il prof. Duccio Tabet."

Littleton, Isaac Thomas, 1921–
The literature of agricultural economics: its bibliographic organization and use. ₁Raleigh₁ North Carolina Agricultural Experiment Station, 1969.

65 p. forms. 23 cm. (North Carolina Agricultural Experiment Station. Tech. bul. no. 191)

A revision of the author's thesis, University of Illinois.

Moscow. TSentral'naﬁa nauchnaﬁa sel'skokhozﬁaĭstvennaﬁa biblioteka.
Производительность труда в сельском хозяйстве зару-

бежных стран; библиографический список иностранной литературы за 1940–1963 гг. ₁Библиографы: Л. С. Авраамова, Т. А. Сурова₁ Москва, 1965.

143 p. 20 cm.

At head of title: Центральная научная сельскохозяйственная библиотека ВАСХНИЛ. Всесоюзный научно-исследовательский институт экономики сельского хозяйства.

Takahashi, Iichirō.
Bibliography on agricultural marketing, in the U. S. Journal of farm economics, vol. 1, no. 1–vol. 44, no. 5, by Iichiro Takahashi and Hiroshi Mori. Tokyo, National Research Institute of Agriculture ₁1964₁

169 p. 21 cm. (National Research Institute of Agriculture, Tokyo. Publication no. 236 ₁i. e. 264₁)

True, Arthur W   1898–
Economics of agriculture of foreign countries and U. S. foreign agricultural trade; a selected list of publications prepared or sponsored by the Economic Research Service, April 1, 1961–March 31, 1966. ₁Compiled by Arthur W. True. Washington₁ Economic Research Service, U. S. Dept. of Agriculture ₁1966₁

iii, 8 p. 26 cm. (₁U. S.₁ Dept. of Agriculture. Economic Research Service₁ ERS-foreign 167)

LIBRARY CATALOGS

Biblioteca Alfredo Guzmán.
Situación actual de la Biblioteca "Alfredo Guzmán." ₁San Miguel de Tucumán₁ 1968.

100 p. illus., ports. 27 cm. (Estación Experimental Agrícola de Tucumán. Publicación miscelánea, no. 28)

Cover title.

Japan. Nōrinshō. Toshokan.
(Nōrinshō Toshokan zōsho mokuroku)
農林省図書館蔵書目録　東京　農林省図書館
昭和45–46(1970–71)

3 v. 26 cm.

Cover title.
CONTENTS: 第1巻　著者名編―第2巻　分類編―第3巻　洋書編

Japan. *Rin'yachō. Rinseibu. Chōsaka.*
林野庁資料室収書目録　林野庁林政部調査課
東京　林野庁　昭和38–39 ₁1963–64₁

2 v. 26 cm.

CONTENTS.―第1巻　農業編・林業編―第2巻　社会科学・雑編・農林業編追録・著者名索引・洋書

Pasto, Colombia. Universidad de Nariño. Instituto Tecnológico Agrícola. Biblioteca.
Publicaciones periódicas recibidas en la Hemeroteca del Instituto Tecnológico Agrícola, por Zoila Guayasamín de López, hemerotecaria. Pasto, Universidad de Nariño, Instituto Tecnológico Agrícola, 1968.

142 l. 28 cm. (Its Serie bibliográfica, no. 6)

United States. National Agricultural Library.
Catalog. 1966/70–
Totowa, N. J., Rowman and Littlefield.

v. in   29 cm. quinquennial.

Issued in pts.

United States. National Agricultural Library.
Dictionary catalog of the National Agricultural Library,

1862–1965. New York, Rowman and Littlefield, 1967–70.

73 v. 29 cm.

At head of title: United States Department of Agriculture.
"Translations of articles, A–Z": v. 73.

PERIODICALS

Aliaga de Vizcarra, Irma.
Guía de publicaciones periódicas agrícolas y conexas de
Bolivia. La Paz, Sociedad de Ingenieros Agrónomos de
Bolivia, 1968.

5, 11 l. 28 cm. (Sociedad de Ingenieros Agrónomos de Bolivia.
Boletín bibliográfico no. 8)

Boalch, Donald Howard.
Current agricultural serials; a world list of serials in
agriculture and related subjects, excluding forestry and
fisheries, current in 1964, edited by D. H. Boalch. Oxford,
1965–

v. 25 cm.
At head of title: International Association of Agricultural Librarians and Documentalists. Association internationale des biblio-
thecaires et documentalistes agricoles.
To be kept up to date by lists published in the Quarterly bulletin
of the International Association of Agricultural Librarians and Documentalists.
CONTENTS.—v. 1. Alphabetical list.

Brünn. Universita. *Knihovna.*
Soupis zemědělských časopisů v Universitní knihovně v
Brně. [Catalogue of agricultural periodicals in the University Library in Brno] Sest.: Dušan Štěpánek a František Vřeský. V Brně, 1964.

50 p. 29 cm. (*Its* Výběrový seznam, 95)

Titles on cover also in Russian and German.

Carinthia. Kammer für Land- und Forstwirtschaft.
Gesamtverzeichnis der in der Landwirtschaftskammer
für Kärnten aufliegenden Zeitungen, Zeitschriften und
Schriftenreihen. (1. Aufl.) Stand 1. Jän. 1968. Klagenfurt (Kammer für Land- und Forstwirtschaft in Kärnten)
1968.

51, xxi p. 30 cm.

Commonwealth Agricultural Bureaux.
Consolidated list of scientific and technical serials regularly seen by the institutes and bureaux of the Commonwealth Agricultural Bureaux. Farnham Royal, Commonwealth Agricultural Bureaux, 1971.

[7], 188 p. 25 cm.

Estación Experimental Agropecuaria Pergamino.
Catálogo de publicaciones periódicas. Dirigió: Eduardo
Ferreira Sobral. [Pergamino, 1964]

224 p. 26 cm. (*Its* Serie bibliográfica, t. 8)

Added t. p.: General catalog of periodical publications.
Pref. in Spanish and English.

Hernández de Caldas, Angela.
Publicaciones periódicas bioagrícolas latinoamericanas; un
directorio, por Angela Hernández de Caldas, con la colaboración de Zoila Guayasamín de López. Pasto [Colombia]
Universidad de Nariño, Instituto Tecnológico Agrícola,
1966.

71 l. 28 cm. (Series bibliográfica, no. 5)

Hernández de Caldas, Angela.
Publicaciones periódicas y organismos agropecuarios
colombianos, 1887–1963. Medellín, Editorial Universidad
de Antioquia, 1964.

50 l. 28 cm.

At head of title: Universidad de Antioquia. Escuela Interamericana de Bibliotecología.

Indian Agricultural Research Institute, *Delhi. Library.*
Catalogue of serials in the Indian Agricultural Research
Institute library, March, 1967, New Delhi. Delhi, Union
Catalog Division, National Science Library, Indian Na-
tional Scientific Documentation Centre; [distributor: In-
dian Agricultural Research Institute Library, 1967]

[18], 660 p. (INSDOC union catalogue series, 4) 24 cm.

Inter-African Bureau for Soils and Rural Economy.
List of periodicals received by the Interafrican Bureau
for Soils (giving usual abbreviations of titles and complete
address of editors). [n. p., 1965]

28 l. 27 cm.

English or French.

International Institute of Tropical Agriculture.
Union list of selected scientific and technical periodicals
in Nigerian libraries. Ibadan, 1970.

171 l. 28 cm.

Konětopský, Antonín, comp.
Soupis docházejících a objednaných zemědělských časopisů v roce 1967. Sest. Antonín Konetopský. V Brně,
1967.

21 l. 30 cm. (Universitní knihovna v Brně. Výběrový seznam,
130)

List Agr : förteckning över löpande utomnordiska tidskrifter
och seriepublikationer i nordiska lantbruks-, skogs, träd-
gårds- och veterinärmedicinska bibliotek : list of current
non-Nordic periodicals and serials in Nordic research libraries of agriculture, forestry, horticulture and veterinary
medicine / [utg. av] Lantbrukshögskolan, Ultunabibliote-
ket. — Uppsala : [Lantbrukshögskolan, Konsulentavd./
Publikationer, distr.], 1974.

473 p. ; 23 cm.

**Moscow. TSentral'naia nauchnaia sel'skokhoziaistvennaia
biblioteka.**
(Inostrannye sel'skokhoziaistvennye zhurnaly)
Иностранные сельскохозяйственные журналы : аннотированный указатель, 1960–1972 гг. / Центральная
научная сельскохозяйственная библиотека ; [ред. А. Т.
Яйкова (отв. редактор) ... et al.]. — 2. изд., перер. и
доп. — Москва : ЦНСХБ, 1973.
471 p. ; 22 cm.
At head of title: Всесоюзная академия сельскохозяйственных
наук имени В. И. Ленина.
Includes indexes.

Mutkurova, Nadezhda.
Чужди периодични издания в библиотеките от систе-
мата на АСН, 1901–1967 ; своден каталог. [Съставители:
Надежда Муткурова, Добрина Николова, Донка Петрова]
София, 1970.

ix, 422 p. 31 cm.

At head of title: Академия на селскостопанските науки. Централна библиотека.

Naples. Università. *Facoltà di agraria.*
Catalogo dei periodici posseduti dalla biblioteca e dagli
Istituti della Facoltà. A cura di Marina Guardati. Napoli,
1966 [i. e. 1967].

427 p. mounted plate. 24 cm.

Naples. Università. Facoltà di agraria.
Catalogo dei periodici posseduti dalla biblioteca e dagli
istituti della Facoltà di agraria. 2. edizione aggiornata al
1970 con 1420 modifiche ed aggiunte. Napoli, 1970 [i. e.
1971].

475 p. mounted plate. 24 cm.

Name of editor, Marina Guardati, at head of title.

Nielsen, Gerda Overgaard, 1917–

Fortegnelse over løbende udenlandske tidsskrifter og serier i Den Kgl. Veterinær- og landbohøjskoles bibliotek og danske jordbrugs- og veterinære institutioner. Foreløbig udg. København, Kgl. Veterinær- og landbohøjskoles bibliotek. 1964.

232 p. 22 cm.

AFRICA

Commonwealth Bureau of Agricultural Economics.

Aspects of agriculture policy and rural development in Africa; an annotated bibliography, prepared by [the] Commonwealth Bureau of Agricultural Economics, Oxford [edited by Margot A. Bellamy]. Farnham Royal, Commonwealth Agricultural Bureaux, 1971.

5 v. 30 cm. (Its Annotated bibliographies. Series B)

Cover title.
CONTENTS: 1. General.—2. North and North East Africa.— 3. East Africa.—4. South and Central Africa.—5. West Africa.

Commonwealth Bureau of Agricultural Economics.

The marketing of agricultural produce in West African countries, with special reference to Ghana: an annotated bibliography, prepared by [the] Commonwealth Bureau of Agricultural Economics. Farnham Royal, Commonwealth Agricultural Bureaux, 1971.

[4] 6 p. 30 cm. (Its Annotated bibliography no. 2)

Dejene, Tekola.

Experiences in rural development: a selected, annotated bibliography of planning, implementing, and evaluating rural development in Africa, by Tekola Dejene and Scott E. Smith. [Washington, Overseas Liaison Committee, American Council on Education] 1973.

48 p. 28 cm. (OLC paper, no. 1)
At head of title: Development from below.

Food and Agriculture Organization of the United Nations. Documentation Center.

Bibliography of FAO documents on Algeria [and other African countries] Roma, 1970–

sheets. 11 x 15 cm.

Microfiche.
CONTENTS: Algeria, Nov. 1971. (B 031).—Botswana, Nov. 1971. (B 019).—Cameroon, Sept. 1971. (B 016).—Chad, Nov. 1971. (B 020).—Dahomey, Nov. 1971. (B 029).—Ethiopia, Nov. 1971. (B 018). 2 sheets.—Ghana, Aug. 1971. (B 009). 2 sheets.—Kenya, Sept. 1971. (B 011). 2 sheets.—Liberia, Nov. 1971. (B 028).—Madagascar, Sept. 1971. (B 007).—Niger, Nov. 1971. (B 021).—Nigeria, Oct. 1971. (B 002 cont.).—Rwanda, Sept. 1971. (B 023).—Sudan, Nov. 1971. (B 017). 3 sheets.—Tanzania, Sept. 1971. (B 024). 2 sheets.—Tunisia, Mar. 1970. (B 001). 2 sheets.—Zambia, Sept. 1971. (B 010). 2 sheets.

Jumba-Masagazi, A H K

Science and technology in East Africa : a bibliography and short commentaries / compiled by A. H. K. Jumba-Masagazi. — Nairobi : East African Academy, Research Information and Publication Service, 1973.

163 p. ; 30 cm. — (Information circular - East African Academy, Research Information and Publication Service ; no. 7)

Lefèvre, P C

Alimentation des populations africaines au sud du Sahara; dépouillement de la bibliothèque de l'I. N. E. A. C. d'après un plan analytique établi par P. C. Lefèvre. Bruxelles, Centre de documentation économique et sociale afri-

caine, 1965.
xiv, 221 p. 23 cm. (Centre de documentation économique et sociale africaine. Enquêtes bibliographiques, 13)
Cover title.
Half title : Bibliographie de l'alimentation des populations africaines au sud du Sahara.

Lefèvre, P C

Les paysannats en Afrique au sud du Sahara. Dépouillement de la bibliothèque de l'I. N. E. A. C. d'après un plan analytique établi par P. C. Lefèvre. Bruxelles, Centre de documentation économique et sociale africaine, 1965.

215 p. 23 cm. (Centre de documentation économique et sociale africaine. Enquêtes bibliographiques, 12)
Cover title.
Half title : Bibliographie des paysannats en Afrique au sud du Sahara.

McLoughlin, Peter F M

Research on agricultural development in East Africa [by] Peter F. M. McLoughlin. New York, Agricultural Development Council [°1967]

111 p. 23 cm.

Neville-Rolfe, Edmund.

Economic aspects of agricultural development in Africa: a selective annotated reading list of reports and studies concerning 40 African countries during the period 1960–1969. Oxford, University of Oxford (Agricultural Economics Research Institute), 1969.

xxiii, [257] p. 29 cm.

Parrot, D

Bibliographie de base pour les écoles d'agriculture d'Afrique tropicale et de Madagascar. Paris (15e), Bureau pour le développement de la production agricole, 202, rue de la Croix-Nivert [1968].

24 p. 27 cm.
At head of title: Secrétariat d'État aux affaires étrangères.
Cover title.
"Tiré à part de la bibliographie, parue dans le 'Courrier de l'enseignant' établie par le Groupe d'appui et de recherches pédagogiques du B. D. P. A. parue dans les numéros 21, 24 et 25 de 'Promotion rurale.'"

BOLIVIA

Aliaga de Vizcarra, Irma.

Bibliografía agrícola boliviana. Recopilación y clasificación realizada por Irma Aliaga de Vizcarra. La Paz, Ministerio de Agricultura, Biblioteca, 1967.

137 p. 22 cm.

——— Suplemento. Recopilación y clasificación realizada por Irma Aliaga de Vizcarra. [La Paz] Ministerio de Agricultura, Biblioteca, 1969–

v. 22 cm.

CONTENTS.—v. 1. 1967–1968.

Bibliografía agrícola boliviana. v. 1–
[Cochabamba, Editorial Universitaria] 1970–

v. 22 cm.

Vols. 1– issued by the Ministerio de Agricultura, with the Facultad de Ciencias Agronómicas, Universidad Mayor de San Simón.

Cardozo Gonzáles, Armando.

Catálogo de la bibliografía agrícola de Bolivia, 1900–1963, de Arturo Costa de la Torre [por] Armando Cardozo. [La Paz] 1970.

14 l. 29 cm. (Sociedad de Ingenieros Agrónomos de Bolivia. Boletín bibliográfico no. 11)

Cover title.
Compiled from Costa de la Torre's Catálogo de la bibliografía boliviana.

Torrico Arze, Armando, 1928–
Bibliografía boliviana de economía agrícola ₁por₁ Armando Torrico Arze ₁e₁ Irma Aliaga de Vizcarra. ₁La Paz₁ 1967.

27 l. 29 cm. (Sociedad de Ingenieros Agrónomos de Bolivia. Boletín bibliográfico no. 6)

BULGARIA

Kekhlibareva, Veselina.
₁Bibliografiia na bŭlgarskata literatura po selsko i gorsko stopanstvo, veterinarna meditsina i dŭrvoobrabotvashta promishlennost—1971₁
Библиография на българската литература по селско и горско стопанство, ветеринарна медицина и дървообработваща промишленост—1971. София, ССА Г. Димитров, 1973.

315 p. 27.5 cm.
At head of title: Централна селскостопанска библиотека.
By V. Kekhlibareva and L. Karaivanova.

CHINA

Chin ling ta hsüeh, Nanking. Nung hsüeh yüan. Nung yeh ching chi hsi.
₁Nung yeh lun wen so yin₁
中國農業論文索引 (1858–1934) ₁吳相湘 劉紹唐主編 台北₁ 傳記文學出版社 ₁民國60 i. e. 1971₁

3 v. 27 cm. (民國史料叢刊 第 13 種)

Reprint of the 1933–35 editions published by the University of Nanking Library, Nanking, with original t. p. of v. 1-2: 農業論文₁
索引 金陵大學農學院農業經濟系農業歷史組(前農業圖書研究部) 編 Agricultural index to periodicals and bulletins in Chinese and in English principally published in China, compiled by the Division of Agricultural History (formerly Research Library), Dept. of Agricultural Economics, College of Agriculture and Forestry, University of Nanking; v. 3: 農業論文索引續編 金陵大學圖書館雜誌小冊部編 Supplement, compiled by the Dept. of Periodicals and Pamphlets, the University of Nanking Library, University of Nanking.

Logan, William J C 1933–
Publications on Chinese agriculture prior to 1949. ₁Compiled by William J. C. Logan; calligraphy and indexing by Peter B. Schroeder₁ Washington, National Agricultural Library, U. S. Dept. of Agriculture, 1966.

ii, 142 p. 26 cm. (U. S. National Agricultural Library. Library list no. 85)

COLOMBIA

Pérez Cordero, Luis de J
Bibliografía del sector agropecuario colombiano ₁por₁ Luis de J. Pérez Cordero. Bogotá, 1967.

ii, 399 p. 28 cm.

Serna Córdoba, Himilce O
Indice agrícola colombiano, 1961–1966, por Himilce O. Serna Córdoba. Medellín ₁Editorial Universidad de Antioquia, 1968₁

xviii, 381 l. 27 cm. (Publicaciones de la E. I. B. Serie: Bibliografías, no. 20)
Tesis (licenciatura en bibliotecología)—Universidad de Antioquia.
"La presente entrega es una continuación del Indice agrícola colombiano, 1951–1960 preparado por Carlos Cadavid A."

COMMUNIST COUNTRIES

Commonwealth Bureau of Agricultural Economics.
The role of private plots in socialist agriculture: annotated bibliography, prepared by ₁the₁ Commonwealth Bureau of Agricultural Economics. Farnham Royal, Commonwealth Agricultural Bureaux, 1971.

₁1₁ iii, 9 p. 30 cm. (Its Annotated bibliography no. 7)

CZECHOSLOVAK REPUBLIC

Jurkovič, Miloš.
Slovenská poľnohospodárska bibliografia. ₁Praha, Československé zemědělské muzeum ÚVTI, 1968₁

462 p. 21 cm. (Prameny historie zemědělství a lesnictví, 5)

Machata, Pavol.
Bibliografia publikačnej činnosti na Vysokej škole poľnohospodárskej v Nitre do roku 1966. V Nitre, Vysoka škola poľnohospodárska, 1971.

2 v. (663 p.) 29 cm.

Prague. Ústřední zemědělská a lesnická knihovna.
Československé socialistické zemědělství v odborné literatuře. (Doporučující bibliografie.) Zprac. ₁kol.₁ Praha, Ústav vědeckotechn inf., rozmn., 1972.

33, ₁1₁ p. 21 cm.
Illustrated t. p.
"Zpracovala: Ústřední zemědělská a lesnická knihovna"

Prague. Vysoká škola zemědělská.
Bibliography.
Prague.

v. 24 cm. annual.
Began with vol. for 1967/68.
Vols. for issued by the university under its English form of name: Agricultural University.

ESTONIA

Estonian S. S. R. *Riiklik Ajaloo Keskarhiiv.*
Ülevaade looma- ja taimekasvatusalastest materjalidest Eesti NSV Riiklikus Ajaloo Keskarhiivis. Koostanud E. Ibius. Tallinn, 1968.

59 p. 20 cm.

EUROPE

Beranová, Magdalena.
Evropské zemědělství v archeologii. Bibliografie 1945–1965. ₁Souběž.₁ překlad do něm.: H. Tichá a A. Schebek. Praha, Archeologický ustav ČSAV, rozmn, 1969.

17, 274, ₁1₁ p. 24 cm. (Archeologické studijní materiály, 7)

Added t. p. in German.

Ludvíková, Václava.
Otázky socialistického zemědělství. Výběrová bibliografie za rok 1967. Sest. Václava Ludvíková. Praha, St. knihovna ČSSR-Ustr. ekom. knihovna, rozmn., 1969.

115, ₁2₁ l. 20 cm.

EUROPEAN ECONOMIC COMMUNITY COUNTRIES

Commonwealth Bureau of Agricultural Economics.
E. E. C. agricultural policy: an annotated bibliography, prepared by ₁the₁ Commonwealth Bureau of Agricultural Economics. Farnham Royal, Commonwealth Agricultural Bureaux, 1971–73.

3 v. 30 cm. (Its Annotated bibliography, no. 5–6. 16)

Cover title.
"Compiled from World agricultural economics and Rural sociology abstracts."
CONTENTS: v. 1. Structural reform.—v. 2. Membership applications.—v. 3. International trade.

Hedges, Brian D
Agriculture in the European Economic Community; an annotated bibliography, 1958–66 ₁by Brian D. Hedges and Reed E. Friend. Washington₁ Economic Research Service, U. S. Dept. of Agriculture ₁1968₁

ii, 77 p. 26 cm. (₁U. S. Dept. of Agriculture. Economic Research Service₁ ERS-foreign no. 213)
Cover title.

Nil, Frans de.
Landbouwwetgeving in de E. E. G.; analytische bibliografie, 1958–1965. Brussel, Belgische Commissie voor Bibliografie, 1969.

viii, 312 p. 20 cm. (Bibliographia Belgica, 106)
"Proefschrift neergelegd bij de—Provinciale Bibliotheekschool van Brabant."

Organization for Economic Cooperation and Development. Library.
La politique agricole. Agricultural policy. ₁Paris, 1970₁
2 v. 27 cm. (Its Bibliographie spécialisée analytique. Special annotated bibliography, 27, 28)
"The bibliography has been selected and annotated by Mrs. Raïssa Tarr."
Series no. of v. 2 corrected by label : 28.

Oslo. Norske Nobelinstitutt. Biblioteket.
Jordbruket i det Europeiske fellesskap. Dokumenter og et utvalg litteratur. Utarb. av Elsa Skarprud. Oslo, 1971.

₁2₁, 8 l. 31 cm.

Yeganiantz, Levon.
Agriculture and trade of the European Economic Community; a selected, annotated bibliography, by Levon Yeganiantz and John Moore. College Park, Agriculture Experiment Station, University of Maryland, 1967.

vi, 84 p. 27 cm. (₁Maryland. Agricultural Experiment Station, College Park₁ Miscellaneous publication, 616)
Maryland Agricultural Experiment Station. Contribution no. 3930.

GERMANY

Bohte, Hans Günther.
Bibliographie des Schrifttums über Agrarstruktur und Landeskultur ⟨Verbesserung der Agrarstruktur⟩ in der Bundesrepublik Deutschland 1949–1970. Berlin, Landschriften-Verlag ₁c1971₁

274 p. 21 cm.

Gercke, Annemarie.
Bibliographie des deutschen Agrarrechts 1945–1965. Hrsg. von Karl Kroeschell und Wolfgang Winkler. Köln, C. Heymann, 1968.

xxiv, 239 p. 21 cm. (Schriftenreihe des Instituts für Landwirtschaftsrecht der Universität Göttingen, Bd. 1)

GHANA

Volta River Authority.
Agricultural development on the Accra-Ho-Keta Plains. Accra ₁Ghana₁ 1972.

12 p. 34 cm. (Its Library list no. 8)

GREAT BRITAIN

Gt. Brit. *Ministry of Agriculture, Fisheries and Food.*
Agricultural and food statistics: a guide to official sources. ₁New ed.₁ London, H. M. S. O., 1969.

v, 119 p., fold. plate. forms. 21 cm. (Studies in official statistics, no. 14) 12/6

McDonald, Donald, 1857–
Agricultural writers from Sir Walter of Henley to Arthur

Young, 1200–1800. Reproductions in facsim. and extracts from their actual writings, enl. and rev. from articles which have appeared in "The field" from 1903 to 1907, to which is added an exhaustive bibliography. New York, B. Franklin ₁1968₁

228 p. illus. 26 cm. (Burt Franklin : bibliography & reference series #217)

Reading, Eng. University. Library.
Accessions of historical farm records revised up to March 1970. Reading (Berks), University of Reading (Library), 1970.

20 leaves. 30 cm.

Reading, Eng. University. Library.
Historical farm records : a summary guide to manuscripts and other material in the University Library collected by the Institute of Agricultural History and the Museum of English Rural Life. — Reading : University of Reading, Library, 1973.
xii, 320 p. ; 25 cm.
Includes index.

HUNGARY

Eke, Pálné.
Magyar agrárföldrajzi bibliográfia, 1961–1966. Hungarian agrogeographical bibliography, 1961–1966. Összeállította Eke Pálné ₁és₁ Enyedi György. Budapest, Magyar Tudományos Akadémia, Földrajztudományi Kutató Intézet, 1968.
93 p. 29 cm.
Cover title.
Pref. and titles also in English.

Gallai, Ervin.
A mezőgazdasági bibliográfiai tájékoztatás kérdései. Budapest ₁Országos Könyvtárügyi és Dokumentációs Tanács₁ 1964.

66 p. 23 cm. (Az Országos Könyvtárügyi és Dokumentációs Tanács kiadványai, 18)

Rau, Jenő.
A mezőgazdasági üzemtan magyar szakirodalma, bibliográfia. ₁Szerk. Lőrincz Gyula. Az anyagot összegyűjtötte Lucza Ferencné és Szabó Andrásné közreműködésével Rau Jenő. Budapest, 1968–

v. 24 cm. (Agrártudományi Egyetem Központi Könyvtárának kiadványai, 18. sz.
Pref. in Hungarian, Russian, English, and German.

INDIA

Indian Council of Agricultural Research. *Library.*
Documentation of agriculture; the bulletin of current references on agriculture in India.
Jan./June 1965–
New Delhi.

v. 34 cm.

National Institute of Community Development.
Agriculture and food production in India; a bibliography. Hyderabad ₁India₁ 1971.

151 p. 34 cm.

"Prepared on the occassion ₁sic₁ of Workshop-cum-Seminar on Rural Institutions and Agricultural Development in the Seventees ₁sic₁."

Wadhwa, D C 1933–
Agrarian legislation in India, 1793–1966 ₁by₁ D. C. Wadhwa. Poona, Gokhale Institute of Politics and Economics ₁c1973–

v. 26 cm. (Gokhale Institute studies no. 61

INDONESIA

Bibliografi ekonomi pertanian Indonesia. Bogor, Panitia Dokumentasi Survey Agro Ekonomi, 1967.

15 p. 33 cm.

"Dikutip dari skripsi jang berdjudul 'Penjelidikan literatur di Pusat Perpustakaan Biologi dan Pertanian "Bibliotheca-Bogoriensis" mengenai sosial ekonomi pertanian di Indonesia,' disusun oleh Sdr. Sjamsiah Marzuki."

Ringkasan publikasi dan laporan penelitian pertanian. th. 1–   Djan. 1971–
Bogor, Panitia Koordinasi Penelitian Pertanian.

v. 24 cm.

JAMAICA

Steer, Edgar S
A select bibliography of reference material providing an introduction to the study of Jamaican agriculture, by Edgar S. Steer. Hope, Jamaica, Agricultural Planning Unit, Ministry of Agriculture and Fisheries, 1970.

40 p. 28 cm.

JAPAN

Bibliography of agricultural sciences in Japan.

[Tokyo] Science and Technology Agency.

no. 26 cm. annual.

Began in 1971. Cf. New serial titles.
Vols. for   published with the cooperation of the Japan Documentation Society and the Japan Association of Agricultural Librarians and Documentalists.

Japan. Kannōkyoku.
(Nōji sankōsho kaidai)
農事参考書解題
東京 国書刊行会 昭和45（1970）
274, 40p 図 22cm

Tōhata, Seiichi, 1899–
(Nōsho ni rekishi ari)
農書に歴史あり 東畑精一著 東京 家の光協
会 昭和48(1973)
268 p. 19 cm.

KIRGHIZISTAN

Экономика сельского хозяйства Киргизии. Библиогр. указатель. (1956–1964). Фрунзе, "Илим," 1968.

256 p. 21 cm.

At head of title: Академия наук Киргизской ССР. Институт экономики. Центральная научная библиотека.
Added t. p. in Kirghiz.
Compiled by L. M. Erman and others.

LATIN AMERICA

Niederböster, Heinrich.
Landwirtschaftliche Fragen Iberoamerikas. Eine Auswahl neuerer Zeitschriftenaufsätze. Hamburg, (Institut für Iberoamerika-Kunde) 1965.

104 p. 21 cm. (Institut für Iberoamerika-Kunde. Reihe Bibliographie und Dokumentation, Heft 8)

MIDDLE EAST

Taylor. Donald C
Research on agricultural development in selected Middle Eastern countries [by] Donald C. Taylor. New York, Agricultural Development Council [1968]

x, 166 p. 23 cm.

ONTARIO

Ontario. Dept. of Agriculture and Food. Farm Economics Co-operatives and Statistics Branch.
A list of current branch publications, January 1971. Toronto, Farm Economics, Cooperatives and Statistics Branch, Ontario Dept. of Agriculture and Food, 1971.

6 l. 28 cm.

Cover title.

PAKISTAN

Siddiqui, Akhtar H
Agriculture in Pakistan; a selected bibliography, 1947–1969. Compiled by Akhtar H. Siddiqui. Rawalpindi, Printed and distributed by the Office of Assistant Director/Agricultural Policy, United States Agency for International Development, Pakistan 1969.

iv, 88 p. 27 cm.

PERU

La Molina, Peru. Estación Experimental Agrícola. Biblioteca.
Bibliografía agrícola peruana existente en la Biblioteca de la Estación Experimental Agrícola de La Molina. Compilada por: Amalia Cavero de Cornejo. Lima, Ministerio de Agricultura, Servicio de Investigación y Promoción Agraria-SIPA, Estación Experimental Agrícola de La Molina, 1967–

v. 28 cm.

ROMANIA

Comitetul Judeţean de Cultură şi Educaţie Socialistă Iaşi.
În sprijinul propagandei agricole în biblioteci. Materiale bibliografice de recomandare. Iaşi, 1972.

52 p. 24 cm.

At head of title: Comitetul Judeţean de Cultură şi Educaţie Socialistă. Biblioteca Municipală „Gheorghe Asachi"—Iaşi.

ROME

White. K   D
A bibliography of Roman agriculture, by K. D. White. Reading, University of Reading (Institute of Agricultural History), 1970.

xxviii, 63 p. 25 cm. (Bibliographies in agricultural history, no. 1)

RUSSIA

Bogatova, Galina Petrovna.
(Fundament sel'skokhoziaĭstvennogo proizvodstva)
Фундамент сельскохозяйственного производства. (XXIV съезд КПСС и основные пути развития сельск. хоз-ва). Рек. указ. литературы. Москва, "Книга," 1973.

72 p. 20 cm.

At head of title: Государственная библиотека СССР имени В. И. Ленина.
By G. P. Bogatova, S. P. Karazeeva and V. A. Nasedkina.

Экономика и организация сельскохозяйственного производства: рекомендательный указатель литературы. [Составитель Г. К. Донская. Редактор А. М. Бочевер] Москва, Книга, 1966.

19 p. 20 cm.

At head of title: Государственная библиотека СССР и Центральная научная сельскохозяйственная библиотека ВАСХНИЛ.

Gorbatov, A   L
(Intensifikatsiia sel'skokhoziaĭstvennogo proizvodstva)
Интенсификация сельскохозяйственного производства. Библиогр. указ. отеч. литературы за 1969–71 гг. Москва, 1972.

104 p. 20 cm.

At head of title: Всесоюзная Академия сельскохозяйственных наук имени В. И. Ленина. Центральная научная сельскохозяйственная библиотека.

Gorbatov, A   L
(Khoziaĭstvennyĭ raschet v sel'skom khoziaĭstve SSSR)
Хозяйственный расчет в сельском хозяйстве СССР. Библиогр. указатель отечеств. литературы за 1965–1967 гг. (Сост. А. Л. Горбатов). Москва, 1968.

86 p. 20 cm.

At head of title: Всесоюзная академия сельскохозяйственных наук имени В. И. Ленина. Центральная научная сельскохозяйственная библиотека.

Gorbatov, A   L
(Proizvoditel'nost' truda v sel'skom khoziaĭstve)
Производительность труда в сельском хозяйстве. Библиогр. указатель отечественной литературы за 1967–1969 гг. в количестве 469 назв. и иностранной за 1966–1969 гг. в количестве 169 назв. (Сост. А. Л. Горбатов). Москва, 1970.

116 p. 20 cm.
At head of title: Всесоюзная академия сельскохозяйственных наук имени В. И. Ленина. Центральная научная сельскохозяйственная библиотека. Справочно-библиографический отдел.

Gorbatov, A   L
Размещение и специализация сельскохозяйственного производства. Библиогр. указатель отечеств. литературы за 1966–1967 гг ... (Сост. А. Л. Горбатов). Москва, 1967.

92 p. 20 cm.
At head of title: Всесоюзная ордена Ленина Академия с.-х. наук имени В. И. Ленина. Центральная научная сельскохозяйственная библиотека. Справочно-библиографический отдел.

Leningrad. Vsesoiuznyĭ institut rastenievodstva. Biblioteka.
(Bibliograficheskiĭ ukazatel' rabot sotrudnikov instituta)
Библиографический указатель работ сотрудников института. (1934–1968). Под ред. акад. Д. Д. Брежнева. Ленинград, 1969–

v. 27 cm.

At head of title, v.   : Всесоюзная академия сельскохозяйственных наук имени В. И. Ленина.
"Составители: Т. С. Миркина (и др.)"

Makarenko, G   A
Книгу—в помощь специалисту сельского хозяйства на производстве. Указатель литературы ... Москва, 1967.

124 p. 21 cm.

At head of title: Всесоюзная ордена Ленина академия сельскохозяйственных наук имени В. И. Ленина. Центральная научная сельскохозяйственная библиотека.
By G. A. Makarenko and V. G. Grigor'eva.

Morachevskaia, Elena Nikolaevna.
Библиография по районированию, размещению и специализации сельского хозяйства. (1960–1966 гг.) Москва, "Наука." 1970.

161 p. 21 cm.
At head of title: Академия наук СССР. Госплан СССР. Совет по изучению производительных сил.

Moscow. TSentral'naia nauchnaia sel'skokhoziaĭstvennaia biblioteka.
Интенсификация сельского хозяйства СССР; общие вопросы. Указатель лит-ры. (Составил А. Л. Горбатов). Москва, 1964.

23 p. 21 cm.

At head of title: Всесоюзная академия сельскохозяйственных наук имени В. И. Ленина.

Moscow. TSentral'naia nauchnaia sel'skokhoziaĭstvennaia biblioteka. *Spravochno-bibliograficheskiĭ otdel.*
Материальная заинтересованность и ее роль в развитии социалистического сельского хозяйства; библиографический список отечественной литературы за 1964–1965 гг. в количестве 548 названий. (Составил А. Л. Горбатов). Москва, 1966.
64 p. 20 cm.
At head of title: Всесоюзная академия с.-х. наук имени В. И. Ленина.

Shchekachev, IU   I
(Nauchnaia organizatsiia upravleniia v sel'skokhoziaĭstvennom proizvodstve)
Научная организация управления в сельскохозяйственном производстве. (Библиогр. указ. отеч. и зарубеж. литературы за 1960–1970 гг.) Москва, 1972.

121 p. 20 cm.
At head of title: Министерство сельского хозяйства РСФСР. Всероссийский научно-исследовательский институт труда и управления в сельском хозяйстве.

Указатель книг, журнальных и газетных статей по сельскому хозяйству за 1912 год. (Подготовлен Ленинградским филиалом Центр. науч. с.-х. библиотеки) по материалам А. Д. Педашенко. Ленинград, 1966–
v. 20 cm.
At head of title, v. 1–   : Всесоюзная ордена Ленина академия сельскохозяйственных наук имени В. И. Ленина. Центральная научная сельскохозяйственная библиотека.
CONTENTS.—т. 1. Сельскохозяйственное образование.

(Ukazatel' knig, zhurnal'nykh i gazetnykh stateĭ po sel'skomu khoziaĭstvu)
Указатель книг, журнальных и газетных статей по сельскому хозяйству за 1915 год. По материалам А. Д. Педашенко. (В 9-ти т.) Т. 1–   Москва—Ленинград, 1973–
v. 20 cm.

SUDAN

McLoughlin, Peter F   M
Research for agricultural development in Northern Sudan to 1967: a classified inventory and analysis (by Peter F. M. McLoughlin.) Frederiction, N. B., P. McLoughlin Associates (1971)

iv, 86, 2 l. 28 cm. (Notes and papers in development, no. 1)

SWEDEN

Uppsala. Universitet. *Litteraturhistoriska institutionen. Avdelningen för litteratursociologi.*
Tidningen Lantarbetaren 1908–1966. Ett register utarbetat av Avdelningen för litteratursociologi med företal av Ewald Jansson och historik av Lars Furuland. Uppsala, Lundequistska bokhandeln (distr.) 1967.

3 v. 32 cm. (Meddelanden utg. av Avdelningen för litteratursociologi vid Litteraturhistoriska institutionen i Uppsala, nr. 2 (:1–2:3)

UNITED STATES

Edwards, Everett Eugene, 1900–
A bibliography of the history of agriculture in the United States, by Everett E. Edwards. New York, B. Franklin (1970)

iv, 307 p. 24 cm. (Selected essays in history, economics, and social science, 152)

Burt Franklin bibliography and reference series, 846.
Reprint of the 1930 ed.

Schlebecker, John T
Bibliography of books and pamphlets on the history of agriculture in the United States, 1607–1967 [by] John T. Schlebecker. Santa Barbara, Calif., A[merican] B[ibliographical] C[enter]—Clio, 1969.

vii, 183 p. 26 cm.

"Published under contract with the Smithsonian Institution."

United States. Dept. of Agriculture. Office of Management Services.
Periodic reports of agricultural economics and statistics. [Prepared by Division of Information, Office of Management Services, U. S. Department of Agriculture. Washington] U. S. Dept. of Agriculture, 1973.

10 p. 26 cm.

VIETNAM

U. S. Engineer Agency for Resources Inventories.
Vietnam agriculture; a selected annotated bibliography, prepared by Engineer Agency for Resources Inventories in cooperation with Vietnam Research and Evaluation Information Center. Bureau for Vietnam, Agency for International Development. [Editors: Janet G. Gee and Mary Anglemyer] Washington, 1970.

v, 58 p. 27 cm.

YUGOSLAVIA

Stancl, Branko.
Bibliografija s prikazima radova članova Instituta od 1945. do 1966. godine. ⟨Đuro Regan: Kratki historijski pregled razvoja Instituta za ekonomiku i organizaciju poljoprivrede Poljoprivrednog fakulteta Sveučilišta u Zagrebu⟩. Zagreb, Institut za ekonomiku i organizaciju poljoprivrede Poljoprivrednog fakulteta Sveučilišta, 1966.

118, [2] p. 24 cm.

AGRICULTURE, COOPERATIVE

Food and Agriculture Organization of the United Nations. Documentation Center.
Agricultural cooperation. Coopération agricole. Cooperación agrícola. Annotated bibliography. Author and subject index. FAO publications and documents (1945–Sep. 1971). [Rome, 1971]

1 v. (various pagings) 28 cm.

Houée, Paul.
Coopération et organisations agricoles françaises. Paris, Éditions Cujas, 1969–70 [v. 1, 1970]

2 v. 24 cm. (Communautés)

Illustrated covers.
Vol. 2 has subtitle: Éléments bibliographiques, 1884–1966.

Kutten, A
Bibliography on physical planning of cooperative and collective agricultural settlements in Israel; a selection of publications in foreign languages, compiled by A. Kutten [and] J. Maos. [Haifa, Technion, Israel Institute of Technology, Faculty of Architecture and Town Planning, 1967]

18 l. 27 cm.

Kutten, A
Bibliography on physical planning of cooperative and collective agricultural settlements in Israel; a selection of publications in foreign languages. [3d ed. Haifa, Tech-

nion-Israel Institute of Technology, Faculty of Architecture and Town Planning, 1970]

51 l. 27 cm.

AGUINALDO Y FAMY, EMILIO

Medina, Isagani R
Preliminary bibliography on Emilio Aguinaldo. [Compiled by Isagani R. Medina] Manila, National Historical Commission, 1969.

76 p. 24 cm.

AIDA FAMILY

Saitama Kenritsu Urawa Toshokan.
(Aida Ke Aizawa Ke monjo mokuroku)
会田家・相沢家文書目録　浦和　埼玉県立浦和図書館　1971.

404 p.　26 cm.　[近世史料所在調査報告　6]

AIR

Hall, L　　A
A bibliography of thermophysical properties of air from 0 to 300 K [by] L. A. Hall. [Washington] U. S. National Bureau of Standards; for sale by the Supt. of Docs., U. S. Govt. Print. Off., 1969.

iii, 121 p. 27 cm. (NBS technical note 383)

POLLUTION

Air Pollution Technical Information Center.
Air pollution aspects of emission sources: a bibliography with abstracts. Research Triangle Park, N. C., Environmental Protection Agency, Air Pollution Control Office; for sale of the Supt. of Docs., U. S. Govt. Print. Off., Washington, 1971–

v. 26 cm. (Air Pollution Control Office publication no. AP-92–94, 96, 105, 107

Publication AP-94–
Air Programs.   Issued by the Office of

CONTENTS: [1] Municipal incineration.—[2] Nitric acid manufacturing.—[3] Sulfuric acid manufacturing.—

[5] Electric power production.—[6] Boilers.—[7] Iron and steel mills.

Air Pollution Technical Information Center.
Air pollution translations: a bibliography with abstracts. [Compiled by] Office of Technical Information and Publications, Air Pollution Technical Information Center. Arlington, Va., U.S. National Air Pollution Control Administration, 1969–

v.   27 cm. (National Air Pollution Control Administration publication no. AP-56)

Air Pollution Technical Information Center.
Beryllium and air pollution: an annotated bibliography [by] Office of Technical Information and Publications, Air Pollution Technical Information Center. Research Triangle Park, N. C., U. S. Environmental Protection Agency, Air Pollution Control Office; for sale by the Supt. of Docs., U. S. Govt. Print. Off., Washington, 1971.

iii, 75 p. 24 cm. (Air Pollution Control Office publication no. AP-83)

Air Pollution Technical Information Center.
Chlorine and air pollution: an annotated bibliography. Research Triangle Park, N. C., Environmental Protection Agency, Office of Air Programs; for sale by the Supt. of

Docs., U. S. Govt. Print. Off., Washington, 1971.

iii, 113 p. 23 cm. (Office of Air Programs publication no. AP-99)

Air Pollution Technical Information Center.

Hydrocarbons and air pollution; an annotated bibliography. Raleigh, N.C., National Air Pollution Control Administration; [for sale by the Supt. of Docs., U.S. Govt. Print. Off., Washington] 1970.

2 v. (1183 p.) 24 cm. (National Air Pollution Control Administration publication no. AP-75)

CONTENTS: Pt. 1. Categories A to E.—Pt. 2. Categories F to M and indexes.

Air Pollution Technical Information Center.

Hydrochloric acid and air pollution: an annotated bibliography [by] Office of Technical Information and Publications, Air Pollution Technical Information Center. Research Triangle Park, N. C., Environmental Protection Agency, Office of Air Programs; for sale by the Supt. of Docs., U. S. Govt. Print. Off., Washington, 1971.

iii, 107 p. 23 cm. (Office of Air Programs publication no. AP-100)

Air Pollution Technical Information Center.

Mercury and air pollution: a bibliography with abstracts. Research Triangle Park, N. C., Environmental Protection Agency, Office of Air Programs; [for sale by the Supt. of Docs., U. S. Govt. Print. Off., Washington] 1972.

v, 50 p. 26 cm. (Office of Air Programs publication no. AP-114)

Air Pollution Technical Information Center.

Nitrogen oxides: an annotated bibliography. Raleigh, N. C., National Air Pollution Control Administration; [for sale by the Supt. of Docs., U. S. Govt. Print. Off.] 1970.

iii, 633 p. 24 cm. (National Air Pollution Control Administration publication no. AP-72)

Air Pollution Technical Information Center.

Odors and air pollution: a bibliography with abstracts. Research Triangle Park, N. C., Environmental Protection Agency, Office of Air Programs; [for sale by the Supt. of Docs., U. S. Govt. Print. Off., Washington] 1972.

v, 257 p. 26 cm. (Office of Air Programs publication no. AP-113)

Air Pollution Technical Information Center.

Photochemical oxidants and air pollution: an annotated bibliography [by] Office of Technical Information and Publications, Air Pollution Technical Information Center. Research Triangle Park, N. C., U. S. Environmental Protection Agency, Air Pollution Control Office; for sale by the Supt. of Docs., U. S. Govt. Print. Off., Washington, 1971.

2 v. (iii, 1529 p.) 23 cm. (Air Pollution Control Office publication no. AP-88)

American Institute of Plant Engineers.

A plant engineer's guide to the literature on air and water pollution. Prepared by American Institute of Plant Engineers with the cooperation of the John Crerar Library, Research Information Service. C. Fred Gurnham, editor. Cincinnati, 1970.

47 p. 28 cm.

Boos, Inge.

Schwermetalle als Luftverunreinigung: Blei, Zink, Cadmium-Heavy metals: lead, zinc, and cadmium; Bibliography. Kolloquium d. VDI-Komm. Reinhaltung d. Luft am 22./23. Febr. 1973 in Düsseldorf; Literaturübersicht (1970-1972)/ bearb. von Inge Boos u. Ursula Rahlenbeck.

Erstellt von d. VDI-Fachdokumentation Reinhaltung d. Luft. — Düsseldorf: VDI-Fachdokumentation Reinhaltung d. Luft, 1973.

80 l.; 29 cm.

English or German.

Cooper, Anna Grossmann.

Sulfur oxides and other sulfur compounds; a bibliography with abstracts. Washington, U. S. Dept. of Health, Education, and Welfare, Public Health Service, Division of Air Pollution; [for sale by the Superintendent of Documents, U. S. Govt. Print. Off.] 1965.

xi, 383 p. 26 cm. (Public Health Service publication no. 1093. Bibliography series, no. 56)

(Metody zashchity okruzhaiushcheĭ prirodnoĭ sredy ot zagriaznenii)

Методы защиты окружающей природной среды от загрязнений. Библиогр. указ. [1967–1971 гг. Сост. Е. Н. Кондрашова, А. А. Галазова, Е. А. Колотушина и др.] Москва, 1972.

170 p. 22 cm.

At head of title: Государственный комитет Совета Министров СССР по науке и технике. Государственная публичная научно-техническая библиотека СССР.

Nekola, Miloslav.

Prachové a plynné exhalace elektráren. Doporučující bibliografie kniž. a čas. literatury. Sest. Miloslav Nekola. Úvod: Břetislav Klobouk. 1. vyd. Praha, UVTEI-St. techn. knihovna, rozmn, 1968.

65 p. 21 cm. ([Prague. Státní technická knihovna] Bibliografie, sv. 127)

Prague. Státní technická knihovna.

Boj proti hluku a exhalacím v průmyslových městech; doporučující bibliografie knižní a časopisecké literatury. [Sest. Jitka Kostková] Praha, 1965.

97 p. 21 cm. (Its Bibliografie, sv. 75)

Qutub, Musa Y

Air pollution, compiled by Musa Qutub. [Chicago, Mid-continent Scientific, c1973]

9 p. 22 cm. (His Environmental reference series, 8)

Subject index to current literature on air and water conservation. -Apr. 1969. [New York] Committee for Air and Water Conservation, American Petroleum Institute.

no. 28 cm. monthly.

Trondheim. Norges tekniske høgskole. *Biblioteket.*

Luftforurensing. Trondheim, 1966.

48 p. 30 cm. (Its Litteraturliste, 31)

Verein Deutscher Ingenieure. *Dokumentationsstelle. Fachdokumentation Reinhaltung der Luft.*

Bibliographie Reinhaltung der Luft 1957-1966. Hrsg. im Auftrage der VDI-Kommission Reinhaltung der Luft von der VDI-Dokumentationsstelle, Fachdokumentation Reinhaltung der Luft, Düsseldorf. Düsseldorf, VDI-Verlag, 1967–

v. 21 cm.

Weiner, Jack, 1910–

Air pollution in the pulp and paper industry [by] Jack Weiner and Lillian Roth. Introd. by W. M. Van Horn. Appleton, Wis., Institute of Paper Chemistry, 1969.

iii, 224 p. 28 cm. (Institute of Paper Chemistry. Bibliographic series, no. 237)

———— ₁Supplement₁ Appleton, Wis., Institute of Paper Chemistry, 1970.

v. 28 cm. (Institute of Paper Chemistry. Bibliographic series, no. 237, suppl. 1–

AIR CONDITIONING
see also Heat; Plumbing

(Bibliograficheskiĭ ukazatel' literatury po konditsioneram, kaloriferam i ventil'iatoram.)
Библиографический указатель литературы по кондиционерам, калориферам и вентиляторам. Москва, 1971.
17 p. 21 cm.
At head of title: Техническое управление. Центральный научно-исследовательский институт информации и технико-экономических исследований по строительному, дорожному и коммунальному машиностроению.

AIR LINE RESERVATIONS

Phillips, Edward.
Bibliography on reservation systems and ticketing 1959–1966. ₁Montreal₁ CN Headquarters Library ₁1967?₁
13 p. 28 cm. (CN Headquarters Library. Special series no. 12)

AIR WARFARE

Santelli, James S
An annotated bibliography of the United States Marine Corps' concept of close air support, by James S. Santelli. Washington, Historical Branch, G-3 Division, Headquarters, U. S. Marine Corps, 1968.
24 p. 26 cm. (Marine Corps historical bibliography)

AIRPLANES

Australia. National Acoustic Laboratories.
Publications on aircraft noise held by N. A. L.; a bibliography with abstracts, compiled by Joan Cordell. Sydney, National Accoustic Laboratories, Dept. of Health, 19
v. 30 cm. (Bibliographic report no. 12
CONTENTS:
—Supplement 3. January 1971–September 1973.

Bulletin signalétique: Série constructions aéronautiques. no 73–74; jan.–déc. 1968. ₁Paris₁
22 no. 25 cm. semimonthly.
Supersedes in part Bulletin signalétique, issued 1965–67 by the Service de documentation scientifique et technique de l'armement, and continues its numbering.
Issues for Jan.–June 1968 published by the Centre de documentation de l'armement; July–Dec. 1968 by its Antenne constructions aéronautiques.

Corridon, Geraldine Antoinette, 1916–
Aircraft in agriculture, 1958–1963; a list of selected references ₁compiled by Geraldine A. Corridon₁ Washington, National Agricultural Library, U. S. Dept. of Agriculture, 1965.
iv, 93 p. 27 cm. (₁U. S. National Agricultural Library₁ Library list no. 65, suppl. 1)
Supplements Bibliography on aviation and economic entomology, by I. L. Hawes, issued as U. S. Dept. of Agriculture. Bibliographical bulletin no. 8, and Aircraft in agriculture; a selected list of references, by N. G. Larson, issued as Library list no. 65.

McLellan, Alden.
The upper atmospheric environment of the supersonic transport: a bibliography. Madison, University of Wisconsin, 1971.
106 p. 28 cm.
Title on spine: SST bibliography.

U. S. *Dept. of Transportation. Library Services Division.*
Aircraft noise and sonic boom; selected references. ₁Compiled by Maria R. Haywood₁ Washington, 1969.
iii, 41 p. 26 cm. (*Its* Bibliographic list no. 2)

U. S. Dept. of Transportation. Library Services Division.
Hijacking; selected readings. Washington, 1971.
vi, 53 p. 26 cm. (Its Bibliographic list no. 5)
Updates Hijacking; selected references, issued in 1969 by U. S. Federal Aviation Administration, Library Services Division.

U. S. Federal Aviation Administration. Library Services Division.
Hijacking; selected references ₁compiled by Ann O'Brien₁ Washington, 1969.
i, 22 p. 26 cm. (*Its* Bibliographic list no. 18)
Cover title.

U. S. *Federal Aviation Agency. Library Services Division.*
Aircraft noise and sonic boom; selected references. ₁Compiled by Louise K. Annus₁ Washington, 1966.
ii, 112 p. 26 cm. (*Its* Bibliographic list no. 13)
Cover title.

U. S. *Library of Congress. Aerospace Technology Division.*
Soviet aircraft circuit breakers; annotated bibliography. ₁Washington₁ 1965.
iii, 18 l. 29 cm. (*Its* ATD report B–65–54)
"Based on Soviet open-source literature available at the Aerospace Technology Division and ₁i. e. of₁ the Library of Congress."

AIRPORTS

King, Richard L
Airport noise pollution: a bibliography of its effects on people and property, by Richard L. King. With a foreword by Jerrold A. Fadem. Metuchen, N. J., Scarecrow Press, 1973.
380 p. 22 cm.

U. S. Dept. of Transportation. Library Services Division.
Airport problems: access and air traffic congestion; selected readings. ₁Compiled by Maria R. Haywood₁ Washington, 1971.
v, 34 p. 26 cm. (**Its** Bibliographic list no. 4)

U. S. *Federal Aviation Administration. Library Services Division.*
Air traffic and airport congestion; selected references. ₁Compiled by Nancy B. Nelsen₁ Washington, Dept. of Transportation, Federal Aviation Administration, 1969.
iii, 30 p. 26 cm. (*Its* Bibliographic list no. 17)
Cover title.

U. S. *Federal Aviation Agency. Library Services Division.*
Access to airports; selected references. ₁Compiled by Louise K. Annus₁ Washington, Federal Aviation Agency, 1966.
7 p. 26 cm. (*Its* Bibliographic list no. 12)
Cover title.
———— Supplement. Washington, Federal Aviation Administration, 1967.
ii, 7 p. 26 cm. (*Its* Bibliographic list no. 12. Suppl.)
Cover title.

AISNE, FRANCE (DEPT.)

Aisne, France (Dept.). Archives départementales.
Guide des archives de l'Aisne. Laon, ₍Archives départementales,₎ 1971.

xl, 286 p. 24 cm.

At head of title: G. Dumas.

AIZAWA FAMILY see under Aida family

AKADEMIE DER WISSENSCHAFTEN, BERLIN

Akademie der Wissenschaften, *Berlin. Hauptbibliothek.*
Gesamtregister der Abhandlungen, Sitzungsberichte, Jahrbücher, Vorträge und Schriften der Preussischen Akademie der Wissenschaften, 1900–1945. ₍Redaktion: Wilhelm Seyffert und Ingeburg Weinitschke₎ Berlin, Akademie-Verlag, 1966.

xxi, 314 p. 25 cm.

Continues O. Köhnke's Gesamtregister über die in den Schriften der Akademie von 1700–1899 erschienenen wissenschaftlichen Abhandlungen und Festreden, which formed v. 3 of the 1900 ed. of A. von Harnack's Geschichte der Königlich Preussischen Akademie der Wissenschaften zu Berlin.

Vezényi, Pál.
Abhandlungen und Sitzungsberichte der Deutschen Akademie der Wissenschaften (Königl. Preussische Akademie) zu Berlin 1900–1960: Bibliographie. München-Pullach, Verlag Dokumentation, 1968.

264 p. 21 cm.

Publications replacing Sitzungsberichte 1939–1945 also included.

AKADEMIE DER WISSENSCHAFTEN, MUNICH

Akademie der Wissenschaften, Munich.
Veröffentlichungen 1932–1970, Bayerische Akademie der Wissenschaften. München, Beck, 1970.

109 p. 22 cm.

AKADEMIĨA NAUK GRUZINSKOĬ SSR, TIFLIS

Akademiĩa nauk Gruzinskoĭ SSR, *Tiflis. Tsentral'naĩa nauchnaĩa biblioteka.*
Библиография изданий Академии наук Грузинской ССР 1957–1960 гг. Тбилиси, Изд. АН Груз. ССР, 1963 ₍вып. дан. 1967₎.

587 p. 26 cm.

AKADEMIĨA NAUK SSSR

Akademiĩa nauk SSSR. *Biblioteka.*
Библиотека Академии наук СССР, 1714–1964; библиографический указатель. ₍Составили Э. П. Файдель и др. Ответственный редактор М. С. Филиппов₎ Ленинград, 1964.

807 p. 22 cm.

Akademiĩa nauk SSSR. *Izdatel'stvo.*
Каталог книг Издательства Академии наук СССР, 1945–1962. ₍Составитель Я. Я. Бычков₎ Москва, Наука, 1965.

367 p. 27 cm.

Mamaeva, L   I
Библиографический указател изданий Коми филиала Академия наук СССР. (1958–1966). Сыктывкар, 1968.

165 p. 20 cm.

At head of title: Академия наук СССР. Коми филиал. Научная библиотека.

Указатель библиографических работ, выполненных библиотеками Академии наук СССР и академий наук союзных республик. Москва, 1957.
110 p.
At head of title: Академия наук СССР. Библиотечная комиссия при Президиуме АН СССР.
Microfilm. 1 reel. 35 mm.

AKADEMIĨA NAUK TURKMENSKOĬ SSR, ASHKHABAD

Nuryev, O   M
₍Bibliografiĩa izdaniĭ Akademii nauk Turkmenskoĭ SSR₎
Библиография изданий Академии наук Туркменской ССР. 1941–1961 гг. Сост. О. Нурыев и А. Я. Степанов. Отв. ред. акад. Т. Б. Бердыев. Редактор А. С. Якуничева. Ашхабад, "Ылым," 1971.

413 p. 22 cm.

At head of title: Академия наук Туркменской ССР. Центральная научная библиотека.
Added t. p. in Turkoman.

Stepanov, A   IA
Библиография изданий Академии наук Туркменской ССР. 1962–1966 гг. Составители: А. Я. Степанов и С. А. Мамедова. Редактор А. Язбердыев. Ашхабад, Ылым, 1970.

301 p. 23 cm.

At head of title: Академия наук Туркменской ССР. Центральная научная библиотека.
Added t. p. in Turkmen.

AKADEMIĨA NAUK URSR, KIEV

Akademiĩa nauk URSR, Kiev.
Каталог видань Української академії наук, 1918–1930. Приготовив і видав Дмитро М. Штогрин. Чікаго, Т-во Укр. бібліотекарів Америки, 1966.

284, 74 p. 23 cm. (Слов'янські біо-бібліографічні матеріяли, т. 1)

Added t. p.: Catalog of publications of The Ukrainian Academy of Sciences, 1918–1930.

Akademiĩa nauk URSR, Kiev.
₍Vydannĩa₎
Видання. 1968–
Київ, Наукова думка.

v. 23 cm. annual.

Prepared by the Academy's Tsentral'na naukova biblioteka.

AKHAĨA REGION, GREECE

Karabias, Notēs.
(Achaïkē vivliographia)
Ἀχαϊκὴ βιβλιογραφία : συμβολὴ πρώτη, 1765–1971 / Νότη Διον. Καραβία. — Ἀθῆναι : Βιβλιοπωλεῖον Καραβία, 1972.

6, 134 p. ; 25 cm. — (Βιβλιοθήκη ἱστορικῶν μελετῶν ; 52)

AKITA, JAPAN (PREFECTURE)

Akita Kenritsu Akita Toshokan.
(Kikuchi bunko Akibayashi bunko Tanaka bunko mokuroku)

菊池文庫・秋林文庫・田中文庫目録 ₍秋田₎ 秋田図書館（秋田県立） 昭和46(1971)

82 p. 26 cm.

Mishima, Tōru.
秋田県郷土史関係目録 逐次刊行物 [三島亮
編 秋田, みしま書房 昭和42 [1967]

150 p. 26 cm.

ALABAMA

Alabama. Planning Reference Service.
A selected bibliography of Alabama county and regional planning and development documents. [Compiled by Mark P. Worsham] Montgomery, Alabama Development Office, 1971.

ix, 140 p. 28 cm.

Mason, Sara Elizabeth.
A list of nineteenth century maps of the State of Alabama. [1st ed.] Birmingham, Ala., Birmingham Public Library, 1973.

253 p. 23 cm.

U. S. *Library of Congress.*
Alabama: the sesquicentennial of statehood; an exhibition in the Library of Congress, Washington, D. C., December 14, 1969 to August 14, 1970. Washington; [For sale by the Supt. of Docs., U. S. Govt. Print. Off.] 1969.

viii, 74 p. illus., facsims., maps, ports. 26 cm. (*Its* [State exhibition catalogs] 24)

ALAIN, pseud. see Chartier, Emile

ALASKA

Alaska. Division of State Libraries.
State publications received.
Juneau.

v. 28 cm.

Harris, Margaret P
A contribution to regional bibliography: Alaska; a pilot study in indexing, by Margaret P. Harris. Fairbanks, Alaska, 1972.

1 v. (various pagings) 28 cm.

Lada-Mocarski, Valerian, 1898–
Bibliography of books on Alaska published before 1868. With an introd. by Archibald Hanna, Jr. New Haven, Yale University Press, 1969.

vii, 567 p. facsims. 29 cm.

Includes the facsimile title pages, detailed description of pagination and collation, and analyses of the contents of over 160 books, with English translation of Russian titles.

ALBACETE, SPAIN (PROVINCE)

Fuster Ruiz, Francisco, 1941–
Fondos bibliográficos albacetenses. Colección de impresos albacetenses conservados en los archivos Histórico Provincial y del Ayuntamiento de Albacete, precedida de una historia de la imprenta en esta provincia. Albacete, Excmo. Ayuntamiento, 1972.

xlvi, 185 p., 1 l., plates. 28 cm.

ALBANIA; ALBANIAN LITERATURE

Legrand, Émile Louis Jean, 1841–1903.
Bibliographie albanaise; description raisonnée des ouvrages publiés en albanais ou relatifs à l'Albanie du quinzième siècle à l'année 1900. Œuvre posthume complétée et publiée par Henri Gûys. Paris, Librairie universitaire, 1912. [Leipzig, Zentralantiquariat der Deutschen Demokratischen Republik, 1973]

viii, 228 p. 22 cm.

Original ed. issued as v. 5 of his Œuvres posthumes.

Shuteriqi, Dhimetër S
Shkrimet Shqipe në vitet 1332–1850 (bibliografi) [nga] Dh. S. Shuteriqi. [Tiranë] Shtëpia Botonjëse N. Frashëri [1965]

233 p. 19 cm.

ALBEE, EDWARD

Amacher, Richard E
Edward Albee at home and abroad; a bibliography. Compiled by Richard E. Amacher and Margaret Rule. New York, AMS Press [1973]

95 p. 23 cm.

ALBERDI, JUAN BAUTISTA

Cordoba, Alberto Octavio, 1891–
Bibliografía de Juan Bautista Alberdi. [Buenos Aires] Distribuidor Abeledo-Perrot [1969, °1968]

394 p. facsim., port. 24 cm. (Biblioteca de la Academia Nacional de Derecho y Ciencias Sociales de Buenos Aires. Serie 2, Obras, no. 2)

ALCOHOL; ALCOHOLISM
see also Drugs

The Alcoholism digest annual. v. 1–
1972/73–
Rockville, Md., Information Planning Associates.

v. illus. 29 cm.

Anderson, Carl Leonard, 1901–
Alcoholism, a selected bibliography, compiled by Carl L. Anderson. Bethesda, Md., U. S. Dept. of Health, Education, and Welfare, Public Health Service, National Institutes of Health, 1964.

13 p. 16 cm. ([U. S.] Public Health Service. Publication no. 1200)

Comité national pour l'étude et la prévention de l'alcoolisme.
Catalogue de la bibliothèque [du] Comité national pour l'étude et la prévention de l'alcoolisme et des autres toxicomanies. Bruxelles, Comité national pour l'étude et al prévention de l'alcoolisme et des autres toxicomanies, C. N. A., chaussée de Vleurgat, 94, 1972.

2 v. 27 cm.
Cover title.
CONTENTS: 1. ptie. Alcool.—2. ptie. Drogues, autres que l'alcool, nicotine y comprise.

International bibliography of studies on alcohol. [Edited by Mark Keller] New Brunswick, N. J., Publications Division, Rutgers Center of Alcohol Studies [1966–

v. 26 cm.

An integral part of the documentation activities of Rutgers Center of Alcohol Studies.

CONTENTS.—v. 1. References, 1901–1950, by S. S. Jordy.

Jugoslavenska bibliografija alkoholizma. [Priredio Vladimir Hudolin uz suradnike: Dagmar Adamović et al. Zagreb, Pliva, 1964]

xix, 190 p. 20 cm.

Keller, Mark, 1907–
CAAAL manual; a guide to the use of the Classified Abstract Archive of the Alcohol Literature [by] Mark Keller, Vera Efron [and] E. M. Jellinek. New Brunswick, N. J., Publications Division, Rutgers Center of Alcohol Studies [1965]

xvii, 155 p. illus. 25 cm.

First published in 1953 under the title: Manual of the Classified Abstract Archive of the Alcohol Literature.

Phillips, Julianne.
Alcoholics Anonymous: an annotated bibliography, 1935–1972. [n. p., Central Ohio Pub. Co., 1973]

63 p. 22 cm.

Popham, Robert E
Culture and alcohol use; a bibliography of anthropological studies, compiled by Robert E. Popham and Carole D. Yawney. Toronto, Addiction Research Foundation, 1967.

52 l. 28 cm. (Addiction Research Foundation. Bibliographic series, no. 1)

Simpson, David Welsh.
Current alcohol studies; a short bibliography. Wellington, Medical Unit, Wellington Hospital, 1968.

ii, 31 p. 34 cm.

Smajkić, Arif.
Alkoholizam kod radnika (bibliografski referat). Sarajevo, 1967.

32 p. 29 cm. (Radovi Instituta za higijenu i socijalnu medicinu Medicinskog fakulteta Univerziteta u Sarajevu, Publikacija, br. 28)

White, Anthony G
Skid row as urban subcommunity, : a bibliography / Anthony G. White ; Mary Vance, editor. — Monticello, Ill. : Council of Planning Librarians, 1974.

7 p. : 28 cm. — (Exchange bibliography - Council of Planning Librarians : 689)

ALCOTT, LOUISA MAY

Gulliver, Lucile, 1882–
Louisa May Alcott; a bibliography. With an appreciation by Cornelia Meigs. New York, B. Franklin [1973]

71 p. 22 cm. (Burt Franklin bibliography and reference series, 292. Selected essays and texts in literature and criticism, 188)

Reprint of the 1932 ed.

Ullom, Judith C
Louisa May Alcott: a centennial for Little women; an annotated, selected bibliography. Compiled by Judith C. Ullom. Washington, Library of Congress; [for sale by the Supt. of Docs., U. S. Govt. Print. Off., 1969.

vii 91 p. illus. 24 cm.

Prepared by the Children's Book Section, Library of Congress, to serve in part as a catalog of the exhibition of Louisa May Alcott items mounted in the Rare Book Division.

ALDINGTON, RICHARD

Moscow. Vsesoiuznaia gosudarstvennaia biblioteka inostrannoĭ literatury.
Ричард Олдингтон; биобиблиографический указатель. [Составитель Б. М. Парчевская] Москва, Книга, 1965.

58 p. 22 cm. (Писатели зарубежных стран)

ALDRIN

Water Resources Scientific Information Center.
Aldrin and endrin in water, a bibliography. Washington

[1972]

iii, 119 p. 27 cm. (Its Bibliography series, WRSIC 72-203)

ALECSANDRI, VASILE

Biblioteca V. A. Urechia.
Vasile Alecsandri. [150 de ani de la naștere]. Catalogul lucrărilor existente în Biblioteca „V. A. Urechia." Întocmit: C. Bădic și S. Codreanu. Galați, 1971.

63 p. with port., errata, 9 l. of facsims. 19 cm.

At head of title: Biblioteca „V. A. Urechia" Galați.

ALEKSEEV, MIKHAIL PAVLOVICH

Finashina, G N
(Mikhail Pavlovich Alekseev)
Михаил Павлович Алексеев. Вступит. статья Ю. Д. Левина. Библиогр. сост. Г. Н. Финашиной. Москва, "Наука," 1972.

128 p., port. 16 cm. (Материалы к биобиблиографии ученых СССР. Серия литературы и языка, вып. 9)

At head of title: Академия наук СССР.

ALESSANDRO, RAFFAELE D'

Schweizerisches Musik-Archiv.
Raffaele d'Alessandro, né le 17 mars 1911, décédé le 17 mars 1959. Liste des œuvres. Zurich, Archives musicales suisses, 1970.

ii, 6 l. 30 cm.

Cover title.
French and German.

ÅLESUND, NORWAY

Helseth, Konrad, 1903–
Litteratur om Ålesund. En bibliografi. [Utg. av] Ålesund folkebibliotek. Ålesund, 1971.

[2] 179 l. 22 cm.

ALEXANDER THE GREAT

Burich, Nancy J
Alexander the Great: a bibliography [by] Nancy J. Burich. [1st ed. Kent, Ohio] Kent State University Press [1970]

xxiii, 153 p. 23 cm.

ALGAE

Algae abstracts: a guide to the literature. Prepared from material supplied by Water Resources Scientific Information Center, Office of Water Resources Research, Department of the Interior, Washington, D. C. New York, IFI/Plenum [1973]

2 v. 29 cm.

CONTENTS: v. 1. To 1969.—v. 2. 1970–1972.

Библиография советской литературы по водорослям за 1936–1940 гг. (с дополнением за предыдущие годы). Составили: М. М. Голлербах [и др.] Ленинград, 1966.

168, [3] p. 22 cm.

At head of title: Академия наук СССР. Всесоюзное ботаническое общество. Библиотека Академии наук СССР.
Added t. p.: Bibliographia algologica sovietica.

Draganov, Stefan Iordanov.
(Bibliografiia i katalog na fosilnite vodorasli v Bŭlgariia)
Библиография и каталог на фосилните водорасли

в България, 1859–1971. Bibliography and catalogue of fossil algae in Bulgaria, 1859–1971. София, Софийски университет "Климент Охридски," 1973.

64 p. 22 cm.

At head of title: Стефан Йорд. Драганов и Николина Г. Ковачева.

Table of contents and introduction also in English.

Draganov, Stefan Iordanov.

Библиография на литературата върху водораслите на България. ⟨1890–1969⟩. София, СУ Климент Охридски, 1971 (библиогр. каре 1972).

72 p. 22 cm.

At head of title: Софийски университет "Климент Охридски." Университетска библиотека. Стефан Йорд. Драганов.

Title also in English: Bibliography of literature on algae in Bulgaria.

Table of contents also in English.

Gollerbakh, Maksimilian Maksimilianovich.

[Vodorosli]

Водоросли. Сводный указ. к отеч. библиогр. по водорослям за 1737–1960 гг. Сост. М. М. Голлербах и Л. К. Красавина. Под ред. [и с предисл.] М. М. Голлербаха. Ленинград, 1971.

623 p. 22 cm.

At head of title: Академия наук СССР. Ботанический институт им. В. Л. Комарова. Библиотека Академии наук СССР.

Graves, Ralph Henry, 1952–

Use of algae in space biology; a guide for student research, by Ralph H. Graves. Washington, Biological Sciences Communication Project, Medical Center, George Washington University, 1969.

vii, 157 p. 23 cm.

Prepared for the Biosciences Programs Division, National Aeronautics and Space Administration.

Halperín, Delia R   de.

Bibliografía preliminar sobre aprovechamiento e industrialización de las algas marinas bentónicas [por] Delia R. de Halperín [y] Alicia L. Boraso. Buenos Aires, Instituto Nacional de Tecnología Industrial, 1971.

152 l. 29 cm. (Centro de Investigación de Biología Marina. Contribución técnica no. 8)

Johnson, Jesse Harlan, 1892–

Bibliography of fossil algae, algal limestones, and the geological work of algae, 1956–1965, by J. Harlan Johnson. Golden, Colorado School of Mines, 1967.

vii, 148 p. 23 cm. (Quarterly of the Colorado School of Mines, v. 62, no. 4)

Krasavina, Liudmila Karlovna.

Библиография советской литературы по водорослям. За 1941–1960 гг. Сост. Л. К. Красавина. Отв. ред. заслуж. деят. науки РСФСР проф. М. М. Голлербах. Ленинград, 1968.

343 p. 21 cm.

At head of title: Академия наук СССР. Ботанический институт им. В. Л. Комарова. Библиотека Академии наук СССР.

Summaries in English and German; table of contents also in English and German.

Tsuda, Roy T

Preliminary bibliography on the marine benthic algae in the central Pacific, Polynesia, and Micronesia, by Roy T. Tsuda. [Honolulu, Hawaii Institute of Marine Biology] 1966.

13 l. 28 cm. (Hawaii Institute of Marine Biology. Technical report no. 10)

ALGEBRAIC CURVES see Curves, Algebraic

ALGER, HORATIO

Gardner, Ralph D   1923–

Road to success: the bibliography of the works of Horatio Alger, by Ralph D. Gardner. Rev. ed. Mendota, Ill., Wayside Press [1971]

133 p. illus. 22 cm.

Published in 1964 under title: Horatio Alger; or, The American hero era.

ALGERIA

Deutsches Institut für Afrika-Forschung.

Algerien, Wirtschaft und Entwicklungsplanung: ausgew. neuere Literatur/ [Bearb.: Ties Möller]. Dokumentations-Leitstelle im ADAF; Dt. Inst. f. Afrikaforschung e. V. im Verbund d. Stiftung Dt. Übersee-Inst. — Hamburg: Dt. Inst. f. Afrikaforschung e. V., Dokumentations-Leitstelle, 1972.

74 l.; 21 cm. — (Dokumentationsdienst Afrika; 5)

Lawless, Richard I

A bibliography of works on Algeria published in English since 1954; compiled by Richard I. Lawless. [Durham], University of Durham Centre for Middle Eastern and Islamic Studies, 1972.

[1], iii, 30 p. 25 cm. (University of Durham. Centre for Middle Eastern and Islamic Studies. Occasional papers series, no. 1) £1.00

Tangier. African Training and Research Centre in Administration for Development. Documentation Centre.

Bibliography on Algeria. Bibliographie sur l'Algérie. Tanger, 1971.

41 l. 28 cm.

English and French.

ALGOL (COMPUTER PROGRAM LANGUAGE)

Granova, G   N

Язык алгол. [Универс. язык программирования]. Рек. обзор литературы. [Москва, "Книга," 1971].

16 p. 16 cm. (Новое в науке и технике)

At head of title: Государственная библиотека СССР имени В. И. Ленина.

ÂLÎ

Atsız, Nihal, 1905–

Âlî bibliyografyası. Hazırlayan: Atsız. İstanbul, M[illî] E[ğitim] B[akanlığı] 1968.

121 p. 24 cm. (Süleymaniye Kütüphanesi yayınları, 3)

"Künhü'l-ahbâr'ın Osmanlı tarihi bölümünden III. Mehmed çağına ait parçanın sadeleştirilmiş şekli": p. 53–112.

'ALÎ SHÎR, MÎR, called AL-NAWÂ'Î

Svidina, Evgeniia Dmitrievna.

Алишер Навои. Биобиблиография. (1917–1966 гг.) К 525-летию со дня рождения. Ташкент, Изд. худож. лит., 1968.

108 p. 20 cm.

At head of title: Государственная библиотека УзССР им. Алишера Навои.

ALICANTE, SPAIN

Albert Berenguer, Isidro.

La imprenta en la provincia de Alicante. 1602–1925. [Alicante₁ Instituto de Estudios Alicantinos. Diputación Provincial de Alicante ₁1971₁

563 p. 22 cm. (Publicaciones del Instituto de Estudios Alicantinos. Serie I, 5)

Alicante, Spain. Archivo Municipal.
Inventario del Archivo Municipal de Alicante (1252–1873). Alicante ₁Fondo Editorial del Excmo. Ayuntamiento₁ 1974.

145 p. 21 cm. (Publicaciones del Fondo Editorial del Excmo. Ayuntamiento de Alicante. Serie Ad Fontes, 6)

At head of title: Vicente Martínez Morellá.

Fresneau Saorín, Augusto, 1912–
Archivo Municipal de Alicante. Indice general de remisiones. Alicante, 1971.

65 p. 22 cm. (Publicaciones del Fondo Editorial del Excmo. Ayuntamiento de Alicante. Serie Ad Fontes, v. 2)

"500 ejemplares.

ALIEN LABOR

Briani, Vittorio.
Emigrazione e lavoro italiano all'estero. Elementi per un repertorio bibliografico generale a cura di Vittorio Briani. Roma, 1967.

vii, 228 p. 24 cm.

At head of title: Ministero degli affari esteri. Direzione generale dell'emigrazione e degli affari sociali.

Denmark. Arbejds- og socialministeriet. Biblioteket.
Udvalg af litteratur vedrørende gæstearbejdere. København K, Arbejds- og Socialministeriernes Bibliotek, Slotsholmsgade 12, 1970.

8 l. 30 cm.

ALIEV, GULIAM ALIEVICH

Makhmudov, G   Z
Г. А. Алиев. Библиография. ₁Вступит. статья д-ра с.-х. наук проф. К. А. Алекперова₁. Баку, Изд. АН АзССР, 1968.

90 p. 16 cm. (Академия наук Азербайджанской ССР. Фундаментальная библиотека. Деятели науки и культуры Азербайджана)

Added t.-p. in Azerbaijani.

ALIEV, MUSA MIRZOEVICH

Aliev, R   A
(M. M. Aliev)
М. М. Алиев. Библиография. ₁Вступит. статья акад. К. А. Ализаде₁. Баку, Изд. АН АзССР, 1969.

76 p. 16 cm. (Академия наук Азербайджанской ССР. Фундаментальная библиотека. Деятели науки и культуры Азербайджана)

Added t. p. in Azerbaijani.
By R. A. Aliev and N. B. Listengarten.

ALIEV, VAGAB SAFAROVICH

В. С. Алиев. Библиография. ₁Вступит. статья акад. С. Д. Мехтиева, с. 5–22₁. Баку, "Элм," 1969.

72 p. 17 cm. (Деятели науки и культуры Азербайджана)

At head of title: Академия наук Азербайджанской ССР. Фундаментальная библиотека.
By E. V. Gurevich and others.
Added t. p. in Azerbaijani.

ALKALI METAL HALIDE CRYSTALS

(Eksitony v shchelochnogaloidnykh kristallakh.)
Экситоны в щелочногалоидных кристаллах. Би-

блогр. за 1929–1970 гг. Тарту, 1971.

48 p. 20 cm.

At head of title: Академия наук Эстонской ССР. Институт физики и астрономии.
By E. Vasil'chenko and others.

ALLEN, JAMES EDWARD

New York (State). State Library, *Albany*.
A guide to the papers of James E. Allen, Jr., President of the University of the State of New York and Commissioner of Education, 1955–1969. ₁Albany₁ 1970.

68 p. 23 cm.

"The Allen papers are a collection of documents drawn from the files of the Commissioner's Office."

ALLENTOWN, PENNSYLVANIA

Halpern, Kathryn D
A preliminary checklist of Allentown and Bethlehem, Pennsylvania imprints, 1813–1876, with a historical introduction, by Kathryn D. Halpern. Washington, 1964.

iv, 89 l. 28 cm.

Typescript (carbon copy)
Thesis (M. s. L. s.)—Catholic University of America.

ALLGÄU

Weitnauer, Alfred, 1905–
Bücher und Aufsätze. (Bibliographie.) Kempten ⟨Allgäu⟩ Verlag für Heimatpflege, 1968.

82 p. 21 cm.

ALLOYS

Alloys index. Jan. 1974–
₁Metals Park, Ohio₁

v. 30 cm. monthly.

"An auxiliary publication to Metals abstracts and Metals abstracts index."
Began with Jan. 1974 issue. Cf. New serial titles.
Vols. for 1974– published jointly by the American Society for Metals and the Metals Society.

Carter, Gesina C
The NBS Alloy Data Center: function, bibliographic system, related data centers, and reference books ₁by₁ Gesina C. Carter ₁and others₁ Washington, U. S. Dept. of Commerce, National Bureau of Standards; for sale by the Supt. of Docs., U. S. Govt. Print. Off., 1968.

1 v. (various pagings) illus., forms. 26 cm. (NBS technical note 464)

(Diagrammy sostoîaniîa troĭnykh metallicheskikh sistem)
Диаграммы состояния тройных металлических систем. 1910–1969 гг. Библиогр. справочник. Москва, "Наука," 1972.

189 p. 21 cm.

On leaf preceding t. p.: Академия наук СССР. Институт металлургии имени А. А. Байкова.
By I. I. Kornilov and others.

Hausner, Henry Herman, 1901–
Bibliography on refractory metals and alloys, 1961–1963, by Henry H. Hausner and Helen C. Friedemann. Reutte, Tyrol, Metallwerk Plansee Aktiengesellschaft, 1964.

ii, 193 p. 19 cm.

Syre, Robert.
A bibliography of refractory metals; compiled by Robert Syre, edited by K. J. Spencer. Maidenhead, Technivision Services; ₁London, Distributed by Technical P.₁, 1968.

iii-xxii, 426 p. 25 cm. (AGARD bibliography no. 5)

ALLWOOD, MARTIN SAMUEL

Allwood, Martin Samuel, 1916–
Bibliography 1942–1968. Books, pamphlets, brochures, and translations, by Martin S. Allwood. Mullsjö, Anglo-American Center, 1968.

(1), 15 l. 28 cm.

ALMANACS

Górska, Barbara.
Katalog kalendarzy XVII–XVIII w. w zbiorach Biblioteki Ossolineum. Wrocław, Zakład Narodowy im. Ossolińskich, 1968.

xi, 269 p. facsims. 24 cm.

At head of title: Zakład Narodowy imienia Ossolińskich. Biblioteka Polskiej Akademii Nauk.

Grand-Carteret, John, 1850–1927.
Les almanachs français; bibliographie, iconographie des almanachs, années, annuaires, calendriers, chansonniers, étrennes, états, heures, listes, livres d'adresses, tableaux, tablettes, et autres publications annuelles éditées à Paris, 1600–1895. Genève, Slatkine Reprints, 1968.

cx, 846 p. illus. 23 cm.

"Réimpression de l'édition de Paris, 1896."

Marwinski, Felicitas.
Almanache, Taschenbücher, Taschenkalender. Weimar (Thüringische Landesbibliothek) 1967.

105 p., several plates. 16 x 25 cm. (Kataloge der Thüringischen Landesbibliothek Weimar, 1)

Pissin, Raimund, 1878–
Almanache der Romantik, hrsg. von Raimund Pissin. Hildesheim, New York, G. Olms, 1970.

xii p., 452 columns. 29 cm.

Reprint of the 1910 ed., which was issued as [Bd. 7] of Veröffentlichungen der Deutschen Bibliographischen Gesellschaft, and as Bd. 5 of Bibliographisches Reportorium.

ALOST, BELGIUM

Stadsarchief Aalst.
Inventaris van het oud archief van de Stad Aalst / door Erik Houtman ; voorwoord van J[an] Buntinx. — Brussel, (Keizerslaan 4) : Archief- en Bibliotheekwezen in België, 1974.

334 p. : ill., tables, facsims. ; 25 cm. — (Archief- en Bibliotheekwezen in België. Inventarissen ; 4)

ALPHA RAYS   see under   Helium

ALPS
see also under   Hiking

Wehrbereichsbibliothek Sechs München.
Die Alpen; Schlagwortkatalog der ausleihbaren Berg-, Ski- und Wanderführer, sowie ergänzende Landschaftsbeschreibungen. Aus dem Syst. Katalog erarbeitet von Paul Gleixner und Waltraut Dollinger. München, 1966.

52 p. 29 cm. (Its Schrifttumsauszug Nr. 67)

ALSACE

Bibliothèque centrale de prêt du Haut-Rhin.
Avec le bibliobus découvrez l'Alsace [par] Bérengère Sins [et] Michèle Stevaux. Catalogue des alsatiques mis à la disposition de ses lecteurs par la Bibliotheque centrale de

prêt du Haut-Rhin. Suivi d'un conte inédit de Henri de Wineck. Avant-propos de Christian Wilsdorf. Colmar [1972?]

150 p. illus. 15 x 21 cm.

12 [Douze] siècles d'histoire du livre: à travers les collections des bibliothèques d'Alsace. exposition, mars, avril, mai 1973, Strasbourg, Mulhouse, Colmar, [publié par la Bibliothèque nationale et universitaire de Strasbourg]. [Strasbourg], [Bibliothèque nationale et universitaire]. 1973.

71 p. 21 cm.

Exhibition catalog.
Errata slips inserted.

Rhin, Haut-, *France (Dept.).* *Archives.*
Inventaire de la sous-série 2J : collection Fernand-J. Heitz. Dressé par Lucie Roux, conservateur, sous la direction de Christian Wilsdorf. Colmar, 1968.

191 p. port. 24 cm.

At head of title: Archives départementales du Haut-Rhin.
"Bibliographie des travaux de F. J. Heitz": p. 19–21.

Specklin, Robert.
L'Alsace, 1000 et 1 [i. e. mille et une] communes; notes pour une documentation préalable. [Strasbourg, CRDP] 1971.

83 p. illus. 28 cm. (Annales du Centre régional de documentation pédagogique de Strasbourg)

ALT, ROBERT

Robert Alt zum 65. Geburtstag. Eine Bibliographie seiner Arbeiten. (Bearb.: Rudi Schulz [u. a.]) Berlin, Pädagogische Zentralbibliothek, 1970.

15 l. 21 cm.

ALTAYSKIY KRAY, RUSSIA

Литература об Алтайском крае. Библиогр. указатель. Барнаул, Алт. кн. изд., 1968.

223 p. 20 cm.

At head of title: Алтайская краевая библиотека.
By M. G. Vokhrysheva, and others.

(Stranit͡sy iz istorii Altai͡a)
Страницы из истории Алтая. Библиогр. указ. Барнаул, [Алт. кн. изд-во], 1971.

79 p. 22 cm.

At head of title: Алтайская краевая библиотека.
"Составители: М. Л. Борцова" [и др.]
By T. A. Polukhin and others.

ALTITUDES

Physiological factors relating to terrestrial altitudes: a bibliography, by L. Yvonne Wulff [and others. Columbus] Ohio State University Libraries; distributed by the Ohio State University Press, 1968.

1 v. (various pagings) 27 cm. (The Ohio State University Libraries publications, no. 3)

RF project no. 2360, Ohio State Research Foundation.

ALUMINUM

アルミニウム技術文献集 昭和41– 年版 [1966–
東京] 日本科学技術情報センター

v. 26 cm. annual.

Machová, Elena.
Výroba a použitie hliníka. Výberový zoznam z domácej a zahraničnej literatúry. Zost.: Elena Machová. Bratislava, Slov. techn. knižnica, cyklostyl, 1968.

65, ₁1₎ p. 21 cm. (Bratislava. Slovenská technická knižnica. Edícia 2. Séria B: Výberové bibliografie)

ALUMINUM SULPHATE

Laszkiewicz, Olga T   M
Manufacture of aluminum sulphate. Compiled by O. T. M. Laszkiewicz. Adelaide, State Library of South Australia, 1970.

9 p. 27 cm. (State Library of South Australia. Research Service Bibliographies. Series 4, no. 133)

ALZEY, GERMANY

Johannes, Detlev.
Alzeyer Bibliographie. Mit Berücksichtigung der im Alzeyer Raum geborenen Dichter und Schriftsteller. Alzey, Verlag der Rheinhessischen Druckwerkstätte (1968).

xiv, 202 p. 24 cm. (Alzeyer Geschichtsblätter. Sonderheft, 2)

AMADÍS DE GAULA

Vaganay, Hugues, 1870–
Amadis en français; essai de bibliographie. Genève, Slatkine Reprints, 1970.

151 p. illus. 31 cm.

"Réimpression de l'édition de Florence, 1906."

AMADO, JORGE

Moscow. Vsesoiûznaîa gosudarstvennaîa biblioteka inostrannoĭ literatury.
Жоржи Амаду; биобиблиографический указатель. ₁Составитель Л. А. Шур₎ Москва, Книга, 1965.

47 p. 22 cm. (Писатели зарубежных стран)

AMAMI ISLANDS

Kagoshima Kenritsu Toshokan. *Amami Bunkan.*
鹿児島県立図書館. 奄美分館
鹿児島県立図書館奄美分館郷土資料目録
昭和44年3月1日現在
鹿児島 鹿児島県立図書館協会奄美支部, 鹿児島県立図
書館奄美分館 昭和44(1969)
158p 26cm

AMATEUR THEATRICALS

Das Laienspiel in der ost- und mitteldeutschen Kulturarbeit ... ₁Hrsg. vom Ministerium für Arbeit, Soziales und Vertriebene des Landes Schleswig-Holstein in Zusammenarbeit mit der Landesarbeitsgemeinschaft für Laienspiel und Laientheater. Kiel₎ 1961.

31 p. 21 cm. (Schriftenreihe zur Förderung der ostdeutschen Kulturarbeit, Heft Nr. 3)

Werkcentrum voor Leketoneel en Creatief Spel.
Alfabetische katalogus studiebibliotheek Het Werkcentrum — Ons Leekenspel. Verklaring van tekens, verantwoording, boeken, tijdschriften. Amsterdam, ₁Herenmarkt 12₎, Het Werkcentrum; ₁Bussum, Gudelalaan 2₎, Ons Leekenspel, ₁1971₎.

1 v. (loose-leaf) 24 cm.

Cover title: Katalogus studiebibliotheek.
"Deze katalogus vermeldt het boekenbezit van Ons Leekenspel te Bussum, het Werkcentrum ₁voor Leketoneel en Creatief Spel₎ in Amsterdam en van Werkschult/Werkcentrum ₁Gronings Instituut

voor Ekspressie en Kommunikatie₎ te Groningen ... per 1 mei 1970 ... Titelbeschrijvingen door Gerda Tendeloo."

AMAZON VALLEY

Banco da Amazonia. *Departamento de Estudos Econômicos.*
Bibliografia BASA, 1943–1968. Belém, Divisão de Documentação e Divulgação, 1968.

14 l. 28 cm. (*Its* Documento no. 6)

AMBER

Kaliningrad, Russia.
(Antar')
Янтарь; месторождения, добыча, обработка, история культуры. Библиографический указатель лит-ры. ₁Составитель Н. Канайлова. Калининград₎ Калининградское книжное изд-во, 1966.

124 p. 14 cm.

At head of title: Калининградская опорная научно-техническая библиотека.

Kaliningradskaîa oblastnaîa biblioteka.
Янтарь—богатство нашего края; аннотированный рекомендательный указатель литературы. ₁Составитель А. Боброва. Калининград₎ Калининградское книжное изд-во, 1965.

21 p. 15 cm. (Знай свой край)

At head of title: Калининградское областное управление культуры. Областная библиотека.

Pietrzak, Teresa.
Bursztyn bałtycki w piśmiennictwie polskim, 1534–1967. Opracowała Teresa Pietrzak. ₁Wyd. 1.₎. Warszawa, Wydawnictwa Geologiczne, 1972.

68 p. 21 cm. (Muzeum ziemi. Opracowania dokumentacyjne, 1)

At head of title: Polska Akademia Nauk. Muzeum Ziemi.

AMERICA

see also Central America; Latin America; North America; South America

Alcedo, Antonio de, 1736–1812.
Bibliotheca americana; catálogo de los autores que han escrito de la América en diferentes idiomas y noticia de su vida y patria, años en que vivieron, y obras que escribieron. Introd. de Jorge A. Garcés G. ₁Quito, 1964–65₎

2 v. 27 cm. (Publicaciones del Museo Municipal de Arte e Historia, v. 32)

Comité Organizador del XXXVI Congreso Internacional de Americanistas.
Bibliografía americanista española, 1935–1963. ₁Recopilación realizada por Fernando de Armas Medina, et al. Editada bajo la dirección de José Alcina Franch₎ Sevilla, 1964.

xxiii, 565 p. 25 cm.

"Con ocasión de reunirse en España el XXXVI Congreso Internacional de Americanistas."

Eberstadt (Edward) and Sons, *New York.*
Americana; being a collection of rare & important books & manuscripts relating to the history of America, including a choice selection of Lincolniana. New York ₁1964₎

171 p. illus., facsims. 28 cm. (*Its* Catalogue 165)

Harrisse, Henry, 1829–1910.
Bibliotheca Americana vetustissima; a description of works relating to America, published between the years 1492 and 1551. Chicago, Argonaut, 1967.

liv, 519, xl, 199 p. facsims. 23 cm.

Reprint of the 1866 New York ed. and its Additions published in Paris, 1872.

Heard, Joseph Norman, 1922–
Bookman's guide to Americana. 3d ed. New York, Scarecrow Press, 1964.

424 p. 22 cm.

Inter-American Statistical Institute.
Bibliography of selected statistical sources of the American nations; a guide to the principal statistical materials of the 22 American nations, including data, analyses, methodology, and laws and organization of statistical agencies. Bibliografía de fuentes, estadísticas escogidas de las naciones americanas; una guía de los principales materiales estadísticos de las 22 naciones americanas incluyendo datos, análisis, metodología y leyes y organización de los organismos de estadística. 1st ed. Washington, 1947. Detroit, Blain-Ethridge Books, 1974.

xvi, 689 p. 24 cm.

Jones, Herschel Vespasian, 1861–1928.
Americana collection of Herschel V. Jones; a check-list, 1473–1926, compiled by Wilberforce Eames. New York, Cooper Square Publishers, 1964.

xii, 220 p. 32 cm.

First published in 1938.
"Serves also as a complement to Mr. Jones's Adventures in Americana, 1492–1897, published in 1928."

Jones, Herschel Vespasian, 1861–1928.
Adventures in Americana, 1492–1897; the romance of voyage and discovery from Spain to the Indies, the Spanish Main, and North America; inland to the Ohio country; on toward the Mississippi; through to California; over Chilkoot Pass to the gold fields of Alaska. Being a selection of books from the library of Herschel V. Jones, Minneapolis, Minnesota. With a pref. by Wilberforce Eames. New York, Cooper Square Publishers, 1964.

2 v. facsims. 32 cm.

First published in 1928.

"With the advice of Wilberforce Eames this catalogue was made by Helen Fagg."

Larned, Josephus Nelson, 1836–1913, *ed.*
The literature of American history; a bibliographical guide, in which the scope, character, and comparative worth of books in selected lists are set forth in brief notes by critics of authority. New York, F. Ungar Pub. Co. ₁1966₁

ix, 588 p. (p. 473–477 advertisement) 27 cm. (American classics) 12.50

Reprint of the 1902 ed.

Muller (Frederik) en Compagnie, *Amsterdam.*
Catalogue of books, maps, plates on America and of a remarkable collection of early voyages. With an alphabetical and a subject index by G. J. Brouwer. ₁Reprint of the ed. Amsterdam 1872–1875₁. Amsterdam, N. Israel, 1966.

viii, 658 p. 22½ cm.

Rich, Obadiah, 1783?–1850.
Bibliotheca Americana nova; a catalogue of books in various languages relating to America, printed since the year 1700, including voyages to the Pacific and round the world and collections of voyages and travels. Compiled principally from the works themselves by O. Rich. Rev. by the addition of two supplements. New York, B. Franklin ₁1967₁

2 v. 24 cm. (Burt Franklin bibliography and reference series ≵43)
"First published London 1835–1846."
CONTENTS.—pt. 1. 1701–1800.—pt. 2. Printed since the year 1800.

Ternaux-Compans, Henri, 1807–1864.
Bibliothèque américaine ou catalogue des ouvrages relatifs à l'Amérique qui ont paru depuis sa découverte jusqu'à l'an 1700. Par H. Ternaux. ₁Réimpression de l'éd. Paris 1837₁. Amsterdam, B. R. Grüner, 1968.

viii, 192 p. 23 cm.

Ternaux-Compans, Henri, 1807–1864.
Bibliothèque américaine; ou, Catalogue des ouvrages relatifs a l'Amérique, qui ont paru depuis sa découverte jusqu's l'an 1700. Chicago, Argonaut, 1968.

viij, 191 p. 23 cm.

"Réimpression de l'édition Paris 1837."

LIBRARY AND EXHIBITION CATALOGS

Brinley, George, 1817–1875.
Catalogue of the American library of the late Mr. George Brinley, of Hartford, Conn. New York, AMS Press ₁1968₁

5 pts. in 2 v. 23 cm.

Reprint of the 1879–93 ed.
Each part has also special t. p.
On spine: Brinley American library auction catalogue.
Consists of the catalogs for the 5 auctions at which the library was sold, an index, and a price list.

The British look at America during the age of Samuel Johnson; an exhibition. Providence, Associates of the John Carter Brown Library, 1971.

vi, 55 p. illus., facsims., map, ports. 27 cm.

Catalogue, by T. R. Adams and J. D. Black, of an exhibition shown in the John Carter Brown Library beginning in April 1971.
"Address by Herman W. Liebert delivered at the 28th annual meeting of the Associates of the John Carter Brown Library April 30, 1971": p. ₁1₁–16.

Brown University. *John Carter Brown Library.*
A collection's progress: two retrospective exhibitions. Providence, Associates of the John Carter Brown Library, 1968.

79 p. illus., facsims., maps. 27 cm.

Supplements the library's catalog of an exhibition, In retrospect, 1923–1949, held in 1949.
Catalogue of two exhibitions; one held at the Grolier Club, New York, Apr. 16–June 1, 1968; the other at the library, Providence, Apr. 5–Sept. 1, 1968.

Geographical Association. *Library.*
The Americas: a list of works added to the Geographical Association Library, 1958–1968. Sheffield, Geographical Association, 1968.

₁1₁, 32 p. maps. 25 cm.

Cover title.
"Forms a supplement to the catalogue North and Latin America which was published in November 1958."

Stevens, Henry, 1819–1886.
Historical nuggets. Bibliotheca Americana; or, A descriptive account of my collection of rare books relating to America. New York, B. Franklin ₁1971₁

xii, 805 p. 19 cm. (Burt Franklin bibliography & reference series, 410. American classics in history and social science, 154)

Half-title and running title: Bibliotheca Americana.
Reprint of v. 1–2 (1862) of the original.

MAPS

Michigan. University. William L. Clements Library.
Research catalog of maps of America to 1860 in the William L. Clements Library, University of Michigan, Ann Arbor, Michigan. Edited by Douglas W. Marshall. Boston, G. K. Hall, 1972.

4 v. 37 cm.

Stevens, Henry Newton, 1855–1930.
Comparative cartography, by Henry Stevens and Roland Tree. London, Map Collectors' Circle, 1967.

12, [2], 305–363 p. 25 cm. (Map Collectors' Circle. Map collectors' series, no. 39)

First published in Essays honoring Lawrence C. Wroth, Portland, Me., 1951.

Tooley, Ronald Vere, 1898–
French mapping of the Americas: the De l'Isle, Buache, Dezauche Succession (1700–1830) by R. V. Tooley. London, Map Collectors' Circle, 1967.

39 p. facsims., maps. 25 cm. (Map Collectors' Circle. Map collectors' series, no. 33)

Tooley, Ronald Vere, 1898–
Printed maps of America, by R. V. Tooley. London, Map Collectors' Circle, 1971–

v. maps. 25 cm. (Map collectors' series, v. 7, no. 68–69, v. 8, no. 80

U. S. *Library of Congress. Map Division.*
A list of maps of America in the Library of Congress. Compiled by P. L. Phillips. Complete and unabridged reprint [of the ed. Washington, 1901]. Amsterdam, Theatrvm Orbis Terrarvm. [1967].

1144 p. 22½ cm.

AMERICAN DRAMA see Drama - United States

AMERICAN FICTION see Fiction - United States

AMERICAN IMPRINTS see United States - Imprints

AMERICAN INDIANS
see also Aztecs; Eskimos; Mayas; and Chippewa, Iroquois, Moravian, Navaho, and Ute Indians

American Indian Research Project.
Oyate iyechinka woglakapi; an oral history collection. Vermillion [S. D.] 1970–

v. 28 cm.

Cover title.
Text in English.
List of taped interviews with the Plains Indians and those non-Indians working actively with them; housed in the Library of the University of South Dakota, Vermillion.

Barrow, Mark V 1935–
Health and disease of American Indians north of Mexico; a bibliography, 1800–1969, compiled by Mark V. Barrow, Jerry D. Niswander, and Robert Fortuine. Gainesville, University of Florida Press, 1972.

xiii, 147 p. 24 cm.

A Bibliography of urban Indians in the United States.
Compiled by Arthur M. Harkins [and others] Minneapolis, Training Center for Community Programs in coordination with Office of Community Programs, Center for Urban and Regional Affairs, University of Minnesota, 1971.

42 l. 28 cm.

Brennan, Jere L
The forgotten American—American Indians remembered; a selected bibliography for use in social work education. Compiled by Jere L. Brennan. New York, Council

on Social Work Education [1972]

ix, 83 p. 23 cm.

Brigham Young University, Provo, Utah. Instructional Development Program.
Bibliography of nonprint instructional materials on the American Indian. Prepared by the Instructional Development Program for the Institute of Indian Services and Research, Brigham Young University. Provo [1972]

v, 221 p. 28 cm.

Center for the Study of Migrant and Indian Education.
Indian education bibliography. Rev. ed. [Toppenish, Wash.] 1971.

72 p. 29 cm.

Durovich, Anna.
Indian education—bibliography. [n. p., 1967]

13 p.

Caption title.
Microfilm print, enlarged. Bethesda, Md., ERIC Document Reproduction Service. 13 p. on [7] l. 22 x 30 cm.

Fenton, William Nelson, 1908–
American Indian and white relations to 1830, needs & opportunities for study; an essay by William N. Fenton. A bibliography by L. H. Butterfield, Wilcomb E. Washburn, and William N. Fenton. New York, Russell & Russell [1971, °1957]

x, 138 p. 23 cm. (Needs and opportunities for study series)

Fowler, Catherine S
Great Basin anthropology ... a bibliography. Compiled by Catherine S. Fowler. Don D. Fowler, editor. Thelma Winnie, associate editor. [Reno, Western Studies Center, University of Nevada System, 1970]

xx, 418 p. col. maps. 28 cm. (Social sciences & humanities publication no. 5)

Freeman, John F
A guide to manuscripts relating to the American Indian in the library of the American Philosophical Society, compiled by John F. Freeman. Murphy D. Smith: editorial consultant. Philadelphia, American Philosophical Society, 1966 [°1965]

x, 491 p. 27 cm. (Memoirs of the American Philosophical Society, v. 65)

Howard, R Palmer, 1912–
A historiography of the five civilized tribes: a chronological approach [by R. Palmer Howard. Oklahoma City, Oklahoma Historical Society] °1969.

20 p. 23 cm.

Idaho. Indian Education.
Books about Indians and reference material. [Rev.] Boise [1971]

175 p. illus. 28 cm.

Cover title.
"Supersedes the 1968 publication."

Index to literature on the American Indian. 1970–
[San Francisco] Indian Historian Press.

v. 24 cm. annual.

"Published for the American Indian Historical Society."

Johnson, Basil.
Bibliography of Indian history books. Toronto, Indian-Eskimo Association of Canada, 1970.

14 p. 28 cm.

Library Services Institute for Minnesota Indians. University of Minnesota.
American Indians; an annotated bibliography of selected library resources. Will Antell — project director. Lee Antell—associate director. ₁Minneapolis, 1970₁

xii, 156 p. 28 cm.

Lynas, Lothian.
Medicinal and food plants of the North American Indians: a bibliography. New York, Library of the New York Botanical Garden, 1972.

21 p. 27 cm.

Marken, Jack Walter, 1922–
The Indians and Eskimos of North America: a bibliography of books in print through 1972, by Jack W. Marken. Vermillion, S. D., Dakota Press, 1973.

ix, 200 p. 22 cm.

Modern native Americans: a selective bibliography. Compiled by Arthur M. Harkins ₁and others₁ Minneapolis, Training Center for Community Programs, University of Minnesota, 1971.

130 l. 28 cm.

Newberry Library, Chicago. Edward E. Ayer Collection.
Narratives of captivity among the Indians of North America; a list of books and manuscripts on this subject in the Edward E. Ayer Collection of the Newberry Library. Ann Arbor, Mich., Gryphon Books, 1971.

x, 120, vii, 49 p. 22 cm.

"Supplement I, by Clara A. Smith": vii, 49 p. at end.
"Facsimile reprint of the 1912 edition."

Newberry Library, Chicago. Edward E. Ayer Collection.
Narratives of captivity among the Indians of North America; a list of books and manuscripts on this subject in the Edward E. Ayer Collection of the Newberry Library. Chicago, Newberry Library. Detroit, Gale Research Co., 1974.
x, 120, vii, 49 p. 22 cm.
Facsim. reprint of the 1912 ed. which was issued as no. 3 of the Publications of the Newberry Library.
"Supplement I, by Clara A. Smith": vii, 49 p. at end.

Snodgrass, Marjorie P
Economic development of American Indians and Eskimos, 1930 through 1967: a bibliography ₁by₁ Marjorie P. Snodgrass. ₁Washington, U. S. Bureau of Indian Affairs; for sale by the Supt. of Docs., U. S. Govt. Print. Off.₁ 1968 ₁i. e. 1969₁

v, 263 p. 26 cm. (Departmental Library. Bibliography series, no. 10)

United States. National Archives and Records Service.
The American Indian; select catalog of National Archives microfilm publications. Washington, 1972.

v, 50 p. 27 cm. (National Archives publication no. 72-27)

ART AND MUSIC

Broyles, Bettye J
Bibliography of pottery type descriptions from the eastern United States, compiled and edited by Bettye J. Broyles. Morgantown, W. Va., 1967.

96 p. map. 28 cm. (Southeastern Archaeological Conference. Bulletin 4)

Dawdy, Doris Ostrander.
Annotated bibliography of American Indian painting. New York, Museum of the American Indian, Heye Foundation, 1968.

27 p. 26 cm. (Contributions from the Museum of the American Indian, Heye Foundation, v. 21, pt. 2)

Javitch, Gregory.
A checklist of American Indian dances, songs, and music in the library of Gregory Javitch. Montreal, 1973.

₁15₁ p. 23 cm.

Martin, F   Ellen.
Indian arts and crafts; bibliography. Compiled by F. Ellen Martin. Tempe, Ariz., 1968.

38 l. 28 cm.

U. S. Indian Arts and Crafts Board.
Bibliography of contemporary American Indian and Eskimo arts and crafts. Washington ₁1964₁

4 p. 27 cm. (Its Bibliography no. 1)

U. S. *Indian Arts and Crafts Board*.
Bibliography of contemporary American Indian and Eskimo arts and crafts. Washington ₁1964?₁

₁4₁ l. 27 cm. (*Its* Bibliography no. 4/6–64)

At head of title: Fact sheet.

Wardwell, Allen.
Annotated bibliography of Northwest Coast Indian art, by Allen Wardwell and Lois Lebov. New York, Library, Museum of Primitive Art, 1970.

25 p. 28 cm. (Primitive art bibliographies, no. 8)

CATALOGS

Field, Thomas Warren, 1820–1881.
An essay towards an Indian bibliography; being a catalogue of books relating to the history, antiquities, languages, customs, religion, wars, literature, and origin of the American Indians, in the library of Thomas W. Field. With bibliographical and historical notes, and synopses of the contents of some of the works least known. Detroit, Gale Research Co., 1967.
iv, 430 p. 23 cm.
Title page includes original imprint: New York, Scribner, Armstrong, 1873.

Thomas Gilcrease Institute of American History and Art, Tulsa, Okla. Library.
The Gilcrease-Hargrett catalogue of imprints. Compiled by Lester Hargrett. Prepared for publication and with an introd. by G. P. Edwards. Foreword by John C. Ewers. ₁1st ed.₁ Norman, University of Oklahoma Press ₁1972₁

xviii, 400 p. 24 cm.

U. S. *Dept. of the Interior. Library*.
Biographical and historical index of American Indians and persons involved in Indian affairs. Boston, G. K. Hall, 1966.

8 v. 36 cm.

A subject index developed in the library of the Bureau of Indian Affairs under Mrs. Anita S. Tilden. In 1949, this library was consolidated with other bureau libraries to form the library of the Department of the Interior where the index is now located. From 1951 to late 1965, Mrs. Eugenia Langford continued the work of the index.

JUVENILE LITERATURE

Byler, Mary Gloyne.
American Indian authors for young readers; a selected bibliography. Compiled and with an introd. by Mary Gloyne Byler. New York, Association on American Indian Affairs ₁1973₁

26 p. 23 cm.

Canada. Dept. of Indian Affairs and Northern Development.
About Indians; a listing of books. Les Indiens; une liste de livres à leur sujet. ₁Ottawa, 1972₁

27 p. illus. 22 cm. (Its IAND publication, no. QS-0461-000-BB-A-1)

Olsen, Diane.
Indians in literature; a selected annotated bibliography for children. ₁Minneapolis₁ University of Minnesota, Training Center for Delinquency Prevention ₁1964₁

15 p.

Microfilm print, enlarged. Bethesda, Md., ERIC Document Reproduction Service. 15 p. on ₁9₁ l. 22 x 30 cm.

Stensland, Anna Lee, 1922–
Literature by and about the American Indian; an annotated bibliography for junior and senior high school students. ₁Urbana, Ill.₁ National Council of Teachers of English ₁1973₁

x, 208 p. 23 cm.

LANGUAGES AND LITERATURE

Cardozo, Lubio.
Bibliografía de la literatura indígena venezolana ₁por₁ Lubio Cardozo, Seminario de literatura Indígena Venezolana. Mérida, Universidad de los Andes, Centro de Investigaciones Literarias, 1970.

122 p. 28 cm.

Cardozo, Lubio.
Contribución a la bibliografía sobre la literatura indígena venezolana. Mérida, Universidad de los Andes, Centro de Investigaciones Literarias, 1966.

15 p. 19 cm. (Universidad de los Andes. Centro de Investigaciones Literarias. CIL, 1)

Hirschfelder, Arlene B
American Indian authors; a representative bibliography. Compiled by Arlene B. Hirschfelder. New York, Association on American Indian Affairs ₁1970₁

45 p. 23 cm.

Magalhães, Erasmo d'Almeida.
Bibliografia descritiva de lingüística indígena brasileira, 1954–1965. São Paulo, Universidade de São Paulo, 1967.

70 l. 21 cm.

Pilling, James Constantine, 1846–1895.
Bibliographies of the languages of the North American Indians. New York, AMS Press ₁1973₁

3 v. 24 cm.

Reprint of the 1887-94 editions, which were published separately and issued as Smithsonian Institution. Bureau of Ethnology. Bulletin no. 1, 5–6, 9, 13–16, 19.
CONTENTS: v. 1. pt. 1. Eskimos. pt. 2. Siouan. pt. 3. Iroquoian. pt. 4. Muskhogean.—v. 2. pt. 5. Algonquian.—v. 3. pt. 6. Athapascan. pt. 7. Chinookan. pt. 8. Salishan. pt. 9. Wakashan.

Pottier, Bernard.
Bibliographie américaniste, linguistique amérindienne ... Paris, Musée de l'homme, 1967–

v. 27 cm.

At head of title: Société des américanistes.

Summer Institute of Linguistics.
Bibliografía del Instituto Lingüístico de Verano en el Perú, junio 1946–junio 1971. Recopilación por Mary Ruth Wise S. Sumarios por Paul Powlison F. ₁Lima₁ Instituto Lingüístico de Verano, 1971.

124 p. 22 cm.

U.S. *Indian Arts and Crafts Board.*
Indian and Eskimo folktales. Washington ₁1967₁

4 p. 27 cm. (*Its* Bibliography no. 3)

LEGAL STATUS, LAWS, ETC.

National Indian Law Library.
Catalogue. v. 1–
1973/74–
₁Boulder, Colo.₁

v. 28 cm. annual.

"An index to Indian legal materials and resources."
Published with the Native American Rights Fund.

Sabatini, Joseph D
American Indian law: a bibliography of books, law review articles, and Indian periodicals, compiled by Joseph D. Sabatini. ₁Albuquerque₁ American Indian Law Center, 1973.

40 p. 23 cm.

PERIODICALS

Price, John A   1933–
U. S. and Canadian Indian periodicals, by John Price. Edited by Richard G. Woods ₁and₁ Arthur M. Harkins. Minneapolis, Training Center for Community Programs, University of Minnesota, 1971.

21 l. 28 cm.

Princeton University. Library.
American Indian periodicals in the Princeton University Library; a preliminary list by Alfred L. Bush and Robert S. Fraser. Princeton, N. J., 1970.

78 p. 28 cm.

ALASKA

Workman, Karen Wood.
Alaskan archaeology: a bibliography. Anchorage, Alaska Division of Parks, 1972.

24 p. 22 cm. (Alaska. Division of Parks. Miscellaneous publications. History and archaeology series, no. 1)

CANADA

British Columbia. Provincial Museum of Natural History and Anthropology, Victoria.
A selected list of publications on the Indians of British Columbia. Rev. ed. Victoria, 1970.

31 p. map. 22 cm.

Kidd, Kenneth E.
Brief bibliography of Ontario anthropology, by Kenneth E. Kidd, Edward S. Rogers ₁and₁ Walter A. Kenyon. ₁Toronto₁ Royal Ontario Museum, University of Toronto ₁°1964₁

20 p. 26 cm. (Art and archaeology occasional paper 7)

Meiklejohn, Christopher.
Annotated bibliography of the physical anthropology and human biology of Canadian Eskimos and Indians. ₁Toronto₁ Dept. of Anthropology, University of Toronto, 1971.

169, xvi l. 28 cm.

Meiklejohn, Christopher.
Bibliography of the physical anthropology and human biology of Canadian Eskimos and Indians, ₁compiled by C. Meiklejohn. Toronto₁ Dept. of Anthropology, University

of Toronto, 1970.

ii, 102, xi l. 28 cm.

Whiteside, Don.
Aboriginal people : a selected bibliography concerning Canada's first people / by Don Whiteside. — Ottawa : National Indian Brotherhood, c1973.

i, 345 p. ; 23 cm.

SOUTH AMERICA

Heller, Joyce de.
Bibliografía de orfebrería prehispánica de Colombia. Bibliography of pre-hispanic goldwork of Colombia. Bogotá, Tall. Gráf. Banco de la República, 1971.

126 p. illus. 39 cm. (Museo del Oro. Estudios. v. 1, no. 1)

Mareski, Sofía.
Bibliografía sobre datos y estudios etnográficos y antropológicos del Paraguay. Estudio bibliográfico preparado en el CPDS por Sofía Mareski y Oscar Humberto Ferraro. Asunción [Centro Paraguayo de Documentación Social, 19]72.

143 p. 27 cm. (Centro Paraguayo de Documentación Social. Documentos y estudios bibliográficos, 2)

Martínez, Héctor.
Bibliografía indígena andina peruana, 1900–1968 [por] Héctor Martíneez, Miguel Cameo C. [y] Jesús Ramírez S. Lima, Ministerio de Trabajo y Comunidades, Instituto Indigenista Peruano, 1968–

v. 29 cm.

Martínez, Héctor.
Bibliografía indígena andina peruana (1900–1968) [por] Héctor Martínez, Miguel Cameo C. [y] Jesús Ramírez S. [Lima, Centro de Estudios de Población y Desarrollo, 1969]

157 p. 29 cm.

Means, Philip Ainsworth, 1892–1944.
Biblioteca Andina [Pt. 1]: essays on the lives and works of the chroniclers, or, the writers of the sixteenth and seventeenth centuries who treated of the pre-Hispanic history and culture of the Andean countries. New Haven, Connecticut Academy of Arts and Sciences. Detroit, Blaine Ethridge -Books, 1973.

276–525 p. illus. 21 cm.

Reprint of the 1928 ed., which was the only part published, issued as v. 29 of Transactions of the Connecticut Academy of Arts and Sciences.

Ortiz, Pedro.
Bibliografía básica de Puno. Lima, 1964.

39 p. 28 cm. (Ministerio de Trabajo y Asuntos Indígenas. Plan Nacional de Integración de la Población Aborigen. Serie bibliográfica, no. 1)

Peru. *Oficina Ejecutiva del Plan Nacional de Integración de la Población Aborigen.*
Serie bibliográfica. no. 1. Lima, 1964.

1 v. 28 cm.

No more published?

UNITED STATES

Jillson, Willard Rouse, 1890–
A selected bibliography on the American Indian: historic and prehistoric in Kentucky. Frankfort, Ky., Roberts Print. Co., 1964.

42 p. 23 cm.

Maine Historical Society. Library.
The Indians of Maine: a bibliographical guide, being largely a selected inventory of material on the subject in the society's library. Compiled by Roger B. Ray. Portland, Me., Maine Historical Society, 1972.

[44] p. 26 cm.

Neuman, Robert W
A bibliography relative to Indians of the State of Louisiana, by Robert W. Neuman and Lanier A. Simmons. Baton Rouge, Louisiana Geological Survey, 1969.

72 p. 23 cm. (Anthropological study no. 4)

Oregon. State Library, *Salem*.
Indians of Oregon; a bibliography of materials in the Oregon State Library. Leroy Hewlett, reference consultant, editor. [Salem, 1969]

125 p. 23 cm.

Winsor, Justin, 1831–1897.
The New-England Indians : a bibliographical survey, 1630–1700 / by Justin Winsor. — Montreal : Osiris Publications, 1973.

35 p. ; 23 cm.

Reprint of the 1895 ed. published by J. Wilson and Son, Cambridge, which was reprinted from the Proceedings of the Massachusetts Historical Society, November, 1895.

WEST INDIES

Chevrette, Valerie.
Annotated bibliography of the precolumbian art and archaeology of the West Indies. New York, Library, Museum of Primitive Art, 1971.

18 p. 28 cm. (Primitive art bibliographies, no. 9)

Vanderwal, Ronald L
An annotated bibliography prepared for 'Prehistory of the West Indies,' Dept. of Extra-Mural Studies, University of the West Indies [by] Ronald L. Vanderwal. Kingston, 1967]

[6] p. 36 cm.

AMERICAN LITERATURE

Under this heading is entered the literature of the United States; when the literature of the United States is included with that of Great Britain it is entered under ENGLISH LITERATURE

see also under Dissertations, Academic

American literature abstracts.

[San Jose, Calif.]

v. 28 cm. semiannual.

"A review of current scholarship in the field of American literature."
Began with Dec. 1967 issue. Cf. New serial titles, 1966/68.

Bonner, John Wyatt.
Bibliography of Georgia authors, 1949–1965. Athens, University of Georgia Press [c1966]

vii, 266 p. 24 cm.

Bronte, Diana Lydia.
A sense of place. [Princeton, N. J.] National Humanities

Series ₁1972₁

38 p. 28 x 15 cm. (A National Humanities Series bibliography)

At head of title: Time out for man.
"Based on the touring National Humanities Series program, A sense of place."

Clark, Harry Hayden, 1901–1971.
American literature: Poe through Garland. New York, Appleton-Century-Crofts ₁1971₁

xii, 148 p. 24 cm. (Goldentree bibliographies in language and literature)

Davis, Richard Beale.
American literature through Bryant, 1585–1830. New York, Appleton-Century-Crofts ₁1969₁

xv, 135 p. 24 cm. (Goldentree bibliographies in language and literature)

DeGruson, Gene.
Kansas authors of best sellers; a bibliography of the works of Martin and Osa Johnson, Margaret Hill McCarter, Charles M. Sheldon, and Harold Bell Wright. Pittsburg, Kansas State College of Pittsburg, 1970 ₁c1969₁

iv, 30 p. illus., facsims. 28 cm.

Etulain. Richard W
Western American literature: a bibliography of interpretive books and articles, by Richard W. Etulain. Vermillion, S. D., Dakota Press. 1972.

xii, 137 p. 22 cm.

Finotti, Joseph Maria, d. 1879.
Bibliographia Catholica Americana; a list of works written by Catholic authors, and published in the United States. New York, B. Franklin ₁1971₁

318, 6 p. 19 cm. (Burt Franklin bibliography & reference, 401. Essays in literature & criticism, 116)

Reprint of the 1872 ed.
"Mathew Carey, a catalogue of his works": p. 268–291, 296–299.
"Addenda et corrigenda": 6 p. (2d group)

Foley. Patrick Kevin, 1856–1937.
American authors, 1795–1895; a bibliography of first and notable editions, chronologically arranged with notes. With an introd. by Walter Leon Sawyer. New York, Milford House, 1969.

xvi, 350 p. 23 cm.

Reprint of 1897 ed.
"Initials and pseudonyms. Anonyms": p. ₁337₁–350.

Gaer, Joseph, 1897–
Bibliography of California literature; fiction of the gold-rush period, drama of the gold-rush period, poetry of the gold-rush period. New York, B. Franklin ₁1970₁

123 p. illus. 24 cm. (Burt Franklin bibliography & reference series, 378. American classics in history & social science, 156)

Gohdes, Clarence Louis Frank, 1901–
Bibliographical guide to the study of the literature of the U. S. A. ₁by₁ Clarence Gohdes. 3d ed., rev. and enl. Durham, N. C., Duke University Press, 1970.

x, 134 p. 24 cm.

Johnson, Merle De Vore, 1874–1935.
Merle Johnson's American first editions. Rev. and enl. by Jacob Blanck. 4th ed. Waltham, Mass., Mark Press, 1965 ₁c1942₁

xviii, 553 p. 24 cm.

"Issued in a limited printing of 500 copies."
Reprint of the 4th ed., 1942.

Jones, Howard Mumford, 1892–
Guide to American literature and its backgrounds since

1890 ₁by₁ Howard Mumford Jones and Richard M. Ludwig. 3d ed., rev. and enl. Cambridge, Harvard University Press, 1964.

xiii, 240 p. 22 cm.

Jones, Howard Mumford, 1892–
Guide to American literature and its backgrounds since 1890 ₁by₁ Howard Mumford Jones and Richard M. Ludwig. 4th ed., rev. and enl. Cambridge, Mass., Harvard University Press, 1972.

xii, 264 p. 22 cm.

Levidova, Inna Mikhaĭlovna.
(Khudozhestvennaĭa literatura SShA)
Художественная литература США ... Библиогр. обзор. Под ред. доц. Н. М. Эйшискиной. Москва, 1968.

61 p. 21 cm. (В помощь работникам библиотек)

At head of title: Всесоюзная государственная библиотека иностранной литературы.

Lightfoot, Jean H
Multi-ethnic literature in the high school: a mental health tool ₁by₁ Jean H. Lightfoot. Rockville, Md., National Institute of Mental Health, Center for Studies of Child and Family Mental Health; ₁for sale by the Supt. of Docs., U. S. Govt. Print. Off., Washington, 1973₁

vii. 43 p. 27 cm. (DHEW publication no. (HSM) 73–9079)

Peet, Louis Harman, 1863–1905.
Handy book of American authors. Detroit, Gale Research Co., 1971.

iv, 317 p. 19 cm. (Crowell's handy information series)

"Facsimile reprint of the 1901 edition ₁published under title: Who's the author?₁"

Columbia, S. C., University of South Carolina Press.
v. illus. 24 cm. annual.
The yearbook of American bibliographical and textual studies.

Rubin, Louis Decimus, 1923–
A bibliographical guide to the study of Southern literature, edited by Louis D. Rubin, Jr. With an appendix containing sixty-eight additional writers of the colonial South by J. A. Leo Lemay. Baton Rouge, Louisiana State University Press ₁1969₁

xxiv, 368 p. 25 cm. (Southern literary studies)

Stone, Herbert Stuart, 1871–1915.
First edition₁s₁ of American authors. A manual for book-lovers, compiled by Herbert Stuart Stone, with an introd. by Eugene Field. Kennebunkport, Me., Milford House, 1970.

xxiv, 223 p. 19 cm.

Reprint of the 1893 ed.

Trübner, Nikolaus, 1817–1884.
Trübner's Bibliographical guide to American literature; a classed list of books published in the United States of America during the last forty years. With bibliographical introd., notes, and alphabetical index. Compiled and edited by Nicolas Trübner. London, Trübner, 1859. Detroit, Republished by the Gale Research Co., 1966.
x, cxlix, 554 p. 23 cm.
CONTENTS.—Bibliographical prolegomena.—Contributions towards a history of American literature ₁by B. Moran₁.—Public libraries in the United States ₁by E. Edwards₁.—Classed list of books.—Alphabetical index.

Turco, Lewis.
The literature of New York; a selective bibliography

of colonial and native New York State authors. [Bing-hamton, New York State English Council, c1970]

xxiii, 96 p. 23 cm. (New York State English Council. Monograph no. 12)

The **White House** library; a short-title list. Washington, White House Historical Association, 1967.

219 p. illus. 23 cm.

Foreword signed: James T. Babb.

BIBLIOGRAPHIES

Havlice, Patricia Pate.
Index to American author bibliographies. Metuchen, N. J., Scarecrow Press, 1971.

204 p. 22 cm.

Nilon, Charles H
Bibliography of bibliographies in American literature, by Charles H. Nilon. New York, R. R. Bowker Co., 1970.

xi, 483 p. 24 cm.

Oslo. Universitet. Bibliotek.
A bibliographical guide to research in American litera-ture and language. Publ. by the Royal university library, Oslo. Comp. by Jan Erik Røed. Oslo, 1971.

20 p. 21 cm.

BIO-BIBLIOGRAPHY

Adams, Oscar Fay, 1855–1919.
A brief handbook of American authors. 7th ed., rev. and enl. Boston, Milford House [1973]

xi, 210 p. 22 cm.

Reprint of the 1884 ed. published by Houghton, Mifflin, Boston.

Adams, Oscar Fay, 1855–1919.
A dictionary of American authors. 5th ed. rev. and enl. Boston, Houghton Mifflin, 1904. Detroit, Gale Research Co., 1969.

viii, 587 p. 23 cm.

Adams, Oscar Fay, 1855–1919.
A dictionary of American authors. Kennebunkport, Me., Milford House, 1970.

444 p. 23 cm.

Reprint of the 1897 ed., an enlargement of his Brief handbook of American authors.

American writers; a collection of literary biographies. Leonard Unger, editor in chief. New York, Scribner [1974-

v.   29 cm.

The biographies were originally published as the University of Minnesota pamphlets on American writers.
Includes bibliographies.
CONTENTS: v. 1. Henry Adams to T. S. Eliot.
        —v. 4. Isaac Bashevis Singer to Richard Wright.

Boyce, Richard Fyfe.
American foreign service authors: a bibliography, by Richard Fyfe Boyce and Katherine Randall Boyce. Me-tuchen, N. J., Scarecrow Press, 1973.

x, 321 p. 22 cm.

Burke, William Jeremiah, 1902–
American authors and books, 1640 to the present day [by] W. J. Burke and Will D. Howe. Rev. by Irving Weiss

and Anne Weiss. 3d rev. ed. New York, Crown Publish-ers [c1972]

719 p. 25 cm.

Paluka, Frank.
Iowa authors: a bio-bibliography of sixty native writers. Iowa City, Friends of the University of Iowa Libraries, 1967.

xi, 243 p. 23 cm.

Schöne, Annemarie.
Abriss der amerikanischen Literaturgeschichte in Tabel-len. Frankfurt a. M., Bonn, Athenäum-Verlag, 1967.

xiv, 300 p. 22 cm. (Athenäum Bücher zur Dichtkunst)

HISTORY AND CRITICISM

Gohdes, Clarence Louis Frank, 1901–
Literature and theater of the States and regions of the U. S. A.; an historical bibliography [by] Clarence Gohdes. Durham, N. C., Duke University Press, 1967.

ix, 276 p. 25 cm.

Leary, Lewis Gaston, 1906–
Articles on American literature, 1950–1967. Compiled by Lewis Leary, with the assistance of Carolyn Bartholet and Catharine Roth. Durham, N. C., Duke University Press, 1970.

xxi, 751 p. 25 cm.

Libman, Valentina A
Russian studies of American literature; a bibliography. Compiled by Valentina A. Libman. Translated by Robert V. Allen. Edited by Clarence Gohdes. Chapel Hill, Uni-versity of North Carolina Press, 1969.

xiv, 218 p. 24 cm. (University of North Carolina. Studies in comparative literature, no. 46)

Marsh, John L   1927–
A student's bibliography of American literature. Com-piled by John L. Marsh. Dubuque, Iowa, Kendall/Hunt Pub. Co. [1971]

x, 100 p. 23 cm.

Resources for American literary study. v. 1–
spring 1971–
[College Park, Md.]

v. 23 cm. semiannual.

Smith, Karen June.
Criticisms of American literature 1960–1970; a select bibliography. Johannesburg, University of Witwatersrand, Dept. of Bibliography, Librarianship and Typography, 1972.

2 v. 30 cm.

Part II by Judy Adrienne Backman.

LIBRARY AND EXHIBITION CATALOGS

The **American** writer in England; an exhibition arranged in honor of the sesquicentennial of the University of Virginia. With a foreword by Gordon N. Ray and an introd. by C. Waller Barrett. Charlottesville, University Press of Vir-ginia [1969]

xxxv, 137 p. illus., facsims., ports. (part col.) 27 cm.

Harvard University. *Library.*
American literature. Cambridge. Mass.: distributed by the Harvard University Press, 1970.

2 v. 29 cm. (*Its* Widener Library shelflist, 26–27)

CONTENTS.—v. **1.** Classification schedule, classified listing by call number, chronological listing.—v. **2.** Author and title listing.

Indiana. University. Lilly Library.
An exhibition of American literature, honoring the completion of the editorial work on the 100th volume approved by the Center for Editions of American Authors, together with eighteenth-century American fiction published abroad, eighteenth-century American editions of some English fiction, eighteenth-century American drama, the first quarter century of fiction written and published in America: 1774–1799; [catalogue, compiled by David A. Randall, Librarian] Bloomington, 1973.

76 p. illus. 28 cm. (**Its** Publication no. 17)

New York (City) Public Library. *Berg Collection.*
First fruits; an exhibition of first editions of first books by American authors, by John D. Gordan. New York, New York Public Library [1968]

25 p. 26 cm.

Reprinted with revisions, from the Bulletin of the New York Public Library, December 1951."
"[The] exhibition, first shown in 1951, is being mounted again in memory of John D. Gordan."

NEGRO AUTHORS

Dakan, Norman E
Black literature. Prepared by: Norman E. Dakan. [San Francisco, Pacific Air Forces] 1970.

v, 69 p. 27 cm. (PACAF basic bibliographies for base libraries)

Drzick, Kathleen.
Annotated bibliography of works relating to the Negro in literature and to Negro dialects [by] Kathleen Drzick, John Murphy [and] Constance Weaver. [Kalamazoo, 1969]

36 l. 28 cm.

Olsson, Martin.
A selected bibliography of black literature : the Harlem Renaissance / by Martin Olsson. — [Exeter, Eng.] : University of Exeter, American Arts Documentation Centre, 1973.

24 p. ; 21 cm. — (American arts pamphlet ; no. 2)

Stanford, Barbara Dodds.
Negro literature for high school students. [Champaign, Ill.] National Council of Teachers of English [1968]

ix, 157 p. 21 cm.

Swisher, Robert.
Black American literature, compiled by Robert Swisher, and Black American folklore, compiled by Jill A. Archer. [Bloomington] Indiana University Libraries, 1969.

25 p. 28 cm. (Focus: Black America bibliography series)

Turner, Darwin T   1931–
Afro-American writers, compiled by Darwin T. Turner. New York, Appleton-Century-Crofts, Educational Division [1970]

xvii, 117 p. 24 cm. (Goldentree bibliographies in language and literature)

TRANSLATIONS

Fukuda, Naomi.
明治・大正・昭和邦訳アメリカ文学書目 A bibliography of translations, American literary works into Japanese, 1868–1967. 福田なをみ編纂 細入藤太郎監修 [東京] 原書房 1968.

17, 239 p. 27 cm.

In colophon: 邦訳アメリカ文学書目

Kunzová, Hela, *comp.*
American literature in Czechoslovakia, 1945–1965; [bibliography. Compiled by Hela Kunzová and Hana Rybáková. English, translation by Roberta F. Samsourová. Edited by Jiřina Tůmová. Prague, Czechoslovak P. E. N., 1966]

77 p. 21 cm.

Repertorio bibliografico della letteratura americana in Italia. A cura del Centro di studi americani, sotto la direzione di Biancamaria Tedeschini Lalli. Roma, Edizioni di Storia e letteratura, 1966–

v. in   25 cm. (Biblioteca di studi americani, 12–13

CONTENTS. v. 1. 1945–1949. Coordinatore: R. Perrault.—v. 2. 1950–1954. Coordinatore: A. Pinto Surdi.

AMERICAN MISSIONARY ASSOCIATION

Amistad Research Center.
Author and added entry catalog of the American Missionary Association archives. Introd. by Clifton H. Johnson. Westport, Conn., Greenwood Pub. Corp. [1970?]

3 v. 32 cm.

CONTENTS.—v. **1.** A–Ez.—v. **2.** Fab–Poo.—v. **3.** Pop–Zz. References to schools and mission stations (p. [893]–932)

AMERICAN PHILOSOPHICAL SOCIETY

American Philosophical Society, Philadelphia.
Serial list of publications. Philadelphia, 1966.

181 p. 22 cm.

AMERICAN POETRY see Poetry - United States

AMERICAN REVOLUTION see United States-History - Revolution

AMERICAN WIT AND HUMOR

Koundakjian, Theodore H
A check list of the Theodore H. Koundakjian collection of native American humor of the nineteenth century, compiled by Theodore H. Koundakjian. Berkeley, Calif., 1970.

142 l. 29 cm.

"Twenty copies have been prepared".

Koundakjian, Theodore H
A revised check list of the Theodore H. Koundakjian collection of native American humor of the nineteenth century. Compiled by Theodore H. Koundakjian. Berkeley, Calif., 1973.

1 v. (various pagings) 28 cm.

"Of this check-list twenty copies have been prepared."

AMPHIBIANS see Herpetology

AMSTERDAM

Amsterdam. *Gemeentelijke-Archiefdienst.*
Inventaris van het archief van de memoriemeesters van de Oude- of St. Nicholaaskerk te Amsterdam. Door P. H. J. van der Laan. Amsterdam, Stadsdrukkerij, 1968.

181 p. 24 cm.

At head of title: Gemeentelijke Archiefdienst Amsterdam.

AN-SKI, S., pseud. see Rappoport, Solomon

ANABAPTISTS

Bahlmann, Paul, 1857–1937.
Die Wiedertaüfer zu Münster. Eine bibliographische Zusammenstellung von P. Bahlmann. Nieuwkoop, B. de Graaf, 1967.

68 p. 21½ cm.

"Nachdruck der Ausgabe Münster, 1894. ₍S. A. aus der Zeitschrift für vaterl. Geschichte und Altertumskunde Westfalens, Bd 51, mit Nachträgen und Register₎"

ANARCHISM

Bettini, Leonardo.
Bibliografia dell'anarchismo ... Firenze, CP, 1972–

v. 23 cm.

CONTENTS: v. 1, t. 1. Periodici e numeri unici anarchici in lingua italiana pubblicati in Italia (1872–1971).

Nettlau, Max, 1865–1944.
Bibliographie de l'anarchie. Préf. d'Élisée Reclus. New York, B. Franklin ₍1968₎

xi, 294 p. 23 cm. (Burt Franklin bibliography and reference series, 219)

"Originally published Paris 1897. Reprinted 1968."

Nettlau, Max, 1865–1944.
Geschichte der Anarchie: Ergänzungsband. Glashütten im Taunus, D. Auvermann, 1972.
56, xxxvi p. 23 cm.
Pt. 2, Biographische und bibliographische Daten, is reprinted from the International Review of Social History, Vol. 14, pt. 2, 1969.
Pt. 3, Personen- und Periodicaregister, is an index to his Der Vorfrühling der Anarchie, Der Anarchismus von Proudhon zu Kropotkin, and Anarchisten und Sozialrevolutionäre.
CONTENTS: 1. Lehning, A. Necrology of Max Nettlau.—2. Nettlau, M. Biographische und bibliographische Daten. — 3. Hunink, M. Personen- und Periodicaregister.

ANASTĀS MĀRĪ, AL-KIRMILĪ

'Awwād, Kūrkīs.
الأب انستاس ماري الكرملي، حياته ومؤلفاته، ١٨٦٦–١٩٤٧.
تأليف كوركيس عواد. بغداد، مطبعة العاني، ١٩٦٦.

303 p. 25 cm.

ANATOMY

Bouchet, Alain.
Titres et travaux scientifiques du Prof. Alain Bouchet. Lyon, ₍69-Saint-Genis-Laval, l'auteur, 7, rue de Corette,₎ 1970.

247 p. illus. 27 cm.

Choulant, Johann Ludwig, 1791–1861.
Geschichte und Bibliographie der anatomischen Abbildung nach ihrer Beziehung auf anatomische Wissenschaft und bildende Kunst; nebst einer Auswahl von Illustrationen nach beruehmten Kuenstlern: Hans Holbein ₍et al.₎ Niederwalluf bei Wiesbaden₎ M. Sändig ₍1971₎
xviii, 203, 122–159 p. illus., col. plate. 30 cm.
"Unveränderter Neudruck der Ausg. von 1852 unter Hinzufügung der 1858 erschienen Ergänzungen des Verfassers."
"Berichtigungen und Ergänzungen zur Geschichte und Bibliographie der anatomischen Abbildung" published in Graphische Incunabeln für Naturgeschichte und Medicin, Leipzig, 1858 (p. 122–159, 2d group).

Haller, Albrecht von, 1708–1777.
Bibliotheca anatomica. Mit einem Vorwort von Gunter Mann. Hildesheim, New York, G. Olms, 1969.

2 v. 23 cm.

Reprint of the Zürich, 1774–77 ed.

Vigh, Béla.
Magyar anatómiai, szövet- és fejlődéstani bibliográfia, 1945–1960. Budapest, Országos Orvostudományi Könyvtár és Dokumentációs Központ, 1965.

259 p. 23 cm.

ANCIENT HISTORY see History, Ancient

ANDERSEN, HANS CHRISTIAN
see also under Danish literature - Translations

Dallas. Public Library.
Andersen's land, terrace exhibit room, Dallas Public Library, October 19–31, 1964. ₍Dallas, 1964₎

₍20₎ p. 22 cm.

"Catalog of editions from the Jean Hersholt collection of the Library of Congress and from the rare book collections of the Dallas Public Library."

Hans Christian Andersen; bibliography of the works translated into Romanian which are published in volume (1886–1965) Bucharest, Romanian Institute for Cultural Relations with Foreign Countries, 1966.

40 p. 20 cm.

Label mounted on t. p.: Introduction and bibliographical presentation elaborated by Dorothea Sasu-Ţimerman.

Jørgensen, Aage.
H. C. Andersen litteraturen. 1875–1968. En bibliografi. Århus, Akademisk Boghandel, 1970.

396 p. 21 cm.
Added t. p.: Hans Christian Andersen literature, 1875–1968.
Foreword in Danish and English.

———— Supplement. ₍Af₎ Jørgen Skjerk. København NV, Eget forlag, Tagensvej 235, 1970.
9 l. 30 cm.

Juel Møller, Sv.
Bidrag til H. C. Andersens bibliografi. København, Det Kongelige Bibliotek, 1966–

v. 25 cm.

CONTENTS.—bd. 1. Bøger på færøsk, grønlandsk, finsk, islandsk, norsk og svensk. 12.- dkr (D 67–19)

ANDERSON, MAXWELL

Texas. University at Austin. Humanities Research Center.
A catalogue of the Maxwell Anderson collection at the University of Texas. Compiled by Laurence G. Avery. ₍Austin₎ University of Texas at Austin; ₍distributed by University of Texas Press, 1968₎

175 p. illus., facsims., port. 26 cm. (Tower bibliographical series, no. 6)

Based on editor's thesis—University of Texas.

ANDERSON, SHERWOOD

White, Ray Lewis.
The Merrill checklist of Sherwood Anderson. Columbus, Ohio, C. E. Merrill Pub. Co. ₍1969₎

iv, 36 p. 19 cm. (Charles E. Merrill program in American literature)

Charles E. Merrill checklists.
Cover title: Checklist of Sherwood Anderson.

ANDERSSON, INGEMAR

Lilliestam, Åke, 1925–
Ingemar Andersson. En bibliografi. ₁Stockholm, författaren, (Kungl. bibl.)₁, 1973.

15 p. 20 cm.

ANDREWS, THOMAS COLEMAN

Oregon. University. *Library.*
Inventory of the papers of T. Coleman Andrews. Eugene, 1967.

28 l. 28 cm. (*Its* Occasional paper no. 5)

ANGA (PAPUAN PEOPLE) see Kukukuku

ÅNGERMANLAND, SWEDEN

Carli, Olof, 1890–
Ångermanlands bibliografi; förteckning över litteratur utkommen före 1940, av O. Carli. Umeå, Skytteanska samfundet ₁1965₁

xiv, 256 p. 24 cm. (Skytteanska samfundets handlingar, no. 4)

ANGLING see Fishing

ANGLO-AMERICAN LAW see Law - Great Britain; Law - United States

ANGLO-SAXON LITERATURE see English literature - To 1700

ANGLO-SAXONS

Heusinkveld, Arthur Helenus.
A bibliographical guide to old English; a selective bibliography of the language, literature, and history of the Anglo-Saxons, compiled by Arthur H. Heusinkveld ₁and Edwin J. Bashe. Folcroft, Pa.₁ Folcroft Library Editions, 1971.
153 p. 26 cm.
"Limited to 150 copies."
Reprint of the 1931 ed., which was issued as v. 4, no. 5, of University of Iowa studies.

ANGOLA

Greenwood, Margaret Joan.
Angola; a bibliography. Cape Town, University of Cape Town, School of Librarianship, 1967.

₁viii₁, 52 p. 23 cm.

ANIMAL INDUSTRY see Livestock

ANIMAL NUTRITION see Feeds and feeding

ANIMALS see Zoology

ANNUALS see Almanacs; Gift-books; Periodical publications

ANNUNZIO, GABRIELE D'

Fondazione Il Vittoriale degli Italiani.
Inventario dei manoscritti di Gabriele d'Annunzio. ₁Brescia₁, 1968.

ix, 391 p. plates. 24 cm. (Quaderni dannunziani, 36/37)

Forcella, Roberto.
D'Annunzio. New York, B. Franklin ₁1973₁

4 v. 18 cm. (Burt Franklin bibliography & reference series, 481. Selected essays and texts in literature and criticism, 196)

Reprint of the 1926–37 ed., v. 1–2 of which were published by Fondazione Leonardo per la cultura italiana, Roma, and issued as no. 25/27 and 37/39 of Guide bibliografiche, and v. 3–4 of which were published by Sansoni, Firenze, and issued as no. 2 and 4 of Guide bibliografiche dell'Istituto nazionale fascista di cultura.
CONTENTS: ₁1₁ 1863–1883.—₁2₁ 1884–1885.—₁3₁ 1886.—₁4₁ 1887.

Ravegnani, Giuseppe, 1895–1964.
D'Annunzio scrittore di lettere. Milano, Quaderni dell'Osservatore, 1971.

243 p. 21 cm. (Quaderni dell'Osservatore, n. 10) L2000

Vecchioni, Mario.
Bibliografia critica di Gabriele D'Annunzio. Pescara-Roma, Edizioni aternine, 1970.

97 p. 28 cm.

Vecchioni, Mario.
Bibliografia musicale. Primo supplemento alla Bibliografia critica di Gabriele D'Annunzio. Pescara-Roma, Edizioni aternine, 1971.

28 p. 20 cm.

ANONYMS AND PSEUDONYMS

Cushing, William, 1811–1895.
Anonyms. A dictionary of revealed authorship. (Reprografischer Nachdruck der Ausg. Cambridge 1889.) Hildesheim, G. Olms, 1969.

829 p. 22 cm.

Gaines, Pierce Welch.
Political works of concealed authorship in the United States, 1789–1810, with attributions. Rev. and enl. ed. Hamden, Conn., Shoe String Press, 1965.

100 p. facsims. 22 cm.

First published in 1959 under title: Political works of concealed authorship during the administrations of Washington, Adams, and Jefferson, 1789–1809.

McGhan, Barry.
Sciencefiction and fantasy pseudonyms, with 1973 supplement. ₁n. p.₁ Misfit Press; ₁may be purchased from H. DeVore, Dearborn, Mich., c1973₁

iv, 34, iii, 21 p. 28 cm.

Sharp, Harold S
Handbook of pseudonyms and personal nicknames, compiled by Harold S. Sharp. Metuchen, N.J., Scarecrow Press, 1972.

2 v. (1104 p.) 22 cm.

Stonehill, Charles Archibald, 1900–
Anonyma and pseudonyma, by Charles A. Stonehill, Junr., Andrew Block, and H. Winthrop Stonehill. 2d ed. New York, Milford House, 1969.

4 v. in 2 (3448 columns) 23 cm.

Reprint of the 1926–27 ed.

ANONYMS AND PSEUDONYMS, CHINESE

Shu, Austin C   W
Modern Chinese authors: a list of pseudonyms, compiled by Austin C. W. Shu. 2d rev. ed. ₁Taipei₁ Distributed by Chinese Materials and Research Aids Service Center, 1971.

84, ₁4₁ p. 27 cm. (Chinese Materials and Research Aids Service Center. Occasional series, no. 9)

ANONYMS AND PSEUDONYMS, FRENCH

Quérard, Joseph Marie, 1797–1865.
Les supercheries littéraires dévoilées, par J.-M. Quérard.

2. éd., considérablement augmentée, publiée par Gustave Brunet et Pierre Jannet. (Reprografischer Nachdruck der Ausg. Paris 1869–89.) Hildesheim, G. Olms, 1965.

3 v. 23 cm.

ANONYMS AND PSEUDONYMS, GERMAN

Rassmann, Christian Friedrich, 1772–1831.
Kurzgefasstes Lexicon deutscher pseudonymer Schriftsteller von der ältern bis auf die jüngste Zeit aus allen Fächern der Wissenschaften [von] Fr. Rassmann. Mit einer Vorrede über die Sitte der literarischen Verkappung von J. W. S. Lindner. Leipzig, W. Nauck, 1830. [Leipzig, Zentralantiquariat der Deutschen Demokratischen Republik, 1971]

viii, 248 p. 20 cm.

ANONYMS AND PSEUDONYMS, GREEK (MODERN)

Ntelopoulos, Kyriakos.
Νεοελληνικὰ φιλολογικὰ ψευδώνυμα. 1. ἔκδ. ᾿Αθῆναι, Κολλέγιον ᾿Αθηνῶν, 1969.

143, [1] p. 21 cm. (Βιβλιοθήκη Κολλεγίου Αθηνῶν. ᾿Εγχειρίδια βιβλιοθηκονομίας, 3)

ANONYMS AND PSEUDONYMS, HEBREW AND YIDDISH

Chajes, Saul, 1884–1935.
אוצר בדויי השם; הוא מפתח השמות הבדויים, של המחברים בספרות ישראל בעברית ובאידית—כנוייהם, סימניהם ונוטריקניהם עם פתרונותיהם—מתקופת הגאונים עד העת החדשה, מאת שאול חיות. [Hildesheim, G. Olms, 1967]

xiv, 335, 10, [1], 66 p. 22 cm.
Added t. p.: Thesaurus pseudonymorum quae in litteratura Hebraica et Judaeo-Germanica inveniuntur.
"Reprografischer Nachdruck der Ausgabe Wien 1933."
(ספרים יוצאים לאור על ידי קרן חפרסים על שם הרב צבי פרץ חיות ז״ל בבית מדרש הרבנים בוינא)

ANONYMS AND PSEUDONYMS, LATIN AMERICAN

Medina, José Toribio, 1852–1930.
Diccionario de anónimos y seudónimos hispanoamericanos. Buenos Aires, Impr. de la Universidad, 1925. Detroit, B. Ethridge, 1973.

2 v. in 1. 23 cm. (Serie Anónimos y seudónimos hispanoamericanos)

"Facsimile edition."
Original ed. issued as no. 26–27 of Publicaciones del Instituto de Investigaciones Históricas, Universidad de Buenos Aires.

Tauro, Alberto, 1914–
Hacia un catálogo de seudónimos peruanos. Lima, Universidad Nacional Mayor de San Marcos [1967]

66 p. 25 cm.

Victorica, Ricardo.
Errores y omisiones del Diccionario de anónimos y seudónimos hispanoamericanos de José Toribio Medina. Buenos Aires, Viau & Zona, 1928. Detroit, B. Ethridge, 1973.

338 p. 23 cm. (Serie anónimos y seudónimos hispanoamericanos)

"Facsimile of a volume in the Maury A. Bromsen Medina Collection in the University of Florida Libraries."

Victorica, Ricardo.
Nueva epanortosis al Diccionario de anónimos y seudónimos de J. T. Medina. Buenos Aires, L. J. Rosso, 1929. Detroit, B. Ethridge, 1973.

207 p. 23 cm. (Serie anónimos y seudónimos hispanoamericanos)

"A slightly reduced facsimile of a volume in the University of Michigan Library."

Villas-Bôas, Pedro.
Pseudônimos de regionalistas e abreviaturas. Pôrto Alegre, Impressora Moliterni, 1967.

26 p. 22 cm.

Villas-Bôas, Pedro.
Pseudônimos rio-grandenses [por] P. Villas Bôas. [Pôrto Alegre] 1970.

61, [12] l. 31 cm.

ANONYMS AND PSEUDONYMS, ROMANIAN

Straje, Mihail, 1901–
Dicţionar de pseudonime, alonime [sic], anagrame, asteronime, criptonime ale scriitorilor şi publiciştilor români. Bucureşti, „Minerva," 1973.

xxiii, 812 p. 20 cm.

ANONYMS AND PSEUDONYMS, RUSSIAN

Petrîaev, Evgeniĭ Dmitrievich.
(Psevdonimy literatorov-sibirîakov)
Псевдонимы литераторов-сибиряков : материалы к "Истории рус. литературы Сибири" / Е. Д. Петряев. — Новосибирск : "Наука," Сиб. отд-ние, 1973.

74 p. ; 22 cm.

At head of title: Академия наук СССР. Сибирское отделение. Институт истории, филологии и философии.

ANOUILH, JEAN

Kelly, Kathleen White.
Jean Anouilh: an annotated bibliography. Metuchen, N. J., Scarecrow Press, 1973.

viii, 132 p. 22 cm. (The Scarecrow author bibliographies, no. 10)

ANREITH, ANTON

Wolf, Hillary.
Anton Anreith: sculptor; a bibliography. Johannesburg, University of the Witwatersrand, Dept. of Bibliography, Librarianship and Typography, 1972.

iv, 27 p. 20 cm.

"Compiled in part fulfilment for the requirements of Diploma in Librarianship, University of the Witwatersrand, Johannesburg."

ANTARCTIC see Polar regions

ANTENNAS (ELECTRONICS)

United States. Library of Congress. Aerospace Technology Division.
Mathematics of antennas; annotated bibliography [by] Leonas Kacinskas. Washington] 1966.

iv, 62 l. 28 cm. (Its ATD report 66–33)

"Compiled from Soviet open sources published 1961–1964."

ANTHEIT, BELGIUM

Belgium. *Archives de l'État, Liège.*
Inventaire analytique des chartes de l'abbaye du Val-Notre-Dame, par Georges Hansotte, conservateur. Bruxelles, 1964.

17 p. 29 cm.

ANTHONY, SCOTT J.

Colorado. State Historical Society. Library.
A calendar of the papers of Scott J. Anthony, 1830–1903; a holding of the Library of the State Historical Society of Colorado. Processed by Jean H. Cramer. Denver, 1967.

14 l. 23 x 29 cm.

ANTHROPOLOGY AND ETHNOLOGY
see also Archaeology; and under
Dissertations, Academic

Abstracts in anthropology. v. 1–
Feb. 1970–
₁Westport, Conn.₁ Greenwood Periodicals.

v. 26 cm. quarterly.

Bunakova, O. V.
Библиография трудов Института этнографии им. Н. Н. Миклухо-Маклая, 1900–1962. Саставители: О. В. Бунакова, Р. В. Каменецкая. Ленинград, Наука, 1967.
281 p. 27 cm.
At head of title: Академия наук СССР. Библиотека Академии наук СССР. Институт этнографии им. Н. Н. Миклухо-Маклая.
Added t. p.: Bibliographie des travaux de l'Institut d'éthnographie Mikloukho-Maclay.
Table of contents also in French.

Conklin, Harold C
Folk classification: a topically arranged bibliography of contemporary and background references through 1971 ₁by₁ Harold C. Conklin. ₁New Haven₁ Dept. of Anthropology, Yale University, 1972.

501 p. 23 cm.

Dokládal, Milan.
Československá anthropologická bibliografie, 1955–1964. Чехословацкая антропологическая библиография. Bibliographie der tschechoslowakischen anthropologischen literatur. Brno, Československa spolecnost anthropologická při Československé akademii věd, 1966–

v. 21 cm.

Table of contents also in German and Russian.

Etnologiske ekstrakter 1970–72. ₁Udg. af NEFA's Dokumentationstjeneste₁. København, NEFA's Forlag, 1972.

63 p. 21 cm. (NEFA dokumentation, 1972, nr. 1)

Field, Henry, 1902–
Bibliography: 1926–1964. Nos. 1–594. ₁Miami? Fla.₁ 1964.

vii, 112 p. 28 cm.

"Includes and supplements ... ₁the compiler's₁ 'Bibliografía,' which was published in Boletín bibliográfico de antropología americana, vol. 9, pp. 325–33, Mexico City, 1948 ... Also included ₁is₁ the complete list of materials microfilmed in the American Documentation Institute."

Field, Henry, 1902–
Bibliography of Soviet archaeology and physical anthropology, 1936–1967, nos. 1–167. ₁Coconut Grove, Fla.₁ 1967.

21 p. 23 cm.

Field, Henry, 1902–
Bibliography of Soviet archaeology and physical anthropology, 1936–1972, nos. 1–189. Coconut Grove, Fla., Field Research Projects, 1972.

v, 20 p. 23 cm.

Frederick W. Crumb Memorial Library.
Some sources of information in anthropology available at the Frederick W. Crumb Memorial Library, State University College, Potsdam, New York. Prepared by Suzanne Hill with the assistance of the Dept. of Anthropology—Sociology. ₁Potsdam, N. Y.₁ 1969.

16 l. 28 cm. (₁Frederick W. Crumb Memorial Library₁ Pub₁lication₁ no. 69–13)

Gallagher, James Joseph, 1919 (Sept. 26)–
An annotated bibliography of anthropological materials for high school use, by James J. Gallagher. New York, Macmillan ₁c1967₁

ix, 135 p. 23 cm.

Human Relations Area Files, inc.
HRAF source bibliography. New Haven, Conn., 1973 ₁c1969₁

1 v. (various pagings) 30 cm.

Keesing, Felix Maxwell, 1902–1961.
Culture change; an analysis and bibliography of anthropological sources to 1952. New York, Octagon Books, 1973 ₁c1953₁

ix, 242 p. 24 cm.

Reprint of the ed. published by Stanford University Press, Stanford, Calif., which was issued as no. 1 of Stanford anthropological series.

Lægdsmand, Karsten.
Bibliografi for folkelivsforskere. Med særlig henblik på de materielle kulturprodukter og næringslivet. Et udvalg. København, Københavns Universitets Fond til Tilvejebringelse af Læremidler, 1968.

432 p. 24 cm.

At head of title: Københavns universitets institut for europæisk folkelivsforskning.

Rountree, Louise Marie.
Multi-cultures; a select multi-ethnic bibliography for the young reader. ₁Salisbury? N. C.₁ 1969.

32 l. 28 cm.

Tippett, Alan Richard.
Bibliography for cross-cultural workers. Compiled by A. R. Tippett. South Pasadena, Calif., William Carey Library ₁c1971₁

252 p. 24 cm.

Vademecum für den Ethnologen. Vademecum for the Anthropologist. (Eine Bibliographie lieferbarer Bücher als Grundlage für die Bibliothek eines Ethnologen.) München, Renner (1967).

48 l. of illus. 21 cm.

Vademecum für den Ethnologen. Vademecum for the anthropologist. (Eine Bibliographie lieferbarer Bücher und Zeitschriften als Grundlage f. d. Bibliothek e. Ethnologen.) 2., völlig neu bearb. u. stark erw. Aufl. München, Renner (1968).

62 l. with illus. 21 cm.

Verzeichnis von Beiträgen zur Anthropologie und Ethnologie, die in 50 jähriger Forschungsarbeit entstanden sind ⟨1916–1966⟩ Den Freunden und Helfern von P. Martin Gusinde ... zu seinem 80. Geburtstag ⟨29. Okt. 1966⟩ und zum 60 jährigen Bestehen der Internationalen Zeitschrift für Völker- und Sprachenkunde "Anthropos" dargeboten vom Anthropos-Institut. ₁Mit Portrait₁ (Mödling, Missionsdruckerei St. Gabriel ₁1966₁)

15 p. 21 cm.

LIBRARY CATALOGS

Harvard University. Peabody Museum of Archaeology and Ethnology. Library.
Catalogue: authors. Boston, G. K. Hall, 1963.
26 v. 37 cm.

"Its outstanding feature is the inclusion of journal articles. For more than 50 years the periodicals have been indexed, as well as compilations such as Festschriften, and the proceedings of congresses."

——————First supplement. Boston, G. K. Hall, 1970.
6 v. 37 cm.
Contains entries from 1963 through the first half of 1969.

——————Second supplement. Boston, G. K. Hall, 1971.
2 v. 27 cm.
Covers entries from the second half of 1969 through the first half
of 1971, and for volumes from the previously uncatalogued libraries
of G. G. MacCurdy, P. A. Means, and S. K. Lothrop.

Harvard University. Peabody Museum of Archaeology and Ethnology. Library.
Catalogue: subjects. Boston, G. K. Hall, 1963.
27 v. 37 cm.
——————Index to subject headings. Boston, G. K. Hall, 1963.
vi, 117 p. 37 cm.

——————First supplement. Boston, G. K. Hall, 1970.
6 v. 37 cm.
Entries represent additions from 1963 through the first half of 1969.

AFRICA

Hertefelt, Marcel d'.
African governmental systems in static and changing conditions. A bibliographic contribution to political anthropology. Tervuren, Musée royal de l'Afrique centrale, 1968.
xxiv, 178 p. 26½ cm.

Holas, Bohumil.
Werke und Artikel über afrikanische traditionelle Kulturen, 1946–1971. ₍Von₎ B. Holas. ₍Vom Französischen durch Peter Mohr übersetzt.₎ Paris, P. Geuthner, 1971.
111 p. port. 21 cm.

AMERICA

Guyot, Mireille.
Bibliographie américaniste: archéologie et préhistoire, anthropologie et ethnohistoire. Paris, Musée de l'homme ₍1969?₎
248 l. 27 cm.
At head of title: Société des américanistes.

Hasler, Juan A
Bibliographia americanistica brevis / Juan A. Hasler. — Medellín, Colombia : Universidad de Antioquia, 1973.
170 p. ; 24 cm.

AUSTRALIA

Craig, Beryl F.
Arnhem Land peninsular region (including Bathurst and Melville Islands) compiled by Beryl F. Craig. Canberra, Australian Institute of Aboriginal Studies, 1966.
viii, 205 p. maps (part fold.) 26 cm. (Australian Institute of Aboriginal Studies, Canberra. Occasional papers in aboriginal studies, no. 8. Bibliography series no. 1)

Craig, Beryl F
Cape York, compiled by Beryl F. Craig. Canberra, Australian Institute of Aboriginal Studies, 1967.
viii, 233 p. maps (part fold.) 26 cm. (Australian Institute of Aboriginal Studies. Occasional papers in aboriginal studies, no. 9. Bibliographical series no. 2)

Craig, Beryl F
Central Australian and western desert regions: an annotated bibliography, compiled by Beryl F. Craig. Canberra, Australian Institute of Aboriginal Studies, 1969.
xi, 351 p. maps. 26 cm. (Australian aboriginal studies, no. 31) (Bibliography series, no. 5)

Craig, Beryl F
Kimberley region: an annotated bibliography; compiled by Beryl F. Craig. Canberra, Australian Institute of Aboriginal Studies, 1968.
x, 209 p. maps (part fold.) 26 cm. (Australian aboriginal studies, no. 13) (Bibliography series, no. 3)

Craig, Beryl F
North-west-central Queensland; an annotated bibliography. Compiled by Beryl F. Craig. Canberra, Australian Institute of Aboriginal Studies, 1970.
xiii, 137 p. illus., map. 27 cm. (Australian Aboriginal studies no. 41) (Bibliography series no. 6)

Marchant, Leslie Ronald.
A list of French naval records and illustrations relating to Australian and Tasmanian aborigines, 1771 to 1828, compiled by Leslie R. Marchant. Canberra, Australian Institute of Aboriginal Studies, 1969.
83 p. 26 cm. (Australian aboriginal studies, no. 21) (Bibliography series, no. 4)

Massola, Aldo.
Bibliography of the Victorian Aborigines, from the earliest manuscripts to 31 December 1970. Melbourne, Hawthorn Press, 1971.
95 p. 25 cm.

BRAZIL

Baldus, Herbert, 1899–
Bibliografia crítica da etnologia brasileira. São Paulo, 1954. Nendeln/Liechtenstein, Kraus Reprint, 1968–70.
2 v. illus., facsims., maps, ports. 25 cm. (Völkerkundliche Abhandlungen, Bd. 3–4)
Vol. 2, a new work, has imprint: Hannover, Kommissionsverlag Münstermann-Druck, 1968.
Vol. 1 has introductory matter in Portuguese and English; vol. 2, in Portuguese, English and German.

Hartmann, Thekla.
Panorama das investigações antropológicas no Brasil. São Paulo, 1968.
29 l. 24 cm.
At head of title: Universidade de São Paulo, Faculdade de Filosofia, Ciências e Letras. Cadeira de Antropologia.
Includes bibliographical references.

ESTONIA

Hagar, Helmut.
A bibliography of works published by Estonian ethnologists in exile, 1945–1965, compiled by Helmut Hagar. Stockholm, Institutum Litterarum Estonicum, 1965.
63 p. 21 cm.

Viires, Ants.
Eesti Nõukogude etnograafia bibliograafia, 1945–1966. Koostanud Ants Viires ja Jüri Linnus. Tallinn, Eesti NSV Teaduste Akadeemia Ajaloo Instituut, 1967.
x, 128 p. 20 cm.

EUROPE

Theodoratus, Robert J 1928–
Europe; a selected ethnographic bibliography, by Robert J. Theodoratus. New Haven, Conn., Human Relations Area Files, 1969.
xi, 544 p. 22 cm. (Behavior science bibliographies)

INDIA

Field, Henry, 1902–
Bibliography on the physical anthropology of the peoples of India, by Henry Field and Edith M. Laird. Coconut

Grove, Fla., Field Research Projects, 1968–70.

2 v. 28 cm.

IRAN

Zamānī, Maḥmūd.

ختاب‌شناسی فرهنگ عامه و مردم شناسی ایران، گردآوری

محمود زمانی. تهران ‏[1972‏]. 1350.

‏(نشریه مؤسسه فرهنگی منطقه‌ئی، شماره 23‏)

CONTENTS: 2. بخش . — . بخش ‏1. زمانی، محمود. فهرست کتابها.
بلوکباشی، علی. فهرست مقاله‌ها.

JAPAN

Cultural anthropology in Japan, by the Committee for the Publication of Cultural Anthropological Studies in Japan. ₍Compiler: Seiichi Izumi. 1st ed. Tokyo₎ Tokyo Electrical Engineering College Press, 1967.

vi, 112 p. 26 cm.

"The present volume is published to serve as a catalogue of selected books and articles published ₍in Japan₎ between 1960 and 1964."

English and Japanese.

KOREA

Knez, Eugene Irving, 1916–

한국人類學에관한 文獻목록   A selected and annotated bibliography of Korean anthropology, by Eugene I. Knez and Chang-su Swanson. ₍國會圖書館司書局 編輯   서울, 수원대, 시판 ₍1968₎

235 p. map. 25 cm.

Appendices (p. 201–233): A. Author index (著者索引)—B. Title index (書名索引)

MEXICO

Genovés Tarazaga, Santiago.

La antropología física en México, 1943–1964; inventario bibliográfico, por Santiago Genovés T. y Juan Comas. ₍1. ed.₎ México, Universidad Nacional Autónoma de México, 1964.

55 p. 24 cm. (Universidad Nacional Autónoma de México. Instituto de Investigaciones Históricas. 1. ser.: Publ. no. 91. Cuadernos del Instituto de Investigaciones Históricas. Serie antropológica, no. 17)

"Contribución a la XXXIII sesión de la American Association of Physical Anthropologists, 22–24 de junio de 1964, México."

Continuation of the bibliographical section of the authors' La antropología física en México, 1943–1959, published in 1960 with the authors' names in reverse order.

MORAVIA

Rousová, Jiřina.

Soupis národopisných příspěvků v regionálních časopisech západní Moravy. Jiřina Rousová a Vlasta Svobodová. ₍Brno, 1967₎

47 p. 21 cm. (Bibliograficka příloha Věstníku NSČ a SNS, č. 10)

NEW GUINEA

Australian National University, *Canberra. Dept. of Anthropology and Sociology.*

An ethnographic bibliography of New Guinea. Canberra, Australian National University Press, 1968.

3 v. 26 cm.

CONTENTS.—v. 1. Author index.—v. 2. District index.—v. 3. Proper names index.

PHILIPPINE ISLANDS

Saito, Shiro.

Preliminary bibliography of Philippine ethnography.

PORTUGAL

Pereira. Benjamim Enes.

Bibliografia analítica de etnografia portuguesa. Lisboa, Instituto de Alta Cultura, 1965.

xv, 670 p. 25 cm.

At head of title: Instituto de Alta Cultura. Centro de Estudos de Etnologia Peninsular.

RUSSIA

Titova, Zoîa Dmitrievna.

Этнография. Библиография рус. библиографий по этнографии народов СССР (1851–1969). Москва, "Книга," 1970.

143 p. 21 cm.

At head of title: Государственная ордена Трудового Красного Знамени публичная библиотека им. М. Е. Салтыкова-Щедрина. З. Д. Титова.

SLOVAKIA

Kubová, Milada.

Bibliografia slovenskej etnografie a folkloristiky za roky 1960–1969. Bratislava, Národopisný ústav SAV, 1971.

104 p. 24 cm.

SUDAN

Garsse, Yvan van.

Ethnological and anthropological literature on the three Southern Sudan provinces Upper Nile, Bahr el Ghazal, Equatoria. ₍Sint Niklaus Waas, Parlaan, 2₎ 1972.

₍1₎, 83 l. 32 cm.

TASMANIA

Plomley, Norman James Brian.

An annotated bibliography of the Tasmanian aborigines ₍by₎ N. J. B. Plomley. London, Royal Anthropological Institute, 1969.

xix, 143 p. 21 cm. (Royal Anthropological Institute. Occasional paper no. 28)

YUGOSLAVIA

Kujundžić, Ivan, *comp.*

Izvori za povijest bunjevačko-šokačkih Hrvata. Sastavio Ivan Kujundžić. Zagreb, Matica hrvatska, 1968.

94, ₍1₎ p. 19 cm. (Matica hrvatska. Izvanredno izdanje)

ANTICOAGULANTS (MEDICINE)

Endo Laboratories. *Medical Dept.*

Anticoagulant therapy, a selected bibliography. Garden City, N. Y., 1968.

48 p. 22 cm.

ANTIDEPRESSANTS

Anti-depressant drug studies, 1955–1966; bibliography and selected abstracts ₍by₎ Aaron Smith ₍and others₎ Research Dept., Haverford State Hospital, Haverford, Pa. Chevy Chase, Md., National Institute of Mental Health; ₍for sale by the Supt. of Docs., U. S. Govt. Print. Off., Washington, 1969₎

iv, 639 p. 26 cm. (Public Health Service publication no. 1905)

ANTIGUA

Tooley, Ronald Vere, 1898–

The printed maps of Antigua, 1689–1889, by R. V. Tooley. London, Map Collectors' Circle, 1969.

11 p., ₍16₎ p. of maps. 25 cm. (Map Collectors' Circle. Map Collectors' series, no. 55)

ANTIOQUIA, COLOMBIA (DEPT.)

Antioquia, *Colombia (Dept.) Departamento Administrativo de Planeación.*
Indice cartográfico: Originales, copias, mapas. Medellín, 1969.
37 l. maps. 27 cm.

Valle, Francisco, fl. 1971–
Bibliografía de autores antioqueños, 1960–1969. Compilada por Francisco Valle. Medellín, Editorial Universidad de Antioquia, 1971.
102 l. 27 cm. (Manuales de bibliografía y documentación colombiana) (Publicaciones de la Escuela Interamericana de Bibliotecología. Serie bibliográfica, no. 29)

"Este trabajo es una actualización de la obra de la licenciada Mary Alvarez Restrepo, 'Bibliografía de autores antioqueños,' desde la creación del departamento hasta 1960."

ANTIQUITIES see Archaeology

ANTISEMITISM

Arditti, Benjamin Joseph, 1897–
(ha-Sifrut ha-antishemit be-Bulgaryah)
הספרות האנטישמית בבולגריה; רשימה ביבליאוגרפית מאת
בנימין ארדיטי. חולון, 1972.
79 p. facsims. 25 cm.

On dust jacket: The antisemitic literature in Bulgaria.
Introd. also in Bulgarian.

Wiener Library, London.
Prejudice: racist-religious-nationalist (compiled and edited by Helen Kehr) London, Vallentine, Mitchell (for the) Institute of Contemporary History, 1971.
ix, 385 p. 23 cm. index. (Wiener Library. Catalogue series, no. 5)

ANTONIO DE SAN JOSÉ, padre

Higinio de Santa Teresa, Brother.
Antonio de San José. Estudios bio-bibliográfico. **Alzo** (Guipúzcoa) (Higinio Gandarias) 1972.
161 p. 25 cm.

ANTRIM, IRELAND (COUNTY)

Antrim County Library.
A subject catalogue of books and some other material relating to County Antrim. 2nd ed. Ballymena (Demesne Ave, Ballymena, Co. Antrim), Antrim County Library, 1969.
(1), 27 p. 26 cm.

ANTWERP (CITY, DIOCESE AND PROVINCE)

Antwerp. Havenbedrijf. Afdeling Studie en Prospectie. Bibliotheek.
Haven van Antwerpen; bibliografie. Antwerpen, 1964.
38 l. 27 cm.

At head of title: Stad Antwerpen, Havenbedrijf, Algemene Directie, Afd. Studie & Prospectie.

Antwerp. Onze Lieve Vrouw (Cathedral). Kathedraal en Diocesaan Archief.
De archieven van het Onze-Lieve-Vrouw Kapittel te Antwerpen, 1124–1801, in het kathedraal en diocesaan archief. (Door) J. van den Nieuwenhuizen. (Antwerpen, Kapittel van de Kathedraalkerk, Groenplaats, 21), (1969).
xvii, 73 l. port., illus., tables, facsim. 28 cm. (Kapittelschriften, 9)

Belgium. Archives de l'État, Antwerp.
Inventaris van de archieven van het Nationaal Komiteit voor Hulp en Voeding, Provincie Antwerpen. Door F. G.

C. Beterans. Brussel, Algemeen Rijksarchief, Ruisbroekstr. 2, 1970.
(iii), 131 p. 30 cm.
At head of title: Ministerie van Nationale Opvoeding en Nederlandse Cultuur en Ministerie van Nationale Opvoeding en Franse Cultuur. Algemeen Rijksarchief en Rijksarchieven in de Provinciën.

Belgium. Archives de l'État, Antwerp.
Inventarissen van hedendaagse archieven van gemeenten. Brussel, Algemeen Rijksarchief, 1973–
v. 30 cm.
"Gegeven door de gemeentebesturen aan het depot van het Rijksarchief te Antwerpen."

Belgium. Archives de l'État, Antwerp.
Inventarissen van kerkarchieven. Brussel, Algemeen Rijksarchief, 197
v. 30 cm.

Brabant, Jozef van.
Oud Antwerps kerkarchief in het Rijksarchief, het Stadsarchief en het Archief der Commissie van Openbare Onderstand te Antwerpen, en in andere instellingen en archieffondsen. Inventarissen en synoptische lijsten. (Door J. van Brabant. Antwerpen, Kapittel van de Kathedraalkerk, Groenplaats, 21), (1972).
xxx, 96 l. facsim. 27 cm. (Oud Antwerps kerkarchief 3) (Kapittelschriften, 11)

L'Escaut et Anvers. Témoignages d'un essor. (Anvers, Crédit communal de Belgique, 1966).
77 p. illus., map, facsims. 20 cm.
"Exposition ... organisée pour célébrer l'ouverture du siège du Crédit communal de Belgique pour la province d'Anvers."

Oud Antwerps kerkarchief. (Antwerpen, Kapittel van de Kathedrallkerk, 1969–
v. illus. 28 cm.

AOSTA, VALLEY OF see under Piedmont

APHERDIANUS, PETRUS see Afferden, Pieter van

APICULTURE see Bee culture

APOLLINAIRE, GUILLAUME

Paris. Bibliothèque nationale.
Apollinaire, Paris, 1969. (22 octobre–30 novembre. Catalogue par Jean Adhémar, Lise Dubief et Gérard Willemetz. Préface par Étienne Dennery.) Paris, Bibliothèque nationale, 1969.
180 p. plates. 20 cm.

APOLOGETICS

Steinschneider, Moritz, 1816–1907.
Polemische und apologetische Literatur in arabischer Sprache zwischen Muslimen, Christen und Juden, nebst Anhängen verwandten Inhalts. (Reprografischer Nachdruck der Ausg. Leipzig 1877.) Hildesheim, Gg. Olms, 1966.
x, 456 p. 21 cm. (Abhandlungen zur Kunde des Morgenlandes, VI, 3)

APPALACHIAN REGION

Appalachian bibliography. Compiled for Appalachian Regional Commission. Morgantown, West Virginia University Library, 1967.
2 v. 29 cm.
CONTENTS.—(1) Authors.—(2) Subjects.

Nelsen, Hart M

Bibliography on Appalachia: a guide to studies dealing with Appalachia in general, and including rural and urban working class attitudes toward religion, education, and social change, by Hart M. Nelsen and Anne K. Nelsen. with the assistance of James K. Miller. ₍Bowling Green, Western Kentucky University, Office of Research and Services, 1967₎

73 1. 28 cm. (Western Kentucky University. College of Commerce. Office of Research and Services. Research bulletin #4)

APPORTIONMENT (ELECTION LAW)

Archibald, Marybelle.

Reapportionment; an annotated bibliography, 1966–1971. ₍Sacramento₎ California State Library, Law Library, 1971.

15 p. 28 cm.

California. *Legislature. Assembly. Legislative Reference Service.*

The general subject of reapportionment. ₍Sacramento?₎ 1965.

39 1. 28 cm.

New Jersey. Law and Legislative Reference Bureau.

Problems of legislative apportionment and districting after Baker v. Carr; a subject bibliography. ₍Trenton, N. J.₎ 1966.

31 p. 31 cm.

White, Anthony G

Representation as an urban problem; a bibliography ₍by₎ Anthony G. White. Mary Vance, editor. ₍Monticello, Ill., Council of Planning Librarians₎ 1973.

11 p. 28 cm. (Council of Planning Librarians. Exchange bibliography, 468)

APPRAISAL see Valuation

APRICOT

Mante, Willi, 1919–

Bibliographie des internationalen Aprikosen-Schrifttums. Bibliography of the international literature on apricots. ₍Von₎ Willi Mante ₍u.₎ Walter Blodig. Berlin (Techn. Univ., Universitätsbibliothek, Abt. Publikationen) 1970.

xxi, 259 p. 21 cm. (Bibliographische Reihe der Technischen Universität Berlin, Bd. 1)

AL-'AQQĀD, 'ABBĀS MAḤMŪD

al-Ḥalwajī, 'Abd al-Sattār 'Abd al-Ḥaqq.

عباس محمود العقاد، نشرة بيليوجرافية بآثاره الفكرية. اعداد عبد الستار عبد الحق الحلوجى. ₍القاهرة₎ مطبعة دار الكتب، 1964.

32, 156 p. 24 cm.

At head of title: الجمهورية العربية المتحدة. وزارة الثقافة والارشاد القومى. دار الكتب.

AQUACULTURE

George Washington University, Washington, D. C. Biological Sciences Communication Project.

Bibliography of aquaculture. ₍Wilmington, N. C.₎ Coastal Plains Center for Marine Development Services, 1971.

vii, 245 p. 28 cm. (Coastal Plains Center for Marine Development Services. Publication 71-4.

AQUARIUMS

Řídká, Bohuslava.

Akvaristika a teraristika; výběr literatury. ₍Zprac. Bohuslava Řídká₎ V Brně. Universitní knihovna, 1971.

8 l. 21 cm. (Bibliografický leták, 165)

AQUATIC BIOLOGY see Marine biology

ARAB COUNTRIES

see also under Asia *(Fodor)*; Dissertations, Academic

'Abd al-Raḥmān, 'Abd al-Jabbār.

دليل المراجع العربية والمعربة، فهرست ببليـــوغرافي يعرف ويقيم المراجع الـ ية والمعربة فى مختلف الموضوعات، والمراجع الاجنبية التى تبحـ ن شؤون العرب. تأليف عبد الجبار عبد الرحمن. ₍الطبعة 1.₎ بصرة، دار الطباعة الحديثة ₍1970₎

12, 556, 5 p. 24 cm.
Added t. p.: Guide to Arabic reference books; an annotated bibliography of books in Arabic, and books in Western languages dealing with the Arabs, by A. J. Abdulrahman.
Introds. in Arabic and English.

American University of Beirut. Economic Research Institute.

A cumulation of a selected and annotated bibliography of economic literature on the Arabic-speaking countries of the Middle East, 1938–1960. Boston, G. K. Hall, 1967.

viii, 358 p. 37 cm.

The publications are in English, French, or Arabic.
Cumulated at the School of Oriental and African Studies, University of London, from the bibliography prepared by the Economic Research Institute, American University of Beirut, with additional entries.

American University of Beirut. *Economic Research Institute.*

A selected and annotated bibliography of economic literature on the Arab countries of the Middle East, 1953–1965. Beirut, 1967.

xvii, 458 p. 24 cm.

"Consolidates the annual "Supplements" to the bibliography which covered the years 1953 up to 1962 and includes materials appearing in the three following years."

al-Amīn, 'Abd al-Karīm, 1926–

دليل المراجع العربية، تأليف عبد الـكـريم الأمين ₍وزاهدة₎ ابراهيم. بغداد، مطبعة شفيق 1970–.

v. 24 cm.

Cover title: Guide to Arabic reference books, by Abdul Karim Alamin ₍and₎ Zahida Ibrahim.

Dār al-Kutub wa-al-Wathā'iq al-Qawmīyah.

The Arab history; a bibliographical list. Cairo, National Library Press, 1966.

292 p. 27 cm.

"₍Includes₎ publications in European languages."
At head of title: United Arab Republic, Ministry of Culture, the National Library & Archives.

Dār al-Kutub wa-al-Wathā'iq al-Qawmīyah. *Idārat al-Bibliyūjrāfiyā.*

التاريخ العربي، قائمة بيليوجرافية. القاهرة، مطبعة دار الكتب، 1968.

592 p. 27 cm.

At head of title: الجمهورية العربية المتحدة. وزارة الثقافة. دار الكتب والوثائق القومية. ادارة البيليوجرافيا.
Cover title: The Arab history, Arabic section; a bibliographical list.

Ḥasīb, Khayr al-Dīn.
(Maṣādir al-fikr al-iqtiṣādī al-'Arabī fī al-'Irāq)

مصادر الفكر الاقتصادي العربي في العراق ﺑﺘﺄﻟﻴﻒ، خير
الدين حسيب. ﺑﺎﻟﻄﺒﻌﺔ 1. بيروت، دار الطليعة للطباعة
والنشر ﺑ1972،

480 p. 24 cm.

Indian Council for Cultural Relations. *Library.*
The Arab world and India; a select bibliography. ﺑDelhi,
1965،

30 l. 27 cm.

Cover title.
"Compiled on the occasion of the Seminar on India and the Arab
World, February 15–20, 1965."

Ljunggren, Florence.
The Arab World index; an international guide to periodical literature in the social sciences and humanities in the
contemporary Arab World, 1960–1964. Compiled and edited
by Florence Ljunggren. Cairo, American University in
Cairo Press, 1967.

xv, 549 p. 24 cm.

Markaz al-Tanmiyah al-Ṣinā'īyah lil-Duwal al-'Arabīyah.
ﺑBibliyūjrāfiyā al-maṭbū'āt al-'Arabīyah،

ببليوجرافيا المطبوعات العربية الصادرة في مجالات التنمية
الصناعية في الدول العربية. ﺑالقاهرة، مركز التنمية الصناعية
للدول العربية ﺑ1971،

430 p. 24 cm.

Markaz al-Tanmiyah al-Ṣinā'īyah lil-Duwal al-'Arabīyah.
ببليوجرافية التنمية الصناعية. ﺑالقاهرة، ﺑ1969–

v. 24 cm.

ﺑسلسلة ببليوجرافيات التنمية الصناعية للعالم العربي، رقم 1،

Cover title.

CONTENTS.— —
1. الفهرس الجغرافي الموضوعي (الموحد) للكتب العربية —

Ule, Wolfgang.
Bibliographie zu Fragen des arabischen Sozialismus, des
Nationalismus und des Kommunismus unter dem Gesichts-
punkt des Islams. In Zusammenarbeit mit der Dokumen-
tationsleitstelle für den Modernen Orient beim Deutschen
Orient-Institut. Hamburg, 1967.

x, 170 p. 29 cm.

At head of title: Deutsches Orient-Institut (Deutsche Orient-
Stiftung)

ARAB-JEWISH RELATIONS see Jewish-Arab
relations

ARABIAN PENINSULA

U. S. Library of Congress. Near East Section.
The Arabian Peninsula; a selected, annotated list of
periodicals, books, and articles in English. Prepared under
the direction of the Near East Section, Division of Orientalia. New York, Greenwood Press ﺑ1969،

xi, 111 p. 27 cm.

Reprint of the 1951 ed.

BIBLIOGRAPHIES

Geddes, Charles L
Analytical guide to the bibliographies on the Arabian
Peninsula ﺑby، C. L. Geddes. ﺑDenver, American Institute
of Islamic Studies, 1974،

50 p. 21 cm. (American Institute of Islamic Studies. Bibliographic series no. 4

ARABIC IMPRINTS

'Awwād, Kūrkīs.
مشاركة العراق في نشر التراث العربي، تأليف كوركيس عواد.
بغداد، مطبعة المجمع العلمي العراقي، 1969.

91 p. 24 cm. ﺑمطبوعات المجمع العلمي العراقي،
«مستل من المجلد السابع عشر من مجلة المجمع العلمي العراقي»

(Dalīl al-kutub al-Miṣrīyah)
دليل الكتب المصرية. جنيف، شركة ترادكسيم ﺑتوزيع مؤسسة
الاهرام، القاهرة، 1972.

503 p. 29 cm.

Franklin Book Programs, inc.
قائمة مطبوعات ١٩٥٣ – ١٩٦٥. القاهرة، مؤسسة فرانكلين
للطباعة والنشر ﺑ1966؟،

231 p. 22 cm.

Maḥmūd, 'Iṣām Muḥammad.
(Maṭbū'āt al-Mawṣil)
مطبوعات الموصل، منذ سنة ١٨٦١ – ١٩٧٠ م. كتب،
كتيبات، مجلات، صحف، نشرات، دوريات. جمع وترتيب
عصام محمد محمود. مراجعة وتقديم عبد الحليم اللاوند.
الموصل، مطبعة الجمهور ﺑ1971،

156 p. facsims. 22 cm.
Page 4 of cover has caption: Mosul printed ﺑsic، from 1861-1970,
by E. M. Mahmood & A. al-Lawand.

**Studi arabistici e arte tipografica araba in Italia dal XV
al XX secolo.** Rabat, Fez, Marrakech, novembre–dicembre
1972. Sotto gli auspici del Ministero marocchino della cultura e dell'insegnamento originario, superiore e secondario e
con la collaborazione dello Istituto italiano di cultura in
Marocco. Roma, Aziende tipografiche eredi dott. G. Bardi,
ﺑ1972،

62, 13 p. 24 cm.

At head of title: Centro per le relazioni Italo-arabe, Roma.

Utah. University. Middle East Library.
Arabic collection: Aziz S. Atiya library for Middle East
studies. Salt Lake City, University of Utah Press ﺑ1968،

xv, 841 p. 29 cm. (Its Catalogue series, v. 1)

ARABIC LANGUAGE

'Awwād, Kūrkīs.
المباحث اللغوية في مؤلفات العراقيين المحدثين، تأليف
كوركيس عواد. بغداد، مطبعة العاني، 1965.

150 p. 25 cm.

ERIC Clearinghouse for Linguistics.
1960–1967 selected bibliography of Arabic. Washington
ﺑ1967،

viii, 71 p. 28 cm.

Ghālī, Wajdī Rizq.
المعجمات العربية، ببليوجرافية شاملة مشروحة، اعداد
وجدي رزق غالي. تقديم حسين نصار. القاهرة، الهيئة
المصرية العامة للتأليف والنشر، 1971.

252 p. 28 cm.

Added t. p.: Arabic dictionaries, an annotated comprehensive bibliography, by Wagdy Rizk Ghali.
Introductions in Arabic and English.

Piamenta, Moshe.
ביבליוגרפיה יסודית לשפה וספרות ערבית מודרנית.

مراجع اساسية فى اللـغـة والادب الـعـربـى الـمـعـاصـر .
בעריכת מ. פיאמנטה וז״א. לוין. ירושלים, האוניברסיטה העברית,
הפקולטה למדעי הרוח, המכון ללימודי אסיה ואפריקה, תשכ״ד
[1963/64]

iv, 15 l. 27 cm.

Cover title.
Added t. p.: Basic bibliography of modern Arabic language and literature.

ARABIC LITERATURE

Contribución para una bibliografía de la literatura árabe del siglo xx. Madrid, Instituto Hispano-Arabe de Cultura, 1966.

58 p. 25 cm. (Cuadernos del "Seminario de Pensamiento Arabe Contemporáneo," 1)

Daqqāq, 'Umar.
مصادر التراث العربي في اللغة والمعاجم والادب والتراجم .
تأليف عمر الدقاق . حلب، المكتبة العربية [1968]

331 p. 25 cm.

Ibn al-Nadīm, Muḥammad ibn Isḥāq, fl. 987.
الفهرست، لابن النديم . بيروت، مكتبة خياط [1966]

278, viii, 361, 43, xxii p. 28 cm. (روائع التراث العربي) (1)

Added t. p.: Kitâb al-Fihrist, mit Anmerkungen, hrsg. von Gustav Flügel.
Photo-offset of the ed. published in Leipzig in 2 v., 1871–72.

Ibn al-Nadīm, Muḥammad ibn Isḥāq, fl. 987.
[al-Fihrist]
كتاب الفهرست، للنديم ابو الفرج محمد بن ابى يعقوب اسحق
المعروف بالوراق . تحقيق رضا—تجدد . [طهران]، يطلب من
مكتبة الاسدى ، 2 [1350 i. e. 1971 or]

3, 425, 4, [1], 169 p. facsims. 29 cm.

Ibn al-Nadīm, Muḥammad ibn Isḥāq, fl. 987.
The Fihrist of al-Nadīm; a tenth-century survey of Muslim culture. Bayard Dodge, editor and translator. New York, Columbia University Press, 1970.

2 v. (xxxiv, 1149 p.) facsims., geneal. table. 24 cm. (Records of civilization: sources and studies, no. 83)

Ibn al-Nadīm, Muḥammad ibn Isḥāq, fl. 987.
كتاب الفهرست، تأليف محمد بن اسحاق نديم . ترجمه م .
رضا تجدد بن على بن زين العابدين مازندرانى . چاپ 1. [تهران]
ابن سينا [1965]

18, 644, 8, 66 p. 25 cm.

Ibn Sūdah, 'Abd al-Salām ibn 'Abd al-Qādir.
دليل مؤرخ المغرب الاقصى، تأليف عبد السلام بن عبد القادر
ابن سودة المرى . الطـبـعـة 2. الدار البيضاء، دار الكتاب ،
1960–65.

2 v. port. 22 cm.

Makkī, Ṭāhir Aḥmad.
دراسة فى مصادر الادب، تأليف طاهر احمد مكى . [الطبعة 1
مصر، دار المعارف [1968–

v. facsims. 24 cm. (المكتبة الادبية)

Added t. p.: Des sources bibliographiques de la littérature arabe, par Ṭaher Aḥmad Makki.

Mu'tamar al-Udabā' al-'Arab, 5th, Baghdad, 1965.
ادباء المؤتمر . جمع مواد الكتاب ونسق معلوماته عبد الرزاق
الهلالى . بغداد، وزارة الثقافة والارشاد، 1966 .

206 p. ports. 24 cm. (12) (سلسلة الكتب الحديثة)

«عقد ببغداد في شهر شباط من عام 1965 مؤتمر الادباء العرب الخامس»

Pons Boigues, Francisco.
Los historiadores y geógrafos arábigo-españoles, 800–1150 A. D.; ensayo de una [sic] diccionario bio-bibliográfico, acompañada [sic] de anotaciones críticas y históricas, descripciones analíticas de las obras. Con apéndices varios, un índice general e índices arábigos precedido de una introducción general. Amsterdam, Philo Press, 1972.

514 p. 24 cm.
Reproduction of the 1898 Madrid ed., published under title: Ensayo bio-bibliográfico sobre los historiadores y geógrafos arábigo-españoles.

al-Rayyis, Sa'dūn.
الادباء العراقيون المعاصرون وانتاجهم [تأليـف] سـعـدون
الريس . [بغداد] وزارة الثقافة والارشاد، مديرية الثقافة العامة
[1965]

102 p. 17 cm. (2 ،سلسلة الثقافة العامة)

«صدر لحية لمؤتمر الادباء العرب الخامس ومهرجان الشعر السادس المنعقدين
في بغداد من 15—25 شباط 1965»

Sezgin, Fuat.
Geschichte des arabischen Schrifttums. Leiden, E. J. Brill, 1967–

v. 23½ cm.

Contents.—Bd. 1. Qur'ānwissenschaften, Hadīt Geschichte, Fiqh, Dogmatik, Mystik bis ca. 430 H.

Sezgin, Fuat.
[Geschichte des arabischen Schrifttums. Arabic]
تاريخ التراث العربي [تأليف] فؤاد سزگين . نقله الى العربية
فهمى ابو الفضل . راجعـه محمود فهمـى حجازى . القاهرة،
الهيئة المصرية العامة للتأليف والنشر 1971– .

v. 28 cm.

Contents : مجلد 1. جزء 1. مكتبيات المحفوظات العربية . المراجع العامة .
علوم القرآن . علم الحديث . —

JEWISH AUTHORS

Moreh, Shmuel.
(Fihris al-maṭbū'āt al-'Arabīyah allatī allafahā aw nasharahā al -udabā' wa-al-'ulamā' al-Yahūd, 1863–1973)
فهرس المطبوعات العربية التي الفها او نشرها الأدباء والعلماء
اليهود، 1863 — 1973 / اعده وقدمه للطبع شموئيل موريه . —
اورشليم : معهد بن تسفي لدراسة الجاليات اليهودية فى الشرق
التابع لمؤسسة ياد اسحق بن تسفي والجامعة العبرية ، 1973 .

221, 11 p. ; 22 cm.

Added title pages in Hebrew and English; Hebrew t. p. has title: Ḥibure Yehudim ba-lashon ha-'aravit, 1863–1973; English t. p. has title: Arabic works by Jewish writers, 1863–1973.

LIBRARY CATALOGS

Stanford University. *Hoover Institution on War, Revolution, and Peace.*
The Library catalogs of the Hoover Institution on War, Revolution, and Peace, Stanford University: catalog of the Arabic collection. Boston, G. K. Hall, 1969.

xi, 902 p. 37 cm.

TRANSLATIONS

Badrān, Husayn.
(al-Thabat al-bibliyujrāfī lil-a'māl al-mutarjamah, 1956–1967)
الثبت البليوجراف للاعمال المترجمة، 1956 — 1967 . اعداد
لجنة من حسين بدران [و] سليمان جرجس [و] فاطمة ابراهيم .

اشراف بدر الديب. ،القاهرة، الهيئــة المصرية العامة للكتاب،
1972.

12, 859 p. 28 cm.

ARABIC MATHEMATICS see Mathematics, Arabic

ARABIC MEDICINE see Medicine, Arabic

ARABIC PERIODICALS see Periodical publications - Arab countries

ARAGON

Gallofre Guinovart, Rafael.
Documentos del reinado de Alfonso III de Aragón, relativos al antiguo reino de Valencia y contenidos en los registros de la Corona de Aragón. ,Valencia, Institución Alfonso el Magnánimo, 1968.

478 p. 25 cm.

ARANHA, JOSÉ PEREIRA DA GRAÇA

Rio de Janeiro. Biblioteca Nacional.
Exposição comemorativa do centenário de nascimento de Graça Aranha. Rio de Janeiro, 1968.

47 p. plates, ports. 28 cm.

ARBITRATION
see also Collective bargaining

Organization for Economic Cooperation and Development. *Library.*
Systèmes d'arbitrage des conflits du travail. Labour arbitration systems. ,Paris, 1967.

v, 106 p. 27 cm. (*Its* Bibliographie spéciale analytique. Special annotated bibliography, 15)

"This bibliography has been compiled and annotated by Mrs. R. Tarr.

Seide, Katharine.
The Paul Felix Warburg union catalog of arbitration; a selective bibliography and subject index of peaceful dispute settlement procedures. Compiled and edited by Katharine Seide. Totowa. N. J., Published for the Eastman Library of the American Arbitration Association by Rowman and Littlefield, 1974.

3 v. 29 cm.
CONTENTS. v. 1. Alphabetical index.—v. 2. Subject index : commercial, international commercial, international public.—v. 3. Subject index : labor, community disputes, uninsured motorist.

U. S. *Dept. of Labor.*
Compulsory arbitration; selected references, 1951–1966. ,Washington, 1966,

6 p. 27 cm.

Caption title.
First published in 1965 by the U. S. Dept. of Labor Library.

ARBUTHNOT, MAY HILL

Harig, Katherine Jean.
A bio-bibliography of May Hill Arbuthnot (1884–1969) with selective annotations. Washington, 1971.

93 l. 28 cm.

Thesis (M. S. in L. S.)—Catholic University of America.

ARCHAEOLOGY
see also Anthropology, and names of specific countries, regions, etc.

Bailey, Lynn Robison, 1937–
From adze to vermilion; a guide to the hardware of history, and the literature of historic sites archaeology, by L. R. Bailey. Pasadena, Calif., Socio-Technical Books, 1971.

xv, 237 p. illus. 22 cm.

Bleck, Rolf-Dieter.
Bibliographie der archäologisch-chemischen Literatur. Weimar (Staatliches Museum für Ur- und Frühgeschichte Thüringens) 1966–

v. 30 cm. (Alt Thüringen. Beihefte)

CONTENTS: ,1, Naturwissenschaftliche Untersuchungen von Kunst- und Kulturgut aller Zeiten, chemische Konservierungsverfahren, Geschichte der chemischen Technik.—2. Chemisch-pyhsikalische Untersuchungen an Kunst- und Kulturgut chemische Konservierungsverfahren, Beiträge zur Kulturgeschichte der Technik.

Bulletin signalétique 526: Art et archéologie-Proche-Orient, Asie, Amérique. v. 24–
1970–
Paris. Centre de documentation due C. N. R. S.

v. 28 cm. quarterly.

Supersedes in part Bulletin signalétique 521: Sociologie, ethnologie. préhistoire et archéologie, and continues its vol. numbering.

Gaudel, Paul.
Bibliographie der archäologischen Konservierungstechnik. 2., erw. Ausg. Berlin, Hessling, 1969.

374 p. 27 cm. (Ergänzungsbände des Berliner Jahrbuchs für Vor- und Frühgeschichte. Bd. 2)

Gomme, *Sir* George Laurence, 1853–1916.
Index of archaeological papers, 1665–1890. New York, B. Franklin ,1965,

2 v. (xi, 910 p.) 22 cm. (Burt Franklin bibliography & reference series, 132)
Reprint of the 1907 ed. published in London.

Hester, Thomas R
Bibliography of archaeology ,by, Thomas R. Hester ,and, Robert F. Heizer. ,Reading, Mass., Addison-Wesley Pub. Co., 1973– ,

v. 28 cm. (Addison-Wesley modular publications, 29. An Addison-Wesley module in anthropology)
CONTENTS: v. 1. Experiments, lithic technology, and petrography.

Hulan, Richard.
A guide to the reading and study of historic site archaeology ,by, Richard Hulan ,and, Stephen S. Lawrence. Columbia, Published for the Conference on Historic Site Archaeology by the Museum of Anthropology, University of Missouri, 1970.

iii, 127 l. 28 cm. (Museum brief #5)

Library Association. *County Libraries Group.*
Readers' guide to books on archaeology (excluding the British Isles). 2nd ed. London, Library Association, 1967.

32 p. 18½ cm. (*Its* Readers' guides, new series, no, 98)

Milan. Politecnico. Istituto di geofisica applicata. Sezione prospezioni archeologiche.
Bibliografia. Roma. Sallustiana, 1968.

16 p. 23½ x 23½ cm.

Cover title.
In Italian and English.

Petsche, Jerome E
Bibliography of salvage archeology in the United States, compiled by Jerome E. Petsche. With a foreword by Joan

O. Brew. Lincoln, Neb., 1968.

iv, 162 p. 26 cm. (River Basin Surveys. Publications in salvage archeology, no. 10)

Sviridova, Inna Nikolaevna.
По следам древних культур; рассказы о книгах. Москва, Книга, 1966.

44, [2] p. illus. 20 cm.

At head of title: И. Н. Свиридова.

Valcárcel Esparza, Carlos Daniel.
El archivo Tello [por] C. D. Valcárcel. Lima, 1966.

76 p. 24 cm.

LIBRARY CATALOGS

Deutsches Archäologisches Institut. Römische Abteilung. Bibliothek.
Kataloge der Bibliothek des Deutschen Archäologischen Instituts, Rom: Autoren- und Periodica Kataloge. Boston, G. K. Hall, 1969.

7 v. 37 cm.

Added t. p.: Catalogs from the library of the German Institute of Archaeology, Rome; author and periodical catalogs.
Foreword also in English.

Deutsches Archäologisches Institut. Römische Abteilung. Bibliothek.
Kataloge der Bibliothek des Deutschen Archäologischen Instituts, Rom: systematischer Katalog. Boston, G. K. Hall, 1969.

3 v. 37 cm.
Added t. p.: Catalogs from the Library of the German Institute of Archaeology, Rome; classified catalog.
CONTENTS: Bd. 1. Rezensionen—Technik u. Materiel.—Bd. 2. Kunstgeschichte—Epigraphik.—Bd. 3. Philosophie—Organisation.

Worcestershire Archaeological Society. *Library.*
Subject catalogue; compiled by R. Mary Sargeant. Worcester, Worcestershire Archaeological Society, 1966.

[3], 41 f. front. (facsim.) table. 33½ cm.

PERIODICALS

Boss, Edward C
Bibliography of archaeological periodicals of the United States, adjacent Canada & Mexico [by Edward C. Boss. McMurray, Pa., 1964]

40 p. maps. 28 cm.

Caption title.

Deutsches Archäologisches Institut. Römische Abteilung. Bibliothek.
Kataloge der Bibliothek des Deutschen Archäologischen Instituts, Rom: Zeitschriften — Autorenkatalog. Boston, G. K. Hall, 1969.

3 v. 37 cm.

Added t. p.: Catalogs from the library of the German Institute of Archaeology, Rome; author catalog of periodicals.
Foreword also in English.

ARCHAEOLOGY, CLASSICAL see Classical Antiquities

ARCHANGEL, RUSSIA (PROVINCE)

Ivankina, L   P
(Arkhangel'skaíà oblast')
Архангельская область. Рек. указ. сов. литературы. [Архангельск], Сев.-Зап. кн. изд-во, 1973.

240 p. 21 cm.

At head of title: Архангельская областная библиотека им. Н. А. Добролюбова.

ARCHERY

Bobbs, Howard.
Bows and arrows : an archery bibliography / by Howard Bobbs and Marcia Muth Miller. — 1st ed. — Santa Fe, N. M. : Sunstone Press, [1974]

22 p. ; 22 cm.

ARCHILA, RICARDO

Freites de Acosta, Alecia.
Ricardo Archila. Caracas, Escuela de Biblioteconomía y Archivos, Facultad de Humanidades y Educación, Universidad Central de Venezuela, 1968.

51 p. port. 16 cm. (Serie bibliográfica, 7)

ARCHIMEDES   see under   Euclides

ARCHITECTS

Brown, Sally May.
Architects and others: an annotated list of people of South African interest appearing in the Royal Institute of British Architects Journal, 1880–1925; a bibliography. Johannesburg, University of the Witwatersrand, Department of Bibliography, Librarianship and Typography, 1969 [i. e. 1970]

[xlv] 23 p. 30 cm.

"Compiled in part fulfilment for the requirements of the Diploma in Librarianship, University of the Witwatersrand, Johannesburg."

Gropius, Wren, Latrobe, Wright. Charlottesville. Published for the American Association of Architectural Bibliographers [by the] University Press of Virginia [1972]

132 p. 24 cm. (American Association of Architectural Bibliographers. Papers. v. 9)

Sharp, Dennis.
Sources of modern architecture: a bibliography. London, published for the Architectural Association by Lund Humphries, 1967.

56 p. front., illus. (incl. ports.), facsims. 30 cm. (Architectural Association, London. Paper no. 2)

Contents list in English, French and German.

Sharp, Dennis.
Sources of modern architecture: a bibliography. [1st ed.] New York, G. Wittenborn [1967]

56 p. facsims., ports. 30 cm. (Architectural Association, London. Paper no. 2)

ARCHITECTURAL ACOUSTICS

Doelle, Leslie L
Acoustics in architectural design (an annotated bibliography on architectural acoustics) by Leslie L. Doelle. Ottawa, 1965.

543 p. illus. 29 cm. (National Research Council, Canada. Division of Building Research. Bibliography no. 29)

Thesis (M. ARCH.)—McGill University.

ARCHITECTURE
see also   Synagogue architecture

Bibliografia di architettura e urbanistica. Prefazione di Vittorio Gregotti. Milano, Libreria La città; Milano, G. Mazzotta, 1971–

v. illus., plates. 19 cm.

Borsi, Franco.
Orientamenti bibliografici. Cattedra di storia dell'archi-

tettura 1. Corso A ... Anno accademico 1971–72. Firenze, G & G, 1972.

33, 600–647 p. 24 cm.

At head of title: Università degli studi di Firenze. Facoltà di architettura. Istituto di storia dell'architettura.

Comolli, Angelo.
Bibliografia storico-critica dell'architettura civile ed arti subalterne. Indice analitico a cura di Bruno della Chiesa. Milano, Labor riproduzioni e documentazioni ₁1964–65₎

4 v. 33 cm.

"Ristampa anastatica. Prima edizione di 200 esemplari. 75."
Facsims. of original titlepages, v. 1–2, have imprint: Roma, Stamperia vaticana, 1788; v. 3–4, Apresso il Salvioni, 1791–92.

Hall, Sir Robert de Zouche, 1904–
A bibliography on vernacular architecture; edited by Robert de Zouche Hall ₁for the Vernacular Architecture Group₎. Newton Abbot, David and Charles, 1972.

191 p. 24 cm. Index.

Kleeman, Walter.
Interior ergonomics—significant dimensions in interior design and planning: a selected bibliography ₁by₎ Walter Kleeman, Jr. ₁Monticello, Ill., Council of Planning Librarians₎ 1972.

43 p. 29 cm. (Council of Planning Librarians. Exchange bibliography, 286)

Library Association. *County Libraries Group.*
Readers' guide to books on architecture. 2nd ed. ₁Durham₎, Library Association (County Libraries Group), 1969.

43 p. 19 cm. (*Its* Readers' guides, new series, no. 106)

Nauchno-issledovatel'skiĭ institut teorii, istorii i perspektivnykh problem sovetskoĭ arkhitektury.
Научно-исследовательские работы НИИ теории, истории и перспективных проблем советской архитектуры, выполненные в 1963–1967 гг. (Сборник аннот.) Москва, Центр науч.-техн. информации по гражд. строительству и архитектуре, 1970.

45 p. 21 cm

At head of title: Государственный комитет по гражданскому строительству и архитектуре при Госстрое СССР.
"Составитель В. Н. Дардик."

Neil, J   Meredith, 1937–
Paradise improved; environmental design in Hawaii, by J. Meredith Neil. Charlottesville, Published for the American Association of Architectural Bibliographers ₁by₎ the University Press of Virginia ₁1972₎

xi, 208 p. illus. 24 cm. (American Association of Architectural Bibliographers. Papers, v. 8)

Park, Helen.
A list of architectural books available in America before the Revolution. New ed., rev. and enl., with a foreword by Adolf K. Placzek. Los Angeles, Hennessey & Ingalls, 1973.

xv, 79 p. illus. 24 cm. (Art & architecture bibliographies, 1)

Originally appeared as an article in the Journal of the Society of Architectural Historians.

Pevzner, D   P
Памятники архитектуры, их сохранение, реставрация и размещение в современной планировке и застройке городов. (Отечеств. и иностр. литература за 1960–1968 гг.) Москва, 1968 ₁обл. 1969₎.

112 p. 26 cm.
At head of title: Госстрой СССР. Центральная научно-техническая библиотека по строительству и архитектуре.
"Библиографический указатель."

Pevzner, D   P
Вопросы теории архитектуры. Отечеств. и иностр. литература за 1960–1969 гг. ₁Библиогр. указатель₎. Москва, 1969.

98 p. 26 cm.

At head of title: Госстрой СССР. Центральная научно-техническая библиотека по строительству и архитектуре.

Phillips, Margaret, 1939–
Guide to architectural information. Lansdale, Pa., Design Data Center ₁1971₎

vi, 89 p. 24 cm.

Roos, Frank John, 1903–1966.
Bibliography of early American architecture; writings on architecture constructed before 1860 in Eastern and Central United States. Urbana, University of Illinois Press, 1968.

389 p. 24 cm.

1943 ed. published under title: Writings on early American architecture.

Rozei, Lola.
ביבליוגרפיה על ארכיטקטורה ובניה בישראל.
Bibliography on architecture and building in Israel ₁compiled and edited by Lola Rozei₎
חיפה, אגודת האינג'ינרים והארכיטקטים בישראל, מרכז הבניה, מדור הדוקומנטציה, 1967.

ii, 51 p. 25 cm.
"Devoted to the first World Congress of Engineers and Architects in Israel ... 1967."

Smith, Denison Langley, 1924–
How to find out in architecture and building; a guide to sources of information, by D. L. Smith. ₁1st ed.₎ Oxford, New York, Pergamon Press ₁1967₎

xii, 232 p. illus. 20 cm. (Commonwealth and international library. Library and technical information division)

Trčková, Blanka.
Umění kolem nás. Výběrová bibliografie z fondu Kraj. knihovny v Čes. Budějovicích, Alšovy Jihočes. galerie na Hluboké a Jihočes. musea v Čes. Budějovicích. České Budějovice, Kraj. knihovna, rozmn., 1969.

₁95₎ p. 5 illus. 29 cm.

TSelikov, Alekseĭ Ivanovich.
Охрана, реставрация и консервация памятников русской архитектуры. (1917–1968 гг.) Библиогр. указатель литературы. Москва, Центр науч.-техн. информации по гражд. строительству и архитектуре, 1970.

32 p. 21 cm.
At head of title: Государственный комитет по гражданскому строительству и архитектуре при Госстрое СССР. Научно-исследовательский институт теории, истории и перспективных проблем советской архитектуры, and other organizations.

Wolf, Heide, *comp.*
Architecture south of the Sahara, 1963–1965; a list of references. Johannesburg, University of the Witwatersrand, Department of Bibliography, Librarianship and Typography, ₁1967₎

₁iv₎, v, 37 l. 29 cm.

LIBRARY AND EXHIBITION CATALOGS

Colegio Oficial de Aparejadores y Arquitectos Técnicos de Cataluña y Baleares.
Catálogo de la biblioteca.

————— Suplemento. (Barcelona) ₁1971₎

56 p. 21 cm.

"Confeccionado por la bibliotecaria del Colegio, Srta. M. Carmella."

Deutsche Bauakademie. *Deutsche Bauinformation. Abteilung Übersetzungen.*

Katalog der Übersetzungen. [Zusammenstellung und redaktionelle Bearbeitung: Hans Gerisch] Berlin, Deutsche Bauinformation, 1965–

v. 30 cm.

At head of title: Deutsche Bauakademie.

Cover title: Katalog der Übersetzungen. Переводы. Translations. Traductions.

"Bestandteil der Deutschen Bau-Enzyklopädie."

CONTENTS.—[1] Sektor 1: Gesellschaftswissenschaftliche Grundlagen des Bauwesens. Sektor 3: Städtebau und Siedlungswesen.—[2] Sektor 5: Industriebau.—[3] Sektor 8: Baudurchführung.

Hanover. Technische Universität. Universitätsbibliothek.

Katalog der Sammlung Haupt. (Buchbestand). Hannover, 1970.

iii, 228 p. 30 cm.

"Bearb. von D. Henkes."

Harvard University. Graduate School of Design. Library.

Catalogue of the Library of the Graduate School of Design, Harvard University. Boston, Mass., G. K. Hall, 1968.

44 v. 37 cm.

———— First supplement. Boston, Mass., G. K. Hall, 1970.

2 v. 37 cm.

Harvard University. Library. Dept. of Printing and Graphic Arts.

Sixteenth-century architectural books from Italy and France; [exhibition] June–September 1971. Cambridge [1971]

[50] p. illus., facsims. 28 cm.

Royal Institute of British Architects, London. Library.

Catalogue of the Royal Institute of British Architects Library. Folkestone, Dawsons, 1972.

2 v. illus. 29 cm.

Reprint of the 1937-38 ed. published by the Royal Institute of British Architects, London.

CONTENTS: v. 1. Author catalogue of books and manuscripts.— v. 2. Classified index & alphabetical subject index of books and manuscripts.

Savez arhitekata Hrvatske.

Bibliografija članaka iz časopisa. [Glavni i odgovorni urednik: Mladen Vodička] Zagreb, Savez arhitekata Hrvatske, 1969–

v. 20 cm. (Stručna biblioteka Saveza arhitekata Hrvatske, god. 9, sv. 11; god. 10, sv. 14)

CONTENTS.—1. Stanovanje.—2. Nastava i odgoj. Sportski objekti.

PERIODICALS

Columbia University. *Libraries. Avery Architectural Library.*

Avery index to architectural periodicals. Boston, G. K. Hall, 1963.

12 v. 37 cm.

———— Supplement. Boston, G. K. Hall, 1965–

v. 37 cm.

Columbia University. Libraries. Avery Architectural Library.

Avery index to architectural periodicals. 2d ed., rev. and enl. Boston, G. K. Hall, 1973–

v. 37 cm.

ARCHIVES
see also Manuscripts

Evans, Frank Bernard, 1927–

The administration of modern archives: a select bibliographic guide. Compiled by Frank B. Evans. Washington, Office of the National Archives, 1970 [i. e. 1971]

xiii, 213 p. 24 cm.

Hepworth, Philip.

Archives and manuscripts in libraries. 2d ed. London, Library Association, 1964.

70 p. illus. 22 cm. (Library Association. Pamphlet no. 18)

Piechota, Regina.

Katalog zagranicznych przewodników i inwentarzy archiwalnych przechowywanych w Bibliotece Naczelnej Dyrekcji Archiwów Państwowych. Oprac. Regina Piechota i Grażyna Ziółkowska. [Wyd. 1.] Warszawa [Państwowe Wydawn. Naukowe, Oddz. w Łodzi] 1968.

55 p. 21 cm.

At head of title: Naczelna Dyrekcja Archiwów Państwowych.

ARCTIC see Polar regions

ARCTIC GRAYLING

Vincent, Robert E

Bibliography of the Arctic grayling, *Thymallus arcticus*, of North America, by Robert E. Vincent. Washington, 1965.

15 p. 27 cm. (U. S. Fish and Wildlife Service. Bureau circular 213)

At head of title: U. S. Dept. of the Interior, Fish and Wildlife Service, Bureau of Sport Fisheries and Wildlife.

ARDENNES, FRANCE (DEPT.)

Ardennes, France (Dept.). Archives départementales.

Guide des Archives des Ardennes [par] Hubert Collin, directeur des Services d'archives des Ardennes. Charleville-Mézières, 1974.

482 p. illus. 24 cm.

Ardennes, *France (Dept.) Archives départementales.*

Répertoire numérique des registres paroissiaux et de l'état-civil antérieurs à 1852, par René Robinet ... Mézières, Direction des services d'archives, 1966.

88 p. 31 cm.

ARECA NUT

Ramachander, P   R

Bibliography on arecanut, up to December 1966. Compiled by P. R. Ramachander & K. V. Ahamed Bavappa. Vittal, Central Arecanut Research Station, 1967.

44, vi p. 24 cm. (Central Arecanut Research Station. Technical bulletin no. 1) unpriced

ARENBERG, HOUSE OF

Descheemaeker, Jacques.

Maison d'Arenberg, inventaire des archives publiques françaises et bibliographie. 92 Neuilly-sur-Seine, l'auteur, 81 bis, rue Perronet, 1968.

52 l. 27 cm.

ARGENTINE IMPRINTS

Argentine Republic. Comisión Asesora del Servicio de Promoción Postal del Libro Argentino.
Servicio de promoción postal del libro argentino; catálogo. ₁Buenos Aires, 1967₁

80 p. 26 cm.

Buenos Aires (*Province*) *Dirección de Cultura.*
1ª ₁i. e. Primera₁ muestra del libro bonaerense; catálogo provisorio. La Plata, 1965.

25 p. 23 cm.

Los Libros. año 1–   jul. 1969–
₁Buenos Aires, Editorial Galerna₁

v. illus. 34 cm. monthly.

LACAP 69–5386

"Un mes de publicaciones en Argentina y el mundo."

BIBLIOGRAPHIES

Geoghegan, Abel Rodolfo.
Bibliografía de bibliografías argentinas, 1807–1970. Edición preliminar. Buenos Aires, Casa Pardo, 1970.

164 p. (p. 131–164 advertisements) 20 cm.

ARGENTINE LITERATURE

Becco, Horacio Jorge, 1924–
Fuentes para el estudio de la literatura argentina. ₁Buenos Aires₁ Centro Editor de América Latina ₁1968₁

62 p. 20 cm. (Enciclopedia de la literatura argentina, 1)

Foster, David William.
Research guide to Argentine literature, by David William Foster and Virginia Ramos Foster. Metuchen, N. J., Scarecrow Press, 1970.

146 p. 22 cm.

ARGENTINE REPUBLIC

Argentine Republic. *Consejo Federal de Inversiones.*
Catálogo de publicaciones, 1959–1966. Buenos Aires, 1966.

245 p. 28 cm.

"El presente catálogo fue preparado por la Biblioteca del Consejo Federal de Inversiones."

Argentine Republic. Consejo Federal de Inversiones.
Desarrollo económico y planificación en la República Argentina; selección bibliográfica, 1930–1972. ₁Compilación y selección: Alfredo Estévez.₁ Buenos Aires, 1972.

394 p. 27 cm. (Its Serie técnica, no. 13)

Argentine Republic. Consejo Federal de Inversiones. Biblioteca.
Bibliografía: los censos argentinos por regiones. Buenos Aires, 1968.

xxviii, 255 p. 28 cm. (Serie Regiones, 2)

"Realizado por Alfredo Estévez, jefe de la Biblioteca del Consejo Federal de Inversiones, con la colaboración de ... Lucía M. R. de Ayos."

Argentine Republic. *Consejo Federal de Inversiones. Biblioteca.*
Bibliografía sobre el desarrollo económico nacional. no. 1–
Buenos Aires, 1965–

v. 28 cm.

Argentine Republic. Consejo Nacional de Desarrollo. Biblioteca.
Bibliografía sobre sistema nacional de planeamiento y acción para el desarrollo. Buenos Aires, 1969–

v. 30 cm.

Instituto Torcuato di Tella. *Centro de Investigaciones Económicas.*
Catálogo de estadísticas publicadas en la República Argentina ₁por₁ Lelia I. Boeri. 2. ed. ₁Buenos Aires₁ Editorial del Instituto ₁1966₁

4 v. (2,041 p.) 27 cm. (*Its* Serie ocre: Economía)

Vols. 3–4; "Ampliación y actualización ... Anexo a la segunda edición."

Marsal, Juan Francisco.
Contribución a una bibliografía del ensayo socio-político argentino y mexicano contemporáneo ₁por₁ Juan F. Marsal. Buenos Aires, Instituto Torcuato di Tella, Centro de Investigaciones Sociales, 1969.

25 l. 29 cm. (Instituto Torcuato di Tella. Centro de Investigaciones Sociales. Documento de trabajo, 66)

Sabor, Josefa Emilia.
Bibliografía básica de obras de referencia de artes y letras para la Argentina, por Josefa E. Sabor y Lydia H. Revello. Buenos Aires, Fondo Nacional de las Artes ₁1969₁

78 p. 23 cm. (Bibliografía argentina de artes y letras. Compilación especial no. 36)

Serie Regiones. no. 1–
Buenos Aires, Consejo Federal de Inversiones, Biblioteca, 1967–

no. 28 cm.

Turco Greco, Carlos A
Catálogo cartográfico de la República Argentina. Consejo Nacional de Investigaciones Científicas y Técnicas. Preparado por Carlos A. Turco Greco. ₁Buenos Aires₁ Editorial Universitaria de Buenos Aires ₁1967₁

262 l. col. maps (part fold.) 32 cm. (Biblioteca de América. Documentos)

United Nations. Development Programme. Oficina del Representante Residente en Argentina.
Estudios technicos sobre Argentina, 1956–1971, preparados por organismos del sistema de las Naciones Unidas segun indicativas del Gobierno de la República. Revision 2. Buenos Aires, 1971.

vi, 66 p. 28 cm.

Uriondo, Oscar Adolfo.
Bibliografía geográfica referente a la República Argentina. Primera contribución. Buenos Aires, 1964.

110 p. 27 cm.

Villascuerna, Inés.
Bibliografía para el estudio histórico de la marginalidad en el Noroeste de Argentina. Buenos Aires, Instituto Torcuato di Tella, Centro de Investigaciones Sociales, 1970.

88 p. 29 cm. (Instituto Torcuato di Tella. Centro de Investigaciones Sociales. Documento de trabajo, 71)

GOVERNMENT PUBLICATIONS

Mesa, Rosa Quintero.
Argentina, compiled by Rosa Quintero Mesa. New York, R. R. Bowker, 1971.

xxxii, 693 p. 29 cm. (Latin American serial documents, v. 5)

LAW see Law - Argentine Republic

ARID REGIONS
see also Deserts

Aminullah, 1930–
Bibliography of C. A. Z. R. I. publications, 1959–1969. Compiled. Jodhpur, Central Arid Zone Research Institute ₁1971?₁

38, iv p. 28 cm.

"Bulletin by the Arid Zone Research Association of India, Jodhpur."

Beersheba, Israel. ha-Makhon le-ḥeker ha-Negev.
Publications, 1960–1970. Beer-Sheva, 1971.

54 l. 28 cm.

Cover title.
At head of title: Prime Minister's Office, National Council for Research & Development, Negev Institute for Arid Zone Research, 1971.

Paylore, Patricia.
Seventy-five years of arid-lands research at the University of Arizona; a selective bibliography. 1891–1965. ₁Tucson₁ Office of Arid Lands Research, University of Arizona ₁1966₁

viii, 95 p. 24 cm.

Smith-Sanclare, Shelby.
A selected annotated bibliography on physical planning in arid lands. ₁Monticello, Ill.₁ Council of Planning Librarians, 1973.

46 p. 29 cm. (Council of Planning Librarians. Exchange bibliography no. 423)

ARISTOTLE

A Bibliography of Aristotle editions 1501–1600. With an introduction and indexes by F. Edward Cranz. ₁1st ed.₁ Baden-Baden, V. Koerner, 1971.

xii, 187 p. 24 cm. (Bibliotheca bibliographica Aureliana, 38)

"Consists of the Aristotle listings of the Index Aureliensis."

Markowski, Mieczysław.
Repertorium commentariorum Medii Aevi in Aristotelem Latinorum quae in Bibliotheca Iegellonica Cracoviae asservantur / composuerunt Miecislaus Markowski, Sophia Włodek ; ₁praca wykonana w Zespole Historii Polskiej Filozofii Średniowiecznej₁. — Wrocław : Zakład Narodowy im. Ossolińskich, 1974.

210 p. ; 24 cm.

At head of title: Polska Akademia Nauk. Instytut Filozofii i Socjologii.

Rhode, Gisela.
Bibliographie der deutschen Aristoteles-Übersetzungen vom Beginn des Buchdrucks bis 1964. Frankfurt a. M., Klostermann (1967)

xiv, 104 p. 21 cm. (Bibliographische Beiträge, Bd. 1)

Schwab, Moïse, 1839–1918.
Bibliographie d'Aristote. New York, B. Franklin, 1967.

380 p. 23 cm. (Burt Franklin bibliography & reference series, 235)

"Originally published, France, 1896."

ARITHMETIC
Smith, David Eugene, 1869–1944.
Rara arithmetica; a catalogue of the arithmetics written before the year MDCI with a description of those in the library of George Arthur Plimpton of New York. ₁4th ed., including A. De Morgan's Arithmetical books, published at London in 1847₁ New York, Chelsea Pub. Co., 1970.

xviii, 725 p. illus., facsims. 21 cm.

Includes the author's "Addenda to Rara arithmetica which described in 1908 such European arithmetics printed before 1601 as were then in the library of the late George Arthur Plimpton" (p. ₁499₁–548) first published in 1939.

ARIZONA

Arizona. Dept. of Economic Planning and Development. Planning Division.
Annotated list of publications, 1968–1972. ₁Phoenix₁ 1972.

1. v. (various pagings) 29 cm.

"Prepared by Office of the Governor through the Planning Division, Department of Economic Planning and Development, State of Arizona."
On cover: State planning notes.

Goodman, David Michael.
Arizona odyssey; bibliographic adventures in nineteenth-century magazines, by David M. Goodman. ₁1st ed.₁ Tempe, Arizona Historical Foundation, 1969.

xvii, 360 p. illus., ports. 29 cm.

Powell, Donald M
Arizona gathering II, 1950–1969; an annotated bibliography ₁by₁ Donald M. Powell. Tucson, University of Arizona Press ₁1973₁

vii, 207 p. 24 cm.

"Outgrowth of a periodic bibliography which has been appearing twice yearly in the Arizona quarterly since 1952."
Includes most of the entries from the author's An Arizona gathering; a bibliography of Arizoniana, 1950–1959, published in 1960.

Wallace, Andrew, *ed.*
Sources & readings in Arizona history; a checklist of literature concerning Arizona's past. With introductory essays by Ramon F. Adams ₁and others₁ Decorations by Anne Merriman Peck. Tucson, Arizona Pioneers' Historical Society, 1965.

xvi, 181 p. illus. 24 cm.

ARKANSAS

Arkansas. Legislative Council.
Studies conducted by State agencies over the past ten years. ₁Little Rock₁ 1971.

19 l. 36 cm. (Its Informational memo no. 149)

Caption title.
Memorandum to Arkansas Legislative Council, from Research Dept., Arkansas Legislative Council.

Arkansas. *Library Commission.*
Arkansas books and materials; a compilation of Arkansas shelf lists of the public libraries of Arkansas. ₁Compiled by LaNell Compton and Lorene Bryant₁ Little Rock, 1967.

224 p. 28 cm.

Arkansas. *Library Commission.*
Arkansiana for high schools. Compiled by Anne Jackson, consultant, high school and public libraries. Rev. Little Rock, 1964.

54 p. 23 cm.

Arkansas. University. *Industrial Research and Extension Center.*
Publications on the State of Arkansas. Marsha A. Walters ₁and₁ Sherry H. Hogan: editors. Linda R. Seamon, compiler. Little Rock, 1967.

2 v. 28 cm. (Its Publication L-4-I—L-4-II)

ARKANSAS. UNIVERSITY

Arkansas. University. *Committee on Research.*
Faculty and staff research publications and other contributions, 1957–1963. ₍Fayetteville₎ University of Arkansas ₍1965?₎

810 p. 28 cm.

"Compiled by the University of Arkansas Library."

ARKHAM HOUSE, SAUK CITY, WISCONSIN

Derleth, August William, 1909–
Thirty years of Arkham House, 1939–1969; a history and bibliography. Prepared by August Derleth. Sauk City, Wis., Arkham House, 1970.

99 p. ports. 20 cm.

ARMAS CHITTY, JOSÉ ANTONIO DE

Lemmo B   , Angelina.
J. A. de Armas Chitty; ₍bibliografía₎ por Angelina Lemmo B. Caracas, Escuela de Biblioteconomía y Archivos, Universidad Central de Venezuela, 1969.

102 p. port. 16 cm. (Escuela de Biblioteconomía y Archivos. Serie bibliográfica, 10)

ARMENIA

Salmaslian, Armenag.
Bibliographie de l'Arménie ₍par₎ A. Salmaslian. Nouv. éd. entièrement rev. et considérablement augm. Erévan, Éditions de l'Académie des sciences de la R. S. S. de l'Arménie, 1969.

468 p. port. 26 cm.

At head of title: Académie des sciences de la R. S. S. de l'Arménie. Bibliothèque fondamentale.
Added t. p. in Armenian.

ARMENIAN IMPRINTS

Davt'yan, Hayk M
Ազխարհաբար դերբը Հայ տպագրության սկզբից մինչև 1850 թվականը. առաջաբան և մատենագիտական ցուցակ ₍դրից₎ Հայկ Դավթյան: Խմբ. Արամ Բարայանի: Երևան, 1964:

141 p. facsims. 20 cm.

At head of title: Հայկական ՍՍՌ Ալ. Մյասնիկյանի անվան Պետական Թեղուրբլիվական Գրադարան:

Eganyan, Zh   H
(Al. F. Myasnikyani anvan Hanrapetakan Gradaranowm ch'eghats sovetahay grk'eri ts'owts'ak)
Ալ. Ֆ. Մյասնիկյանի անվան Հանրապետական Գրադարանում չեղած սովետահայ գրքերի ցուցակ, 1917–1967: ₍Կազմեցին Ժ. Հ. Եղանյան և Ս. Ն. Մադիկյան։ Խմբագրեց և Ս. Մարգարյոն₎ Ա. Ֆ. Մյասնիկյանի անվան Հանրապետական Գրադարան, Կոմպլեկտավորման Բաժին, 1969:

119 p. 20 cm.

Hayastani Hanrapetakan Gradaran .
Ցուցակ փոխանակման ֆոնդի գրքերի: Երևան, 1967:

141 l. 30 cm.

At head of title: Հայկական ՍՍՀ Կուլտուրայի Մինիստրություն։ Ալ. Մյասնիկյանի անվան Հանրապետական Գրադարան:
Cover title.
Caption title: Ցուցակ Հայաստանի Հանրապետական Գրադարանի փոխանակման ֆոնդի:

Korkotyan, K'narik.
Հայ տպագիր դերբը Կոստանդնուպուլսում, 1567–1850 թթ. Երևան, 1964:

At head of title: Հայկական ՍՍՌ Կուլտուրայի Մինիստրություն Ալ. Մյասնիկյանի անվան Հանրապետական Գրադարան: «Գրքահայ տպագրությնների ժամանակագրական ցուցակ»: p. ₍105₎–₍150₎

ARMENIAN LITERATURE

Grigor'îân, Kamsar Nersesovich.
Армянская литература в русских переводах. (1786–1917). Сост. и авт. предисл. К. Н. Григорян₍!₎ Ереван, Изд. Ереванского ун-та, 1969.

164 p. 20 cm. (Ереванский государственный университет. Кабинет литературных связей. Библиографическая серия, вып. 1)

Rhowbinian, Rh
Սովետահայ գրական-գեղարվեստական ժողովածուներ. մատենագիտություն, 1961–1965: ₍Կազմեց Ռ. Ռուբինյան₎ Խմբագիր Գ. Ալաբանյան₎ Երևան, 1966:

167 cm. 20 cm.

At head of title: Հայկական ՍՍՀ Կուլտուրայի Մինիստրություն Ալ. Մյասնիկյանի անվան Հանրապետական Գրադարան:
Lists also some Russian titles.
Index and summary in Russian.

ARMS AND ARMOR

John Woodman Higgins Memorial Library.
Catalogue of books. Worcester ₍1969?₎

vii, 120 p. illus. 26 cm.

Collection cataloged by Albert G. Anderson, Jr.

ARNDT, ERNST MORITZ

Herling, Manfred.
Ernst Moritz Arndt, 1769–1969. Katalog d. Auststellg. zum 200. Geburtstag Ernst Moritz Arndts. ₍Von₎ Manfred Herling ₍u.₎ Horst-Diether Schroeder. Greifswald, Ernst-Moritz-Arndt-Universität (1969)

94 p. illus. 19 cm.

Loh, Gerhard.
Arndt-Bibliographie. Verzeichnis d. Schriften von u. über Ernst Moritz Arndt. Festgabe z. 200. Geburtstage von Ernst Moritz Arndt. Hrsg. von d. Ernst-Moritz-Arndt-Univ. Greifswald. (Berlin) Deutscher Verl. d. Wissenschaften ₍zu bezehen: Greifswald, Ernst-Moritz-Arndt-Universität₎ 1969.

307 p. 24 cm.

Schäfer, Karl Heinz.
Ernst Moritz Arndt; ein bibliographisches Handbuch 1769–1969, von Karl Heinz Schäfer und Josef Schawe. Bearb. und eingel. von Karl Heinz Schäfer. Bonn, L. Röhrscheid, 1971.

xi, 806 p. 23 cm. (Veröffentlichungen des Stadtarchivs Bonn. Bd. 8)

ARNE, THOMAS AUGUSTINE and MICHAEL

Parkinson, John A
An index to the vocal works of Thomas Augustine Arne and Michael Arne, by John A. Parkinson. Detroit, Information Coordinators, 1972.

82 p. 23 cm. (Detroit studies in music bibliography, 21)

ARNIM, LUDWIG ACHIM, FREIHERR VON

Mallon, Otto, 1893–
Arnim-Bibliographie. (Reprografischer Nachdruck der

Ausg. Berlin, 1925) Hildesheim, Gg Olms, 1965.

196 p. 22 cm.

ARNOLD, BENEDICT

Gocek, Matilda A
Benedict Arnold; a reader's guide and bibliography, by Matilda A. Gocek. Monroe, N. Y., Library Research Associates, 1973.

28 p. 23 cm.

ARNOLD, MATTHEW

Davis, Arthur Kyle, 1897–
Matthew Arnold's letters; a descriptive checklist. Charlottesville, Published for the Bibliographical Society of the University of Virginia [by] University Press of Virginia [1968]

xlv, 429 p. illus., port. 25 cm.

Smart, Thomas Burnett.
The bibliography of Matthew Arnold, compiled and edited by Thomas Burnett Smart. New York, B. Franklin, [1968]

x, 90 p. 23 cm. (Burt Franklin bibliography and reference series, 159)

Reprint of the 1892 ed.

ARRÁIZ, ANTONIO

Caracas. Universidad Católica Andrés Bello. Seminario de Literatura Venezolana.
Contribución a la bibliografía de Antonio Arráiz, 1903–1963. [Caracas, Gobernación del Distrito Federal, 1969]

100 p. port. 21 cm. (Colección Bibliografías, 3)

Cover title: Bibliografía Antonio Arráiz.
"Investigación realizada por las alumnas Teresita Alvarez V. [et al.] durante el año académico 1966–67 [y el año 1967–68] ... bajo la dirección del profesor Efraín Subero."

ARRIETA, RAFAEL ALBERTO

López, Susana Beatriz.
Contribución a la bibliografía de Rafael Alberto Arrieta. Buenos Aires, Fondo Nacional de las Artes [1969]

102 p. illus. 22 cm. (Bibliografía argentina de artes y letras. Compilación especial no. 37)

ART
see also Aesthetics; Performing arts; and under Dissertations, Academic

Ahlstrand, Jan Torsten, 1938–
Böcker om konst. Ett kommenterat urval. Lund, Bibliotekstjänst; [Solna, Seelig] 1968.

83, (1) p. 21 cm. (Btj-serien, 7)

Art. Kunst.
1972–
Basel, Helbing & Lichtenhahn; Available from International Publications Service Collings, New York.

v. 21 cm. annual.

"International bibliography of art book."
English, French, and German.

Australian Society for Education Through Art.
Art education bibliography; a list of books concerned with the theories and philosophies of art education. [Adelaide, 1967]

47 p. 20 cm.

Produced in South Australia for the 2nd Biennial Assembly of the Australian Society for Education Through Art.

Barnaveli, Teĭmuraz Vasil'evich.
Аннотированная библиография печатных трудов сотрудников Института истории грузинского искусства Академии наук Грузинской ССР. 1941–1968 гг. Сост. Т. Барнавели. Тбилиси, "Мецниереба," 1970.

337 p. 22 cm.
Added t. p. in Georgian.
On leaf preceding t. p.: Академия наук Грузинской ССР. Институт истории грузинского искусства.

Bleha, Josef.
Průvodce výtvarně uměleckými bibliografiemi, slovníky a informativními příručkami. Zprac. Josef Bleha. Praha, St. knihovna ČSR-Ústř, bibliogr. středisko, rozmn., 1971.

180 p. 20 cm. (Prameny bibliografie a informativní literatury. č. 3)

Title also in Russian, German, English, and French; English title: Guide-book through art-bibliographies, dictionaries and reference books.

Carrick, Neville.
How to find out about the arts; a guide to sources of information. [1st ed.] Oxford, New York, Pergamon Press [1965]

xi, 164 p. illus. 20 cm. (The Commonwealth and international library, 2250)

Dobruská, Naděžda.
Vzájemné vztahy barvy světla a barevnosti prostředí. Doporučující bibliografie knižní a čas. literatury. Sest. Naděžda Dobruská. Předml.: Ladislav Chalupský. Praha, UVTEI, rozmn., 1970.

63 p. 21 cm. (Prague. Státní technická knihovna. Bibliografie, sv. 150)

Dove, Jack.
Fine arts. London, Bingley, 1966.

88 p. 22½ cm. (The Readers guide series)

Fehl, Philipp P
A bibliographical guide to the study of the history of art, by Philipp P. Fehl. Chapel Hill [N. C.] 1965.

48 l. 28 cm.

Georgi, Charlotte.
The arts and the world of business; a selected bibliography. Metuchen, N. J., Scarecrow Press, 1973.

123 p. 22 cm.

Goldman, Bernard, 1922–
Reading and writing in the arts: a handbook. Detroit, Wayne State University Press, 1972.

163 p. 22 cm.

Kiell, Norman.
Psychiatry and psychology in the visual arts and aesthetics, a bibliography. Madison, University of Wisconsin Press, 1965.

xiv, 250 p. 25 cm.

LeDoux Library.
Books of interest to the artist. Eunice [La.] 1970.

[5] l. 28 cm. (Its Bibliography 1)

Lucas, Edna Louise, 1899–
Art books; a basic bibliography on the fine arts [by] E. Louise Lucas. Greenwich, Conn., New York Graphic Society [1968]

245 p. 22 cm.

"Based on the bibliographies previously prepared [by the author] under the title: The Harvard list of books on art."

Mexico (City). Universidad Nacional. Instituto de Investigaciones Estéticas.
Bibliografía del Instituto de Investigaciones Estéticas, 1966–1968, por Danilo Ongay Muza. [1. ed.] México, 1969.

33 p. illus., facsims. 24 cm.

"Suplemento 2 del núm. 38 de los Anales del Instituto de Investigaciones Estéticas."

Moscow. Institut istorii iskusstv.
Библиография изданий института. (1944–1966 гг.). Москва, 1967.

170 p. 21 cm.

At head of title: Министерство культуры СССР. Институт истории искусств.
Compiled by N. A. Naroushvili.

New York. Metropolitan Museum of Art.
Publications of the Metropolitan Museum of Art, 1870–1964, a bibliography. Compiled by Albert TenEyck Gardner, associate curator of American paintings and sculpture. [New York] 1965.

vi, 72 p. 21 cm.

Novinky uměnovědné literatury.
[Praha] Státní knihovna ČSR.

v. 21 cm. 4 no. a year.

Continues Novinky literatury. Společenské vědy. Řada VII: Umění.
Issued by Státní knihovna ČSR, Ústřední bibliografické středisko.

Ostroĭ, Ol'ga Semenovna.
Изобразительное и прикладное искусство. Библиогр. рус. библиографии. Москва, "Книга," 1969.

213 p. 22 cm.

At head of title: Государственная ордена Трудового Красного Знамени публичная библиотека имени М. Е. Салтыкова-Щедрина. О. С. Остроĭ.

Prague. Francouzská knihovna.
Výtvarnictví—Architektura. Praha, [nákl. vl.], rozmn., 1968.

68 p. 29 cm. (Seznamy příručních knihoven, 1)
Caption title.
At head of title: Státní knihovna ČSSR. Francouzská knihovna.

Saskatchewan. Provincial Library, Regina. Bibliographic Services Division.
Art and architecture. Regina, 1972.

93 p. 22 cm.

Thompson, Helen (MacPherson) 1905–
Manual arts and crafts, prepared by Helen M. Thompson. [San Francisco, Pacific Air Forces] 1965.

viii, 188 p. 27 cm. (PACAF basic bibliographies)

Uses of Newer Media in Art Education Project.
Reproductions and paperback books on art. Washington, National Art Education Association, 1967.

64 p. 24 cm.

"No. 3 in a series of publications sponsored by the Uses of Newer Media Project of the National Art Education Association."

Výběrová bibliografie k dějinám umění. České a slovenské knihy. Učeb. text pro nástavbové studium kulturně výchovné práce na stř. knihovnických školách a kult. zařízení

nár. výborů. Sets. [kol.] Praha, SNTL, rozmn. St 6, 1970.

61, [1] p. 29 cm.

At head of title: Osvětový ústav v Praze.
By Olga Alexandrová and others.

Zykmundová, Anna.
Moderní výtvarné umění. Základní díla ve fondech Univ. knihovny v Brně. Sest. Anna Zykmundová. Brno, Univ. knihovna, rozmn., 1968.

10, [1] p. 21 cm. (Bibliografický leták. Universitní knihovna v Brně, 156)

BIBLIOGRAPHIES

Besterman, Theodore, 1904–
Art and architecture; a bibliography of bibliographies. Totowa, N. J., Rowman and Littlefield, 1971.

216 p. 20 cm. (His The Besterman world bibliographies)

BIO-BIBLIOGRAPHY

Bucharest. Biblioteca Centrală de Stat.
Aniversări culturale 1972. Prezentări biobibliografice. București, 1972.

344 p. 21 cm.

At head of title: Biblioteca Centrală de Stat a Republicii Socialiste România.

Queensland. Public Library, Brisbane. Country Extension Service.
Art: history and criticism [prepared by the] Country Extension Service, State Library of Queensland. Brisbane, Country Extension Service, State Library of Queensland, 1972.

92 p. 28 cm.

LIBRARY AND EXHIBITION CATALOGS

California. State College, *Long Beach. Library.*
Card catalog main entries representing international museum and gallery exhibitions. By Warner Olsen, art cataloger. [Long Beach] 49er Shops, California State College [1967]

129 l. 22 x 29 cm.

Dār al-Kutub wa-al-Wathā'iq al-Qawmīyah.
Fine arts, subject catalogue. Cairo, National Library Press, 1962–67.

2 v. (591 p.) 28 cm. 2.59

At head of title: United Arab Republic. Ministry of Culture and National Guidance. National Library, Cairo.
Added t. p.: الفنون الجميلة، فهرس موضوعى
Vol. 2 includes author indexes.

Florence. Kunsthistorisches Institut.
Katalog des Kunsthistorischen Instituts in Florenz. Boston, G. K. Hall, 1964.
9 v. 37 cm.
Added t. p. and introd. in English.

———— Erster Nachtragsband. Boston, G. K. Hall, 1968.
2 v. 37 cm.
Added t. p. and introd. in English.

Ghent. Rijksuniversiteit. Bibliotheek.
Aanwinsten: kunst. ontspanning en sport. Samengesteld door G. Milis-Proost. Gent. Centrale Bibliotheek van de Rijksuniversiteit. [Rozier 9], 197

v. 30 cm.

Harvard University. Fine Arts Library.
Catalogue of the Harvard University Fine Arts Library, the Fogg Art Museum. Boston, G. K. Hall, 1971.

15 v. 37 cm.

Vol. 15: Catalogue of auction sales catalogues.

Herrmann, Frank.
The English as collectors; an exhibition of books selected by Frank Herrmann. London, National Book League, 1972.

76 p. 21 cm.

Exhibition held May 8th to May 27th 1972, National Book League.

Michael Pabst Antiquariat und Kunsthandlung.
Katalog. ₍Illustr.₎ Wien ₍1968-69₎

2 v. illus. 21 cm.

At head of title of v. 2: Eine Auswahl von Werken österreichischer Künstler, ca. 1890-1940.
CONTENTS: 1. Literatur und Kunst des 20. Jahrhunderts.—2. Vom Jugendstil zum Expressionismus.

National Book League, *London.*
Art books: an annotated list; based on an exhibition at the Tate Gallery, Autumn 1968. London, National Book League; Tate Gallery, 1968.

136 p. 22 cm.

Ottawa. National Gallery of Canada. Library.
Catalogue of the Library of the National Gallery of Canada. Boston, G. K. Hall, 1973.

8 v. 37 cm.

Added t. p. in French: Catalogue de la Bibliothèque de la Galerie nationale du Canada.

Paris. Bibliothèque Forney.
Catalogue matières: arts-décoratifs, beaux-arts, métiers, techniques. Paris, Société des amis de la Bibliothèque Forney, 1970–

v. 31 cm.

Paris. Bibliothèque nationale. Département des estampes.
Catalogue des ouvrages relatifs aux beaux-arts du Cabinet des estampes de la Bibliothèque nationale (Série Y). ₍Par Marcel Roux. Introduction par François Courboin.₎ Paris, F. de Nobele, 1970.

xii, 372 p. 23 cm. (Archives de l'art français, nouv. période, t. 11)

"Reproduction en fac-similé de l'édition faite à Paris, par E. Champion, en 1921."—Bibl. de la Fr.

South Kensington Museum, *London. National Art Library.*
Universal catalogue of books on art. New York, B. Franklin ₍1964₎

3 v. 26 cm. (Burt Franklin bibliography and reference series, #47)

Edited by J. H. Pollen.
Reprint of the 1870-77 ed., published under title: First proofs of the Universal catalogue of books on art.

CONTENTS.—V. 1. A to K.—v. 2. L to Z.—v. 3. Supplement.

Syndicat national des éditeurs (France). Groupe des éditeurs des livres d'art.
Catalogue des livres d'art français. Paris ₍1970₎

368 p. illus., col. plates. 21 cm.

Victoria and Albert Museum, South Kensington. National Art Library.
Catalogue: author catalogue. Boston, G. K. Hall, 1972.

10 v. 37 cm.

Victoria and Albert Museum, South Kensington. National Art Library.
National Art Library catalogue, Victoria and Albert Museum, London, England. Boston, G. K. Hall, 1972–

v. 37 cm.

CONTENTS:
₍2₎ Catalogue of exhibition catalogues.

PERIODICALS

Paris. Bibliothèque Forney.
Catalogue d'articles de périodiques, arts décoratifs et beaux-arts. Bibliothèque Forney, Paris. Boston, G. K. Hall, 1972.
4 v. 36 cm.
Added t. p.: Catalog of periodical articles, decorative and fine arts, Bibliothèque Forney, Paris.
"From 1919 to 1950, only particularly relevant articles were selected and analyzed. Since 1950, periodical holdings have been systematically catalogued ..."

AFRICA

International African Institute.
A bibliography of African art; compiled at the International African Institute by L. J. P. Gaskin under the direction of Guy Atkins. London, International African Institute, 1965.

x, 120 p. 28½ cm. (Africa bibliography series B)

Isaacs, Marion.
The South African Impressionist painters; a select bibliography. Johannesburg, University of the Witwatersrand, Dept. of Bibliography, Librarianship and Typography, 1973.

90 p. 30 cm.

Mirvish, Doreen Belle.
South African artists 1900–1958; a bibliography. ₍Cape Town₎ University of Cape Town Libraries, 1970.

40 p. 23 cm. (University of Cape Town. School of Librarianship. Bibliographical series)

AUSTRIA

Verband der Antiquare Österreichs.
Österreich in Kunst und Literatur. ₍Wien, 1965₎

32 p. 30 cm. (Its Verzeichnis der im Rahmen der österreichischen Buchwoche veranstalteten Gemeinschafts-Ausstellung, 1965)

CANADA

Reid, Dennis R
A bibliography of the Group of Seven ₍by₎ Dennis Reid. Ottawa, National Gallery of Canada, 1971.

80 p. 22 x 31 cm.

CHINA

Chu, Ts'un-li, 1444–1513.
(T'ieh wang shan hu)
鐵網珊瑚　朱存理撰　₍台北₎　國立中央圖書館
₍民國 59 i. e. 1970₎

3 v. (1380 p.) 21 cm. (藝術賞鑒選珍)

景印國立中央圖書館藏舊抄本
CONTENTS.—上　書品　卷1-5—中　書品　卷6-10—下　藏品　6 卷

Kaplan, Sidney M 1912–
The art of China; systematic bibliography and reading

assignments covering periods from earliest times through the Sung Dynasty [by] Prof. Kaplan. [Columbus? Ohio, 1967]

[44] l. 29 cm.

Tu, Mu, 1458–1525.
(T'ieh wang shan hu)
鐵網珊瑚 [20 卷] 都穆撰 [台北] 國立中央
圖書館 [民國 59 i. e. 1970]

676 p. 21 cm. (藝術賞鑒選珍)

景印國立中央圖書館藏舊抄本

COMMONWEALTH OF NATIONS

National Book League, *London.*
Arts in the Commonwealth. London, 1965.

16 p. 22 cm.

"Annotated reading list ... prepared for the Commonwealth books exhibition at Marlborough House in October, 1965."

National Book League, London.
Literature and the arts of the Commonwealth, [by the] National Book League with the Commonwealth Institute. London, National Book League, 1972.

90 p. 21 cm.

"Prepared for the Commonwealth Book Fair held at the Commonwealth Institute from 13 October to 5 November 1972."

"Supplementary list; late entries": 4 p., inserted.

GERMANY

Badstübner-Gröger, Sibylle.
Bibliographie zur Kunstgeschichte von Berlin und Potsdam. Berlin, Akademie-Verlag, 1968.

xiii, 320 p. 28 cm. (Schriften zur Kunstgeschichte, Heft 13)

Stadtbibliothek Bielefeld.
Westfälische Kunst bis zum Barock; ein Literaturverzeichnis. [Bearb.: Wolfgang Beyrodt] Bielefeld, 1970.

63 p. 21 cm.

ITALY

Bibliografia del libro d'arte italiano. Roma, C. Bestetti [1952–64]

2 v. in 3. illus., facsims., plates. 20 cm.

CONTENTS.—[v. 1.] 1940–1952, a cura di E. Aeschlimann.—v. 2. 1952–1962. 2 v.

LATIN AMERICA

Smith, Robert Chester, 1912– ed.
A guide to the art of Latin America. Edited by Robert C. Smith and Elizabeth Wilder. New York, Arno Press, 1971.

v, 480 p. 24 cm.

Reprint of the 1948 ed.

NEPAL

Bernier, Ronald M
A bibliography of Nepalese art [by] Ronald M. Bernier. [1st ed. Kathmandu] Voice of Nepal; [distributor: Educational Enterprise, 1970]

46 p. 22 cm.

NEW GUINEA

Newton, Douglas, 1920– *comp.*
Bibliography of Sepik District art annotated for illustrations. [New York, Library, Museum of Primitive Art] 1965–

v. 28 cm. (Primitive art bibliographies, no. 4)

NIGERIA

Ben-Amos, Paula.
Bibliography of Benin art. New York, Library, Museum of Primitive Art, 1968.

17 p. 28 cm. (Primitive art bibliographies, no. 6)

RUSSIA

Белорусское искусство. вып. 1–
Минск, Книжная палата БССР, 1965–

v. 20 cm.

"Биобиблиографический справочник."
Issued by Sektor iskusstva of Gosudarstvennai͡a biblioteka BSSR im. V. I. Lenina.

Leningrad. Publichnai͡a biblioteka.
(Iskusstvo—vsem)
Искусство—всем. Москва, "Книга," 1972.

207 p. 20 cm. (Беседы о книгах)

At head of title: Государственная публичная библиотека им. М. Е. Салтыкова-Щедрина.
"Составитель: Э. Э. Найдич."

Ostroĭ, Ol'ga Semenovna.
(Russkie spravochnye izdanii͡a po izobrazitel'nomu i prikladnomu iskusstvu)
Русские справочные издания по изобразительному и прикладному искусству. Аннот. указ. Москва, "Книга," 1972.

280 p. 22 cm.

Ostroĭ, Ol'ga Semenovna.
(Sto dvadt͡sat' pi͡at' knig po russkomu i sovetskomu iskusstvu)
125 книг по русскому и советскому искусству. Рек. библиогр. указ. Ленинград, "Художник РСФСР," 1972.

139 p. with illus. 21 cm.

Ruchimskai͡a, E A
Книги по искусству. Рек. указатель для сред. школы. [С 1960 по 1966 гг.] Москва, "Дет. лит.," 1967.

64 p. with illus. 20 cm. (Школьная библиотека)

Для средней школы.
At head of title: Дом детской книги.

Voi͡akina, Svetlana Mikhaĭlovna.
[Sovetskoe izobrazitel'noe iskusstvo]
Советское изобразительное искусство. Рек. указ. литературы в помощь самообразованию молодежи. Москва, "Книга," 1972.

100 p. 20 cm. (В мире прекрасного)

At head of title: Государственная библиотека имени В. И. Ленина. С. М. Воякина.

Zubov, I͡Uriĭ Sergeevich.
(Bibliografii͡a iskusstva)
Библиография искусства. Под ред. доц. Ю. С. Зубова. [Учебник для библ. фак. ин-тов культуры]. Москва, "Книга," 1973.

303 p. 21 cm.

At head of title: Ю. С. Зубов, Е. П. Погорелая, А. А. Туровская.

Zykmundová, Anna, *comp.*
Ohlas ruských revolučních avantgard v Československu v letech 1920–1938. Sest. Anna Zykmundová. ₍V Brně₎ 1967.

34 p. 21 cm. (Universitní knihovna v Brně. Výběrový seznam, 133)

SAXONY-ANHALT

Harksen, Sibylle.
Bibliographie zur Kunstgeschichte von Sachsen-Anhalt. Berlin, Akademie-Verlag, 1966.

x, 431 p. 28 cm. (Schriften zur Kunstgeschichte ₍Bd. 11₎)

SWEDEN

Lundqvist, Maja.
Svensk konsthistorisk bibliografi. Sammanställd ur den tryckta litteraturen till och med år 1950. Bibliography to Swedish history of art. Literature issued up to and including 1950. Stockholm, Almqvist & Wikcell, 1967.

xxxi, (2), 432 p. 27 cm. (Stockholm studies in history of art, 12)

THURINGIA

Möbius, Helga.
Bibliographie zur thüringischen Kunstgeschichte. Berlin, Akademie-Verlag, 1974.

227 p. 28 cm. (Schriften zur Kunstgeschichte, Heft 16)

TURKEY

Aslanapa, Oktay.
Selçuklu sanatı bibliyografyası. ₍Oktay Aslanapa ve yardımcıları tarafından hazırlanmıştır₎ İstanbul, Yapı ve Kredi Bankası, 1971.

47 p. 28 cm.

UNITED STATES

Foster, Donald LeRoy, 1928–
A checklist of U. S. Government publications in the arts, by Donald L. Foster. ₍Urbana, University of Illinois, Graduate School of Library Science₎ 1969.

48 p. 29 cm. (University of Illinois. Graduate School of Library Science. Occasional papers, no. 96)

McCoy, Garnett.
Archives of American art; a directory of resources. New York, Bowker, 1972.

ix, 163 p. 23 cm.

Whitehill, Walter Muir, 1905–
The arts in early American history; an essay by Walter Muir Whitehill. A bibliography by Wendell D. Garrett and Jane N. Garrett. Chapel Hill, Published for the Institute of Early American History and Culture at Williamsburg, Va., by the University of North Carolina Press ₍1965₎

xv, 170 p. 24 cm. (Needs and opportunities for study series)

ART, BYZANTINE

Bibliographie de l'art byzantin et post-byzantin, 1945–1969.
Athènes, Comité national hellénique de l'association internationale d'études du sud-est européen, 1970.

115 p. 24 cm.

"Publié à l'occasion du IIème congrès international des études balkaniques et sud-est européennes."

Hjort, Øystein.
Byzans. ₍Bibliografi til byzantinsk kunst udvalgt og kommenteret af Øystein Hjort og Jørgen Schou-Christen-

sen₎. ₍København₎ Kunstakademiets Bibliothek, 1966.

1 v. (loose leaf) 30 cm.

ART, GOTHIC

Boskovits, Miklós, *ed.*
L'art du gothique et de la renaissance, 1300–1500; bibliographie raisonnée des ouvrages publiées en Hongrie. Budapest ₍Comité national hongrois d'histoire de l'art₎ 1965.

2 v. (540 p.) 23 cm.

At head of title: Institut d'histoire de l'art de l'Université "Eötvös Lóránd" et le Bureau central de propagande des Musées hongrois.

CONTENTS.—1. ptie. Généralités. Topographie, urbanisme, protection des monuments. Architecture.—2. ptie. Sculpture. Peinture et gravure. Arts décoratifs.

ART, JEWISH

Mayer, Leo Ary, 1895–1959.
Bibliography of Jewish art. Edited by Otto Kurz. Jerusalem, Magnes Press, Hebrew University, 1967.

374 p. 25 cm. 25.00

Mayer, Leo Ary, 1895–1959.
Bibliography of Jewish art ₍by₎ L .A. Mayer; edited by Otto Kurz. Jerusalem, Magnes P.; ₍London₎ Oxford U. P., 1967.

374 p. 24½ cm.

ART, MEDIEVAL

Scheller, Robert Walter Hans Peter.
A survey of medieval model books ₍by₎ R. W. Scheller. Haarlem, Erven F. Bohn, 1963 ₍i. e. 1964₎

xi, 215 p. illus. 24 cm.

"Published by Teylers tweede genootschap."

ART, MODERN
see also   Expressionism; Surrealism

Bildende Kunst 1850–1914 ₍i. e. achtzehnhundertfünfzig bis neunzehnhundertvierzehn₎; Dokumentation aus Zeitschriften des Jugendstil, hrsg. von Gerhard Bott. Berlin, Gebr. Mann ₍c1970–

v. 29 cm.

Hesse, Gritta.
Kunst der jungen Generation; ein Literaturverzeichnis und biographisches Nachschlagewerk. ₍Berlin₎ Amerika-Gedenkbibliothek, Berliner Zentralbibliothek, 1968–

v. 21 cm.

"Dieses Verzeichnis wurde von Gritta Hesse und Hille Schneider zusammengestellt."

Lietzmann, Hilda.
Bibliographie zur Kunstgeschichte des 19. Jahrhunderts; Publikationen der Jahre 1940–1966. Mit Referaten von K. Lankheit, F. Novotny und H. G. Evers. München, Prestel-Verlag, 1968.

234 p. illus., ports. 25 cm. (Studien zur Kunst des neunzehnten Jahrhunderts, Bd. 4)

Mattos, Maria Virgínia Bastos de.
Semana de arte moderna: 50 anos; bibliografia. ₍São Paulo₎ Universidade de São Paulo, Depto. Biblioteconomia e Documentação, Hemeroteca, 1972–

v. 22 cm.

CONTENTS: 1. Artigos de jornais.

Zykmundová, Anna.
Umělecké směry 20. století. Soupis lit. z fondu Univ. knihovny Brno. Sest. Anna Zykmundová. Brno, Univ. knihovna, t. G, 1970.

44 p. 21 cm. (Výběrový seznam, č. 161)

ART, ORIENTAL

Canberra, Australia. National Library.
Asian art and Asian books; catalogue of an exhibition drawn by the National Library from Australian collections to mark the 28 Congress of Orientalists in Canberra, January 6 to 12, 1971. ₍Canberra₎ 1971.

vi, 31 p. illus. 26 cm.

PERIODICALS

Bijutsu Kenkyūjo, Tokyo.
(Tōyō bijutsu bunken mokuroku)
東洋美術文献目録　定期刊行物所載古美術文献　美術
研究所編纂

東京　柏林社書店（発売）　昭和42(1967)
570, 34p　27cm

Tōkyō Kokuritsu Bunkazai Kenkyūjo. *Bijutsubu.*
日本東洋古美術文献目録　東京国立文化財研究
所美術部₍美術研究所₎編　東京　中央公論美術出
版　昭和44 (1969)
698 p. 27 cm.

ART, RENAISSANCE　see under　Art, Gothic

ART SALES

Paris. Bibliothèque Forney.
Catalogue des catalogues de ventes d'art. Bibliothèque Forney, Paris. Boston, G. K. Hall, 1972.

2 v. 35 cm.

Added t. p.: Catalog of the catalogs of sales of art, Bibliothèque Forney, Paris.
Pref. also in English.
CONTENTS: v. 1. Collectionneurs A-Z. Dates 1930.—v. 2. Dates 1931. Lieux A-Z.

ART THERAPY

Centre international de documentation concernant les expressions plastiques. Bibliothèque.
Liste des acquisitions, 1970–1971. Paris ₍1970–

v. 27 cm.

Pacey, Philip.
Remedial art: a bibliography. ₍Hatfield, Hertis₎. 1972.

₍87₎ p. 30 cm.

ARTIFICIAL INSEMINATION

Искусственное осеменение сельскохозяйственных животных; указатель отечественной литературы за 1859–1963 гг. в количестве 3343 названий. ₍Редактор М. Н. Алямовская₎ Москва, 1965.

412 p. 21 cm.

At head of title: Всесоюзная академия с.-х. наук имени В. И. Ленина. Центральная научная сельскохозяйственная библиотека. Справочно-библиографический отдел.

ARTIFICIAL SATELLITES　see Satellites, Artificial

ARTISANS　see　Handicrafts

ARUNDEL CASTLE

Steer, Francis W
Arundel Castle archives; edited by Francis W. Steer. Chichester (Sussex) West County Council, 1968–

v. 25 cm.

Handlists never issued separately.
CONTENTS.—v. 1. Interim handlists, nos. 1–12.

ARYANS

Mayrhofer, Manfred, 1926–
Die Indo-Arier im alten Vorderasien. Mit einer analytischen Bibliographie. Wiesbaden, Harrassowitz, 1966.

160 p. with illus., 1 map, 1 front. 24 cm.

ARZE, JOSÉ ANTONIO

Arze, José Roberto.
Ensayo de una bibliografía del Dr. José Antonio Arze. ₍1. ed.₎ Cochabamba, Bolivia ₍Editorial Universitaria₎ 1968.

81 p. facsims., ports. 18 cm.

ASBESTOS

Sachedina, Roshanara.
A bibliography of asbestos in Tanzania. Dodoma, Mineral Resources Division, 1966.

4 p. 25 cm.

ASIA
see also　Middle East, and under Dissertations, Academic

(Ajia keizai kankei bunken mokuroku)
アジア・アフリカ総合研究組織
アジア経済関係文献目録
東京　アジア経済研究所　1968
215p　26cm　（アジア・アフリカ文献解題　1）

Ajia Keizai Kenkyūjo shuppanbutsu, tsūkan dai 749-gō.

Asia Society.
Asia: a guide to paperbacks. Ainslie T. Embree, editor, Jackson H. Bailey ₍and others₎ Rev. ed. ₍New York₎ 1968.

iii, 178 p. 23 cm.

Published in 1964 under title: A guide to paperbacks on Asia.

Asia Society.
A guide to paperbacks on Asia. Selected and annotated ₍by₎ Ainslie T. Embree, editor, Jackson H. Bailey ₍and others₎. New York₎ 1964.

1 l., 89 p. 23 cm.

Bau, Milli, 1911–
Asien. (Leben, Denken, Schaffen seiner Völker.) Ein Wegweiser durch das Schrifttum. (München, Asien-Verlag M. Bau) 1967.

95 p. 19 cm.

Birnbaum, Eleazar.
Books on Asia from the Near East to the Far East; a guide for the general reader, selected and annotated by Eleazar Birnbaum. ₍Toronto₎ University of Toronto Press ₍1971₎

xv, 341 p. 24 cm.

Bulletin of Far Eastern bibliography. v. 1–5; Feb. 1936–1940. New York, AMS Press ₍1968₎

5 v. 29 cm.

Reprint of a periodical published in Washington by the Committees on Far Eastern Studies of the American Council of Learned Societies and edited by E. H. Pritchard.

Cwik, Hans-Jürgen.
Deutschsprachige Publikationen des Jahres 1969 über Asien und Ozeanien. Publications of 1969 on Asia and Oceania in German language. Zusammengestellt von Hans-Jürgen Cwik. Hamburg, Institut für Asienkunde, Dokumentations-Leitstelle, 1971.

ii, 70 p. 30 cm. (Documentatio Asiae, Nr. 1)

Dobson, W A C H ed.
The contribution of Canadian universities to an understanding of Asia and Africa. Contribution des universités canadiennes à la connaissance de l'Asie et de l'Afrique. Edited by W. A. C. H. Dobson. With a foreword by Henry D. Hicks. Ottawa, Canadian National Commission for Unesco ₍1964?₎

iv, 70 p. 24 cm.

Dobson, W A C H ed.
The contribution of Canadian universities to an understanding of Asia and Africa. Contribution des universités canadiennes á la connaissance de l'Asie et de l'Afrique, edited by W. A. C. H. Dobson. 2d ed. rev. and enl. ₍Ottawa, Canadian National Commission for Unesco, 1967?₎

iv, 160 p. 23 cm.

A bibliographical directory of scholars.
Text bilingual, English and French.

Documents on Asian affairs: select bibliography. v. 1–1957–
New Delhi, Indian Council of World Affairs and Indian School of International Studies.

v. 26 cm. (Indian Council of World Affairs. Library. Bibliographical series)

Superseded by Indian Council of World Affairs. Documentation on Asia.
Vols. 2– prepared by Documents Section, Indian School of International Studies.

Eastern Michigan University. Library.
Children's books on Asia; a selected list from the Eastern Michigan University Library. Compiled and annotated by Alice Wu. Edited by Ann Andrew. ₍Ypsilanti, Mich.₎ 1972.

15 p. 29 cm. (Its Bibliography series, no. 28)

Ehrman, Edith.
Preliminary bibliography on East Asia for undergraduate libraries. Edith Ehrman, project editor; Ward Morehouse, project director. New York, Foreign Area Materials Center, 1967.

x, 475 p. 28 cm.

Compiled under the auspices of the Center for International Programs and Services, State Education Dept., University of the State of New York, as part of a project being undertaken by the Foreign Area Materials Center, New York.

Embree, Ainslie Thomas.
Asia; a guide to basic books. Compilers and annotators: Ainslie T. Embree ₍and others₎. New York₍ Asia Society, 1966.

57 p. 23 cm.

Fodor, Michael.
The East; books in Western languages on Asian and Arabic countries. London, IFLA/FIAB for the Unesco Orient-Occident Major Project, 1965.

viii, 107 p. 20 cm.

Cover title: Books on the East.
Title-page, introduction and text in English, French and Spanish.

Friederici, Karl.
Bibliotheca Orientalis. A complete list of books, papers, serials, essais, etc. published from the year 1876 to 1883 on the history, languages, religions, antiquities and literature of the East. Amsterdam, Oriental Press, 1967.

8 pts. in 1 v. 23 cm.

Added t. p.: Bibliotheca Orientalis. Vollständige Liste der vom Jahre 1876 bis 1883 erschienenen Bücher, Broschuren, Zeitschriften, usw. über die Sprachen, Religionen, Antiquitäten, Literaturen und Geschichte des Ostens.
"Neudruck der Ausgabe Leipzig, London 1876–1883."

Fujii, Masao, 1912–
アジア諸国の工業化 ₍藤井正夫・玉置正美・島義治著 東京₎ アジア経済研究所 ₍1965₎

vii, 287 p. 21 cm. (文献解題シリーズ 第10集)

アジア経済研究所出版物 通巻第426号

Gillin, Donald G
East Asia: a bibliography for undergraduate libraries ₍by₎ Donald Gillin, Edith Ehrman ₍and₎ Ward Morehouse. Williamsport, Pa., Bro-Dart Pub. Co., 1970.

xvi, 130 p. 29 cm. (Foreign Area Materials Center, University of the State of New York. Occasional publication no. 10)

Gosling, Lee Anthony Peter, 1927–
Maps, atlases, and gazetteers for Asian studies: a critical guide, by L. A. Peter Gosling. New York, State Education Dept., 1965.

vi, 27 p. 28 cm. (Foreign Area Materials Center, University of the State of New York. Occasional publication no. 2)

Hobbs, Cecil Carleton, 1907–
Understanding the peoples of southern Asia: a bibliographical essay. ₍Urbana₎ 1967.

58 p. 28 cm. (University of Illinois. Graduate School of Library Science. Occasional papers, no. 81)

Caption title.

Hobbs, Cecil Carlton, 1907–
Writings on southern Asia, 1942–1968, by Cecil Hobbs. ₍Washington, 1968₎

46 l. 26 cm.

Inforasia. v. 1–
Jan./ Mar. 1974–
₍Shirasato-machi (Chiba prefecture), Japan, Japan English Service₎

v. 27 cm. quarterly.

"An international quarterly bibliography of new books and non-print resources in English related to Asia."

Kerner, Robert Joseph, 1887–1956.
Northeastern Asia, a selected bibliography; contributions to the bibliography of the relations of China, Russia, and Japan, with special reference to Korea, Manchuria, Mongolia, and eastern Siberia, in Oriental and European languages. New York, B. Franklin ₁1968₎

2 v. 23 cm. (Burt Franklin bibliography & reference series, 255)
Reprint of the 1939 ed.

Kovář, Blahoslav.
Asie, Afrika, Latinská Amerika; bibliografie českých a slovenských knih, 1961–1964. V Praze, Národní knihovna, 1964.

78 p. 21 cm. (Bibliografický katalog ČSSR. České knihy, 1964. Zvláštní seš., 6)

Meyer, Milton Walter.
Asia: an introductory bibliography. Milton W. Meyer, compiler. 3d ed., rev. Los Angeles, 1968.

iii, 75 p. 28 cm.

Meyer, Milton Walter.
Asian bibliography. Milton W. Meyer, compiler. 2d ed., rev. Los Angeles? 1967.

1 v. (various pagings) 28 cm.

Mundus. v. 1–
1965–
Stuttgart, Wissenschaftliche Verlagsgesellschaft.

v. 24 cm. quarterly.

"Review of German research contributions on Asia, Africa and Latin America."
In English.

National Book League, *London.*
The Commonwealth in South and South East Asia: an annotated list. London, National Book League, 1969.

₁2₎, 32 p. 22 cm.

Issued by the National Book League and the Commonwealth Institute.

Quenzel, Carrol Hunter, 1906–
A bibliography of books, periodicals, and recordings pertaining to Asia, in the Library of Mary Washington College of the University of Virginia. Compiled by Carrol H. Quenzel ₁at the request of the Committee on Local Arrangements for the Southeastern Regional meeting of the Association for Asian Studies, February 3–4, 1967₎ Fredericksburg. Va., 1966.

ix, 160 l. 28 cm.

(Rekishi no meicho)
歴史の名著　日本人篇　歴史科学協議会編　東京
校倉書房　1970.

246 p. 18 cm.

Rühlmann, Gerhard.
Die orientalische Archäologie an der Martin-Luther-Universität Halle-Wittenberg ⟨1948–1969⟩. Bibliogr. Übersicht über d. Publikationstätigkeit d. Mitarbeiter. Halle ⟨S.⟩ (Martin-Luther-Universität. Sektion Orient- u. Altertumswissenschaften) 1970.

xviii, 61 p. 21 cm.

Ternaux-Compans, Henri, 1807–1864.
Bibliothèque asiatique et africaine, ou catalogue des ouvrages relatifs à l'Asie et à l'Afrique qui ont paru depuis la découverte de l'imprimerie jusqu'en 1700, par H. Ternaux-Compans. ₁Réimpression de l'édition Paris, 1841₎. Amsterdam, B. R. Grüner, 1968.

vi, 350 p. 22 cm.

Tokushu Bunko Rengō Kyōgikai.
特殊文庫連合協議会
特殊文庫所蔵
マイクロフィルム連合目録
東京　昭和42(1967)
273, 53p　26 cm

Tōyōshi Kenkyū Rombun Mokuroku Henshū Iinkai.
(Nihon ni okeru Tōyōshi rombun mokuroku)　日本における東洋史論文目録　東洋史研究論文目録編集委員会編　東京　日本学術振興会　丸善発売　昭和 39–42 ₁1964–67₎
4 v. 27 cm.
Added title in colophon: Japanese studies on Asian history; a catalogue of articles concerning the history of Asia (excluding Japan) in periodicals and other collective publications appeared in Japan from c. 1880 to 1962.

Vol. 4 has special title: 著者名索引

Tsien, Tsuen-hsuin, 1909–
East Asia: checklist of literature proposed for micropublishing. ₁Von₎ T. H. Tsien. Zug, Inter Documentation Company, ₁1967?₎

₁56₎ p. 21 cm.

United States. Dept. of the Army. Army Library.
Japan: analytical bibliography with supplementary research aids and selected data on: Okinawa, Republic of China (Taiwan), Republic of Korea. Washington, U. S. Dept. of the Army; ₁for sale by the Supt. of Docs., U. S. Govt. Print. Off.₎ 1972.

x, 371 p. illus., maps (11 fold. col. in pocket) 26 cm.

U. S. *Office of Education. Educational Materials Center.*
South and Southeast Asia; a bibliography. ₁2d report₎ July 16, 1965. ₁Washington, Office of Education, U. S. Dept. of Health, Education, and Welfare, 1966₎

11 p. 26 cm.

Yang, Winston L　Y
Asian resources in American libraries; essays and bibliographies. Edited by Winston L. Y. Yang and Teresa S. Yang. With contributions by John T. Ma ₁and others₎ And an Appendix by Yukihisa Suzuki. New York ₁Foreign Area Materials Center, University of the State of New York₎ 1968.

ix, 122 p. 28 cm. (University of the State of New York. Foreign Area Materials Center. Occasional publication no. 9)

BIBLIOGRAPHIES

Nunn, Godfrey Raymond, 1918–
Asia: a selected and annotated guide to reference works ₁by₎ G. Raymond Nunn. Cambridge, Mass., M. I. T. Press ₁1971₎

xiii, 223 p. 24 cm.

Nunn, Godfrey Raymond, 1918–
East Asia; a bibliography of bibliographies, by G. Raymond Nunn. ₁Honolulu₎ East West Center Library, 1967.

x, 92 l. 28 cm. (Occasional papers of East West Center Library, no. 7)

Nunn, Godfrey Raymond, 1918–
South and Southeast Asia; a bibliography of bibliographies, by G. Raymond Nunn. ₍Honolulu₎ East West Center Library, 1966.

v, 59 l. 28 cm. (Occasional papers of East-West Center Library, no. 4)

Yunesuko Higashi Ajia Bunka Kenkyū Sentā, *Tokyo.*
Bibliography of bibliographies of East Asian studies in Japan. ₍Editor: Kimpei Goto₎ Compiled and published by Centre for East Asian Cultural Studies. ₍Tokyo₎ 1964.

iv, 190, xvi p. 21 cm. (Centre for East Asian Cultural Studies. Bibliography no. 3)

"Compiled as a supplement to the relevant parts of ... A survey of Japanese bibliographies concerning Asian studies."

Yunesuko Higashi Ajia Bunka Kenkyū Sentā, *Tokyo.*
A survey of bibliographies in Western languages concerning East and Southeast Asian studies. ₍Tokyo₎ Centre for East Asian Cultural Studies ₍°1966–

v. 21 cm. (Centre for East Asian Cultural Studies. Bibliography no. 4–

EXHIBITION CATALOGS

Barcelona. Biblioteca Central.
Catálogo de la Exposición Bibliográfica Oriental. Galería de Exposiciones de la Biblioteca Central, Barcelona, mayo–junio de 1972. Organizada por la Asociación Española de Orientalistas con la colaboración de la Biblioteca Central de Cataluña, la Biblioteca y Seminario de Papirología de la Facultad Teológica de San Cugat del Vallés y el Museo Etnológico de Barcelona. Barcelona ₍1973₎

45 p. 25 cm.

Chicago. University. Committee on Far Eastern Studies.
Far East: an exhibition of resources in the University of Chicago Library ₍at₎ the Joseph Regenstein Library, March–June, 1973. ₍Chicago, 1973₎

₍35₎ p. illus. 22 cm.

International Colloquium on Luso-Brazilian Studies. *6th, Cambridge, Mass. and New York, 1966.*
Europe informed; an exhibition of early books which acquainted Europe with the East. Cambridge, Massachusetts: Harvard College Library; New York, New York: New York Public Library, Columbia University Library, Library of the Hispanic Society of America. ₍Cambridge? 1966₎

x, 192 p. illus., facsims. 23 cm.

LIBRARY CATALOGS

Akademiiā nauk SSSR. Biblioteka.
(Spravochnaiā literatura po stranam Azii i Afriki)
Справочная литература по странам Азии и Африки. Сводный каталог иностр. фондов Б-ки АН СССР и Гос. публ. б-ки им. М. Е. Салтыкова-Щедрина. 1945–1968. Под ред. Т. А. Вагановой и С. С. Булатова. Ленинград, 1972.
534 p. 20 cm.

California. University. *Library. East Asiatic Library.*
Subject catalog. Boston, G. K. Hall, 1968.

6 v. 37 cm.

East India Company (*English*) *Library.*
A catalogue of the library of the Hon. East-India Company. ₍New York₎ B. Franklin ₍1969₎

2 v. 24 cm. (Burt Franklin bibliography & reference series, 288)

Vol. 1, reprint of the 1845 ed.; v. 2, A supplemental catalogue, reprint of the 1851 ed.

Harvard University. *Library.*
China, Japan, and Korea; classification schedule, classified listing by call number, alphabetical listing by author or title, chronological listing. Cambridge, Distributed by Harvard University Press, 1968.

494 p. 20 cm. (*Its* Widener Library shelflist, no. 14)

Harvard University. *Library.*
Southern Asia: Afghanistan, Bhutan, Burma, Cambodia, Ceylon, India, Laos, Malaya, Nepal, Pakistan, Sikkim, Singapore, Thailand, Vietnam. Cambridge; Distributed by Harvard University Press, 1968.

iv, 543 p. 29 cm. (*Its* Widener Library shelflist, 19)

Kōbe Daigaku. Keizai Keiei Kenkyūjo.
(Kōbe Daigaku Keizai Keiei Kenkyūjo shozō Ajia Afurika tosho mokuroku)
神戸大学経済経営研究所所蔵アジア・アフリカ図書目録 ₍神戸₎ 神戸大学経済経営研究所 1965 ₍i.e. 1966₎

88, 14 p. 26 cm.

London. University. *School of Oriental and African Studies. Library.*
Library catalogue. Boston, G. K. Hall, 1963.
28 v. 37 cm.
CONTENTS.—v. 1–8. Author catalogue.—v. 9–13. Title index.—v. 14–21. Subject catalogue.—v. 22. Catalogue of manuscripts and microfilms.—v. 23–27. Chinese catalogue.—v. 28. Japanese catalogue.
——— First supplement. Boston, G. K. Hall, 1968.
16 v. 37 cm.
CONTENTS.—v. 1–3. Author catalogue. Catalogue of manuscripts and microfilms.—v. 4–6. Title index.—v. 7–12. Subject catalogue.—v. 13–14. Chinese catalogue, authors.— v. 15. Chinese catalogue, titles.—v. 16. Chinese catalogue, subjects. Japanese catalogue.

Lyons. Bibliothèque de la ville.
Catalogue du fonds oriental de la Bibliothèque municipale de Lyon, par Yvonne Lebègue-La Perrière. ₍Paris, Ministère de l'éducation nationale₎ 1970–

v. 27 cm. ₍Recensement des livres anciens des bibliothèques françaises. Travaux préparatoires, 4

CONTENTS: fasc. 1, Du Maroc aux Indes orientales: historiens, géographes, voyageurs.

Pittsburgh. University. East Asian Library.
Catalog of microfilms of the East Asian Library of the University of Pittsburgh. Compiled by Thomas C. Kuo and John W. Chiang. ₍Pittsburgh₎ 1971.

iii, 253 p. 29 cm. (University of Pittsburgh libraries bibliographic series, no. 7)

English, Chinese, or Japanese.

Technische Hogeschool, Delft. Bibliotheek.
Het Verre Oosten; gids van boeken, tijdschriften en documentaire grammofoonplaten over China, Japan, Korea etc. aanwezig in de Bibliotheek van de Technische Hogeschool te Delft, samengesteld door C. A. van den Berg-Van de Geer. Delft, 1970.

ix, 70 p. 21 cm.

Added t. p.: The Far East.

ASIA, CENTRAL

Inter-documentation Company, *Zug.*
Central Asia: periodicals, bibliographies, political history (civil war), Uzbek literature; a checklist. ₍Editor: Garé

LeCompte. Zug, 1966?₁

15 l. 29 cm. (Basic collections in micro edition)

ASIA, SOUTH

Case, Margaret H
South Asian history, 1750–1950; a guide to periodicals, dissertations, and newspapers [by] Margaret H. Case. Princeton, N. J., Princeton University Press, 1968.

xiii, 561 p. 25 cm.

Datta, Rajeshwari.
Guide to South Asian material in the libraries of London, Oxford & Cambridge by R. Datta. 2nd ed. Cambridge, University (Centre of South Asian Studies), 1966.

[3], 18 f. 30 cm.

De Benko, Eugene.
Research sources for South Asian studies in economic development; a select bibliography of serial publications, by Eugene de Benko and V. N. Krishnan. East Lansing, Asian Studies Center, Michigan State University, 1966.

xi, 97 p. 28 cm. (Asian Studies Center occasional paper, no. 4)

Hay, Stephen N
Preliminary bibliography on South Asia for undergraduate libraries [by] Stephen N. Hay, Edith Ehrman [and] Ward Morehouse. New York, University of the State of New York, State Education Dept., Foreign Area Materials Center, 1967.

ix, 393 p. 28 cm.

Low, Donald Anthony.
Government archives in South Asia: a guide to national and state archives in Ceylon, India and Pakistan; edited by D. A. Low, J. C. Iltis and M. D. Wainwright. London, Cambridge U. P., 1969.

xii, 355 p. fold. plate. 23 cm.

Menge, Paul E
Government administration in South Asia; a bibliography [by] Paul E. Menge. Washington, Comparative Administration Group, American Society for Public Administration [1968]

iii, 100 p. 28 cm. (Papers in comparative public administration. Special series, no. 9)

Meyer, Milton Walter.
South Asia : an introductory bibliography / Milton W. Meyer. — Los Angeles : Dept. of History, California State University, 1972.

14 p. ; 28 cm.

South Asia: a bibliography for undergraduate libraries [by] Louis A. Jacob [and others] Williamsport, Pa., Bro-Dart Pub. Co., 1970.

xvi, 103 p. 29 cm. (University of the State of New York. Foreign Area Materials Center. Occasional publication no. 11)

U. S. *Dept. of the Army.*
South Asia; a strategic survey. Washington, 1966.

vii, 175 p. maps (5 fold. col. in pocket) 26 cm.

ASIA, SOUTHEAST

Berton, Peter Alexander Menquez, 1922–
Soviet works on Southeast Asia; a bibliography of non-periodical literature, 1946–1965 [by] Peter Berton [and] Alvin Z. Rubinstein. With a contribution by Anna Allott.

Los Angeles, University of Southern California Press, 1967.

201 p. 23 cm. (University of Southern California. School of Politics and International Relations. Far Eastern and Russian research series, no. 3)

Bonew, *Mme.*
Premiers éléments bibliographiques relatifs aux problèmes actuels du Sud-Est de l'Asie (établie par Madame Bonew). Bruxelles, Centre d'étude du Sud-Est asiatique, 1966.

515 p. 28 cm.

Cordier, Henri, 1849–1925.
Bibliotheca Indosinica. Dictionnaire bibliographique des ouvrages relatifs à la péninsule indochinoise. New York, B. Franklin [1967]
5 v. in 3. 27 cm. (Burt Franklin Bibliographic & reference series. 106)
"Originally published Paris 1912[–32 as] Publications de l'École française d'Extrême-Orient [v. 15–18, 18 bis]"
Forms with the author's Bibliotheca Sinica and his Bibliotheca Japonica a Bibliographie des pays d'Extrême-Orient. Cf. Postface.
CONTENTS.—v. 1. Préface. Birmanie. Assam. Siam. Laos.—v. 2–3. Péninsule malaise. Indochine française.—v. 4–5. Indochine française (suite) Cambodge. Laos. Tchampa. Dernières additions. Postface. Index.

Erickson, Gerald E
Southeast Asia, prepared by Gerald E. Erickson. [n. p., Pacific Air Forces] 1965.

vii, 95 p. 27 cm. (PACAF basic bibliographies)

Ichikawa, Kenjirō.
Southeast Asia viewed from Japan; a bibliography of Japanese works on Southeast Asian societies, 1940–1963. Compiled for the London-Cornell project. Ithaca, N. Y., Southeast Asia Program, Dept. of Asian Studies, Cornell University, 1965.

112 p. 28 cm. (Cornell University. Southeast Asia Program. Data paper no. 56)

Johnson, Donald Clay, 1940–
A guide to reference materials on Southeast Asia, based on the collections in the Yale and Cornell University libraries. New Haven, Yale University Press, 1970.

xi, 160 p. 26 cm. (Yale Southeast Asia studies, 6)

Loofs, Helmut Herman Ernst.
Elements of the megalithic complex in Southeast Asia; an annotated bibliography [by] H. H. E. Loofs. Canberra, Centre of Oriental Studies in association with Australian National University Press [1968]

ix, 114 p. map. 25 cm. (Australian National University, Canberra. Centre of Oriental Studies. Oriental monograph series no. 3)

Meyer, Milton Walter.
Southeast Asia : an introductory bibliography / Milton W. Meyer. — [Los Angeles? : s. n.], 1971.

36 p. ; 28 cm.

Morrison, Gayle.
A guide to books on Southeast Asian history, 1961–1966. Gayle Morrison, comp., Stephen Hay, ed. [Santa Barbara, Calif., American Bibliographical Center [1969]

viii, 105 p. 27 cm. (Bibliography and reference series, no. 8)

Nan-yang ta hsüeh. Nan-yang yen chiu so.
(Nan-yang yen chiu Chung wên ch'i k'an tzŭ liao so yin)
南洋研究中文期刊資料索引 Index to Chinese periodical literature on Southeast Asia, 1905–1966. Singapore, 南洋大學南洋研究所編印 Institute of Southeast

Asia, Nanyang University, 1968.

363 p. 27 cm.

Prefatory matter and table of contents also in English.

Pedersen, Ole Karup.
Litteratur om Sydøstasien. Historie og moderne samfundsforhold. 2. revid. udg. København, Mellemfolkeligt Samvirke, 1966.

14 l. 30 cm.

Shu, Austin C   W
Twentieth century Chinese works on Southeast Asia, a bibliography. Compilation and translation by Austin C. W. Shu and William W. L. Wan. Check-edited by T. W. Kwok. [Honolulu] East-West Center, 1968.

iii, 201 l. 28 cm. (Occasional papers of Research Publications & Translations. Annotated bibliography series, no. 3)

Books, pamphlets, and articles; with authors' names romanized and in characters; titles romanized, in characters, and in English translation.

Based chiefly on Hsü Yün-ch'iao's Preliminary bibliography of Southeast Asian studies, published in Nan-yang yen chiu. The bulletin, v. 1 (1959), p. 1–169, and on Li Yih-yüan's Studies on overseas Chinese in East Asia; a catalog of books and articles in Chinese and Japanese, published in Chung yang yen chiu yüan. Min tsu hsüeh yen chiu so, Nan-kang, Formosa. Chung yang yen chiu yüan min tsu hsüeh yen chiu so chi k'an, v. 18 (1964), p. 143–235.

Southeast Asia: a bibliography for undergraduate libraries [by] Donald Clay Johnson [and others] Williamsport, Pa., Bro-Dart Pub. Co., 1970.

xviii, 59 p. 29 cm. (University of the State of New York. Foreign Area Materials Center. Occasional publication no. 13)

Southeast Asia Treaty Organization.
SEATO publications. Bangkok, Thailand, 1965.

13 p. 28 cm.

Tregonning, K   G
Southeast Asia; a critical bibliography [by] Kennedy G. Tregonning. Tucson, University of Arizona Press [1969]

103 p. 28 cm.

United States. Dept. of the Army. Army Library.
Peninsular Southeast Asia; a bibliographic survey of literature: Burma, Cambodia, Laos, Thailand. Washington, Dept. of the Army; [for sale by the Supt. of Docs., U. S. Govt. Print. Off.] 1972.

xi, 424 p. col. maps (3 fold. in pocket) 26 cm. $8.75

U. S. *Library of Congress. Orientalia Division.*
Southeast Asia; an annotated bibliography of selected reference sources in Western languages, compiled by Cecil Hobbs, head, South Asia Section. Rev. and enl. Washington, [For sale by the Superintendent of Documents, U. S. Govt. Print. Off.] 1964.

v, 180 p. 27 cm.

U. S. *Library of Congress. Orientalia Division.*
Southeast Asia; an annotated bibliography of selected reference sources in Western languages. Compiled by Cecil Hobbs. Rev. and enl. New York, Greenwood Press [1968]

v, 180 p. 32 cm.

Reprint of the 1964 ed.

LIBRARY CATALOGS

Ajia Keizai Kenkyūjo, *Tokyo.*
Union catalogue of documentary materials on Southeast Asia. 東南アジア関係資料総合目録 Tokyo, Institute of Asian Economic Affairs; アジア経済研究所 1964.

5 v. in 1. 26 cm. (アジア経済研究所出版物 通巻第350–354号)

CONTENTS. — v. 1. General and Southeast Asia in general. — v. 2. India (I) The social sciences.—v. 3. India (II) The humanities and natural sciences.—v. 4. Other countries in Asia.—v. 5. Index.

Illinois. Northern Illinois University, De Kalb. Library.
List of recent Southeast Asia acquisitions in the Swen Franklin Parson Library. Compiled by Southeast Asia Librarian and Center for Southeast Asian Studies. De Kalb, 1968.

65 l. 29 cm.

Illinois. Northern Illinois University, De Kalb. Library.
Revised list of Southeast Asia holdings in the Swen Franklin Parson Library. Compiled by Southeast Asia Library & Center for Southeast Asian Studies. De Kalb, 1968.

285 l. 29 cm.

United States. Library of Congress. Orientalia Division.
Southeast Asia subject catalog. Boston, G. K. Hall, 1972–

v. 37 cm.

ASIAN-AFRICAN POLITICS   see   Afro-Asian politics

ASIAN IMPRINTS

California. University. *Library. East Asiatic Library.*
Author-title catalog. Boston, G. K. Hall, 1968.

13 v. 37 cm.

CONTENTS.—v. 1. Radicals 1 — to 9:4 伏—v. 2. Radicals 9:5 佳 to 30:3 名—v. 3. Radicals 30:4 否 to 38 嬾—v. 4. Radicals 39 子 to 57 彌—v. 5. Radicals 58 棄 to 72 日本文—v. 6. Radicals 72 日本稿 to 75:4 杲—v. 7. Radicals 75:4 東 to 85:6 洒—v. 8. Radicals 85:7 洚 to 113:4 祇—v. 9. Radicals 113:5 祖 to 140:8 菲—v. 10. Radicals 140:9 葆 to 162 邏—v. 11. Radicals 163 邑 to 186 香—v. 12. Radicals 187 馬 to 214 龠 Kana & Han'gŭl. Alphabetical supplement A to G.—v. 13. Alphabetical supplement H to Z.

Union catalogue of Asian publications 1965–1970. Edited by David E. Hall. Compiled under the auspices of the Orientalists' Group, Standing Conference of National and University Libraries. Sponsored by and edited at the School of Oriental and African Studies, University of London. London, Mansell, 1971.

4 v. 36 cm.

United States. Library of Congress.
Far Eastern languages catalog. Boston, G. K. Hall, 1972.

22 v. 37 cm.

U. S. Library of Congress. Library of Congress Office, Djakarta.
Accessions list, Indonesia, Malaysia, Singapore, and Brunei. v. 1–
July 1964–
Djakarta.

v. 28 cm.

Frequency varies.

At head of title, 1964–May/June 1969: The Library of Congress Public Law 480 Project; July/Aug. 1969–   The Library of Congress National Program for Acquisitions and Cataloging.

Title varies: July 1964–July/Aug. 1970, Accessions list, Indonesia.

Vols. for 1964–May/June 1969 issued by the office under its earlier name: American Libraries Book Procurement Center, Djakarta.

——————— Cumulative list of serials. Jan. 1964/Sept. 1966–
Djakarta.

> v. 28 cm. annual.
> At head of title. Jan. 1964/Sept. 1966–1964/68: The Library of Congress Public Law 480 Project.
> Vols. for June 1964/Sept. 1966–1964/68 issued by the office under its earlier name: American Libraries Book Procurement Center, Djakarta.
> Kept up to date by supplements.
> Vol. for Oct. 1966/Dec. 1967 bound with v. 2 of the main work.

ASIAN LANGUAGES AND LITERATURE see Oriental languages and literature

ASIAN STUDIES

Bibliography of Asian studies. 1969–
[n. p.] Association for Asian Studies.

> v. 26 cm.
> Previously issued as a part of the Journal of Asian studies.

British Columbia. University. Asian Studies Division.
A bibliography of indexes and abstracts on Asian studies in the Library of University of British Columbia. Vancouver, 1972.

> ii, 47 l. 27 cm. (Its List of catalogued books. Supplement no. 4) (University of British Columbia Library. Reference publication no. 39)

Cumulative bibliography of Asian studies, 1941–1965: subject bibliography. Boston, Mass., G. K. Hall, 1970.

> 4 v. 27 cm.
> Cumulates part of a succession of publications begun ca. 1934 as Lists by the American Council of Learned Societies Devoted to Humanistic Studies' Committee on Far Eastern Studies, continued 1936–40 as the council's Bulletin of Far Eastern bibliography, and from 1941 issued in the Journal of Asian studies (until 1956 Far Eastern quarterly) under titles: Far Eastern bibliography (until 1956), and Bibliography of Asian studies (after 1956).
> The name of the body issuing the bibliography since 1941 (Association of Asian Studies) appears on t. p.
> CONTENTS.—v. 1. Asia–China-H.—v. 2. China-I–India-L.—v. 3. India-M—Korea-L.—v. 4. Korea-M—Vietnam, Cambodia and Laos.

Livotova, Ol'ga Émanuilovna.
Востоковедение в изданиях Академии наук, 1726–1917; библиография. Москва, Наука; Глав. ред. восточной лит-ры, 1966.

> 142 p. 22 cm.
> At head of title: Академия наук СССР. Институт народов Азии. О. Э. Ливотова, В. Б. Португаль.

Opitz, Fritz.
Die Ostasienforschung in der Bundesrepublik Deutschland. Hamburg (Institut für Asienkunde) 1967.

> 61 p. 21 cm. (Mitteilungen des Instituts für Asienkunde Hamburg, Nr. 18)

Pearson, James Douglas, 1911–
Oriental and Asian bibliography; an introduction with some reference to Africa [by] J. D. Pearson. Hamden, Conn., Archon Books, 1966.

> xvi, 261 p. 23 cm.

Pearson, James Douglas, 1911–
Oriental and Asian bibliography: an introduction with some reference to Africa [by] J. D. Pearson. London, Lockwood, 1966.

> xvi, 261 p. 22½ cm.

ASIANS IN THE UNITED STATES see also under Dissertations, Academic

Engelberg, Linda.
Ethnic groups in the United States: a bibliography of books and articles of groups in Hawaii and on the mainland: Chinese, Filipinos, Hawaiians, Japanese, Koreans, Samoans. Prepared by Linda Engelberg and Joan Hori. [Honolulu] University of Hawaii, Sinclair Undergraduate Library, 1972.

> [14 p. 28 cm.

Fujimoto, Isao.
Asians in America: a selected annotated bibliography, by Isao Fujimoto, Michiyo Yamaguchi Swift, and Rosalie Zucker. [Davis, Calif.] 1971.

> x, 205 p. 28 cm. (University of California, Davis. Asian American Studies Division. Working publication no. 5)

Kitano, Harry H   L
Asians in America; a selected bibliography for use in social work education. Compiled by Harry H. L. Kitano. New York, Council on Social Work Education [1971]

> vii, 79 p. 24 cm.

ASIATIC SOCIETY, CALCUTTA

Asiatic Society, *Calcutta.*
Index to the publications of the Asiatic Society, 1788–1953. Compiled by Sibadas Chaudhuri. Calcutta, 1956–

> v. in 25 cm. (Its Journal. Extra number. 3d ser., v. 22–23
> CONTENTS.—v. 1, pt. 1. Asiatick researches. Journal (3 series up to 1953). Memoirs. Miscellaneous publications. pt. 2. Bibliotheca Indica series. Proceedings and year-books. Miscellaneous notes in the Journal of the Society. Miscellaneous publications.

ASIMOV, ISAAC

Miller, Marjorie M
Isaac Asimov: a checklist of works published in the United States, March 1939–May 1972, by Marjorie M. Miller. With a note by Isaac Asimov. [1st ed. Kent, Ohio] Kent State University Press [1972]

> xiii, 98 p. 23 cm. (The Serif series: bibliographies and checklists, no. 25)

Tepper, Matthew Bruce.
The Asimov science fiction bibliography. Compiled by M. B. Tepper. Santa Monica, Chinese Ducked Press, 1970.

> 1 v. (unpaged) 22 cm.

ASPHALT

Mullens, Marjorie C
Selected annotated bibliography on asphalt-bearing rocks of the United States and Canada, to 1970, by Marjorie C. Mullens and Albert E. Roberts. Washington, U.S. Govt. Print. Off., 1972.

> iv, 218 p. illus. 24 cm. (Geological Survey bulletin 1352)

ASRATIAN, ÉZRAS ASRATOVICH

Simonov, Pavel Vasil'evich.
Эзрас Асратович Асратян. Вступ. статья П. В. Симонова. Библиография составлена Г. Н. Финашиной. Москва, Наука, 1967.

> 91 p. port. 17 cm. (Материалы к биобиблиографии ученых СССР. Серия биологических наук: Физиология, вып. 9)

ASSAMESE LITERATURE

Shastri, P   N   1923–
The Writers Workshop handbook of Assamese literature [by] P. N. Shastri & P. Lal. Calcutta, Writers Workshop,

v. 23 cm. c1972–

Title on spine: Assamese literature.
Running title: The WW handbook of Assamese literature.
"A Writers Workshop greybird book."

ASTAUROV, BORIS L'VOVICH

Goriacheva, R   I
(Boris L'vovich Astaurov)
Борис Львович Астауров. Вступит. статья П. Ф. Рокицкого. Библиогр. сост. Р. И. Горячевой и А. Л. Тепеницыной. Москва, "Наука," 1972.

67 p. port. 16 cm. (Материалы к биобиблиографии ученых СССР. Серия биологических наук: Генетика, вып. 2) (Биобиблиография ученых СССР)

ASTROLOGY

McGurk, Patrick.
Astrological manuscripts in Italian libraries (other than Rome). London, Warburg Institute, 1966.

xxx, 111 p. plates. 24 cm. (London. University. Warburg Institute. Catalogue of astrological and mythological illuminated manuscripts of the Latin Middle Ages, 4)

ASTRONAUTICS
see also Space sciences

Aerospace bibliography. 3d- ed. Washington, For sale by the Supt. of Docs., U. S. Govt. Print. Off. [1966]–

v. illus. 26 cm.

The first 2 editions were each issued in 3 pts. and published separately with special titles.
Third ed. compiled by the National Aerospace Education Council for the Educational Programs Division of the National Aeronautics and Space Administration; 4th ed.– by the council for the Administration.

Beard, Robert Brookes.
Soviet cosmonautics 1957–1969: a bibliography of articles published in British periodicals and of British and foreign books, by Robert Beard. Swindon, (Wilts.), R. Beard, 1970.

43 p. 26 cm.

Bulletin signalétique: Série engins, espace. no. 73–94; jan.–déc. 1968. [Paris] Centre de documentation de l'armement.

22 no. 25 cm. semimonthly.

Supersedes in part Bulletin signalétique, issued 1965–67 by the Service de documentation scientifique et technique de l'armement, and continues its numbering.

Filipowsky, Richard F
Space communications: theory and applications; a bibliography ... 1958–1963. Compiled by Richard F. Filipowsky and Louise C. Bickford. Washington, Scientific and Technical Information Division, National Aeronautics and Space Administration; [for sale by the Superintendent of Documents, U. S. Govt. Print. Off.] 1965.
4 v. 26 cm. (NASA SP-7022(01)–7022(04))
"Compiled by the Federal Systems Division, IBM, for the National Aeronautics and Space Administration under contract no. NASw-981."
CONTENTS.–v. 1. Modulation and channels.–v. 2. Coding and detection theory.–v. 3. Information processing and advanced techniques.–v. 4. Satellite and deep space applications.

Космос рядом с нами; рекомендательный указатель литературы для молодежи. [Составители: О. А. Ермолаева и др.] Москва, Книга, 1967.

93 p. illus., facsim. 22 cm.

On verso of t. p.: Государственная библиотека СССР им. В. И. Ленина. Центральная политехническая библиотека.

Liapunov, Boris Valerianovich.
[Liudi, rakety, knigi]

Люди, ракеты, книги. [Обзор литературы]. Москва, "Книга," 1972.

95 p. with illus. 20 cm.

Реферативный журнал: Исследование космического пространства.
Москва.

v. 27 cm. monthly.

"Отдельный выпуск."
Series 62 of Реферативный журнал.
Began in 1964. Cf. Letopis' periodicheskikh izdanii SSSR, Apr. 1963–Apr. 1965.
Vols. for 1964–66 issued by Institut nauchnoi informatsii of the Akademiia nauk SSSR; 1967– by Vsesoiuznyi institut nauchnoi i tekhnicheskoi informatsii of Gosudarstvennyi komitet po nauke i tekhnike.

Sergeeva, N   A
Дорога в космос. Рек. указ. литературы. Москва, "Знание," 1971.

31 p. 20 cm. (В помощь лектору)

United States.   National Aeronautics and Space Administration.   Scientific and Technical Information Office.
NASA patent abstracts bibliography. Jan. 1972–

Washington.

v. 27 cm. semiannual. (NASA SP)

Vols. for Jan. 1972– issued in two sections (e. g., section 1: Abstracts; section 2: Indexes)

BIBLIOGRAPHIES see Aeronautics - Bibliographies

ASTRONOMY

Abt, Helmut A
Bibliography of stellar radial velocities, by Helmut A. Abt and Eleanor S. Biggs. Compiled at the Kitt Peak National Observatory. New York, Printed by Latham Process Corp., 1972.

vii, 502 p. 29 cm.

Akademiia nauk URSR, *Kiev. Biblioteka.*
Астрономія на Україні, 1918–1962 рр.; бібліографічний покажчик. За ред. І. Г. Колчинського. Київ [Наукова думка] 1965.

160, [4] p. 22 cm.

At head of title: Академія наук Української РСР. Державна публічна бібліотека. Т. А. Азарнова, Н. О. Шемець.

Astronomy and astrophysics abstracts. v. 1–
1969–
Berlin, New York, Springer-Verlag.

v. 26 cm. semiannual.

Supersedes Astronomischer Jahresbericht.
Vols. for 1969– published for Astronomisches Rechen-Institut, Heidelberg.

Astrophysical abstracts. v. 1–
Aug. 1969–
London, New York, Gordon and Breach Science Publishers.

v. 27 cm. 4 no. a year.

Brown, Basil J   W
Astronomical atlases, maps & charts; an historical & general guide [by] Basil Brown. London, Dawsons of Pall Mall, 1968.

200 p. illus., charts, maps. 25 cm.

"First published in London, 1932."

Collinder, Per Arne, 1890–
Astronomical works and papers printed in Sweden between 1881 and 1898. Bibliography and historical notes [by] P. Collinder. Stockholm, Almqvist & Wiksell, 1966.

323–339 p. 24 cm. (Arkiv för astronomi, bd. 4, nr. 19)

Uppsala astronomiska observatorium. Meddelande, n:o 159.

Elvove, Solomon, 1923–
Astronomical data in machine readable form. Washington, U. S. Naval Observatory, 1967.

[10] p. 26 cm. (U. S. Naval Observatory. Circular no. 114)

Caption title.
Supersedes Circular no. 111, 4 January 1966.

Elvove, Solomon, 1923–
Astronomical data in machine readable form. Washington, U. S. Naval Observatory, 1970.

[11] p. 27 cm. (United States. Naval Observatory. Circular no. 128)

Supersedes Circular 114, 16 January 1967.

[**Hamann, Günther**]
Das Werden eines neuen astronomischen Weltbildes im Spiegel alter Handschriften und Druckwerke. Ausstellung zum 500. Geburtsjahr v. Nicolaus Copernicus ⟨*Thorn/Torun 19. Febr. 1473, †Frauenburg/Frombork 24. Mai 1543⟩. Veranst. v. d. Österr. Akad. d. Wiss. in Gemeinschaft mit d. Österr. Nationalbibliothek im Rahmen des v. d. Österr. UNESCO-Kommission initiierten "Copernicus-Jahres." Geöffnet v. Mai bis Okt. 1973 im Prunksaal d. Österr. Nationalbibliothek. Wien. (Führer durch die Ausstellung:

Günther Hamann [und] Konradin Ferrari d'Occhieppo.) (Wien, Österr. Akad. d. Wiss., 1973.)

47 p. 21 cm.

Johns, Gerald.
Astronomical literature in the Ernst Zinner collection, San Diego State College Library; a checklist. Compiled by Gerald Johns. [San Diego] Friends of the Library, San Diego State College, 1969.

66 p. illus., ports. 22 cm.

Kemp, D   Alasdair.
Astronomy and astrophysics; a bibliographical guide [by] D. A. Kemp. Foreword by H. A. Brück. London, Macdonald Technical & Scientific; [Hamden, Conn.] Archon Books, 1970.

xxiii, 584 p. 26 cm. (The Macdonald bibliographical guides)

Kilmartin, P   M
The Magellanic Clouds; a bibliography, 1951–1972, compiled by P. M. Kilmartin. Wellington, Carter Observatory, 1973.

68 p. 22 cm. (Carter Observatory. Wellington, N. Z. Astronomical bulletin, no. 79)

Korzeniewska, Iwona.
Bibliografia prac astronomów polskich za lata 1923–1963. Warszawa, Polskie Tow. Astronomiczne, 1964.

iii, 221 p. 29 cm.

Lalande, Joseph Jérôme Le Français de, 1732–1807.
Bibliographie astronomique; avec l'histoire de l'astronomie depuis 1781 jusqu'à 1802. Amsterdam, J. C. Gieben, 1970.

viii, 966 p. 24 cm.

"Réimpression de l'édition Paris, 1803."

Lavrova, Nataliia Borisovna.
Библиография русской астрономической литературы 1800–1900 гг. Под. ред. Д. Я. Мартынова и П. Г. Куликовского. Москва, Изд. Моск. ун-та, 1968.

386 p. 21 cm. (Труды Государственного астрономического института имени П. К. Штернберга, т. 37)

Library Association. County Libraries Group.
Readers' guide to books on astronomy. 2nd ed. London, Library Association, 1969.

19 p. 19 cm. (Its Readers' guide, new ser., no. 107)

Matulaityté, S
Astronomai; bibliografiné rodyklé. Moksl. red. ir iž. straipsnio aut.: P. Slavénas. Vilnius, 1965.

79 p. 20 cm. (Tarybu Lietuvos mokslinikai)

At head of title: Lietuvos TSR Valstybiné respublikiné biblioteka. S. Matulaityté.
Added title pages in Russian and English.
Table of contents also in Russian and English; summaries in Russian and English.

Merman, S   A
Достижения современной радиоастрономии. Рек. список литературы. Москва, "Знание," 1968.

13 p. 19 cm. (В помощьлектору)

At head of title: Всесоюзное общество "Знание." Центральная политехническая библиотека.

Moore, Patrick.
Astronomy and space research. London, National Book League, 1969.

22 p. 22 cm.

Nasedkina, Vera Aleksandrovna.
[Bol'shaia Vselennaia]
Большая Вселенная. Рек. указ. литературы. Москва, "Книга," 1971.

76 p. 20 cm.

Ordina, G   P
Звезды открывают тайны. [Сост. Г. П. Ордина] Рек. обзор литературы. [Москва, "Книга," 1968].

17 p. 17 cm. (Новое в науке и технике, вып. 21)

Cover title.
Caption title: Звезды раскрывают тайны.
"Государственная ордена Ленина библиотека СССР имени В. И. Ленина. Центральная политехническая библиотека."

Pingree, David Edwin, 1933–
Sanskrit astronomical tables in the United States [by] David Pingree. Philadelphia, American Philosophical Society, 1968.

77 p. 30 cm. (Transactions of the American Philosophical Society, new ser., v. 58, pt. 3)

Sen, Samarendra Nath, 1918–
A bibliography of Sanskrit works on astronomy and mathematics, by S. N. Sen, with the research assistance of A. K. Bag and S. Rajeswar Sarma. New Delhi, National Institute of Sciences of India [1966–

v. 23 cm. (National Commission for the Compilation of History of Sciences in India. Source materials series)
Bibliographical references included in "Abbreviations for the manuscript catalogues," and "Abbreviations of periodicals": v. 1, p. xi–xxiii.
CONTENTS.—pt. 1. Manuscripts, texts, translations & studies.

Tochio, Takeshi, 1929–
(Kokon tosho shūsei in'yōsho mokuroku kō, rekishōihen)

古今圖書集成引用書目錄稿　暦象彙編　栃尾武
編　町田　桜美林大学文学部中国語中国文学研究
室　汲古書院（発売）　1972-

    v. illus. 25 cm.

    CONTENTS: ₍1₎-₍2₎ 乾象典

Wattenberg, Diedrich.
    Forschungen und Publikationen zur Geschichte der Astro-
nomie in der Deutschen Demokratischen Republik. Eine
Bibliographie ⟨1949–1969⟩. Mit 4 Taf. Berlin-Treptow
(Archenhold-Sternwarte) 1969.

    138 p. illus. 21 cm. (Veröffentlichungen der Archenhold-Stern-
warte Berlin-Treptow, Nr. 2)

Yang, Shih.
    Man probes the universe. Foreword by Estelle M. Per-
rault. ₍Eunice₎ Ledoux Library, Louisiana State University at Eunice, 1970.

    10 l. 28 cm. (LeDoux Library. Bibliography 2)

    PERIODICALS

São Paulo, Brazil (City)　Universidade. *Instituto Astronômico e Geofísico. Biblioteca.*
    Catálogo das publicações periódicas existentes na Biblio-
teca do Instituto Astronômico e Geofísico, desde 1886 até
1962. São Paulo, 1964.

    xvi, 383 p. 24 cm.

ASTROPHYSICS see Astrology

ATHEISM

Arendaş, Margareta.
    În sprijinul propagandei ateist-ştiinţifice. Bibliografie
pentru lectori şi conferenţiari. Oradea, Biblioteca munici-
palä Oradea. 1972.

    12 l. 26 cm.

Chevalier, Bernadette.
    L'athéisme dans le monde moderne de 1955 à mars 1969.
Bibliographie analytique. Genève ₍1969₎.

    ii, 47 p. 30 cm.

    "Diplôme de l'École de bibliothécaires."

Kaushanskiĭ, Pavel L'vovich.
    О новых работах по научному атеизму. (Краткая
библиогр.) Москва, 1970.

    44 p. 20 cm. (В помощь лектору)

    At head of title: Общество "Знание" РСФСР. Научно-методи-
ческий совет по пропаганде научного атеизма. П. Л. Каушан-
ский.

Kopylova, V　　　N
    В. И. Ленин об атеизме и религии. Книги, журн.
статьи и статьи из сборников на рус. яз. за 1958–1968 гг.
Москва, 1969.

    38 p. 20 cm. (Библиографические и методические материалы
в помощь областным, краевым и республиканским библиотекам)

Leŭ, E　　　I
    Праўда пра рэлігію: рэкамендацыйны спіс літаратуры.
₍Складальнікі: Е. І. Леу, В. М. Сіленка, І. Ул. Смыкава₎
Мінск, 1969.

    3 pamphlets in portfolio. 20 cm.

    Cover title.
    At head of title: Дзяржаўная бібліятэка БССР імя У. І. Леніна.

Основы научного атеизма: рекомендательный указатель
литературы. ₍Составители: Г. Н. Белавенцева и др. Редактор Ю. М. Тугов₎ Москва, Книга, 1966.

    181 p. 22 cm.

    At head of title: Государственная библиотека СССР им. В. И.
Ленина.

Poškutė, B
    Mokslas ir religija. Rekomenduojamosios literatūros
rodyklė. Vilnius, 1968.

    75 p. 20 cm.

Zinātniski ateistiskai propagandai. Bibliogrāfija un
metodiskas rekomendācijas. Rīgā, 1971.

    59 p. 20 cm.

    At head of title: Viļa Lāča Latvijas PSR Valsts bibliotēka. Zināt-
niski metodiskā un bibliogrāfiskā darba nodaļa.
    Title also in Russian: В помощь научно-атеистической пропа-
ганде.
    By B. Arnicāne and others.
    Latvian and Russian.

ATHLETICS see Physical education; Sports

ATHOS, MOUNT

Ntelopoulos, Kyriakos.
    ₍Symvolē stē vivliographia tou Hagiou Orous₎
    Συμβολὴ στὴ βιβλιογραφία τοῦ Ἁγίου Ὄρους· αὐτοτελεῖς
ἐκδόσεις, 1701–1971. Ἀθῆναι, 1971.

    69 p. 23 cm. (₍Βιβλιογραφικὲs ἔρευνες, 1₎)

ATLANTIC REGION see North Atlantic region

ATLASES

Alexander, Gerard L
    Guide to atlases: world, regional, national, thematic; an
international listing of atlases published since 1950, by
Gerard L. Alexander. Metuchen, N. J., Scarecrow Press,
1971.

    671 p. 22 cm.

Koeman, Cornelis.
    Atlantes Neerlandici. Bibliography of terrestrial, mari-
time and celestial atlases and pilot books, published in the
Netherlands up to 1880. Compiled and edited by C. Koeman. Amsterdam, Theatrum Orbis Terrarum, 1967-₍71₎

    5 v. illus. 31 cm.

Polska Akademia Nauk. Instytut Geografii.
    National and regional atlases: sources, bibliography, arti-
cles. Prepared by Jolanta Drecka, Halina Tuszyńska
-Rękawek, under the direction of Stanisław Leszczycki. ₍2d
ed.₎ Warsaw, 1964.

    155 p. 3 fold. col. maps (in pocket) 21 cm. (Dokumentacja geo-
graficzna, nr. 1)

    Preface also in Russian.
    Presented at the 20th International Geographical Congress.
    First ed. published in 1960 under title: National atlases, sources,
bibliography, articles.

————— Supplement for 1963–1967, prepared by Halina
Tuszyńska-Rękawek, Jolanta Drecka, under the direction of
Stanisław Leszczycki. Warsaw, 1968.

    73 p. 21 cm. (Dokumentacja geograficzna, zesz. 1)

    Prepared for the 21st International Geographical Congress.

————— ₍Supplement₎ for 1968–1971, prepared by Halina
Tuszyńska-Rękawek and Stanisław Leszczycki. Warszawa,

1972.

92 p. 21 cm. (Dokumentacja geograficzna, zesz. 3)
Preface also in Russian.
Prepared for the 22d International Geographical Congress.

Riedlová, Marie.
Přírodovědné a zemědělské atlasy ve fondech Státní vědecké knihovny v Olomouci. Zprac. Marie Riedlová. Olomouc, St. věd. knihovna, rozmn., 1969.

28, ₁1₁ p. 29 cm. (Publikace Státní vědecké knihovny v Olomouci, čis. 3/1969)

Walsh, James Patrick, *comp.*
General world atlases in print; a comparative analysis, compiled by S. Padraig Walsh. 1966 ed. New York, R. R. Bowker Co. ₁1966₁

66 p. 22 cm.

Walsh, James Patrick, comp.
General world atlases in print, 1972–1973; a comparative analysis, compiled by S. Padraig Walsh. ₁4th ed., enl.₁ New York, Bowker ₁1973₁

ix, 211 p. 23 cm.

LIBRARY AND EXHIBITION CATALOGS

Canada. Public Archives. National Map Collection.
Atlases published in the Netherlands in the rare atlas collection. Atlas publiés aux Pays-Bas se trouvant dans la collection d'atlas rares. Compiled and edited by Lou Seboek. ₁Ottawa₁ 1973.
xvi, 132 p. 28 cm.
Dutch or Latin; introductory material in English and French.
"No. 1 in a provisional series describing the atlases in the National Map Collection by country of origin."

Greenwich, Eng. National Maritime Museum. Library.
Atlases & cartography. London, H. M. S. O., 1971.

2 v. (xi, 1166 p.) 12 plates, illus., charts, facsims., maps, port. 25 cm. index. (Its Catalogue of the library, v. 3)

London, Ont. University of Western Ontario. Library.
Atlases in University collections. London, Ont. ₁1971₁
ii, 59 l. 22 x 28 cm.

Manchester, *Eng. Public Libraries. Commercial Library & Information Dept.*
National and economic atlases available in the Commercial Library. Manchester, Manchester Public Libraries, 1968.
₁1₁, 14 p. 25 cm. (*Its* Business bibliographies, 5)

United States. Library of Congress. Map Division.
A list of geographical atlases in the Library of Congress, compiled by Philip Lee Phillips. Amsterdam, Theatrum Orbis Terrarum, 1971.

4 v. in 2 23 cm.

Reprint of the first 4 vols. of the 6 vol. Washington, 1909–1920 ed.

United States. Library of Congress. Map Division.
United States atlases; a list of national, state, county, city, and regional atlases in the Library of Congress. Compiled by Clara Egli Le Gear. New York, Arno Press, 1971.

viii, 445 p. 24 cm.

Reprint of the 1950 ed.
Cover title: United States atlases in the Library of Congress.

Utrecht. Rijksuniversiteit. Geografisch Instituut.
400 ₁i. e. vier honderd₁ jaar atlas. Catalogus van de tentoonstelling Geografisch Instituut, Rijksuniversiteit

Utrecht, 1 oktober–27 november 1970. ₁Amsterdam, Theatrum Orbis Terrarum, 1970₁

₁36₁ p. 21 cm.

ATMOSPHERE, UPPER

Italy. Consiglio nazionale delle ricerche. Istituto di fisica dell'atmosfera.
Elenco delle pubblicazioni. 2. edizione aggiornata al 15 ottobre 1969. Roma, Istituto di fisica dell'atmosfera, 1969.

43 p. 24½ cm. (IFA-PV, n. 34)

Edited by F. M. Vivona.

ATOM; ATOMIC ENERGY
see also   Nuclear physics

Anthony, L   J
Sources of information on atomic energy, by L. J. Anthony. ₁1st ed.₁ Oxford, New York, Pergamon Press ₁1966₁

x, 245 p. 24 cm. (International series of monographs in library and information science, v. 2)

Argentine Republic. Comisión Nacional de Energía Atómica.
Catálogo de informes publicados. Buenos Aires, 1971.

54 p. 30 cm.

Argentine Republic. *Comisión Nacional de Energía Atómica.*
Lista de informes publicados por la Comisión Nacional de Energía Atómica. Buenos Aires, 1967.

₁10₁ p. 27 cm.

Atomindex.

Vienna, International Atomic Energy Agency.

v. in   21 cm.   semimonthly.

Continues List of references on nuclear energy issued by International Atomic Energy Agency.

Australia. Atomic Energy Commission. Research Establishment.
List of report publications. Lucas Heights, 1970.

90 p. 30 cm.

Berton, Micheline.
Applications scientifiques des explosions nucléaires. ₁Saclay, Service de documentation du C. E. A., Centre d'études nucléaires de Saclay₁ 196
v. 27 cm. (v. 3: 30 cm.) (Bibliographie CEA no
At head of title, v. 3: Centre d'études de Bruyères-le-Chatel.
Vol. 3 has title: Applications pacifiques des explosions nucléaires.
Summaries in English.
CONTENTS:
—ptie. 2. Géologie, séismologie, étude des sols, fracture des roches.—
ptie. 3. Mines, chimie, extraction de gaz et de pétroles.
—— Applications pacifiques des explosions nucléaires. Géologie, séismologie, comportement des sols et des roches;
₁additif à la bibliographie no 66. Saclay, Service central de documentation du C. E. A., Centre d'études nucléaires de Saclay; vente et diffusion à La Documentation française. Secrétariat général du Gouvernement, Direction de la documentation, Paris₁ 1969
200 p. 30 cm. (Bibliographie CEA–BIB–152)
At head of title: Centre d'études de Bruyères-le-Chatel.

Bulletin signalétique 165: Physique atomique et moléculaire.
v. 34–   1973–
Paris, Centre national de la recherche scientifique, Centre de documentation.

v. 30 cm.

Supersedes in part Bulletin signalétique 160. Structure de la matière I—physique de l'état condensé, physique atomique et moléculaire, spectroscopie.

Euro abstracts. v. 8–
Jan. 1970–
[Brussels]

v. 30 cm.

Continues Euratom information.
Dutch, French, German or Italian and English.
Published by the Commission of the European Communities, Directorate-General Dissemination of Information.

France. *Commissariat à l'énergie atomique.*
Liste récapitulative des textes C. E. A. publiés dans la presse scientifique, 1962–1964. [Gif-sur-Yvette (S.-et-O.) Commissariat à l'énergie atomique, Centre d'études nucléaires de Saclay, Service de documentation] 1965.

573 p. 27 cm. (*Its* Série "Bibliothèque", BIB. 1005)

At head of title: Service central de documentation.

International Atomic Energy Agency.
Peaceful uses of nuclear explosions. (Comp. by V. Ionescu.) Vienna, Internat. Atomic Energy Agency, 1970.

466 p. 24 cm. (*Its* Bibliographical series, no. 38)

United States. Atomic Energy Commission.
A bibliography of basic books on atomic energy. [Oak Ridge, Tenn.] United States Atomic Energy Commission, Office of Information Services, 1971.

ii, 58 p. illus. 22 cm. (The World of the atom series, WAS-002)

U. S. *Atomic Energy Commission.*
Books on atomic energy for adults and children. [Oak Ridge, Tenn.] U. S. Atomic Energy Commission, Division of Technical Information [1969]

48 p. illus., ports. 22 cm. (*Its* Understanding the atom series)

United States. Atomic Energy Commission.
Index to AEC information booklets. [Oak Ridge, Tenn., U. S. Atomic Energy Commission, Office of Information Services, 1972]

iii, 66 p. illus. 22 cm.

Cover title.
Supersedes its Index to the Understanding the atom series.

U. S. *Atomic Energy Commission.*
Index to the Understanding the atom series. [Oak Ridge, Tenn.] U. S. Atomic Energy Commission, Division of Technical Information [1967]

10 p. 22 cm. (Understanding the atom)

U. S. *Atomic Energy Commission.*
Index to the understanding the atom series. [Oak Ridge, Tenn., U. S. Atomic Energy Commission, Division of Technical Information, 1968]

12 p. 22 cm. (Understanding the atom)

U. S. *Atomic Energy Commission.*
Index to the Understanding the atom series. [Oak Ridge, Tenn.] U. S. Atomic Energy Commission, Division of Technical Information [1970]

iii, 33 p. illus. 22 cm. (*Its* Understanding the atom series)

U. S. *Atomic Energy Commission.*
Reading resources in atomic energy. [Oak Ridge, Tenn.] U. S. Atomic Energy Commission, Division of Technical

Information [1968]

iv, 20 p. 22 cm. (Understanding the atom)

West, Robert G
Plowshare; a selected, annotated bibliography of the civil, industrial, and scientific uses for nuclear explosions, compiled by Robert G. West [and] Robert C. Kelly. Oak Ridge, Tenn., U. S. Atomic Energy Commission, Division of Technical Information Extension; [available from the National Technical Information Service, Springfield, Va.] 1971.

vii, 359 p. 27 cm.

———— [Supplement 1–] Compiled by Robert C. Kelly. Oak Ridge, Tenn., U. S. Atomic Energy Commission, Technical Information Center; [available from the National Technical Information Service, Springfield, Va.] 1972–

v. 27 cm.

LIBRARY CATALOGS

International Atomic Energy Agency. Library.
IAEA library catalogue of books. 1968/70–
Vienna.

v. 30 cm. (International Atomic Energy Agency. IAEA)

"A technical report published by the International Atomic Energy Agency."
Vols. for are cumulations of the library's IAEA library new acquisitions.

International Atomic Energy Agency. Library.
IAEA Library, new acquisitions. v. 12, no. 7–v. 13, no. 8.; July 1970–Aug. 1971. Vienna.

2 v. 25 cm. monthly.

Continues its Recent acquisitions.
Continued by its New acquisitions in the IAEA and UNIDO libraries.

International Atomic Energy Agency. Library.
New acquisitions in the IAEA and UNIDO libraries. v. 13, no. 9–
Sept. 1971–
Vienna.

v. 25 cm. monthly.

Continues its IAEA Library, new acquisitions.
Vols. for Sept. 1971– include the new acquisitions in the United Nations Industrial Development Organization Library.

Kokuritsu Kokkai Toshokan, *Tokyo.*
Catalogue of foreign atomic energy reports acquired by the National Diet Library. v. 1– 1966/67–
Tokyo.

v. 26 cm. annual.

Report year ends Mar. 31.

Cover title, 1966/67– ：外国原子力関係機関刊行資料目録

PERIODICALS

Denmark. *Atomenergikommissionen. Biblioteket.*
Tidsskriftkatalog. 2. udg. Risø, 1965.

3, 102 p. 29 cm.

Denmark. *Atomenergikommissionen. Biblioteket.*
Tidsskriftkatalog. 3. udg. Risø, 1967.

3, 108 p. 29 cm.

Denmark. *Atomenergikommissionen. Biblioteket.*
Tidsskriftkatalog. 5. udg. Risø, Atomenergikommissionen, 1969.

3, 118 p. 29 cm.

ATOMIC FUEL see Nuclear fuels

ATOMIC POWER INDUSTRY

Bioenvironmental effects associated with nuclear power plants; a selected bibliography. Compiled by Ramona A. Mayer ₁and others₎ Columbus, Ohio, Battelle, Columbus Laboratories, 1972.

iii, 292 p. 28 cm.

"Prepared under Battelle Memorial Institute Columbus Laboratories, U. S. Atomic Energy Commission contract W–7405–3ng–92 (Task 23)."

International Atomic Energy Agency.
Nuclear power economics; ₁bibliography₎ Vienna, 1964.

144 p. 24 cm. (*Its* Bibliographical series, no. 13)

Foreword in English, French, Russian, and Spanish.

Rossouw, S   F
Nuclear power economics; a bibliography covering 1965–1966, compiled by S. F. Rossouw. **Pretoria, Atomic Energy Board, 1968.**

70 p. 30 cm. (Atomic Energy Board. PEL 167)

South Africa. *Atomic Energy Board. Liaison and Information Division.*
Nuclear power economics, a bibliography covering 1963–1965. Compiled by S. F. Rossouw. ₁Pretoria? Pelindaba, 1966₎

115 l. 30 cm.

ATOMIC SPECTRA

Fuhr, J   R
Bibliography on atomic line shapes and shifts (1889 through March 1972) ₁by₎ J. R. Fuhr, W. L. Wiese, and L. J. Roszman. ₁Washington₎ National Bureau of Standards; ₁for sale by the Supt. of Docs., U.S. Govt. Print. Off.₎ 1972.

x, 154 p. 26 cm. (NBS special publication 366)

Hagan, Lucy.
Bibliography on atomic energy levels and spectra, July 1968 through June 1971 ₁by₎ Lucy Hagan and W. C. Martin. Washington, National Bureau of Standards; for sale by the Supt. of Docs., U.S. Govt. Print. Off., 1972.

iv, 102 p. 27 cm. (National Bureau of Standards special publication 363)

Moore, Charlotte Emma, 1898–
Bibliography on the analyses of optical atomic spectra ₁by₎ Charlotte E. Moore. ₁Gaithersburg, Md.₎ U. S. National Bureau of Standards; for sale by the Supt. of Docs., U. S. Govt. Print. Off., Washington, 1968–69.

4 v. 27 cm. (National Bureau of Standards special publication 306, 306–2, 306–3, 306–4)

ATOMIC WEAPONS

Germany (*Federal Republic, 1949–   *) *Bundestag. Wissenschaftliche Abteilung.*
Kernwaffen und internationale Sicherheit; Auswahlbibliographie. Bonn, 1967.

77 p. 30 cm. (*Its* Bibliographien, Nr. 14)

Germany (*Federal Republic, 1949–   *) *Bundestag. Wissenschaftliche Abteilung.*
Nukleare Sicherheitspolitik der einzelnen Staaten; Auswahlbibliographie. ₁Bonn₎ 1968.

39 p. 30 cm. (*Its* Bibliographien, Nr. 15)

"Die Bibliographie wurde im Referat Fachdokumentation von Herrn Dr. Wolfram-Georg Riggert bearbeitet."

Nagasaki Kenritsu Nagasaki Toshokan.
(Gensuibaku kankei shimbun kiji sakuin)
原水爆関係新聞記事索引　県立長崎図書館蔵
昭和20年8月-昭和45年12月　長崎　長崎県立長崎
図書館　昭和46(1971)

294 p. 26 cm.

U. S. *Dept. of the Army.*
Nuclear weapons and NATO; analytical survey of literature. Washington, 1970.

viii, 450 p. illus. (part fold.), maps (part fold. col.) 27 cm.

U. S. *Dept. of the Army.*
Nuclear weapons and the Atlantic alliance; a bibliographic survey. Washington, 1965.

vi, 193 p. 1 fold. col. map. 26 cm.

AUBE, FRANCE (Dept.)

Aube, *France (Dept.). Archives départementales.*
Répertoire numérique de la série O (administration communale, voirie, dons et legs), dressé par Jean Andrieux ₁et al.₎ Sous las direction de Gildas Bernard. Troyes, Impr. La Renaissance, 1969.

881 p. fold. col. map. 32 cm.

On spine: Répertoire numérique détaillé de la série O.

Aube, France (Dept.). Archives départementales.
Répertoire numérique de la série R (affaires militaires), 1800–1939. Dressé par Gildas Bernard ... Troyes, 21, rue Étienne-Pédron, 1970.

235 p. plates. 31 cm.

Société académique de l'Aube.
Répertoire numérique des archives déposées par la Société académique de l'Aube (sous-série 2 J) dressé par Pierre Piétresson de Saint-Aubin et Gildas Bernard. Troyes, Impr. la Renaissance, 1966.

160 p. plates. 24 cm.

At head of title: Archives départementales de L'Aube.

AUBURN, NEW YORK

Kabelac, Karl Sanford.
Book publishing in Auburn, New York, 1851–1876; an introduction and an imprints bibliography. **Aurora, N. Y., 1969.**

iii, 136 l. 29 cm.

Thesis—State University College, Oneonta, N. Y.
Photocopy of typescript.

AUDEN, WYSTAN HUGH

Bloomfield, Barry Cambray.
W. H. Auden, a bibliography; the early years through 1955, by B. C. Bloomfield. With a foreword by W. H. Auden. Charlottesville, Published for the Bibliographical Society of the University of Virginia ₁by₎ the University Press of Virginia ₁1964₎

xix, 171 p. 24 cm.

Bloomfield, Barry Cambray.
W. H. Auden: a bibliography 1924–1969 ₁by₎ B. C. Bloomfield and Edward Mendelson. 2d ed. Charlottes-

ville, Published for the Bibliographical Society of the University of Virginia, by the University Press of Virginia ₍1972₎

xvi, 420 p. port. 26 cm.

AUDIO-VISUAL EDUCATION
see also Radio in education; Television in education; and under Dissertations, Academic - Education

Bethancourt, Marcella.
A selected bibliography of print and nonprint media in the audiovisual field, by Marcella Bethancourt ₍and₎ Pamelia Eck. Tempe, Bureau of Educational Research and Services, Arizona State University, 1971.

40 p. 28 cm. (₍Arizona. State University, Tempe. Bureau of Educational Research and Services₎ Educational services bulletin no. 38)

Coppen, Helen Elizabeth.
Survey of British research in audio-visual aids; compiled by Helen E. Coppen. 2nd ed. London, National Committee for Audio-Visual Aids in Education, Educational Foundation for Visual Aids, 1968.

₍4₎, 163 p. 22 cm.

———— Supplement 1, 1968. London, National Committee for Audio-Visual Aids in Education, Educational Foundation for Visual Aids ₍1969₎

49 p. 22 cm.

———— Supplement no. 2, 1969. London, National Committee for Audio-Visual Aids in Education, Educational Foundation for Visual Aids ₍1970₎

44 p. 22 cm.

Danmarks radio. Biblioteket.
Massemedier, radio og fjernsyn. En bibliografi. Udarb. på grundlag af anskaffelser i Danmarks Radios Bibliotek 1960–1969. København V, Eget forlag, eksp.: Rosenørns Allé 22, 1970.

76 l. 30 cm.

Davis, Harold S
Instructional media center; an annotated bibliography, by Harold S. Davis and David J. Crotta. Cleveland, Educational Research Council of America ₍1971₎

32 p. 22 cm.

Educational Media Council.
Educational media index. A project of the Educational Media Council. New York, McGraw-Hill ₍1964₎

14 v. 26 cm.
Includes bibliographies.
CONTENTS.—v. 1. Pre-school and primary, grades K–3.—v. 2. Intermediate, grades 4–6.—v. 3. Art and music.—v. 4. Business education and training.—v. 5. English language.—v. 6. Foreign language.—v. 7. Guidance, psychology, and teacher education.—v. 8. Health-safety and home economics.—v. 9. Industrial and agricultural education.—v. 10. Mathematics.—v. 11. Science and engineering.—v. 12. Geography and history.—v. 13. Economics and political science.—v. 14. Master title index.

European research in audio-visual aids; editor J. A. Harrison. London, published by the National Committee for Audio-Visual Aids in Education on behalf of the Council of Europe, 1966 ₍i. e. 1967₎

2 v. 23 cm.

CONTENTS.—pt. 1. Bibliography.—pt. 2. Abstracts.

France. *Institut pédagogique national.*
Bibliographie sommaire en langue française sur les techniques audio-visuelles appliquées à l'éducation. Édition 1962. Paris, l'Institut ₍196–₎

80 p. 27 cm. (*Its* Catalogues, répertoires et bibliographies)

———— Complément 1962–1964. Paris, l'Institut ₍196–₎

39 p. 27 cm. (*Its* Catalogues, répertoires et bibliographies)

Green, Edward J
An annotated bibliography of visual discrimination learning ₍by₎ Edward J. Green ₍and₎ Joan A. O'Connell. New York, Teachers College Press, Teachers College, Columbia University ₍1969₎

vi, 171 p. 23 cm.

Harrison, John Allen.
Recherches consacrées aux moyens audio-visuels en Europe ... sous la direction de J. A. Harrison. Londres, Strasbourg, Conseil de l'Europe, 1967.

2 v. 23 cm.

At head of title: Conseil de la coopération culturelle du Conseil de l'Europe.
Issued also in English under title: European research in audio-visual aids.
CONTENTS.—1. ptie. Bibliographie.—2. ptie. Sommaires.

Jennings, P   M
Audio-visual aids: a classical catalogue, compiled by P. M. Jennings. 3rd ed. Slough (Bucks.), published for the Orbilian Society by Centaur Books, 1966.

70 p. 21½ cm.

Previous editions issued by the Orbilian Society under title: A classical catalogue of publications suitable for use in schools.

Jones, Milbrey L., 1948–
Sources of audiovisual materials ₍by₎ Milbrey L. Jones. Washington, Office of Education, U. S. Dept. of Health, Education, and Welfare; for sale by the Supt. of Docs., U. S. Govt. Print. Off., 1967₎

14 p. 27 cm.

Latchaw, Truly Trousdale.
Audio-visual guidance materials; an annotated bibliography and directory of Minnesota sources. ₍St. Paul, Dept. of Education₎ 1965.

xlviii, 278 p. 26 cm. (Minnesota guidance series)

Latchaw, Truly Trousdale.
Audio-visual guidance materials; an annotated bibliography and directory of Minnesota sources. St. Paul, State Dept. of Education, 1970.

lxxvii, 484 p. 28 cm. (Minnesota guidance series)

Limbacher, James L
A reference guide to audiovisual information, by James L. Limbacher. New York, Bowker, 1972.

ix, 197 p. 23 cm.

National Audio-Visual Aids Centre. *Experimental Development Unit.*
Survey of British research in audio-visual aids: part 1. Bibliography. part 2. Abstracts. London, National Committee for Audio-Visual Aids in Education; Educational Foundation for Visual Aids ₍1965₎

75 p. 22 cm. (*Its* Report no. 3)

Oswald, Ida.
An annotated bibliography on audiovisual instruction in professional education, by Ida Oswald with the assist-

ance of Linda Petersen. New York, Council on Social Work Education ₁1966₁

lx, 61 p. 23 cm.

Rufsvold, Margaret Irene, 1907–
Guides to newer educational media: films, filmstrips, kinescopes, phonodiscs, phonotapes, programed instruction materials, slides, transparencies, videotapes ₁by₁ Margaret I. Rufsvold and Carolyn Guss. 2d ed. Chicago, American Library Association, 1967.

vi, 62 p. 24 cm.

First published in 1961 under title: Guides to newer educational media: films, filmstrips, phonorecords, radio, slides, television.

Rufsvold, Margaret Irene, 1907–
Guides to educational media; films, filmstrips, kinescopes, phonodiscs, phonotapes, programed instruction materials, slides, transparencies, videotapes ₁by₁ Margaret I. Rufsvold and Carolyn Guss. 3d ed. Chicago, American Library Association, 1971.
lx, 116 p. 23 cm.
First ed. published in 1961 under title: Guides to newer educational media: films, filmstrips, phonorecords, radio, slides, television; 2d ed. published in 1967 under title: Guides to newer educational media: films, filmstrips, kinescopes, phonodiscs, phonotapes, programed instruction materials, slides, transparencies, videotapes.

Taggart, Dorothy T 1917–
A guide to sources in educational media and technology / by Dorothy T. Taggart. — Metuchen, N. J. : Scarecrow Press, 1975.

viii, 156 p. ; 22 cm.

U. S. Library of Congress. Education and Public Welfare Division.
New technology in education; selected references. ₁Compiled by Lilla M. Pearce and Helen A. Miller₁ Prepared for the Subcommittee on Science, Research, and Development of the Committee on Science and Astronautics, U. S. House of Representatives. Washington, U. S. Govt. Print. Off., 1971.

ix, 140 p. 24 cm.

Westdeutscher Rundfunk. Bibliothek.
Hörfunk. Fernsehen. Bildung. Ein Literaturverz. (Bearb. von Gudrun Biessmann. Stand: 1. März 1971.) (₁Köln₁ Westd. Rundfunkbibliothek) 1971.

239 p. 21 cm. (Kleine Rundfunkbibliothek, Heft 2)

Young, Earl H
Audio-visual equipment and materials; a guide to sources of information and market trends ₁by Earl H. Young₁ Washington, U. S. Business and Defense Services Administration; for sale by the Supt. of Docs., U. S. Govt. Print. Off., 1969.

iii, 15 p. 23 cm.

AUDIOLOGY

Hnatiow, Gail.
Evoked response audiology: a bibliographic review ₁by₁ Gail Hnatiow ₁and₁ John P. Reneau. Madison, Central Wisconsin Colony and Training School, 1968.

91 p. 29 cm. (Central Wisconsin Colony and Training School. Research proceedings. Monograph supplement, v. 1)

AUDITING

Institute of Internal Auditors.
Bibliography of internal auditing, 1950–1965. New York, 1967.

v. 106 p. 23 cm.

AUĖZOV, MUKHTAR OMARKHANOVICH

(Bibliograficheskiĭ ukazatel' po tvorchestvu M. O. Auėzova)
Библиографический указатель по творчеству М. О. Ауэзова. ₁В 2-х т.₁ Алма-Ата, ₁"Наука",₁ 1972–

v. 22 cm.

At head of title, v. 1– : Академия наук Казахской ССР. Институт литературы и искусства им. М. О. Ауэзова.
Russian and Kazakh.
By L. M. Auėzova and others.

AUGUSTA, GEORGIA

Rowland, Arthur Ray, 1930–
A guide to the study of Augusta and Richmond County, Georgia, by A. Ray Rowland. Augusta, Ga., Richmond County Historical Society, 1967.

69 p. 23 cm.

AUGUSTINE, SAINT ·

Institut des études augustiniennes.
Fichier augustinien; Institut des études augustiniennes, Paris, fichier-auteurs. Boston, G. K. Hall, 1972.

2 v. 36 cm.

Added t. p.: Augustine bibliography; Institut des études augustiniennes, Paris, author catalog.

Institut des études augustiniennes.
Fichier augustinien; Institut des études augustiniennes, Paris, fichier-matières. Boston, G. K. Hall, 1972.

2 v. 36 cm.

Added t. p.: Augustine bibliography; Institut des études augustiniennes, Paris, subject catalog.

AUGUSTINIAN CANONS. WINDESHEIM CONGREGATION

Sint-Truiden, Pieter van, 1609–1674.
Petri Trudonensis Catalogus scriptorum Windeshemensium. Editus cura: W. Lourdaux, E. Persoons. Leuven, Universitaire uitg., 1968.

264 p. 25 p. (Universiteit te Leuven. Publicaties op het gebied van de geschiedenis en de filologie. 5e Reeks, Deel 3)

AUGUSTINIANS

Zumkeller, Adolar, 1915–
Manuskripte von Werken der Autoren des Augustiner-Eremitenordens in mitteleuropäischen Bibliotheken. Würzburg, Augustinus-Verlag, 1966.

764 p. 22 cm. (Cassiciacum, Bd. 20)

AUROBINDO, SRI see Ghose, Aurobindo

AUSTEN, JANE

Keynes, *Sir* Geoffrey Langdon, 1887–
Jane Austen; a bibliography, by Geoffrey Keynes. New York, B. Franklin ₁1968₁

xxv, 289 p. illus., ports. 23 cm. (Burt Franklin bibliography and reference series, no. 158)

On spine: Bibliography of Jane Austen.
Reprint of the 1929 ed.

Keynes, Sir Geoffrey Langdon, 1887–
Jane Austen: a bibliography, by Geoffrey Keynes. Fol-

croft, Pa., Folcroft Press ₍1969₎

    xxv, 280 p. illus. 23 cm.

    Reprint of the 1929 ed.

Roth, Barry, 1942–

    An annotated bibliography of Jane Austen studies, 1952–1972 ₍by₎ Barry Roth ₍and₎ Joel Weinsheimer. Charlottesville. Published for the Bibliographical Society of the University of Virginia ₍by₎ the University Press of Virginia ₍1973₎

    ix, 272 p. 24 cm.

AUSTRALASIA

Mander-Jones, Phyllis, 1896–

    Manuscripts in the British Isles relating to Australia, New Zealand, and the Pacific. Editor: Phyllis Mander-Jones. Canberra, Australian National University Press, 1972.

    xxiii, 697 p. 26 cm.

    "Sponsored by the National Library of Australia and the Australian National University."

Mander-Jones, Phyllis, 1896–

    Manuscripts in the British Isles relating to Australia, New Zealand, and the Pacific. Honolulu, University Press of Hawaii ₍c1972₎

    xxiii, 697 p. 26 cm.

    "Sponsored by the National Library of Australia and the Australian National University."

Sydney. Public Library of New South Wales. *Mitchell Library.*

    Catalogue of manuscripts of Australasia and the Pacific in the Mitchell Library, Sydney. Sydney, Trustees of the Public Library of New South Wales, 1967–

    v. 27 cm.

    CONTENTS.—₍1₎ Series A. Manuscripts catalogued between 1945 and 1963.—

AUSTRALIA
see also   Australasia

Australia. Dept. of Trade and Industry. Central Library.

    Australian trade; a select reading list of material held in the Central Library. ₍Canberra₎ 1972.

    18 l. 30 cm.

Australia. *Dept. of Trade and Industry. Industry Economics Branch.*

    Bibliography on manufacturing industry in Australia. ₍Canberra?₎ 1968.

    25 l. 30 cm.

Australian immigration; a bibliography and digest. no. ₍1₎–1966–

    Canberra, Dept. of Demography, Australian National University.

    v. 27 cm.

Australian National University, *Canberra. Dept. of International Relations.*

    Select bibliography of Australia's foreign relations. Rev. ₍Canberra₎ 1968.

    22 p. 34 cm.

Borchardt, Dietrich Hans, 1916–

    Australian bibliography; a guide to printed sources of information ₍by₎ D. H. Borchardt. ₍2d ed.₎ Melbourne, Canberra ₍etc.₎ Cheshire ₍1966₎

96 p. 22 cm.

Canberra, Australia. National Library.

    An exhibition in honour of Sir John Ferguson, arranged by the National Library of Australia for the thirteenth biennial conference of the Library Association of Australia, August 1965. Canberra, National Library of Australia, 1965.

    viii, 23 p. facsims., col. plates, port. 24 cm.

    "The catalogue has been compiled and the exhibition arranged by David Thomas, Violet Gibson, Pauline Fanning, and Lindsay Cleland of the Reference Division."

Canberra, Australia. National Library.

    Select reading list on Canadian-Australian relations. Canberra, 1966.

    61 l. 26 cm.

Dutton, Henry Hampden, 1879–1932.

    Australiana collection; catalogue. Adelaide, Theodore Bruce & Co. Pty. Limited, 1966.

    vii, 60 p. illus., port. 24 cm.

Finlayson, Jennifer Ann S

    Historical statistics of Australia; a select list of official sources ₍by₎ Jennifer Finlayson. Canberra, Dept. of Economic History, Research School of Social Sciences, Australian National University, 1970.

    ix, 55 p. 25 cm.

Gibbney, Herbert James.

    A biographers' index of parliamentary returns (New South Wales, Queensland & Victoria) 1850–1889, compiled by H. J. Gibbney & N. Burns. Canberra, Department of History (Australian Dictionary of Biography) Institute of Advanced Studies, Australian National University, 1969.

    xiii, 180 p. 26 cm.

Hince, Kenneth.

    Sale catalogue of Australiana from the library of Dame Mabel Brookes. Arranged for sale by Kenneth Hince. ₍Catalogue preparation: Kenneth Hince.₎ Melbourne, The Author, 77 Bourke Street, 1968.

    69 p. illus. 24 cm.

Hudson, W   J

    Australia's external relations: towards a bibliography of journal articles, by W. J. Hudson. East Melbourne, Australian Institute of International Affairs ₍1971₎

    44 p. 24 cm.

    Cover title.

    "Reprinted from the December, 1970, and April, 1971, issues of the Institute's journal, The Australian outlook."

Lancaster, Henry Oliver, 1913–

    Bibliography of vital statistics in Australia and New Zealand ₍by₎ H. O. Lancaster. Sydney, Australasian Medical Pub. Co., 1964.

    67 p. 24 cm.

    This work, which is reprinted from the Australian journal of statistics, v. 6, no. 2, 1964, p. 33–99, has also the paging of the original.

Lionel Lindsay Gallery.

    Catalogue of the library of the Lionel Lindsay Gallery Toowoomba, compiled by staff of the University of Queensland Library for the Director of the Gallery, Mr. W. R. F. Dolton. ₍St. Lucia, Q.₎ University of Queensland Library, 1969.

    71 p. 26 cm.

Reiner, Ernst.
Literaturbericht über Australien und Neuseeland. 1938–1963. Gotha, Leipzig, Haack VEB, 1967.

294 p. 20 cm. (Geographisches Jahrbuch, Bd. 62)

Sutherland, Bruce, 1904–
Australiana in the Pennsylvania State University Libraries. University Park, Pennsylvania State University Libraries, 1969.

x, 391 p. illus., map. 28 cm. (₁Pennsylvania. State University. Libraries₁ Bibliographical series, no. 1)

HISTORY

Canberra, Australia. National Library.
Guide to collections of manuscripts relating to Australia. Canberra, 1965–

1 v. (loose-leaf) 31 cm.

Cover title: Manuscripts relating to Australia : guide to collections.

Canberra, Australia. National Library. Manuscript Section.
Manuscript material relating to immigrant voyages to Australia. Canberra, 1964.

32 p. 25 cm.

Davidson, Rodney.
A book collector's notes on items relating to the discovery of Australia, the first settlement and the early coastal exploration of the continent. ₁North Melbourne₁ Cassell Australia ₁1970₁

138 p. illus., facsims., maps. 25 cm.

Loveday. Peter.
Bibliography of selected manuscripts relating to Australian politics since 1890 held in the Mitchell Library, Sydney. ₁By₁ Peter Loveday and Helen Nelson. ₁Sydney, University of Sydney₁ Dept. of Govt. and Public Administration, 1964.

1 v. (unpaged) 25 cm.

O'Hara, John, comp.
Journal articles on Australian history. ₁Compiled by John O'Hara and Stephen Foster. Armidale, N. S. W.₁ University of New England, Dept. of History, 1970.

ii, 100 p. 34 cm.

Ward, Patricia Bruce, 1921–
Teaching through the library : a selection of resources for Australian history, 1770–1900, by Patricia B. Ward. Sydney, School Library Association of New South Wales, 1971.

iii, 21 p. 22 cm. (School Library Association of New South Wales. Occasional papers, no. 8)

IMPRINTS

Booksellers' reference book.
1965–
Melbourne, D. W. Thorpe Pty.

v. 25 cm.

LAW see Law - Australia

MAPS

Australia. *Dept. of National Development.*
Index to Australian resources maps of 1940–59. Canberra, 1961 ₁i. e. 1962₁

241 p. col. maps. 24 cm.

————Supplement for 1960–64. Canberra, 1966.

viii, 250 p. col. maps. 24 cm.

Australia. *Division of National Mapping.*
Map catalogue; 1 : 100,000 series, 1 : 250,000 series. ₁Canberra, 1969?₁

1 v. (loose-leaf) 30 cm.

Australian maps.

Canberra, National Library of Australia.

no. 25 cm. quarterly.

Began with Jan./Sept. 1968 issue.

Canberra, Australia. National Library.
Index atlas to maps in series in the Map Collection, National Library of Australia. Canberra, 1966–

v. (loose-leaf) chiefly col. maps. 42 x 69 cm.

Scales vary.
Kept up to date by amendment pages.

CONTENTS.—₁1₁ pt. 1. Australia. pt. 2. New Guinea.

Tooley, Ronald Vere, 1898–
Early maps of Australia, the Dutch period; being examples from the collection of R. V. Tooley, with bibliographical notes. London, Map Collectors' Circle, 1965.

27 p. maps. 25 cm. (Map Collectors' Circle. Map collectors' series, no. 23)

Tooley, Ronald Vere, 1898–   *comp.*
One hundred foreign maps of Australia, 1773–1887 ₁by R. V. Tooley₁ London, Map Collectors' Circle, 1964.

₁16, ₁28₁ p. facsim., maps. 25 cm. (Map collectors' series, no. 12)

Tooley, Ronald Vere, 1898–
Printed maps of Australia, being a catalogue of a collection, by R. V. Tooley. London, Map Collectors' Circle, 1970–

v. maps. 25 cm. (Map collectors' series, v. 6, no. 60

AUSTRALIA, WESTERN see Western
Australia

AUSTRALIAN ABORIGINES see
Anthropology - Australia

AUSTRALIAN LITERATURE

Blake, Leslie James.
Australian writers ₁by₁ L. J. Blake. ₁Adelaide₁ Rigby ₁1968₁

viii, 208 p. 22 cm.

Johnston, Grahame.
Annals of Australian literature. Melbourne, New York, Oxford University Press, 1970.

xi, 147 p. 23 cm.

Mackaness, George, 1882–
Bibliomania; an Australian book collector's essays. ₁Sydney₁ Angus and Robertson ₁1965₁

199 p. illus., facsims., ports. 23 cm.

Miller, Edmund Morris, 1881–1964.
Australian literature from its beginnings to 1935 : a de-

scriptive and bibliographical survey of books by Australian authors in poetry, drama, fiction, criticism and anthology with subsidiary entries to 1938, by E. Morris Miller. Facsimile ed. Sydney, Sydney University Press, 1973.

2 v. (xi, 1074 p.) 25 cm.
Initiated and commenced by the late Sir John Quick.
"Alphabetical list of non-Australian authors of novels associated with Australia": v. 2, p. 966–971.

AUSTRIA

Austria. Statistisches Zentralamt.
Publikationen. 1960/70–
₍Wien₎

v. 23 cm.

Supersedes its Verzeichnis der Veröffentlichungen des österreichischen Statistischen Zentralamtes.

Behrmann, Lilly-Ralou.
Bibliographie zur Aussenpolitik der Republik Österreich seit 1945. (Stand: 31. Dez. 1971) ₍Von₎ Lilly-Ralou Behrmann, Peter Proché ₍und₎ Wolfgang Strasser. Wien, W. Braumüller ₍c1974₎

505 p. 24 cm. (Schriftenreihe der österreichischen Gesellschaft für Aussenpolitik und Internationale Beziehungen, Bd. 7)

Hungary. Központi Statisztikai Hivatal. Könyvtár és Dokumentációs Szolgálat.
Külföldi statisztikai adatforrások. 1973–
Budapest, Statisztikai Kiadó Vállalat.

v. 29 cm.

"A Központi Statisztikai Hivatal Könyvtárának katalógusa."

Notring der Wissenschaftlichen Verbände Österreichs.
Wissenschaftliche Periodica und Buchreihen Österreichs. Hrsg. vom Notring d. Wissenschaftl. Verbände Österreichs aus Anlass seines 20 jähr. Bestehens. Wien, 1969.

31 p. 21 cm.

Stock, Karl Franz.
Bibliographien der Österreichischen Bundesländer. Auswahlverzeichnis. Von Karl F. Stock. Graz, Universitätsbibliothek, 1966.

62 p. 29 cm.

HISTORY

Bridge, F R
The Habsburg monarchy 1804–1918: books and pamphlets published in the United Kingdom between 1818–1967; a critical bibliography. London, University of London (School of Slavonic and East European Studies), 1967.

₍1₎ ii, 82 p. 22 cm.

Österreichische historische Bibliographie. Austrian historical bibliography. 1965–
Santa Barbara, Calif., Clio Press.

v. 23 cm. annual.

Vienna. Nationalbibliothek.
50 ₍Fünfzig₎ Jahre österreichische Zeitgeschichte. Ausstellung d. Österr. Nationalbibliothek zum Gedenken an die Übernahme in das Eigentum d. Republik u. die Benennung als "Nationalbibliothek" im Jahre 1920. Prunksaal, 11. Mai bis 15. Okt. 1970. (Gestaltung d. Ausstellung: Otto Koller ₍und₎ Walter G. Wieser. Red. des Katalogs: Walter G. Wieser.) Wien, Österr. Nationalbibliothek, 1970.

56 p. 21 cm.

AUSTRIA, UPPER

Marks, Alfred, 1921–
Bibliographie zur oberösterreichischen Geschichte. 1954–1965 / von Alfred Marks ; hrsg. vom Oberösterreichischen Landesarchiv. — Wien ; Köln ; Graz : Böhlau in Komm., 1972.

viii, 429 p. : 24 cm.   Au 73-22-12
"Ergänzungsband zu den Mitteilungen des Oberösterreichischen Landesarchivs."
Continues 4 works of the same title by E. Strassmayr covering the period 1891–1953.

AUSTRIAN LITERATURE

Giebisch, Hans, 1888–
Bio-bibliographisches Literaturlexikon Österreichs, von den Anfängen bis zur Gegenwart ₍von₎ Hans Giebisch ₍und₎ Gustav Gugitz. Wien, Brüder Hollinek ₍1964₎

viii, 516 p. 25 cm.

Grossberg, Mimi, 1905–
Österreichische Autoren in Amerika. Geschick u. Leistung d. österr. literarischen Emigration ab 1938 in den Vereinigten Staaten. Eine Ausstellung, veranst. vom Amerika-Haus, Wien in Zsarb. mit d. Dokumentationsstelle f. Neuere Österr. Literatur. (Katalogred.: Mimi Grossberg u. Viktor Suchy.) (Wien, Dokumentationsstelle f. Neuere Österr. Literatur) 1970.

19 l. 16 x 23 cm.

Das Österreichische Buch. Schöne Bücher aus fünf Jahrhunderten. Австрийская книга. Книжные сокровища пяти столетий. (Hrsg. vom Hauptverband des Österreichischen Buchhandels anlässlich der Buchausstellungen in Moskau und Leningrad im Jahre 1969. Wien) Hauptverband des Österreichischen Buchhandels (1969)

71 p. 18 cm.

BIBLIOGRAPHIES

Stock, Karl Franz.
Personalbibliographien österreichischer Dichter und Schriftsteller; von den Anfängen bis zur Gegenwart ₍von₎ Karl F. Stock, Rudolf Heilinger ₍und₎ Marylène Stock. Mit Auswahl einschlägiger Bibliographien, Nachschlagewerke, Sammelbiographien, Literaturgeschichten und Anthologien. Pullach bei München, Verlag Dokumentation, 1972.

xxiii, 703 p. 22 cm.

AUSTRO-PRUSSIAN WAR, 1866

Válka 1866 ₍i. e. Tisíc osmset šedesát šest₎ Výběrová regionální bibliogr. Hradec Králové, Kraj. muzeum, t. ₍MTZ, Trutnov₎ 1968.

89, ₍7₎ p. port. 21 cm. (Fontes Musei Reginaehradecensis, 5)

"Památce profesora Josefa Simona."
Prefatory material also in German.

AUTHORSHIP

Fialová, Božena.
Jak psát vědeckou práci. Soupis literatury. Zprac. Božena Kyjovská. Brno, Univ. knihovna, t. G 07, Blansko, 1971.

₍6₎ p. 21 cm. (Bibliografický leták, č. 160)

AUTOBIOGRAPHY see Biography

AUTOGRAPHS

Musikantiquariat Hans Schneider.
Musikerautographen / Tutzing : Schneider ₍c1973₎
109 p. : facsims. ; 24 cm. — (Its Katalog ; Nr. 180)

Szladits, Lola L
Documents: famous & infamous; selected from the Henry W. and Albert A. Berg Collection of English and American Literature, by Lola L. Szladits. ₍New York₎ New York Public Library, 1972.
34 p. illus. 26 cm.

AUTOMATION
see also   Computers

Davis, L
Automation—social aspects, a list of selected references, compiled by L. Davis. Melbourne, State Library of Victoria, 1967.
47 p. 25 cm. (Research service bibliographies, 1967, no. 2)

Supplement to Research service bibliography, 1965, no. 6.

Gros, Eugene.
Russian books on automation and computers, compiled by E. Gros. London, Scientific Information Consultants ₍1967₎
₍3₎, 92 p. 24½ cm.

"Contains literature either published, or announced for publication, in 1965 and 1966."

Harrison, Annette.
Bibliography on automation and technological change and studies of the future. ₍Santa Monica, Calif., Rand Corp.₎ 1966.
20 p. 28 cm. (₍Rand Corporation. Paper₎ P-3365)

International Labor Office.
Social aspects of automation. A bibliography of material available in the International Labour Office. Geneva, 1966.
iv, 167 p. 30 cm. ₍(International Labor Office. Document₎ AUT/DOC/2 (Revised))
At head of title: International Labour Office, Automation Programme.

International Labor Office. *International Occupational Safety and Health Information Centre.*
Health and safety aspects of automation and technological change, a collection of abstracts, 1956 to 1962. ₍Washington₎ U. S. Dept. of Labor, Manpower Administration, Office of Manpower, Automation and Training ₍1964₎
v, 181 p. 26 cm.

Kandová, Jitka.
Optimální řízení a Pontrjaginův princip maxima. (Lit. rešerše.) Zprac. J. Kandová. Praha, Ekon. ústav ČSAV, rozmn., 1968.
61 p. 20 cm. (Ekonomicko-matematicka laboratoř při Ekonomickém ústavu ČSAV. Informační publikace, č. 26)

K'o hsüeh chi shu wen hsien so yin: Tzu tung hua yü t'ung hsün.
科学技术文献索引　自动化与通訊 Kexue jishu wenxian suoyin. 总第31- 期 1965 年 1 月 –
₍北京₎ 中国科学技术情报研究所

no. in　v.　27 cm.　monthly.

Continues 科学技术文献索引 (期刊部分) 自动化与通訊 and 科学技术文献索引 (特件文献部分) 自动化与通訊
Vols. for 1965-　prepared by 中国科学技术情报研究所 (with 中国科学院自动化研究所 Jan.-May 1965; 邮电部邮电科学研究院 Jan.-Sept. 1965; 邮电部邮电科学技术情报研究所 Oct. 1965- ）

Kussow, Omar.
Instructional materials on productivity and automation: An annotated bibliography, by Omar Kussow. A descriptive list of films, by William Dunwiddie. Madison, Center for Productivity Motivation, School of Commerce, University of Wisconsin, 1965.
14 p. 23 cm.

Organization for Economic Cooperation and Development. *Library.*
Automation. Paris, 1964.
iv, 38 p. 29 cm. (*Its* Bibliographie spéciale analytique, 2 (39))
Introductory matter in French and English.

Przeglad dokumentacyjny, 1970. Warszawa, Instytut Automatyki Polskiej Akademii Nauk, 1971.
98 p. 24 cm. (Prace Instytutu Automatyki PAN, zesz. 98)

Rupešová, Miloslava.
Použití analogových a číslicových počítačů při řízení výrobních pochodů. Výběrová bibliografie kniž. a čas. literatury. Sest. Miloslava Rupešová. Předml.: V. Strejc. 1. vyd. Praha, UVTEI, rozmn., 1967–
v. 21 cm.
CONTENTS.—díl 1. Pochody metalurgické a chemické.

Sedlák, Jan.
Automatizační prostředky. Výběrová bibliografie knižní a čas. lit. Sest. Jan Sedlák. 1. vyd. Praha, UVTEI-St. techn. knihovna, rozmn., 1968–
v. 21 cm. (Prague. Státní technická knihovna. Bibliografie, sy. 131)
CONTENTS.—1. Číslicové a analogové počítače.

AUTOMATION IN DOCUMENTATION see Information storage and retrieval systems

AUTOMOBILES

Beck, Eugene H
Automobile parking; selected references, 1962–1964. Washington, Highway Research Board, 1965.
56 p. 25 cm. (Highway Research Board. Bibliography 37)
National Research Council. Publication 1325.
"Compiled by the U. S. Bureau of Public Roads Library ... by Eugene H. Beck and Dawn E. Willis with the assistance of Edward D. Colognie."

Boleszny, Ivan.
Automobiles; a classified list of books in the Public Library of South Australia, compiled by I. Boleszny. Adelaide, Public Library of South Australia, 1966.
125 p. 27 cm. (Research Service bibliographies. Series 4, no. 76)

Henry, Marybeth.
Motor vehicle emissions: a bibliography. Monticello, Ill., Council of Planning Librarians, 1972.
38 p. 28 cm. (Council of Planning Librarians. Exchange bibliography 275)

Jones, D   C   1933–

Bibliography on driver licensing; final report, by D. C. Jones [and] S. K. Stouffer. Research Triangle Park, N. C., Research Triangle Institute, Operations Research and Economics Division, 1970.

37 p. 27 cm.

"Prepared for the U. S. Department of Transportation, National Highway Safety Bureau, under Contract no. FH–11–7253."

Kessler, Mary Z

Abandoned vehicles: a selected bibliography. Compiled by Mary Z. Kessler. Rev. and supplemented by Nan C. Burg. Mary Vance, editor. [Monticello, Ill., Council of Planning Librarians] 1972.

13 p. 28 cm. (Council of Planning Librarians. Exchange bibliography, 296)

Kessler, Mary Z

Automobile parking: a selected list of references [compiled by] Mary Z. Kessler. [Monticello, Ill., Council of Planning Librarians, 1971]

23 l. 28 cm. (Council of Planning Librarians. Exchange bibliography, 228)

Library Association. County Libraries Group.

Readers' guide to books on automobile engineering. 2nd ed. London, Library Association (County Libraries Group), 1969.

47 p. 19 cm. (Its Readers' guides, new series, no. 112)

Mobile Homes Manufacturers Association. Public Relations Division.

Mobile home industry; bibliography [July, 1965, through September, 1970] Chicago, Ill., Mobile Homes Manufacturers Association [1971, °1970]

10 p. (incl. cover) 28 cm.

National Research Council. *Highway Research Board.*
Headlight glare. Washington, 1968.

60 p. 25 cm. (*Its* Bibliography no. 46)

National Academy of Sciences, Washington, D. C.   Publication 1556.

National Research Council. *Highway Research Board.*
Night visibility, selected references. Washington, 1967.

16 p. 25 cm. (*Its* Bibliography, no. 45)

National Research Council. Publication 1501.

Paterson, George David Lennox.

Rolls-Royce motor cars, 1903–1969: a bibliography, compiled by G. D. L. Paterson. Crewe (Cheshire), Rolls-Royce Ltd., 1969.

[2], 17 l. 30 cm.

Schipf, Robert G

Automotive repair and maintenance [by] Robert G. Schipf. Littleton, Colo., Libraries Unlimited, 1973.

119 p. 24 cm. (Spare time guides: information sources for hobbies and recreation, no. 1)

U. S. *Bureau of Public Roads. Library.*
Parking; selected references, 1966. Washington, Highway Research Board, Division of Engineering, National Research Council, National Academy of Sciences, 1967.

25 p. 25 cm. (Bibliography, no. 44)

National Research Council. Publication 1445.

U. S. *Bureau of Public Roads. Library.*
Parking: selected references, 1967. Washington, Highway Research Board, National Research Council, 1968.

31 p. 25 cm. (National Research Council. Highway Research Board. Bibliography no. 47)

National Academy of Sciences. Publication 1611.

U. S. *Bureau of Public Roads. Library.*
Parking: selected references, 1968. Washington, Highway Research Board, National Research Council, 1969.

21 p. 25 cm. (National Research Council. Highway Research Board. Bibliography no. 50)

National Academy of Sciences. Publication 309–01787–4.

Victoria, Australia. State Library, Melbourne. Research Dept.

Driver education in high schools. Melbourne, 1970.

9 l. 26 cm.

SAFETY MEASURES

Michigan. University. Highway Safety Research Institute.

The 1970 international automobile safety bibliography of literature through January 1970. Joseph C. Marsh IV, editor. New York, Distributed by Society of Automotive Engineers [c1970]

xv, 604 p. 29 cm.

Compiled as a contribution to the 1970 International Automobile Safety Conference.

New York (*State***).** *Dept. of Motor Vehicles. Research Library.*
New York State safety car project; bibliography. [Albany] 1966.

58 p. 27 cm.

United States. National Highway Traffic Safety Administration.

Air bags. Washington [1973]

46 p. 27 cm. (Its Special bibliography no. 5)

Cover title.
"DOT HS 801 033. Air bag restraint systems."

United States. National Highway Traffic Safety Administration.

Seat/safety belts. Washington [1973]

80 p. 27 cm. (Its Special bibliography no. 2)

AVALANCHES

Knapp, George L

Avalanches, including debris avalanches; a bibliography. Edited by George L. Knapp. Washington, Water Resources Scientific Information Center; [available from the National Technical Information Service, Springfield, Va.] 1972.

iv, 87 p. 27 cm. (Bibliography series, WRSIC 72–216)

"Produced wholly from the information base comprising only Selected water resources abstracts (SWRA)."

AVIATION   see Aeronautics

AVIATION MEDICINE

Aerospace medicine and biology; a continuing bibliography with indexes. Jan./Mar. 1964–
Washington, Scientific and Technical Information Division, National Aeronautics and Space Administration; [available

from the Clearinghouse for Federal Scientific and Technical
Information, Springfield, Va.;

v. 28 cm. (NASA SP-7011)

Supersedes an earlier publication with the same title, issued
1952–63.
Subtitle varies.

"Compiled through the cooperative efforts of the Aerospace Medi-
cine and Biology Bibliography Project of the Library of Congress
(LC), the American Institute of Aeronautics and Astronautics
(AIAA), and NASA."

Japan. Kōkū Igaku Jikkentai.
(Kōkū jiko ni kansuru kōkū igaku bunken mokuroku)
航空事故に関する航空医学文献目録 Bibliogra-
phy of aviation accident in medical aspects. ［東京］ 航
空医学実験隊 Aero Medical Laboratory. 1965.

210 p. 25 cm. (Its 医実文献目録 no. 2)

Sergeev, Aleksandr Aleksandrovich.
Отечественная литература по авиационной, высокогор-
ной и космической биологии и медицине. Библиография. Ленинград, "Наука," Ленингр. отд-ние, 1969.

190 p. 27 cm.

United States. Office of Aviation Medicine.
Index to FAA Office of Aviation Medicine reports: 1961
through 1971 [by] J. Robert Dille [and] Marcia H. Grimm.
Washington, 1972.

24 p. illus. 27 cm. (Its FAA-AM-72-1)

AVIGNON

Autrand, Aimé.
Répertoire numérique des archives municipales d'Avignon; documents de l'epoque révolutionnaire. Répertoire
par A. Autrand. Inventaire partiel et table par L. Duhamel et J. de Font-Réaulx. Avignon Archives de Vau-
cluse, 1955.

xx, 119 p. 82 cm.
Running title: Archives municipales d'Avignon.
"Répertoire numérique des archives municipales d'Avignon: période révolutionnaire" (p. [v]–xx) comprises series A through I, K, L
and N through R.
"Inventaire-sommaire des archives municipales d'Avignon: période
révolutionnaire" (p. [1]–110) comprises articles A 1–5, B 1–14, D 1–28
and D II 1–2.

AZERBAIJAN

Kerimova, D IŪ
26 бакинских комиссаров. (Библиография). Баку,
1968.

69 p. 19 cm.
At head of title: Министерство культуры Азербайджанской
ССР. Азербайджанская государственная республиканская библио-
тека им. М. Ф. Ахундова.

Kuliev, N M
История Азербайджана. (1920–1961). Библиография.
Баку, "Элм," 1970.

287 p. 22 cm.

At head of title: Академия наук Азербайджанской ССР.
Фундаментальная библиотека.
Added t. p. in Azerbaijani.

Великий Октябрь и Азербайджан. (1917–1967). Библиография. Баку, Изд. АН АзССР, 1967.

172 p. 21 cm.

At head of title: Академия наук Азербайджанской ССР. Фунда-
ментальная библиотека.
Added t. p. in Azerbaijani.
By N. M. Kuliev and others.

AZEVEDO, ARIO L.

Azevedo, Ario L
Contribuição para uma relação cronológica da bibliografia
publicada. Lourenço Marques, 1964.

8 l. 30 cm. (Instituto de Investigação Científica de Moçambique.
Centro de Documentação. Doc. inf., no. 8)

AZTECS

Harkányi, Katalin.
The Aztecs; bibliography. Compiled by Katalin Harkányi. [San Diego, Calif., 1971]

30 l. 28 cm.

"A relatively complete list of the library's holdings on the
Aztecs of Mexico."

B

BA, AMADOU HAMPATÉ

Sow, Alfâ Ibrâhîm.
Inventaire du Fonds Amadou-Hampâté Bâ, répertorié à Abidjan en 1969 par Alfâ Ibrâhîm Sow. Paris, C. Klincksieck, Université de Paris X, Laboratoire d'ethnologie et de sociologie comparative, 1970.

85 p. 22 cm.

"₍Classification₎ par matières ... ₍des₎ principaux titres des documents que M. Amadou-Hampâté Bâ détient dans ses achives d'Abidjan."

BABYLONIAN INSCRIPTIONS see
Inscriptions, Cuneiform

BACCHELLI, RICCARDO

Vitale, Maurizio.
Bibliografia degli scritti di Riccardo Bacchelli. 1909–1970. Milano-Napoli, R. Ricciardi, 1971.

xiv, 208 p. 23½ cm.

2d ed.

BACKHOUSE FAMILY

Durham, Eng. University. Durham Colleges. Dept. of Palaeography and Diplomatic.
List of the Backhouse papers. Durham, 1973.

ii. 114 l. 30 cm.

BACOVIA, GEORGE

Chiscop, Liviu.
George Bacovia. 1881–1957. Biobibliografie. Cuvînt înainte de prof. univ. dr. doc. Dan Simonescu. Bacău, Comitetul de cultură şi educaţie socialistă, Biblioteca municipală, 1972.

367 p. with illus. and facsims., port. on leaf. 21 cm.

BÁCS-KISKÚN, HUNGARY

Fenyvessi, Anna (Góhér)
Megyénk felszabadulása, 1944; bibliográfia és dokumentumgyűjtemény ₍Szerk.: Fenyvessiné Góhér Anna₎ Kecskemét, Katona József Megyei Könyvtár, 1965.

79 p. illus. 20 cm.

BACTERIOPHAGE

Raettig, Hansjürgen.
Bakteriophagie. 1957–1965. Stuttgart, G. Fischer, 1967.

2 v. 20 cm. (Literatur-Dokumentation. Reihe 1, T. 2)

Added t. p.: Bacteriophagy.

CONTENTS.—T. 1. Einführung. Sachregister. Stichwort-Index.—T. 2. Bibliographie.

BAGER, EINAR

Modéer, Kjell Å   1939–
Einar Bagers bibliografi. ₍Av₎ Kjell Å. Modéer. Utg. av

Malmö fornminnesförening. Malmö, Utgivaren, 1972.

34, (1) p. illus. 22 cm.

"Tillägnas Einar Bager av Malmö Fornminnesförening på hans 85 -årsdag den 19 april 1972."

BAHRĪANYI, IVAN

Voĭchyshyn, Ĭūliĭa.
(Ivan Bahrĭanyĭ)
Іван Багряний; літературно-бібліографічна студія. Вступне слово Константина Біди. Вінніпег, 1968.

86 p. 24 cm. (Українська вільна академія наук. Серія: Література, ч. 10)

Added t. p.: Ivan Bahriany.

BAIN, ANDREW GEDDES

Evenden, Dawn Eva.
Andrew Geddes Bain; a bibliography. Johannesburg, University of the Witwatersrand, Dept. of Bibliography, Librarianship and Typography, 1971.

iii, 29 p. 30 cm.

"Compiled in part fulfilment for the requirements of the Diploma in Librarianship, University of the Witwatersrand."

BAJA CALIFORNIA

Barrett, Ellen C
Baja California; a bibliography of historical geographical, and scientific literature relating to the peninsula of Baja California and to the adjacent islands in the Gulf of California and the Pacific Ocean. Los Angeles, Bennett & Marshall, 1957–67.

2 v. maps (on lining papers) facsim., port. 26 cm.

Book 2 has imprint: Los Angeles, Westernlore Press.

CONTENTS.—book 1. 1535–1956—book 2. 1535–1964. Chronological index, 1535–1964 (p. ₍169₎–217)

—— Baja California bibliography, 1965–1966; a supplement, by Katherine M. Silvera. La Jolle, Calif., Baja Californianos of the Friends of the University of California San Diego Library, 1968.

42 p. 25 cm.

BAKER FAMILY

Durham, Eng. University. *Durham Colleges. Dept. of Palaeography and Diplomatic.*
The Baker Baker papers. Durham, Eng., The Prior's Kitchen, The College, 1964–

v. 33 cm.

CONTENTS.—v. 1. List of documents relating to Boulby alum works.—v. 2. General letters and papers, 1561–1759.—v. 3. List of general letters and papers, 1760–1787. v. 5. List of general letters and papers, 1846–1891.

BAKING

American Society of Bakery Engineers.
Decennial index to publications, 1955–1964. Chicago ₍1965₎

74 p. 29 cm.

Subject index to the society's Proceedings of the annual meeting, its Bulletin (no. 140–177), and its Engineers' information service reports (no. 27–41). Continues the society's Index to publications, 1924–1954.

Gentry, Dwight L
Bakery products. Rev. by Elizabeth Janezeck. Washington, Small Business Administration, 1964.

8 p. 27 cm. (Small business bibliography no. 19)

Caption title.
"Originally published as Small business bulletin no. 19."

BAKKEN, HALLVARD S.

Flo, Olav, 1922–
Bibliografi over Hallvard S. Bakkens forfatterskap. 1900—26. oktober—1970. Bergen, 1970.

25 l. 30 cm.

BALATON, LAKE, HUNGARY

Helikon Könyvtár. *Balatoni Gyüjtemény.*
A keszthelyi Helikon-Könyvtár Balatoni Gyüiteménye. ₍Összeállította Berlász Jenő és Varga Béláné₎ Budapest, 1959–65.

2 v. 20 cm. (Az Országos Széchényi Könyvtár kiadványai, 43, 62)

Vol. 2 has title: A keszthelyi Helikon Könyvtár Balatoni Gyüjteménye könyvtárjegyzék.

BĂLCESCU, NICOLAE

Nestorescu-Bălceşti, Horia.
Nicolae Bălcescu. Contribuţii biobibliografice. Cu un studiu introductiv de Dan Berindei. Bucureşti, Editura enciclopedică română, Editura militară, 1971.

xxxix, 300 p. with illus., ports. and facsims. 21 cm.

BALKAN PENINSULA
see also under Dissertations, Academic

Bibliografie československé balkanistiky.
Brno, Universita J. E. Purkyně.

v. 29 cm. (Materiály k dějinám a kultuře střední a jihovýchodní Evropy) (Učební texty vysokých škol)

Began with vol. for 1945/65.
Vols. for   issued by Fakulta filosofická of Universita J. E. Purkyně.

Bibliographie d'études balkaniques. v. ₍1₎–
1966–
Sofia.

v. 29 cm. annual.

Issued by Académie bulgare des sciences, Institut d'études balkaniques, Centre international de recherches scientifiques et de documentation.

Horecky, Paul Louis, 1913–
Southeastern Europe; a guide to basic publications. Paul L. Horecky, editor. Chicago, University of Chicago Press ₍1969₎

xxii, 755 p. 25 cm.

BALKARIA see under Kabardia

BALLADS

Eberhard, Wolfram, 1909–
Taiwanese ballads; a catalogue. ₍Taipei, Orient Cultural Service₎ 1972.

ix, 171 p. 21 cm. (Asian folklore and social life monographs, v. 22) (Tung fang wên ts'ung)

Holzapfel, Otto.
Die mittelalterliche skandinavische Volksballade. Eine Bibliographie. Marburg/L., (Volkskunde-Forum) 1969.

77 p. with illus. 21 cm. (Volkskundeforum. Bibliographie, 3)

Jeanroy, Alfred, 1859–1953.
Bibliographie sommaire des chansonniers français du Moyen Age (manuscrits et éditions). New York, B. Franklin ₍1971₎

viii, 78 p. 19 cm. (Burt Franklin bibliography & reference series, 423. Essays in literature and criticism, 139)
Reprint of the 1918 ed.
Supplements Bibliographie des chansonniers français des XIIIe et XIVe siècles, by G. Raynaud.
"Additions et rectifications à la liste des chansons de G. Raynaud": p. ₍63₎–72.

London. Stationers' Company.
An analytical index to the ballad-entries (1557–1709) in the registers of the Company of Stationers of London. Compiled by Hyder E. Rollins. Foreword by Leslie Shepard. Hatboro, Pa., Tradition Press. 1967 ₍°1924₎

xv, 324 p. 24 cm.

Half title: Index to the ballad-entries in the Stationers' registers.

Raynaud, Gaston, 1850–1911.
Bibliographie des chansonniers français des XIII° et XIV° siècles, comprenant la description de tous les manuscrits, la table des chansons classées par ordre alphabétique de rimes, et la liste des trouvères. Paris, F. Vieweg. 1884. ₍Osnabrück. Biblio Verlag. 1971₎

2 v. in 1. 22 cm.

Raynaud, Gaston, 1850–1911.
Bibliographie des chansonniers français des XIII° et XIV° siècles ... New York, B. Franklin ₍1972₎

2 v. in 1 23 cm. (Burt Franklin bibliography & reference series, 469. Music history and reference series, 2)

Reprint of the 1884 ed.
CONTENTS: t. 1. Description des manuscrits.—t. 2. Table des chansons. Liste des trouvères.

BALLANTYNE, ROBERT MICHAEL

Quayle, Eric.
R. M. Ballantyne: a bibliography of first editions. London, Dawsons, 1968.

128 p. 10 plates, illus., facsims., ports. 23 cm.

BALLET see Dance

BALLINGER, MARGARET LIVINGSTONE

Udeman, Elsa.
The published works of Margaret Livingstone Ballinger; a bibliography. Johannesburg, University of the Witwatersrand, Dept. of Bibliography, Librarianship, and Typography, 1968.

₍x₎ 63 p. 30 cm.

BALMER, LUC

Luc Balmer. Werkverzeichnis. Zürich, Schweizerisches Musik-Archiv, 1970.

8 l. 30 cm.

Cover title.
French and German.

BALNEOLOGY see Health resorts, watering-places, etc.

BALTIC LANGUAGES

Kubicka, Weronika.
Języki bałtyckie; bibliografia. Baltic languages; bibli-

ography. Łódź, 1967–

v. 29 cm. (Wydawnictwa bibliograficzne Biblioteki Uniwersyteckiej w Łodzi, 10)

Preface also in English.
Bibliography: v. 1, p. v–xxiii.

CONTENTS.—cz. 1. Językoznawstwo bałtyckie.

BALTIC STATES
see also under Finland *(Harvard)*

Hanover. Niedersächsische Landesbibliothek.
Katalog des Schrifttums über die baltischen Länder. Hannover, 1971.

2 v. (vi, 722 p.) 21 cm.

Hollander, Bernhard A
Bibliographie der baltischen Heimatkunde: ein Wegweiser f. d. heimatkundl. Unterricht in Lettland u. Estland/ von Bernhard Hollander. Hrsg. von d. Ges. f. Geschichte u. Altertumskunde zu Riga. — Nachdr. [d. Ausg.] Riga, Kymmel, 1924. — Hannover-Döhren: v. Hirschheydt, 1972.

104 p.; 20 cm.

Pantzer, Gerhard von, 1913–1966.
Personen- und familienkundliche Literatur in baltischen Zeitschriften. 1948–1960. Köln, [Wahner Str. 2, Isabella v. Pantzer] 1970.

52 p. 21 cm. (Baltische Ahnen- und Stammtafeln. Sonderheft Nr. 10)

Toronto. University. Library.
Baltic material in the University of Toronto Library; a bibliography compiled by Elvi Aer [and others. Toronto] Printed for the Association of Baltic Studies and the University of Toronto Library by the University of Toronto Press [1972]

125 p. 25 cm.

BALTIMORE COUNTY, MARYLAND

Baltimore Co., Md.
Baltimore County publications. 2d ed. [Towson? Md., 1972]

23 p. 23 cm.

Cover title.
"Prepared by Richard Parsons, Baltimore County Public Library, with the cooperation of the Office of Information & Research, Baltimore County, Maryland."

BALTIMORE METROPOLITAN AREA

Maryland. Morgan State College, *Baltimore. Urban Studies Institute.*
Baltimore metropolitan area urban affairs bibliography. Baltimore, 1967.

iv, 70 l. 28 cm.

BALZAC, HONORÉ DE

Hara, Masao, 1927–

原　政夫

日本におけるバルザック書誌

東京　駿河台出版社　1969

209p　図版　22cm

Institutul Romîn pentru Relaţiile Culturale cu Străinătatea.
Honoré de Balzac: bibliographie des oeuvres traduites en roumain et parues en volumes, 1852–1965. Anatole France:

bibliographie des oeuvres traduites en roumain et parues en volumes, 1904–1964. Bucarest, Institut roumain pour les relations culturelles avec l'étranger, 1965.

19 p. 20 cm.

Cover title.

Paevskaiâ, Anastasiiâ Vladimirovna.
Оноре Бальзак; библиография русских переводов и критической литературы на русском языке, 1830–1964. Москва, Книга, 1965.

426 p. illus., facsims., port. 23 cm.

At head of title: Всесоюзная государственная библиотека иностранной литературы. А. В. Паевская, В. Т. Данченко.

BALZAC, JEAN LOUIS GUEZ, SIEUR DE

Beugnot, Bernard, 1932–
Jean-Louis Guez de Balzac, bibliographie générale. Montréal, Presses de l'Université de Montréal, 1967.

173 p. 22 cm.

————— Supplément 1–
Montréal, Presses de l'Université de Montréal, 1969–

v. 22 cm.

BANDUNG, INDONESIA. UNIVERSITAS NEGERI PADJADJARAN

Pudjiadi, R
Penerbitan2 staf pengadjar Institut Keguruan dan Ilmu Pendidikan, Bandung 1954–1964, disusun oleh R. Pudjiadi [dan] Ratna Wilis Dahar. [Bandung, 1964?]

35 l. 21 cm.

BANGLADESH

Kayastha, Ved P
The crisis on the Indian subcontinent and the birth of Bangladesh: a selected reading list. Compiled and edited by Ved P. Kayastha. Rev. and enl. ed. [Ithaca, N. Y.] South Asia Program, Cornell University, 1972.

vii, 142 p. 28 cm. (South Asia occasional papers and theses, 1)

BANK OF ENGLAND

Stephens, Thomas Arthur, 1852–1925.
A contribution to the bibliography of the Bank of England. New York, A. M. Kelley, 1968.

xiii, 200 p. 22 cm. (Reprints of economic classics)

Reprint of the 1897 ed.

BANK VAN LENING TE DELFT

Delft. Gemeentearchief.
Inventaris van het archief van de commissarissen over de Bank van Lening te Delft, 1676–1923, door D. Van Duijn. Aangevuld en herz. door I. W. L. A. Caminada. Inventaris 1960. Delft, 1970.

23 l. 29 cm.

BANKING

American Bankers Association. *Marketing Dept.*
A selective, annotated bank marketing bibliography. New York [1968]

vii, 103 p. 28 cm.

Burgess, Norman.
How to find out about banking and investment. [1st ed.]

Oxford, New York, Pergamon Press [1969]

xii, 300 p. 20 cm. (The Commonwealth and international library. Libraries and technical information division)

Canadian Bankers' Association.
 A bibliography of Canadian banking. Une bibliographie sur la banque au Canada. [Toronto, 1971?]

35 p. 26 cm.

English and/or French.

Chihō Kin'yūshi Kenkyūkai.
 日本金融機関史 文献目録　地方金融史研究会編 [東京] 全国地方銀行協会 1967.

170 p. 26 cm.

Krasensky, Hans.
 Zwölf Jahre Österreichische Bankwissenschaftliche Gesellschaft. Wien, Manz, 1965.

52 p. 24 cm. (Schriftenreihe der Österreichischen Bankwissenschaftlichen Gesellschaft, Heft 25)

Shukla, Madan Mohan.
 Banks and banking in India, with special reference to bank nationalisation; a select list of articles. Compiled by Madan Mohan Shukla, Jagmal Singh Chauhan [and] Vinod Kumar Maheshwari. [1st ed.] Delhi, New Star Publishers [1970]

283 p. 23 cm.

Singh, Mohinder, M. A.
 Facets of social control and nationalisation of banks in India; a selected annotated bibliography. Compiled by Mohinder Singh; assisted by J. F. Pandya and M. C. Shah. Foreword by Ishwar Dayal. Ahmedabad, Balgovind Prakashan [1970]

136 p. 22 cm.

Von Dohlen, John L
 Research in bank management: a selected annotated bibliography, by John L. Von Dohlen. Prepared under the supervision of J. L. Dake and A. W. Stalnaker. [Atlanta, Industrial Management Center, Georgia Institute of Technology] 1970.

iii, 41 l. 20 cm.

Yüan, K'un-hsiang, *comp.*
 貨幣金融論文分類索引　袁坤祥　馬景賢編輯
 A classified index to articles on money and banking (1945–65), compiled by Frank K. S. Yuan [and] Ma Ching-hsien. Taipei, [美國亞洲學會中文研究資料中心] 1967.

xliii, 329 p. 27 cm. (中文研究資料中心研究資料叢書第3號 Chinese Materials and Research Aids Service Center. Research aids series, no. 3)

Text in Chinese, with English introduction by Robert L. Irick.

BANKING LAW

U. S. Congress. House. Committee on Banking and Currency.
 List of publications issued by Committee on Banking and Currency: hearings, reports, and committee prints, 39th–91st Congresses (1865–1970). 91st Congress, 2d session. Washington, U. S. Govt. Print. Off., 1970.

viii, 151 p. 24 cm.

At head of title: Committee print.

BANKS ISLANDS, NEW HEBRIDES

Krauss, Noel Louis Hilmer, 1910–
 Bibliography of the Banks Islands, Western Pacific, by N. L. H. Krauss. Honolulu, 1971.

10 p. 23 cm.

BANTUS

Ellis, Barbaralyn.
 Religion among the Bantu in South Africa: a list of works published after 1956. Compiled by Barbaralyn Ellis. Johannesburg, University of the Witwatersrand, Department of Bibliography, Librarianship and Typography, 1968.

iv, 15 l. 30 cm.

BAPTISM

Gill, Athol.
 A bibliography of Baptist writings on Baptism, 1900–1968. Rüschlikon-Zürich, Baptist Theological Seminary, (1969).

184 p. 21 cm. (Bibliographical aids, no. 1)

BAR ASSOCIATIONS

Parness, Jeffrey A
 Citations and bibliography on the unified bar in the United States; an American Judicature Society research report, by Jeffrey A. Parness. Chicago, American Judicature Society, 1973.

32 p. 28 cm.

Leaf, summarizing new developments in bar unification since press time, inserted at end.

BAR-ILAN UNIVERSITY see Ramat-Gan, Israel. Bar-Ilan University

BARANSKIĬ, NIKOLAĬ NIKOLAEVICH

Finashina, G   N
 Николай Николаевич Баранский. (1881–1963). Вступит. статья Ю. Г. Саушкина. Библиогр. сост. Г. Н. Финашиной и Р. И. Кузьменко. Москва, "Наука," 1971.

120 p. 17 cm. (Материалы к биобиблиографии ученых СССР. Серия географических наук, вып. 4)

BARANYA, HUNGARY
see also under Pécs, Hungary

Baranya Megyei Könyvtár. Szerzeményező és Feldolgozó Csoport.
 Baranyáról, múltról, máról; ajánló könyvjegyezék a Baranya Megyei Könyvtár helyismereti állományából. [Írta és összeállította a Megyei Könyvtár Szerzeményező és Feldolgozó Csoportja] Pécs, 1968.

28 p. illus. 20 cm. (A Baranya Megyei Tanács Megyei Könyvtárának kiadványai, 10)

BARBADOS

Boston. Public Library.
 Bibliotheca Barbadiensis; a catalog of materials relating to Barbados, 1650–1860 in the Boston Public Library. Boston, 1968.

27 p. 21 cm.

Campbell, Tony.
 The printed maps of Barbados from the earliest times

to 1873. London, Map Collectors' Circle, 1965.

24 p. 25 maps. 25 cm. (Map collectors' series, no. 21)

Handler, Jerome S
A guide to source materials for the study of Barbados history, 1627–1834, by Jerome S. Handler. Carbondale, Southern Illinois University Press [c1971]

xvi, 205 p. 25 cm.

BARBERTON, SOUTH AFRICA

Bartlett, Sandra.
Barberton; a selective bibliography, compiled by Sandra Bartlett. Johannesburg, Department of Bibliography, Librarianship and Typography, University of the Witwatersrand, 1972.

[2], iv, 37 p. 29 cm.

BARBUSSE, HENRI

Moscow. Vsesoiûznaiâ gosudarstvennaiâ biblioteka inostrannoĭ literatury.
Анри Барбюс; биобиблиографический указатель. [Составитель А. В. Паевская. Автор вступ. статьи Ф. С. Наркирьер. Ответственный редактор М. Я. Яхонтова] Москва, Книга, 1964.

192 p. port. 22 cm. (Писатели зарубежных стран)

BARCELONA (PROVINCE)

Barcelona (*Province*) *Diputación Provincial.*
Catálogo de publicaciones de la Diputación Provincial de Barcelona y de sus instituciones y servicios [por] María José Buxó-Dulce de Voltes. Barcelona, 1966.

xvi, 182 p. 24 cm.

Comisión Mixta de Coordinación Estadística de Barcelona.
Inventario de información cartográfica de la Provincia de Barcelona; efectuado en 31 de diciembre de 1969. Barcelona, Comisión Mixta de Coordinación Estadística, 1970.

217 p. illus. 21 x 30 cm. (Its Serie Bibliografías, no. 1)

BARI (CITY)

Giovine, Alfredo.
Bibliografia barese. (Saggio aggiornato fino al 1967). Bari, 1968.

159 p. 24½ cm. (Biblioteca dell'Archivio delle tradizioni popolari baresi)

BARK

Ross, William D
Bibliography of bark. Compiled by William D. Ross. Corvallis, Forest Research Laboratory, Oregon State University, 1966.

56 p. 23 cm. ([Oregon. State University, Corvallis. Forest Research Laboratory] Bibliographical series 6)

BARLACH, ERNST

Kröplin, Karl Heinz.
Ernst-Barlach-Bibliographie./ bearb. von Karl-Heinz Kröplin. — Berlin: Dt. Staatsbibliothek, 1972.

66 p.; 21 cm. — (Deutsche Staatsbibliothek. Bibliographische Mitteilungen, 25)

BARLEY

Commonwealth Bureau of Plant Breeding and Genetics, *Cambridge, Eng.*
Breeding barley for resistance to scald. Farnham Royal (Bucks.) Commonwealth Agricultural Bureaux [1967]

[2], 16 p. 24 cm. (*Its* Annotated bibliography, 1)

BARNIKOL, ERNST

Meckert, Udo.
Bibliographie Ernst Barnikol, 1916–1964. Halle, Akademischer Verlag, 1964.

31 p. 21 cm.

BAROJA Y NESSI, PIO

Odriozola, Antonio.
Bibliografía de Pío Baroja y catálogo de la exposición bibliográfica en el centenario de su nacimiento. Vigo, 1972.

[24] p. 23 cm.

"Exposición bibliográfica del 4 al 12 de diciembre de 1972, Nueva sala de exposiciones, Caja de Ahorros Municipal de Vigo."

BARRIE, SIR JAMES MATTHEW

Cutler, Bradley Dwyane, 1904–
Sir James M. Barrie, a bibliography, with full collations of the American unauthorized editions, by B. D. Cutler. New York, B. Franklin [1968]

242 p. facsims. 23 cm. (Burt Franklin bibliography and reference series, 155)

Reprint of the 1931 ed.

BARUCH, ISMAR

U. S. Civil Service Commission.
The Ismar Baruch collection of Civil Service papers, 1836–1953. [Washington] 1967.

v, 17 p. 23 cm.

BASAVA

Gunjal, S   R   1932–
ಬಸವ ಸಾಹಿತ್ಯ ದರ್ಪಣ; ಕನ್ನಡ-ತೆಲುಗು-ತಮಿಳು-ಸಂಸ್ಕೃತ-ಹಿಂದೀ-ಮರಾಠೀ-ಉರ್ದು-ಇಂಗ್ಲಿಷ್-ಫ್ರೆಂಚ್ ಭಾಷೆಗಳಲ್ಲಿ ಬಸವಣ್ಣನವರನ್ನು ಕುರಿತು ರಚಿತವಾದ ಗ್ರಂಥಗಳ ವಿವರಣಾತ್ಮಕ ಸೂಚಿ. [ಸಂಪಾದಕ] ಎಸ್. ಆರ್. ಗುಂಜಾಳ. [1. ಆವೃತ್ತಿ] ಬೆಂಗಳೂರು, ಬಸವ ಸಮಿತಿ [1967–

v. 23 cm.   (ಬಸವ ಸಮಿತಿ ಸಂಶೋಧನ ಗ್ರಂಥಮಾಲೆ, 1
In Kannada.

BASHKIR LITERATURE

Gaĭnullin, Midkhat Fazlyevich .
Писатели Советской Башкирии. Биобиблиогр. справочник. Уфа, Башкнигоиздат, 1969.

408 p. with illus. 21 cm.

At head of title: М. Гайнуллин, Г. Хусаинов.

BASQUE LITERATURE

San Martín Ortiz de Zárate, Juan, 1922–
Escritores euskéricos; catálogo biobibliográfico de escritores contemporáneos en vascuence. Bilbao, Editorial La Gran Enciclopedia Vasca, 1968.

183 p. illus., facsims., ports. 17 cm.

———— ———— Apéndice: correcciones y adiciones a la 1. ed., por Juan San Martín. Bilbao, Editorial La Gran Enciclopedia Vasca, 1969.

38 p. 16 cm.

Vinson, Julien, 1843–1926 or 7.
Essai d'une bibliographie de la langue basque. Oosterhout, Anthropological Publications, 1970.

2 v. in 1 (xlviii, 818 p.) facsims. 25 cm.

"Réimpression de l'édition de Paris, 1891 et 1898."

BASQUE PROVINCES

Auch, France. Bibliothèque municipale.
Inventaire du fonds espagnol et basque (legs Branet) [par] Georges Courrou, bibliothécaire de la ville d'Auch ... Auch, Bibliothèque municipale, 1964–

v. 27 cm.

Catálogo de la Exposición de Libros vascos antiguos y raros celebrada en la Biblioteca Provincial de Vizcaya con motivo de la IV Asamblea de Instituciones de Cultura de las Diputaciones. Bilbao, setiembre de 1970. [Bilbao, 1970?]

53 p. 25 cm. (Publicaciones de la Exma. Diputación Provincial de Vizcaya)

Cuzacq, René.
Nouvelles études basques et huitième répertoire d'articles divers (Bayonne, Landes, études régionales) Mont-de-Marsan, J. Lacroste, 1966.

71 p. 21 cm.

BASQUES

Idaho. University. Library.
The Basque collection: a preliminary checklist. Compiled by Charles A. Webbert. [Moscow] 1971.

iv l., 100 p. 28 cm. (Its Publication no. 9)

McCall, Grant.
Bibliography of materials relating to Basque-Americans. [Reno] Distributed by the Basque Studies Program, University of Nevada System [1968?]

21 l. 28 cm.

Nevada. University. *Desert Research Institute.*
Bibliography of materials relating to Basque-Americans; a publication of the Basque Studies Program. Reno [1968?]

17 l. 29 cm.

BASTOGNE, BELGIUM

Belgium. Archives de l'État, Arlon.
Inventaire des archives de l'Hôpital et de la Maison des Trinitaires à Bastogne, 1237–1783, par Roger Petit. Bruxelles, Archives générales du Royaume, 1971.

294 p. 25 cm.

At head of title: Ministère de l'éducation nationale et de la culture française et Ministère de l'éducation nationale et de la culture néerlandaise. Archives générales du Royaume et Archives de l'État dans les provinces.

BATH, ENGLAND

Bath Municipal Libraries.
Bath guides, directories and newspapers in the Reference Library. Revised ed. Bath, Bath Reference Library, 1967.

[24] p. 21 cm.

BATS

Linhart, Samuel B
A partial bibliography of the vampire bats (Desmodus, Diphylla, Diaemus). Compiled by Samuel B. Linhart. Denver, Denver Wildlife Research Center, 1971.

iv, 53 p. 27 cm.

English or Spanish.
"[Issued] in cooperation with Office of Agriculture and Fisheries, Bureau of Technical Assistance, U. S. Agency for International Development."

BATTISS, WALTER W.

Van Bruggen, Lee.
Walter Battiss : a bibliography / compiled by Lee van Bruggen. — Johannesburg : University of the Witwatersrand, Dept. of Bibliography, Librarianship and Typography, 1972.

vii, 17 p. ; 30 cm.

BAUDELAIRE, CHARLES PIERRE

Cargo, Robert T
Baudelaire criticism, 1950–1967; a bibliography with critical commentary [by] Robert T. Cargo. University, University of Alabama Press [°1968]

xii, 171 p. illus. 21 cm.

Fongaro, Antoine.
Deux années d'études baudelairiennes (juillet 1966–juin 1968). Avec un avant-propos par Antoine Fongaro et une introduction par Ll. J. Austin. Matériel bibliographique recueilli et publié par Antoine Fongaro, Gianni Mombello, et Patrizia Rocchi. Torino, Società editrice internazionale, 1970.

106 p. 24 cm.

"Supplemento al n. 39 di Studi francesi, settembre–dicembre 1969."

Vanderbilt University, Nashville. Center for Baudelaire Studies.
Baudelaire and Poe, an exhibition in conjunction with the inauguration of the Center for Baudelaire Studies, April ninth to thirtieth, 1969. [Nashville, 1969]

16 p. 22 cm.

BAUXITE

Bardossy, György.
Bibliographie des travaux concernant les bauxites publiés en francais, anglais, russe et allemand. ⟨1965–1968⟩. Preparée par Gy. Bardossy. Zagreb, Académie yougoslave des sciences et des arts, 1971.

34 p. 24 cm. (Travaux du Comité international pour l'étude des bauxites, des oxydes et des hydroxydes d'aluminium, no 8)

BAVARIA

Baader, Clemens Alois, 1762–1838.
Lexikon verstorbener baierischer Schriftsteller des achtzehnten und neunzehnten Jahrhunderts. Ausgearb. von Clemens Alois Baader. Hildesheim, New York, G. Olms, 1971.

2 v. 22 cm.

Reprint of the ed. published in Augsburg in 1824–25.

Bavaria. Hauptstaatsarchiv.
Lehrausstellungen im Hauptstaatsarchiv München 1965–1967. (Bearb.: Karl Otto Ambronn [u. a.]) (Kallmünz über Regensburg: Lassleben in Komm.) 1967.

76 p., xiv p. of illus. 21 cm. (Mitteilungen für die Archivpflege in Bayern. Sonderheft 5)

Krausen, Edgar.
Die handgezeichneten Karten im Bayerischen Hauptstaatsarchiv sowie in den Staatsarchiven Amberg und Neuburg a. d. Donau bis 1650. Neustadt a. d. Aisch, Degener, 1973.

xxxvi, 298 p. facsims., 20 plates. 21 cm. (Bayerische Archivinventare, Heft 37)

Wagner, Friedrich, 1887–
Bibliographie der bayerischen Vor- und Frühgeschichte, 1884–1959. Wiesbaden, O. Harrassowitz, 1961.

xxix, 334 p. 25 cm. (Bibliographien, hrsg. von der Kommission für Bayerische Landesgeschichte bei der Bayerischen Akademie der Wissenschaften, Bd. 6)

Wild, Joachim.
Beiträge zur Registerführung der bayerischen Klöster und Hochstifte im Mittelalter. Kallmünz Opf., M. Lassleben, 1973.
viii, 119 p. 25 cm. (Münchener historische Studien. Abteilung geschichtl. Hilfswissenschaften, Bd. 12) (Münchener Universitäts-Schriften. Philosophische Fakultät)
A revision of the author's thesis, Munich, 1969.

BAX, SIR ARNOLD EDWARD TREVOR

Parlett, Graham.
Arnold Bax, a catalogue of his music; compiled by Graham Parlett. London, Triad Press, 1972.

52 p. port. 23 cm.

Limited ed. of 150 copies;

BAY PSALM BOOK see under Bible. Old Testament. Psalms

BEACHES

Dolan, Robert.
Selected bibliography on beach features and related nearshore processes, compiled by Robert Dolan ₍and₎ James McCloy. Baton Rouge, Louisiana State University Press, 1965.

vi, 59 p. 29 cm. (Louisiana State University studies. Coastal studies series, no. 11)

Mitchell, James Kenneth, 1930–
A selected bibliography of coastal erosion, protection and related human activity in North America and the British Isles. ₍Toronto, Dept. of Geography, University of Toronto₎ 1968.

66 p. 28 cm. (Natural hazard research. Working paper no. 4)

BEACONSFIELD, BENJAMIN DISRAELI, 1ST EARL OF see Disraeli, Benjamin

BEAGLEHOLE, JOHN CAWTE

Walton, Margery.
John Cawte Beaglehole; a bibliography. ₍Compiled by Margery Walton, Julia Bergen and Janet Paul. Wellington, N. Z.₎ Alexander Turnbull Library, 1972.

47 p. port. 18 cm.

BEANS

Campinas, Brazil. Instituto Argonômico do Estado de São Paulo. Biblioteca.
Bibliografia brasileira do feijão (Phaseolus vulgaris L.).

Viçosa, Imprensa Universitária, Universidade Federal de Viçosa, 1971.
iv, 105 p. 28 cm.
At head of title: Secretaria da Agricultura do Estado de São Paulo. Coordenadoria da Pesquisa Agropecuaria. Instituto Agronômico. Biblioteca. Universidade Federal de Viçosa—Minas Gerais. Biblioteca Central.

Inter-American Center for Documentation and Agriculture Information.
Bibliografía frijol (Phaseolus spp.). Ed. acumulada. Turrialba, Costa Rica, Centro Interamericano de Documentación e Información Agrícola, 1972.

viii, 299 p. 28 cm. (Its Bibliografías, no. 4)

Edition for 1965, compiled by A. M. Paz de Erickson, issued under title: Frijol (Phaseolus spp.)

Moscow. TSentral'naia nauchnaia sel'skokhoziaĭstvennaia biblioteka. *Leningradskoe otdelenie.*
Фасоль.; библиографический указатель отечественной литературы в количестве 524 названий за 1888–1963 гг. Ленинград, 1961.

60 p. 21 cm.

BEAUCAIRE

Du Guerny, Yannig.
Répertoire numérique des Archives communales de Beaucaire, séries anciennes et séries modernes, par Y. Chassin DuGuerny. Avant-propos de Jean Sablou. Nîmes, Archives du Gard, 1970.

140 p. plates. 24 cm.

BEAUMONT, WILLIAM

Washington University, *St. Louis. Libraries. Library of the School of Medicine.*
Index to the Wm. Beaumont, M. D., 1785–1853, manuscript collection. Compiled by Phoebe A. Cassidy ₍and₎ Roberta S. Sokol. Introd. by Estelle Brodman. ₍St. Louis₎ Washington University School of Medicine, 1968.

165 p. facsim., geneal. tables, port. 22 x 28 cm.

BECHER, JOHANNES ROBERT

Berlin. Stadtbibliothek.
Johannes R. Becher. Zum 10. Todestag am 11. Okt. (Zusammengestellt von Ewald Birr. Red. Bearb.: Adolf Weser u Hilde Weise.) Berlin, Berliner Stadtbibliothek, 1968.

70 p. 21 cm. (Bibliographische kalenderblätter. Sonderblatt 22)

BECHUANALAND see Botswana

BECKETT, SAMUEL

Federman, Raymond.
Samuel Beckett: his works and his critics; an essay in bibliography ₍by₎ Raymond Federman and John Fletcher. Berkeley, University of California Press, 1970.

xiii, 383 p. 25 cm.

Knowlson, James.
Samuel Beckett: an exhibition held at Reading University Library, May to July 1971. Catalogue by James Knowlson. Foreword by A. J. Leventhal. London, Turret Books, 1971.

123 p. 25 cm.

Samuel Beckett, 1 (2). 2. livr. Paris, Lettres modernes, 1971.

1 v. (unpaged) 18 cm. (Calepins de bibliographie, no 2) (Lettres modernes)

"Chaque livraison annule et remplace la précédente."
CONTENTS: Essai de bibliographie des œuvres de Samuel Beckett (1929–1966) par R. J. Davis.—Essai de bibliographie des études en langues française et anglaise consacrées à Samuel Beckett (1931–1966) par J. R. Bryer et M. J. Friedman.—Complément (1929–1969) par P. C. Hoy.—Avec une esquisse de bibliographie des études en autres langues (1953–1969)

Samuel Beckett, 1 (2). 2. livr. Paris, Lettres modernes, 1972.

1 v. (unpaged) 18 cm. (Calepins de bibliographie, no 2) (Lettres modernes)

"Chaque livraison annule et remplace la précédente."
CONTENTS: Davis, R. J. Essai de bibliographie des œuvres de Samuel Beckett (1929–1966).—Bryer, J. R. et Friedman, M. J. Essai de bibliographie des études en langues française et anglaise consacrées à Samuel Beckett (1931–1966).—Hoy, P. C. Complément (1929–1970).—Esquisse de bibliographie des études en d'autres langues (1953–1970)

Tanner, James T   F
Samuel Beckett; a checklist of criticism, by James T. F. Tanner and J. Don Vann. [1st. ed. Kent, Ohio] Kent State University Press [1969]

vi, 85 p. 23 cm. (The Serif series: bibliographies and checklists, no. 8)

BEDELL, CATHERINE MAY

Washington (State). University. Library.
Catherine May : an indexed register of her congressional papers, 1959–1970 in the Washington State University Library. — Pullman : Washington State University, 1972.

32 p. : ill. ; 28 cm.

BEDFORDSHIRE, ENGLAND

Conisbee, L   R
A Bedfordshire bibliography, with some comments and biographical notes [by] L. R. Conisbee. [Luton? Eng.] Bedfordshire Historical Record Society [1962]

333 p. 25 cm.

—————— Second supplement [by] L. R. Conisbee. [Luton? Eng.] Bedfordshire Historical Record Society [1971]

128 p. 24 cm.

BEE CULTURE

Harbo, John.
Annotated bibliography on attempts at mating honeybees in confinement, by J. Harbo. Gerrards Cross, Bee Research Association, 1971.

[1], 16 leaves. 28 cm. (Bee Research Association. Bibliography no. 12)

Johansson, Tage Sigvard Kjell, 1919–
Apicultural literature published in Canada and the United States [by] T. S. K. Johansson and M. P. Johansson. [New York?] 1972.

103 p. 22 cm.

BEECH

Iwano, Mikado, 1904–
(Buna no bunken to sono shōroku)

ぶなの文献とその抄録　岩野三門編

東京　日本ぶな材協会　昭和44 (1969)

130p　21cm

1958 ed. published under title: Buna ni kansuru bunkenshū.

Liese, Walter, 1926–
Buchenholz-Dokumentation. Bearb. von W. Liese [u. a.] auf Anregung der Deutschen Gesellschaft für Holzforschung im Auftrage des Bundesministeriums für Ernährung, Landwirtschaft und Forsten. Hamburg, Wiedebusch in Kommission, 1967–

v. 30 cm. (Mitteilungen der Bundesforschungsanstalt für Forst- und Holzwirtschaft Reinbek b. Hamburg, Nr. 66
CONTENTS.—T. 1. Biologische Eigenschaften, Pathologie und Holzschutz.

BEELAERTS FAMILY

Netherlands (Kingdom, 1815–   ). Rijksarchief, The Hague.
Inventaris van het familiearchief Beelaerts van Emmichoven, 1417–1912, door H. Tissing, volontaire Algemeen Rijksarchief. ['s-Gravenhage] 1965.

135 l. coat of arms, geneal. tables, map, port. 30 cm.

Seal of the Algemeen Rijksarchief, Hague, on cover.

BEETHOVEN, LUDWIG VAN

Berlin. Deutsche Staatsbibliothek. Musikabteilung.
Die Beethoven-Sammlung in der Musikabteilung der Deutschen Staatsbibliothek. Verz. Autographe, Abschriften, Dokumente, Briefe. (Zusammengestellt von Eveline Bartlitz. Berlin, Deutsche Staatsbibliothek, 1970).

x, 229, 3, 25 p. 21 cm.

Breitkopf und Härtel.
Ludwig van Beethoven. Thematisches Verzeichnis. Von Gustav Nottebohm. Nebst der Bibliotheca Beethoveniana. Von Emerich Kastner. Erg. von Theodor Frimmel. Leipzig, Breitkopf & Härtel, 1925. (Unveränderter Nachdruck.) (Leipzig, Zentralantiquariat der Deutschen Demokratischen Republik, 1968.)
220, vi, 84 p. 28 cm.

Breitkopf und Härtel.
Ludwig van Beethoven. Thematisches Verzeichnis. Nebst der Bibliotheca Beethoveniana von Emerich Kastner, erg. von Theodor Frimmel. Wiesbaden, M. Sändig [1969]
220, vi, 84 p. music. 22 cm.
Reprint of ed. published by Breitkopf & Härtel in 1925 which was a reprint of the 2d ed., 1868.
"Bibliotheca Beethoveniana; Versuch einer Beethoven-Bibliographie, von Emerich Kastner. 2. Aufl., mit Ergänzungen und Fortsetzung von Theodor Frimmel": vi, 84 p. at end.

Elvers, Rudolf, 1924–
Ludwig van Beethoven 1770–1970. Autographe aus d. Musikabt. d. Staatsbibliothek Preussischer Kulturbesitz. (Ausstellg. 1.–30. Dez. 1970 im Mendelssohn-Archiv der Staatsbibliothek. Bearb. von Rudolf Elvers u. Hans-Günter Klein.) Berlin (-Dahlem, Staatsbibliothek Preussischer Kulturbesitz) 1970.
18 l. with illus. 15 x 19 cm. (Staatsbibliothek Preussischer Kulturbesitz. Ausstellungskataloge, 1)

Gyimes, Ferenc.
Ludwig van Beethoven a magyar könyvtárakban és gyűjteményekben; bibliográfia. [Összeállította: Gyimes Ferenc és Vavrinecz Veronika] Budapest, Állami Gorkij Könyvtár, 1970–

v. port. 21 cm.

CONTENTS: Beethoven-irodalom.

Stuttgart. Stadtbücherei.
Ludwig van Beethoven zum 200. Geburtstag. Noten, Schallplatten, Bücher aus d. Beständen d. Musikabt. (Zusammengestellt von Brigitte Willberg.) Stuttgart, Stadtbücherei (1970).

106 p. 21 cm.

Vienna. Historisches Museum.
Ludwig van Beethoven. Leben, Schaffen, Umwelt. (Bearb. d. Ausstellung u. des Kataloges: Heinz Schöny.) (Wien) Eigenverl. des Museums (1970).

56 p., 8 p. of illus. 21 cm. (Its Sonderausstellung, 28)

Catalog of the exhibition held at the Historisches Museum in Vienna, Sept.–Dec. 1970.

Wuppertal. Städtische Musikbibliothek.
Beethoven. Bestand d. Städt. Musikbibliothek Wuppertal 1970. Literatur, Noten, Schallplatten. (Wuppertal, Städtische Musikbibliothek, 1970.)

36 p. 19 cm.

BEETS

McCready, Rolland Martin, 1915–
Bibliography of research on utilization of sugar beets, 1949–1965, in the Western Utilization Research and Development Division, Agricultural Research Service, United States Department of Agriculture. (Prepared by R. M. McCready. Albany, Calif., 1966.

27 p. 27 cm. ((U. S. Agricultural Research Service) ARS74–33)

BÉGUIN, ALBERT

Grotzer, Pierre.
Les écrits d'Albert Béguin. Essai de bibliographie. Neuchâtel, La Baconnière, 1967.

135 p. 23 cm. (Langages. Documents)

BEL'CHIKOV, NIKOLAĬ FEDOROVICH

Akademiĭa nauk SSSR.
Николай Федорович Бельчиков. Вступ. статья А. П. Овчаренко. Библиография составлена Р. И. Кузьменко. Москва, Наука, 1965.

87 p. port. 17 cm. (Материалы к биобиблиографии ученых СССР. Серия литературы и языка, вып. 6)

BELFAST

Stevenson, Noragh.
Belfast before 1820: a bibliography of printed material. Belfast, Belfast Library & Society for Promoting Knowledge, 1967 (i. e. 1968)

(7), 64 p. 25 cm.

"Submitted in part requirement for the University of London Diploma in Librarianship, 1963."

BELGIAN CONGO see ZAIRE

BELGIUM

Archives de l'État à Huy.
Inventaire des archives communales déposées aux Archives de l'État à Huy, par H. (i. e. E.) Tellier & P. Bauwens, attachés. (Bruxelles) Archives générales du Royaume, 1968–

v. 30 cm.

Archives de l'État à Huy.
Inventaire des archives des cures déposées aux Archives de l'État à Huy. Par E. Tellier & P. Bauwens. Bruxelles, Archives générales du Royaume, (Galerie Ravenstein, 78), 1969–

v. tables. 30 cm.

Baeyens, Richard.
Documentatie over België, Selectieve en analytische bibliografie. Brussel, Belgisch Instituut voor voorlichting en documentatie, (Montoyerstr., 3), 1970.

x, 171 p. 25 cm.

Issued also under title: Documentation sur la Belgique.

Baeyens, Richard.
Documentation sur la Belgique. Bibliographie sélective et analytique. Bruxelles, Institut belge d'information et de documentation, (r. Montoyer, 3), 1970.

x, 159 p. 25 cm.

Issued also in Dutch under title: Documentatie over België.

Beaufays, Jean.
Selection bibliographique de l'histoire de la Belgique 1918–1939. Bibliographie introductive à l'histoire de la deuxième guerre mondiale du point de vue belge. Bruxelles, 1968.

89 p. 21 cm.

Belder, Josef de, 1933–
Bibliografie van de geschiedenis van België: 1865–1914 (Door) J. de Belder (en) J. Hannes. Bibliographie de l'histoire de Belgique. Leuven, Nauwelaerts; Paris, Béatrice-Nauwelaerts, 1965.

301 p. 24½ cm. (Centre interuniversitaire d'histoire contemporaine. Cahiers, 38)

Belgium. Archives de l'Etat, Bruges.
Catalogus van kaarten en plannen (bewaard op het) Stadsarchief van Brugge. Opgemaakt door A. Schouteet. Brugge, Stad Brugge, 1972.

xvi, 71 p. illus., diagrs., maps. 24 cm. (Brugse geschiedbronnen, 2)

Belgium. *Archives de l' État, Liège.*
Inventaire des archives communales déposées aux Archives de l'État à Liège. Bruxelles, 19

v. 29 cm.

Vol. 9 by Georges Hansotte.

Belgium. Archives de l'État, Liège.
Inventaires d'archives d'entreprises. Bruxelles, (Archives générales du Royaume), rue de Ruysbroeck, 2, 1971.
153 p. 30 cm.
At head of title: Ministère de l'éducation nationale et de la culture française, et Ministère de l'éducation nationale et de la culture néerlandaise. Archives générales du Royaume et Archives de l'État dans les provinces.
Includes bibliographical references.
CONTENTS: Hansotte, G. Inventaire des archives de la Société anonyme des charbonnages de Bonne-Espérance, Batterie et Violette.—Pleyns, J. Inventaire des archives du journal d'annonces "l'Information, les annonces liègeoises."—Rouhart-Chabot, J. Inventaire des archives des Verreries nouvelles d'Aigremont: supplément.—Pleyns, J. Archives d'entreprises allemandes mises sous séquestre après la guerre 1914–1918.—Hansotte, G. Inventaire des archives de l'entreprise textile de la famille Dethier à Hodimont dites "Fonds Dethier."

Belgium. *Archives générales du royaume.*
Inventaire des archives de l'Administration centrale et supérieure de la Belgique et du Conseil de gouvernement, par Marie-Rose Thielemans, conservateur. Bruxelles, 1964.

xviii, 159 p. 25 cm.

Dargent, J   L
Bibliographie des thèses et mémoires géographiques belges (par) J. L. Dargent Supplément 1959–1965. Bruxelles, Commission belge de bibliographie, 1966.

xlv, 64 p. 21 cm. (Bibliographia Belgica, 92)

Institut belge d'information et de documentation.
Catalogus ₍van de publicaties van het₎ Belgisch Instituut voor Voorlichting en Documentatie. Brussel, Montoyerstr., 3, ₍1970₎.

37 p. 23 x 11 cm.

Nicodème, Jacques.
Répertoire des inventaires des archives conservées en Belgique, parus avant le 1ᵉʳ janvier 1969. Repertorium van inventarissen van archieven in België bewaard, verschenen vóór 1 januari 1969. Préf. par C. Wyffels. Bruxelles ₍Commission belge de bibliographie₎ 1970.

121 p. 25 cm. (Bibliographia Belgica 107)

Archives et bibliothèques de Belgique. Numéro spécial 2.

Nieuwenhuysen, Andrée van.
Relevé d'archives roumaines relatives à l'histoire de la Belgique, précédé d'un aperçu historique. Bruxelles, Archives générales du Royaume, 1973.

vi, 70 p. 24 cm. (Miscellanea archivistica. 1)

At head of title: Archives générales du Royaume et Archives de l'État dans les provinces.

Publications scientifiques de l'État. Choix de publications récentes éditées par: les Archives générales du Royaume, la Bibliothèque royale de Belgique, l'Institut d'aéronomie spatiale de Belgique, l'Institut royal météorologique de Belgique, l'Institut royal du patrimoine artistique, l'Institut royal des sciences naturelles de Belgique, le Jardin botanique de l'État, le Musée royal de l'Afrique centrale, les Musées royaux d'art et d'histoire, les Musées royaux des beaux-arts de Belgique, l'Observatoire royal de Belgique. (Exposition organisée à la Bibliothèque Albert Iᵉʳ, Bruxelles du 11 au 15 janvier 1966). (Bruxelles) ₍Bibliothèque royale de Belgique₎ 1966.

54 p. 27 cm.

Stuttgart. Stadtbücherei.
Belgien: Land und Leute, Kunst und Künstler, Kultur- und Kunststätten, Werk und Leben der Dichter; ein Bücherverzeichnis zur Belgischen Woche 1963. ₍Von Gudrun Schweickhardt bearb. Stuttgart, Kulturamt, 1963₎

35 p. illus., col. plates. 22 cm.

"Das kleine Auswahl-Verzeichnis enthält das in der Stadtbücherei Stuttgart vorhandene deutschsprachige Belgien-Schrifttum."

Les Travaux d'histoire locale. Conseils aux auteurs.
——— Compléments. ₍Par₎ M₍aurice-A₎₍urélien₎ Arnould, J₍ean₎ Fichefet, M₍aurits₎ Gysseling ₍e. a.₎ (Bruxelles), Pro Civitate, (Crédit communal de Belgique, r. de la Banque, 13), 1969–

v. illus., maps, tables. 24 cm. (Pro Civitate. Collection Histoire. Série in -8°, no 22

Vandewoude, Emiel J L M 1923–
Inventaire des archives relatives au développement extérieur de la Belgique sous le règne de Léopold II, par Emile Vandewoude. Bruxelles, 1965.

lx, 298 p. facsims., port. 29 cm. (Archives générales du Royaume. Archives des palais royaux, no 1)

Wetenschappelijke publikaties van het Rijk. Keuze uit de jongste publikaties uitgegeven door het Algemeen Rijksarchief, het Instituut voor Ruimte-Aeronomie van België ₍e. a.₎ ₍Tentoonstelling in de Albert I- Bibliotheek, Brussel, van 11 tot 15 januari 1966₎ Brussel ₍Koninklijke Biblio-

theek van België, Keizerslaan 4₎ 1966.

54 p. 27 cm.

IMPRINTS
see also under Netherlands - Imprints

Cockx-Indestege, Elly.
Belgica typographica 1541–1600. Catalogus librorum impressorum ab anno MDXLI ad annum MDC in regionibus quae nunc Regni Belgarum partes sunt. ₍Auctores₎ Elly Cockx-Indestege et Geneviève Glorieux. Nieuwkoop, B. de Graaf, 1968–

v. 29 cm. (Nationaal Centrum voor de Archeologie en de Geschiedenis van het Boek, 2)

BELGRAD

Živanović, Milan Ž
Библиографија српске књижевне задруге 1892–1967. ⟨₍Саставио и₎ "Уз библиографију" ₍написао₎⟩ Милан Ж. Живановић. Иницијал СКЗ нацртао Јован Јовановић. Београд, Српска књижевна задруга, 1967.

lxxxviii, 443 p. illus., ports., facsims. 19 cm. (Српска књижевна задруга, коло 60, књ. 409)

BELGRANO, MANUEL

Biblioteca Municipal Pública del Partido de General Pueyrredón.
Bibliografía sobre Manuel Belgrano; adhesión al bicentenario de su nacimiento y sesquicentenario de su muerte. Mar del Plata, 1970.

13 l. 36 cm.

BELKNAP, GEORGE EUGENE and REGINALD ROWAN

U. S. *Library of Congress. Manuscript Division.*
George Eugene Belknap, Reginald Rowan Belknap: a register of their papers in the Library of Congress. Washington, Library of Congress, 1969.

5, 8 l. 27 cm.

"Naval Historical Foundation collection."

BELL, DANIEL

Tamiment Library.
A guide to Daniel Bell's files on the Communist Party (U. S. A.), Socialist Party, and labor unions. ₍New York, 1970₎

8 p. 28 cm. (Its Bulletin, no. 46)

Caption title.

On cover: New York University Libraries.

BELL, WILLIAM ABRAHAM

Colorado. State Historical Society. Library.
A calendar of the papers of William Abraham Bell, 1841–1921; a holding of the Library of the State Historical Society of Colorado. Processed by Lee Scamehorn. Denver, 1970.

iv, 84 l. 23 x 29 cm.

BELORUSSIA see White Russia

BENEDICTINES. CONGRÉGATION DE SAINT-MAUR

Lama, Carl von, 1841–1920.
Bibliothèque des écrivains de la Congrégation de Saint-

Maur, ordre de Saint-Benoît en France ₍par₎ Charles de Lama. Genève, Slatkine Reprints, 1971.

261 p. 22 cm.

"Réimpression de l'édition de Munich, 1882."

BENGALI LITERATURE

Haq, Shamsul.
বাংলা সাহিত্য: গ্রন্থপঞ্জী, ১৯৪৭-১৯৬৯. ₍লেখক₎ শামসুল হক. ঢাকা, পাকিস্তান জাতীয় গ্রন্থ কেন্দ্র ₍1970₎

14, 470 p. 22 cm.

In Bengali.

Mukherji, Jagomohon.
Bengali literature in English; a bibliography. ₍1st ed.₎ Calcutta, M. C. Sarkar ₍1970₎

xv, 108, 7 p. 18 cm.

"Supplement, July 1967 to December 1969": 7 p. (3d group)

BENGALI PERIODICALS see Periodical publications - Pakistan

BENNETT, ARNOLD

Emery, Norman.
Arnold Bennett (1867–1931): a bibliography. Hanley, Stoke-on-Trent, Central Library, 1967.

iii, 6 f. 25½ cm. (Horace Barks Reference Library. Bibliographical series no. 3)

A List of his writings presented to H. S. Bennett on his eightieth birthday, 15 January 1969. London, Cambridge U. P., 1969.

15 p. 2 ports. 21 cm.

BENNY, JACK

Smith, David Rollin, 1940–
Jack Benny checklist: radio, television, motion pictures, books and articles, by David R. Smith. Los Angeles, University of California Library, 1970.

33 l. 29 cm.

BENOIT, PIERRE ANDRÉ

Les Livres réalisés par P. A. Benoit, 1942–1971. 26 mars–25 avril 1971, Musée Fabre, Montpellier. Montpellier, Musée Fabre, 1971.

118 p. illus. 23 cm.

Cover title.
Exhibition catalog.

BENONI, SOUTH AFRICA

Moffat, Felicity Janet.
Benoni magisterial district; a bibliography compiled by Felicity Janet Moffat. Johannesburg: University of the Witwatersrand, 1972.

vi, 53 p. l. 30 cm.

BEOWULF

Fry, Donald K
Beowulf, and The fight at Finnsburh; a bibliography ₍by₎ Donald K. Fry. Charlottesville, Published for the Bibliographical Society of the University of Virginia ₍by₎

University Press of Virginia ₍1969₎

xx, 222 p. 25 cm.

Tinker, Chauncey Brewster, 1876–1963.
The translations of Beowulf; a critical bibliography. New York, Gordian Press, 1967.

147 p. 23 cm. (Yale studies in English, 16)

Reprint of the 1903 ed., a portion of the author's thesis, Yale University.

Tinker, Chauncey Brewster, 1876–1963.
The translations of Beowulf; a critical bibliography. New York, B. Franklin ₍1968₎

147 p. 22 cm. (Burt Franklin bibliography & reference series, 90)

Reprint of the 1903 ed.

BERENSON, BERNHARD

Mariano, Nicky, *ed*.
The Berenson archive; an inventory of correspondence, compiled by Nicky Mariano, on the centenary of the birth of Bernard Berenson, 1865–1965. Florence, Italy, Villa I Tatti, Harvard University Center for Italian Renaissance Studies; distributed by Harvard University Press, Cambridge, 1965.

xii, 122 p. facsim., port. 24 cm.

BERGEN, NORWAY. UNIVERSITETET

Bergen, Norway. Universitetet. *Biblioteket*.
Publikasjoner. 1948–1965. Generalregister. Bergen, Universitetsforlaget, 1967.

68 p. 25 cm.

A continuation of Bergens museums publikasjoner 1825–1948, published in 1955.

BERGMAN, SHMUEL HUGO

Shohetman, Baruch, 1890–1956.
כתבי שמואל הוגו ברגמן: ביבליוגרפיה, 1967-1903. מאת ברוך שוחטמן ושלמה שונמי. ירושלים, הוצאת ספרים ע״ש ״ל מאגנס, האוניברסיטה העברית ₍המכירה הראשית: יבנה, תל-אביב₎ 728 ₍1968₎

12, 88, xi p. port. 23 cm. 5.00

Added t. p.: The writings of Shmuel Hugo Bergman: a bibliography, 1903–1967.
Introductory material also in English.

BERGSON, HENRI LOUIS

Gunter, Pete Addison Y 1936–
Henri Bergson : a bibliography / by P. A. Y. Gunter. — Bowling Green, Ohio : Philosophy Documentation Center, Bowling Green University, ₍1974₎

457 p. ; 24 cm. — (Bibliographies of famous philosophers ; 1)

BERKELEY, GEORGE, BP. OF CLOYNE

Jessop, Thomas Edmund, 1896–
A bibliography of George Berkeley, by T. E. Jessop. With an inventory of Berkeley's manuscript remains by A. A. Luce. New York, B. Franklin ₍1968₎

xi, 99 p. 23 cm. (Burt Franklin bibliography and reference series, 234)

Philosophy monograph series, 21.

Jessop, Thomas Edmund, 1896-
A bibliography of George Berkeley, by T. E. Jessop. With inventory of Berkeley's manuscript remains, by A. A. Luce. 2d ed. (rev. and enl.).   The Hague, M. Nijhoff, 1973

xx, 155 p.   25 cm.   (International archives of the history of ideas, 66)

BERKSHIRE, ENGLAND

Reading, Eng.   Public Libraries.
Local collection catalogue of books and maps relating to Berkshire.   Reading, Central Public Library, 1958.

259 p.   25 cm.

————————Supplement; books added 1956–1966.   Reading, Central Public Library, 1967.

84 p.   25 cm.

BERLIN

Berlin.   Amerika-Gedenkbibliothek. *Berlin-Abteilung.*
Berlin und die Berliner; ein Bücherverzeichnis, zusammengestellt von der Berlin-Abteilung der Amerika-Gedenkbibliothek/Berliner Zentralbibliothek.   ₍Bearbeiter des Kataloges: Karlheinz Engel₎   Berlin, 1965.

48, ₍8₎ p.   illus., ports. 21 cm.

Berlin.   Stadtbibliothek.
Berlin und Umgebung — unsere sozialistische Heimat. Auswahlbibliographie.   (Berlin) Berliner Stadtbibliothek, 1971.

23 p.   21 cm.

"Zusammengestellt von Dr. Günther Jarosch anlässlich der Ausstellung Wir lieben und gestalten unsere sozialistische Heimat."

Berlin (West Berlin).   Senat.   Bibliothek.
Berlin-Bibliographie.   In der Senatsbibliothek bearb. Mit einem Vorwort von Hans Herzfeld und Rainer Stromeyer.   Berlin, New York, De Gruyter, 1965–
v.   24 cm.   (Historische Kommission zu Berlin.   Bibliographien, Bd. 1, 4   (Veröffentlichungen der Historischen Kommission zu Berlin, Bd. 15, 43
Errata slip inserted.
CONTENTS: Bd. ₍1₎ Zopf, H. und Heinrich, G.   Bis 1960.—Bd. ₍2₎ Scholz, U. und Stromeyer, R.   1961 bis 1966.

Bremen.   Volksbüchereien.
Berlin.   Ein Literaturverzeichnis.   (Bibliographische Bearbeitung: Werner Reinhold.   Bremen) Volksbüchereien der Freien Hansestadt Bremen (1967).

39 p.   19 cm.

Historische Kommission zu Berlin.
Bibliographien.   Bd. 1–
Berlin, De Gruyter, 1965–

v.   24 cm.   (*Its* Veröffentlichungen)

BERLIN, IRVING

Jay, Dave, *pseud.*
The Irving Berlin songography; 1907–1966.   New Rochelle, N. Y., Arlington House ₍ᶜ1969₎

172 p.   21 cm.

BERLINER, RUDOLF

Müller, Theodor, 1892–
Rudolf Berliner; Bibliographie, zum 14. April 1966. ₍München, 1966₎

22 p.   24 cm.

Published to honor Rudolf Berliner on the occasion of his 80th birthday.

BERLIOZ, HECTOR

Arts Council of Great Britain.
Berlioz and the romantic imagination: an exhibition organized by the Arts Council and the Victoria and Albert Museum on behalf of the Berlioz Centenary Committee in cooperation with the French Government, 17 October to 14 December.   London, Arts Council, 1969.
xxiv, 147 p.   illus. (some col.), facsims., plan, ports. (incl. 1 col.). 26 cm.   index.
"Catalogue edited by Elizabeth Davison."

Paris.   Bibliothèque nationale.
Hector Berlioz, Paris, 1969.   ₍Exposition inaugurée le 5 mars.   Catalogue par François Lesure, avec la collaboration de Yane Fromrich-Bonéfant.   Préface par Étienne Dennery.₎   Paris, Bibliothèque nationale, 1969.

188 p.   illus.   20 cm.

BERMUDA ISLANDS

Bermuda Library, Hamilton, Bermuda Islands.
Bermudiana, bibliography.   ₍Hamilton, Bermuda Islands, 1971₎

26 p.   illus.   21 cm.

Palmer, Margaret.
The printed maps of Bermuda.   London, Map Collectors' Circle, 1965.

19 p.   24 plates.   25 cm.   ₍Map collectors' series, no. 19)

BERNANOS, GEORGES

Jurt, Joseph.
Georges Bernanos, 1; essai de bibliographie des études en langue française consacrées à Georges Bernanos durant sa vie.   1. livr.   Paris, Lettres modernes, 1972–

v.   18 cm.   (Calepins de bibliographie, no 4)   (Lettres modernes)

On spine: Bernanos 1 (1)
"Chaque livraison annule et remplace la précédente."
CONTENTS: t. 1. 1926–1948.

BERNARD, CLAUDE

Grmek, Mirko Dražen.
Catalogue des manuscrits de Claude Bernard, avec la bibliographie de ses travaux imprimés et des études sur son œuvre, par M. D. Grmek.   Avant-propos par M. Bataillon et E. Wolff.   Introduction par L. Delhoume et P. Huard. Paris, Masson & Cⁱᵉ, 1967.

420 p.   24 cm.

BEROES, PEDRO

Vannini de Gerulewicz, Marisa.
Pedro Beroes.   Caracas, Escuela de Biblioteconomía y Archivos, Facultad de Humanidades y Educación, Universidad Central de Venezuela, 1967.

77 p.   port.   16 cm.   (Serie bibliográfica, 4)

BERRIES
Geday, Gusztáv.
A bogyósgyümölcsüek hazai irodalma, 1920–1966.   Összeállította Geday Gusztáv.   Szerkesztőbizottság: Bognár S., et al.   Felelős szerkesztő: Kozma Pál.   Budapest, 1968.

78 p.   24 cm.   (Kertészeti egyetem kiadványai)

Pref. in Hungarian, English, and Russian.

BERRYMAN, JOHN

Kelly, Richard J
John Berryman: a checklist. Compiled by Richard J. Kelly. With a foreword by William Meredith and an introd. by Michael Berryhill. Metuchen, N. J., Scarecrow Press, 1972.

xxxvi, 105 p. port. 22 cm. (The Scarecrow author bibliographies, no. 8)

Stefanik, Ernest C
John Berryman, a descriptive bibliography ₍by₎ Ernest C. Stefanik, Jr. ₍Pittsburgh₎ University of Pittsburgh Press, 1974.

xxix, 285 p. port. 24 cm. (Pittsburgh series in bibliography)

BERZELIUS, JÖNS JAKOB, FRIHERRE

Holmberg, Arne, 1889–
Bibliografi över J. J. Berzelius, utg. av Kungl. Svenska vetenskapsakademien genom Arne Holmberg. Stockholm, 1933–67.

6 v. 23 cm.

Added t. p. in French.

CONTENTS.—1. del. Tryckta arbeten av och om Berzelius.—Supplement. 3 v.—2. del. Manuskript.—Supplement. 1 v.

BESSON, LOUIS

Darnajoux, Hervé.
Bibliographie des articles de M. Louis Besson, par H. Darnajoux. Paris, Direction de la météorologie nationale, 1965.

8 p. 27 cm. (Bibliographie signalétique hebdomadaire sélectionnée. Supplément no 3)

BETEL NUT see Areca Nut

BETHELL, PINCKNEY C. and WILLIAM D.

Colorado. State Historical Society. Library.
A calendar of the papers of Pinckney C. and William D. Bethell, 1848–1901: a holding of the Library of the State Historical Society of Colorado. Processed by Lee Scamehorn. Denver, 1968.

32 l. 23 x 29 cm.

BETHLEHEM, PENNSYLVANIA see under Allentown, Pennsylvania

BEUEL, GERMANY

Neu, Heinrich, 1906–
Das Schrifttum über die Stadt Beuel; eine Bibliographie von Heinrich Neu. Beuel, Stadtverwaltung, 1969.

42 p. 21 cm. (Studien zur Heimatgeschichte der Stadt Beuel, Heft 12)

BEVERAGES

Noling, A   W
Beverage literature: a bibliography. Compiled by A. W. Noling. Metuchen, N. J., Scarecrow Press, 1971.

865 p. 22 cm.

BEWICK, THOMAS and JOHN
Bain, Iain.
Thomas Bewick, engraver, of Newcastle, 1753–1828: a check-list of his correspondence and other papers. ₍Baldock

(Herts.), Iain Bain, 1970₎.

46 p. illus., facsims. 22 cm.

Caption title.
Book jacket title: A checklist of the manuscripts of Thomas Bewick.
"Reprinted from The Private library, with addenda."

Hugo, Thomas, 1820–1876.
The Bewick collector; a descriptive catalogue of the works of Thomas and John Bewick ... London, L. Reeve, 1866. Detroit, Singing Tree Press, 1968.

xxiii, 562 p. illus. 22 cm.

———————— Supplement ... London, L. Reeve, 1868. Detroit, Singing Tree Press, 1968.

xxxii, 353 p. illus. 22 cm.

Hugo, Thomas, 1820–1876.
The Bewick collector; a descriptive catalogue of the works of Thomas and John Bewick. New York, B. Franklin ₍1970₎

xxiii, 562 p. illus. 23 cm. (Burt Franklin bibliography & reference series, 314)

Art history & art reference, 33.
Reprint of the 1866 ed.

———— ———— A supplement ... New York, B. Franklin ₍1970₎

xxxii, 353 p. illus. 23 cm. (Burt Franklin bibliography & reference series, 314)

Art history & art reference, 33.
Reprint of the 1868 ed.

BEYER, WILHELM RAIMUND

Buhr, Manfred.
Wilhelm Raimund Beyer, eine Bibliographie ₍von₎ Manfred Buhr, Joseph E. Drexel ₍und₎ Werner Jakusch. ₍Mit Faksimiles und Abbildungen₎ Wien, Frankfurt, Zürich, Europa-Verlag (1967)

79 p. 21 cm.

BEYLE, MARIE HENRI see Stendhal

BIALIK, HAYYIM NAHMAN

Jerusalem. Hebrew University. Jewish National and University Library.
(Ḥayim Naḥman Byalik)

חיים נחמן ביאליק; תערוכה למלאת מאה שנה להולדתו ₍נערכה על-ידי מחלקת כתבי-היד והארכיונים של בית-הספרים הלאומי והאוניברסיטאי. הקטלוג הוכן על-ידי בית הספרים הלאומי והאוניברסיטאי בשתוף עם מוסד ביאליק, ירושלים והוצאת דביר, תל-אביב. ירושלים, 1972₎

74 p. illus. 23 cm.
Cover title: Chaim Nachman Bialik.
Exhibition held at the Berman Hall, Jewish National and University Library, 1972.

Jeshurin, Ephim H   1885–1967.
חיים-נחמן ביאליק ביבליאגראפיע.
Chaim Nachmen Bialik bibliography.
צוזאמענגעשטעלם פון יעפים ישורין.
Buenos Aires, Ateneo Literario en el Iwo, 1964.

15 p. 18 cm.

"סעפאראט-אפדרוק פון ... חיים-נחמן ביאליק, אויסגעקליבענע שריפטן."

BIAŁYSTOK, POLAND (VOIVODESHIP)
Białostockie Towarzystwo Naukowe.
Bibliografia regionu białostockiego. Bibliography of the

Białystok Region (Poland) ₁Opracował zespół bibliograficzny Białostockiego Towarzystwa Naukowego przy współudziale Biblioteki Wojewódzkiej w Białymstoku, Muzeum w Białymstoku oraz Oddziału Białostockiego Polskiego Towarzystwa Historycznego₁ Białystok ₁Państwowe Wydawn. Naukowe₁ 1964–

v. 25 cm.

At head of title, v. 1– : Muzeum w Białymstoku.
Vol. 1 by U. Lewicka and J. Pochodowicz.
"Supplement do tomu V 'Rocznika białostockiego.' "

BIAŁYSTOK REGION

Katalog Tek Glinki. Oprac. Teresa Zielinska. Warszawa, Ministerstwo Kultury i Sztuki, 1969–

v. 30 cm. (Ośrodek Dokumentacji Zabytków. Biblioteka Muzealnictwa i Ochrony Zabytków. Seria B., t. 26)

CONTENTS: cz. 1. Katalog osobowy.

BIBLE

Coldham, Geraldine Elizabeth.
A bibliography of Scriptures in African languages, compiled by Geraldine E. Coldham. London, British and Foreign Bible Society, 1966.

2 v. 25 cm.

CONTENTS.—v. 1. Polyglot. Acholi—Mousgoum.—v. 2. Mpama—Zulu.
"A revision of the African sections of the Darlow and Moule 'Historical catalogue of printed editions of the Holy Scripture', with additions to 1964."

Falk, Franz, 1840–1909.
Bibelstudien, Bibelhandschriften und Bibeldrucke in Mainz vom achten Jahrhundert bis zur Gegenwart. Amsterdam ₁Nieuwe Herengracht 35₁ Rodopi, 1969.

vi, 338 p. 22 cm.

Reprint of the Mainz, 1901 ed.

Goris, Jan Albert, 1899–
Het boek van Joachim van Babylon. Hetwelk bevat het oprecht verhaal van zijn leven en dat van zijn beroemde huisvrouw Suzanna, kort geleden ontdekt in de opgravingen van Nat-tah-nam en voor het eerst zorgvuldig vertaald en uitgegeven door een liefhebber der oudheid. ₁Door₁ Marnix Gijsen. Amsterdam, Meulenhoff ₁Nederland₁ 1969.

176 p. 21 cm.

Guide to Bibles in print. 1966–
Austin ₁Tex.₁ R. Gordon and Associates.

v. 22 cm. annual.

Compiler and editor: 1966– G. Hester.

Herbert, Arthur Sumner.
Historical catalogue of printed editions of the English Bible: 1525–1961; revised and expanded from the edition of T. H. Darlow and H. F. Moule, 1903, by A. S. Herbert. London, British & Foreign Bible Society; New York, The American Bible Society, 1968.

xxxi, 549 p. 26 cm.

Revised and expanded edition of vol. 1 of Historical catalogue of printed editions of Holy Scripture in the Library of the British and Foreign Bible Society.

Det Kongelige Vajsenhus.
Det kongelige Vajsenhus' bibel- og salmebogssamling m. m. Registreret af P. E. Arnstrøm. København K, Det Kongelige Vajsenhus' Elevforening "Det Gode Minde," Nr. Farimagsgade 51, 1969.

29 p. 22 cm.

Cover title: Bibel- og salmebogssamling.

Nickels, Peter.
Targum and New Testament. A bibliography together with a New Testament index. Rome, Pontifical Biblical Institute, 1967.

xi, 88 p. 21½ cm. (Scripta Pontificii Istituti Biblici, 117)

O'Callaghan, Edmund Bailey, 1797–1880.
A list of editions of the Holy Scriptures and parts thereof printed in America previous to 1860. With introd. and bibliographical notes by Edmund Bailey O'Callaghan. Albany, Munsell & Rowland, 1861. Detroit, Republished by Gale Research Co., 1966.

liv, 415 p. facsims. 24 cm.

Panzer, Georg Wolfgang Franz, 1729–1805.
Ausführliche Beschreibung der ältesten Augspurgischen Ausgaben der Bibel mit litterarischen Anmerkungen. ₁Herdr. van de uitg. Nürnberg, 1780₁. Amsterdam, Grüner, 1971.

158 p. 23 cm.

Polska bibliografia biblijna adnotowana. 1964/68–

Warszawa, Akademia Teologii Katolickiej.

v. 24 cm.

Spurgeon, Charles Haddon, 1834–1892.
Commenting & commentaries: two lectures, a catalogue of Bible comentaries and expositions, by C. H. Spurgeon. ₁New ed.₁; together with a complete textual index to his sermons. London, Banner of Truth Trust, 1969.

ix, 224 p. 23 cm.

Wares, Alan Campbell.
Bibliography of the Wycliffe Bible Translators, Compiled by Alan C. Wares. Santa Ana, Calif., Wycliffe Bible Translators, 1970.

xxii, 84 p. 21 cm.

LIBRARY AND EXHIBITION CATALOGS

American Bible Society.
The many faces of the Bible; an exhibition commemorating the sesquicentennial of the American Bible Society, April 17 through October 9, 1966. Washington, D. C., The Washington Cathedral Rare Book Library, 1966.

41 p. illus. 28 cm.

"Prepared jointly through the offices of the American Bible Society and Washington Cathedral."

Berkowitz, David Sandler, 1913–
In remembrance of creation; evolution of art and scholarship in the Medieval and Renaissance Bible. Waltham, Mass., Brandeis University Press ₁1968₁

xviii, 141, ₁160₁ p. illus., facsims. 29 cm. (Publications of the Society of Bibliophiles at Brandeis University, no. 3)

"Catalogue of an exhibition to commemorate the twentieth anniversary of Brandeis University held at the Rapaporte Treasure Hall, Brandeis University Library, May 4th through June 11th, 1968."

Berteele, Jozef M
De bijbel vroeger en nu. Tentoonstelling. (Ingericht door de Bijbelkringen van Kortrijk, de Oekumenische Kring, de Stadsbibliotheek). Stadsbibliotheek te Kortrijk van 5 april tot 3 mei 1969. (Samenstelling catalogus: J. M. Berteele ₁&₁ Paul Vancolen) ₁Kortrijk, Stadsbiblio-

theek, Guido Gezellestraat₁ 1969.

22 p. 22 cm.

Houston, Tex. University.
University of Houston exhibition of Bibles and related materials, Christmas 1970. Houston, 1970.

₁24₁ p. illus., facsims. (2 col.) 32 cm.

"Notes prepared by Mrs. Marian Orgain, curator of special collections."

Memorial Bible House Library of Scriptures.
Memorial Bible House, Library of Scriptures, Canberra; a short account of the books contained in the library with a descriptive catalogue of the Scriptures in Oceanic languages. Canberra ₁1967₁

75 p. col. maps. 27 cm.

"Memorial Bible House: supplementary list of Oceanic Scriptures" (₁4₁ leaves) inserted.

St. Mary's Seminary, Oscott, Eng.
Catalogue of the Bible collections in the Old Library at St. Mary's, Oscott, c. 1472–c. 1850; edited by G. F. Pullen. Sutton Coldfield (New Oscott, Sutton Coldfield, Warwickshire), St. Mary's Seminary, 1971.

ii–xxii, 208, ₁12₁ p. facsims., ports. 24 cm. (Its Catalogue pt. 2)

Texas. University. *Humanities Research Center.*
The Holy Bible at the University of Texas, by David R. Farmer. ₁Austin, 1967₁

71 p. illus., facsims. 25 cm.

A revision and an expansion of the 1960 catalogue; The Holy Bible, an exhibit, by Edwin T. Bowden.
A description of some Bibles in the collections of the Humanities Research Center and of the Library.

Washington, D. C. Cathedral of St. Peter and St. Paul. *Rare Book Library.*
In the beginning was the word. Washington, 1965.

71 p. illus., facsims., ports. 28 cm.

"Opening exhibition of written and printed Biblical and liturgical texts from the eighth century to the present. May sixteenth to October fifteenth, nineteen hundred and sixty-five."

Washington, D. C. Cathedral of St. Peter and St. Paul. *Rare Book Library.*
Presidential inaugural Bibles; catalogue of an exhibition, November 17, 1968 through February 23, 1969. ₁Washington, 1969₁

49, ₁27₁ p. illus., facsims., ports. 26 cm.

MANUSCRIPTS

Antonioli Martelli, Valeria.
Manoscritti biblici ebraici decorati provenienti da biblioteche italiane pubbliche e private. Catalogo della mostra ordinata presso la Biblioteca trivulziana, Castello Sforzesco, Milano, 2/28 marzo 1966, a cura di Valeria Antonioli Martelli e Luisa Mortara Ottolenghi; con prefazioni di Carlo Bernheimer, Roberto Bonfil ₁e₁ Cecil Roth. Milano, Edizioni dell'ADEI-WIZO ₁1966₁

101 p. facsims. (part col.), plates (part col.) 24 cm.
Prefaces in Italian and English.

Chicago. University. Library.
New Testament manuscript traditions. An exhibition based on the Edgar J. Goodspeed collection of the University of Chicago Library. The Joseph Regenstein Library. January-March, 1973. ₁Chicago, 1973₁

₁52₁ p. 25 cm.

Gregory, Casper René, 1846–1917.
Die griechischen Handschriften des Neuen Testaments. Leipzig, J. C. Heinrich'sche Buchhandlung, 1908. ₁Leipzig, Zentralantiquariat der Deutschen Demokratischen Republik, 1973₁

v, 366 p. 22 cm.

PERIODICALS

Elenchus bibliographicus biblicus.
Rome, Biblical Institute Press.

v. 24 cm. annual.

Began with v. 49, 1968; previously included in Biblica.
Editor: P. Nober.

Langevin, Paul Émile.
Bibliographie biblique. Biblical bibliography. Biblische Bibliographie. Bibliografia biblica. Bibliografía bíblica. 1930–1970. Québec, Presses de l'Université Laval, 1972.

xxviii, 935 p. 27 cm.

Metzger, Bruce Manning, *ed.*
Index to periodical literature on Christ and the Gospels, compiled under the direction of Bruce M. Metzger. Leiden, E. J. Brill, 1966.

xxiii, 602 p. 25 cm. (New Testament tools and studies, v. 6)

St. John's University, Collegeville, Minn.
Library index to Biblical journals. Edited by Thomas Peter Wahl. Established by Raymond Breun. Collegeville, Minn., St. John's University Press, 1971.

1 v. (unpaged) 24 cm.

"July 1970. Fifth edition."

BIBLE. OLD TESTAMENT

Grossfeld, Bernard.
A bibliography of Targum literature. Cincinnati, Hebrew Union College Press, 1972 ₁i. e. 1973₁

xxvii, 132 p. 29 cm. (Bibliographica Judaica, no. 2 ₁i. e. 3₁)

Jerusalem. Hebrew University. *Institute of Jewish Studies.*
תדריך ביבליוגרפי לבחינות הגמר במקרא. ירושלים, האוניברסיטה העברית בירושלים, הפקולטה למדעי הרוח, החוג למקרא. תשכ"ה, ₁19₁65.

14 l. 28 cm.

Jerushalmi, Joseph.
אישים וספרים במקרא; ביבליוגרפיה. מאמרים מכתבי עת וקבצים עבריים ₁מאת₁ יוסף ירושלמי. חיפה, לסטודנט. 731 ₁1970 or 71₁

v, 125 p. 24 cm.

On verso of t. p.: Bibliography of persons and books in the Bible; articles from Hebrew periodicals and collections.

North, Robert Grady, 1916–
Exégèse pratique des petits prophètes postexiliens. Bibliographie commentée, 950 titres. English summary. Rome, Biblico, 1969.

228 p. illus. 24 cm.

At head of title: Robert North.

Society for Old Testament Study.
A decade of Bible bibliography; the book lists of the Society for Old Testament Study, 1957–1966. Edited by G. W. Anderson. Oxford, Blackwell, 1967.

ix, 706 p. 21 cm.

(Ta'arukhat Tanakh bi-defus uve-omanut)

תערוכת תנ״ך בדפוס ובאמנות. ישראל, תש״ל; קטלוג. ‏תל-אביב,
‏1970,

61 p. (p. 55–61 advertisements) 22 cm.

Cover title.

‏"יום סניף החברה לחקר המקרא בתל-אביב ... תערובה זאת בה ... כל
מה שנדפס בארץ על החנ״ך מיום קום המדינה."

BIBLE. OLD TESTAMENT. PSALMS

Eames, Wilberforce, 1855–1937.
A list of editions of the Bay Psalm book or New England version of the Psalms. New ed., with a facsim. reprint of the 1st ed. of the Bay Psalm book, printed by S. Daye at Cambridge in New England in 1640. New York, Burt Franklin ₁1973₎

20 ₁297₎ p. 22 cm. (Burt Franklin bibliography & reference series, 473. Philosophy and religious history monographs, 122)

Eames' List is a reprint of the 1885 ed. published in New York.

Minis, Cola.
Bibliographie zu den Altmittel- und Altniederfränkischen Psalmen und Glossen. ₁Von₎ C. Minis. Amsterdam, Rodopi, 1971.

84 p. 23 cm. (Beschreibende Bibliographien, Heft 2)

BIBLE. NEW TESTAMENT

Clifford E. Barbour Library.
A periodical and monographic index to the literature on the Gospels and Acts. Based on the files of the École biblique in Jerusalem. Pittsburgh ₁1971₎

xxiv, 336 p. 28 cm. (Bibliographia tripotamopolitana, no. 3)

Pages 331–336 and other pages at the end of each section blank for notes.
Introductory matter in English and French.

Malatesta, Edward.
St. John's Gospel, 1920–1965. A cumulative and classified bibliography of books and periodical literature on the fourth Gospel, compiled by Edward Malatesta. Rome, Pontifical Biblical Institute, 1967.

xxviii, 205 p. 24 cm. (Analecta Biblica, 32)

Mattill, Andrew Jacob, 1924–
A classified bibliography of literature on the Acts of the Apostles, compiled by A. J. Mattill and Mary Bedford Mattill. Leiden, E. J. Brill, 1966.

xviii, 513 p. 25 cm. (New Testament tools and studies, v. 7)

Scholer, David M
A basic bibliographic guide for New Testament exegesis ₁by₎ David M. Scholer. South Hamilton, Mass., Gordon-Conwell Bookcentre ₁1971₎

56 l. 29 cm.

Scholer, David M
A basic bibliographic guide for New Testament exegesis, by David M. Scholer. 2d ed. Grand Rapids, Eerdmans ₁1973₎

94 p. 21 cm. $2.25

BIBLIOGRAPHIES

Hurd, John Coolidge.
A bibliography of New Testament bibliographies. New York, Seabury Press, 1966.

75 p. 28 cm.

BIBLICAL GREEK   see   Greek language, Biblical

BIBLIOGRAPHICAL EXHIBITIONS   see Bibliography - Exhibition catalogs

BIBLIOGRAPHY
see also   Books; Documentation; Reference books

BEST BOOKS

General bibliographies only; bibliographies of selected books on a specific subject are entered under the subject.

Bertalan, Frank J
The junior college library collection. General editor: Frank J. Bertalan. 1st ed. Newark, N. J., Bro-Dart Foundation, 1968.

xiii l, 396, ₁108₎ p. 29 cm.

Bertalan, Frank J
The junior college library collection. General editor: Frank J. Bertalan. Associate editor: Jessie Kitching. 1970 ed. Newark, N. J., Bro-Dart Foundation, 1970.

xiv, 503, ₁129₎ p. 29 cm.

Everyman's library.
The reader's guide to Everyman's library, compiled by A. J. Hoppé. Further revised ed. London, Dent, New York, Dutton, 1966.

xiv, 434 p. 18½ cm. (Everyman's library, 889)

Everyman's library.
The reader's Guide to Everyman's Library, compiled by A. J. Hoppé. Further revised ₁ed.₎. London, Dent, 1971.

ix, 468 p. 19 cm. (Everyman's library, no. 1889) (Everyman paperback)

Fjeldgaard, Ellen, 1936– *comp.*
Hjem og fritid. Bøger for familien. Udarb. af: Ellen Fjeldgaard, Astrid Hoffmeyer, og Hans Chr. Larsen. Vignetter: Birthe Bruun. København, Bibliotekscentralen, 1966.

32 p. illus. 20 cm.

Fogelberg, Kerstin, 1939–
Har ni läst ... Ett urval böcker i populära intresseområden. Av Kerstin Fogelberg och Ingrid Nilsson. Lund, Bibliotekstjänst, 1967.

51 p. 21 cm. (Btj-serien, 3)

France. *Ministère de la coopération.*
Indications bibliographiques à l'usage des bibliothèques africaines et malgaches. Paris, Ministère de la coopération ₁1969?₎

x, 264 p. 21 cm.

Guida alla formazione di una biblioteca pubblica e privata. Catalogo sistematico e discografia. Con un commento di Delio Cantimori, una lettera di Salvatore Accardo e una documentazione sull'esperienza di Dogliani. Torino, G. Einaudi, 1969.

xxvii, 681 p. 18 cm. (Piccola biblioteca Einaudi, 123)

Ḥammādī, Muḥammad Rushdī.
₁Li-kay takūna ... min: qādāt al-fikr₎

لكى تكون ... من: قادة الفكر ، تأليف محمد رشدى حمادى .
القاهرة، عيسى البابى الحلبى ،1972،

543 p. 24 cm.

Holl, Oskar.
Wissenschaftskunde. Pullach bei München, Verlag Dokumentation ،c1973،

2 v. (363 p.) 19 cm. (Uni-Taschenbücher, 286/287 Interdisziplinär)

The **Home** guide to books. no. 1–
1965–
Cedar Rapids, Iowa, Carlyn Pub. Co.

no. 22 cm.

Jāmi'at al-Kuwayt. *Murāqabat al-Maktabāt.*
نشرة المكتبة. رقم 1– اكتوبر 1966–
الكويت،

v. 83 cm.

Added title: Library bulletin.
Arabic or English.
No. 1 issued by the university's al-Maktabah al-Ra'īsīyah.

Kieran, John, 1892–
Books I love; being a selection of 100 titles for a home library, with added comment on other books, many authors and the delights of reading. ،1st ed.، Garden City, N.Y., Doubleday, 1969.

xvi. 200 p. 22 cm.

Közművelődési könyvtárak összesített törzsanyagjegyzéke,
1959–1964. Budapest, OSZK Könyvtártudományi és Módszertani Központ, 1967–

v. 20 cm. (A Könyvtártudományi és Módszertani Központ kiadványai, 17)

CONTENTS.—1. Szépirodalom.

Lobet, Marcel.
Classiques de l'an 2.000. (Nivelles), Éditions de la Francité, (1970).

212 p. 23 cm.

Lombardo Toledano, Vicente, 1894–
Obras fundamentales de la literatura y la música del mundo occidental. ،1. ed. México, Ediciones Lombardo, 1965،

42 p. 20 cm.

Lombardy. Assessorato alla cultura, informazione e partecipazione.
Guida per una biblioteca economica. ،Milano, 1972،

xi, 341 p. 19 cm.

At head of title: Regione Lombardia.

Louisiana. State Library, *Baton Rouge.*
Break-through with books; a booklist for adult correctional institutional libraries. Baton Rouge, 1970.

67 l. 28 cm.

Louisiana. *State Library, Baton Rouge.*
Designed for you by your State Library, 1966–1967. ،Baton Rouge, 1966،

20 p. 22 cm.

McGinniss, Dorothy A
Guide to the selection of books for your secondary school library. Title selections by Dorothy A. McGinniss. ،Somerville, N. J., Baker & Taylor Co. ،1968،

viii, 264 p. port. 28 cm.

McGinniss, Dorothy A
Guide to the selection of books for your secondary school library; titles selected by Dorothy A. McGinniss. ،1972–73 ed. Somerville, N. J., Baker & Taylor Co., 1972،

xxiii, 329 p. 29 cm.

———— ———1973 supplement. ،Somerville, N. J., Baker & Taylor Co., 1972، c1973.

xxiii, 108 p. 28 cm.

Moorman, Lawrence, comp.
Value sources / Lawrence Moorman, Marilyn Moorman. — Dubuque, Iowa : Kendall / Hunt Pub. Co., ،1974،

xii, 279 p. : ill. : 28 cm.

National Association of Independent Schools. Library Committee.
Books for secondary school libraries. 4th ed. New York, R. R. Bowker Co., 1971.

viii, 308 p. 24 cm.

First-3d ed. published under title: 4000 books for secondary school libraries.

National Association of Independent Schools. Library Committee.
4000 books for secondary school libraries; a basic list. New York, R. R. Bowker Co., 1968.

230 p. 23 cm.

Fourth ed. published in 1971 under title: Books for secondary school libraries.

National Book League, *London.*
Commonwealth celebrities' choice. London, National Book League, 1966.

19 p. 21½ cm.

New York Library Association. *Children's and Young Adult Services Section.*
College preparatory reading list. Rev. ed. ،Woodside, N. Y., 1968،

23 p. 22 cm.

Opening day collection. Prepared under the supervision of Richard K. Gardner, editor, Louise F. Lockwood, associate editor, Kenneth McLintock ،and others، assistant editors. 3d ed. Middletown, Conn., Choice, 1974.

iv, 59 p. illus. 28 cm.

Ordódy, Mária.
A nagy közművelődési könyvtárak kézikönyvei; ajánló jegyzék ،írta، Ordódy Mária ،és، Pálvölgyi Endre. Budapest, Népművelési Propaganda Iroda, 1967.

163 p. 21 cm. (A Könyvtártudományi és Módszertani Központ kiadványai, 23)

Pauk, Walter.
Reading for success in college. Oshkosh, Wis., Academia Press ،1968،

iv, 82 p. 23 cm.

Petersson, Stina.
Tid att läsa; förslag på kärleksromaner, detektivromaner, reseskildringar, böcker om djur och natur m. m. ،3. omarb. uppl. Lund, Bibliotekstjänst, 1971،

69 p. 19 cm. (Btj-serien, 35)

111

Petersson, Stina.
Tid att läsa : förslag på kärleksromaner, detektivromaner,, reseskildringar, böcker om djur och natur m. m. / av Stina Petersson. — 4. omarb. uppl. — Lund : Bibliotekstjänst, 1974.

68 p. ; 19 cm. — (Btj-serien ; 56)

Includes index.
ISBN 91-7018-096-2 : kr47.00

Pirie, James W 1913-
Books for junior college libraries; a selected list of approximately 19,700 titles, compiled by James W. Pirie. Chicago, American Library Association, 1969.

x, 452 p. 29 cm.

Public Library Association. *Starter List for New Branch & New Libraries Collection Committee.*
Books for public libraries; selected titles for small libraries and new branches. New York, R. R. Bowker Co., 1970.

xvii, 194 p. 24 cm.

Public Library Association. Starter List for New Branch & New Libraries Collection Committee.
Books for public libraries : nonfiction for small collections / compiled by the Starter List for New Branch & New Libraries Collection Committee of the Public Library Association, a division of the American Library Association. — 2d ed. — New York : R. R. Bowker Co., 1975.

xv, 220 p. ; 24 cm.

Public library catalog. Edited by Gary L. Bogart and Estelle A. Fidell. 6th ed., 1973. New York, H. W. Wilson Co., 1974.

x, 1543 p. 26 cm. (Standard catalog series)

First-4th ed. issued by H. W. Wilson Co. under title: Standard catalog for public libraries.
Companion volumes to H. W. Wilson Company's Fiction catalog.

Reading round the world; a set of international reading lists. Edited by Frank Gardner & M. Joy Lewis. ₁Hamden, Conn., published by₁ Archon Books on behalf of IFLA ₁1969₁

200 p. 23 cm.

Compiled by members of the Libraries in Hospitals Section of the International Federation of Library Associations.

Reading round the world: a set of international reading lists; compiled by members of the International Federation of Library Associations and edited by Frank Gardner & M. Joy Lewis. London, Bingley on behalf of the I. F. L. A., 1969.

200 p. 23 cm.

Compiled by members of the Libraries in Hospitals Section of the International Federation of Library Associations.

Rivière, Philippe.
La bibliothèque idéale. 5. éd. revue et augm. Paris, Éditions universitaires ₁1970₁

402 p. 20 cm. (La Bibliothèque idéale)

Senior high school library catalog. Edited by Rachel Shor and Estelle A. Fidell. 9th ed. New York, H. W. Wilson Co., 1967.

xii, 1251 p. 27 cm. (Standard catalog series)

On spine: With Catholic supplement.
Previous editions issued by H. W. Wilson Co. under title: Standard catalog for high school libraries.
Kept up to date by annual supplements.

Senior high school library catalog. Edited by Estelle A. Fidell and Toby N. Berger. 10th ed. New York, H. W. Wilson Co., 1972.

xii, 1214 p. 27 cm. (Standard catalog series)

First-8th ed. published under title: Standard catalog for high school libraries.
Kept up to date by annual supplements.

Smith, Jane Fulton.
An area list of reserved book collections in college libraries. ₁Poughkeepsie, N. Y.₁ Southeastern New York Library Resources Council, 1969.

iv, 79 p. 29 cm.

On cover: New York State. Reference & Research Library Resources Program. Research Resources for the Hudson Valley.

Søholm, Ejgil.
Ti tusind titler. F₁olkebibliotekernes₁ u₁denlandske₁ V₁andrebogsamling₁ grundkatalog. Udarb. af Ejgil Søholm og Jens Raahauge Nielsen. Arhus, Statsbiblioteket, 1968.

155 p. 30 cm.

Sonnenschein, William Swan, 1855-1931.
The best books; a reader's guide and literary reference book, being a contribution towards systematic bibliography, by William Swan Sonnenschein (William Swan Stallybrass) With an introd. by Francesco Cordasco. 3d ed., entirely rewritten. London, G. Routledge, 1910-35. Detroit, Gale Research Co., 1969.

6 v. (3759 p.) 23 cm.

CONTENTS.—pt. I. A, Theology. B, Mythology and folklore. C, Philosophy.—pt. II. D, Society. E, Geography.—pt. III. F, History and historical biography. G, Archaeology and historical collaterals.—pt. IV. H, Natural science. H*, Medicine and surgery. I, Arts and trades.—pt. V. K, Literature and philology.—pt. VI. Index, including synopsis of classification, etc., by Frances H. S. Stallybrass. Preface, by W. T. S. Stallybrass. List of British publishers, learned societies, etc., by Lawrence H. Dawson.

U. S. *Information Agency.*
Books for prestige presentation. Washington, U. S. Information Agency, Information Center Service, 1968.

12 p. 27 cm. (*Its* Subject bibliography no. 12/68)

U. S. *Information Agency.*
Books for prestige presentation. Washington, 1969.

11 p. 27 cm. (*Its* Subject bibliography no. 8/69)

University Microfilms, Ann Arbor, Mich.
Xerox college library program; a comprehensive book service for the academic library. Ann Arbor ₁1969?₁

ix, 457 p. 28 cm.

Vzorový katalóg pre osvetové knižnice na Slovensku. ₁Zostavil: Michal Kováč a kol. Zodpovedná redaktorka Mária Lehotská₁ 2., prepracované a doplnené vyd. ₁V Martine₁ Matica slovenska, 1966-69.

4 v. 25 cm.

CONTENTS: zv. 1. Náučná literatúra; výber kníh z vydaní za roky 1945-1964.—zv. 2. Krásna literatúra; výber kníh z vydaní za r. 1945-1965.—zv. 3. Literatúra pre deti; výber kníh z vydaní za roky 1945-65.—zv. 4. Literatúra pre mládež; výber z knižných vydaní od roku 1945-1965.

Wheeler, Helen Rippier.
A basic book collection for the community college library, by Helen Wheeler. ₁Hamden, Conn.₁ Shoe String Press, 1968.

x, 317 p. 26 cm.

Wigny, Pierre Louis.
La nouvelle bibliothèque de l'honnête homme. Publiée sous la direction de Pierre Wigny. Anvers, Impr. Excelsior, (₍pour₎ le Fonds Mercator, à l'initiative de la Banque de Paris et des Pays-Bas, Bruxelles), 1968.

803 p. 24 cm.

A revision of the work previously published under title: La bibliothèque de l'honnête homme.

Wilson, H. W., *firm, publishers.*
Junior high school library catalog, edited by Rachel Shor and Estelle A. Fidell. 1st ed. New York, 1965.

768 p. 27 cm. (Standard catalog series)

———————Supplement. 1966–
New York.

v. 26 cm. annual.

Wilson, H. W., *firm, publishers.*
Public library catalog. Edited by Estelle A. Fidell. 5th ed., 1968. New York, 1969.

viii, 1646 p. 27 cm. (*Its* Standard catalog series)

First–4th ed. published under title: Standard catalog for public libraries.

Wilson, James Albert, 1928–
A self-directed reading program in society, business, and man; 'Kulter, Kitsch, and Klatsch'. By James A. Wilson ₍and₎ Joan P. McLean. Pittsburgh, Graduate School of Business, University of Pittsburgh ₍1968₎

57 l. 29 cm.

BIBLIOGRAPHIES

General bibliographies of bibliographies and of the subject Bibliography.

Avicenne, Paul.
Bibliographical services throughout the world, 1960–1964. ₍Paris₎ UNESCO ₍1969₎

228 p. 21 cm. (UNESCO bibliographical handbooks, 11)

Besterman, Theodore.
A world bibliography of bibliographies and of bibliographical catalogues, calendars, abstracts, digests, indexes, and the like. 4th ed. rev. and greatly enl. throughout. Lausanne, Societas bibliographica ₍1965–66₎

5 v. (8425 columns) 28 cm.

Vol. 5: Index.

Canberra, Australia. National Library. *Australian Bibliographical Centre.*
Bibliographies and bibliographical services for Australian public libraries, a select list. Canberra, Australian Advisory Council on Bibliographical Services, 1961.

vii, 26 p. 25 cm.

Československá akademie věd. *Základní knihovna.*
Seznam encyklopedií, biografií a bibliografií. 2. vyd. Sest. Milada Jedličková. Praha, 1965.

303 p. 20 cm.

Collison, Robert Lewis.
Bibliographies, subject and national: a guide to their contents, arrangement and use ₍by₎ Robert L. Collison. 3rd ed., revised & enlarged. London, Lockwood, 1968.

xviii, 203 p. 23 cm.

Courtney, William Prideaux, 1845–1913.
A register of national bibliography, with a selection of the chief bibliographical books and articles printed in other countries. New York, B. Franklin ₍1967₎

3 v. in 2. 23 cm. (Burt Franklin bibliography & reference series, no. 134)

Reprint of the edition published 1905–12.

Deutscher Bibliotheksverband. Bezirksgruppe Rostock. Arbeitsgruppe Bibliographische Arbeit.
Verzeichnis der im Bezirk Rostock laufend gehaltenen Bibliographien. ₍Bearbeiter: Elfriede Rohde₎ Rostock, Universitätsbibliothek, 1970.

63 p. 21 cm.

Downs, Robert Bingham, 1903–
American library resources; a bibliographical guide, by Robert B. Downs. Boston, Gregg Press, 1972 ₍c1951₎

428 p. 29 cm. (The Library reference series. Librarianship and library resources)

Reprint of the ed. published by the American Library Association, Chicago. Sponsored by the American Library Association Board on Resources of American Libraries.

Downs, Robert Bingham, 1903–
Bibliography; current state and future trends, edited by Robert B. Downs and Frances B. Jenkins. Urbana, University of Illinois Press, 1967.

vii, 611 p. 24 cm. (Illinois contributions to librarianship, no. 8)

"Appeared originally in the Janaury and April 1967 issues of Library trends." Includes bibliographies.

Gábor, František.
Bibliografia bibliografií ŠVK v Košiciach za roky 1956–1970. Zost.: František Gábor. Košice, ŠVK, rozmn., 1971.

3 v. 20 cm. (Bibliografické správy ŠVK Košice, čís. 2719/1971)

Glynn, J   H
Index to bibliographies compiled in the Research Service, State Library of South Australia. Series 4, 1964–1967, compiled by J. H. Glynn. Adelaide, State Library of South Australia, 1967.

21 p. 26 cm. (Research Service bibliographies. Series 4, no. 97)

Greifswald. Universität. *Bibliothek.*
Verzeichnis der an der Universitätsbibliothek Greifswald laufend gehaltenen Bibliographien. ₍Bearbeitung: Frieder Löffler₎ Greifswald, 1967.

27 p. 21 cm. (Veröffentlichungen der Universitätsbibliothek Greifswald, 3)

Gudovshchikova, I   V
Общая международная библиография библиографии. Учеб. пособие по курсу "Общая иностр. библиография." Ленинград, 1969.

105 p. with illus. 21 cm.

At head of title: Министерство культуры РСФСР. Ленинградский государственный институт культуры имени Н. К. Крупской.

Guild, Reuben Aldridge, 1822–1899.
The librarian's manual; a treatise on bibliography, comprising a select and descriptive list of bibliographical works; to which are added, sketches of publick libraries. Illustrated with engravings. New York, C. B. Norton, 1858. Detroit, Grand River Books, 1971.

10, 304 p. illus. 22 cm.

Halle. Universitäts- und Landesbibliothek Sachsen-Anhalt. Abteilung Information und Dokumentation.
Der Bestand des bibliographischen Handapparates der Abteilung Information und Dokumentation der Universitäts- und Landesbibliothek Sachsen-Anhalt in Halle (Saale) ; Auswahl. Zusammengestellt und bearb. von Karl Klaus Walther, Johanna Eleonore Pape und Heidrun Wöllenweber. Halle (Saale) Universitäts- und Landesbibliothek Sachsen-Anhalt, 1972.

46 p. 22 cm. (Schriften zum Bibliotheks- und Büchereiwesen in Sachsen-Anhalt, 37)

Harvard University. *Library.*
Bibliography and bibliography periodicals. Cambridge, Distributed by the Harvard University Press, 1966.

1066 p. 29 cm. (Widener Library shelflist no. 7)

Heydrich, Jürgen.
Bibliographie der Bibliographien für Leitbibliotheken. 5. Ausg. Köln, Zentralkatalog d. Landes Nordrhein-Westfalen, 1972.

ix, 13 p. 21 cm.

Internationale Bibliographie des Buch- und Bibliothekswesen, mit besonderer Berücksichtigung der Bibliographie. n. F. 1.–15. Jahrg.; 1926–40. Leipzig, O. Harrassowitz. Nendeln, Kraus Reprint, 1969.

15 v. in 7. 26 cm.

"Jahresbibliographie des Zentralblattes für Bibliothekswesen." Supersedes Bibliographie des Bibliotheks- und Buchwesens. Editors: 1926–29 Rudolf Hoecker, Joris Vorstius.

John Crerar Library, *Chicago.*
A list of bibliographies of special subjects, July, 1902. New York, B. Franklin [1968]

502 p. 27 cm. (Burt Franklin bibliography and reference series, 210)

Reprint of the 1902 ed.

Kaĭnarova, Mariía Atanasova.
Обща международна библиография на библиографията. Съвременно състояние и проблеми. (София) Нар. библ. Кирил и Методий [1970].

58 p. 20 cm.

Kringlen, Stein.
Grunnkurs i bibliografi; annotert fortegnelse med en kort innføring. Foreløpig utg. Oslo, Statens bibliotekskole, 1964.

87 l. 30 cm.

Lewy, Kaethe.
מדריך לביבליונרפיות כלליות ולספרי עזר. מאת קטה לוי. ירושלים. האוניברסיטה העברית. בית הספר לספרנות. 727
[1966 or 7]

xi, 155 p. 25 cm.

IL 6.00 (8. האוניברסיטה העברית. בית-הספר לספרנות. פרסומים, מס.)
Added t. p.: Guide to general bibliographies and reference books.

Malclès, Louise Noëlle.
Manuel de bibliographie. 2. éd. entièrement refondue et mise à jour. Paris, Presses universitaires de France, 1969 [°1963]

366 p. 25 cm.

Malclès, Louise Noëlle, 1900–
Notions fondamentales de bibliographie. 5e édition revue et mise à jour. Paris, École nationale supérieure de bibliothécaires, 1969.

ii, 60 p. 27 cm.

At head of title: Direction des bibliothèques et de la lecture publique. Certificat d'aptitude aux fonctions de bibliothécaire.

Malclès, Louise Noëlle.
Notions fondamentales de bibliographie. 5. éd. revue et mise à jour (1969). Paris, École nationale supérieure des bibliothèques, 1972.

i, 60 p. 27 cm.

Millares Carlo, Agustín, 1893–
Prontuario de bibliografía general. Maracaibo, Venezuela, Universidad del Zulia, Dirección de Cultura, 1966.

140 p. facsims., port. 23 cm.

Munch-Petersen, Erland.
Kilder til litteratursøgning. Et annoteret udvalg af bibliografier og kataloger. København, (Gad), 1973.

303 p. 20 cm. (Danmarks biblioteksskoles skrifter, 9)

Munch-Petersen, Erland.
Udenlandsk bibliografi og danske kataloger. I tilslutning til "A guide to Danish bibliography." København, Danmarks Biblioteksskole (Bibliotekscentralen) 1968.

121 p. 20 cm.

Nikolaev, Valeriĭ Alekseevich.
Общая библиография библиографий; учебное пособие по курсу "Общая библиография." Москва, 1964.

21 p.

At head of title: Министерство культуры РСФСР. Московский государственный институт культуры. Николаев, В. А.

Microfilm. 1 reel. 35 mm.

Ottervik, Gösta, 1911–
Bibliografier. Kommenterad urvalsförteckning med särskild hänsyn till svenska förhållanden. 3., omarb. och väsentligt utökade uppl. Lund, Bibliotekstjänst, 1966.

255 p. 25 cm. (Sveriges allmänna biblioteksförenings handböcker, 13)

Platt, Peter.
A guide to book lists and bibliographies for the use of schools. 3rd revised ed. London, School Library Association, 1969.

vi, 41 p. 25 cm. (School Library Association. Book lists)

Previous eds. compiled by Wilfred Leonard Saunders under title: A guide to book lists and bibliographies for the use of school librarians.

RAS newsletter. no. 1–
New York, Science Associates/International, inc., 1974–

no. 28 cm.

"A quarterly listing of selected bibliographies and reading lists not included in Readers advisory service."

Readers advisory service: Selected topical booklists. no. 1–

New York, Science Associates/International, inc., 1974–

no. 29 cm.

Riedlová, Marie.
Bibliografické ročenky a retrospektivní bibliografie. Výběr čes. a slov. bibliografií 1945–1970. Sest. Marie Riedlová. Olomouc, St. věd. knihovna, rozmn., 1972.

55, [1] p. 29 cm. (Publikace Státní vědecké knihovny v Olomouci, čís. 3/1972)

Saskatchewan. Provincial Library, Regina. Bibliographic Services Division.
Bibliographies & booklists compiled by the Provincial Library. Regina, 1973.

8 p. 22 cm.

Schneider, Georg, 1876–1960.
Handbuch der Bibliographie. 5. Aufl. Stuttgart, A. Hiersemann, 1969 [°1968]

ix, 674 p. 24 cm.

Reprint of the 4th edition published in Leipzig by K. W. Hiersemann in 1930.

Silvestri, Gerhard.
Einführung in die Bibliographie. Wien, Österreichisches Institut für Bibliotheksforschung, 1966.

36 p. 29 cm. (Leitfäden zur Bibliotheksprüfung, Heft 3)

Silvestri, Gerhard.
Einführung in die Bibliographie. Zusammengestellt von Gerhard Silvestri. 2., erg. Aufl. Wien (Österreichisches Institut für Bibliotheksforschung) 1968.

iv, 36 l. 30 cm. (Leitfäden zur Bibliotheksprüfung, Heft 3)

Silvestri, Gerhard.
Einführung in die Bibliographie. ⟨Bibliographien u. Nachschlagewerke.⟩ Zsgest. v. Gerhard Silvestri unter Mitarb. v. J. Mayerhöfer [u. a.] 3., verb. Aufl. Wien (Österr. Inst. f. Bibliotheksforschung) 1973.

vi, 88 l. 30 cm. (Leitfäden zur Bibliotheksprüfung, Heft 3)

Soupis bibliografií.
[Praha] Státní knihovna ČSR.

v. in 21 cm. annual. (Novinky literatury: Přehledy informativní literatury)

Began with vol. for 1965.
Caption title : Soupis bibliografií přírůstek a informace o novinkách českých, slovenských a zahraničních bibliografií.

Totok, Wilhelm.
Handbuch der bibliographischen Nachschlagewerke [von] Wilhelm Totok, Rolf Weitzel [und] Karl-Heinz Weimann. 3., erw., völlig neu bearb. Aufl. Frankfurt a. M., Klostermann (1966)

xxiv, 362 p. 25 cm.

Totok, Wilhelm.
Handbuch der bibliographischen Nachschlagewerke. Hrsg. von Wilhelm Totok, Karl-Heinz Weimann und Rolf Weitzel. 4., erw., völlig neu bearb. Aufl. Frankfurt am Main, V. Klostermann [c1972]

xxxiv, 367 p. 25 cm.

At head of title: Totok-Weitzel.
Table of contents and "Bibliographische Terminologie" in English, French and German.

U. S. *Library of Congress. General Reference and Bibliography Division.*
Guide to Soviet bibliographies; a selected list of references. Compiled by John T. Dorosh. New York, Greenwood Press [1968]

v, 158 p. 29 cm.

Reprint of the 1950 ed.

Webber, Winslow Lewis, 1898–
Books about books, by Winslow L. Webber. A bio-bibliography for collectors. Ann Arbor, Mich., Gryphon Books, 1971.

168 p. 22 cm.

"Facsimile reprint of the 1937 edition."

Webber, Winslow Lewis, 1898-
Books about books; a bio-bibliography for collectors, by Winslow L. Webber. Boston, Hale, Cushman & Flint, 1937. Detroit, Gale Research Co., 1974.

168 p. 18 cm.

White, Alex Sandri.
Fact-finding made easy; a new guide to informational sources, by A. Sandri White. New, updated ed. Allenhurst, N. J., Aurea Publications [1967]

129 l. 30 cm.

BIBLIOGRAPHIES, NATIONAL

Jones, Helen Gertrude (Dudenbostel) 1908–
United States of America national bibliographical services and related activities in 1965–1967, compiled by Helen Dudenbostel Jones. Chicago, Reference Services Division, American Library Association, 1968.

v, 56 p. 23 cm.

Krendlová, Helena.
Národné bibliografie vo fondoch Bibliografickej čitárne Univerzitnej knižnice v Bratislave. Zost. H. Krendlová. Bratislava, Univ. knižnica, rozmn., 1968–69.

2 v. 21 cm. (Katalógy univerzitnej knižnice v Bratislave, 4/1969)

CONTENTS: 1. Slovanské národné bibliografie.—2. Súpis národných bibliografií ostatných štátov.

Kubíček, Jaromír.
Národní bibliografie. Soupis nár. bibilografií k období 1945–1970 z fondů Univ. knihovny v Brně. Zprac. Jaromír Kubíček. Brno, Univ. knihovna, rozmn., 1970.

43 l. 20 cm. (Na pomoc knihovníkům a čtenářům, 46)

U. S. *Library of Congress. General Reference and Bibliography Division.*
Current national bibliographies. Compiled by Helen F. Conover. New York, Greenwood Press [1968]

iv, 132 p. 29 cm.

Reprint of the 1955 ed.

BIO-BIBLIOGRAPHIES

Hamberger, Georg Christoph, 1726–1773.
Zuverlässige Nachrichten von den vornehmsten Schriftstellern vom Anfange der Welt bis 1500. Mit einer Vorrede von Johann Matthias Gesner. Hildesheim, G. Olms, 1971.

4 v. 20 cm.

Reprint of the ed. published in Lemgo by J. H. Meyer in 1756–64.

Hennicke, Karl August.
Beiträge zur Ergänzung und Berichtigung des Jöcher'-

schen Allegemeinen Gelehrten-Lexikon's und des Meusel'-schen Lexikon's der von 1750 bis 1800 verstorbenen teutschen Schriftsteller. (Reprografischer Nachdruck der Ausg. Leipzig, Vogel, 1811–1812.) Hildesheim, G. Olms, 1969.

3 v. in 1. 23 cm.

Cover title: Ergänzungen zu Jöcher und Meusel.

Rathlef, Ernst Ludwig, 1709–1768.
Geschichte jeztlebender Gelehrten, als eine Forsetzung des Jeztlebenden Gelehrten Europa. Hrsg. von Ernst Ludewig Rathlef. Hildesheim, New York, G. Olms, 1972.

12 v. in 3. 18 cm.

Reprint of the Celle, 1740–47 ed.
Vol. 3 (parts 9–12) ed. by J. C. Strodtmann.
Continuation of G. W. Götten's Das jetzt-lebende Gelehrte Europa; continued by J. C. Strodtmann's Beytraege zur Historie der Gelahrheit.

BOOKS ISSUED IN SERIES

Baer, Eleanora A
Titles in series; a handbook for librarians and students, by Eleanora A. Baer. 2. ed. New York, Scarecrow Press, 1964.

2 v. (1530 p.) 23 cm.

————— Supplement to the 2d ed. ₁1st₎– Metuchen, N. J., Scarecrow Press, 1967–

v. 23 cm.

Ku, Hsiu.
(Hui k'o shu mu)
彙刻書目　顧修撰　朱學勤補　₍台北₎　廣文書局　₍民國61 i. e. 1972₎

10 v. (10, 6, 2840 p.) 19 cm. （書目五編）

影印光緒12(1886)年朱氏增訂重編本原書20冊不分卷

——續彙刻書目　羅振玉撰　₍台北₎　廣文書局　₍民國61 i. e. 1972₎

3 v. (10, 4, 1098 p.) 19 cm. （書目五編）

Pestel, Maurice van.
Répertoire des collections étrangères en cours de publication. 2ème éd. Repertorium van de lopende buitenlandse reekswerken. 2de uitg. ₍Bruxelles₎ Bibliothèque royale de Belgique, ₍bd de l'Empereur, 4₎, 1970.

286 p. 30 cm.

At head of title: Bibliothèque royale de Belgique. Koninklijke Bibliotheek van België. M. van Pestel.

Richard Abel & Company.
A series catalog; a title listing of current series and sets. Compiled from the Richard Abel & Company automated standing order system. 1st prelim. ed. Portland, c1971.

v, 466 p. 28 cm.

Richard Abel & Company.
A series catalog; a listing of current series and sets compiled from the Richard Abel & Company automated standing order system with a classed subject index. General editor: Don Stave. Portland, ₍Or., 1973₎

xiii, 890 p. 28 cm.

Williams, Sam P
Reprints in print-serials, 1966, covering reprints of scholarly serials and monographs in series in print and available as of December 31, 1966, compiled and edited by Sam P. Williams. Dobbs Ferry, N. Y., Oceana Publications, 1967.

iv, 377 p. 24 cm.

Williams, Sam P
Reprints in print-serials, 1969; covering reprints of scholarly serials and monographs in series in print and available as of December 31, 1969. Compiled and edited by Sam P. Williams. ₍2d ed.₎ Dobbs Ferry, N.Y., Oceana Publications, 1970.

577 p. 24 cm.

EARLY PRINTED BOOKS

Bibliographies of early printed books of a specific country or on a particular subject are entered under the appropriate place or subject heading

see also Bibliography - Rare books; Incunabula

Cameron, William James.
Robert Addison's library; a short-title catalogue of the books brought to Upper Canada in 1792 by the first missionary sent out to the Niagara frontier by the Society for the Propagation of the Gospel, compiled by William J. Cameron and George McKnight with the assistance of Michaele-Sue Goldblatt. Hamilton, Ont., printed at McMaster University for the Synod of the Diocese of Niagara, 1967.

xliv, 98 p. illus. facsims. 28 cm.

Esposito, Enzo.
Annali di Antonio De Rossi stampatore in Roma (1695–1755). Firenze, L. S. Olschki, 1972.

xxxi, 645 p. 22 plates. 25½ cm. (Biblioteca di bibliografia italiana, 67)

Fournival, Richard de, *fl.* 1246–1260.
La biblionomia de Richard de Fournival du manuscrit 636 de la Bibliothèque de la Sorbonne. Texte en facsimilé avec la transcription de Léopold Delisle ₍par₎ H. J. de Vleeschauwer. Pretoria, 1965.

₍79₎ 1. 25 cm. (Mousaion; livres et bibliothèques, 62)

Text in Latin; commentary in French.

Frankfurter gelehrte Anzeigen.
Frankfurter gelehrte Anzeigen 1772; Auswahl. ₍Hrsg. von Hans-Dietrich Dahnke und Peter Müller. 1. Aufl.₎ Leipzig, Reclam. 1971.

483 p. 17 cm. (Reclams Universal-Bibliothek, Bd. 374)

Giessen. Universität. *Bibliothek.*
Die Postinkunabeln der Universitätsbibliothek Giessen. Beschrieben von Hermann Schüling. Giessen, Universitätsbibliothek, 1967.

x, 533 p. with 1 illus. 23 cm. (*Its* Berichte und Arbeiten, 10)

Goldschmidt, Ernst Philip.
Medieval texts and their first appearance in print. New York, Biblo and Tannen, 1969.

144 p. illus. 21 cm. (Supplement to the Bibliographical Society's Transactions, no. 16)

Reprint of the 1943 ed.

Gt. Brit. *Foreign Office. Library.*
A short title catalogue of books printed before 1701 in the Foreign Office Library; compiled by Colin L. Robertson. London, H. M. S. O., 1966.

ix, 177 p. 24½ cm.

Hase, Martin von, 1901–
Bibliographie der Erfurter Drucke von 1501–1550. 3. erw. Aufl. Nieuwkoop, B. de Graaf, 1968 [1969]

248 p. with illus. 31 cm.

"Zuerst im Börsenblatt für den Deutschen Buchhandel—Frankfurter Ausgabe—, Jahrgang 1966, Nr. 99 und dann in 2. verbesserter und erweiterter Auflage im 'Archiv für Geschichte des Buchwesens,' Band VIII, Lieferung 3/4 1967 veröffentlicht."

Hazen, Allen Tracy, 1904–
A catalogue of Horace Walpole's library, by Allen T. Hazen. New Haven, Yale University Press, 1969.

3 v. illus. 26 cm.

Index Aureliensis; catalogus librorum sedecimo saeculo impressorum. Aureliae Aquensis, 196 – ᶜ1962– [v. 1, 1965]

v. 25 cm. (Bibliotheca bibliographica Aureliana, 7, 11, 13–

Issued in pts., 1962– , as "editio princeps," and in bound volumes, 1965– , as "editio altera."

Klosterneuburg, Austria (Monastery of Augustinian canons) Bibliothek.
Klosterneuburger Altdrucke (1501–1520). Nieuwkoop, B. de Graaf, 1966.

xv, 224 p. 22½ cm. (Jahrbuch des Stiftes Klosterneuburg, VIII, 1)

Kropfinger-von Kügelgen, Helga.
Europäischer Buchexport von Sevilla nach Neuspanien im Jahre 1586: mit 4 Taf./ von Helga Kropfinger-von Kügelgen. Bücher des 16. Jahrhunderts in Puebla de los Angeles/ von Efraín Castro Morales. Die Biblioteca Palafoxiana in Puebla/ von Johann Specker. Vorw. [z. Gesamtwerk] von Erwin Walter Palm. — Wiesbaden: Steiner, 1973.

145 p.: ill.; 29 cm. (Das Mexiko-Projekt der Deutschen Forschungsgemeinschaft, 5)

On spine: Europäische Bücher in Neuspanien zu Ende des 16. Jahrhunderts.

Kühn, Fritz, 1883 (Oct. 11)–1968.
Die Varnhagensche Bibliothek. Gesamtverzeichnis. (Bearb. von Fritz Kühn.) Iserlohn (Ev[angelische] Kirchengeimeinde) 1966.

152 p. with illus. 21 cm. (Schriftenreihe vom Haus der Heimat, Bd. 10)

Lincoln Cathedral. Library.
Catalogue of foreign books in the Chapter Library of Lincoln Cathedral, compiled by William Herbert Kynaston. [East Ardsley, Eng.] EP Publishing, 1972.

xi, 82 p. facsims. 23 cm.

"Reprint of the 1937 edition text, with corrections and additions."

Lipen, Martin, 1630–1692.
Bibliotheca realis philosophica. Hildesheim, G. Olms, 1967.

2 v. (1504 p.) 30 cm.

"Reprografischer Nachdruck der Ausgabe Frankfurt a. M. 1682."

MacDonald, Robert H
The library of Drummond of Hawthornden; edited with an introduction by Robert H. MacDonald. Edinburgh, Edinburgh University Press, 1971.

xii, 245 p., 18 plates. illus., facsims., maps, ports. 29 cm.

Madrid. Biblioteca Nacional.
Catálogo colectivo de obras impresas en los siglos XVI al XVIII existentes en las bibliotecas españolas. Ed. provisional. Madrid, 1972–

v. 31 cm.

At head of title: Ministerio de Educación y Ciencia. Dirección General de Archivos y Bibliotecas.
CONTENTS: 1– Siglo XVI.

Milan. Università. Facoltà di giurisprudenza. Biblioteca.
La cinquecentine dell'Università di Milano ... Milano, Stabilimento tipografico A. Cordani, 1969.

2 v. illus. 24½ cm.

At head of title: Università degli studi di Milano. Biblioteche della Facoltà di giurisprudenza, lettere e filosofia. Giuliana Sapori.

CONTENTS: 1. Dal 1501 al 1550. Precede un elenco degli incunabili.—2. Dal 1551–1599.

Muller, Jean.
Aussereuropäische. Druckereien im 16. Jahrhundert; Bibliographie der Drucke, [von] Jean Muller [und] Ernst Róth. [1. Aufl.] Baden-Baden, Verlag Librairie Heitz, 1969.

176 p. facsims. 24 cm. (Bibliotheca bibliographica Aureliana, 22)

Newcastle-upon-Tyne. University. Library.
A list of the post-incunabula in the University Library, Newcastle upon Tyne; compiled by William Smith Mitchell. Newcastle upon Tyne, University of Newcastle upon Tyne, 1965.

[3], 70 p. 26 cm.

Padua. Biblioteca Antoniana.
The library of the Franciscans of the Convent of St. Antony, Padua, at the beginning of the fifteenth century, by K. W. Humphreys. Amsterdam, Erasmus Booksellers, 1966.
206 p. 25 cm. (Studies in the history of libraries and librarianship, v. 3)
Safaho monographs, v. 4.
"The two inventories printed in [this work] ... are contained in two volumes in the Biblioteca Antoniana in Padua, manuscripts 572 and 573. Ms. 572 consists of 44 folios describing the contents of the Library and the Sacristy in 1396–7. Only the book-lists are printed here from fols. 9 to 22. Ms. 573 has 66 folios listing the books in the Library in 1449."

Paris. Université. Bibliothèque.
Catalogue de la réserve XVIᵉ siècle (1501–1540) de la bibliothèque de l'Université de Paris, par Charles Beaulieux, bibliothécaire. New York, B. Franklin [1969]

2 v. illus. 24 cm. (Burt Franklin bibliography and reference series, 258)

Vol. 2: Supplément et suite (1541–1550) avec ... une table générale (1501–1550)
Reprint of the edition published in Paris, 1909–1910.

Payne, Olive.
The libraries of Daniel Defoe and Phillips Farewell; Olive Payne's sales catalogue (1731) edited by Helmut Heidenreich. Berlin, [H. Heidenreich] 1970.

xlix, 209 p. facsim. 22 cm.

Includes facsim. of original t.p.: Librorum ex bibliothecis Philippi Farewell, D. D. et Danielis De Foe, Gen., Catalogus: or, A catalogue of the libraries of the reverend and learned Philips Farewell ... and of the ingenious Daniel De Foe.

Royal Grammar School, Guildford, Eng.
The chained library of the Royal Grammar School, Guildford, catalogue; compiled by Gwendolen Woodward and R. A. Christophers; with an introduction by R. A. Christophers. Guildford, Royal Grammar School, Guild-

ford, 1972.

[5], 80, [5] p. illus. 24 cm.

Ruelens, Charles Louis, 1820–1890.
Annales plantiniennes depuis la fondation de l'Imprimerie plantinienne à Anvers jusqu'a la mort de Chr. Plantin, 1555–1589, par C. Ruelens & A. de Backer. New York, B. Franklin, 1967.

iii, 324, 15 p. port. 23 cm. (Burt Franklin bibliography and reference series, 127)

Reprint of the ed. published in Paris, 1866.
"Table des éditions par ordre alphabétique": p. [1]–15 (at end)

Savelli, Rodolfo.
Catalogo del fondo Demetrio Canevari della Biblioteca civica Berio di Genova / a cura di Rodolfo Savelli. — Firenze : La nuova Italia, [1974]

lv, 476 p. ; 24 cm. — (Pubblicazioni del Centro di studi del pensiero filosofico del Cinquecento e del Seicento in relazione ai problemi della scienza del Consiglio nazionale delle ricerche : Serie 2, Strumenti bibliografici ; 1)

Scotland. National Library, Edinburgh.
A short-title catalogue of foreign books printed up to 1600; books printed or published outside the British Isles now in the National Library of Scotland and the Library of the Faculty of Advocates, Edinburgh. Edinburgh, H.M. Stationery Off., 1970.

viii, 545 p. 25 cm.

Soupisy tisků 16. stol. z fondů Universitní knihovny v. Brně. Sest. Vladislav Dokoupil za spolupráce Jaroslava Vobra. Brno, Univ. knihovna, rozmn., 1970–

v. 29 cm.

CONTENTS:
sv. 6. Tisky 16. stol. v Universitní knihovně v Brně. 8 v.—sv. 7. Tisky 16. století z knihoven dominikánů a kapucínů ve Znojmě, křižovníků na Hradišti u Znojma a piaristů v Mikulově.

Spain. Ministerio de Asuntos Exteriores. Biblioteca.
Obras antiguas impresas (siglos XVI, XVII y XVIII) de la biblioteca del Ministerio de Asuntos Exteriores / [por Miguel Santiago Rodríguez y Consuelo del Castillo Bravo]. — [Madrid : Ministerio de Asuntos Exteriores, 1972].

128 p. ; 24 cm.

Šturdíková, Marta.
Katalóg tlačí 16. storočia františkánskej knižnice v Illohovci. Zost. Marta Šturdíková, úvod Štefan Valentovič. 1. vyd. Martin, Matica slovenská, rozmn., 1970.

113, [2] p. 21 cm. (Slovenské knižnice, zv. 6)

Added t. p. in Latin.

Supplément provisoire à la "Bibliographie lyonnaise" du président Baudrier ... Paris. Bibliothèque nationale. 1967–

v. 26 cm. (Recensement des livres anciens des bibliothèques françaises. Travaux préparatoires, 2

At head of title: Centre lyonnais d'histoire et de civilisation du livre.
Fasc. 1 by Y. de La Perrière.

Trondheim. Katedralskolen.
Katalog over rektor Kleists boksamling ved Trondheim katedralskole. Utarb. av Wilhelm K. Støren. Oslo, Universitetsforlaget, 1972.

184 p. 23 cm. (Norsk bibliografisk bibliotek, bd. 47)

Västerås domkyrka. Biblioteket.
Västerås domkyrkas bibliotek år 1640. Efter Petrus Olai Dalekarlus' katalog. Genom Åke Åberg. Västerås, Stifts- och landsbibliotek; [Västmanlands läns tidning (distr.)], 1973.

151 p. 20 cm. (Acta Bibliothecæ Arosiensis, 6)

First ed. published in 1640 under title: Bibliotheca, sive Catalogus librorum templi [et] consistorij Cathedralis Arosiæ.

Venosa. Biblioteca civica.
Le cinquecentine. Venosa, A cura dell'Amministrazione comunale, 1968.

[49] l. 82 cm.

Willer, Georg, 1514 or 15–1631 or 32.
Die Messkataloge Georg Willers. [Hrsg.:] Georg Willer. — Reprograf. Nachdr. d. Ausg. 1564–1 — Hildesheim, New York: Olms, 1972–

v. 20 cm. — (Die Messekataloge des sechzehnten Jahrhunderts, Bd. 1

CONTENTS: [1] Herbstmesse 1564 bis Herbstmesse 1573.

Williams, Sir Harold Herbert, 1880–1964.
Dean Swift's library, with a facsimile of the original sale catalogue and some account of two manuscript lists of his books. Folcroft, Pa., Folcroft Press [1969]

viii, 93, 16 p. 23 cm.

Reprint of the 1932 ed.
Title page of the sale catalog, compiled by George Faulkner, reads: A catalogue of books, the library of the late Rev. Dr. Swift, Dean of St. Patrick's, Dublin. To be sold by auction ... Dublin, Printed for G. Faulkner, 1745.

Wofford College, Spartanburg, S. C. Library.
Seventeenth century imprints. Compiled and edited by Alan B. Johns. Spartanburg, Wofford Library Press, 1971.

21 l. illus. 28 cm. (Wofford College Library. Special collections checklist, no. 6)

EXHIBITION CATALOGS

American Antiquarian Society, Worcester, Mass.
A society's chief joys; an exhibition from the collections of the American Antiquarian Society. Worcester [Mass., 1969]

137 p. illus., facsims., col. port. 27 cm.

Catalog of an exhibition held at the Grolier Club, New York, April 15–May 31, 1969.

American Antiquarian Society, Worcester, Mass.
A society's chief joys; an introduction to the collections of the American Antiquarian Society. With a foreword by Walter Muir Whitehill. Worcester [c1969]

30, [124] p. illus., facsims., ports. (1 col.) 28 cm.

"Entries and illustrations prepared for the catalogue of ... temporary exhibitions [at the Grolier Club] are reproduced in this book as a matter of permanent record."

Brussels. Bibliothèque royale de Belgique.
Les richesses de la bibliophilie belge. II. Exposition à la Bibliothèque Albert 1er, [Bruxelles], du 22 octobre au 20 novembre 1966. [Bruxelles], Société des bibliophiles et iconophiles de Belgique, 1966.

105 p. illus., facsim. 25 cm. bfr 100.–

At head of title: Société des bibliophiles et iconophiles de Belgique.

California. University. *University at Los Angeles. Library.*
101 notable gifts; the importance of private support for the university libraries: an exhibit in the Research Library,

University of California, Los Angeles, October 8 to November 11, 1964. ₁Los Angeles, 1964₁

13 p. facsims. 23 cm.

Chicago. University. *Library.*

A catalogue to an exhibition of notable books and manuscripts from the collections of the University of Chicago Library. Prepared for the dedication of the Joseph Regenstein Library, October thirty-first, nineteen hundred and seventy. ₁Chicago, 1970₁

95 p. illus., facsims. 27 cm.

On spine: An exhibition for the dedication of the Joseph Regenstein Library, the University of Chicago.

Coburg (City). Landesbibliothek.

Druckschriften der Reformation; Ausstellung der Landesbibliothek Coburg vom 27.5.–15.6. 1973 im Silbersaal des Schlosses Ehrenburg. ₁Ausstellung und Katalog: Jürgen Erdmann₁ Coburg, 1973.

35 p. illus. 24 cm.

Courtrai, Belgium. Bibliothèque publique de la ville.

Beelden uit eigen bezit. Catalogus van de tentoonstelling. (Stadsbibliotheek te Kortrijk van 11 november tot 31 december 1969. Samenstelling catalogus: J. M. Berteele ₁&₁ Paul Vancolen). Kortrijk, ₁Guido Gezellestr.₁, 1969.

41 p. illus. 22 cm.

Desgraves, Louis.

Figures de bibliophiles bordelais, exposition organisée à la Bibliothèque municipale de Bordeaux pour ... le centième anniversaire de la fondation de la Société des bibliophiles de Guyenne, 1866–1966. Catalogue par Louis Desgraves ... Octobre 1966. Bordeaux, Bibliothèque municipale, 1966.

93 p. illus. 25 cm.

Genoa. Biblioteca civica Berio.

Mostra di manoscritti e libri rari della Biblioteca Berio. Genova, 9 maggio–8 giugno 1969. Catalogo. Genova, SAGEP. ₁1969₁.

213 p. illus. plates. 24 cm.

Hirth, Mary.

Cyril Connolly's one hundred modern books from England, France, and America, 1880–1950. Catalog by Mary Hirth with an introd. by Cyril Connolly. An exhibition: March–December 1971. ₁Austin₁ Humanities Research Center, University of Texas at Austin ₁c1971₁

120 p. illus. 20 x 26 cm.

Jerusalem. Hebrew University. *Jewish National and University Library.*

Aspects of the contribution of Charles E. Feinberg to the Jewish National and University Library. ₁Jerusalem, 1969₁

iv, 41, 11 p. illus., facsims. 24 cm. N. T.

Added t. p.: מבט על תרומותיו של צ'רלס א. פיינברג לבית-הספרים הלאומי והאוניברסיטא.

"Hebrew text": 11 p. at end.
Catalog of an exhibition in honor of Charles E. Feinberg's 70th birthday held at the Jewish National and University Library, Oct. 1969.

John and Mable Ringling Museum of Art, Sarasota, Fla. Library.

Rare books of the 16th, 17th and 18th centuries from the Library of the Ringling Museum of Art, Sarasota, Florida. An exhibition prepared by Valentine L. Schmidt and presented by the Ringling Museum November 3–23, 1969. ₁Sarasota, Fla., 1969₁

32 p. illus. 26 cm.

Livres et estampes de la Bibliothèque municipale de Nice; ₁exposition à la₁ Galerie de la Marine, juin 1969. Premier festival international du livre. ₁Nice, Galerie de la Marine, 1969₁

103 p. plates. 17 x 22 cm.
At head of title: Jumelage Nice/Édimbourg.
"La plupart ₁des livres₁ viennent ... d'être exposés à Édimbourg, du 19 août au 14 septembre 1968."
"Parallèlement à cette exposition et faisant corps avec elle, la Galerie de la Marine présente un choix de livres et d'estampes, provenant des Bibliothèques publiques d'Édimbourg."

Morlanwelz, Belgium. Musée de Mariemont.

Exposition organisée à l'occasion de la visite des membres du Grolier Club de New-York au Musée de Mariemont le 28 mai. 1967. Morlanwelz Mariemont, (Belgium), Musée de Mariemont, ₁1967.₁

19 p. illus., plates. 24 cm.

Morlanwelz, Belgium. Musée de Mariemont. *Bibliothèque.*

Prestige de la Bibliothèque ₁du Musée de Mariemont₁. (Exposition, Morlanwelz-Mariemont), Musée de Mariemont, 6 mai–31 octobre 1967. (Catalogue). (Morlanwelz-Mariemont), Musée de Mariemont, 1967.

95 p. illus., facsims. 25 cm. (Trésors inconnus du Musée de Mariemont, 2)

Oxford. University. *Bodleian Library.*

The Bodleian Library and its friends; catalogue of an exhibition held 1969–1970. Oxford ₁Eng.₁ Bodleian Library ₁1970₁

88 p. illus., facsims. 22 cm.

Label mounted on t. p.: Supplied by Worldwide Books, Boston, Massachusetts.

La Première bibliothèque canadienne: la Bibliothèque des jésuites de la Nouvelle-France. 1632–1800. The first Canadian library: the Library of the Jesuit College of New France. ₁Ottawa, Information Canada, 1972₁

62 p. illus. 23 cm.

Catalog of an exhibition held at the National Library of Canada, Ottawa, 1972.
English and French.

Rio de Janeiro. Biblioteca Nacional.

O livro raro em seus diversos aspectos. Catálogo organizado pela bibliotecaria Iracema Celeste Rodrigues Monteiro. Rio de Janeiro, 1972.

58 p. plates (part col.) 23 cm.

"Exposição comemorativa do Ano Internacional do Livro, planejada pela Seção de Livros Raros, organizada pela Seção de Exposições e inaugurada em novembro de 1972."

Rosenwald, Lessing Julius, 1891–

A selection of printed books, manuscripts, miniatures, prints and drawings in the Lessing J. Rosenwald Collection, "Alverthorpe," Jenkintown, Pa., exhibited on the occasion of the visit of the Association internationale de bibliophilie, October 3, 1971. ₁Jenkintown, 1971₁

38 p. plan. 21 cm.

Some treasures of the Bancroft Library celebrating the dedication of the enlarged and remodeled library, May 6th, 1973. ₁Berkeley₁ Friends of the Bancroft Library, University of California, 1973.

85 p. illus. 27 cm. (The series of keepsakes, issued by the Friends of the Bancroft Library, no. 21)

Strasbourg. Bibliothèque nationale et universitaire.

Cent ans d'acquisitions, catalogue, 4 décembre 1971–15 janvier 1972. Strasbourg, Bibliothèque nationale et universitaire, 1971.

iv, 91 p. 26 cm.

At head of title: Exposition.

Toronto. Public Libraries.
One hundred books since 1471; an exhibition of fine printing from the collections of the Toronto Public Library. ₍Catalogue. Toronto, 1967₎

31 p. illus. 22 x 28 cm.

Exhibition held Feb. 6–Mar. 4, 1967.

Ukrainian incunabula, manuscripts, early printed and rare books. ₍Cambridge₎ Houghton Library, 1970.

₍8₎ p., 39 p. of facsims. 24 cm.

Virginia. University. *Library.*
The Atcheson Laughlin Hench collections of manuscripts and rare books; an exhibition selected from M. Hench's gifts to the Library, winter 1966–1967. ₍Charlottesville? 1967?₎

1 v. (unpaged) 17 cm.

Washington University, *St. Louis. Libraries. George N. Meissner Rare Book Dept.*
Recent additions to the book and manuscript collections; an exhibition, December 8, 1967–March 8, 1968. St. Louis ₍1968?₎

₍19₎ p. illus. 19 cm.

Wolfenbüttel. Herzog-August-Bibliothek.
Barocke Bücherlust: aus d. Sammlungen d. Herzog August Bibliothek Wolfenbüttel; Ausstellung in d. histor. Räumen d. Wolfenbütteler Schlosses vom 13. Sept.–5. Nov. 1972/ ₍Katalog: Paul Raabe unter Mitw. von Karl-Heinz Habersetzer₎. — Wolfenbüttel: Herzog-August-Bibliothek, 1972.
142 p.: ill.; 26 cm. (Its Ausstellungskataloge, Nr. 6)

MICROSCOPIC AND MINIATURE EDITIONS

Dawson's Book Shop, Los Angeles.
Miniature books: 1966–1971. Compiled by Fern Dawson Shochat ₍and others₎ Los Angeles ₍1971₎

1 v. (unpaged) illus. 22 cm.

"Lists 15 to 33 with index."

Engström, Gösta.
Om miniatyrböcker. Stockholm, Sällskapet Bokvännerna, 1966.

71 p. illus. 16 cm. (Bokvännens miniatyrserie, 22)

Koopman, Harry Lyman, 1860–1937.
Miniature books. Los Angeles, Dawson's Book Shop, 1968.

viii, 103 p. 48 mm.

400 copies printed by Grabhorn-Hoyem, San Francisco, with type and ornamental blue borders designed by Bruce Rogers.

OUT-OF-PRINT BOOKS

Xerox University Microfilms.
Out-of-print book catalog : authors. — ₍Ann Arbor, Mich.₎ : Xerox University Microfilms, 1974.

16 sheets (1222 p.) ; 11 x 15 cm.

Microfiche.

Title from heading area.
Title on jacket : Catalog of out-of-print books.

PAPERBACK EDITIONS

Catalogue de collections au format de poche.

Paris, Cercle de la librairie.

v. 19 cm. annual.

Cover title   : Catalogue de livres au format de poche.

District News Company.
Paperback book catalog; elementary, junior & senior high, college. Cottage City, Md., Education Dept. District News Co. ₍1972₎

24 p. 28 cm.

Gedin, Per I   1928–
Den nya boken. En presentation och analys av pocketboken. ₍Av₎ Per I. Gedin. Stockholm, Prisma; ₍Seelig₎ 1966.

115, (1) p. (6) plates, illus. 19 cm. (Prisma)

Huguet, Jean, 1925–
La Bibliothèque idéale de poche ₍par₎ Jean Huguet et Georges Belle. Paris, Éditions universitaires, 1966.

359 p. 18 cm.

Huguet, Jean, 1925–
La bibliothèque idéale de poche ₍par₎ Jean Huguet ₍et₎ Georges Belle. 2. éd. rev. et augm. Paris, Éditions universitaires ₍1969₎

314 p. 20 cm. (La Bibliothèque idéale)

Paperbound books in print. Mar. 1971–
₍New York. Bowker₎

no. 28 cm. 3 no. a year.

"A title, author & subject index."
Formerly published as a numbered issue of the Month ahead/Paperbound books in print.

Reginald, R
Cumulative paperback index, 1939-1959; a comprehensive bibliographic guide to 14,000 mass-market paperback books of 33 publishers issued under 69 imprints, by R. Reginald and M. R. Burgess. Detroit, Gale Research Co. ₍1973₎

xxiv, 362 p. 29 cm.

Tölle, Manfred.
Taschenbuch-, Paperback- und Schulausgaben moderner Literatur. ₍Stand vom 31.12. 1969₎ Stuttgart, E. Klett ₍1970₎

146 p. 23 cm. (Der Deutschunterricht. Beiheft zu Jahrg. 22/ 1970)

RARE BOOKS
see also Children's literature - Rare books; Illuminated books; Incunabula; Manuscripts

Biltz, Karl, 1830–1901.
Neuer deutscher Bücherschatz. Verzeichnis einer an Seltenheiten ersten Ranges reichen Sammlung von Werken der deutschen Literatur des xv. bis xix. Jahrhunderts. Mit bibliographischen Bemerkungen und einem Anhang: Das wiederaufgefundene Wittenberger Gesangbüchlein vom Jahre 1526. (Reprografischer Nachdruck der Ausg. Berlin 1895.) Hildesheim, Gg. Olms, 1967.

264 p. 20 cm.

Birley, *Sir Robert,* 1903–
Eton College library: one hundred books selected and annotated by Robert Birley. Eton (Bucks.), Eton College, 1969.

41 p. 22 cm.

Černá-Šlapáková, Marie Ludmila.
Vzácné staré knihy ve Státní technické knihovné v Praze. Výběr přípr., úvodem a výkladém opatřila Marie L. Černá-Šlapáková. Předml.: Antonín Derfl. 1. vyd. Praha, SPN, t. ST 2, 1971.

344, ₃₃₎ p. ₇₆₎ p. of plates. 25 cm. (Edice Publikace státních vědeckých knihoven)

Summary in Russian, English, French and German.

欽定天祿琳琅書目·續目　彭元瑞撰　₍台北₎　廣文書局 ₍1968₎

5 v. (10, 6, 104, 1810 p.) 19 cm. (書目續編 26)
據光緒10 (1884) 長沙王先謙刊本影印

CONTENTS.—1-2. 欽定天祿琳琅書目 10 卷　于敏中等奉敕撰—3-5. 欽定天祿琳琅書目後編 20 卷　彭元瑞等奉敕撰—天祿琳琅書目續目目次　廣文編譯所編 (v. 1, p. 1-104)

Coimbra. Universidade. Biblioteca.
Catálogo dos reservados da Biblioteca Geral da Universidade de Coimbra. ₍Coimbra₎ 1970.

xvi, 753 p. facsims. 25 cm. (Acta Universitatis Conimbrigensis)

Ehrman, Albert.
Mss and printed books presented by Mr. and Mrs. Albert Ehrman to the Friends of the National Libraries, the British Museum, and other libraries from 1925 to 1970. ₍Oxford, Eng., Printed by Alden & Mowbray, 1970₎

19 p. illus., port. 22 cm.

Erweiterte Oberschule "Geschwister Scholl." Bibliothek.
Kostbarkeiten aus Freibergs ältester Bibliothek. Ein Streifzug in Bildern durch d. histor. Bibliothek d. Erw. Oberschule "Geschwister Scholl" in Freiberg, von Hans-Christian Neumann. Freiberg, Stadt- u. Bergbaumuseum (1970).

86 p. with illus. 21 cm. (Freiberger Bilder, Heft 6)

Gallardo, Bartolomé José, 1776–1852.
Ensayo de una biblioteca española de libros raros y curiosos. Ed. facsímil. Madrid, Editorial Gredos ₍1968₎

4 v. 28 cm. (Biblioteca románica hispánica. 9. Facsímiles, 1)

Facsím. of the 1863-89 ed.

Guru Nanak University. Library.
Classified catalogue of rare books and manuscripts available in the library, November 24, 1971. Amritsar ₍1971₎

1 v. (various pagings) 28 cm.

English, Hindi, Panjabi, and Urdu.

Harrisse, Henry, 1829–1910.
Excerpta Colombiniana. Bibliographie de quatre cents pièces gothiques, françaises, italiennes, et latines du commencement du XVI⁹ siècle non décrites jusqu'ici; précédée d'une histoire de la Bibliothèque colombine et de son fondateur. Genève, Slatkine Reprints, 1971.

lxxv, 315 p. illus. 23 cm.

"Réimpression de l'édition de Paris, 1887."

Henry E. Huntington Library and Art Gallery, *San Marino, Calif.*
Great books in great editions. Selected and described by Roland Baughman and Robert O. Schad. ₍Rev. ed.₎ San Marino, 1965.

65 p. illus., facsims. 25 cm.

"Original edition ... was a catalogue of an exhibition held in 1940 at the Huntington Library."

Hove, Eng. Public Library.
123: a catalogue of rare and valuable books in the Hove Public Library. including incunabula, facsimiles, books from modern fine printing presses and fine bindings; compiled by Jack Dove, Borough Librarian and Curator. Hove ₍Sussex₎ Hove Public Library, 1969.

45 p. 4 plates, illus., facsims 21 cm.

Hrkalović, Janko.
Каталог ретких српских књига 1741–1941. Саставио Јанко Хркаловић. ⟨Дејан Медаковић: О аутору овог Каталога⟩. Београд, Издање аутора, 1971.

229, ₍1₎ p. 23 plates with facsims. 22 cm.

Huang, P'i-lieh, 1763–1825.
蕘圃藏書題識 ₍10卷　補遺　刻書題識₎　黃丕烈撰　繆荃荪₍sic₎等輯 ₍臺北₎　廣文書局 ₍1967₎

4 v. (8, 9, 1084 p.) 19 cm.　(書目叢編 3)
據民國8 (1919) 年刊本影印

———————續₍錄 4卷₎ 王大隆輯 ₍臺北₎ 廣文書局 ₍1967₎

8, 2, 258 p. 19 cm.　(書目叢編 4)
據民22 (1933) 秀水王氏學禮齋刊本影印
蕘圃雜著目錄：p. 215-252.

Ihre, Johan, 1707–1780, *praeses.*
Om orsakerna till böckers sällsynthet. Akademisk avhandling, 1741–1743. Övers. från latinet jämte inledning och kommentar av Gösta Engström. Göteborg, Universitetbiblioteket, 1967.

106, (1) p. illus. 25 cm. (Acta Bibliothecae Universitatis Gothoburgensis, 8)

Translation of De caussis raritatis librorum.

Illinois. University at Urbana-Champaign. Library. Rare Book Room.
Catalog. Boston, G. K. Hall, 1972.

11 v. 37 cm.

Karlsruhe. Badische Landesbibliothek.
Kostbare Einbände, seltene Drucke : aus d. Schatzkammer d. Bad. Landesbibliothek : Neuerwerbungen 1955 bis 1974 / Franz Anselm Schmitt. — Karlsruhe : Badenia-Verlag, 1974.

96 p. : Ill. (some col.) ; 24 cm.

Le Petit, Jules, 1845–1915.
Bibliographie des principales éditions originales d'écrivains français du xv au xviii siècle. Ouvrage contenant environ 300 fac-similés de titres des livres décrits. New York, B. Franklin ₍1966₎

vii, 689 ₍i. e. 583₎ p. illus., facsims. 27 cm. (Burt Franklin bibliography and reference series, 120)

"Originally published Paris: 1888; reprinted 1966."

Luxemburg (City). Bibliothèque nationale. Département de la réserve précieuse.

Les acquisitions du Département de la réserve précieuse, en 1971. Luxembourg, 1972.

18 l. illus. 30 cm.

Mo, Yu-chih, 1811–1871.

(Lü-t'ing chih chien ch'uan pen shu mu)

郘亭知見傳本書目 〔16卷〕 莫友芝撰 〔臺北〕 廣文書局 〔民國61 i.e. 1972〕

2 v. (10, 4, 666 p.) 19 cm. (書目五編)

Reprint ed.

Mo, Yu-chih, 1811–1871.

宋元舊本書經眼錄 〔3卷〕 莫友芝撰 〔臺北〕 廣文書局 〔1967〕

8, 2, 302 p. 20 cm. (書目叢編12)

據同治 12 (1873) 年莫繩係刊本影印
附錄 (p. 179–302): 卷1 書衣筆識—卷 2 金石筆識

New York (City). Public Library. Rare Book Division.

Dictionary catalog of the Rare Book Division. Boston, G. K. Hall, 1971–

v. 37 cm.

At head of title: The New York Public Library, Astor, Lenox & Tilden Foundations, the Research Libraries.

Niimi, Hiroshi, 1905–1945.

新美 寛

本邦残存典籍による輯佚資料集成 新美寛編 鈴木隆一補
京都 京都大学人文科学研究所 昭和43 (1968)

2 冊 27 cm

Parenti, Marino, 1900–1963.

Rarità bibliografiche dell'Ottocento. Materiali e pretesti per una storia della tipografia italiana nel secolo decimonono. Firenze, Sansoni, 1953–64.

8 v. illus., ports., facsims. (part col.) 26 cm. (Contributi alla Biblioteca bibliografica italica, 3, 13, 16, 19, 22, 24–25, 27)

Vol. 1: 3. ed. rifatta e di molto ampliata.
No more published. Vol. 8: Deb-Erc.

Philadelphia. Library Company.

Bibliothesauri; or, Jewels from the shelves of the Library Company of Philadelphia, being a catalogue of a selection of rare, old, curious, valuable, important, unusual, beautiful, influential, and historic books in the fields of religion, law, science, medicine, history, travel, art and literature, to which is prefixed a brief introduction by Edwin Wolf 2nd. Philadelphia, 1966.

68 p. illus. 23 cm.

Pierpont Morgan Library, *New York.*

A review of acquisitions, 1949–1968. With a foreword by Henry S. Morgan, and pref. by Arthur A. Houghton, Jr. New York, 1969.

xiv, 186 p. 49 plates, port. 28 cm.

Pinto de Mattos, Ricardo, 1839?–1882.

Manual bibliographico portuguez de livros raros, classicos e curiosos, revisto e prefaciado pelo Camillo Castello Branco. Catálogo descritivo em ordem alfabético sob au-

tores, com notas biográficas, descrevendo em detalhe suas obras com anotações críticas, desde o século dezesseis até o meio do século décimo nono. Amsterdam, Gérard Th. van Heusden, 1971.

582 p. 23 cm.

Ricci, Seymour de, 1881–1942.

The book collector's guide; a practical handbook of British and American bibliography. New York, B. Franklin [1970]

xviii, 648 p. 24 cm. (Essays in literature & criticism, 62)

Burt Franklin bibliography & reference series, 327.
Reprint of the 1921 ed.

Rosenbach Company, *firm, booksellers.*

The collected catalogues of Dr. A. S. W. Rosenbach, 1904–1951. Index by Don Ward. New York, Arno Press [1968, °1967]

10 v. illus., facsims., port. 24 cm.

Originally issued as sales catalogs; now reissued and grouped in subject categories.

CONTENTS.—v. 1–3. Americana.—v. 4–6. Rare books and manuscripts.—v. 7.—English literature and Shakespeare.—v. 8. Rare books, manuscripts, literature exhibitions, and essays.—v. 9. To Dr. R.—v. 10. Index.

Rothschild, Nathan James Edouard, *baron* **de,** 1844–1881.

Catalogue des livres composant la bibliothèque de feu M. le baron James de Rothschild [par] Emile Picot. New York, B. Franklin [1967]

5 v. illus., facsims., plates (part col.) port. 26 cm. (Burt Franklin bibliography and reference series, 96)

Compiled chiefly by Rothschild and completed by E. Picot. 3,382 items.
Reprint of the ed. published in Paris, 1884–1920.

CONTENTS.—t. 1. Théologie. Jurisprudence. Sciences et arts. Belles-lettres.—t. 2. Belles-lettres.—t. 3. Histoire. Supplément.—t. 4. 2. Supplément. Appendice: Table des personnages qui figurent dans les ballets portés au présent Catalogue.—t. 5. 3. Supplément. Table alphabétique générale.

Scotland. National Library, Edinburgh.

Notable accessions since 1925; a book of illustrations. Edinburgh, 1965.

[128] p. illus. 25 cm.

South Carolina. University. *Library.*

Rare book collection in the McKissick Memorial Library, the University of South Carolina. Edited by Davy-Jo Stribling Ridge, chief reference librarian. Columbia, 1966.

396 p. col. illus. 24 cm.

First published in 1952 under title: Rare books in the McKissick Library, by E. D. English.

Southampton, Eng. Public Libraries.

A catalogue of the Pitt Collection. [Southampton] Southampton Corp., 1964.

133 p. 24 cm.

At head of title: City of Southampton Public Libraries Committee.
On cover: A catalogue of books: The Pitt Collection, City of Southampton Public Libraries.

Steenstrup, Norman V

Mine bøger og håndskrifter. [Af] Norman V. Steenstrup. Hjallese, Forfatteren, Hans Appels Vej 14, 1969.

46 p. illus. 21 cm.

Sterne, Laurence, 1713–1768.

A facsimile reproduction of a unique catalogue of Laurence Sterne's library. With a pref. by Charles Whibley. London, J. Tregaskis; New York, E. H. Wells, 1930. [New York, AMS Press, 1973]

94 p. 23 cm.

Includes t. p. of original ed. which reads: A catalogue of a curious and valuable collection of books, amonk which are included the entire library of the late revered and learned Laurence Sterne ... which will begin to be sold exceeding cheap (the prices printed in the catalogue) on Tuesday, August 23, 1768 ... by J. Todd and H. Sotheran.

Sylva (J. A. Telles da) (Firm)
Manuscritos & [i. e.] livros valiosos. Lisboa [1971–

v. illus. 25 cm.

Têng, Pang-shu, *chin shih* 1898.
群碧樓善本書目 [6卷] 鄧邦述撰 [台北] 廣文書局 [1967]

10, 2, 48, 390 p. 20 cm. (書目續編31)
原書雖與寒瘦山房鬻存善本書目合刻於1930年 兩目實互不相涉 茲分別影印裝訂
————Another issue.
2 v. (10, 2, 48, 390 p.) in 1.

Têng, Pang-shu, *chin shih,* 1898.
寒瘦山房鬻存善本書目 [7卷] 鄧邦述撰 [台北] 廣文書局 [1967]

2 v. (10, 2, 40, 596 p.) 20 cm. (書目續編32)

原書雖與群碧樓善本書目合刻於1930年 兩目實互不相涉 茲分別影印裝訂

350 [i. e. Trois cent cinquante] livres illustrés, illustratifs, ou illustre, du dix-septième au dix-neuvième siècle. [Paris] P. Berès [1972?]

1 v. (unpaged) illus. (part col.), maps. 26 cm.

"Catalogue 64."

Tung, K'ang, 1867–
書舶庸譚 [4卷] 董康撰 [臺北] 廣文書局 [1967]

8, 2, 308 p. 20 cm. (書目叢編19)

據民19 (1930) 年大東書局石印本影印

United States. Library of Congress. Rare Book Division.
Some guides to special collections in the Rare Book Division. Washington, Library of Congress, 1974.

12 p. 23 cm.

Venice. Biblioteca nazionale marciana.
Mostra di 110 [i. e. centodieci] edizioni rare della Biblioteca nazionale marciana. Venezia, 1965–66. [Venezia, 1965?]

117 p. illus. 20 cm.

At head of title: VII centenario della nascita di Dante; V centenario dell'introduzione della stampa in Italia.

Wang, Wên-chin.
文祿堂訪書記 [5卷] 王文進撰 [臺北] 廣文書局 [1967]

2 v. (8, 2, 540 p.) 20 cm. (書目叢編15)

據民31 (1942) 文祿堂印本影印

Webster, Paul Francis.
The small, select library of Paul Francis Webster; six hundred years of significant literature 1299–1899. Beverly Hills, Calif., 1972.

1 v. (unpaged) facsims. 26 cm.

Winchester College, Winchester, Eng. Warden and Fellows' Library.
A short-title list of printed books in [the] Strong Room. Winchester, Fellows' Library, 1973 [i. e. 1974]

[2], 22 l. 30 cm. (Fellows' Library publications no. 1)

Wise, Thomas James, 1859–1937.
The Ashley library; a catalogue of printed books, manuscripts, and autograph letters collected by Thomas J. Wise. With a new pref. by Simon Nowell-Smith. Folkestone [Kent] Dawsons of Pall Mall, 1971.

11 v. illus., facsims., ports. 27 cm.

Catalog of the author's library of 1st editions of the famous English poets and dramatists from Elizabethan times until the present.
"[In] this reprint ... [of the 1922–36 ed.] against all the entries of printed books received by the British Museum have been supplied the Ashley shelf-marks in the library of the Museum ... The occasional short notes written into entries, and the occasional deletions, have been taken from the marked set only accessible to readers in the reading room."

Yeh, Ch'i-hsün, 1908–
拾經樓紬書 葉啓勳纂 [臺北] 廣文書局 [1967]

8, 2, 364 p. 20 cm. (書目叢編16)

Original t. p. reads: 拾經樓紬書錄三卷
據丁丑 (1937) 長沙葉氏拾經樓印本影印

REPRINTS

Announced reprints. v. 1–
Feb. 1969–
Washington, Microcard Editions.

v. 28 cm. quarterly.

Guide to reprints. 1967–
Washington, Microcard Editions.

v. 28 cm. annual.

Editor: 1967– A. J. Diaz.

[Tokusen meicho fukkoku zenshū, Kindai Bungakukan, sakuhin kaidai]
特選名著複刻全集 近代文学館 作品解題 [名著複刻全集編集委員会編 東京 日本近代文学館 昭和46 i. e. 1971]

178 p. illus. 22 cm.

Williams, Sam P
Reprints in print-serials, 1966, covering reprints of scholarly serials and monographs in series in print and available as of December 31, 1966, compiled and edited by Sam P. Williams. Dobbs Ferry, N. Y., Oceana Publications, 1967.

iv, 377 p. 24 cm.

UNFINISHED BOOKS

Corns, Albert Reginald, 1875–
A bibliography of unfinished books in the English language, with annotations, by Albert R. Corns and Archibald Sparke. New York, B. Franklin [1969]

xvi, 255 p. 22 cm. (Burt Franklin bibliography & reference series, 260)

Title on spine: Unfinished books in the English language. Reprint of the 1915 ed.

UNIVERSAL BIBLIOGRAPHIES

Brunet, Jacques Charles, 1780–1867.
Manuel du libraire et de l'amateur de livres, contenant 1° Un nouveau dictionnaire bibliographique ... 2° Une table en forme de catalogue raisonné ... 5ᵉ éd. originale entièrement refondue et augmentée d'un tiers par l'auteur ... Paris, G.-P. Maisonneuve & Larose, 1965–66.

6 v. illus. 23 cm.

Reprint of the edition published in 1860–65, Firmin-Didot, Paris.

———————— Supplément, contenant 1° Un complément du Dictionnaire bibliographique de M. J.-Ch. Brunet ... 2° La table raisonnée des articles au nombre d'environ 10,000, décrits au présent supplément, par MM. P. Deschamps et G. Brunet ... Paris, G.-P. Maisonneuve & Larose, 1966.
2 v. in 1. 23 cm.

Reprint of the edition published in 1878–80, Firmin-Didot, Paris. Also numbered as v. 7–8 on spine.

Ebert, Friedrich Adolf, 1791–1834.
A general bibliographical dictionary, from the German of Frederic Adolphus Ebert. Oxford, University Press, 1837. Detroit, Gale Research Co., 1968.

4 v. (xvii, 2052 p.) 23 cm.

Translation of Allgemeines bibliographisches Lexikon.

CONTENTS.—v. 1. A–E.—v. 2. F–L.—v. 3. M–P.—v. 4. Q–Z.

Gesner, Konrad, 1516–1565.
Bibliotheca universalis und Appendix. Osnabrück, O. Zeller, 1966.

2 v. 33 cm. (Milliaria, 5)

Facsimile. Original t. p. reads: Bibliotheca vniuersalis: siue, Catalogus omnium scriptorum locupletissimus in tribus linguis, Latina, Graeca & Hebraica, extantium & non extantiū, ueterum & recentiorum in hunc usq, diem, doctorum & indoctorum, publicatorum & in bibliothecis latentium ... Tigvri, Apvd Christophorvm Froschouerum, mense Septembri anno MDXLV.
Author arrangement; continued by a subject arrangement in 2 v.: Pandectarum sive partitionum universalium Conradi Gesneri ... libri XXI and Partitiones theologicae, pandectarum universalium Conradi Gesneri liber ultimus. The two volumes were published in 1548 and 1549 respectively.

CONTENTS: [1] Bibliotheca vniuersalis.—[2] Appendix Bibliothecae Conradi Gesneri. Epitome Bibliothecae Conradi Gesneri, conscripta primum a Conrado Lycosthene Rubeaquensi: nunc denuo recognita & ... locupletata per Iosiam Simlervm.

Mareschal, Philibert.
La guide des arts et sciences, et promptuaires de tous livres tant composez que traduicts en françois. Genève, Slatkine Reprints, 1971.

421 p. 22 cm.

"Réimpression de l'édition de Paris, 1598."

BIBLIOTHERAPY

Association of Hospital and Institution Libraries. Committee on Bibliotherapy.
Biblio-therapy: methods and materials. [Prepared by] Committee on Bibliotherapy, (Mildred T. Moody, chairman) and Subcommittee on the Troubled Child, (Hilda K. Limper, chairman), Association of Hospital and Institution Libraries. Chicago, American Library Association, 1971.

vi, 161 p. 23 cm.

Riggs, Corinne W
Bibliotherapy; an annotated bibliography. [Newark, Del., International Reading Association] 1968.

22 p. 22 cm. (IRA annotated bibliography no. 16)

Riggs, Corinne W
Bibliotherapy: an annotated bibliography. Compiled by Corinne W. Riggs. Ramon Ross, general editor. Newark, Del., International Reading Association, 1971.

26 p. 22 cm. (IRA annotated bibliography series)

U. S. *Veterans Administration. Medical and General Reference Library.*
We call it bibliotherapy; an annotated bibliography on bibliotherapy and the adult hospitalized patient, 1900–1966. [Compiled by Rosemary Dolan] Washington, 1967.

iii, 50 p. 27 cm. (*Its* Bibliography 10–1)

1952 ed. issued under title: Bibliotherapy; 1958 and 1962 editions, under title: Bibliotherapy in hospitals.

BIEDENKOPF, GERMANY

Biedenkopf, Ger. Staatsarchiv.
Stadtarchive: Stadt Biedenkopf (mit Urkundenbestand X 1: Stadt Biedenkopf) Bearb. von Reinhard König unter Beteiligung von I. Auerbach. Mit Unterstützung der Historischen Kommission für Hessen und Waldeck. Marburg, Staatsarchiv, 1971.

x, 277 p. 30 cm. (Repertorien des Hessischen Staatsarchivs Marburg, Bestand 330)

BIEL, SWITZERLAND

Jung-Küffer, Jeannine.
Bibliographie zur Geschichte der Stadt Biel von ihren Anfängen bis 1815. Diplomarb. der Vereinigung Schweizerischer Bibliothekare. [Biel] 1968.

iii, 61 l. 30 cm.

BIERCE, AMBROSE GWINETT

Gaer Joseph, 1897–
Ambrose Gwinett Bierce, bibliography and biographical data. New York, B. Franklin [1968]

102 p. 24 cm. (Burt Franklin bibliography and reference series, no. 161)

On spine: Bibliography of Ambrose Bierce.
Reprint of 1935 ed.

Gaer, Joseph, 1897–   ed.
Ambrose Gwinett Bierce, bibliography and biographical data. Folcroft, Pa., Folcroft Press [1969]

102 l. 35 cm.

Reprint of the 1935 ed., which was issued as Monograph 4 of California Literary Research Project.

BIG SANDY VALLEY, KENTUCKY

Jillson, Willard Rouse, 1890–
A bibliography of the Big Sandy Valley; citations of printed and manuscript sources touching upon its history, geology, coal, oil, gas, shale, clay, sandstone, limestone, and mining industries, with annotations. Frankfort, Ky., Roberts Print. Co., 1964.

42 p. 23 cm.

BIG THICKET NATIONAL PARK, TEXAS
Kress, Alexander.
Ralph Yarborough: the Big Thicket's advocate in Congress; an annotated Congressional record bibliography, 1962–1970. Austin, Tex. [1970]

80 p. illus., group port. 22 cm.

BILHARZIASIS   see   Schistosomiasis

BILINGUALISM

Mackey, William Francis.
Bibliographie internationale sur le bilinguisme, préparée sous la direction de William F. Mackey. International bibliography on bilingualism. Quebec, Presses de l'Université Laval, 1972.

xxviii, 337, 209, 203 p. 27 cm.

"Published for the International Center for Research on Bilingualism."
French or English.

Wales. University. University College, Swansea. Dept. of Education.
Bilingualism: a bibliography of 1000 references with special reference to Wales. [New ed.]. Cardiff, University of Wales Press, 1971.

95 p. 22 cm. (Welsh studies in education, v. 5)

Previous ed. published as 'Bibliography of bilingualism.' 1960.

BINET, JEAN

Schweizerisches Musik-Archiv.
Jean Binet, né le 17 octobre 1893, mort le 24 février 1960. Liste des oeuvres. Zurich, Archives musicales suisses, 1970.

iii, 17 l. 30 cm.

Cover title.
French and German.

BIOCHEMISTRY

Copenhagen. Universitet. *Biokemisk institut A.*
Publikationer. Publications, 1962–1965. København, 1966.

10 p. 25½ cm.

Courtois, Jean Émile.
Titrés et travaux scientifiques de Jean-Émile Courtois ... Lons-le-Saunier, impr. M. Declume, 1970.

68 p. 27 cm.

Heenan, W   F
An information guide to selected books of biochemistry and related subjects. Compiled by W. F. Heenan. [Washington, George Washington University] 1968.

109 p. 28 cm. (George Washington University. Biological Sciences Communication Project. BSCP communiqué 30–68)

Oslo. Universitet. *Institutt for klinisk biokjemi.*
Institute of Clinical Biochemistry, Rikshospitalet, University of Oslo, Oslo, Norway. First report and list of publications covering the 5 year period from the opening of the institute January 1st 1961 to December 31st 1965. Oslo [1966]

18 p. 21 cm.

Tóth, Miklós, 1938–
Magyar biokémiai és biofizikai, bibliográfia, 1945–1960. Budapest, Országos Orvostudományi Könyvtár és Dokumentációs Központ, 1966.

iv, 440 p. 24 cm.

PERIODICALS

Chemical-biological activities. v. 1–
Jan. 11, 1965–
Easton, Pa., American Chemical Society.

v. in   illus. 29 cm. biweekly.

Vol. 1, no. 1 preceded by a number dated Sept. 1962, called Sample issue.
"A publication of the Chemical Abstracts Service."

BIOGRAPHY
see also Bibliography - Bio-
bibliographies and subdivision
Bio-bibliography under particular
subjects and under names of places.

Adlerberth, Roland.
Människan i blickpunkten: memoarer och biografier; ett urval. [Lund, Bibliotekstjänst, 1965]

54 p. 21 cm. (Bibliotekstjänsts bokurval nr 51)

Allinson, A   A
Biography and autobiography [by] A. A. Allinson and F. E. Hotchin. Melbourne, Cheshire [1969]

42 p. illus. 20 cm. (14–16: a reading guide)

Bode, Ingrid.
Die Autobiographien zur deutschen Literatur, Kunst und Musik 1900–1965. Bibliographie und Nachweise der persönlichen Begegnungen und Charakteristiken. Stuttgart, Metzler (1966)

x, 308 p. 24 cm. (Repertorien zur deutschen Literaturgeschichte, Bd. 2)

Dargan, Marion.
Guide to American biography. Foreword by Dumas Malone. Westport, Conn., Greenwood Press [1973, c1949–52]

2 v. in 1 (viii, 510 p.) 22 cm.

Reprint of the ed. published by the University of New Mexico Press, Albuquerque.
CONTENTS: pt. 1. 1607–1815.—pt. 2. 1815–1933.

Dimpfel, Rudolf A
Biographische Nachschlagewerke: Adelslexika, Wappenbücher; systematische Zusammenstellung für Historiker und Genealogen, von Rudolf Dimpfel. 2., um ein Namenregister verm. Aufl. Wiesbaden, M. Sändig [1969]

148 p. 22 cm.

"Ergänzter Neudruck der Ausgabe 1922."

Institut für Zeitgeschichte, Munich. Bibliothek.
Biographischer Katalog. Boston, G. K. Hall, 1967.

viii, 764 p. 37 cm.

Added t. p.: Biographical catalog.

Johnson, Robert Owen.
An index to profiles in the New Yorker. Metuchen, N. J., Scarecrow Press, 1972.

vi, 190 p. 22 cm.

Kokuritsu Kokkai Toshokan, *Tokyo. Sankō Shoshibu.*
人物文献索引 人文編 昭和20–39 年刊行分 [国立国会図書館参考書誌部編] Tokyo, 国立国会図書館 National Diet Library [1967]

388 p. 26 cm.

本索引は当館所蔵の各種邦文資料の… 刊行物中から作成した

National Book League, *London.*
Biographies and autographies 1968. London, National Book League, 1969.

35 p. 22 cm.

Nicholsen, Margaret E
People in books; a selective guide to biographical literature arranged by vocations and other fields of reader interest, by Margaret E. Nicholsen. New York, H. W. Wilson Co., 1969.

xviii, 498 p. 27 cm.

Nohrström, Kyllikki.
Elämäkertoja ja muistelmia; kirjaluettelo. Helsinki, Suomen Kirjastoseura, 1964.

151 p. 21 cm.

Oettinger, Eduard Maria, 1808–1872.
Bibliographie biographique universelle. Dictionnaire des ouvrages relatifs à l'histoire de la vie publique et privée des personnages célèbres de tous les temps et de toutes les nations, depuis le commencement du monde jusqu'à nos jours. (Reprogr. Nachdr. 2. Ausg. Brussel 1854.) Hildesheim, Dr. Gerstenberg, 1971.

2 v. in 1 (iv p., 2192 columns) 25 cm.

Riedlová, Marie.
Biografické slovníky. Soupis publikací z fondů St. věd. knihovny v Olomouci. Sest. Marie Riedlová. Olomouc, St. věd. knihovna, rozmn., 1969.

64, [1] p. 29 cm. (Publikace Státní vědecké knihovny v Olomouci, čís. 6/1969)

Riedlová, Marie, *comp.*
Česká životopisná literatura vydaná v letech 1963–1967. [Sest. Marie Riedlová. V Olomouci, 1968]

201 p. 30 cm. (Publikace státní vědecké knihovny v Olomouci, 8/1968)

Saskatchewan. Provincial Library, Regina. Bibliographic Services Division.
People in books: a bibliography. Regina, Sask., 1972.

206 p. 28 cm.

Shaw, Thomas Shuler, 1906–
Index to profile sketches in New Yorker magazine, 1925–1970. 2d, rev. ed. Boston, F. W. Faxon, 1972.

x, 206 p. 23 cm. (Useful reference series, no. 98)

"Revision of Index to profile sketches in New Yorker magazine ... which covered those appearing in volume 1, number 1, February 21, 1925 to volume 16, number 1, February 17, 1940, bringing it up to date to volume 46, number 1, February 21, 1970."

Slocum, Robert B
Biographical dictionaries and related works; an international bibliography of collective biographies ... [by] Robert B. Slocum. Detroit, Gale Research Co. [1967]

xxiii, 1056 p. 24 cm.

———— Supplement. Detroit, Gale Research Co. [1972]

xiii, 852 p. 24 cm.

United States. Library of Congress. General Reference and Bibliography Division.
Biographical sources for the United States. Compiled by Jane Kline. Boston, Gregg Press, 1972.

v, 58 p. 27 cm. (The Library reference series. Basic reference sources)

Reprint of the 1961 ed. published by the General Reference and Bibliography Division, Library of Congress, Washington.

Westphal, Margarethe.
Die besten deutschen Memoiren. (Lebenserinnerungen u. Selbstbiographien aus 7 Jahrhunderten.) [Von] M. Westphal. Unveränd., berecht. Nachdr. d. Ausg. (Leipzig, Koehler u. Volckmar,) 1923. München-Pullach, Berlin, Verl. Dokumentation, 1971.

423 p. 19 cm. (Kleine Literaturführer, Bd. 5)

Wofford College, Spartanburg, S. C. Library.
Bibliography. Compiled by Elizabeth Sabin. Edited by Frank J. Anderson. Spartanburg [S. C.] Wofford Library Press, 1970.

30[l. 29 cm. (Wofford College Library. Special collections checklist, no. 4)

JUVENILE LITERATURE

Golland, Keith S
Biographies for children: a select list; compiled by Keith S. Golland and edited by R. W. Thompson. 4th ed. Romford, Ex., Havering Libraries, 1967.

[3], 123, xxii p. 25½ cm.

Kerr, Laura J 1916–
Who's where in books; an index to biographical material. Compiled by Laura J. Kerr. Ann Arbor, Michigan Association of School Librarians [1971]

vi, 313 p. 23 cm.

New York (*State*) *Bureau of Elementary Curriculum Development.*
Famous Americans for young Americans; a bibliography for grade 4. [Rev.] Albany, 1966.

56 p. 23 cm.

"While the original publication was appropriate for grades 5 and 6, this bibliography pertains more specifically to the fourth grade social studies program."

Silverman, Judith, 1933–
An index to young readers' collective biographies; elementary and junior high-school level. New York, R. R. Bowker Co., 1970.

ix, 282 p. illus. 27 cm.

Stanius, Ellen J
Index to short biographies: for elementary and junior high grades. Compiled by Ellen J. Stanius. Metuchen, N. J., Scarecrow Press, 1971.

348 p. 22 cm.

BIOLOGY
see also Marine biology ; Microbiology

Arnaud, Patrick.
Bibliographie générale de biologie antarctique et subantarctique (Cétacés exceptés). General bibliography of antarctic and subantarctic biology (excluding Cetacea). Par Patrick Arnaud, Françoise Arnaud [et] Jean-Claude Hureau. [Paris, Impr. de l'Institut géographique national, 1967]

xvi, 180 p. map. 27 cm. (Comité national français des recherches antarctiques. CNFRA, no 18)

At head of title: Territoire des terres australes et antarctiques françaises.
English, French, Spanish, and Russian.

Bioresearch index. no. 1–   Jan. 1967–
Philadelphia, BioSciences Information Service of Biological Abstracts.

no. in   v. 28 cm. monthly.

Supersedes Bioresearch titles.

Bioresearch titles. Sept. 1965–Dec. 1966. Philadelphia, BioSciences Information Service of Biological Abstracts.

2 v. in 5. 28 cm. monthly.

Superseded by Bioresearch index.

Creager, Joan G
Guidelines and suggested titles for library holdings in undergraduate biology, edited by Joan G. Creager. ₁Washington₁ Commission on Undergraduate Education in the Biological Sciences, 1971.

iv, 65 p. 23 cm. (Commission on Undergraduate Education in the Biological Sciences. Publication no. 32)

Current index to conference papers in life sciences. **v. 1–**
Sept. 1969–
₁New York₁ CCM Information Corp.

v. 26 cm. monthly.

Vols. for 1969–   prepared by World Meetings Information Center.

Ewald, Gustav.
Führer zur biologischen Fachliteratur; Bibliographien der Biologie. Stuttgart, G. Fischer, 1973.

173 p. illus., plates. 19 cm. (Uni-Taschenbücher, 211. Biologie)

Honfi, Ferenc.
Biológiai tantárgypedagógiai bibliográfia ₁összeállitotta Honfi Ferenc és Miklovicz Afpád₁ Nyiregyháza, Magyar Pedagógiai Társaság Szabolcs-Szatmári Tagozata, 1971.
57 p. 21 cm.
At head of title: A magyar Pedagógiai Társaság Szabolcs-Szatmári Tagozata és a Nyiregyházi Tanárképző Főiskola kiadványa.
A bibliography of relevant articles published in A biologia tanitása between 1962–1970.

Hurlburt, Evelyn M
Radioisotope experiments in high school biology; an annotated selected bibliography ₁by₁ Evelyn M. Hurlburt. Prepared under the auspices of the United States Atomic Energy Commission, Division of Nuclear Education and Training. ₁Oak Ridge, Tenn., A. E. C., Division of Technical Information₁ 1966.
iii, 20 p. 22 cm.
An abridged version of Radioisotope techniques for instruction in the biological sciences.

Kerker, Ann E
Biological and biomedical resource literature ₁by₁ Ann E. Kerker and Henry T. Murphy. Lafayette, Ind., Purdue University, 1968.

ix, 226 p. 28 cm.

"Based in part on the former bibliography ... Literature sources in the biological sciences ₁by A. E. Kerker and E. M. Schlundt₁"

Key to Turkish science: biological sciences. v. 1–
Dec. 1969–
Yenişehir-Ankara, Türdok.

v. 24 cm.

At head of title: TBTAK. Scientific and Technical Research Council of Turkey.

Novinky literatury: Biologie. 1973–
Praha ₁Státní knihovna ČRS₁

v. 21 cm. 4 no. a year.

Continues Novinky literatury. Přírodní vědy. Řada biologická.

Økland, Jan, 1931–
Bibliografi over hydrobiologi. ⟨Bøker, skrifter og tidsskrifter.⟩ ₁Utg. av₁ Universitetet i Oslo. Limnologisk institutt. Oslo 1969.

59 l. 30 cm.

Organization for Economic Cooperation and Development.
Scientific fundamentals of the eutrophication of lakes and flowing waters, with particular reference to nitrogen and phosphorus as factors in eutrophication. Les bases scientifique de l'eutrophisation des lacs et des eaux courantes sous l'aspect particulier du phosphore et de l'azote comme facteurs d'eutrophisation.
———— Annex: bibliography. Annexe. bibliographie.
Paris, 1970.

61 p. 30 cm.

Pásztor, György.
A tanárképző főiskolák állattani-, növénytani tanszékek oktatói biológiai tárgyú tantárgypedagógiai munkáinak bibliográfiája, 1948–1970. A Művelődésügyi Minisztérium Pedagógusképző Osztálya mellett működő Biológiai Szakbizottság megbizásából összeállították: Pásztor György ₁és₁ Wéber Mihály. ₁Budapest, Országos Pedagógiai Könyvtár és Múzeum, 1970₁
51 p. 19 cm.
Cover title: Biológiai tantárgypedagógiai bibliográfia.

Sachregister der Abwasserbiologie. Zu den Bänden 1–13 der Münchner Beiträge zur Abwasser-, Fischerei- und Flussbiologie und zu den Bänden 1 und 2 des Handbuches der Frischwasser- und Abwasserbiologie. München, Wien, Oldenbourg, 1967.
136 p. 24 cm. (Münchner Beiträge zur Abwasser-, Fischerei-und Flussbiologie, Bd. 14)
"Im Jahre 1966 erschienene Arbeiten der Bayerischen Biologischen Versuchsanstalt München und Wielenbach (Demoll-Hofer-Institut) und des Zoologisch-Parasitologischen Instituts der Tierärztlichen Fakultät der Universität München, zusammengestellt von G. Heuschmann-Brunner": p. ₁133₁–136.

A Series of special bibliographies. **no. 1–**
Philadelphia, BioSciences Information Services of Biological Abstracts ₁1968–

no. 28 cm.

Smith, Roger Cletus, 1888–
Guide to the literature of the life sciences ₁by₁ Roger C. Smith ₁and₁ W. Malcolm Reid. 8th ed. Minneapolis, Burgess Pub. Co. ₁c1972₁

vi, 166 p. 26 cm.

Earlier editions published under title: Guide to the literature of the zoological sciences.

Stromenger, Zuzanna.
Współczesna biologia; poradnik bibliograficzny. Warszawa, Biblioteka Narodowa, 1969.

86 p. 21 cm.

At head of title: Biblioteka Narodowa. Instytut Bibliograficzny. Zuzanna Stromenger, Henryk Adler.

Vienna. Universität. *Histologisch-Embryologisches Institut.*
Liste der Publikationen aus dem Histologisch-Embryologischen Institut der Universität Wien seit 1956. (Wien, Selbstverlag des Histologisch-Embryologischen Institutes der Universität Wien, 1969.)

20 p. 25 cm.

BIBLIOGRAPHIES

Besterman, Theodore, 1904–
Biological sciences; a bibliography of bibliographies. Totowa, N. J., Rowman and Littlefield, 1971 [i. e. 1972]

471 p. 20 cm. (His The Besterman world bibliographies)

PERIODICALS

Bergen, Norway. Universitetet. *Biblioteket.*
Biologiske tidsskrifter. Bibliografi over Universitetets bestand av utenlandske periodica i biologiske fag med grenseområder. [Bergen] 1967.

2 l., 70 p. 25 cm.

Bibliotheca Bogoriensis.
Daftar madjalah ilmiah Indonesia jang terdapat di Pusat Perpustakaan Biologi dan Pertanian "Bibliotheca-Bogoriensis" dan Institut Pertanian Bogor. Bogor [1967?]

37 p. 32 cm. (Its Seri bibliografi. no. 3)
———— Suplemen. List of Indonesian periodicals in the Central Library for Biology and Agriculture "Bibliotheca Bogoriensis" and Bogor Agricultural University. Supplement. Bogor [1969]

8 p. 32 cm. (Its Serie bibliografi, no. 13)

Biological Council.
Abbreviated titles of biological journals: a list culled with permission from The world list of scientific periodicals with indications of the abbreviations recommended by the U. S. A. Standards Institute where these differ. 3rd ed.: compiled by P. C. Williams on behalf of the Biological Council. London, Biological Council, 1968.

viii, 47 p. 23 cm.

BioSciences Information Service of Biological Abstracts.
Biological abstracts list of serials with title abbreviations. 19 –69. [Philadelphia]

v. 28 cm. annual.

Continued by the service's BIOSIS list of serials with coden, title abbreviations, new, changed and ceased titles.

BioSciences Information Service of Biological Abstracts.
BIOSIS list of serials with coden, title abbreviations, new, changed and ceased titles. 1970– Philadelphia.

v. 28 cm. annual.

Continues the service's Biological abstracts list of serials with title abbreviations.
Title varies slightly.

International Council of Scientific Unions. *Abstracting Board.*
Some characteristics of primary periodicals. in the domain of the biological sciences. Paris, Conseil international des unions scientifiques, Bureau des résumés analytiques,

1967.

84 p. tables. 27 cm.

Oregon. University. *Library.*
Biological serials. Eugene, 1966.

172 p. 28 cm. (University of Oregon Library occasional paper no. 4)

Oslo. Universitet. Bibliotek.
Utenlandske periodika i Norge. Biologi. Oslo, 1968.

vi, 107 l. 30 cm.

At head of title: Norsk samkatalog.
First ed. published in 1953 under title: Samkatalog over tidsskrifter. Medisin med grenseområder.
Second rev. ed. published in 1958 under title: Samkatalog over periodika: medisin med grenseområder.
Beginning with the 3d ed. (1967) published under title: Utenlandske periodika i Norge.

BIONICS
see also   Cybernetics

Anisimova, T   N
Бионика. Библиогр. указ. отеч. и иностр. литературы. 1958–1968. Сост. Т. Н. Анисимова. Москва, "Наука," 1971.

168 p. 27 cm.

On leaf preceding t. p.: Академия наук СССР. Научный совет по комплексной проблеме "Кибернетика." Сектор сети специальных библиотек.

Бионика.

Новосибирск, Гос. публичная науч.-техн. библиотека Сибирского отд-ния Академии наук СССР.

v. 21 cm. monthly.

"Информационно-библиографический бюллетень."
Began 1967.

Bogomolova, Ekaterina Mitrofanovna.
Библиографический указатель. [Составитель: Екатерина Митрофановна Богомолова] Москва, 1965.

39 p. 20 cm. (Лектору о бионике)

Новая наука-бионика.
At head of title: Общество "Знание" РСФСР.

Campbell, Alan.
Bionics and biocybernetics. [Washington] Aerospace Technology Division, Library of Congress, 1968.

iv, 366 p. illus. 27 cm. (ATD report 68–77–108–4)

Largely abstracts of Soviet open-source literature covering the period 1965–1968.

BIRDS   see   Ornithology

BIRTH CONTROL
see also   Abortion

Bibliography of family planning & population. v. 1– July 1972–
Cambridge, Eng., Simon Population Trust.

v. 25 cm. bimonthly.

Chowdhury, Uma, 1926–
Annotated bibliography on family planning communication. New Delhi, Central Family Planning Institute

[1970]

[9], 154 p. 22 cm. (CFPI monograph series, no. 4)

Family planning educational materials; an annotated bibliography of selected items. Chapel Hill, Carolina Population Center, 1968.

89 p. 22 cm.

"Edited by Educational Materials Unit, Carolina Population Center."

Kasdon, David L

International family planning, 1966–1968; a bibliography, by David L. Kasdon. Chevy Chase, Md., National Institute of Mental Health; [For sale by the Supt. of Docs., U .S. Govt. Print. Off., Washington] 1969.

v, 62 p. 24 cm. (Public Health Service publication no. 1917)

"A publication of the National Clearinghouse for Mental Health Information."

Kenyon, Carleton W

A selective bibliography on population control—abortion, birth control, euthanasia, and sterilization. Compiled by Carleton Kenyon. Sacramento, California State Library, Law Library, 1966.

17 p. 28 cm.
Cover title.

————Supplement, compiled by Lorna Flescher. Sacramento. California State Library, Law Library, 1969.

6 p. 28 cm.

Muyden-Floor, Miriam G   van.

Literatuurrapport over vrijwillige sterilisatie [door] Miriam G. van Muyden-Floor. [Zeist] Nederlands Instituut voor Sociaal Seruologisch Onderzoek, 1970.

33, [5] l. 30 cm. (Nederlands Instituut voor Sociaal Sexuologisch Onderzoek. Literatuur rapport, 2)

Tietze, Christopher, *ed.*

Bibliography of fertility control, 1950–1965. New York, National Committee on Maternal Health [1965]

iv, 108 p. 22 cm. ([National Committee on Maternal Health] Publication no. 23)

Watts, Mary Elizabeth, 1911–

Selected references for social workers on family planning; an annotated list. Compiled by Mary E. Watts. [Washington] U. S. Dept. of Health, Education, and Welfare, Children's Bureau, 1968.

23 p. 26 cm.

Watts, Mary Elizabeth, 1911–

Selected references for social workers on family planning; an annotated list. Compiled by Mary E. Watts. Rev. Rockville, Md., U. S. Maternal and Child Health Service; [for sale by the Supt. of Docs., U. S. Govt. Print. Off., Washington] 1971.

38 p. 27 cm. (Public Health Service publication no. 2154)

INDIA

Bhatia, Brajesh.

Family life and population education, compiled and edited by Brajesh Bhatia [and] M. M. L. Goyal. New Delhi, National Institute of Family Planning [1971]

23 p. 24 cm. (National Institute of Family Planning. Bibliography series, 1)

Bibliography of cost benefit studies on family planning in India and IUCD studies in India. Bombay, Demographic Training and Research Centre [1970]

21 p. 28 cm.

Cover title.
CONTENTS: A bibliography of cost benefit studies on family planning in India, by K. B. Suri and S. P. Mohanty.—A bibliography of IUCD studies in India, by Asha Bhende.

Kapil, Krishan K   1933–

A bibliography of sterilization and KAP studies in India, by Krishan K. Kapil and Devendra N. Saksena. Bombay, Demographic Training and Research Centre [1968]

38 p. 28 cm.

Patankar, Tara.

A bibliography of fertility studies in India. Bombay, Demographic Training and Research Centre [1969]

38 p. 30 cm.

INDONESIA

Perkumpulan Keluarga Berencana Indonesia. Pusat Latihan dan Penelitian Nasional. Perpustakaan.

Suatu bibliografi beranotasi dari: bahan-bahan tentang keluarga berencana dan kependudukan di Indonesia dan bidang-bidang yang berhubungan dengan itu, yang ada di Perpustakaan Pusat Latihan dan Penelitian Nasional/Perkumpulan Keluarga Berencana Indonesia. Jakarta, 1973.

75 l. 34 cm.

BISMARCK, OTTO, FURST VON

Born, Karl Erich.

Bismarck-Bibliographie. Quellen und Literatur zur Geschichte Bismarcks und seiner Zeit. Hrsg. von Karl Erich Born. Bearbeitet von Willy Hertel unter Mitarbeit von Hansjoachim Henning. (Köln und Berlin) Grote (1966)

259 p. 24 cm.

BISSCHOPPELIJKE SEMINARIE TE GENT

Bisschoppelijke Seminarie te Gent.

Inventaris van het archief van het Bisschoppelijk Seminarie te Gent: Fondsen Hiëronymieten, Seminarie, Fundatie Lemmens-Broeckx en Fundatie Goethals. [Door] J. Roegiers. Brussels, [Algemeen Rijksarchief], Ruisbroekstr., 2, 1970.

xvii, 93 p. 30 cm.
"Het Seminarie-archief is verdeeld over drie archiefdepots: het Seminarie, het Rijksarchief en het Bisdom te Gent."

BITUMEN   see under   Pavements

BITZIUS, ALBERT

Arm, Erna.

Bibliographie der schweizerischen und deutschen Erstausgaben und Erstdrucke des literarischen Werkes Jeremias Gotthelfs ⟨Albert Bitzius⟩, 1797–1854. [Bern,] Vereinigung Schweizerischer Bibliothekare, 1970.

i, xix, 68 l. 3 plates (facsims.) 30 cm.

"Diplomarbeit."

BLACHER, BORIS

Akademie der Künste, Berlin. Archiv.

Boris Blacher. [Ausstellung des Archives der Akademie

der Künste innerhalb der Veranstaltungen der Abteilung Musik anlässlich des 70. Geburtstages von Boris Blacher; Akademie der Künste Berlin, 6. Januar–18. Februar 1973. ₁Ausstellung und Katalog: Walther Huder. Berlin, Druck: Brüder Hartmann, 1973₁

45, ₁11₁ p. illus. 22 cm.

BLACK, HUGO LAFAYETTE

Meador, Daniel John.
Mr. Justice Black and his books ₁by₁ Daniel J. Meador. Charlottesville, University Press of Virginia ₁1974₁

x, 200 p. ports., facsims. 26 cm.

BLACK MUSLIMS

Williams, Daniel T
The Black Muslims in the United States: a selected bibliography, by Daniel T. Williams and Carolyn L. Redden. ₁Tuskegee, Ala.₁ Hollis Burke Frissell Library, Tuskegee Institute, 1964.

19 l. 28 cm.

BLACK SEA

Brünn. Krajská lidová knihovna.
Sovětské Černomoří. Výběrová bibliogr. Brno, Knihovna Jiřího Mahena, rozmn., 1972.

45, ₁1₁ p. 21 cm. (Na cestu do SSSR)

Laking, Phyllis N
The Black Sea, its geology, chemistry, biology; a bibliography, by Phyllis N. Laking. Woods Hole, Mass., Woods Hole Oceanographic Institution, 1974.

xiv, 368 p. 24 cm. (Woods Hole Oceanographic Institution. Contribution no. 3330)

BLACK STUDIES   see   Afro-American Studies

BLAGOEV, DIMITŬR

Mutafova, M
(Dimitŭr Blagoev)
Димитър Благоев. 115 години от рождението му. (Библиографска справка). ₁Състави: М. Мутафова₁ Шумен, 9171 ₁i. e. 1971₁

23 p. 21 cm.

At head of title: Окръжна библиотека—Шумен. Отдел "Справочно-библиографско и информационно обслужване и краезнание."

BLAKE, WILLIAM

Bentley, Gerald Eades, 1930–
A Blake bibliography; annotated lists of works, studies, and Blakeana ₁by₁ G. E. Bentley, Jr., and Martin K. Nurmi. Minneapolis, University of Minnesota Press ₁1964₁

xix, 393 p. illus. 25 cm.

Cambridge. University. Fitzwilliam Museum.
William Blake: catalogue of the collection in the Fitzwilliam Museum, Cambridge; edited by David Bindman. Cambridge, Heffer, 1970.

vii, 88 p., 44 plates. illus. (incl. 1 col.), facsims., ports. 23 x 26 cm.

Westminster City Libraries.
William Blake: catalogue of the Preston Blake Library presented by Kerrison Preston in 1967 ₁compiled by Phyllis Goff₁. London, Westminster City Libraries, 1969.

₁127₁ p. 26 cm. index.

BLANCO, EDUARDO

Caracas. Universidad Católica Andrés Bello. Escuela de Letras. Centro de Investigaciones Literarias.
Contribución a la bibliografía de Eduardo Blanco, 1838–1912. ₁Caracas, Gobernación del Distrito Federal, 1971₁

82 p. port. 20 cm. (Colección Bibliografías, 9)

Cover title: Bibliografía Eduardo Blanco.
"Realizado por María Luisa Alzuru de Palacios ₁et al.₁ ... bajo la dirección del profesor Efraín Subero."

BLAST-FURNACES

British Iron & Steel Industry Translation Service.
The blast furnace: a bibliography of translated articles. London, Iron and Steel Institute ₁1966₁.

12 p. 26 cm.

BLASTING   see under Boring

BLAŽEK, OLDŘICH

Opatřil, Stanislav.
Oldřich Blažek, 1903–1942. Bibliografii prací připravili Stanislav Opatřil a Kamil Horňak. Brno, 1966.

60 p. 20 cm. (Život a dílo čs. pedagogů, č. 5)

Státní pedagogická knihovna v Brně. Publikace. č. 265.

BLEACHING

American Society for Testing and Materials. Committee D–12.15.05.
Bibliographical abstracts on evaluation of fluorescent whitening agents, 1929–1968. Prepared by L. E. Weeks ₁and others₁ Philadelphia ₁1972₁

33 p. 28 cm. (ATSM special technical publication no. 507)

West, Clarence Jay, 1886–1953.
Bleaching ₁by₁ Clarence J. West and W. B. Weber. ₁Appleton, Wis., Institute of Paper Chemistry₁ 1955 ₁i. e. 1956₁

441 p. 28 cm. (Appleton, Wis. Institute of Paper Chemistry. Bibliographic series, no. 183)

———————Supplement 1–   ₁By Lillian Roth and Jack Weiner. ₁Appleton, Wis., Institute of Paper Chemistry₁ 1965–

v. 28 cm.

BLEKSLEY, ARTHUR

Burnton, Ruth.
Arthur E. H. Bleksley; a bibliography. Johannesburg, University of the Witwatersrand, Department of Bibliography, Librarianship and Typography, 1970.

₁xi₁, 41 p. 30 cm.

Cover title: The work of Arthur E. H. Bleksley.
Compiled in part fulfilment for the requirements of the Diploma in Librarianship, University of Witwatersrand.

BLIND

Index of publications issued by International Research Information Service through summer 1970. New York, American Foundation for the Blind, 1970.

38 p. 29 cm.

Cover title.

———— Addendum ... through spring 1973. New York, American Foundation for the Blind, 1973.

9 l. 29 cm.

Index of publications issued by International Research Information Service through June 1971. New York, American Foundation for the Blind, 1971.

40 p. 28 cm.

International Research Information Service.
Bibliography of mobility research and mobility instrumentation research (a provisional bibliography) New York, American Foundation for the Blind, 1964.

30 p. 28 cm.

Seattle. Public Library. *Division for the Blind and the Physically Handicapped.*
Selected bibliographies on blindness. [Prepared by Seattle Public Library, Division for the Blind and the Physically Handicapped, and the Institutional Library Services Division, Washington State Library. Seattle? 1967]

10 p. 28 cm.

Wien, Virginia.
Bibliography of the blind. Lansing, Michigan Dept. of Education, State Library [1966]

13 p. 28 cm. ([Michigan. State Library, Lansing] Bibliography for educators no. 13)

BLIND, BOOKS FOR THE

Cobb, Parris G
Tape catalogue, 1970; a listing of books recorded on magnetic tape by volunteer readers in our studios and available for use by the blind and physically handicapped. Compiled by Parris G. Cobb. Salt Lake City, Utah State Library Commission, Division for the Blind and Physically Handicapped [1970]

vi, 252 p. illus. 29 cm.

Crane Library.
Library materials for the blind and partially sighted available from the Crane Library, compiled by J. McRee Elrod. Vancouver, 1972.

lxxix, 105 p. 28 cm.

Denmark. Statens bibliotek for blinde.
Fortegnelse over lydbøger. 1956/1971. København, Statens Bibliotek for Blinde, Eksp.: Rønnegade 1, København Ø, 1972.

315 p. 21 cm.

Denmark. Statens trykkeri og bibliotek for blinde.
Fortegnelse over lydbøger i Statens trykkeri og bibliotek for blinde 1956/1965. København [1966]

160 p. 22 cm.

———— Tillæg 1966. København [1966]

40 p. 22 cm.

Deutscher Verband Evangelischer Büchereien.
Grossdruckbücher. Ausw. f. sehbehinderte Leser. (Red.: Annette Blanke, Elfriede Conrad [und] Leselotte Stern.)

[u. a.] (Göttingen) 1969.

47 p. 25 cm. (Beiheft zu "Der Evangelische Buchberater," 3)

For younger readers; braille and talking books. 1964/65–
[Washington]

v. illus. 28 cm.

Vols. for 1964/65–   published for the Library of Congress, Division for the Blind and Physically Handicapped by the American Foundation for the Blind.

Horn, Thomas D
Books for the partially sighted child [by] Thomas D. Horn and Dorothy J. Ebert. Champaign, Ill., National Council of Teachers of English [1965?]

79 p. 24 cm.

Cover title.
"Reprinted from Elementary English."

Landau, Robert A
Large type books in print, edited by Robert A. Landau & Judith S. Nyren. New York, R. R. Bowker Co., 1970.

xxi, 193 p. 29 cm.

Linderberg, Kerstin, 1928–
Böcker med stor stil. En förteckning i urval. Ny, omarb. uppl. Lund Bibliotekstjänst, 1967.

30 p. 21 cm. (Btj-serien, 2)

Michigan. *Blind and Physically Handicapped Library.*
A catalog of braille, large-print, magnetic-tape, microfilm, talking books, held in Michigan schools and other cooperating agencies. Lansing, 1969.

123 p. 28 cm.

Michigan. Blind and Physically Handicapped Library.
A catalog of braille, large-print, magnetic-tape, talking books, held in Michigan schools and other cooperating agencies. Lansing, 1971.

208 p. 22 x 28 cm.

Michigan. *State Library Division. Blind and Physically Handicapped Section.*
Magnetic tape titles recorded by volunteers and on deposit at the library for the Blind and Physically Handicapped Section of the State Library Division. Lansing, Michigan Dept. of Education, Bureau of Educational Services, 1968.

51 p. 28 cm.
On cover: Catalog of books on magnetic tape.
To be used in conjunction with tape catalogs issued by the Library of Congress, Division for the Blind and Physically Handicapped.

Sweden. Rikscentralen för pedagogiska hjälpmedel åt synskadade.
Katalog. Studiebiblioteket. Upprättad mars 1973 ... Solna, Rikscentralen för pedagogiska hjälpmedel åt synskadade (Tomtebodaskolan), [1972].

(69) l. 30 cm.

U. S. Library of Congress. Division for the Blind and Physically Handicapped.
Cassette books [catalog] Washington, 1971.

vii, 75 p. 27 cm.

Supersedes the catalog entitled Cassettes 1 issued in 1968.

United States. Library of Congress. Division for the Blind and Physically Handicapped.
Cassette books; [catalog] 2d ed. Washington, Library of Congress, 1974.

iii, 146 p. 26 cm.

Supersedes the catalog entitled Cassettes 1 issued in 1968.

U. S. Library of Congress. Division for the Blind and Physically Handicapped.
Talking books to profit by. Washington [1971]

11 p. 27 cm.

Västerås, Sweden. Stifts- och landsbiblioteket.
Talbokskatalog. Kommenterad förteckning över talböcker i Stifts- och landsbiblioteket. Västerås, 1966.

127, [1] p. 21 cm.

Yelland, Michael, *ed.*
Large and clear: a list of large-type books, edited by M. Yelland. London, Library Association, 1965 [i. e. 1966]

31 p. 22 cm. (Library Association. Special subject list, no. 47)

BLIND, PERIODICALS FOR THE

U. S. *Library of Congress. Division for the Blind and Physically Handicapped.*
Magazines: braille and recorded. Washington, 1968.

12 l. 27 cm.

BLIND-DEAF

Löwe, Armin.
Bibliographie des Taubblindenwesens. Bibliography on deaf-blindness. [Von] Armin Löwe [u.] Benno Westermann. Dortmund, E. Beschel, 1969.

46 p. 21 cm. (Schriften zur Sonderpädagogik. Reihe B: Originalerbeiten, Heft 5)

Washington (State). State Library, Olympia.
The deaf-blind; a selected bibliography. [Olympia] 1971.

11 l. 28 cm.

BLOCH, CLAUDE CHARLES

United States. Library of Congress. Manuscript Division.
Claude Charles Bloch, Julius Augustus Furer, John Franklin Shafroth, William Harrison Standley: a register of their papers in the Library of Congress. Washington, Library of Congress, 1973.

iii, 6, 10, 4, 11 p. 27 cm.

"Naval Historical Foundation collection."

BLOCK-BOOKS see under Manuscripts, Indic, [Japanese, Mongolian, and Tibetan]

BLOOD

Dávid, József.
Magyar haematológiai és transzfúziós bibliográfia, 1945–1960. [Budapest] Országos Orvostudományi Könyvtár és Dokumentációs Központ, 1964.

vii, 472 p. 24 cm.

Fibrinolysis, Thrombolysis, and blood clotting: a bibliography. 1966–
[Washington, U. S. Govt. Print. Off.]

v. 26 cm.

Issued monthly with annual cumulations.
Began in 1965 with no annual cumulation for that year.
Vols. for   issued by Committee on Thrombolytic Agents, National Heart Institute in cooperation with National Library of Medicine.

Hauptmann, Erik.
Jugoslavenska hematološka bibliografija. Priredili: Erik Hauptmann i Inga Črepinko. Zagreb, "Pliva," [1969]–

v. 20 cm.

Leningradskiĭ nauchno-issledovatel'skiĭ institut gematologii i perelivaniĭa krovi.
Список научных работ, выполненных сотрудниками Ленинградского института гематологии и переливания крови. (1932–1968 гг.) Ленинград, 1969.

249 p. 23 cm.

At head of title: Министерство здравоохранения РСФСР.
1.50rub

Maupin, Bernard, 1910–
Blood platelets 1971; an annotated bibliography. Amsterdam, Excerpta Medica, 1973.

viii, 293 p. 25 cm.

Maupin, Bernard, 1910–
Blood platelets 1972; an annotated bibliography. Amsterdam, Excerpta Medica [New York, Distributed in the U. S. by American Elsevier Pub. Co.] 1973.

viii, 300 p. 24 cm.

BLUMGARTEN, SOLOMON

Jeshurin, Ephim H   1885–1967.
יהואש ביבליאגראפיע. צוזאמענגעשטעלט פון יעפים ישורין,
ניו-יארק, 1965. [בוענאס איירעס] יוסף ליפשיץ-פאנד פון דער
ליטעראטור-געזעלשאפט ביים ייווא, 1965.

18 p. 18 cm.

Cover title.
Added cover title: Ieholash bibliography.
"סעפאראט-אפדרוק פון 25סטן באנד מוסטערווערק פון דער יידישער
ליטעראטור; יהואש, לידער, מעשלאך, משלים."

BOARS AND BOATING

Boat Owners Association of the United States.
Boating publications log. [Washington] Boat/U. S. Book and Publication Service, °1966.

81 p. 23 cm.

Library Association. *County Libraries Group.*
Readers' guide to books on sailing, cruising, and motorboating. [London] 1964.

23 p. 19 cm. (*Its* Readers' guide, new ser., no. 77)

Cover title: Sailing, cruising, and motorboating.
"Compilation undertaken by the Librarian and staff of Dorset County Library."

Parshin, S   A
(Molodym liubiteliam sudostroeniia i vodno-motornogo sporta)
Молодым любителям судостроения и водно-моторного спорта; аннотированный указатель литературы. [Составитель С. А. Паршин] Москва, 1972.

60 p. 20 cm. (В помощь техническому творчеству молодежи)

At head of title: Министерство культуры РСФСР. Государственная республиканская юношеская библиотека РСФСР имени 50-летия ВЛКСМ.

Van Wageningen, Jennifer Marjorie, 1944–
Concrete boats, ships and yachts, compiled by J. M. van Wageningen. Adelaide, State Library of South Australia, 1970.

12 p. 27 cm. (Research Service bibliographies, series 4, no. 127)

Van Wageningen, Jennifer Marjorie, 1944–
Construction of fibreglass reinforced plastic boats. Compiled by J. M. van Wageningen. Adelaide, State Library of South Australia, 1969.

27 p. 26 cm. (Research Service bibliographies, series 4, no. 125)

Watts, Tessa R
Sailing; selected by Tessa R. Watts. London, National Book League ₁1972₎

40 p. 21 cm.

On cover: Sailing; an annotated list, 1972.

BOCCACCIO, GIOVANNI

Bacchi della Lega, Alberto, 1848–1924.
Serie delle edizioni delle opere di Giovanni Boccacci latine, volgari, tradotte e transformate. Bologna, Forni, 1967.

162 p. 25 cm.

Half title: Bibliografia boccaccesca.
"Ristampa anastatica della edizione di Bologna, Romagnoli, 1875."

BOCCHERINI, LUIGI

Gérard, Yves.
Thematic, bibliographical, and critical catalogue of the works of Luigi Boccherini, compiled by Yves Gérard under the auspices of Germaine de Rothschild; translated by Andreas Mayor. London, New York, Oxford University Press, 1969.

xix, 716 p. facsims., music, plates. 26 cm.

On spine: Catalogue of the works of Luigi Boccherini.
"Companion volume to Boccherini: his life and work by Germaine de Rothschild."

BODEGRAVEN, NETHERLANDS

Hervormde Gemeente te Bodegraven.
Inventaris van de archieven der Hervormde gemeente te Bodegraven, 1513–1952, door G. M. van Aalst. ₁'s-Gravenhage₎ Algemeen Rijksarchief, 1969.

85 l. 29 cm.

BODKIN, THOMAS

Denson, Alan.
Thomas Bodkin: a bio-bibliographical survey with a bibliographical survey of his family. Dublin, Bodkin Trustees; Kendal (Westmd.), A. Denson, 1966.

₁2₎, 236 p. 34 cm.

BØDTCHER, LUDVIG ADOLPH

Jørgensen, Aage.
Ludvig Bødtcher. En biliografi. Højbjerg, Eget forlag, Kragelunds Allé 10, 1971.

9 l. 21 cm.

BOER WAR, 1899–1902 see South African War

BOETZELAER FAMILY

Netherlands (Kingdom, 1815–). Rijksarchief in Utrecht, Utrecht.
Inventaris archieven Van Boetzelaer, door E. P. Polak-De Booy. ₁Utrecht₎ Rijksarchief Utrecht, 1965.

268 p. illus., geneal. tables. 29 cm.

BOGENSE, DENMARK

Denmark. Landsarkivet for Fyn.
Bogense kommunale arkiv 1869–1970. ₁Udarb. af Kirsten Helle Pedersen₎. Odense, Eksp.: Jernbanegade 36, 1973.

28 l. 29 cm. (Its Arkivregistratur)

BOGOTÁ, COLOMBIA

Medina, José Toribio, 1852–1930.
La imprenta en Bogotá, 1739–1821. Amsterdam, N. Israel, 1964.

101 p. 22 cm. (Reprint series of José Toribio Medina's bibliographical works, 11)

Original ed. published in Santiago de Chile, 1904.

BOHEMIA

Publikace Zemského statistického úřadu Království Českého (1897–1918) ₁Odpovědný pracovník Jaroslav Podzimek₎. Praha, ₁Vydalo Oborové informační středisko pro statistiku a účetnictví Výzkumného ústavu statistiky a účetnictví₎ 1968.

58 p. 21 cm. (Vyzkumný ústav statistiky a účetnictví. Oborové informační středisko. Rešerše, č. 17)

BÖHME, RUDOLF

Dresden. Stadt- und Bezirksbibliothek.
Bibliographie Rudolf Böhme. Selbständige Schriften, Zeitschriftenaufsätze, Rezensionen, Bibliographien. Anlässl. s. 65. Geburtstages hrsg. Dresden, 1972.

28 l. 21 cm.

BOHUSLÄN, SWEDEN

Gothenburg, Sweden. Stadsbiblioteket. *Länsavdelningen.*
Litteratur om Bohuslän. Omarb. uppl. Göteborg, 1967.

44 p. 21 cm.

BOKEMEYER, HEINRICH

Kümmerling, Harald.
Katalog der Sammlung Bokemeyer. Kassel, Bärenreiter ₁1970₎

423 p. illus., facsims., music. 30 cm. (Kieler Schriften zur Musikwissenschaft, Bd. 18)

BOLÍVAR, VENEZUELA (STATE)

Venezuela. Universidad Central, *Caracas. Escuela de Biblioteconomía y Archivos.*
Muestra antológica del libro de Guayana. Caracas, Facultad de Humanidades y Educación, Universidad Central de Venezuela, 1964.

25 p. 23 cm.

"Catálogo de la exposición organizada por la Escuela de Biblioteconomía y Archivos ... como homenaje de la U. C. V. a la conmemoración del bicentenario de Ciudad Bolívar."

BOLIVIA

Costa de la Torre, Arturo.
Catálogo de la bibliografía boliviana; libros y folletos, 1900–1963. La Paz, 1966 [i. e. 1968–

v. 24 cm.

Mesa, Rosa Quintero.
Bolivia. New York, Bowker, 1972.

xxxiii, 156 p. 29 cm. (Latin American serial documents, v. 6)

Muñoz Reyes, Jorge, 1904–
Bibliografía geográfica de Bolivia. La Paz, Academia Nacional de Ciencias de Bolivia, 1967.

170 p. 23 cm. (Academia Nacional de Ciencias de Bolivia. Publicación no. 16)

Torrico Arze, Armando, 1928–
Bibliografía boliviana de colonización [por] Armando Torrico Arze [e] Irma Aliaga de Vizcarra. La Paz, 1967.

7 l. 29 cm. (Sociedad de Ingenieros Agrónomos de Bolivia. Boletín bibliográfico no. 7)

BIBLIOGRAPHIES

Siles Guevara, Juan, 1939–
Bibliografía de bibliografías bolivianas. [La Paz] Ministerio de Cultura, Información, y Turismo, Impr. del Estado, 1969.

38 p. 19 cm. (Cuadernos de bibliografía, no. 1)

BÖLL, HEINRICH

Deutsche Akademie für Sprache und Dichtung.
Das Werk Heinrich Bölls in Übersetzungen: zur Verleihung d. Nobelpreises f. Literatur 1972; Ausstellung in d. Hess. Landes- u. Hochschulbibliothek, Darmstadt vom 23. Nov. 1972–31. Jan. 1973/ Deutsche Akademie für Sprache und Dichtung. — Darmstadt: Dt. Akad. f. Sprache u. Dichtung; Darmstadt: Hess. Landes- u. Hochschulbibliothek, 1972.

11 l.; 30 cm.

BOLL-WEEVIL

Mitlin, Luceille Liston.
Boll weevil, *Anthonomus grandis* Boh., abstracts of research publications, 1961–65. Compiled by Luceille Liston Mitlin and Norman Mitlin. [Washington] Agricultural Research Service, U. S. Dept. of Agriculture [1968]

iv, 32 p. 26 cm. (U. S. Dept. of Agriculture. Miscellaneous publication no. 1092)
Continuation of Cotton boll weevil (Anthonomus grandis Boh.) abstracts of research publications, 1843–1960, by Henry A. Dunn, issued as Miscellaneous publication no. 985.

BOLOGNA, ITALY

Bologna. Comune (1116–1506), Reggimento (1506–1786). A cura della xi Commissione territoriale della F. I. S. A., Bologna. Milano, Fondazione italiana per la storia amministrativa, 1967.

26 p. tables. 27 cm. (Acta Italica, 2)
Edited by Gianfranco Orlandelli.

BOLZANO, JAN KŘTITEL

Křivský, Pavel.
Jan Křtitel Bolzano, 1777–1859 : literární pozůstalost / zprac. Pavel Křivský. — Praha : Lit. archív Památníku

nár. písemnictví, 1972.

7 p. ; 21 cm. — (Edice inventářů ; čís. 251)

BONGS, ROLF

Bongs, Ursula.
Rolf Bongs; ein bibliographisches Verzeichnis 1925–1972. [Zusammenstellung: Ursula und Rolfson Bongs]. Düsseldorf, Stadtbücherei, 1972.

12 p. 21 cm.

BONIFACIO, CORSICA

Bonifacio, Corsica. Archives municipales.
Répertoire sommaire des archives municipales de Bonifacio, XVIe siècle-début du XXe ... Bastia, Fédération d'associations et groupements pour les études corses, 1971.

32 p. 27 cm. (Cahiers Corsica, 15–16)
At head of title: Claude Valleix (père André-Marie, O. F. M.)

BONIN ISLANDS

Shigen Chōsajo.
(Ogasawara ni kansuru bunken mokuroku)
小笠原に関する文献目録 [東京] 科学技術庁資源調査所 昭和43(1968)
33 p. 26 cm. (科学技術庁資源調査所資料 第5号)

BONN, GERMANY

Höroldt, Dietrich.
Bonner Bibliographie und Literaturbericht 1965–1970, bearb. von Dietrich Höroldt, Paul Melchers [und] Otto Wenig. Bonn, L. Röhrscheid, 1972.

237 p. port. 23 cm. (Veröffentlichungen des Stadtarchivs Bonn. Bd. 9)

BONNARD, GEORGES ALFRED

Vaud. Bibliothèque cantonale et universitaire, Lausanne. Département des manuscrits.
Inventaire du fonds Georges Bonnard, IS 1952, par Marianne Perrenoud. Lausanne, Bibliothèque cantonale et universitaire, 1969.

17 l. 30 cm. (Its Inventaire des fonds manuscrits, 7)

BÖÖK, FREDRIK

Arvidsson, Rolf, 1920–
Fredrik Bööks bibliografi 1898–1967. Stockholm, Norstedt, 1970.

(4), 353, (1) p. 23 cm.

BOOK-COLLECTING see Bibliography - Early printed books; Bibliography - Rare books; Incunabula

BOOK DESIGN

Myers, Robin.
A handlist of books and periodicals on British book design since the war to accompany the Galley Club exhibition of book design 45–66, selected by Will Carter. London, Galley Club, [1967]

[2], 12 p. 27 x 14½ cm.

National Book League, *London.*
Textbook design exhibition, 1966: catalogue of an exhibi-

tion of books published between May 1962 and May 1965 and chosen for the National Book League by G. Fielden Hughes, Ruari McLean and Kenneth Pinnock. London, National Book League [1966]

[72] p. illus. 18½ cm.

BOOK PRESERVATION see Books - Conservation and restoration

BOOK SELECTION, REVIEWS, ETC.
see also Bibliography - Best books

Gallup, Jennifer.
Reference guide to book reviews; a checklist of sources in the humanities, social sciences, and fine arts, prepared by Jennifer Gallup. Vancouver, University of British Columbia Library, 1968.

19 l. 28 cm. (Reference publication no. 24)

Gallup, Jennifer.
Reference guide to reviews; a checklist of sources in the humanities, social sciences, and fine arts. Vancouver, University of British Columbia Library, 1970.

38 p. 23 cm. (University of British Columbia. Library. Reference publication no. 31 (revision of no. 24))

1968 ed. published under title: Reference guide to book reviews; a checklist of sources in the humanities, social sciences, and fine arts.

Gray, Richard A
A guide to book review citations; a bibliography of sources, compiled by Richard A. Gray. [Columbus] Ohio State University Press [1969, °1968]

viii, 221 p. 22 cm. (The Ohio State University Libraries publications, no. 2)

Matos, Antonio, *ed.*
Guía a las reseñas de libros de y sobre Hispanoamérica. Río Piedras, P. R., 1965.

xii, 311 p. 28 cm.

Added t. p: Hispanic America through book reviews; a guide to reviews of books from and about Hispanic America.

Perkins, Flossic L
Book and non-book media; annotated guide to selection aids for educational materials [by] Flossie L. Perkins. Urbana, Ill., National Council of Teachers of English [1972]

ix, 298 p. 21 cm.

A revision of the 1967 ed. of Book selection media by Ralph Perkins.

Perkins, Ralph.
Book selection media; a descriptive guide to 175 aids for selecting library materials. Champaign, Ill., National Council of Teachers of English [1966]

xi, 188 p. 22 cm.

Perkins, Ralph.
Book selection media; a descriptive guide to 170 aids for selecting library materials. Revision. Champaign, Ill., National Council of Teachers of English, 1967.

xxiii, 168 p. 22 cm.

BOOK TRADE see Publishing and bookselling

BOOKBINDING

Dühmert, Anneliese.
Buchpflege, eine Bibliographie. Stuttgart, M. Hettler, 1963.

209 p. 25 cm.

"Auf Veranlassung der Einbandkommission des Vereins Deutscher Bibliothekare."
"Es wurde der Zeitraum von 1910 bis 1960 erfasst."

BOOKKEEPING see Accounting

BOOKS
see also Bibliography

Gothenburg, Sweden. Stadsbiblioteket.
Böcker om böcker [Utg. av Stadsbiblioteket, Göteborg. Göteborg [1968]

[1], 11 p. 21 cm.

"Denna katalog omfattar böckerna i Elgströmska samlingen i Göteborgs stadsbibliotek."

Hart, Horace.
Bibliotheca typographica in usum eorum qui libros amant: a list of books about books. With an introd. by George Parker Winship. Ann Arbor, Mich., Gryphon Books, 1971.

xi, 112 p. 22 cm.

Facsim. reprint of the 1933 ed.
"This list contains books in English only."

Pratt, Roland Davies.
A thousand books on books: a selection of English books on bookmaking, book-selling and book-collecting [by] R. D. Pratt. Weston-Super-Mare (Som.), R. D. Pratt, 1967.

96 p. 19½ cm.

Steinberg, Heinz.
Forschungsobjekt Buch. Untersuchungen zur Sozialpsychologie des Lesens. Eine Literaturzusammenstellung. Berlin, Amerika-Gedenkbibliothek, 1969.

134 p. 21 cm.

Vorstius, Joris, 1894–1964.
Die Erforschung des Buch- und Bibliothekswesens in Deutschland 1933–1945. Systematische Bibliographie der Bücher und Zeitschriftenaufsätze mit Erläuterungen. Aus dem Nachlass hrsg. von Siegfried Joost. Amsterdam, Verlag der Erasmus Buchhandlung, 1969.

xiv, 235 p. 27½ cm. (Safaho-Monographien, Bd. 6)

"Gedruckt in 400 Exemplaren."

CONSERVATION AND RESTORATION

Dragunova, Galina Nikolaevna.
(Sokhrannost' bibliotechnykh fondov)
Сохранность библиотечных фондов. Выборочный аннот. указ. отеч. и зарубеж. литератуы. Сост. Г. Н. Драгунова и Е. А. Азарова. Москва, 1972.

65 p. 20 cm.

At head of title: Всесоюзная государственная библиотека иностранной литературы. Отдел зарубежного библиотековедения.

Janda, Jozef.
Ochrana knižničného fondu. Sprac. Jozef Janda. Bratislava, Slov. techn. knižnica, rozmn., 1972.

116, [1] p. 20 cm. (Bratislava. Slovenská technická knižnica. Edícia: Metodické pomôcky SITK. Séria B: Bibliografie, č. 14)

Summary also in Russian, German, and English.

PRICES

Valuable books; a price guide for old and not so old books. Mesilla Park, N.M., Price Guide Pub. Co., 1973-

v.   22 cm.

CONTENTS: v. 1. Fiction.

PRIVATELY PRINTED

Dobell, Bertram, 1842-1914.
Catalogue of books printed for private circulation. Collected by Bertram Dobell and now described and annotated by him. London, Published by the author 1906. Detroit, Republished by Gale Research Co., 1966.

238 p. 24 cm.

Glasgow School of Art.
The page right printed; an exhibition of the work of the private presses from William Morris to the present day [held at] Glasgow School of Art, 1st-12th May 1973. [Glasgow] Glasgow School of Art, 1973.

42 p. illus., facsims. 26 cm.

Limited ed. of 400 copies of which the first 100 are numbered.

Martin, John, 1791-1855.
Bibliographical catalogue of privately printed books. 2d ed. New York, B. Franklin [1970]

xxv, 593 p. facsim. 23 cm. (Burt Franklin bibliography and reference series, 357)

Reprint of the 1854 ed.

Private press books. 1959-
North Harrow [Eng.] Private Libraries Association.

v. 22 cm.

Ridler, William.
British modern press books: a descriptive check list of unrecorded items. London, Covent Garden Press, 1971.

iii-xvi, 310 p. 25 cm.

BOOKS ISSUED IN SERIES see Bibliography - Books issued in series

BOOKS OF HOURS see Hours, Books of

BOOKSELLERS' CATALOGS see Catalogs, Booksellers'

BOOKSELLING see Publishing and bookselling

BOONE, DANIEL

Miner, William Harvey, 1877-1934.
Daniel Boone: contribution toward a bibliography of writings concerning Daniel Boone. New York, B. Franklin [1970]

ix, 32 p. 19 cm. (Burt Franklin bibliography & reference series, 853)

American classics in history & social sciences, 186.
On spine: Bibliography of Daniel Boone.
Reprint of the 1901 ed.

BOOTS AND SHOES

Gillespie, Karen R
Footwear, by Karen R. Gillespie. Revision. Washing-

ton, Small Business Administration, 1965 [i. e. 1966]

16 p. 26 cm. (Small business bibliography no. 63)

BORGEN, JOHAN

Deichmanske bibliotek, *Oslo.*
Johan Borgen: En litteraturliste. [Oslo] 1966.

7 p. 21 cm. (Publikum møter våre forfattere, nr. 1)

BORGOÑA, JUAN DE

Smith, Virginia Carlson.
Juan de Borgoña and his school: a bibliography, by Virginia Smith. Los Angeles, Hennessey & Ingalls, 1973.

vi, 41 p. port. 28 cm. (Art & architecture bibliographies, no. 2)

BORING

Aleksenko, N   I
[Burovzryvnye raboty na podzemnykh i otkrytykh gornykh rabotakh]
Буровзрывные работы на подземных и открытых горных работах. [Библиогр. указ. отеч. и зарубеж. книжной, журн. и пат. литературы за 1968–1971 гг. I кв. Сост. Алексенко Н. И., Швецова В. Г., Агладзе Ю. Е.] Москва, 1971.

278 p. 23 cm.

At head of title: Министерство цветной металлургии СССР. Центральный научно-исследовательский институт информации и технико-экономических исследований цветной металлургии.

Prague. Státní technická knihovna.
Vrtací a trhací technika v dolech a lomech; výběrová bibliografie knižní a časopisecké literatury. [Sest. Jan Picek. Redaktor: Naděžda Dobruská] Praha, 1964.

117 p. 21 cm. (*Its* Bibliografie, sv. 61)

BORLÄNGE, SWEDEN

Wingborg, Olle, 1928-
Litteratur om Borlänge och Stora Tuna; en bibliografi över ett kommunblock. [Falun, Dalarnas fornminnes- och hembygdsförbund, 1965]

166 p. 22 cm. (Dalarnas fornminnes- och hembygdsförbunds skrifter, 14)

BORNEO

Leigh, Michael B
Checklist of holdings on Borneo in the Cornell University Libraries, compiled by Michael B. Leigh with the assistance of John M. Echols. Ithaca, N. Y., Southeast Asia Program, Dept. of Asian Studies, Cornell University, 1966.

62 l. 27 cm. (Cornell University. Dept. of Asian Studies. Southeast Asia Program. Data paper no. 62)

BORNHOLM

Denmark. *Landsarkivet for Sjælland, Lolland, Falster og Bornholm.*
Bornholmske kirkebøger. København, 1968.

8, 57 p. 30 cm. (*Its* Foreløbige arkivregistraturer)

BORROW, GEORGE HENRY

Wise, Thomas James, 1859-1937.
A bibliography of the writings in prose and verse of

George Henry Borrow, by Thomas J. Wise. ₁1st ed. reprinted₁ London, Dawsons of Pall Mall, 1966.

xxii, 316 p. front., facsims. 22½ cm.

Facsimile reprint of 1st ed., London, Richard Clay, 1914.

BORSOD, HUNGARY

Bodgál, Ferenc.
Borsod megye néprajzi irodalma. Budapest, Múzeumok Központi Propaganda Irodája, 1958–70.

2 v. 21 cm. (A Miskolci Herman Ottó Múzeum néprajzi kiadványai, 1)

Vol. 2, published by Herman Ottó Múzeum, Miskolc, lacks series statement.

Kluger, Lászlóné.
Borsod megye fejlődése, 1945–1964, a megyei lapok tükrében; cikkbibliográfia. Miskolc, ₁II. Rákóczi Ferenc Könyvtár₁ 1966.

437 p. map. 25 cm. (Könyvtári füzetek, 2)

Summary in German and Russian.

BOSKOVICE, CZECHOSLOVAK REPUBLIC (CITY)

Skutil, Jan.
Archív města Boskovic. 1463–1945 (1953). Katalog. Inventář. ₁Autoři:₁ Jan Skutil—Lubomír Chalupa. Blansko, ONV, t. G 07, 1973.

59, ₁1₁ p. 30 cm.

At head of title: Okresní archív Blansko.

BOSMAN, HERMAN CHARLES

De Saxe, Shora Gertrude.
Herman Charles Bosman: a bibliography, compiled by Shora Gertrude De Saxe. Johannesburg, University of the Witwatersrand, Dept. of Bibliography, Librarianship and Typography, 1971.

v, 42 p. 30 cm.

Thesis (Diploma in Librarianship)—University of Witwatersrand.

BOSNIA AND HERZEGOVINA

Akademija nauka i umjetnosti Bosne i Hercegovine. *Biblioteka.*
Pregled izdanja bivšeg Naučnog društva i Akademije nauka i umjetnosti Bosne i Hercegovine, 1953–1968. Izrađeno u Biblioteci Akademije nauka i umjetnosti Bosne i Hercegovine. Urednik Ethem Čamo. Sarajevo, Akademija nauka i umjetnosti Bosne i Hercegovine, 1968.

39 p. 24 cm. (Akademija nauka i umjetnosti Bosne i Hercegovine. Posebna izdanja, knj. 10)

Added t. p. in French.

Hadžiosmanović, Lamija.
Bibliografija Prve muslimanske nakladne knjižare i štamparije (Muhameda Bekira Kalajdžića). Sarajevo, Udruženje Ilmije u SR BiH, 1967.

45, ₁1₁ p. 24 cm.

BŌSŌ PENINSULA

Shinra, Aiko.
(Bōsō kenkyū bunken sōran)

新羅　愛子

房総研究文献総覧

千葉　京葉企画社　昭和44(1969)

129p　25cm

付　房総研究略史

BOSSUET, JACQUES BÉNIGNE

Bourseaud, H   M   1856–
Histoire et description des manuscrits et des éditions originales des ouvrages de Bossuet, avec l'indication des traductions qui en ont été faites et des écrits auxquels ils ont donné lieu à l'époque de leur publication. Nouv. éd. rev. et augm. Genève, Slatkine Reprints, 1971.

xxxvii, 232 p. 22 cm.

"Réimpression de l'édition de Saintes, 1898."

BOSWELL, JAMES

Kerslake, John F
Mr. Boswell. London, National Portrait Gallery, 1967.

1 v. (unpaged) 22 cm.

Label on t. p.: supplied by Worldwide Books, Inc., New York, N. Y.

BOTANICAL GARDENS

MacPhail, Ian, 1923–
Hortus botanicus; the botanic garden & the book: fifty books from the Sterling Morton Library exhibited at the Newberry Library for the fiftieth anniversary of the Morton Arboretum. Compiled by Ian MacPhail. Introductory essay by Joseph Ewan. ₁Meriden, Conn., Printing: Meriden Gravure Co.₁ 1972.

119 p. illus. 21 cm.

Catalog of the exhibition held April 11–May 31, 1972.

BOTANY
see also   Plants

Current advances in plant science. v. 1–
July 1972–
Oxford, Eng., Sciences, Engineering, Medical, & Business Data, ltd.

v. 23 cm. monthly.

"A subject categorised listing of titles in plant science compiled from the current literature."

Horticultural Society of New York. (*Founded 1900*)
Printed books, 1481–1900, in the Horticultural Society of New York. A listing by Elizabeth Cornelia Hall. New York, 1970.

xiii, 279 p. 24 cm.

Inter-documentation Company, *Zug.*
Botany. Zug, Switzerland, 1966.

47 p. 21 cm. (Basic collections in micro edition)

Jackson, Benjamin Daydon, 1846–1927.
Guide to the literature of botany; being a classified selection of botanical works, including nearly 6000 titles not given in Pritzel's "Thesaurus." New York, Hafner Pub. Co., 1964.

xl, 626 p. 24 cm.

"Originally published in 1881 ... Reprinted under license from the Linnean Society of London."

Küchler, August Wilhelm, 1907–
International bibliography of vegetation maps. Edited by A. W. Küchler. ₁Lawrence, University of Kansas Libraries, 1965–70₁

4 v. 26 cm. (University of Kansas publications. Library series, no. 21, 26, 29, 36)

CONTENTS: v. 1. North America.—v. 2. Europe.—v. 3. U. S. S. R., Asia, & Australia.—v. 4. Africa, South America, and the world (general).

Linné, Carl von, 1707–1778, praeses.
Auctores botanici. Botanic authors. In dissertatione propositi, quam sub praesidio Caroli Linnaei ad publicum examen defert Augustinus Loo. Stockholm, Rediviva; ₁Nordiska bokhandeln (distr.)₁ 1970.

₍5₎, 20 p. 20 cm. (Suecica rediviva, 13)

Facsim. of 1759 ed.
Diss.—Uppsala (A. Loo, respondent)

Linné, Carl von, 1707–1778, praeses.
Botaniska författare. (Auctores botanici.) Akademisk avhandling under Linnés presidium. Uppsala, 1759. Övers. från latinet av Telemak Fredbärj och Albert Boerman. Uppsala, Almqvist & Wiksell, 1973.

17 p. 23 cm. (His Valda avhandlingar, nr. 63)

Diss.—Uppsala (A. Loo, respondent)

Linné, Carl von, 1707–1778.
Caroli Linnæi Bibliotheca botanica recensens libros plus mille de plantis huc usque editos, secundum Systema auctorum naturale in classes, ordines, genera et species dispositos, additis editionis loco, tempore, forma, lingua etc. cum explicatione Fundamentorum botanicorum pars prima. München, W. Fritsch; ₁New York, Stechert-Hafner Service Agency₁ 1968.
₁165₁, 35 p. 17 cm. (Historiae scientiarum elementa, fasc. 4)

Facsimile reprint of Amsterdam ed., 1736.

Moscow. Glavnyĭ botanicheskiĭ sad. *Nauchnaia biblioteka.*
Фотопериодизм растений; библиографический указатель литературы 1910–1963 г.г. Составители: Т. Н. Соколова, Т. В. Сакова. Под ред. Н. Н. Константинова. Москва, Наука, 1965.

364 p. 23 cm.

At head of title: Академия наук СССР. Сектор сети специальных библиотек. Главный ботанический сад. Научная библиотека.

Nissen, Claus, 1901–
Die botanische Buchillustration. Ihre Geschichte und Bibliographie. 2. Aufl. Durchgesehener und verb. Abdruck der zweibändigen Erstaufl., ergänzt durch ein Supplement. Stuttgart, Hiersemann, 1966.

3 v. in 1. 31 cm.

Nissen, Claus, 1901–
Die botanische Buchillustration; ihre Geschichte und Bibliographie. Supplement. Stuttgart, A. Hiersemann, 1966.

vii, 97 p. 31 cm.

"Sonderdruck von Band III des Werkes 'Die botanische Buchillustration,' 2. Auflage (durchgesehener und verbesserter Abdruck der zweibändigen Erstauflage von 1951, ergänzt durch ein Supplement)."

Sherff, Earl Edward, 1886–
An annotated list of my botanical writings; a bibliographic list, with notations of observed errata, needed emendations, and additions of taxa described by the author too late for inclusion in the original publications. Bloomington, Ill., Published by the author for the Earl Edward Sherff Botanical Library, Illinois Wesleyan University, 1964.

48 p. 26 cm.

Skytte-Christiansen, M
Bibliografiske hjælpemidler til det botaniske studium. Ved M. Skytte Christiansen. 2. udg. København, Botanisk Centralbibliotek, Gothersgade 130, 1971.

169 l. 30 cm.

BIBLIOGRAPHIES

Swift, Lloyd H 1920–
Botanical bibliographies; a guide to bibliographic materials applicable to botany, by Lloyd H. Swift. Minneapolis, Burgess Pub. Co. ₁1970₁

xxxvii, 804 p. 23 cm.

ECOLOGY

Bibliografia litosocjologiczna Polski, 1964–1966. Warszawa ₁Zakład Fitosocjologii Stosowanej Uniwersytetu Warszawskiego₁ 19

v. 29 cm. (Materiały Zakładu Fitosocjologii Stosowanej U. W. nr. 19)

At head of title, v. : Aniela Matuszkiewicz.

CONTENTS.—
cz. 3. 1964–1966.

Tüxen, Reinhold, 1899–
Bibliographia phytosociologica syntaxonomica. Hrsg. v. Reinhold Tüxen. Lehre, Cramer, 1971–

pt. 24 cm.

CONTENTS: Lfg. 1. Bolboschoenetea maritimi. Lfg. 2. Lemnetea. Lfg. 3. Spartinetea. Lfg. 4. Violetea calaminariae. Lfg. 5. Zosteretea marinae. Lfg. 6. Ammophiletea. Lfg. 7. Salicetea herbaceae. Lfg. 8. Epilobietea angustifolii.

PERIODICALS
Hunt Botanical Library.
B–P–H; Botanico-Periodicum-Huntianum. Editors: George H. M. Lawrence ₁and others₁ Pittsburgh, 1968.

1063 p. 29 cm.

PRE-LINNEAN WORKS

Arber, Agnes (Robertson) 1879–1960.
Herbals, their origin and evolution; a chapter in the history of botany, 1470–1670. 2d ed. rewritten and enl. Darien, Hafner, 1970.

xxiv, 325 p. 157 illus., facsims., ports. 22 cm.

Facsimile of the 1938 ed.

Early botanical books; an exhibit celebrating the centennial of the Arnold Arboretum, 1872–1972 ₁held₁ May 21, 1972–June 9, 1972 ₁at₁ the Houghton Library, Harvard University. ₁Catalogue prepared by Pamela Bruns and others₁ Cambridge, Mass. ₁Houghton Library, Harvard University. 1972₁
52 p. illus. 24 cm.
In cooperation with the Arnold Arboretum Library.

AFRICA

Association pour l'étude taxonomique de la flore d'Afrique tropicale.
Relevé des travaux de phanérogamie systématique et des

taxons nouveaux concernant l'Afrique au sud du Sahara et Madagascar. Index of the papers on systematic phanerogamy and of the new taxa concerning Africa south of the Sahara and Madagascar. Bruxelles, 1971.

68 p. 22 cm. (A. E. T. F. A. T. index, 1970)

De Wet, Madeleine.
A bibliography of South African *Stapelieae*. ₍Cape Town₎ University of Cape Town, School of Librarianship, 1964.

vi, 97 p. 23 cm. (University of Cape Town. School of Librarianship. Bibliographical series)

"Presented in partial fulfilment of the requirements for the higher certificate in librarianship, January 1963."

AMERICA

Küchler, August Wilhelm, 1907–
Vegetation maps of North America. Compiled by A. W. Küchler and Jack McCormick. Naarden ₍Ruysdaelplein 35,₎ Van Bekhoven, 1971.

467 p. 25 cm. (His International bibliography of vegetation maps, v. 1)

Reprint of the 1965 ed., published by University of Kansas as no. 21 of their Library series under title: International bibliography of vegetation maps.

Schuster, Joseph L   1932–
Literature on the mesquite (*Prosopis* L.) of North America; an annotated bibliography, edited by Joseph L. Schuster. ₍Lubbock, Texas Tech University₎ 1969.

84 p. 23 cm. (International Center for Arid and Semi-arid Land Studies. Special report no. 26)

Torrey Botanical Club.
Index to American botanical literature, 1886–1966. Boston, G. K. Hall, 1969.

4 v. 37 cm.

A reproduction of an index published serially since 1886 in the Bulletin of the Torrey Botanical Club.

ASIA, SOUTHEAST

A Bibliography of the botany of Southeast Asia. Washington, 1969.

1 v. (unpaged) 28 cm.

Reed, Clyde Franklin, 1918–
Bibliography to floras of Southeast Asia; Burma, Laos, Thailand (Siam), Cambodia, Viet Nam (Tonkin, Annam, Cochinchina), Malay Peninsula, and Singapore, by Clyde F. Reed. Baltimore, 1969.

191 p. map. 23 cm.

AUSTRALIA

Lovett, B   H
The geographical distribution of native plants in South Australia and the Northern Territory: an index to articles in selected South Australian periodicals, compiled by B. H. Lovett. Adelaide, State Library of South Australia, 1970–

v. 27 cm. (Research Service bibliographies, series 4, no. 136)

BRAZIL

Alemão, Francisco Freire, 1797–1874.
Os manuscritos do botânico Freire Alemão; catálogo e transcrição, por Darcy Damasceno e Waldir da Cunha. ₍Rio de Janeiro, Biblioteca Nacional₎ Divisão de Publicações e Divulgação, 1964.

372 p. illus. 27 cm. (Anais da Biblioteca Nacional, v. 81)

Angely, João, 1917–
Bibliografia vegetal do Paraná; bibliografia botânica do Paraná. Bibliografia dos typos da flora do Paraná 5.174 spp., comentada. Curitiba ₍Edições Phyton₎ 1964.

304 p. 32 cm. (Coleção Saint-Hilaire, v. 6)

CUBA

Samkova, Hana.
Bibliografía botánica cubana (teórica y aplicada) con énfasis en la silvicultura, por Hana Samkova y Věroslav Samek. La Habana, Academia de Ciencias de Cuba, Instituto de Biología, 1967.

36 p. 27 cm. (Serie biológica no. 1)

EUROPE

Hamann, Ulrich, 1931–
Bibliographie zur Flora von Mitteleuropa; eine Auswahl der neueren floristischen und vegetationskundlichen Literatur sowie allgemeiner Arbeiten über Geobotanik, Systematik, Morphologie, Anatomie, Cytologie ... zusammengestellt von Ulrich Hamann und Gerhard Wagenitz. München, C. Hanser, 1970.

328 p. 24 cm.

GERMANY

Gottwald, Norbert.
Register der Hessischen Floristischen Briefe 1952–1968. Darmstadt, Institut für Naturschutz, 1971.

180 l. 30 cm. (Institut für Naturschutz Darmstadt. Schriftenreihe. Beiheft 22)

GREAT BRITAIN

Kent, Douglas H   comp.
Index to botanical monographs: a guide to monographs and taxonomic papers relating to phanerogams and vascular cryptogams found growing wild in the British Isles. Compiled by Douglas H. Kent. London, published for the Botanical Society of the British Isles by Academic P, 1967.

xi, 163 p. 24 cm.

Systematics Association.
Bibliography of key works for the identification of the British fauna and flora; edited for the association by G. J. Kerrich, R. D. Meikle and Norman Tebble. 3rd ed. London, Systematics Association, 1967.

vii, 186 p. 21½ cm. (*Its* Publication no. 1)

Previous editions edited by J. Smart.

LITHUANIA

Šapiraitė, Sara, 1905–
Lietuvos botanikos bibliografija. 1800–1965. Mokslinis red. K. Brundza. Vilnius, 1971.

528 p. 22 cm.

At head of title: Lietuvos TSR Mokslų Akademijos Centrinė biblioteka. S. Šapiraitė.
Added t. p.: Библиография ботаники Литвы.
Prefatory matter and table of contents also in Russian.

MORAVIA

Řídká, Bohuslava.
Květena jižní Moravy. Sest. Bohuslava Řídká. Brno, Univ. knihovna, rozmn., 1969.

18, [1] p. 21 cm. (Brünn. Universita. Knihovna. Výběrový seznam, čis. 149)

NEVADA

Tueller, Paul T 1934–

The vegetation of Nevada; a bibliography [by] Paul T. Tueller, Joseph H. Robertson [and] Ben Zamora. Reno, Agricultural Experiment Station, Max C. Fleischmann College of Agriculture, University of Nevada, 1971.

iii, 29 p. 28 cm.

NORWAY

Kleppa, Peter, 1903–

Norsk botanisk bibliografi 1814–1964. Utg. av Norsk botanisk forening og Universitetsbiblioteket i Oslo. Oslo, Universitetsforl., 1973.

334 p., 6 l. 25 cm. (Universitetsbiblioteket i Oslo. Skrifter, 2)

OCEANIA

Ferguson, Ian Keith, 1938–

Index to Australasian taxonomic literature for 1968, compiled by I. K. Ferguson. Utrecht, Netherlands, International Bureau for Plant Taxonomy and Nomenclature, 1970.

62 p. 24 cm. (Regnum vegetabile, v. 66)

Sachet, Marie Hélène.

Island bibliographies: Micronesian botany, Land environment and ecology of coral atolls, Vegetation of tropical Pacific islands, by Marie-Hélène Sachet and F. Raymond Fosberg. Compiled under the auspices of the Pacific Science Board. [Washington] National Academy of Sciences, National Research Council, 1955.

v, 577 p. 23 cm. (National Research Council. Publication 335)

———— Supplement. Washington, National Academy of Sciences, 1971.

ix, 427 p. 28 cm.

PAKISTAN and KASHMIR

Kazmi, S M A

Bibliography on the botany of West Pakistan and Kashmir and adjacent regions, by S. M. A. Kazmi. Edited by Henry Field and Edith M. Laird. Miami, Fla., Field Research Projects, 1970–

v. 28 cm.

CONTENTS.—1. Taxonomy.

RUSSIA

Demesheva, G A

(Botanicheskaía literatura Kazakhstana)

Ботаническая литература Казахстана. 1937–1965 гг. Алма-Ата, 1971.

425 p. 21 cm.

Levina, Fanni Íakovlevna.

Геоботаника в ботаническом институте им. В. Л. Комарова АН СССР. 1922–1964. Ленинград, "Наука," Ленингр. отд-ние, 1971.

319 p. with illus., 6 l. of ports. 22 cm.

Osipchik, L A

Советская литература по флоре и растительности Белоруссии. Библиография. 1919–1968 гг. Минск, 1970.

433 p. 21 cm.

At head of title: Академия наук Белорусской ССР. Фундаментальная библиотека им. Я. Коласа. Всесоюзное ботаническое общество. Белорусское отделение. "Составители: Л. А. Осипчик и В. С. Гельтман."

Skal'naía, G D

[Rastitel'nyĭ mir Kirovskoĭ oblasti]

Растительный мир Кировской области. Указ. литературы. Киров, 1971.

76 p. 20 cm.

At head of title: Кировская областная библиотека имени А. И. Герцена. Библиографический отдел. Г. Д. Скальная.

Vorob'eva, T A

Растительность и растительные ресурсы Западной Сибири; библиография 1909–1962 гг. Составила Т. А. Воробьева при участии В. П. Соколовой и А. А. Конограй. Москва, Наука, 1964.

151 p. 27 cm.

At head of title: Академия наук СССР. Сибирское отделение. Государственная публичная научно-техническая библиотека. Библиографический отдел.

BOTANY, MEDICAL

Bibliotheca Bogoriensis.

Bibliografi mengenai tanaman obat'an di Indonesia. (Bibliography on medicinal plants in Indonesia). Bogor [1969]

46 p. 33 cm. (Seri bibliografi, no. 14)

BOTSWANA

Balima, Mildred Grimes.

Botswana, Lesotho, and Swaziland; a guide to official publications, 1868–1968, compiled by Mildred Grimes Balima, African Section. Washington, General Reference and Bibliography Division, Library of Congress; [for sale by the Supt. of Docs., U. S. Govt. Print. Off.] 1971.

xvi, 84 p. 27 cm.

Middleton, Coral.

Bechuanaland, a bibliography. [Cape Town] University of Cape Town, School of Librarianship, 1965.

iv, 37 p. 23 cm. ([Cape Town] University of Cape Town. School of Librarianship. Bibliographical series)

"Presented in partial fulfilment of the requirements for the higher certificate in librarianship, University of Cape Town."

Mohome, Paulus.

A bibliography on Bechuanaland, compiled by Paulus Mohome [and] John B. Webster. Syracuse, N. Y., Bibliographic Section, Program of Eastern African Studies, Syracuse University, 1966.

58 p. 28 cm. (Program of Eastern African Studies. Occasional bibliography, no. 5)

———— Supplement, compiled by John B. Webster, Paulus Mohome [and] M. Catherine Todd. Syracuse, N. Y.,

Bibliographic Section, Program of Eastern African Studies, Syracuse University, 1968.

x, 38 p. 28 cm. (Program of Eastern African Studies. Occasional bibliography, no. 12)

Preface in English and French.

The National bibliography of Botswana. v. 1– 1969–

[Gaberones] Botswana National Library Service.

v. 33 cm. semiannual.

Stevens, Pamela.
Bechuanaland: bibliography. ₍Cape Town₎ University of Cape Town, School of Librarianship, 1947 ₍i. e. 1964₎

iv, 27 p. 23 cm. (₍Cape Town₎ University of Cape Town. School of Librarianship. Bibliographical series)

First published in 1947 under title: Bibliography of Bechuanaland. "Presented in partial fulfilment of the requirements for the higher certificate in librarianship."

Willet, Shelagh M
A checklist of recent reference books on Lesotho, Botswana, and Swaziland. Compiled by Shelagh M. Willet. ₍Grahamstown, Dept. of Librarianship, Rhodes University₎ 1971.

6 l. 26 cm. (₍Rhodes University, Grahamstown, South Africa. Dept. of Librarianship₎ Bibliographical series, no. 1)

BOUILLON FAMILY   see under   Rohan family

BOURINOT, ARTHUR STANLEY

Ottawa. National Library.
Arthur S. Bourinot. ₍Catalogue prepared by Joyce Banks₎ Ottawa, 1971.

30, 30 p. ports. 23 cm.

English and French.

BOWLES, PAUL

McLeod, Cecil R
Paul Bowles: a checklist, 1929–1969 ₍by₎ Cecil R. McLeod. ₍Flint, Mich.₎ Apple Tree Press ₍°1970₎

vii, 24 p. port. 23 cm.

BOY SCOUTS

Monté, Luis.
Bibliografía scout (180 obras comentadas). Madrid, S. I. P. E.; distribuye: Expo. Scout, Salamanca ₍1967₎

55 p. 22 cm.

BRABANT (PROVINCE)

Belgium. Archives générales du Royaume.
Inventaire des archives du cadastre du Brabant avant 1865, par Armand Grunzweig ₍et₎ Alexandre Notebaert. Bruxelles, Archives générales du Royaume, rue de Ruysbroeck, 2–6, 1971.

vii, 134 p. 30 cm.

BRACKENRIDGE, HUGH HENRY

Heartman, Charles Frederick, 1883–
A bibliography of the writings of Hugh Henry Brackenridge prior to 1825. Compiled by Charles F. Heartman. New York, B. Franklin ₍1968₎

37 p. illus., facsims., port. 23 cm. (Burt Franklin bibliography & reference series, 231)

Reprint of the 1917 ed.

BRAGINSKIĬ, IOSIF SAMUILOVICH

Komissarov, D   S
Иосиф Самуилович Брагинский. Вступ. статья Д. С. Комиссарова. Библиография составлена С. Л. Милибанд и Л. В. Турсуновой. Душанбе, 1966.

92 p. port. 17 cm. (Академия наук Таджикской ССР. Центральная научная библиотека. Материалы к биобиблиографии ученых Таджикистана, вып. 8)

BRAHMS, JOHANNES

Simrock, N., firm, Berlin.
The N. Simrock Thematic catalog of the works of Johannes Brahms. Thematisches Verzeichniss sämmtlicher im Druck erschienenen Werke von Johannes Brahms. New introd., including addenda and corrigenda by Donald M. McCorkle. New York, Da Capo Press, 1973.

L, 175 p. music. 26 cm. (Da Capo Press music reprint series)

Reprint of the 1897 ed., in German.

BRAILLE   see   Blind, Books for the; Blind, Periodicals for the

BRAIN - DIEASES   see Neurology

BRAIN DRAIN

Argentine Republic. Congreso. Biblioteca.
Emigración de profesionales. técnicos y científicos argentinos; bibliografía. ₍Buenos Aires₎ 1966.

13 p. 28 cm. (Serie Asuntos varios, no. 6)

Beijer, G
Brain drain. Auszug des Geistes. Exode des cerveaux. A selected bibliography on temporary and permanent migration of skilled workers and high-level manpower, 1967–1972. G. Beyer. The Hague, Nijhoff, 1972.

84 p. 24 cm. (European demographic monographs, 3)

English, French, or German.

Boschi, Renato Raul.
Bibliografia internacional comentada sôbre imigração e retôrno de pessoal qualificado. Rio de Janeiro ₍Instituto Brasileiro de Relações Internacionais₎ 1971.

45 l. 28 cm. (Projeto Retôrno. Doc₍umento₎ no. 1)

Research Policy Program.
Brain drain and brain gain. A bibliography on migration of scientists, engineers, doctors and students. Lund, 1967.

48 p. 23 cm.

Scobie, Marrigje.
Migration and return of highly qualified manpower: a bibliography of recent publications 1965–1971 ₍by₎ Marrigje J. A. Scobie. Oslo ₍Norwegian Research Council for Science and the Humanities₎ 1971.

13 l. 30 cm. (Norwegian Research Council for Science and the Humanities. Institute for Studies in Research and Higher Education. Notat 8)

Mimeographed.

BRAITHWAITE, WILLIAM STANLEY

Syracuse University. Library. Manuscript Collections.
William Stanley Braithwaite; a register of his papers in the Syracuse University Library. Prepared by John S. Patterson. ₍Syracuse, N. Y.₎ 1964.

18 l. port. 28 cm. (Its Manuscript register series, register no. 7)

BRANDED MERCHANDISE

Uhr, Ernest B
Brands: a selected and annotated bibliography ₍by₎ Ernest B. Uhr and William A. Wallace. ₍Chicago, American Marketing Association, 1971, c1972₎

v, 56 p. 23 cm. (AMA bibliography series, no. 18)

BRANDENBURG

Schreckenbach, Hans Joachim.
Bibliographie zur Geschichte der Mark Brandenburg. Weimar, Böhlau, 1970–

v. 25 cm. (Veröffentlichungen des Staatsarchivs Potsdam, Bd. 8–

BRĂTESCU-VOINEŞTI, IOAN ALEXANDRU

Trandafir, Rachila.
Ioan Alexandru Brătescu-Voineşti. (1868–1946). Bibliografie selectivă. ₍Coordonator: Victor Petrescu. Coperta colecţiei: Emil Florin Grama₎. Tîrgovişte, 1973.

96 p. 21 cm. (Personalităţi ale culturii dîmboviţene)

At head of title: Comitetul de Cultură şi Educaţie Socialistă Dimboviţa. Biblioteca Municipală Tîrgovişte.
"Întocmirea bibliografiei: Rachila Trandafir, Stela Marin."

BRAZIL

see also under Portugal

Brazil. *Ministério do Planejamento e Coordenação Geral.*
Catálogo das publicações do MINIPLAN. Rio de Janeiro, 1968–

v. 30 cm.

Canstatt, Oskar, 1842–1912.
Repertório crítico da literatura teuto-brasileira. Tradução de Eduardo de Lima Castro. Revisão e notas de Hans Jürgen W. Horch. Rio de Janeiro, Editôra Presença, 1967.

294 p. 21 cm. (Coleção germânica, 3)

Translation of: Kritisches Repertorium der deutsch-brasilianischen Literatur (Berlin, 1902). Nachtrag zum kritischen Repertorium der deutschbrasilianischen Literatur (Berlin, 1906).
"Suplemento ao repertório crítico da bibliografia alemã-brasileira," por Oscar Canstatt: p. ₍163₎–220.

Ferreira, Carmosina N
Bibliografia seletiva sobre desenvolvimento econômico no Brasil ₍por₎ Carmosina N. Ferreira, Lieny do Amaral Ferreira ₍e₎ Elizabeth Tolomei Moletta. Rio de Janeiro, IPEA/Doc., 1972.

96 p. 29 cm. (Instituto de Planejamento Econômico e Social. Setor de Documentação. Série bibliográfica, no. 1)

Garraux, Anatole Louis, 1833–1904.
Bibliographie Brésilienne. Catalogue des ouvrages français et latins. Relatifs au Brésil (1500–1898). ₍Réimpression de l'éd. Paris, 1898₎. Amsterdam, Grüner, 1971.

400 p. 23 cm.

Gillett, Theresa.
Catalog of Luso-Brazilian material in the University of New Mexico libraries. Compiled by Theresa Gillett and Helen McIntyre. Metuchen, N. J., Scarecrow Press, 1970.

xiv, 961 p. 22 cm.

Heimer, Franz-Wilhelm.
Neuere Studien zur Politik Brasiliens, 1960–1967 ₍i. e. neunzehnhundertsechzig–neunzehnhundertsiebenundsechzig₎ In Zusammenarbeit mit Maria de Lourdes Heimer und Mara Jorge Ramos. ₍Freiburg i. Br., Arnold-Bergstraesser-Institut für Kulturwissenschaftliche Forschung, 1968₎

ix, 91 p. 24 cm. (Bibliographien zur Politik und Gesellschaft lateinamerikanischer Länder, Bd. 1)
Introduction in German and Spanish.

Knopp, Anthony.
Brazil books; a guide to contemporary works. ₍New York₎ Center for Inter-American Relations ₍1970?₎

20 p. 22 cm.

Levine, Robert M *ed.*
Brazil: field research guide in the social sciences. Robert M. Levine, editor. ₍New York₎ Institute of Latin American Studies, Columbia University, 1966.

vi, 298 p. 23 cm.

Moraes, Rubens Borba de, 1899–
Bibliografia brasileira do período colonial; catálogo comentado da obras dos autores nascidos no Brasil e publicadas antes de 1808. São Paulo, 1969.

xxii, 437 p. facsims. 24 cm. (Publicação do Instituto de Estudos Brasileiros, 9)

Musso Ambrosi, Luis Alberto.
Bibliografía uruguaya sobre Brasil; libros y folletos referentes al Brasil o de autores brasileños, impressos en el Uruguay, por Luis Alberto Musso. Nota preliminar del Dr. Albino J. Peixoto, Jr. Montevideo, 1967.

99 p. 24 cm. (Publicaciones del Instituto de Cultura Uruguayo-Brasileño, 17)

Richardson, Ivan L
Bibliografia brasileira de administração pública e assuntos correlatos ₍por₎ Ivan L. Richardson. Rio de Janeiro, Fundação Getúlio Vargas, Serviço de Publicações, 1964.

xxii, 840 p. 24 cm.
Portuguese or English.

BIO-BIBLIOGRAPHY

Reis, Antônio Simões dos, 1899–
Bibliografia brasileira. Rio, Organização Simões, 1966–

v. 18 cm.

GOVERNMENT PUBLICATIONS

Brazil. *Ministério da Educação e Cultura. Serviço de Documentação.*
Catálogo das publicações do Serviço de Documentação, 1947–1965. Organizado pelos bibliotecários Xavier Placer, Edson Nery da Fonseca e José Alcides Pinto. ₍Rio de Janeiro₎ 1965.

156 p. 22 cm.

Mesa, Rosa Quintero.
Brazil, compiled by Rosa Quintero Mesa. Ann Arbor, Mich., University Microfilms, 1968.

viii, 2, 343, 12 p. 29 cm. (Latin American serial documents, v. 2)
Prepared under a grant from the Ford Foundation to the University of Florida Libraries.

HISTORY

Boxer, Charles Ralph, 1904–
Some literary sources for the history of Brazil in the eighteenth century, by C. R. Boxer. Oxford, Clarendon P., 1967.

36 p. 22 cm. (The Taylorian lecture, 1967)

Graham, Richard, 1934–
Brazil in the London Times, 1850–1905; a guide ₁by₁ Richard Graham ₁and₁ Virginia Valiela. ₁Carbondale? Ill., Seminar on the Acquisition of Latin American Library Materials, 1969₁

vii, 101 p. 28 cm. (Seminar on the Acquisition of Latin American Library Materials. SALALM bibliography, 1)

Martínez Ortiz, José.
Documentos manuscritos y obras varias impresas referentes a la historia del Brasil, existentes en Valencia (España). ₁Valencia₁ Instituto de Estudios Americanistas, Institución Alfonso el Magnánimo, 1969.

65 p. 18 cm.

The documents and books listed are preserved in the Biblioteca Universitaria de Valencia and the Biblioteca Municipal de Valencia.

Sodré, Nelson Werneck, 1911–
O que se deve ler para conhecer o Brasil. 3. ed. ₁Rio de Janeiro₁ Civilização Brasileira ₁1967₁

394 p. 21 cm. (Retratos do Brasil, v. 34)

Souza, Antonio de.
Manuscritos do Brasil nos arquivos de Portugal e da Espanha ₁por₁ Antônio de Souza Júnior. Rio de Janeiro, Imprensa do Exército, 1969.

67 p. 23 cm.

IMPRINTS

Bibliografia brasileira mensal.

₁Rio de Janeiro₁ Instituto Nacional do Livro.

v. 27 cm.

Began with Nov. 1967 issue.

Rio de Janeiro. Instituto Nacional do Livro.
Exposição do livro brasileiro contemporâneo, organizada pelo Instituto Nacional do Livro e pela Biblioteca Central da Universidade de Essex. U. K. Brazilian book exhibition, arranged by the National Book Institute of Brazil and Essex University Library. Colchester (Essex), University of Essex, 1969.

ix, 217 p. 21 x 33 cm.

Sindicato Nacional dos Editôres de Livros.
Edições brasileiras: Frankfurt Book Fair. Rio de Janeiro, 1970.

101 p. 22 cm.

BRAZIL, NORTHEAST

Banco do Nordeste do Brasil, Fortaleza. Departamento de Estudos Econômicos do Nordeste.
Sumário dos trabalhos publicados pelo BNB. ₁2. ed.₁ Fortaleza, 1966.

41 l. 28 cm.

Banco do Nordeste do Brasil, Fortaleza. Departamento de Estudos Económicos do Nordeste.
Sumários dos trabalhos publicados pelo BNB. ₁Preparado por Juracy Portela Pimentel. 3 ed., rev. e ampliada₁ Fortaleza, 1969.

88 l. 28 cm.

Brazil. Superintendência do Desenvolvimento do Nordeste. Departamento de Administração Geral. Biblioteca.
Bibliografia sôbre a SUDENE e o Nordeste. Recife, 1969.

385 p. 23 cm.

Brazil. *Superintendência do Desenvolvimento do Nordeste. Departamento de Administração Geral. Biblioteca.*
Catálogo das publicações editadas pela SUDENE ₁1959–1969₁ Recife, 1969.

133 p. illus. 23 cm.

Brazil. Superintendência do Desenvolvimento do Nordeste. Divisão de Cartografia.
Bibliografia cartográfica do Nordeste. Recife, Divisão de Documentação, 1965.

209 p. 23 cm.

Rio de Janeiro. Biblioteca Nacional.
Nordeste brasileiro; catálogo da exposição. Rio de Janeiro, Divisão de Publicações e Divulgação, 1970.

86 p. illus. 23 cm.

"Exposição organizada pela Seção de Exposições e inaugurada em 24 de novembro de 1970."

BRAZILIAN LITERATURE

Carpeaux, Otto Maria, 1900–
Pequena bibliografia crítica da literatura brasileira. 3. ed. revista e aumentada. ₁Rio de Janeiro₁ Editôra Letras e Artes, 1964.

335 p. 21 cm.

Carpeaux, Otto Maria, 1900–
Pequena bibliografia crítica da literatura brasileira. Rio de Janeiro, Ed. de Ouro, 1968.

335 p. port. 16 cm. (Biblioteca mentor cultural)

Moraes, Jomar.
Bibliografia crítica da literatura maranhense. São Luís, ₁Departamento de Cultura do Maranhão₁ 1972.

xix, 122 p. 23 cm.

Rio de Janeiro. Biblioteca Nacional.
Modernismo brasileiro: bibliografia, 1918–1971. Organizada por Xavier Placer. Rio de Janeiro, Divisão de Publicações e Divulgação, 1972.

401 p. 21 cm. (Coleção Rodolfo Garcia. Série B—Catálogos e bibliografias)

BRAZING

Wayne State University, *Detroit. Center for Application of Science and Technology.*
Brazing and brazing alloys; a bibliography. Washington, Technology Utilization Division, Office of Technology Utilization, National Aeronautics and Space Administration; ₁for sale by the Clearinghouse for Federal Scientific and Technical Information, Springfield, Va.₁ 1967.

v, 52 p. 23 cm. (NASA SP-5026)

BRECHT, BELGIUM

Beterams, Frans Gaston Coleta, 1913–
Inventaris van de gemeentearchieven van Brecht. Door G. Beterams. Brussel, Algemeen Rijksarchief, Ravenstein-galerij 78, 1968.

298 p. maps, tables. 25 cm.

At head of title: Ministerie van Nationale Opvoeding en Cultuur. Algemeen Rijksarchief (en) Rijksarchief te Antwerpen.

BRECHT, BERTOLT

Bertolt-Brecht-Archiv.
Bestandsverzeichnis des literarischen Nachlasses. (1. Aufl.) Berlin, Aufbau-Verlag, 1969–

v. 22 cm.

CONTENTS.—Bd. 1. Stücke, bearb. von H. Ramthun.

Bielefeld. Stadtbücherei.
Bertolt Brecht. Werke und Sekundärliteratur aus den Beständen der Stadtbücherei Bielefeld. Zusammengestellt anlässlich der Aufführung von "Der aufhaltsame Aufstieg des Arturo Ui" an den Städtischen Bühnen Bielefeld. Bielefeld, 1967.

27 p. 21 cm.

Otto, Werner, 1922–
Versuch einer Aufstellung von Vertonungen zu Brecht-Stücken. Berlin, Deutsche Staatsoper, Dramaturgie, 1966.

13 l. 30 cm.

Petersen, Klaus-Dietrich.
Bertolt Brecht. Leben und Werk. Ein Bücherverzeichnis. Einführung, Zeittafel und Bibliographie ⟨1957–1964⟩ von Klaus-Dietrich Petersen. Mit einem Beitrag von Johannes Klein. Dortmund, Stadtbücherei, 1966.

142 p., 2 fronts. 21 cm. (Dichter und Denker unserer Zeit, Folge 35)

Petersen, Klaus-Dietrich.
Bertolt-Brecht-Bibliographie. Mit einem Geleitwort von Johannes Hansel. Bad Homburg v. d. H., Berlin, Zürich, Gehlen (1968).

87 p. 19 cm. (Bibliographien zum Studium der deutschen Sprache und Literatur, Bd. 2)

Volgina, A   A
Бертольт Брехт. Биобиблиогр. указатель. Москва, "Книга," 1969.

168 p. 24 cm. (Писатели зарубежных стран)

At head of title: Всесоюзная государственная библиотека иностранной литературы.

BREMEN

Bremen. Volksbüchereien.
Bremen im Buch. Ein Literaturverzeichnis zum Jubiläumsjahr 1965, der 1000-jährigen Wiederkehr des Verleihung der Marktrechte an Bremen. (Bearbeitung Heinrich Lühring) Bremen, Volksbüchereien (1965)

63 p. illus. 19 cm.

BRENNAN, CHRISTOPHER JOHN

Chaplin, Harry F.
A Brennan collection; an annotated catalogue of first editions, inscribed copies, letters, manuscripts and association items, collected and collated by Harry F. Chaplin. Sydney,

Wentworth Press, 1966.

81 p. illus., facsim., port. 26 cm. (Studies in Australian bibliography, no. 15)

BRENTANO, CLEMENS

Clemens Brentano. Ausstellg. 22. Juni–20. Sept. 1970. (Katalogbearb: Jürgen Behrens (u. a.) Mit 2 Farbtaf., 16 Schwarzweiss-Abb. u. 7 Abb. im Text.) Bad Homburg vor d. Höhe, Gehlen (1970).

167 p. illus. 21 cm.

At head of title: Freies Deutsches Hochstift, Frankfurter Goethe-museum.

Mallon, Otto, 1893–
Brentano-Bibliographie. ⟨Clemens Brentano, 1778 bis 1842⟩ (Reprografischer Nachdruck der Ausg. Berlin 1926) Hildesheim, Olms, 1965.

289 p. 22 cm.

Walldorf, Hazel.
Clemens Brentano; a bibliography to supplement Mallon, 1926. Johannesburg, University of the Witwatersrand, Department of Bibliography, Librarianship and Typography, 1971.

(x), 62 p. 30 cm.

"Compiled in part fulfilment for the requirements of the Diploma in Librarianship, University of the Witwatersrand."

BRESCIA, ITALY

Peroni, Vincenzo, 1746–1810.
Biblioteca bresciana. Opera postuma di Vincenzo Peroni ... Bologna, Forni, 1968.

3 v. port. 17 cm.

Facsim. of the Brescia, 1818–23 ed.

BRETON, ANDRÉ

Sheringham, Michael.
André Breton: a bibliography. London, Grant and Cutler, 1972.

122 p. 21 cm. index. (Research bibliographies and checklists, 2)

BRETTER, EMIL

Hellmuth-Brauner, Vladimír.
Emil Bretter (1857–1919); Literární pozůstalost. Praha, Literární archív Památníku národního písemnictví, 1972.

8 p. 21 cm. (Edice inventářů, čís. 240)

BREWING

Sedlmayr, Fritz.
Die "prewen" Münchens seit 1363 bis zur Aufhebung der Lehensverleihung durch den Landesfürsten ⟨1814⟩. Gesammelt von Fritz Sedlmayr. Ausgearb. von Lore Grohsmann. Nürnberg, Carl (1969).

xii, 257 p. 24 cm.

Šteinerová, Svatava, comp.
Bibliografie dějin čs. pivovarství. Excerpováno z knih a časopisů v Knihovně Národního technického muzea. Sest. Svatava Šteinerova s kolektivem. Praha, 1966.

241 p. 21 cm. (Rozpravy Národního technického muzea v Praze. Populárně-vědecká řada, 22)

Rejtharová, Alena.
Pivovarnické časopisy v knihovním fondu Státní vědecké knihovny v Plzni. Plzeň, Státní vědecká knihovna, 1972.

20 p. 21 cm. (Bibliografie technické literatury, 13)

BŘEZINA, OTOKAR, pseud.   see   Jebavý, Václav

BRICE, GERMAIN   see under   Corrozet, Gillies

BRICEÑO PEROZO, MARIO

Ramírez Báez, Carmen Celeste.
Mario Briceño Perozo. Caracas, Escuela de Biblioteconomía y Archivos, Facultad de Humanidades y Educación, Universidad Central de Venezuela, 1970.

282 p. port. 16 cm. (Serie bibliográfica, 12)

BRICKS

Gunst-De Paepe, Claudine.
Bricks, brickmaking and brickworks. A select bibliography for the period 1962-1970. Books, conference papers, articles, patents, standards. 1216 entries. Compiled by Cl(audine) Gunst-De Paepe and E(dward) H. Lapeysen. (Mechelen, H. Dessain), 1970.

149 p. illus. 21 cm.

Drafted by the Nationaal Centrum voor Wetenschappelijke en Technische Dokumentatie.

BRILON, GERMANY

Stadtarchiv Brilon.
Inventar des Stadtarchivs Brilon, bearb. von Alfred Bruns. Münster/Westf., Aschendorff ₍1970-

v. fold. map (in pocket) 24 cm. (Inventare der nichtstaatlichen Archive Westfalens, n. F., Bd. 4)

BRISTOL, ENGLAND

Bristol, Eng. Archives Office.
Guide to the Bristol Archives Office, City and County of Bristol, by Elizabeth Ralph, City Archivist; with a foreword by W. J. Hutchinson. Bristol, Bristol Corporation, 1971.

xiii, 132, ₍4₎ p. facsims., map. 26 cm. index.

BRITISH COLUMBIA

Lowther, Barbara Joan Sonia Horsfield, 1932-
A bibliography of British Columbia; laying the foundations, 1849-1899, by Barbara J. Lowther with the assistance of Muriel Laing. ₍Victoria, B. C., University of Victoria, 1968₎

xii, 328 p. 29 cm.

Okanagan Regional Library
British Columbia books. ₍3d ed. Kelowna, B. C., 1971₎

47 p. 28 cm.

Cover title.
Caption title: Books about British Columbia and books by British Columbia authors in the stock of the Okanagan Regional Library, May 1971.
Edition for 1965 published under title: British Columbia.

Smith, Robert Dennis Hilton, 1903-
Northwestern approaches; the first century of books, by R. D. Hilton Smith. Foreword by Samuel Rothstein. Victoria, B. C., Adelphi Book Shop, 1969.

67 p. illus., facsims. 24 cm.

BRITISH COMMONWEALTH OF NATIONS   see   Commonwealth of Nations

BRITISH GUIANA   see   Guyana

BRITISH HONDURAS

Bath, Sérgio.
Notas para uma bibliografia sobre Belize, Honduras Britânica. México, Embaixada do Brasil, 1966.

₍21₎ l. 29 cm.

"40 exemplares mimeografados."

Minkel, Clarence W   1928-
A bibliography of British Honduras, 1900-1970, by Clarence W. Minkel and Ralph H. Alderman. [East Lansing, Latin American Studies Center, Michigan State University, ᶜ1970₎

vii, 93 p. 23 cm. (Latin American Studies Center. Michigan State University. Research report, no. 7)

BRITISH IN SOUTH ASIA

Cambridge. University. Centre for South Asian Studies.
Cambridge South Asian archive; records of the British period in South Asia relating to India, Pakistan, Ceylon, Burma, Nepal and Afghanistan held in the Centre of South Asian Studies, University of Cambridge; compiled and edited by Mary Thatcher. London, Mansell Information Publishing, 1973.

xi, 346 p. 23 cm.

BRITTEN, BENJAMIN

Boosey & Hawkes, ltd., London.
Benjamin Britten; a complete catalogue of his published works. ₍Rev. ed.₎ London, 1973.

52 p. facsims., port. 26 cm.

BRNO, CZECHOSLOVAK REPUBLIC

Brünn. Universita. *Knihovna.*
Brno v obrazech; průvodce obrazovým materiálem Universitní knihovny v Brně. Sest. Věra Bednářová. V Brně, 1964.

72 p. 21 cm. (*Its* Výběrový seznam, 88)

BROADSIDES
see also Chap-books

Coupe, William A.
The German illustrated broadsheet in the seventeenth century. Historical and iconographical studies ₍by₎ William A. Coupe. Baden-Baden, Heitz, 1966-67.

2 v. with illus. 24 cm. (Bibliotheca bibliographica Aureliana, 17, 20)

Edmond, John Philip, 1850-1906, *comp.*
Catalogue of English broadsides, 1505-1897. New York, B. Franklin ₍1968₎

xi, 526 p. 27 cm. (Burt Franklin bibliography and reference series #139)

At head of title: Bibliotheca Lindesiana.
Catalogue of a special collection in the library of James Lindsay, Lord Crawford, first published in 1898.

Halle, J., *firm, booksellers, Munich.*
Newe Zeitungen. Relationen, Flugschriften, Flugblätter, Einblattdrucke von 1470 bis 1820. ([Nachdruck der Ausgabe München, 1929] Katalog 70) Nieuwkoop, B. de Graaf. 1967.

xii, 408 p. with illus. 23 cm.

Prussia. *Kommission für den Gesamtkatalog der Wiegendrucke.*
Einblattdrucke des xv. [i. e. fünfzehnten] Jahrhunderts; ein bibliographisches Verzeichnis. Nendeln/Liechtenstein, Kraus Reprint, 1968.

xix, 553 p. 24 cm. (Sammlung bibliothekswissenschaftlicher Arbeiten, 35./36. Heft (II. Ser., 18./19. Heft))

Reprint of the edition published in Halle a. S. by E. Karras in 1914.

United States. Library of Congress. Rare Book Division.
Catalog of broadsides in the Rare Book Division. Boston, G. K. Hall, 1972.

4 v. 37 cm.

Introd. signed by Frederick R. Goff, chief, Rare Book Division. CONTENTS: v. 1. Geographic shelflist catalog.—v. 2. Author/title catalog: A-M.—v. 3. Author/title catalog: N-Z.—v. 4. Chronological catalog.—v. 5.

BROD, MAX

Kayser, Werner.
Max Brod: [Mit unveröffentlichten Briefen Max Brods an Hugo u. Olga Salus u. an Richard Dehmel]/ von Werner Kayser u. Horst Gronemeyer unter Mitarb. von Lando Formanek. Eingel. von Willy Haas u. Jörg Mager. — Hamburg: Christians, 1972.

193 p.; 22 cm. (Hamburger Bibliographien; Bd. 12)

BROFFERIO, ANGELO

Bottasso, Enzo.
Angelo Brofferio; mostra bibliografica nel centenario della morte. Catalogo a cura di Enzo Bottasso. Torino, Biblioteca civica di Torino, 1966.

87 p. illus. 22 cm. (Manuali e saggi di bibliografia, 2)

BRONNER, FRANZ XAVER

Radspieler, Hans.
Franz Xaver Bronner. Bearb. von Hans Radspieler. Hrsg. von der Kantonsbibliothek und vom Staatsarchiv des Kantons Aargau. Aarau, 1964.

[12] 31 p. port. 21 cm. (Aargauische Bibliographien und Repertorien, 1)

BRONSHTAYN, YEHEZKEL see Brownstone, Ezekiel

BRONTË FAMILY
see also under Eliot, George

Brontë Society. *Museum and Library, Haworth.*
Catalogue of the Museum & Library, the Brontë Society. Compiled by J. Alex. Symington. New York, B. Franklin [1968]

199 p. illus., facsims., maps, ports. 23 cm. (Burt Franklin bibliography and reference series #153)

Reprint of the 1927 Haworth ed.

BROOKE, RUPERT

Schroder, John.
Catalogue of books and manuscripts by Rupert Brooke, Edward Marsh & Christopher Hassall, collected, compiled and annotated by John Schroder, with a frontispiece by Joan Hassall. Cambridge, Rampart Lions Pr., 1970.

134 p., 11 plates. 1 illus., facsims., port. 30 cm.

BROOKE-POPHAM, SIR ROBERT

Oxford. University. Rhodes House Library.
Papers of Sir Robert Brooke-Popham, MSS Afr. s 1120, kept in Rhodes House Library, Oxford. [Prepared by P. A. Empson. Oxford, 1968?]

[23] l. 33 cm.

At head of title: Oxford University colonial records project.

BROOMÉ, BERTIL

Willers, Uno Erik Wilhelm, 1911–
Bertil Broomé; en bibliografi 23 juni 1973. [Redigerad av Uno Willers] Stockholm, 1973.

37 p. 24 cm. (Acta Bibliothecae Regiae Stockholmiensis, 17)

BROWNE, SIR THOMAS

Keynes, *Sir* **Geoffrey Langdon,** 1887–
A bibliography of Sir Thomas Browne Kt. M. D., by Geoffrey Keynes. 2nd ed. revised and augmented. Oxford, Clarendon P., 1968.

iii-xv, 203 p. 4 plates, illus., facsims., ports. 26 cm.

BROWNING, ELIZABETH BARRETT and ROBERT

Barnes, Warner.
A bibliography of Elizabeth Barrett Browning. Austin, Humanities Research Center] University of Texas; [distributed by University of Texas Press, 1967]

179 p. facsims., ports. 26 cm.

Baylor University, *Waco, Tex.* **Library.** *Armstrong Browning Library.*
The Pied Piper of Hamelin in the Armstrong Browning Library, Baylor University, Waco, Texas. A catalogue of materials related to Browning's poem, including a list of items on exhibit in the library during January and February, 1969. Prepared under the editorial supervision of Jack W. Herring, director. Waco [1968?]

27 p. illus., facsims. 24 cm. (Baylor University Browning interests, no. 20)

Broughton, Leslie Nathan, 1877–1952.
Robert Browning: a bibliography, 1830–1950, by Leslie Nathan Broughton, Clark Sutherland Northup [and] Robert Brainard Pearsall. New York, B. Franklin [c1970]

xvi, 446 p. 24 cm. (Burt Franklin bibliography & reference series, 315. Essays in literature and criticism, 50)

On spine: Bibliography of Robert Browning, 1830–1950.
"New edition [with a new pref. by R. B. Pearsall]"

East, Sally Keith Carroll.
Browning music; a descriptive catalog of the music related to Robert Browning and Elizabeth Barrett Browning in the Armstrong Library. 1972. Waco, Tex., Armstrong Browning Library, 1973.

xv, 414 p. facsims. 24 cm.

Peterson, William S
Robert and Elizabeth Barrett Browning : an annotated bibliography, 1951–1970 / by William S. Peterson. — New York : Browning Institute, 1974.

xiii, 209 p. ; 24 cm.

Texas. University. *Humanities Research Center.*
Catalogue of the Browning collection, compiled by Warner Barnes. ₍Austin, 1966₎

120 p. facsims. 25 cm. (*Its* Bibliographical series ₍3₎)

Wise, Thomas James, 1859–1937.
A bibliography of the writings in prose and verse of Elizabeth Barrett Browning, by Thomas J. Wise. ₍1st ed. reprinted₎ Folkestone, Dawsons, 1970.

xv, 247 p. illus., facsims., ports. 23 cm.

First published in 1918.

Wise, Thomas James, 1859–1937.
A complete bibliography of the writings in prose and verse of Robert Browning, by Thomas J. Wise. Folkestone, Dawsons, 1971.

₍1₎, 9, 260 p., 10 plates. illus., facsims. 23 cm.

Reprint of the London, 1897 ed.

BROWNSTONE, EZEKIEL

Jeshurin, Ephim H 1885–1967.
יחזקאל בראנשטיין ביבליאגראפיע. צוזאמענגעשטעלט פון יעפים ישורין. תל-אביב. המנורה, 1965.

13 p. 18 cm.
Cover title.
Added cover title: E. Brownstone bibliography.

BRUGES, BELGIUM

Vanhoutryve, André.
Bibliografie van de geschiedenis van Brugge. Handzame, Uitgaven Familia et Patria, 1972.

xv, 708 p. 24 cm.

BRUNEI see under Malaysia

BRUNN see Brno

BRUNNER, OTTO

Wolgast, Günther.
Verzeichnis der Schriften: Professor Otto Brunner, 1923–1966. Zusammengestellt von Günther Wolgast. Hamburg, 1966.

73 p. 21 cm.

BRUSSELS

Danckaert, Lisette.
L'évolution territoriale de Bruxelles. La cartographie de ± 1550 à 1840. Bruxelles, Arcade, 1968.

164 p. plans, tables. and album (6 plates) 28 cm. (Publications du Centre national d'histoire des sciences, 2)

Includes summary in English and Dutch.

BRUSSELS. UNIVERSITÉ NOUVELLE

Despy-Meyer, Andrée.
Inventaire des archives de l'Université nouvelle de Bruxelles, 1894–1919, déposées aux Archives de l'Université de Bruxelles. Bruxelles, (bd de l'Empereur, 4), 1973.

52 p. 25 cm. (Archives et bibliothèques de Belgique. Inventaires, 1)

BRYANSK, RUSSIA (PROVINCE)

Bentsel', G N
(Literatura o Brianskoĭ oblasti)
Литература о Брянской области за 1968 год. ₍Сост. Г. Н. Бенцель, Р. К. Пожаринская₎ Брянск, 1972.

175 p. 20 cm.

At head of title: Брянская областная библиотека. Библиографический отдел.

Bentsel', G N
(Literatura o Brianskoĭ oblasti)
Литература о Брянской области за 1969 год. ₍Сост. библиографы Г. Бенцель, Р. Пожаринская₎. Брянск, 1972.

196 p. 20 cm.

Литература о Брянской области. ₍В 3-х вып.₎ Библиогр. указатель. ₍Вып. 1₎– Брянск, ₍Приок. кн. изд., Брян. отд-ние₎, 1970–

v. 16 cm.

Pozharinskaia, R K
Литература о Брянской области. Библиогр. указатель за 1967 г. ₍Сост. Р. К. Пожаринская и Е. Н. Чернова₎. Брянск, ₍Приок. кн. изд., Брян. отд-ние₎, 1970.

139 p. 20 cm.

BRYANT, WILLIAM CULLEN

Sturges, Henry Cady, *b.* 1846, *comp.*
Chronologies of the life and writings of William Cullen Bryant, with a bibliography of his works in prose and verse, compiled by Henry C. Sturges. To which is prefixed a memoir of the poet by Richard Henry Stoddard. New York, B. Franklin ₍1968₎

cxxvii p. port. 23 cm. (Burt Franklin bibliography and reference series, no. 164)

Reprint of the 1903 ed.

BRYOLOGY

Murray, Barbara M
Catalog of bryophytes and lichens of the central Brooks Range, Alaska : a literature review / Barbara M. Murray. — ₍Anchorage₎ : University of Alaska Museum; 1974.

46 leaves ; 28 cm.

Rosario, Romualdo M del.
Bibliography of Philippine bryology, by Romualdo M. del Rosario and Nieva V. del Rosario. Manila ₍National Museum₎ 1967.

19 p. 26 cm. (Museum publication no. 3)

BRYOZOA

Bassler, Ray Smith, 1878–
Bryozoa (generum et genotyporum index et bibliographia). ₍By₎ R. S. Bassler. Den Haag, W. J. Junk, 1970.

229 p. 23 cm. (Fossilium catalogus, I ; Animalia, pars 67)

Reprint of the 1934 ed.

BÜCHNER, GEORG

Schlick, Werner.
Das Georg Büchner-Schrifttum bis 1965; eine internationale Bibliographie. Hildesheim, G. Olms, 1968.

226 p. 23 cm.

BUCKWHEAT

Frantseva, A IA
Гречиха; библиографический список отечественной литературы за 1961–1966 гг. в количестве 553 названий. ₍Составитель А. Я. Францева₎ Москва, 1966.

67 p. 20 cm.

At head of title: Всесоюзная академия сельскохозяйственных наук имени В. И. Ленина. Центральная научная сельскохозяйственная библиотека. Справочно-библиографический отдел.

BUDAPEST

Budapest. *Fővárosi Levéltár.*
A Fővárosi Levéltár térképei, 1705–1918; repertórium. Összeállította: Farkas Elemérné. ₍Kiadja: a Művelődésügyi Minisztérium Levéltári Osztálya₎ Budapest, Művelődésügyi Minisztérium Levéltári Osztálya, Levéltárak Országos Központja, 1964.

v, 300 p. 28 cm. (Levéltári leltárak, 31)

Summary in French and Russian.

Budapest. *Fővárosi Levéltár.*
Testületek, (céhek és ipartársulatok) egyházi szervek, családok, személyek, gyüjtemények. ₍Az egyes fejezetek szerzői: Bácskai Vera, Felhő Ibolya és Bónis György₎ Budapest, Művelődésügyi Minisztérium Levéltári Igazgatóságának megbizásából, Magyar Országos Levéltár, 1969.

166 p. 29 cm. (Levéltári alapleltárak, 2. Budapest Főváros Levéltára, 5)

Tolnai, György.
A Tanácsköztársaság Budapestje a korabeli lapok tükrében; bibliográfia, írta és szerk. Tolnai György. Budapest, Fővárosi Szabó Ervin Könyvtár, 1969.

ix, 686 p. 29 cm.

BUDAPEST. MŰSZAKI EGYETEM

Budapest. Műszaki Egyetem. *Központi Könyvtár.*
Az audio-vizuális oktatás ujabb szakirodalma a budapesti Műszaki Egyetem Központi Könyvtárában; címjegyzék. ₍Összeállította Spányi Balázsné₎ Budapest, 1965.

26 p. 25 cm.

Hodinka, László.
A Budapesti Műszaki Egyetem történetének bibliográfiája ₍írta₎ Hodinka László, Karolyi Zsigmond ₍és₎ Végh Ferenc. ₍Budapest, Budapesti Műszaki Egyetem, 1969₎

2 v. (678 p.) 20 cm. Budapesti Műszaki Egyetem Központi Könyvtára műszaki tudománytörténeti kiadványok, 20 sz.)

BUDDHISM

Abe, Ryūichi.
六地藏寺法寶藏典籍について　阿部隆一著
₍常澄村₎ 六地藏寺 ₍1967₎

35 p. 21 cm.

Aichi Gakuin Daigaku. Toshokan.
(Yokoseki bunko mokuroku)
横関文庫目録　愛知学院大学図書館所蔵　名古屋　愛知学院大学図書館　昭和46(1971)

75 p. 26 cm.

Beautrix, Pierre.
Bibliographie de la littérature prajñāpāramitā. Bruxelles, Institut belge des hautes études bouddhiques, ₍chaussée de Louvain, 696₎, (1971).

ix, 58 l. 26 cm. (Publications de l'Institut belge des hautes études bouddhiques. Série Bibliographies, no 3)

Beautrix, Pierre.
Bibliographie du bouddhisme. Bruxelles, Institut belge des hautes études bouddhiques, ₍chaussée de Louvain, 696₎, ₍1971

v. 26 cm. (Publications de l'Institut belge des hautes études bouddhiques. Série Bibliographies, no 2)

Beautrix, Pierre.
Bibliographie du bouddhisme Zen. Bruxelles, Institut belge des hautes études bouddhiques, (r. de l'Orient, 74), (1969).

iv, 114 p. 26 cm. (Publications de l'Institut belge des hautes études bouddhiques. Série Bibliographies, no 1)

(Bukkyō no meicho)
仏教の名著　12選　笠原一男編　東京　学陽書房 1973.

292 p. 19 cm. (名著入門ライブラリー)

Chattopadhyaya, Alaka.
Catalogue of Indian (Buddhist) texts in Tibetan translation, Kanjur & Tanjur; alphabetically rearranged ₍by₎ Alaka Chattopadhyaya in collaboration with Mrinalkanti Gangopadhyaya ₍and₎ Debiprasad Chattopadhyaya. Calcutta, Indo-Tibetan Studies; ₍selling agents: Firma K. L. Mukhopadhyaya, 1972–

v. 22 cm.

Chung-hua hsüeh shu yüan. Fo chiao wen hua yen chiu so.
(Erh shih nien lai fo chiao ching shu lun wen so yin)
二十年來佛教經書論文索引　₍陽明山₎　中華學術院佛教文化研究所 ₍編₎ 印　₍華岡書城經銷　民國61 i.e. 1972₎

311 p. illus. 21 cm. (中華大典)

Added colophon title: Catalogue of Chinese Buddhist articles and books published in Taiwan during the last 20 years.

Held, Hans Ludwig, 1885–
Deutsche Bibliographie des Buddhismus. Hildesheim, New York, G. Olms, 1973.

viii, 190 p. 20 cm.

Reprint of the 1916 ed., published by Hans Sachs-Verlag, Munich.

Institut belge des hautes études bouddhiques.
Série Bibliographies. no 1–

Bruxelles ₍1969–

no. 26 cm. (Its Publications)

Ryūkoku Daigaku Daigakuin Shinshū Kenkyūkai.

〔Shinshūgaku kankei gakujutsu kenkyū rombun moku-roku〕

真宗学関係学術研究論文目録　自昭和31年1月
至昭和44年12月　龍谷大学大学院真宗研究会編
京都　龍谷大学大学院真宗研究会　昭和45(1970)

63, 50 p.　21 cm.

Saeki, Ryōken, 1880-1962.

(Immyō sahō hensen to chojutsu)

因明作法変遷と著述　佐伯良謙和上遺稿　斑鳩
町(奈良県)　法隆寺　昭和44(1969)

182 p. (on double leaves)　port.　31 cm.

Tōhoku Daigaku, Sendai, Japan.　Hōbungakubu.

(Chibetto Daizōkyō sōmokuroku)

西藏大藏経總目録　東北帝国大学法文学部編
東京　名著出版　昭和45(1970)

2, 2, 701, 124 p.　27 cm.

編者: 宇井伯壽等
東北帝国大学 昭和9年の複製
Added t. p.: A complete catalogue of the Tibetan Buddhist cannons
(Bkaḥ-hgyur and Bstan-ḥgyur)
西藏大藏経總目録索引　A catalogue-index of the Tibetan Buddhist

canons (Bkaḥ-ḥgyur and Bstan-ḥgyur): p. 1-124 (4th group)

Yoo, Yushin.

Buddhism: a subject index to periodical articles in
English, 1728-1971. Metuchen, N. J., Scarecrow Press,
1973 ₍c1972₎

xxii, 162 p.　22 cm.

BUDEVSKA, ADRIANA

Dzholova, Penka.

Адриана Будевска. 〈Препоръч. библиогр. по случай
90 г. от рождението ѝ〉. (Ред. Зара Ангелова). Бургас,
Окр. библ., 1968.

47 p. with ports.　20 cm.

BUDGET

Chackerian, Richard.

Selected bibliography on public budgeting.　Seattle, Bureau of Governmental Research and Services, University of
Washington, 1968.

6 l.　28 cm.

Harper, Roger Michael.

Budget and cost control in commercial enterprises, compiled by R. M. Harper.　Adelaide, Public Library of South
Australia, 1966.

23 p.　27 cm.　(Public Library (Research Service bibliographies.
Series 4, no. 75)

Hawaii State Library.

PPB bibliography; Hawaii State library system 1970.
Honolulu, Office of Library Services, Teacher Assist Center, State of Hawaii ₍1971₎

53 p.　22 cm.

Knight, Kenneth W

The literature of state budgeting in Australia, Canada,
and the United States of America: a survey and select
bibliography, ₍by₎ Kenneth W. Knight.　₍St. Lucia, Q.₎
University of Queensland Press ₍1970₎

51 p.　22 cm.

Pennsylvania.　State Library, *Harrisburg.*

Planning, programming, budgeting system; a selected
bibliography of recent articles and monographs available
in the Pennsylvania State Library.　Compiled by Marjory
H. Hetrick.　Harrisburg, General Library Bureau, Pennsylvania State Library, 1969.

4 l.　29 cm.

Shore, Barry.

The equipment replacement aspects of capital budgeting;
a bibliography.　₍Madison, University of Wisconsin, Bureau
of Business Research & Service, 1970?₎

40 l.　28 cm.　(Wisconsin project reports, v. 3, no. 5)

Washington (State).　State Library, *Olympia.*

Performance budgeting bibliography: including planning,
programming, budgeting.　₍Olympia₎ 1969.

6 l.　28 cm.

BUDGETS, PERSONAL

Hitotsubashi Daigaku, *Tokyo.　Tōkei Shiryō Seibi Sentā.*
一橋大学統計資料整備センター
家計調査資料目録　　一橋大学統計資料整備
センター．一橋大学経済研究所資料係編
〔国立〕　一橋大学統計資料整備センター．一橋大学
経済研究所資料係　昭和43(1968)

73p　25 cm

Title also in English: Bibliography of statistical data on family
budgets.

BUDRY, PAUL

**Vaud.　Bibliothèque cantonale et universitaire, Lausanne.
Département des manuscrits.**

Inventaire du fonds Paul Budry (1883-1949), IS 2134,
par Marianne Perrenoud.　Lausanne, Bibliothèque cantonale
et universitaire, 1970.

36 l.　30 cm.　(Its Inventaire des fonds manuscrits, 8)

BUENOS AIRES (PROVINCE)

**Archivo Histórico de la Provincia de Buenos Aires Dr.
Ricardo Levene.**

Catálogo de los documentos del Archivo.　La Plata, 1967-
₍i. e. 1968-

v. illus.　27 cm.　(Publicaciones del Archivo Histórico de la
Provincia Doctor Ricardo Levene)

CONTENTS: 1. Catálogo del Tribunal de Cuentas y Contaduría de
la Provincia; incluye catálogo de la Sección Libros de la Legislatura
de Buenos Aires.—2. Indice de mapas, planos y fotografías de la
Sección Ministerio de Obras Públicas.

BUFFALOES

Almeida, Norma Martins de.

Búfalo (*Bubalus, Bubalis*).　Cruz das Almas, 1968.

22 l.　28 cm.　(Instituto de Pesquisas e Experimentação Agro-

pecuarias do Leste. Lista bibliográfica, no. 7)

BUGGE, ANDERS RAGNAR

Sommerfeldt, Wilhelm Preus, 1881–1957.
Professor dr. phil. Anders Bugges forfatterskap. Ved
W. P. Sommerfeldt. Oslo, Universitetsforlaget, 1969.

34 p. ports. 23 cm. (Sjuande november-bibliografiane, nr. 1)

Norsk bibliografisk bibliotek, bd. 42, hefte 1.

BUILDING
see also under Dissertations,
Academic

Abstracts bangunan. Apr. 1970–
₁Bandung₁ Lembaga Penjelidikan Masalah Bangunan.

v. illus. 30 cm. monthly (irregular)

Antonenko, V V
Облицовщику. Рек. указатель литературы. Москва,
"Книга," 1968.

23 p. 17 cm. (В помощь рабочим строительной промышленности, вып. 3(11))

Balberova, L A
(Setevoe planirovanie v stroitel'stve)
Сетевое планирование в строительстве. Библиогр.
указатель литературы за 1966–1968 гг. и половину 1969
г. Москва, 1969.

108 p. 21 cm.
At head of title: Госстрой СССР. Гипротис.
By L. A. Balberova, I. A. Pavlova, and K. S. Vorob'eva.

Baukombinat Dresden. Technische Bibliothek.
Katalog der Technischen Bibliothek: Fachbücher. Dresden, VEB (B) Baukombinat ₁1965₁

78 p. 21 cm.

Bentley, Howard B
Building construction information sources. Detroit, Gale
Research Co. ₁1964₁

181 p. 23 cm. (Management information guide, 2)

Bibliografia budownictwa. Piśmiennictwo krajowe. 1970–

₁Warszawa, Centralny Ośrodek Informacji Budownictwa₁

v. 25 cm. monthly.

Building climatology. List of literature. Stockholm, Svensk
byggtjänst (distr.) 1967.

v. 30 cm. (Rapport från Byggforskningen. 1967: 33)

Contents.—

pt. 3. Heat.

Construction references. no. 1–
Jan./June 1970–
London, Dept. of the Environment.

no. 30 cm. semiannual.

Formed by the union of Consolidated accessions list and Consolidated building references to articles in periodicals, issued by Gt. Brit. Ministry of Public Building and Works. Library.

Dargan Bullivant Associates.
CIRIA index of technical publications; compiled and designed by Dargan Bullivant Associates. London, Construction Industry Research and Information Association, 1968.

1 v. (unpaged) facsims. 30 cm.

Drischel, Otto.
Generalsachregister zu allen Schriften der Forschungsgesellschaft für den Wohnungsbau ⟨FGW⟩ 1956–31. Juli
1962. Zusammengestellt von Otto Drischel. Wien (Forschungsgesellschaft für den Wohnungsbau) 1963.
120 l. 30 cm.
"Forschungsgesellschaft für den Wohnungsbau. Arbeitsunterlage,
A 640."
——————Nachtrag. 1.–
Wien, 1965–
Forschungsgesellschaft für den Wohnungsbau.

Garston, Eng. Building Research Station.
Publications and films, 1967. Watford (Herts.), Building Research Station ₁1968₁

23 p. 30 cm.

Kramárová, A
Vonkajšie povrchové úpravy stavebných konštrukcií.
Výber. zozn. z domácej a zahraničnej literatúry. Zost.:
A. Kramárová. Bratislava, Slov. techn. kniž. nica, rozmn.,
1970.

₁1₁, 85, ₁2₁ p. 21 cm. (Bratislava. Slovenská technická knižnica.
Edícia 2. Séria B: Výberové bibliografie)

Kramárová, A
Výškové budovy. Zost.: A₁lžbeta₁ Kramárová. Bratislava, Slov. techn. kniž., rozmn., 1969.

2 v. 21 cm. (Bratislava. Slovenská technická knižnica. Edícia
2. Séria B: Výberové bibliografie)

CONTENTS: 1. Výberová bibliografia knižnej a časopiseckej
literatúry.—2. Výberový zoznam z domácej a zahraničnej literatúry.

Latta, J K
Annotated bibliography on construction management and
site control, by J. K. Latta. Ottawa, National Research
Council, Division of Building Research, 1964.

ii, 18 l. 28 cm. (₁National Research Council, Canada. Division
of Building Research₁ Bibliography no. 28)

Latta, J K
Annotated bibliography on construction management and
site control, by J. K. Latta. Rev. by Y. Fortier. Ottawa,
Division of Building Research, National Research Council,
1970.

1 v. (various pagings) 28 cm. (₁National Research Council,
Canada. Division of Building Research₁ Bibliography 28)

Machová, Elena.
Progresívne metódy riadenia a organizácie stavebníctva.
Výber. bibl. kniž. a čas. lit. Zost. Elena Machová. Bratislava, Slov. techn. knižnica, rozmn., 1969.

83, ₁2₁ p. 20 cm. (Bratislava. Slovenská technická knižnica.
Edícia 2. Séria B: Výberové bibliografie)

National Research Council, Canada. *Division of Building
Research.*
List of ₁and index to₁ publications, 1947–1965. ₁Ottawa,
1965₁

99 p. 21 cm.

Cover title.
Lists all available publications of the Division and those pertaining to building issued by the National Research Council prior to
the formation of the Division.

Научная организация труда в строительстве (НОТ).
Библиогр. аннот. указатель литературы по строительству
и архитектуре за 1962–1968 гг. Изд. 2-е, переработ. и

дом. Москва, [ЦНТИ по гражд. строительству и архитектуре], 1969.

104 p. 22 cm.

Новости технической литературы: Строительство и архитектура. 1971–

Москва, Изд-во лит-ры по строительству.

v. 29 cm. biweekly.

Supersedes Библиографический указатель текущей отечественной литературы по строительству и архитектуре and Библиографический указатель текущей иностранной литературы по строительству и архитектуре.

Issued by TSentral'naîa nauchno-tekhnicheskaîa biblioteka po stroitel'stvu i arkhitekture and TSentral'nyĭ institut nauchnoĭ informatsii po stroitel'stvu i arkhitekture.

(Novosti tekhnicheskoĭ literatury. Stroitel'stvo i arkhitektura. Razdel A. Seriîa VIII: Organizatsiîa, mekhanizatsiîa i proizvodstvo stroitel'no-montazhnykh rabot)

Новости технической литературы. Строительство и архитектура. Раздел А. Серия VIII: Организация, механизация и производство строительно-монтажных работ.

Москва, Центр. ин-т науч. информации по строительству и архитектуре.

v. 22 cm. 12 no. a year.

"Библиографическая информация."

Some information previously (–1972) published in Новости технической литературы. Строительство и архитектура. Раздел А. Серия II–IV.

Title varies: –1972, Новости технической литературы. Строительство и архитектура. Раздел А. Серия VIII: Производство строительных и монтажных работ.

Issues for   prepared by Informatsionno-bibliograficheskiĭ otdel of TSNTB po stroitel'stvu i arkhitekture.

(Novosti tekhnicheskoĭ literatury. Stroitel'stvo i arkhitektura. Razdel A. Seriîa XIII: Upravlenie stroitel'stvom, ékonimika stroitels'tva)

Новости технической литературы. Строительство и архитектура. Раздел А. Серия XIII: Управление строительством, экономика строительства. 1973–

Москва, Центр. ин-т науч. информации по строительству и архитектуре.

v. 22 cm.

"Библиографическая информация."

Information previously published in Новости технической литературы. Строительство и архитектура. Раздел А. Серия I.

(Novosti tekhnicheskoĭ literatury. Stroitel'stvo i arkhitektura. Razdel A. Seriîa IX: Stroitel'nye konstruktsii, stroitel'naîa fizika)

Новости технической литературы. Строительство и архитектура. Раздел А. Серия IX: Строительные конструкции, строительная физика.

Москва, Центр. ин-т науч. информации по строительству и архитектуре.

v. 22 cm. 12 no. a year.

"Библиографическая информация."

Some information previously (–1972) published in Новости технической литературы. Строительство и архитектура. Раздел А. Серия VIII.

Title varies: –1972, Новости технической литературы. Строительство и архитектура. Раздел А. Серия IX: Теория и расчет конструкций и сооружений, строительная физика.

Issues for   prepared by Informatsionno-bibliograficheskiĭ otdel of TSNTB po stroitel'stvu i arkhitekture.

Pevzner, D   P

Объемно-блочное домостроение. Отечеств. и иностр. литература за 1966–1969 гг. (сентябрь). [Сост. библиограф Д. П. Певзнер]. Москва, 1969.

49 p. 24 cm.

At head of title: Госстрой СССР. Центральная научно-техническая библиотека по строительству и архитектуре.

Polska bibliografia budownictwa. [Autorzy: Marta Kłyszewska, Rafał Kozłowski, Zbigniew Staniszewski. Wyd. 1.] Warszawa, Arkady, 1967–

v. 25 cm.

Table of contents in v. 1–   also in English and Russian.

Purzycki, Julian.

Bibliografia prac naukowo-badawczych Instytutu Techniki Budowlanej, opublikowanych w latach 1945–1964. Warszawa, 1965.

121, 12 p. 29 cm.

At head of title: Instytut Techniki Budowlanej. Działowy Ośrodek Informacji Naukowo-Technicznej. Julian Purzycki, Hanna Nowakowa.

Royal Institute of British Architects, _London._

CI/SfB classified list of essential references. London, R. I. B. A., 1968.

40 p. 30 cm.

Rozhkaln, É   L

(Ésteticheskaîa organizatsiîa proizvodstvennoĭ sredy)

Эстетическая организация производственной среды. [Библиогр. указ. отеч. и иностр. литературы ...] Москва, 1972.

94 p. 20 cm. (В помощь художнику-конструктору) (Библиографическая информация)

Cover title.

At head of title: Государственный комитет Совета Министров СССР по науке и технике. Всесоюзный научно-исследовательский институт технической эстетики.

By É. L. Rozhkaln and V. M. Soldatov.

Samuolienė, G

Visuomeniniai pastatai.—Žemės ūkio pastatai. Bibliografinė rodyklė. Vilnius, 1972.

333 p. 22 cm.

At head of title: Lietuvos TSR Valstybinė respublikinė biblioteka. Respublikinė mokslinė techninė biblioteka.

Title also in Russian: Общественные здания, сельскохозяйственные здания.

Siegert, Justin.

Anleggsmaskiner. Utarb. ved Justin Siegert. Trondheim, NTH-trykk, 1968.

22 p. 30 cm. (Norges tekniske høgskoles biblioteker. Litteraturliste 38)

Trondheim. Norges tekniske høgskole. Biblioteket.

Fukt- og varmeisolering. Trondheim, 1967.

18 p. 30 cm. (Its Litteraturliste, 35)

U. S. Dept. of Labor. Library.

The construction industry; selected references, 1960–1969. [Washington] U. S. Dept. of Labor, 1970.

13 p. 27 cm. (Its Current bibliographies no. 2)

U. S. _General Services Administration. Central Office Library._

Buildings bibliography. [Washington] General Services Administration, Office of Administration; [for sale by the Supt. of Docs., U. S. Govt. Print. Off.] 1968.

79 p. 26 cm.

Vojanová, Eva.

Literatura pro stavebníky. Bibliografie z fondu Kraj.

knihovny Maxima Gorkého v Ústí nad Labem. Zprac. Eva Vojanová. Ústí nad Labem, Kraj. knihovna M. Gorkého, rozmn., 1973.

73, [1] p. 29 cm.

Ward, Jack W
Construction information source and reference guide; listings of texts, manuals, handbooks associations, societies, institutes, periodicals, publishers & book sources, by Jack W. Ward. 3d ed. Phoenix, Ariz., Construction Publications, 1973.

190 p. 28 cm.

PERIODICALS

Fraunhofer-Gesellschaft zur Förderung der Angewandten Forschung. *Dokumentationsstelle für Bautechnik, Stuttgart.*
Bestandsliste der Periodica, Oktober 1964. Stuttgart, 1964.

iv, 140 p. 21 cm.

BUILDING AND LOAN ASSOCATIONS

Institut für Städtebau, Wohnungswirtschaft und Bausparwesen (Arnold-Knoblauch-Institut)
Bibliographie des deutschsprachigen Bausparschiftums. Bonn, Domus-Verlag [1965–

v. 24 cm. (*Its* Schriftenreihe, Bd. 2

CONTENTS.—Bd. 1. 1924 bis 1944.

BUILDING LAWS

Hess, Walter A
Bibliographie zum Bau-, Boden- und Planungsrecht der Schweiz, 1900–1967. Bibliographie du droit des constructions, du droit foncier et du droit relatif à l'aménagement du territoire en Suisse, 1900–1967. Bearb. von Walter A. Hess. Hrsg. von der Schweizerischen Gesellschaft für Koordination und Förderung der Bauforschung. Zürich, Verlag Bauforschung, 1968.
xxviii, 259 p. 24 cm. (Schriftenreihe der Schweizerischen Gesellschaft für Koordination und Förderung der Bauforschung, Bd. 2)

BUILDING MATERIALS

Bibliograficheskiĭ ukazatel' literatury po oborudovaniiŭ dlía proizvodstva stroitel'nykh materialov.
Библиографический указатель литературы по оборудованию для производства строительных материалов. Москва, 1971.
28 p. 21 cm.
At head of title: Техническое управление. Центральный научно-исследовательский институт информации и технико-экономических исследований по строительному, дорожному и коммунальному машиностроению.

Centre scientifique et technique du bâtiment.
Liste bibliographique [sur l'habitat dans les pays chauds] Paris, 1972–

pamphlets in v. 30 cm.

CONTENTS: [1] Fondations sur sols gonflants. Utilisation du bambou, canne à sucre, riz dans la construction. L'urbanisme dans les pays chauds. Industrialisation de la construction. Bois tropicaux. Bétons, ciments. Architecture dans les pays chauds: ouvrages généraux, numéros spéciaux et ouvrages par pays. Architecture dans les pays chauds: le logement.

Davis, L *comp.*
Pisé, adobe and cob; a list of selected references, compiled by L. Davis. Melbourne, State Library of Victoria, 1966.

25 p. 26 cm. (State Library of Victoria Research Dept. Research service bibliographies, 1966, no. 1)

Deutscher Ausschuss für Stahlbeton.
Die Versuchsberichte des Deutschen Ausschusses für Stahlbeton; Inhaltsübersicht der Hefte 1 bis 230, von O. Graf und H. Deutschmann. Berlin, W. Ernst, 1973.

51 p. 30 cm. (Deutscher Ausschuss für Stahlbeton, Heft 231)

Jansson, Ingvar.
Timber joints; a selected bibliography, based on items referred to at the TRADA–CIB Symposium on Joints in Timber Structures, held in March 1965. [Stockholm] National Swedish Institute for Building Research; [distribueras av Svensk byggtjänst, 1965]
1 v. (various pagings) 29 cm. (National Swedish Institute for Building Research. Report 23)

Machová, Elena.
Vnútrozávodná doprava v stavebníctve. Výber. zoznam z domácej a zahraničnej lit. Zost. E. Machová. Bratislava, Slov. techn. knižnica. rozmn., 1970.

83, [3] p. 21 cm. (Bratislava. Slovenská technická knižnica. Edícia 2. Séria B: Výberové bibliografie)

Ostrava, Czechoslovak Republic (City) Státní vědecká knihovna.
Využití elektrárenských odpadů ve stavebnictví; výberová bibliografie. [Sest. Marie Kurečková] Ostrava, 1964.

52 p. 29 cm. (*Its* Publikace. Řada II, čís. 877)

Poškuté, B
Lietuvos TSR statybinės medžiagos; bibliografiné rodyklė. Vilnius, 1966.

138 p. 20 cm.

At head of title: Lietuvos TSR Valstybiné respublikiné biblioteka. B. Poškuté.

Tirak'íân, G K
Библиографический указатель рефератов патентов по отрасли, помещенных в РЖ ВИНИТИ. [Составители: Г. К. Тиракьян, Е. Д. Карпекина, Н. И. Куколкина]. Москва, 1970.

36 p. 16 x 26 cm. (Центральный научно-исследовательский институт информации и техникоэкономических исследований по строительному, дорожному и коммунальному машиностроению. Серия 2: Оборудование для производства строительных материалов)

At head of title: Министерство строительного, дорожного и коммунального машиностроения. Техническое управление.

BUILDING SOCIETIES see Building and loan associations

BUILDINGS, PREFABRICATED

Efektivnost a ekonomie prefabrikace a prefabrikovaných staveb; výběrová bibliografie. [Sest. Božena Legátová] Ostrava, 1966.

123 l. 29 cm. (Státní vědecká knihovna v Ostravě. Publikace. Řada II, čís. 411)

Kramárová, A
Výstavba a údržba panelových stavieb : výberový zoznam z domácej a zahraničnej lit. / zost. A. Kramárová. — Bratislava : Slov. techn. knižnica, 1973–

v. ; 21 cm. — ([Bratislava. Slovenská technická knižnica] : Edícia 2 : Séria B Výberové bibliografie)

Trondheim. Norges tekniske høgskole. *Biblioteket.*
Prefabrikasjon og husbygging. Trondheim, 1967.

39 l. 30 cm. (*Its* Litteraturliste, 32)

BUKHARIN, NIKOLAI IVANOVICH

Heitman, Sidney.
Nikolai I. Bukharin; a bibliography, with annotations, including the locations of his works in major American and European libraries. Compiled and edited by Sidney Heitman. Stanford, Hoover Institution on War, Revolution and Peace, Stanford·University, 1969.

181 p. 27 cm. (Hoover Institution bibliographical series, 37)

BUKOWINA

Beck, Erich, 1929–
Bibliographie zur Landeskunde der Bukowina. Literatur bis zum Jahre 1965. München, Verlag des Südostdeutschen Kulturwerkes, 1966.

xxiii, 378 p. 24 cm. (Veröffentlichungen des Südostdeutschen Kulturwerkes. Reihe B ⟨Wissenschaftliche Arbeiten⟩ Bd. 19)

BUKOWSKI, CHARLES

Dorbin, Sanford M
A bibliography of Charles Bukowski. Los Angeles, Black Sparrow Press, 1969.

93 p. 25 cm.

BULGARIA
see also Communism - Bulgaria and under Turkey (*Mikhov*)

Atseva, Vera I
Тракия, Родопите и Средногорието във възрожденската книжнина. Указател на литература. (Състав … Ред. Въла С. Декало). Пловдив, Нар. библ. Ив. Вазов, 1971.

vi, 644 p. 22 cm.

Busse, Nataliía V
Новая система руководства народным хозяйством Народной Республики Болгарии. Литература за 1964–июнь 1968 гг. ₁Сост. Н. В. Буссе. Вступит. статья канд. экон. наук Р. Н. Евстигнеева₁. Москва, 1970.

xii, 155 p. 20 cm.

At head of title: Академия наук СССР. Институт научной информации и фундаментальная библиотека по общественным наукам.

Cherniâvskii, Georgii Iosifovich.
Советская и международная периодика о Болгарии. 1917–1944 г.г. Истор. библиогр. София, Нар. библ. Кирил и Методий, 1970 (библиогр. каре 1971).

178 p. 28 cm.

At head of title: Г. И. Чернявский, П. С. Сохань.

Cherniâvskii, Georgii Iosifovich.
Советская печать о Болгарии. XI. 1917–IX. 1944 гг. Истор. библиогр. София, Нар. библ. Кирил и Методий, 1970.

380 p. 30 cm.

At head of title: Г. И. Чернявский, П. С. Сохань.

Kŭnchev, Stefan I
Българо-немски културни отношения. 1806–1966. Библиогр. (Израб. от. Стефан Кънчев и Траян Радев. Ред. Стефан Ив. Станчев). София, Нар. библ. Кирил и Методий, 1968.

222 p. 30 cm.
At head of title: Народна библиотека "Кирил и Методий."
Added t. p.: Bulgarisch-deutsche Kulturbeziehungen.
Summary in German.

Pundeff, Marin V
Bulgaria; a bibliographic guide, by Marin V. Pundeff. Washington, Slavic and Central European Division, Reference Department, Library of Congress; ₁for sale by the Superintendent of Documents, U. S. Govt. Print. Off.₁ 1965.

ix, 98 p. 26 cm.

Pundeff, Marin V
Bulgaria; a bibliographic guide, by Marin V. Pundeff. Washington, Slavic and Central European Division, Library of Congress, 1965. New York, Arno Press, 1968.

ix, 98 p. 27 cm.

Решенията на Юлския пленум в действие. Библиогр. Ред. Велчо Ковачев. София, БКП, 1970.

112 p. 20 cm.

Compiled by P. Drŭgmedzhieva and others.

Szolginiowa, Wanda.
Bułgaria w piśmiennictwie polskim, 1944–1963. Warszawa, 1965.

216 p. 21 cm. (Prace Instytutu Bibliograficznego, nr. 5)

Preface also in Bulgarian and English.

Traikov, Veselin Nikolov, 1921–
България в чуждата литература 1954–1963; библиографски указател. София, 1965.

219 p. 24 cm. (Поредица "Булгарика")

At head of title: Народна библиотека "Кирил и Методий." Веселин Трайков.

HISTORY

Drŭgmedzhieva, Petía Trifonova.
90 години от освобождението на България от османско иго; библиография. ₁Съставила Петя Т. Дюгмеджиева. Редактор Бонка Тодорова Петкова₁ София, 1968.

86 p. 21 cm.

At head of title: Народна библиотека "Кирил и Методий."

Plovdiv, Bulgaria. Narodna biblioteka "Ivan Vazov."
Дейци от Пловдивския край загинали в антифашистката борба, 1923–1944 год: библиографски указател. ₁Изработила Славка Г. Ломева₁ Пловдив, 1964.

121 p. 20 cm.

At head of title: Народна библиотека "Иван Вазов," Пловдив. Справочно-библиографски и информационен отдел.

Raikov, Bozhidar Nikolov.
(Aprilskoto vŭstanie, otrazeno v bŭlgarskiîa i chuzhdiîa periodichen pechat ot 1876 g.)
Априлското въстание, отразено в българския и чуждия периодичен печат от 1876 г. Библиогр. (Ред. К. Възвъзова и Ан. Вълчева. Съставител Божидар Райков). ₁Т.₁ 1–   София, Нар. библ. кирил и Методий, 1973–
v. 25 cm. 2.33 lv (v. 1)
At head of title: Народна библиотека "Кирил и Методий."
Added t. p.: The April uprising as reported by the Bulgarian and foreign press in 1876.
Prefatory matter also in English.

(Septemvriiskoto narodno antifashistko vŭstanie)
Септемврийското народно антифашистко въстание—1923

г. Библиогр. (Под ред. на Велчо Ковачев). София, Партиздат, 1973.

431 p. 20.5 cm.

Cover title: Септември 1923.
By P. T. Dîugmedzhieva and others.

Sofia. Narodna biblioteka.
Априлско въстание 1876 г.; препоръчителна библиография по случай 90-годишнината на въстанието. ₁Шиляна Аврамова и др.₎ София, 1966.

90 p. illus., facsims., ports. 24 cm.

At head of title: Народна библиотека "Кирил и Методий." Градска библиотека, София.

Sofia. Narodna biblioteka.
(Khiliada i trista godini Bŭlgariîa)
1300 години България. Темат. препоръч. библиогр. (Ред. Анелия Вълчева и Крумка Шарова). София, Нар. библ. Кирил и Методий, 1973.

365 p. 24.5 cm.

By G. G. Draganov and others.

LAW see Law - Bulgaria

BULGARIAN IMPRINTS

Български книгопис. 1969–
София, Народна библиотека "Кирил и Методий."

v. 28 cm.

"Годишен указател на българските книги, нотни, графически и картографически издания."

BIBLIOGRAPHIES

Petkova, Zornitsa Malcheva.
(Bibliografiîa na bŭlgarskata bibliografiîa. 1944–1969)
Библиография на българската библиография. 1944–1969. (Израб. Зорница Малчева Петкова). София, Нар. библ. Кирил и Методий, 1971.

603 p. 20 cm.

BULGARIAN LANGUAGE AND LITERATURE

Bulgarian books; International Book Fair, Cairo, 1970. ₁Sofia₎ Hemus; Balgarska Kniga ₁1970?₎

46 p. illus. 21 cm.

Български писатели–69; юбилейно издание. ₁Редактор Григор Григоров. Съставители Тодор Янчев, Иван Сарандев₎ София, Българска книга, 1969.

178 p. illus., ports. 21 cm.

Dîugmedzhieva, Petîa Trifonova.
Младият герой в съвременната българска литература; материали в помощ на библиотекарите, комсомолските дружества и книгоразпространителите. ₁Съставители П. Дюгмеджиева, П. Едрева, Л. Тодорова. Редактор И. Василев₎ София, Наука и изкуство, 1967.

102 p. 20 cm. (pbk.)
At head of title: Централен организационен комитет. Национална читателска конференция.

Dîugmedzhieva, Petîa Trifonova.
(Sŭvremenni bŭlgarski pisateli)
Съвременни български писатели. Препоръч. библиогр. (Ред. Любен Георгиев). (София) Нар. библ. Кирил и Методий (1972).

312 p. 25 cm.

At head of title: Централен комитет на Профсъюза на работниците от полиграфическата промишленост и културните институти. Секция за библиотекарите.
By P. Dîugmedzhieva, A. Karadzhova and S. Angelov.

Gerlinghoff, Peter.
Bibliographische Einführung in das Studium der neueren bulgarischen Literatur. ⟨1850–1950.⟩ Meisenheim am Glan, Hain, 1969.

108 p. 23 cm.

International book fair Cairo '72; Bulgarian books. ₁Sofia, Hemus, 1972₎

41 p. 16 x 23 cm.

Ivanov, Stefan Krumov.
Антифашистката борба на българския народ, отразена в художествената и мемоарната литература; препоръчителна библиография. София, Наука и изкуство, 1964.

89 p. 20 cm.

At head of title: Стефан Иванов, Петя Дюгмеджиева.

Ivanova, Liliîana.
(Bŭlgarski ezik i literatura)
Български език и литература. Препоръч. библиогр. в помощ на учителите по бълг. език и литература. ₁С предг. от София Филипова₎. София, Нар. библ. Кирил и Методий и др., 1973.

392 p. 29 cm.

At head of title: Народна библиотека "Кирил и Методий." Окръжна библиотека—гр. Ловеч.

Kîurkchieva, Elena.
Алманах ₁на издателство₎ "Български писател." 1948–1968. (Библиогр. Израб. Елена Кюркчиева и Елена Огнянова) (София, Бълг. писател) ₁1971₎

192 p. with facsims. 29 cm.

Krŭsteva, Ivanka.
Поети и писатели, родени в Михайловградски окръг; библиография. ₁Изработили: Иванка Кръстева, Венета Ряхова₎. Михайловград, 1968.

79 p. ports. 20 cm.

At head of title: Окръжна методична библиотека.

TRANSLATIONS

Dîugmedzhieva, Petîa Trifonova.
(Chuzhdestranni pisateli na bŭlgarski ezik)
Чуждестранни писатели на български език. 1945–1971. Био-библиогр. указател. (Състав. П. Дюгмеджиева и Ст. Иванов. Ред. ₁с предг.₎ Венко Христов). София, Нар. библ. Кирил и Методий, 1973.

812 p. 24 cm.
At head of title: Народна библиотека "Кирил и Методий." Централен комитет на Профсъюза на работниците от полиграфическата промишленост и културните институти. Секция на библиотекарите.

Nicoloff, Assen.
Bulgarian folklore and fine literature translated into English, French and German; a selected bio-bibliography, by Assen Niciloff. Cleveland, 1971.

79 p. 29 cm.

Oreshkova, Zdravka P
Съветска художествена литература в България, 1955–1965; биобиблиографический справочник. София, Нар. библиотека "Кирил и Методий," 1967.

505 p. 20 cm.
At head of title: Здравка Орешкова, Стефан Кънчев, Сийка

Танчева.
On cover: Народна библиотека "Кирил и Методий."

Traĭkov, Veselin Nikolov, 1921–
Българска художествена литература на чужди езици; библиографски указател, 1823–1962. София, Наука и изкуство, 1964.

378 p. illus., facsims. 25 cm.

At head of title: Български библиографски институт "Елин Пелин." Веселин Трайков.

BŬLGARSKA AKADEMIIÂ NA NAUKITE, SOFIA

Mishaĭkov, Ivan.
100 years Bulgarian academic books, 1869–1968; catalogue of the books and periodicals of the Bulgarian Academy of Agricultural Sciences in Bulgaria. ₍Compiled by: Ivan Mishaĭkov and Yordan Hristov. Ed. Kiril Manov₎. Sofia, Pub. House of the Bulgarian Academy of Sciences, 1969.

184 p. 20 cm.

Mishaĭkov, Ivan.
100 години българска академична книга. 1869–1968. Каталог на изданията и списанията на БАН и на АСН в България. (Състав. Иван Мишайков и Йордан Христов. Ред. Кирил Манов.) София, БАН, 1969.

192 p. 20 cm.

BULLFIGHTING

Carmena y Millán, Luis, 1845–1903.
Tauromáquia. Apuntes bibliográficos ... (Apéndice a la Bibliografía de la tauromáquia) Madrid, Imp. de José M. Ducazcal, 1888. ₍Madrid, Unión de Bibliófilos Taurinos, 1971₎

68 p. 27 cm.

"Doscientos ejemplares, numerados del 1 al 200 y nominados, y diez ejemplares sin nominar ni numerar ... Ejemplar no. 20."

BULMER, WILLIAM

Isaac, Peter Charles Gerald.
A second checklist of books, pamphlets and periodicals printed by William Bulmer ₍compiled by Peter C. G. Isaac₎ Wylam, Allenholme Press, 1973.

₍1₎, 39 leaves. 30 cm.

BULST, WALTHER

Düchting, Reinhard.
Bibliographie Walther Bulst. (Walther Bulst zum 70. Geburtstag. ₍Von₎ Reinhard Düchting ₍und₎ Wolfgang Wiemann.) Heidelberg, L. Schneider, 1969.

29 p. with port. 24 cm.

BUNYAN, JOHN

Greaves, Richard L
An annotated bibliography of John Bunyan studies, compiled by Richard L. Greaves. Pittsburgh, Pa., Clifford E. Barbour Library, Pittsburgh Theological Seminary ₍1972₎

84 p. 28 cm. (Bibliographia tripotamopolitana, no. 5)

Tibbutt, H   G
Bunyan's standing to-day, by H. G. Tibbutt. ₍Elstow, Eng.₎ Elstow Moot Hall, 1966.

26 p. 21 cm. (Elstow Moot Hall. Leaflet 8)

BURGOS, SPAIN

Mansilla, Reoyo, Demetrio.
Catálogo documental del archivo Catedral de Burgos (804–1416) ... Madrid, etc. ₍Consejo Superior de Investigaciones Científicas. Instituto "Enrique Flórez"₎ 1971.

5 l., 585 p. 26 cm. (Monumenta hispaniae sacra. Subsidia: v. 2)

BURGSTEINFURT

Fürstliches Archiv zu Burgsteinfurt.
Inventar des Fürstlichen Archivs zu Burgsteinfurt, bearb. von Alfred Bruns und Wilhelm Kohl. Hrsg. von Alfred Bruns. Münster Westf., Aschendorff ₍1971–
v. illus., fold map. 24 cm. (Inventare der nichtstattlichen Archive Westfalens, n. F., Bd. 5
Also issued as v. 73 of Das Bentheimer Land.
CONTENTS: A Allgemeine Regierungssachen der Grafschaften Bentheim und Steinfurt.

BURIAT LANGUAGE

Dugarov, Nima Budaevich.
Библиография литературы по бурятскому языкознанию. Составитель Н. Б. Дугаров. Улан-Удэ, 1964.

164 p. 20 cm.

At head of title: Академия наук СССР. Сибирское отделение. Бурятский комплексный научно-исследовательский институт.

BURIAT-MONGOLIA

Buriat A. S. S. R. Respublikanskaiâ biblioteka.
Литература о Бурятской АССР. Рек. указатель. Улан-Удэ, Бурят. кн. изд., 1968.

227 p. 20 cm.

At head of title: Республиканская библиотека Бурятской АССР им. М. Горького.
By R. B. Azheeva and others.

BURIATS   see under   Mongolia

BURKE, EDMUND

Todd, William Burton.
A bibliography of Edmund Burke ₍by₎ William B. Todd. London, Hart-Davis, 1964.

312 p. facsims., port. 23 cm. (The Soho bibliographies, 17)

BURMA

Bernot, Denise.
Bibliographie birmane, années 1950–1960 ... Paris, Éditions du Centre national de la recherche scientifique, 1968.

231 p. 27 cm. (Atlas ethno-linguistique. 3. série: Bibliographies)

Trager, Frank N
Burma: a selected and annotated bibliography ₍by₎ Frank N. Trager, with the assistance of Janelle Wang ₍and others₎ New Haven, Human Relations Area Files Press, 1973.

xii, 356 p. 22 cm. (Behavior science bibliographies)

Edition of 1956 prepared by the Burma Research Project of New York University and published under title: Annotated bibliography of Burma.

Whitbread, Kenneth.
Catalogue of Burmese printed books in the India Office Library. London, H. M. Stationery Off., 1969.

xi, 231 p. 25 cm.

At head of title: Foreign and Commonwealth Office.

BURNEY FAMILY

Hemlow, Joyce.
A catalogue of the Burney family correspondence, 1749-1878, by Joyce Hemlow, with Jeanne M. Burgess and Althea Douglas. New York, New York Public Library [1971]

xxix, 458 p. illus. 27 cm.

BURNS

Feller, Irving, 1925-
International bibliography on burns; for better patient care, research, and teaching. [Ann Arbor, Mich., American Burn Research Corp., 1969]

xxi, 341 p. 29 cm.

———— 1970- supplement. [Ann Arbor, Mich., American Burn Research Corp., 1970-

v. 28 cm.

BURNS, ROBERT

Egerer, J   W
A bibliography of Robert Burns [by] J. W. Egerer. Edinburgh, Oliver & Boyd, 1964.

xiii, 396 p. 23 cm.

Egerer, J   W
A bibliography of Robert Burns [by] J. W. Egerer. Carbondale, Ill., Southern Illinois University Press [1965, °1964]

xiii, 396 p. 23 cm.

Ross, John Dawson, 1853-1939.
The story of the Kilmarnock Burns. Stirling [Scot.] E. Mackay, 1933. [New York, AMS Press, 1973]

89 p. facsim. 19 cm.

Roy, George Ross, 1924-
Robert Burns; an exhibition, February 1971. Catalogue and introductory note by G. Ross Roy. DeKalb, Swen Franklin Parson Library, Northern Illinois University [1971]

viii, 51 p. facsims. 24 cm.

BURR, AARON

Tompkins, Hamilton Bullock, 1843-1921.
Burr bibliography; a list of books relating to Aaron Burr. New York, B. Franklin [1970]

89 p. 23 cm. (Burt Franklin bibliography & reference series, 316)

On spine: A bibliography of Aaron Burr.
Reprint of the 1892 ed.

Tompkins, Hamilton Bullock, 1843-1921.
Burr bibliography; a list of books relating to Aaron Burr. Brooklyn, Historical Print. Club, 1892. [New York, AMS Press, 1973]

47 p. 23 cm.

Wandell, Samuel Henry, 1860-1943.
Aaron Burr in literature; books, pamphlets, periodicals, and miscellany relating to Aaron Burr and his leading political contemporaries, with occasional excerpts from publications, bibliographical, critical, and historical notes, etc. Introd. by Walter F. McCaleb. Port Washington, N. Y., Kennikat Press [1972]

xx, 302 p. illus. 23 cm.
Reprint of the 1966 ed.

BURROUGHS, EDGAR RICE

Heins, Henry Hardy, 1923-
A golden anniversary bibliography of Edgar Rice Burroughs, compiled and edited by Henry Hardy Heins. Complete ed., rev. West Kingston, R. I., D. M. Grant, 1964.

418 p. illus., facsim., ports. 26 cm.

BURTON, SIR RICHARD FRANCIS

Penzer, Norman Mosley, 1892-
An annotated bibliography of Sir Richard Francis Burton, к. c. м. g., by Norman M. Penzer. Preface by F. Grenfell Baker. Reprinted. London, Dawsons of Pall Mall, 1967.

xvi, 351 p. illus. 22 cm.

Penzer, Norman Mosley, 1892-
An annotated bibliography of Sir Richard Francis Burton, by Norman M. Penzer. Pref. by F. Grenfell Baker. New York, B. Franklin [1970]

xvi, 351 p. illus., facsims., port. 24 cm. (Essays in literature & criticism, 66)

Burt Franklin bibliography & reference series, 337.
Reprint of the 1923 ed.

BURUNDI

Nahayo, Simon.
Contribution à la bibliographie des ouvrages re'atifs au Burundi ⟨Afrique centrale⟩. Genève, 1971.

iii, ix, 68 l. 30 cm.

"Travail présenté à l'Institut d'études sociales de Genève, École de bibliothécaires, en vue de l'obtention du diplôme."

BUS LANES

International Union of Public Transport.
Voies réservées aux autobus. Bus lanes. Busspuren. Bibliographie. Bruxelles, UITP, 1972.

24 l. 27 cm.

BUSHMAN LANGUAGES

Levy, Leah.
A preliminary list of publications referring to the non-Bantu Click languages. [Cape Town] Dept. of African Languages, School of African Studies, University of Cape Town, 1968.

21, [2], 14 l. 33 cm. (Communications from the School of African Studies. New series, no. 33)

BUSHMEN

Willet, Shelagh M.
The Bushman; a select bibliography, 1652-1962, by Shelagh M. Willet. Johannesburg, University of the Witwatersrand, Dept. of Bibliography, Librarianship and Typography, 1965.

ii, 37 l. 30 cm.

BUSINESS
see also Commerce; International business enterprises; Small business; and under Dissertations, Academic

Alexander, Raphael.

Business pamphlets and information sources; a guide to currently available pamphlets, reprints, and paperbacks in the field of business, and to organizations and government agencies which are sources of business information, arranged by subject. Edited by Raphael Alexander. New York, Exceptional Books [1967]

72 p. 23 cm.

Allen, David E *comp.*

Business books translated from English, 1950–1965, compiled by David E. Allen, Jr. Reading, Mass., Addison-Wesley Pub. Co. [1966]

xiv, 414 p. 29 cm.

Business books in print: subject index, author index, title index. 1973–

New York, R. R. Bowker, Co.

v. 29 cm.

California. University. University at Los Angeles. Graduate School of Business Administration. Division of Research.

Current business research, UCLA 1969–70; a survey of recent research. [Los Angeles, 1970]

69 p. 23 cm.

Cole, Arthur Harrison, 1889–

Measures of business change; a Baker Library index, by Arthur H. Cole, with the assistance of Virginia Jenness and Grace V. Lindfors. Westport, Conn., Greenwood Press [1974, c1952]

xii, 444 p. 23 cm.

Reprint of the ed. published by R. D. Irwin, Chicago.

Coman, Edwin Truman, 1903–

Sources of business information, by Edwin T. Coman, Jr. Rev. ed. Berkeley, University of California Press, 1964.

xii, 330 p. 24 cm. (University of California bibliographic guides)

Executive's guide to information sources; a detailed listing for management personnel of 2,300 business and business-related subjects, with a record of periodicals, organizations, bureaus, directories, bibliographies, and other sources concerned with each topic. Detroit, Gale Research Co. [°1965]

3 v. (2467 p.) 23 cm.

Galambos, Louis.

American business history. Washington, Service Center for Teachers of History [°1967]

32 p. 23 cm. (Service Center for Teachers of History. Publication no. 70)

Georgia State University. Bureau of Business and Economic Research.

Report of publications by the faculty of the School of Business Administration, Georgia State University. 1970/71–

[Atlanta]

v. 23 cm.

Harvard University. *Graduate School of Business Administration. Baker Library.*

Business literature: an annotated list for students and businessmen. [Boston] 1968.

139 p. 23 cm. (*Its* Reference list, no. 25)

"A revision of References list no. 17."
First published in 1947 under title: Textbooks in the field of business (Reference list no. 1); 1952, 1955, and 1959 editions under title: Business literature: a reading list for students and businessmen (Reference list no. 17)

Harvard University. Graduate School of Business Administration. Baker Library.

Business reference sources; an annotated guide for Harvard Business School students. Lorna M. Daniells, compiler. [Boston] 1971.

108 p. 23 cm. (**Its** Reference list no. 27)

1963 ed. published under title: Selected reference sources; 1965 ed. under title: Selected business reference sources.

Harvard University. *Graduate School of Business Administration. Baker Library.*

Selected business reference sources. [Boston] 1965.

72 p. 23 cm. (*Its* Reference list, no. 24)

Hollander, Stanley C 1919–

Management consultants and clients, compiled by Stanley C. Hollander with the assistance of Stephen R. Flaster. East Lansing, Division of Research, Graduate School of Business Administration, Michigan State University, 1972.

xxii, 541 p. 24 cm. (MSU business studies)

First ed. published in 1963 under title: Business consultants and clients.

Inoue, Hitoshi, 1933–

(Kaigai kigyō jōhō no tebiki)

海外企業情報の手引き 井上如, 河島正光著

東京 日本経済新聞社 昭和45(1970)

191p 18cm (日経文庫)

Janezeck, Elizabeth G

Basic library reference sources for business use, by Elizabeth G. Janezeck. Washington, Small Business Administration, 1966.

8 p. 26 cm. (Small business bibliography no. 18)

Janezeck, Elizabeth G

Basic library reference sources [by Elizabeth G. Janezeck. Rev.] Washington, Small Business Administration [1970]

11 p. 26 cm. (Small business bibliography no. 18)

Issued in 1966 under title: Basic library reference sources for business use.

Schreier, James W

The entrepreneur and new enterprise formation; resource guide [compiled by James W. Schreier and John L. Komives. Milwaukee, Center for Venture Management] 1973.

xxiii, 193 p. 28 cm.

An updated, expanded version of The entrepreneur and new enterprise formation, by E. E. Anderson and J. L. Komives.

A Selected list of books and periodicals in the field of business. [1st]– ed.; 1966–

East Lansing, Bureau of Business and Economic Research, Graduate School of Business Administration, Michigan State University.

v. 23 cm. biennial.

Compiler: 1966– W. S. Stoddard.

Sources on business topics. no. 1–

Minneapolis, Graduate School of Business Administration, University of Minnesota, 1965–

no. 23 cm.

Trejo, Arnulfo D
Bibliografía comentada sobre administración de negocios
y disciplinas conexas, con un directorio descriptivo de al-
gunas instituciones importantes en la especialidad, por
Arnulfo D. Trejo, con la colaboración de Erlinda Chávez
Barriga ⌈y⌉ Isabel Olivera Rivarola. Prólogo: Alan B.
Coleman. ⌈México⌉ Centro Regional de Ayuda Técnica-
México, Agencia para el Desarrollo Internacional ⌈1964⌉
xvi, 155 p. 23 cm.

Trejo, Arnulfo D
Bibliografía comentada sobre administración de negocios
y disciplinas conexas; con un directorio descriptivo de algunas instituciones importantes en la especialidad, por
Arnulfo D. Trejo. Con la colaboración de Erlinda Chávez
Barriga. Prólogo de Alan B. Coleman. ⌈2. ed., aumentada
y corr.⌉ Reading Mass., Addison-Wesley Pub. Co. ⌈1967⌉
xxi, 232 p. 24 cm. (Administración de empresas)

Vaisto, Erkki.
Suomen liiketaloustieteellinen kirjallisuus 1971. Business
literature in Finland 1971. Helsinki, Kauppakorkeakoulun
Kirjasto, 1972.
⌈iii⌉, 10 p. 30 cm. (Kauppakorkeakoulun kirjaston julkaisuja. 4)

English and Finnish.

Wade-Cochran, Julienne.
A guide to library materials for business research: indexes, periodicals, references. ⌈University ed.⌉ Editorial
review-board: Henry R. Anderson ⌈and others⌉ Don W.
Arnold, editor. DeKalb, Ill., Consortium for Applied Research and Development ⌈1971⌉
73 l. 28 cm.

Washington (State) University. *Graduate School of Business Administration.*
List of publications. Seattle ⌈1968⌉
ii, 15 p. forms. 28 cm. (*Its* Occasional paper, 18)

Young (Arthur) and Company.
Sources of world tax & business information. Edited
by H. Bartlett Brown. Rev. ed. ⌈New York⌉ 1968.
vi, 74 p. 23 cm.

Ziegler, Maria.
Spezialliteratur über Konjunkturumfragen. ⟨A bibliography about business surveys⟩ Zusammengestellt von
M⌈aria⌉ Ziegler. (München, Ifo-Inst. f. Wirtschaftsforschung, CIRET-Informations- u. Dokumentationszentrum)
1968.
xii, 152 l. 30 cm. (CIRET-Studien, Nr. 10)

Introduction also in English.

LIBRARY CATALOGS

**Harvard University. Graduate School of Business Admin-
istration. Baker Library.**
Subject catalog of the Baker Library, Graduate School of
Business Administration, Harvard University. Boston,
G. K. Hall, 1971.
10 v. 37 cm.

PERIODICALS

Directories International, inc.
Business media guide international: Africa & Middle East
edition. Editor: Christine G. Levite. Evanston, Ill., 1973.

1 v. (various pagings) illus. 28 cm.
On spine: Business media: Africa & Middle East.

Directories International, inc.
Business media guide international: Asia & Russia edition. Editor: Christine G. Levite. Evanston, Ill., 1973.
1 v. (various pagings) illus. 29 cm.
On spine: Business media: Asia & Russia.

Directories International, inc.
Business media guide international: Europe edition. Editor: Kathleen C. Parrin. Evanston, Ill., 1973–
v. illus. 29 cm.
On spine: Business media: Europe.

**Harvard University. Graduate School of Business Admin-
istration. Baker Library.**
Current periodical publications in Baker Library. 1971/
72–
⌈Boston⌉
v. 28 cm. annual.
Supersedes its Current journals in Baker Library.

Ledbetter, William.
A directory of American business periodicals / William
Ledbetter, L. W. Denton. — Columbus, Ohio : Grid, inc.,
⌈1974⌉
iii, 167 p. ; 28 cm.

Research index.
⌈Wallington, Eng.⌉ Business Surveys ltd.
v. in 36 cm. biweekly.
"A comprehensive reference to articles and news items of financial
interest."
Began in Aug. 1965. Cf. Brit. nat. bibl., 1965.

BUSINESS EDUCATION

Business and office education: instructional materials; ⌈final
report⌉ Columbus, Center for Vocational and Technical
Education, Ohio State University; for sale by the Supt. of
Docs., U. S. Govt. Print. Off., Washington, 1972.
viii, 117 p. 28 cm. (⌈Ohio. State University, Columbus. Center
for Vocational and Technical Education⌉ Bibliography series no. 9)
"A compilation of abstracts from Abstracts of instructional materials in vocational and technical education, 1967–1971."

**Harvard University. Graduate School of Business Ad-
ministration.**
Bibliography, cases, and other materials for the teaching
of business administration in developing countries: Africa
and the Middle East. Andrew R. Towl, director of project: Grace V. Lindfors, editor. Boston, 1969.
vii, 456 p. 28 cm.

Harvard University. *Graduate School of Business Administration.*
Bibliography, cases and other materials for the teaching
of business administration in developing countries: Latin
America. Andrew R. Towl, director of project. Ruth C.
Hetherston, editor. Boston, 1966.
xv, 366 p. 28 cm.

Harvard University. *Graduate School of Business Administration.*
Bibliography, cases and other materials for the teaching

of business administration in developing countries: South and Southeast Asia. Andrew R. Towl, director of project; Grace V. Lindfors, editor. Boston, 1968.

viii, 408 p. form. 28 cm.

Harvard University. *Graduate School of Business Administration.*
Bibliography, cases, and other materials for the teaching of business administration in developing countries; comparative index. Grace V. Lindfors, editor; Charles N. Gebhard, computer analyst; Andrew R. Towl, director of project. Boston, 1969.

xxi, 328 p. 28 cm.

On spine: Developing countries; comparative index.
Index to three publications published under the general title: Bibliography, cases, and other materials for the teaching of business administration in developing countries—Latin America, 1966; South and Southeast Asia, 1968; and Africa and the Middle East, 1969.

Harvard University. *Graduate School of Business Administration.*
Bibliography, cases and other materials for the teaching of multinational business. Harvey P. Bishop: director of project. Grace V. Lindfors: editor. Boston, 1964.

xi, 283 p. 28 cm.

Ohio. State University, Columbus. Center for Vocational and Technical Education.
Distributive education; instructional materials. A compilation of abstracts from Abstracts of instructional materials in vocational and technical education, 1967–1971. Columbus; For sale by the Supt. of Docs., U. S. Govt. Print. Off., Washington, 1972.

viii, 140 p. 28 cm. (Its Bibliography series no. 10)

Rahe, Harves, 1914–
Accounting-bookkeeping-recordkeeping research index; a comprehensive list of research studies in the teaching of accounting, bookkeeping, and recordkeeping from 1923 to 1966. New York, Gregg Division, McGraw-Hill [°1967]

v, 46 p. 23 cm.

BUSINESS ETHICS

Atkins, John Leslie.
Industrial espionage and trade secrets: a bibliography; ed. by J. L. Atkins. Coventry, Cadig Liaison Centre 1972.

[4], 17 leaves. 30 cm.

Christian, Portia, 1908–
Ethics in business conduct: selected references from the record—problems, attempted solutions, ethics in business education [by] Portia Christian with Richard Hicks. Detroit, Gale Research Co. [°1970]

156 p. 23 cm. (Management information guide, 21)

Cover title: Ethics in business conduct; a guide to information sources.

Popielarz, Donald T
Ethics in business; an annotated bibliography, prepared by Donald T. Popielarz under the supervision of Robert J. Holloway. Minneapolis, Graduate School of Business Administration, University of Minnesota, 1965, °1966.

12 p. 23 cm. (Sources on business topics, no. 1)

Van Vlack, Philip W
Economic ethics bibliography; ethical studies [by Philip W. Van Vlack, Charles L. Sewrey and Charles E. Nielsen] Brookings, S. D., Economics Dept., Agricultural Experiment Station, 1964.

104 p. 23 cm. ([South Dakota. Agricultural Experiment Station, Brookings] Bulletin 524)

BUSINESS FORECASTING see Economic forecasting

BUSTAMANTE, CARLOS MARIA DE

O'Gorman, Edmundo, 1906–
Guía bibliográfica de Carlos María de Bustamante. Trabajo realizado por el Seminario de Historiografía de la Facultad de Filosofía y Letras, bajo la dirección del doctor Edmundo O'Gorman . [1. ed.] México, Centro de Estudios de Historia de México, 1967.

277 p. 23 cm.

At head of title: Universidad Nacional Autónoma de México.

BUTLER, SAMUEL

Harkness, Stanley Bates.
The career of Samuel Butler, 1835–1902; a bibliography, by Stanley B. Harkness. New York, B. Franklin [1968]

154 p. 32 cm. (Burt Franklin bibliography & reference series, 111)

Reprint of the 1955 ed.

Hoppé, A   J
A bibliography of the writings of Samuel Butler (author of "Erewhon") and of writings about him, by A. J. Hoppé. With some letters from Samuel Butler to F. G. Fleay, now first published. New York, B. Franklin [1968]

xv, 184 p. facsims. 24 cm. (Burt Franklin: bibliography and reference series 178)

Originally published 1925.

BUTTERFLIES

Field, William Dewitt, 1914–
A bibliography of the catalogs, lists, faunal and other papers on the butterflies of North America north of Mexico arranged by state and province (Lepidoptera: Rhopalocera) [by] William D. Field, Cyril F. dos Passos, and John H. Masters. Washington, Smithsonian Institution Press; [for sale by the Supt. of Docs., U.S. Govt. Print. Off.] 1974.

104 p. 26 cm. (Smithsonian contributions to zoology, no. 157)

BUXTON, CLARENCE EDWARD VICTOR

Oxford. University. Rhodes House Library.
Papers of C. E. V. Buxton; Mss Brit. Emp. s 390. [Prepared by P. A. Empson. Oxford?, 1972?]

33 l. 26 cm.

At head of title: Oxford University colonial records project.

BYELORUSSIA see White Russia

BYKOVS'KYĬ, LEV

Bykovs'kyĭ, Lev.
(U sluzhbakh ukraïns'kiĭ knyzhtsi)
У службах українській книжці; біо-бібліографія.
Денвер, Колорадо, 1972.

275 p. illus. 28 cm.

At head of title: Український бібліологічний інститут.
Added t. p.: My life and works.

BYNNER, WITTER

Lindsay, Robert O
Witter Bynner; a bibliography, by Robert O. Lindsay.
Albuquerque, University of New Mexico Press, 1967.

viii, 112 p. 23 cm. (University of New Mexico publications. Library series, no. 2)

BYRON, GEORGE GORDON NOËL BYRON, BARON

Carl H. Pforzheimer Library, New York.
Byron on the continent; a memorial exhibition, 1824–1974, February–April 1974. [New York, 1974]

85 p. 23 cm.

Catalog of an exhibition sponsored by the Pforzheimer Library and New York Public Library and held at the latter.

First Edition Club, London.
Bibliographical catalogue of first editions, proof copies & manuscripts of books by Lord Byron, exhibited at the fourth exhibition held by the First Edition Club, January 1925. [Folcroft, Pa.] Folcroft Library Editions, 1974.

xvii, 97 p. facsims. 29 cm.

Reprint of the 1925 ed. printed for the First Edition Club, London.

BYZANTINE STUDIES

Československá akademie věd. *Ústav dějin evropských socialistických zemí.*
Bibliografie československé byzantologie. Praha, 1966.

2 v. (x, 367 p.) 20 cm. (Bibliografické příručky, sv. 1–2)

Cover title: Bibliographie de la byzantinologie tchécoslovaque (y compris les travaux des byzantinistes étrangers actifs en Tchécoslovaquie)

Lemerle, Paul Émile, 1903–
Titres et travaux de Paul Émile Lemerle. Limoges, impr. A. Bontemps, 1966.

24 p. 24 cm.

Additions and corrections in MS.

PERIODICALS

London. University. *Institute of Classical Studies.*
A survey of periodicals relevant to Byzantine studies in several London libraries. London, University of London (Institute of Classical Studies) 1968.

xi, 20 p. 28 cm.

C

CABELL, JAMES BRANCH

Brewer, Frances Joan.
James Branch Cabell; a bibliography of his writings, biography and criticism. With a foreword by James Branch Cabell. Freeport, N. Y., Books for Libraries Press [1971, ⁰1957]

206 p. 23 cm.

Holt, Guy, 1892–1934.
A bibliography of the writings of James Branch Cabell. Folcroft, Pa., Folcroft Press [1969]

73 p. port. 22 cm.

Reprint of the 1924 ed., which was issued as no. 3 of The Centaur bibliographies of modern American authors.

Holt, Guy, 1892–1934.
A bibliography of the writings of James Branch Cabell. Philadelphia. Centaur Book Shop, 1924. New York, Haskell House Publishers, 1972.

73 p. port. 23 cm.

Original ed. issued as no. 3 of The Centaur bibliographies of modern American authors.

CABOT, JOHN and SEBASTIAN

Winship, George Parker, 1871–1952.
Cabot bibliography, with an introductory essay on the careers of the Cabots based upon an independent examination of the sources of information. New York, B. Franklin [1967]

iii, 180 p. 22 cm. (Burt Franklin bibliographical and reference series, #99)

American classics in history and social science, #14. Reprint of the 1900 ed.

CABRAL, PEDRO ALVARES

Rio de Janeiro. Biblioteca Nacional.
v [i. e. Quinto] centenário do nascimento de Pedro Alvares Cabral, 1468–1968, exposição comemorativa. Rio de Janeiro, 1968.

48 p. illus., ports. 24 cm.

"Organizada com a colaboração do Instituto Histórico e Geográfico Brasileiro e do Ministério das Relações Exteriores."

CADDIS-FLIES

Fischer, F   C   J
Trichopterorum catalogus, by F. C. J. Fischer. Amsterdam, Nederlandsche Entomologische Vereeniging, 1966–

v. 24 cm.

CONTENTS.

v. 7. Leptoceridae, Pars 2.

CADMIUM

Water Resources Scientific Information Center.
Cadmium in water; a bibliography. Washington [1973]

iv, 231 p. 27 cm. (Its Bibliography series, WRSIC 73–209)

CAIRO

Zakī, 'Abd al-Raḥmān.
مراجع تاريخ القاهرة منذ انشائها الى اليوم [تاليف] عبـد الرحمن زكى. القاهرة، الجمعية الجغرافية المصرية، 1964.

19, 21 p. 24 cm.

Added t. p.: A bibliography of the literature of the city of Cairo. Includes publications in Arabic and Western languages.

CAIRO. JĀMI'AT AL-QĀHIRAH. KULLĪYAT AL-ĀDĀB

Cairo. Jāmi'at al-Qāhirah. *Kulliyat al-Ādāb.*
الرسائل العلمية لدرجتى الماجستير والدكـــتوراه، 1932 – 1966. [الجيزة] مطبعة جامعة القاهرة، 1967.

86 p. 26 cm.

CALABRIA

Borretti, Mario.
Contributo per una bibliografia storica calabrese (1945–1964). Cosenza, MIT, 1968.

343 p. 24 cm.

Cardi, Luigi.
Calabria. A cura di Luigi Cardi. Napoli, Tip. La buona stampa, 1970.

211 p.; table nserted. 21½ cm. (Collana di bibliografie geografiche delle regioni Italiane, v. 14)

At head of title: Consiglio nazionale delle ricerche. Comitato per le scienze storiche, filologiche e filosofiche.

Mazzoleni, Jole.
Fonti per la storia della Calabria nel Viceregno (1503–1734) esistenti nell'Archivio di stato di Napoli. Napoli, EDISUD. 1968.

452 p. 25 cm.

Zavarroni, Angelo, 1710–1767.
Bibliotheca calabra. [Di] Angelo Zavarrone. Bologna, Forni, 1967.

232 p. 22 cm.

Facsim. of the Naples, 1753 ed.

CALDERÓN DE LA BARCA, PEDRO

Calderón de la Barca studies, 1951–69; a critical survey and annotated bibliography. [General editors: Jack H. Parker and Arthur M. Fox. Toronto] University of Toronto Press [1971]

xiii, 247 p. 26 cm.

"A project of the Research Committee of Spanish Group Three of the Modern Language Association of America."

CALENDAR, ROMANIAN

Dunăreanu, Elena.
Calendarele românești sibiene (1793–1970). Sibiu, 1970.

340 p., 35 l. of facsims. 24 cm.

At head of title: Biblioteca „Astra" Sibiu.
"Lucrare elaborată în cadrul Serviciului de Informare Bibliografică."

CALENDARS   see Almanacs

CALIFORNIA
see also Baja California and under
Oregon *(Southern Oregon)*

Cowan, Robert Ernest, 1862-1942.
A bibliography of the history of California, 1510-1930, by
Robert Ernest Cowan and Robert Granniss Cowan. San
Francisco, Printed by J. H. Nash, 1933-64.

4 v. (v, 926 p.) 30 cm.

Vol. 4, by R. G. Cowan, published in Los Angeles.

Edwards, Elza Ivan, 1897-
Desert voices; a descriptive bibliography, by E. I. Edwards.
With photos. and foreword by Harold O. Weight. Westport,
Conn., Greenwood Press [1973, c1958]

xxviii, 215 p. illus. 23 cm.

Reprint of the ed. published by Westernlore Press, Los Angeles.

Gaer, Joseph, 1897-   ed.
Bibliography of California literature: pre-gold rush
period. New York, B. Franklin [1970]

69 p. 22 cm. (Burt Franklin bibliography & reference, 389.
American classics in history and social science, 164)

Reprint of the 1935 ed.

Goodman, John Bartlett.
An annotated bibliography of California county histories:
the first one hundred-eleven years, 1855-1966, with introd.
and The first California county history. Los Angeles, 1966.

[2 v. (557 l.) facsims., maps. 29 cm.

Photo-copy of typescript with marginal manuscript notes, additions, and revisions.

CONTENTS.—v. 1. Alameda to Nevada.—v. 2. Orange to Yuba.

Heizer, Robert Fleming, 1915-
A bibliography of California archaeology. Compiled by Robert F. Heizer and Albert B. Elsasser, with the assistance of C.
William Clewlow, Jr. Berkeley, University of California, Dept.
of Anthropology, 1970.

ii, 78 p. 28 cm. (Contributions of the University of California Archaeological Research Facility, no. 6)

Leister, D   R
California politics and problems, 1964-1968; a selective
bibliography, by D. R. Leister. Berkeley, Institute of Governmental Studies, University of California, 1969.

33 l. 28 cm.

A supplement to California politics and problems, 1900-1963, by
David A. Leuthold, published in 1965.

Leuthold, David A
California politics and problems, 1900-1963; a selective
bibliography, by David A. Leuthold with the assistance of
William M. Reid and William Macauley. Berkeley, Institute of Governmental Studies, University of California,
1965.

vii, 64 p. 28 cm.

Revzan, Lawrence H
Sources of information relevant to California's water,
recreation, transportation, education, and housing pro-

grams, by Lawrence H. Revzan and J. Michael Kavanagh.
[Los Angeles, 1967]

130 l. 29 cm. (Institute of Government and Public Affairs, University of California, Los Angeles. MR-104)

Rocq, Margaret Miller.
California local history; a bibliography and union list of
library holdings, edited by Margaret Miller Rocq for the
California Library Association. 2d ed., rev. and enl. Stanford, Calif., Stanford University Press, 1970.

xv, 611 p. map. 29 cm.

1950 ed. compiled by the California Library Association.

Stoughton, Gertrude K
The books of California; an introduction to the history
and the heritage of this State as revealed in the collection
in the Pasadena Public Library assembled by Nellie May
Russ, by Gertrude K. Stoughton. Los Angeles, W. Ritchie
Press, 1968.

ix, 213 p. illus. 24 cm.

BIBLIOGRAPHIES

Weber, Francis J
A bibliography of California bibliographies, by Francis
J. Weber. Introd. by Doyce B. Nunis, Jr. Los Angeles,
W. Ritchie Press ['1968]

vii, 30 p. facsims. 24 cm.

Weber, Francis J
A select bibliographical guide to California history,
1863-1972. Compiled and annotated by Francis J. Weber.
Los Angeles, Dawson's Book Shop [1972]

ix, 89 p. 19 cm.

IMPRINTS

Conlan, Eileen M
A checklist of California imprints for the year 1870, with
a historical introduction, by Eileen M. Conlan. Washington, 1967.

vi, 150 l. 28 cm.

Thesis (M. s.)—Catholic University of America.
Typescript (carbon copy)

Drury, Clifford Merrill, 1897-
California imprints, 1846-1876, pertaining to social, educational, and religious subjects. A bibliography of 1099
titles: books, pamphlets, broadsides, periodicals, newspapers, and manuscripts; each described, annotated, and
located. [Glendale, Calif., Distributed for the author by
A. H. Clark Co.] 1970.

220 p. 25 cm.

Kidd, Deborah Dove.
A check list of California non-official imprints for the
year 1872, with a historical introduction. Washington,
1967.

iv, 172 l. 28 cm.

Thesis (M. s. L. s.)—Catholic University of America.

MAPS

California. *Dept. of Water Resources.*
Topographic mapping in California; [index. Sacra-
mento] 1965.

x, 154 p. fold. maps. 28 cm. (*Its* Bulletin no. 79-64)

"List[s] all maps produced on the standard quadrangle format by the U. S. Geological Survey and other agencies."
"Current as of January 1965."

Chapin, Edward L
A selected cartobibliography of Southern California, by Edward Lloyd Chapin, Jr. [Los Angeles?] 1950.

xix, 451 l. illus. 21 cm.

Thesis (M. A.)—U. C. L. A.

Tooley, Ronald Vere, 1898–
California as an island; a geographical misconception illustrated by 100 examples from 1625 to 1770, by R. V. Tooley. London, Map Collectors' Circle [1964]

28 p. maps. 25 cm. (Map collectors' series, no. 8)

CALIFORNIA. LEGISLATURE

California. *Legislature. Assembly. Legislative Reference Service.*
Bibliography of the California Legislature. Prepared at the request of the Assembly Committee on Elections and Reapportionment. Sacramento, 1965.

19 l. 28 cm.

California. State Library, Sacramento. Government Publications Section.
California legislative publications charts. Sacramento, 1965.

6, 16, 2 l. 28 cm.

"Based on material presented at two workshops conducted by the Government Publications Section of the California State Library in the Marin County Civic Center on March 1, 1965, and in the Burbank Public Library on March 15, 1965."

CALIFORNIA. STATE COLLEGE, SAN JOSE

California. State College, *San Jose. Library.*
San Jose State College faculty and staff bibliography to 1966. San Jose, 1967.

90 p. 27 cm. (*Its* Library bibliography series, no. 1)

"Designed to supplement the Faculty and staff bibliography, 1951–1962, which was edited by professor Robert Woodward."

CALIFORNIA. UNIVERSITY. CALIFORNIA ARCHAEOLOGICAL SURVEY

Heizer, Robert Fleming, 1915-
Check list and index to reports of the University of California Archaeological Survey, nos. 32 (1955) to 74 (1968); check list of contributions of the Archaeological Research Facility of the Department of Anthropology, nos. 1 (1965) to 14 (1972); other information on activities of the survey and facility, 1948-1972 [by] Robert F. Heizer. Berkeley [University of California] Archaeological Research Facility, 1972.

80 p. 28 cm. (Reports of the University of California Archaeological Survey, no. 75)

CALIFORNIA CONDOR

Rehfus, Ruth.
California condor (*Gymnogyps californianus*); the literature since 1900. Compiled by Ruth Rehfus. Washington, U. S. Dept. of the Interior, Dept. Library, 1968.

16 p. 28 cm. ([U. S. Dept. of the Interior. Library [Bibliography no. 7)

CALLAN, JOHN LANSING

U. S. *Library of Congress. Manuscript Division.*
John Lansing Callan, John Crittenden Watson; a register of their papers in the Library of Congress. Washington, Library of Congress, 1968.

6, 8 l. 26 cm.

"Naval Historical Foundation collection."

CALVADOS, FRANCE (DEPT.)

Calvados, *France (Dept.) Archives départementales.*
L'Activité industrielle et la vie ouvrière dans le Calvados sous le Second Empire, catalogue des documents exposés par le Service éducatif des Archives départementales du Calvados, Caen, 1965–1966. Caen, Centre régional de documentation pedagogique, 1965.

7 l. 27 cm. (Annales du Centre régional de documentation pédagogique de Caen)

Calvados, France (Dept.). Archives départementales.
Répertoire numérique de la sous-série 3 Q. Enregistrement 1790–1900, dressé par Serge de Poorter et François Hummel sous la direction de Gildas Bernard. Caen, Archives départementales, 1973.

237 p. 23 cm.

CAMALDOLITES

Ziegelbauer, Magnoald, 1689–1750.
Centifolium Camaldulense, sive notitia scriptorum Camaldulensium; quam ceu prodromum exceptura est bibliotheca patrum Camaldulensium seu operum ad historiam, disciplinam, et ascesin Sac. Ord. Camald. attinentium collectio tomis VI. Comprehensa; cujus bibliothecae, seu collectionis accurandae hic ad calcem praevius exhibetur conspectus auctore P. Magnoaldo Ziegelbaur. Farnborough (Hants.), Gregg P., 1967.
[10], 96 p. 33 cm.

CÁMARA DE COMERCIO, BOGOTÁ

Ramírez Vargas, María Teresa.
La Cámara de Comercio de Bogotá y sus publicaciones / por María Teresa Ramírez Vargas y Susan Casement. — [s. l. : s. n., 1974]

115 leaves ; 22 x 33 cm.

At head of title: Red Colombiana de Información y Documentación y Documentación Económica—II reunión, junio 20–28 de 1974 (RECIDE II–DE-no. 2)
English and Spanish.
Includes indexes.

CAMBODIA

Association des écrivains khmers. Bibliothèque.
Catalogue des auteurs et des livres publiés au Cambodge. v. 1–   1966–
Phnom-Penh.

v. 27 cm.

In French.

Fisher, Mary L
Cambodia: an annotated bibliography of its history, geography, politics, and economy since 1954 [by] Mary L. Fisher. [Cambridge, Mass.] Center for International Studies, Massachusetts Institute of Technology, 1967.

v, 66 p. 27 cm.

CAMDEN, ENGLAND

Lavell, Cherry.
Beginning in local history in Camden: a basic booklist; ₍compiled by Cherry Lovell for the Camden History Society₎. London, London Borough of Camden, Libraries and Arts Department, 1972.

₍3₎, 28 p. 21 cm.

CAMDEN SOCIETY, LONDON see under Royal Historical Society, London

CAMELIDAE

Cardozo Gonzáles, Armando.
Bibliografía de los camélidos ₍por₎ Armando Cardozo. ₍La Paz, Empresa Editora Universo₎ 1968.

35 p. 21 cm. (Estación Experimental Ganadera de Patacamaya. Boletín experimental, no. 32)

Cover title.
"Una edición revisada de la bibliografía aparecida en el libro Auquénidos."

CAMERON, JOHN

Swinne, Axel Hilmar.
John Cameron, Philosoph und Theologe (1579–1625); bibliographisch-kritische Analyse der Hand- und Druckschriften, sowie der Cameron-Literatur. Marburg, N. G. Elwert, 1968.

xi, 367 p. illus., facsims., port. 21 cm. (Schriften des Instituts für Wissenschaftliche Irenik der Johann Wolfgang Goethe Universität Frankfurt am Main, 1)

CAMEROON

Dippold, Max F
Une bibliographie du Cameroun; les écrits en langue allemande ₍par₎ Max F. Dippold. Préf. de M.-S. Eno Belinga. Burgau, Impr. O. Boeck, 1971.

xix, 343 p. 22 cm. (Publication de l'Institut de coopération sociale)

CAMÕES, LUIZ DE

Leitão, Ivany Souza.
Bibliografia camoniana do Centro de Cultura Portuguesa ₍por₎ Ivany Souza Leitão ₍e₎ Carlos Neves d'Alge. Fortaleza, Imprensa Universitária da Universidade Federal do Ceará, 1972.

62 p. 23 cm.

Martins, Antônio Coimbra.
IV ₍i. e. Cuarto₎ centenario de Os Lusíadas de Camões, 1572–1972. Exposición bibliográfica e iconográfica, Madrid 1972, 21 de noviembre–10 de diciembre. ₍Valencia, 1972₎

xxvi, 358 p. plates (part col.) 26 cm.

At head of title: Biblioteca Nacional de Madrid. Fundación Calouste Gulbenkian.

Martins, Antônio Coimbra.
Os Lusiadas van Camões. Vierhonderdste verjaring 1572–1972. (Tentoonstelling). Brussel, Koninklijke Bibliotheek Albert I, 6 mei–30 juni 1972. (Catalogus vertaald door Willem Bossier en Jean Ottevaerre ₍e. a.₎) ₍Brussel₎, De Vrienden van Portugal, ₍A. Huysmanslaan, 85₎, 1972.

239 p. ports., illus., facsims. 26 cm.

Martins, Antônio Coimbra.
"Os Lusíades" de Camões, quatrième centenaire, exposition bibliographique et iconographique, Paris, 1er mars–23 avril 1972. ₍Catalogue par Antonio Coimbra Martins. Préface par Joaquim Veríssimo Serrão.₎ Paris (16°). Centre culturel portugais, 51. Av. d'Iéna, 1972.

215 p. illus., plates (part col.), errata. 25 cm.

On cover: Quatrième centenaire de Os Lusiadas de Camões, 1572/1972.

Rio de Janeiro. Biblioteca Nacional.
Os Lusíadas, 1572–1972; catálogo da exposição. ₍Rio de Janeiro₎ Divisão de Publicações e Divulgação, 1972.

69 p. illus. 24 cm.

"Exposição comemorativa do 4o. centenário de Os Lusíadas (1572–1972) organizada pela Seção de Exposições e inaugurada em abril de 1972."

Rio de Janeiro. Gabinete Português de Leitura.
Catálogo da Exposição camoniana do Real Gabinete Português de Leitura do Rio de Janeiro, comemorativa do quarto centenário da edição de Os Lusiadas. Seguido de notas bio-bibliográficas sobre a cultura portuguesa do século XVI. Organizado por Artur Forte de Faria de Almeida, chefe da Biblioteca. Rio de Janeiro, 1972.

207 p. facsims. 23 cm.

CAMPO LARGO, BRAZIL

Costa, Odah Regina Guimarães.
Arquivo da Paróquia de Campo Largo da Piedade ₍por Odah Regina Guimarães Costa e Maria Ignês Mancini De Boni₎ Curitiba, Universidade Federal do Paraná, Instituto de Ciências Humanas, Departamento de História, 1972.

56 p. 23 cm. (Boletim da Universidade Federal do Paraná, Instituto de Ciências Humanas, Departamento de História, no. 17)

CAMPUS PLANNING see College facilities

CAMUS, ALBERT

Fitch, Brian T
Albert Camus, 1 (2); essai de bibliographie des études en langue française consacrées à Albert Camus (1937–1967), par Brian T. Fitch et Peter C. Hoy. 2. livr. Paris, Lettres modernes, 1969.

1 v. (unpaged) 18 cm. (Calepins de bibliographie, no 1) (Lettres modernes)

"Chaque livraison annule et remplace la précédente."

Fitch, Brian T
Albert Camus, 1 (3); essai de bibliographie des études en langue française consacrées à Albert Camus (1937–1970), par Brian T. Fitch et Peter C. Hoy. 3. livr. Paris, Lettres modernes, 1972.

1 v. (unpaged) 18 cm. (Calepins de bibliographie, no 1) (Lettres modernes)

"Chaque livraison annule et remplace la précédente."

Hoy, Peter C
Camus in English, an annotated bibliography of Albert Camus's contributions to English and American periodicals and newspapers (1945–1968) ₍by₎ Peter C. Hoy. 2nd revised and enlarged edition. Paris, Lettres modernes, 1971.

1 v. (unpaged) 18 cm. (Biblio notes, 4)

Roeming, Robert F
Camus: a bibliography. Compiled and edited by Robert F. Roeming. Madison, University of Wisconsin Press, 1968.

298 p. 25 cm.

CAMUS, JEAN PIERRE

Descrains, Jean.
Bibliographie des œuvres de Jean-Pierre Camus, évêque de Belley (1584–1652) ... [Paris (2ᵉ),] Société d'étude du XVIIᵉ siècle, [24, Bd Poissonnière,] 1971.

84 p. diagrs. (1 fold.) 25 cm. (Publications de la Société d'étude du XVIIᵉ siècle, 1)

CANADA
see also under Australia (Canberra) and Dissertations, Academic

Alexandrin, Barbara.
Bibliography of the material culture of New France [by] Barbara Alexandrin and Robert Bothwell. [Ottawa, National Museums of Canada, 1970]

vii, 32 p. 25 cm. (Publications in history, no. 4)

Amtmann, Bernard.
Contributions to a short-title catalogue of Canadiana. Montreal, 1971–

v. 29 cm.

CONTENTS: v. 1. A1–C2575.—v. 2. C2576–H843.—v. 3. H344–P1137.—v. 4. P1138–Z11.

Berry, John Widdup, 1939–
Social psychology of Canada; an annotated bibliography, edited by J. W. Berry [and] G. J. S. Wilde. Assisted by Cathy Evans [and] Pat Evans. Supported by the Canada Council. Kingston [Ont.] 1971.

iv, 96 p. 28 cm.

Campbell, Henry Cummings, 1919–
How to find out about Canada, edited by H. C. Campbell. [1st ed.] Oxford, New York, Pergamon Press [1967]

xiv, 248 p. illus. 20 cm. (The Commonwealth and International library. Libraries and technical information division.)

Canada. *Dept. of Manpower and Immigration.*
Immigration, migration and ethnic groups in Canada; a bibliography of research 1964–1968. Immigration, migration et groupes ethniques au Canada; une bibliographie de recherches 1964–1968. Ottawa, 1969.

xiv, 56 p. illus., forms. 25 cm.

"Fourth volume in the series of Bibliography for research of citizenship, immigration and ethnic groups in Canada."
Introductory material in English and French.

Canada. Public Archives.
Access programme to public records, significant accessions July 1969–August 1970, compiled by J. Atherton. Ottawa, Public Archives of Canada, Manuscript Division, 1970.

11, 13 p. 22 cm. (Public Archives of Canada. Manuscript Division. Bulletin no. 2)

Added t. p.: Programme d'accès aux fonds officiels.
English and French.

Canada. *Public Archives.*
Check-list of parish registers. Répertoire des registres paroissiaux. Compiled by Marielle Campeau. Ottawa, Public Archives of Canada, Manuscript Division, 1969.

21 p. 22 cm.

Cover title.
English or French.

Canadiana Library. List. Liste. [Montreal, 1967–

v. 25 cm.

On cover: The library and man and his world.
Text bilingual, English and French.
CONTENTS: List 1. Books.—List 2. Periodicals.

Carleton University, *Ottawa. Library.*
Sources of information for research in Canadian political science and public administration; a selected and annotated bibliography prepared for the Dept. of Political Science and the School of Public Administration. Ottawa, 1964.

25 l. 28 cm.

Cover title.
1958 ed. published under title: Sources of information for research in Canadian public administration.

Chalifoux, Jean Pierre.
Bibliographie sur des questions actuelles. [Montréal] Bibliothèque, Centre d'études canadiennes-françaises, McGill University, 1968.

[84] l. 30 cm.

Directory of Canadian archival repositories. Annuaire des archives canadiennes. 1971–
[Ottawa?] Archives Section, Canadian Historical Association.

v. 25 cm.

English and French.

Fulford, Robert.
Read Canadian: a book about Canadian books; edited by Robert Fulford, David Godfrey and Abraham Rotstein. Toronto, James Lewis & Samuel, 1972.

xi, 275 p. 19 cm.

Langhammer, Else Birgit, 1922–
The William Palmer Witton Canadiana collection, by Birgit Langhammer, for University of Toronto, School of Library Science. Hamilton, 1967.

24, 14, [13] l. 28 cm.

Longley, Richmond Wilberforce.
Bibliography of climatology for the Prairie Provinces 1957–1969. Bibliography editors: Richmond W. Longley [and] John M. Powell. Edmonton, University of Alberta Press, 1971.

64 p. 23 cm. (University of Alberta. Studies in Geography. Bibliographies, 1)

Motiuk, Laurence.
A reading guide to Canada in world affairs. 1945–1971; compiled by Laurence Motiuk and Madeline Grant. [Toronto] Canadian Institute of International Affairs [c1972]

x, 313 p. 28 cm.

National Book League, *London.*
Commonwealth in North America: an annotated list. London, National Book League, 1969.

[1], 21 p. 22 cm.

Issued by the National Book League and the Commonwealth Institute.

Page, Donald M
A bibliography of works on Canadian foreign relations, 1945–1970, compiled by Donald M. Page. ₁Toronto₁ Canadian Institute of International Affairs, 1973.

441 p. 28 cm.

Peel, Bruce Braden, 1916–
A bibliography of the Prairie Provinces to 1953. ₁Toronto₁ University of Toronto Press ₁1956₁

xix, 680 p. 26 cm.

———————Supplement. ₁Toronto₁ University of Toronto Press, 1963.

x, 130 p. 26 cm.

Ryder, Dorothy E
Canadian reference sources; a selective guide. Dorothy E. Ryder, editor. Ottawa, Canadian Library Association, 1973.

x, 185 p. 25 cm.

St. James Public Library.
A bibliography of Canadiana. Centennial ed. ₁St. James, Manitoba₁ 1967.

1 v. (various pagings) 36 cm.

Snow, Kathleen Mary, 1918–
Canadian materials for schools ₁by₁ Kathleen M. Snow ₁and₁ Philomena Hauck. Toronto, McClelland and Stewart ₁c1970₁

200 p. 24 cm.

Stewart, Alice R
The Atlantic Provinces of Canada; union lists of materials in the larger libraries of Maine. Compiled by Alice R. Stewart. Orono, Me., University of Maine Press, 1965.

vi, 85 p. 23 cm. (University of Maine studies, 2d ser., no. 82)

University of Maine bulletin, v. 68, no. 28.

Stewart, Alice R
The Atlantic Provinces of Canada; union lists of materials in the larger libraries of Maine. Compiled by Alice R. Stewart. 2d ed. Orono, New England-Atlantic Provinces-Quebec Center, University of Maine, 1971.

70 p. 23 cm.

Stuart-Stubbs, Basil.
Maps relating to Alexander Mackenzie: a keepsake distributed at a meeting of the Bibliographical Society of Canada, Jasper Park, June, 1968 ₁by₁ B. Stuart-Stubbs. n. p., 1968?

₁33₁ l. 12 maps. 29 cm.

BIBLIOGRAPHIES

Bhatia, Mohan.
Bibliographies, catalogues, checklists and indexes of Canadian provincial government publications. Saskatoon, University of Saskatchewan, Library, 1970.

16 l. 29 cm.

Bhatia, Mohan.
Canadian federal government publications: a bibliography of bibliographies. Saskatoon, University of Saskatchewan, 1971.

33 l. 28 cm.

Bhatia, Mohan.
Canadian provincial government publications: bibliography of bibliographies. Rev. and enl. ed. Saskatoon, University of Saskatchewan, Library, 1971.

19 l. 28 cm.

Lochhead, Douglas.
Bibliography of Canadian bibliographies. Index compiled by Peter E. Grieg. 2d ed. rev. and enl. ₁Toronto₁ University of Toronto, published in association with the Bibliographical Society of Canada ₁1972₁
xiv, 312 p. 24 cm.
Added t.p. in French: Bibliographie des bibliographies canadiennes.
English or French.
First ed. (1960) compiled by Raymond Tanghe.

BIO-BIBLIOGRAPHY

Morgan, Henry James, 1842–1913.
Bibliotheca canadensis: or, A manual of Canadian literature. Ottawa, Printed by G. E. Desbarats, 1867. Detroit, Gale Research Co., 1968.

xiv, 411 p. 24 cm.

GOVERNMENT PUBLICATIONS

Canada. *Bureau of Statistics. Library.*
Historical catalogue of Dominion Bureau of Statistics publications, 1918–1960. Catalogue rétrospectif des publications du Bureau fédéral de la statistique. Ottawa, DBS Library ₁and₁ Canada Year Book Division, 1966 ₁i. e. 1967₁

xiv, 298 p. 23 cm.

Henderson, George Fletcher.
Federal royal commissions in Canada, 1867–1966; a checklist. ₁Toronto₁ University of Toronto Press ₁1967₁
xvi, 212 p. 25 cm.

Symansky, Judith.
Canadian federal Royal Commissions of interest to business libraries 1955–1970; with an appendix of provincial Royal Commissions, compiled by Ena Lazarus. ₁Montreal₁ McGill University. Graduate School of Library Science, 1972.

iii, 35 l. 28 cm. (Graduate School of Library Science, McGill University. Occasional papers, 3)

Cover title: Canadian Royal Commissions of interest to business libraries.

HISTORY

Beaulieu, André.
Guide d'histoire du Canada ₁par₁ André Beaulieu, Jean Hamelin ₁et₁ Benoît Bernier. Québec, Presses de l'Université Laval, 1969.

xvi, 540 p. 23 cm. (Les Cahiers de l'Institut d'histoire, 13)

1965 ed. published under title: Guide de l'étudiant en histoire du Canada.

Canada. Public Archives.
General inventory: manuscripts. Inventaire général: manuscrits. Ottawa, 1971-
v. 28 cm.

English and French.
CONTENTS: v. 1. mg 1-mg 10.
—v. 4. mg 22-mg 25.—v. 5. mg 26-mg 27.

Canada. *Public Archives.*
Preliminary inventory; manuscript group 17: religious archives. ₁Ottawa₁ Public Archives of Canada, Manuscripts Division, 1967.

v, 17 p. 26 cm.

English or French.

Canada. *Public Archives.*
Preliminary inventory; manuscript group 18, pre-conquest papers. ₁Ottawa, R. Duhamel, Queen's printer₁ 1964.

67 p. 25 cm.

At head of title: Public Archives of Canada, Manuscripts Division.

Canada. *Public Archives.*
Preliminary inventory. Manuscript group 30, twentieth century manuscripts. ₁Ottawa, Queen's Printer₁ 1966.

v, 87 p. 26 cm.

Issued by the Manuscript Division of the Public Archives.

Faribault, Georges Barthélemi, 1789–1866.
Catalogue d'ouvrages sur l'histoire de l'Amérique et en particulier sur celle du Canada, de la Louisiane, l'Acadie, et autres lieux. Rédigé par G. B. Faribault. ₁East Ardsley, Yorkshire, Eng.₁ S. R. Publishers; ₁New York₁ Johnson Reprint Corp., 1966.

207 p. 22 cm.

Facsim. of the ed. published in Québec.

Hamelin, Jean.
Guide de l'étudiant en histoire du Canada ₁par₁ Jean Hamelin ₁et₁ André Beaulieu. Préf. de Marcel Trudel. ₁Québec, Presses de l'Université Laval, 1965₁

iv, 274 l. 28 cm.

Irish University Press.
Index to British Parliamentary papers on Canada and Canadian boundary, 1800–1899. ₁Dublin, 1974₁
xxv, 159 p. 25 cm. (Indexes to the IUP 1000-volume series of British parliamentary papers)
On spine: British parliamentary papers.

Lande, Lawrence M
Confederation pamphlets, a check-list—liste abrégée ₁by Lawrence Lande₁ Montreal, McGill U. P., 1967.

67 p. facsims. 28 cm. (Lawrence Lande Foundation for Canadian Historical Research. ₁Pamphlet₁ no. 8)

Morley, William F   E
The Atlantic Provinces; Newfoundland, Nova Scotia, New Brunswick, Prince Edward Island, by William F. E. Morley. ₁Toronto₁ University of Toronto Press ₁1967₁

137 p. facsims., maps. 26 cm. (Canadian local histories to 1950: a bibliography, v. 1)

Thibault, Claude.
Bibliographia Canadiana. Don Mills, Ont., Longman Canada, 1973.

lxiv, 795 p. 24 cm.

English and French.
Includes index.

IMPRINTS

Barbeau, Victor, 1896–
Dictionnaire bibliographique du Canada français /

Victor Barbeau et André Fortier. — Montréal : Académie canadienne-française, 1974.

246 p. ; 32 cm.

Canadian books in print. Catalogue des livres canadiens en librairie. 1967–
₁Toronto₁ University of Toronto Press.

v. in   26 cm.

English or French.
Published for the Canadian Books in Print Committee.

Dulong, Gaston.
Bibliographie linguistique du Canada français. Québec, Presses de l'Université Laval, 1966.

xxxii, 166 p. 23 cm. (Bibliothèque française et romane. Série E: Langue et littérature françaises au Canada, 1)

Quebec (*Province*) *Dept. of Cultural Affairs. Arts and Letters Branch.*
Liste des titres de volumes en langue française, publiés par les éditeurs canadiens au cours de l'année 1965. ₁Québec, 1967₁

₁13₁ l. 28 cm.

At head of title: Ministère des affaires culturelles du Québec. Service des lettres et du livre.

Subject guide to Canadian books in print. 1973–
₁Toronto₁ University of Toronto Press.

v. 26 cm. annual.

Toronto. Public Libraries.
The Canadian catalogue of books published in Canada, about Canada, as well as those written by Canadians, with imprint 1921–1949; consolidated English language reprint edition, with cumulated author index. Canada, Toronto Public Libraries, 1967.

1 v. (various pagings) 25 cm.

JUVENILE LITERATURE

Alberta Teachers' Association. English Council.
Canadian books for schools; a centennial listing. Edmonton, English Council and School Library Council of the Alberta Teachers' Association, 1968.

63 p. 21 cm.

Canada. *Dept. of External Affairs. Information Division.*
A list of Canadian books for young people; for the guidance of those responsible for the selection of books for school libraries. ₁Ottawa, Queen's Printer₁ 1969.

29 p. 23 cm.

Cover title: Books about Canada.
"Published by the Information Division of the Department of External Affairs in co-operation with the National Library of Canada."

LAW see Law – Canada

LIBRARY CATALOGS

Boston. Public Library.
Canadian manuscripts in the Boston Public Library; a descriptive catalog. Boston, G. K. Hall, 1971.

v, 76 p. 26 cm.

Glenbow-Alberta Institute. Library.
Catalogue of the Glenbow Historical Library. Boston, Mass., G. K. Hall, 1973.

4 v. 37 cm.

Harvard University. *Library.*
Canadian history and literature; classification schedule, classified listing by call number, alphabetical listing by author or title, chronological listing. Cambridge; Distributed by the Harvard University Press, 1968.

411 p. 29 cm. (*Its* Widener Library shelflist, 20)

McGill University, *Montreal. Library.*
The Lawrence Lande collection of Canadiana in the Redpath Library of McGill University; a bibliography collected, arranged, and annotated by Lawrence Lande. With an introd. by Edgar Andrew Collard. Montreal, Lawrence Lande Foundation for Canadian Historical Research, 1965.

xxxv, 301 p. facsims., maps (part fold.) 36 cm.

On cover: A bibliography of Canadiana.
Issued in a case with a mounted reproduction of the frontispiece in A. Cluny's The American traveller. London, 1769.

McGill University, Montreal. Library.
Rare and unusual Canadiana; first supplement to the Lande bibliography [compiled by Lawrence Lande] Montreal, McGill University, 1971.

xx, 779 p. facsims. 29 cm. (Lawrence Lande Foundation for Canadian Historical Research. [Publications] no. 6)

Limited ed. of 500 signed copies.
Facsim. of broadside "Ménagerie annexioniste" laid in.

Montreal. Université. Bibliothèque centrale. Service des collections particulières.
Catalogue de la collection François-Louis-Georges Baby, rédigé par Camille Bertrand. Préf. de Paul Baby et introd. par Lucien Campeau. Montréal, Bibliothèques de l'Université de Montréal, 1971.

2 v. (viii, 1235 p.) 36 cm. (Publications du Service des collections particulières)
On spine: Collection Baby.

Ottawa. National Gallery of Canada. *Library.*
Canadian Collection; author catalogue. [Ottawa, 1965]

[98] l. 34 cm.

Ottawa. National Gallery of Canada. Library.
Canadiana; in the Library of the National Gallery of Canada. Rev. ed. Ottawa, 1967.

1 v. (unpaged) 34 cm.

Introd. in English and French. Entries in French for French language publications.

———— Supplement, 1968. Ottawa, 1968.

v 1., 37 p. 34 cm.

Ruth Konrad Collection of Canadiana.
The Ruth Konrad Collection of Canadiana; a descriptive catalogue, edited by Albert A. Spratt. [Mississauga, Ont.] Mississauga Public Library Board, 1971.

100 p. port. 23 cm.

Cover title: The Ruth Konrad Collection of Canadiana in the Mississauga Public Library.

MAPS

May, Betty.
County atlases of Canada; a descriptive catalogue. Atlas de comtés canadiens; catalogue descriptif, compiled by Betty May. Assisted by Frank McGuire [and] Heather Maddick. [Ottawa] National Map Collection, Public Archives of Canada, 1970.

xii, 192 p. illus., maps. 28 cm.
Introduction in English and French.

Thomas, Morley K
Guide to the climatic maps of Canada, by M. K. Thomas and S. R. Anderson. [Toronto] Dept. of Transport, Meteorological Branch, 1967.

v, 79 p. 28 cm. ([Canada. Meteorological Branch] CLI-1-67)

CANADA. ROYAL CANADIAN MOUNTED POLICE

Arora, Ved Parkash.
Royal Canadian Mounted Police; a bibliography [compiled by Ved P. Arora] Regina, Bibliographic Services Division, Provincial Library, 1973.

iv, 42 p. 28 cm.

CANADA, NORTHERN

Montreal. École des hautes études commerciales. Centre de recherches arctiques.
Catalogue des coupures de presse [de la] collection Gardner. Montréal 1967–

v. 28 cm.
Cover title.
Introd. in French and English.
CONTENTS: no 1. Transports et communications: Territoires-du-Nord-Ouest et Arctique.—no 2. Végétaux et animaux: Territoires-du-Nord-Ouest et Arctique.—no 3. Exploration et recherche scientifique: Territoires-du-Nord-Ouest et Arctique.—no 4. Indiens et Esquimaux: Territoires-du-Nord-Ouest et Arctique.—no 5. Défense: Territoires-du-Nord-Ouest et Arctique.—no 6. Villes et frontières: Territoires-du-Nord-Ouest et Arctique.—no 7. Mines: Territoires-du-Nord-Ouest et Arctique.—no 8. Divers: Territoires-du-Nord-Ouest et Arctique.—no 9. Divers: Terre-Neuve.—
no 11. Travail: Terre-Neuve.—no 12. Pâtes et papiers: Terre-Neuve.—no 13. Santé et hôpitaux: Terre-Neuve.—no 14. Agriculture: Terre-Neuve.—no 15. Histoire: Terre-Neuve.—no 16. Animaux sauvages: Terre-Neuve.—no 17. Défense: Terre-Neuve.—no 18. Développement économique: Terre-Neuve.—no 19. Pêcheries: Terre-Neuve.

Quebec (City). Université Laval. Centre d'études nordiques.
Une décennie de recherches au Centre d'études nordiques, 1961–1970; résumés des principaux travaux publiés et manuscrits. Québec, Université Laval, 1971.

113 l. 28 cm. (Its Collection Bibliographie, no 4)

CANADIAN LITERATURE

Bell, Inglis Freeman, 1917–
Canadian literature, Littérature canadienne, 1959–1963. A checklist of creative and critical writings. Bibliographie de la critique et des œuvres d'imagination. Edited by Inglis F. Bell and Susan W. Port. [Vancouver] Publications Centre, University of British Columbia, 1966.
140 p. illus. 24 cm.

"A Canadian literature supplement."
Title and pref. bilingual, English and French.
Headings in English for English-Canadian literature and in French for French-Canadian literature.
"Amended cumulation of the annual lists from Canadian literature."—Pref.

Canadian Cultural Information Centre.
Canadian literary awards. Ottawa, 1966–

v. 23 cm.

Cover title.
Text bilingual, English and French.
Added t. p. in French: Prix littéraires Canadiens.

CONTENTS.—pt. 1. Governor General's literary awards.

Ottawa. National Library.
Manitoba authors. Ecrivains du Manitoba. Ottawa, 1970.

1 v. (unpaged) illus., ports. 21 cm.

English and French.

Rhodenizer, Vernon Blair, 1886–   *comp.*
Canadian literature in English. [Montreal, Printed by Quality Press, °1965]

1055 p. 24 cm.

—————— Index to Vernon Blair Rhodenizer's Canadian Literature in English, compiled by Lois Mary Thierman. Edmonton, Printed by La Survivance [1968?]

ix, 469 p. 24 cm.

Watters, Reginald Eyre.
A checklist of Canadian literature and background materials, 1628–1960, in two parts: first, a comprehensive list of the books which constitute Canadian literature written in English; and second, a selective list of other books by Canadian authors which reveal the backgrounds of that literature. 2d ed., rev. and enl. [Toronto, Buffalo] University of Toronto Press [1972]

xxiv, 1085 p. 24 cm.

Watters, Reginald Eyre.
On Canadian literature, 1806–1960; a check list of articles, books, and theses on English-Canadian literature, its authors, and language, compiled by Reginald Eyre Watters [and] Inglis Freeman Bell. [Toronto] University of Toronto Press [1966]

ix, 165 p. 25 cm.

FRENCH

British Columbia. University. Library.
A checklist of printed materials relating to French-Canadian literature, 1763–1968. Liste de référence d'imprimés relatifs à la littérature canadienne-française [by] Gérard Tougas. 2d ed. Vancouver, University of British Columbia Press [1973]

xvi, 174 p. 24 cm.

Preliminary material in English and French.

Chalifoux, Jean Pierre.
Liste de sources bibliographiques relatives à la littérature canadienne-française. [Montréal] La Bibliothèque, Centre d'études canadiennes-françaises, McGill University, 1967.

[26] l. 28 cm.

"Deuxième édition revue."

CANAHUA   see under   Quinoa

CANALS

Kelbrick, Norman.
Canals: a select reading list. Cheltenham, Gloucestershire Technical Information Service, 1971.

[2], 9 p. 20 cm.

CANARY ISLANDS

Broekema, C
Maps of the Canary Islands published before 1850; a checklist compiled by C. Broekema. London, The Map Collectors Circle, 1971.

24 p. illus. 25 cm. (Map collectors' series v. 8, no. 74)

Vizcaya Cárpenter, Antonio.
Tipografía canaria; descripción bibliográfica de las obras editadas en las Islas Canarias desde la introducción de la imprenta hasta el año 1900. Santa Cruz de Tenerife, 1964.

xcii, 726 p. illus., facsims., ports. 26 cm. (Consejo Superior de Investigaciones Científicas. Instituto de Estudios Canarios en la Universidad de La Laguna. Bibliografías locales, no. 2)

CANCER
see also   Tumors

Anderson Hospital and Tumor Institute, *Houston, Tex. Medical Library.*
Nursing literature on cancer. 1958–1964; bibliography. [Houston, 1965]

[16] l. 28 cm.

Addendum, 1958–1965 ([7] l., inserted)

Koenig, Elizabeth A   H
Cancer and virus, a guide and annotated bibliography to monographs, reviews, symposia, and survey articles with emphasis on human neoplasm, 1950–63 [by] Elizabeth Koenig. Washington [U. S. Dept. of Health, Education, and Welfare, Public Health Service, National Cancer Institute]; for sale by the Superintendent of Documents, U. S. Govt. Print. Off. [1966]

vi, 94 p. 24 cm. (Public Health Service publication no. 1424)

Paul, Rolf.
Krebs-Chemotherapeutika. ⟨Zytostatika exkl. Hormone und Radionuklide.⟩ Literaturnachweis. (Jülich, Kernforschungsanlage, Zentralbibliothek, 1966)

290 l. 30 cm. (Bibliographische Reihe der Kernforschungsanlage Jülich, Nr. 12)

U. S. *National Cancer Institute.*
Reading on cancer; an annotated bibliography, prepared by Research Information Branch, National Cancer Institute. [Rev. Washington] U. S. Dept. of Health, Education, and Welfare, Public Health Service, National Institutes of Health; [for sale by the Superintendent of Documents, U. S. Govt. Print. Off., 1964]

iv, 16 p. 24 cm. (Public Health Service publication no. 457. Public health bibliography series no. 14)

U. S. *National Cancer Institute.*
Reading on cancer; an annotated bibliography, prepared by Research Information Branch, National Cancer Institute. [Rev. Washington] U. S. National Institutes of Health, for sale by the Supt. of Docs., U. S. Govt. Print. Off., [1969]

iv, 23 p. 24 cm. (Public Health bibliography series, no. 14)
Public Health Service publication no. 457.

United States. National Cancer Institute. Program Analysis and Communication Office. Information Unit.
Partial bibliography on human cancer involving viruses (covering period of January 1966 through December 1969) Bethesda, Md. [1970]

71 p. 27 cm.

CANILLEROS, MIGUEL MUÑOZ DE SAN PEDRO, CONDE DE

Martínez Quesada, Juan.
Bibliografía de las publicaciones históricas de Miguel Muñoz de San Pedro, conde de Canilleros (1922–1965) Recopilada por Juan Martínez Quesada. Prólogo de Alfonso Díaz de Bustamante y Quijano. Valencia, 1966.

59 p. 21 cm.

CANOES AND CANOEING

Saskatchewan. Provincial Library, Regina. Bibliographic Services Division.
Canoeing; a bibliography. Regina, 1973.

16 p. 22 cm.

Saskatchewan. Provincial Library, Regina. Bibliographic Services Division.
Canoes and canoeing; a bibliography. Regina, Sask., 1972.

43 p. 22 cm.

CANTAL, FRANCE (DEPT.)

Cantal, France (Dept.). Archives départementales.
Répertoire de la série G, clergé séculier d'Ancien régime, suivi du Répertoire de la sous-série 346 F, collection Chabau, par Léonce Bouyssou ... Aurillac, Archives départementales, 1972.
173 p. 24 cm.

Cantal, *France (Dept.).* *Archives départementales.*
Répertoire numérique de la série S; travaux publics et transports, 1800–1940. Établi par Michel Blarez, sousarchiviste, sous la direction de Léonce Bouyssou, directeur des Services d'archives du Cantal. Aurillac, Impr. moderne, 1969.

232 p. 32 cm.

CANTH, ULRIKA VILHELMINA JOHNSSON

Kannila, Helle.
Minna Canthin kirjallinen tuotanto; henkilöbibliografia. Helsingissä, Otava [1967]

88 p. 19 cm.

CAPE COLOURED PEOPLE see Colored people (South Africa)

CAPE OF GOOD HOPE
see also under Madagascar *(France)*

Berning, J M
A select bibliography on the 1820 Settlers and settlement, compiled by J. M. Berning. Grahamstown, 1820 Settlers National Monument Foundation, 1970.

[iv], 8 p. 21 cm.

Schrire, D
The Cape of Good Hope, 1782–1842, from De la Rochette to Arrowsmith. Being some notes on the development of the early mapping of European-occupied South Africa by English cartographers, by D. Schrire. London, Map Collectors' Circle, 1965.

16 p. maps (1 fold.) 25 cm. (Map Collectors' Circle. Map Collectors' series, no. 17)

ČAPEK, KAREL and JOSEF

Pilná, Věra.
Karel Čapek. 1890–1938. Bibliogr. a ukázky z jeho tvorby 30. let. Vyprac. Věra Pilná. Praha, Měst. knihovna, rozmn., [1969].

57, [2] p. illus., facsims. 29 cm. (Metodické texty a bibliografie M. K.)

Vacina, Ladislav.
Karel Čapek-Josef Čapek. Výběrová bibliogr. Sest. Ladislav Vacina. Náchod, Okr. knihovna, rozmn., 1970.

45, [1] p. 29 cm.

ČAPEK, KAREL MATĚJ

Ryšánková, Helena.
Karel Matěj Čapek-Chod. Personální bibliografie. Sest. Helena Ryšánková. Plzeň, Knihovna města Plzně, t. Stráž 107, Cheb, 1972.

27, [1] p. 21 cm. (Beletristé Západočeského kraje)

CAPITAL

Buenos Aires. Bolsa de Comercio. *Biblioteca.*
Revaluación de activos, bibliografía. [Buenos Aires] 1966.

10 l. 28 cm.

Organization for Economic Cooperation and Development. *Library.*
Marché des capitaux. Capital markets. [Paris] Organisation de coopération et de développement économiques, 1969.

v, 147 p. 27 cm. (*Its* Bibliographie spéciale analytique. Special annotated bibliography, 22)

Cover title.
"Prepared and written by Mrs. R. Tarr."

CAPITAL INVESTMENTS

Akademiia nauk SSSR. *Fundamental'naia biblioteka obshchestvennykh nauk.*
Капиталовложения в народное хозяйство СССР. Основные фонды промышленности и их использование. Указатель советской литературы, 1945–1964. [Составители: Т. П. Андрущенко, Е. Б. Марголина. Ответственный редактор Е. В. Бажанова. Москва, Наука, 1966]

161 p. 22 cm.

Andrić, Stanislava.
Bibliografija o sistemu investiranja. Sastavile: Stanislava Andrić, Dubravka Kunštek, Marija Sever-Zebec. Zagreb, Ekonomski institut, 1972.

110 p. 22 cm.

CAPITAL PUNISHMENT

New Jersey. *Commission to Study Capital Punishment.*
Bibliography. [Trenton, 1964]

31 l. 28 cm.

Issued also as p. 24–51 of the commission's Report.

CAPUANA, LUIGI

Raya, Gino, 1906–
Bibliografia di Luigi Capuana. (1839–1968). Roma, Ciranna, 1969.

282 p. illus., plates. 24 cm. (Collana "Lettere nella storia," 4)

CAPUCHIN NUNS

Felice da Mareto, Father, 1909–
Le cappuccine nel mondo. (1538–1969). Cenni storici e bibliografia. A cura di Felice da Mareto. Parma, Libreria francescana editrice, 1970.

viii, 478 p. plates. 24½ cm. (Biblioteca storico-religiosa, 1)

CARACAS, VENEZUELA

Briceño Perozo, Mario.
Documentos para la historia de la fundación de Caracas existentes en el Archivo General de la Nación. Caracas, A. G. N., 1969.

757 p. facsims. 23 cm. (Biblioteca venezolana de historia, 7)

A calendar of documents including extensive citations from the original texts with the orthography and punctuation modernized.

Caracas (Archdiocese). Archivo.
Catálogo general del Archivo Arquidiocesano de Caracas, por Jaime Suriá, director del Archivo Arquidiocesano. Madrid, Escuelas Profesionales "Sagrado Corazón de Jesús", 1964.

79 p. 20 cm.

Medina, José Toribio, 1852–1930.
La imprenta en Caracas, 1808–1821. Amsterdam, N. Israel, 1964.

29 p. 22 cm. (Reprint series of José Toribio Medina's bibliographical works, 8)

Original ed. published in Santiago de Chile, 1904.

CARBOHYDRATES

Химия углеводов; библиографический указатель, 1961–1964. [Составители: А. И. Усов, Л. В. Бакиновский, Л. П. Иванико. Отв. редактор А. И. Усов] Москва, Наука, 1966.

327 p. 23 cm.

At head of title: Академия наук СССР. Сектор сети специальных библиотек. Объединенная библиотека при Институтах химии природных соединений и молекулярной биологии.

CARBON FIBERS

Atkins, John Leslie.
Carbon fibres—so far: an interim bibliography, edited by J. L. Atkins. Coventry (Warwickshire), Cadig Liaison Centre, Reference Library, 1970.

[3], 12 leaves. 30 cm.

CARBON MONOXIDE

Cooper, Anna Grossman.
Carbon monoxide; a bibliography with abstracts. Washington, U. S. Dept. of Health, Education, and Welfare, Public Health Service; [for sale by the Superintendent of Documents, U. S. Govt. Print. Off.] 1966.

viii, 440 p. 26 cm. (Public Health Service publication no. 1503. Bibliography series no. 68)

CARDIGANSHIRE, WALES

Jones, Glyn Lewis.
Llyfryddiaeth Ceredigion, 1600–1964. A bibliography of Cardiganshire. Aberystwyth (Card.), Llyfrgell Ceredigion, 1967.

3 v. 26 cm.
CONTENTS.—v. 1. Ardaloedd Ceredigion—Cardiganshire localities.—v. 2–3. Awduron Ceredigion—Cardiganshire authors.

———— Atodiad. 1964–68. Supplement. Aberystwyth (Card.), Llyfrgell Ceredigion, 1970.

[10], xv, 178 p. 25 cm.

CARDIOVASCULAR SYSTEM

Faidutti, Bernard.
Titres et travaux scientifiques du Dr Bernard Faidutti ... [69–Caluire, l'auteur, 9, montée des Soldats,] 1969.

321 p. illus. 27 cm.

Ghyczy, Kálmán.
Magyar kardiológiai, angiológiai, szív- és érsebészeti bibliografia, 1945–1960. Összeállította: Ghyczy Kálmán és Kuntner Mária. Budapest, Országos Orvostudományi Könyvtár és Dokumentációs Központ, 1965.

vi, 455 p. 24 cm.

Institute for Advancement of Medical Communication. *Cardiovascular Literature Project.*
Index-handbook of cardiovascular agents [by] Isaac D. Welt [director] New York, Published for the Institute for Advancement of Medical Communication [by] Blakiston Division, McGraw-Hill, 1960–69 [v. 1, 1963]
4 v. in 6. 29 cm.
Vol. 2 issued as Publication 821 of the National Research Council with imprint: Washington, National Academy of Sciences—National Research Council, 1960.
Vol. 4, by I. D. Welt and M. P. D. Martin, has imprint: Metuchen, N. J., Scarecrow Press. It was supported by research grant HE 09466 from the National Heart Institute, National Institutes of Health, U. S. Public Health Service, Dept. of Health, Education, and Welfare.

CONTENTS.—v. 1. 1931–1950.—v. 2. 1951–1955.—v. 3. 1956–1959.—v. 4. 1960–1963. 2 pts.

Ravin, Abe, 1908–
International bibliography of cardiovascular auscultation and phonocardiography; journal articles 1820–1966, books, theses, dissertations, phonodiscs 1819–1968. Compiled by Abe Ravin and Florence K. Frame. New York, American Heart Association, 1971.

x, 318 p. 27 cm. (American Heart Association. Monograph no. 31)

United States. Atomic Energy Commission. Technical Information Center.
Cardiac pacemakers and mechanical hearts; a bibliography of radioisotope power sources. [Washington] Available from the National Technical Information Service, U. S. Dept. of Commerce, Springfield, Va.] 1973.

ii, 32, 13 p. 28 cm.

U. S. *National Aeronautics and Space Administration. Scientific and Technical Information Division.*
Ballistocardiography, a bibliography; a compilation of references to papers, reports, monographs, reviews, and books, of both domestic and foreign origin, which appeared during the period 1877–1964. Washington; [For sale by the Superintendent of Documents, U. S. Govt. Print. Off.] 1965.

iii, 46 p. 26 cm. [NASA SP-7021]

"FAA AM 65–15."
Based on bibliographies compiled by W. R. Scarborough and other members of the staff of the Federal Aviation Agency.

CARDS   see   Gambling

CARGO HANDLING

Kramárová, A   comp.
Prekladacie zariadenia pri vodnej doprave; výberový zoznam z domácej a zahraničney literatury. Zostavila: A. Kramárova. Spolupracoval: Peter Majerník. Bratislava, Slovenská technická knižnica, 1965.

60 p. 21 cm.

CARIBBEAN AREA
see also West Indies and under
Dissertations, Academic

Caribbean bibliographic series. no. 1–
San Juan, University of Puerto Rico Press, 1970–

no. 25 cm.

No. 1–   issued by the Institute of Caribbean Studies, University of Puerto Rico.

Comitas, Lambros.
Caribbeana 1900–1965, a topical bibliography. Editorial research assistant: Carol Feist Dickert. Consultant on Netherlands Caribbean: Annemarie de Waal Malefijt. Seattle, Published for Research Institute for the Study of Man [by] University of Washington Press [1968]

L, 909 p. map (on lining papers) 26 cm.

Institute of Jamaica, Kingston. Library.
Bibliography of the West Indies (excluding Jamaica) by Frank Cundall, Secretary and Librarian of the Institute of Jamaica. Kingston, Institute of Jamaica, 1909. New York, Johnson Reprint Corp., 1971.

179 p. 23 cm.

National Book League, *London.*
The Commonwealth in the Caribbean: an annotated list. London, National Book League, 1969.

[2], 16 p. 22 cm.

Issued by the National Book League and the Commonwealth Institute.

Ragatz, Lowell Joseph, 1897–
A guide for the study of British Caribbean history, 1763–1834, including the abolition and emancipation movements, compiled by Lowell J. Ragatz. New York, Da Capo Press, 1970.

viii, 725 p. 24 cm.

Classified and annotated.
Reprint of the 1932 ed.

CARIBBEAN LITERATURE

Engber, Marjorie.
Caribbean fiction and poetry. New York, Center for Inter-American Relations [c1970]

86 p. 22 cm.

Merriman, Stella E
Commonwealth Caribbean writers; a bibliography. Compiled by Stella E. Merriman and Joan Christiani. Georgetown, Guyana [Public Library] 1970.

iv, 98 p. 28 cm.

CARINTHIA

Zopp, Friedrich.
Kärntner Bibliographie. Das Schrifttum über Kärnten aus den Jahren 1962–1965. ⟨Mit Nachtr. 1945–1961.⟩ Klagenfurt, Geschichtsverein f. Kärnten, 1970.

272 p. 24 cm.

CARLQUIST, GUNNAR

Arvidsson, Rolf, 1920–
Bibliografi över Gunnar Carlquists tryckta skrifter. [Lund, författaren] 1966.

23, (1) p. 25 cm.

CARLYLE, THOMAS

Dyer, Isaac Watson, 1855–1937.
A bibliography of Thomas Carlyle's writings and ana. New York, B. Franklin [1968]

xii, 587 p. port. 24 cm. (Burt Franklin bibliography and reference series, #177)

Reprint of the 1928 ed.

Dyer, Isaac Watson, 1855–1937.
A bibliography of Thomas Carlyle's writings and ana. New York, Octagon Books, 1968.

xiii, 587 p. 24 cm.

Reprint of the 1928 ed.

Shepherd, Richard Herne, 1842–1895.
The bibliography of Carlyle; a bibliographical list, arranged in chronological order of the published writings in prose and verse of Thomas Carlyle (from 1820 to 1881). New York, Haskell House Publishers, 1970.

xi, 60 p. 23 cm.

Reprint of the 1881 ed.

CARMELITES

Carmelites. Institutum Carmelitanum.
L'Institutum Carmelitanum; attività scientifica ed editoriale dal 1951 al 1971. Roma, 1971.

50 p. 22 cm.

Simeón de la Sagrada Familia, padre.
Panorama storico-bibliografico degli autori teresiani. Roma, Edizioni del Teresianum, 1972.

130 p. 22 cm. (Bibliotheca Carmelitica. Serie 3: Subsidia, 5)

At head of title: Simeone della S. Famiglia.
Originally published in Archivum bibliographicum Carmelitanum, 1970–1971, n. 12–13.

CARNEGIE, ANDREW

U. S. *Library of Congress. Manuscript Division.*
Andrew Carnegie: a register of his papers in the Library of Congress. Washington, 1964.

21 p. 26 cm.

CARO, JOSEPH

Israel. *Misrad ha-ḥinukh veha-tarbut.*
"ארבע מאות שנה שלחן ערוך" שכ"ה–תשכ"ה; תערוכת ובל.

אייר-סיון תשכ"ה, קרית האוניברסיטה העברית. ירושלים. קטלוג. העורכים: י. רוטשילד וי. תא-שמע. ירושלים, 1965.

16 p. 18 cm.

At head of title: משרד החינוך והתרבות, המחלקה לתרבות תורנית. בית הספרים הלאומי והאוניברסיטאי, ירושלים.

Pref. in Hebrew and English.

CAROLINA see North Carolina; South Carolina

CARPETS

U. S. *Agricultural Research Service.*
An annotated list of literature references on carpets and rugs, 1940 to 1963 [compiled and annotated by Martha L. Hensley. Washington] 1965.

38 p. 26 cm.

CARRERAS Y CANDI, FRANCISCO

Bultó Blajot, María Rosa.
Francisco Carreras Candi: notas biográficas y bibliografía de un gran historiador, por María Rosa Bultó Blajot. Repertorio de cartas reales conservadas en el Instituto Municipal de Historia. II: 1458–1479, por Juan-F. Cabestany Fort. Barcelona, 1967.

316 p. illus. 24 cm. (Instituto Municipal de Historia. Documentos y estudios, 17)

Includes bibliographies.

CARROLL, LEWIS see Dodgson, Charles Lutwidge

CARTAGENA, COLOMBIA

Medina, José Toribio, 1852–1930.
La imprenta en Cartagena de las Indias, 1809–1820. Amsterdam, N. Israel, 1964.

70 p. 22 cm. (Reprint series of José Toribio Medina's bibliographical works, 12)

Original ed. published in Santiago de Chile, 1904.

CARTAGENA, SPAIN

Spain. *Dirección General de Archivos y Bibliotecas.*
Selección de bibliografía cartagenera; catálogo de la exposición conmemorativa de la inaguración de la Casa de la Cultura. [Madrid, 1967]

1 v. (unpaged) illus., facsims., port. 22 cm. (Serie Casas de la Cultura)

CARTER, ELLIOTT COOK

New York (City). Public Library. Music Division.
Elliott Carter: sketches and scores in manuscript; a selection of manuscripts and other pertinent material from the Americana Collection of the Music Division, the New York Public Library, on exhibition December 1973 through February 1974 in the Vincent Astor Gallery, Library & Museum of the Performing Arts, the New York Public Library at Lincoln Center. [New York] New York Public Library, Astor, Lenox and Tilden Foundations [1973]

64 p. illus. 24 cm.

CARTHUSIANS

Petreius, Theodorus, 1569–1640.
Bibliotheca Cartusiana, sive Illustrium sacri Cartusiensis ordinis scriptorum catalogus. Auctore Theodoro Petreio. Accesserunt origines omnium per orbem Cartusiarum, quas eruendo publicavit Aubertus Miraeus. Farnborough, Gregg, 1968.

[34], 316, [1], 75 p. 18 cm.

Facsimile reprint of Cologne ed., 1609.

CARTOGRAPHY

see also Atlases; Maps; Nautical charts

Bonacker, Wilhelm.
Kartenmacher aller Länder und Zeiten. Stuttgart, H. Hiersemann, 1966.

243 p. 28 cm.

Introductory text in German and English.
"Angewandte Kürzungen des Schrifttums": p. 22–23.

Deutscher Kartographentag, 20th, Stuttgart, 1971.
Ausstellungskatalog. Kartographentag Stuttgart 1971. Zusammenstellung und Red.: Walter Leibbrand. Stuttgart, Dt. Ges. f. Kartographie e. V., Ortsverein Stuttgart (1971)

89 l. of maps with text. 24 cm.

Fordham, *Sir* **Herbert George,** 1854–1929.
Studies in carto-bibliography, British and French, and in the bibliography of itineraries and road-books. London, Dawsons, 1969.

x, 180 p. 2 plates, 1 illus., facsim., map. 23 cm.

Reprint of the Clarendon Press ed., Oxford, 1914.

Henshall, J   M
Sir H. George Fordham, carto-bibliographer, by J. M. Henshall. London, Map Collectors' Circle, 1969.

30, 28 p. coat of arms, map, port. 25 cm. (Map collectors' series, v. 6, no. 51)

Includes Christopher Saxton of Dunningley, by Sir George Fordham.

Paris. Bibliothèque nationale. Département des cartes et plans.
La Terre et son image, 100 chefs-d'œuvre de la cartographie, de Marco Polo à La Pérouse, exposition organisée à l'occasion du cent cinquantième anniversaire de la Société de géographie, [25] novembre ... 1971 [–8 janvier 1972. Paris. Catalogue par Edmond Pognon, avec la collaboration de Monique de La Roncière, Marie Antoinette Vannereau et Henri Hugonnard-Roche.] Paris, Bibliothèque nationale, 1971.

Porter, Philip Wayland, 1928–
A bibliography of statistical cartography [by] Philip W. Porter. [Minneapolis] Dept. of Geography, University of Minnesota [1964]

66 l. illus. 28 cm.

Ristow, Walter William, 1908–
Guide to the history of cartography; an annotated list of references on the history of maps and map-making. Compiled by Walter W. Ristow. Washington, Geography and Map Division, Library of Congress; [for sale by the Supt. of Docs., U. S. Govt. Print. Off.] 1973.

96 p. 24 cm.

First and 2d editions issued by the Library's Map Division under title: A guide to historical cartography.

Steward, Harry.
Education and training in the mapping sciences: a working bibliography. New York, American Geographical Society, 1969.

xi, 60 l. 30 cm.

Theatrum orbis terrarum. Die Erfassung des Weltbildes zur Zeit d. Renaissance u. des Barocks. (Ausstellung. Katalog: E. Bernleithner ₍u. a.₎). Hrsg. v. Gerhart Egger. Wien, Österr. Museum f. Angewandte Kunst, 1970.
104 p., 72 p. of illus. 24 cm. (Schriften der Bibliothek des Österreichischen Museums für Angewandte Kunst, 5)

"Die ausgestellten Objekte stammen nur zum Teil aus Bibliothek und Sammlungen des Österreichischen Museums."

United States. Library of Congress. Geography and Map Division.
The bibliography of cartography. Boston, G. K. Hall, 1973.

5 v. 37 cm.

A reproduction of a card bibliography in the Geography and Map Division, which contains an estimated 90,000 entries for works published from the early 19th century through 1971.

U. S. *Library of Congress. Map Division.*
Three-dimensional maps; an annotated list of references relating to the construction and use of terrain models, compiled by Walter W. Ristow. 2d ed., rev. and enl. Washington ₍For sale by the Superintendent of Documents, U. S. Govt. Print. Off.₎ 1964 ₍i. e. 1965₎

x, 38 p. 27 cm.

Watkins, Jessie B
Selected bibliography on maps in libraries: acquisition, classification, cataloging, storage, uses. Compiled by Jessie B. Watkins. ₍Syracuse, N. Y.₎ Syracuse University, 1965.

17 l. 28 cm.

CARTY, WILLIAM EDWARD

Washington (State) State University, Pullman. *Library. Manuscript-Archives Division.*
William Edward Carty: an indexed register of his papers, 1898–1963, in the Washington State University Library. Pullman, 1967.

42 p. 27 cm.

CASAS, BARTOLOMÉ DE LAS, BP. OF CHIAPA

Mejía Sánchez, Ernesto.
Las Casas en México; exposición bibliográfica conmemorativa del cuarto centenario de su muerte, 1566–1966. ₍1. ed.₎ México, Universidad Nacional Autónoma de México, 1967.

169 p. facsims., port. 18 cm. (Anejos al Boletín de la Biblioteca Nacional, 2)

At head of title: Instituto Bibliográfico Mexicano. Biblioteca Nacional.

CASCUDO, LUÍS DA CÂMARA

Lima Filho, Diógenes da Cunha.
Bibliografia de Luís da Câmara Cascudo. Natal, 1965.

14 p. port. 24 cm.

Mamede, Zila.
Luís da Câmara Cascudo: 50 anos de vida intelectual,

1918–1968; bibliografia anotada. Natal, Fundação José Augusto, 1970.

2 v. in 3 (1043 p.) port. 24 cm.

CASE INSTITUTE OF TECHNOLOGY, CLEVELAND

Case Archive.
The Case Archive and record service ₍by₎ Herbert R. Young. ₍Cleveland, Case Institute of Technology-₎ Dept. of Institute Relations, 1964.

19 p. 28 cm.

On cover: Index to Case Archives.

CASEY, SILAS

U. S. *Library of Congress. Manuscript Division.*
Silas Casey, Stanford Caldwell Hooper; a register of their papers in the Library of Congress. Washington, Library of Congress, 1968.

5, 9 l. 27 cm.

"Naval Historical Foundation collection."

CASPIAN SEA

Gîul', K   K
Библиографический аннотированный справочник по Каспийскому морю. Баку, "Элм," 1970.

217 p. with diagrs. 22 cm.

At head of title: Академия наук Азербайджанской ССР. Институт Географии. Фундаментальная библиотека. К. К. Гюль, П. В. Жило, В. М. Жирнов.

Gîul, K   K
Каспийское море. Реферативный сборник. Москва, 1970.

236 p. 27 cm.

At head of title: Всесоюзный институт научной и технической информации Государственного комитета Совета Министров СССР по науке и технике и Академии наук СССР. Институт географии Академии наук Азербайджанской ССР. Гюль К. К., Лаппалайнен Т. Н., Полушкин В. А.

CASSAVA

Mattos, Carmélia Regina de.
Mandioca (Manihot utiliasima). Compilada por Carmélia Mattos e Herbene Valença. Cruz das Almas, Brasil, 1969.

31 l. 28 cm. (Instituto de Pesquisas e Experimentação Agropecuárias do Leste. Lista bibliográfica no. 16)

CASSIUS, JAROSLAV KOLMAN, pseud. see Kolman, Jaroslaw

CAST-IRON

Ghee, M   P
Working of nodular cast iron, compiled by M. P. Ghee. Adelaide, State Library of South Australia, 1971.

10 p. 26 cm. (Research service bibliographies, series 4, no. 150)

CASTE

Dōshisha Daigaku, Kyoto. Jimbun Kagaku Kenkyūjo.
(Dōshisha Daigaku Jimbun Kagaku Kenkyūjo shozō buraku mondai bunken mokuroku)

同志社大学人文科学研究所々蔵　部落問題文献
目録　京都　同志社大学人文科学研究所　昭和44
(1969)

96 p.　26 cm.

CASTLE, WILLIAM RICHARDS

Herbert Hoover Presidential Library.
William R. Castle papers. ₍West Branch, Iowa, 1971?₎

67 l.　28 cm.

CASTOR-BEAN

Almeida, Norma Martins de.
Mamona; bibliografia das publicações que se encontram
na biblioteca dêste Instituto. compilado por Norma M. de
Almeida. Cruz das Almas, 1967.

20 l.　32 cm.　(Instituto de Pesquisas e Experimentação Agropecuárias do Leste. Lista bibliográfica no. 8)

CASTRIOT, GEORGE see Kastriōtes, Geōrgios

CASTRO, BRAZIL

**Paraná, Brazil (State). Universidade Federal. Departa-
mento de História.**
Arquivos da cidade de Castro. Curitiba, 1972.

129 p.　23 cm.　(Its Boletim, no. 16)

CATALAN IMPRINTS

Instituto Nacional del Libro Españól.
Llibres en català. Barcelona, 1967.

173 p.　24 cm.

Instituto Nacional del Libro Español.
Llibres en Català. Barcelona, 1968.

282 p.　25 cm.

Half title: Catàleg de llibres en català.

CATALOGING, LIBRARY see Library science - Processing

CATALOGS, BOOKSELLERS' AND PUBLISHERS'

Growoll, Adolf, 1850–1909.
Book trade bibliography in the United States in the
nineteenth century, by Adolph Growoll. New York, B.
Franklin ₍1969₎

lxxvii, 79 p.　24 cm.　(Burt Franklin bibliography and reference
series #89)

Reprint of the 1939 ed.
"Catalogue of all the books printed in the United States" (79 p.)
has special t. p., a reproduction of the original, Boston, 1804, except
for the omission of article "A" with which the original title begins.

CONTENTS.—pt. 1. The beginnings of booktrade bibliography.
Bookseller's associations, 1801–1892. Side-lights on the early conditions of the book-trade. The first book-trade catalogue. Book-
trade helps, 1801–1897. Chronological list of catalogues, book-trade
and literary journals. Sketches of some American bookseller-bib-
liographers.—pt. 2. Catalogue of all the books printed in the United
States ... Published by the bookseller's in Boston, January, 1804.

McKay, George Leslie, 1895–
American book auction catalogues, 1713–1934; a union

list. Compiled by George L. McKay. With an introd. by
Clarence S. Brigham. Including supplements of 1946 and
1948. Detroit, Gale Research Co., 1967.

xxxii, 560 p.　facsims.　23 cm.

Title page includes original imprint: New York, New York Public
Library, 1937.
"Reprinted with additions from the Bulletin of the New York
Public Library, 1935–1936."

Mouchová, Saša.
Bibliografický soupis knih vydaných v letech 1965–1967.
Sest. Saša Mouchová.—Bibliografický soupis reproduckí
vydaných v letech 1965–1967. Sest. Jitka Mědílková.
Uspoř. Rudolf Lužík. Praha, Odeon, t. Rudé právo, 1971.

221, ₍3₎ p.　20 cm.

On spine: Bibliografický soupis knih a reprodukcí vydaných
Odeonem v letech 1965–1967.

Richter, Günter, fl. 1965–　　*ed.*
Verlegerplakate des xvi. und xvii. Jahrhunderts bis zum
Beginn des Dreissigjährigen Krieges. Wiesbaden, Pressler,
1965.

42 p., 22 plates (in portfolio)　43 cm.

Sale catalogues of libraries of eminent persons. General
editor: A. N. L. Munby. London, Mansell Information/
Publishing Ltd; Sotheby Parke-Bernet Publications, Ltd,
1971–
v.　25 cm.
"The catalogues have been reproduced wherever possible from
priced and annotated copies."
CONTENTS: v. 1. Munby, A. N. L.　Poets and men of letters.—

v. 3. Gemmet, R. J.　Poets and men of letters.—v. 4. Watkins, D. J.
Architects.- v. 5. Parks, S.　Poets and men of letters.—v. 6. Wool-
ford, J.　Poets and men of letters.

Schmidová-Hornišová, Eva.
Bibliografia produkcie vydavateľstva Mladé letá za roky
1950–1969. Zostavila Eva Schmidová-Hornišová. ₍Brati-
slava Mladé letá, 1971₎

525 .　25 cm.

CATALOGS, COLLEGE

Schroeder, Konrad, 1941–
Vorläufiges Verzeichnis der in Bibliotheken und Archiven
vorhandenen Vorlesungsverzeichnisse deutschsprachiger
Universitäten aus der Zeit vor 1945. Saarbrücken, An-
glistisches Institut der Universität des Saarlandes, 1964.

1 v. (unpaged)　21 cm.

CATALONIA

Colomer Preses, Ignasi Maria.
Els mapes antics de les terres catalanes des del segle XI
₍per₎ Mossèn Colomer. Granollers, Editorial Montblanc,
1967.

101 p.　maps (1 fold.)　17 cm.　(Biblioteca excursionista, v. 7.
Sèrie cartogràfica, no. 1)

Comisión Mixta de Coordinación Estadística de Barcelona.
Bibliografía económica de Cataluña 1960–1969. ₍Barce-
lona, 1971?₎

116 p.　21 cm.　(Its Serie bibliográfica, no. 2)

Feliu i Monfort, Gaspar.
Bibliografía de historia económica de Cataluña, 1950–
1970, por Gaspar Feliu Monfort. ₍Barcelona, 1971₎

165 p. 22 cm. (Fondo Cultural de la Caja de Ahorros Provincial de la Diputación de Barcelona. ₁Publicaciones₁ 11)

Giralt y Raventós, Emilio, 1927–
Bibliografia dels moviments socials a Catalunya, país Valencià i les Illes. Dirigida per E. Giralt i Raventós amb la col·laboració de A. Balcells. A. Cucó, J. Termes ... Barcelona, Lavínia ₁1972₁

xiv, 832 p. 22 cm.

BIO-BIBLIOGRAPHY

Elías de Molins, Antonio, 1850–1909.
Diccionario biográfico y bibliográfico de escritores y artistas catalanes del siglo XIX. Hildesheim, New York, G. Olms, 1972.

2 v. illus. 25 cm.   GDB***

Reprint of the edition published in Barcelona in 1889-1895.

Torres Amat, Félix, Bp., 1772–1847.
Memorias para ayudar a formar un diccionario crítico de los escritores catalanes (Barcelona, 1836). Barcelona, Curial, 1973.

xliii, 719 p. 23 cm. (Documents de cultura-facsímils, no. 1)

—— Suplemento al Diccionario crítico de los escritores catalanes (Burgos, 1849) per Joan Corminas. Barcelona, Curial, 1973.

368 p. 23 cm. (Documents de cultura-facsímils, no. 2)

CATAPHORESIS see Electrophoresis

CATECHISMS

Eames, Wilberforce, 1855–1937.
Early New England catechisms; a bibliographical account of some catechisms published before the year 1800, for use in New England. Worcester, Mass., Press of C. Hamilton, 1898. Detroit, Singing Tree Press, 1969.

111 p. 22 cm.

"Read, in part, before the American Antiquarian Society, at its annual meeting in Worcester, October 21, 1897."

Eames, Wilberforce, 1855–1937.
Early New England catechisms; a bibliographical account of some catechisms published before the year 1800, for use in New England. New York, B. Franklin ₁1971?₁

iv, 111 p. 23 cm. (Burt Franklin bibliography and reference series, no. 78)

Reprint of the 1898 ed.

CATERINA DA SIENA, SAINT

Zanini, Lina.
Bibliografia analitica di s. ₁i. e. santa₁ Caterina da Siena, 1901–1950. Roma, Edizioni cateriniane, 1971.

viii, 251 p. 24 cm.

At head of title: Centro nazionale di studi cateriniani.

CATERING see Restaurants

CATHOLIC CHURCH

Boyle, Leonard E
A survey of the Vatican archives and its medieval holdings, by Leonard E. Boyle. Toronto, Pontifical Institute of Medieval Studies, 1972.

iv, 250 p. 25 cm. (Pontifical Institute of Mediaeval Studies. Subsidia mediaevalia, 1)

Cernitori, Giuseppe.
Biblioteca polemica degli scrittori che dal 1770 sino al 1793 hanno o difesi, o impugnati i dogmi della Cattolica Romana Chiesa: opera di D. Giuseppe Cernitori. Farnborough (Hants.), Gregg, 1967.

₁10₁, 266 p. 21½ cm.

Facsimile reprint of the 1793 ed.

Halkin, Léon Ernest, 1906–
Les archives des nonciatures. Bruxelles, Institut historique belge de Rome; Rome, Academia Belgica, 1968.

91 p. 25 cm. (Bibliothèque de l'Institut historique belge de Rome, fasc. 14)

Hurter, Hugo, 1832–1914.
Nomenclator literarius theologiae Catholicae theologos exhibens aetate, natione, disciplinis distinctos. Edidit et commentariis auxit H. Hurter. New York, B. Franklin ₁197–?₁

5 v. in 6. 24 cm. (Burt Franklin bibliographical and reference series, no. 39)

Reprint of vols. from various editions published 1906-26.
CONTENTS: t. 1. Aetas prima. Ab aerae Christianae initiis ad theologiae scholasticae exordia (1109) 4. ed. cura F. Pangerl.—t. 2. Aetas media. Ab exordiis theologiae scholasticae usque ad celebratum Concilium Tridentinum, ab anno 1100–1563. 2. ed. emendata et plurimum aucta.—t. 3. Aetas recens: post celebratum Concilium Tridentinum seculum primum, ab anno 1564–1663. 3. ed. plurimum aucta et emendata.—t. 4. Aetas recens: seculum secundum post celebratum Concilium Tridentinum, ab anno 1664–1763. 3. ed. plurimum aucta et emendata.—t. 5. Aetas recens: pars 1. Seculum tertium post celebratum Concilium Tridentinum, ab anno 1764–1869. pars 2. Theologos complectens novissimos, ab anno 1870–1910. 3. ed. plurimum aucta et emendata. 2 v.

Mierzwinski, Theophil T 1924–
What do you think of the priest? A bibliography on the Catholic priesthood. Compiled and edited by Theophil T. Mierzwinski. With a foreword by John F. Whealon. ₁1st ed.₁ New York, Exposition Press ₁1972₁

95 p. 22 cm. (An Exposition-university book)

Posoborowe publikacje teologiczne w Polsce. Praca zbiorowa pod red. J. Myśkowa i B. Przybyszewskiego. Warszawa, Akademia Teologii Katolickiej, 1969.

437 p. 24 cm.

Venezuela. Biblioteca Nacional, Caracas.
Catálogo de libros de la Exposición Catequística. Con un estudio histórico y bibliográfico por Lucila L. de Pérez Díaz. Cuernavaca, México, Centro Intercultural de Documentación, 1970.

74 p. 23 cm. (Sondeos, no. 24)

"260 ejemplares."
Both the essay and the catalog were originally published in the periodical Adsum, Caracas, 1943.

CONTENTS.—Presentación, por P. Grases.—Revista de los libros principales que formaron la Exposición Catequística de la Biblioteca Nacional, con algunos apuntes históricos y bibliográficos, por L. L. de Pérez Díaz.—Exposición Catequística de la Biblioteca Nacional de Venezuela; fichero completo de los libros expuestos en la Biblioteca Nacional de Caracas, con motivo del Primer Congreso Catequístico Nacional.

LITURGY AND RITUAL

Charles Louis de Bourbon, Duke of Parma, 1799–1883.
Bibliothèque liturgique: Description des livres de liturgie

imprimés aux XVe et XVIe siècles, faisant partie de la bibliothèque de S. A. R. Mgr Charles-Louis de Bourbon, par Anatole Alès. New York, B. Franklin [1970]

2 v. in 1. 22 cm. (Burt Franklin bibliography & reference series, 377. Philosophy monograph series, 41)
Running title: Bibliothèque de Charles-Louis de Bourbon.
Reprint of the main work published in Paris, 1878, and of the supplement published in Paris, 1884.

Darmstadt. Hessische Landes- und Hochschulbibliothek.

Die liturgischen Handschriften der Hessischen Landes- und Hochschulbibliothek Darmstadt, beschrieben von Leo Eizenhöfer und Hermann Knaus. Wiesbaden, O. Harrassowitz, 1968.

382 p. col. plate. 23 cm. (Die Handschriften der Hessischen Landes- und Hochschulbibliothek Darmstadt, Bd. 2)

Falk, Franz, 1840–1909.

Die deutschen Mess-Auslegungen von der Mitte des fünfzehnten Jahrhunderts bis zum Jahre 1525. Amsterdam, Rodopi, 1969.

ix, 53 p. facsim. 22 cm.

Photomechanical reprint of the Köln, 1889 ed.

Gamber, Klaus.

Codices liturgici latini antiquiores. Secunda editio aucta. Freiburg/Schweiz, Universitätsverlag, 1968.

2 v. (651 p.) 26 cm. (Spicilegii Friburgensis subsidia, vol. 1)

Janini, José.

Manuscritos litúrgicos de la Biblioteca Nacional. Catálogo por José Janini y José Serrano. Con la colaboración de Anscario M. Mundo. Madrid, Dirección General de Archivos y Bibliotecas, 1969.

xxviii, 332 p. illus. (part col.), facsims. 25 cm.

Olivar, Alexandre.

Els manuscrits litúrgics de la Biblioteca de Montserrat. Monestir de Montserrat, 1969.

211 p. 24 cm. (Scripta et documenta, 18)

Pierpont Morgan Library, *New York.*

Liturgical manuscripts for the Mass and the Divine Office, by John Plummer. With an introd. by Anselm Strittmatter. New York, 1964.

53 p. 24 facsims. 26 cm.

Catalog of manuscripts selected for exhibition in the Pierpont Morgan Library, Jan. 14–Mar. 21, 1964.

Radó, Polikárp, 1899–

Libri liturgici manuscripti bibliothecarum Hungariae et limitropharum regionum quos recensuit Polycarpus Radó. Primae partis editio revisa et aucta cui et toti operi adlaboravit Ladislaus Mezey. Budapest, Akadémiai Kiadó, 1973.

639 p. 25 cm.

Salmon, Pierre, Aug. 23, 1896–

Les manuscrits liturgiques latins de la Bibliothèque vaticane ... Città del Vaticano, Biblioteca apostolica vaticana, 1968–72.

5 v. 25 cm. (Studi e testi, 251, 253, 260, 267, 270)

CONTENTS: 1. Psautiers, antiphonaires, hymnaires, collectaires, bréviaires.—2. Sacramentaires, épistoliers, évangéliaires, graduels, missels.—3. Ordines Romani, pontificaux, rituels, cérémoniaux.—4. Les livres de lectures de l'office. Les livres de l'office du chapitre. Les livres d'heures.—5. Liste complémentaire. Tables générales.

Zaccaria, Francesco Antonio, 1714–1780.

Bibliotheca ritualis, concinnatum opus a Francisco Antonio Zaccaria. New York, B. Franklin [1964]

2 v. in 3. 26 cm. (Burt Franklin bibliography and reference series, 58)
Reprint of the ed. published in Rome, 1776–1781.
CONTENTS.—t. 1. De libris ad sacros utriusque Ecclesiae Orientalis, et occidentalis ritus pertinentibus.—t. 2. De librorum ritualium explanatoribus. Pars altera supplementa continens, praemisso Joannis Maldonati inedito De caeremoniis tractatu, cui praeter adnotationes adcedit gemina editoris dissertatio. 2 v.

PERIODICALS

The Catholic periodical and literature index.

Haverford, Pa., Catholic Library Association.

v. 29 cm.

Began with July/Aug. 1968 issue. Cf. New serial titles.
Continues the Catholic periodical index.
Absorbed the Guide to Catholic literature.

CATHOLIC CHURCH IN AUSTRIA

Catholic Church. *Apostolic Nunciature (Austria)*
Nuntiaturberichte. Wien, H. Böhlaus Nachf., 1970–

v. 24 cm. (Publikationen des österreichischen Kulturinstituts in Rom, 2. Abt.: Quellen, Reihe 2)

CONTENTS.—Bd. 1. Der Schriftverkehr zwischen dem päpstlichen Staatssekretariat und dem Nuntius am Kaiserhof Antonio Eugenio Visconti, 1767–1774.

CATHOLIC CHURCH IN CALIFORNIA

Weber, Francis J

A select bibliographical guide to California Catholic periodical literature, 1844–1973. Compiled and annotated by Francis J. Weber, Los Angeles, Dawson's Book Shop [1973]

viii, 118 p. 19 cm.

Weber, Francis J

A select bibliography to California Catholic literature, 1856–1974 / compiled and annotated by Francis J. Weber. — Los Angeles : Dawson's Book Shop, [1974]

x, 70 p. : 19 cm.

Weber, Francis J

A select guide to California Catholic history, by Francis J. Weber. Los Angeles, Westernlore Press, 1966.

xxvii, 227 p. illus., port. 22 cm.

CATHOLIC CHURCH IN CANADA

History collection: Canadian catholic church. Collection d'histoire: L'Église catholique canadienne. Catalogue no. 1–
1971–
Saskatoon, St. Thomas More College.

v. 22 cm.

CATHOLIC CHURCH IN ENGLAND

St. Mary's Seminary, Oscott, Eng.
Recusant books at St. Mary's, Oscott. New Oscott, Warwickshire, 1964–

v. illus. 24 cm.
On cover: The Oscotian.
Bibliography: v. 1, p. 1–[v]

CONTENTS: pt. 1. 1518–1687:
—— ——— Short-title index. ₍New Oscott, Warwickshire,
1967–
v. 24 cm.
Caption title.
On cover: The Oscotian.
CONTENTS: pt. 1, section 1. 1518–1687.

CATHOLIC CHURCH IN ITALY

Marinelli, Olga.
Le confraternite di Perugia dalle origini al sec. xix;
bibliografia delle opere a stampa. Perugia, Edizioni "Gra-
fica" ₍1965₎

1035 p. 25 cm.

"Estratto dagli Annali della Facoltà di lettere e filosofia ₍dell'Università di Perugia₎, vol. II e seguenti."

CATHOLIC CHURCH IN THE NETHERLANDS

Katholiek Documentatie Centrum.
Archieven van het Katholiek Documentatie Centrum; een
reeks inventarissen, uitg. onder red. van A. F. Manning,
W. A. A. Mes ₍en₎ J. H. Roes. Nijmegen, 1973–

v. illus. 22 cm.

CATHOLIC LITERATURE

Bernard, Jack F
A guide to Catholic reading ₍by₎ Jack F. Bernard and
John J. Delaney. Garden City, N. Y., 1966.

vi, 392 p. 22 cm.

Carey, Marie Aimee.
A bibliography for Christian formation in the family.
Glen Rock, N. J., Paulist Press ₍1964₎

175 p. 19 cm. (Deus books)

The **Catholic** book in Poland, 1945–1965; classified catalogue.
₍Prepared by Maria Pszczółkowska. Translated by Danuta
Karcz and Jolanta Ronikier₎ Warszawa, Ars Christiana,
1966.

544 p. 21 cm.

Translation of Książka katolicka w Polsce, 1945–1965.

Falk, Franz, 1840–1909.
Die Druckkunst im Dienste der Kirche, zunächst in
Deutschland, bis zum Jahre 1520. Amsterdam, Rodopi
(Nieuwe Herengracht 35) 1969.

108 p. 22 cm. (Görres-Gesellschaft zur Pflege der Wissenschaft
im Katholischen Deutschland. Vereinsschrift 2)

Reprint of the 1879 ed. published in Cologne.

Książka katolicka w Polsce, 1945–1965; spis bibliograficzny.
₍Opracowanie: Maria Pszczółkowska.₎ Warszawa, Ars
Christiana, 1966.

463 p. illus. 21 cm.

Le Livre catholique en Pologne, 1945–1965; liste bibliographique. ₍Traduction: Jan Ostrowski et Halszka Wiśniow-
ska₎ Warszawa, Ars Christiana, 1967.

522 p. 21 cm.

Translation of: Książka katolicka w Polsce. 1945–1965.

McCabe, James Patrick.
Critical guide to Catholic reference books. With an introd. by

Russell E. Bidlack. Littleton, Colo., Libraries Unlimited, 1971.

287 p. 24 cm. (Research studies in library science, no. 2)

Based on the author's thesis, University of Michigan.

Rennhofer, Friedrich.
Bücherkunde des katholischen Lebens; bibliographisches
Lexikon der religiösen Literatur der Gegenwart. Wien,
Brüder Hollinek ₍1961₎

xii, 360 p. 25 cm.

—— ——— Nachtrag (1960–1965) Wien, Brüder Hollinek
₍1967–

v. 25 cm.

CATILINA, LUCIUS SERGIUS

Criniti, Nicola.
Bibliografia catilinaria. Milano, Vita e pensiero, 1971.

84 p. 22 cm. (Pubblicazioni dell'Università cattolica del S. Cuore.
Saggi e ricerche. Serie 3: Scienze storiche, 6)

CATS

Necker, Claire.
Four centuries of cat books; a bibliography, 1570–1970.
Metuchen, N. J., Scarecrow Press, 1972.

vii, 511 p. 22 cm.

CATTANEO, CARLO

Armani, Giuseppe.
Gli scritti su Carlo Cattaneo. Saggio di una bibliografia
(1836–1972). Pisa, Nistri-Lischi, 1973.

243 p. 22 cm. (Domus mazziniana, Pisa. Collana scientifica, 13)

CATTLE see Livestock

CAUCASIAN LANGUAGES

Aliroev, I IŪ
Библиография по нахскому языкознанию. ₍Авт. предисл. и сост. И. Ю. Алироев₎. Грозный, Чечено-Ингуш.
кн. изд., 1968.

95 p. 20 cm.

At head of title: Чечено-Ингушский научно-исследовательский
институт истории, языка, литературы и экономики при Совете
Министров ЧИАССР.

CAUCASUS

Miansarov, Mikhail Misropovich, 1830–1880.
Bibliographia Caucasica et Transcaucasica. ₍Door₎ M.
Miansarof. Amsterdam, Meridian Publishing Co., 1967.

xiii, 814 p. 22½ cm.

Unabridged reprint of St. Petersburg ed., 1874–1876.
In Russian.

CAVES see Speleology

CAVITATION

Chadwick, U R M
Bibliography on cavitation in fluids, ₍by₎ (Miss) U. R. M.
Chadwick. London, H. M. S. O., 1966.

₍3₎, 21 p. 30 cm. (United Kingdom Atomic Energy Authority.
Reactor Group. TRG information series, no. 518)

Trondheim. **Norges tekniske høgskole.** *Biblioteket.*
Kavitasjon. Trondheim, 1967.

23 p. 29 cm. (*Its* Litteraturliste 33)

CAZI, JOSIP

Bio-bibliografija Josipa Cazija. Lektura i oprema: Brane
Crlenjak. Vukovar, Općinsko sindikalno vijeće; Centar za
kulturu Radničkog sveučilišta, 1969.

57, ₁1₁ p. with port. 21 cm.

CEARÁ, BRAZIL (STATE)

Souza, Maria da Conceição.
Estudos bibliográficos cearenses. Fortaleza, Imprensa
Universitária da Universidade Federal do Ceará, 1973–

v. 22 cm. (Biblioteca de cultura. Série A: Documentário,
v. 7)

CONTENTS: v. 1. Livros e folhetos.

CECCHI, EMILIO

Scudder, Giuliana.
Bibliografia degli scritti di Emilio Cecchi. A cura di
Giuliana Scudder. Roma, Edizioni di storia e letteratura,
1970.

316 p. plates. 25 cm. (Sussidi eruditi, 24)

CELA, CAMILO JOSÉ

Huarte Morton, Fernando.
Bibliografía de Viaje a la Alcarria de Camilo José Cela.
Guadalajara, Diputación Provincial, 1972.

72 p. 23 cm.

Huarte Mortón, Fernando.
Ensayo de una bibliografía de "La familia de Pascual
Duarte." Madrid, 1968.

62–105 p. facsims. 19 cm.

Cover title.
"Sobretiro de los Papeles de Son Armadans, no. 142, enero de
1968."

CELLULOSE

Roth, Lillian.
Chemical modification of cellulose ₁by₁ Lillian Roth and
Jack Weiner. Appleton, Wis., Institute of Paper Chemistry,
1966–67.

3 v. 28 cm. (Appleton, Wis. Institute of Paper Chemistry.
Bibliographic series, no. 228–229, 234)

CONTENTS.—1. Cross-linking.—2. Chemical and radiation grafting.—
3. Esters and ethers.

CELTIC LITERATURE

Harvard University. Library.
Celtic literatures; classification schedule, classified listing by
call number, chronological listing, author and title listing.
Cambridge, Mass.; Distributed by the Harvard University Press,
1970.

192 p. 29 cm. (Its Widener Library shelflist, 25)

CELTS

Scotland. National Library, Edinburgh.
Celtica. Edinburgh, 1967.

v, 56 p. illus. 25 cm. (Its catalogue no. 6)
Errata slip inserted.

CEMENT

Stenger, Ferdinand.
Selected bibliography of cement and concrete technology.
Denver, ₁U. S. Bureau of Reclamation, Office of Engineer-
ing Reference, Library Branch₁ 1965.

23 p. 27 cm. (₁U. S. Bureau of Reclamation. Office of Engineering Reference. Library Branch₁ Bibliography no. 243)

BIBLIOGRAPHIES

Cement and Concrete Association. *Library.*
A bibliography of bibliographies on cement and concrete:
an arrangement of all the published bibliographies compiled
by the Library of the Cement and Concrete Association during the period 1946–1967. London, Cement and Concrete
Association, 1968.

₁2₁, 3, 8 p. 30 cm.

CENSUS
see also United States - Census

U. S. *Library of Congress. Census Library Project.*
National censuses and vital statistics in Europe, 1918–
1939: an annotated bibliography, with 1940–1948 supplement. Prepared by Henry J. Dubester, chief. Detroit,
Gale Research Co., 1967.

vii, 215, v, 48 p. 24 cm.

At head of title: United States Department of Commerce ...
Bureau of the Census ... United States Library of Congress ...
Reference Department ...
Title page includes original imprint: Washington, 1948.

U. S. *Library of Congress. Census Library Project.*
National censuses and vital statistics in Europe, 1918–
1939; an annotated bibliography, prepared by Henry J.
Dubester, chief. New York, B. Franklin ₁1969₁

vii, 215, v, 48 p. 24 cm. (Selected essays in history, economics, &
social science, 79)

Burt Franklin bibliography & reference series, 239.
"Originally published 1948."
"National censuses and vital statistics in Europe, 1940–1948 supple-
ment": p. ₁1₁–v, 1–48 (3d and 4th groups, respectively)

CENTO, ITALY

Fanti, Mario, comp.
Gli archivi capitolare e parrocchiale di S. Biagio di Cento.
Inventario a cura di Mario Fanti. Bologna, Presso la
Deputazione di storia patria, 1972.

vii, 225 p. plates. 24 cm. (Deputazione di storia patria per le
province di Romagna. Documenti e studi, v. 9)

CENTRAL AMERICA
Rodríguez, Mario, 1922–
A guide for the study of culture in Central America; humani-
ties and social sciences, by Mario Rodríguez and Vincent C.
Peloso. Washington, Pan American Union, 1968.

vii, 88 p. 28 cm. (₁Pan American Union. Division of Philosophy and Letters₁ Basic bibliographies, 5)

CENTRIFUGES

Browning, Phyllis M
Preparative ultracentrifuge applications; an annotated
bibliography, compiled by Phyllis M. Browning. Palo

Alto, Calif., Spinco Division of Beckman Instruments
₁1969₎

v, 117 p. 28 cm.

Ultracentrifuge applications. 1969–
Palo Alto, Calif., Spinco Division of Beckman Instruments, inc.

v. 28 cm. annual.

Compiler: 1969–   P. M. Browning.

CENTRO INTERAMERICANO DE INVESTIGACIÓN Y DOCUMENTACIÓN SOBRE FORMACIÓN PROFESIONAL

Centro Interamericano de Investigación y Documentación sobre Formación Profesional.
Catálogo de publicaciones CINTERFOR, 1964–1970. Montevideo, 1970.

75 p. 26 cm.

Centro Interamericano de Investigación y Documentación sobre Formación Profesional.
Catálogo de publicaciones CINTERFOR, 1964–1971. Montevideo, 1971.

92 p. 26 cm.

CEPHALOSPORIN

Brierley, R   V
The cephalosporins, by R. V. Brierley and E. J. Scott. Brentwood (Essex), Selected Dissemination Information Ltd ₁1970₎.

₁41₎ leaves. 30 cm.

CERAMICS
see also   Glass; Tiles

Hench, L   L
A bibliography of ceramics and glass; L. L. Hench, editor. Gainesville, Fla., 1967.

v, 85 p. 28 cm. (Florida. University, Gainesville. Engineering and Industrial Experiment Station. Bulletin series no. 126)

Engineering progress at the University of Florida, v. 21, no. 1. "A State technical services monograph."

Krakow.   Akademia Górniczo-Hutnicza.   Instytut Ceramiki Specjalnej i Ogniotrwałej.
Prace.
1–
₁Kraków₎ 1973–

no. 24 cm. (Zeszyty naukowe Akademii Górniczo-Hutniczej im. Stanisława Staszica. Ceramika)

Stephani, Claus.
Töpferkunst der Deutschen in Rumänien. Bibliographie. ₁Riehen,₎ Keramik-Freunde der Schweiz, 1972.

56 p. 21 cm. (Keramikfreunde der Schweiz. Neujahrsgabe, 1972)

PERIODICALS

Binns-Merrill Library.
Periodicals and serial publications. 1968–
Alfred.

v. 28 cm.

Supersedes its Serial publications.

CEREMONIES

Landwehr, John.
Splendid ceremonies; state entries and royal funerals in the Low Countries, 1515–1791. A bibliography. Nieuwkoop, De Graaf; Leiden, Sijthoff, 1971.

276 p. with illus. 27 cm.

ČERMÁK, DOMINIK

Křivský, Pavel.
Dominik Čermák (1835–1890). Lit. pozůstalost. Zprac. Pavel Křivský. Praha, Lit. archív Památníku nár. písemnictví, rozmn. Ruch, Liberec, 1971.

14, ₁1₎ p. 21 cm. (Edice inventářů, čís. 235)

ČERNÝ, TOMÁŠ

Kirschnerová, Jana.
Tomáš Černý (1840–1909); literární pozůstalost (fragment). Praha, Literární archív Památníku národniho písemnictví, 1971.

3 p. 21 cm. (Edice inventářů, čís. 197)

CERVANTES SAAVEDRA, MIGUEL DE

Drake, Dana B
Miguel de Cervantes Saavedra; a critical bibliography, by Dana B. Drake. ₁Blacksburg? Va.₎ 1968–

v. 22 cm.

"Based on a dissertation presented ... at the University of North Carolina at Chapel Hill."

CONTENTS.—v. 1. The novelas ejemplares.

Monterey, Mexico.   Instituto Tecnológico y de Estudios Superiores.   Biblioteca.
Catálogo abreviado de la Colección Cervantina "Carlos Prieto" del Instituto Tecnológico y de Estudios Superiores de Monterrey, por Andrés Estrada Jasso. ₁1. ed.₎ Monterrey, 1965.

viii, 111 p. 24 cm. (Publicaciones del Instituto Tecnológico y de Estudios Superiores de Monterrey. Serie: Catálogos de Biblioteca, 1)

Rius y de Llosellas, Leopoldo, 1840–1898.
Bibliografía crítica de las obras de Miguel de Cervantes Saavedra. New York, B. Franklin ₁1970₎

3 v. illus., ports. 24 cm. (Essays in literature & criticism, 72)

Burt Franklin Bibliography & reference series, 840. Reprint of the edition published in Madrid, 1895–1905.

ČESKÝ KRUMLOV, CZECHOSLOVAK REPUBLIC (OKRES)

Navrátil, František.
Soupis vlastivědné literatury okresu Český Krumlov. České Budějovice, Jihočes. muzeum, rozmn. Kraj. knihovna, 1970.

₁430₎ p. 29 cm.

CEYLON
see also under   Pakistan *(Selected reading lists)*

Birman, D A
(Bibliografiĭa Tseĭlona)
Библиография Цейлона. 1917–1967. Москва, "Наука," 1973.

38 p. 21 cm.

At head of title: Академия наук СССР. Институт востоковедения. Институт научной информации по общественным наукам. By D. A. Birman and M. N. Kafitina.

Goonetileke, H A I
A bibliography of Ceylon; a systematic guide to the literature on the land, people, history and culture published in Western languages from the sixteenth century to the present day [by] H. A. I. Goonetileke. Foreword by J. D. Pearson. Zug, Switzerland, Inter Documentation Co. [°1970]

2 v. (lxxx, 865 p.) 21 cm. (Bibliotheca Asiatica, 5)

Macdonald, Teresa.
Union catalogue of the Government of Ceylon publications held by libraries in London, Oxford and Cambridge. London, Mansell, 1970.

[6] p., 75 columns. 26 cm.

At head of title: Centre of South Asian Studies, University of Cambridge.

U. S. *Library of Congress. American Libraries Book Procurement Center, Delhi.*
Accessions list, Ceylon. v. 1–
Mar. 1967–
New Delhi.

v. 28 cm. quarterly.

At head of title: The Library of Congress Public Law 480 Project.

LAW see Law - Ceylon

CHADWICK, HECTOR MUNRO and NORA KERSHAW

A list of the published writings of Hector Munro Chadwick and his wife Nora Kershaw Chadwick presented to Nora Kershaw Chadwick on her eightieth birthday, 28 January 1971. [Edinburgh, Distributed by the National Library of Scotland, 1971]

28 p. ports. 22 cm.

Limited ed. of 300 copies.

CHAFFEE, EDMUND BIGELOW

Syracuse University. Library. Manuscript Collections.
Edmund B. Chaffee, an inventory of his papers in Syracuse University Library. Compiled by Walter Timms. Syracuse, N. Y., 1968.

xiii, 185 p. 28 cm. (Its Manuscript inventory series. Inventory no. 11)

CHAGAS' DISEASE

Olivier, Margaret C
A bibliography on Chagas' disease (1909–1969) by Margaret C. Olivier, Louis J. Olivier [and] Dorothy B. Segal. Washington, U. S. Govt. Print. Off., 1972.

vii, 633 p. 26 cm. (Index-catalogue of medical and veterinary zoology. Special publication no. 2)

At head of title: United States Department of Agriculture.

CHAGHATAYAN LITERATURE see Jagataic literature

CHAĬKOVSKIĬ, PETR IL'ICH

Tschaikowsky-Studio.
Systematisches Verzeichnis der Werke von Pjotr Iljitsch Tschaikowsky; ein Handbuch für die Musikpraxis. Hamburg, Musikverlag H. Sikorski [c1973]

112 p. 27 cm.

CHAMBERS, WASHINGTON IRVING

U. S. *Library of Congress. Manuscript Division.*
Washington Irving Chambers; a register of his papers in the Library of Congress. Washington, 1967.

15 l. 27 cm.

"Naval Historical Foundation Collection."

CHAMPIER, SYMPHORIEN

Allut, Paul, b. ca. 1800.
Étude biographique et bibliographique sur Symphorien Champier. [Réimpression de l'éd. de Lyon, 1859]. Nieuwkoop, De Graaf, 1972.

xxiv, 435 p. with illus. 22 cm.

CHANDLER, RAYMOND

Bruccoli, Matthew Joseph, 1931–
Raymond Chandler; a checklist, by Matthew J. Bruccoli. [1st ed. Kent, Ohio] Kent State University Press [1968]

ix, 35 p. 23 cm. (The Serif series: bibliographies and checklists [no. 2])

CHANSON DE ROLAND

Seelmann, Emil Paul, 1859–1915.
Bibliographie des altfranzösischen Rolandsliedes mit Berücksichtigung nahestehender Sprach- und Litteraturdenkmale. Wiesbaden, M. Sändig [1969]

xiii, 113 p. 22 cm.

Reprint of the ed. published in Heilbronn by Gebr. Henninger in 1888.

CHANTS (PLAIN, GREGORIAN, ETC.)

Bryden, John Rennie, 1913–
An index of Gregorian chant, compiled by John R. Bryden and David G. Hughes. Cambridge, Harvard University Press, 1969.

2 v. 27 cm.

Bibliography: v. 1, p. xiii–xv.

CONTENTS.—v. 1. Alphabetical index.—v. 2. Thematic index.

Feininger, Laurence Karl Johann, 1909–
Repertorium cantus plani ... Tridenti, Societas universalis Sanctae Ceciliae, 1969–

v. 24 cm.

Pref. signed: Laurentius Feininger.
"Descriptio atque inventarium collectionis Laurentii Feininger."
Errata slip inserted in v. 1.
CONTENTS: 1. Antiphonaria.

Klimisch, Mary June.
A cumulative index of Gregorian chant sources, by M. Jane Klimisch. Yankton, S. D., Sacred Music Resource

Center, Mount Marty College, 1973.

31 p. 28 cm. (Sacred Music Resource Center Project. Progress report 2)

CHAP-BOOKS

Harvard University. *Library.*
Catalogue of English and American chapbooks and broadside ballads in Harvard College Library. Compiled by Charles Welsh and William H. Tillinghast. Detroit, Singing Tree Press, 1968.

xi, 171 p. 24 cm. (Library of Harvard University. Bibliographical contributions, no. 56)
Reprint of the 1905 ed. with a new introductory note by Leslie Shepard.

Marília, Brazil. Faculdade de Filosofia, Ciências e Letras.
Catálogo da coleção de literatura de cordel, Faculdade de Filosofia, Ciências e Letras de Marília. Coligida sob os auspícios da Fundação Ford, por Sol e Maria Tereza Biderman. ₁Marília, Brazil₁ 1970.

79 l. 33 cm.

Neuburg, Victor E
Chapbooks: a bibliography of references to English and American chapbook literature of the eighteenth and nineteenth centuries, by Victor E. Neuburg. London, Vine Press, 1964.

88 p. facsims. 23 cm.

Neuburg, Victor E
Chapbooks: a guide to reference material on English, Scottish and American chapbook literature of the eighteenth and nineteenth centuries, ₁by₁ Victor E. Neuberg. 2nd ed. London, Woburn Press, 1972.

x, 81 p. 23 cm.

Thomson, Frances Mary.
Newcastle chapbooks in Newcastle upon Tyne University Library: ₁a catalogue, by₁ Frances M. Thomson. Newcastle-upon-Tyne, Oriel P., 1969.

109 p. illus. 21 cm. (University library publications)

CHAPLIN, RALPH

Washington State Historical Society.
Inventory of the Ralph Chaplin collection. ₁Tacoma₁ 1967.

iv, 30 p. port. 22 cm.

CHAR, RENÉ

Benoit, Pierre André.
Bibliographie des œuvres de René Char de 1928-1963, par P. A. Benoit. ₁Ribaute-les-Tavernes, Gard₁ Le Demi-jour, 1964.

08 p. illus. 25 cm.

CHARACTERS AND CHARACTERISTICS

Greenough, Chester Noyes, 1874-1938.
A bibliography of the Theophrastan character in English with several portrait characters. Prepared for publication by J. Milton French. Westport, Conn., Greenwood Press ₁1970, ©1947₁

xii, 347 p. 27 cm. (Harvard studies in comparative literature, 18)

CHARENTE, FRANCE (DEPT.)

Belanger, Michel.
La documentation en Charente: guide pour l'étude départementale. ₁Angoulême, C. D. D. P. de la Charente, 1973₁

126 p. 21 cm.

CHARITIES

Adams, Herbert Baxter, 1850-1901.
Notes on the literature of charities. Baltimore, Publication agency of the Johns Hopkins University, 1887. ₁New York, Johnson Reprint Corp., 1973₁

48 p. 22 cm.

Pages also numbered 284-324.
Original ed. issued as no. 8 of Municipal government, history, and politics, which forms the 5th series of Johns Hopkins University studies in historical and political science.

Granier, Camille, 1858-
Essai de bibliographie charitable. New York, B. Franklin ₁1968₁

vii, 449 p. 24 cm. (Burt Franklin bibliography & reference series, 200)

"First published Paris 1891."

CHARLESTON, SOUTH CAROLINA

Dunn, Barbara Butts.
Check list of Charleston, South Carolina, imprints for the years 1826-1830, with a historical introduction. 1967.

iv, 127 l. 28 cm.

Typescript (carbon copy)
Thesis (M. S. L. S.)—Catholic University of America.

Koenig, Mary Odelia, 1915-
A check list of Charleston, South Carolina imprints for the years 1819-1825, with a historical introduction, by M. Odelia Koenig. 1969.

iv, 106 l. 28 cm.

Thesis (M. S. in L. S.)—Catholic University of America.
Typescript (carbon copy)

CHARLIER DE GERSON, JEAN see Gerson, Joannes

CHARTERIS, LESLIE

Alexandersson, Jan, 1934-
₁Leslie Charteris och Helgonet, under 5 decennium. Bio-bibliografi. ₁Av₁ Jan Alexandersson ₁och₁ Iwan Hedman. Strängnäs, ₁Dast Magazine₁, ₁1972₁.

93 p. illus. 30 cm.

CHARTIER, ÉMILE

Alain à Lorient, exposition du centenaire ... ₁Hôtel de ville de Lorient, 23 mars-14 avril 1968.₁ Lorient, Hôtel de ville, 1968.

₁10₁ p. illus. 28 x 12 cm.

Illustrated cover.
Preface by Théo Henry.

CHARTS see Nautical charts

CHASIDISM see Hasidism

CHASSÉ, CHARLES

Finistère, *France (Dept.). Archives départementales.*
Répertoire numérique de la sous-série 97 J, fonds Charles
Chassé, dressé par Alexis Le Bihan ... Quimper, Archives
départementales du Finistère, 1969.

51 p. 24 cm.

Pages also numbered 249–296.
"Extrait du Bulletin de la Société archéologique du Finistère,
tome xciv, 1968."

CHATEAUBRIAND, FRANÇOIS AUGUSTE RENÈ, VICOMTE DE

Paris. Bibliothèque nationale. Département des imprimés.
Catalogue des ouvrages de Chateaubriand [publié par] E.
Dacier. New York, B. Franklin [1970]

70 p. 22 cm. (Burt Franklin bibliography & reference series, 394.
History, economics and social science, 222)

E. Dacier collaborated in the editing of the 27th vol. of the Catalogue général des livres imprimés de la Bibliothèque nationale. Auteurs, from which this is an extract.
Reprint of 1906 ed.

CHAUCER, GEOFFREY

Baugh, Albert Croll, 1891–
Chaucer, compiled by Albert C. Baugh. New York, Appleton-Century-Crofts [1968]

xv, 128 p. 24 cm. (Goldentree bibliographies in language and
literature)

Crawford, William R.
Bibliography of Chaucer, 1954–63, by William R. Crawford. Seattle, University of Washington Press [1967]

xliv, 144 p. 23 cm. (University of Washington publications in
language and literature, v. 17)

"First supplement to D. D. Griffith's Bibliography of Chaucer,
1908–1953."

Martin, Willard Edgar, 1906–
A Chaucer bibliography, 1925–1933, by Willard E. Mar-
tin, Jr. Durham, N. C., Duke University Press, 1935.
[New York, AMS Press, 1973]

xii, 97 p. 23 cm.
Original ed. issued in series: Duke University publications.
A second supplement to Eleanor P. Hammond's "Chaucer: a bibliographical manual," published in 1908. The first supplement, compiled by D. D. Griffith and published in 1926, covers the period from
1908–1924 and is entitled "A bibliography of Chaucer." The present
bibliography follows Griffith's classification and includes supplementary items to the two earlier compilations.

CHAUNCY, CHARLES

Ford, Paul Leicester, 1865–1902.
Bibliotheca Chaunciana: a list of the writings of Charles
Chauncy. New York, B. Franklin [1971]

30 p. 22 cm. (Burt Franklin bibliography & reference series 442.
History of education 9)

Reprint of the 1884 ed., which was issued as no. 6 of Elzevir Club
series.

CHAVEZ, CESAR ESTRADA

Fodell, Beverly, 1930–
Cesar Chavez and the United Farm Workers; a selective
bibliography. Detroit, Wayne State University Press,
1974.

103 p. 23 cm.

"A revision and expansion of the bibliography, Cesar Chavez and
the United Farm Workers, privately printed by the Archives of
Labor History and Urban Affairs of Wayne State University in
January 1970."

CHAVÍN, PERU

Espejo Núñez, Julio V
Bibliografía arqueológica de Chavín [por] Julio Espejo
Núñez. Lima [1964]

[13]–40 p. 25 cm.

Cover title.
"Separata: Boletín bibliográfico, publicado por la Biblioteca Central de la Universidad Nacional Mayor de San Marcos, vol. xxxvi,
nos. 1–2 ... 1964."

CHEB REGION, CZECHOSLOVAK REPUBLIC

Männer, Valentin.
Index für Egerländer Volks- u[nd] Heimatkunde. [Am-
berg, Egerer Landtag e. V., 1971]

201 p. 21 cm.

CHEEVER, JOHN

Payne, Warren E
A checklist of the published works of John Cheever,
1930–1968 [by] Warren E. Payne. [n. p.] ᵉ1969.

34 l. 28 cm.

Photocopy of typescript.

CHEKIANG, CHINA   see under   Kiangsu

CHEMICAL BONDS

Anfimova, L   D
[Khimicheskaîa sviâz' v poluprovodnikakh]
Химическая связь в полупроводниках. Краткий биб-
лиогр. указ. литературы. Минск, 1971.

143 p. 20 cm.

At head of title: Академия наук Белорусской ССР. Институт
физики твердого тела и полупроводников.
"Составители: Л. Д. Анфимова, В. М. Колосовская."

CHEMICAL ENGINEERING

Bourton, Kathleen.
Chemical and process engineering unit operations: a
bibliographical guide [by] Kay Bourton; foreword by Sir
Harold Hartley. London, Macdonald & Co., 1967.

xxv, 534 p. tables. 25 cm. (The Macdonald bibliographical
guides)

Bourton, Kathleen.
Chemical and process engineering unit operations; a
bibliographical guide [by] Kay Bourton. Foreword by
Sir Harold Hartley. New York, IFI/Plenum, 1968.

xxv, 534 p. 25 cm. (Bibliographical guide series)

Brown, Russell, 1920–
How to find out about the chemical industry, by Russell
Brown and G. A. Campbell. [1st ed.] Oxford, New York,
Pergamon Press [1969]

xiii, 219 p. illus. 20 cm. (The Commonwealth and international
library. Libraries and technical information division)

Moscow. Publichnaîa biblioteka.
Молодежь на стройках большой химии; беседа о
книгах. [Составители: О. Дробинин, Н. Размахнина,
И. Черемисинова. Редактор М. Лупова] Москва,
Книга, 1964.

26, [2] p. 17 cm.
At head of title: Государственная библиотека СССР имени В. И.
Ленина.

Smith, Anne M comp.

Brief guide to reference materials in chemical engineering in the Library of the University of British Columbia. compiled by Anne M. Smith. Rev. by R. J. Brongers. Vancouver, University of British Columbia Library, 1969.

17 p. 23 cm. (University of British Columbia Library. Reference publication no. 30)

Šteinerová, Svatava, comp.

Bibliografie dějin čs. chemického průmyslu a přidružených výrob. Praha, 1967.

201 p. 21 cm. (Rozpravy Národního technického muzea v Praze, 31)

On label mounted on t. p.: Zpracovala Svatava Šteinerová s kolektivem spolupracovníků.

CHEMICAL KINETICS

Bibliography of chemical kinetics and collision processes; an annotated bibliography of gas-phase reaction rates and low-energy cross sections of atoms, ions, and small molecules. Prepared under the direction of Adolf R. Hochstim, ed. By M. Berman ₁and others₁ New York, IFI/Plenum, 1969.

ix, 953 p. 29 cm.

"The major part of the book has been photo-reproduced from computer printout."

Sinnott, George A

Bibliography of ion-molecule reaction rate data (January 1950–October 1971) ₁by₁ George A. Sinnott. ₁Gaithersburg, Md.₁ National Bureau of Standards; ₁for sale by the Supt. of Docs., U. S. Govt. Print. Off., Washington₁ 1973.

vi, 66 p. 26 cm. (National Bureau of Standards special publication 381)

Stern, Marvin J

Heavy-atom kinetic isotope effects; an indexed bibliography ₁by₁ Marvin J. Stern and Max Wolfsberg. Washington, National Bureau of Standards; for sale by the Supt. of Docs., U. S. Govt. Print. Off., 1972.

iv, 34 p. 26 cm. (National Bureau of Standards special publication 349)

Westley, Francis.

A bibliography of kinetic data on gas phase reactions of nitrogen, oxygen, and nitrogen oxides.

—— A supplementary bibliography of kinetic data on gas phase reactions of nitrogen, oxygen, and nitrogen oxides. ₁Washington₁ U. S. National Bureau of Standards; ₁for sale by the Supt. of Docs., U. S. Govt. Print. Off.₁ 1973.

xii, 79 p. 26 cm. (NBS special publication 371)

Westley, Francis.

Chemical kinetics in the C-O-S and H-N-O-S systems: a bibliography—1899 through June 1971. ₁Washington, National Bureau of Standards; for sale by the Supt. of Docs., U.S. Govt. Print. Off.₁ 1972.

x, 62 p. 26 cm. (NBS special publication 362)

CHEMICAL WARFARE

Meeker, Thomas A

Chemical/biological warfare. Compiled by Thomas A. Meeker. Los Angeles. Center for the Study of Armament and Disarmament. California State University ₁1972?₁

vii, 27 p. 22 cm. (Classroom study series, v. 1, no. 2)

CHEMISTRY

see also Biochemistry; Geochemistry

Akadémiia navuk BSSR, *Minsk. Fundamental'naia bibliâtêka.*

Химия в изданиях ученых Белоруссии; библиографический указатель литературы, 1945–1963 гг. ₁Составитель А. Д. Василевская. Редактор Г. Н. Артюшевский₁ Минск ₁Наука и техника₁ 1964.

225 p. 21 cm.

Bibliografía brasileira de tecnologia. v. 1–

1968/69–

Rio de Janeiro ₁Instituto Brasileira de Bibliografía e Documentação₁

v. 28 cm.

"Química e química tecnológica."

Библиография трудов сотрудников лабораторий Института общей и неорганической химии АН УССР в Одессе, 1945–1966 гг. ₁Отв. редактор М. Б. Шустова₁ Киев, Наук. думка, 1967.

47 p. 20 cm.

At head of title: Академия наук Украинской ССР. Институт общей и неорганической химии. Лаборатории в Одессе.

Bibliographies of chemists. v. 1–

1971–

₁Santa Monica, Calif₁ Intra-Science Research Foundation.

v. 28 cm.

Borel, Pierre, 1620?–1689.

Bibliotheca chimica; seu, Catalogus librorum philosophicorum hermeticorum. Mit einem Vorwort von Rudolf Schmitz. Hildesheim, G. Olms, 1969.

254 p. 14 cm.

At head of title: Petrus Borellius.
"Reprografischer Nachdruck der Ausgabe Heidelberg 1656."

Bottle, R T

The use of chemical literature, edited by R. T. Bottle. 2nd ed. London, Butterworths, 1969.

xii, 294 p., 2 plates. illus., facsims. 22 cm. (Information sources for research and development)

Burman, Charles Raymond.

How to find out in chemistry; ₁a guide to sources of information, by₁ C. R. Burman. ₁1st ed.₁ Oxford, New York, Pergamon Press ₁1965₁

vii, 220 p. facsims. 23 cm. (The Commonwealth and international library of science, technology, engineering, and liberal studies. Libraries and technical information division, v. 3)

Burman, Charles Raymond.

How to find out in chemistry ₁by₁ C. R. Burman. ₁2d ed.₁ Oxford, New York, Pergamon Press ₁1966₁

ix, 226 p. facsims. 20 cm. (The Commonwealth and international library. Libraries and technical information division)

Chemischer Informationsdienst: anorganische und physikalische Chemie. 1–2. Jahrg.; Jan. 1970–28. Dez. 1971. Weinheim/Bergstrasse, Verlag Chemie.

2 v. 21 cm. weekly.

Issued by Gesellschaft Deutscher Chemiker.
Merged with Chemischer Informationsdienst: organische Chemie to form Chemischer Informationsdienst.

Gefter, Evgenii Leonidovich.

(Metody raboty s khimicheskoĭ literaturoĭ)

Методы работы с химической литературой. Москва, "Химия," 1972.

63 p. 20 cm.

Jusková-Chudíková, Magda.
Doplnková literatúra k vyučovaniu chémie na ZDŠ a SVŠ. Odporúč. bibliografia. Bratislava, Slov. pedag. knižnica, rozmn., 1968.

36, [2] p. 20 cm.

Leipziger Kommissions- und Grossbuchhandel.
Literaturkatalog Chemie. [Hrsg. vom Leipziger Kommissions- und Grossbuchhandel in Gemeinschaft mit dem Ministerium für Kultur et al. Leipzig, 1967]

193 p. 20 cm.

Liu, Regina S   R
Searching chemical literature; a library guide, by Regina S. R. Liu. Honolulu, University of Hawaii Library, 1969.

iv, 117 p. 29 cm.

Martinson, H
[Bibliografii︠a︡ nauchnykh trudov sotrudnikov Instituta khimii]
Библиография научных трудов сотрудников Института химии (1947–1972) / сост. Х. Мартинсон. — Таллин, [АН ЭССР], 1973.

409 p. ; 20 cm.

Mellon, Melvin Guy, 1893–
Chemical publications, their nature and use [by] M. G. Mellon. 4th ed. New York, McGraw-Hill [1965]

xi, 324 p. illus. 24 cm.

Nowak, Alois.
Fachliteratur des Chemikers. Einführung in ihre Systematik und Benutzung, mit einer Übersicht über wichtige Werke. (Mit einer Einführung in die Dokumentation.) 2., überarb. und erg. Aufl. Berlin, Deutscher Verlag der Wissenschaften, 1967.

192 p. 22 cm.

Ostrava, Czechoslovak Republic (City)   Státní vědecká knihovna.
Chemie pro technickou praxi; výběr literatury. [Zpracovatel: Marie Kurečková. V Ostravě] 1965.

37 p. 20 cm. (*Its* Publikace. Řada II, čís. 387)

Petrov, I︠U︡   I
Предметно-библиографический указатель по методам исследования, анализа и контроля в химии и химической технологии. Под ред. канд. техн. наук Г. П. Головинского. Сост. канд. хим. наук Ю. И. Петров, С. К. Шахова. Москва, 1968.

507 p. 26 cm. (Экспресс-информация)

At head of title: Государственный комитет Совета Министров СССР по науке и технике. Академия наук Союза ССР. Всесоюзный институт научной и технической информации. Отдел химии. Сектор экспресс-информации.

Roth-Scholtz, Friedrich, 1687–1736.
Bibliotheca chemica; oder, Catalogus von Chymischen-Büchern. Hildesheim, New York, G. Olms, 1971.

5 v. in 1. illus. 17 cm.

Reprint of the Nuremberg, 1727–29 ed.

Ruske, Walter.
Verlag Chemie 1921–1971. Im Auftrage des Verlags Chemie verfasst von Walter Ruske. [Weinheim, Verlag Chemie, °1971]

79, 159 p. illus., facsims., ports. 26 cm.

Semishin, Vasiliĭ Ivanovich.
Литература по периодическому закону Д. И. Менделеева (1869–1969). Москва, "Высш. школа," 1969.

240 p., port. 20 cm.

Strel't︠s︡ova, V
Библиография научных работ сотрудников Института физико-органической химии АН БССР за 1931–1967 гг. Минск, 1970.
161 p. 21 cm.
At head of title: Филиал Фундаментальной библиотеки им. Я. Коласа при Институте ФОХ АН БССР.
By V. Strel't︠s︡ova and A. V. Belova.

Terent'ev, Aleksandr Petrovich.
Химическая литература и пользование ею. Москва, Химия, 1964.

318 p. 22 cm.

At head of title: А. П. Терентьев и Л. А. Яновская.

Terent'ev, Aleksandr Petrovich.
Химическая литература и пользование ею. 2., перер. и доп. изд. Москва, Химия, 1967.

326 p. illus. 22 cm.

At head of title: А. П. Терентьев, Л. А. Яновская.

Wisconsin. University. *Library.*
Chemical, medical, and pharmaceutical books printed before 1800, in the collections of the University of Wisconsin Libraries. Edited by John Neu. Compiled by Samuel Ives, Reese Jenkins, and John Neu. Madison, University of Wisconsin Press, 1965.

viii, 280 p. 25 cm.

Includes titles in the Denis I. Duveen collection in chemistry and alchemy, which the university acquired in 1951.

BIBLIOGRAPHIES

Библиография иностранной библиографии по химии.
[Составили: Э. А. Молодцова, Н. А. Никифоровская, А. Г. Рытов. Отв. редакторы: А. Ю. Шагалов и В. П. Алексеева] Ленинград, Наука [Ленинградское отд-ние] 1966–1971.

2 v. 23 cm.

At head of title: Академия наук СССР. Ордена трудового красного знамени Библиотека Академии наук СССР.
By E. A. Molodt︠s︡ova, and others.
Vol. 2 published by Izdatel'skiĭ otdel Biblioteki AN SSSR.

CONTENTS: вып. 1. Отдельно изданные библиографические указатели и прикнижная библиография, 1930–1964 гг.—вып. 2. Библиографическая периодика и журналы, имеющие раздел библиографии.

Библиография советской библиографии по химии и химической технологии. 1917–1965. Ленинград, "Наука," Ленингр. отд-ние, 1968.

382 p. 22 cm.

At head of title: Академия наук СССР. Ордена Трудового Красного Знамени библиотека Академии наук СССР.
By E. A. Molodt︠s︡ova and others.

HISTORY

Moss, Roger W
The Morgan collection in the history of chemistry; a checklist. Compiled by Roger W. Moss, Jr. Athens, Ohio University Library, 1965.

vii, 178 p. facsims., port. 28 cm.

Cover title: J. W. Morgan collection; a checklist.

Szőkefalvi-Nagy, Zoltán.
Ajánló bibliográfia a magyarországi vegyészet története tanulmányozásához. Budapest, Magyar Vegyészeti Múzeum, 1969.

58 p. 20 cm. (Magyar Vegyészeti Múzeum közleményei, 2. évf., 1. sz.)

PERIODICALS
see also under Engineering -
Periodicals

Access. 1969–
ₜColumbus, Ohioₗ Chemical Abstracts Service, American Chemical Society.

v. 28 cm.

"Key to the source literature of the chemical sciences."
Supersedes the American Chemical Society's List of periodicals abstracted by Chemical abstracts.

American Chemical Society. Chemical Abstracts Service.
Chemical Abstracts Service source index. 1970–
ₜEaston, Pa.ₗ American Chemical Society.

v. 28 cm.

Supersedes Access.

American Chemical Society. Chemical Abstracts Service.
Chemical Abstracts Service source index quarterly. 1970, issue 4–
Easton, Pa., American Chemical Society.

v. 28 cm.

The 4th issue of each year is a cumulation for the 12 month period Oct. to Sept.
Supersedes Access quarterly.

Arkharova, I͡Unii͡a Zakharovna.
(Osnovnye inostrannye periodicheskie izdanii͡a po khimii v bibliotekakh Leningrada)
Основные иностранные периодические издания по химии в библиотеках Ленинграда. Сводный каталог. Сост. Ю. З. Архарова. Под ред. О. Н. Григорова. Ленинград, 1972.

171 p. 22 cm.

At head of title: Библиотека Академии наук СССР. Ленинградское областное правление Всесоюзного химического общества им. Д. И. Менделеева.

Boska, Krystyna.
Katalog czasopism zagranicznych: chemia i dziedziny pokrewne, z lat 1945–1965, znajdujących sie w bibliotekach Łodzi, Pabianic, Tomaszowa, Mazowieckiego, Zgierza, Opracowała Krystyna Boska. ₜWyd. 1.ₗ Łódź, Nakł. Politechniki Łódzkiej, 1966.

xi, 220 p. 24 cm. (Politechnika Łódzka. Materiały bibliograficzne)

Chemical abstracts information file. July 1965–
Columbus, Ohio, Chemical Abstracts Service, Ohio State University.

v. 29 cm.

(Khimii͡a i khimicheskai͡a promyshlennostʹ)
Химия и химическая промышленность. Указ. период. и продолжающихся изд. Москва, 1972.
326 p. 29 cm. (Международная система научной и технической информации)
At head of title: Международный центр научной и технической информации.
By I. F. Kuznetsova and others.
Russian, German, Hungarian, Polish, Rumanian, Slovak, Czech, Bulgarian and Mongolian.

Sassoon, Gabriel Jacques.
Current Japanese journals containing articles on pure chemistry, by G. J. Sassoon. London ₜBritish Museumₗ 1971.

iii, 22 p. 25 cm. Index. (National Reference Library of Science and Invention. Occasional publications)

Sassoon, Gabriel Jacques.
Current Japanese journals containing articles on pure chemistry, by G. J. Sassoon. 2nd ed. London, ₜBritish Museumₗ, 1972.

iii, 22 p. 25 cm. Index. (National Reference Library of Science and Invention. Occasional publications)

Zeitschriftenverzeichnis mit Titelabkürzungen und Verlagsorten. Weinheim/ Bergstr., Verl. Chemie (1970).

46 p. 21 cm.

At head of title: VtB, Verfahrenstechnische Berichte.
"... eine Neuauflage unseres 1955 erstmals erschienenen und in den Jahren 1962 und 1966 vervollständigten Zeitschriftenverzeichnisses ..."

CHEMISTRY, AGRICULTURAL see Agricultural chemistry

CHEMISTRY, ANALYTIC
see also Chromatographic analysis;
Radioactivation analysis

Bilten dokumentacije. Serija D 6: Analitička hemija.
Bulletin of documentation. Series D 6: Analytical chemistry. g. 1–
jan. 1971–
Beograd, Jugoslovenski centar za tehničku i naučnu dokumentaciju.

v. 30 cm. monthly.

Efremov, German Vasilʹevich.
Литература по неорганическому химическому анализу; пособие для студентов. ₜЛенинградₗ 1964.

55 p. 22 cm.

At head of title: Ленинградский государственный университет имени А. А. Жданова. Г. В. Ефремов.

Efremov, German Vasilʹevich.
Литература по неорганическому химическому анализу. Пособие для студентов и науч. сотрудников. Изд. 2., доп. ₜЛенинградₗ Химия, 1967.

75 p. 22 cm.

Halbleiterwerk Frankfurt/Oder. Abteilung Dokumentation.
Analytische Chemie. Stahnsdorf, 1968.

2 v. (56 p.) 21 cm.

Jolly, Stephen Claude.
Official, standardised and recommended methods of analysis.
———— Supplement; compiled and edited for the Analytical Methods Committee of the Society for Analytical Chemistry, by S. C. Jolly. London, Society for Analytical Chemistry, 1967.

xiv, 424 p. illus. 26 cm.

Kabanova, O   L
Электрохимические методы анализа неорганических веществ в водных растворах. Библиогр, указатель (1955–1966 гг.) Москва, "Наука," 1969.
256 p. 26 cm.

On leaf preceding t. p.: Академия наук СССР. Ордена Ленина институт геохимии и аналитической химии им. В. И. Вернадского. Сектор сети специальных библиотек.
By O. L. Kabanova, G. F. Kalinina, and E. A. Lukashevich.

Klug. Ottó.
Nagyfrekvenciás mérésmódszerek az analitikai és fizikai kémiában; bibliográfia. High-frequency measuring methods in the analytical and physical chemistry; bibliography. Budapest, 1964.

2 v. (vi, 340 l.) 29 cm. (Fémipari Kutató Intézet kiadványai, 6. sz.)

Table of contents and titles of bibliographical items in Hungarian and English.

Luijten, Johannes Gerardus Antonius.
A bibliography of organotin analysis, compiled by J. G. A. Luijten. ₁Rev. ed. Greenford, Eng.₁ Tin Research Institute ₁1970₁

48 p. 24 cm. (Tin Research Institute. ₁Publication₁ 417)

Texas Transportation Institute, College Station.
Spectrochemical analysis, spectroscopy, spectrophotometers, spectrophotometry, photometry, reflectometry, colorimetry, tri-stimulus color, chromatography. ₁College Station, 1966₁

8 l. 28 cm. (Bibliography: Survey of library facilities project, 66-3)
Cover title.
Cooperative research: 2-8-54-1.
Sponsored by the Texas Highway Dept. in cooperation with Dept. of Commerce, Bureau of Public Roads.

CHEMISTRY, INORGANIC

Latvijas Padomju Sociālistiskās Republikas Zinātņu akadēmija. *Neorganiskās ķīmijas institūts.*
Исследования Института неорганической химии за 20 лет. Библиография. 1946–1966. ₁Предисловия О. К. Кукурса и др.₁ Рига, "Зинатне," 1968.

197 p. 20 cm.

At head of title: Академия наук Латвийской ССР. Институт неорганической химии.

CHEMISTRY, MEDICAL

Ellis, Gwynn Pennant.
Medicinal chemistry reviews: a select bibliography ₁by₁ G. P. Ellis. London, Butterworths, 1972.

ix, 170 p. 24 cm.

Shorter version first published in Progress in medicinal chemistry, v. 6.

CHEMISTRY, ORGANIC

Chemischer Informationsdienst: Organische Chemie. 1.–

Jahrg.; Jan. 1970–
Weinheim/Bergstrasse, Verlag Chemie.

v. 21 cm. weekly.

"Herausgeber: Gesellschaft Deutscher Chemiker und Farbenfabriken Bayer AG."

Debrecen, Hungary. Tudományegyetem. *Szerves Kémiai Intézet.*
Debreceni Kossuth Lajos Tudományegyetem Szerves Kémiai Intézete és a Magyar Tudományos Akadémia Antibiotikum Kémiai Kutató Csoport dolgozóinak munkássága 1966-ig. Debrecen, 1966.

40 p. 29 cm.

General organic crystal structures; bibliography 1935–69. Edited by Olga Kennard and David G. Watson. Utrecht, N. V. A. Oosthoek for the Crystallographic Data Centre Cambridge and the International Union of Crystallography ₁1970₁

xxiii, 413 p. 24 cm. (Molecular structures and dimensions, 1)

Pichugina, G   S
Нефтехимический синтез; рекомендательный указатель литературы. ₁Составитель: Г. С. Пичугина₁. Москва, Книга, 1967.

23 p. 17 cm. (Рабочему—о новой технике, вып. 3 (22))

At head of title: Государственная публичная научно-техническая библиотека СССР. Государственная ордена Трудового красного знамени публичная библиотека им. М. Е. Салтыкова-Щедрина.

Wolski, Edward.
Chemistry of organometallic compounds; annotated bibliography. ₁Washington₁ Aerospace Technology Division, Library of Congress, 1966–

v. 28 cm. (ATD report 66-47

"Based on Soviet-bloc open sources available in the Library of Congress and covering the period from 1 January to 31 December 1964."

CONTENTS.—pt. a. Organosilicon and organogermanium chemistry.

CHEMISTRY, TECHNICAL

Bratislava. Slovenská vysoká škola technická. Chemickotechnologická fakulta.
Bibliografia. Bratislava, Chemickotechnologická fakulta SVŠT. rozmn., ₁1969₁

1 v. (unpaged) 25 cm.

Bulletin signalétique 8: Chimie II—chimie appliquée, métallurgie. v. 22–29; 1961–68. Paris, Centre de documentation du C. N. R. S.

8 v. in 13. 28 cm. monthly.

Supersedes in part Bulletin signalétique, issued 1940–60, and continues its vol. numbering.
Superseded by Bulletin signalétique 880: Chimie appliquée, génie chimique, céramique, eaux, corps gras, papier, pollution atmosphérique, and by Bulletin signalétique 740: Métaux, metallurgie.

Bulletin signalétique 880: Chimie appliquée, génie chimique, céramique, eaux, corps gras, papier, pollution atmosphérique. v. 30–
1969–
Paris, Centre de documentation du C. N. R. S.

v. 28 cm. monthly.

Supersedes in part Bulletin signalétique 8: Chimie II—chimie appliquée, métallurgie, and continues its vol. numbering.

Bulletin signalétique 880: Génie chimique, industries chimique et parachimique.

Paris, Centre national de la recherche scientifique, Centre de documentation.

v. 30 cm.

Continues Bulletin signalétique 880: Chimie appliquée, génie chimique, céramique, eaux, corps gras, papier, pollution atmosphérique.

Экстракция неорганических соединений. Библиогр. указ. ₁Отв. ред. чл.-кор. АН СССР Ю. А. Золотов₁. Москва, "Наука," 1971.

2 v. 26 cm.
At head of title: В. В. Багреев ₁и др.₁
On leaf preceding t. p.: Академия наук СССР. Ордена Ленина Институт геохимии и аналитической химии им. В. И. Вернадского. Сектор сети специальных библиотек.
CONTENTS: ₁1₁ 1945–1962.—₁2₁ 1963–1967.

Francis, Alfred West.
Handbook for components in solvent extraction [by] Alfred W. Francis. New York, Gordon and Breach [1972]

ix, 534 p. 24 cm.

Library Association. *County Libraries Group.*
Readers' guide to books on chemical technology. 2nd ed. London, Library Association (County Libraries Group). 1966.

32 p. 18½ cm. (*Its* Readers' guides, new ser., no. 88)

Moscow. Publichnaȋa biblioteka.
Книги по химизации народного хозяйства; рекомендательные списки для районных и сельских библиотек. [Составители: Г. П. Богатова, О. И. Дробинин, И. П. Черемисинова] Москва, Книга, 1964.

23 p. 17 cm.

At head of title: Государственная библиотека СССР имени В. И. Ленина.

Vissh khimiko-tekhnologicheski institut.
(Sbornik na nauchnite trudove na prepodavatelite ot Visshiĭa khimiko-tekhnologicheski institut)
Сборник на научните трудове на преподавателите от Висшия химико-технологически институт—София, излезли от печат до края на 1971 г. [Библиогр. указатл]. София, ВХТИ, 1972.

863 p. 23 cm.

At head of title: Комитет за наука, технически прогрес и висше образование.

CHER, FRANCE (DEPT.)

Cher, France (Dept.). Archives.
Répertoire numérique, B 4339 à B 5120, par Paul Cravayat ... Précédé d'une introduction par Jean-Yves Ribault ... Bourges, Archives départementales, 1970.

124 p. 24 cm.

At head of title: Archives départmentales du Cher. Série B. Cours & juridictions de l'Ancien Régime.

CHESAPEAKE BAY

The Chesapeake Bay bibliography, by Susan O. Barrick and others. Gloucester Point, Virginia Institute of Marine Science, 1971–

v. 28 cm. (Special scientific report no. 58 of the Virginia Institute of Marine Science)

"IRRPOS project report no. 3; Sea Grant Program report no. 3; and Task order no. 1 of the National Aeronautics and Space Administration."
CONTENTS: v. 1. The James River.

CHESS

Sakharov, Nikolaĭ Ivanovich.
Шахматная литература СССР. Библиография. (1775–1966). Москва, "Книга," 1968.

208 p. 21 cm.

CHESSMAN, CARYL WHITTIER

Largo, Andrew O
Caryl Whittier Chessman, 1921–1960: essay and critical bibliography. Compiled by Andrew O. Largo. San Jose, Calif., Bibliographic Information Center for the Study of Political Science, 1971.

15 p. 28 cm. (Bibliographic Information Center for the Study of Political Science. Occasional papers series no. 2)

CHESTER, COLBY MITCHELL

United States. Library of Congress. Manuscript Division.
Colby Mitchell Chester, William Freeland Fullam, Samuel McGowan, Henry Croskey Mustin: a register of their papers in the Library of Congress. Washington, Library of Congress, 1973.

iii, 4, 6, 7, 5 p. 27 cm.

"Naval Historical Foundation collection."

CHESTERTON, GILBERT KEITH

Sullivan, John, 1904–
Chesterton continued: a bibliographical supplement; together with some uncollected prose and verse by G. K. Chesterton. London, University of London P., 1968.

xiv, 120 p. illus., facsims. 23 cm.

Sullivan, John, 1904–
Chesterton continued; a bibliographical supplement. Together with some uncollected prose and verse by G. K. Chesterton. New York, Barnes & Noble [1969, °1968]

xiv, 120 p. illus., facsims. 23 cm.

Supplement to the author's G. K. Chesterton: a bibliography.

Wahlert Memorial Library.
Gilbert Keith Chesterton; an exhibition catalogue of English and American first editions on the occasion of the centenary of his birth, 1874–1974, along with appreciations and tributes to the man and his works by friends and critics. Dubuque, Ia., 1974.

47 p. illus. 22 cm.

CHIANGSU see Kiangsu

CHICAGO

Rothman, Richard.
Social studies related to the physical structuring of Chicago: a bibliography. Mary Vance, editor. Monticello, Ill., Council of Planning Librarians, 1972.

35 p. 28 cm. (Council of Planning Librarians. Exchange bibliography, 260)

CHICANOS see Mexican-Americans

CHICHESTER, ENGLAND (DIOCESE)

Chichester, *Eng.* (*Diocese*)
A catalogue of the records of the bishop, archdeacons and former exempt jurisdictions; compiled by Francis W. Steer and Isabel M. Kirby, with a foreword by the Rt. Rev. the Lord Bishop of Chichester and a preface by Marc Fitch. Chichester, West Sussex Record Office, 1966.

xxiii, 268 p. 25½ cm. (*Its* Records, v. 1)

Chichester, *Eng.* (*Diocese*)
A catalogue of the records of the Dean and Chapter, Vicars Choral, St. Mary's Hospital, colleges and schools, compiled by Francis W. Steer and Isabel M. Kirby, with a foreword by the Very Reverend the Dean of Chichester. Chichester, West Sussex County Council, 1967.

xviii, 102 p. tables. 25 cm. (*Its* Records, v. 2) 50/-

Chichester, Eng. (Diocese). Record Office.
Handlist of parish registers, bishops' transcripts and modern transcripts in the Diocesan Record Office. Chichester [Eng.] 1973.

22 1. 21 x 30 cm. (Its Lists and Indexes, no. 7)

Chichester, Eng. (Diocese). Record Office.
A handlist of the Bishops' transcripts, 1567–1936. Chichester (Sussex), West Sussex County Council, 1970.

[1], 37 p. 25 cm.

CHILD PSYCHIATRY

Bryson, Carolyn Q
Early childhood psychosis: infantile autism, childhood schizophrenia and related disorders; an annotated bibliography, 1964 to 1969. Prepared by Carolyn Q. Bryson and Joseph N. Hingtgen. Rockville, Md., National Institute of Mental Health [1971]

vii, 127 p. 27 cm. (U. S. Dept. of Health, Education, and Welfare. Publication no. (HSM) 71-9062)

Tavistock Institute of Human Relations, London.
Annotated list of publications, 1946–1970. London, Tavistock Centre [1970].

[1], 97 p. 22 cm.

At head of title: Tavistock Institute of Human Relations and the Tavistock Clinic.

CHILD PSYCHOLOGY

Canberra, Australia. National Library.
The pre-school child; a list of Australian works. [Canberra] 1967.

24 p. 25 cm.

Iowa. University. *Institute of Child Behavior and Development.*
Fifty years of research, 1917–1967. Iowa City, University of Iowa, 1967.

vii, 129 p. 23 cm.

Kinder fordern uns heraus. ... Bücher wollen helfen. Ein Auswahlverz. d. Berliner Stadtbüchereien. (Hrsg. im Auftr. d. Senators f. Schulwesen. Bearb.: Annemarie Kaiser [u. a.]) (Berlin, Amerika-Gedenk-Bibliothek [1970].)

48 p. several l. of illus. 21 cm.

Kinder fordern uns heraus; ... Bücher wollen helfen. Ein Auswahlverzeichnis der Berliner Stadtbüchereien. [Bearbeiter: T. Kusel et al.] Neuaufl. [Berlin, Amerika-Gedenk-bibliothek] 1973.

48 p. illus. 21 cm.

Leopold, Werner F., 1896–
Bibliography of child language, by Werner F. Leopold. New York, AMS Press [1970]

v, 115 p. 24 cm. (Northwestern University humanities series, v. 28)

Reprint of the 1952 ed.

Leopold, Werner F 1896–
Bibliography of child language. Rev. and augmented by Dan Isaac Slobin. Bloomington, Indiana University Press [1972]

xviii, 202 p. 25 cm. (Indiana University studies in the history and theory of linguistics)

Lucker, Elisabeth.
Elternpädagogik und Psychohygiene. Mit einem Anhang zum elternpädagogischen Schrifttum. Weinheim(/ Bergstr.) u. Berlin, Beltz (1967).

147 p. 21 cm.

Michigan. University. Research Center for Group Dynamics.
Bibliography of research in children, youth, and family life. Ann Arbor, 1969.

17 p. 23 cm.

Michigan. University. Research Center for Group Dynamics.
Bibliography of research in children, youth, and family life. Ann Arbor, 1970.

19 p. 23 cm.

I Problemi dei giovani. Analisi della letteratura italiana, proposte di studio ulteriore. [n. p.], Amministrazione per le attività assistenziali italiane ed internazionali, 1969.

302 p. illus. 24 cm. (Indagini e documentazioni sociali, 1)

Project Head Start.
Bibliography on early childhood. Washington, 1970.

19, 16 p. 27 cm.

Schmidt, Heiner.
Bibliographie zur literarischen Erziehung. Gesamtverzeichnis 1900 bis 1965. Selbständige Schriften, Monographien, Beiträge aus Sammelwerken und Aufsätze ... (Zürich, Einsiedeln, Köln,) Benziger, (1967).

xii, 820 p. 22 cm.

Stevenson, Harold William, 1924– *comp.*
Studies of children's learning; a bibliography [by] Harold Stevenson. [Goleta? Calif.] Psychonomic Journals [1968]

192-218 p. 28 cm. (Psychonomic monograph supplements, v. 2, no. 11)

CHILDREN
see also Youth

Cass, Joan E *comp.*
Some books about children (Autobiographies and novels); selected and annotated by Joan E. Cass. Supplementary list. London, Child Care, 1966–

v. 24 cm.

Council on Social Work Education.
An annotated bibliography of books and short stories on childhood and youth. New York [°1968]

vi, 52 p. 28 cm.

World Organization for Early Childhood Education. *Sveriges nationalkommitté.*
Böcker om barn. Barnavård och barnpsykologi. Ett kommenterat urval av en arbetsgrupp under ordförandeskap av Lisa Smedberg. Lund, Bibliotekstjänst; [Solna, Seelig] 1968.

41 p. 21 cm. (Btj-serien, 8)

*CARE AND WELFARE
see also Pediatrics*

Canadian Welfare Council. *Research Branch.*
The day care of children, an annotated bibliography. Rev. Ottawa, 1969.

68 1. 28 cm.

Children's Bureau Clearinghouse for Research in Child Life.
Bibliography on the battered child. [Rev. Washington, 1969]

22 p. 26 cm.

Deutsches Jugendinstitut.
Modellbibliothek für Jugendämter; ein Verzeichnis. ₁München, 1970₎

v, 106 p. 25 cm.

Jones, Dorothy Mounce, 1908–   *comp.*
Children who need protection, an annotated bibliography, compiled by Dorothy M. Jones. ₁Washington₎ U. S. Dept. of Health, Education, and Welfare, Welfare Administration, Children's Bureau; for sale by the Superintendent of Documents, U. S. Govt. Print. Off., 1966.

75 p. 24 cm.

Prepared in the Department Library, U. S. Dept. of Health, Education, and Welfare.

Merriam, Alice H
A selected bibliography on day care services, compiled and annotated by Alice H. Merriam. ₁Washington₎ U. S. Dept. of Health, Education, and Welfare, Welfare Administration, Children's Bureau ₁1965₎

94 p. 26 cm.

Morlock, Maud.
Homemaker services, history and bibliography. ₁Washington₎ U. S. Dept. of Health, Education, and Welfare, Welfare Administration, Children's Bureau; for sale by the Superintendent of Documents, U. S. Govt. Print. Off., 1964.

vi, 116 p. 24 cm. (₁U. S.₎ Children's Bureau. Publication no. 410)

Olst, A   C   M   van.
Nederlandse bibliografie over jeugdgezondheidszorg ₁1945–1965₎ Door A. C. M. van Olst. Met een ten geleide door J. H. de Haas. Leiden, Afdeling Sociale Hygenie, Nederlands Instituut voor Praeventieve Geneeskunde, 1966.

80 p. 20 cm.

Oregon. *Governor's Committee on Children and Youth.*
Bibliography of materials received relative to children and youth. Portland, 1968–

v. 28 cm.

Project on Cost Analysis in Children's Institutions.
Cost and time studies in child welfare and related subjects, a bibliography. Edited by Robert Elkin. Washington ₁U. S. Dept. of Health, Education, and Welfare, Welfare Administration, Children's Bureau₎ 1965.

vii, 32 p. 27 cm.

U. S. *Children's Bureau.*
Children's Bureau publications. 1912/May 1964–

₁Washington₎

v. 23 cm.

"An index to publications by number, title, author, and subject."

United States. National Institute of Mental Health.
Selected references on the abused and battered child. ₁Rockville, Md.; For sale by the Supt. of Docs., U. S. Govt. Print. Off., Washington, 1972₎

11 p. 26 cm. (DHEW publication no. (HSM) 73–9034)

LAW
    see also Illegitimacy

United States. Children's Bureau. Division of Juvenile Delinquency Service.
Legal bibliography for juvenile and family courts ₁by₎

William H. Sheridan, assistant director ₁and₎ Alice B. Freer, program analyst. ₁Washington₎ U. S. Dept. of Health, Education, and Welfare Administration, Children's Bureau; ₁for sale by the U. S. Superintendent of Documents, U. S. Govt. Print. Off.₎ 1966.

46 p. 26 cm.

—— A supplement. ₁Washington₎ U. S. Dept. of Health, Education, and Welfare, Office of Youth Development; ₁for sale by the Supt. of Docs., U. S. Govt. Print. Off. 1973₎

iv, 18 p. 26 cm. (DHEW publication non. (SRS) 73–26001)

Cover title: Juvenile and family courts; a supplement.

United States. Youth Development and Delinquency Prevention Administration.
Juvenile and family courts; a legal bibliography ₁by William H. Sheridan and Alice B. Freer.   Washington, 1971₎

iii, 110 p. 26 cm. (DHEW publication no. (SRS) 72-26001)

Cover title.

Contains the 1966 ed. of Legal bibliography for juvenile and family courts, issued by U.S. Children's Bureau, Division of Juvenile Delinquency Service, and 4 annual supplements.

Von Pfeil, Helena P
Juvenile rights since 1967 : an annotated, indexed bibliography of selected articles and books / by Helena P. Von Pfeil ; foreword by Monrad Paulsen ; pref. by William Fort, Bette Browne. — South Hackensack, N.J. : F. B. Rothman, 1974.

xvii, 199 p. ; 29 cm.

CHILDREN, DELINQUENT   see   Juvenile delinquency

CHILDREN, HANDICAPPED   see   Handicapped children

CHILDREN OF MIGRANT LABORERS

Center for the Study of Migrant and Indian Education.
Migrant education bibliography. 2d ed. ₁Toppenish, Wash.₎ 1971.

99 p. illus. 29 cm.

CHILDREN'S LITERATURE

Lists of books for children on specific subjects are entered under the subjects.

see also   Mentally handicapped children, ₁Slow learning children, Socially handicapped children₎ Books for

Carlsen, G   Robert, 1921-
Books and the teen-age reader; a guide for teachers, librarians, and parents, by G. Robert Carlsen.   Rev. and updated.   New York, Harper & Row ₁c1971₎

247 p. 22 cm.

Cass, Joan E
Books for the under fives; introduction and notes by Joan E. Cass.   London, National Book League, 1970.

24 p. illus. 13 cm.

Child Study Association of America. *Children's Book Committee.*
Children's books of the year 1969. ₁New York, 1970₎

45 p. 22 cm.

Child Study Association of America. *Children's Book Committee.*
Reading with your child through age 5. ₍New York, 1970₎

viii, 30 p. illus. 23 cm.

Child Study Association of America. Children's Book Committee.
Reading with your child through age 5. Rev. ed. ₍New York₎ Child Study Press ₍1971, c1972₎

viii, 40 p. illus. 23 x 10 cm.

Children's Book Council, New York.
Children's books: awards & prizes. ₍New York, 1969₎

₍32₎ p. 28 cm.

Previous editions prepared by Westchester Library System.

Children's Book Council of Victoria.
Books for children; a select list; 4th ed. Victoria, Children's Book Council, 1966.

91 p. 22 cm.

Children's book review. v. 1–
Feb. 1971–
₍Wormley, Eng., Five Owls Press₎

v. illus. 26 cm. bimonthly.

Issues for Apr. 1971– include separately paged section: Children's book review: occasional list, no. 1–

Children's Book Review Service.
Children's book review service. v. 1–
Sept. 1972–
Brooklyn.

v. 28 cm. monthly.

Children's books for schools and libraries. 1966/67–

New York, R. R. Bowker Co.

v. 21 cm. annual.

Supersedes in part Publishers' library bindings in print.

Children's books in print. 1969–
London, Whitaker.

v. 25 cm. annual.

Children's books in print. 1969–
New York, R. R. Bowker Co.

v. 29 cm. annual.

Supersedes Children's books for schools and libraries.

—— Subject guide. 1970–
New York, R. R. Bowker Co.

v. 29 cm. annual.

Children's literature in education. 1–
Mar. 1970–
₍London₎ Ward Lock Educational.

no. illus. 26 cm. 3 no. a year.

Cianciolo, Patricia J
Picture books for children. Patricia Jean Cianciolo, editor, and the Picture Book Committee. Chicago, American Library Association, 1973.

xiii, 159 p. illus. 25 cm.

Colwell, Eileen H
First choice: a basic book list for children; edited by Eileen Colwell, L. Esmé Green and F. Phyllis Parrott, for the Youth Libraries Group of the Library Association. London, L. A., 1968.

120 p. 21 cm.

Douglas, Alison M comp.
Primarily for presents: a choice of books for children ₍by₎ Alison M. Douglas. Birmingham, Library Association (Youth Libraries Group), 1970.

₍17₎ p. illus. 22 cm. (Library Association. Youth Libraries Group. Pamphlet, no. 7)

Eakin, Mary K
Good books for children; a selection of outstanding children's books published 1950–65, compiled by Mary K. Eakin. 3d ed. Chicago, University of Chicago Press ₍1966₎

xv, 407 p. 24 cm.

Selected from the Bulletin of the Center for Children's Books.

The **Elementary** school library collection, phases 1–2–3. General editor: Mary V. Gaver. 2d ed. Newark, N. J., Bro-Dart Foundation ₍1966₎

xvi, 1108 p. 32 cm.

—— Supplement. 2d ed. Newark, N. J., Bro-Dart Foundation ₍c1966₎

viii, ₍1100₎–1293 p. 32 cm.

The **Elementary** school library collection; a guide to books and other media, phases 1–2–3. General editor: Mary V. Gaver. 4th ed. Newark, N. J., Bro-Dart Foundation, 1968.

xx, 625 p. 32 cm.

—— Supplement. 4th ed. Newark, N. J., Bro-Dart Foundation, 1969.

vi, 98 p. 32 cm.

The **Elementary school library collection**; a guide to books and other media, phases 1–2–3. General editor: Mary V. Gaver. Assisted by Dorothy Fix ₍and others₎ 5th ed. Newark, N. J., Bro-Dart Foundation, 1970.

xxii, 710 p. 32 cm.

—— Fifth edition supplement. Newark, N. J., Bro-Dart Foundation, 1970.

ix, 193 p. 32 cm.

The **Elementary school library collection**; a guide to books and other media, phases 1–2–3. General editor: Mary V. Gaver, assisted by Eileen Conlon ₍and others₎ Newark, N. J., Bro-Dart Foundation, 1971.

xxvi, 831 p. 32 cm.

The **Elementary school library collection**; a guide to books and other media, phases 1-2-3. General editor: Mary V. Gaver. Assisted by Dorothy Fix ₍and others₎ 7th ed. Newark, N.J., Bro-Dart Foundation, 1972.

xxvi, 821 p. 32 cm.

The **Elementary school library collection, phases 1-2-3**; a guide to books and other media. Mary V. Gaver, general editor. Phyllis Van Orden, associate editor. Assisted by Dorothy Fix ₍and others₎ 8th ed. New Brunswick, N.J., Bro-Dart Foundation, 1973.

xxviii, 780 p. 32 cm.

Englund, David, 1928–
Böcker för bokrummet. En kommenterad grundförteck-

ning för skolbiblioteken på mellan- och högstadiet. Redigerad av Maja Lisa Näslund. Lund, Bibliotekstjänst, 1966.

131 p. 21 cm. (Bibliotekstjänsts bokurval, 60)

Feminists on Children's Media.
Little Miss Muffet fights back; recommended non-sexist books about girls for young readers. [New York, c1971]

48 p. illus. 23 x 10 cm.

Fisher, Janet.
5 to 8. [Birmingham, Eng.] Library Association. Youth Libraries Group [1972?]

43 p. illus. 21 cm. (Library Association. Youth Libraries Group. Pamphlet no. 12)

Frank, Josette, 1893–
Your child's reading today. New and rev. ed. Garden City, N. Y., Doubleday, 1969.

xvi, 368 p. 25 cm.

Friends, Society of. *American Friends Service Committee.*
Books for friendship; a list of books recommended for children. 4th ed. [Philadelphia, 1968]

46 p. illus. 23 cm.

First published in 1953 under title: Books are bridges.

Glade, Melba.
Windows to the magic world of books / Melba Glade. — [Ogden? Utah] : Glade, [1974]

231 p. : ill. ; 28 cm.

Griffin, Louise.
Multi-ethnic books for young children; annotated bibliography for parents and teachers. [Washington, National Association for the Education of Young Children, 1971?]

74 p. illus. 26 cm. (An ERIC-NAEYC publication in early childhood education)

Harrison, Nancy.
Reading aloud to the family. London, National Book League, 1970.

30 p. 21 cm.

Distributed in the U.S. and Canada by Richard Abel & Co.

Harrison, Nancy.
The story hour: reading aloud for all ages, selected by Nancy Harrison. London, National Book League, 1972.

46 p. 21 cm.

Haviland, Virginia, 1911–
Children's books of international interest; a selection from four decades of American publishing. Virginia Haviland, editor. Chicago, American Library Association, 1972.

x, 69 p. 21 cm.

Hempstead Public Library. Foreign Language Center for Children.
Annotated bibliography. Hempstead, N. Y., 1970.

vi, 106 p. 22 cm.

Hewins, Caroline Maria, 1846-1926.
A mid-century child and her books. New York, Macmillan, 1926. Detroit, Singing Tree Press, 1969.

xi, 136 p. facsims. 21 cm.

"Alphabet ... reproduced from Peter Piper's practical principles of plain and perfect pronunciation": p. 123-136.

Hill, Janet.
Books for children: the homelands of immigrants in Britain: Africa, Cyprus, India and Pakistan, Ireland, Italy, Poland, Turkey, the West Indies. London, Institute of Race Relations; Distributed by Research Publications Services, 1971.

85 p. 21 cm. (Institute of Race Relations. Special series)

Huus, Helen, 1913–
Children's books to enrich the social studies; for the elementary grades. Rev. ed. Washington, National Council for the Social Studies [c1966]

xiii, 201 p. illus. 23 cm. (National Council for the Social Studies, Bulletin no. 32)

Jam'īyat al-Maktabāt al-Madrasīyah.
الفهرس المصنف للكتب المختارة للمكتبات المدرسية، من ١٩٦٣/٦٢ الى ١٩٦٨/٦٧. [القاهرة] توزيع دار الفكر العربى، ١٩٦٩.

318 p. 24 cm.

At head of title: جمعية المكتبات المدرسية
Added t. p.: Classified list of selected books for school libraries, 1962/63-1967/68.

Jeffery, J. Betty.
Growing up with books; selected by J. Betty Jeffery. London, published for National Library Week by the National Book League, 1966.

5-38 p. 22 cm.

Jeffery, J   Betty.
Growing up with books; selected by J. Betty Jeffery. 2nd ed. London, National Book League, 1969.

39, p. 22 cm.

Jeffery, J   Betty.
Growing up with books; selected by J. Betty Jeffery. London, National Book League, 1972.

42 p. 21 cm.

Keating, Charlotte Matthews.
Building bridges of understanding. Cover and section pages illustrated by Pat Morris. Tucson, Ariz., Palo Verde Pub. Co., 1967.

xvii, 134 p. 24 cm.

Keating, Charlotte Matthews.
Building bridges of understanding between cultures. Tucson, Ariz., Palo Verde Pub. Co. [1971]

xiii, 233 p. 24 cm.

Kelley, Marjorie E   1932-
In pursuit of values: a bibliography of children's books, by Marjorie E. Kelley. New York, Paulist Press [1973]

44 p. illus. 23 cm.

Kent, *Eng. Education Committee.*
Catalogue of recommended books and publications for secondary schools: English. [New ed.] Maidstone (Kent), County Education Offices, 1966.

57 p. 25 cm.

Kircher, Clara J
Behavior patterns in children's books: a bibliography, compiled by Clara J. Kircher. Washington, Catholic University of America Press ₁1966₁

v, 132 p. 24 cm.

"A replacement for Character formation through books."

Kujoth, Jean Spealman.
Best-selling children's books. Metuchen, N.J., Scarecrow Press, 1973.

305 p. 22 cm.

Larrick, Nancy.
A parent's guide to children's **reading. Rev. and enl.** 3d ed. New York, Pocket Books ₁1969₁

xvii, 334 p. illus. 18 cm.

Library Association. *County Libraries Group.*
Readers' guide to books on attitudes and adventure. 2nd ed.; ₁compiled by Sheila Ray and Colin Ray₁ London, Library Association (County Libraries Group), 1968.

29 p. 19 cm. (*Its* Readers' guide. New ser., no. 103)

Cover title: Attitudes and adventure.

Library Association. Youth Libraries Group.
Fiction, faction: books for the family, 1971. Birmingham, Library Association ₁Youth Libraries Group₁ 1971.

₁2₁ 16 p. illus. 22 cm. index (Its pamphlet no. 9)

Library Association. Youth Libraries Group.
Stories to read and to tell. ₁Birmingham, Eng., 1974?₁

20 p. 22 cm. (Its Pamphlet, 13)

Library Association. Youth Libraries Group.
Stories to tell: a list compiled by members of the Youth Libraries Group, London and Home Counties Branch, and edited by Mary Junor. London, Library Association (Youth Libraries Group), 1968.

31 p. 22 cm. (Its Pamphlet, no. 2)

Library Association. Youth Libraries Group. North West Branch.
Books for all time; a guide to current editions of classics for young people, compiled by the North West Branch, Youth Libraries Group of the Library Association. Birmingham, Combridge Jackson Ltd., 1973.

123 p. illus. 22 cm.

Linderberg, Kerstin, 1928–
Skönlitteratur för ungdom. Urval. 3., ₁väsentligt utökade₁ uppl. Lund, Bibliotekstjänst, 1966.

111 p. illus. 21 cm. (Bibliotekstjänsts bokurval, nr. 55)

Previous selection compiled by Mary Ørvig.

Les Livres de l'enfance du xv⁰ au xix⁰ siècle. Préf. de Paul Gavault. ₁London₁ Holland Press ₁1967₁

xx, 446 p. plates. 29 cm.

Reprint of 1930 ed.

McGinniss, Dorothy A
Guide to the selection of books for your elementary school library, prepared by Dorothy A. McGinniss. ₁Hillside,

N. J.₁ Baker & Taylor Co. ₁1967₁

viii, 353 p. 28 cm.

McGinniss, Dorothy A
Guide to the selection of books **for your elementary** school library, prepared by Dorothy A. McGinniss. ₁Sommerville, N. J.₁ Baker & Taylor ₁1968₁

viii, 457 p. forms. 28 cm.

McGinniss, Dorothy A
Guide to the selection of books for your elementary school library, 1971–72. Titles selected by Dorothy A. McGinniss. ₁3d ed. Somerville, N. J., Baker & Taylor Co., 1971₁

xvi, 309 p. forms. 28 cm.
Title on spine: Baker & Taylor's guide to the selection of books for your elementary school library.

————————1972 supplement. ₁Somerville, N. J., Baker & Taylor Co., 1972₁

xxi, 109 p. forms. 28 cm.

McGinniss, Dorothy A
Guide to the selection of books for your elementary school library. Prepared by Dorothy A. McGinniss. 1973–74 ed. ₁Somerville, N. J.₁ Baker & Taylor Co. ₁1972, c1973₁

xxvii, 309 p. 28 cm.

Macháčková, Marcela.
Knihy pro děti v roce 1969. Výběrová anotovaná bibliogr. dětské lit. Připr. Marcela Macháčková. Praha, Měst. knihovna, rozmn., 1970.

53, ₁1₁ p. 29 cm. (Metodické texty a bibliografie MK v Praze)

Maib, Frances.
List of suggested literature books. ₁Moscow, College of Education₁ University of Idaho, 1965.

25 l. 29 cm.

Cover title: Selected books to read aloud to children: elementary grades.

Maine. State Library, *Augusta. Office of the Children's Specialist.*
A basic buying list of children's books, pre-school through 9th grade. Augusta, 1966.

vii, 257 p. 28 cm.

Marantz, Kenneth.
A bibliography of children's art literature; an annotated bibliography of children's literature designed to stimulate and enrich the visual imagination of the child. Compiled by Kenneth Marantz. Washington, National Art Education Association, 1965.

17 p. 18 x 19 cm.

Mortimer, Sheila M
What shall I read? a select list of quality books for children, compiled and edited by Sheila M. Mortimer. London, Library Association, 1973.

163 p. 22 cm.

Moses, Montrose Jonas, 1878-1934.
Children's books and reading. New York, M. Kennerley. Ann Arbor, Mich., Gryphon Books, 1971 ₁c1907₁

272 p. 22 cm.

Moss, Elaine.
Children's books of the year 1970, annotated and selected

by Elaine Moss. [London] Hamish Hamilton in association with the National Book League and the British Council [1971]

96 p. 22 cm.

Moss, Elaine.
One hundred books for children 1966–67. 2nd ed., with supplement: 25 books for children: January–June, 1968, selected by Elaine Moss. London, National Book League, 1968.

24 p. 22 cm.

Moss, Elaine.
Paperbacks for children—two to eleven; selected and annotated by Elaine Moss. London, National Book League, [1973].

21 p. 21 cm. (National Book League. Publication, no. 73:6:1)

Munich. Internationale Jugendbibliothek.
Die Besten der Besten: Bilder-, Kinder- und Jugendbücher aus 57 Ländern oder Sprachen. Hrsg. von Walter Scherf als Veröffentlichung der Internationalen Jugendbibliothek. München, Verlag Dokumentation; [R. R. Bowker Co., New York] 1971.

189 p. 22 cm. (Its Kataloge, 3)

Added t. p.: The best of the best; picture, children's, and youth books from 57 countries or languages.

Munich. Internationale Jugendbibliothek.
Preisgekrönte Kinderbücher. Children's prize books. Ein Katalog d. Internat. Jugendbibliothek über 67 Preise. Hrsg. u. mit e. Einf. vers. von Walter Scherf. München [vielm.] Pullach u. Berlin, Verl. Dokumentation, 1969.

xi. 238 p. 22 cm.

Text in German and English.

Natali, Zara.
Problems encountered by characters in children's fiction, 1945–1965; an annotated bibliography. Johannesburg, Dept. of Bibliography, Librarianship and Typography, University of the Witwatersrand, 1967.

iv, 90 p. 29 cm.

Thesis (diploma in librarianship)—University of the Witwatersrand.

National Book League, *London.*
School library fiction. London, National Book League, 1966–

v. 22 cm.

CONTENTS.—v. 1. Historical fiction.—v. 2. Children and adults.—v. 3. Mystery and adventure.

National Council of Teachers of English.
Adventuring with books; a book list for elementary schools. Prepared by Elizabeth Guilfoile, editorial chairman, and the Committee on the Elementary School Book List of the National Council of Teachers of English. [New York] New American Library [1966]

256 p. illus. 18 cm. (A Signet book, T2914)

National Council of Teachers of English.
Adventuring with books; 2,400 titles for pre-K–grade 8. Prepared by Shelton L. Root, Jr., and a committee of the National Council of Teachers of English. 2d ed. New York, Citation Press, 1973.

xiii, 395 p. 21 cm.

National Council of Teachers of English.
Your reading; a book list for junior high schools, prepared by Charles B. Willard, editorial chairman, and the Committee on the Junior High School Book List of the National Council of Teachers of English. [New York] New American Library [1966]

222 p. illus., facsims. 18 cm. (A Signet book, T2915)

Neesam, Malcolm.
Into space. [Birmingham, Eng., Library Association, Youth Libraries Group, 1972]

16 p. 21 cm. (Storylines, no. 2)

New Brunswick. *Dept. of Education.*
Supplementary reading list for New Brunswick junior high schools. Fredericton, 1968.

72 p. 25 cm.

New Brunswick. *Dept. of Education.*
Supplementary reading list for New Brunswick elementary schools. Fredericton, 1969.

98 p. 25 cm.

New York *(City)* *Board of Education.*
Suggested readings in the literatures of Africa, China, India, Japan. New York [1968]

124 p. 22 cm. (Its Curriculum bulletin. 1967–68 ser., no. 13)

Nichols, Margaret S
Multicultural bibliography for preschool through second grade: in the areas of Black, Spanish-speaking, Asian American, and native American cultures [by] Margaret S. Nichols [and] Margaret N. O'Neill. Stanford, Calif., Multicultural Resources, 1972.

40 p. 25 cm.

Okanagan Regional Library.
Books for boys and girls. [Kelowna, B. C. Okanagan Regional Library, 1966]

[8] p. 22 cm.

Ott, Helen Keating.
Helping children through books; a selected booklist for the seventies. Bryn Mawr, Pa., Church and Synagogue Library Association, 1974.

i, 16 p. 29 cm. (Church and Synagogue Library Association. CSLA bibliography)

An updated version of a bibliography prepared for use at a workshop held during the 1973 annual conference of the Church and Synagogue Library Association, July 1973, Portland, Or.

Owen, Betty M
Smorgasbord of books : titles junior high readers relish / Betty M. Owen. — New York : Citation Press, 1974.

87 p. ; 20 cm.

Paperbound book guide for elementary schools. 1966–
New York, R. R. Bowker.

v. 22 cm.

Pittsburgh. Carnegie Library.
Stories to tell to children; a selected list. 8th ed., rev. and edited by Laura E. Cathon, Marion McC. Haushalter [and] Virginia A. Russell. Margaret Hodges, consultant.

₁Pittsburgh₁ Published for Carnegie Library of Pittsburgh Children's Services by the University of Pittsburgh Press ₁1974₁

xI, 145 p. illus. 21 cm.

Ray, Sheila G   (Bannister)
Readers' guide to books on attitudes and adventure. London, Library Association (County Libraries Group), 1965.

18 p. 18½ cm. (Readers' guides, new ser., no. 86)

'A selection of books for young adults'—Cover note.
"Compiled by Mrs. C. H. Ray (née Miss Sheila Bannister) ... and Mr. C. H. Ray."

Roscoe, Sydney.
John Newbery and his successors, 1740-1814; a bibliography by S. Roscoe. Wormley, Five Owls Press, 1973.

xxxi, 461, ₁32₁ p. 1 col. illus., facsims., map. 24 cm.

Roscoe, Sydney.
Newbery—Carnan—Power: a provisional check-list of books for the entertainment, instruction and education of children and young people, issued under the imprints of John Newbery and his family in the period 1742-1802, by S. Roscoe. ₁London, Dawsons of Pall Mall₁ 1966.

viii, 81 p. plates (facsims.) 33 cm.

Rosenberg, Judith K
Young people's literature in series: fiction; an annotated bibliographical guide ₁by₁ Judith K. Rosenberg & Kenyon C. Rosenberg. Littleton, Colo., Libraries Unlimited, 1972.

176 p. 24 cm.

Rosenberg, Judith K
Young people's literature in series: publishers' and non-fiction series: an annotated bibliographical guide ₁by₁ Judith K. Rosenberg & Kenyon C. Rosenberg. Littleton, Colo., Libraries Unlimited, 1973.

280 p. 24 cm.

Saint-Albin, Jacques de.
Livres à transformations parus en langue française, classés selon les procédés, par J. de Saint-Albin. Paris, Comité national de la gravure française, Cabinet des estampes de la Bibliothèque nationale, 1968.

219-254 p. plates. 27 cm. (Nouvelles de l'estampe, 1968, no 6)

Saskatchewan. Provincial Library, Regina. Bibliographic Services Division.
Fiction for young readers. Regina, 1973.

55 p. 21 cm.

Saskatchewan. Provincial Library, Regina. Bibliographic Services Division.
Picture books for young children. Regina, 1973.

35 p. 21 cm.

School Library Association. Primary Schools Sub-Committee.
Books for primary children: an annotated list; compiled by the Primary Schools Sub-committee of the S.L.A. and edited by Berna Clark. 3rd ed. London, School Library Association, 1969.

vi, 113 p. 25 cm.

First ed. published as Primary school library books by the Primary Schools Book Panel of the School Library Association, 1960.

The **School** library journal book review. 1968/69– New York, R. R. Bowker Co.

v. 29 cm. annual.

Period covered by each vol. ends May 31.

South Australia. *Libraries Board.*
Books for young people; an annotated list. Adelaide ₁1963–64; v. 1, 1964₁

2 v. illus. 22 cm.

CONTENTS.—pt. 1. Up to 9 years. 9 to 13 years. 3d ed.—pt. 2. 13 to 17 years. 2d ed.

South Australia. *Libraries Board.*
Books for young people; an annotated list. ₁4th ed.₁ Adelaide, 1966–

v. 22 cm.

CONTENTS.—pt. 1. Up to 13 years.

South Australia. *Libraries Board.*
Books for young people; a guide to Christmas buying. ₁Adelaide, 1969₁

24 p. 21 cm.

South Australia. Libraries Board.
Books for young people; a guide to Christmas buying. ₁Adelaide₁ ₁1970₁

24 p. 21 cm.

South Australia. Libraries Board.
Books for young people; a guide to Christmas buying. ₁Adelaide, 1972₁

24 p. 21 cm.

South Australia. Libraries Board.
Books for young people; a guide to Christmas buying. ₁Adelaide, 1973₁

23 p. 22 cm.

Special Committee of the National Congress of Parents and Teachers and the Children's Services Division, American Library Association.
Let's read together; books for family enjoyment. 3d ed. Chicago, American Library Association, 1969.

xi, 103 p. 21 cm.

Sutherland, Zena, comp.
The best in children's books; the University of Chicago guide to children's literature, 1966-1972. Chicago, University of Chicago Press ₁1973₁

xii, 484 p. 24 cm.

"Book reviews were previously published in the Bulletin of the Center for Children's Books."

Thompson, Evelyn S   1899–
Distinguished children's books. Compiled and edited by Evelyn S. Thompson. ₁Houston, Tex.₁ 1967 ₁*1968₁

454 p. port. 28 cm.

Toronto. Public Libraries.
Books for youth: a guide for teen-age readers, edited by Catherine C. Robertson ₁and others₁ With an introd. by H. C. Campbell. 3d ed. ₁Toronto₁ 1966.

v, 154 p. illus. 28 cm.

First ed. 1940, 2d ed. 1956, issued by Circulation Division, Toronto Public Library.

Toronto. Public Libraries.
Catalogue of replacement books for children's library collections. [Toronto] 1966.

190 p. 26 cm.

Toronto. Public Libraries. Boys and Girls Services.
Books for boys and girls. Toronto, Boys and Girls Division, Toronto Public Libraries, 1966.

[6] p. 22 cm.

Toronto. Public Libraries. *Boys and Girls Services.*
Books for boys and girls. Edited by Marguerite Bagshaw, head of Boys and Girls Services, Toronto Public Library, assisted by Doris Scott. With an introd. by Henry C. Campbell. [4th ed.] Toronto, Ryerson Press [1966]

301 p. illus. 21 cm.

Udenlandske børnebøger. Red. af Marja-Liisa Heise. Udg. af De Storkøbenhavnske Folkebibliotekers Samarbejdsudvalg. København, (Bibliotekscentralen), 1969.

5, 111 p. 21 cm.

United Nations Educational, Scientific and Cultural Organization.
A world of children's books; a selective international bibliography. Le monde des livres pour enfants; bibliographie internationale sélective. Paris, Unesco, 1972.

148 p. 28 cm.

English and French.

Walker, Elinor, ed.
Book bait; detailed notes on adult books popular with young people. 2d ed. Chicago, American Library Association, 1969.

v, 129 p. 21 cm.

Warren, Dorothea.
Fiction, verse and legend: a guide to the selection of imaginative literature for the middle and secondary school years; compiled by Dorothea Warren and Griselda Barton. London, School Library Association, 1972.

vi, 68 p. 25 cm. (School Library Association. Book lists)

Wood, Kenneth Albert.
Buy, beg or borrow: a choice of books for children Birmingham, Library Association (Youth Libraries Group), 1969.

[15] p. illus. 22 cm. (YLG Pamphlet no. 5)

World Organization for Early Childhood Education.
Understanding of others; a bibliography of children's books which promote positive attitudes about people and present wholesome human relations and feelings about various cultural groups. [2d ed. Copenhagen] 1966.

17 p. 21 cm.

Yorkshire, Eng. West Riding. County Library.
100 children's books of 1970. Wakefield, 1971.

[16] p. illus. 21 cm.

BIBLIOGRAPHIES

Boudreau, Ingeborg.
Aids to choosing books for children. New York, Children's Book Council [1967]

folder ([6] p.) 28 cm.

Caption title.
Compiled by Ingeborg Boudreau, in consultation with Augusta Baker and others.

Boudreau, Ingeborg.
Aids to choosing books for children. New York, Children's Book Council [1969]

19 p. 23 cm.

Copenhagen. Statens pædagogiske studiesamling.
Katalog over bibliotekets litteratur vedrørende børns og unges læsning. København, 1970.

46 columns, 4 p. 30 cm.

Redigeret af Vibeke Stybe.

Jones, Milbrey L   1948–
Book selection aids for children and teachers in elementary and secondary schools [by Milbrey L. Jones. Washington, Office of Education, U. S. Dept. of Health, Education, and Welfare; for sale by the Superintendent of Documents, U. S. Govt. Print. Off., 1966]

16 p. 27 cm.

Ladley, Winifred C   1904–
Sources of good books and magazines for children; an annotated bibliography. Compiled by Winifred C. Ladley. Rev. Newark, Del., International Reading Association, 1970.

18 p. 22 cm. (IRA annotated bibliography)

Ray, Colin H   1921–
Background to children's books, selected by Colin Ray. London, National Book League, 1971.

24 p. 21 cm.

Ray, Colin H   1921–
Background to children's books, selected by Colin Ray. [New ed.] London, National Book League, 1974.

18 p. 22 cm.

BIO-BIBLIOGRAPHY

De Montreville, Doris.
Third book of junior authors. Edited by Doris de Montreville and Donna Hill. New York, H. W. Wilson Co., 1972.

320 p. illus. 27 cm. (The Authors series)

"Continues the work of Stanley J. Kunitz and Howard Haycraft in The junior book of authors ... 1951, and of Muriel Fuller in More junior authors, 1963." Includes a cumulative index to the 3 works (p. 314–320)

Ofek, Uriel.
עולם צעיר; אנציקלופדיה לספרות ילדים [מאת] אוריאל אופק. רמת־גן, מסדה [1970]

766 columns. illus., facsims., ports. 27 cm.

On verso of t. p.: Young world: encyclopaedia of children's literature.

HISTORICAL FICTION
Charlton, Kenneth.
Recent historical fiction for secondary school children. Revised and rewritten [ed.]. London, Historical Association, 1969.

32 p. 22 cm. (Teaching of history pamphlet, no. 18)

Francis, Shelagh.

Time past: historical fiction for young people; compiled by Shelagh Francis, John L. Hirst. ₁Chester,₁, ₁Cheshire County Council, Libraries and Museums,₁, ₁Chester Public Library₁, 1972.

43 p. illus. 21 cm.

Hotchkiss, Jeanette.

European historical fiction and biography for children and young people. 2d ed. Metuchen, N. J., Scarecrow Press, 1972.

272 p. 22 cm.

1967 ed. published under title: European historical fiction for children and young people.

Hotchkiss, Jeanette.

European historical fiction for children and young people. Metuchen, N. J., Scarecrow Press, 1967.

148 p. 22 cm.

New Zealand Library Association. *Children's and Young People's Section.*

Historical fiction. ₁A list of books for older children₁ ₁Wellington₁ New Zealand Library Association, 1967.

folder (₁7₁ p.)¹ 19 cm.

HISTORY AND CRITICISM

Haviland, Virginia, 1911–

Children's literature: a guide to reference sources. Washington, Library of Congress; ₁for sale by the Superintendent of Documents, U. S. Govt. Print. Off.₁ 1966.

x, 341 p. illus. 24 cm.

Compiled by Virginia Haviland, Elisabeth Wenning Davidson, and Barbara Quinnam of the Children's Book Section.

—————— First supplement, compiled by Virginia Haviland, with the assistance of Margaret N. Coughlan. Washington, Library of Congress, 1972–

v. 24 cm.

Library Association. Youth Libraries Group.

Books about children's literature: a booklist prepared by the Committee of the Youth Libraries Group, and edited by Marcus Crouch. Revised ed. London, Library Association, 1966.

36 p. 21 cm.

Wegehaupt, Heinz.

Bibliographie der in der DDR von 1949–1971 erschienenen theoretischen Arbeiten zur Kinder- und Jugendliteratur/ im Auftr. d. DDR-Zentrums f. Kinderliteratur zusammengestellt von Heinz Wegehaupt. Berlin: Kuratorium Sozialist. Kinderliteratur d. DDR; Berlin: DDR-Zentrum f. Kinderliteratur, 1972.

78 p. 30 cm.
Cover title: Bibliographie erschienener theoretischer Arbeiten zur Kinder- und Jugendliteratur.

Wegehaupt, Heinz.

Theoretische Literatur zum Kinder- und Jugendbuch; bibliographischer Nachweis von den Anfängen im 18. Jahrhundert bis zur Gegenwart nach den Beständen der Deutschen Staatsbibliothek, Berlin. Theoretical supplementary literature to children's and young people's books. Bearb. von Heinz Wegehaupt. Mit Vorwort von Horst Kunze. München-Pullach, Verlag Dokumentation, 1972.

xviii, 448 p. 22 cm.
Added t. p. Introduction, and table of contents in English.

LIBRARY AND EXHIBITION CATALOGS

Connecticut. Southern Connecticut State College, *New Haven. Library.*

The Carolyn Sherwin Bailey historical collection of children's books: a catalogue. Researched, compiled, and edited by Dorothy R. Davis. ₁New Haven₁ Southern Connecticut State College, 1966.

232 p. illus., facsims. 23 cm.

Fieler, Frank B

The David McCandless McKell collection: a descriptive catalog of manuscripts, early printed books, and children's books, by Frank B. Fieler, assisted by John A. Zamonski and Kenneth W. Haas, Jr. Boston, G. K. Hall, 1973.

ix, 243 p. 27 cm.

Floyd, Jean L

Bookwave recommended reading for teenagers; an annotated catalogue of books and periodicals. Compiled and edited by Jean L. Floyd. Assisted by M. Tarcisia ₁and others₁ Kingston, Jamaica, 1970.

140 p. 22 cm.

Hammersmith, Eng. Public Libraries.

Early children's books; a catalogue of the collection in the London Borough of Hammersmith Public Libraries. ₁Hammersmith₁ 1965.

121 p. 33 cm.

Harris Public Library, *Preston, Eng.*

A catalogue of the Spencer Collection of early children's books and chapbooks: presented to the Harris Public Library, Preston, by Mr. J. H. Spencer, 1947; compiled by David Good, with an introduction by Percy H. Muir. Preston, Harris Public Library, 1967.

xi, 307 p. 22 cm.

International exhibition of children's books. ₁Organised by Children's Book Trust, New Delhi, 21 April to 7 May 1967. New Delhi, printed by the Indraprastha Press, 1967.

68 p. illus. 28 cm.

—————— List of books. ₁New Delhi, Printed by the Indraprastha Press, 1967₁

82 p. 28 cm.

Munich. Internationale Jugendbibliothek.

Länderkatalog. Boston, G. K. Hall, 1968.

4 v. 37 cm.

Added t. p.: International Youth Library, Munich. Language Sections Catalog.
Editorial matter also in English.
"Die vorliegenden Kataloge verzeichnen den Bestand der Bibliothek mit Ausnahme eines Teiles der Zugänge in den Jahren 1949–1957; diese Bestände sind in einem gesonderten Arbeitskatalog zu finden."

CONTENTS.—Bd. 1. A Österreich-D Deutschland (A-K)—Bd. 2. D Deutschland (L-Z)-E Spanien.—Bd. 3. EIR Irland-RA Argentinien.—Bd. 4. RC China-ZA Südafrikanische Republik. Sekundärliteratur.

National Book League, *London.*

British children's books: ₁catalogue of an exhibition₁ 3rd ed. London, National Book League, 1967.

96 p. 21½ cm.

National Book League, London.

British children's books. 4th ed. London, N.B.L., 1972.

102 p.   22 cm.

Catalogue of an exhibition.

National Book League, London.
Children's books of yesterday; a catalogue of an exhibition held at 7 Albemarle Street, London during May 1946. Compiled by Percy H. Muir, with a foreword by John Masefield.   New ed., rev. and enl.   Detroit, Singing Tree Press, 1970.

v, 211 p.   23 cm.

National Book League, *London.*
School library books: non-fiction ₍catalogue of an exhibition₎ 1965.   London, National Book League ₍1966₎

338 p.   22 cm.

National Book League, *London.*
School library books: non fiction.   ₍2d ed.₎   London, 1969.

351 p.   22 cm.

"Catalogue and exhibition."

Saskatchewan.   Dept. of Education.   Program Development Branch.
Sing out for books; Saskatchewan school library book display, 1969 ₍catalogue₎, prepared by the Supervisor of School Libraries.   Regina, 1969.

75 p.   28 cm.

Saskatchewan.   Dept. of Education.   Program Development Branch.
Sing out for books; Saskatchewan school library book display, 1970, prepared by the Supervisor of School Libraries, Saskatchewan Dept. of Education.   Regina, Program Development, General Education Branch, Saskatchewan Dept. of Education, 1970.

vi, 29 p.   illus.   28 cm.

United States.   Library of Congress.   Children's Book Section.
The wide world of children's books; an exhibition for International Book Year. An annotated catalog, compiled by Virginia Haviland, head, Children's Book Section.   Washington ₍for sale by the Supt. of Docs., U.S. Govt. Print. Off.₎ 1972.

iv, 84 p.   illus.   13 x 19 cm.

The exhibition and catalog include items from the Library's collection, representing 38 countries.

Victoria and Albert Museum, South Kensington.   Library.
Victorian children's books, selected from the Library of the Victoria and Albert Museum, London; ₍catalogue of₎ an exhibition at the Bibliothèque royale, Brussels, 29 September–13 November 1973, arranged for Europalia 73 Great Britain by the National Book League in co-operation with the British Council.   London, National Book League, 1973.
3–107 p.   illus.   21 x 23 cm.

Wandsworth, Eng.   Public Libraries.
The Wandsworth collection of early children's books; (catalogue prepared by Doris Aubrey).   (London), Wandsworth Public Libraries, 1972.

(3), 263 p.   25 cm.

Warringah Shire. *Library.*
Catalogue of children's books.   ₍no. 1–   ₎   Sydney, Warringah Shire Library, 1967.

83, 63 p.   28 cm.

Wayne State University, *Detroit.   Libraries.*
The Eloise Ramsey collection of literature for young people, a catalogue, compiled by Joan Cusenza.   Detroit, 1967.

389 p.   23 cm.

RARE BOOKS

Chelyshev, Boris Dmitrievich.
В поисках редких книг.   ₍Для детей₎.   Москва, "Просвещение," 1970.

111 p. with illus.   20 cm.

Justin G. Schiller, ltd.
Children's books from four centuries including original drawings, manuscripts, and related juvenilia.   New York ₍c1973₎

1 v. (unpaged)   illus.   25 cm.   (**Its** Catalogue 29)

McKee, Ruth V
McKee's price guide to children's literature, 1970; including prices on related reference books, biographies, and bibliographies, by Ruth V. McKee.   ₍Wayzata? Minn.₎ Waytonka Press ₍c1970₎

74 p.   22 cm.

Rosenbach, Abraham Simon Wolf, 1876–1952.
Early American children's books, by A. S. W. Rosenbach, with bibliographical descriptions of the books in his private collection.   Foreword by A. Edward Newton.   New York, Kraus Reprint Corp., 1966.

lix, 354 p.   illus. (part col.), facsims.   27 cm.

Reprint of the 1933 ed.

Rosenbach, Abraham Simon Wolf, 1876-1952.
Early American children's books, by A. S. W. Rosenbach, with bibliographical descriptions of the books in his private collection. Foreword by A. Edward Newton.   New York, Dover Publications ₍1971₎

lix, 354 p.   illus., facsims.   24 cm.

Reprint of the 1933 ed.

Schatzki, Walter, 1899-
Children's books, old and rare. Foreword by Leslie Shepard. New York.   Detroit, Gale Research Co., 1974.

46 p.   illus.   23 cm.

"Catalogue number one."
Reprint of the 1941 ed. published by the author under title: Old and rare children's books.

Toronto.   Public Libraries. *Boys and Girls Services.*
A chronicle of Boys and Girls House and a selected list of recent additions to the Osborne collection of early children's books, 1542–1910, and the Lillian H. Smith collection, 1911–1963.   ₍Toronto, 1964₎

29 p.   illus.   26 cm.

"Prepared to commemorate the opening of the new Boys and Girls House, Toronto Public Library, Toronto, Canada, May, 1964."

United States.   Library of Congress.   Children's Book Section.
Americana in children's books : rarities from the 18th and 19th centuries : an exhibition catalog of items chosen and annotated by the Children's Book Section. — Washington : Library of Congress, 1974.

iii, 28 p. : ill. ; 15 cm.

"Mounted in the Library of Congress Rare Book Room, November 1974–January 1975."

Welch, D'Alté Aldridge, 1907-1970.
A bibliography of American children's books printed prior to 1821. ₁Barre? Mass.₁ American Antiquarian Society and Barre Publishers, 1972.

lxvi, 516 p. 27 cm.

"Originally published in six parts in the Proceedings of the American Antiquarian Society."

Welch, D'Alté Aldridge, 1907-1970.
A bibliography of American children's books printed prior to 1821. ₁Worcester, Mass.₁ American Antiquarian Society, 1972.

lxvi, 516 p. 27 cm.

Originally published in the Proceedings of the American Antiquarian Society: A–C, Apr. 1963: D–G, Oct. 1963; H, Oct. 1954; I–O Oct. 1965: P–R, Apr. 1967; S–Z, Oct. 1967.

TRANSLATIONS

Rabban, Elana.
Books from other countries, 1968–1971. ₁Chicago, American Association of School Libraries₁ 1972.

48 p. 27 cm.

Storybooks International, inc., *Locust Valley, N. Y.*
Translated children's books offered by publishers in the U. S. A. ₁Locust Valley₁ 1968.

83 p. 22 cm.

CHILDREN'S LITERATURE, AFRIKAANS

Pienaar, Lydia, *comp.*
Basic children's books: a list for a South African library; Supplement. Cape Town, City Libraries, 1967.

134–224 p. 25 cm.

Afrikaans and English.

Pienaar, Lydia.
Basic children's books; a list for a South African library. 3d rev. ed.

———— Supplement. Basiese kinderboeke 'n lys vir 'n Suid-Afrikaanse biblioteek. Bylae. ₁Cape Town₁ Cape Town City Libraries, 1970.

l, 24 l. 26 cm.

English or Afrikaans.

Pienaar, Lydia.
Basic children's books: a list for a South African library. Basiese kinderboeke: 'n lys vir 'n Suid-Afrikaanse biblioteek, compiled by Lydia Pienaar. ₁4th rev. ed.₁ ₁Cape Town₁ Cape Town City Libraries, 1972.
₁2₁ p., ₁307₁ leaves in various pagings. 26 cm.
English or Afrikaans.
———— Supplement. Bylae, compiled by Lydia Pienaar. ₁Cape Town₁ Cape Town City Libraries, 1973–
v. 26 cm.
English or Afrikaans.

South Africa. *Dept. of Education, Arts and Science. Division Library Services.*
Keurlys van boeke vir tegniese kolleges, hoër tegniese, hoër handel- en hoër huishoudskole asook spesiale skole. Select list of books for technical colleges, technical high, commercial high and domestic high schools as well as special schools. Pretoria, the Department, 1966.
xiii, 198 p. 30 cm. (*Its* List, no. 1)

CHILDREN'S LITERATURE, ARABIC

Sha'lān, Jamāl 'Abd al-Hamīd.
(al-Fihris al-muṣannaf lil-kutub al-mukhtārah lil-maktabāt al-madrasīyah min 1968/69 ilá 1972/73)
الفهرس المصنف للكتب المختارة للمكتبات المدرسية من ١٩٦٩/٦٨ الى ١٩٧٣/٧٢ / اعداد جمال عبد الحميد شعلان. — القاهرة: دار وهدان، ₁1974؟₁

286 p. ; 25 cm.

At head of title: Jam'īyat al-Maktabāt al-Madrasīyah.

CHILDREN'S LITERATURE, AUSTRALIAN

Anderson, Hugh.
The singing roads; a guide to Australian children's authors and illustrators, arranged and edited by Hugh Anderson. 3rd ed. Surry Hills ₁N. S. W.₁ Wentworth Press, 1970–

v. ports. 26 cm.

Children's Book Council of Victoria.
Australian children's books; a select list. 3rd ed. ₁Melbourne, 1967₁

39 p. illus. 22 cm.

Children's Book Council of Victoria.
Australian childrens books; a select list. 4th ed. ₁Melbourne₁ Childrens Book Council of Victoria ₁1970₁

36 p. illus. 22 cm.

Muir, Marcie.
A bibliography of Australian children's books. London, Deutsch, 1970.

3–1038 p., 24 plates. illus., (some col.), facsims. (some col.) 25 cm. (A Grafton book)

CHILDREN'S LITERATURE, CANADIAN

McDonough, Irma, *comp.*
Profiles from In review, Canadian books for children. Ottawa, Canadian Library Association, 1971.

iii, 56 p. ports. 23 cm.

CHILDREN'S LITERATURE, CATALAN

Rovira, Teresa.
Bibliografía histórica del libro infantil en catalán. Madrid, Asociación Nacional de Bibliotecarios, Archiveros y Arqueólogos (1972)

xxvii, 189 p. illus., plates. 24 cm. (Biblioteca profesional de ANABA. Bibliografías, 1)

At head of title: Teresa Rovira. Mª del Carme Ribé.

CHILDREN'S LITERATURE, CHINESE

The Chinese in children's books ₁in₁ the New York Public Library ₁prepared by Angela Au Jong and others. New York, Taplinger Pub. Co.₁ 1973 ₁c1965₁

30 p. 20 cm.

CHILDREN'S LITERATURE, CUBAN

Muriedas, Mercedes.
Bibliografía de la literatura infantil cubana, **siglo XIX.**

La Habana, Departamento Juvenil, Biblioteca Nacional José Martí, 1969–

v. 23 cm. (Colección Textos para narradores)

CHILDREN'S LITERATURE, CZECH

Czechoslovak Republic. *Státní nakladatelství dětské knihy.* Bibliografický soupis, 1949–1963. ₍Zprac. Jan Šnobr₎ Praha, 1966.

651 p. illus. (part col.) 20 cm.

At head of title: Státní nakladatelství dětské knihy, Praha.

Czechoslovak Republic. Státní nakladatelství dětské knihy. Bibliografický soupis 1964–1968. Státní nakl. dětské knihy. Praha. Zprac. Miroslav Petrtýl. Předml.: Jaroslav Seifert. Václav Stejskal: Pokus o socialistickou kulturní revoluci, doslov. 1. vyd. Praha, Albatros, t. Tisk 3, Čes. Těšín, 1970.

421, ₍3₎ p. ₍6₎ p. of col. plates. 20 cm.

At head of title: Státní nakladatelství dětské knihy, Praha.

Přehled české literatury pro mládež. V Praze, Státní pedagogická knihovna Komenského, ústřední pedagogická knihovna ČSSR.

v. 30 cm. annual.

Compiler: A. Holubová.

CHILDREN'S LITERATURE, DUTCH

Centrale Vereniging voor Openbare Bibliotheken. Bureau Boek en Jeugd. Boek en jeugd; jeugdlectuurgids voor gezin en school, samengesteld door en onder verantwoordelijkheid van het Bureau Boek en Jeugd te 's-Gravenhage. 's-Gravenhage, Leopold, 1972.

205 p. 21 cm.

CHILDREN'S LITERATURE, ENGLISH see Children's literature

CHILDREN'S LITERATURE, FRENCH

Bron, Claude. Romanciers choisis pour l'enfance et l'adolescence. Auteurs contemporains de langue française. Neuchâtel, H. Messeiller, (1972).

215 p. ports. 21 cm.

La Carrière du livre d'enfant à l'école et à la maison, avril 1969, Maison de la culture d'Amiens, catalogue. Amiens, Maison de la culture, 1969.

₍II₎, 105 p. 27 cm. (Éclat du livre, 3)

Cover title.
Exhibition catalog.

Duché, Didier Jacques, 1916– Bibliothèque idéale des enfants. Paris, Éditions universitaires, 1967.

479 p. 18 cm.

France. *Institut pédagogique national.* Des livres, des disques, un choix pour les bibliothèques scolaires, pour vos enfants de 4 à 16 ans … ₍Paris,₎ Services d'édition et de vente des productions de l'Éducation nationale, 1968.

115 p. illus. 24 cm. (Institut pédagogique national. Répertoires, bibliographies, catalogues)

International Board on Books for Young People. Section française. Dictionnaire des écrivains pour la jeunesse: auteurs de langue française. ₍Paris, Seghers, 1969₎

214 p. 17 cm. (Dictionnaire Seghers)

Quebec (*Province*) *Bureau des bibliothèques scolaires.* Choix d'albums pour les maternelles et les enfants de 6 à 8 ans. ₍Québec, Service d'information du Ministère de l'éducation, 1966₎

91 p. 23 cm.

Samuel Lajeunesse, Odile. Les Livres pour les jeunes enfants 6 ans –8 ans, étude bibliographique, sélective et critique … Paris, Association nationale du livre français à l'étranger, ₍1967 ?₎

75 l. 27 cm.

Samuel Lajeunesse, Françoise. Les Livres pour enfants de 8 à 10 ans, étude bibliographique, sélective et critique … Paris, Association nationale du livre français à l'étranger, 1967.

₍48₎ l. 27 cm.

Samuel Lajeunesse, Françoise. Les Livres pour enfants de 10 à 12 ans, étude bibliographique, sélective et critique … Paris, Association nationale du livre français à l'étranger, 1967.

₍60₎ l. 27 cm.

CHILDREN'S LITERATURE, GERMAN

Binder, Lucia. Lexikon der Jugendschriftsteller in deutscher Sprache. Hrsg. v. Lucia Binder. (Wien, Leinmüller ₍1968₎)

219 p. 21 cm. (Schriften zur Jugendlektüre, Bd. 6)

"Sonderdruck aus Die Barke, 1968."

Dummer, Gisela. Der Grundbestand; Bücher für den Aufbau von Jugendbüchereien und Schülerbüchereien ₍bearb. von Gisela Dummer, Mechthild Fehre und Gertrud Mielitz. Rendsburg, Büchereiwesen in Holstein e. V., Büchereizentrale₎ 1965.

105 p. 21 cm.

Frankfurt am Main. Universität. *Institut für Jugendbuchforschung.* Jugendliteratur heute. Hrsg. von Klaus Doderer. Frankfurt/M., Institut für Jugendbuchforschung der Hochschule für Erziehung an der Wolfgang Goethe-Universität. ₍Wienheim, Beltz in Kommission₎ 1965.

64 p. 21 cm.

Germany (*Democratic Republic. 1949–*) *Zentralinstitut für Bibliothekswesen.* Materialien für die Kinderbibliotheksarbeit. 1. Liste empfehlenswerter Kinderbücher für die Systematik-Altersgruppe I. 2. Staffelungsschlüssel für Kerntitel. ₍Berlin₎ Zentralinstitut für Bibliothekswesen. 1966.

15 p. 21 cm.
Cover title.
Reprinted from Mitteilungen und Materialien. 1966, Heft 1.
"Liste empfehlenswerter Kinderbücher für die Systematik-Altersgruppe II"
(11 p.) inserted. Reprinted from Mitteilungen und Materialien. 1966, Heft 4.

Hatzold, Ilse.
Deutscher Jugendbuchpreis. 1966–1970. (Bearbeitung: Ilse Hatzold ₍u.₎ Gerda Kohler. Katalog.) (München) Arbeitskreis f. Jugendliteratur (1970).

70 p. 22 cm.

International Institute for Children's, Juvenile and Popular Literature.
1000+1 ₍Tausendundein₎ Buch. (Herausgeber: Internationales Institut für Kinder-, Jugend- und Volksliteratur) (Wien, Verlag für Jugend und Volk ₍1967₎).

96 p. 21 cm.

International Institute for Children's, Juvenile and Popular Literature.
1000 & 1 ₍i. e. Tausendundein₎ Buch. Redigiert von R. Bamberger. Wien, Jugend & Volk, 1970.

96 p. 21 cm.

Lange, Marianne.
Das richtige Buch für unser Kind. (Herausgeber: Demokratischer Frauenbund Deutschlands.) (Berlin, Volk u. Wissen 1966.)

56 p. with illus. 21 cm. (Schriftenreihe Elternhaus und Schule)

Preisgekrönte Kinder- und Jugenbücher, 1954–1961. ₍Herausgeber: Institut für Wissenschaft und Kunst. Wien, Verlag für Jugend und Volk, 1962?₎

85 p. illus. (part col.) 23 cm.

Schmidt, Heiner.
Jugendbuch im Unterricht. Inhaltliche Erschliessung des Jugendschrifttums. Zugleich ein kritischer Gesamtüberblick 1950 bis 1965. Unter Mitarbeit von Willi Röwekamp. (2. neubearb. Aufl.) Duisburg, Eidens; Weinheim, Beltz (1966)

500 p. 21 cm.

First ed. published in 1960 under title: Schulpraktische Jugendlektüre.

Simon, Ilse.
Die neue Kinderliteratur in der Unterstufe. (Bearb. Neuaufl.) Berlin, Volk u. Wissen, 1965.

104 p. with illus. 22 cm.

Vaterland, Kinderland, gute Heimat für gross und klein. Empfehlgn. f. literar. Veranstaltgn. zum 20. Jahrestag der DDR. (Zusammengestellt von Marion Bierwagen und Ingeborg Rohnstock. Berlin, Kinderbuchverl., Berliner Stadtbibliothek, 1969)

58 p. illus. 20 cm.

Vom Leben der Kinder in anderen Ländern. (Bibliographie.) (Leipzig, Stadt- und Bezirksbibliothek, 1967.)

27 p. with illus. 21 cm.

Wegehaupt, Heinz.
Deutschsprachige Kinder- und Jugend-literatur der Arbeiterklasse von den Anfängen bis 1945; Bibliographie, zusammengestellt von Heinz Wegehaupt. ₍1. Aufl.₎ Berlin, Kinderbuchverlag ₍1972₎

103 p. 24 cm. (Resultate)

Wegweiser für Lehrer und Erzieher. (Bibliographie. Zusammengestellt von Bernhard Kerbs ₍u. a.₎) (Berlin, Kinderbuchverlag, 1968.)

28 p. with illus. 24 cm.

Zehn Jahre Deutscher Jugendbuchpreis, 1956–1965. (Bearbeitung des Katalogteils: Ingeborg Dettmar, Irmgard Rothweiler. München) Arbeitskreis für Jugendschrifttum (1966)

103 p. 21 cm.

CHILDREN'S LITERATURE, HEBREW

Iḥud ha-kevutsot veha-kibutsim. *ha-Maḥlakah le-ḥinukh.*
ספרי קריאה לבני הכיתות ב'-י"ב. ₍תל-אביב₎ איחוד הקבוצות והקיבוצים, המחלקה לחינוך, 1965.

24 p. 24 cm.

Israel. ha-Va'adah le-sifre keri'ah.
מדריך לספרי קריאה לילדים; קטלוג מנומק ומפתחות. ₍המערכת: הוה ויזל, משה חלפן וגירה פרדקין₎ תל-אביב, יהדיו, 731 ₍1970₎

176 p. illus. 24 cm.

At head of title: משרד החינוך והתרבות, המזכירות הפדגוגית לחינוך יסודי ולהבצרת מורים, הועדה לספרי קריאה.

Regev, Menachem.
ספרות ילדים, מהותה ובחינותיה; ביבליוגרפיה בלווית הערות ₍מאת₎ מנחם רגב. ירושלים, מרכז ההדרכה לספריות ציבוריות, 1967.

83 p. 25 cm.

Added t. p.: Juvenile literature—various aspects: an annotated bibliography.

World Zionist Organization. *Dept. of Education and Culture in the Diaspora.*
ביבליוגרפיה לגננות ורשימות ציוד. ירושלים, המחלקה לחינוך ולתרבות בגולה, 1966.

13 l. 28 cm.

CHILDREN'S LITERATURE, HUNGARIAN

Kepes, Ágnes.
Új beszélő könyvtár; az ifjúsági olvasmányok ajánló jegyzéke, összeallította Kepes Ágnes és Szász Eta. Budapest, Móra Ferenc Könyvkiadó, 1969.

726 p. illus. 21 cm.

CHILDREN'S LITERATURE, ITALIAN

Colonnetti, Laura.
Cari libri. Guida alla lettura di opere italiane e straniere per i ragazzi della scuola media. Pubblicazione della Fondazione Alberto Colonnetti a cura di Laura Colonnetti. Torino, Rattero, 1968.

xxxii, 451 p. 21 cm.

Martinez, Eugenia.
Leggere. Guida critico-bibliografica al libro per la gioventù. 2. edizione ampliata e aggiornata. Firenze, F. Le Monnier, 1969.

x, 361 p. 21½ cm.

Sacchetti, Lina.
Letture; guida alle letture degli alunni della scuola dell'obbligo. Firenze, Giunti Bemporad Marzocco ₍1968, c1967₎

2 v. 22 cm.

Includes bibliographies.

CONTENTS: v. 1. Narrativa, poesia e mito.—v. 2. Divulgazione storica e scientifica.

Il Segnalibro. Manuale del bibliotecario per ragazzi. Firenze, Centro didattico nazionale di studi e documentazione, 1970.

418 p. illus. 24 cm.

CHILDREN'S LITERATURE, JAPANESE

Manhattan Donnell Library Center.
Japanese children's books on exhibition in the Central Children's Room. ₁New York₁ New York Public Library ₁1972?₁

30 p. illus. 18 cm.

Catalog of an exhibition held at Donnell Library Center, New York Public Library, Oct. 18–Nov. 4, 1972.

CHILDREN'S LITERATURE, KIRGHIZ

Ishenov, Saĭnidin.
Киргизская детская литература. (1926–1966 гг.) Био-библиографический справочник. Фрунзе, "Мектеп," 1969.
184 p. with illus. 21 cm.
At head of title: Министерство культуры Киргизской ССР. Республиканская детская библиотека.
Added t. p.: Кыргыз балдар адабияты.
By S. Ishenov, I. P. Smolĭânskiĭ, and A. A. Timina.
Kirgiz and Russian.

CHILDREN'S LITERATURE, LATVIAN

Dambrāne, Emīra.
Grāmatas bērniem un jaunatnei, 1940–1965. ₁Sakārtojusi Emīra Dambrāne₁ Rīgā, Liesma, 1965.

300 p. 17 cm.

Dambrāne, Emīra.
Ko lasīt bērniem, 1.–4. klašu skolēniem. ₁Sastādījusi E. Dambrāne₁ Rīgā, Latvijas valsts izdevniecība, 1960.

127 p. 17 cm.

CHILDREN'S LITERATURE, LITHUANIAN

Jurevičiūtė, I
Vaikų literatūra; bibliografija, 1940–1964. Vilnius, Vaga, 1965.

308 p. 21 cm.

Stasiukaitienė, E
Pasakos. Vadovas po pasakas mergaitēms ir berniukams, visiems pasakų mēgējams. Vilnius, 1968.

113 p. with illus. 20 cm.

At head of title: Lietuvos TSR Valstybinė respublikinė biblioteka. Vaikų literatūros skyrius. E. Stasiukaitienė.

CHILDREN'S LITERATURE, MOLDAVIAN

Rekhtman, F
Скрипторий Молдовей повестинд копиилор. ₁Индиче аднотате пентру елевий класелор примаре₁. Кишинэу, ₁"Лумина"₁, 1968.

41 p. with illus. 17 cm.
At head of title: Министерул културий ал РСС Молдовенешть. Бибиотека републиканэ пентру копий "А. С. Пушкин."

CHILDREN'S LITERATURE, NORWEGIAN

Bøker for skolebiblioteker; 10-årskatalog, 1957–66, utvalget ved Kirke-undervisningsdepartementets rådgivende komité for skolebiblioteker. Utg. av Kirke- og undervisningsdepartementet. ₁Oslo₁ Statens bibliotekstilsyn, 1973.

260 p. 21 cm.

Gode barnebøker. 250 utvalgte nye og eldre barnebøker. Utsendt af Norsk kulturråd. ₁Oslo, 1969₁

48 p. illus. 20 cm.

Hagemann, Sonja.
Barnelitteratur i Norge. 1850–1914. Oslo, Aschehoug, 1970.

302 p. 23 cm.

CHILDREN'S LITERATURE, PERSIAN

Kānūn-i Parvarish-i Fikrī-i Kūdakān va Nawjavānān.
(Kitābnāmah)
كتابنامه ، فهرست كتابهای موجود در كتابخانه‌های كانون
پرورش فكری كودكان و نوجوانان. تهران ، انتشارات كانون
پرورش فكری كودكان و نوجوانان 1972– ‫1351.

v. 29 cm.

CHILDREN'S LITERATURE, POLISH

Skrobiszewska, Halina.
Uśmiech, przygoda, fantazja; poradnik bibliograficzny dla młodzieży od 11 do 15 lat. Warszawa, 1973.

127 p. illus. 12 x 18 cm.

At head of title: Biblioteka Narodowa. Instytut Bibliograficzny.

CHILDREN'S LITERATURE, RUSSIAN

Dom detskoĭ knigi.
Твои новые книги; библиографический указатель для школьников среднего и старшего возраста. ₁Составитель З. Д. Короза₁ Москва, Детская лит-ра, 1965.

111 p. illus. 21 cm.

Dzīâkanava, Zofīâ Uladzimiraŭna.
Дзіцячая література БССР. Рэк. паказальнік літературы. 1961–1965. ₁Прадмова М. Яфімава₁ Мінск, 1967.

96 p. 20 cm.

At head of title: Дзяржаўная бібліятэка БССР імя У. І. Леніна. Навукова-метадычны аддзел бібліятэказнаўства.

Khuze, Ol'ga Fedorovna.
Сто тысяч почему; рекомендательный библиографический указатель книг для школьников 4–6-х классов. ₁О книгах рассказала О. Ф. Хузе₁ Ленинград, Детская лит-ра; Ленинградское отд-ние, 1967.

53 p. illus. 22 cm.

At head of title: Ленинградский дом детской книги.

Leningradskiĭ dom detskoĭ knigi.
Твои новые книги; библиографический указатель для учащихся среднего и старшего возраста. ₁Составитель А. Я. Трабский₁ Ленинград, Детская лит-ра, 1964.

109 p. illus. 20 cm.

Nedashkovskaíà, Z   **P**

ĮChto chitat' detíàmĮ

Что читать детям. 5–8 кл. ĮБиблиогр. указательĮ. Москва, "Книга," 1970.

96 p. 20 cm.

Ol'shevskaíà, L   **A**

(O russkoĭ klassike dlíà deteĭ)

О русской классике для детей. (Метод.-библиогр. пособие для руководителей чтения, работающих с учащимися 7–8-х кл.) Москва, "Книга," 1971.

126 p. 20 cm.

At head of title: Государственная публичная библиотека им. М. Е. Салтыкова-Щедрина.   Л. А. Ольшевская.

Razorenova, Ada Valentinovna.

Твоя книжная полка. ĮМоскваĮ Молодая гвардия, 1966.

62 p. 14 cm. (Библиотечка "Вступающему в комсомол")

At head of title: А. Разоренова, И. Кернес.

Sinikina, S   **S**

Книжка про книжки. (Что читать первокласснику). Москва, "Книга," 1970.

15 p. with illus. 20 cm.

At head of title: Государственная ордена Ленина библиотека СССР им. В. И. Ленина.

Sinikina, S   **S**

Книжка про книжки. (Что читать учащимся 2–3-х кл.) Москва, "Книга," 1970.

30 p. with illus. 20 cm.

At head of title: Государственная ордена Ленина библиотека СССР им. В. И. Ленина.

Virolaĭnen, Laura Aleksandrovna.

Лучшие книги зарубежных писателей; рекомендательный аннотированный указатель литературы для учащихся 7–8 классов. ĮСоставитель Л. А. Виролайнен. Редактор Л. М. ФедюшинаĮ Ленинград, 1964.

102 p. 21 cm.

At head of title: Министерство культуры РСФСР. Государственная публичная библиотека им. М. Е. Салтыкова-Щедрина.

CHILDREN'S LITERATURE, SCANDINAVIAN

Skjønsberg, Kari.

Fortegnelse over litteratur i Norge, Sverige og Danmark om barns og unges fritidslesning. Oslo, Universitetsforlaget, 1967.

52 p. 23 cm. (Scandinavian university books)

CHILDREN'S LITERATURE, SLOVAK

Sliacky, Ondrej.

Bibliografia slovenskej literatúry pre deti a mládež 1918–1944. 1. vyd. Bratislava, Mladé letá, t. Východoslov. tlač., Košice, 1970.

272, Į2Į p. 20 cm. (Otázky detskej literatúry)

Sliacky, Ondrej.

Bibliografia slovenskej literatúry pre mládež, 1945–1964. ĮVyd. 1. BratislavaĮ Mladé letá Į1965Į

333 p. 21 cm. (Otázky detskej literatúry)

Slovník slovenských spisovateľov pre deti a mládež. Zost. Ondrej Sliacky. 1. vyd. Bratislava, Mladé letá, t. Východo-

doslov. tlač., Košice, 1970.

428, Į2Į p. 21 cm. (Otázky detskej literatúry)

CHILDREN'S LITERATURE, SPANISH

Libros para los quince años. Barcelona, Editorial Nova Terra, 1969.

96 p. 23 cm.

On cover: Escuela activa de padres.
"Selección de lecturas ... elaborada en las escuelas 'Talitha' y Costa i Llobera.' Han colaborado José Hilario Gómez del Cerro" Įet al.Į

Spain. *Comisión de Información y Publicaciones Infantiles y Juveniles.*

Selección de revistas y libros infantiles y juveniles. Madrid ĮMinisterio de Información y Turismo, Dirección General de PrensaĮ 1965.

70 p. 21 cm.

CHILDREN'S LITERATURE, SWEDISH

Auraldsson, Kerstin, 1931–

Småbarnsböcker : ett urval bilderböcker, ramsor, sagor och berättelser / av Kerstin Auraldsson. — 2. omarb. uppl. — Lund : Bibliotekstjänst, 1974.

76 p. : ill. ; 19 cm. — (Btj-serien ; 58)

Genell Storm, Elisabeth.

Vad kommer sen? Vill du läsa mera om Pippi Långstrump, Bill och många andra. ĮSammanställd av Elisabeth Genell Storm och Charlotte BrattströmĮ Lund. Bibliotekstjänst; ĮSolna, SeeligĮ 1968.

48 p. illus. 21 cm. (Btj-serien, 12)

Klingberg, Göte.

Kronologisk bibliografi över barn- och ungdomslitteratur utgiven i Sverige 1591–1839. Stockholm, Föreningen för svensk undervisningshistoria, 1967.

242, (1) p. illus. 24 cm. (Årsböcker i svensk undervisningshistoria, v. 118)

Summary in English.

Loman, Anna, 1923–

Vad kommer sen? Barnbokserier aktuella 1971. 2. omarb. uppl. Lund. Bibliotekstjänst; (Solna : Seelig) 1971.

51 p. illus. 21 cm. (Btj-serien, 38)

Näslund, Maja Lisa.

Lågstadiets klassbibliotek; litteraturförteckning. ĮLund, 1965Į

79 p. 22 cm. (Bibliotekstjänsts bokurval, 50)

Nilsson, Kerstin, 1940–

Från hästar till frimärken. 500 bra faktaböcker för barn. Urval. Lund, Bibliotekstjänst; ĮSolna, SeeligĮ 1970.

72 p. illus. 21 cm. (Btj-serien, 26)

Sveriges allmänna biblioteksförening. Specialgruppen för barn- och tonårsverksamhet.

6 Įi. e. SexĮ års bästa barnböcker 1965–1970. Ett kvalitetsurval sammanställt av SAB:s specialgrupp för barn- och tonårsverksamhet. Lund, Bibliotekstjänst; ĮSolna, SeeligĮ 1971.

72 p. 19 cm. (Btj-serien, 39)

"Denna bibliografi anknyter till 20 års bästa barnböcker 1944-1964 ¡av A. Lidén¡"

Taranger, Anton, 1917–
1.500 ¡i. e. Femton hundra¡ titlar för skolans boksamlingar. En kommenterad grundförteckning för mellan- och högstadiet. Lund, Bibliotekstjänst, 1970.

270 p. 21 cm. (Btj-serien, 27)

CHILDREN'S LITERATURE, URDU

Ibne Insha.
Literature for children in Urdu. ¡Karachi¡ National Book Centre of Pakistan ¡1967¡

39 p. 22 cm. Rs 2

CHILDREN'S PERIODICALS

Dobler, Lavinia G
The Dobler world directory of youth periodicals, by Lavinia G. Dobler. New York, Schulte Pub. Co., 1966.

xi, 37 p. 23 cm.

"Successor to The Dobler international list of periodicals for boys and girls."

Dobler, Lavinia G
The Dobler world directory of youth periodicals. Compiled and edited by Lavinia Dobler ¡and¡ Muriel Fuller. 3d enl. ed. New York, Citation Press, 1970.

108 p. 23 cm.

"Successor to The Dobler international list of periodicals for boys and girls."

Madison, *Wis. Board of Education. Dept. of Curriculum Development.*
Magazines for elementary grades. Madison, 1965.

27 l. 29 cm.

Spain. *Comisión de Información y Publicaciones Infantiles y Juveniles.*
Prensa infantil y juvenil: pasado y presente. ¡Textos y documentación: Jesús María Vázquez et al. Legislación: Manuel Camacho y de Ciria¡ Madrid, 1967.

122 p. 21 cm.

CHILDREN'S PLAYS

Brix, Vibeke.
Børnedramatik 1955-1970. En bibliografi. København, Bibliotekscentralen, 1972.

45 l. 30 cm.

Kreider, Barbara.
Index to children's plays in collections. Metuchen, N.J., Scarecrow Press, 1972.

138 p. 22 cm.

Vill du spela teater? En kommenterad katalog över barnpjäser uppställd i intresseområden. Lund, Bibliotekstjänst; ¡Solna, Seelig¡, 1969.

128 p. illus. 21 cm. (Btj-serien, 21)

CHILDREN'S POETRY

Brewton, John Edmund, 1898-
Index to poetry for children and young people, 1964-1969; a title, subject, author, and first line index to poetry in collections for children and young people. Compiled by John E. and Sara W. Brewton, and G. Meredith Blackburn III. New York, Wilson, 1972.

xxx, 575 p. 26 cm.

"A supplement to Index to children's poetry."

Morris, Helen (Soutar) 1909–
Where's that poem? An index of poems for children, arranged by subject, with a bibliography of books of poetry and an introduction on the teaching of poetry, by Helen Morris. Oxford, Blackwell, 1967.

xxxv, 300 p. 19½ cm.

Shaw, John MacKay.
Childhood in poetry; a catalogue, with biographical and critical annotations, of the books of English and American poets comprising the Shaw Childhood in Poetry Collection in the Library of the Florida State University. With lists of the poems that relate to childhood, notes, and index. Detroit, Gale Research Co. ¡1967–68, c1967¡

5 v. 29 cm.

Vol. 5.: Indexes.

————— Supplement. Detroit, Gale Research Co. ¡1972¡

3 v. 29 cm.

Subero, Efraín, 1931–
Bibliografía de la poesía infantil venezolana. Caracas, Banco del Libro, 1966.

118 p. 22 cm.

Thompson, Denys, 1907–
Poetry for children / selected by Denys Thompson. — London : National Book League, 1973.

8 p. ; 21 cm. — (Publication - National Book League with the Poetry Society ; no. 73:3:1)

CHILDREN'S REFERENCE BOOKS

Dierks, Margarete (Nax)
Vom Bilderbuch zum Arbeitsbuch. Eine Studie von Margarete Dierks im Auftrag des Instituts für Jugendbuchforschung in Frankfurt. Reutlingen, Ensslin u. Laiblin (1965).

71 p. with illus. 21 cm.

Landman, Juanita Mathie.
Bibliography for elementary school teachers, levels K-9, by Juanita M. Landman. ¡Darien, Conn., Teachers Pub. Corp., 1968¡

80 p. 23 cm.

Library Association of Australia. *Children's Libraries Section. Victorian Division.*
Children's encyclopaedias; a second survey of encyclopaedias used by children in Australia. ¡Melbourne¡ 1966.

27 p. 34 cm.

Lock, Clara Beatrice Muriel, 1914–
    Reference material for young people. ₍Hamden, Conn.₎ Archon Books ₍1967₎

    189 p. 23 cm. (The Readers guide series)

Lock, Clara Beatrice Muriel, 1914–
    Reference material for young people, by Muriel Lock. London, Bingley, 1967.

    189 p. 22½ cm. (The Readers guide series)

Lock, Clara Beatrice Muriel, 1914–
    Reference material for young people ₍by₎ Muriel Lock. Sydney, Bennett ₍1967₎

    189 p. 23 cm. (The Readers guide series)

Lock, Clara Beatrice Muriel, 1914-
    Reference material for young people. Rev. and enl. ed. by Muriel Lock, with the assistance of Shelagh Francis & Maureen White. ₍Hamden, Conn.₎ Linnet Books ₍1971₎

    532 p. 23 cm.

Lock, Clara Beatrice Muriel, 1914-
    Reference material for young people, rev. and enl. ed. by Muriel Lock; with the assistance of Shelagh Francis and Maureen White. London, Bingley, 1971.

    532 p. 23 cm. £4.75

Peterson, Carolyn Sue, 1938-
    Reference books for elementary and junior high school libraries. Metuchen, N.J., Scarecrow Press, 1970.

    191 p. 22 cm.

Stanley, Caroline, 1911–
    Reference tools 1968-1969: a bibliography based on the acquisitions of the Educational Materials Center from January 1968 through July 1969. ₍Washington₎ U. S. Office of Education; ₍for sale by the Supt. of Docs., U. S. Govt. Print. Off., 1969₎

    iii, 5 p. 27 cm.

CHILE; CHILEAN LITERATURE

Aránguiz Donoso, Horacio.
    Bibliografía histórica (1959–1967) ₍por₎ Horacio Aránguiz Donoso ₍et al.₎ Santiago de Chile, Universidad Católica de Chile, Instituto de Historia, 1970.

    84 p. 27 cm.

Briseño, Ramón, b. 1814.
    Estadística bibliográfica de la literatura chilena, 1812–1876. Estudio preliminar de Guillermo Feliú Cruz. Edición facsimilar de la principe de 1862, realizada por la Biblioteca Nacional bajo los auspicios de la Comisión Nacional de Conmemoración del Centenario de la muerte de Andrés Bello. Santiago de Chile ₍Biblioteca Nacional₎ 1965–66.

    3 v. ports. (1 col.) 28 cm.

    CONTENTS.— t. 1. 1812–1859. Impresos chilenos. Obras sobre Chile. Escritores chilenos.— t. 2. 1860–1876. Prensa chilena por órden alfabético. Prensa chilena por órden cronolójico. Prensa periodística chilena. Bibliografía chilena en el país, desde 1812 hasta 1859 inclusive. Bibliografía chilena en el extranjero, desde 1860 hasta 1876 inclusive. Curiosidades bibliográfico-chilenas.— t. 3. 1810–1876. Adiciones y ampliaciones, por R. Silva Castro. Introd. de G. Feliú Cruz.

Feliú Cruz, Guillermo, 1901–
    Notas para una bibliografía sobre viajeros relativos a Chile. Santiago de Chile, Editorial Universitaria, 1965.

    281 p. port. 27 cm.

Medina, José Toribio, 1852–1930.
    Biblioteca hispano-chilena, 1523–1817. Amsterdam, N. Israel, 1965.

    3 v. facsims., ports. 23 cm. (Reprint series of José Toribio Medina's bibliographical works, 17)

    Original ed. published in Santiago de Chile, 1897–1899.

    CONTENTS.— t. 1. Siglo XVI–XVII.— t. 2. Sin fecha determinada, siglo XVII. Siglo XVIII (1701–1768).—t. 3. 1769–1800. Sin fecha determinada, siglo XVIII. Siglo XIX. Sin fecha determinada, siglo XIX.

Moraga Neira, René.
    Bibliografía económica de Chile; guía de publicaciones periódicas, libros, folletos e informes técnicos publicados por instituciones chilenas de carácter económico entre los años 1960 y 1968 ₍par₎ René Moraga Neira ₍y₎ Paulina Sanhueza Vargas. Santiago de Chile, Banco Central de Chile, Biblioteca, 1969.

    v, 196 p. 27 cm.

Santiago de Chile. Biblioteca Nacional.
    Bibliografía de las memorias de grado sobre literatura chilena, 1918–1967. Santiago de Chile, 1969.

    39 p. 25 cm.

CHIMPANZEES

Rohles, Frederick H
    The chimpanzee; a topical bibliography, edited by Frederick H. Rohles, Jr. 2d ed. ₍Manhattan? Kan., 1972?₎

    viii, 468 p. 28 cm.

    Prepared in cooperation with the Primate Information Center, Regional Primate Research Center, University of Washington, Seattle.

CHINA
    see also under Dissertations, Academic

Berton, Peter Alexander Menquez, 1922-
    Contemporary China; a research guide, by Peter Berton and Eugene Wu. Edited by Howard Koch, Jr. Prepared for the Joint Committee on Contemporary China of the American Council of Learned Societies and the Social Science Research Council. Stanford, Calif., Hoover Institution on War, Revolution, and Peace, 1967.

    xxix, 695 p. 26 cm. (Hoover Institution bibliographical series, 31)

Catalog of current research publications on modern China.

    ₍Taipei₎ Modern China Historical Materials Center, Institute of International Relations, Republic of China.

    v. 27 cm. bimonthly.

    Began in 1966. Cf. New serial titles.
    Absorbed by Issues and studies, July 1969.

Chang, Chun-shu, 1934-
    Premodern China; a bibliographical introduction. ₍Ann Arbor, Center for Chinese Studies, University of Michigan₎ 1971.

    iii, 183 p. 23 cm. (Michigan papers in Chinese studies, no. 11)

Chen, C   M
An index to Chinese archaeological works published in the Peoples Republic of China, 1949–1965, by C. M. Chen [and] Richard B. Stamps. East Lansing, Asian Studies Center, Michigan State University, 1972.

ix, 75 p. map. 28 cm. (East Asia series, no. 3)

Chesneaux, Jean.
Introduction aux études d'histoire contemporaine de Chine, 1898–1949; [guide de recherches. Par] Jean Chesneaux [et] John Lust. Paris, Mouton, 1964 [i. e. 1965]

148 p. 27 cm. (Matériaux pour l'étude de l'Extrême-Orient moderne et contemporain. Travaux, 2)

Running title: Introduction à l'histoire contemporaine de Chine.

Chiu, Rosaline Kwan-wai.
Language contact and language planning in China (1900–1967); a selected bibliography, and a pref. by William F. Mackey. Quebec, Published for the International Center for Research on Bilingualism [by] Les Presses de l'Université Laval, 1970.

xviii, 273 p. 25 cm.

Authors and titles in characters and in romanization.

Chu, Mu-chieh, 1516 or 7–1586.
授經圖 [20 卷] 朱睦㮮撰 [台北] 廣文書局 [1968]

10, 4, 280 p. 20 cm. (書目續編 35)

據道光 19 (1839) 年李氏惜陰軒叢書本重印
易書詩春秋禮各 4 卷

(Chūgoku bunka kankei bunken mokuroku)
アジア・アフリカ総合研究組織
中国文化関係文献目録
東京 アジア経済研究所 1968
80p 26 cm （アジア・アフリカ文献解題 2）

Ajia Keizai Kenkyūjo shuppanbutsu, tsūkan dai 750-gō.

中国関係日本文雑誌論説記事目録 [東京 近代中国研究センター編集発行] 1964–

v. 26 cm.

CONTENTS.—1. 外事警察報北京週報・燕塵—2. 支那時報東亞情報調査月報・特調班月報

Chung-hua min kuo kuo chi kuan hsi yen chiu so, T'ai-pei.
(Chung-hua min kuo kuo chi kuan hsi yen chiu so yen chiu lun wên so yin)
中華民國國際關係研究所研究論文索引 （自民國五十年十月起至五十五年六月止） Index of research papers prepared and published by Institute of International Relations, Republic of China (October 1961–June 1966). 臺北 中華民國國際關係研究所編印 [1966?]
78, 44 p. 20 x 27 cm.

Chung-hua wen hua fu hsing yün tung t'ui hsing wei yüan hui.
(Chung-hua wen hua tsung lun shu mu)
中華文化總論書目 中華文化總論論文目錄索引
臺北 中華文化復興運動推行委員會編輯出版

[民國 62 i. e. 1973]

14. 70 p. 26 cm.

Chung yang t'u shu kuan, T'ai-pei.
A bibliography of books on China in western languages in the collection of NCL. 國立中央圖書館館藏西文漢學書目 臺北 中華叢書編審委員會 臺灣書局總經銷 民國 59 [1970]

4. 211 p. 21 cm. (Its 國立中央圖書館目錄叢刊第 2 輯) (中華叢書)

Chung yang t'u shu kuan, T'ai-pei.
(Chung-kuo chin êrh shih nien wên shih chê lun wên)
中國近二十年文史哲論文 分類索引 [臺北]
國立中央圖書館編輯出版 [民國 59 i. e. 1970]

xi [i. e. xxxx], 852 p. 27 cm.

Cordier, Henri, 1849–1925–
Bibliotheca Sinica. Dictionnaire bibliographique des ouvrages relatifs à l'Empire chinois. 2. éd. rev., corr., et considérablement augm. New York, B. Franklin [1968]
6 v. in 5. illus., facsims. 27 cm. (Burt Franklin bibliography & reference series, 250)
Reprint ed. Vols. 1–5 originally published in Paris, 1904–1924; v. 6 compiled by East Asiatic Library, Columbia University and originally published in New York, 1953.
CONTENTS: v. 1–4. La Chine proprement dite. Les étrangers en Chine. Relations des étrangers avec les Chinois. Les Chinois chez les peuples étrangers. Les pays tributaires de la Chine. Additions et corrections.—v. 5. Supplément et index (fascicule Ier; no more published)—v. 6. Author index (second supplement volume)

Gálik, Marián.
Preliminary research-guide: German impact on modern Chinese intellectual history. Hrsg. von Wolfgang Bauer. München, Seminar für Ostasiatische Kultur- und Sprachwissenschaft, 1971.

120 l. 30 cm.

Preface in English, German, and Chinese.

Gardner, Charles Sidney, 1900–   comp.
A union list of selected western books on China in American libraries. Compiled by Charles S. Gardner. 2d ed. rev. and enl. New York, B. Franklin [1970]

xi, 111 p. 23 cm. (Selected essays in history, economics & social science, 143)

Burt Franklin bibliography & reference series, 345.
On spine: Western books on China.

Hall, William P   J
A bibliographical guide to Japanese research on the Chinese economy (1958–1970), by W. P. J. Hall. Cambridge, Mass., East Asian Research Center, Harvard University; distributed by Harvard University Press, 1972.

xiii, 100 p. 28 cm. (Harvard East Asian monographs, 46)

Harris, Richard, 1914–
Modern China. 2nd ed. London, National Book League in association with the Book Development Council, 1965.

20 p. 21½ cm. (National Book League. Reader's guide)

Hartwell, Robert.
A guide to sources of Chinese economic history, A. D. 618–1368. [Chicago] Committee on Far Eastern Civilizations, University of Chicago [°1964]

xv, 257 p. 23 cm.

Herman, Theodore, 1913–
The geography of China: a selected and annotated bibliography. New York, State Education Dept., 1967.

44 p. 28 cm. (Foreign Area Materials Center, University of the State of New York. Occasional publication no. 7)

Herzer, Christine.
Die Volksrepublik China; eine annotierte Zeitschriftenbibliographie 1960–1970. Wiesbaden, O. Harrassowitz [c1971]

346 p. 25 cm. (Schriften des Instituts für Asienkunde in Hamburg, Bd. 31)

Hoffmann, Rainer.
Bücherkunde zur chinesischen Geschichte, Kultur und Gesellschaft. München, Weltforum Verlag [c1973]

ix, 518 p. 22 cm. (Arnold-Bergstraesser-Institut. Materialien zu Entwicklung und Politik, 2)

Kindai Chūgoku Kenkyū Iinkai.
(Chūgoku kankei tosho mokuroku)
中国関係図書目録　和文・1957–1970. [東京]
東洋文庫近代中国研究委員会　1971.

189 p. 26 cm. N.T.

Kobylinski, Hanna, 1907–
Litteratur om Østasien: Kina og Japan. Annoteret bibliografi. København, Mellemfolkeligt Samvirke, 1972.

135 p. 22 cm. (MS bibliografier, 2:1)

Danish, Norwegian, or Swedish.

Kokusai Bunka Kaikan, Tokyo. Toshokan.
China. Tokyo, International House of Japan Library, 1972.

115 p. 21 cm. (Its Acquisition list no. 2)

Liu, Chun-jo, 1922–
Controversies in modern Chinese intellectual history; an analytic bibliography of periodical articles, mainly of the May fourth and post-May fourth era. Cambridge, Published by the East Asian Research Center, Harvard University; distributed by Harvard University Press, 1964.

vii, 207 p. 28 cm.

London, Ont. Public Library and Art Museum.
China. Rev. ed. London, Ont., London Public Library and Art Museum, 1966.

[3] p. illus. 22 cm.

Lust, John.
Index Sinicus: a catalogue of articles relating to China in periodicals and other collective publications, 1920–1955, compiled by John Lust with the assistance of Werner Eichhorn. Cambridge, Eng., W. Heffer [1964]

xxx, 663 p. 26 cm.

Supplementing H. Cordier's Bibliotheca Sinica & T. L. Yuan's China in Western literature.

Lyons. Bibliothèque de la ville.
La Chine découverte par les Européens; début XVIIe–début XIXe siècle, exposition, 13 juin–30 juillet 1972. Bibliothèque de la ville de Lyon. Lyon, Bibliothèque de la ville de Lyon, 1972.

1 v. (unpaged) ill. 26 cm.

Niijima, Atsuyoshi, 1928–　ed.
現代中国入門―何を読むべきか―新島淳良・野村浩一編　東京　勁草書房　昭和40 [1965]

281. 12 p. illus. 17 cm. (中国新書　11)

Oslo. Norske Nobelinstitutt. *Biblioteket.*
Folkerepublikken China etter 1957. Litteratur i Nobelinstituttets bibliotek. Utarb. av Ågot Brekke. Oslo, 1968.

20 l. 29 cm.

Oslo. Norske Nobelinstitutt. Biblioteket.
Folkerepublikken China etter 1957. Litteratur i Nobelinstituttets bibliotek. 2. utg. Ajourført til juli 1971 av Elsa Skarprud. Oslo, 1971.

24 l. 30 cm.

Per lo studio della rivoluzione cinese. [Roma, 1971]

576 p. illus., ports. 21 cm. (Ideologie, v. 4, n. 13–14)

"Fascicolo speciale dedicato alla rivoluzione cinese."

CONTENTS: Contributo a una bibliografia italiana sulla rivoluzione cinese (1945–1970).—Testi di revisionisti sovietici.—Saggi su alcuni aspetti della rivoluzione cinese.

Quah, Rosalind.
Library resources in Singapore on contemporary mainland China. [Singapore] Institute of Southeast Asian Studies [1971]

11 l. 28 cm. (Institute of Southeast Asian Studies. Library bulletin, no. 1)

Saran, Vimla, 1930–
Documentation on China, 1963–1965. Edited by Vimla Saran. New Delhi, Published under the auspices of School of International Studies, Jawahar Lal Nehru University, 1971.

iv, 346 p. 26 cm.

Saskatchewan. Provincial Library, Regina. Bibliographic Services Division.
Books on China. Regina, Provincial Library, 1973.

33 p. 22 cm.

Siemers, Günter.
China vom Opiumkrieg bis zur Gegenwart : eine einführende Bibliographie = China from the Opium War to the present : an introductory bibliography / Günter Siemers. — Hamburg : Institut für Asienkunde, Dokumentations-Leitstelle Asien, 1974.

ix, 264 p. ; 30 cm. — (Dokumentationsdienst Asien ; Reihe A, 4)

Foreword in English and German.

Soong, James Chu-yul.
Chinese materials on microfilm available from the Library of Congress. Washington, Center for Chinese Research Materials, Association of Research Libraries, 1971.

xiii, 82 p. 27 cm. (Association of Research Libraries, Center for Chinese Research Materials. Bibliographical series, no. 11)

Originally presented as the author's thesis (M. S. in L. S.), Catholic University of America.

Spriggle, Howard.
China: old and new. [1st ed. Darby? Pa.] H. Spriggle Publishers, 1970.

94 l. illus. 29 cm.

Tsien, Tche-hao.
La République populaire de Chine, revue des revues. Rédacteurs: M. Tsien Tche-hao ... M⁽ᵐᵉ⁾ J. Tsien ... Strasbourg, Centre de recherches sur l'U. R. S. S. et les pays de l'Est, 1966.

55 p. 25 cm.

U. S. *Bureau of the Census.*
The population and manpower of China: an annotated bibliography, by Foreign Manpower Research Office, Bureau of the Census. New York, Greenwood Press ₍1968₎

ix, 132 p. 29 cm.

Reprint of the 1958 ed.

U. S. Dept. of the Army.
Communist China: a bibliographic survey. Washington; ₍For sale by the Supt. of Docs., U. S. Govt. Print. Off.₎ 1971.

x, 253 p. illus., col. maps (2 fold. in pocket) 26 cm.

U. S. *Dept. of the Army.*
Communist China: a strategic survey; a bibliography. ₍Washington, For sale by the Superintendent of Documents, U. S. Govt. Print. Off.₎ 1966.

viii, 143 p. illus., col. maps. 26 cm.

U. S. *Dept. of the Army.*
Communist China: ruthless enemy or paper tiger? New York, Greenwood Press ₍1969₎

vi, 137 p. illus., fold. maps. 26 cm.

Reprint of the 1962 ed.

ARMED FORCES

Rhoads, Edward J   M
The Chinese Red Army, 1927–1963; an annotated bibliography, by Edward J. M. Rhoads, in collaboration with Edward Friedman, Ellis Joffe ₍and₎ Ralph L. Powell. Cambridge, East Asian Research Center, Harvard University; distributed by Harvard University Press, 1964.
xiv, 188 p. 26 cm. (Harvard East Asian monographs, 16)
"Study ... carried under a contract with the Department of Defense."

BIBLIOGRAPHIES

Ch'iao, Yen-kuan.
₍Shu mu ssu pien hsü lu₎
書目四編叙錄　喬衍琯撰　₍臺北₎　廣文書局
₍民國 59 i. e. 1970₎

1 v. (various pagings) 25 cm.

Chung yang t'u shu kuan, T'ai-pei.
(Shu mu chü yao)
書目舉要　₍國立中央圖書館選輯　臺北₎　中華叢書編審委員會　₍臺灣書店總經銷　民國 53 i. e. 1964₎

72 p. 19 cm. (中華叢書)

Feng, Ping-wen.
₍Ch'üan kuo t'u shu kuan shu mu hui pien₎
全國圖書館書目匯編　馮秉文編　北京　中華書局 1958. ₍Washington, D. C., Center for Chinese Research Materials, Association of Research Libraries, 1971₎

144 p. 22 cm.

Added cover title: A bibliography of bibliographies compiled by Chinese libraries (Ch'üan-kuo t'u-shu kuan shu-mu hui-pien).

Original ed. issued in series:

Yao, Ming-ta, 1905–1942.
中國目錄學年表　姚名達著　₍臺北₎　臺灣商務印書館 ₍1967₎

2, 2, 17, 175, 17 p. 18 cm. (人人文庫 337–338)

BIOGRAPHY

Ch'ang, Pi-tê.
(T'ai-wan kung ts'ang tsu p'u chieh t'i) 台灣公藏族譜解題　昌彼得編纂　₍台北₎　國立中央圖書館 民國 58 ₍1969₎

4, 12, 106 p. 19 cm.

Chung yang t'u shu kuan, *T'ai-pei.*
明人傳記資料索引　國立中央圖書館編　₍臺北₎ 民國 54–55 ₍1965–66₎

2 v. in 1. 26 cm.

Wang, Pao-hsien.
歷代名人年譜總目　王寶先編纂　₍臺中₎　東海大學圖書館　民國 54 ₍1965₎

46, 353 p. 21 cm. (圖書館學小叢書 Library science series)

Added title on verso of t. p.: An Index to chronological biographies of eminent Chinese.

On cover: 香港　龍門書店發行

Yamane, Yukio, 1921–
日本現存明代地方志傳記索引稿　山根幸夫主編 小川尚・松山康子協編　₍東京₎　東洋文庫明代史研究室 1964.

12, 718 p. 25 x 36 cm.

FOREIGN RELATIONS

Hanabusa, Nagamichi, 1902–
英　　修　道
中国関係条約取極目録　英修道編
東京　電応通信　昭和44 (1969)
422p 22cm

Johnston, Douglas M
Agreements of the People's Republic of China, 1949–1967: a calendar, by Douglas M. Johnston and Hungdah Chiu. Cambridge, Harvard University Press, 1968.

xvii, 286 p. 25 cm. (Harvard studies in East Asian law, 3)

Saran, Vimla, 1930–
Sino-Soviet schism: a bibliography, 1956–1964. London, Asia Publishing House, 1971.

xvii, 162 p. 25 cm.

"Issued under the auspices of the School of International Studies, Jawaharal Nehru University."

Saran, Vimla, 1930–
Sino-Soviet schism, a bibliography, 1956–1964. New York, Asia Pub. House ₍1971₎

xv, 162 p. 25 cm.

"Issued under the auspices of the School of International Studies, Jawaharlal Nehru University."

GOVERNMENT PUBLICATIONS

Lei, Chin.

(Chung-hua min kuo cheng fu kung pao fen lei hui pien tsung mu)

中華民國政府公報分類彙編總目 Government gazettes of the Republic of China, 1912–1914: A grand table of contents. 〔雷瑨輯〕 Washington, D.C., Center for Chinese Research Materials, Association of Research Libraries, 〔1971?〕

vii, 173 p. 27 cm. (Association of Research Libraries. Center for Chinese Research Materials. Bibliographical series no. 9)

Text in Chinese, with prefatory matter in English.

HISTORY

Chang, Li-chih, 1900–
〔Cheng shih kai lun〕

正史概論 著作者張立志 〔臺1版 臺北，商務印書館 〔民國 53 i. e. 1964〕

14, 146 p. 19 cm. (國學小叢書)

Chung yang yen chiu yüan. Chin tai shih yen chiu so, Nan-kang, Formosa.

(Chung-kuo hsien tai shih tzŭ liao tiao ch'a mu lu)

中國現代史資料調查目錄 中央研究院近代史研究所編 〔郭廷以 李毓澍主編 張玉法等編輯 臺北〕 民國 57–58 〔1968–69〕

11 v. (double leaves) 26 cm.

CONTENTS: 1. 報紙・雜誌・公報 1902–1949.—2. 一般資料部份 1894–1923.—3. 一般資料部份 1924–1936.—4. 一般資料部份 1937–1945.—5. 一般資料部份 (1937–1945) (1946–1949)

—6. 總理係中山—7. 總裁將中正 革命人物（上）—8. 革命人物（續） 抗戰及剿共忠烈錄—9–10. 外交檔案部份 1901–1926.—11. 附錄 （檢查表）

Franke, Wolfgang, 1912–
An introduction to the sources of Ming history. Kuala Lumpur, University of Malaya Press 〔distributed by Oxford University Press, London〕 1968.

xxv, 347 p. 26 cm.

"Enlarged and completely revised edition of ... 〔the author's〕 Preliminary notes on the important Chinese literary sources for the history of the Ming dynasty, 1368–1644 〔published in 1948〕"

Hervouet, Yves.
Bibliographie des travaux en langues occidentales sur les Song parus de 1946 à 1965. En appendice: Bibliographie des travaux en langue russe, par Ludmila Kuvshinnikova. Bordeaux, SO–BO–DI, 1969.

xxi, 139, 28 p. 19 cm. (Collection sinologique de l'Université de Bordeaux, v. 1)

Hsieh, Kuo-chên, 1901–

晚明史籍考 〔20卷〕 謝國楨輯 〔臺北〕 藝文印書館 〔1068〕

3 v. (1198 p.) 22 cm.

Originally published in 1933 by the 國立北平圖書館

Kao, Ssŭ-sun, *chin shih* 1184.

史略 〔6卷〕 子略 〔4卷 目錄〕 高似孫撰 台北 廣文書局 民國57 〔1968〕

10, 3, 258, 2, 166 p. 19 cm. （書目續編39–40） 210.00

Colophon title.

史略據古逸叢書 1884 年景刊本影印 子略據四明叢書 1932 年刊本影印

坿楊守敬經籍訪古志跋：p. 255–258.

K'uang, Li-an.

〔Wei Chin Nan-pei-ch'ao shih yen chiu lun wen shu mu yin te〕

魏晉南北朝史研究論文書目引得 鄺利安編著 〔臺北〕 臺灣中華書局 〔民國 60 i. e. 1971〕

6, 8, 246 p. 21 cm.

"An introduction to theses on the study of the dynasty of Wei and Chin and that of the dynasty of South and North China": p. 3–6 (1st group)

Liao, Chi-lang, 1938–

(Liang Chin shih pu i chi k'ao) 兩晉史部遺籍考 廖吉郎著 〔臺北 嘉新水泥公司文化基金會 民國 59 i. e. 1970〕

4, 5, 3, 236 p. 21 cm. （嘉新水泥公司文化基金會研究論文第 213 種） （嘉新水泥公司文化基金會叢書）

Sung, Hsi.

宋史研究論文與書籍目錄 史學研究目錄第一種 宋晞編 A classified list of Chinese articles and books on the Sung history, by Shee Sung. 〔陽明山〕 中華學術院 中國文化學院 史學研究所 民國 55 〔1966〕

III, 82, II, 13 p. 27 cm.

Wang, Chi, 1930–
Chinese history: selected works in English; a preliminary bibliography. Washington, Dept. of History, Georgetown University, 1970 〔i. e. 1971〕

105 p. 26 cm.

Yamane, Yukio, 1921–

(Gendai shi kenkyu bunken mokuroku)

元代史研究文献目録 山根幸夫 大嶋立子編 浦和 山根幸夫 東京 汲古書院（発売） 1971.

213 p. 25 cm.

On p. 〔4〕 of cover: A classified bibliography of articles and books concerning the Yüan period in Japanese and Chinese.

Yamane, Yukio, 1921–

(Shingai kakumei bunken mokuroku)

辛亥革命文献目録 山根幸夫編 東京 東京女子大学東洋史研究室 汲古書院（発売） 1972.

96 p. 25 cm.

Yu, Ping-kuen.

(Chung-kuo shih hsüeh lun wen yin te)

中國史學論文引得 Chinese history: Index to learned articles. 余秉權編 〔香港〕 香港亞東學社 Hong Kong East Asia Institute, 1963–70.

2 v. 27 cm.

Vol. 2 has series statement: Harvard-Yenching Library bibliographical series 1.
Text in Chinese, with prefatory matter also in English.

CONTENTS: v. ₁1₁ 1902–1962 (據香港大學馮平山圖書館所藏期刊及縮影膠片)—v. 2. 1905–1964 (歐美所見中文期刊文史哲論文綜錄)

HISTORY, LOCAL

Ch'en, K'uei.
(Chi jui lou shu mu)
稽瑞樓書目 ₁4卷₁ 陳揆撰 ₁台北₁ 廣文書局 ₁民國61 i.e. 1972₁
10, 2, 236 p. 20 cm. (書目五編)
Reprint of the 1877 ed., issued in series: 滂喜齋叢書

Kokuritsu Kokkai Toshokan, *Tokyo.* *Sankō Shoshibu.* *Ajia Afurikaka.*
国立国会図書館. 参考書誌部アジア・
アフリカ課
日本主要図書館・研究所所蔵
中国地方志総合目録
東京 国立国会図書館参考書誌部 昭和44(1969)
350p 26cm

In Chinese and Japanese; title also in English: Union catalogue of Chinese local gazetteers in 14 major libraries and research institutes in Japan.

Leslie, Donald, 1922–
Catalogues of Chinese local gazetteers ₁by₁ Donald Leslie and Jeremy Davidson. Canberra, Dept. of Far Eastern History, Research School of Pacific Studies, Australian National University ₁1967₁
xxxix, 125 p. maps. 25 cm. (Guide to bibliographies on China and the Far East)

Lowe, Joseph Dzen-Hsi, *comp.*
A catalog of the official gazetteers of China in the University of Washington, compiled by Joseph Dzen-Hsi Lowe. Zug, Inter Documentation Co. AG ₁°1966₁
vii, 72 p. 21 cm. (Bibliotheca Asiatica, no. 1)
Catalog of collection in the University of Washington Library.

Pittsburgh. **University.** *East Asian Library.*
The Chinese local history, a descriptive holding list. Compiled by Thomas C. T. Kuo, assisted by John Chiang & Francis Chow. ₁Pittsburgh₁ 1969.
87 l. 28 cm.

Tōyōgaku Bunken Sentā Renraku Kyōgikai.
中国地方誌連合目録 東洋学文献センター連絡協議会編 東京 東洋文庫 1964 ₁i. e. 昭和40 (1965)₁
267 p. 26 cm.
On cover: 収蔵機関 東洋文庫・東京大学東洋文化研究所京都大学人文科学研究所内閣文庫

Yamane, Yukio, 1921–
(Nihon genzon Mindai chihōshi mokuroku)
日本現存明代地方志目録 山根幸夫 細野浩二編 増補 東京 東洋文庫明代史研究室 1971.

41 p. 25 cm.

IMPRINTS *see Chinese imprints*

LAW *see Law - China*

MAPS

Kokuritsu Kokkai Toshokan, *Tokyo.*
中国本土地図目録 国立国会図書館及び東洋文庫所蔵資料 ₁西村庚編 東京, 極東書店 昭和42 ₁1967₁
104 p. 26 cm.
Colophon inserted.

Williams, Jack Francis.
China in maps, 1890–1960; a selective and annotated cartobibliography. ₁Seattle?₁ 1966.
viii, 301 l. maps. 30 cm.
Thesis (M. A.)—University of Washington.

PERIODICALS

Hitotsubashi Daigaku, Tokyo. **Keizai Kenkyūjo.**
₁Chūgoku, Chōsen kankei shozō zasshi mokuroku₁
中国・朝鮮関係所蔵雑誌目録 ₁東京₁ 一橋大学経済研究所 1966.
95 p. 25 cm. (Its 特殊文献目録シリーズ no. 12)
昭和40(1965)年12月末現在
この目録の編集を担当したのは…常川静子である

POLITICS AND GOVERNMENT

Fraser, Stewart E
China—the Cultural Revolution, its aftermath and effects on education and society: a select and partially annotated bibliography, by Stewart E. Fraser ₁and₁ Hsu Kuang-liang. London, University of London Institute of Education, 1972.
₁2₁, 102 p. 21 cm. (Education libraries bulletin, suppl. 16)

Jiang, Joseph.
Chinese bureaucracy and government administration, an annotated bibliography. ₁Honolulu₁ Research Translations, East-West Center, 1964.
ii, 157 l. 28 cm. (Occasional papers of the Institute of Advanced Projects. Annotated bibliography series no. 1)
Books, pamphlets, and articles primarily by Chinese; with authors' names romanized and in characters; titles romanized, in characters, and in English translation.

Michigan. **University.** **Asia Library.**
(Mi-hsi-kên ta hsüeh Ya-chou t'u shu kuan hung wei ping chi wên hua ta ko ming)
密西根大學亞洲圖書館紅衞兵暨文化大革命資料目錄 湯廼文 馬惟一₁合編₁ Source materials on Red Guards and the great proletarian cultural revolution. Compiled by Raymond N. Tang and Wei-yi Ma. Ann Arbor, 1969.
v, 332 l. 29 cm.
At head of title: Asia Library, The University of Michigan, The University Library.
In Chinese, with preface in English.
Mimeographed.

Soong, James Chu-yul.
Red Guard publications: a checklist (RG-9). [Prepared by James Chu-yul Soong, with the assistance of Chung-ping Wang] Washington, Center for Chinese Research Materials, Association of Research Libraries [1970]

30 p. 28 cm. (Association of Research Libraries. Center for Chinese Research Materials. Bibliographical series, no. 6)

Yu lien yen chiu so, Kowloon.
(Hung wei ping tzŭ liao mu lu)
紅衞兵資料目錄 [九龍] 友聯研究所 [1970]
70 p. 26 cm.

Added cover title: Catalogue of Red Guard publications held by URI (Chinese edition).

CHINESE IMPRINTS

Chang, Chün-hêng, *chü jên*, 1894.
適園藏書志 [16卷] 張鈞衡撰 [台北] 廣文書局 [1969]

2 v. (10, 2, 108, 792 p.) 20 cm. (書目續編 30)

據民 5 (1916) 南林張氏家塾刻本複印 原書無目次今補輯篇目...以利檢索

Chang, Ju-yü.
[Ch'ün shu k'ao so]
群書考索 前集66卷 後集65卷 續集56卷 別集25卷 附索隱 [章如愚撰 台北 新興書局 民國 60 i. e. 1971]

8 v. (20, 5548 p.) 21 cm.

Reprint of 明正德戊辰 (1508) 劉氏慎獨齋校刻本

Ch'ên, Chên-sun, *fl.* 1211-1249.
直齋書錄解題 [22卷] 陳振孫撰 [台北 廣文書局 [1968]

3 v. (10, 7, 1332 p.) 20 cm. (書目續編 24)

據重刻武英殿聚珍版本仿印

Chiang, Kuang-hsü, 1813-1860.
東湖叢記 [6卷] 蔣光煦撰 [臺北 廣文書局 [1967]

8, 2, 15, 896 p. 20 cm. (書目叢編 6)

據雲自在龕叢書光緒 9 (1883) 年刊本影印

Chiao, Hung, 1541-1620.
(Kuo shih ching chi chih)
國史經籍志 [6卷] 焦竑輯 [台北 廣文書局 [民國 61 i. e. 1972]

3 v. (10, 8, 894 p.) 20 cm. (書目五編)

Reprint of the 1851 ed., issued in series: 粵雅堂叢書

(Ch'üan kuo hsin shu mu.)
全国新书目 Quan-guo xinshumu. National bibliography. 1950: 总第 [1]-286 期 1951 年 1/3 月 -1966 年 7 月 16 日 Washington, Reprinted by Center for Chinese Research Materials, Association of Research Libraries [1972]

17 v. in 20. 29 cm.

In Chinese.

Reprint, with added t. p.: National bibliography (Ch'üan-kuo hsin shu-mu) comp. by wen-hua pu. Ch'u-pan shih-yeh kuan-li chü. Pan-pen t'u-shu kuan, of 全国新书目 Quan-guo xinshumu (1950-58 have title only in characters) issued with various frequency in 北京 by 文化部出版事业管理局版本图书馆 (called 1950 中央人民政府出版總署圖書期刊司; 1951-Oct. 1954 中央人民政府出版總署圖書館; Nov. 1954-Apr. 1957 文化部出版事業管理局圖書館) No. 3-4, 138-149 are wanting in the reproduction.

(Chung-hua min kuo ch'u pan t'u shu mu lu) 中華民國出版圖書目錄 民國 59 年 1 月號 – [1970–台北 國立中央圖書館

no. 27 cm. monthly.

Supersedes The monthly list of Chinese books. Title also in English, 1970- : Chinese bibliography.

崇文總目輯釋 [5卷 補遺 坿錄 王堯臣 歐陽修等奉敕撰 錢東垣 錢侗 [等] 撰 i. e. 輯釋 臺北 廣文書局 [1968]

2 v. (10, 6, 846 p.) 20 cm. (書目續編 21)

Originally published in the 汗筠齋叢書 with date 嘉慶 4 (1799) under title: 崇文總目 咸豐 3 (1853) 刊入粵雅堂叢書 茲以粵雅本校刊精審據以影印

Chung yang t'u shu kuan, T'ai-pei.
(Chung-hua min kuo ch'u pan t'u shu mu lu hui pien)
中華民國出版圖書目錄彙編 國立中央圖書館編 臺北 民國 53 [1964]

2 v. in 1. 27 cm.

本目錄係根據本館歷年所編中華民國出版圖書目錄彙編而成所著錄之圖書以 38 年 ... 至 52 年底 ... 送繳本館者爲限

———— 續輯 [臺北 國立中央圖書館編印 民國 59 [1970]

2 v. 27 cm.

本目錄所著之圖書以 53 年 1 月至 57 年 6 月底依出版法送繳本館者爲限

CONTENTS.—[1] 續輯—[2] 續輯索引

Huang, Yü-chi, 1629-1691.
千頃堂書目 [32卷] 黃虞稷撰 [臺北 廣文書局 [1967]

6 v. (8, 20, 23, 2266 p.) 20 cm. (書目叢編 1)

據適園叢書民 2 (1913) 年刊本影印

Juan, Yüan, 1764-1849.
(Wên hsüan lou ts'ang shu chi) 文選樓藏書記 [6卷 阮元撰 [台北 廣文書局 [民國 58 i. e. 1969]

3 v. (10, 4, 876 p.) in 1. 19 cm. (書目三編 56)

據中央圖書館藏李慈銘校訂·會稽李氏越縵堂烏絲欄鈔
本影印

Kan, P'eng-yün, b. 1861.

(Ch'ung ya t'ang shu lu)

崇雅堂書錄　廿鵬雲編　[台北]　廣文書局
[民國61 i. e. 1972]

4 v. (10, 12, 1244 p.) 19 cm. (書目五編)

Reprint of the 1935 ed.
CONTENTS: 書錄 15卷—碑錄 5卷—碑錄補 4卷

漢籍叢書所在目錄　東洋学文献センター連絡協議会
[編　東京　東洋文庫] 1965 [i. e. 1966]

8, 90, 43 p. 26 cm.

收藏機関　東洋文庫·東京大学東洋文化研究所·京都大学人
文科学研究所国立国会図書館内閣文庫静嘉堂文庫·天理図書
館

Kao, Po-ho.

浦陽藝文考　高伯和著　臺北　立志書局總經銷
民國57 [1968]

1, 5, 13, 190 p. 21 cm.

Colophon title.

Ku, Kuang-ch'i, 1776–1835.

(Ssu shih chai chi wai shu pa chi ts'un)

思適齋集外書跋輯存　[顧廣圻撰]　方志商
[2卷　廿鵬雲撰　台北]　廣文書局　[民國61 i. e.
1972]

10, 2, 120, 4, 84 p. 19 cm. (書目五編)

Cover title.
Reprint ed.

Liu, Hsien-hsin, 1896–1932.

(Hsü chiao ch'ou t'ung i)

續校讎通義　劉咸炘撰　[臺北]　廣文書局
[民國61 i. e. 1972]

10, 4, 236 p. 19 cm. (書目五編)

本書為劉氏續堂學誠校讎通義
影印民國17(1928)年劉氏自刻本原書2冊不分卷

Lu, Ching, 1856–1928.

(Ssu k'u Hu-pei hsien cheng i shu t'i yao)

四庫湖北先正遺書提要　[4卷]　附遺書存目 [4
卷 札記]　盧靖輯 [盧弼輯校　臺北]
[民國61 i. e. 1972]

2 v. (10, 2, 530 p.) 20 cm. (書目五編)

Reprint of the 1922 ed.

Lu, Hsin-yüan, 1834–1894.

儀顧堂題跋 [16卷]　陸心源著 [台北]　廣文書
局 [1968]

2 v. (10, 4, 772 p.) 20 cm. (書目續編29)
據1890年刊本影印

———儀顧堂續跋 [16卷 台北, 廣文書局] [1968]

2 v. (718 p.) 20 cm. (書目續編29)
據1892年刊本影印

Lu, Hsin-yüan, 1834–1894.

皕宋樓藏書志 [120　卷]　續志 [4卷]　陸心源
編 [台北]　廣文書局 [1968]

12 v. (10, 1, 16, 4, 5578 p.) 19 cm. (書目續編28)
據1883年十萬卷樓刊本影印
坿 皕宋樓藏書源流放　島田翰撰: v. 1, p. 16.
——————Another issue.　平裝
22 v. (10, 1, 16, 4, 5578 p.) in 7.

Miao, Ch'üan-sun, 1844–1919.

藝風藏書記·續記　繆荃孫撰 [臺北]　廣文書局
[1967]

2 v. (8, 3, 5, 752 p.) 20 cm. (書目叢編11)

據光緒辛丑 (1901) 癸丑 (1913) 原刊本影印

CONTENTS.—上　藝風藏書記八卷—下　藝風藏書續記
八卷

Mo, Po-chi, 1878–

五十萬卷樓藏書目錄初編 [22卷]　莫伯驥撰
[臺北]　廣文書局 [1967]

11 v. (8, 2, 2862 p.) 20 cm. (書目叢編14)

據民25 (1936) 東莞莫氏自印本影印

The Monthly list of Chinese books. 新書簡報　第1-9
卷 民國49年9月-民國58年11月 [1960-69]
台北　國立中央圖書館

9 v. 26 cm. monthly.

Suspended July 1967-June 1968.
Issues for Feb.-Nov. 1969 have no vol. numbering but constitute
v. 9.
Chinese title varies: July-Dec. 1968, 新書目錄—1969, 國立中央
圖書館新書目錄
Vols. for July 1968-69 issued in Chinese.
Superseded by 中華民國出版圖書目錄

National bibliography of new books; selected issues. [Hono-
lulu] East-West Center, 1966.

2 v. 28 cm. (Occasional papers of Research Translations, Institute of Advanced Projects, East-West Center. Translation series, no.
17–18)
Translation of no. 8–11, Apr. 16–June 15, 1965 (serial no. 256–259)
of Ch'üan kuo hsin shu mu, compiled by the Library of the Publishing Industry Supervisory Bureau, Ministry of Culture, Peking.

P'êng, Kuo-tung.

重修清史藝文志·彭國棟纂修 [臺北]　臺灣商
務印書館 [1968]

3, 4, 338 p. 21 cm.

(Po-shan shu ying)

盍山書影　宋本第一輯 [元本第二輯　江蘇省立國
學圖書館編　臺北　廣文書局　民國59 i. e. 1970]

92, 221 l. (chiefly facsims.) 26 cm. (書目四編)

Reprint of 民國18 (1929) 國學圖書館石印本

(Sung Chin Yüan pên shu ying)

宋金元本書影 [瞿啓甲編　識語4卷　丁祖蔭撰

臺北　廣文書局　民國 59 i. e. 1970」

　　1 v. (chiefly facsims.)　26 cm.　(書目四編)

　　At head of title in colophon: 鐵琴銅劍樓
　　Reprint of 鐵琴銅劍樓瞿氏刊本

Yang, Chia-lo.
　　(Min kuo i lai ch'u pan hsin shu tsung mu)
　　民國以來出版新書總目提要　楊家駱著　「台北
　　縣新店鎮」　中國辭典館復館籌備處　「民國 60 i. e.
　　1971」
　　　2 v. (2, 2192 p.)　20 cm.

　　　Colophon title: 民國以來出版新書總目提要初編
　　　On spine: A comprehensive catalogue of books published since
　　　the focusing of the Republic.
　　「圖書年鑑」原分上下二冊　原上冊為「圖書事業志」現未重
　　印　原下冊為「新書總目提要」　卽今所重印的民國以來出版新書
　　總目提要初編

Yeh, Te-hui, 1864-1927.
　　(Kuan ku t'ang shu mu ts'ung k'o)
　　觀古堂書目叢刻　葉德輝等 [sic] 撰　「台北」　廣
　　文書局　「民國 61 i. e. 1972」
　　　8 v. (10, 10, 2278 p.)　19 cm.　「書目五編」
　　　景印民國8(1919)年觀古堂刻本原書15種48卷內一種不分卷

Yüeh, K'o, 1173?-ca. 1240.
　　九經三傳沿革例　岳珂撰　「台北」　廣文書局
　　「1968」
　　　1 v. (various pagings)　19 cm.　(書目續編 23, 27, 34, 41-44)

　　　Contents.—九經三傳沿革例　岳珂撰—遂初堂書目　尤袤
　　撰—百宋一廛賦注　顧廣圻撰　黃丕烈注—敪刻唐宋祕本
　　書目　黃虞稷　周在浚撰—澹生堂藏書約　祁承㸁撰—流通
　　古書約　曹溶撰—藏書紀要　孫從添撰

EARLY PRINTED WORKS

Ch'ao, Kung-wu.
　　群齋讀書志 [20卷]　晁公武撰　「姚應績編　王
　　先謙校正　臺北　廣文書局」 [1967]
　　　4 v. (10, 28, 1618 p.)　19 cm.　(書目續編 22)

　　　Original t. p. reads: 晁氏郡齋讀書志二十卷　趙氏坿志二卷
　　　據光緒甲申 (1884) 長沙王氏刊本影印

Ch'ao, Kung-wu.
　　郡齋讀書志 [20卷]　晁公武撰 「姚應績編
　　王先謙校正　台北」 廣文書局 [1967]
　　　6 v. (10, 28, 1618 p.) in 2.　19 cm.　(書目續編 22)

　　　Original t. p. reads: 晁氏郡齋讀書志二十卷　趙氏坿志二卷
　　　據光緒甲申 (1884) 長沙王氏刊本影印

Chung yang t'u shu kuan, T'ai-pei.
　　「Hsien ts'un Sung jen chu shu mu lu」
　　現存宋人著述目略　編輯者國立中央圖書館　臺
　　北　中華叢書編審委員會　臺灣書店總經銷　1971」
　　　8, 294 p.　21 cm.　(國立中央圖書館目錄叢刊第7種) (中華
　　叢書)

　　　Colophon title.

Kuo li ku kung po wu yüan.
　　(Kuo li ku kung po wu yüan p'u t'ung chiu chi)　國
　　立故宮博物院普通舊籍目錄　「臺北　民國 59 i. e.
　　1970」
　　　1, 2, 8, 316 p.　22 cm.

內閣藏書目錄　「8卷」　張萱 [等] 撰　「台北」　廣文
書局 [1968]
　　　2 v. (10, 2, 566 p.)　19 cm.　(書目續編 25)

　　　據民國 2 (1913) 適園叢書本影印

P'an, Ch'êng-pi, ed.
　　(Ming tai pan pên t'u lu ch'u pien)
　　明代版本圖錄初編　「12卷」　潘承弼　顧廷龍同
　　纂　「臺北縣永和鎮」　文海出版社　「民國 60 i. e.
　　1971」
　　　540 p.　facsims.　20 cm.

Shibue, Chūsai, 1805-1858.
　　[Keiseki hōkoshi. Chinese]
　　經籍訪古志　「澀江抽齋」　森立之撰　「台北」
　　廣文書局　「民國 56 i. e. 1967」
　　　8, 2, 247 p.　20 cm.　(書目叢編 18)

　　　Reprint of 日本昭和 10 (1935) 影印稿本

Suzuki, Yoshijirō, 1901-
　　鈴木　由次郎
　　漢書藝文志
　　　東京　明德出版社　昭和43 (1968)
　　　312 p　20 cm　(中国古典新書)

Yang, Shih-ch'i, 1365-1444.
　　(Wen-yüan ko shu mu)
　　文淵閣書目　「20卷」　楊士奇撰　「台北」　廣文
　　書局　「民國 58 i. e. 1969」
　　　10, 4, 860 p.　20 cm.　(書目三編 48)

　　　Reprint of the ed. published by 桐川顧氏. in series: 讀畫齋叢書; 戊戊
　　　with new introd.

Yi Chŏngjo, *King of Korea,* 1752-1800.
　　群書標記　「正祖著　시종?」　學文閣　「新韓書
　　林供給 1970」
　　　370, 8 p.　23 cm.

　　　Photo-offset from 弘齋全書卷 179-184.
　　　Colophon inserted.
　　　100 部限定版

LIBRARY CATALOGS

Chicago. University. Library. Far Eastern Library.
　　Author-title catalog of the Chinese collection.　Boston, G. K.
　　Hall, 1973.
　　　8 v.　37 cm.

　　　At head of title: Catalogs of the Far Eastern Library, University of Chicago,
　　Chicago, Illinois.

Chicago. University. Library. Far Eastern Library.
　　Classified catalog and subject index of the Chinese and
　　Japanese collections.　Boston, G. K. Hall, 1973.

6 v. 37 cm.

At head of title: Catalogs of the Far Eastern Library, University of Chicago, Chicago, Illinois.

Columbia University. *Libraries. East Asiatic Library.*
Quarterly bibliography of new titles in Chinese, East Asian Library, Columbia University. v. 1-3, no. 3; Oct. 1963–Nov. 1965. ₍New York₎

3 v. 22 x 28 cm.

Title also in Chinese: 哥倫比亞大學東亞圖書館中文新書目

Kyūshū Daigaku, Fukuoka, Japan. Toshokan. Kyōyōbu Bunkan.
(Kyūshū Daigaku Fuzoku Toshokan Kyōyōbu Bunkan kanseki mokuroku)

九州大学附属図書館教養部分館漢籍目録　福岡　九州大学附属図書館教養部分館　昭和46(1971)

101, 32, 5 p. 27 cm.

Naikaku Bunko, Tokyo.
(Naikaku Bunko kanseki bunrui mokuroku)

内閣文庫漢籍分類目録　改訂　東京　内閣文庫　昭和46(1971)

1 v. 27 cm.

North Carolina. University. *Library.*
List of Chinese books and periodicals in the Far Eastern collection of the University of North Carolina Library at Chapel Hill. ₍Chapel Hill, 1965–

v. in 28 cm.

Stanford University. *Hoover Institution on War, Revolution, and Peace.*
The library catalogs of the Hoover Institution on War, Revolution, and Peace, Stanford University; catalog of the Chinese collection. Boston, G. K. Hall, 1969.

13 v. 37 cm.

Running title: The Hoover Institution catalog of the Chinese collection.
Authors and titles in Chinese and romanized forms.

Toyo Bunko, Tokyo.
A classified catalogue of pamphlets in foreign languages in the Toyo Bunko, acquired during the year 1917–1971. Tokyo, 1972.

ii, 328 p. 26 cm.

Added t. p. in Japanese.

Tōyōgaku Bunken Sentā Renraku Kyōgikai.
(Kanseki bunrui mokuroku)　漢籍分類目録　₍編輯者·東洋学文献センター連絡協議会　代表者·辻直四郎　東京　東洋文庫　昭和42–　i. e. 1967–

v. 26 cm.

CONTENTS.—₍1₎　集部　東洋文庫之部

Tōyōgaku Bunken Sentā Renraku Kyōgikai.
(Kanseki sōsho shozai mokuroku)

漢籍叢書所在目録　収蔵機関　東洋文庫·東京大学東洋文化研究所·京都大学人文科学研究所·国立国会図書館·内閣文庫·静嘉堂文庫·天理図書館

東洋学文献センター連絡協議会₍編輯　東京　東洋文庫₎　1965₍i.e. 1966₎

8, 99, 43 p. 26 cm.

Tung, Shih-kang.
Chinese microfilms in Princeton University: a checklist of the Gest Oriental Library. Washington, Center for Chinese Research Materials, Association of Research Libraries, 1969.

57 p. 29 cm. (Association of Research Libraries. Center for Chinese Research Materials. Bibliographical series, no. 2)

Virginia. University. Library.
The Ellen Bayard Weedon Chinese collection at the University of Virginia. Catalogue of the Ma Kiam Library, by Ng Tung King. Edited by Roy Land. Charlottesville, 1965.

17, 5, 30, ₍9₎ l. 22 x 28 cm.
Introductory matter in English and Chinese; catalogue in Chinese.

Added t. p.: 維基尼亞大學額稜唎瑤魏登中文藏書馬鑑圖書館目錄

CHINESE IN ASIA

Li, I-yüan.
東亞華僑研究參考書目　李亦園₍編₎　Studies on overseas Chinese in East Asia; a catalogue of books and articles in Chinese and Japanese, compiled by Yih-yuan Li. ₍臺北₎　中央研究院民族學研究所　Institute of Ethnology, Academia Sinica, 1964.

143–235 p. 27 cm.
Cover title.
In Chinese with foreword in English.

Nevadomsky, Joseph-john.
The Chinese in Southeast Asia; a selected and annotated bibliography of publications in Western languages, 1960-1970, by Joseph-john Nevadomsky and Alice Li. Berkeley, Center for South and Southeast Asia Studies, University of California, 1970.

xvi, 119 l. 28 cm. (Center for South and Southeast Asia Studies, University of California. Occasional paper no. 6)

CHINESE IN HAWAII

Lowe, Chuan-hua, 1902–
The Chinese in Hawaii: a bibliographic survey, by C. H. Lowe. Taipei, Printed by China Print. ₍1972₎

vi, 148 p. 1 fold. map. 23 cm.

CHINESE IN THE UNITED STATES

Cowan, Robert Ernest, 1862–1942.
Bibliography of the Chinese question in the United States, by Robert Ernest Cowan and Boutwell Dunlap. San Francisco, A. M. Robertson, 1909. ₍San Francisco, R and E Research Associates, 1970₎

68 l. 22 cm.

Hansen, Gladys C 1925–
The Chinese in California: a brief bibliographic history, selected by Gladys C. Hansen. Annotated by William F. Heintz. ₍Portland, Or.₎ R. Abel, 1970.

140 p. illus. 27 cm. (Bibliographic series, no. 1)

This work is based on material in the Californiana collection, Dept. of Rare Books and Special Collections, San Francisco Public Library, covering the period 1850 through 1968.

Ng, Pearl.
Writings on the Chinese in California. ₍San Francisco, R' and E Research Associates, 1972₎

vii, 118 p. 28 cm.

Thesis (M. A.)—University of California, 1939.

CHINESE INSCRIPTIONS see Inscriptions, Chinese

CHINESE LANGUAGE

Hsieh, Ch'i-k'un, 1737–1802.
(Hsiao hsüeh k'ao)
小學考 ₍50 卷₎ 謝啓昆撰 ₍台北₎ 廣文書局 ₍民國 58 i. e. 1969₎

10 v. (₍46₎, 2458 p.) in 2. 19 cm. (書目三編 65)

Reprint of 清光緒 14 (1888) 杭州浙江書局刊本

Saeki, Tomi, 1910–
(Sōdai bunshū sakuin)
宋代文集索引 佐伯富編 〔京都〕 京都大學 東洋史研究會 1970.

9, 845, 18p. 22cm. （東洋史研究叢刊之 24）

Added t. p.: Index to wen-chi of the Sung period.

Ting, Chieh-min.
方言考 丁介民著 ₍臺北₎ 臺灣中華書局 ₍1969₎

1, 2, 9, 158 p. 22 cm.

Wang, William S-Y 1933–
CLIBOC: Chinese linguistics bibliography on computer, compiled by William S-Y. Wang and Anatole Lyovin. Cambridge ₍Eng.₎ University Press, 1970.

513 p. 3 maps (part col. in pocket) 23 cm. (Princeton-Cambridge studies in Chinese linguistics, 1)

Wu, Shou-li.
閩南語史研究文獻目錄—吳從宜(守禮)先生華甲紀念 ₍吳昭婉等輯 臺北 1969₎

44 p. port. 21 cm.

Cover title.
Added title on p. ₍4₎ of cover: List of works by Wu Shou-li.
PARTIAL CONTENTS.—從宜先生生平簡述—從宜先生編著年表—閩南方言研究文獻目錄 續編 吳守禮著

Yang, Winston L Y
A bibliography of the Chinese language, compiled by Winston L. Y. Yang and Teresa S. Yang. New York, American Association of Teachers of Chinese Language and Culture; distributed by Paragon Book Gallery, New York, 1966.

xiv, 171 p. 26 cm.

CHINESE LITERATURE

Chin, T'an.
(Wen jui lou ts'ang shu mu lu)
文瑞樓藏書目錄 ₍12卷₎ 金檀撰 ₍台北₎ 廣

文書局 ₍民國 61 i. e. 1972₎

10, 4, 308 p. 19 cm. （書目五編）

Running title: 文瑞樓書目
Reprint of the 1811 ed., issued in series: 讀畫齋叢書

Kanaoka, Shōkō, 1930–
(Tonkō shutsudo bungaku bunken bunrui mokuroku)
敦煌出土文學文獻分類目錄 附解説 スタイン本・ペリオ本 金岡照光編 ₍東京₎ 東洋文庫敦煌文獻研究委員會 1971.

251 p. 26 cm. （西域出土漢文文獻分類目錄 4）

On p. ₍4₎ of cover: Classified catalogue of literary and popular works in Chinese in Tun-huang documents from Stein and Pelliot collections.

Nishimura, Genshō, 1944–
(Nihon genson Shinjin bunshū mokuroku)
日本現存清人文集目錄 西村元照編 京都 東洋史研究会 朋友書店（発売） 1972.

438 p. 26 cm.

Cover title; title also in English: A catalogue of Wênchi in Ching Dynasty existing in Japan.

Pei-ching t'u shu kuan.
(Kuan ts'ang chieh fang ch'ü ch'u pan wên i tso p'in shu mu)
館藏解放区出版文艺作品书目 北京 北京图书館編印 1958. ₍Hong Kong, 萬有圖書公司 1971?₎

213 p. 21 cm.

Yamane, Yukio, 1921–
(Nihon genson Genjin bunshū mokuroku)
日本現存 元人文集目錄 山根幸夫, 小川尚編
浦和 山根幸夫 東京 汲古書院（発売） 1970
66p 25cm

Yamane, Yukio, 1921–
日本現存明人文集目錄 山根幸夫・小川尚編 東京 大安印刷 1966.

150, iv p. 25 cm.

Yang, Shou-ching, 1839–1915.
日本訪書志 ₍16卷₎ 楊守敬撰 ₍臺北₎ 廣文書局 ₍1967₎

4 v. (8, 3, 1062 p.) 20 cm. （書目叢編 17）

據光緒辛丑 (1901) 年刊本影印

₍**Yao, Chin-yüan₎ chü jen,** 1843, comp.
₍Ch'ing tai chin hui shu mu₎
銷燬抽燬書目 英廉等編 禁書總目 軍機處編 違礙書目 臺北 廣文書局 民國 61 ₍1972₎

₍18₎, 44, 136, 66 p. 19 cm. （書目五編）

Colophon title.
1957 ed. published by 上海商務印書館 under the compiler's name 姚覲元 and the collective title: 清代禁燬書目
Reprint of the ed., issued in series: 咫進齋叢書; with new introd.

BIO-BIBLIOGRAPHY

Chung yang t'u shu kuan, T'ai-pei.
Directory of contemporary authors of the Republic of China. [Taipei], National Central Library, 1970.

318 p. 21 cm. (國立中央圖書館目錄叢刊第 6 輯) (中華叢書)

In colophon: 中華民國當代文藝作家名錄　編輯者國立中央圖書館　出版者中華叢書編審委員會　總經銷　臺灣書局
Chinese and/or English.

Liang, Jung-jo.
中國文學百家傳　第 1 輯　梁容若著　台中　私立東海大學　Tunghai University; 中央書局經售 1966.

8, 3, 4, 406 p. illus., facsims., ports. 21 cm.

Colophon and binder's title: 文學十家傳 Biographies of ten Chinese authors.

CONTENTS.—杜甫--白居易--韓愈--柳宗元--歐陽修--蘇軾--陸游--袁枚--黃遵憲--梁啓超

Liang, Jung-jo.
(Tso chia yü tso p'in)
作家與作品　梁容若著　[臺中]，私立東海大學中央書局經售 [1971]

208 p. 22 cm.

Added colophon title: Authors and selected writings.

PERIODICALS

Hsien tai wên hsüeh ch'i k'an lien ho tiao ch'a hsiao tsu.
Contemporary Chinese literature: a list of periodicals, 1902–1949. Washington, D. C., Reprinted by Center for Chinese Research Materials, Association of Research Libraries, 1968.

vii, 110 p. 9 x 28 cm.

Original t. p. reads: 中國現代文學期刊目錄　初稿　現代文學期刊聯合調查小組編　上海文藝出版社　1961 (中國現代文學史資料叢書　甲種)
In Chinese.

Onoe, Kanehide.
(Sen-kyūhyaku-sanjūnendai Chūgoku bungei zasshi)
1930年代中国文芸雑誌　尾上兼英編　東京　東京大学東洋文化研究所付属東洋学文献センター刊行委員会　昭和46- (1971-

v. 21 cm. (東洋学文献センター叢刊　第14- 輯)

TRANSLATIONS

Chung yang t'u shu kuan, T'ai-pei.
(Chung i wai wen t'u shu mu lu)
中譯外文圖書目錄　國立中央圖書館編輯　臺北　中華叢書編審委員會　臺灣書局總經銷　民國61 [1972]

10, 1117 p. 21 cm. (國立中央圖書館目錄叢刊第11輯) (中華叢書)
Colophon title.
本目錄所收譯書自民國卅八年...至民國五十九年二月止

Wylie, Alexander, 1815–1887.
Notes on Chinese literature: with introductory remarks on the progressive advancement of the art; and a list of translations from the Chinese into various European lan-

guages, by A. Wylie. 2d ed. New York, Paragon Book Reprint Corp., 1964.

xxxx, 307 p. 24 cm. (Paragon reprint oriental series, 19)

CHINESE STUDIES

Fairbank, John King, 1907–
Japanese studies of modern China; a bibliographical guide to historical and social-science research on the 19th and 20th centuries, by John King Fairbank, Masataka Banno [and Sumiko Yamamoto. Cambridge, Harvard University Press, 1971, °1955]

xviii, 331 p. 25 cm. (Harvard-Yenching Institute studies, 26)

Hongkong. Chinese University. Institute of Advanced Chinese Studies and Research.
(Hsin Ya yen chiu so yen chiu wên hsien) 新亞研究所研究文獻類目 [九龍　新亞研究所 1969]

2, 2, 1, 84 p. 21 cm.

Title on p. [4] of cover: Index to essays, lectures, & research works, 1953–1969.

Leslie, Donald, 1922–
Author catalogues of western sinologists [by] Donald Leslie and Jeremy Davidson. Canberra, Dept. of Far Eastern History, Research School of Pacific Studies, Australian National University [1966]

lvii, 257 p. 25 cm. (Guide to bibliographies on China and the Far East)

Ogawa, Kandō.
小川　貫道
漢學者傳記及著述集覽
東京　名著刊行会　昭和45 (1970)
781p 図版 22cm

監修者：小柳司気太
関書院　昭和10年刊の複製

Weitzman, David L
Chinese studies in paperback [by] David L. Weitzman. Berkeley, Calif., McCutchan Pub. Co. [1968, °1967]

vi, 82 p. 23 cm.

CHINY (COMTÉ) see under Luxemburg, Belgium

CHIOCCHETTI, EMILIO

Consolati, Giuseppe.
Bibliografia di p. Emilio Chiocchetti, filosofo trentino (Moena, 1880–1951) ... A cura di Giuseppe Consolati, Trento, Archivio dei Francescani. Trento, Arti grafiche Saturnia, 1968.

86 p. illus. 24 cm. (Circolo culturale moenese. Quaderno, 2)

CHIPPEWA INDIANS

Minnesota Historical Society.
Chippewa and Dakota Indians; a subject catalog of books, pamphlets, periodical articles, and manuscripts in the Minnesota Historical Society. St. Paul, 1969.

1 v. (unpaged) 28 cm.

CHLORINE

Smith, Ralph G   1920–
Chlorine: an annotated bibliography; a selection of references from 1824 to 1971 on the medical, toxicological, industrial hygiene, and environmental aspects of exposure to chlorine. Prepared by Ralph G. Smith and the Department of Occupational & Environmental Health, Wayne State University, Detroit, Michigan, for the Chlorine Institute, inc., New York, New York, 1971. [New York, 1972]

1 v. (unpaged) 23 cm.

CHOCEŇ, CZECHOSLOVAK REPUBLIC

Nezbeda, Vilém.
Bibliografie Choceňska s tematickým soupisem nejdůležitějších článků a statí. Choceň, Archív Městského národního výboru, 1964.

33 p. 29 cm.

CHOPIN, FRYDERYK FRANCISZEK

Brown, Maurice John Edwin.
Chopin: an index of his works in chronological order [by] Maurice J. E. Brown. 2nd, revised ed. London, Macmillan, 1972.

xvii, 214 p. music. 23 cm.

Michałowski, Kornel.
Bibliografia chopinowska, 1849–1969. Chopin bibliography. Kornel Michałowski. [Wyd. 1. Kraków] Polskie Wydawn. Muzyczne [1970]

267 p. illus. 24 cm. (Towarzystwo im. Fryderyka Chopina. Documenta Chopiniana, 1)

Prefatory matter, table of contents, and legends also in English

Towarzystwo imienia Fryderyka Chopina, Warsaw. Biblioteka.
Książki i czasopisma. Warszawa, 1969.

314 p. 21 cm. (Towarzystwo imienia Fryderyka Chopina. Katalog zbiorów)

Towarzystwo imienia Fryderyka Chopina, Warsaw. Biblioteka.
Nuty. [Oprac. Janina Ohrt]. Warszawa, 1969.

275 p. 21 cm. (Towarzystwo imienia Fryderyka Chopina, Warsaw. Katalog zbiorów)

Towarzystwo imienia Fryderyka Chopina, Warsaw. Fototeka.
Korespondencja F. Chopina, ludzi jego epoki i ludzi związanych z tradycją Chopinowską. Warszawa, 1969.

77 p. 21 cm. (Towarzystwo imienia Fryderyka Chopina. Katalog zbiorów)

Towarzystwo imienia Fryderyka Chopina, Warsaw. Fototeka.
Utwory Fryderyka Chopina; autografy, szkice, kopie, pierwodruki, druki zabytkowe. Utwory innych kompozytorów. Warszawa, 1969.

136 p. 21 cm. (Towarzystwo imieni a Fredyryka Chopina. Katalog zbiorów)

Added t. p.: Frederic Chopin's works.
Prefatory matter also in English.

Towarzystwo imienia Fryderyka Chopina, Warsaw. Muzeum.
Ikonografia, pamiątki i sztuka użytkowa. Warszawa, 1970.

156 p. 21 cm. (Towarzystwo imienia Fryderyka Chopina. Katalog zbiorów)

Prefatory matter also in English.

CHORAL MUSIC see Vocal music

CHOU, SHU-JEN

Shen, P'eng-nien, bibliographer, comp.
(Lu Hsün yen chiu tzu liao pien mu)
魯迅研究資料編目 沈鵬年輯 [上海] 上海文艺出版社 1958. [香港? 1971?]

ix, 516 p. 22 cm.

Original ed. issued in series: 中国现代文学史資料丛書[甲种]

CHOU, YANG

Maruyama, Noboru, 1931–
(Shū Yō cho yaku rombun Shū Yō hihan bunken mokuroku)
周揚著訳論文 周揚批判文献目録 丸山昇編
[東京] 東京大学東洋文化研究所附属東洋学文献センター 昭和44[1969]

52 p. 21 cm. (東洋学文献センター叢刊 第4輯)

CHRISTENSEN, POVL

Holst, Poul.
Povl Christensen. En bibliografi. [Illustrationerne af Povl Christensen] Ringkøbing [Forening for Boghaandværk] A. Rasmussens Bogtrykkeri; [Eksp.: Strube, Strubes Forlag] 1968.

158 p. illus. 25 cm.

CHRISTIAN-ALBRECHTS-UNIVERSITÄT see Kiel. Universität

CHRISTIAN ART AND SYMBOLISM

Gurruchaga, Juan.
Indice bibliográfico de publicaciones belenistas y temas afines. Recopilación, traducción y sinopsis: Juan Gurruchaga, Rafael Gutiérrez [y] Juan Carlos Martín. Portada: Juan Salsamendi. [San Sebastián] Asociación Belenista de Guipúzcoa [1967]

ix, 249 p. illus. 25 cm.

Preface in various languages.

Schneider Berrenberg, Rüdiger.
Kreuz, Kruzifix: eine Bibliographie/ Rüdiger Schneider Berrenberg. — München: Schneider Berrenberg, 1973.

317 p.; 21 cm.

CHRISTIAN UNION see Ecumenical movement

CHRISTIANITY
see also Theology

Adorno, Francesco.
Il pensiero greco-romano e il cristianesimo. Orientamenti bibliografici a cura di Francesco Adorno. Bari, Laterza, 1970.

vii, 110 p. 18 cm. (Piccola biblioteca filosofica Laterza. ₍Nuova Ser.₎, 49)

Anderson, Gerald H.
Christianity in southeast Asia: a bibliographical guide: an annotated bibliography of selected references in Western languages, edited by Gerald H. Anderson. New York, Missionary Research Library, 1966.

ix, 69 p. map. 28 cm.

Chao, Jonathan T'ien-en.
A bibliography of the history of Christianity in China (a preliminary draft). Waltham, Mass., Faculty-in-Preparation, China Graduate School of Theology ₍1970₎

iv, 54 p. 22 cm. (CGST research project no. 3)

In colophon: 中國基督教史書目初編 編者趙天恩 出版者 中國神學研究院

Preface in Chinese.

Christian Council of Malawi.
Christian literature survey, June 1966. ₍Blantyre, 196

v. 33 cm.

Cover title.
CONTENTS:
v. 2. Catalogue of books in the languages of Malawi.

Encounter with books; a guide to Christian reading. Edited by Harish D. Merchant. Downers Grove, Ill., Inter-Varsity Press ₍°1970₎

xxvii, 262 p. 21 cm.

Grier, William James.
The best books: a guide to Christian literature ₍by₎ W. J. Grier. London, Banner of Truth Trust, 1968.

175 p. 19 cm.

McLean, George F *comp.*
An annotated bibliography of philosophy in Catholic thought, 1900–1964, edited by George F. McLean. New York, F. Ungar Pub. Co. ₍1967₎

xiv, 371 p. 22 cm. (Philosophy in the 20th century: Catholic and Christian. v. 1)

McLean, George F *comp.*
A bibliography of Christian philosophy and contemporary issues, edited by George F. McLean. New York, F. Ungar Pub. Co. ₍1967₎

viii, 312 p. 22 cm. (Philosophy of the 20th century: Catholic and Christian, v. 2)

Metodio da Nembro, Father.
Quattrocento scrittori spirituali. Milano, Centro studi Cappuccini lombardi, 1972.

xvi, 465 p. 24 cm. (Centro studi Cappuccini lombardi. ₍Pubblicazioni₎, 18)

At head of title: Metodio da Nembro (Carobbio Mario).

National Book League, *London.*
Christianity in books; a guide to current Christian literature. London, 1964.

141 p. 22 cm.

Von Oeyen, Robert R
Philippine Evangelical Protestant and independent Catholic churches; an historical bibliography of church records, publications, and source material located in the greater Manila area ₍by₎ Robert R. Von Oeyen, Jr. ₍Quezon City₎ Asian Center, University of the Philippines, 1970.

v, 80 l. 27 cm. (Asian Center, University of the Philippines. Bibliography series, no. 1)

CHRISTMAS

Library Association. Youth Libraries Group.
Christmas stocking. ₍Birmingham, Eng., 1973?₎

16 p. 22 cm. (Its Pamphlet, no. 14)

Long, Sidney.
And all the dark make bright like day; Christmas books, 1960–1972. ₍Boston, Mass., Horn Book, 1972₎

15 p. illus. 20 cm.

Cover title.
"A selective list of Christmas books that have been reviewed in The Horn book since 1960."

CHROMATOGRAPHIC ANALYSIS

American Society for Testing and Materials. Subcommittee D–20.70 on Analytical Methods. Section D–20.70.04 on Gel Permeation Chromatography.
Bibliography on liquid exclusion chromatography (gel permeation chromatography) / sponsored by Section D–20.70.04 on Gel Permeation Chromatography of Subcommittee D–20.70 on Analytical Methods, American Society for Testing and Materials. — Philadelphia : ASTM, 1974.
93 p. ; 23 cm. — (Atomic and molecular data series ; AMD 40)

Bibliography of column chromatography, 1967–1970 and survey of applications. ₍Editors₎ Zdeněk Deyl ₍and others₎ Amsterdam, New York, Elsevier Scientific Pub. Co., 1973.

xix, 1067 p. 25 cm. (Journal of chromatography. Supplementary volume no. 3)

Bibliography of paper and thin-layer chromatography, 1961–1965 and survey of applications ₍by₎ Karel Macek ₍and others₎ Amsterdam, New York, Elsevier Pub. Co., 1968.

1041 p. 24 cm.

"Journal of chromatography, supplementary volume 1968."
Continues Bibliography of paper chromatography, 1957–1968.

Bibliography of paper and thin-layer chromatography, 1966–1969 and survey of applications ₍by₎ Karel Macek ₍and others₎ Amsterdam, New York, Elsevier Pub. Co., 1972.

xvi, 901 p. 25 cm. (Journal of chromatography. Supplementary volume, no. 2)

Gas and liquid chromatography abstracts. 1970–
London, Institute of Petroleum.

v. 26 cm. annual.

Continues Gas chromatography abstracts.
Vols. for 1970– sponsored by the Gas Chromatography Discussion Group, Institute of Petroleum.

Gas chromatography—mass spectrometry abstracts. v. 1– Jan./Mar. 1970–
₍London₎ Science & Technology Agency.

v. 25 cm. quarterly.

Haywood, B J
Thin-layer chromatography; an annotated bibliography, 1964–1968, by B. J. Haywood. ₍Ann Arbor, Mich., Ann

Arbor Science Publishers, 1968.

284 p. 24 cm.

Laboratorio di cromatografia, *Rome.*

Il Laboratorio di cromatografia. Struttura, argomenti di ricerca, contributi scientifici a stampa. Roma, Consiglio nazionale delle ricerche, 1968.

9 p. plates. 25½ cm.

At head of title: Consiglio nazionale delle ricerche.
Edited by G. Agricola.

Litvinova, É   M

Газовая хроматография. Библиогр. указатель отечеств. и зарубежной литературы. (1961–1966 гг.) Ч. 1–2. Москва, "Наука," 1969.

2 v. 26 cm.

At head of title: Академия наук СССР. Институт органической химии им. Н. Д. Зелинского. Сектор сети специальных библиотек.

CONTENTS.—ч. 1. Теория, аппаратура, методы.—ч. 2. Анализ смесей, применение в химии, биологии, медицине и в промышленности.

Preston, Seaton Tinsley, 1921–

A comprehensive bibliography and index to the literature on gas chromatography, by Seaton T. Preston, Jr. and Geneva Hyder. Evanston, Ill., Preston Technical Abstract Co. [1965]

537 p. 24 cm.

Preston Technical Abstracts Company, *Evanston, Ill.*

A termatrex index to the literature on gas chromatography, 1952 to 1964 (inclusive). [Evanston, Ill., 1965]

8, 233 p. 28 cm.

Scott, Ronald McLean, 1933–

Thin-layer chromatography abstracts, 1968–1971 [by] Ronald M. Scott. Ann Arbor, Mich., Ann Arbor Science Publishers, 1972.

395 p. 24 cm.

On spine: TLC abstracts 1968–1971.
"Carries forward the project begun with Thin-layer chromatography, an annotated bibliography, 1964–1968."

Scott, Ronald McLean, 1933–

Thin-layer chromatography abstracts, 1971–1973 [by] Ronald M. Scott and Münime Lundeen. Ann Arbor, Mich., Ann Arbor Science Publishers [1973]

589 p. 24 cm.

Signeur, Austin V

Guide to gas chromatography literature, by Austin V. Signeur. New York, Plenum Press, 1964–67.

2 v. 28 cm.

Thin-layer chromatography abstracts. v. 1–
Jan./Feb. 1971–
[London] Science & Technology Agency.

v. 25 cm. bimonthly.

Waksmundzki, Andrzej, comp.

Bibliografia prac polskich autorów z zakresu chromatografii i elektroforezy za lata 1947–1964. Oprac.: Andrzej Waksmundzki, Regina Schreiter. [Wyd. 1.] Łódź [Państwowe Wydawn. Naukowe, Oddz. w Łodzi] 1970.

202 p. 34 cm. (Lubelskie Towarzystwo Naukowe. Prace Wydziału Matematyczno-Fizyczno-Chemicznego)

CHRYSOSTOMUS, JOANNES, SAINT, PATRIARCH OF CONSTANTINOPLE

Aldama, José Antonio de.

Repertorium pseudochrysostomicum. Collegit J. A. de Aldama … Paris, Éditions du Centre national de la recherche scientifique, 1965.

xviii, 241 p. 24 cm. (Documents, études et répertoires, publiés par l'Institut de recherche et d'histoire des textes, 10)

Burger, Douglas Clyde, 1938–

A complete bibliography of the scholarship on the life and works of Saint John Chrysostom. Evanston, Ill., 1964.

134 l. 28 cm.

Codices Chrysostomici graeci … Paris, Éditions du Centre national de la recherche scientifique, 1968–

v. 25 cm. (Documents, études et répertoires, 13–

CONTENTS. — 1. Codices Britanniae et Hiberniae descripsit Michel Aubineau. (F 68–5188)—2. Codices Germaniae descripsit Robert E. Carter. (F 68–5188)

CH'U TZ'Ŭ

Chiang, Liang-fu, ed.

(Ch'u tz'ŭ shu mu wu chung)

楚辭書目五種   姜亮夫著   [台北]   泰順書局
[1970?]

3, 18, 479, 21 p. illus., facsims., fold. map. 21 cm.

Cover title.

Reprint of the 1961 ed. published by 北京中華書局 with 第5
部楚辭論文目錄 deleted.

CHUANG-TZŬ see under LAO-TZŬ

CHUNG-SHAN HSÜEH SHU WÊN HUA CHI CHIN TUNG SHIH HUI

Chung-shan hsüeh shu wên hua chi chin tung shih hui.
(Chung-shan hsüeh shu wên hua chi chin tung shih hui yu kuan jên shih chu tso)

中山學術文化基金董事會有關人士著作目錄

[臺北   中山學術文化董事會   民國]58 i. e. 1969]

4, 2, 150 p. 26 cm.

Colophon title: 中山學術文化基金董事會有關人士著作
目錄

CHUNG YANG YEN CHIU YÜAN

Chung yang yen chiu yüan.
(Chung yang yen chiu yüan yüan shih chi yen chiu jên yüan chu tso mu lu)

中央研究院士及研究人員著作目錄   附:中央研究
院出版品目錄   中華民國建國六十年紀念   南港
[中央研究院編輯出版]   民國60 [1971]

732 p. 27 cm.

Title on p. [4] of cover: Titles and publications of academicians and research staffs of the Academia Sinica.

CHURCH, JAMES EDWARD see under Snow
(Poulton)

CHURCH

Chiesa locale. Roma, Edizioni pastorali, [1972?]

61 p. 23½ cm. (Quaderni di aggiornamento bibliografico. Serie Teologia pastorale, 4)

CHURCH AND EDUCATION

Little, Lawrence Calvin, 1897–
Religion and public education: a bibliography. Lawrence C. Little, compiler. Pittsburgh, University of Pittsburgh, Program in Religious Education, School of Education, 1966.

v, 203 p. 29 cm.

Little, Lawrence Calvin, 1897–
Religion and public education; a bibliography. Lawrence C. Little, compiler. 3d ed., rev. and enl. Pittsburgh, University of Pittsburgh Book Center, 1968.

v, 214 p. 28 cm.

CHURCH AND STATE

Veilleux, Bertrand.
Bibliographie sur les relations entre l'Église et l'état au Canada français, 1791–1914. Montréal, Bibliothèque, Centre d'études canadiennes-françaises, Université McGill, 1969.

92 l. 29 cm.

Compiled for the Centre d'études canadiennes-françaises.

CHURCH ARCHITECTURE

Poscharsky, Veronika.
Bibliographie des Kirchenbaues und der kirchlichen Kunst der Gegenwart. Im Auftrag des Institutes für Kirchenbau und Kirchliche Kunst der Gegenwart. Marburg/Lahn, 1963–64.

4 v. 21 cm.

CHURCH CALENDAR

Marwinski, Felicitas.
Zu einem glückseligen neuen Jahr gedruckt. 43 Wand- u. Wappenkalender aus d. Jahren v. 1568–1781 beschrieben, erläutert u. mit e. Namen- u. Sachregister versehen v. Felicitas u. Konrad Marwinski. Weimar, (Nationale Forschungs- u. Gedenkstätten [d. klassischen deutschen Literatur]) 1968.

101 p., 5 plates. 22 cm.

CHURCH COUNCILS   see   Councils and synods

CHURCH HISTORY   see   Ecclesiastical history

CHURCH MUSIC
    see also Hymns

Daniel, Ralph T
The sources of English church music, 1549–1660; compiled by Ralph T. Daniel and Peter Le Huray. London, Stainer and Bell for the British Academy, 1972.

2 v. (x, 159 p.) music. 25 cm. (Early English church music. Supplementary volume 1)

Gombosi, Marilyn, *comp.*
Catalog of the Johannes Herbst Collection. Edited by Marilyn Gombosi. Chapel Hill, University of North Carolina Press [1970]

xix, 255 p. facsims., music. 24 cm.

Thematic catalog of Moravian Church music copied by Johannes Herbst.

Metcalf, Frank Johnson, 1865–1945.
American psalmody; or, Titles of books containing tunes printed in America from 1721 to 1820. Compiled by Frank J. Metcalf. New introd. by Harry Eskew. New York, Da Capo Press, 1968.

x, 54 p. facsims. 24 cm. (Da Capo Press music reprint series)

"This Da Capo Press edition is an unabridged republication of the first edition published in New York in 1917."

Wilkes, Roger.
English cathedrals and collegiate churches and chapels: their music, musicians and musical establishments: a select bibliography. London, Friends of Cathedral Music [1968].

[2], 12 p. 21 cm.

CHURCH OF SCOTLAND

Scotland. Record Office.
Records of the Church of Scotland; preserved in the Scottish Record Office and General Register Office, Register House Edinburgh. Glasgow, Scottish Record Society, 1967.

34 p. 22 cm. (Scottish Record Society, v. 94)

CHURCH SLAVIC LITERATURE

Chernysheva, N   F
(Katalog russkikh knig kirillovskoĭ pechati)
Каталог русских книг кирилловской печати XVI–XVIII вв. Москва, 1972.

37 p. 20 cm.

Cover title.
At head of title: Министерство культуры РСФСР. Государственная публичная историческая библиотека.

Kubans'ka-Popova, M   M
Києво-Печерський державний історико-культурний заповідник; стародруки XVI–XVIII ст. Катадог. Автор тексту та упорядник М. М. Кубанська-Попова. Київ, Мистецтво, 1971.

78 p. 59 plates. 23 cm.

Pekarskiĭ, Petr Petrovich, 1828–1872.
(Opisanie slavi͡ano-russkikh knig i tipografiĭ)
Описаніе славяно-русскихъ книгъ и типографій 1698–1725 годовъ. Санктпетербургъ, Общественная польза, 1862. [Cambridge, Oriental Research Partners, 1972]

ii, 694, xxv p. 23 cm. (His Наука и литература въ Россіи при Петрѣ Великомъ, т. 2)

Zernova, Antonina Sergeevna, 1883–
Сводный каталог русской книги кирилловской печати XVIII века. Москва, 1968.

567 p. 21 cm.
At head of title: Государственная ордена Ленина библиотека СССР имени В. И. Ленина. Отдел редких книг.
Compiled by A. S. Zernova and T. N. Kameneva.

CHURCHILL, SIR WINSTON LEONARD SPENCER

Woods, Frederick.
A bibliography of the works of Sir Winston Churchill

-кɢ, ᴏᴍ, ᴄʜ. 2nd revised ed. London, Kaye & Ward, 1969.

398 p., 5 plates. illus., port. 23 cm.

Woods, Frederick.
A bibliography of the works of Sir Winston Churchill, K. G., O. M., C. H. by Frederick Woods. ₍2d ed. rev. Toronto₎ University of Toronto Press ₍1969₎

398 p. port. 23 cm.

CHUVASHIAN LITERATURE

I͡Ur'ev, Mikhail Ivanovich.
Чăваш писателĕсем. Био-библиографи справочникĕ. Шупашкар, Чăваш АССР кĕнеке изд-ви, 1968.

370 p. ports. 21 cm.

CINCINNATI. UNIVERSITY

Schueler, Frances S 1928–
University of Cincinnati faculty publications and creative works, 1965 and 1966. ₍Compiled by Frances S. Schueler and Mary E. Kirkpatrick. Cincinnati₎ University of Cincinnati, 1967.

64 p. 23 cm.

CINEFLUOROGRAPHY

McDonagh, K **M**
Cinefluorography. Compiled by K. M. McDonagh. Adelaide, State Library of South Australia, 1968.

47 p. 26 cm. (State Library of South Australia. Research Service. Bibliographies, ser. 4, no. 116)

CINEMA see Moving-pictures

CIRCADIAN RHYTHMS

U. S. *Federal Aviation Administration. Library Services Division.*
Circadian rhythms; selected references ₍compiled by Louise Annus Heller₎ Washington, 1968.

82 p. 26 cm. (*Its* Bibliographic list no. 15)

CIRCUS

Amsterdam. Universiteit. *Bibliotheek.*
Catalogus van de circus-bibliotheek. Nagelaten door K. D. Hartmans. ₍Amsterdam, Universiteitsbibliotheek (Singel 423)₎ 1968–

v. port 24 cm. (*Its* Speciale catalogi, nieuwe serie, no. 4)

Brabec, Jan.
Artistik. Auswahl-Bibliographie. Von Jan Brabec ₍und₎ (Julius) Markschiess-van Trix. Berlin, Deutsche Staatsbibliothek, 1968.

III, 147 p. with illus. 21 cm.

Toole-Stott, Raymond.
A bibliography of books on the circus in English from 1773 to 1964. Derby, Eng., Harpur, distributors ₍1964₎

80 p. 22 cm.

Cover title: English circus books.
Errata slip inserted.

Ulrich, Walter, 1897–
Bibliographie der deutschen Circus- und Varieté-Litera-

tur. Die Artistik in Schrifttum und Kunst. Abgeschlossen mit 1. Halbjahr 1966. (Wien, Orbis-Zeitungsdienst, 1966)

24 p. 21 cm. (Schriftenreihe der Internationalen Gesellschaft der Circus-Historiker, Heft 7)

CÍSAŘOVÁ, ANNA KOLÁŘOVÁ

Křivský, Pavel.
Anna Císařová-Kolářová. (1887–1963.) Literární pozůstalost. Zprac. Pavel Křivský. Praha, Památník nár. písemnictví. rozmn., 1970.

8, ₍1₎ p. 20 cm. (Edice inventářů, čís. 219)

At head of title: Literární archív Památníku národního písemnictví v Praze.

CITIES AND TOWNS
see also Metropolitan areas; Suburbs; Urbanization

Antinoro-Polizzi, Joseph A
Ghetto and suburbia; an urban reference guide ₍by₎ Joseph Antinoro-Polizzi ₍and₎ Joseph Vincent Versage. ₍1st ed.₎ Rochester, N. Y., Great Lakes Press; ₍distributed by Sociological Associates, 1973₎

xvi, 400 p. illus. 22 cm.

Australian Institute of Urban Studies.
Bibliography of urban studies in Australia ₍prepared by₎ Australian Institute of Urban Studies. Second volume, 1969–1971. Canberra City, Australian Institute of Urban Studies, 1972.

vii, 107 p. 30 cm.

First vol., 1966–1968, edited by G. Walkley, was published in 1971.

Bibliographie zur Stadtgeographie: deutschsprachige Literatur 1952–1970 ₍von₎ Peter Schöller ₍et al.₎ Paderborn, F. Schöningh, 1973.

xvi, 139 p. 30 cm. (Bochumer geographische Arbeiten, Heft 14)

Bryfogle, R **Charles,** 1941–
Urban problems: a bibliography for a secondary school geography course ₍by₎ R. Charles Bryfogle. Mary Vance, editor. Monticello, Ill., Council of Planning Librarians, 1971.

66 p. 28 cm. (Council of Planning Librarians. Exchange bibliography, 196)

Cover title.

—————— A bibliography of non-print and audio-visual materials for a secondary school geography course, supplement to Exchange bibliography no. 196 ₍by₎ R. Charles Bryfogle. Mary Vance, editor. Monticello, Ill., Council of Planning Librarians, 1972.

64 p. 28 cm. (Council of Planning Librarians. Exchange bibliography, 259)

Danckaert, Lisette.
Negentien Belgische steden in kaart en prent. ₍Tentoonstelling georganiseerd in samenwerking met het Gemeentekrediet van België in Brussel, Albert 1-Bibliotheek, van 10 januari tot 18 februari 1968₎ Brussel ₍Koninklijke Bibliotheek, Keizerslaan 4₎ 1968.

vi, 95, ₍26₎ p. illus., maps, plans. 26 x 19 cm. (Catalogus nr. 27)

Also issued in French edition under the title: Plans et vues de dix-neuf villes Belges.

Davidson, Claud M
Rural and suburban towns: spatial characteristics of change in population and functional structure, by Claud M. Davidson. Mary Vance, editor. Monticello, Ill., Council of Planning Librarians, 1972.

18 p. 28 cm. (Council of Planning Librarians. Exchange bibliography, 272)

Dollinger, Philippe.
Bibliographie d'histoire des villes de France, préparée par Philippe Dollinger ... Philippe Wolff ... Avec la collaboration de Simonne Guenée ... Paris, C. Klincksieck, 1967.

756 p. map. 24 cm.

At head of title: Commission internationale pour l'histoire des villes.

Fritschler, A   Lee, 1937–
Urban affairs bibliography; a guide to the literature in the field [by] A. Lee Fritschler, B. Douglas Harman [and] Bernard H. Ross. 2d ed. Washington, School of Government and Public Administration, American University, 1970.

iv, 94 p. 28 cm.

Index kommunalwissenschaftlicher Literatur: Bücher.
Index of publications on local government and urban studies: books. Nr. 1–
Mai 1970–
Wien, Kommunalwissenschaftliches Dokumentationszentrum.

no. 21 x 29 cm. 2 no. a year.

At head of title: KDZ.

Index to current urban documents.   v. 1–
July/Oct. 1972–
Westport, Conn., Greenwood Press.

v. 26 cm. quarterly.

Keyser, Erich, 1893–1968.
Bibliographie zur Städtegeschichte Deutschlands, unter Mitwirkung zahlreicher Sachkenner hrsg. von Erich Keyser. Köln, Böhlau, 1969.

ix, 404 p. col. map (in pocket) 24 cm. (Acta Collegii Historiae Urbanae Societatis Historicorum Internationalis)

On spine: Städtebibliographie Deutschlands.

Liniger-Goumaz, Max.
Villes et problèmes urbains de la République démocratique du Congo, bibliographie. Genève, les Éditions du Temps, 1968.

86 l. 27 cm.

Shandanova, Lilîana.
(Sotsialno-ikonomicheskoto razvitie na grada, petnadeseti-devetnadeseti v.)
Социално-икономическото развитие на града, XV–XIX в. : библиогр. обзор на бълг. книжнина / [състав. Лиляна Шанданова и Стефка Ангелова ; под ред. на Николай Тодоров и Веселин Трайков]. — София : БАН, 1974.

221 p. ; 22 cm.
At head of title: Българска академия на науките. Институт за балканистика. Международен център за научни изследвания и документация.
Includes index.

Smith, Suzanne M
An annotated bibliography of small town research, prepared by Suzanne M. Smith. Madison, Dept. of Rural Sociology, University of Wisconsin, 1970.

vii, 137 l. 28 cm.

Stelter, Gilbert Arthur, 1933–
Canadian urban history; a selected bibliography, compiled by Gilbert A. Stelter. Sudbury, Laurentian University Press, 1972.

ii, 61 p. 28 cm. (Laurentian University. Social science research publication no. 2)

Tal'man, Rina Osipovna.
Города Таджикистана; указатель литературы. [Составитель Р. О. Тальман. Отв. редактор Н. Н. Негматов] Душанбе, Ирфон, 1967.

87 p. illus. 20 cm.

At head of title: Государственная республиканская библиотека Таджикской ССР им. Фирдоуси. Библиографический отдел.

Tashkend.   Gosudarstvennaîa publichnaîa biblioteka.
Города Узбекистана; указатель литературы. [Составитель С. И. Кейзер] Ташкент, Гос. изд-во Узбекской ССР, 1964.

95 p. 20 cm.

At head of title: Государственная республиканская библиотека УзССР им. А. Навои.

U. S. *Air Force Academy.   Library.*
The States and the urban crisis. [Colorado Springs] 1969.

46 p. 21 cm. (*Its* Special bibliography series, no. 43)

U. S. *Dept. of Housing and Urban Development.*
Selected readings on urban affairs; a limited selection of current books which are pertinent to urban affairs. Washington [1967]

20, 5 p. 26 cm.

Usan, M   N
(Zarubezhnye goroda)
Зарубежные города. Каталог иностр. карт и атласов. Москва, 1972.

103 p. 20 cm. free

At head of title: Государственная библиотека СССР имени В. И. Ленина. Отдел картографии.
By M. N. Usan and L. A. Khobotova.

Voronezh, Russia (City)   Oblastnaîa biblioteka.
Города Воронежской области; указатель литературы. [Составитель А. Ванина] Воронеж, Центрально-Черноземное книжное изд-во, 1965.

46 p. 20 cm.

At head of title: Областное управление культуры. Областная библиотека им. И. С. Никитина.
"К 50-летию советской власти."

Walkley, Gavin.
Bibliography of urban studies in Australia. Preliminary ed. Canberra, Australian Institute of Urban Studies, 1969.

[viii], 116 p. 30 cm.

Walkley, Gavin.
Bibliography of urban studies in Australia. First edition, 1966–1968. Edited by Gavin Walkley with the assistance of Barbara Goodhew. Canberra, National Library of

grafie. Les grandes agglomérations en Belgique. Bibliographie analytique sélective. Brussel, Belgische Commissie voor Bibliografie, 1966.

3 v. (lxiii, 755 p.) tables. 20½ cm. (Bibliographia Belgica, 91)

Wallace, Rosemary H
International bibliography and reference guide on urban affairs, edited by Rosemary H. Wallace. Ramsey, N. J., Ramsey-Wallace Corp., 1966.

iii, 92 l. 28 cm.

Waterhouse, Alan.
Urban development in Mediaeval Europe: a bibliography. Monticello, Ill., Council of Planning Librarians, 1971.

20 l. 28 cm. (Council of Planning Librarians. Exchange bibliography 232)

White, Anthony G
City types, : a selected bibliography / Anthony G. White ; Mary Vance, editor . — Monticello, Ill. : Council of Planning Librarians, 1974.

5 p. ; 28 cm. — (Exchange bibliography - Council of Planning Librarians ; 687)

Wurman, Richard Saul, 1935–
Making the city observable. Minneapolis, Walker Art Center [1971]

96 p. illus. 29 cm. (Design quarterly [80])

Žebrytė, Jonė.
Pažinkime gimtąjį kraštą : literatūros rodyklė / J. Zebryte. — Vilnius : Lietuvos TSR Kulturos ministerija, 1974.

277 p. ; 22 cm.

At head of title: Lietuvos TSR Valstybinė respublikinė biblioteka.

PERIODICALS

Index kommunaler Zeitschriften. Ausg. 1-
Okt. 1970–
[Wien, Kommunalwissenschaftliches Dokumentationszentrum]

v. 21 x 30 cm.

At head of title, 1970–   : KDZ.

Svenska stadshistoriska institutet.
Register över stadshistorisk litteratur 1945–1963 behandlad i de stadshistoriska revyerna 1947–1970. Stockholm, Stadshistoriska institutet; Eksp.: Svenska kommunförbundet, (distr.) 1972.

78 p. 30 cm.

PLANNING
   see also Housing; Regional planning;
   Urban renewal

Association of Engineers and Architects in Israel. *Building Centre, Haifa.*
A bibliography on town and country planning in Israel, 1949–1964. Prepared on the occasion of the 27th World Congress for Housing and Planning, Jerusalem, 21–28 June 1964.

ביבליוגרפיה על תכנון פיסי בישראל, 1949–1964 ... חיפה, אגודת האינג׳נרים והארכיטקטים בישראל. מרכז הבניה. 1964.

20 p. 25 cm.

Barr, Charles W
Australian planning and development: a selected bibliography [by] Charles W. Barr. [Monticello, Ill., Council of Planning Librarians] 1973.

26 p. 29 cm. (Council of Planning Librarians. Exchange bibliography 505)

Bestor, George Clinton.
City planning; a basic bibliography of sources and trends [by] George C. Bestor and Holway R. Jones. Sacramento, California Council of Civil Engineers and Land Surveyors, 1966.

xv, 195 p. 28 cm.

Bestor, George Clinton.
City planning bibliography; a basic bibliography of sources and trends, by George C. Bestor and Holway R. Jones. 3d ed. New York, American Society of Civil Engineers, 1972.

xv, 518 p. 23 cm.

Published in 1962 and 1966 under title: City planning.

Branch, Melville Campbell, 1913–
Comprehensive urban planning; a selective annotated bibliography with related materials, by Melville C. Branch. Beverly Hills, Calif., Sage Publications [1970]

477 p. 24 cm.

Budapest. *Fővárosi Levéltár.*
A Fővárosi Levéltárban őrzött építési tervek jegyzéke; a budai és az óbudai levéltár építési tervei. Összellitotta: Farkas Elemérné. Budapest, Művelődésügyi Minisztérium Levéltári Osztálya, 1965.

2 v. (xxxiii, 556 p.) 29 cm. (Levéltári jegyzékek 8)
Summary also in German, French, and Russian.

Canadian Council on Urban and Regional Research.
Urban & regional references; [références] urbaines & régionales, 1945–1962. [Ottawa, 1964]
1 v. (loose-leaf) forms. 30 cm.
Preliminary pages in English and French; listings in English or French.

—— ———— Supplement.
Ottawa.
v. 26 cm. annual.
English or French.

Canadian Council on Urban and Regional Research.
Urban and regional references; [références] urbaines and regionales, 1945–1969. Ottawa [1970]

xi, 796 p. 27 cm.

"A cumulation of the preceding six numbers listing materials that appeared between World War II and 1970 plus selected earlier documents."
Preliminary pages in English and French; listings in English or French.

Carroll, Michael Anthony.
An exploration of the relationship between urban planning and human behavior: toward the identification of professional responsibilities, by Michael A. Carroll. [Monticello, Ill., Council of Planning Librarians] 1968.

22 l. 29 cm. (Council of Planning Librarians. Exchange bibliography 60)
Caption title.
Thesis (M. A.)—University of Illinois.

Cockburn, Cynthia.
A bibliography on planning education. London, Centre for Environmental Studies, 1970.

43 p. 30 cm. (Centre for Environmental Studies. Information papers, 13)

Dembowska, Zofia.
Bibliografia zagadnień struktury przestrzemnej jednostek osadniczych i ośrodków miejskich. Warszawa, Państwowe Wydawn. Naukowe, 1967.

139 p. 24 cm. (Instytut Podstawowych Problemów Planowania Przestrzennego Politechniki Warszawskiej. Materiały i studia)

Duisburg. Stadtbücherei.
Raum und Stadt. Ein Auswahlverzeichnis zu Problemen der Raum- und Stadtplanung. (Bearb. von Wilhelm Lübbe.) Duisburg, Stadtbücherei (1969).

97 p. 21 cm.

Eastern Michigan University. Library.
City and regional planning; an annotated bibliography of books and U. S. documents in the University Library. Compiled by Hannelore B. Rader. [Ypsilanti, Mich., 1970-

v. 29 cm. (Its Bibliography series, no. 6

Ehler, Charles N
Environmental systems planning and management: a preliminary sorting of literature [by] Charles N. Ehler. Monticello, Ill. [Council of Planning Librarians] 1972.

64 p. 29 cm. (Council of Planning Librarians. Exchange bibliography 251)

Fadeeva, G   P
(Tendentsii razvitiia krupnykh gorodskikh aglomeratsii)
Тенденции развития крупных городских агломераций. (Библиогр. указ. отеч. и иностр. информ. материалов 1967–1971 гг.) [Сост. Г. П. Фадеева]. Москва, 1972.
60 p. 21 cm.
At head of title: Центр научно-технической информации по гражданскому строительству и архитектуре. Справочно-информационный фонд.

Guia de pesquisa de habitação e urbanismo. 1968–
Rio de Janeiro.

v. 30 cm.

Vols. for 1968-   compiled by the Instituto Brasileiro de Bibliografia e Documentação for the Serviço Federal de Habitação e Urbanismo.

Guttenberg, Albert Z
Environmental reform in the United States: the Populist-Progressive era and the New Deal, by Albert Z. Guttenberg. [Monticello, Ill., Council of Planning Librarians, 1969]

15 l. 28 cm. (Council of Planning Librarians. Exchange bibliography 85)

Harrison, James D
An annotated bibliography on environmental perception with emphasis on urban areas [by] James D. Harrison. [Monticello, Ill., Council of Planning Librarians, 1969]

41 l. 29 cm. (Council of Planning Librarians. Exchange bibliography 93)

Howard, William Arby, 1931–
Remote sensing of the urban environment, a selected bibliography, compiled by William A. Howard. [Monticello, Ill., Council of Planning Librarians, 1969]

6 l. 28 cm. (Council of Planning Librarians. Exchange bibliography 60)

Kraemer, Kenneth L
The systems approach in urban administration-planning, management, and operations, by Kenneth L. Kraemer with the collaboration of Ralph J. Lewis. [Monticello, Ill., Council of Planning Librarians, 1968]

60 l. 28 cm. (Council of Planning Librarians. Exchange bibliography 49)

Misra, Surya Kant.
Building and planning in developing countries; a partially annotated bibliography. [By S. K. Misra] Stockholm, National Swedish Institute for Building Research, 1967.

71 p. 30 cm. (Rapport från byggforskningen, 28:1967)

Nippon Toshi Keikaku Gakkai.
(Toshi keikaku bunken mokuroku)
都市計画文献目録 〔東京〕 日本都市計画学会 1969.

286p. 22cm.

Obudho, Robert A
Urbanization, city, and regional planning of metropolitan Kisumu, Kenya: bibliographical survey of an East African city [by] Robert A. Obudho and Constance E. Obudho. Monticello, Ill., Council of Planning Librarians, 1972.

26 p. 28 cm. (Council of Planning Librarians. Exchange bibliography 278)

Ottersen, Signe Ruh.
Readings on natural beauty; a selected bibliography. Compiled by Signe Ruh Ottersen. Washington, U. S. Dept. of the Interior, Dept. Library, 1967.

iii, 94 p. 27 cm. ([U. S. Dept. of the Interior. Library] Bibliography no. 1)

Peng, George T   C
New town planning design and development; comprehensive reference materials [by] George T. C. Peng [and] Nakul S. Verma. Lincoln, University of Nebraska, 1971.

108 p. 21 cm.

Powell, David R
New towns bibliography [by] David R. Powell and Nan C. Burg. [Monticello, Ill., Council of Planning Librarians] 1972.

34 p. 29 cm. (Council of Planning Librarians. Exchange bibliography 249)

Cover title.
Introd. abstracted from New communities for Pennsylvania? By D. R. Powell.

Queensland. Dept. of the Co-ordinator-General of Public Works.
Bibliography of regional & urban studies; general and Australian references. [Brisbane] 1970.

1 v. (various pagings) 33 cm.

Australia for the Australian Institute of Urban Studies, 1971.

vii, 78 p. 30 cm.

"Preliminary edition [1966–1968] published 1969."

Ridder, Edmond de.
Grote agglomeraties in België. Analytische keuzebiblio-

(Sotsial'nye problemy gradostroitel'stva i arkhitektury)
Социальные проблемы градостроительства и архитектуры. Библиогр. указ. сов. литературы. 1967–1970 гг. Москва, 1971.

102 p. 24 cm.

At head of title: Научно-исследовательский институт теории, истории и перспективных проблем советской архитектуры Госгражданстроя. Центральная научно-техническая библиотека по строительству и архитектуре Госстроя СССР.

Edited by A. F. Krasheninnikov.

Spain. Ministerio de la Vivienda.
Catálogo de documentos informativos y resúmenes monográficos, 1960–1969. ₁Madrid, Servicio Central de Publicaciones₁ Ministerio de la Vivienda ₁19

v. 22 cm.

CONTENTS:
2. Urbanismo: Ordenación del territorio y planificación urbana.

Spearritt, Peter.
Selected writings of Sydney planning advocates, 1900–1947: a preliminary bibliography. Canberra, Metropolitan Research Trust, 1973.

vi, 21 l. 30 cm.

Town Planning Institute, *London*.
Planning research; a register of research of interest to those concerned with town and country planning, recording work commenced or completed during the period 1948 to 1963. 2d ed. London, 1965.

xxviii, 226 p. 31 cm.

Town Planning Institute, *London*.
Planning research: a register of research for all those concerned with town and country planning. 3rd ed. recording work commenced or completed during the period 1964–1967. London, Town Planning Institute, 1968.

xxviii, 236 p. 30 cm.

U. S. *Dept. of Housing and Urban Development.*
New communities; a bibliography. Washington; For sale by the Supt. of Docs., U. S. Govt. Print. Off. ₁1970₁

iv, 84 p. 26 cm.

U. S. Dept. of Housing and Urban Development. Library.
Environment and the community; an annotated bibliography. Washington, U. S. Dept. of Housing and Urban Development; for sale by the Supt. of Docs., U. S. Govt. Print. Off., 1971.

iii, 66 p. 27 cm.

U. S. *Housing and Home Finance Agency. Library.*
New communities; a selected, annotated reading list. ₁Washington₁ 1965.

24 p. 26 cm.

Železnikar, Iva.
Dokumentacijski pregled raziskovalne dejavnosti v SR Sloveniji (Regionalno prostorsko in urbanistično planiranje) Izdelal in priredil: Urbanistični inštitut SR Slovenije. Sestavila: Iva Železnikar s sodelovanjem Mire Lojk. Redakcija: Vinko Mlakar. Ljubljana, 1969.

v, 180 l. 29 cm. (Socialistična republika Slovenija. Biro za regionalno prostorsko planiranje. ₁Publikacija₁ 24)

Železnikar, Iva.
Slovenska urbanistična bibliografija za leto 1965. Kri-

tični pregled knjig, periodike, študijskega gradiva in načrtov s področja urbanizma ter bližnjih panog. Pripravila I. Železnikar. Ljubljana, Urbanistični inštitut SR Slovenije, 1966.

₁2₁, 80 l. 29 cm.

Železnikar, Iva.
Slovenska urbanistična bibliografija za leto 1966 in 1967. Sestavila Iva Železnikar s sodelovanjem Tanje Stefanciosa. Ljubljana, Urbanistični inštitut SR Slovenije, 1969.

vii, 148 l. 29 cm.

CITRUS   see Fruit

CITY CHURCHES

White, Anthony G
Religion as an urban institution: a selected bibliography ₁by₁ Anthony G. White. Monticello, Ill., Council of Planning Librarians, 1973.

11 p. 29 cm. (Council of Planning Librarians. Exchange bibliography 450)

CITY TRAFFIC

Chu, Chen.
Environmental effects of urban road traffic: an annotated bibliography. London, Centre for Environmental Studies, 1972.

77 p. 30 cm. index. (Centre for Environmental Studies. Information papers, 20)

Dobruská, Naděžda.
Dělba dopravní práce a řešení dopravy ve městech. Doporučující bibliogr. knižní a čas. lit. Sest. Naděžda Dobruská. Úvod: Jaroslav Vandas. 1. vyd. Praha, UVTEI-St. techn. knihovna, rozmn., 1968.

72 p. 21 cm. (Prague. Státní technická knihovna. Bibliografie, sv. 128)

Garbrecht, Dietrich.
Pedestrian movement: a bibliography. ₁Monticello, Ill., Council of Planning Librarians₁ 1971.

27 l. 28 cm. (Council of Planning Librarians. Exchange bibliography 225) $3.00

CIUDAD BOLÍVAR, VENEZUELA

Grases, Pedro, 1909–   comp.
Impresos de Angostura, 1817–1822; facsímiles. Caracas, Presidencia de la República, 1969.

117 p. facsims. 32 cm.

ČIURLIONIS, MIKALOJUS KONSTANTINAS

Čiurlionytė-Karužienė, Valerija.
Mikalojus Konstantinas Čiurlionis; bibliografija. Vilnius, Vaga, 1970.

682 p. 21 cm.

At head of title: Valerija Čiurlionytė-Karužienė, Simonas Egidijus Juodis, Vladas Žukas.

CIVIL DEFENSE

Florida. University, *Gainesville, Information Center for Civil Defense.*
Catalog of holdings as of January 1, 1967. ₁Gainesville₁

1967–

1 v. (loose-leaf) 28 cm.

At head of title: Architectural and engineering development.

Human Sciences Research, inc.
Civil defense bibliography, January 1966; a compilation of references relevant to the study of societal recovery from nuclear attack. [McLean, Va., 1966]

vii, 76 p. 29 cm.

Malwad, N   M
Civil defence: an annotated bibliography, 1960–1968. Compiled by N. M. Malwad. Trombay, India, Bibliography Unit, Library & Technical Information Section, Bhabha Atomic Research Centre, 1970.

vi, 244 p. 29 cm.

U. S. *Clearinghouse for Federal Scientific and Technical Information.*
Civil defense; a report bibliography. [Springfield, Va.] 1965.

1 v. (unpaged) 26 cm.

U. S. *Dept. of the Army. Army Library.*
Civil defense: 1960–67; a bibliographic survey. Washington. Dept. of the Army; [for sale by the Supt. of Docs., U. S. Govt. Print. Off.] 1967.

vi, 124 p. illus. 26 cm.

U. S. *Federal Aviation Agency. Library Services Division.*
Defense readiness: selected references. Washington, 1964.

iv, 37 p. 27 cm. (*Its* Bibliographic list no. 11)

CIVIL ENGINEERING

Information 70: a select list of publications and films. Watford, Building Research Station [1969]

59 p. 30 cm.

Institution of Civil Engineers, London.
Index to publications, January 1965 to December 1969. London (Great George St., S. W. 1), Institution of Civil Engineers, 1971.

[4], 114 p. 23 cm.

Liège. Université. *Centre d'études, de recherches et d'essais scientifiques des constructions du génie civil.*
Vingt années du Centre d'études, de recherches et d'essais scientifiques du génie civil. (Liège), Centre d'études, de recherches et d'essais scientifiques du génie civil, 1967.

63 p. 27 cm. (*Its* Mémoires, nouv. sér., no 20)

Smirnova, E   A
(Ekspluatatsiîa iskusstvennykh sooruzheniĭ)
Эксплуатация искусственных сооружений. Темат. указ. отеч. литературы 1968–1971 гг. [Сост. Е. А. Смирнова]. Москва, "Транспорт," 1973.

40 p. 20 cm.

At head of title: Министерство путей сообщения СССР. Центральная научно-техническая библиотека.

Tibbetts, D. C.
A bibliography on cold weather construction, compiled by D. C. Tibbetts. Rev. by G. G. Boileau. Ottawa, Division of Building Research, National Research Council, 1965.

1 v. (various pagings) 28 cm. (National Research Council, Canada. Division of Building Research. Bibliography no. 10)

BIBLIOGRAPHIES

Fraunhofer-Gesellschaft zur Förderung der Angewandten Forschung. *Dokumentationsstelle für Bautechnik, Stuttgart.*
Fortschritte im Bauwesen durch Auswertung des Schrifttums; Literaturzusammenstellungen. 2. Aufl. Stuttgart, 1965.

vii, 64 p. 20 cm.

Cover title.
Pref. also in English.

PERIODICALS

Abstract and index publications for the building industry. Stockholm, Institutet för byggdokumentation, 1969.

(1), 56 l. 30 cm. (Institutet för byggdokumentation. Rapport 1969:2)

Civil engineering periodicals index. v. 1–
Jan. 1964–
New Delhi [M. Kapila]

no. 24 cm. monthly (except July)

CIVIL LAW

Bibliographie des traductions des codes de droit privé des états membres du Conseil de l'Europe et de la Conférence de La Haye de droit international privé. Bibliography of translations of codes of private law in member states of the Council of Europe and the Hague Conference on Private International Law. Strasbourg, Conseil de l'Europe, 1967.

355 p. 24 cm.
Issued by the Council's European Committee on Legal Cooperation; compiled by Mme. G. van der Espt.

Trybulski, Zbigniew.
Bibliografia prawa i postępowania cywilnego; literatura, orzecznictwo. Warszawa, Wydawn. Prawnicze, 19

v. 25 cm.

CONTENTS:
t. 8. 1965–1969.

CIVIL RIGHTS

Armstrong, Douglas.
A selective bibliography on human and civil rights, compiled by Douglas Armstrong and Marian Dworaczek. [Toronto] Ontario Ministry of Labour, Research Library, 1973.

20 l. 28 cm.

Baskin, Alex.
The American Civil Liberties Union papers: a guide to the records, A.C.L.U. cases 1912–1946. Stony Brook, N.Y., Archives of Social History, 1971.

iii, 87 l. 28 cm.

Erçman, Sevinç.
Bibliographie concernant la Convention européenne des droits de l'homme. Bibliography relating to the European convention on human rights. [Strasbourg? Conseil de l'Europe, 1973]

ix, 129 p. 30 cm.

"This bibliography has been prepared by S. Erçman."

Ginger, Ann Fagan.
Human rights organizations and periodicals directory, 1973. Ann Fagan Ginger, editor. Berkeley, Meiklejohn Civil Liberties Institute [1973]

24 p. 28 cm.

International Institute of Human Rights.
Bibliothèque minimum dans le domaine des droits de l'homme. A basic library of books on human rights. Préparée à l'occasion du Festival international du livre, Nice 19 ᵒ qu [sic] 25 mai 1972. Strasbourg [1972]

10 p. 30 cm.

Ontario. Ministry of Labour. Research Branch. Library.
Human rights: a bibliography of government documents held in the Library, compiled by M. Dworaczek. [Toronto] Ontario Ministry of Labour Research Library, 1973.

34 p. 28 cm.

United States. Congress. Senate. Committee on the Judiciary. Subcommittee on Constitutional Rights.
List of publications, 1955–1972. Washington, U. S. Govt. Print. Off., 1972.

13 p. 24 cm.

At head of title: 92d Congress, 2d session. Committee print.

Wright, Robert Ernest Middleton, 1930–
Human rights: a booklist [compiled by R. E. M. Wright]. Worthing (Sussex), Worthing College of Further Education (College Library), 1968.

[4], 10 p. 1 illus. 26 cm.

JUVENILE LITERATURE

Detroit. Public Library. Children's Service.
Human rights; a list of books for boys and girls. [Compiled by the Children's Service of the Detroit Public Library. Rev. ed.]. Detroit, Public Library, 1966.

[16] p. 23 cm.

CIVIL SERVICE

National Civil Service League.
The disadvantaged and Government jobs: a bibliography. Washington, Manpower Press; [distributed by] Consortium Press [1973]

48 p. 29 cm.

First published by the League in 1970.

U. S. Civil Service Commission.
Guide to Federal career literature. [Washington; For sale by the Supt. of Docs., U. S. Govt. Print. Off.] 1969.

32 p. col. illus. 26 cm.

U. S. Civil Service Commission.
Guide to Federal career literature. [Washington; For sale by the Supt. of Docs., U. S. Govt. Print. Off., 1971]

28 p. 27 cm.

United States. Civil Service Commission.
Guide to Federal career literature. [Washington; For sale by the Supt. of Docs., U. S. Govt. Print. Off., 1972]

34 p. 26 cm.

U. S. *Civil Service Commission.*
Position classification and pay in the Federal Government. Washington, 1970.

63 p. 26 cm. (Personnel bibliography series no. 31)

United States. Civil Service Commission.
Position classification and pay in the Federal Government. Washington: [for sale by the Supt. of Docs., U. S. Govt. Print. Off.] 1973.

48 p. 27 cm. (Personnel bibliography series no. 50)

U. S. Civil Service Commission. Library.
Employee benefits and services. Washington, 1970.

150 p. 26 cm. (Its Personnel bibliography series, no. 33)

Cover title.
"Supplements two earlier numbers in the Personnel bibliography series, Federal employment: benefits, leave practices, and services, and Federal employment: retirement, insurance, and medical care, both issued in 1964."

United States. Civil Service Commission. Library.
Employee benefits and services. Washington; [for sale by the Supt. of Docs., U. S. Govt. Print. Off.] 1972 [i. e. 1973]

60 p. 27 cm. (Its Personnel bibliography series no. 47)

Supplements Personnel bibliography no. 33 published in 1970.

United States. Civil Service Commission. Library.
The Federal civil service — history, organization, and activities. Washington; [For sale by the Supt. of Docs., U. S. Govt. Print. Off.] 1971 [i. e. 1972]

55 p. 27 cm. (Its Personnel bibliography series, no. 43)

Cover title.
Supplement to The Federal civil service—history, organization, and activities, by E. Woodruff, 1962.

United States. Civil Service Commission. Library.
State, county, and municipal personnel publications. Washington; [For sale by the Supt. of Docs., U. S. Govt. Print. Off.] 1972.

79 p. 27 cm. (Its Personnel bibliography series no. 48)

CIVILIZATION

Berlin. Amerika-Gedenkbibliothek.
Konturen der Zukunft. (Bearb. von Bodo Gropius u. a.) Berlin, 1967.

39 p. 21 cm.

Eade, John Christopher.
Bibliographical essay on studies in eighteenth-century European culture in Australia since 1958. Prepared by J. C. Eade. [Sydney] Sydney University Press for the Australian Academy of the Humanities [1970]

39 p. 24 cm.

Ecsedy, Andorné.
Újkor [bibliográfia. Szerk. és írta Ecsedy Andorné és Gáliczky Éva] Budapest, Fővárosi Szabó Ervin Könyvtár, 1966–

v. 20 cm. (Történelmi ismeretterjesztő és szépirodalmi művek ajánló bibliográfiája)

Indiana. University. Lilly Library.
The Ian Fleming collection of 19th–20th century source material concerning Western civilization together with the originals of the James Bond-007 tales ₍catalogue. Bloomington, 1971 ?₎

53 p. illus. 28 cm. (Lilly Library publication no. 12)

On cover: Ian Lancaster Fleming.

National Council for the Social Studies. *World Civilization Booklist Committee.*
World civilization booklist; supplementary reading for secondary schools. Morris Gall, chairman; Arthur E. Soderlind, co-chairman. Washington ₍°1968₎

xii, 234 p. 23 cm. (National Council for the Social Studies. Bulletin 41)

Outgrowth of NCSS bulletin no. 31 which appeared under the title World history book list published in 1959.

CIVILIZATION, GRECO-ROMAN

Akademie der Wissenschaften, Berlin. Institut für Griechisch-Römische Altertumskunde.
Veröffentlichungen des Instituts für Griechisch-Römische Altertumskunde, sowie seiner Mitarbeiter, 1955–1964. Berlin, 1965.

72 p. 21 cm.

Ashbridge, Jean.
Classical studies: background reading for secondary schools: an annotated booklist: selected by Jean Ashbridge and R. A. Hubbard in consultation with the Joint Association of Classical Teachers. London, National Book League, 1968.

25 p. 22 cm.

Includes a section on Roman Britain.

Vidman, Ladislav.
Bibliografie řeckých a latinských studií v Československu za léta 1951–1960. Bibliographia studiorum graecorum et latinorum in Bohemoslovenia MCMLI–MCMLX. Praha, Státní knihovna ČSSR, 1966.

146 p. 21 cm. (Bibliografický katalog ČSSR. České knihy 1966. Zvláštní seš. 1)

Prefaratory matter and table of contents also in Latin.

PERIODICALS

Dunedin, N. Z. University of Otago. Library.
Check-list of classical periodicals in New Zealand libraries. ₍Dunedin₎ University of Otago, 1970.

29 p. 26 cm.

Cover title.
1967 edition issued by University of Otago Dept. of Classics.

CIVILIZATION, GREEK

Demetrius, James Kleon.
Greek scholarship in Spain and Latin America. With an introd. on the history of Greek scholarship in Spain by Lluis Nicolau D'Olwer, and a pref., by Phil Conley. Chicago, Argonaut, 1965.

144 p. 22 cm.

CIVILIZATION, HISPANIC

Utrecht. Rijksuniversiteit. *Spaans, Portugees en Ibero—Amerikaans Instituut.*
Spain, Portugal and Latin America: catalogue of a collection of works in the field of Ibero-American literature and of works relating to the Spanish and Portuguese speaking countries, published in Eastern Europe. Utrecht, Bibliotheek der Rijksuniversiteit te Utrecht, 1965.

iv, 70 l. 25 cm.

CLARE, JOHN

A Check list of books by and about John Clare (chiefly from a private collection). Wilbarston ₍Eng.₎ Pilgrim Publications, 1970.

20 p. port. 22 cm.

Cover title: The poet Clare.

The **Poet** Clare. Market Harborough (Leics.), Pilgrim Publications, 1970.

3 leaves and pamphlet (₍5₎, 20 p.) in pocket. port. 28 cm.

Cover title.
"An address to a copy of Clare's poems": leaf ₍3₎
The pamphlet consists of "A check list of books by and about John Clare (chiefly from a private collection)"

CLARINET AND CLARINET MUSIC

Errante, F Gerard.
A selective clarinet bibliography. Compiled by F. Gerard Errante. Oneonta, N. Y., Swift-Dorr Publications, c1973.

82 p. 29 cm.

Gillespie, James E
Solos for unaccompanied clarinet: an annotated bibliography of published works, by James E. Gillespie, Jr. Detroit, Information Coordinators, 1973.

79 p. 23 cm. (Detroit studies in music bibliography, 28)

CLARK, KENNETH BANCROFT

Jenkins, Betty.
Kenneth B. Clark; a bibliography. ₍Compilers: Betty Jenkins, Lorna Kent and Jeanne Perry. 1st ed. New York, Metropolitan Applied Research Center, 1970₎

v, 60 p. 28 cm.

CLARK, SIR KENNETH MACKENZIE

Slythe, R Margaret.
Kenneth Clark, Lord Clark of Saltwood: bibliography research R. Margaret Slythe. Revised ed. Bournemouth, Bournemouth and Poole College of Art, 1971.

24 p. facsim. 22 cm. (Guides to the published work of art historians, no. 1)

Previous ed. published as Sir Kenneth Clark, 1968.

Slythe, R Margaret.
Sir Kenneth Clark; edited by R. Margaret Slythe. Bournemouth, Bournemouth and Poole College of Art ₍1968₎

24 p. 21 cm. (Guides to the published work of art historians, no. 1)

Stagg, Lynette Eleanor.
Sir Kenneth MacKenzie Clark, 1903–   ; a bibliogra-

phy of his published works including letters to "The Times", compiled by Lyn Eleanor Stagg. Johannesburg, University of the Witwatersrand, Department of Bibliography, Librarianship and Typography, 1969.

ₓᵥᵢ, 80 p. 30 cm.

Compiled in part fulfilment for the requirements of the Diploma in Librarianship, University of the Witwatersrand.

CLASS DISTINCTION   see   Social Classes

CLASSICAL ANTIQUITIES

Bibliografia d'archeologia classica. 1. ed. Roma, L'erma di Bretschneider, 1969.

139 p. 24 cm.

CLASSICAL LITERATURE
see also   Greek literature; Latin
literature

Catalogo delle edizioni di testi classici esistenti nelle biblioteche degli istituti stranieri di Roma. Roma, 1969.

xix, 544 p. 25 cm.

At head of title: Unione Internazionale degli Istituti di archeologia, storia e storia dell'arte in Roma.
Edited by B. Guidi, A. Zaretti.

Clarke, Adam, 1760?–1832.
A bibliographical dictionary; plus, The bibliographical miscellany (a supplement to the dictionary) With a foreword by Francesco Cordasco. Metuchen, N. J., Mini-Print Corp., 1971.

1 v. (unpaged) 31 cm.

Reprint of the 1802–04 and 1806 ed.

Gwinup, Thomas.
Greek and Roman authors; a checklist of criticism ₍by₎ Thomas Gwinup and Fidelia Dickinson. Metuchen, N. J., Scarecrow Press, 1973.

x, 194 p. 22 cm.

Hazel, John.
A list of Greek and Latin texts in print; compiled by J. Hazel. London (31 Gordon Sq., W. C. 1), Joint Association of Classical Teachers, Committee on Editions of Classical Texts, 1971.

₍1₎, 19 p. 20 cm.

"The third version of the list originally compiled by Mr. G. I. F. Tingay in 1966."

Kroh, Paul.
Lexikon der antiken Autoren. Stuttgart, A. Kröner ₍c1972₎

xvi, 675 p. 18 cm. (Kröners Taschenausgabe, Bd. 366)

Marouzeau, Jules, 1878–1964.
Dix années de bibliographie classique; bibliographie critique et analytique de l'antiquité gréco-latine pour la période 1914–1924. New York, B. Franklin ₍1969₎

2 v. (xv, 1286 p.) 24 cm. (Collection de bibliographie classique)
Burt Franklin bibliography and reference series, no. 227.
A continuation of Scarlat Lambrino's Bibliographie de l'antiquité classique, 1886–1914. Continued by l'Année philologique ... 1924/26–

"Originally published 1927–28. Reprinted 1969."
CONTENTS.—1. ptie. Auteurs et textes.—2. ptie. Matières et disciplines.

Moss, Joseph William, 1803–1862.
A manual of classical bibliography: comprising a copious detail of the various editions of the Greek and Latin classics, and of the critical and philological works published in illustration of them, with an account of the principal translations, into English, French, Italian, Spanish, German, etc. 2d ed. Port Washington, N. Y., Kennikat Press ₍1969₎

2 v. 23 cm.

Reprint of the 1837 ed.

Palmer, Henrietta Raymer, 1867–
List of English editions and translations of Greek and Latin classics printed before 1641, by Henrietta R. Palmer. With an introd. by Victor Scholderer. ₍Folcroft, Pa.₎ Folcroft Library Editions, 1970.
xxxii, 119 p. 26 cm.
"150 copies."
Reprint of the 1911 ed., issued in series: Bibliographical Society, London. Publications.

Stock, Leo.
Literaturverzeichnis für den Latein- und Griechischunterricht. Frankfurt ⟨M.⟩ Norddeutsche Verlagsanstalt Goedel, 1966–68.

2 v. 21 cm.

CONTENTS.—T. 1. Latein, bearb. von L. Stock.—T. 2. Griechisch, bearb. von M. Schilling.

TRANSLATIONS

Beardsley, Theodore S   1936–
Hispano-classical translations printed between 1482 and 1699, by Theodore S. Beardsley, Jr. Pittsburgh, Pa., Duquesne University Press, 1970.

xi, 176 p. 24 cm. (Duquesne Studies. Philological series, 12)

Modern Humanities Research Association monograph.

Parks, George Bruner, 1890–
The Greek and Latin literatures. Editors: George B. Parks and Ruth Z. Temple. New York, Ungar ₍1968₎

xix, 442 p. 27 cm. (The Literatures of the world in English translation: a bibliography, v. 1)

Smith, Frank Seymour.
The classics in translation; an annotated guide to the best translations of the Greek and Latin classics into English, by F. Seymour Smith. With a pref. by Henry Bartlett Van Hoesen. New York, B. Franklin ₍1968₎

307 p. 23 cm. (Burt Franklin bibliography & reference series, 240)

Essays in literature & criticism, 14.
Reprint of the 1930 ed.

CLASSICAL PHILOLOGY
see also   Greek philology; Latin
language; and under Dissertations,
Academic

American classical review. v. 1–
Feb. 1971–
New York, The City University of New York.

v. 26 cm. bimonthly.

Elkjær, Kjeld, 1916–
Danmark og antiken. Bibliografi over danske hjælpemidler til studiet af den klassiske oldtid. ₍Af₎ Kjeld Elkjær og Per Krarup. ₍Udg. af₎ Klassikerforeningen. 2. udg. ved Kjeld Elkjær og Georg Mondrup. København, Gyldendal, 1968.

139 p. 22 cm.

Engelmann, Wilhelm, 1808–1878.
Bibliotheca philologica; oder, alphabetisches Verzeichniss derjenigen Grammatiken, Wörterbücher, Chrestomathieen, Lesebücher und anderer Werke, welche zum Studium der griechischen und lateinischen Sprache gehören, und vom Jahre 1750, zum Theil auch früher, bis zur Mitte des Jahres 1852 in Deutschland erschienen sind. Hrsg. von Wilhelm Engelmann. Nebst einer systematischen Uebersicht. 3., umgearb. und verb. Aufl. [Walluf bei Wiesbaden] M. Sändig [1972]
v, 236 p. 21 cm.
Reprint of the 1853 ed. published in Leipzig.

Hübner, Emil, 1834–1901.
Bibliographie der klassischen Alterthumswissenschaft: Grundriss zu Vorlesungen über d. Geschichte u. Encyklopädie d. klass. Philologie/ Ernst Willibald Emil Hübner. — Nachdr. d. 2., verm. Aufl. Berlin 1889 — Hildesheim, New York: Olms, 1973.
xiii, 434 p.; 19 cm.
First ed. published in 1876 under title: Grundriss zu Vorlesungen über die Geschichte und Encyklopädie der classischen Philologie.

Leeds, Eng. University. Institute of Education. Library.
Catalogue of the National Collection of Greek and Latin school text-books (1800 onwards) [by] William B. Thompson and J. D. Ridge. [Leeds (Yorkshire)] University of Leeds (Institute of Education), 1970–
v. 30 cm.
CONTENTS: pt. 1. Dictionaries. Grammars. Vocabularies. Notes and miscellanea. Courses. Composition manuals (prose and verse). Readers. Selections.

Library of the Hellenic and Roman Societies and the Institute of Classical Studies.
A selection of additions to the library 1968–1969. London, University of London, 1969.
23 p. 22 cm.

Norton, Mary E
A selective bibliography on the teaching of Latin and Greek, 1920–69 [by] Mary E. Norton. New York, ERIC Clearinghouse on the Teaching of Foreign Languages [1971]
45 p. 27 cm.

Ooteghem, Jules van.
Bibliotheca graeca et latina. A l'usage des professeurs des humanités gréco-latines. [Par] J. Van Ooteghem. 3e éd. [Namur, Wesmael-Charlier]; [pour les] Éditions de la revue "Les Études classiques," Namur, (1969).
[vi], 387, 107 p. 23 cm.

Pökel, Wilhelm.
Philologisches Schriftsteller-Lexikon. (Unveränderter reprografischer Nachdruck der Ausg. Leipzig 1882.) Darmstadt, Wissenschaftliche Buchgesellschaft, 1966.
viii, 328 p. 24 cm.

Pöschl, Viktor.
Bibliographie zur antiken Bildersprache. Unter Leitung von Viktor Pöschl bearb. von Helga Gärtner und Waltraut Heyke. Heidelberg, C. Winter, 1964.
xvi, 674 p. 25 cm. (Bibliothek der klassischen Altertumswissenschaften. Neue Folge. 1. Reihe)
At head of title: Heidelberger Akademie der Wissenschaften.

Semi, Francesco.
Manuale di filologia classica. Con repertorio di termini linguistici e filologici a cura di Paolo Zonelli. Padova, Liviana, 1969 [i. e. 1970].
viii, 372 p. illus. 24 cm.

PERIODICALS

Brearley, Denis George, 1940–
A union list of classical periodicals in the university libraries of Ottawa, compiled by Denis G. Brearley. [Ottawa] University of Ottawa, Bibliothèque centrale/Central Library, 1970.
v, 107 leaves. 28 cm.
Lists holdings of Carleton University Library, Saint Paul University Library, and University of Ottawa Libraries.

CLASSIFICATION OF BOOKS see Library Science - Processing

CLAUDEL, PAUL

Bibliographie des œuvres de Paul Claudel. Paris, Les belles lettres [1973]
191 p. 24 cm. (Annales littéraires de l'Université de Besançon, 144. Centre de recherches de littérature française (XIXe et XXe siècles) [Publications] v. 10)

Hubert, Marie Clotilde.
Paul Claudel, 1868–1955. Préface de Pierre-Henri Simon ... [Catalogue par Marie-Clotilde Hubert. Avant-propos par Étienne Dennery.] Paris, Bibliothèque nationale, 1968.
xxiv, 174 p. plates. 21 cm.

Labriolle, Jacqueline de.
Claudel and the English speaking world, a critical bibliography. Edited and translated [from the French ms.] by Roger Little. London, Grant and Cutler, 1973.
173 p. 23 cm. (Research bibliographies & checklists, 6)

CLAVIJERO, FRANCISCO JAVIER

Pasquel, Leonardo.
Bibliografía de Clavijero. [México, Editorial Citlaltépetl, 1971]
157 p. illus. 18 cm. (Colección Suma veracruzana. Serie Bibliografía)

CLAY

Reichard, Ernő.
A tégla- és cserépipar irodalma; tájékoztató és ajánló bibliográfia. Budapest, Épitőanyagipari Központi Kutató Intézet, 1964.
203 p. 23 cm.

CLEANING

Weeks, Lloyd E
Bibliographical abstracts on evaluation of brightening agents for detergent usage [1929–1961] Prepared by L. E. Weeks, J. L. Staubly and W. A. Millsaps. Philadelphia, American Society for Testing and Materials, 1964.
v, 26 p. 23 cm. (American Society for Testing and Materials. Special technical publication no. 177–A)

Willett, Ronald Paul, 1933–
Laundry and drycleaning: coin-operated and nonauto-

matic ₍by₎ R. P. Willett and J. R. Grabner. Revision. Washington, Small Business Administration, 1965.

8 p. 26 cm. (Small business bibliography no. 22)

Caption title.
"Originally issued as Small business bulletins no. 22, Automatic laundries, and 40, Laundry and dry cleaning."

Willett, Ronald Paul, 1933–
Laundry and drycleaning: coin-operated and nonautomatic ₍by₎ R. P. Willett and J. R. Grabner. Revision. Washington, Small Business Administration, 1966.

8 p. 26 cm. (Small business bibliography no. 22)

CLEMENS, SAMUEL LANGHORNE
see also under Dissertations, Academic

Asselineau, Roger.
The literary reputation of Mark Twain from 1910 to 1950; a critical essay and a bibliography. Westport, Conn., Greenwood Press ₍1971₎

240 p. 23 cm. (Publications de la Faculté des lettres de l'Université de Clermont. Fasc. hors-sér.)
Reprint of the 1954 ed.
Originally presented as the author's thesis, Université de Paris.

Institutul Romîn pentru Relatiile Culturale cu Străinăta-tea.
Mark Twain in Romania; bibliography of the Romanian translations published in volume and in magazines, 1888–1966. Bucharest, Romanian Institute for Cultural Relations with Foreign Countries 1967.

47 p. 20 cm.

Johnson, Merle De Vore, 1874–1935.
A bibliography of the works of Mark Twain, Samuel Langhorne Clemens: A list of first editions in book form and of first printings in periodicals and occasional publications of his varied literary activities. Rev. and enl. Westport, Conn., Greenwood Press ₍1972, c1935₎

xiii, 274 p. 22 cm.

Webb, David S
Mark Twain holdings in the Missouriana Library, compiled by David S. Webb and Paul O. Selby. Kirksville, Northeast Missouri State College, 1968.

62, 3, ₍24₎ l. 28 cm.

A catalogue of the Missouriana Library, Pickler Memorial Library, Northeast Missouri State College.

CLEVELAND, GROVER

U. S. *Library of Congress. Manuscript Division.*
Index to the Grover Cleveland papers. Washington, ₍For sale by the Superintendent of Documents, U. S. Govt. Print. Off.₎ 1965.

xi, 345 p. 29 cm. (*Its* Presidents' papers index series)

CLEVELAND, JOHN

Morris, Brian Robert.
John Cleveland (1613–1658): a bibliography of his poems, by Brian Morris. London, Bibliographical Society, 1967.

vii, 61 p. front. (port.). 25½ cm. (Bibliographical Society publication 1065)

CLIMATOLOGY
see also Meteorology

Budapest. Országos Műszaki Könyvtár és Dokumentációs Központ.
Klimatizálás. Budapest, 1968.

70 p. 20 cm. (*Its* A tudomány és technika újdonságai magyar nyelven; ajánló bibliográfia, 31. sz.)

Chandler, Tony John.
Selected bibliography on urban climate, prepared by T. J. Chandler. Geneva, Secretariat of the World Meteorological Organization, 1970.

383 p. 28 cm. (WMO no. 276.TP.155)

Hacia, Henry.
An annotated bibliography of climatic atlases and charts of the world. Silver Spring, Md., U. S. Environmental Data Service, 1970.

2 v. 26 cm.

"EDS/BM-79."

CONTENTS.—v. 1. Land areas.—v. 2. Oceans, seas, and islands.

Wilcocks, Julia Ruth Nadene.
The application of statistical methods to climatology: a selective bibliography. Johannesburg, University of the Witwatersrand, Department of Bibliography, Librarianship and Typography, 1971.

₍8₎, 38 p. 29 cm.

CLIPPINGS (BOOKS, NEWSPAPERS, ETC.)

Havlín, Otakar.
Výstřižková dokumentace ve Státním ústředním archivu. 1900–1946. Tematický rejstřík. Zprac. O. Havlín. Praha, St. ústř. archiv, rozmn., 1969.

19, 444, ₍2₎ p. 29 cm. (Inventáře a katalogy fondů Státního ústředního archivu v Praze, 19)

CLOCKS AND WATCHES

Franklin Institute, *Philadelphia. Library.*
Horological books and pamphlets in the Franklin Institute Library, compiled by Walter A. R. Pertuch and Emerson W. Hilker. 2d ed. Philadelphia ₍1968₎

109 l. 28 cm.

CLOTHING see Costume

CLOUDS

Murray, Francis W 1921–
An annotated bibliography of dynamic cloud modeling ₍by₎ F. W. Murray. Santa Monica, Calif., Rand Corp., 1968.

iii, 37 p. 28 cm. (Rand Corporation. Memorandum RM-5582-ESSA)

Research supported by the Environmental Science Services Administration, Dept. of Commerce, under contract no. E-37-67(n).

———— Supplement. Santa Monica, Calif., Rand Corp., 1968–

v. 28 cm. (Rand Corporation. Memorandum RM-5582/1-ESSA)

Ormsby, J P
An annotated bibliography on interpretation of clouds

and cloudiness by means of satellite photographs, 1965–1969
[by] J. P. Ormsby and B. E. Dethier. Ithaca, New York
State College of Agriculture, 1970.

76 p. 23 cm. (Cornell University Agricultural Experiment Station. Bulletin 1031)

Stepanova, Nina Alekseevna, 1906–
An annotated bibliography on cloudiness in the U. S. S. R.,
by Nina A. Stepanova. Washington, U. S. Environmental
Data Service, 1967.

v. 66 p. maps. 27 cm.

Cover title.
"WB/BS-6."
"Sponsored by Air Weather Service, Environmental Technical Applications Center, U. S. Air Force."
Compiled from available sources in the U. S. Weather Bureau Library and in the Library of Congress, issued prior to Dec. 1964.

CLOUGH, ARTHUR HUGH

Gollin, Richard M
Arthur Hugh Clough; a descriptive catalogue; poetry,
prose, biography, and criticism, by Richard M. Gollin,
Walter E. Houghton, and Michael Timko. [New York]
New York Public Library [1967]

117 p. port. 26 cm.

"Reprinted, with additions and revisions, from the Bulletin of the New York Public Library, July 1960, November 1966, January–March 1967."

CLOUTIER FAMILY

Louisiana. Northwestern State College of Louisiana,
Natchitoches. Russell Library.
The Cloutier collection, Louisiana Room, Russell Library;
a calendar with explanatory preface by Katherine F.
Bridges, Louisiana Librarian. Natchitoches, 1966.

35 l. 29 cm.

COAL; COAL MINING

Akimova, É   P
[Vorkuta ugol'naiá]
Воркута угольная. Указатель литературы за 1965–
1969 гг. Воркута, 1970.

107 p. 21 cm.

At head of title: Комбинат "Воркутауголь." Опорная научно
-техническая библиотека при ДНТЭП.
"Составили: Э. П. Акимова, В. Ф. Павленко."

Australia. Commonwealth Scientific and Industrial Research Organization. Division of Coal Research.
List of publications, January 1, 1952–December 31, 1966.
Chatswood, N. S. W., CSIRO Division of Mineral Chemistry [1966?]

46 p. 24 cm.

Averitt, Paul, 1908-
Bibliography and index of U.S. Geological Survey publications relating to coal, 1882-1970, by Paul Averitt and Lorreda
Lopez. Washington, U.S. Govt. Print. Off., 1972.

v, 173 p. 24 cm. (Geological survey bulletin 1377)

"Supersedes Circular 86."
Supt. of Docs. no.: I 19.3:1377

Belgium. *Archives de l'État, Liège.*
Inventaire des archives des Charbonnages de Gosson-

Kessales, par Georges Hansotte. Bruxelles, 1969.

17 p. 30 cm.

At head of title: Ministère de l'Éducation nationale. Archives
générales du Royaume. Archives de l'État à Liège.

Gilbert, Oscar E
Bibliography of Alabama coal, by Oscar E. Gilbert, Jr.,
and W. Everett Smith. University, Ala., Division of
Economic Geology, 1972.

55 p. 23 cm. (Geological Survey of Alabama. Circular 77)

Glass, Gary B
Bibliography of Wyoming coal, by Gary B. Glass and Richard
W. Jones. Laramie, Geological Survey of Wyoming, 1974.

163 p. maps. 23 cm. (Geological Survey of Wyoming. Bulletin 58)

Gukanova, E   A
Научные основы перевода предприятий угольной промышленности на новую систему планирования и материального стимулирования. Библиогр. указатель отечеств и зарубежной литературы. 1965–1968 гг. (1-е полугодие). [Сост. Гуканова Е. А.] Москва, 1968.

107 p. 20 cm. (Справочно-информационный фонд угольной
промышленности)

At head of title: Министерство угольной промышленности
СССР. Центральный научно-исследовательский институт экономики и научно-технической информации угольной промышленности. Центральная научно-техническая библиотека угольной
промышленности.

Kentucky. University. Geological Survey.
Bibliography of coal in Kentucky. Lexington, 1970.

vi, 73 p. map. 28 cm. (Its Series X. Special publication 19)

Kieffer, F   V
A bibliography of surface coal mining in the United
States to August, 1971, by F. V. Kieffer. Columbus, Ohio,
Forum Associates, 1972.

xi, 71 p. 22 cm.

Munn, Robert F
The coal industry in America; a bibliography and guide
to studies [by] Robert F. Munn. Morgantown, West Virginia University Library, 1965.

x, 230 p. 24 cm.

Palkova, V   IA
[Mekhanizatsiia vyemki ugol'nykh plastov pri pomoshchi strugov]
Механизация выемки угольных пластов при помощи
стругов. Библиогр. указ. отеч. и зарубеж. литературы
за 1968–1970 гг. [Сост. Палкова В. Я.] Москва, 1971.

55 p. 20 cm. (Справочно-информационный фонд угольной
промышленности)

At head of title: Министерство угольной промышленности
СССР. Центральный научно-исследовательский институт экономики и научно-технической информации угольной промышленности. Центральная научно-техническая библиотека угольной
промышленности.

**Perm', Russia (City). Nauchno-issledovatel'skiĭ ugol'nyĭ
institut.**
[Annotatsii nauchno-issledovatel'skikh rabot za 1971 god]
Аннотации научно-исследовательских работ за 1971
год. Пермь, 1972.

30 p. 21 cm.

At head of title: Министерство угольной промышленности СССР.

Ube Shiritsu Toshokan. Kyōdo Shiryōkan.
(Tankō shiryō mokuroku)
炭鉱史料目録　宇部市立図書館付設郷土資料館

宇都 昭和43(1968)
32 p. 22 cm.

United States. Atomic Energy Commission. Technical Information Center.
Coal processing : gasification, liquefaction, desulfurization : a bibliography, 1930–1974. — ₁Oak Ridge, Tenn.₁ : U. S. Atomic Energy Commission, Office of Information Services, Technical Information Center ; ₁Springfield, Va. : available from the National Technical Information Service, U. S. Dept. of Commerce₁, 1974.
vi, 757 p. ; 28 cm.

COASTS
see also Beaches

Cammack, John H
Bibliography of offshore and estuarine areas of Alabama with selected annotations, by John H. Cammack, Thomas J. Joiner, and Robert D. Schneeflock. University, Ala., Geological Survey, 1971.
vi, 50 p. illus. 23 cm. (Geological Survey of Alabama. Circular 69)
"Prepared in cooperation with the University of Alabama, University of South Alabama, and the South Alabama Regional Planning Commission."

Coastal Plains Center for Marine Development Services.
Coastal zone environmental bibliographies. Wilmington, N. C., 1973–
v. 28 cm. (Its Publication 73-1-

Walker, Harley Jessie, 1921–
Publications from coastal and marine research at Louisiana State University. Compiled by H. J. Walker. Baton Rouge, Museum of Geoscience, Louisiana State University, 1972.
32 p. 22 cm. (Mélanges, no. 6)

COBBETT, WILLIAM

Gaines, Pierce Welch.
William Cobbett and the United States, 1792–1835; a bibliography with notes and extracts by Pierce W. Gaines. Worcester, Mass., American Antiquarian Society, 1971.
xxi, 249 p. illus. 25 cm.

Pearl, Morris Leonard.
William Cobbett; a bibliographical account of his life and times, by M. L. Pearl. With a foreword by G. D. H. Cole. ₁Folcroft, Pa.₁ Folcroft Press, 1970.
vii, 266 p. 24 cm.
"Limited to 150 copies."
Reprint of the 1953 ed.

Pearl, Morris Leonard.
William Cobbett; a bibliographical account of his life and times, by M. L. Pearl. With a foreword by G. D. H. Cole. Westport, Conn., Greenwood Press ₁1971₁
vii, 266 p. 23 cm.
Reprint of the 1953 ed.

COBDEN, RICHARD

West Sussex, *Eng. County Records Office*.
The Cobden and Unwin papers: a catalogue; edited by Patricia Gill. Chichester (Sx.), West Sussex County Council, 1967.
v, 50 p. 25 cm.

West Sussex, *Eng. County Record Office*.
The Cobden papers; a catalogue, edited by Francis W. Steer. Chichester, West Sussex County Council, 1964.
xi, 125 p. illus., fold. geneal. tables. 25 cm.
On spine : Catalogue of the Cobden papers.

COCHRANE, HENRY CLAY

United States Marine Corps Museum.
Register of the Henry Clay Cochrane papers, 1809–1957, and undated, in the United States Marine Corps Museum, Quantico, Virginia, by C. F. W. Coker. ₁Quantico, Va.₁ 1968.
86 p. 23 cm. (Marine Corps Museum, Quantico, Va. Manuscript register series, no. 1)

COCKERELL, THEODORE DRU ALISON

Weber, William Alfred, 1918–
Theodore Dru Alison Cockerell, 1866–1948, by William A. Weber. Boulder, University of Colorado Press, 1965.
124 p. port. 26 cm. (University of Colorado studies. Series in bibliography, no. 1)

COCONUT

Bibliotheca Bogoriensis.
Bibliografi mengenai kelapa (Cocos nucifera L.) di Indonesia. (Bibliography on coconuts in Indonesia) Bogor ₁1968₁
33 p. 22 cm. (Its Seri bibliografi, no. 10, 1968)

Mattos, Carmelia Regina de.
Côco (Cocos nucifera L.); bibliografia das publicações que se encontram na Biblioteca dêste Instituto. Compilada por Carmelia Mattos, Dalva Natal e Herbene Rosa. Cruz das Almas, Brasil, 1970.
28 l. 29 cm. (Instituto de Pesquisas e Experimentação Agropecuárias do Leste. Lista bibliográfica, no. 20)

COCTEAU, JEAN

Orléans, France. Bibliothèque municipale.
Jean Cocteau, l'oiseleur, le Groupe des Six, Bibliothèque municipale d'Orléans. ₁17 octobre–22 novembre 1970.₁ Orléans, Bibliothèque municipale, Maison de la culture d'Orléans et du Loiret, 1970.
₁37₁ p. illus. 16 cm.
Exhibition catalog.

Société des amis du Musée des beaux-arts de Nantes.
Hommage à Jean Cocteau ... Nantes, 21 mai au 15 juin 1964. ₁Préfaces par Georges Auric, Julien Lanoe et René Bertrand₁ Nantes, Musée des beaux-arts, 1964.
63 p. plates. 24 cm.
"Exposition organisée par la Société des amis du Musée des beaux arts."
Illustrated cover.
"Supplément au catalogue": 8 p. inserted.

CODING THEORY

Dénes, József.
Kódelméleti bibliográfia. Készült a Központi Fizikai

Kutató Intézet és a Távközlési Kutató Intézet kódelméleti szemináriuma keretében 1968–ban. ₍Budapest, 1968₎

152 p. 28 cm.

COELENTERATA   see   Zoantharia

COELHO NETTO, HENRIQUE

Coelho Netto, Paulo, 1902–
Bibliografia de Coelho Netto, por Paulo Coelho Netto com a colaboração de Neuza do Nascimento Kuhn. Brasília, Instituto Nacional do Livro, 1972.

326 p. illus. 21 cm. (Instituto Nacional do Livro. Coleção Documentos, 4)

COFFEE

Viçosa, Brazil. Universidade Federal. Biblioteca Central. Seção de Bibliografia e Documentação.
Bibliografia do café (1952–1972); levantamento bibliográfico do material existente sobre café no acervo da Biblioteca Central da U. F. V. Viçosa, 1973.

vi, 124 p. 23 cm. (Universidade Federal de Viçosa. Biblioteca Central. Série Bibliografias especializadas, 3)

COIMBRA

Loureiro, José Pinto.
Bibliografia coimbrã. Coimbra, Câmara Municipal, 1964.

343 p. 24 cm.

COIMBRA. UNIVERSIDADE

Coimbra. Universidade. Biblioteca.
Catálogo da exposição bibliográfica, 1926–1966. ₍Coimbra₎ Biblioteca Geral da Universidade, 1966.

xviii, 729 p. 24 cm.

"Catálogo ... da actividade intelectual do corpo docente, dos técnicos e dos servidores da Universidade de Coimbra, registrando as obras publicadas ... no período que vai de 1926 a 1966."

COINS   see   Numismatics

COLD REGIONS   see   Polar regions

COLEMAN, JOHN WINSTON

Coleman, John Winston, 1898–
The collected writings of J. Winston Coleman, Jr. Introd. by Holman Hamilton. Lexington, Ky., Winburn Press, 1969.

ix, 112 p. plates, ports. 22 cm.

CONTENTS.—Bibliography.—Biographical sketches.—Poems.

COLERIDGE, SAMUEL TAYLOR

Savage, Basil.
Samuel Taylor Coleridge, 1772–1834: a list of books in print; ₍compiled by Basil Savage₎. London, St Panoras Library, 1972.

₍17₎ p. 11 x 23 cm.

Shepherd, Richard Herne, 1842–1895.
The bibliography of Coleridge; a bibliographical list, arranged in chronological order, of the published and privately-printed writings in verse and prose of Samual Taylor Coleridge, including his contributions to annuals, magazines, and periodical publications, posthumous works, memoirs, editions, etc. by Richard Herne Shepherd. Rev., corr., and enl. by W. F. Prideaux. ₍Folcroft, Pa.₎ Folcroft Press, 1970.

x, 95 p. 23 cm.
"Limited to 150 copies."
Reprint of the 1900 ed.

COLETTE, SIDONIE GABRIELLE

Cornand, Monique.
Colette: Paris, ₍10 mai–15 septembre₎ 1973, Bibliothèque nationale, ₍catalogue par Monique Cornand et Madeleine Barbin; avec la collaboration de Marie-Laure Chastang; préface par Étienne Dennery₎. Paris, Bibliothèque nationale, 1973.

xvi, 215 p. illu. 24 cm.

COLHOUN, EDMUND ROSS

U. S. *Library of Congress. Manuscript Division.*
Edmund Ross Colhoun; Charles O'Neil: a register of their papers in the Library of Congress. Washington, Library of Congress, 1967.

8, 9 l. 27 cm.

"Naval Historical Foundation collection."

COLLECTIVE BARGAINING

Hudson, Bennett.
Collective bargaining in higher education; a selected, annotated bibliography, by Bennett Hudson and James L. Wattenbarger. Gainesville, Institute of Higher Education, University of Florida, 1972.

16 l. 29 cm.

Kleingartner, Archie.
Professional and quasi-union organization and bargaining behavior; a bibliography. ₍Los Angeles, Institute of Industrial Relations, University of California, 1972₎

74 p. 28 cm.

Rothman, William A
A bibliography of collective bargaining in hospitals and related facilities, 1959–1968 ₍by₎ William A. Rothman. Ann Arbor, Institute of Labor and Industrial Relations, University of Michigan-Wayne State University, 1970.

106 p. 24 cm.

Rothman, William A
A bibliography of collective bargaining in hospitals and related facilities, 1969–1971 ₍by₎ William A. Rothman. Ann Arbor, Institute of Labor and Industrial Relations, The University of Michigan—Wayne State University, 1972.

127 p. 24 cm.

On spine: Collective bargaining in hospitals, 1969–1971.

Shimaoka, Helene R
Selected references on public employee collective bargaining, with emphasis on the State level, by Helene R. Shimaoka. ₍Honolulu₎ Industrial Relations Center, University of Hawaii, 1971.

iii, 47 p. 23 cm. (Industrial Relations Center. University of Hawaii. Occasional publications, 81)

On cover: Bibliography: public employee collective bargaining.

Shimaoka, Helene R

Topic coded titles on public employee collective bargaining, with emphasis on state and local levels, by Helene R. Shimaoka. 2d ed. ₁Honolulu₁ Industrial Relations Center, University of Hawaii, 1972.

55 p. 23 cm. (University of Hawaii. Industrial Relations Center. Occasional publications, 87)

United States. Division of Public Employee Labor Relations.

Current references and information services for policy decision-making in state and local government labor relations: a selected bibliography. ₁By Gilbert E. Donahue₁ Washington, 1971.

vii, 88 p. 27 cm.

COLLECTIVE FARMS

Biró, Ferenc.

Jövedelem és jövedelemrészesedés a termelőszövetkezetekben. ₁Összeállitotta: Biró Ferenc és Tóth Mátyás. Szerk. Barna Béláné₁ Budapest, Károlyi Mihály Országos Mezőgazdasági Könyvtár és Dokumentációs Központ, 1964.

91 p. illus. 21 cm. (Szakirodalmi tanácsadó, 20)

Gorbatov, A   L

История коллективизации сельского хозяйства СССР. Библиогр. указатель отечеств. литературы ... Москва, 1968.

88 p. 20 cm.

At head of title: Всесоюзная ордена Ленина Академия сельскохозяйственных наук имени В. И. Ленина. Центральная научная сельскохозяйственная библиотека.
"Составил А. Л. Горбатов."

COLLECTIVE SETTLEMENTS, ISRAELI   see   Kibbutz

COLLEGE CATALOGS   see   Catalogs, College

COLLEGE FACILITIES

California. State Colleges. Division of Institutional Research.

How big? a review of the literature on the problems of campus size. Los Angeles, 1970.

vi, 74 p. 28 cm. (Its Monograph no. 8)

Council of Educational Facility Planners.

Selected references for planning higher education facilities ₁by Carroll W. McGuffey and others₁ Edited by Kenneth R. Widdall, executive secretary. ₁Columbus, Ohio₁ 1968.

95 p. 28 cm.

D'Amico, Louis Anthony, 1920–

The spatial campus: a planning scheme with selected and annotated bibliography, by Louis A. D'Amico and William D. Brooks. Bloomington, School of Education, Indiana University, 1968.

iii, 118 p. 23 cm. (Bulletin of the School of Education, Indiana University, v. 44, no. 5)

ERIC Clearinghouse on Educational Facilities.

Planning in higher education; an interpretive bibliog-

raphy. Prepared by Norman P. Isler. Madison, ERIC Clearinghouse on Educational Facilities, University of Wisconsin, 1969.

6 v. 28 cm.
"Contract with the U. S. Office of Education ... OEC-1-7-07883-5005."
CONTENTS: pt. 1. Facilities and space utilization.—pt. 2. Campus planning.—pt. 3. Special facilities in higher education planning.—pt. 4. Case histories in campus planning.—pt. 5. Financial aspects of higher education planning.—pt. 6. The community and junior college.

New York (*State*). *University. Office of Planning in Higher Education.*

Campus and facilities planning in higher education: the process and the personnel; an annotated bibliography. ₁Developed by Philip S. Phelon₁ Albany, 1968.

iii, 18 p. 28 cm.

Parsons, Kermit Carlyle, 1927–

An annotated bibliography on university planning and development. compiled by Kermit C. Parsons ₁and₁ Jon T. Lang. New York, Society for College and University Planning, 1968 ₁i. e. 1969 or 70, ᶜ1969₁

158 p. 28 cm.
"First edition was published by the Council of Planning Librarians as Exchange bibliography no. 22 ... In ... 1964 a revised edition ... was published as Exchange bibliography no. 30. The present edition includes approximately 350 new listings and an alphabetical author-item title index."

COLLEGE STUDENTS   see   Students

COLLEGE TEACHING

Bucharest. Universitatea. Biblioteca Centrală. Sectorul de Documentare.

Probleme de pedagogie universitară contemporană. Bibliografie selectivă. București, 1972.

xxxi, 286 p. 21 cm.

At head of title: Biblioteca Centrală Universitară București. Sectorul de Documentare Universitară.
"Lucrare elaborată ... în cadrul Serviciului de Informare şi Documentare condus de Ileana Băncilă."

Hall, John, 1943–

University teaching methods: a select bibliography ₁compiled by J. Hall and D. E. Jones, indexed by P. Foster. 2d ed. Sheffield₁ University of Sheffield, 1973.

76 p. 30 cm.

At head of title: Sheffield University Library. Information Service.

Prior, Harm.

Kritische Bibliographie zur Hochschuldidaktik: 200 kommentierte Bücher u. Aufsätze/ Harm Prior. — Hamburg: Arbeitskreis f. Hochschuldidaktik 1971.

ii, 220 p.; 21 cm. — (Blickpunkt Hochschuldidaktik; Heft 17)

COLLEGE UNIONS   see   Student unions

COLLINS, CHARLES

Scollard, Robert Joseph.

A bibliography of the writings of Charles Collins / compiled by Robert J. Scollard ; with an introd. by J. Francis Mallon. — Toronto : Basilian Press, 1974.

24 p. : facsim. ; 22 cm. — (Basilian historical bulletin ; 9)

COLLINS, GREENVILLE

Verner, Coolie.
Captain Collins' Coasting pilot; a carto-bibliographical analysis. London, Map Collectors' Circle, 1969.

47 p. facsims., maps. 25 cm. (Map collectors' series, no. 58)

COLLINS, WILKIE

Parrish, Morris Longstreth, 1867–1944.
Wilkie Collins and Charles Reade: first editions described with notes, by M. L. Parrish with the assistance of Elizabeth V. Miller. New York, B. Franklin [1968]

x, 354 p. illus., facsims., ports. 24 cm. (Burt Franklin: bibliography and reference series, no. 186)

On spine: Bibliography of Wilkie Collins and Charles Reade. Reprint of the 1940 ed.

COLLIOURE, FRANCE

Archives départementales des Pyrénées-Orientales.
Inventaire analytique de la sous-série 3 B (Amirauté de Collioure, 1691–1790). Rédigé par Jean-Gabriel Gigot ... Perpignan, Direction des Services d'archives, 1968.

283 p. 24 cm.

At head of title: Département des Pyrénées-Orientales. Archives départementales.

COLOGNE

Cologne. Statistisches Amt.
Veröffentlichungen des Statistischen Amtes der Stadt Köln 1946 bis 1970; eine Bibliographie. Köln, 1971.

48 p. 21 cm.

Hartzheim, Joseph, 1694–1763.
Bibliotheca Coloniensis, in qua vita et libri typo vulgati et manuscripti recensentur omnium Archidioeceseos Coloniensis. Farnborough, Gregg P., 1967.

[456] p. 32 cm.

Kölner archivalische Kostbarkeiten: Ausstellung z. Einweihung d. neuen Hauses d. Histor. Archivs d. Stadt Köln vom 9. Dez. 1971–25. Febr. 1972/ [Bearb. d. Kataloges: Hugo Stehkämper.] — Köln: Histor. Archiv d. Stadt Köln [1971].

68 p., 15 l., insert., 15 col. ill.; 24 cm.

COLOMBIA

Bernal Villa, Segundo.
Guía bibliográfica de Colombia de interés para el antropólogo. [1. ed. Bogotá, Ediciones Universidad de los Andes, 1969 [cover 1970]

782 p. maps. 25 cm.

At head of title: Universidad de los Andes. Departamento de Antropología.

Colombia. *Departamento Administrativo Nacional de Estadística.*
Trayectoria bibliográfica del Departamento Administrativo Nacional de Estadística, 1952–1966. Publicación preparada por Armando Moreno Mattos, jefe de la División de Información. Bogotá, 1967.

10 l. 27 cm.

Florén Lozano, Luis, 1913–
Obras de referencia y generales de la bibliografía colombiana. Medellín, Editorial Universidad de Antioquia, 1968.

204, 22 l. 28 cm. (Publicaciones de la E. I. B. Serie: Bibliografía no. 28)

At head of title: Universidad de Antioquia. Escuela Interamericana de Bibliotecología.

Madrid. Museo Naval.
Catálogo de los documentos referentes a la independencia de Colombia existentes en el Museo Naval y Archivo de Marina "Bazán." Madrid, Consejo Superior de Investigaciones Científicas, Instituto Histórico de Marina, 1969.

xvii, 223 p. 25 cm.

Ocampo López, Javier.
Historiografía y bibliografía de la emancipación del Nuevo Reino de Granada. [1. ed.] Tunja, Universidad Pedagógica y Tecnológica de Colombia, 1969.

555 p. 24 cm. (Ediciones La Rana y el águila)

Piedrahíta P [   ], Dora.
Indice económico colombiano, 1967–1970 / compilado por Dora Piedrahíta P. — Medellín : Editorial Universidad de Antioquia, 1973.
v, 132 leaves ; 28 cm. — (Publicaciones de la E. I. B. : Serie Bibliografías ; no. 23)
At head of title: Universidad de Antioquia. Escuela Interamericana de Bibliotecología.
Continues Indice económico colombiano, 1960–1966, by M. C. Suaza Vargas.

Suaza Vargas, María Cristina.
Indice económico colombiano, 1960–1966. Medellín [Editorial Universidad de Antioquia, 1968]

xi, 263 l. 27 cm. (Publicaciones de la E. I. B. Serie: Bibliografías, no. 23)

Tesis (licenciatura en bibliotecología)—Universidad de Antioquia. "Continuación del Indice económico colombiano, 1951–1960."

Watson, Gayle Hudgens.
Colombia, Ecuador, and Venezuela: an annotated guide to reference materials in the humanities and social sciences. Metuchen, N. J., Scarecrow Press, 1971.

279 p. 22 cm.

"Outgrowth of the thesis done at the Graduate School of Library Science at the University of Texas at Austin."

Ziervogel, Barbara.
Kolumbien. Neuere Studien 1958–1969. (Bielefeld) Bertelsmann-Universitätsverl. (1969).
ix, 85 p. 24 cm. (Materialien des Arnold-Bergstrüsser-Instituts für Kulturwissenschaftliche Forschung, Bd. 25)

Bibliographien zur Politik und Gesellschaft lateinamerikanischer Länder.

GOVERNMENT PUBLICATIONS

Bibliografía oficial colombiana. no. 1–
1964–
Medellín, Escuela Interamericana de Bibliotecología.

no. in v. 28 cm.

Mesa, Rosa Quintero.
Colombia, compiled by, Rosa Quintero Mesa. Ann Arbor, Mich., University Microfilms, 1968.

xv, 137, 3 p. 29 cm. (Latin American serial documents, v. 1)

Prepared under a grant from the Ford Foundation to the University of Florida Libraries.

Peraza Sarausa, Fermín, 1907–
Publicaciones oficiales colombianas, por Fermín Paraza y José Ignacio Bohórquez C. Gainesville, Fla., 1964.

iv, 31 l. 28 cm. (Biblioteca del bibliotecario, 69)

IMPRINTS

Texas. University. Library. Latin American Collection.
Recent Colombian acquisitions. no. 1; 1962/64. Austin.

60 l. 28 cm.

Continued by the publication with the same title issued by the body under the later name of the university: **Texas. University at Austin.**

Texas. University at Austin. Library. Latin American Collection.
Recent Colombian acquisitions. no. 2–
Aug. 1965/Dec. 1968–
Austin.

no. 28 cm.

Continues the publication with the same title issued by the body under the earlier name of the university: **Texas. University.**

LAW see Law - Colombia

MAPS

Cortés, Vicenta.
Catálogo de mapas de Colombia. Madrid, Ediciones Cultura Hispánica, 1967.

337 p. facsims. 21 cm.

Kapp, Kit S
The early maps of Colombia up to 1850, by Kit S. Kapp. London, Map Collectors' Circle, 1971.

32 p. maps. 25 cm. (Map collectors' series, 8th vol., no. 77)

COLOMBIAN LITERATURE

Orjuela, Héctor H
Fuentes generales para el estudio de la literatura colombiana; guía bibliográfica [por] Héctor H. Orjuela. Bogotá, 1968.

xl. 863 p. 24 cm. (Publicaciones del Instituto Caro y Cuervo. Series bibliográfica, 7)

COLOMBO, CRISTOFORO

Aboal Amaro, José Alberto.
Catálogo sistemático de la Biblioteca Colombina de Montevideo, República Oriental del Uruguay. Montevideo, Ediciones de la Biblioteca, 1966.
144 p. 25 cm. (Publicaciones de la Biblioteca Colombina)
"Edición privada de 100 ejemplares. Ejemplar número 74."
"La colección de libros, folletos, revistas, boletines, memorias, mapas, etc., relacionada con don Cristóbal Colón, Américo Vespucio, el descubrimiento de América y el origen de su nombre, que formaba parte del repositorio de la Colombina, se guarda, ahora, en la Biblioteca de la Universidad [del Estado de Nueva York en Stony Brook]."
"Suplemento" (p. [123]–144) lists material transferred to the Museo Histórico Nacional de Montevideo in 1960 and material acquired by the Biblioteca Colombina after the transfer to the State University at Stony Brook.

Major, Richard Henry, 1818–1891.
The bibliography of the first letter of Christopher Columbus, describing his discovery of the New World. Amsterdam, Meridian, 1971, [1972].

84 p. with illus. 23 cm.

Reprint of the London, 1872 ed.

COLONIZATION

Collotti Pischel, Enrica.
L'Internationale communiste et les problèmes coloniaux. 1919–1935. [Par] Enrica Collotti Pischel [et] Chiara Robertazzi. Paris, La Haye, Mouton & Co., 1968.

584 p. 24 cm. (Matériaux pour l'histoire du socialisme international. 2. série: Essais bibliographiques, 2)

Wisconsin. University. *Land Tenure Center. Library.*
Colonization and settlement: a partially annotated bibliography. Madison, Wis., [Land Tenure Center, University of Wisconsin] 1965.

45, viii p. 28 cm. (Training and methods series, 5)

COLOR

Dzięgielewski, Tadeusz.
Bibliografia dotycząca kolorystyki w budownictwie przemysłowym. Oprac. Tadeusz Dzięgielewski, Klara Hermelińska. Warszawa, 1967.

142 p. 29 cm. (Instytut Urbanistyki i Architektury. Seria prac własnych zesz. 150)

At head of title: Instytut Urbanistyki i Architektury.

Kelly, Kenneth Low, 1910–
Colorimetry and spectrophotometry: a bibliography of NBS publications, January 1906 through January 1973 [compiled by] Kenneth L. Kelly. [Washington] National Bureau of Standards; [for sale by the Supt. of Docs., U.S. Govt. Print. Off.] 1974.
51 p. 26 cm. (NBS special publication 393)

COLOR-PRINTING

Moore, Nicholas Lister, 1946–
Electronic colour scanners: a select bibliography; compiled by N. L. Moore. [Hatfield], [Hertis], [1972].

49 p. 30 cm.

COLORADO

Colorado. *Division of State Archives and Public Records.*
Checklist [of] Colorado publications received. v. 1–
Oct./Dec. 1964–
Denver.

v. in 28 cm. quarterly.

Masthead title, 1964– Checklist of Colorado public documents.

Colorado. University. *Bureau of Governmental Research and Service.*
A selected bibliography of Colorado State and local government, by Morris J. Schur, research assistant. Boulder, 1964.

viii, 99 p. illus. (1 in pocket) 23 cm.

A List of Colorado State publications.

Denver, Colorado State Library.

v. in 28 cm.

"A selected checklist."
Compiler: S. L. Judd.

COLORED PEOPLE (SOUTH AFRICA)

Jacobson, Evelyn.
The Cape Coloured: a bibliography, compiled by Evelyn

Jacobson. 2nd imp. Cape Town. University of Cape Town Libraries. 1972.

[7], 50 p. 23 cm. (University of Cape Town Libraries. Bibliographical series)

"Presented in partial fulfillment of the requirements for the Higher Certificate in Librarianship, 1945."

Taylor, Cecily Johanna.
Coloured education; a bibliography. Cape Town, University of Cape Town Libraries, 1970.

[viii], 21 p. 23 cm. (University of Cape Town. School of Librarianship. Bibliographical series)

Presented in partial fulfilment of the requirements for the Higher Certificate in Librarianship, 1966.

COLUMBIA RIVER

Water Resources Scientific Information Center.
A selected annotated bibliography on Columbia & Snake Rivers. Compiled for the State of Washington, Dept. of Ecology. Olympia, Wash., Dept. of Ecology, 1973.

iii, 357 p. 28 cm. (Water Resources Information System. WRIS information bulletin no. 6)

COLUMBUS, CHRISTOPHER see Colombo, Cristoforo

COLUMBUS, OHIO

Redmond, John Oliver.
A checklist of Columbus, Ohio, imprints for the years 1833–1841; with a historical introduction. 1966.

iv, 109 l. 29 cm.

Typescript (carbon copy)
Thesis (M. s. in L. s.)—Catholic University.

COMENIUS, JOHANN AMOS

Bečková, Marta.
Komeniana, vydaná knižně od roku 1945. Sest. Marta Bečková. Praha, 1967.

56 l. 20 cm.

At head of title: Státní pedagogická knihovna Komenského v Praze (Ústřední pedagogická knihovna ČSSR)
Introductory matter also in Russian, English, German, and French.

CONTENTS.—Spisy Komenského.—Literatura o Komenském.

Berlász, Piroska.
Comenius Magyarországon kiadott műveinek lelőhely-bibliográfiája. [Az anyagot gyűjtötte: Berlász Piroska és Horánszky Nándor. Szerk.: Kondor Imre] Budapest, 1970.

91 p. facsims. 26 cm. (Neveléstörténeti bibliográfiák, 1)

Added t. p.: Bibliographia operum Comenii in Hungaria typis mandatorum ad loca ubi asservantur composita.

Kalkušová, Slávka.
Jan Amos Komenský. Soupis lit. z fondů Kraj. knihovny v Čes. Budějovicích. České Budějovice, Kraj. knihovna, rozmn., 1970.

20 p. 29 cm.

"U příležitosti 300. výročí úmrtí J. A. Komenského."

Körbrová, Zuzana.
Komeniana v Městské knihovně. Zuzana Körbrová. Praha, Městská knihovna, rozmn., 19

v. 20 cm.

Malinová, Miluše.
Jan Ámos Komenský. Soupis knih z fondu St. věd. knihovny v Hradci Králové. Sest. Miluše Malinová. Hradec Králové, St. věd. knihovna, rozmn., 1970.

26 p. 20 cm. (Publikace SVK, č. 6/70)

Osińska, Wanda.
Jan Amos Komenský w Polsce; repertorium prac Komeńskiego, znajdujących się w polskich księgozbiorach. Wrocław, Zakład Narodowy im. Ossolińskich, 1972.

174 p. illus., facsims. 24 cm. (Źródła do dziejów nauki i techniki, t. 12)

Svojtková, Věra.
Pedagogický ústav J. A. Komenského. Československá akademie věd, 1954–1969. [Sestavila Věra Svojtková] Praha, PÚ JAK ČSAV, 1969.

256 p. 21 cm.

COMIC BOOKS, STRIPS, ETC.

France. Centre régional de documentation pédagogique, Bordeaux.
Les Bandes dessinées [du 19 janvier au 21 mars 1970. Catalogue par Pierre Pascal.] Bordeaux, C. R. D. P., 75, cours d'Alsace-Lorraine, 1970.

122 p. illus., 8 plates. 18 cm.

Exhibition catalog.

Inleiding tot het Belgisch stripverhaal. (Tentoonstelling, Albert I-Bibliotheek van 29 juni tot 25 augustus 1968) Brussel, 1968.

xix, 80 p. illus. 26 cm. ([Catalogi van tentoonstellingen gehouden in de Albert I-Bibliotheek te Brussel, nr. 30])

Issued also under title: Introduction à la bande dessinée belge.

Kaukoranta, Heikki.
Suomalaiset sarjakuvajulkaisut. Teck nade serier i Finland. Comic books in Finland. 1904–1966. Helsinki, 1968.

xxi, 78 (2) p. 23 cm. (Helsingin yliopiston kirjaston julkaisuja, 84)

Kempkes, Wolfgang.
Bibliographie der internationalen Literatur über Comics. International bibliography of comics literature. Hrsg. von Wolfgang Kempkes. München-Pullach, Verlag Dokumentation, 1971.

213 p., [10] p. of illus. 21 cm.

Foreword, and table of contents also in English.

Kempkes, Wolfgang.
Bibliographie der internationalen Literatur über Comics. International bibliography of comics literature. 2. verb. Aufl. New York, R. R. Bowker Co., 1974 [c1973]

293 p. illus. 21 cm.

In the 1st ed. (1971) the English title appeared first on t. p.

Kempkes, Wolfgang.
Bibliographie der internationalen Literatur über Comics. International bibliography of comics literature/ Wolfgang Kempkes. — 2., verb. Aufl. — Pullach/München: Verlag

Dokumentation, 1974.

293 p.: ill.; 22 cm.

Introduction and preface and table of contents also in English.

Kempkes, Wolfgang.
International bibliography of comics literature. Bibliographie der internationalen Literatur über Comics. New York, R. R. Bowker Co., 1971.

213 p. illus. 22 cm.

English and German.

Overstreet, Robert M
The comic book price guide. 1st– ed.; 1970– Cleveland, Tenn.

v. illus. 22 cm.

"Books from 1933—present included."

Shuppan Kagaku Kenkyūjo.
(Jiryū ni notta "komikkubon")
時流に乗った"コミック本" 東京 出版科学研.
究所 昭和44(1969)

21 p. 26 cm. (解説シリーズ 108)

COMMERCE
see also Business

Arnold, Joyce M
Bibliography for libraries established in export promotion centers, by Joyce M. Arnold. [n. p.] 1965.

ii, 36 l. 29 cm.

Catalogue of free foreign trade directories. Nottingham, Trade Guide Publications, 1966.

24 p. illus. 23 cm.

Commercial index. v. 1– Jan. 1966–
[Calcutta]

v. 25 cm. monthly.

Contracting Parties to the General Agreement on Tariffs and Trade. *International Trade Centre.*
Répertoire bibliographique: Sélection de statistiques du commerce international. Genève, 1967.

iv, vi, 150 p. 28 cm.

At head of title: GATT. Centre du commerce international.
On cover: Statistiques du commerce international.

Dlesková, Vlasta.
Knižní literatura z oboru politické ekonomie, světového hospodářství, mezinárodních organizací, vztahů a pod. Zprac. Vlasta Dlesková a kol. Praha, Oborové středisko VTEI Výzkumného ustavu pro zahraniční obchod, 1971.

135 p. 29 cm. (Základní bibliografie zahraničního obchodu, 2 díl, 14 dodatek)

Gt. Brit. *Board of Trade. Economic Research Unit.*
Competition, monopoly and restrictive practices: a select bibliography. London: H. M. S. O., 1970.

[3], 127 p. 31 cm.

Compiled by the Economic Research Unit, with the assistance of the Economics Division of the Board of Trade Library.

International Trade Centre.
Compendium of sources: international trade statistics; an analytical compilation of foreign trade statistics published by international agencies and national governments the world over, with an introduction on their use in market research. Geneva, GATT International Trade Centre, 1967.

150 p. 29 cm.

Nauchnoizsledovatelski institut po vŭnshna tŭrgoviiâ.
(Bibliografiiâ na trudovete na NII za vŭnshna turgoviiâ)
Библиография на трудовете на НИИ за външна търговия, 1963–1972. София, Научноизследователски институт за външна търговия, 1972.

47 p. 29 cm.

Organization for Economic Cooperation and Development.
Library.
Les rélations commerciales Est-Ouest. East-West trade relations. [Paris] 1966.

v, 95 p. 27 cm. (*Its* Bibliographie spéciale analytique 7 (44))

Organization of American States.
Bibliografiá de comercio exterior. Bogotá, 1968.

73 l. 29 cm.

Ostrava, Czechoslovak Republic (City) Státní vědecká knihovna.
Obchodní interiér a exteriér; bibliografie. [Sest.: Jaroslava Lehká] Ostrava, 1967.

69 l. 29 cm. (*Its* Publikace. řada II, č. 415)

Przegląd dokumentacyjny z zakresu handlu wewnętrznego.
r. 22– 1972–
Warszawa, Instytut Handlu Wewnętrznego, Ośrodek Informacji Naukowo-Technicznej i Ekonomicznej.

v. 20 x 29 cm. quarterly.

Continues Przegląd bibliograficzny z zakresu handlu wewnętrznego.

Sandström, Curt, 1943–
Företagsekonomisk dokumentation 1960–1970. Av C[urt] Sandström och C[hrister] Ullvetter. Göteborg, Forskning och information, [1971].

39, (211) p. 30 cm.

Segers, Agnes.
Het industrieel aspect in het Engels commercialistisch mercantilisme, 1660–1727. L'aspect industriel dans le commercialisme mercantiliste anglais. Der industrielle Aspekt im englischen kommerziellen Merkantilismus. The industrial aspect of English commercial mercantilism. Brussel, Belgische Commissie voor Bibliografie, 1973.

x, 176 p. 21 cm. (Bibliographia Belgica, no. 119)
Introd. in English, Flemish, French, and German.

Smith, George Mayo.
World wide business publications directory, by George M. Smith and Herbert J. Smith. New York, Simon and Schuster [1971]

xvi, 593 p. 26 cm.

Uhlig, Zofia.
Przewodnik po literaturze z zakresu ekonomiki, organizacji i techniki handlu. Warszawa, Zakład Wydawn. CRS, 1966.

63 p. 21 cm. (Biblioteka spółdzielni zaopatrzenia i zbytku)

Wojciechowska, Wanda.
Księgi adresowe, katalogi międzynarodowych targów i wystaw w zbiorach Informacji techniczno-ekonomicznej. ₁Oprac. zespół pod kierunkiem Zbigniewa Stolarskiego w składzie: Wanda Wojciechowska, Maria Pfeffer, Franciszek Wyszyński.₁. Warszawa, 1968.

136 p. 21 cm. (Centralny Instytut Informacji Naukowo-Technicznej i Ekonomicznej. Informacje, wskazówki, wytyczne, 10/68)

At head of title: Centralny Instytut Informacji Naukowo-Technicznej i Ekonomicznej.

BIBLIOGRAPHIES

Besterman, Theodore, 1904–
Commerce: manufactures and labour; a bibliography of bibliographies. Totowa, N. J., Rowman and Littlefield, 1971 ₁i. e. 1972₁

2 v. (823 p.) 20 cm. (His The Besterman world bibliographies)

CATALOGS

Taehan Muyŏk Chinhŭng Kongsa. Muyŏk Tosŏgwan.
資料目錄 ₁서울₁ 大韓貿易振興公社貿易圖書館 1965–67.

2 v. 26 cm.

Added t. p.: Kotra Library catalogue.

Tōkyō Toritsu Hibiya Toshokan.
近藤記念海事財団文庫目錄 付·書名索引 ₁東京₁ 昭和41 ₁1966₁

57 p. illus. 26 cm.

On cover: 東京都立日比谷図書館蔵

Unione italiana delle camere di commercio, industria e agricultura. Biblioteca.
Catalogo dei volumi e delle pubblicazioni periodiche italiane ed estere nella Biblioteca dell'Unione, 1966. Roma, Azienda beneventana tip. editoriale ₁1966₁
169 p. 24 cm.
—— Catalogo della Biblioteca dell'Unione: supplemento dello schedario per argomenti. Roma, Azienda beneventana tip. editoriale ₁1966₁
38 p. 24 cm.

PERIODICALS

International Trade Centre.
Annotated directory of regional and national trade and economic journals. Geneva, 1971.

vii, 153 p. 27 cm.

Library Association. Reference, Special and Information Section. Western Group.
Union list of current commercial periodicals, edited by Anthony Baker. London, 1968.

xi, 43 p. 22 cm.

Montreal. Ecole des hautes études commerciales. Bibliothèque.
Catalogue des périodiques ₁compilé par Vasile Tega₁. Montréal, 1970–

v. 22 x 28 cm.

CONTENTS: v. 1. Périodiques autres que ceux des gouvernements et des organismes internationaux.

COMMERCIAL EDUCATION see Business education

COMMERCIAL LAW

California. State Library, *Sacramento. Law Library.*
Recent material on debtor's rights and problems: a selective bibliography. Sacramento, 1967.

9 p. 28 cm.

Ezer, Mitchel J
Uniform commercial code bibliography, 1967, by Mitchel J. Ezer. ₁1st ed.₁ Philadelphia, Joint Committee on Continuing Legal Education of the American Law Institute and the American Bar Association ₁1967₁

xvi, 90 p. 22 cm.

"More than just a supplement to the bibliography published in 1966."

Ezer, Mitchel J
Uniform commercial code bibliography, 1969, by Mitchel J. Ezer. ₁1st ed.₁ Philadelphia, Joint Committee on Continuing Legal Education of the American Law Institute and the American Bar Association ₁1969₁

xvi, 120 p. 22 cm.

Ezer, Mitchel J
Uniform commercial code bibliography ₁by₁ Mitchel J. Ezer. Philadelphia, Joint Committee on Continuing Legal Education of the American Law Institute and the American Bar Association ₁1972₁

xxx, 539 p. 26 cm.

"December 31, 1970, was the cutoff point in compiling the bibliography."
Kept up to date by pocket supplements.

International Trade Centre.
A guide to sources of information on foreign trade regulations. Geneva, 1969.

v, 119 p. 21 x 27 cm.

Marke, Julius J
Commercial law: information sources ₁by₁ Julius J. Marke and Edward J. Bander. Detroit, Gale Research Co. ₁1970₁

220 p. 23 cm. (Management information guide, 17)

Roebuck, Derek.
A legal bibliography, by D. Roebuck and A. Szakats. Wellington, New Zealand Society of Accountants 1968.

7 p. 25 cm.

Sprudzs, Adolf.
Legal aspects of Yugoslav foreign trade; a selected bibliography, compiled by Adolf Sprudzs in consultation with Djurica Krstić. Chicago, 1968.

iii, 27 p. 27 cm. (University of Chicago Law School Library publications: Bibliographies and guides to research, no. 3)

COMMERCIAL PRODUCTS

Food and Agriculture Organization of the United Nations. Documentation Center.
Index; Indice, 1945–1966: commodities; produits; productos basicos. ₁Rome₁ 1969.

1 v. (various pagings) 28 cm.

Megathlin, Donald E
A bibliography on new product planning, compiled by Donald E. Megathlin and Winnifred E. Schaeffer. 2d ed. Chicago, American Marketing Association ₍°1966₎

x, 62 p. 23 cm. (AMA bibliography series, no. 5)

Simon, G   A
New product development and sale. Revised by G. A. Simon and F. V. Fortmiller. Washington, Small Business Administration, 1963 ₍i. e. 1964₎

11 p. 26 cm. (Small business bibliography no. 4)

Caption title.
"Originally issued as Small business bulletin no. 4."

Warsaw. Instytyt Ekonomiki i Organizacji Przemysłu. *Ośrodek Informacji i Dokumentacji Naukowo-Technicznej.*
Metody analizy potrzeb w zakresie artykułów zaopatrzenia materiałowo-technicznego oraz problemy pokrewne. Warszawa, 1965.

69 p. 29 cm. ₍*Its* Tematyczne zestawienie dokumentacyjne, nr. 44₎

PERIODICALS

Consumers index to product evaluations and information sources. v. 1–
winter 1974–
₍Ann Arbor, Pierian Press₎

v. 28 cm. quarterly.

International Trade Centre.
Annotated directory of product and industry journals. Geneva, 1970.

xi, 359 p. 27 cm.

At head of title: UNCTAD–GATT.

COMMON MARKET   see   European Economic Community

COMMONWEALTH OF NATIONS
see also   Great Britain - Colonies

Horne, A   J
The Commonwealth today; a select bibliography on the Commonwealth and its constituent countries ₍by₎ A. J. Horne. Foreword by Sir Kenneth Bradley. ₍London₎ Library Association, 1965.

107 p. 22 cm. (Library Association. Special subject list no. 45)

Morrell, William Parker, 1899–
British overseas expansion and the history of the Commonwealth: a select bibliography, by W. P. Morrell. 2nd ed. fully revised. London, Historical Association, 1970.

48 p. 22 cm. (Helps for students of history, no. 63)

National Book League, *London.*
Commonwealth biography. London, National Book League, 1966.

22 p. 21½ cm.

National Book League, *London.*
Commonwealth history. London, National Book League with the Commonwealth Institute, 1968.

32 p. 22 cm.

National Book League, *London.*
The Commonwealth in books. London, 1964.

126 p. 22 cm.

National Book League, *London.*
The Commonwealth in Europe: an annotated list. London, National Book League and the Commonwealth Institute, 1969.

₍1₎, 18 p. 22 cm.

National Book League, *London.*
The Commonwealth in general: an annotated list. London, National Book League, 1969.

₍1₎, 18 p. 22 cm.

Issued by the National Book League and the Commonwealth Institute.

National Book League, *London.*
The Commonwealth today. London, National Book League with the Commonwealth Institute, 1968.

31 p. 22 cm.

National Book League, *London.*
Commonwealth travel and description. London, National Book League, 1966.

16 p. 21½ cm.

National Book League, *London.*
Politics in the Commonwealth. London, National Book League, 1966.

24 p. 21½ cm.

National Book League, *London.*
Trade and development in the Commonwealth. London, National Book League with the Commonwealth Institute, 1968.

14 p. 22 cm.

Readers guide to the Commonwealth. 1970–
₍London₎ National Book League.

v. 21 cm.

Prepared by the National Book League, the Commonwealth Institute and the Foreign & Commonwealth Office.

Technical co-operation; a monthly bibliography. v. 1–

Jan. 1964–
₍London₎

v. 30–34 cm. monthly.

Issues no. 1–   of 1964 published by the Library of the Dept. of Technical Co-operation; 19   –70 by the Library of the Ministry of Overseas Development; 1971–   by the Overseas Development Administration.

——— Supplement. 1964–

₍London₎
v. 29–33 cm.

Issues no. 1–2 of 1964 published by the Library of the Dept. of Technical Co-operation; no. 3 of 1964–no. 2 of 1970 by the Library of the Ministry of Overseas Development; no. 3 of 1970–   by the Overseas Development Administration.

JUVENILE LITERATURE
National Book League, *London.*
Children's books on the Commonwealth. London, National Book League, 1966.

36 p. 21½ cm.

National Book League, *London.*
Children's books on the Commonwealth. London, National Book League with the Commonwealth Institute, 1968.

35 p. 22 cm.

COMMUNICABLE DISEASES
see also under Institut Pasteur d'Algérie

Perkins, Lee, 1942–
Drug resistant diseases. ₍Washington₎ Aerospace Technology Division, Library of Congress, 1968.
51, 30 l. 26 cm. (ATD report 68–92)
Abstracts of articles appearing in Soviet-bloc and other publications from Jan. 1, 1964 to date.
"Prepared in response to a request from the Medical Intelligence Office, Office of the Surgeon General, Department of the Army."
"MEDLARS bibliography in malaria 1964 to date": p. 1–30 (2d group)

COMMUNICATION
see also Information science; Mass media; and under Dissertations, Academic

Behn, Hans Ulrich.
Presse, Rundfunk, Fernsehen in Asien und Afrika. Eine Bibliographie in- und ausländischer Fachliteratur ⟨Zeitschriftenartikel, Monographien, Bücher⟩. ₍Bonn, Friedrich-Ebert-Stiftung, 1966₎
117 p. 29 cm. (Studien und Berichte aus dem Forschungsinstitut der Friedrich-Ebert-Stiftung)

Carter, Robert M
Communication in organizations; an annotated bibliography and sourcebook ₍by₎ Robert M. Carter. Detroit, Gale Research Co. ₍1972₎
ix, 272 p. 23 cm. (Management information guide, 25)

Hills, Jacqueline.
A review of the literature on primary communications in science and technology. London, Aslib, 1972.
₍3₎, 36 p. 30 cm. (Aslib. Occasional publications, no. 9)

"A review prepared on behalf of the Office for Scientific and Technical Information."
"Distributed in Canada, the USA, and the Philippines by Chicorel Library Publishing Co., New York."

Indice corrente de comunicações. set. 1970–
São Paulo, Universidade de São Paulo, Departamento de Biblioteconomia e Documentação.
no. 22 cm. semiannual.

Myren, Delbert Theodore, 1925–
Bibliography: communications in agricultural development ₍by₎ Delbert T. Myren. ₍México, 1965₎
ix, 101 p. 23 cm.

Rogers, Everett M
Bibliography on the diffusion of innovations, by Everett M. Rogers. East Lansing, Dept. of Communication, Michigan State University, 1966.
113 p. 28 cm. (Michigan State University, Dept. of Communication, College of Communication Arts. Diffusion of innovations research report no. 4)
"This bibliography ₍one product of the Diffusion Documents Center at Michigan State University₎ was partially supported by the U. S. Agency for International Development as a research project, Diffusion of innovations in rural societies, Contract csd–725."

Rutgers University, *New Brunswick, N. J. Bureau of Information Sciences Research.*
Bibliography of research relating to the communication of scientific and technical information. New Brunswick, N. J., Rutgers University Press, 1967.
xxxii, 732 p. 23 cm.
On spine: Communication of scientific and technical information, a bibliography:

Source, inc.
Source catalog. ₍Chicago, Ill., Swallow Press, 1971–
v. illus. 28 cm.
CONTENTS: no. 1. Communications.

South Carolina. State College, *Orangeburg. Communications Dept.*
Library holdings for courses in communications. Orangeburg, 1965.
189 l. 28 cm.

Trondheim. Norges tekniske høgskole. *Biblioteket.*
Teknisk informasjon og kommunikasjon. Utarb. som elevarbeid av Karin Hellandsjø. Trondheim, 1966.
8 l. 30 cm. (*Its* Litteraturliste, 26)

Voos, Henry.
Organizational communication; a bibliography. New Brunswick, N. J., Rutgers University Press, 1967.
251 p. 23 cm.

Weber, Dianne.
Teleconferencing; a bibliography, compiled by Dianne Weber, under the direction of Katherine Shervis. Computer programming by Richard G. Wolfe and Roger Voytecki. Madison, EDSAT Center, University of Wisconsin, 1971.
42 p. 28 cm. (EDSAT publication series, no. 2)

Wersig, Gernot.
Inhaltsanalyse. Einführung in ihre Systematik und Literatur. ₍2 Beiträge.₎ (Berlin) Spiess (1968).
160 p. 21 cm. (Schriftenreihe zur Publizistikwissenschaft, 5)

Yu, Ping-kuen.
History of communications, a grand table of contents, compiled by Ping-kuen Yu. Washington, Center for Chinese Research Materials, Association of Research Libraries, ₍1970₎
xii, 57 p. 22 x 28 cm. (Association of Research Libraries. Center for Chinese Research Materials. Bibliographical series, no. 4)
Reprint of the prefatory matters and tables of contents from six works entitled: 交通史總務編·交通史郵政編·交通史電政編·交通史路政編·交通史航政編 and 交通史航空編 compiled by 交通鐵道部交通史編纂委員會

PERIODICALS

Austria. *Generaldirektion für die Post- und Telegraphenverwaltung. Bibliothek.*
Zeitschriftenverzeichnis. Stand 1. Mai 1968. Wien, Generaldirektion für die Post- und Telegraphenverwaltung ₍1968₎
ii, 59 l. 30 cm.

COMMUNISM
see also Socialism

Berlin. Stadtbibliothek. Abteilung Allgemeinbildende Bibliotheken.
Auf den Spuren des Roten Oktober, hohe Leistungen zu Ehren der DDR. Materialsammlung für Bibliothekare, Lehrer und Erzieher. ₍Red. Bearb.: M. Bierwagen. Berlin, Zentralinstitut für Bibliothekswesen₎ 1967.

63 p. 21 cm.

Библиография общественно-политической литературы. Учебник для библиотеч. фак. ин-тов культуры. Изд. 2-е, испр. и доп. ч. 1– Москва, "Просвещение," 1968–

v. 22 cm.

At head of title, v. 1– : Московский государственный институт культуры. Л. А. Левин ₍и др.₎

The Bibliographical bulletin of current Marxology; trial issue. ₍Editor: Jerzy Rudzki₎ Warszawa, Państwowe Wydawn. Naukowe, 1965.

176 p. 24 cm.

Issued by Instytut Filozofii i Socjologii, Polska Akademia Nauk.

Burmistrova, Tat'iana IÚl'evna.
Обзор советской литературы о социалистическом интернационализме. Материалы Всесоюз. конференции "Теорет. вопросы соц. интернационализма." Москва, "Знание," 1968.
25 p. 28 cm.
At head of title: Всесоюзное общество "Знание." Научный совет по комплексной проблеме "Закономерности развития общественных отношений и духовной жизни общества" Институт философии АН СССР. Сектор научного коммунизма.

Cohen, Jack, *writer on Marxism.*
A reader's guide to the study of Marxism, by Jack Cohen and James Klugmann. London, Communist Party (Education Dept.) ₍1966₎

₍1₎, 82 p. 22 cm.

Communism, conspiracy and treason. Sydney, Tidal Publications ₍1968₎

21 p. 18 cm.

Dŭgmedzhieva, Petŭa Trifonova.
Единство на световното комунистическо и работническо движение. (Препоръч. библиогр. Под ред. на Велчо Ковачев). (София, Нар. библ. Кирил и Методий, 1969).

05 p. 21 cm.

At head of title: Отдел препоръчителна библиография.
By P. Dŭgmedzhieva, V. Trenkova, A. Karadzhova.

Dutschke, Rudi.
Ausgewählte und kommentierte Bibliographie des revolutionären Sozialismus von K. Marx bis in die Gegenwart. Heidelberg, Druck- und Verlagskooperative ₍1969₎

40 p. 15 cm. (Kleine Agitations-broschüren, Nr. 1)

(Formirovanie novogo cheloveka)
Формирование нового человека. Рек. указ. литературы. Москва, "Книга," 1973.

77 p. 20 cm.

At head of title: Государственная публичная историческая библиотека РСФСР.
"Составители: Г. Д. Ушакова ₍и др.₎"

Grishina, G   I
₍Sovremennaia nauchno-tekhnicheskaia revoliutsiia i sozdanie fundamenta kommunizma₎
Современная научно-техническая революция и создание фундамента коммунизма. Рек. указ. литературы. Москва, "Книга," 1972.

177 p. 20 cm.

At head of title: Государственная библиотека СССР им. В. И. Ленина)

Haque, Serajul.
Economy of the Socialist countries; a select bibliography. Edited by Alauddin Talukder. Dacca, Bangladesh Institute of Development Economics, 1972.

iv, 57 p. 24 cm.

Husár, Jozef.
Úvod do bibliografie klasikov marxizmu-leninizmu. ₍Vyd. 1.₎ Martin, Matica slovenská, 1965.

99 p. 24 cm. (Edícia: Teória a dokumentácia bibliografie, č. 2)

Ježek, Alexandr.
V. I. Lenin a proletářský internacionalismus. Bibliogr. ke 100. výročí narozenin V. I. Lenina. Sest. Alexandr Ježek. Praha, Měst. knihovna, rozmn., 1970.

100, ₍1₎ p. 29 cm.

Kolarz, Walter.
Books on communism, a bibliography. 2d ed. New York, Oxford University Press, 1964 ₍ᶜ1963₎

viii, 568 p. 19 cm.

First ed., 1959, by R. N. C. Hunt.

Korea (*Republic*). *Kukťo T'ongirwŏn.*
(Kongsanjuŭi kwan'gye tosŏ mongnok) · 공산주의관계 도서목록 ₍서울₎ 국토통일원 1969.

578 p. 26 cm.

Ленин и современность. (Рек. указатель литературы). ₍Вступит. статья и науч. ред. д-ра философ. наук Л. Н. Суворова₎. Москва, "Книга," 1969.
223 p. 20 cm.
At head of title: Государственная библиотека СССР имени В. И. Ленина. Государственная публичная библиотека имени М. Е. Салтыкова-Щедрина. Государственная публичная историческая библиотека.
By E. M. Teper and others.

Marxisticko-leninské principy stranické práce. Doporučující bibliografie na pomoc stranickému vzdělávání, střední stupeň. Red. J. Hanzálek. Znojmo, ONV-odb. kultury, rozmn., 1973.

21 p. 20 cm.

At head of title: Okresní knihovna ve Znojmě.

Matica slovenská, Turčiansky sv. Martin. Knihovedný odbor.
Stranícké sjazdy a knižnice; súpis literatúry o práci knižníc pred straníckymi sjazdami a po nich z našich i zahraničných knihovníckych časopisov. ₍Autor: Kolektiv prac. KOMS₎ Martin, Matica Slovenská, 1966.

45 p. 24 cm.

"Záväzok pracovníkov Knihovedného odboru Matice slovenskej k XIII. sjazdu KSČ."

(Mirovoe kommunisticheskoe dvizhenie—avangard antiimperialisticheskoi bor'by)
Мировое коммунистическое движение—авангард анти-

империалистической борьбы. Рек. указ. литературы. Москва, "Книга," 1972.

128 p. 20 cm.

At head of title: Государственная публичная историческая библиотека РСФСР.
By M. I. Artemova and others.

Misharina, Vladilena Vasil'evna.
Против буржуазной идеологии. [Ленинские принципы критики]. Рек. указ. литературы. Москва, "Книга," 1971.

96 p. 20 cm.

At head of title: Государственная библиотека СССР. имени В. И. Ленина. В. Мишарина, И. Свиридова, Г. Донская.

Moscow. Publichnaïa biblioteka.
Основы научного коммунизма; рекомендательный указатель литературы. [Составитель Ю. М. Тугов] Москва, Книга, 1965.

93 p. 22 cm.

At head of title: Государственная библиотека СССР имени В. И. Ленина.

Над раскрытым томом Ленина. Библиогр. пособие для молодежи. Москва, "Книга," 1969.

111 p. 20 cm.

At head of title: Государственная ордена Ленина библиотека СССР имени В. И. Ленина.
By L. Popova, and others.

Основы политических знаний. Рек. указатель литературы. Москва, "Книга," 1968.

112 p. 20 cm.

At head of title: Государственная ордена Ленина библиотека СССР имени В. И. Ленина.
By V. V. Misharina and others.

Papírník, Miloš.
Bibliografický průvodce ke klasikům marxismu-leninismu. [2., doplněné vyd.] Praha [Státní pedagogické nakl.] 1965.

128 p. 21 cm. (Publikace státních vědeckých knihoven)

At head of title: Státní knihovna ČSSR. Ústřední vědeckometodický kabinet knihovnictví. Miloš Papírník.

Persits, Moiseĭ Aronovich.
Soviet works on history of contemporary international workers' movement published in 1965–1969 [by] M. A. Persits. Moscow, "Nauka" Pub. House, Central Dept. of Oriental Literature, 1970.

24 p. 21 cm. (Studies by Soviet historians for the period 1965–1969)

"XIII International Congress of Historical Sciences, Moscow, August 16–23, 1970."

(Rabochiĭ klass—glavnaïa dvizhushchaïa sila revoliutsionnoĭ bor'by za mir, demokratiïu i sotsializm)
Рабочий класс—главная движущая сила революционной борьбы за мир, демократию и социализм. Рек. указ. литературы. Москва, "Книга," 1971.

79 p. 20 cm.

At head of title: Государственная публичная историческая библиотека РСФСР.
By M. I. Artemova and others.

Ruffmann, Karl Heinz.
Kommunismus in Geschichte und Gegenwart; ausgewähltes Bücherverzeichnis. Bearb. in Verbindung mit Werner John [et al.] von Karl-Heinz Ruffmann. [1. Aufl. Herausgeber: Bundeszentrale für Politische Bildung] Bonn

[1964]
285 p. 18 cm. (Schriften der Bundeszentrale für Politische Bildung)
"Stand : Herbst 1964."
On spine: Bücherverzeichnis Kommunismus.

Ruffmann, Karl Heinz.
Kommunismus in Geschichte und Gegenwart. Ausgew. Bücherverz. Bearb. in Verb. mit Werner John u. a. von Karl-Heinz Ruffmann. (2., wesentl. erw. Aufl.) (Bonn, Bundeszentrale f. Politische Bildung, 1966.)

453 p. 18 cm. (Schriften der Bundeszentrale für Politische Bildung)
"Stand : Herbst 1966."
On spine : Bücherverzeichnis Kommunismus.

Sakharov, I   V
С Интернационалом. (Интернационалисты в революциях и войнах). Рек. указ. литературы. Москва, "Книга," 1971.

128 p. 20 cm.

At head of title: Государственная публичная библиотека имени М. Е. Салтыкова-Щедрина. И. В. Сахаров, Е. М. Тепер.

Šolcová, Marta, *comp.*
Díla představitelů SDDSR(b) v českých překladech, 1918–1938. [Sest.: Marta Šolcová a Ludmila Ženožičková. V Olomouci, Státní vědecka knihovna, 1967]

35 p. 30 cm. (Publikace Státní vědecké knihovny v Olomouci, 9/1967)

Cover title.

Список литературы кандидатского минимума по марксистско-ленинской философии (для нефилософских специальностей) [Отв. редакторы. В. Т. Калтахчян, М. И. Конкин]. Москва, Мысль, 1969.

7 p. 20 cm.

At head of title: Министерство высшего и среднего специального образования СССР. Отдел преподавания общественных наук.

Starostin, Nikolaĭ Dem'íanovich.
(Sotsialisticheskaïa revoliutsiïa i sovremennost')
Социалистическая революция и современность. Библиогр. обзор. Москва, "Книга," 1973.

110 p. 20 cm.

Starshinova, M   S
Воспитание нового человека. Книги и статьи из журналов, продолжающихся изд., сборников на рус. языке за 1967–1970 гг. Москва, 1970.

54 p. 20 cm. (Библиографические и методические материалы навстречу XXIV съезду КПСС)
At head of title: Государственная ордена Ленина библиотека СССР имени В. И. Ленина. Информационно-библиографический отдел.

Sviridova, Inna Nikolaevna.
(Strany sotsializma : zakonomernosti, problemy i tendentsii razvitiïa)
Страны социализма: закономерности, проблемы и тенденции развития. Рек. указ. литературы. Москва, "Книга," 1973.

144 p. 20 cm.

At head of title: Государственная библиотека СССР имени В. И. Ленина. И. Н. Свиридова, Н. В. Якимова.

Teper, Efim Markovich.
(Klassovye boi v stranakh kapitala)
Классовые бои в странах капитала : беседы о книгах / [Е. М. Тепер]. — Москва : Книга, 1973.

31 p. ; 20 cm. — (Мир, труд, коммунизм ; вып. 89)

Tugov, ĨUriĩ Mikhaĩlovich.
Коммунизм и личность. ₍Библиогр. обзор₎. Москва, "Книга," 1968.

56 p. 20 cm. (Беседа о книгах)

United States. Library of Congress. Legislative Reference Service.
World communism; a selected annotated bibliography (bibliographic materials through September 1963) Prepared at the request of the Subcommittee to Investigate the Administration of the Internal Security Act and Other Internal Security Laws of the Committee on the Judiciary, United States Senate. Washington, United States Govt. Print. Off., 1964–₍72₎

2 v. 24 cm. (88th Cong., 2d sess. Senate. Document no. 69)
Vol. 2, prepared by the Congressional Research Service, Library of Congress, has title: World communism, 1964–1969, a selected bibliography.

Vol. 2 issued as Committee print, 92d Congress, 1st session.

—————— An addendum to Senate document no. 69. Washington, U. S. Govt. Print. Off., 1964.

379–410 p. 24 cm. (88th Cong., 2d sess. Senate. Document no. 69, pt. 2)

Vigor, Peter Hast.
Books on communism and the Communist countries: a selected bibliography; edited by P. H. Vigor. ₍3rd ed.₎. London, Ampersand, 1971.

444 p. 23 cm.

Вопросы библиографии общественно-политической литературы; сборник статей. ₍Под ред. Л. А. Левина₎ Москва, Книга, 1967.

172, ₍4₎ p. 20 cm.

At head of title: Московский государственный институт культуры.

Vučka, Milan.
Komunistické a dělnické strany v českých časopisech roku 1970. Bibliografie. Sest. Milan Vučka. Praha, St. Knihovna ČSR-Nár. knihovna, rozmn., 1971.

75, ₍1₎ p. 20 cm.

Základní otázky vědeckého komunismu. Výběrová bibliogr. ke stř. stupni stranického vzdělávání "Základy marxismu-leninismu." Red. Jan Hanzálek. Znojmo, ONV-odb. kultury, rozmn., 1973.

16 p. 29 cm.

Cover title: Základy vědeckého komunismu.
At head of title: Okresní knihovna ve Znojmě.

LIBRARY CATALOGS

Berlin. Institut für Marxismus-Leninismus. Bibliothek.
Die Bibliothek des Instituts für Marxismus-Leninismus beim Zentralkommittee der SED. Ein Sammelbd. (Red.: Bruno Kaiser u. Lothar Groll.) Berlin (Institut f. Marxismus-Leninismus beim ZK d. SED) 1969.

237 p. illus. 22 cm.

Marx Memorial Library.
Catalogue. London, Marx Memorial Library, 1971–

v. 26 cm.

Cover title.
CONTENTS: v. 1. Marxist classics. — v. 2. Social and political theory.
v. 4. Philosophy.

AFRICA

Paolozzi, Ursula.
Communism in sub-Saharan Africa; an essay with bibliographic supplement. Washington, American University. Center for Research in Social Systems, 1969.

v, 44 p. 28 cm.

BULGARIA

Boĩadzhieva, Mariĩa.
Българската Комунистическа партия—ръководител и организатор на БНА; препоръчителна библиография. ₍Изработи: Мария Бояджиева. Редактор Димитър Фотев₎ София, 1965.
48 p. 20 cm.
At head of title: Централен дом на Народната армия. Централна армейска библиотека.
"Библиографията се издава в чест на двадесетгодишнината от социалистическата революция и БНА."

Bŭlgarska Komunisticheska partiĩa.
История на БКП, 1885–1944; библиография. Материали, публикувани след 9 септ. 1944 г. ₍Библиографията изработиха: Иван Цолов, Велчо Ковачев, Йота Данчева. Библиографията съдържа материали, публикувани до 1 септ. 1964 г. София, 1965.

566 p. 21 cm.

Dancheva, Iota.
Българската комунистическа партия в чуждата литература. 1885–1967. Библиогр. указател. (Израб. Йота Данчева и Михаил Лазаров). София, Партиздат, 1971.

480 p. 21 cm.

At head of title: Народна библиотека "Кирил и Методий."

Девети конгрес на БКП; препоръчителна библиография в помощ на библиотекари, пропагандисти и участници в учебни звена на партийната просвета. ₍Библиографията подготвиха: Ст. Иванов и др. Редактор Ст. Иванов₎ София, Нар. библиотека "Кирил и Методий," 1967.

135 p. 20 cm.

Dimovska, Diana.
80 години от създаването на Българската комунистическа партия в Ямболски окръг. Препоръч. библиогр. (Състав. Д. Димовска. Ред. М. Беленозов). Ямбол, Окр. библ., 1971.

63 p. 20 cm.

At head of title: Окръжна библиотека—Ямбол.

Dĩugmedzhieva, Petĩa Trifonova.
80 години Българска комунистическа партия. Библиогр. материали и разработки. София, Нар. библ. Кирил и Методий, 1971.

146 p. 22 cm.

At head of title: Народна библиотека "Кирил и Методий." Отдел Препоръчителна библиография.
By P. T. Dĩugmedzhieva, E. V. Vasileva and A. A. Karadzhova.

История на Софийската партийна организация, 1885–1944; библиография. ₍Съставители: Велчо Ковачев и др.₎ София, БКП, 1967.

561 p. 21 cm.

Okrŭzhna metodicheska biblioteka—Kŭrdzhali.
(Под знамето на партията към комунизъм)
Под знамето на партията към комунизъм; препоръчителна бибилиография. Кърджали, Окръжна биб-

лиотека, 1970.

37 p.　20 cm.

Sofia. Narodna biblioteka.
Решенията на Априлския пленум в действие; библиография. ₁Изработиха П. Едрева и др. Редактор Петър Цанев₁. София, Изд-во на Българската Комунистическа партия, 1966.

209 p.　20 cm.

At head of title: Народна библиотека "Кирил и Методий."

Vŭleva, Lena ΓA
Под знамето на марксизма-ленинизма. ⟨Препоръч. библиогр.⟩ ₁из историята на Хасковската окр. парт. организация₁. (Ред. Ст. Атанасов). Хасково, Окр. библ. Хр. Смирненски, 1971.

115 p. with ports.　22 cm.

At head of title: Окръжна библиотека "Хр. Смиренски." Справочно-библиографски отдел.

CHINA

Cole, Allan Burnett, 1914–
Fifty years of Chinese communism: selected readings with commentary, by Allan B. Cole and Peter C. Oleson. ₁2d ed.₁ Washington, Service Center for Teachers of History ₁1969₁

50 p.　23 cm.　(Service Center for Teachers of History. Publication no. 47)

First published in 1962 under title: Forty years of Chinese communism.

CZECHOSLOVAK REPUBLIC

Brünn. Krajská lidová knihovna.
50 ₁i. e. Padesát₁ let KSČ v Jihomoravském kraji. Výběrová bibliografie z knih vyd. tiskem po 2. světové válce. Brno, Knihovna J. Mahena, rozmn., 1971.

29, ₁1₁ p.　20 cm.

Krupičková, Vlasta, comp.
Soupis disertačních a habilitačních prací k dějinám KSČ a ČSSR od počátku dělnického hnutí do současnosti; ₁informační přehled z let 1955–1965₁ Praha, 1966.

111 p.　29 cm.　(Bibliografické pomůcky Knihovny Ústavu dějin KSČ)

At head of title: Ustav dějin Komunistické strany Československa. Knihovna.

Kubíček, Jaromír.
Sjezdové materiály KSČ a sborníky historických dokumentů k dějinám Československa v letech 1918–1971. ₁Výběr lit.₁ Zprac. Jaromír Kubíček. Brno, Univ. knihovna, rozmn., 1972.

38, ₁1₁ l.　21 cm.　(Universitníknihovna v Brně. Výběrový seznam, 172)

Lenc, Václav.
14. ₁i. e. Čtrnáctý₁ sjezd KSČ. Bibliografický soupis sjezdových materiálů. Sest. Václav Lenc, Danuše Vlasáková. Praha, St. knihovna ČSR – Ústř. ekon. knihovna, rozmn., 1971.

9, ₁1₁ p.　21 cm.

Machánková, Ružena.
Bibliografia k dejinám komunistického hnutia na Slovensku. Knižná a článková tvorba za roky 1945–1970. 1. vyd. Bratislava, Pravda, t. Pravda, Žilina, 1972.

455, ₁3₁ p.　21 cm.

Maur, Jan.
Založení KSČ v plzeňském tisku a v naší literatuře. Zprac. Jan Maur a František Pěchouček. Plzeň, St. věd. knihovna, rozmn. Stráž 3, Karlovy Vary, 1971.

34, ₁3₁ p.　21 cm.　(Státní vědecká knihovna Plzeň. Společenské, přírodní a užité vědy, 2)

Mrázek, Libor.
Vznik a působení KSČ na Liberecku za 1. republiky. Výběr záznamů z regionálního tisku 1945–1960. Sest. Libor Mrázek. Excerpce: Věra Moravcová, Helena Švančarová a sestavovatel. Liberec, Věd. a lid. knihovna, rozmn., 1971.

57, ₁1₁ l.　20 cm.　(Publikace VLK. Řada A, čís. 108)

Padesát let bojů, práce, vítězství. Výběr z knižní produkce čes. a slov. nakl. k 50. výročí založení Komunistické strany Československa. Praha, Kniž. velkoobchod, t. Rudé právo, Brno, 1971.

85, ₁1₁ p.　22 cm.

50 ₁i. e. PADESÁT₁ let KSČ. Bibliografie pomocných pramenů k oslavám 50. výročí založení KSČ (doplňky leden-březen 1971). Zprac. ₁kol.₁ Red. Marta Šolcová. Olomouc, St. věd. knihovna, rozmn., 1971.

22 p.　29 cm.　(Publikace Státní vědecké knihovny v Olomouci, čís. 3/1971)

50 ₁i. e. Padesát₁ let Komunistické strany Československa. (Bibliografie prací vydaných k 50. výročí založení KSČ) Praha, Ústav československých a světových dějin ČSAV, Ústav marxismuleninismu ÚV KSČ, 1972.

115 p.　21 cm.　(Sbírka: Práce Oddělení vědeckých informací ÚČSD ČSAV v Praze, čís. 1)

Předvoj nového života. Výběrová bibliogr. ₁a lit. ukázky₁ k 50 výročí KSČ. Zprac. kol. Praha, Měst. knihovna, rozmn., 1970.

121, ₁2₁ p.　29 cm.　(Metodické texty a bibliografie Městské knihovny)

GERMANY

Beyer, Willy, 1909–
50 ₁i. e. Fünfzig₁ Jahre Novemberrevolution 1918; Auswahlbibliographie zur Geschichte der Novemberrevolution 1918 und zur Gründung der Kommunistischen Partei Deutschlands in den heutigen Bezirken Halle und Magdeburg in den Jahren 1919/20. Halle, Universitäts- und Landesbibliothek Sachsen-Anhalt, 1968.

20 p.　21 cm.　(Schriften zum Bibliotheks- und Büchereiwesen in Sachsen-Anhalt, 26)

Subtitle corrected from: Auswahlbibliographie Novemberrevolution 1918 und zur Geschichte …

Militärakademie Friedrich Engels. Sektion Gesellschaftswissenschaften.
Lebendige Tradition; Lebensbilder deutscher Kommunisten und Antifaschisten. ₁1. Aufl. Berlin₁ Militärverlag der Deutschen Demokratischen Republik ₁1974₁

2 v.　illus.　20 cm.　(Kleine Militärgeschichte. Biographien)

Sozialistische Einheitspartei Deutschlands.
Unter der roten Fahne; Auswahlbibliographie zur Geschichte der deutschen Arbeiterbewegung. ₁Herausgeber:₁ Sozialistische Einheitspartei Deutschlands, Bezirksleitung Frankfurt (Oder); Stadt- und Bezirksbibliothek Frankfurt (Oder), Abteilung Ausleihe und Literaturpropaganda; ₁und₁ Zentralinstitut für Bibliothekswesen, Berlin. ₁Berlin, 1962–68₁

3 v. illus., ports. 21 cm.

Vol. 2–3: Herausgeber: Zentralinstitut für Bibliothekswesen, Berlin, und Stadt- und Bezirksbibliothek Frankfurt (Oder)

HUNGARY

Budapest. Fővárosi Szabó Ervin Könyvtár.
Budapest munkásmozgalmának válogatott irodalma, 1919 augusztus 1–1945 február 13. ₁Főszerk. Zoltán József. 2. átdolg. kiad.₁ Budapest, 1965.

478 p. plates. 25 cm.

First ed. published in 1959 under title: Budapest munkásmozgalma, 1919–1945.

Gáliczky, Éva.
Történelem, forradalom; a magyar munkászmozgalom történetéről megjelent legujabb könyvek ajánló bibliográfiája. Budapest, Fővárosi Szabó Ervin Könyvtár, 1966.

63 p. 21 cm.

ITALY

Camurani, Ercole.
Bibliografia del P. L. I. ₁n. p.₁ Partito Liberale Italiano ₁1968₁

247 p. 22 cm.

LATIN AMERICA

Sable, Martin Howard.
Communism in Latin America, an international bibliography: 1900–1945, 1960–1967 ₁by₁ Martin H. Sable with the assistance of M. Wayne Dennis. Los Angeles, Latin American Center, University of California, 1968.
ii, 220 p. 23 cm. (University of California. Latin American Center. Reference series, no. 1–A)
Complements and brings up to date Communism in Latin America, a bibliography: the post-war years (1945–1960) by L. Lauerhass.
Preface in English and Spanish.

LATVIA

Latvijas Komunistiskā partija. *Centrālā Komiteja. Partijas vēstures institūts.*
Latvijas Komunistiskās partijas vēstures bibliogrāfija, 1893–1919. Rīgā, Latvijas valsts izdevnieciba, 1964.

509 p. 23 cm.

At head of title: Latvijas KP CK Partijas vēstures institūts, PSKP CK Marksisma-ļeņinisma institūta filiāle.

ROMANIA

Biblioteca Municipală Timişoara. Serviciul Bibliografic.
Literatură social-politică. Documente de partid şi de stat. 1968/72. ₁În biblioteca municipală Timişoara₁. Catalog tematic selectiv. Întocmit: Hortensia Baica. Timişoara, 1973.

39 p. 30 cm.

Suceava, Romania. Biblioteca Municipală.
Partidul Comunist Român 1921–1971. Bibliografie selectivă. Suceava, 1971.

36 p. with figs. 20 cm.

RUSSIA

Barashkova, Valentina Sergeevna.
О научных основах партийной пропаганды. Рек. указатель литературы. Москва, "Книга," 1971.

113 p. 20 cm.

At head of title: Государственная публичная историческая библиотека РСФСР.
By V. S. Barashkova, IŪ. I. Stukov, and A. I. Urusov.

Fedorova, L   I
История партийных организаций Урала; указатель литературы, изданной в 1956–1964 гг. ₁Составитель Л. И. Федорова₁. Свердловск, Средне-Уральское книжное изд-во, 1967–

v. 22 cm.

At head of title, v. 1– : Свердловская государственная публичная библиотека им. В. Г. Белинского.

Gileva, Elena Ivanovna.
Краткий аннотированный указатель вспомогательных материалов в помощь изучающим историю КПСС. Москва, 1965.

79 p. 22 cm.

At head of title: Московский институт народного хозяйства имени Г. В. Плеханова. Кафедра истории КПСС. Е. И. Гилева, В. Г. Ерсмин.

История Воронежской областной партийной организации. 1892–1966 гг. Библиогр. указатель. Воронеж, Центр.-Чернозем. кн. изд., 1969.

96 p. 20 cm.

At head of title: Воронежское областное управление культуры. Областная библиотека имени И. С. Никитина. Партийный архив Воронежского обкома КПСС.
By R. G. Demidov and others.

Knizhnik, Ivan Sergeevich, 1878–
(Chto chitat' po obshchestvennym naukam)
Что читать по общественным наукам; систематический указатель коммунистической и марксистской литературы 1917–1923 г. г. Издание 2-ое, переработанное и дополненное. Ленинград, "Прибой," 1924. ₁Twickenham, Middx., Anthony C. Hall, 1972₁
504 p. 23 cm. (Slavonic studies reprints, no. 3) (Пособие для библиотекарей, лекторов, членов марксистских кружков и для самообразования)
First ed. published in 1923 under title: Систематический указатель литературы по общественным наукам.

Ksenzova, T   E
Библиография к примерной тематике всесоюзных общественно-политических чтений. Москва, "Знание," 1970.
46 p. 20 cm.
At head of title: Всесоюзное общество "Знание." Научно-методический совет по пропаганде исторических наук. Навстречу XXI съезду КПСС.

Литература по истории КПСС: каталог-проспект. ₁Редактор Г. Пропина₁ Москва, Изд-во полит. лит-ры, 1964.

78 p. illus., facsims. 17 cm.

McNeal, Robert Hatch, 1930–
Guide to the decisions of the Communist Party of the Soviet Union, 1917–1967. Указатель решений Коммунистической Партии Советского Союза, 1917–1967. ₁By₁ Robert H. McNeal. ₁Toronto₁ University of Toronto Press ₁c1972₁
xlix, 326 p. 26 cm.
English introd. with Russian text.

Mikelinskaité, P
Grožinė literatūra studijuojantiems TSKP istoriją; rekomenduojamosios literatūros rodyklė. Vilnius, 1965.

116 p. 20 cm.

At head of title: Lietuvos TSR Valstybinė respublikinė biblioteka.
P. Mikelinskaité.

Misharina, Vladilena Vasil'evna.

Ленинское учение о партии. Рек. указатель литературы. Москва, "Книга," 1970.

80 p. 20 cm.

At head of title: Государственная ордена Ленина библиотека СССР имени В. И. Ленина.

Moscow. Gosudarstvennaĭa publichnaĭa istoricheskaĭa biblioteka.

Идеологическая работа КПСС — могучее оружие в борьбе за коммунизм; рекомендательный указатель литературы в помощь пропаганде решений июньского, 1963 г., пленума ЦК КПСС. ₍Составители Л. А. Котельникова и Н. А. Шокина₎ Москва, Книга, 1964.

169 p. 22 cm.

(Primernaĭa tematika kontrol'nykh rabot po kursu nauchnogo kommunizma dlĭa zaochnykh vysshikh uchebnykh zavedeniĭ, zaochnykh fakul'tetov i otdeleniĭ vuzov)
Примерная тематика контрольных работ по курсу научного коммунизма для заочных высших учебных заведений, заочных факультетов и отделений вузов. ₍Отв. редактор Б. П. Агафонов₎ Москва, Мысль, 1973.

30 p. 20 cm.

Примерная тематика контрольных работ по курсу научного коммунизма для заочных высших учебных заведений, заочных факультетов и отделений вузов. ₍Отв. редакторы Е. А. Ануфриев, И. Ф. Мяятников, Н. Ф. Непочатых₎ Москва, Мысль, 1966.

30 p. 20 cm.
At head of title: Министерство высшего и среднего специального образования СССР. Управление преподавания общественных наук.

(Programma mira i sozidaniĭa)
Программа мира и созидания. Рек. указ. литературы в помощь изучающим материалы и решения XXIV съезда КПСС. Москва, "Книга," 1971.

73 p. 20 cm.

At head of title: Государственная библиотека СССР имени В. И. Ленина.
By M. N. Gubareva and others.

(Resheniĭa dvadtĭsat' chetvertogo s"ezda KPSS i semnadtĭsatogo s"ezda KP Tadzhikistana—v zhizn'!)
Решения XXIV съезда КПСС и XVII съезда КП таджикистана—в жизнь! (Метод. и библиогр. материалы в помощь массовым б-кам). Душанбе, 1971.

54 p. 20 cm.

At head of title: Государственная республиканская библиотека им. А. Фирдоуси.
Russian and Tajik.
Title also in Tajik: Қарорҳои съезди XXIV КПСС ва съезди XVII ПК Точикистон—дар амал!
By R. Rakhmatullaeva and others.

Russia ₍1923– U. S. S. R.₎ Gosud... nyĭ komitet po pechati.
Сводный ... выпуск общественно-политической литературы. 19...
₍Москва₎ Союзкнига.

v. 23 cm.

Cover title, 1965– : Общественно-политическая литература.

Russia (*1923– U. S. S. R.*). *Ministerstvo vysshego i srednego spetsial'nogo obrazovaniĭa. Otdel prepodavaniĭa obshchestvennykh nauk.*

Список литературы для подготовки к кандидатским экзаменам по истории КПСС. Москва, "Мысль," 1968.

13 p. 20 cm.
Cover title.
Edited by I. E. Gorelov, V. M. Savel'ev and G. A. Chigrinov.

Russia (*1923– U. S. S. R.*) *Upravlenie prepodavaniĭa obshchestvennykh nauk.*

Примерная тематика контрольных работ по курсу основ научного коммунизма для заочных высших учебных заведений, заочных факультетов и отделений вузов. ₍Ответственные редакторы В. Т. Калтахчан и В. И. Панченко₎ Москва, Высшая школа, 1964.

38 p. 20 cm.
At head of title: Министерство высшего и среднего специального образования СССР.

Russia (*1923– U. S. S. R.*) *Upravlenie prepodavaniĭa obshchestvennykh nauk.*

Примерный список литературы кандидатского минимума по истории КПСС. ₍Ответственные редакторы: К. М. Темирбаев, Г. А. Конюхов₎ Москва, Мысль, 1964.

22 p. 20 cm.

(Sotsial'no-politicheskoe razvitie sovetskogo obshchestva na sovremennom étape)
Социально-политическое развитие советского общества на современном этапе : рек. указ. литературы / науч. ред. канд. ист. наук В. К. Иванов ; ₍составители, Л. А. Котельникова ... et al.₎. — Москва : Книга, 1974.

78 p. ; 21 cm.
At head of title: Государственная публичная историческая библиотека РСФСР.

UKRAINE

Mashotas, Vladimir Vladimirovich, *comp.*

Комуністична партія Західної України; бібліографічний покажчик матеріалів і публікацій за 1919–1967 рр. ₍Львів, Каменяр, 1969₎

439 p. 21 cm.

At head of title: В. В. Машотас.
On leaf preceding t. p.: Львівська бібліотека Академії наук УРСР.

UNITED STATES

Bibliography on the Communist problem in the United States. New York, Da Capo Press, 1971 ₍c1955₎

xiii, ₍1₎, 474 p. 28 cm. (Civil liberties in American history)

Seidman, Joel Isaac, 1906–

Communism in the United States; a bibliography. Compiled and edited by Joel Seidman, assisted by Olive Golden and Yaffa Draznin. Ithaca ₍N. Y.₎ Cornell University Press ₍1969₎

xii, 526 p. 29 cm.

Tamiment Library.

American Trotskyism, 1928–1970. ₍New York, 1971₎

1 v. (unpaged) 28 cm. (Bulletin of the Tamiment Library, no. 47)

Caption title.
Text prepared by J. Goldberg.

YUGOSLAVIA

Vrtačič, Ludvik.

Einführung in den jugoslawischen Marxismus-Leninis-

mus; Organisation, Bibliographie. Dordrecht, D. Reidel
[1964, °1963]

ix, 208 p. fold. map. 23 cm. (Sovietica; Veröffentlichungen des Osteuropa-Instituts, Universität Freiburg/Schweiz)

COMMUNISM AND RELIGION

Bent, Ans J   van der.
The Christian Marxist dialogue. An annotated bibliography. Der Dialog zwischen Christen und Marxisten. Eine kommentierte Bibliographie. Le dialogue entre chrétiens et marxistes. Une bibliographie analytique. 1959–1969. [By] Ans J. van der Bent. Geneva, World Council of Churches, 1969.

vi, 90 p. 29 cm.

Stange, Douglas C
The nascent Marxist-Christian dialogue: 1961–1967—a bibliography, by Douglas C. Stange. [New York, American Institute for Marxist Studies, 1968]

27 p. 29 cm. (American Institute for Marxist Studies. Bibliographical series, no. 5)

Cover title.
In English, French, German, Italian, or Spanish.

COMMUNIST EDUCATION

Vangermain, Heinz, 1924–
Die Einflussnahme der Arbeiterklasse auf die sozialistische Erziehung der Schüler. ([Von] Heinz Vangermain [u.], Fritz Machler. Berichtszeitraum: 1961–1970.) Berlin, Pädagogische Zentralbibliothek, 1970.

37 p. 21 cm. (Pädagogische Zentralbibliothek. Auswahlbibliographie, 1970, 2)

COMMUNIST ETHICS

Egle, L
Mans laikabiedrs. Ieteicamās literatūras rādītājs. Rīgā, 1972.

32 p. 20 cm.

At head of title: Vija Lāča Latvijas PSR Valsts biblioteka. Zinātniski metodiskā un bibliogrāfiskā darba nodaļa.
"Sastādītāja: L. Egle."
Title also in Russian: Мой современник. Рекомендательный указатель литературы.

Pavlova, L   I
Нравственные ценности нашего современника. Рек. указ. литературы. Москва, "Книга," 1971.

96 p. 20 cm.

At head of title: Министерство культуры СССР. Государственная библиотека СССР имени В. И. Ленина.

COMMUNIST INTERNATIONAL

Prague. Ústav dějin Komunistické strany Československa. Knihovna.
Soupis literatury k dějinám Komunistické internacionály. Sest.: Vlasta Krupičková. Praha, 1964.

iii, 121 p. 29 cm. (Its Bibliografické pomůcky)

Sworakowski, Witold S
The Communist International and its front organizations; a research guide and checklist of holdings in American and European libraries, by Witold S. Sworakowski. Stanford, Calif., Hoover Institution on War, Revolution, and Peace, 1965.

493 p. 27 cm. (Hoover Institution bibliographical series, 21)

COMMUNITY

Argentine Republic. Congreso. Biblioteca. Referencia General.
Desarrollo de la comunidad. Buenos Aires, 1967.

8 l. 28 cm. (Lista de materiales informativos, no. 15)

Brown, Ruth E
Community action programs: an annotated bibliography [by] Ruth E. Brown. Monticello, Ill., Council of Planning Librarians, 1972.

37 p. 28 cm. (Council of Planning Librarians. Exchange bibliography 277)

Chai, Alice Y
Community development in Korea; a bibliography of works in the Korean language. Compiled and annotated by Alice Y. Chai. [Honolulu] East-West Center, 1968.

ii, 67 l. 28 cm. (Occasional papers of Research Publications & Translations. Annotated bibliography series, no. 5)

Gamberg, Herbert.
The escape from power: politics in the American community (a monograph and selected bibliography) [Monticello, Ill., Council of Planning Librarians, 1969]

ii, 59 l. 28 cm. (Council of Planning Librarians. Exchange bibliography 106)

Hawley, Willis D
The study of community power; a bibliographic review [by] Willis D. Hawley & James H. Svara. Santa Barbara, Calif, ABC-Clio [1972]

viii, 123 p. 23 cm.

Jackson, Kathleen O'Brien.
Annotated bibliography on school-community relations. Compiled and annotated by Kathleen O'Brien Jackson. Eugene, Or., ERIC Clearinghouse on Educational Administration, 1969.

viii, 20 p. 28 cm. (ERIC Clearinghouse on Educational Administration. Bibliography series, no. 14)

Mendes, Richard H   P
Bibliography on community organization for citizen participation in voluntary democratic associations [by] Richard H. P. Mendes. [Washington] President's Committee on Juvenile Delinquency and Youth Crime; [for sale by the Superintendent of Documents, U. S. Govt. Print. Off.] 1965.

ii, 98 p. 26 cm.

Oregon. University. Bureau of Municipal Research and Service.
Issues in the community: an annotated bibliography of selected community problems in Oregon. [Eugene] 1967.

274 p. 28 cm.

U. S. Dept. of Health, Education, and Welfare. Library.
Community planning for health, education, and welfare; an annotated bibliography. Compiled for the Bureau of Family Services [by Dorothy M. Jones] Washington, U. S. Bureau of Family Services; [for sale by the Supt. of Docs., U. S. Govt. Print. Off., 1967]

viii, 57 p. 23 cm.

Wellman, Barry Stephen.
Community—network—communication: an annotated bibliography [edited by] Barry Wellman and Marilyn Whit-

aker. Monticello, Ill., Council of Planning Librarians, 1972.

138 p. 28 cm. (Council of Planning Librarians. Exchange bibliography 282, 283)

COMMUNITY AND COLLEGE

Fink, Ira Stephen.
Campus/community relationships: an annotated bibliography, compiled by Ira Stephen Fink and Joan Cooke. New York, Society for College and University Planning, 1971.

63 p. 28 cm.

Stuttgart. Universität. Projektgruppe UNIFO.
Universität. Stadt: Literaturanalyse u. Literaturdokumentation/ gefertigt im Auftr. d. Arbeitsgruppe Standort d. Univ. Dortmund. Projektgruppe UNIFO im Sonderforschungsbereich 63 (Hochschulbau) Städtebaul. Inst., Univ. Stuttgart. ₁Bearb.: Becker, Ruth u. a.₁ — Stuttgart: Städtebaul. Inst., Univ. Stuttgart. 1971.

17, ix, 521 p.; 21 cm.

COMMUNITY COLLEGES   see Junior colleges

COMMUNITY NEWSPAPERS

Hathorn's suburban press. 1971–
₁Chicago₁ Associated Release Service.

v. 24 x 30 cm.

"The Nation's guide to suburban markets."

COMO, ITALY

Archivio di Stato di Como.
Guida dell'Archivio di Stato di Como. A cura di Gabriella Poli Cagliari. Como, Camera di commercio, industria, artigianato e agricoltura, 1971.

106 p. plates. 23½ cm.

COMORO ISLANDS

Gorse, Jean.
Territoire des Comores; bibliographie ₁établie par M. Gorse, avec la collaboration de Mlle Sauvalle₁ Paris, Bureau pour le développement de la production agricole ₁1964?₁

iv, 75 l. 27 cm.

COMPANIES   see Corporations

COMPARATIVE EDUCATION   see Education, Comparative

COMPARATIVE LITERATURE   see Literature, Comparative

COMPLEX COMPOUNDS

Complexes and organometallic structures ₁bibliography 1935–69₁ Edited by Olga Kennard and David G. Watson. Utrecht, N. V. A. Oosthoek for the Crystallographic Data Centre Cambridge and the International Union of Crystallography ₁1970₁

xxiii, 264 p. 24 cm. (Molecular structures and dimensions, 2)

"Prepared at the Crystallographic Data Centre ... Cambridge."
Errata sheet inserted.

COMPOSERS

Canadian Music Centre, Toronto.
Reference sources for information on Canadian composers. Ouvrages de références sur les compositeurs canadiens. ₁Toronto₁ 1970.

11 l. 22 x 28 cm.

At head of title: Canadian Music Centre. Centre musical canadien.

COMPUTER TRANSLATING   see Translating

COMPUTERIZED TYPESETTING

Graham, Joseph Turnbull, 1930–
Computer typesetting: a select bibliography; compiled by J. T. Graham. Hatfield (Herts.) Hertfordshire County Council Technical Library and Information Service, 1966.

₁1₁, 39, iv p. 21½ cm.

Cover title.
"A HERTIS publication."
At head of title: Watford College of Technology.

Graham, Joseph Turnbull, 1930–
Computer typesetting, 1966–68: a select bibliography, compiled by J. T. Graham. Hatfield, Hertis, 1969.

₁4₁, 60 p. 21 cm.

Cover title.
On t. p. Watford College of Technology.
"A HERTIS publication."
Updated version of Computer typesetting compiled in 1966.

U. S. *Federal Electronic Printing Committee.*
A bibliography on electronic composition. Prepared for the Joint Committee on Printing, United States Congress. Washington, U. S. Govt. Print. Off., 1970.

iii, 58 p. 24 cm.

At head of title: 91st Congress, 2d session, Joint Committee Print.

COMPUTERS
see also Electronic data processing; Information storage and retrieval systems

Anderson, Richard H   1932–
A selective bibliography of computer graphics ₁by₁ R. H. Anderson. Santa Monica, Calif., Rand Corp. ₁1971₁

i, 33 p. 28 cm. (₁Rand Corporation. Paper₁ P–4629)

Annotated bibliography of the literature on resource sharing computer networks ₁by₁ R. P. Blanc ₁and others₁ Washington, National Bureau of Standards; ₁for sale by the Supt. of Docs., U.S. Govt. Print. Off.₁ 1973.

iv, 90 p. 26 cm. (National Bureau of Standards special publication 384)

Barnes, Colin I
Computer applications: a select bibliography compiled by Colin I. Barnes. Hatfield (Herts.), Hatfield College of Technology ₁1967₁

₁1₁, 66, viiip. 21 cm.

"A Hertis Publication."
Covers material published Jan. 1965–Dec. 1966.

C/I/L patent abstracts. v. 1–
July/Aug. 1969–

₍New York₎ Science Associates/International.

v. illus. 28 cm. bimonthly.

"Computer/information/library."

Gajkowicz-Dędys, Danuta.
Sieci komórkowe; bibliografia. Warszawa, 1973.

58 p. 24 cm. (Prace CO PAN, 110)

"Na prawach rękopisu."
Summary in English.

GIER System Library.
Index. København, Regnecentralen, 1969.

₍32₎ l. 80 cm.

Great Britain. British Council.
Some British books on computers; a select and annotated list. ₍London₎ British Council and National Book League ₍1972₎

35 p. 21 cm.

Knight, Geoffrey.
Computer software. Edited by Geoffrey Knight, Jr. Washington, Cambridge Communications Corp., ᶜ1968.

vii, 462, 16 p. 29 cm.

"This collection is compiled from Information processing journal and is a continuation of ... Cumulative computer abstracts."

Library Association. County Libraries Group.
Readers' guide to books on computers and data processing ₍compiled by Martin Woodrow₎ 2d ed. ₍Newton, Library Association (County Libraries Group), 1972₎

42 p. 19 cm. (Its Readers' guides, new series no. 128)

First ed. published in 1968 under title: Readers' guide to books on computers and E. D. P.

Library Association. *County Libraries Group.*
Readers' guide to books on computers and E. D. P. London, L. A. (County Libraries Group), 1968.

48 p. 19 cm. (Readers guide, new series, no. 104)

Morrill, Chester.
Computers and data processing: information sources; an annotated guide to the literature, associations, and institutions concerned with input, throughput, and output of data. Detroit, Gale Research Co. ₍1969₎

275 p. 22 cm. (Management information guide, 15)

Murphy, Janet.
COM-computer output microfilm; a selected bibliography compiled by J. Murphy. ₍Hatfield₎ Hertis, 1974.

₍38₎ p. 30 cm.

Polska Akademia Nauk. *Zakład Analogii.*
Komunikaty Zakładu Analogii na Konferencję Techniki Analogowej, Gliwice, wrzesień 1965 r.: Zastosowanie maszyn analogowych w przemyśle; zestawienie bibliograficzne. Warszawa, 1965.

24 p. 30 cm.

Cover title.
At head of title: Instytut Automatyki Polskiej Akademii Nauk.

Pritchard, Alan.
A guide to computer literature; an introductory survey of the sources of information. ₍Hamden, Conn.₎ Archon Books & C. Bingley ₍1969₎

130 p. 23 cm.

Pritchard, Alan.
A guide to computer literature: an introductory survey of the sources of information. London, Bingley, 1969.

130 p. 23 cm.

Pritchard, Alan.
A guide to computer literature; an introductory survey of the sources of information. 2d ed., rev. and expanded. ₍Hamden, Conn.₎ Linnet Books ₍1972₎

194 p. 23 cm.

Pritchard, Alan.
A guide to computer literature: an introductory survey of the sources of information. 2nd ed., revised and expanded. London, Bingley, 1972.

194 p. 23 cm.

Quarterly bibliography of computers and data processing.
no. 1–
Apr. 1971–
₍Phoenix, Applied Computer Research₎

no. 28 cm.

"A cumulative index to computer literature."

Rom, Ruth.
ספרים על מחשבים אלקטרוניים ועל שיטות חשובות; מבחר מאוספי ספריות הטכניון, נערך ע״י רות רום. חיפה, הטכניון, מכון טכנולוגי לישראל, 725, הספריה, 1965₎

56 p. 21 cm. (פרסומי ספרית הטכניון, ב-2)

Added t. p.: Books on computers and computing methods; a selective list of books in the Technion libraries.

Steiwer, Gaston.
Books on computation; new titles and reprints 1967/68, edited by Gaston Steiwer. Aarhus, Akademisk Boghandel, 1968.

144 p. 23 cm.

Stichting het Nederlands Studiecentrum voor Administratieve Automatisering.
International computer bibliography: a guide to books on the use, application and effect of computers in scientific, commercial, industrial and social environments. Manchester, National Computing Centre in co-operation with Stichting Het Nederlands Studiecentrum voor Administratieve Automatisering, Amsterdam, 1968.

₍508₎ p. 30 cm.

TRW software series: index to publications in print. no. 1–
July 1974–
Redondo Beach, Calif., TRW Systems Group, Systems Engineering and Integration Division.

no. 28 cm.

"Supersedes ... TRW software bibliography."

U. S. *Office of State Technical Services.*
Computers; selected bibliographic citations announced in U. S. Government research and development reports, 1966. Washington, State Technical Services, 1968.

ii, 86 p. 26 cm. (*Its* STS 108)

Vondráková, Jana.
Organizace a provoz výpočtových středisek. Výběrová

bibliografie knižní a časopisecké literatury. [Sest. Jana Vondráková a Václav Žilinský] Praha, Ústředí vědeckých, technických a ekonomických informací; Státní technická knihovna, 1970.

50 p. 21 cm. (Prague. Státní technická knihovna. Bibliografie, sv. 159)

Walkowicz, Josephine L
Benchmarking and workload definition: a selected bibliography with abstracts [by] Josephine L. Walkowicz. [Washington] National Bureau of Standards; [for sale by the Supt. of Docs., U. S. Govt. Print. Off.] 1974.

43 p. 26 cm. (NBS special publication 405)

PERIODICALS

Dorling, Alison Rosemary.
A guide to abstracting journals for computers and computing, by A. R. Dorling. London, National Reference Library of Science and Invention, Bayswater Division, 1972.

[1], 13 p. 25 cm. (National Reference Library of Science and Invention. Occasional publications)

Watters, Denys Hayes.
An enriched KWOC index to computer periodical literature. [n. p., 1971]

v, 65 p. 29 cm.

A world list of computer periodicals. Manchester, National Computing Centre, 1970.

[1], 102 p. illus. 30 cm.

CONCENTRATION CAMPS see World War, 1939-1945 - Prisoners and prisons

CONCERTO see under Symphony

CONCRETE
see also Cement

Al'tshuler, D   IA
[Prilozhenie mekhaniki razrushenila k issledovanilu betonnykh konstruktsil s treshchinami]
Приложение механики разрушения к исследованию бетонных конструкций с трещинами. Аннот. библиогр. указатель литературы за период 1964-1969 г. Ленинград, 1970.

118 p. 20 cm.
At head of title: Министерство энергетики и электрификации СССР. Главтехстройпроект. Всесоюзный научно-исследовательский институт гидротехники имени Б. Е. Веденеева. Отдел патентов и научно-технической информации. Лаборатория специальных исследований инженерных конструкций.

Al'tshuler, D   IA
[Treshchinoobrazovanie v zhelezobetonnykh konstruktsifakh]
Трещинообразование в железобетонных конструкциях. Аннот. библиогр. указатель зарубежной литературы за 1964-1969 гг. Ленинград, "Энергия," Ленингр. отд-ние, 1970.

60 p. 20 cm.
At head of title: Министерство энергетики и электрификации СССР. Главтехстройпрект. Всесоюзный научно-исследовательский институт гидротехники имени Б. Е. Веденеева and other organizations.

American Concrete Institute. Committee 209.
Shrinkage and creep in concrete, annotated. Prepared by ACI Committee 209, Creep and Shrinkage in Concrete: Adam M. Neville, Chairman [and others] Detroit, American Concrete Institute [1967-72]

2 v. 28 cm. (ACI bibliography no. 7, 10)
CONTENTS: [1] 1905-1966.—[2] 1966-1970.

American Concrete Institute. Committee 224, Cracking.
Causes, mechanism, and control of cracking in concrete, 1911-1970: annotated. [Detroit, American Concrete Institute, 1971]

92 p. 28 cm. (ACI bibliography no. 9)

American Concrete Institute. *Committee 412.*
Plain and reinforced concrete arches, annotated. Prepared as part of the work of ACI Committee 412, Plain and Reinforced Arches: James Michalos, chairman [and others] Detroit, American Concrete Institute [1966]

v, 34 p. 28 cm. (ACI bibliography no. 6)

Barskova, N   A
[Mekhanicheskala obrabotka betona i estestvennogo kamnia]
Механическая обработка бетона и естественного камня. Аннот. библиогр. указатель зарубежной литературы ... Ленинград, 1970.

48 p. 20 cm.

At head of title: Министерство энергетики и электрификации СССР, and other organizations.

Cohn, M   Z
Limit design for reinforced concrete structures; an annotated bibliography, by M. Z. Cohn. [Detroit, American Concrete Institute, 1970]

88 p. 28 cm. (ACI bibliography no. 8)

Épshteĭn, V   S
[Temperaturnye polia i termonaprfazhennoe sostofanie]
Температурные поля и термонапряженное состояние массивных бетонных конструкций. Аннот. библиогр. указатель. Ленинград, "Энергия," Ленингр. отд-ние, 1969.

49 p. 20 cm
At head of title: Министерство энергетики и электрификации СССР. Главтехстройпроект. Всесоюзный научно-исследовательский институт гидротехники имени Б. Е. Веденеева, and other organizations.

Gartner, Otakar.
Betonové nádrže a vodojemy. [Výběr lit.] Sest. Otakar Gartner a Dagmar Němcová. Brno, St. techn. knihovna, t. G 01, 1971.

54, [1] p. 21 cm. (Výběrový seznam, 4/1970)

Herzlíková, Vlasta.
Lehké betony. Seznam lit. Sest. Vlasta Herzlíková a Milan Matoušek. Brno, St, věd. knihovna-St. techn. knihovna, t. G 11, Dolní Kounice, 1970.

46, [1] p. 21 cm. (Brünn. Státní technická knihovna. Výběrový seznam, 3/1969)

Ячеистые бетоны. Библиогр. указатель литературы за 1960-1966 г. Ленинград, Сектор науч.-техн. информации, 1967.

204 p. 21 cm.

At head of title: Государственный комитет по гражданскому строительству и архитектуре при Госстрое СССР. Ленинградский зональный научно-исследовательский и проектный институт типового и экспериментального проектирования жилых и общественных зданий. Научно-техническая библиотека.

Joint ACI-ASCE Committee 441: Reinforced Concrete Columns.
Reinforced concrete columns, annotated. Boris Bresler,

chairman. Detroit, American Concrete Institute ₁1965₁

122 p. 28 cm. (ACI bibliography, no. 5)

Kramárová, A
Pórobetón v stavebníctve. Výberový zoznam z domácej a zahraničnej literatúry. Zost. A. Kramárová. Bratislava, Slov. techn. knižnica, cyklostyl., 1968.

₁2₁, 76, ₁1₁ p. 21 cm. (Bratislava. Slovenská technická knižnica. Edícia 2. Séria B: Výberové bibliografie)

Li, Shu-t'ien, 1900–
Chronological and classified bibliography on prestressed concrete piling and associated technology, 1946–1966. ₁Rapid City, S. D.₁ 1966.

viii, 70 l. 28 cm. (*His* Monographs on prestressed concrete piling technology, 10)

Li, Shu-t'ien, 1900–
Chronological bibliography on concrete quality control, 1957–1972/3. Compiled and edited under the direction of Shu-t'ien Li. ₁Rapid City, S. D.₁ 1973.

v, 62 l. 28 cm.

Minina, E   IA
₁Mekhanicheskie kharakteristiki betona₁
Механические характеристики бетона. Аннот. библиогр. указатель. Ленинград, 1970.

56 p. 20 cm.
At head of title: Министерство энергетики и электрификации СССР. Главтехстройпроект. Всесоюзный научно-исследовательский институт гидротехники имени Б. Е. Веденеева. Отдел патентов и научно-технической информации. Отдел бетонных и железобетонных конструкций гидросооружений.

Paunova, Anna.
Строителният метод ".Лифт слеб"; библиография, 1958–1967. ₁Съставител Анна Паунова. Редактор Георги Костов₁ София, 1968.

52 p. 20 cm.

On cover: Симпозиум на тема "Метода повдигащи плочи при строителството на многоетажни сгради"; доклади по проблемите на проектирането, изпълнението и развитието на строителството на многоетажни сгради по метода повдигащи плочи, Варна, 1968. Строителен метод Lift slab; библиография.

Tafrov, S   N
₁Vozdukhovovlekaiûshchie dobavki v gidrotekhnicheskom betone₁
Воздухововлекающие добавки в гидротехническом бетоне. Информ. справка зарубежной литературы за 1960–1968 гг. Ленинград, "Энергия," Ленингр. отд-ние, 1969.

51 p. 20 cm.
At head of title: Министерство энергетики и электрификации СССР. Главтехстройпроект. Всесоюзный научно-исследовательский институт гидротехники имени Б. Е. Веденеева. Отдел научно-технической информации.
By S. N. Tafrov and R. I. Kaminarova.

Texas Transportation Institute, College Station.
Concrete shrinkage and thermal expansion. ₁College Station, 1966₁

26 l. 28 cm. (Bibligraphy: Survey of library facilities project, 66–1)

Cover title.
Cooperative research: 2-8-54-1.
Sponsored by the Texas Highway Dept. in cooperation with Dept. of Commerce, Bureau of Public Roads.

Tkachenko, Glafira Mikhaïlovna.
₁Omonolichivanie stykov sbornykh zelezobetonnykh konstrukfsii₁
Омоноличивание стыков сборных железобетонных конструкций. Аннот. библиогр. указатель. Отечеств. и зарубежная литература 1963–1967 гг. ₁Сост. Г. М.

Ткаченко₁. Ленинград, "Энергия," Ленингр. отд-ние, 1969.

72 p. 20 cm.
At head of title: Министерство энергетики и электрификации СССР. Главтехстройпроект. Всесоюзный научно-исследовательский институт гидротехники имени Б. Е. Веденеева. Отдел патентов и научно-технической информации.

CONDEMNED BOOKS

Ditchfield, Peter Hampson, 1854–1930.
Books fatal to their authors. New York, B. Franklin ₁1970₁

xx, 244 p. 19 cm. (Burt Franklin Research & source works series, 495)

Drûbin, German Rafailovich.
Книги, восставшие из пепла. Москва, Книга, 1966.

181 p. illus., facsims., ports. 20 cm.

Farrer, James Anson, 1849–1925.
Books condemned to be burnt. ₁Folcroft, Pa.₁ Folcroft Library Editions, 1972.

xi, 206 p. 24 cm.

Reprint of the 1892 ed. issued in series: The Book-lover's library.

Germany (Federal Republic, 1949–   ). Bundesprüfstelle für Jugendgefährdende Schriften.
Gesamtverzeichnis der in der Liste der jugendgefährdenden Schriften befindlichen Bücher, Hefte, Periodika und sonstigen Prüfobjekte. 10. Aufl. Stand: 31. Dezember 1971. Bonn-Bad Godesberg: Bundesprüfstelle f. Jugendgefährdende Schriften ₁1972–

v. 15 cm.

Hart, William Henry, *d.* 1888.
Index expurgatorius Anglicanus: or, A descriptive catalogue of the principal books printed or published in England, which have been suppressed, or burnt by the common hangman, or censured, or for which the authors, printers, or publishers have been prosecuted. New York, B. Franklin ₁1969₁

290 p. 23 cm. (Burt Franklin bibliography & reference series, 302)

Reprint of the 1872–78 ed.

Lopez, Pasquale.
Sul libro a stampa e le origini della censura ecclesiastica. Napoli, Regina, 1972.

133 p. plates. 25 cm. (Collana historica, 1)

Palo Alto, Calif. Public Library.
Pressures from right & left. ₁Compiled by A. K. Pickrem, Coordinator of Readers' Services. Palo Alto, 1964₁

36 p. 22 cm.

Reusch, Franz Heinrich, 1825–1900.
Der Index der verbotenen Bücher. Ein Beitrag zur Kirchen- und Literaturgeschichte. Neudruck der Ausg. Bonn 1883–₁1885₁ Aalen, Scientia-Verlag, 1967.

2 v. in 3. 24 cm.

Sauvy, Anne.
Livres saisis à Paris entre 1678 et 1701. D'après une étude préliminaire de Motoko Ninomiya. La Haye, M. Nijhoff, 1972.

430 p. 25 cm. (Archives internationales d'histoire des idées, 50)

CONFEDERATE STATES OF AMERICA

Beers, Henry Putney, 1907–
Guide to the archives of the Government of the Confederate States of America. Washington, National Archives, General Services Administration; [for sale by the Supt. of Docs., U. S. Govt. Print. Off.] 1968.

ix, 536 p. facsim. 24 cm. (National Achives publication no. 68–15) 3.75

Companion vol. to Guide to Federal archives relating to the Civil War.

Harwell, Richard Barksdale.
The Confederate hundred; a bibliophilic selection of Confederate books, by Richard Harwell. [Urbana, Ill.] Beta Phi Mu, 1964.

xxiii, 58 p. facsims. 24 cm. (Beta Phi Mu. Chapbook no. 7)

Harwell, Richard Barksdale, *ed.*
Confederate imprints in the University of Georgia Libraries. Edited by Richard B. Harwell. Athens, University of Georgia Press, 1964.

xi, 49 p. facsims. 23 cm. (University of Georgia Libraries. Miscellanea publications, no. 5)

CONFIDENTIAL COMMUNICATIONS

Epstein, Lisa.
Newsman's privilege, an annotated bibliography, 1967–1973. [Sacramento, California State Library, Law Library, 1973.

19 p. 28 cm.

CONFUCIANISM

Wêng, Fang-kang, 1733–1818.
經義考補正 [12卷] 通志堂經解目錄 翁方綱撰 [臺北] 廣文書局 [1968]

10, 5, 496 p. 20 cm. (書目續編 37–38)

據粵雅堂叢書道光 30 (1850) 及咸豐 3 (1853) 刊二書影印

Yi, Ch'un-hŭi.
李朝書院文庫目錄 《李朝書院文庫目錄考》 李春熙編 [大韓民國國會圖書館司書局編輯 시울] 大韓民國國會圖書館 [1969]

40, 184, 12, 35 p. 26 cm.

CONGO (BRAZZAVILLE)

Perrot, Cl
République du Congo-Brazzaville; répertoire bibliographique. Établi par Cl. Perrot avec la collaboration de Hélène Sauvalle. [Paris, Bureau pour le développement de la production agricole, 1966?]

112 l. 27 cm.

CONGO (DEMOCRATIC REPUBLIC) see Zaire

CONGRÉGATION DE SAINT-MAUR see Benedictines. Congrégation de Saint-Maur

CONGREGATION OF THE MISSION see Vincentians

CONGRESSES AND CONVENTIONS

Coorman, Daniël.
Proeve van retrospectieve bibliografie van verslagen en mededelingen van congressen in België: 1875–1957. Voorlopige uitg. Essai de bibliographie rétrospective de comptes rendus et communications de congrès en Belgique: 1875–1957. Éd. provisoire. Brussel [Huidevetterstraat 80–84] Belgische Commissie voor Bibliografie, 1967 [i. e. 1968]

2 v. (xi, 527 p.) 21 cm. (Bibliographia Belgica, 100)

Ghent. Rijksuniversiteit. Bibliotheek. Catalografische Dienst.
Centrale catalogus van de congresliteratuur [aanwezig in de] Rijksuniversiteit te Gent. Colloquia, congressen, symposia e. d. Samengesteld door de Catalografische Dienst van de Centrale Bibliotheek onder leiding van E. Wille. Informatieverwerking: M. Lagasse-Verplanken. Gent, Centrale Bibliotheek van de Rijksuniversiteit, 1973.

183, 133 p. 33 cm.

Hove, Julien van.
Repertoire des comptes rendus de congrès, 1963–1966 [par] Julien van Hove, avec la collaboration des membres de la commission. Bruxelles, Commission belge de bibliographie, 1968.

380 p. 21 cm. (Bibliographia Belgica, 103)

Added t. p.: Repertorium van de verslagen en mededelingen van congressen, 1963–1966.

Vasilevskaĭa, A   D
Научные съезды, конференции и совещания в БССР. 1919–1968. Библиогр. указатель. Минск, 1970.

306 p. 21 cm.

At head of title: Академия наук Белорусской ССР. Фундаментальная библиотека им. Я. Коласа.
By A. D. Vasilevskaĭa and L. I. Zbralevich.

Yearbook of international congress proceedings. 1st ed.; 1960/67–
Brussels, Union of International Associations.

v. 26 cm. (Union of International Associations. Publication)

"Bibliography of reports arising out of meetings held by international organizations."
On spine, 1960/67–   : International meeting reports.

CONGRESSIONAL HEARINGS see Legislative hearings

CONGREVE, WILLIAM

Tennessee. University. Libraries.
The John C. Hodges Collection of William Congreve in the University of Tennessee Library: a bibliographical catalog. Compiled by Albert M. Lyles and John Dobson. Knoxville, 1970.

xiv, 135 p. illus., port. 24 cm. (Its Occasional publication, no. 1)

CONJURING

Hall, Trevor H
Old conjuring books: a bibliographical and historical study with a supplementary check-list [by] Trevor H. Hall.

London, Duckworth, 1972.

xvi, 228, [9] p. facsims., port. 24 cm.

Hall, Trevor H

Old conjuring books; a bibliographical and historical study with a supplementary check-list [by] Trevor H. Hall. New York, St. Martin's Press [1973]

xvi, 228 p. illus. 25 cm.

Heyl, Edgar G

Cues for collectors [by] Edgar Heyl. Chicago, Ireland Magic Co., 1964.

64 p. illus., facsims., port. 22 cm.

Potter, Jack, 1903–

The master index to magic in print; covering books and magazines in the English language published up to and including December 1964; edited by Micky Hades. Calgary, M. Hades Enterprises, 1967–

v. (loose-leaf) 30 cm.

Kept up to date by additions and revisions.

Winder, Roland.

Check list of the older books on conjuring in the library of Roland Winder as at December, 1966. [Leeds? Eng., 1966?]

32 p. illus., facsims., port. 26 cm.

Cover title: R. W. check list.

CONRAD, JOSEPH

Ehrsam, Theodore George.

A bibliography of Joseph Conrad. Compiled by Theodore G. Ehrsam. Metuchen, N. J., Scarecrow Press, 1969.

448 p. 22 cm.

London. Polish Library.

The Joseph Conrad Collection in the Polish Library in London: catalogue (nos. 1–399); compiled by Jadwiga Nowak. London, Polish Library, 1970.

59 p. facsims. 22 cm.

Teets, Bruce E   1914–

Joseph Conrad: an annotated bibliography of writings about him. Compiled and edited by Bruce E. Teets and Helmut E. Gerber. De Kalb, Northern Illinois University Press [1971]

xi, 671 p. 25 cm. (An Annotated secondary bibliography series on English literature in transition, 1880–1920)

CONSERVATION
see also Wildlife conservation

Biblioteksentralen, A/1, Oslo. Bibliografisk avdeling.

Naturvern. Litteraturliste. Utarb. av Tore Hernes. Oslo, 1970.

20 p. 21 cm. (Blant bøker, nr 22)

Carvajal, Joan.

Conservation education; a selected bibliography, compiled by Joan Carvajal and Martha E. Munzer. Danville, Ill., Interstate Printers & Publishers [1968]

xii, 98 p. 23 cm. (Conservation Education Association. Education: key to conservation)

———— Supplement. Danville, Ill., Interstate Printers &

Publishers [1971]

vi, 38 p. 23 cm.

Cocks, J   Fraser.

A bibliography of manuscript resources relating to natural resources and conservation in the Michigan Historical Collections of the University of Michigan, compiled by J. Fraser Cocks, III. [Ann Arbor, Mich.] 1970.

14 l. 28 cm.

Conservation Education Association. Publication Committee.

Environmental conservation education; a selected annotated bibliography. Compiled for the Conservation Education Association. Danville, Ill., Interstate Printers & Publishers [1974]

70 p. 28 cm. (Conservation Education Association. Education: key to conservation, key no. 0)

"Includes most of the books listed in the CEA bibliography [compiled by J. Carvajal and M. E. Munzer] published in 1968 and the supplement published in 1971."

Dokumentation für Umweltschutz und Landschaftspflege.

11.-
Jahrg., n. F.; 1971–
[Stuttgart] W. Kohlhammer.

v. 30 cm. quarterly.

Continues Mitteilungen zur Landschaftspflege issued by: Germany (Federal Republic, 1949–). Bundesanstalt für Naturschutz und Landschaftspflege.
"Herausgegeben von der Bundesanstalt für Vegetationskunde, Naturschutz und Landschaftspflege."

Knîazeva, E   N

(Chelovek i sreda)

Человек и среда. Материалы к теме. Список литературы на рус. яз. преимущественно за 1968–1971 гг. [Сост. библиограф Князева Е. Н.] Москва, 1972.

32 p. 19 cm.

Cover title.
At head of title: Государственная библиотека СССР имени В. И. Ленина. Информационно-библиографический отдел.

Morkūnaitė, Ž

Tarybų Lietuvos gamta ir jos apsauga; rekomenduojamos literatūros rodyklė. Vilnius, 1966.

101 p. 20 cm.

At head of title: Lietuvos TSR Valstybinė respublikinė biblioteka. Introduction also in Russian.
"Gamtos apsauga Tarybų Lietuvoje," by K. Balevičius (Lithuanian and Russian, with summary in English): p. 7–27.

Nasedkina, Vera Aleksandrovna.

Внимание—природа. Рек. указатель литературы. Москва, "Книга," 1970.

97 p. 20 cm.

At head of title: Государственная ордена Ленина библиотека СССР имени В. И. Ленина. В. А. Наседкина.

National Book League, London.

Man and environment. London, National Book League in association with the Nature Conservancy [1970].

31 p. 22 cm.

Ozerova, Galina Aleksandrovna.

Берегите природу! [Аннот. указатель] Составитель Г. А. Озерова. [Москва, "Книга," 1967].

16 p. 20 cm. (Мир, труд, коммунизм, вып. 12)

Caption title.
At head of title: Государственная ордена Трудового красного Знамени публичная библиотека им. М. Е. Салтыкова-Щедрина.

Paulsen, David F
Natural resources in the governmental process; a bibliography selected and annotated [by] David F. Paulsen. Tucson, University of Arizona Press [1970]

99 p. 23 cm. (University of Arizona. Institute of Government Research. American Government studies, no. 3)

Rounds, Sandra M
A bibliography on environmental problems. Compiled by Sandra M. Rounds and Jo-Ann Michalak. [Bloomington?] Reference Dept., Indiana University Library, 1970.

15 p. 28 cm.

"Listing of the books and periodicals to be found in the Indiana University Main Library building ... Include[s] only those books which are related to the subjects that will be discussed at Indiana University on April 22, 1970, during the Environmental Teach-In."

Wahlberg, Sven, 1920–
Naturen och människan. Ett urval böcker, tidskrifter, 1 judbildband och smalfilmer. [Av] Sven och Marianne Wahlberg. I samarbete med Svenska naturskyddsföreningen. Lund, Bibliotekstjänst, 1970.

30 p. 21 cm. (Btj-serien, 25)

Wahlberg, Sven, 1920–
Naturen och människan. Ett urval böcker, tidskrifter, ljubildband och smalfilmer. [Av] Sven och Marianne Wahlberg. 2 omarb. uppl. I samarbete med Svenska naturskyddsföreningen. Lund, Bibliotekstjänst, 1972.

42 p. 21 cm. (Btj-serien. 41)

Watt, Lois Belfield.
Environmental-ecological education: a bibliography of fiction. nonfiction and textbooks for elementary and secondary schools. compiled by Lois B. Watt and Myra H. Thomas. Boulder, Colo. [Clearinghouse for Social Studies/Social Science Education]; for sale by the Supt. of Docs., U. S. Govt. Print. Off., Washington, 1971.

34 p. 29 cm. (ERIC Clearinghouse for Social Studies/Social Science Education. Reference series, no. 5)

LIBRARY CATALOGS

Denver. Public Library. Conservation Library.
Catalog of the Conservation Library. Denver Public Library. — Boston : G. K. Hall, 1974.

6 v. ; 37 cm.

CONTENTS: Catalog of books. Serials. 2 v.—Special indexing file. 4 v.

CONSTANT, BENJAMIN

Catalogo delle opere di Benjamin Constant publicate in lingua italiana in Italia e in Svizzera. Milano, novembre 1967. Centre français d'études et d'information, Consolato generale di Svizzera. [n. p., 1967?].

6 p. 21 cm.

CONSTITUTIONAL CONVENTIONS

Browne, Cynthia E
State constitutional conventions from independence to the completion of the present Union, 1776-1959; a bibliography, compiled by Cynthia E. Browne. Introd. by Richard H. Leach. Westport, Conn., Greenwood Press [1973]

xl, 250 p. 24 cm.

Chicago State College.
A selected bibliography on constitutional conventions, pre-

pared by Chicago State College: John A. Rackauskas [and others, and] Eastern Illinois University: Betty Heartbank, Verne Stockman [and] B. J. Szerenyi. [Chicago, 1970?]

12 p. 28 cm. (A Publication of the Public Information Committee on the Sixth Illinois Constitutional Convention, pt. 1)

Montana. Constitutional Convention Commission.
Selected bibliography. [Helena, 1971?]

5 p. 28 cm. (Montana Constitutional Convention memorandums, memorandum no. 7)

At head of title: Montana Constitutional Convention. 1971-1972.

New York (State). State Library. *Albany. Legislative Reference Library.*
Constitutional revision in the Empire State; a bibliography. Albany, 1967.

8 p. 28 cm. (Convention series, no. 1)

CONSTITUTIONAL LAW

Correa Saavedra, Mario.
Bibliografía del derecho constitucional. [Santiago de Chile, C. E. Gibbs A.] 1967.

352 p. 19 cm.

Popović, Milijan, 1938–
Građa za bibliografiju teorije države i prava. Prevela na francuski Madeleine Stevanov-Charlier. Novi Sad, Pravni fakultet—Zavod za naučno-istraživački rad, 1972.

xii, 386, [2] p. 24 cm.

Added t, p.: Matériaux bibliographiques de la théorie générale de l'État et du droit.
Serbo-Croatian and French.

CONSTRUCTION   see   Building

CONSUMERS

Bibliography on marketing to low-income consumers. Washington, U. S. Dept. of Commerce, Business and Defense Services Administration, in cooperation with the National Marketing Advisory Committee Task Force of the U. S. Dept. of Commerce; For sale by the Supt. of Docs., U. S. Govt. Print. Off., 1969.

49 p. 26 cm.

Interested parties contributed references to the clearinghouse established at the University of Minnesota.

Canada. *Parliament. Library. Reference Branch.*
Consumers and consumer problems; select bibliography/ Le consommateur et ses problèmes; bibliographie sélective. Ottawa, 1967.

23 l. 28 cm.

At head of title: 27th Parliament.
Caption title.
Text in English and French.

Marketing and the low income consumer. [Rev. ed.] Washington, U. S. Bureau of Domestic Commerce; for sale by the Supt. of Docs., U. S. Govt. Print. Off. [1971]

65 p. 26 cm.

"A United States Department of Commerce publication."
1969 ed. issued under title: Bibliography on marketing to low-income consumers.

National Association of Manufacturers of the United States of America. *Market Development/Distribution Dept.*
TIPS: techniques in product selection; a handbook of

information on consumer products & services. New York ₁1968₁

iv, 124 p. illus. 28 cm.

Saskatchewan. Provincial Library, Regina. Bibliographic Services Division.
Consumer education; a bibliography. Regina, 1973.

18 p. 22 cm.

U. S. Office of Consumer Affairs.
Consumer education bibliography, prepared by the Office of Consumer Affairs and the New York Public Library. ₁Washington; For sale by the Supt. of Docs., U. S. Govt. Print. Off., 1971.

vii, 192 p. 23 cm.

Yonkers, N. Y. Public Library.
Consumer education bibliography. Washington, For sale by the Supt. of Docs., U. S. Govt. Print. Off. ₁1969₁

x, 170 p. 24 cm.

"Prepared for the President's Committee on Consumer Interests."

CONTINI, GIANFRANCO

Breschi, Giancarlo.
Bibliografia degli scritti di Gianfranco Contini. Firenze, Società dantesca italiana, 1973.

77 p. 25 cm.

CONTRACTS

Farrell, David M
The contracting out of work; an annotated bibliography, by David M. Farrell. Kingston, Ont., Industrial Relations Centre, Queen's University, 1965.

v, 61 p. 24 cm. (Industrial Relations Centre, Queen's University at Kingston, Ont. Bibliography series, no. 1)

CONYBEARE, FREDERICK CORNWALLIS

Mariès, Louis.
Frederick Cornwallis Conybeare (1856–1924); notice biographique et bibliographie critique. New York, B. Franklin ₁1970₁

154 p. 23 cm. (Burt Franklin bibliography and reference series, 388)

Pages also numbered as 186–332 of Revue des études arméniennes. Reprint of the edition published in Paris, 1926.

COOK, SIR ALBERT RUSKIN

Albert Cook Library.
Albert Ruskin Cook, 1870–1951; a select bibliography prepared on the occasion of the centenary celebrations March 6–8, 1970, Kampala, with chronology. Kampala ₁Uganda₁ 1970.

11 p. 15 cm.

COOK, JAMES

Dunedin, N. Z. Public Library.
Captain James Cook; a select bibliography compiled from the collection at Dunedin Public Library. ₁Dunedin₁ 1969.

14 l. 26 cm.

Holmes, Sir Maurice, 1885–
Captain James Cook; a bibliographical excursion. New

York, B. Franklin ₁1968₁

103 p. facsims. 23 cm. (Literature of discovery, exploration, and geography, 4)

Burt Franklin bibliography and reference series, 262.
Title on spine: Bibliography of Captain Cook.
Reprint of the 1952 ed., a revised and expanded ed. of An introduction to the bibliography of Captain James Cook, R. N.

New South Wales. Library.
Bibliography of Captain James Cook, R. N., F. R. S., circumnavigator. Editor: M. K. Beddie. 2d ed. Sydney ₁Council of the Library of New South Wales₁ 1970.

xvi, 894 p. 25 cm.

First ed. published in 1928 by the Mitchell Library of the Public Library of New South Wales.

Sydney. Public Library of New South Wales. *Mitchell Library.*
Bibliography of Captain James Cook, R. N., F. R. S., circumnavigator. New York, B. Franklin ₁1968₁
172 p. 24 cm. (Burt Franklin bibliography and reference series no. 176)
Reprint of the 1928 ed.
"Comprising the collections in the Mitchell Library and General Reference Library, the private collections of William Dixson, Esq., and J. A. Ferguson, Esq., and items of special interest in the National Library, Canberra, the Australasian Pioneers' Club, Sydney, and in the collection of the Kurnell Trust."

COOKERY
see also   Food

Berckel, Hortense W   van.
De buitenlandse keuken in Nederland; bibliografie van boeken over buitenlandse kookkunst verschenen nà 1945, samengesteld door Hortense W. van Berckel. ₁Amsterdam, Bibliotheek- en Documentatieschool₁ 1969.

vi, 30 l. 30 cm.

"Werkstuk 2e cyclus Bibliotheek- en Documentatieschool, Amsterdam."

Bitting, Katherine (Golden) 1869–1937.
Gastronomic bibliography. San Francisco, 1939. Ann Arbor, Mich., Gryphon Books, 1971.

xiii, 718 p. illus., facsims., ports. 22 cm.

Cook, Margaret.
America's charitable cooks: a bibliography of fundraising cook books published in the United States (1861–1915). Kent, Ohio, 1971.

315 p. illus. 24 cm.

Library Association. County Libraries Group.
Readers' guide to books on cookery ₁compiled by Mrs. G. M. Cox₁. Newton, Library Association (County Libraries Group), 1971.

28 p. 19 cm. (Its Reader's guides, new series no. 124)

Lowenstein, Eleanor.
Bibliography of American cookery books, 1742–1860. ₁3d ed₁ Worcester ₁Mass.₁ American Antiquarian Society, 1972.

xii, 132 p. 25 cm.

"Based on Waldo Lincoln's American cookery books, 1742–1860."

Ryšánková, Helena, comp.
Kuchařky; výběrová bibliografie. ₁Sest. Helena Ryšánková₁. Plzeň, 1968.

43 l. 21 cm. (Krajská knihovna Plzeň. Malé bibliografie, sv. 34)

Uhler, John Earle.
The Rochester Clarke bibliography of Louisiana cookery, edited by John E. and Glenna Uhler. Plaquemine, La., Iberville Parish Library [1966]

89 p. 22 cm.

Lists works collected by Rochester Clarke and supplemental material.

COOLING TOWERS

Akulova, Lîûdmila Grigor'evna.
Градирни. Аннот. библиогр. справочник. Ленинград, "Энергия," Ленингр. отд-ние, 1968–

v. 22 cm.

At head of title, v. : Министерство энергетики и электрификации СССР. Главтехстройпроект. Всесоюзный научно-исследовательский институт гидротехники имени Б. Е. Веденеева. Л. Г. Акулова, Л. Э. Родэ.

Contents.—
2. Иностранная литература.

COOPER, JAMES FENIMORE

Spiller, Robert Ernest, 1896–
A descriptive bibliography of the writings of James Fenimore Cooper, by Robert E. Spiller & Philip C. Blackburn. New York, B. Franklin [1968]

ix, 259 p. facsims. 23 cm. (Burt Franklin bibliography & reference series, 242)

"Originally published, 1903."

COOPERATION; COOPERATIVE SOCIETIES
see also Agriculture, Cooperative

Basal, S C 1923–
Documentation on co-operative development. Edited S. C. Basal. Jaipur, Co-operative Dept., Rajasthan [1968?]

iv, i, 117, 5 p. 24 cm. (Sahkari vyavahar pustakmala, 14)

Buczkowska, Maria.
Bibliografia wydawnictw książkowych i ważniejszych artykułów dotyczących spółdzielczości pracy za lata 1954–1969. Warszawa, Zakład Wydawnictw CRS, 1972.

158 p. 24 cm.

At head of title: Centralny Związek Spółdzielczości Pracy. Maria Buczkowska, Barbara Pierzchałowa.

Georgetown, Guyana. Public Library.
Bibliography on co-operatives. Prepared by Public Free Library in collaboration with Co-operatives Division, Ministry of Economic Development. Georgetown, Public Free Library, 1971.

ix, 64 p. 28 cm.

International Co-operative Alliance. *Regional Office and Education Centre for South-East Asia.*
Annotated bibliography of literature produced by the co-operative movements in South-east Asia. New Delhi [1964–

1 v. (loose-leaf) 27 cm.

———— Supplement.
New Delhi.

v. 30 cm. semiannual.

International Labor Office. *Library.*
Cooperation. Rev. ed. Geneva, 1964.

102 p. (*Its* Bibliographical contributions, no. 23. Contributions

bibliographiques, no. 23)

First published in 1958 under title: Bibliography on cooperation.

Jastrzębski, Wojciech.
Bibliografia orzecnictwa i piśmiennictwa z zakresu prawa spółdzielczego za lata 1961–1966. Warszawa, Zakład Wydawnictw CRS, 1972.

122 p. 24 cm. (Spółdzielczy Instytut Badawczy. Seria bibliograficzna 7)

La Plata. Universidad Nacional. *Instituto de Estudios Cooperativos.*
Catálogo de la ii [i. e. Segunda] exposición universitaria de libro cooperativo, organizada por el Instituto de Estudios Cooperativos, 29 de junio–4 de julio, 1964. La Plata, 1964.

97 p. 23 cm.

At head of title: Universidad Nacional de la Plata. Facultad de Ciencias Económicas.

Maggiolo V , Lorenzo.
Bibliografía sobre cooperativas [por] Lorenzo Maggiolo [y] Augusto Celis M. Valencia, Ediciones de la Universidad de Carabobo, 1968.

65 p. 23 cm.

On cover: Universidad de Carabobo. Facultad de Ciencias Económicas y Sociales. Centro de Planificación y Desarrollo Económico. Sección de Cooperativas.

Peru. Oficina Nacional de Desarrollo Cooperativo. Biblioteca.
Catálogo de publicaciones de la ONDECOOP, 1965–1971. [Lima, 1972]

ii, 52 p. 28 cm. (Cenacoop. Serie bibliográfica, no. 5)

"Incluye todas las publicaciones realizadas por la ONDECOOP y su antecesor INCOOP ... y que forman parte del patrimonio de la Biblioteca."
"Persona responsable de esta edición: Alicia Ibáñez."

Pinho, Diva Benevides.
Cooperativismo: seleção bibliográfica. São Paulo ISPECO [1967?]

38 p. 23 cm.

Originally published in part 4 of the author's thesis Cooperativas e desenvolvimento econômico, Universidade de São Paulo, 1962.

Shatil, Joseph E
Bibliography (temporary) of studies of rural cooperation in Israel. Prepared by Joseph E. Shatil. [Jerusalem] 1965.

46 p. 28 cm.

At head of title: State of Israel, Ministry of Labor, Department of Cooperation.

Smethurst, John B
A bibliography of co-operative societies' histories / compiled by John B. Smethurst. — Manchester : Co-operative Union Ltd., [1974]

[10], 122 p. ; 34 cm.

Whitney, Howard S
Bibliography on cooperatives and social and economic development, prepared by Howard S. Whitney and Hassan A. Ronaghy, with the assistance of Adlowe L. Larson, Wayne H. Weidemann [and] Mary Jean McGrath, in cooperation with the International Cooperative Development Service of the Agency for International Development. Madison, International Cooperative Training Center, University Extension Division, University of Wisconsin [1964]

79 p. 29 cm.

COOTE, GEORGE GIBSON

Glenbow-Alberta Institute.
George Gibson Coote papers, 1907–1956. Calgary, Glenbow Archives, 1969.

31 p. 28 cm. (Glenbow archives series, no. 4)

COPENHAGEN

Copenhagen. Kommunebibliotekerne.
Københavns bibliografi; litteratur om København til 1950, ved Svend Thomsen, Drude Lange ₍og₎ Irmelin Nordentoft. ₍København₎ 1957–60.

3 v. 22 cm.

————————Supplement. København, 1967–

v.

CONTENTS.—1. 1951–1965, ved S. Thomsen.

COPERNICUS, NICOLAUS

Baranowski, Henryk.
Bibliografia Kopernikowska, 1509–1955. Opracował Henryk Baranowski. ₍New York, Lenox Hill Pub. & Dist. Co., 1970₎

448 p. facsims. 22 cm. (Burt Franklin: bibliography and reference series 303. Science classics 5)

At head of title: Polska Akademia Nauk. Komitet Historii Nauk. Preface also in French.

Biskup, Marian.
Regesta Copernicana. Wrocław, Zakład Narodowy im. Ossolińskich, 1973.

241 p. illus. 25 cm. (Studia Copernicana, 7)

At head of title: Polska Akademia Nauk. Zakład Historii Nauki i Techniki.
Preface also in French and Russian.

Chapin, Seymour L
Nicolaus Copernicus, 1473-1973; his revolutions and his revolution. Catalogue of an exhibition of manuscripts & books, with an historical essay by Seymour L. Chapin. ₍Los Angeles, Printed by Plantin Press, 1973₎

49 p. illus. 29 cm.

Exhibition held at the Linderman Library, Lehigh University, Bethlehem, Pa., Sept.-Nov. 1973.

Łódź, Poland. Miejska Biblioteka Publiczna.
Copernicana w zbiorach Miejskiej Biblioteki Publicznej. (wybór) ₍Oprac. Malgorzata Basińska₎. Łódź, 1971.

30 p. 24 cm.

At head of title: Miejska Biblioteka Publiczna im. L. Waryńskiego w Łodzi.

ĆOPIĆ, BRANKO

Библиографија целокупних дела Бранка Ћопића. Београд, Просвета, 1964.

clxvii p. 19 cm.

Preface signed: Станка Костић.

COPPER

Copper abstracts. v. 1–
1970–
₍The Hague?₎

v. 30 cm.

"Selected abstracts of recent literature."

Malhotra, Subhash C
Bibliography on copper smelting, by Subhash C. Malhotra. ₍Salt Lake City, Printed by Insight Print. & Graphics₎ 1973.

xxiii, 271 p. illus. 24 cm.

COPYING PROCESSES
see also Xerography

Bard Laboratories.
Bibliographies on reprography. ₍Amherst, N. H., 1969₎

10 v. 28 cm.

Caption title.

CONTENTS.—section 1–2. Thermographic processes.—section 3 & 5. Physical microencapsulation. Liquid crystals.—section 4. Chemical encapsulation (molecular complexes) 2 v.—section 6. Physical means for imaging.—section 7. Recording papers.—section 8–10. Organic photoconductors. Photoelectrochemical processes. Electrostatic developers.—section 11–13. Photopolymerization and photodepolymerization. Binder free silver halide systems. Explosive materials for photo-imaging.—section 14–16. Pressure marking systems. Mimeograph. High speed printing.—section 17. Free radical systems.

————Supplement. 1970–
Amherst, N. H.

v. 28 cm.

Gőrnerová, Anna.
Reprografia v informačných strediskách. Zost.: Anna Gőrnerová, Pavol Pohánka. Bratislava, Slov. techn. knižnica, rotaprint, 1968.

91, ₍1₎ p. 20 cm. (Edícia: Metodické pomôcky SITK. Séria B: Bibliografie, č. 6)

Summary also in Russian and German.

Jones, Rennie C
The application of copying processes to work with current records and historical manuscripts; selected references, compiled by Rennie C. Jones. ₍Melbourne₎ State Library of Victoria, 1966.

35 p. 26 cm. (Victoria. State Library. Research bibliographies 1966, no. 7)

Pretoria. State Library.
Bibliography of reprography. Bibliografie oor reprografie. Pretoria, the Library, 1970.

₍viii₎ 42 p. 23 cm. (Pretoria. State Library. Bibliographies, no. 15)

Text in English and Afrikaans.

COPYRIGHT

Huang. Paul Te-Hsien.
Bibliography on copyright. ₍Halifax, N. S., 1971₎

vi, 61, i, 15 l. 29 cm.

Huang, Paul Te-Hsien.
Bibliography on copyright, compiled by Te-Hsien Huang. ₍2d ed. Halifax, 1972₎

vi, 118 l. 28 cm.

Huang, Paul Te-Hsien.
Union list of copyright publications in West European libraries. Catalogue collectif des ouvrages sur la propriété intellectuelle dans les bibliothèques de l'Europe occidentale. Bibliographisches Verzeichnis zum Urheberrecht anhand des Bestandes von 11 West Europäischen Bibliotheken, com-

piled by Te-Hsien Huang. Halifax, 1974.
xii, 621 p. 28 cm.
English, French, and German.

White, Anthony G
Copyrights, : a selected bibliography / Anthony G. White ; Mary Vance, editor. — Monticello, Ill. : Council of Planning Librarians, 1974.

9 p. ; 28 cm. — (Exchange bibliography - Council of Planning Librarians ; 686)

PERIODICALS

Roberts, Matt, 1929-
Copyright: a selected bibliography of periodical literature relating to literary property in the United States. Metuchen, N.J., Scarecrow Press, 1971.

416 p. 22 cm.

CORN see Grain; Maize

CORNEILLE, PIERRE

Le Verdier, Pierre Jacques Gabriel, 1854-
Additions à la Bibliographie cornélienne, par P. Le Verdier et É. Pelay. New York, B. Franklin [1970]

xi, 251 p. 21 cm. (Burt Franklin bibliography & reference, 392. Theatre and drama series, 18)

Reprint of the edition published in Rouen, 1908.
"Ce livre est né de l'Exposition cornélienne, réunie à Rouen, au mois de juin 1906, à l'occasion du troisième centenaire de la naissance de Pierre Corneille."

CORNWALLIS, CHARLES CORNWALLIS, 1st MARQUIS

Reese, George Henkle.
The Cornwallis papers; abstracts of Americana. Compiled by George H. Reese. Charlottesville, Published for Virginia Independence Bicentennial Commission [by] University Press of Virginia [1970]

xiv, 260 p. 24 cm. (Virginia Independence bicentennial publication no. 2)

CORPORATION LAW

10 [i. e. **Zehn**] Jahres-Spiegel des Aktienwesens, 1956–1965; Aktienwesen und Wirtschaftsentwicklung im Spiegel der Fachpresse. Hamburg, Trede [°1966]

143 p. 30 cm.

At head of title: Die Aktiengesellschaft; Zeitschrift für das gesamte Aktienwesen.

CORPORATIONS

American Society of Corporate Secretaries.
Reference list for corporate secretaries. Published for the use of the society and its members. New York [1968]

12 p. 28 cm.

Donaldson, Gordon, 1922-
Corporate and business finance; a classified bibliography of recent literature, compiled by Gordon Donaldson and Carolyn Stubbs. [Boston] Baker Library, Graduate School of Business Administration, Harvard University, 1964.

85 p. 25 cm. (Baker Library, Graduate School of Business Administration, Harvard University. Reference list no. 22)

Kansai Daigaku, Osaka. Keizai Seiji Kenkyūjo.
(Shashi dantaishi mokuroku)

関西大学.経済・政治研究所

社史・団体史目録

吹田 1968
88p 21cm

Rodhe, Knut, 1909-
Litteraturanvisningar för internationäll bolagsrätt. 4. uppl. Lund, Juridiska föreningen i Lund; Studentlitteratur (distr.), 1973.

23 p. 23 cm.

At head of title: Handelshögskolan i Stockholm, Rättsvetenskapliga institutionen.

Sperry, Robert, 1933-
Mergers and acquisitions: a comprehensive bibliography. [Washington, Mergers & Acquisitions, inc., 1972]

vii, 223 p. 29 cm.

At head of title: Mergers & acquisitions, the journal of corporate venture.

Tōkyō Daigaku. Keizaigakubu.
(Eigyō hōkokusho mokuroku)

営業報告書目録—戦前之部—東京　東京大学経済学部　昭和45(1970)

117 p. 25 cm. [和書主題別目録　7]

Toronto. Public Libraries.
Early Canadian companies; a guide to sources of information in the Toronto Public Libraries on selected Canadian companies over 100 years old. Compiled by Barbara B. Byers, Gabriel Pal and members of the staff of the Business Reference Section, City Hall Branch, Toronto Public Library. Toronto, 1967.

32 p. facsims. 23 cm.

CORRESPONDENCE SCHOOLS AND COURSES

Holmberg, Börje.
Studies in education by correspondence. A bibliography, edited by Börje Holmberg. Publ. by Hermods on behalf of the Educational committee of CEC (the European Council for Education by Correspondence). Malmö, Hermods, 1968.

72 p. 20 cm.

CORROSION AND ANTI-CORROSIVES

Dobruská, Naděžda.
Koroze dopravních prostředků; výběrová bibliografie knižní a časopisecké literatury. Praha, [UVTEI] 1970.

95 p. 21 cm. (Státní technická knihovna v Praze. Bibliografie, sv. 149)

At head of title: Ústředí vědeckých, technických a ekonomických informací. Státní technická knihovna v Praze, nositelka řádu republiky.

Philipp, Hans-Joachim.
Organische Inhibitoren der Metallkorrosion. Bearb. von Hans-Joachim Philipp, Karlheinz Richter [und] Manfred Seidel. Berlin, Verlag Technik (1967).

205 p. 21 cm. (Bibliothek der Technischen Universität Dresden. Bibliographische Arbeiten, Nr. 2)

Spindler, Harald.
Korrosion und Korrosionsschutz unter tropischen Klimabedingungen. Eine Bibliographie für die Jahre 1960–1969. [Von] H. Spindler. (Dresden, Techn. Univ., Bibliothek [1970].)

146 p. 21 cm. (Bibliothek der Technischen Universität Dresden. Bibliographische Arbeiten, Nr. 5)

Vallée, Marie Geneviève.
Influence des radiations sur la corrosion, par Marie-Geneviève Vallée, en collaboration avec M. Mouhot. [Gif-sur-Yvette (S.-et-O), Commissariat à l'énergie atomique, Service de documentation] 1964.

53 p. 27 cm. (Commissariat à l'énergie atomique. Série "Bibliographies," no 16)

On cover: Centre d'études nucléaires de Saclay.

CORROZET, GILLES

Bonnardot, Alfred, 1808–1884.
Gilles Corrozet et Germain Brice. Études bibliographiques sur ces deux historiens de Paris. (Réimpr. de l'éd. de Paris, 1880.) Genève, Slatkine Reprints, 1971.

iv, 69 p. 23 cm.

CORSI, EDWARD

Syracuse University. Library. Manuscript Division.
Edward Corsi; inventory of his papers. Compiled by Roberta Thibault. Syracuse, N. Y., 1969.

32 l. port. 28 cm. (Manuscript inventory series, inventory no. 13)

CORSO, GREGORY

Wilson, Robert Alfred Jump, 1922–
A bibliography of works by Gregory Corso, 1954–1965, compiled by Robert A. Wilson. New York, Phoenix Book Shop, 1966.

v, 40 p. 22 cm. (The Phoenix bibliographies, no. 2)

CORTÉS, HERNANDO

Valle, Rafael Heliodoro, 1891–1959.
Bibliografía de Hernán Cortés. New York, B. Franklin [1970]

viii, 209 p. illus. 19 cm. (Burt Franklin bibliography and reference, 386. Literature of discovery, exploration & geography series, 7)

Reprint of the 1953 ed.

COSER, LEWIS A.

Hill, Suzanne.
Lewis Coser; [list of publications] Potsdam, N. Y., State University College, 1970.

2 l. 28 cm. (Frederick W. Crumb Memorial Library. Publication no. 70-4)

COST

Crouse, Robert L
Value engineering/analysis bibliography [by] Robert L. Crouse. [Rev. ed.] n. p., Available from Society of American Value Engineers [1967]

xxviii, 198 p. 28 cm.

Hertfordshire, *Eng. Technical Library and Information Service.*
Value engineering bibliography. Hatfield (Herts.), Hatfield College of Technology, 1966.

[1], 28 p. 21 cm.

Mitchell, Bruce, 1944–
Benefit-cost analysis: a select bibliography [by] Bruce Mitchell and Joan Mitchell. [Monticello, Ill., Council of Planning Librarians, 1972]

44 p. 28 cm. (Council of Planning Librarians. Exchange bibliography 267)

Ruokonen, Kyllikki.
Arvoanalyysi; uudempaa kotimaista ja ulkomaista kirjallisuutta. Value analysis; recent Finnish and foreign literature. Helsinki, Kauppakorkeakoulun kirjasto, 1972.

[1], 10 p. 30 cm. (Kauppakorkeakoulun kirjaston julkaisuja, 2)

Sherwin Neal and Associates.
Bibliography on cost engineering-process industries June 1970/71. Henley-on-Thames (14 Friday St., Henley-on-Thames, Oxon. RG9 1AJ), Richard S. Gothard & Co. Ltd, [1971].

[3], 22 leaves. 29 cm.

COSTA, JOAQUÍN

Cheyne, George J G
A bibliographical study of the writings of Joaquín Costa, 1846–1911 [by] George J. G. Cheyne. London, Tamesis Books, 1972.

iii-xix, 189, [24] p. facsims., ports. 25 cm. (Coleccion Tamesis. Serie A: Monografias, 24)

COSTA RICA

Lines, Jorge A 1891–
Anthropological bibliography of aboriginal Costa Rica. Bibliografía antropológica aborigen de Costa Rica. [By] Jorge A. Lines. Provisional edition. San José, Tropical Science Center, 1967.

xiv, 190 p. front. 22 cm. (Tropical Science Center. Occasional paper no. 7. Estudio ocasional no. 7)

COSTER, CHARLES DE

Moscow. Vsesoiuznaia gosudarstvennaia biblioteka inostrannoi literatury.
Шарль де Костер; биобиблиографический указатель. [Составители: В. Т. Данченко, В. А. Паевская] Москва, Книга, 1964.

70 p. port. 21 cm. (Писатели зарубежных стран)

COSTUME

American Home Economics Association. Textiles and Clothing Section.
Aesthetics and clothing; an annotated bibliography. Washington, American Home Economics Association [1972]

viii, 159 p. 28 cm.

Anthony, Pegaret.
Costume: a general bibliography, by Pegaret Anthony and Janet Arnold. London, The Victoria & Albert Museum in association with the Costume Society, 1966.

[1], 49 p. 28 cm. (Bibliography no. 1)

Bergler, Georg.
Bibliographie der Mode und der Textilwirtschaft. Essen, Girardet (1971).

125 p. 21 cm. (Schriften der Nürnberger Akademie für Absatzwirtschaft)

Berlin. Kunstbibliothek.
Katalog der Lipperheideschen Kostümbibliothek. Neubearb. von Eva Nienholdt und Gretel Wagner-Neumann. (Fotos: Karl H. Paulmann. 2., völlig neubearb. u. verm. Aufl.) Berlin, Mann, 1965.

2 v. (xix, 1166 p.) 31 cm.

DeBolt, Don.
Men's and boys' wear stores. Washington, Small Business Administration, 1968.

8 p. illus. 27 cm. (Small business bibliography no. 45)

Eicher, Joanne Bubolz.
African dress; a select and annotated bibliography of Subsaharan countries. [East Lansing] African Studies Center, Michigan State University, 1969.

xi, 134 p. map. 23 cm.

Gillespie, Karen R
Apparel and accessories for women, misses, and children, by Karen B. Gillespie. Revision. Washington, Small Business Administration, 1965.

19 p. 26 cm. (Small business bibliography no. 50)

Caption title.
"Originally issued as Small business bulletin no. 50."

Hiler, Hilaire, 1898–
Bibliography of costume; a dictionary catalog of about eight thousand books and periodicals, compiled by Hilaire and Meyer Hiler. Edited by Helen Grant Cushing, assisted by Adah V. Morris. New York, B. Blom [1967]

xl, 911 p. 24 cm.

Reprint of the 1939 edition.

Janezeck, Elizabeth G
Men's and boys' clothing. Rev. by Elizabeth Janezeck. Washington, Small Business Administration, 1965.

12 p. 26 cm. (Small business bibliography, no. 45)

Caption title.
Previously issued in 1961 by Ralph S. Burkholder, as Small business bulletin bibliography no. 45.

Lazar, Vicky.
Costume and fashion in South Africa 1652–1910; a bibliography [2nd imp.] [Cape Town] University of Cape Town Libraries, 1970.

[vii] 30 p. 23 cm. (University of Cape Town. School of Librarianship. Bibliographical series)

Levy, June Rosine.
African traditional garb of the native tribes of Southern Africa [a bibliography] Johannesburg, University of the Witwatersrand, Dept. of Bibliography, Librarianship and Typography, 1972.

iii, 74 p. 29 cm.

Library Association. County Libraries Group.
Readers' guide to books on costume. 2d ed. [London] 1972.

30 p. 19 cm. (Its Readers' guide, new series, no. 126)

Morris, Miriam.
Dress and adornment of the head; an annotated bibliography, by Miriam Morris and Eleanor Kelley. [Baton Rouge] School of Home Economics, Louisiana State University, 1970.

ii, 33 p. 28 cm. (Home economics research report, no. 1)

Snowden, James.
European folk dress; a guide to 555 books and other sources of illustrations and information. London, Victoria and Albert Museum, Dept. of Textiles, for the Costume Society, 1973.

69 l. 30 cm. (Bibliography, no. 2)

CÔTE D'IVOIRE see Ivory Coast

COTESWORTH FAMILY

Gateshead, Eng. Public Libraries.
Cotesworth MSS. Gateshead (Central Library, Prince Consort Rd, Gateshead, Co. Durham NE8 4LN), Gateshead Public Libraries, 1971.

[2]. 12 leaves. 30 cm.

COTTON

Bibliotheca Bogoriensis.
Bibliografi mengenai kapas di Indonesia. Bogor, 1967.

22 p. 33 cm. (Its Seri bibliografi, no. 1)

Brouwer, C   J
Bibliography on cotton irrigation, compiled by C. J. Brouwer and L. F. Abell. Wageningen, The Netherlands, International Institute for Land Reclamation and Improvement, 1970.

41 p. 25 cm. (International Institute for Land Reclamation and Improvement. Bibliography 8)

Murray, Jay Clarence, 1929–
A selected annotated bibliography on cotton breeding and genetics, 1950–1964, by Jay C. Murray and Laval M. Verhalen. [Stillwater, Okla.] 1965.

115 p. 28 cm. (Oklahoma State University Experiment Station. Processed series, P–508)

Woodbury, Charles Jeptha Hill, 1851–1916.
Bibliography of the cotton manufacture. New York, B. Franklin [1970]

213 p. 23 cm. (Burt Franklin bibliography & reference series, 338. Selected essays in history, economics & social science, 135)

Reprint of the 1909–10 ed.

COULOMMIERS, FRANCE see under Meaux

COUNCILS AND SYNODS

Sawicki, Jakub.
Bibliographia synodorum particularium. Collegit Jaco-

bus Theodorus Sawicki. E Civitate Vaticana, S. Congregatio de Seminariis et Studiorum Universitatibus, 1967.

xxx, 379 p. 25 cm. (Monumenta iuris canonici. Series C: Subsidia, v. 2)

COUNSELING

Freeman, Ruth (St. John) 1901–
Counseling, a bibliography (with annotations) by Ruth St. John Freeman and Harrop A. Freeman. New York, Scarecrow Press, 1964.

986 p. 22 cm.

COUNTY GOVERNMENT see Local government

COUPLINGS

Nagy, Géza.
Tengelykapcsolók; bibliográfia. Budapest, 1966.

412 p. 21 cm. (Budapesti Müszaki Egyetem Központi Könyvtára. Tudományos müszaki bibliográfiak, 7. sz.)

COURLAND see under Livonia

COURTRAI, BELGIUM

Belgium. Archives de l'Etat, Courtrai.
Inventarissen van archieven van kerkfabrieken. Door E. Warlop. Brussel, Algemeen Rijksarchief (Ruisbroekstraat 2), 1969–

v. 29 cm.

Warlop, E
Ontledingen van de oorkonden bewaard in de "Farde A. de Poorter" ⟨1141–1789⟩. Door E. Warlop. Brussel ₍Algemeen Rijksarchief₎ 1969.

33 p. 30 cm.

At head of title: Ministerie van Nationale Opvoeding en Cultuur.

COURTS
see also Judges; Jury

Borås, Sweden. Stadsbiblioteket.
Förteckning över mikrofilmade domböcker i Älvsborgs län. Borås, 1968.

(2), 164 l. 30 cm.

———— Supplement. Borås, 1971.

36 l. 30 cm.

Fremlin, Ronald H
Modern judicial administration; a selected and annotated bibliography. Edited by Ronald H. Fremlin. ₍Reno, Nev., Court Studies Division, National College of the State Judiciary, 1973₎

vii, 359 p. 24 cm.

Jackson, Barbara.
Congestion and delay in the courts; an annotated bibliography, 1967–1971. Sacramento, California State Library, Law Library, 1971.

12 p. 28 cm.

National College of the State Judiciary. Court Studies Division.
Congestion and delay; a selected and annotated bibliography. Reno, Nev. ₍1972₎

7 l. 28 cm.

National College of the State Judiciary. Court Studies Division.
Court administration; a selected and annotated bibliography. Reno, Nev. ₍1972₎

12 l. 28 cm.

Tompkins, Dorothy Louise (Campbell) Culver.
Court organization and administration; a bibliography. Compiled by Dorothy Campbell Tompkins. Berkeley, Institute of Governmental Studies, University of California, 1973.

vii, 200 p. 28 cm.

United States. National Archives and Records Service.
List of pre-1840 Federal district and circuit court records : based on the "Report on evaluation and procedure for project to microfilm pre-1840 Federal court records," by Irwin S. Rhodes / compiled by R. Michael McReynolds. — Washington : The National Archives, National Archives and Records Service, General Services Administration, 1972.

vii, 11 p. ; 27 cm. — (Special list - National Archives and Records Service ; no. 31)

United States. National Archives and Records Service.
Preliminary inventory of the records of the Supreme Court of the United States : record group 267 / compiled by Marion Johnson. — ₍Rev.₎ — Washington : National Archives & Records Service, General Services Administration, 1973.

vii, 17 p. ; 27 cm. — (Preliminary inventory - National Archives and Records Service ; 139)

Previous ed. issued by National Archives.
Includes the records of the Court of Appeals in Cases of Capture, 1780-1787.

Zarefsky, David.
Complete handbook on the administration of justice; a reference manual for debaters and others interested in the subject, by David Zarefsky, Thomas B. McClain ₍and₎ Douglas Andrews. Skokie, Ill., National Textbook Co. ₍1971₎

316 p. 24 cm.

On spine: The administration of justice.

COUSINS, JAMES HENRY and MARGARET E.

Denson, Alan.
James H. Cousins (1873–1956) and Margaret E. Cousins (1878–1954) : a bio-bibliographical survey; compiled by Alan Denson; family reminiscences and an autobiographical note by William D. Cousins, foreword by Padraic Colum. Kendal (Westmd.), A. Denson, 60 Low Fellside, 1967.

₍2₎, 350 p. 35 cm.

Limited ed. of 100 copies.

COZZENS, JAMES GOULD

Meriwether, James B
James Gould Cozzens: a checklist. Compiled by James B. Meriwether. Introd. by James Gould Cozzens. Detroit, Gale Research Co. ₍1972₎

85 p. illus. 23 cm.

"A Bruccoli-Clark book."

Michel, Pierre, 1934–
James Gould Cozzens. An annotated checklist. ₍Brussels₎, Center for American Studies (Bibliothèque royale Albert I, bd. de l'Empereur, 4), ₍1971₎.

123 p. 23 cm.

Michel, Pierre, 1934–
James Gould Cozzens; an annotated checklist. ₁1st ed. Kent, Ohio₁ Kent State University Press ₁c1971₁
123 p. 22 cm. (The Serif series: bibliographies and checklists, no. 22)

CRABS

Butler, T   H
A bibliography of the Dungeness crab, *Cancer magister* Dana, by T. H. Butler. ₁Ottawa, Queen's Printer₁ 1967.
12 p. 28 cm. (Fisheries Research Board of Canada. Technical report no. 1)

Tagatz, Marlin E
Annotated bibliography on the fishing industry and biology of the blue crab, Callinectes sapidus ₁by₁ Marlin E. Tagatz and Ann Bowman Hall. Seattle, National Marine Fisheries Service; for sale by the Supt. of Docs., U. S. Govt. Print. Off., Washington, 1971.
94 p. 26 cm. (NOAA technical report NMFS SSRF–640)
"A United States Department of Commerce publication."

CRAFTS   see   Handicrafts

CRAIG,   EDWARD   GORDON

Fletcher, Ifan Kyrle, 1872–
Edward Gordon Craig: a bibliography, by Ifan Kyrle Fletcher and Arnold Rood. London, Society for Theatre Research, 1967.
117 p. plate, port. 22 cm.

CRANE,   HART

Gotham Book Mart & Gallery.
Hart Crane; a catalog of his works. ₁New York, 1972₁
12 p. 26 cm.

Lohf, Kenneth A
The literary manuscripts of Hart Crane, compiled by Kenneth A. Lohf. ₁Columbus₁ Ohio State University Press ₁1967₁
xx, 151 p. facsims. 23 cm. (Calendars of American literary manuscripts)

Schwartz, Joseph.
Hart Crane: an annotated critical bibliography. New York, D. Lewis ₁ᶜ1970₁
xi, 276 p. 23 cm.

Schwartz, Joseph.
Hart Crane: a descriptive bibliography ₁by₁ Joseph Schwartz and Robert C. Schweik. ₁Pittsburgh₁ University of Pittsburgh Press ₁1972₁
xxiv, 168 p. illus. 25 cm. (Pittsburgh series in bibliography)

CRANE,   STEPHEN
see also under   Hawthorne, Nathaniel

Bruccoli, Matthew Joseph, 1931-
Stephen Crane, 1871-1971; an exhibition from the collection of Matthew J. Bruccoli. ₁Columbia₁ Dept. of English, University of South Carolina, 1971.
17 p. facsims. 22 cm. (University of South Carolina. Dept. of English. Bibliographical series, no. 6)

Katz, Joseph.
The Merrill checklist of Stephen Crane. Columbus, Ohio, C. E. Merrill Pub. Co. ₁1969₁
iv, 41 p. 19 cm. (Charles E. Merrill program in American literature)
Charles E. Merrill checklists.

Stallman, Robert Wooster, 1911–
Stephen Crane; a critical bibliography, by R. W. Stallman. ₁1st ed.₁ Ames, Iowa State University Press, 1972.
xxxxii, 642 p. 23 cm.

Williams, Ames William.
Stephen Crane; a bibliography, by Ames W. Williams and Vincent Starrett. New York, B. Franklin ₁1970, ᶜ1948₁
xi, 161 p. illus., ports. 24 cm. (Burt Franklin: bibliography and reference series 298. Essays in literature & criticism 89)

CREASEY,   JOHN

John Creasey in print 1970. ₁n. p.; Printed for J. Creasey and Hodder & Stoughton, ᶜ1969₁
73 p. illus. 22 cm.
Label mounted on p. ₁4₁ of cover: New York, Walker.

CREATIVITY

Arasteh, A   Reza.
Creativity in the life-cycle. By A. Reza Arasteh. Leiden, E. J. Brill, 1968–
v. 25 cm.

Hlavsa, Jaroslav.
Psychologie kreativity; bibliografie do roku 1970. Praha, Kabinet pro výzkum a uplatnění kreativity, Strojírenský institut při VÚSTE, 1972.
360 l. 31 cm.
Title also in English: The psychology of creativity.
Introduction and table of contents also in English.

Michigan Cooperative Curriculum Program. *Committee on Creativity.*
Bibliography on creativity. 1st revision. Lansing, Dept. of Public Instruction, 1964.
27 p. 28 cm.

Razik, Taher A
Bibliography of creativity studies and related areas, by Taher A. Razik. Buffalo, State University of New York ₁1965₁
iv, 451 p. 23 cm.

CREDIT

Kniffin, Fred W
Retail credit and collections, by Fred W. Kniffin. Revision. Washington, Small Business Administration, 1964.
12 p. 26 cm. (Small business bibliography no. 31)

Kniffin, Fred W
Retail credit and collections, by Fred W. Kniffin. Revision. Washington, Small Business Administration, 1966.
8 p. 26 cm. (Small business bibliography no. 31)

CREELEY, ROBERT

Novik, Mary.
Robert Creeley; an inventory, 1945–1970. With a foreword by Robert Creeley. ₍Kent, Ohio₎ Kent State University Press ₍1973₎

xvii, 210 p. 23 cm. (The Serif series: bibliographies and checklists, no. 28)

Novik, Mary.
Robert Creeley; an inventory, 1945–1970. With a foreword by Robert Creeley. Montreal, McGill-Queen's University Press, 1973.

xvii, 210 p. 23 cm.

CREUSE, FRANCE (DEPT.)

Carriat, Amédée.
Dictionnaire bio-bibliographique des auteurs du pays creusois et des écrits le concernant, des origines à nos jours. Guéret, Impr. Lecante & les Presses du Massif central, 1964–

v. 25 cm.

Creuse, France (Dept.). Archives départementales.
Guide des archives de la Creuse ₍par₎ Henri Hemmer, directeur des services d'archives de la Creuse. Guéret, 1972.

164 p. 25 cm.

CRICKET

Polden, K   J
Cricket: a list of books about cricket in the State Library of South Australia, compiled by K. J. Polden. Adelaide, State Library of South Australia, 1967.

29 p. 26 cm. (Research Service bibliographies, series 4, no. 96)

Taylor, Alfred D
The catalogue of cricket literature, by Alfred D. Taylor. Wakefield, S. R. Publishers, 1972.

vi, ₍1₎, 115 p. 21 cm.

Reprint of 1st ed., London, Merritt and Hatcher, 1906.

CRIME AND CRIMINALS
see also under   Dissertations, Academic

Adams, Ramon Frederick, 1889–
Burs under the saddle; a second look at books and histories of the West ₍by₎ Ramon F. Adams. ₍1st ed.₎ Norman, University of Oklahoma Press ₍1964₎

x, 610 p. 23 cm.

Adams, Ramon Frederick, 1889–
Six-guns and saddle leather; a bibliography of books and pamphlets on western outlaws and gunmen, compiled by Ramon F. Adams. New ed., rev. and greatly enl. ₍Norman, University of Oklahoma Press, 1969₎

xxv, 808 p. 25 cm.

Bibliografia sui delinquenti anormali psichici. A cura di F. Ferracuti ₍et al.₎. Introduzione di Nicola Reale e Girolamo Tartaglione. Roma, Centro nazionale di prevenzione e difesa sociale, Sezione criminologica, 1967.

200 p. 24 cm. ₍Serie studi di criminologia, n. 2)

California. State Library, *Sacramento. Law Library*.
Fair trial and free press; a bibliography. ₍Sacramento₎ 1967.

10 p. 28 cm.

Cambridge. University. *Institute of Criminology*.
Bibliographical series. no. 1–
Cambridge ₍1966₎–

v. 30 cm.

Cumming, *Sir* John Ghest, 1868–1958.
A contribution towards a bibliography dealing with crime and cognate subjects. 3d ed. Montclair, N. J., Patterson Smith, 1970.

xiv, 107 p. 23 cm. (Patterson Smith reprint series in criminology, law enforcement, and social problems. Publication no. 103)

Half-title: Bibliography dealing with crime.
Reprint of the 3d ed. published in 1935 with corrections.

Ferracuti, Franco.
Intelligenza e criminalità; bibliografia. Intelligence and criminality; bibliography. Milano, Giuffrè, 1966.

xxi, 61 p. 22 cm. (Scritti di criminologia e diritto criminale, 2)

Added titles and text (introduction) in Spanish, French, and German.

Fox, Richard George.
The extra Y chromosome and deviant behavior; a bibliography ₍by₎ Richard G. Fox. ₍Toronto₎ Centre of Criminology, University of Toronto, 1970.

21 l. 28 cm.

An Inventory of surveys of the public on crime, justice and related topics, by Albert D. Biderman ₍and others₎. Washington₎ National Institute of Law Enforcement and Criminal Justice; for sale by the Supt. of Docs., U. S. Govt. Print. Off., 1972.

1 v. (various pagings) 26 cm.

Tompkins, Dorothy Louise (Campbell) Culver.
White collar crime; a bibliography, compiled by Dorothy Campbell Tompkins. Berkeley, Institute of Governmental Studies, University of California, 1967.

vii, 85 p. 23 cm.

Vandiver, Richard.
A selected bibliography of paperback books on crime. Compiled by Richard Vandiver, with the assistance of Jacqueline Lewis. ₍Carbondale, Center for the Study of Crime, Delinquency and Corrections, Southern Illinois University₎ 1970.

33 p. 20 cm. (Inscape)

BIBLIOGRAPHIES

Sellin, Johan Thorsten, 1896–
A bibliographical manual for the student of criminology, by Thorsten Sellin ₍and₎ Leonard D. Savitz. ₍New York₎ National Research and Information Center on Crime and Delinquency ₍1965₎

1 v. (unpaged) 28 cm.

Cover title.
Half title: A bibliographic manual for the student of criminology.
"First ... published in 1935."
"Reprinted from the International bibliography on crime and delinquency. Volume 1, no. 3."

CRIMINAL LAW AND PROCEDURE
see also Parole; Probation

Becker, Harold K
Law enforcement; a selected bibliography, by Harold K. Becker ₍and₎ George T. Felkenes. Metuchen, N. J., Scarecrow Press, 1968.

257 p. 22 cm.

Böhmer, Georg Wilhelm, 1761–1839.
Handbuch der Litteratur des Criminalrechts. In seinen allgemeinen Beziehungen, mit besondrer Rücksicht auf Criminalpolitik nebst wissenschaftlichen Bemerkungen. Amsterdam, Rodopi (Nieuwe Herengracht 35), 1970.

xlviii, 888 p. 22½ cm.

Reprint of the Göttingen 1816 ed.

California. University. Institute of Governmental Studies.
Administration of criminal justice, 1949-1956; a selected bibliography. Compiled by Dorothy Campbell Tompkins ₍Institute of Governmental Studies₎ Montclair, N.J., Patterson Smith, 1970.

xi, 351 p. 23 cm. (Patterson Smith reprint series in criminology, law enforcement, and social problems. Publication no. 102)

Reprint of the 1956 ed.

California. University. *Institute of Governmental Studies.*
Bibliography of crime and criminal justice, 1927–1931. Compiled by Dorothy Campbell Culver. Montclair, N. J., Patterson Smith, 1969.

xl, 413 p. 24 cm. (Patterson Smith reprint series in criminology, law enforcement, and social problems. Publication no. 99)

"Originally published 1934."
"Reprinted with corrections."

California. University. *Institute of Governmental Studies.*
Bibliography of crime and criminal justice, 1932–1937. Compiled by Dorothy Campbell Culver. Montclair, N. J., Patterson Smith, 1969.

xxxi, 391 p. 24 cm. (Patterson Smith reprint series in criminology, law enforcement, and social problems. Publication no. 100)

"Originally published 1939."
"Reprinted with corrections."

California. University. *Institute of Governmental Studies.*
Sources for the study of the administration of criminal justice, 1938-1948; a selected bibliography. Compiled by Dorothy Campbell Tompkins ₍Institute of Governmental Studies₎ Montclair, N. J., Patterson Smith, 1970.

294 p. 23 cm. (Patterson Smith reprint series in criminology, law enforcement, and social problems. Publication no. 101)

Reprint of the 1949 ed.

Canada. *Parliament. Library. Reference Branch.*
Crime and criminal justice; select bibliography. Ottawa, 1967.

25 l. 28 cm.

At head of title: 27th Parliament.
Caption title.
Text in English and French.

Clerc, François.
Contribution à la bibliographie des travaux consacrés à la procédure pénale en Suisse. Neuchâtel, Université, 1966.

139 p. 24 cm. (Mémoires de l'Université de Neuchâtel, t. 29)

Janiszewska-Talago, Elzbieta.
Polska bibliografia penitencjarna, 1963–1969. Warszawa, Wydawn. Prawnicze, 1972.

141 p. 21 cm. (Prace Ośrodka Badań Przestępczości)

Jescheck, Hans Heinrich.
Quellen und Schrifttum des Strafrechts. Hrsg. von Hans-Heinrich Jescheck ₍und₎ Klaus H. A. Löffler. ₍Stand: 1. 1. 1972₎ München, Beck, 1972–

v. 29 cm.

At head of title: Max-Planck-Institut für Ausländisches und Internationales Strafrecht, Freiburg im Breisgau.
CONTENTS: Bd. 1. Europa.

Łukawski, Wiesław.
Orzecznictwo SN i bibliografia do przepisów Kodeksu karnego, Kodeksu karnego wykonawczego i Kodeksu postepowania karnego. Okres od 1. I. 1972 r. do 31. XII. 1972 r. Warszawa, Wydawn. Prawnicze, 1973.

205 p. 21 cm. (Biblioteka Palestry, 3)

Marcus, Marvin.
Criminal justice: bibliography. Atlanta, School of Urban Life, Georgia State University ₍1971₎

i, 53 l. 28 cm.

Najgebauer, Zygmunt.
Bibliografia prawa i postępowania karnego; literatura, orzecznictwo. Warszawa, Wydawn. Prawnicze, 1969–71.

2 v. 25 cm.

At head of title: Zygmunt Najgebauer, Feliks Prusak.
CONTENTS: ₍t. 1.₎ 1944–1964.—t. 2. 1965–1969.

Porte-Petit Candaudap, Celestino.
Programa de la parte general del derecho penal. Prólogo de Luis Garrido. ₍2. ed.₎ México, Universidad Nacional Autónoma de México, 1968.

914 p. 23 cm.

São Paulo, Brazil (State). Tribunal de Alçada Criminal. Biblioteca.
Catálogo. 1970–
₍São Paulo₎

v. 22 cm.

Tompkins, Dorothy Louise (Campbell) Culver.
The confession issue from McNabb to Miranda; a bibliography, compiled by Dorothy C. Tompkins. Berkeley, Institute of Governmental Studies, University of California, 1968.

v, 100 p. 23 cm.

Tompkins, Dorothy Louise (Campbell) Culver.
Sentencing the offender; a bibliography, compiled by Dorothy Campbell Tompkins. Berkeley, Institute of Governmental Studies, University of California, 1971.

vii, 102 p. 23 cm.

"Supplements, in part, ₍the author's₎ Administration of criminal justice, 1949-1956; a selected bibliography," issued in 1956 by the Institute of Governmental Studies, University of California.

Villaseca Delano, Adriana.
Indice bibliográfico de derecho penal ₍por₎ Adriana Villaseca Delano ₍y₎ Carmen Méndez Urrutia. ₍Santiago de Chile₎ Editorial Jurídica de Chile ₍1971₎

448 p. 23 cm.

At head of title: Universidad Católica de Chile. Facultad de Ciencias Jurídicas, Políticas y Sociales. Escuela de Derecho de Santiago.

CRIPPLES   see   Physically handicapped

CRITICAL PATH ANALYSIS

Hampshire Technical Research Industrial Commercial Service.
A bibliography of critical path methods. Southampton, Hampshire Technical Research Industrial Commercial Service, 1966.

₍7₎, 72 p. 22 cm.

Hampshire Technical Research Industrial Commercial Service.
A bibliography of critical path methods. 2nd ed. Southampton (Hants.), Hampshire Technical Research Industrial Commercial Service, 1969.

₍2₎, iii, 52 p. 22 cm.

Laszkiewicz, Olga T   M
Critical path scheduling. Compiled by O. T. M. Laszkiewicz. Adelaide, State Library of South Australia, 1968.

33 p. 26 cm. (Research Service bibliographies, ser. 4, no. 114)

"Supplement to Research Service Bibliography Series 4, no. 17."

Latta, J   K
Annotated bibliography on critical path programming, by J. K. Latta. Ottawa, National Research Council, Division of Building Research, 1964.

24 l. 28 cm. (₍National Research Council, Canada. Division of Building Research₎ Bibliography no. 27)

Texas Transportation Institute, *College Station.*
Critical path method; an annotated bibliography. College Station, Texas, Texas A&M University ₍1964₎

19 l. 28 cm.

Cover title.
"Prepared ... in connection with Project 2-8-54-1, Survey of library facilities for a proposed research area, in cooperation with the Texas Highway Department and the Department of Commerce, Bureau of Public Roads."

CRITICAL POINT

Michaels, Stella.
Equilibrium critical phenomena in fluids and mixtures; a comprehensive bibliography with key-word descriptors ₍by₎ Stella Michaels, Melville S. Green, and Sigurd Y. Larsen. Washington, U. S. National Bureau of Standards: for sale by the Supt. of Docs., U. S. Govt. Print. Off., 1970.
iv, 231 p. 27 cm. (National Bureau of Standards special publication 327)

CRITICISM   see   Literary criticism

CROATION IMPRINTS

Prpic, George J
The Croatian publications abroad after 1939; a bibliography, by George J. Prpic. Cleveland, Published by the author in co-operation with the Institute for Soviet and East European Studies, John Carroll University, 1969.

x, 66 p. illus., maps. 28 cm.

Prpić, George J
Hrvatske knjige i knjižice u iseljeništvu. Croatian books and booklets written in exile, by George J. Prpić and Hilda Prpić. ₍Cleveland, Institute for Soviet and East European Studies, John Carroll University₎ 1973.

xix, 73 p. illus. 26 cm.

CROATION PHILOLOGY   see   Serbo-Croatian philology

CROCIONI, GIOVANNI

Anceschi, Giuseppe.
Bibliografia degli scritti di Giovanni Crocioni. A cura di Giuseppe Anceschi. Reggio Emilia, 1970.

31 p. 24 cm.

Borsari, Silvano, *ed.*
L'opera di Benedetto Croce; bibliografia. Napoli, Nella sede dell'Istituto, 1964.

x, 618 p. port. 29 cm.

At head of title: Istituto italiano per gli studi storici.

CROUSAZ, JEAN PIERRE DE

Vaud. Bibliothèque cantonale et universitaire, *Lausanne. Département des manuscrits.*
Inventaire des archives Jean-Pierre de Crousaz, 1663–1750 (IS 2024), par Marianne Perrenoud. Lausanne, Bibliothèque cantonale et universitaire, 1969.

84 l. 30 cm. (*Its* Inventaires des fonds manuscrits, 6)

CROY, MARIE, PRINCESSE DE

Belgium. Archives de l'État, Mons.
Inventaire des papiers de la princesse Marie de Croy, par R. Wellens. Bruxelles, Archives générales du Royaume, 1970.

48 p. 30 cm.

At head of title: Ministère de l'éducation nationale et de la culture française, et Ministère de l'éducation nationale et de la culture néerlandaise. Archives générales du Royaume et Archives de l'État dans les provinces.

CRUIKSHANK, GEORGE

Cohn, Albert Mayer.
George Cruikshank; a catalogue raisonné, by Albert M. Cohn. ₍New York₎ Collectors Editions ₍1969₎

xvi, 375 p. illus., port. 29 cm.

Reprint of the 1924 ed.

CRUSADES

Harvard University. *Library.*
Crusades: classification schedule, classified listing by call number, alphabetical listing by author or title, chronological listing. Cambridge, Mass., 1965.

23, 19, 19 p. 28 cm. (*Its* Widener Library shelflist ₍v. 1₎)

CRUSHING MACHINERY

Drobová, Irena.
Drvnie, mletie a triedenie materiálov; výberový zoznam z domácej a zahraničnej literatúry. Zostavila I. Drobová. ₍Edícia 2.₎ Bratislava, 1966.

98 p. 20 cm.

At head of title: Slovenska technická knižnica v Bratislave.

CRYOGENICS

Codlin, Ellen M
Cryogenics and refrigeration; a bibliographical guide (by) Ellen M. Codlin. Foreword by K. Mendelssohn. New York, IFI/Plenum, 1968–

v. 25 cm. (Bibliographical guide series)

Codlin, Ellen M
Cryogenics and refrigeration: a bibliographical guide (by) Ellen M. Codlin; foreword by K. Mendelssohn. London, Macdonald, 1968–(70)

2 v. 26 cm. (The Macdonald bibliographical guides)

Duffy, William, 1930–
Low temperature physics; a KWIC index to the conference literature, 1958–1969 (by) William Duffy, Jr., and James A. Miller. (Santa Clara, Calif.) University of Santa Clara Press (1970)

287 p. 29 cm.

Vlčková, Božena.
Kryogenika. Technika nízkych teplôt. /Výberový súpis literatúry./ Zost. a úvod (nap.) Božena Vlčková. Košice, ŠVK. rotaprint, 1971.

61, (1) p. 20 cm. (Bibliografické správy ŠVK Košice. čie. 2693/1971)

CRYPTOGRAPHY

Galland, Joseph Stanislaus.
An historical and analytical bibliography of the literature on cryptology. New York, AMS Press (1970, c1945)

viii, 209 p. 24 cm. (Northwestern University studies in the humanities, no. 10)

CRYSTALLOGRAPHY

Bulletin signalétique 161: Structure de la matière II—cristallographie. v. 30–
1969–
Paris, Centre de documentation du C. N. R. S.

v. 28 cm. monthly.

Supersedes in part Bulletin signalétique 6: Structure de la matière-cristallographie, solides, fluides, atomes, ions, molécules, and continues its vol. numbering.

International Union of Crystallography. *Commission on Crystallographic Teaching.*
Crystallographic book list. Edited by Helen D. Megaw. With the assistance of H. Curien (and others. Cambridge, Eng.) 1965.

xii, 83 p. 24 cm.

International Union of Crystallography. *Commission on Crystallographic Computing.*
World list of crystallographic computer programs. 2d ed. Edited by David P. Shoemaker. (Rotterdam, Bronderoffset) 1966.

50 p. 27 cm.

First ed., 1962, has title: I. U. Cr. world list of crystallographic computer programs.

CRYSTALS

Eastman Kodak Company.
Liquid crystal bibliography. (Rochester, N. Y.) c1973.

27 sheets. illus. 11 x 15 cm. (Kodak publication no. JJ-193)

Microfiche.
Sheets inserted in pockets fastened to a spiral binder (18 cm.)
Title from binder.
On p. (4) of binder: Eastman Organic Chemicals.

Kourilo, John J
Ultrahigh pressure studies and crystal growth techniques: analytical survey (by John J. Kourilo. Washington) Aerospace Technology Division, Library of Congress, 1966.

v, 58 l. 28 cm. (ATD report 66–56)
"Based on Soviet-Satellite open sources published in 1963. It is a continuation of AID reports (annotated bibliographies) U–64–46, 26 May 1964, on 'Growth of single crystals' and 62–170, 24 October 1962, on 'Silicone carbide'."

Molecular structures and dimensions. Ed. by Olga Kennard and David G. Watson. Published for the Crystallographic Data Centre Cambridge and the International Union of Crystallography. Utrecht, Oosthoek (1970–

v. 24 cm.

"Prepared at the Crystallographic Data Centre ... Cambridge."

CONTENTS.—v. 1. General organic crystal structures.—v. 2. Complexes and organometallic structures.

Образование кристаллов. Библиогр. указатель. 1945–1968. Москва, "Наука," 1970.

2 v. 27 cm.

At head of title: Академия наук СССР. Ордена Трудового Красного Знамени институт кристаллографии. Сектор сети специальных библиотек.
By TS. M. Shapiro, and others.

CUBA

Brünn. Krajská lidová knihovna.
Kubánská revoluce : bibliogr. a biografická pomůcka. — Brno : Knihovna J. Mahena, 1974.

56 p. ; 20 cm.

Fort, Gilberto V   1929–
The Cuban revolution of Fidel Castro viewed from abroad; an annotated bibliography, compiled by Gilberto V. Fort. (Lawrence) University of Kansas Libraries, 1969.

xvi, 140 p. 26 cm. (University of Kansas publications. Library series, 34)

Plasencia Moro, Aleida.
Bibliografía de la Guerra de los Diez Años. Compilada por Aleida Plasencia. La Habana, Departamento Colección Cubana, 1968.

388 p. 28 cm.

At head of title: Biblioteca Nacional José Martí.

Revolutionary Cuba; a bibliographical guide. 1966–

Coral Gables, Fla., University of Miami Press.

v. 21 cm. annual (Research Institute for Cuba and the Caribbean, University of Miami. Research study series.)
Supersedes Anuario bibliográfico cubano.
Vols. for 1966– issued by the Research Institute for Cuba and the Caribbean.
Compiler: 1966– F. Peraza.

Suchlicki, Jaime.
The Cuban revolutionary; a documentary bibliography, 1952–1968. Coral Gables, Fla., Research Institute for Cuba and the Caribbean, University of Miami, 1968.

83 l. 28 cm.

Trelles y Govín, Carlos Manuel, 1866–1951.
Bibliografía social cubana. ₍Introd. y notas por Israel Echevarría. La Habana₎ Biblioteca Nacional José Martí ₍1969₎

x, 50–106, xi–xxxiii p. 21 cm.

Originally published in: Cuba. Delegado al 1. Congreso Internacional de Economía Social, Buenos Aires, 1924. El primer Congreso Internacional de Economía Social celebrado en Buenos Aires. Habana, 1925.

Valdés, Nelson P
The Cuban revolution; a research-study guide (1959–1969) by Nelson P. Valdés and Edwin Lieuwen. ₍1st ed.₎ Albuquerque, University of New Mexico Press ₍1971₎

xii, 230 p. 25 cm.

CUBAN LITERATURE

Ford, Jeremiah Denis Matthias, 1873–1958.
A bibliography of Cuban belles-lettres, prepared by Jeremiah D. M. Ford and Maxwell I. Raphael. New York, Russell & Russell ₍1970₎

x, 204 p. 25 cm.

"Harvard Council on Hispano-American Studies."
Reprint of the 1933 ed.

CUMBERLAND, ENGLAND

Durham, Eng. University. Durham Colleges. Dept. of Palaeography and Diplomatic.
Howard family documents: list of deeds and manorial documents relating to Cumberland, formerly at Naworth Castle, now deposited in the Department of Palaeography and Diplomatic ₍compiled by C. R. Hudleston₎. Durham, University of Durham (Department of Palaeography and Diplomatic), 1970.
2 v. 33 cm.

Durham, Eng. University. Durham Colleges. Dept. of Palaeography and Diplomatic.
Howard family documents; list of miscellaneous papers relating to Cumberland, formerly at Naworth Castle, now deposited in the Department of Palaeography and Diplomatic, South Road, Durham. ₍Compiled by C. R. Hudleston. Durham₎ 1968.

125 l. 34 cm.

Hodgson, Henry Wigston.
A bibliography of the history and topography of Cumberland & Westmorland; compiled by Henry W. Hodgson. Carlisle (Cumberland), Joint Archives Committee for Cumberland, Westmorland and Carlisle, 1968.

301 p. 26 cm. (Joint Archives Committee for Cumberland, Westmorland & Carlisle. Record Office. Publication no. 1)

CUMMINGS, EDWARD ESTLIN
Eckley, Wilton.
The Merrill checklist of E. E. Cummings. Columbus, Ohio, Merrill ₍1970₎

iv, 32 p. 19 cm. (Charles E. Merrill program in American literature)

Charles E. Merrill checklists.
Title on cover: Checklist of E. E. Cummings.

CUNHA, EUCLYDES DA

Reis, Irene Monteiro, 1924–
Bibliografia de Euclides da Cunha. Rio de Janeiro, Instituto Nacional do Livro, 1971.

xxv, 417 p. illus. 22 cm. (Coleção Documentos, 2)

CUNNINGHAM, JAMES VINCENT

Gullans, Charles B
A bibliography of the published works of J. V. Cunningham, by Charles Gullans. Los Angeles, University of California Library, 1973.

44 p. 28 cm.

CURIOSA see Erotica

CURITIBA, BRAZIL

Cardoso, Jayme Antonio.
Arquivo da Câmara Municipal de Curitiba ₍por Jayme Antonio Cardoso₎. Arquivo da Sé Metropolitana e Paróquia de N. Sra. da Luz de Curitiba ₍por Odah Regina Guimarães Costa₎. Curitiba, 1968.
90 p. 23 cm. (Faculdade de Filosofia, Ciências e Letras. Departamento de História. Boletim no. 6) (Boletim da Universidade Federal do Paraná)
"Comemorativo do III Centenário do Pelourinho de Curitiba."
Errata slip inserted.

CURRENCY see Finance

CURVES, ALGEBRAIC

Sokolov, Nikolaĭ Petrovich.
(Algebraicheskie krivye tret'ego i chetvertogo poriadkov)
Алгебраические кривые третьего и четвертого порядков. Библиогр. указ. Киев, "Наук. думка," 1973.

199 p. 20 cm.

At head of title: Академия наук Украинской ССР. Институт математики. Н. П. Соколов, Е. С. Столова.

CUSHING, LEONARD F. see under Snow, Elliot

CYBERNETICS
see also Bionics

Alam, Fazlul.
Cybernetics: automation, computers, control, ergonomics, information theory, and machine translation: a subject guide, with the assistance of Hasina Alam. Provisional ed. London, New Science Publications, 1968.

v, 110 l. 28 cm. (Guide to the information sources)

Beliaevskaia, M I
Наука о творческом мышлении. (Эвристика). ₍Рек. обзор литературы. Москва, "Книга," 1969₎.
31 p. 17 cm. (Новое в науке и технике, вып. 28)

At head of title: Государственная ордена Ленина библиотека СССР имени В. И. Ленина. Центральная политехническая библиотека.

Rost, Gottfried.
Kybernetik und Gesellschaft. Eine bibliographische Information über die Bedeutung der Kybernetik für die gesellschaftswissenschaftlichen Disziplinen. Bearb. von Gottfried Rost und Annemarie Hahn. Leipzig (Deutsche Bücherei) 1965.

47 p. 21 cm. (Bibliographischer Informationsdienst der Deutschen Bücherei, Nr. 8)

CYCLES

Wilson, Louise (Loeffler) 1931–
Catalogue of cycles, by Louise L. Wilson. Pittsburgh, Foundation for the Study of Cycles ₍ᵉ₎1964–

v. illus. 24 cm.

Bibliography : pt. 1, p. 311–353.

CONTENTS.—pt. 1. Economics.

CYRILLUS, SAINT, OF THESSALONICA

Zaĭkov, Boris.
Към светла бъднина върви. Библиогр. материали и худож. произведения за чествуване на Кирил и Методий и 24 май. (Състав. Борис Зайков и Мирка Николова). София, Нар. библ. Кирил и Методий, 1971.

128 p. with illus. and music. 1 l. of illus. 21 cm.

CYSTIC FIBROSIS

Jaeger Gille, Edith, 1930–
Zystische Pankreasfibrose, Mukoviszidose: Dysporia-entero-broncho-pancreatica congenita familiaris, genetisch bedingte Vorderdarmschwäche, erbl. Nichtgedeihen d. Kinder (in Ausnahmefällen auch d. Erwachsenen), Exokriopathie: C. F.; eine Sammlung d. Weltliteratur von 1813 bis 1970, geordnet nach alphabet. Autorenverz. sowie med. Gesichtspunkten, Klinik, Genetik, Biochemie u. Mikrobiologie/ von Edith Jaeger Gille. — Berlin-Lichterfelde, Boothstr. 23: ₍Selbstverl.₎ 1971.

195 p.; 22 cm.

CZECH IMPRINTS

Knězek, Libor.
Bibliografia Vydavateľstva Slovenský spisovateľ 1950–1970. 20 rokov vzniku. Zost.: Libor Knězek. Úvodom: Ján Števček. 1. vyd. Bratislava, Slov. spis., t. Tlač. SNP, Lipt. Mikuláš, 1970.

388, ₍3₎ p. 20 cm.

Prague. Městská lidová knihovna.
20 ₍i. e. Dvacet₎ let ČSSR v naučné literatuře; výberová bibliografie. ₍Autor: Olga Jirečková₎ Praha, 1965.

43 l. 20 cm. (*Its* Metodické texty a bibliografie)

Riedlová, Marie, comp.
Výběr literatury ke kursům a cyklům Lidové akademie. ₍Sest. Marie Riedlová za spolupráce Svatavy Prečanové. V Olomouci, Státní vědecká knihovna, 1968₎

43 p. 20 cm. (Publikace Státní vědecké knihovny v Olomouci, 7/1968)

Cover title.

Vobr, Jaroslav.
Soupis jihlavských tisků českých knížek lidového čtení a populárně-naučné literatury z 18. a 19. století. Jihlava, Muzeum Vysočiny, rozmn. Dům kultury ROH, 1969.

128, ₍2₎ p. 20 cm.

Vobr, Jaroslav.
Soupis knížek lidového čtení z fondů Universitní knihovny v Brně. Zprac. Jaroslav Vobr. Brno, Univ. knihovna, rozmn., 1973.

105, ₍1₎ l. 20 cm. (Výběrový seznam, č. 179)

CZECH LANGUAGE

Gabor, František.
Terminologické normy. Súborná bibliografia čs. názvoslovných noriem za r. 1945–1967. Zost. František Gábor. Košice, Štát. ved. knižnica, cyklostyl, 1967.

2 v. (₍2₎, 394, ₍1₎ l.) 20 cm. (Bibliografické zprávy ŠVK, Košice, čís. 101/1967)

Tylová, Milena.
Publikační činnost pracovníků Ústavu pro jazyk český ČSAV za léta 1963–1967 : bibliografický soupis / zpracovala Milena Tylová. — Praha : Ústav pro jazyk český ČSAV, 1968.

132 p. ; 20 cm.

CZECH LITERATURE

Balášová, Olga.
Bibliografie české literární vědy, 1945–1955; práce o české literatuře. ₍1. vyd. Praha₎ Státní pedagogické nakl. ₍1964₎

xii, 692 p. 25 cm. (Vysokoškolské příručky)

At head of title : Olga Balášová ₍et al.₎
"Z prací Bibliografického oddělení Ústavu pro českou literaturu ČSAV."

Brünn. Universita. *Knihovna.*
Základy estetiky (III. semestr) ; výběr literatury ke kurzu Brněnské lidové university vědy, techniky a umění 1964/65. Literaturu se signaturami knih z fondů Universitní knihovny v Brně vybrala Božena Kyjovská-Fialová, přehlédl Artur Závodský. V Brně, 1964.

4 l. 21 cm. (*Its* Bibliografický leták, 132)

Československá akademie věd. *Ústav pro českou literaturu.*
Slovník českých spisovatelů. ₍Redigovali Rudolf Havel a Jiří Opelík. 1. vyd.₎ Praha, Československý spisovatel, 1964.

625 p. ports. 21 cm.

Kleskeňová, Dagmar.
Soupis sborníků veršů, prózy a písní, vhodných pro vystoupení školní mládeže v kulturních pořadech v předvolební kampani. Připr. Dagmar Kleskeňová. Brno. St. pedagog. knihovna, rozmn., 1971.

9 l. 30 cm. (Bibliografický leták, čís. 250)

Kunc, Jaroslav.
Česká literární bibliografie, 1945–1963; soupis článků, statí a kritik z knižních publikací a periodického tisku let 1945–1963 o dílech soudobých českých spisovatelů. V Praze, Státní knihovna ČSSR, 1963–68.

3 v. in 4. 21 cm. (Bibliografický katalog. České knihy, seš. 6/1963, seš. 5/1964, 7/1964, seš. 4/1967)

Subtitle varies slightly.
Vol. 3 covers the period 1945–1966.

—— —— Rejstříky k. I.–III. dílu. Zpracovaly: Julie Kuncová, Hilda Lechovcová, a Marie Stöcklová. V Praze, Státní knihovna ČSR, 1968.

482 p. 21 cm.

Macháček, Vítězslav.
50 ₁i. e. Padesát₎ českých autorů posledních padesáti let.
1. vyd. Praha, Čs. spis., t. ST 2, 1969.

211, ₁4₎ p. 22 cm.

Mikuškovičová, Jiřina.
Z literární produkce české a části slovenské literatury za
léta 1948–1966; výběrová bibliografie. České Budějovice,
1966.

78 p. 30 cm.

At head of title: Krajská knihovna České Budějovice.

Prague. Městská lidová knihovna.
20 ₁i. e. Dvacet₎ let ČSSR v krásné literature; bibliografie a výběr ukázek. ₁Autor: Zdeňka Čermáková₎ Praha,
1965.

69 l. 29 cm. (*Its* Metodické texty a bibliografie)

Spisovatelé o sobě. Výběrová bibliografie. Brno, Knihovna
Jiřího Mahena, rozmn., 1972–73.

2 v. 20 cm.

CONTENTS: 1. čeští spisovatelé.—2. Slovenští spisovatelé.

Voráčová, Marta.
Základní fond krásné literatury pro menší lidové knihovny. Sest. Marta Voráčová. Olomouc, St. věd. knihovna,
rozmn., 1970.

57, ₁1₎ p. 29 cm. (Publikace Státní vědecké knihovny v Olomouci,
čís. 7/1970)

TRANSLATIONS

Broukalová, Zdenka, comp.
Česká kniha v cizině, 1939–1965. Zprac.: Zdenka Broukalová a Olga Malá. ₁Praha₎ Státní knihovna ČSR, 1968.

297 p. 21 cm. (Bibliografický katalog ČSSR. České knihy 1968.
Zvláštní seš. 7)

Československá kniha v zahraniči; ₁senam knih českých a
slovenských autorů, vydaných v zahraničí v letech 1961–
1965. Praha₎ Dilia ₁1966₎

52 p. 20 cm.

Cover title.
Prefatory matter in French and Russian.

Künzel, Franz Peter.
Übersetzungen aus dem Tschechischen und dem Slowaki-
schen ins Deutsche nach 1945 bei Verlagen der Bundesrepublik Deutschland, der Bundesrepublik Österreich, der
Schweizerischen Eidgenossenschaft und der Tschechoslowakischen Sozialistischen Republik. Eine Bibliographie.
München, Ackermann-Gemeinde, 1969–

v. 21 cm.

TRANSLATIONS - BIBLIOGRAPHIES

Sýkorová, Milena.
Soupis bibliografií překladů literárních děl do češtiny a
slovenštiny. Brno, Universitní knihovna, 1972.

42 l. 21 cm. (Bibliografický leták, 173)

CZECH PERIODICALS see Periodical
publications - Czechoslovak Republic

CZECHOSLOVAK REPUBLIC
see also Communism - Czechoslovak
Republic

Bibliografie československé statistiky. 1966–
Praha, Výzkumný ústav statistiky a účetnictví, Oborové
informační středisko.

v. 20 cm. (Výzkumný ústav statistiky a účetnictví. Oborové informační středisko. Rešerše)

Compiler : 1966–   J. Podzimek.

Bibliografie československého archivnictví 1957–1966.
Zprac. Miloš Kouřil ₁et al. Vyd. 1. Praha₎ Archivní
správa Ministerstva vnitra ČSR, 1970.

279 p. 24 cm.

Introd. also in French, German, and Russian; table of contents in
French, German, and Russian.

Cejpová, Zdena.
Československá společnost po druhé světové valce. Výběr
lit. o sociální struktuře čs. společnosti. Sest. Zdena Cejpová.
Praha, knihovna Ústavu dějin socialismu, rozmn., 1968.

226 p. 29 cm. (Bibliografie a informace knihovny Ústavu dějin
socialismu, č. 9, 1968)

Cejpová, Zdena, *comp.*
Československo, 1945–1966; západní bohemika a slovacika.
Sest.: Zdena Cejpová. ₁Praha₎ 1966.

198 p. 21 cm. (Bibliografie a informace Knihovny Ústavu dějin
KSČ, č 2)

"Pouze pro vnitřní potřebu."

Cejpová, Zdena.
Československo 1945–1967. Západní bohemika a slovacika.
1. dodatek. Sest. Zdena Cejpová. ₁1. vyd.₎ Praha, Knihovna ústavu dějin KSČ, 1967.

73, ₁4₎ p. 20 cm. (Bibliografie a informace knihovny Ústavu
dějin KSČ, č. 5, 1967)

Dvacet let ČSSR; výběrový seznam puvodních českých a
slovenských knih a ruských knih a článků o ČSSR. ₁Zprac.:
Zdeněk Franc et al.₎ Praha, Státní knihovna ČSR, 1965.

375 p. 21 cm. (Bibliografický katalog ČSSR. České knihy.
Ročník 1965. Zvláštní seš, 2)

Added t. p.: Двадцать лет ЧССР.
Czech and Russian.

Gold, H   K
An annotated bibliography on the climate of Czechoslo-
vakia, by H. K. Gold and Henry Hacia. Silver Spring,
Md., U. S. Environmental Data Service; ₁may be procured
from the Clearinghouse for Federal Scientific & Technical
Information, Springfield, Va.₎ 1968.

vii, 47 p. map. 27 cm. (U. S. Environmental Data Service.
WB/BC-99)

Halaša, Andrej.
Ekonomická politika Komunistickej strany Československa. Odporúčajúca bibliografia. Autor: Andrej Halaša
a kol. Úvod: Pavol Chudý — Samuel Žarnovický. 1.
vyd. Martin, Matica slovenská, rozmn., 1972.

69, ₁2₎ p. 24 cm. (Edícia: Odporúčajúce bibliografie)

Jediná cesta. Výběrová bibliogr. k 50. výročí ČSSR. Zprac.
kol. Odpovědný redaktor: Hana Pessrová a Eva Krejčová.
Praha, Kniha, 1968.

245, ₍4₎ p. plates. 21 cm.

Ježek, Alexandr.
Protifašistický odboj za druhé světové války; bibliografie článků z ilegálního periodického tisku vydávaného na území protektorátu a slovenského státu a z legálního periodického tisku na osvobozeném území v letech 1939–1945. Zprac. Alexandr Ježek. Praha, Knihovna Ústavu dějin socialismu, 1969.

₍ 3 v. 20 cm. (Bibliografie a informace knihovny Ústavu dějin socialismu, č. 12)

Materiály k retrospektivní bibliografii české etnografie a folkloristiky. Rediguje Richard Jeřábek. ₍Vyd. 1.₎ Brno ₍UJEP₎ 1965–

v. 29 cm.

At head of title, v. 1– : Universita J. E. Purkyně v Brně. Fakulta filosofická. Katedra etnografie a folkloristiky.

CONTENTS.—sv. 1. Soupis bibliografií české a slovenské etnografie a folkloristiky vydaných v letech 1945–1963. Sestavila Alena Jeřábková.

Matica slovenská, Turčiansky sv. Martin. Bibliografický odbor.
Bibliografia článkov z komunistických a odborárskych novín a časopisov za roky 1938–1945; slovenská časť. Zostavili: Lena Galandová, Blažej Laco, Zora Luptáková. V Martine, 1964.

217 p. 24 cm.

"Pre internú potrebu politických a vedeckých pracovníkov."

Palivec, Viktor.
České regionální bibliografie; přehled publikací a článků z let 1945–1965. Zprac. Viktor Palivec. V Praze, Státní knihovna ČSSR, 1966.

56 p. 21 cm. (Bibliografický katalog ČSSR. České knihy, 1966, zvláštní seš. 8–prosinec 1966)

Podzimek, Jaroslav.
Bibliografie československé statistiky a demografie, 1945–1968. 1. vyd. Praha, Výzkum. ustav stat. a účetnictví, 1969–

v. 21 cm.

Introduction and table of contents also in English.

CONTENTS.—Díl 1. Statistika. sv. 1–2.—Díl 2. Demografie. sv. 1

Renč, Karel.
Z rudého tisku. Výběrová bibliografie článků z Pochodně 1920–1938. Zprac. Karel Renč a Vlasta Hamplová. Hradec Králové, St. věd. knihovna, rozmn., 1971.

201, ₍1₎ p. 29 cm. (Publikace SVK v Hradci Králové, č. 2/71)

Steflíčková, Jarmila.
Jihomoravský kraj 1945–1970. Příspěvek k regionální bibliografii. Sest. Jarmila Šteflíčková a Helena Bayerová. Brno, Knihovna Jiřího Mahena, rozmn., 1970.

50, ₍1₎ p. 21 cm.

Cover title: 25 ₍i. e. Dvacet pět₎ let JMK.

Strnad, Miroslav.
Liberec a Jablonec nad Nisou. Soupis monografií o okresech Liberec a Jablonec n/N. a čas. vycházejících v obou okresech ve fondech Věd. a lid. knihovny v Liberci. Sest. Miroslav Strnad. Liberec, Věd. a lid. knihovna, rozmn., 1969.

152, ₍1₎ p. 29 cm. (Edice: Publikace Vědecké a lidové knihovny v Liberci. Řada A: Bibliografie, č. 90)

Sturm, Rudolf.
Czechoslovakia, a bibliographic guide. Washington, Library of Congress, 1967. New York, Arno Press, 1968.

xii, 157 p. 27 cm.

"Prepared under the sponsorship of the Slavic and Central European Division."

Sturm, Rudolf.
Czechoslovakia, a bibliographic guide. Washington, Library of Congress; ₍for sale by the Supt. of Docs., U. S. Govt. Print. Off.₎ 1967 ₍i. e. 1968₎

xii, 157 p. 26 cm.

"Prepared under the sponsorship of the Slavic and Central European Division."

Voráčová, Marta.
Na pomoc práci národních výborů. Výběr publ. a časopiseckých čl. k Rezoluci konf. nár. výborů okresu Olomouc, konané 6. června 1972. Sest. Marta Voráčová. Olomouc, St. ved. knihovna, rozmn., 1972.

25 p. 29 cm. (Publikace Státní vědecké knihovny v Olomouci 20/1972)

Zaťko, Peter.
Ekonomika miestneho hospodárstva. Sprac. Peter Zaťko. Metod. spolupráca Ján K. Garaj. 1. vyd. Bratislava, SPN, rozmn. Západoslov. tlač. 42, 1968.

41, ₍189₎ p. 20 cm. (Ekonomické aktuality. Bibliografický zpravodaj. Ústredná ekonomická knižnica, Bratislava, 1968, č. 1)

In portfolio.

Zykmundová, Anna.
Soupis nejdůležitějších politických dokumentů a článků uveřejněných v Rudém právu v roce 1969. Zpracovali A. Zykmundová a J. Kubíček. V Brně, Universitní knihovna, 1970.

116 l. 21 cm. (Výběrový seznam, 154)

BIBLIOGRAPHIES

Czerny, Robert.
Einführung in die tschechoslowakische Bibliographie bis 1918; praktische Übersicht der Informationsquellen. ₍1. Aufl.₎ Baden-Baden, V. Koerner, 1971.

128 p. 24 cm. (Bibliotheca bibliographica Aureliana, 28)

28. ₍Dvacátý osmý₎ říjen v československých novodobých dějinách. Vyhlášení samostatnosti státu Čechů a Slováků 1918. Den znárodnění 1945. Schválení Zákona o československé federaci 1968. Výběr z knižní a časopisecké produkce let 1970, 1971, 1972 a první poloviny roku 1973. Brno, Knihovna Jiřího Mahena, rozmn., 1973.

82, ₍2₎ p. 20 cm.

HISTORY

Engová, Helena.
Bibliografie k dějinám ČSR a KSČ 1917–1938. Historiografická produkce za léta 1945–1967. Zprac. Helena Engová, Miloš Měšťánek, ₍který také naps. předml. a₎ Květa Náhlovská. Praha, Knihovna Ústavu dějin socialismu, 1968.
4 v. 20 cm. (Bibliografie a informace knihovny Ústavu dějin socialismu, č. 8)
Vol. 4: Biografické materiály.

Mazur, Arnošt.
Národnostní vývoj na území ČSSR se zvláštním zaměřením na Slezsko a ostravskou průmyslovou oblast. Výběrová bibliografie. Zprac. Arnošt Mazur. Ostrava, Profil, rozmn. MTZ 25, Opava, 1969.

2 v. 20 cm. (Publikace Slezského ústavu ČSAV v Opavě, sv. 61)

Parrish, Michael.
The 1968 Czechoslovak crisis; a bibliography, 1968–1970. ₍Santa Barbara, Calif., American Bibliographical Center, 1971₎
41 p. 28 cm. (Bibliography and reference series, no. 12)

Únor 1948 ₍i. e. **Tisíc devětset čtyřicet osm₎** Výběrová bibliografie z fondů M₍ěstské₎ k₍nihovny₎ v Praze. Sest. kol. Praha, Městská knihovna, rozmn., 1971.
58, ₍1₎ p. 29 cm. (Metodické texty a bibliografie Městské knihovny v Praze)

LAW   see   Law - Czechoslovak Republic

D

DĄBROWSKA, MARIA SZUMSKA

Korzeniewska, Ewa.
Maria Dabrowska ₁1889–1965₁ poradnik bibliograficzny. Warszawa, Biblioteka Narodowa, 1969.

50 p. 21 cm.

At head of title: Biblioteka Narodowa. Instytut Bibliograficzny.

DAHLBERG, EDWARD

Billings, Harold Wayne, 1931–
A bibliography of Edward Dahlberg, by Harold Billings. Introd. by Edward Dahlberg. ₁Austin₁ Humanities Research Center, University of Texas at Austin ₁1971₁

122 p. illus. 24 cm. (Tower bibliographical series, no. 8)

DAIRYING
see also Milk

Chmelař, František, *comp.*
Zvýšení dojivosti a obsahu bílkovin v kravském mléce; soupis literatury. Sest.: František Chmelař a Dušan Štepánek. V Brně, 1966.

16 p. 21 cm. (Universitní knihovna v Brně. Výběrový seznam, 111)

Manchester, Alden Coe, 1922–
The economics of dairy marketing; an annotated bibliography, compiled by Alden C. Manchester. ₁Washington₁ U. S. Dept. of Agriculture, Economic Research Service ₁1966₁

ii, 138 p. 26 cm. (₁U. S. Dept. of Agriculture. Economic Research Service₁ ERS–290)

Moscow. TSentral'naia nauchno-tekhnicheskaia biblioteka pishchevoi promyshlennosti. Nauchno-bibliograficheskii otdel.
Производство диетических молочных продуктов и продуктов детского питания. (Аннот. библиогр. указатель отечеств. и зарубежной литературы за 1965–1968 гг. и 1 кв. 1969 г.) Москва, 1969.

156 p. 20 cm.

At head of title: Министерство пищевой промышленности СССР. Центральная научно-техническая библиотека пищевой промышленности.

U. S. *Dept. of Agriculture. Economic Research Service. Dairy Group.*
Research publications on dairy marketing economics, an annotated bibliography. ₁Washington₁ 1967.

31 p. 26 cm.

Wolf, Alois Francis, 1899–
A bibliography on costs, margins and efficiency in marketing dairy products, compiled by A. F. Wolf. ₁Washington₁ U. S. Dept. of Agriculture, Economic Research Service, Marketing Economics Division, 1965.

64 p. 26 cm.

DAKOTA INDIANS see under Chippewa
    Indians

DAKOTA, SOUTH see South Dakota

DALARNA, SWEDEN

Wingborg, Olle, 1928–
Litteratur om Dalarna. Utg. av Dalarnas biblioteksförbund. Falun, Utgivaren (Stads- och länsbiblioteket.) 1969–

v. 24 cm. (Dalarnas fornminnes- och hembygdsförbunds skrifter, 15

CONTENTS.—Del 1. Artiklar och uppsatser ingående i periodiska publikationer.

DALMATIA

Valentinelli, Giuseppe, 1805–1874.
Bibliografia della Dalmazia e del Montenegro. Bologna, Forni, 1967.

vii, 339 p. 21 cm.

Reprint of the Zagreb, 1855 ed.

DALTON, JOHN

Smyth, Albert Leslie.
John Dalton, 1766–1844: a bibliography of works by and about him, by A. L. Smyth. Manchester, Manchester U. P. ₁1966₁

xvi, 114 p. 11 plates. (incl. ports., facsims.) 25½ cm.

DÄMIRCHIZADÄ, ÄBDULÄZÄL MÄMMÄD OGHLU

Färzälilev, M   N
Ә. М. Дәмирчизадә. Библиографија. Бакы, "Елм," 1970.

65 p. 16 cm. (Азәрбајчанын елм вә мәдәнијјәт хадимләри)

At head of title: Азәрбајчан ССР Елмләр Академијасы. Әсаслы Китабхана.
Added t. p. in Russian.

DAMS

Aleksandrovskiĭ, K   A
₁Gidravlika nizhnego b'efa vodoslivnykh plotin srednego napora
Гидравлика нижнего бьефа водосливных плотин среднего напора. Аннот. библиогр. указатель отечеств. и зарубежной литературы за 1965–1969 гг. Ленинград, "Энергия," Ленингр. отд-ние, 1970.
107 p. 20 cm.
At head of title: Министерство энергетики и электрификации СССР. Главтехстройпроект. Всесоюзный научно-исследовательский институт гидротехники им. Б. Е. Веденеева. Отдел патентов и научно-технической информации.

Gaĭdina, A   A
Расчеты напряженного состояния, деформаций, порового давления и устойчивости плотин из местных материалов. (Информ. справка об отечеств. и зарубежной литературе за 1963–1968 гг.) Ленинград, "Энергия,"

Ленингр. отд-ние, 1969.

20 p. 20 cm.

At head of title: Министерство энергетики и электрификации СССР. Главтехстройпроект. Всесоюзный научно-исследовательский институт гидротехники имени Б. Е. Веденеева. Отдел научно-технической информации.

Karpyshev, Evgeniĭ Sergeevich.
(Spravochno-bibliograficheskiĭ katalog po geologii osnovaniĭ plotin)
Справочно-библиографический каталог по геологии оснований плотин. ₍Составили Е. С. Карпышев и Е. И. Барановская₎. Москва, Энергия, 1967.
123 p. 27 cm. (Материалы по проектированию гидротехнических узлов. Серия 2: Изыскания)
At head of title: Гидропроект.
Added t. p.: Министерство энергетики и электрификации СССР. Всесоюзный ордена Ленина проектно-изыскательский и научно-исследовательский институт Гидропроект имени С. Я. Жука.

Samersova, A   V
Плотиностроение. Информ. справка об отечеств. литературе ... Ленинград, "Энергия," Ленингр. отд-ние, 1968.

40 p. 20 cm.

At head of title: Министерство энергетики и электрификации СССР. Главтехстройпроект. Всесоюзный научно-исследовательский институт гидротехники имени Б. Е. Веденеева. Отдел научно-технической информации.
By A. V. Samersova and N. N. Shufertova.

DANCE
see also Folk-songs, dances and music

American Association for Health, Physical Education, and Recreation. *National Section on Dance.*
Compilation of dance research, 1901–1964. Edited by Esther E. Pease, chairman, Research Committee. Washington, American Association for Health, Physical Education, and Recreation ₍1964₎

52 p. 23 cm.

Vol. 1, "Compiled by Fannie Helen Melcer" on label mounted on t. p.
"Supplement to the Compilation of dance research, 1901–1963 ₍i. e. 1964₎"
Sponsored by the association's Dance Division, a later name of its National Section on Dance.

Forrester, Felicitée Sheila.
Ballet in England: a bibliography and survey, c. 1700–June 1966, by F. S. Forrester; with a foreword by Ivor Guest. London, Library Association, 1968.

224 p. 5 plates, 2 illus., 3 facsims. 22 cm. (Library Association. Bibliographies, no. 9)

González Climent, Anselmo.
Bibliografía flamenca. ₍Madrid₎ Escelicer ₍1965₎

260 p. 19 cm.

González Climent, Anselmo.
Segunda bibliografía flamenca ₍por₎ Anselmo González Climent y José Blas Vega. Edición Angel Caffarena. Málaga, Librería Anticuaria "El Guadalhorce" ₍1966₎

237 p. 25 cm. (Ediciones de libros de Málaga, 11)

310 copies printed. "300 ejemplares, numerados del 1 al 300 sobre papel Registro ... Ejemplar no. 150."

Lange, Roderyk.
Bibliografia zagadnień sztuki tanecznej z lat 1963–1964. Oprac. Roderyk Lange. Warszawa, Centralna Poradnia Amatorskiego Ruchu Artystycznego, 1969.

189 p. 24 cm. (Biblioteka metodyczna)

Leslie, Serge.
A bibliography of the dance collection of Doris Niles & Serge Leslie; annotated by Serge Leslie, edited by Cyril Beaumont. London, C. W. Beaumont; ₍'Dancing Times, Ltd.'₎ 1966

v. 22½ cm.

Magriel, Paul David, 1906–
A bibliography of dancing; a list of books and articles on the dance and related subjects. New York, B. Blom ₍1966₎

229 p. illus. 26 cm.
Reprint of the 1936 edition.

New York (City). Public Library.
When all the world was dancing; rare and curious books from the Cia Fornaroli collection, by Marian Eames. New York ₍1971₎

16 p. illus. 23 cm.

Petermann, Kurt.
Sowjetische Tanzliteratur. Ein annotiertes Bücherverzeichnis der in der Deutschen Staatsbibliothek zu Berlin und im Deutschen Tanzarchiv des Institutes für Volkskunstforschung in Leipzig gesammelten Schriften sowjetischer Autoren. Mit einem Anhang: Sowjetische Tanzliteratur in deutschen Übersetzungen. (Titelübersetzungen und Annotationen: Heinz Legler.) Leipzig, Institut für Volkskunstforschung beim Zentralhaus für Kulturarbeit, 1967.

58 p. 21 cm.

Petermann, Kurt.
Der Tanz in der Sowjetunion. Annotierte Titelübersicht aus sowjetischen Zeitschriften. Berichtszeit: Januar bis Juni 1970. ₍Zusammenstellung und Bearb.: Kurt Petermann. Die Titelübersetzungen und Kurzreferate der russischsprachigen Aufsätze: Wolfgang Staerkenberg. ₍Leipzig₎ Zentralhaus für Kulturarbeit der DDR, Deutsches Tanzarchiv, 1970.

73 p. 29 cm. (Tanzwissenschaftliche Information, Nr. 1)

Van Zile, Judy.
Dance in India; an annotated guide to source materials. Providence, Asian Music Publications, 1973.

xi, 129 p. 23 cm. (Asian music publications. Series A: Bibliographies and research aids, no. 3)

DANILOV, SOFRON PETROVICH

Basharin, Georgiĭ Prokop'evich.
Софрон Данилов. Био-библиогр. указатель. Под ред. З. Т. Тюнгюрядова. Якутск, Якуткнигоиздат, 1969.

43 p. with port. 19 cm.

At head of title: Якутская республиканская библиотека им. А. С. Пушкин ₍sic₎.
By G. P. Basharin and G. S. Tarskiĭ.

DANISH LANGUAGE

Danske sprog- og litteraturselskab, Copenhagen.
Skrifter udg. af det Danske sprog- og litteraturselskab, 1911–1971. ₍Udarb. af Albert Fabritius₎ København, 1971.

59 p. 26 cm.

Jacobsen, Henrik Galberg.
Dansk sprogrøgtslitteratur 1900–1955 / Henrik Galberg

Jacobsen. — København : ₍Gyldendal₎, 1974.

222 p. ; 24 cm. — (Dansk Sprognævns skrifter ; 7)

DANISH LITERATURE
see also Denmark - Imprints

Dansk skønlitterært forfatterleksikon, 1900–1950. Bibliografisk redaktion: Svend Dahl. Medredaktører: Ludvig Bramsen og Mogens Haugsted; biografisk redaktion: Povl Engelstoft. København, Grønholt Pedersen, 1959–64.

3 v. 25 cm.

Dansk skønlitteratur i 60'erne og på tærsklen til 70'erne. Flensborg, Dansk centralbibliotek for Sydslesvig; Eksp.: Kragelund, Padborg, 1971.

71 p. illus. 23 cm.

"Udgivet ... i anledning af udstillingen 28. oktober til 20. november 1971."

Erslew, Thomas Hansen. 1803–1870. Almindeligt forfatter-lexicon for Kongeriget Danmark, med tilhørende bilande fra før 1814 til efter 1858. København, Rosenkilde og Bagger, 1962–63.

3 v. port. 23 cm.
"Fotografisk optryk."

——————— Supplement: 1841–til efter 1858. København, Rosenkilde og Bagger, 1962–63.

v. 23 cm.

——————— Navneregister ₍udarb. af I. E. Dittmann og A. P. Möller₎ København, Rosenkilde og Bagger, 1965.

524 p. 23 cm.

Jørgensen, Aage.
Contributions in foreign languages to Danish literary history 1961–1970. A bibliography. Aarhus, Akademisk Boghandel, 1971.

44 p. illus. 23 cm.

Jørgensen, Aage.
Dansk litteraturhistorisk bibliografi 1971. København, Akademisk forlag, 1972.

56 p. 23 cm.

Romaner, noveller, skuespil, digte. 2. udg. København, Bibliotekscentralen, 1966.

101 p. 22 cm.

Vor tids Hvem skrev hvad, 1914–1964. ₍Udarb. af Niels Chr. Lindtner₎ København, Politikens forlag, 1964.

2 v. illus., facsims., ports. 18 cm. (Politikens håndbøger, nr. 98)

Vor tids Hvem skrev hvad. Efter 1914. Udarbejdet af Niels Chr. Lindtner. Red.: Knud Sandvej. 3. udg. København, Politiken, 1968.

2 v. illus. 18 cm.

TRANSLATIONS

Bredsdorff, Elias.
Danish literature in English translation, with a special Hans Christian Andersen supplement; a bibliography. Westport, Conn., Greenwood Press ₍1973₎

198 p. 19 cm.

Reprint of the 1950 ed. published by E. Munksgaard, Copenhagen.

Lindtner, Niels Christian, 1929–
Verdenslitteratur på dansk; et udvalg af oversættelser og litteratur-historiske behandlinger af verdenslitteraturens klassikere, ved Niels Chr. Lindtner og Erland Munch-Petersen. København, Danmarks biblioteksskole; i kommission hos G. E. C. Gad, 1965.

251 p. 21 cm. (Danmarks biblioteksskoles skrifter, nr. 1)

DANTE ALIGHIERI

Aachen. Stadtbibliothek.
Ausstellung der Dante-Sammlung, Dezember 1965–Februar 1966; Katalog. Aachen, 1965.

27 p. 30 cm.
Cover title: Dante.

Auckland, N. Z. University. *Library.*
Dante and his times; the Jellie Collection. ₍Auckland₎ 1964.

19 p. 21 cm. (*Its* Bibliographical bulletin, 1)

Berlin. Deutsche Staatsbibliothek.
Katalog der Dante-Bibliothek von Friedrich Schneider im Besitz der Deutschen Staatsbibliothek. Zusammengestellt von Horst und Edith Heintze. Berlin, 1965.

viii, 183 p. plates, ports. 24 cm.
Cover title: Dante-Katalog.

Cologne. Universitäts- und Stadtbibliothek.
Dante: Sammlung Reiners. ₍Bearb. von Grete Solbach₎ Köln, 1971.

113 p. 21 cm.

Felice da Mareto, Father, 1909–
Bibliografia dantesco-francescana. A cura di Felice da Mareto. Parma, Libreria francescana editrice, 1972.

125 p., incl. 5 mounted plates. 24 cm. (Biblioteca storico-religiosa, 2)

Fondazione Marco Besso. *Rome.*
Edizioni delle opere di Dante nella biblioteca della Fondazione. Catalogo a cura di Antonio Martini. Roma, 1967.

215 p. illus. 24 cm. (*Its* Collana, 1)

Fucilla, Joseph Guerin, 1897–
Forgotten Danteiana; a bibliographical supplement, by J. G. Fucilla. New York, AMS Press ₍1970, °1939₎

iv, 52 p. 23 cm. (Northwestern University studies in the humanities, no. 5)

Golenishcheva-Kutuzova, I   **V**
Данте в СССР; библиография переводов и критической литературы 1918–1964 гг. ₍Составитель И. В. Голенищева-Кутузова₎. Москва, 1965.

39 p. 22 cm.

At head of title: Академия наук СССР. Фундаментальная библиотека общественных наук имени В. П. Волгина."
"К 700-летию со дня рождения Данте Алигьери."

Marraro, Howard Rosario, 1897–
Bibliografia dantesca americana dal Settecento al 1921 ₍di₎ Howard R. Marraro. Venezia, Stamperia di Venezia, 1965.

277 p. 25 cm.

Cover title.

"Estratto dagli Atti dell'Istituto veneto di scienze, lettere ed arti. Anno accademico 1964–65. Tomo CXXIII. Classe di scienzemorali e lettere."

Morreale de Castro, Margherita, 1922–
Apuntes bibliográficos para el estudio del tema Dante en España hasta el s. XVII ₍por₎ Margherita Morreale. Bari, Editoriale universitaria, ₍1967₎.

44 p. 24 cm.

"Estratto dagli Annali del corso di lingue e letterature straniere dell'Università di Bari. v. VIII, 1967."

Rome (City) Centro nazionale per il catalogo unico delle biblioteche italiane e per le informazioni bibliografiche.
Dante Alighieri, MCCLXV–MCMLXV. Roma, 1965.

101 p. facsims., plates. 36 cm.

"Il presente volume è costituito nella massima parte dalla voce 'Alighieri Dante,' quale compare nel volume terzo del Primo catalogo collettivo delle biblioteche italiane, Alda-Almed (Roma, 1965)."

Saginati, Liana.
La collezione dantesca della Biblioteca civica Berio di Genova ₍di₎ Liana Saginati ₍e₎ Giacomina Calcagno. Presentazione di Giuseppe Piersantelli. Firenze, L. S. Olschki, 1966.

xii, 506 p. facsims., plates, ports. 26 cm. (Biblioteca di bibliografia italiana, 46)

MANUSCRIPTS

Biblioteca medicea laurenziana.
Mostra di codici danteschi. Firenze, L. S. Olschki, 1966.

14 p. 9 facsims. (1 col.) 22 cm.

"La scelta ed il presente catalogo sono opera del Dott. Filippo Di Benedetto."

Mostra di codici ed edizioni dantesche (20 aprile–31 ottobre 1965). Firenze, R. Sandron, 1965.

xxviii, 278 p. 26 plates (part col.) 24 cm. (Comitato nazionale per le celebrazioni del VII centenario della nascita di Dante. Catalogo, 1)

Stuttgart. Landesbibliothek.
Dante Alighieri, 1265–1321. Handschriften, Bildnisse und Drucke des 14. bis 16. Jahrhunderts, vornehmlich aus den Schätzen der Württembergischen Landesbibliothek. (Katalogbearbeitung: Peter Amelung) Stuttgart, Italienisches Kulturinstitut; Württembergische Landesbibliothek; Kulturamt, 1965.

47 p. with illus. 24 cm.

DANUBE RIVER AND VALLEY

Janićijević, Jovan, *comp.*
Jugoslovenska literatura o Dunavu 1945–1965. Sastavio Jovan Janićijević. Beograd, Jugoslovenski bibliografski institut, 1966.

₍3₎, 63 p. 29 cm. (Bibliografska građa, 1)

DANZIG
see also under Prussia

Bibliografia Pomorza Gdańskiego.
Gdańsk, Państwowe Wydawn. Naukowe.

v. 24 cm. annual. (Biblioteka Gdańska Polskiej Akademii Nauk. Seria katalogów i bibliografii)

Began with vol. for 1964.

Issued by Biblioteka Gdańska of Polska Akademia Nauk.
Compilers: W. Andrusiak, B. Ramotowska, and A. Świderska.

Wojewódzkie Archiwum Państwowe w Gdańsku.
Archiwum miasta Gdańska: przewodnik po zespołach. 1253–1945. Opracowały Teresa Węsierska-Biernatowa, Janina Czaplicka ₍i₎ Maria Sławoszewska. ₍Wyd. 1.₎ Warszawa Naczelna Dyrekcja Archiwów Państwowych. ₍Łódź. Państwowe Wydawn. Naukowe, Oddz. w Łodzi₎ 1970.

96 p. illus., facsims. 24 cm.

DAR ES SALAAM. UNIVERSITY COLLEGE

Dar es Salaam. University College.
Report on research. 1967–
₍Dar es Salaam₎

v. 33 cm. annual.

Report for 1967/68–   covers academic year.

DARÍO, RUBÉN

Havana. Biblioteca Nacional José Martí. *Centro de Información Humanística.*
Bibliografía Rubén Darío, en homenaje al centenario de su nacimiento. La Habana, 1967.

vii, 11 p. 27 cm.

Jirón Terán, José.
Bibliografía general de Rubén Darío (julio 1883–enero 1967). ₍Managua, Editorial San José₎ 1967.

128 p. 26 cm. (Publicaciones del centenario de Rubén Darío)

"Tirada aparte de Cuadernos universitarios."

Lozano, Carlos.
Rubén Darío y el modernismo en España, 1888–1920; ensayo de bibliografía comentada. New York, Las Américas Pub. Co., 1968 ₍°1967₎

xxii, 158 p. 23 cm.

Woodbridge, Hensley Charles, 1923–
Rubén Darío, a selective classified and annotated bibliography / compiled by Hensley C. Woodbridge. Metuchen, N. J. : Scarecrow Press, 1975.

xiv, 231 p. ; 22 cm.

A revised and updated version of the author's Rubén Darío: a critical bibliography, published in Hispania, v. 50–51, 1967 and 1968.

DART, RAYMOND ARTHUR

Fischer, Ilse.
Professor Raymond Arthur Dart; a bibliography of his works. Johannesburg, University of the Witwatersrand, Department of Bibliography, Librarianship and Typography, 1969.

₍xiv₎ 37 p. 30 cm.

Compiled in part fulfilment for the requirements of the Diploma in Librarianship, University of the Witwatersrand.

DARTMOOR, ENGLAND
Somers Cocks, John Vernon.
The Dartmoor bibliography, non-fiction; compiled by J. V. Somers Cocks. Exeter, Dartmoor Preservation Association, 1970.

vi, 65 p. 21 cm. (Dartmoor Preservation Association. Publication no. 6)

DARWIN, CHARLES ROBERT

Freeman, R   B
The works of Charles Darwin; an annotated bibliographical handlist, by R. B. Freeman. London, Dawsons of Pall Mall, 1965.

x, 81 p. illus., facsims., plan. 23 cm.

DATA PROCESSING see Electronic data processing; Information storage and retrieval systems

DAUDET, ALPHONSE

Brivois, Jules Jean Baptiste Lucien, 1832–1920.
Essai de bibliographie des œuvres de M. Alphonse Daudet avec fragments inédits. New York, B. Franklin [1970]

vi, 143 p. 19 cm. (Burt Franklin bibliography & reference series, 370)

Essays in literature & criticism, 91.
Reprint of the edition published in Paris, 1895.

DAUKŠA, MIKALOJUS

Lebedys, Jurgis.
Mikalojaus Daukšos bibliografija. Vilnius, "Vaga," 1971.

151 p. 21 cm.

DAUPHINÉ, FRANCE

Allard, Guy, 1635–1716.
Bibliothèque du Dauphiné. [Nouv. éd. revue & augmentée] Genève, Slatkine Reprints, 1970.

340 p. 22 cm.

"Réimpression de l'édition de Grenoble, 1797."

Nigay, Gilbert.
Les Alpes françaises, le Dauphiné et Grenoble, économie et géographie humaine, bibliographie sommaire ... établie par M. Gilbert Nigay ... Grenoble, Association des amis de l'Université de Grenoble [1967?]

v. 1 (unpaged) 21 cm.

DÁVALOS, JUAN CARLOS

Rossi, Iris.
Contribución a la bibliografía de Juan Carlos Dávalos. Buenos Aires, Fondo Nacional de las Artes [1966]

91 p. ports. 22 cm. (Bibliografía argentina de artes y letras. Compilaciones especiales)

"Correspondiente al no. 23."

DAVIČO, OSKAR

Библографија Оскара Давича. ⟨Станка Костин: Увод⟩. Београд, "Просвета," 1969.

cxlvii, [3] p. 19 cm.

DAVIS, JEFFERSON

Louisiana Historical Association.
Calendar of the Jefferson Davis postwar manuscripts. New York, B. Franklin [1970]

ii l., 325 p. 29 cm. (American classics in history & social science, 121) (Burt Franklin bibliography & reference series, 329)

Reprint of the 1943 ed.

DAVIS FAMILY

Brubaker, Robert L
The David Davis family papers, 1816–1943; a descriptive inventory, by Robert L. Brubaker. Springfield, Illinois State Historical Library, 1965.

60 p. geneal. table. 25 cm. (Manuscripts in the Illinois State Historical Library, no. 3)

DAVY, SIR HUMPHRY

Fullmer, June Z
Sir Humphry Davy's published works [by] June Z. Fullmer. Cambridge, Harvard University Press, 1969.

viii, 112 p. 23 cm.

DAWSON, SIR JOHN WILLIAM

Kolodny, Joyce E
A preliminary list of the official papers of Sir John William Dawson, bundle 2, accession 927 1885–1892, by Joyce E. Kolodny. With a foreword by John C. L. Andreassen. Montreal, University Archives, McGill University, 1970.

14 l. 28 cm.

McGill University, Montreal. Archives.
A preliminary list of the official papers of Sir John William Dawson, bundle 3, accession 927, 1854–1857, by Lois Gerth. With a foreword by John C. L. Andreassen. Montreal, 1971.

i, 18 l. 28 cm.

McGill University, Montreal. Archives.
A preliminary list of the official papers of Sir John William Dawson, bundle 6, accession 927, 1855–1858, by Hazel Hutchison. With a foreword by John C. L. Andreassen. Montreal, 1971.

v, 12 p. 28 cm.

McGill University, Montreal. Archives.
A preliminary list of the official papers of Sir John William Dawson, bundle 7, accession 927, 1857–1858, by Ena G. Lazarus. With a foreword by John C. L. Andreassen. Montreal, 1971.

ii, 28 l. 28 cm.

Stilman, Ruth.
A preliminary list of the official papers of Sir John William Dawson, bundle 1, accession 927, 1856–1891. With a foreword by John C. L. Andreassen. Montreal, University Archives, McGill University, 1970.

19 l. 28 cm.

DAY, ARTHUR GROVE

Day, Arthur Grove, 1904–
What did I do right? An auto-bibliography, by A. Grove Day. Honolulu, Priv. print. [by White Knight Press] 1974.

70 p. 22 cm. (White Knight chapbook)

DAY-LEWIS, CECIL

Handley-Taylor, Geoffrey.
C. Day-Lewis, the poet laureate; a bibliography. Compiled by Geoffrey Handley-Taylor and Timothy d'Arch Smith. With a letter of introd. by W. H. Auden. Chicago, St. James Press, 1968.

xii, 42 p. facsims., ports. 24 cm.

DAYTON, OHIO

Becker, Carl M
A bibliography of sources for Dayton, Ohio, 1850–1950; cooperative Dayton history project. Compiled and edited by Carl M. Becker, Jacob H. Dorn [and] Paul G. Merriam. Dayton, Ohio, Wright State University, 1971.

210 l. 28 cm.

DDT

U. S. *National Agricultural Library. Pesticides Information Center.*
DDT ⟨1,1-dichloro-2,2-bis (P-chlorophenyl) ethylene⟩ a list of references selected and compiled from the files of the Pesticides Information Center, National Agricultural Library, 1960–1969. Beltsville, Md., National Agricultural Library, 1970.

iii, 143 p. 27 cm. ([U. S. National Agricultural Library] Library list no. 97)

DEACONS

Guitard, André.
Bibliographie sur le diaconat (janvier 1966–décembre 1969), compilée par André Guitard et Rolland Litalien. Montréal, Office national du clergé, 1970.

72 p. 28 cm. (His Bibliographie sur le sacerdoce, 6)

DEAD SEA SCROLLS

Jongeling, Bastiaan.
A classified bibliography of the finds in the desert of Judah 1958–1969. [By] B. Jongeling. Leiden, Brill, 1971.

xiv, 140 p. 25 cm. (Studies on the texts of the desert of Judah, v. 7)

Yizhar, Michael.
Bibliography of Hebrew publications on the Dead Sea scrolls, 1948–1964. Cambridge, Harvard University Press, 1967.

48 p. 24 cm. (Harvard theological studies, 23)

DEAF

Fellendorf, George W
Bibliography on deafness; a selected index: The Volta review, 1899–1965 [and] the American annals of the deaf, 1847–1965. George W. Fellendorf, editor. [1st ed.] Washington, Alexander Graham Bell Association for the Deaf [1966]
148 p. 23 cm.
———————— Supplement 1966–1972. Washington, Alexander Graham Bell Association for the Deaf [1973]
viii, 37 p. 23 cm.

Lagati, Salvatore.
Bibliografia italiana sull'educazione dei sordi. Libri peri-

odici, scuole, specialisti. Milano, S. E. R. T., 1972.

115 p. 21½ cm.

On spine: 1.

Lerman, Alan.
Vocational adjustment and the deaf: a guide and annotated bibliography. Washington, Alexander Graham Bell Association for the Deaf [1965]

60 p. 28 cm.

Wien, Virginia.
Bibliography of the deaf. Lansing [1966]

14 p. 28 cm. ([Michigan. State Library, Lansing] Bibliography for educators no. 14)

DEAF-BLIND see Blind-deaf

DEATH
see also under Incunabula *(Falk)*

Eckert, William G 1926–
On death. William G. Eckert, editor. Thomas T. Noguchi, co-editor. [n. p., International Reference Organization in Forensic Medicine, 1967?]

10, 44 p. 20 cm.

Kutscher, Austin H 1951–
A bibliography of books on death, bereavement, loss and grief: 1935–1968. Compiled by: Austin H. Kutscher, Jr., and Austin H. Kutscher. New York, Health Sciences Pub. Co. [c1969]

84 p. 26 cm.

Vernick, Joel J
Selected bibliography on death and dying [by] Joel J. Vernick. [Prepared by Information Office, National Institute of Child Health and Human Development. Bethesda, Md.] U. S. National Institutes of Health; for sale by the Supt. of Docs., U. S. Govt. Print. Off., Washington [1969?]

v, 61 p. 26 cm.

DEBATE

Kruger, Arthur N
A classified bibliography of argumentation and debate, by Arthur N. Kruger. New York, Scarecrow Press, 1964.

400 p. 22 cm.

DEBUSSY, CLAUDE

Abravanel, Claude.
Claude Debussy; a bibliography. Detroit, Information Coordinators, 1974.

214 p. 23 cm. (Detroit studies in music bibliography, 29)

DECROLY, OVIDE

Belgium. *Ministère de l'éducation nationale et de la culture.*
Hommage à Ovide Decroly: bibliographie de son œuvre. Hulde aan Ovide Decroly; bibliografie van zijn werk. [Bruxelles] 1964.

48 p. port. 21 cm.

DEDMAN, JOHN JOHNSTONE

Canberra, Australia. National Library. Manuscript Section.
John Dedman; a guide to his papers in the National Library of Australia. Canberra, 1970.

25 l. 27 cm.

DEFOE, DANIEL

Boston. Public Library.
A catalog of the Defoe collection in the Boston Public Library. With a pref. by John Alden. Boston, G. K. Hall, 1966.

vi, 200 p. 26 cm.

The collection begun by W. P. Trent was purchased by the Boston Public Library in 1929. The holdings are shown by reproduced catalog cards.

Moore, John Robert, 1890–
A checklist of the writings of Daniel Defoe. 2d ed. [Hamden, Conn.] Archon Books, 1971.

xviii, 281 p. 23 cm.

Smith, Robert Dennis Hilton, 1903–
Crusoe 250, being a catalogue in celebration of the 250th anniversary of Robinson Crusoe. [Compiled by R. D. Hilton Smith] Victoria, B. C., Adelphi Book Shop, 1970.

119 p. illus., facsims., port. 24 cm.

Edition of 500 copies.

DE GAULLE, CHARLES see Gaulle, Charles de

DEKKER, EDWARD DOUWES

Oshis, V V
Мультатули. Библиогр. указ. [Сост. и авт. вступит. статьи В. В. Ошис.] Москва, "Книга," 1971.

40 p. 22 cm. (Писатели зарубежных стран)

At head of title: Всесоюзная государственная библиотека иностранной литературы.

DEKKER, THOMAS

Allison, Antony Francis.
Thomas Dekker, c. 1572–1632, a bibliographical catalogue of the early editions (to the end of the 17th century), by A. F. Allison. Folkestone, Dawsons, 1972.

143 p. facsims. 23 cm. index. (Pall Mall bibliographies, no. 1)

DELARAGEAZ, LOUIS HENRI

Vaud. Bibliothèque cantonale et universitaire, Lausanne. Département des manuscrits.
Inventaire des archives de Louis-Henri Delarageaz, IS 3681, par Marianne Perrenoud et Olivier Pavillon. Lausanne, Bibliothèque cantonale et universitaire, 1971.

188 l. 30 cm. (Its Inventaires des fonds manuscrits, 10)

DELAWARE

Checklist of official Delaware publications. v. 1–
Jan. 1968–
Dover, State Library Commission.

v. 28 cm.

Reed, Henry Clay, 1899–
A bibliography of Delaware through 1960, compiled by H. Clay Reed and Marion Björnson Reed. Newark, Published for the Institute of Delaware History and Culture by the University of Delaware Press, 1966.

vi, 196 p. 25 cm.

"500 copies printed."

Rink, Evald, 1916–
Printing in Delaware, 1761–1800; a checklist. Wilmington, Del., Eleutherian Mills Historical Library, 1969.

214 p. illus. 25 cm.

DELAWARE BAY

Comprehensive bibliography on Delaware Bay, by Mark Plunguian [and others] Newark, College of Marine Studies, University of Delaware, 1973.

170 p. 28 cm. (Delaware Bay report series, v. 10)

DELAWARE, LACKAWANNA AND WESTERN RAILROAD COMPANY

Syracuse University. Library. Manuscript Collections.
Delaware, Lackawanna, and Western Railroad Company; a register of the corporate records of the Lackawanna division of the Erie-Lackawanna Railroad Company in the Syracuse University Library. Edited by Howard L. Applegate [and] Lyall D. Squair. New York, 1964.

vii, 32 l. 28 cm. (Its Manuscript register series, register no. 6)

DELCHEV, GOTSE

Skopje, Yugoslavia. Narodna i univerzitetska biblioteka.
Гоце Делчев; библиографија. [Составил В. Димитров] Скопје, 1964.

48 p. 20 cm.

DE LEON, DANIEL

Johnson, Oakley C 1890–
Writings by and about Daniel de Leon; a bibliography, by Oakley C. Johnson and Carl Reeve. [New York, American Institute for Marxist Studies] 1966.

26 l. 28 cm. (American Institute for Marxist Studies. Bibliographical series, no. 3)

DEMARIA, GIOVANNI

Gli Scritti di Giovanni Demaria. Padova, CEDAM, 1964.

19 p. 24 cm.

At head of title: Bibliografia economia italiana.

DEMBLIN, B., pseud. see Teitelbaum, B.

DEMOGRAPHY see Population

DEMOSTHENES

Canfora, Luciano.
Inventario dei manoscritti greci di Demostene. Padova, Antenore, 1968.

103 p. 21 cm. (Proagōnes: collezione di studi e testi. Studi, 9)

DENK, PETR, pseud.

Brünn. Státní pedagogická knihovna.
Petr Denk, 1902–1955. Bibliografii prací připravil Kamil Horňák. ₁V Brně, 1964₁

104 l. 20 cm. (Život a dílo čs. pedagogů, č. 3)

DENMARK

Copenhagen. Kongelige Bibliotek.
Denmark: literature, language, history, society, education, arts; a select bibliography ₁of books and articles in the English language₁ København, The Royal Library, 1966.

6, 151 p. 24 cm.

Cover title: Denmark: country, people, culture.

Dania polyglotta. new ser., 1–   1969–
Copenhagen ₁Royal Library₁

v. 24 cm. annual.

"Literature on Denmark in languages other than Danish & books of Danish interest published abroad."
Supersedes Dania polyglotta; répertoire bibliographique annuel des ouvrages, articles, résumés etc., en langues étrangères parus en Danemark.

Denmark. *Rigsarkivet.*
Matriklerne 1664 og 1688. Ved J. O. Bro-Jørgensen. Udg. af Rigsarkivet. København, 1968.

vi, 169 p. 30 cm.

"Nærværende publikation slutter sig således som en specialregistratur til Vejledende arkivregistraturer XII."
At head of title: Specialregistraturer.

Denmark. *Rigsarkivet.*
Skrifter udgivet af Rigsarkivet 1852–1968. København, 1968.

8 p. 30 cm.

Denmark. Udenrigsministeriet.
Publikationer i handelskontorernes publikationscentral. ₁Ny udg.₁ København, Udenrigsministeriets handelskontorer, 1971.

22 p. 21 cm.

Cover title.
At head of title: Udenrigsministeriets erhvervstjeneste.

Dybdahl, Vagn.
Handels- og industrihistorisk litteratur 1952–1965. Århus, Erhvervsarkivet, 1966.

63 p. 25 cm.

Reprint from Fortid og Nutid, bd. XXII, 1966.

Houmøller, Sven.
Biografiske tidsskriftartikler. Register til Danske blandede Tidsskrifter ⟨1855–1912⟩ og Dansk Tidsskrift-Index ⟨1915–49⟩. København, Bibliotekscentralen, 1971.

145 p. 25 cm.

Svennevig, Palle.
Danske kommissionsbetænkninger 1850–1970. København, Folketingets Bibliotek og oplysningstjeneste, Eksp.: Christiansborg, København K, 1972.

8, 616 p. 23 cm.

BIBLIOGRAPHIES

Munch-Petersen, Erland.
A guide to Danish bibliography. Compiled by Erland Munch-Petersen. Assisted by Frederic J. Mosher. Copenhagen, Royal School of Librarianship, 1965.

140 p. 20 cm.

HISTORY

Bruun, Henry.
Dansk historisk Bibliografi 1913–1942. Udg. af Den danske historiske Forening. København, Rosenkilde og Bagger, 1966–

v. 24 cm.

CONTENTS.—Bd. 1. Indledning, politisk Historie samt Stats- og Kulturforhold til og med Erhvervsliv.

Dansk historisk årsbibliografi. 1967–

København ₁Aarhuus stiftsbogtrykkerie₁

v. 23 cm.

Chiefly Danish.
"Udgivet af Den Danske historiske forening og Dansk historisk fællesforening i samarbejde med Det Kgl. Bibliotek."

Denmark. *Landsarkivet for Nørrejylland.*
Fortid i skrift. Vejledning til arkivets udstilling ved Paul G. Ørberg. Viborg ₁1967₁

47 p. illus. 22 cm.

Denmark. *Landsarkivet for Nørrejylland.*
Håndskriftsamlingen. ₁Udarbejdet af Poul Rasmussen₁ Viborg, Landsarkivet, 1969.

156 p. 30 cm. (*Its* Arkivregistraturer, 2)

Denmark. Rigsarkivet.
Oversigt over private personarkiver i Rigsarkivet. København, 1972.

5, 274 p. 21 cm. (Foreløbige arkivregistraturer, ny serie, nr. 3)

Denmark. Rigsarkivet.
Oversigt over Rigsarkivets nyere arkiver. Ved C. Rise Hansen. København, Rigsarkivet, 1972–

v. 22 cm. (Its Foreløbige arkivregistraturer, ny serie, nr. 4)

CONTENTS: 1. Justitsministeriet, Ministeriet for kirke- og undervisningsvæsenet, Kirkeministeriet, Undervisningsministeriet, Ministeriet for kulturelle anliggender, med derunder hørende institutioner.

Tiedje, Alfred.
Danmark under besættelsen. En bogliste fra biblioteket. 2. omarb. og revid. udg. Udarb. af A. Tiedje, Jørgen Hæstrup ₁og₁ Aage Trommer. København, Bibliotekscentralen, 1968.

16 p. 17 cm.

IMPRINTS

Dahl, Svend, 1887–1963.
Den store mønsterkatalog. Under medvirken af A. Tiedje. ₁København₁ Bibliotekscentralen, 1965–73.

2 v. 23 cm.

Vol. 2 has added t. p. in English.
Vol. 2 has preface and contents in Danish and English.
CONTENTS: ₁1₁ Dansk faglitteratur før 1941 i udvalg.—2. Dansk faglitteratur 1941–1955 i udvalg.

Nyere dansk faglitteratur. Et udvalg af bøger på dansk udkommet 1941–1965. København. Bibliotekscentralen. 1967.

311 p. 23 cm.

Nyere dansk faglitteratur. Et udvalg af bøger udkommet efter 1945. 2. udg. København, Bibliotekscentralen, 1969.

364 p. 23 cm.

LAW see Law - Denmark

DENTISTRY
see also under Dissertations, Academic

Asbell, Milton Baron.
A bibliography of dentistry in America. 1790–1840, by Milton B. Asbell. [Cherry Hill, N. J., Printed for the author by Sussex House Publications. 1973]

ix, 107, [1] p. illus. 19 x 23 cm.

Imprint supplied from label mounted on p. [108]

Associazione italiana di radiologia odontostomatologica.
La letteratura radio-stomatologica italiana ... Milano, IDOS, [1968]–

v. 27 cm.

CONTENTS: v. 1. Indice bibliografico dei lavori italiani di radiologia odonto-stomatologica dai primordi al 1966.

Crowley, C   George.
Dental bibliography: a standard reference list of books on dentistry published throughout the world from 1536 to 1885. Arranged chronologically, and supplemented with a complete cross-reference to authors. Compiled by C. Geo. Crowley. Amsterdam, Liberac, 1968.

180 p. 23 cm.

David, Théophile, 1851–1892.
Bibliographie française de l'art dentaire. Amsterdam, Liberac, 1970.

viii, 307 p. 23 cm.

Reprint of the Paris 1889 ed.

Hess, Jean Claude, 1926–
Titres et travaux scientifiques ... Clermont-Ferrand, Impr. France Quercy-Auvergne, 1966.

48 p. 27 cm.

Isaza Restrepo, Irma.
Indice odontológico colombiano, 1887–1966. [Medellín, Editorial Universidad Antioquia. 1968]

xx, 336 l. 28 cm. (Publicaciones de la E. I. B. Serie: Bibliografías, no. 21)

Tesis (licenciada en bibliotecología)—Universidad de Antioquia.

Milan. Università. Istituto di clinica odontoiatrica e stomatologica.
Pubblicazioni Istituto di clinica odontoiatrica e stomatologica dell'Università di Milano. (Direttore: prof. Oscar Hoffer). Anni accademici 1965–66, 1966–67, 1967–68. Trieste, Tip. G. Coana, 1969.

45 p. 24 cm.

Rosa, Malvina Vianna.
A orientação bibliográfica na Faculdade de Odontologia,

UFRGS. Pôrto Alegre, Departamento de Educação e Cultura, 1968.

7 l. diagrs. 33 cm.

At head of title: Universidade Federal do Rio Grande do Sul. Departamento de Educação e Cultura & Associação Riograndense de Bibliotecários.
"I Jornada Sul Riograndense de Biblioteconomia e Documentação ... Tema 5: Informação científica."

Smith, Phyllis M
The rare books collection of the Dental Library, University of Toronto and the Harry R. Abbott Memorial Library, compiled by Phyllis M. Smith. [Toronto, Univ. of Toronto] 1966.

37 p. 25 cm.

At head of title: Royal College of Dental Surgeons of Ontario.

U. S. *National Institutes of Health. Division of Dental Health.*
Catalog: publications, reprints, films, exhibits. Bethesda, Md., U. S. Dept. of Health, Education, and Welfare, Bureau of Health Manpower, Division of Dental Health, Information Office [1968]

iv, 24 p. 23 cm. (Public Health Service publication no. 1784)

DEPAUW UNIVERSITY, GREENCASTLE, INDIANA

Greencastle, Ind. Archives of DePauw University and Indiana Methodism.
Select bibliographic guide to the Archives of DePauw University and Indiana Methodism. Compiled by David J. Olson. [Greencastle, Ind., DePauw University] 1972.

13 p. 24 cm.

DE QUINCY, THOMAS

Manchester, Eng. Public Libraries. *Moss Side Branch.*
Thomas De Quincey; a bibliography based upon the De Quincey collection in the Moss Side Library. Compiled by J. A. Green. New York, B. Franklin [1968]

vii, 110 p. 23 cm. (Burt Franklin bibliography and reference series, 150)

Reprint of the 1908 ed.

DERBYSHIRE, ENGLAND

Derby Borough Libraries. Local History Dept.
Family papers in the Local History Department. Derby, Derby Borough Libraries, 1971.

[1], 18 p. 22 cm. (Guides to the resources of the local history collection)

On cover: Derby Borough Libraries centenary 1871–1971.

Derby Borough Libraries. Local History Dept.
Manuscript books in the local history collection (select list). Derby, Derby Borough Libraries, 1971.

[3], 20 p. 22 cm. (Guides to the resources of the local history collection)

On cover: Derby Borough Libraries centenary 1871–1971.

Derbyshire, Eng. County Library.
Derbyshire: books and other material available in the County Library. Matlock. Derbyshire County Library, 1971.

[8], 107 p. 1 illus. 23 cm.

Handford, Charles Clifford, 1890–
Some maps of the county of Derby, 1577–1850, by Charles C. Handford. Derby, 'Derbyshire Miscellany,' 1971.

₍4₎, 50, vi p., 2 plates. 26 cm. index. (Derbyshire Miscellany. Supplement 11)

DERMATOLOGY

Bulletin signalétique 348: Dermatologie. v. 33–

1972–
Paris, Centre national de la recherche scientifique, Centre de documentation.

v. 30 cm. monthly.

Kabelková, Zdenka.
Dermatovenerologie. Výběr lit. z fondu Univ. knihovny v Brně. Sest. Zdenka Kabelková. Předml.: Jaroslav Horáček. Brno, Univ. knihovna, t. G 07, Blansko, 1970.

81, ₍1₎ p. 21 cm. (Výběrový seznam, č. 160)

Texier, Lucien.
Titres et travaux du Dr Lucien Texier. ₍Nouvelle édition.₎ Bordeaux. impr. Biscaye frères, ₍l'auteur, 8, rue Porte Basse,₎ 1971.

123 p. illus. 27 cm.

DESCARTES, RENÉ

Sebba, Gregor.
Bibliographia Cartesiana, a critical guide to the Descartes literature, 1880–1960. The Hague, M. Nijhoff, 1964.

xv, 510 p. illus. 24 cm. (Archives internationales d'histoire des idées, 5)

DESCHWANDEN, JOSEF WOLFGANG VON

Jaeggli, Alvin E
Katalog des Nachlasses von Josef Wolfgang von Deschwanden (1819–1866) Professor für darstellende Geometrie und erster Direktor des Eidgenössischen Polytechnikums in Zürich, zusammengestellt und kommentiert von Alvin Jaeggli. Zürich ₍Eidgenössische Technische Hochschule₎ 1969.

III, 43 l. port. 30 cm. (Eidgenössische Technische Hochschule Zürich. Schriftenreihe der Bibliothek, 12)

DESEGREGATION see Discrimination

DESERTS

₍Pustyni Turkmenii i ikh khoziaĭstvennoe osvoenie₎
Пустыни Туркмении и их хозяйственное освоение. Указ. литературы (1950–1965). Сост. А. Язбердыев, Л. К. Караджаева, Л. И. Клиппа и А. Я. Степанов. Гл. ред. акад. Т. Б. Бердыев. Отв. ред. акад. М. П. Петров. Ашхабад, "Ылым," 1972.

435 p. 22 cm.
At head of title: Академия наук Туркменской ССР. Центральная научная библиотека.
Added t. p. in Turkoman.

DESIGN see Industrial design

DE SOLA, ABRAHAM

McGill University, Montreal. Archives.
Abraham de Sola papers; a guide to the microfilm. Prepared by Mrs. Emmanuel Miller. With a foreword by

John C. L. Andreassen. Montreal, 1970.

89 l. 28 cm.

Limited ed. of 200 copies.

DESSEWFFY FAMILY

Hungary. Országos Levéltár.
A Dessewffy család levéltára; repreórium. Összeállította: Bakács István. Budapest, Művelődésügyi Minisztérium Levéltári Osztálya, 1967.

275 p. 29 cm. (Levéltári leltárak, 38)
Summary in Russian, French, and German.

DETECTIVE STORIES see Fiction - Detective

DETROIT, MICHIGAN

Koerner, Alberta G   Auringer.
Detroit and vicinity before 1900; an annotated list of maps. Compiled by Alberta G. Auringer Koerner. Washington, Library of Congress; ₍for sale by the Supt. of Docs., U. S. Govt. Print. Off.,₎ 1968.

iv, 84 p. maps. 24 cm.

"Most of the described maps are in the collections of the Geography and Map Division of the Library of Congress."

DEUTSCHE FORSCHUNGSGEMEINSCHAFT

Deutsche Forschungsgemeinschaft (Founded 1949)
Publikationenverzeichnis zu den von der Deutschen Forschungsgemeinschaft geförderten Forschungsvorhaben. Bd. 1–
1964–
₍Bad Godesberg₎

v. 22 cm. annual.

DEUTSCHER KULTURBUND

Baum, Hans Werner.
25 ₍i. e. Fünfundzwanzig₎ Jahre Deutscher Kulturbund. Ein Literaturverz. (Berlin) Berliner Stadtbibliothek, 1970.

24 p. 21 cm.

DEVELOPING COUNTRIES see Underdeveloped areas

DEVON, ENGLAND

Devon, Eng. Record Office.
Brief guide. County Hall, Exeter (Devon) Devonshire County Record Office ₍1969₎–

v. 23 cm.

Cover title.
CONTENTS: pt. 1. Official and ecclesiastical.

Smith, L   M   Ruse.
The hundred of Heytor: a guide to the printed sources relating to South Devon, issued during National Library Week 2. ₍Compiled by L. M. Ruse Smith₎ Torquay, Pub-

lic Library, 1967.

[1], 26 p. 21½ cm.

DEWEY, JOHN

Boydston, Jo Ann, 1924–
    John Dewey; a checklist of translations, 1900–1967. Compiled and edited by Jo Ann Boydston, with Robert L. Andresen. Carbondale, Southern Illinois University Press [1969]

xxxi, 123 p. 21 cm.

DHARMA   see under   Hindu law

DIABETES

Tucker, Harold Atherton, 1916–
    Oral antidiabetic therapy, 1956–1965: with particular reference to tolbutamide (Orinase), by H. A. Tucker. Springfield, Ill., C. C. Thomas [1965]

ix, 676 p. 24 cm.

An annotated bibliography.

DIALECTICAL MATERIALISM

Bocheński, Innocentius M   1902–
    Guide to Marxist philosophy; an introductory bibliography. Edited by Joseph M. Bochenski and [others]. 1st ed.] Chicago, Swallow Press [1972]

81 p. 23 cm.

Brünn. Universita. *Knihovna.*
    Základy filosofie; výběr literatury ke kursu Brněnské lidové university vědy, techniky a umění v zimním a letním běhu 1964/65. Literaturu se signaturami knih z fondů Universitni knihovny v Brně vybrala Anna Zykmundová, přehlédl Hanuš Steiner. V Brně, 1964.

9 l. 21 cm. (*Its* Bibliografický leták, 184)

Lachs, John.
    Marxist philosophy; a bibliographical guide. Chapel Hill, University of North Carolina Press [1967]

xiv, 166 p. 23 cm.

Литература по марксистско-ленинской философии и научному коммунизму; каталог-проспект. Москва, Изд-во полит. лит-ры, 1964.

47 p. 20 cm. (Для системы политического просвещения)

Russia (1923–   U. S. S. R.). Ministerstvo vysshego i srednego spetsial'nogo obrazovaniia. Otdel prepodavaniia obshchestvennykh nauk.
    (Primernaia tematika kontrol'nykh rabot po marksistsko-leninskoi filosofii)
    Примерная тематика контрольных работ по марксистско-ленинской философии. Для заочных высших учебных заведений и заочных отделений вузов. [Отв. редакторы: М. И. Конкин, Ю. И. Москалев] Москва, Мысль, 1973.

31, [1] p. 20 cm.

Russia (*1923–   U. S. S. R.*) *Upravlenie prepodavaniia obshchestvennykh nauk.*
    Примерная тематика контрольных и курсовых работ по марксистско-ленинской философии для заочных высших учебных заведений и заочных отделений вузов. [Ответ-

ственный редактор С. М. Орлов] Москва, Изд-во полит. лит-ры, 1964.

78 p. 20 cm.

At head of title: Министерство высшего и среднего специального образования СССР.

Список литературы кандидатского минимума по марксистско-ленинской философии (для нефилософских специальностей) [Отв. редакторы: Л. Г. Князева, С. М. Орлов]. Москва, Мысль, 1965.

13 p. 20 cm.

At head of title: Министерство высшего и среднего специального образования СССР. Управление преподавания общественных наук.

Ziat'kova, Liudmila Ivanovna.
    [Molodezhi o filosofii]
    Молодежи о философии. Рек. указ. литературы. Москва, "Книга," 1971.

93 p. 20 cm.

At head of title: Государственная библиотека СССР имени В. И. Ленина.

Ziat'kova, Liudmila Ivanovna.
    [Teoriia poznaniia i sovremennaia nauka]
    Теория познания и современная наука. Рек. указ. литературы. Москва, "Книга," 1972.

76 p. 20 cm.

At head of title: Государственная библиотека СССР имени В. И. Ленина. Л. И. Зятькова.

DIAMONDS

Akademiia nauk SSSR. *Sektor seti spetsial'nykh bibliotek.*
    Синтез и физические свойства алмаза; библиографический указатель, 1934–1961. [Составители К. В. Флинт и Н. В. Слесарева. Ответственный редактор М. О. Клия] Москва, Наука, 1965.

119 p. 22 cm.

At head of title: Академия наук СССР. Сектор сети специальных библиотек. Библиотека Института кристаллографии.

Do descobrimento dos diamantes, e diferentes methodos, que se tem praticado na sua extracção. Rio de Janeiro, Biblioteca Nacional, Divisão de Publicações e Divulgação, 1964.

251 p. 27 cm. (Anais da Biblioteca Nacional, v. 80)

"Memória ... oriunda dos manuscritos da ... Coleção Martins."

CONTENTS.—Do descobrimento dos diamantes, e diferentes methodos, que se tem praticado na sua extracção.—Da venda dos diamantes para os países estrangeiros.—Documentos referidos no discurso antecedente.

Vsesoiuznyi nauchno-issledovatel'skii institut sinteza mineral'nogo syr'ia.
    [Sintez i fizicheskie svoistva almaza]
    Синтез и физические свойства алмаза; библиографический указатель, 1962–1965 гг. Под общей ред. В. П. Бутузова, Л. Н. Хетчикова. Москва, ОНТИ ВИЭМС, 1967.

64 p. 27 cm. (Библиографическая информация)

At head of title: Министерство геологии СССР. Всесоюзный научно-исследовательский институт синтеза минерального сырья.

DIARIES

London's diaries. [Catalogue of an exhibition in London]. London, National Book League [1970].

[1], 24 p. 21 cm.

On cover: London's diaries from Samuel Pepys to Harold Nicolson.

DIAS, ANTÔNIO GONÇALVES

Bibliografia gonçalvina, centenário de Antônio Gonçalves Dias, 1864–1964. ₍São Luís, Brasil₎ Departamento de Cultura do Estado, 1964.

45 p. 24 cm.

Maranhão, *Brazil (State)* *Departamento de Cultura.*
Catalogo da exposição comemorativa do 1º centenário da morte de Gonçalves Dias, 1864–1964. Maranhão, 1964.

14 p. 23 cm.

DÍAZ MIRÓN, SALVADOR

Pasquel, Leonardo.
Bibliografía diazmironiana. ₍México, Editorial Citlaltépetl, 1966₎

xi, 63 p. facsims, ports. 18 cm. (Colección, Suma veracruzana. Serie Bibliografía)

DÍAZ RODRÍGUEZ, MANUEL

Caracas. Universidad Católica Andrés Bello. Seminario de Literatura Venezolana.
Contribución a la bibliografía de Manuel Díaz Rodríguez, 1871–1927. ₍Caracas, Gobernación del Distrito Federal, between 1967 and 1970₎

156 p. port. 20 cm. (Colección Bibliografías, 2)

Cover title: Bibliografía Manuel Díaz Rodríguez.
"Trabajo de investigación realizado durante los años académicos 1965–66 y 1966–67 por los siguientes alumnos: Luisa Bello ₍et al.₎ bajo la dirección del profesor Efraín Subero."

DÍAZ SÁNCHEZ, RAMÓN

Bonet de Sotillo, Dolores.
Ramón Díaz Sánchez. Caracas, Escuela de Biblioteconomía y Archivos, Facultad de Humanidades y Educación, Universidad Central de Venezuela, 1967.

71 p. port. 16 cm. (Serie bibliográfica, 5)

Caracas. Universidad Católica Andrés Bello. Seminario de Literatura Venezolana.
Contribución a la bibliografía de Ramón Díaz Sánchez, 1903–1968. ₍Caracas, Gobernación del Distrito Federal, 1970₎

249 p. port. 21 cm. (Colección Bibliografías, 5)

Cover title: Bibliografía Ramón Díaz Sánchez.
"Trabajo de investigación realizado durante los años académicos 1965–66, 1966–67 y 1968–69 por los siguientes alumnos: Manuel Jiménez Rubia ₍et al.₎ bajo la dirección del profesor Efraín Subero."

DIBDIN, THOMAS FROGNALL

Jackson, William Alexander, 1905–1964.
An annotated list of the publications of the Reverend Thomas Frognall Dibdin, D. D., based mainly on those in the Harvard College Library, with notes of others. Cambridge, Houghton Library, 1965.

63 p. facsims, port. 31 cm.

On spine: Jackson on Dibdin.
500 copies.

O'Dwyer, Edward John.
Thomas Frognall Dibdin: bibliographer & bibliomaniac extraordinary, 1776–1847 ₍by₎ E. J. O'Dwyer. Pinner (Mddx.), Private Libraries Association ₍1967₎.

45 p. front. (port.), facsims. 22 cm.

DICKENS, CHARLES

Charles Dickens, 1812–1870. Exposition organisée par le British Council en commémoration du centième anniversaire de la mort de Dickens. Bibliothèque générale de l'Université de Liège du 18 mars au 27 mars 1970. ₍Liège?, 1972?₎

1 v. (unpaged) 22 cm.

Duţu, Alexandru.
Dickens in Rumania; a bibliography for the 150th anniversary ₍by Alexandru Duţu and Sorin Alexandrescu₎ Bucharest, National Commission of the Rumanian People's Republic for UNESCO, 1962.

6 p. illus. 20 cm.

Eckel, John C   1858–
The first editions of the writings of Charles Dickens, their points and values; a bibliography, by John C. Eckel. Rev. and enl. New York, Haskell House, 1972.

xvi, 272 p. illus. 23 cm.

Eckel, John C   1858–
The first editions of the writings of Charles Dickens and their values; a bibliography. ₍Folcroft, Pa.₎ Folcroft Library Editions, 1973.

xviii, 296 p. illus. 24 cm.

Reprint of the 1913 ed. published by Chapman & Hall, London.

Gold, Joseph, 1933–
The stature of Dickens; a centenary bibliography. ₍Toronto₎ Published for University of Manitoba Press by University of Toronto Press ₍1971₎

xxix, 236 p. illus., port. 24 cm.

Cover title: Dickens; a centenary bibliography.

Gt. Brit. *British Council.*
Charles Dickens, 1812–1870: a centenary book exhibition. London, British Council, 1970.

18 p. 21 cm.

Catalog of a book exhibition arranged by the British Council.

Institutul Romîn pentru Relaţiile Culturale cu Străinătatea.
Charles Dickens: bibliography of the Romanian translations published in volume (1898–1966) Bucharest, 1967.

31 p. 20 cm.

Kitton, Frederic George, 1856–1904.
Dickensiana; a bibliography of the literature relating to Charles Dickens and his writings. New York, Haskell House Publishers, 1971.

xxxii, 510 p. port. 23 cm.

Reprint of the 1886 ed.

Kitton, Frederic George, 1856–1904.
The minor writings of Charles Dickens; a bibliography and sketch. New York, Haskell House Publishers, 1970.

xi, 260 p. 22 cm.

Reprint of the 1900 ed.

Ryan, John Sprott, *ed.*
Charles Dickens and New Zealand; a colonial image. Selected from the periodical publications of Charles Dickens, by J. S. Ryan. With historical and biographical notes by A. H. Reed. Wellington, A. H. and A. W. Reed for the Dunedin Public Library; San Francisco, Tri-Ocean Books [1965]

184, viii, 64 p. illus., facsims., map, port. 23 cm.

"Charles Dickens, 1812–1870: catalogue, Alfred and Isabel Reed Dickens collection, Dunedin Public Library, New Zealand, compiled by Brian McPherson" (viii, 64 p.) has special t. p.

Shepherd, Richard Herne, 1842–1895.
The bibliography of Dickens; a bibliographical list, arranged in chronological order, of the published writings in prose and verse of Charles Dickens (from 1834 to 1880) [Folcroft, Pa.] Folcroft Press [1970]

viii, 107 p. 24 cm.

Reprint of the 1880 ed.

Texas. University at Austin. Humanities Research Center.
A catalogue of the VanderPoel Dickens collection at the University of Texas. Compiled by Lucile Carr. [2d ed. Austin] University of Texas at Austin; [distributed by University of Texas Press, 1968]

xi, 274 p. illus., facsims., ports. 26 cm. (Tower bibliographical series, no. 1)

First ed. published in 1961 under title: Catalogue of the Dickens collection at the University of Texas.

Venner, Richard Henry.
Charles Dickens: a brief reader's guide, compiled by R. H. Venner, with introductions by N. V. Tilley. Nottingham, Nottinghamshire County Library, 1970.

[1], 18 p. facsims. 21 cm.

W. J. Carlton, a tribute, with a list of his writings on Dickens. [London, Dickens Fellowship, 1973]

[1], 6 p. 21 cm.

"K. J. F. privately printed."

DICKEY, JAMES

Ashley, Franklin.
James Dickey ... ; a checklist. Ashley. Introd. by James Dickey. Detroit, Gale Research Co., 1972.

xiii, 98 p. illus. 23 cm.

"A Bruccoli-Clark book."

Glancy, Eileen.
James Dickey: the critic as poet; an annotated bibliography with an introductory essay. Troy, N. Y., Whitston Pub. Co., 1971.

107 p. 23 cm.

DICKINSON, EMILY

Buckingham, Willis J
Emily Dickinson, an annotated bibliography; writings, scholarship, criticism, and ana, 1850–1968. Edited by Willis J. Buckingham. Bloomington, Indiana University Press [1970]

xii, 322 p. 24 cm.

Clendenning, Sheila T
Emily Dickinson; a bibliography, 1850–1966, by Sheila T. Clendenning. [1st. ed. Kent, Ohio] Kent State University Press [1968]

xxx, 145 p. 22 cm. (The Serif series: bibliographies and checklists)

Emily Dickinson bulletin.
Brentwood, Md.

no. 28 cm.

Began in 1968. Cf. New serial titles, July 1969.

DICKINSON, JACOB MCGAVOCK

Tennessee. State Library and Archives, *Nashville. Manuscript Division.*
The Jacob McGavock Dickinson papers. Rev. Nashville. 1964.

35 p. geneal. table. 28 cm. (*Its* Registers, no. 1)

Cover title.
Published by the division under its earlier name: Manuscript Section.

DICTIONARIES see Encyclopedias and dictionaries

DIDEROT, DENIS

London. University. Birkbeck College. Library.
Diderot: handlist of books by and about Denis Diderot in the [Birkbeck] College Library, edited by Ann Knock. [London] Birkbeck College Library. 1973.

[1], 11 p. 30 cm. (*Its* Library publication no. 33)

Tourneux, Maurice, 1849–1917.
Les manuscrits de Diderot conservés en Russia, catalogue dressé par M. Maurice Tourneux. Genève, Slatkine Reprints, 1967.

42 p. 23 cm.

DIEGO, ELISEO

García-Carranza, Araceli.
Bibliografía de Eliseo Diego. [Compilada por Aracely García-Carranza, Depto. Colección Cubana] La Habana, 1970.

24 p. 23 cm.

Cover title: Eliseo Diego.
"Con motivo de la participación de Eliseo Diego en el ciclo de conferencias Vida y obra de poetas cubanos."

DIEM, CARL

Zeidler, Johannes.
Bibliographie Carl Diem. (Bearbeitung: J. Zeidler und B. Lau. Herausgeber:) Carl-Diem-Institut (an der Deutschen Sporthochschule Köln). (Schorndorf b. Stuttgart, Hofmann, 1968.)

78 p. 25 cm.

DIESEL LOCOMOTIVES see Locomotives

DIEUDONNÉ, JEAN ALEXANDRE

Dieudonné, Jean Alexandre, 1906–
Notice sur les travaux scientifiques de M. Jean Dieudonné.

₍Gap, impr. Louis-Jean,₎ 1968.

33 p. 27 cm.

DIFFUSION

Taniel, Gérard.
Diffusion thermique. ₍Gif-sur-Yvette, Commissariat à l'énergie atomique, Centre d'études nucléaires de Saclay, Service de documentation₎ 1964.

24 p. 27 cm. (Commissariat à l'énergie atomique. Série "Bibliographies" no 45)

Summary in English.

DIGBY, SIR KENELM

Huston, Kenneth Garth, 1926–
Sir Kenelm Digby; checklist ₍by K. Garth Huston₎ Los Angeles, 1969.

25 p. 20 cm.

Alternate pages blank.
"100 copies printed ... at the Plantin Press, Los Angeles."
"Locations listed in checklist are of copies collated, not a census of known copies."—Note added in ms. to "List of abbreviations."

DIGESTIVE ORGANS

Patel, Jean Claude.
Titres et travaux scientifiques ...   Paris, Masson et Cᵢᵉ, 1965.

31 p. 27 cm.

DIHIGO, JUAN MIGUEL

Dihigo y López Trigo, Ernesto, 1896–
Bibliografía de Juan Miguel Dihigo y Mestre. ₍La Habana, Tall. del Archivo Nacional, 1964₎

90 p. 25 cm.

DIJKSTRA, WALING GERRITS

Kalma, J   J
Waling Dykstra-bibliografy; hwat der oer W. Dykstra skreaun is, de brieven fan en aan him, syn hânskriften op de Prov. Bibliotheek to Ljouwert ₍fan₎ J. J. Kalma en S. Sybrandy. ₍Ljouwert, Fryske Akademy₎ 1970.

48 p. 21 cm. (Minsken en boeken, nr. 12) (Utjefte fan de Fryske Academy, Ljouwert, nr. 38)

DILTHEY, WILHELM

Herrmann, Ulrich, 1939–
Bibliographie Wilhelm Dilthey. Quellen und Literatur. Weinheim (/Bergstr.) Berlin, Basel, Beltz (1969).

xiv, 237 p. 21 cm. (Pädagogische Bibliographien. Reihe A, Bd. 1)

DIMITROV, GEORGI

Koleva, Veselina.
₍Georgi Dimitrov v Severozapadna Bŭlgariîa₎
Георги Димитров в Северозападна България. ⟨Библиогр.⟩. (Науч. ред. ₍с предг.₎ Васил Харизанов). София, Наука и изкуство (Враца, печ. В. Александров) 1972.

4, 111 p. with ports. and facsims. 20 cm.

On cover: Окръжни библиотеки Враца, Видин, Михайловград.
By V. Koleva, L. Filipova and S. Shtipkova.

Kotseva, Mariîa.
(Georgi Dimitrov)
Георги Димитров. 1882–1972. (Препоръчителна библиография). ₍Изработили: Мария Коцева, Катя Сидева₎ Стара Загора, Дом за политическа просвета при ОК на БКП, 1972.

106 p. illus., port. 19 cm.

At head of title: Окръжна библиотека "Захари Княжевски."

Savova, Elena.
Георги Димитров. Библиогр. (Под ред. на Христо Христов). ₍С предг. от Т. Д. Павлов₎ София, БКП 1968.

430 p. 25 cm. 3.23

Preface, introduction and table of contents also in Russian, German, and French.

DIMITROV, VLADIMIR

Okrŭzhna biblioteka—Kyustendil.
(Vladimir Dimitrov-Maistora)
Владимир Димитров-Майстора; библиография. Кюстендил, 1972.

34 p. illus. 20 cm.

DIMOND, ANTHONY JOSEPH

Alaska. University. *Library. Archives and Manuscript Collections.*
Anthony J. Dimond; an inventory of his papers in the Archives and Manuscript Collections of the University of Alaska Library. Compiled by Paul McCarthy. College, Archives and Manuscript Collections, University of Alaska Library, University of Alaska, 1968.

26 l. port. 28 cm.

DINXPERLO, NETHERLANDS

Kobes, D   W
Inventaris van het oud-archief der gemeente Dinxperlo ₍door D. W. Kobes₎ ₍Dinxperlo, 1968?₎

12 l. 30 cm.

DIPHENYLHYDANTOIN

Bogoch, Samuel.
The broad range of use of diphenylhydantoin; bibliography and review ₍by₎ Samuel Bogoch ₍and₎ Jack Dreyfus. ₍New York₎ Dreyfus Medical Foundation ₍ᶜ1970₎

xv, 169 p. 28 cm.

DIPLOMACY see International law and relations

DIRECTORIES

Directories of specific subjects or places are entered under the appropriate subject headings or place names.

see also Encyclopedias and dictionaries

Henderson, G   P
   Current European directories: annotated guide to international, national, city and specialised directories and similar reference works for all countries of Europe; compiled & edited by G. P. Henderson. Beckenham (Kent), C. B. D. Research Ltd., 1969.

   xvi, 222 p. 30 cm.

   English, French or German.

Legátová, Božena.
   Soupis knižních publikací z fondu SVK ₍Státní vědecká knihovna₎ Ostrava. Adresáře. Sest. Božena Legátová. Ostrava, SVK, rozmn., 1970.

   48 p. 20 cm. (Státní vědecká knihovna v Ostravě. Publikace, řada 1, čís. 153)

DISADVANTAGED see Socially handicapped

DISARMAMENT

Germany (Federal Republic, 1949–   ). Bundestag. Wissenschaftliche Dienste.
   Mutual and Balanced Force Reductions (MBFR). Beiderseitige ausgewogene Truppenreduzierungen (Sommer 1968–1971). Auswahlbibliographie. Bonn, 1971.

   19. p. 30 cm. (Its Bibliographien, Nr. 27)

   "Die Bibliographie wurde im Fachbereich II von Wolfram-Georg Riggert bearbeitet."

Meeker, Thomas A
   SALT: an alternative to the Soviet-American arms race. Compiled by Thomas A. Meeker. Los Angeles, Center for the Study of Armament and Disarmament, California State University ₍c1972₎

   vii, 33 p. 22 cm. (Classroom study series, v. 1, no. 1)

DISCOVERIES (IN GEOGRAPHY)

Navarrete, Martín Fernández de, 1765–1844.
   Biblioteca marítima española; obra póstuma. New York, B. Franklin ₍1968₎

   2 v. 23 cm. (Literature of discovery, exploration, & geography, 2)

   Burt Franklin bibliography & reference series, 244.
   "Originally published: 1851. Reprinted: 1968."

Washburn, Wilcomb E
   The age of discovery, by Wilcomb E. Washburn. Washington, Service Center for Teachers of History ₍1966₎

   26 p. 23 cm. (Service Center for Teachers of History. Publication no. 63)

DISCRIMINATION IN EDUCATION

Bolner, James.
   Racial imbalance in public schools; a basic annotated bibliography. ₍Baton Rouge₎ Institute of Government Research, Louisiana State University, 1968.

   iii, 73 p. 28 cm.

Hall, John S
   Implementing school desegregation; a bibliography. Compiled by John S. Hall. Eugene, ERIC Clearinghouse on Educational Administration, 1970.

   23 p. 28 cm. (ERIC Clearinghouse on Educational Administration. Bibliography series, no. 16)

MacDonald, Angel Alexandra Margaret.
   A contribution to a bibliography on university apartheid; a bibliography. Cape Town, University of Cape Town Libraries, 1972.

   iv, 29 p. 23 cm. (University of Cape Town Libraries. Bibliographical series)

St. John, Nancy Hoyt.
   Annotated bibliography on school racial mix and the self concept, aspirations, academic achievement, and interracial attitudes and behavior of Negro children, compiled by Nancy St. John and Nancy Smith. ₍Cambridge₎ School Integration Research, Graduate School of Education, Harvard University, 1966.

   77 l. 28 cm.

Weinberg, Meyer, 1920–
   School integration; a comprehensive classified bibliography of 3,100 references. Chicago, Integrated Education Associates, 1967.

   iv, 137 p. 22 cm.

DISCRIMINATION IN EMPLOYMENT

Institute of Labor and Industrial Relations (University of Michigan–Wayne State University). Research Division.
   Document and reference text; an index to minority group employment information. ₍Ann Arbor₎ 1967.

   viii, 602, ₍30₎ p. 28 cm.

   "Produced under contract with the Equal Employment Opportunity Commission."

   —————— 1971 supplement. Joe A. Miller and Steven C. Gold, editors. ₍Ann Arbor, 1971₎

   1 v. (various pagings) 28 cm.

Pinto, Patrick R
   Problems and issues in the employment of minority, disadvantaged, and female groups: an annotated bibliography ₍by₎ Patrick R. Pinto and Jeanne O. Buchmeier. Minneapolis, Industrial Relations Center, University of Minnesota, 1973.

   62 p. 23 cm. (University of Minnesota. Industrial Relations Center. Bulletin 59)

U. S. Civil Service Commission. Library.
   Equal opportunity in employment. Washington; ₍For sale by the Supt. of Docs., U. S. Govt. Print. Off.₎ 1971 ₍i. e. 1972₎

   135 p. 27 cm. (Its Personnel bibliography series, no. 38)
   Cover title.

"Updates Personnel bibliography no. 29 (1968), and a related section in no. 11 (1963) ... includes material received in the Library in 1969 and 1970."

United States.   Civil Service Commission. Library.
Equal opportunity in employment.   Washington; ₁For sale by the Supt. of Docs., U. S. Govt. Print. Off.₁ 1973.

170 p. 27 cm. (*Its* Personnel bibliography series, no. 49)

Cover title.

"This bibliography supplements Personnel bibliography no. 38 (1971). It covers material received in the ... Library during 1971 and 1972."

U. S. *Federal Aviation Administration.   Library Services Division.*
Equal employment opportunity; selected references. ₁Compiled by Dorothy J. Poehlman₁ Washington, 1968.

i, 7 p. 27 cm. (*Its* Bibliographic list no. 16)

Von Furstenberg, George M   1941–
Discrimination in employment: a selected bibliography ₁by₁ George M. von Furstenbert ₁i. e. Furstenberg₁ With the assistance of William S. Cartwright. Mary Vance, editor. ₁Monticello, Ill., Council of Planning Librarians₁ 1972.

24 p. 28 cm. (Council of Planning Librarians. Exchange bibliography, 297)

Washington (State) State Library, *Olympia.*
Minorities and discrimination with reference to employment practices; a selected bibliography. ₁Olympia, 1967?₁

8 l. 27 cm.

Cover title.

"A selective bibliography of books in the Washington State Library."

DISCRIMINATION IN HOUSING

Boyce, Byrl N
Minority groups and housing; a bibliography, 1950–1970. Selected and edited under the direction of Byrl N. Boyce ₁and₁ Sidney Turoff. ₁Morristown, N. J.₁ General Learning Press ₁1972₁

202 p. 24 cm.

1968 ed. by S. D. Messner.
"A D. H. Mark publication."

Messner, Stephen D
Minority groups and housing; a selected bibliography, 1950–67. Selected and edited under the direction of Stephen D. Messner. ₁Storrs, Center for Real Estate and Urban Economic Studies, University of Connecticut, 1968₁

vii, 60 p. 28 cm. (University of Connecticut. Center for Real Estate and Urban Economic Studies. General series, no. 1)

U. S. *Dept. of Housing and Urban Development. Library.*
Equal opportunity; a bibliography of research on equal opportunity in housing. ₁Washington; For sale by the Supt. of Docs., U. S. Govt. Print. Off., 1969₁

24 p. 26 cm.

Cover title.

DISCRIMINATION IN SPORTS

Thompson, Richard, 1924–
Race discrimination in New Zealand — South African sports tours: a bibliography. Christchurch, N. Z., Dept. of Psychology and Sociology, University of Canterbury, 1966.

23 p. 26 cm. (University of Canterbury. Dept. of Psychology and Sociology. Research project 11)

Thompson, Richard, 1924–
Race discrimination in New Zealand—South African sports tours: a revised bibliography. Christchurch, N. Z., Dept. of Psychology and Sociology, University of Canterbury, 1972.

59 l. 30 cm. (University of Canterbury. Dept. of Psychology and Sociology. Research project 23)

DISRAELI, BENJAMIN, 1ST EARL OF BEACONSFIELD

Stewart, Robert Wilson, 1935–
Benjamin Disraeli: a list of writings by him, and writings about him, with notes, by R. W. Stewart. Metuchen, N. J., Scarecrow Press, 1972.

278 p. 22 cm. (The Scarecrow author bibliographies, no. 7)

DISSERTATIONS, ACADEMIC

Under this heading are entered bibliographies of theses, dissertations, reports, etc., submitted for graduate degrees. Other academic writings and publications of specific universities or similar bodies are entered under the names of the institutions. Dissertations on a specific subject are entered only in section 2. SUBJECTS below; general lists of dissertations accepted by a specific institution are entered in section 3. COUNTRIES, STATES.

BIBLIOGRAPHIES

Black, Dorothy M   comp.
Guide to lists of master's theses, compiled by Dorothy M. Black. Chicago, American Library Association, 1965.

144 p. 24 cm.

1. General

Dissertation abstracts international. v. 1–
1938–
₁Ann Arbor, Mich.₁ University Microfilms.

v. in   21–29 cm.

Frequency varies.
Title varies: 1938–51, Microfilm abstracts.—1952–June 1969, Dissertation abstracts.
Vols. 16–25 include a 13th no.: American doctoral dissertations (called in v. 16–23, Index to American doctoral dissertations), previously issued separately as Doctoral dissertations accepted by American universities; later issued separately.
Vols. for July 1966–   issued in two sections: A; the humanities and social sciences and B; the sciences and engineering.

INDEXES:
Author index.
Vols. 1–22, 1938–51. (Issued by the Georgia Chapter, Special Libraries Association) 1 v.
General index.
Vols. 1–29, 1938–June 1969. 9 v. in 11.

Dissertation digest. B.
₁Ann Arbor, Mich., University Microfilms₁

no. 21 cm.

Dissertations listed are abstracted in forthcoming issues of section B of Dissertation abstracts international.

Jaipur, India (Rajasthan)   University of Rajasthan.
Library.
Catalogue of theses and dissertations available in the Rajasthan University Library. Jaipur, 1966.

vii, 316 l. 27 cm.

Johnson, R   S
Foreign theses in British libraries; compiled by R. S. Johnson. Cardiff (The Library, University College, Cardiff), Standing Conference of National and University Libraries, 1971.

27 p. 21 cm.

Liège. Université. Bibliothèque.
Répertoire des thèses de doctorat européennes. année 1969–1970. Louvain, A. Dewallens ₁1970?₁

1 v. (unpaged) 22 x 28 cm.

At head of title: Université de Liège. Bibliothèque générale.

Proehl, Friedrich-Karl.
Verzeichnis ausgewählter Hochschulschriften 1945 bis 1963. Hamburg (Stiftung Wissenschaft und Presse) 1966.

47 p. 24 cm.

Yüan, T'ung-li, 1895–
A guide to doctoral dissertations by Chinese students in continental Europe, 1907–1962. ₁Washington, 1964₁

154 p. 27 cm.

Cover title.
"Reprinted from Chinese culture quarterly, vol. v, no. 3, 4, and vol. vi, no. 1."

2. Subjects

AERONAUTICS

Sokoll, Alfred Hermann.
Hochschulschriften zur Aero- und Astronautik; deutschsprachige Bibliographie 1910–1965, hrsg. von Alfred H. Sokoll. München, Alkos Verlag, ₁1968₁

vii, 134 p. 21 cm. (Bibliothek der Aero- und Astronautik, Bd. 6)

AFRICA

Bratton, Michael.
American doctoral dissertations on Africa, 1886–1972. Compiled by Michael Bratton and Anne Schneller, for the African Studies Association, Research Liaison Committee. Waltham, Mass. ₁African Studies Association, Research Liaison Committee, 1973₁

xx, 165 p. 23 cm.

Dinstel, Marion.
List of French doctoral dissertations on Africa, 1884–1961. With indexes by Mary Darrah Herrick. Boston, G. K. Hall, 1966.

v, 336 p. 27 cm.

At head of title: Boston University Libraries.

Kettle, M   R
Leeds writings on Africa, compiled by M. R. Kettle. ₁Leeds, Eng.₁ University of Leeds, African Studies Unit ₁1970₁

40 p. 21 cm.

Paris. Université. *Faculté de droit et des sciences économiques. Centre de documentation africaine.*
Thèses et mémoires africanistes soutenus et déposés, année 1967. ₁Paris,₁ Département de droit et économie des pays d'Afrique, 1968.

33 l. 27 cm.

Rial, Jacques.
Inventaire des thèses suisses consacrées à l'Afrique au sud du Sahara, à l'Éthiopie et à Madagascar, 1897–1970. ₁2. éd.₁ Berne, Commission nationale suisse pour l'Unesco, 1972 ₁i. e. 1973₁

35 p. 21 cm.

Standing Conference on Library Materials on Africa.
Theses on Africa, accepted by universities in the United Kingdom and Ireland. Cambridge ₁Eng.₁ W. Heffer ₁1964₁

x, 74 p. 24 cm.

AGRICULTURE

Guayasamín de López, Zoila.
Tesis de grado de ingenieros agrónomos colombianos,

1917–1968. Pasto ₁Colombia₁ Universidad de Nariño, Instituto Tecnológico Agrícola, Biblioteca y Hemeroteca Agrícolas, 1968 ₁cover 1969₁

205 p. 27 cm. (Serie bibliográfica, no. 7) (Universidad de Nariño. Instituto Tecnológico Agrícola. Publicación 8)

Hladká, L

Bibliografický súpis záverečných zpráv, dizertačných a habilitačných prác v Ústrednej pôdohospodárskej knižnici. Spracovala L. Hladká. Nitra, 1966.

109 p. 30 cm. (Edícia: Bibliografické príručky)

At head of title: Ústredna podhospodárska knižnica.

Indian Agricultural Research Institute, Delhi.

Bibliography of theses, submitted for associateship of I. A. R. I. and M. Sc. and Ph. D. degrees of the I. A. R. I. Post-Graduate School, 1938–1969. ₁Compiled by Shri A. S. Ahsan and others₁ New Delhi, 1970.

172 p. 28 cm. (I. A. R. I. Library bibliographical series, 3)

Indian Council of Agricultural Research. *Library.*

Classified list of theses ₁available in I. C. A. R. Library₁. New Delhi, 1967.

64, iv, vii, 7 p. 29 cm.

Inter-American Center for Documentation and Agriculture Information.

Indice latinoamericano de tesis agrícolas: Convenio IICA/ZN/ROCAP. Turrialba, Costa Rica, Centro Interamericano de Documentación e Información Agrícola, 1972.

xvii, 718 p. 28 cm. (Bibliotecología y documentación, no. 20)

Malugani, María Dolores, *comp.*

Tesis de la Escuela para Graduados, 1948–1968; resúmenes. Compilada por María Dolores Malugani ₁y₁ Alfredo Alvear. 2. ed. rev. y ampl. Turrialba, Costa Rica, Instituto Interamericano de Ciencias Agrícolas, Biblioteca y Servicio de Documentación, 1969.

ii, 234 p. 27 cm. (Bibliotecología y documéntación, no. 3)

AMERICAN LITERATURE

Woodress, James Leslie.

Dissertations in American literature, 1891–1966 ₁by₁ James Woodress. Newly rev. and enl. with the assistance of Marian Koritz. Durham, N. C., Duke University Press, 1968.

xii, 185 p. 25 cm.

ANTHROPOLOGY

Montemayor, Felipe.

28 ₁i. e. Veintiocho₁ años de antropología: tesis de la Escuela Nacional de Antropología e Historia ₁1944–1971, por₁ Felipe Montemayor G. México, Instituto Nacional de Antropología e Historia, 1971.

615 p. 23 cm.

"Catálogo ... de las tesis de antropología presentadas en la Escuela."

ARAB COUNTRIES

Selim, George Dimitri, 1931–

American doctoral dissertations on the Arab world, 1883–1968. Compiled by George Dimitri Selim, Near East Section, Orientalia Division. Washington, Library of Congress; for sale by the Supt. of Docs., U. S. Govt. Print. Off., 1970.

xvii, 103 p. 24 cm.

AREA STUDIES

Cruger, Doris M.

A list of American doctoral dissertations on Africa, covering 1961/62 through 1964/65; France, covering 1933/34 through 1964/65; Italy, covering 1933/34 through 1964/65. Compiled by Doris M. Cruger. Ann Arbor, Mich., Xerox, University Microfilms Library Services, 1967.

36 p. 23 cm.

"Listing of doctoral dissertations on Africa was designed as a supplement to a list published in 1962 by the African Section of the Library of Congress."

Cruger, Doris M.

A list of doctoral dissertations on Australia, covering 1933/34 through 1964/65; Canada, covering 1933/34 through 1964/65; New Zealand, covering 1933/34 through 1964/65. Compiled by Doris M. Cruger. Ann Arbor, Mich., Xerox, 1967.

20 p. 24 cm.

ART EDUCATION

Lanier, Vincent.

Doctoral research in art education. ₁Eugene, Or.₁ 1968.

101 p. 23 cm.

"Sponsored by United States Office of Education ₁and₁ University of Oregon."

ASIA

Bishop, Enid.

Australian theses on Asia; a union list of higher degree theses accepted by Australian universities to 31 December 1970. Canberra, Faculty of Asian Studies, Australian National University, 1972.

35 p. 25 cm. (Australian National University, Canberra. Faculty of Asian Studies. Occasional paper, 12)

Bloomfield, Barry Cambray.

Theses on Asia; accepted by universities in the United Kingdom and Ireland, 1877–1964; compiled by B. C. Bloomfield. London, Cass, 1967.

xi, 127 p. table. 25½ cm.

Illinois. Northern Illinois University, De Kalb. Center for Southeast Asian Studies.

Theses on Southeast Asia presented at Northern Illinois University, 1960–1971; an annotated bibliography. De Kalb, 1972.

iii, 13 p. 23 cm.

Jackson, James C

Recent higher degree theses on social, political and economic aspects of Southeast Asia, presented in the Universities of the United Kingdom and in the Universities of Malaya and Singapore. Hull, University of Hull (Department of Geography), 1966 ₁i. e. 1967₁.

₁1₁, iii, f, ₁14₁ f. 34 cm. (University of Hull. Dept. of Geography. Miscellaneous Series, no. 6)

Kozicki, Richard J 1929–

South and Southeast Asia: doctoral dissertations and masters' theses completed at the University of California at Berkeley 1906-1968, by Richard J. Kozicki and Peter Ananda. Berkeley, Center for South and Southeast Asia Studies, University of California, 1969.

viii, 49 l. 28 cm. (Center for South and Southeast Asia Studies, University of California. Occasional paper, no. 1)

Pennington, Juliana.
The University of Southern California doctoral dissertations and master's theses on East and Southeast Asia, 1911–1964. Compiled by Juliana Pennington and Paul Marsh, under the direction of Peter Berton. Introd. by Theodore H. E. Chen. Los Angeles, Asian-Slavic Studies Center, University of Southern California, 1965.

54 l. 28 cm.

SarDesai, D   R
Theses and dissertations on Southeast Asia; an international bibliography in social sciences, education, and fine arts ₍by₎ D. R. Sardesai ₍and₎ Bhanu D. Sardesai, with cooperation of: Alexander Bendik ₍and others₎ Zug, Inter Documentation ₍c1970₎

iv, 176 p. 21 cm. (Bibliotheca Asiatica, 6)

Shulman, Frank Joseph, 1943–
Doctoral dissertations on South Asia, 1966–1970; an annotated bibliography covering North America, Europe, and Australia. Compiled and edited by Frank J. Shulman. Ann Arbor, Center for South and Southeast Asian Studies, University of Michigan, 1971.

xvii, 228 p. 23 cm. (Michigan papers on South and Southeast Asia, 4)

Stucki, Curtis W
American doctoral dissertations on Asia, 1933–June 1966; including appendix of master's theses at Cornell University, 1933–June 1968, by Curtis W. Stucki. Ithaca, N. Y., Southeast Asia Program, Cornell University, 1968.

304 p. 28 cm. (Cornell University. Southeast Asia Program. Data paper no. 71)

Syracuse University.
An annotated bibliography of theses and dissertations on Asia accepted at Syracuse University, 1907–1963. Compiled under the direction of Donn V. Hart. Syracuse, N. Y., Syracuse University Library, 1964.

xii, 46 p. 23 cm.

The, Lian.
Treasures and trivia; doctoral dissertations on Southeast Asia accepted by universities in the United States. Compiled by Lian The and Paul W. van der Veur. ₍Athens, Ohio₎ Ohio University, Center for International Studies, 1968.

xiv, 141 l. 28 cm. (Papers in international studies. Southeast Asia series, no. 1)

ASIANS

Ong, Paul M
Theses and dissertations on Asians in the United States, with selected references to other overseas Asians / compiled by Paul M. Ong, William Wong Lum, with assistance from Keiko Komura, Joyce Sakai, Ferris Yayesaki ; cover by Shelton Yip. — Davis : Asian American Studies, Dept. of Applied Behavioral Sciences, University of California, 1974.

vii, 113 p. ; 28 cm.

Published in 1970 under title: Asians in America.

BALKAN PENINSULA

Scherer, Anton.
Südosteuropa-Dissertationen, 1918–1960. Eine Bibliographie deutscher, österreichischer und schweizerischer Hochschulschriften. Graz, Wien, Köln, Böhlau, 1968.

221 p. 23 cm.

BUILDING

Gero, John S
Post-graduate research theses in the Dept. of Architectural Science: compiled by John S. Gero. ₍Sydney₎ University of Sydney. Dept. of Architectural Science ₍1971₎

60 p. 30 cm. (Education report ER3)

Gero, John S
Undergraduate architectural science theses, 1970, University of Sydney ₍by₎ John S. Gero. Sydney, Dept. of Architectural Science, University of Sydney ₍1971₎

30 p. 30 cm. (Education report, ER 2)

BUSINESS

Michigan. State University, East Lansing. *Bureau of Business and Economic Research.*
Directory of doctoral degrees in economics and business in the Graduate School of Business Administration, Michigan State University, 1948–1965. East Lansing, 1966.

29 p. 23 cm.

CANADA

Fraser, J   Keith.
List of theses and dissertations on Canadian geography; liste des theses et dissertations sur la geographie du Canada. Compiled by J. Keith Fraser and Mary C. Hynes. Ottawa, Lands Directorate, Dept. of the Environment, 1972.

vi, 114 p. 28 cm. (Geographical paper, no. 51)

English and French.

Koester, Charles Beverley, 1926–
A bibliography of selected theses on ₍i. e. in₎ the library of the University of Alberta (Edmonton) relating to western Canada, 1915–1965, compiled for Western Canada Research project by C. B. Koester. Edmonton, 1965.

21 l. 28 cm.

Meyer, W   C
Cumulative list of theses on Canadian geography. Liste des thèses sur la géographie du Canada. Compiled by W. C. Meyer. Ottawa, Geographical Branch, Dept. of Energy, Mines and Resources, 1966.

₍5₎, 57 p. 27 cm. (Bibliographical series/Série bibliographique, 34) 0.50

Woodward, Frances.
Theses on British Columbia history and related subjects in the Library of the University of British Columbia. Rev. and enl. Vancouver, University of British Columbia Library, 1971.

57 p. 23 cm. (University of British Columbia Library. Reference publication no. 35)

CARIBBEAN AREA

Baa, Enid M
Theses on Caribbean topics, 1778–1968. Compiled by Enid M. Baa. San Juan, Institute of Caribbean Studies, University of Puerto Rico, 1970.

v, 146 p. 24 cm. (Caribbean bibliographic series no. 1)

Hills, Theo L
Caribbean topics; theses in Canadian University libraries, compiled by Theo L. Hills. ₍3d ed. Montreal, Centre for Developing-Area Studies, McGill University, 1971₎

21 l. 28 cm.

CHINA

Gordon, Leonard H   D   1928–
Doctoral dissertations on China; a bibliography of studies in Western languages, 1945–1970. Compiled and edited by Leonard H. D. Gordon and Frank J. Shulman. Seattle, Published for the Association for Asian Studies by the University of Washington Press [1972]

xviii, 317 p. 24 cm. (Association for Asian Studies. Reference series, no. 1)

CLASSICAL PHILOLOGY

Thompson, Lawrence Sidney, 1916–
A bibliography of American doctoral dissertations in classical studies and related fields, by Lawrence S. Thompson. [Hamden, Conn.] Shoe String Press, 1968.

xii, 250 p. 22 cm.

CLEMENS, SAMUEL LANGHORNE

Selby, Paul Owen, 1890–
Theses on Mark Twain, 1910–1967. Compiled by P. O. Selby. Kirksville, Missouriana Library, Northeast Missouri State College, 1969.

1 v. (unpaged) 29 cm.

COMMUNICATION

Spiess, Volker.
Verzeichnis deutschsprachiger Hochschulschriften zur Publizistik. 1885–1967. Berlin, Spiess; München-Pullach [Pullach/Isartal] u. Berlin, Verl. Dokumentation (1969).

231 l. 20 cm.

CRIME

University Microfilms, Ann Arbor, Mich.
A bibliography of doctoral research on crime and law enforcement. Ann Arbor, Mich. [1972?]

70 p. 23 x 11 cm.

DENTISTRY

Minas Geraes, Brazil. Universidade Federal. *Faculdade de Odontologia. Biblioteca.*
Bibliografia de teses apresentadas às faculdades de odontologia do Brasil. Pref. por Luzia Penido de Rezende. Belo Horizonte, 1967.

71 l. 32 cm.

Preface and introduction in English and Portuguese.

DRAMA; THEATER

Litto, Fredric M   1939–
American dissertations on the drama and the theatre; a bibliography [by] Fredric M. Litto. [1st ed. Kent, Ohio] Kent State University Press [1969]

ix, 519 p. 29 cm.

Mikhail, E   H
Dissertations on Anglo-Irish drama; a bibliography of studies, 1870–1970 [by] E. H. Mikhail. Totowa, N. J., Rowman and Littlefield [1973]

x, 73 p. 23 cm.

EARTH SCIENCES

Youngblood, Irma.
Theses and dissertations of the New Mexico Institute of Mining and Technology, 1931–1969. Compiled by Irma Youngblood [and] Henry H. Koehn. Socorro, N. M., State Bureau of Mines and Mineral Resources, 1970.

20 p. 28 cm. (New Mexico. State Bureau of Mines and Mineral Resources. Circular 107)

ECOLOGY

University Microfilms, Ann Arbor, Mich.
A bibliography of doctoral research on ecology and the environment. [Ann Arbor, 1972?]

92 p. 23 x 11 cm.

ECONOMICS

Akademiiā nauk URSR, Kiev. Instytut ekonomiky.
Указатель диссертационных работ, выполненных и защищенных в Институте экономики АН УССР, 1946–1965 гг. [Составители: Е. Н. Панченко, Н. П. Бойко. Отв. редактор А. А. Радченко]. Киев, Наук. думка, 1967.

82 p. 21 cm. 0.14

Buenos Aires. Universidad. Facultad de Ciencias Económicas. Biblioteca.
Tesis doctorales aprobadas, desde el 1º de enero hasta el 31 de diciembre de 1968; [resúmenes] Buenos Aires, 1970.

47 p. 20 cm. (Serie de divulgación bibliográfica económica, no. 43)

Ekonomické dizertačné a habilitačné práce v ČSSR a diplomové práce na Slovensku. 1963/64–
Bratislava, Slovenské pedagogické nakl.

v. 21 cm. annual. ([Bratislava] Ústredná ekonomická knižnica. Ekonomické aktuality. Bibliografický zpravodaj)

Issued by Ústredná ekonomická knižnica in Bratislava.
Compiler: 1963/64–   B. Procházka.

Milišić, Đorđe.
Bibliografija doktorskih disertacija iz oblasti ekonomskih nauka. Sastavio Djordje Milišić. Beograd, Jugoslovenski institut za ekonomska istraživanja, 1967.

515–539, xii, [1] p. 24 cm. (Jugoslovenski institut za ekonomska istraživanja. Radovi, 10)

"Objavljeno u časopisu Ekonomist, broj 1–4 za 1966."

Procházka, Boris.
Ekonomické dizertácie a habilitácie v ČSSR. Diplomové a postgraduálne práce na Slovensku v školskom roku 1970/71. Zost. Boris Procházka. 1. vyd. Bratislava, SPN, rozmn. Západoslov. tlač., 1972–

1 v. (loose-leaf) 20 cm.

At head of title: Ústredná ekonomická knižnica Bratislava.
In portfolio.
Introduction and table of contents also in Russian, English, German, and French.

Washington (*State*). *Dept. of Commerce and Economic Development. Business and Economic Research Division.*
Directory of graduate thesis studies from Washington State business and economics schools, 1960–1968. Olympia, 1969.

ii, 125 p. 28 cm.

Wood, W   Donald, 1920–
Canadian graduate theses 1919–1969; an annotated bibliography (covering economics, business and industrial relations), by W. D. Wood, L. A. Kelly [and] P. Kumar. Kingston, Ont., Industrial Relations Centre, Queen's University, 1970.

xiv, 483 p. 24 cm. (Bibliography series, no. 4)

EDUCATION

Cordasco, Francesco, 1920–   *comp.*
Educational sociology: a subject index of doctoral dissertations completed at American universities, 1941–1963. Compiled by Francesco Cordasco and Leonard Covello. New York, Scarecrow Press, 1965.

226 p. 22 cm.

DeCrow, Roger.
Adult education dissertation abstracts: 1963–1967. Roger DeCrow and Nehume Loague, editors. Prepared for the ERIC Clearinghouse on Adult Education. Washington, Adult Education Association of the USA [1971?]

311 p. 26 cm.

Delhi. Central Institute of Education.
Summaries of M. Ed. reports.
Delhi.

v. 22 cm. annual. (Its C. I. E. studies in psychology and education)

Title varies: , Summaries of reports submitted by the students for the degree of Master of Education.

Dossick, Jesse John, 1911–
Doctoral research at the School of Education, New York University, 1890–1970; a classified list of 4,336 dissertations with some critical and statistical analysis, by Jesse J. Dossick. New York, New York University Press, 1972.

xii, 236 p. 26 cm.

Herndon, Myrtis E
Theses and dissertations related to comparative/international education, physical education, sport, and dance. Compiled and edited by: Myrtis E. Herndon. Hiram, Ohio, Dept. of Physical Education for Women, Hiram College [1974]

vi, 459 p. 22 cm.

Leicester, Eng. University. School of Education.
Research theses presented for higher degrees in education at the University of Leicester, 1957–68. Leicester, University of Leicester School of Education [1969].

[15], 86 p. 30 cm.

Cover title.

———— Supplement 1968–69. [Leicester, Eng., 1969?]

29 p. 30 cm.

Malang, Indonesia (City). Institut Keguruan dan Ilmu Pendidikan.
Ringkasan-tesis I. K. I. P. Malang. Malang, Biro I, Institut Keguruan [dan] Ilmu Pendidikan Malang, 1971.
407 p. 28 cm.
"Penerbitan seri pertama."
On cover: Abstracts of master's theses.
Indonesian or English.

National Council of Educational Research and Training.
Educational investigations in Indian universities, 1939–1961; a list of theses and dissertations approved for doctorate and master's degrees in education. [New Delhi, 1966]

286 p. 25 cm.

National Council of Educational Research and Training.
Educational investigations in Indian universities, 1962–

1966: a list of theses and dissertations for doctorate and master's degrees in education. Compiled by Satnam Singh. [New Delhi] 1968.

x, 304 p. 31 cm.

Parker, Franklin, 1921–
Adult education; a partial bibliography of 360 [i. e. 358] partially annotated American doctoral dissertations. Norman, Okla., 1964.

35 p. 28 cm.

Parker, Franklin, 1921–
American dissertations on foreign education; a bibliography with abstracts. Troy, N. Y., Whitston Pub. Co., 1971–

v. 24 cm.

CONTENTS: v. 1. Canada.—v. 2. India.

Parker, Franklin, 1921–
Audio-visual education research: a bibliography of 356 doctoral dissertations, compiled by Franklin Parker and Herman L. Totten. [Norman? Okla., 1966]

19 p. 28 cm.

Smith, Leonard Glenn, 1939–
History of education, philosophy of education, and comparative education; an annotated bibliography of doctoral dissertations accepted at the University of Oklahoma, 1932–1964, by L. Glenn Smith and Franklin Parker. Norman, College of Education, University of Oklahoma, 1964.

41 l. 28 cm.

Wikstrom, Thomas N
West Virginia graduate research studies in education, 1894–1965; a bibliographical listing, prepared under the direction of William K. Hamilton, by Thomas N. Wikstrom. Charleston, West Virginia Dept. of Education, 1965.

150 p. 23 cm.

ENGLAND

Baker, Gillian.
East Anglian history—theses completed [compiled by Gillian Baker. Norwich], University of East Anglia, Centre of East Anglian Studies, 1972.

[8], 23 p. 22 cm.

Hall, John, 1943–
Sheffield University theses relating to Yorkshire and Derbyshire, 1920–1970, compiled by J. Hall and R. Wells. Sheffield, Sheffield University Library, 1971.

[1], 11 p. 33 cm. (University of Sheffield. Library. Information service guides, 5/71)

ENGLISH LANGUAGE AND LITERATURE

Altick, Richard Daniel, 1915–
Guide to doctoral dissertations in Victorian literature, 1886–1958. Compiled by Richard D. Altick and William R. Matthews. Westport, Conn., Greenwood Press [1973, c1960]

vii, 119 p. 23 cm.

Reprint of the ed. published by the University of Illinois Press, Urbana.

A **Directory** of dissertations on English produced by Indian scholars. 1967–
Bombay, Orient Longmans.

v. 22 cm.

"Published on behalf of the Indian Association for English Studies."

English-Teaching Information Centre, London.
Theses and dissertations related to the teaching of English to speakers of other languages, deposited with British universities, 1961–72. London, English-Teaching Information Centre, 1973.

[5], 90 p. 21 cm.

Kushwaha, Mahesh Singh, 1938–
English research in India [by] M. S. Kushwaha. Lucknow, Swastika Publications [1972–

v. 23 cm.

McNamee, Lawrence Francis.
Dissertations in English and American literature; theses accepted by American, British, and German universities, 1865–1964, by Lawrence F. McNamee. New York, Bowker, 1968.
xi, 1124 p. 25 cm.
———— Supplement. 1–
1964/68–
New York, Bowker.
v. 26 cm.

EUROPE, EASTERN

Seydoux, Marianne.
Répertoire des thèses concernant les études slaves, l'U. R. S. S. et les pays de l'Est européen, et soutenues en France de 1824 à 1969, par Marianne Seydoux ... Mieczysław Biesiekierski ... Paris (6e), Institut d'études slaves, 9, rue Michelet, 1970.

150 p. 26 cm. (Travaux publiés par l'Institut d'études slaves, 30)

FISH

Sport Fishing Institute.
Bibliography of theses on fishery biology; a compilation of graduate theses on fishery biology and related subjects. Edited by Robert M. Jenkins, assistant executive vice president. [Washington] 1959.
80 p. 23 cm.
———— First supplement, 1959–1971. Edited by Robert G. Martin. Washington, 1972.
42 p. 23 cm.

FORESTS AND FORESTRY

Florida. University, *Gainesville. School of Forestry.*
Theses in forestry and related subjects accepted at the University of Florida through June, 1966. Gainesville, 1967.

194 p. 23 cm. (*Its* Miscellaneous publication)

Robert G. Stanley, editor.

Polskie Towarzystwo Leśne.
Wykaz stopni i tytułów naukowych nadanych w dziedzinie leśnictwa i drzewnictwa polskiego w latach 1918–1964. [Opracowali: Bohdan Szymański, Stanisław Markowski] Warszawa, Państwowe Wydawn. Rolnicze i Leśne, 1966.

86 p. 21 cm.

Preface also in Russian, French, English, and German.

Smith, Bernice Ferrier.
Theses in forestry. [Seattle] Institute of Forest Products, University of Washington, 1967.

36 p. 22 x 29 cm. ([Washington (State). University. Institute of Forest Products] Library series. Contribution no. 3)

FRANCE

Paris. École des chartes.
Position des thèses soutenues pour obtenir le diplôme d'archiviste-paléographe. Table générale, 1849–1966. Paris, École des chartes, 1967.

ii, 255 p. 24 cm.

FRENCH STUDIES

Campagnoli, Ruggero.
Guida alle tesi di laurea in lingua e litteratura francese. Tratta dalle lezioni del prof. Liano Petroni. Bologna, R. Pàtron, 1971.

79 p. 20½ cm. (Collana di sussidi didattici, 1)

At head of title: Ruggero Campagnoli, A. Valeria Borsari.

Taylor, Alan Carey.
Current research in French studies at universities and university colleges in the United Kingdom, 1969–1970, compiled by A. Carey Taylor. London (c/o A. C. Taylor, Birkbeck College, Malet St., W. C. 1), Association of University Professors of French, [1970]

[2], 185 p. 26 cm.

Taylor, Alan Carey.
Current research in French studies at universities and university colleges in the United Kingdom, 1970/1971, compiled for the Association of University Professors of French and the Society for French Studies in association with the Modern Humanities Research Association by A. Carey Taylor. London, Association of University Professors of French, 1971.
viii, 92 p. 26 cm.

GEOGRAPHY

Browning, Clyde Eugene, 1927–
A bibliography of dissertations in geography, 1901 to 1969: American and Canadian universities [by] Clyde E. Browning. Chapel Hill, University of North Carolina, Dept. of Geography [1970]

ix, 96 p. 23 cm. (Studies in geography, no. 1)

Based chiefly on the dissertation lists published in the Professional geographer.

London, Ont. University of Western Ontario. Dept. of Geography.
Completed graduate and undergraduate theses 1947–1971. 3d ed. [London, Ont., University of Western Ontario] 1971.

34 l. 28 cm.

Marsden, B   S
Bibliography of Australasian geography theses; preliminary ed.: 1933–1971 [by] B. S. Marsden and E. E. Tugby. Brisbane, University of Queensland, Dept. of Geography [1973?]

xx, 77 p. 30 cm.

GEOLOGY

Berg, Richard B   1937–
Index of graduate theses on Montana geology. Compiled by R. B. Berg. Butte, Montana College of Mineral Science and Technology, 1971.

iii, 48 p. maps (2 fold. col. in pocket) 28 cm. (State of Montana. Bureau of Mines and Geology. Special publication 53)

Childers, Barbara S
Abstracts of theses concerning the geology of Utah to 1966, compiled and edited by Barbara S. Childers, assisted by Bernice Y. Smith. Salt Lake City, Utah Geological and Mineralogical Survey, 1970.

233 p. 28 cm. (Utah. Geological and Mineralogical Survey. Bulletin 86)

Chronic, Byron John.
Bibliography of theses in geology, 1958–1963, by John Chronic and Halka Chronic. Washington, American Geological Institute [c1964]

1 v. (unpaged) 29 cm.

Etheridge, Michael Anthony.
Theses in Australian universities 1969–70: abstracts, compiled by M. A. Etheridge and A. J. Irving. Canberra, Australian Government Publishing Service, 1972.

102 p. 25 cm. ([Australia. Bureau of Mineral Resources, Geology and Geophysics] Report no. 165)

Hilly, Jean.
Répertoire général des sujets de thèses de géologie en cours d'étude au 1er mars 1965. [Réalisé et dirigé par Jean Hilly] Paris [1965]

134 p. 23 cm.

At head of title: Centre national de la recherche scientifique. Commission de géologie, paléontologie et géologie appliquée.

Kirkby, Edward A
Index to Michigan geologic theses, by E. A. Kirkby. Lansing [Geological Survey Division, Dept. of Conservation] 1967.

33 p. 22 cm. (Michigan. Geological Survey. Circular 7)

Ward, Dederick C
Bibliography of theses in geology, 1965–1966, by Dederick C. Ward and T. C. O'Callaghan. [Washington] American Geological Institute [1969]

v, 255 p. 23 cm.

Continuation of a series of bibliographies started by Byron John Chronic and Halka Chronic in 1958.

Ward, Dederick C
Bibliography of theses in geology, 1967–1970. Edited by Dederick C. Ward. [Boulder, Colo., Geological Society of America, 1973]

vii, 160, I–274 p. 24 cm. (Geological Society of America. Special paper, 143)
"A cooperative project of the American Geological Institute, the Geological Society of America, and the Geoscience Information Society."
Continuation of a series of bibliographies started by Byron John Chronic and Halka Chronic in 1958.

GHANA

Kafe, Joseph Kofi.
Ghana: an annotated bibliography of academic theses 1920–1970 in the Commonwealth, the Republic of Ireland and the United States of America. Boston, Hall, 1973.

xxviii, 219 p. 27 cm.

HISTORY

Kuehl, Warren F   1924–
Dissertations in history; an index to dissertations completed in history departments of United States and Canadian universities, by Warren F. Kuehl. [Lexington] University of Kentucky Press, 1965–[72] .

2 v. 29 cm.

CONTENTS: [1] 1873–1960.—v. 2. 1961–June 1970.

Lücke, Peter R
Sowjetzonale Hochschulschriften aus dem Gebiet der Geschichte, 1946–1963. Zusammengestellt und eingeleitet von Peter R. Lücke. Hrsg. vom Bundesministerium für Gesamtdeutsche Fragen. Bonn [1965]

98 p. 21 cm.

HOME ECONOMICS

American Home Economics Association.
Art, housing, furnishings and equipment. 1966–

Washington.

v. 28 cm. (Home economics research abstracts, 4)

"Compiles abstracts of masters' theses and doctoral dissertations completed in graduate schools of home economics."

American Home Economics Association.
Home economics education. 1966–
Washington.

v. 28 cm. (Home economics research abstracts, 5)

"Compiles abstracts of masters' theses and doctoral dissertations completed in graduate schools of home economics."

American Home Economics Association.
Textiles and clothing. 1966–
Washington.

v. 28 cm. (Home economics research abstracts, 3)

"Compiles abstracts of masters' theses and doctoral dissertations completed in graduate schools of home economics."

American Home Economics Association.
Titles of dissertations and theses completed in home economics. 1968/69–
Washington.

v. 28 cm. annual.

At head of title, 1968/69–   Home economics research.
Similar information appeared in Journal of home economics, 1964–69.

Shearer, Jane K
Research related to design, housing and equipment, home furnishings, and interior design, 1942–1965; titles of theses, selected and compiled by Jane K. Shearer. Washington, American Home Economics Association [1966]
94 p. 28 cm.
Cover title.
"Compiled from titles of completed theses in home economics and related fields in colleges and universities of the United States, published by the U. S. Department of Agriculture and U. S. Office of Education, 1942 to 1963, and by the American Home Economics Association, 1963 to 1965."

INDONESIA

Pusat Dokumentasi Ilmiah Nasional.
Karja mengenai Indonesia. Djakarta [1969]

ii, 10 l. 34 cm.

IRELAND

Belfast. Queen's University. *Institute of Irish Studies.*
Theses on subjects relating to Ireland presented for higher degrees 1950–1967. Belfast, Queen's University of Belfast, 1968.

[28] leaves. 26 cm.

ITALY

Cinquant'anni di storia economica a Ca' Foscari. Ca' Foscari, anno accademico 1969–70. Padova, Tip. poligrafica moderna, 1970.

112 p. 24 cm. (Università di Venezia, Facoltà di economia e commercio, Istituto di storia economica Gino Luzzatto. Studi e ricerche, 1)

JAPAN AND KOREA

Cornwall, Peter G
Unpublished doctoral dissertations relating to Japan, accepted in the universities of Australia, Canada, Great Britain, and the United States, 1946–1963, compiled by Peter G. Cornwall. [Ann Arbor? Mich., 1965?]

53–88 p. 23 cm.

Caption title.
Cover title: Unpublished dissertations on Japan, 1946–1963.
Running title: Doctoral dissertations on Japan, 1946–1963.
Prepared under the auspices of the Center for Japanese Studies, University of Michigan.
"Reprinted from the Association for Asian Studies Newsletter, vol. x, no. 2, December 1964."

Shulman, Frank Joseph, 1943–
Japan and Korea; an annotated bibliography of doctoral dissertations in Western languages, 1877–1969. Compiled and edited by Frank J. Shulman for the Center for Japanese Studies, University of Michigan. Chicago, American Library Association, 1970.

xix, 340 p. 28 cm.

JEWISH STUDIES

Bihl, Wolfdieter.
Bibliographie der Dissertationen über Judentum und jüdische Persönlichkeiten, die 1872–1962 an österreichischen Hochschulen ⟨Wien, Graz, Innsbruck⟩ approbiert wurden. Wien, Notring der wissenschaftlichen Verbände Österreichs, 1965.

51 p. 24 cm.

Doctoral dissertations and master's theses accepted by American institutions of higher learning. 1963/64–
New York, Yivo Institute for Jewish Research.

v. 29 cm. (Guides to Jewish subjects in social and humanistic research)

"Compiled for the YIVO Clearinghouse for Social and Humanistic Research in the Jewish Field."
Compiler: 1963/64–　　　W. Ravid.

Kirsch, Guido, 1889–
Judaistische Bibliographie. Ein Verzeichnis der in Deuschland und der Schweiz von 1956 bis 1970 erschienenen

Dissertationen und Habilitationsschriften. Basel, Stuttgart, Helbing & Lichtenhahn, 1972.

104 p. 23 cm.

JUNIOR COLLEGES

Parker, Franklin, 1921– *comp.*
The community junior college; bibliography of 519 United States doctoral dissertations. Austin, Tex. [1964]

38 l. 29 cm.

Caption title.
"Curriculum vitae": 21 leaves inserted.

Parker, Franklin, 1921–
The junior and community college: a bibliography of doctoral dissertations, 1918–1963. Compiled by Franklin Parker and Anne Bailey, in cooperation with William K. Ogilvie. Washington, American Association of Junior Colleges [1965]

47 p. 28 cm.

Roueche, John E
A bibliography of doctoral dissertations, 1964–1966, compiled by John E. Roueche. Washington, American Association of Junior Colleges [1967]

17 p. 28 cm.

KANSAS

Socolofsky, Homer Edward, 1922–
Kansas history in graduate study; a bibliography of theses and dissertations. Compiled by Homer E. Socolofsky. [Revision] Topeka, Kansas State Historical Society, 1970.

58 p. 23 cm.

LATIN AMERICA

Chaffee, Wilber A
Dissertations on Latin America by U. S. historians, 1960–1970; a bibliography, by Wilber A. Chaffee, Jr., and Honor M. Griffin. Austin, Institute of Latin American Studies, University of Texas at Austin, 1973.

xi, 62 p. 23 cm. (Guides and bibliographies series: 7)

Rubin, Selma F
Survey of investigations in progress in the field of Latin American studies, compiled for the Inter-American Bibliographical and Library Association and the Pan American Foundation by Selma F. Rubin. Washington, Dept. of Educational Affairs, Pan American Union [1965]

103 p. 21 cm.

Texas. University. Institute of Latin-American Studies.
Seventy-five years of Latin American research at the University of Texas; masters theses and doctoral dissertations 1893–1958, and publications of Latin American interest 1941–1958. Westport, Conn., Greenwood Press [1971]

67 p. facsims. 23 cm. (Its Latin American studies, 18)
Reprint of the 1959 ed.

Texas. University at Austin. Institute of Latin American Studies.
Latin American research and publications at the Univer-

sity of Texas at Austin, 1893-1969. Austin, 1971.

viii, 187 p. 23 cm. (Guides and bibliographies series: 3) (pbk.)

"Issued to commemorate the 30th anniversary of the establishment of the Institute of Latin American Studies."

LIBRARY SCIENCE

Das **Buch- und Bibliothekswesen** im Spiegel der Jahresverzeichnisse der deutschen Hochschulschriften, 1885–1961; eine Bibliographie. [Jena] Gesellschaftswissenschaftliche Beratungsstelle der Universitätsbibliothek Jena, 1964.

vi, 50 p. 30 cm. (Bibliographische Mitteilungen der Universitätsbibliothek Jena, Nr. 6)

Lozano Rivera, Uriel.
Resúmenes de tesis presentadas por los candidatos al título de licenciado en bibliotecología de 1960 a 1966. Medellín, Colombia, Editorial Universdad de Antioquia, 1967.

viii, 109 l. 27 cm. (Publicaciones de la E. I. B. Serie: Bibliografías)

Lozano Rivera, Uriel.
Resúmenes de tesis presentadas por los candidatos al título de licenciado en bibliotecología de 1967 a junio de 1969. Uriel, Lozano Rivera, editor. Medellín, Colombia, Editorial Universidad de Antioquia, 1969.

x, 38 l. 27 cm. (Publicaciones de la E. I. B. Serie: Bibliografías, no. 19)

At head of title: Universidad de Antioquia. Escuela Interamericana de Bibliotecología.

Lozano Rivera, Uriel.
Resúmenes de tesis presentadas por los candidatos al título de licenciado en bibliotecología de 1960–1970. Uriel Lozano Rivera, editor. Medellín, Colombia, Editorial Universidad de Antioquia, 1972.

xiii, 126 l. 27 cm. (Publicaciones de la E. I. B. Serie: Bibliografías, no. 19)

"La presente edición ... actualiza las entregas anteriores correspondientes a 1960-1966 y 1967-1969."

Schlachter, Gail A
Library science dissertations, 1925-1972; an annotated bibliography [by] Gail A. Schlachter [and] Dennis Thomison. Littleton, Colo., Libraries Unlimited, 1974.

293 p. 24 cm. (Research studies in library science, no. 12)

LINGUISTICS

Dissertations in linguistics. 1957/63-1957/64. [Washington, Center for Applied Linguistics.

2 v. 23 cm. annual.

Editor: -1957/64, A. E. Shaughnessy.
L. C. set imperfect: 1957/63 issue wanting.

Rutherford, Phillip R
A bibliography of American doctoral dissertations in linguistics, 1900–1964, compiled by Phillip R. Rutherford. Washington, Center for Applied Linguistics, 1968.

iv, 139 p. 23 cm.

LITERATURE

Bacigalupo, Anna.
Consigli pratici per una tesi di letterature straniere. [Milano], La goliardica, 1967.

8, 144 p. 21 cm.

Naaman, Antoine Youssef.
Guide bibliographique des thèses littéraires canadiennes

de 1921 à 1969 [par] Antoine Naaman. Préf. de Jean Houpert. Montréal, Éditions Cosmos [1970]

338 p. 24 cm.

MACHINERY

Strojárske a metalurgické zavody, Dubnica nad Váhom.
Zoznam kandidátskych, dizertačných, habilitačných a diplomových prác SMZ Dubnica 1962–1970. Dubnica nad Váhom, vyd. OBIS pri SMZ, rozmn., 1970.

57, [2] p. 14 x 21 cm. (Its Edícia III. Séria B)

MEDICINE

Arkhangel'skiĭ gosudarstvennyĭ meditsinskiĭ institut.
(Annotirovannyĭ katalog dissertatsiĭ sotrudnikov instituta)
Аннотированный каталог диссертаций сотрудников института. (1932–1972 гг.) Сост. проф. А. А. Киров. Архангельск, 1972.

218 p. 20 cm.

At head of title: Министерство здравоохранения РСФСР.

Catholic University of America. *Library.*
Nursing theses 1932–1961; an alphabetical listing and keyword index. Prepared by the Catholic University of America Libraries in cooperation with the School of Nursing, on the occasion of the 35th anniversary of the founding of the School of Nursing. [Washington] 1970.

1 v. (unpaged) 31 cm.

"Fred Blum, Head, Special Services Dept., Editor. Nellie Lee Powell, Head, Nursing Library."

Jinnah Postgraduate Medical Center. *Basic Medical Sciences Division.*
Thesis summaries, 1966–1968. Karachi, 1969.

xi, 50 p. 25 cm.

Kanazawa Daigaku. **Igakubu.**
(Gakuiroku)
学位録　大正15年度–昭和36年度　[金沢]　金沢大学医学部　[1972?]
142 p. 21 cm.

Tartu. Ülikool. *Teaduslik Raamatukogu.*
Tartu Ülikooli Arstiteaduskonnas 1892-1917 kaitstud väitekirjad; bibliograafia. [Koostaja V. Leek] Tartu, 1965.

56 p. 22 cm.

In German or Russian.
Added t. p.: Диссертации, защищенные на Медицинском факультете Тартуского университета (romanized: Dissertatsii, zashchishchennye na Meditsinskom fakul'tete Tartuskogo universiteta)

Woźniewski, Zbigniew, comp.
Rozprawy na stopień doktora medycyny polskich wydziałów lekarskich; okres międzywojenny. Oprac. Zbigniew Woźniewski. [Wyd. 1.]. Warszawa, Państwowy Zakład Wydawnictw Lekarskich, 1969.

106 p. facsims. 24 cm.

METAL-WORK

Gentzsch, Gerhard.
Umformtechnik; Dissertationsreferate, 1945–1967. Düsseldorf, VDI-Verlag, 1968.

160 p. 21 cm.

MILITARY ART AND SCIENCE

Millett, Allan Reed.
Doctoral dissertations in military affairs: a bibliography. Selected and compiled by Allan R. Millett and B. Franklin Cooling III. Manhattan, Kansas State University Library, 1972.

v, 153 p. 28 cm. (Kansas State University Library bibliography series, no. 10)

MINNESOTA

Ostrem, Walter Martin.
A bibliography of theses on Minnesota history, including theses on subjects relating to Minnesota history. Mankato, Minn., 1966.

104 l. 28 cm.

MUSIC

Adkins, Cecil.
Doctoral dissertations in musicology. Edited by Cecil Adkins. 5th ed. Philadelphia, American Musicological Society, 1971.

xii, 203 p. 24 cm.

First ed. issued by the Joint Committee of the Music Teachers National Association and the American Musicological Society; 2d-4th editions compiled by Helen Hewitt.

De Lerma, Dominique-René.
A selective list of masters' theses in musicology. Compiled for the American Musicological Society by Dominique-René de Lerma. [1st ed.] Bloomington, Ind., Denia Press, 197

42 p. 28 cm.

Hartley, Kenneth R.
Bibliography of theses and dissertations in sacred music, by Kenneth R. Hartley. Detroit, Information Coordinators, 1966 [°1967]

viii, 127 p. 23 cm. (Detroit studies in music bibliography, 9)

Schaal, Richard.
Verzeichnis deutschsprachiger musikwissenschaftlicher Dissertationen 1961–1970, mit Ergänzungen zum Verzeichnis 1861–1960. Kassel, Bärenreiter, 1974.

91 p. 24 cm. (Musikwissenschaftliche Arbeiten, Nr. 25)

Texas Music Educators Association.
A bibliography of master's theses and doctoral dissertations in music completed at Texas colleges and universities, 1919–1972. — [Rev. ed.] — [Houston] : Texas Music Educators Association, 1974.

iv, 152 p. ; 23 cm.

NEGROES

West, Earle H
A bibliography of doctoral research on the Negro, 1933–1966. Compiled by Earle H. West. [Washington] Xerox, 1969.

vii, 134 p. 29 cm.

NEW ZEALAND

Rodger, Margaret Diana, 1941– comp.
Theses on the history of New Zealand, compiled by Margaret D. Rodger and K. A. Pickens. Palmerston North, Massey University, 1968–72.

4 v. 22 cm. (Massey University. Library series no. 1–4)

CONTENTS: pt. 1. Biographical studies.—pt. 2. Political history.—pt. 3. Social history.—pt. 4. Economic, agricultural and industrial history.

OCEANIA

Dickson, Diane.
World catalogue of theses on the Pacific Islands, compiled by Diane Dickson and Carol Dossor. Canberra, Australian National University Press, 1970.

xii, 123 p. 22 cm. (Pacific monographs)

Dickson, Diane.
World catalogue of theses on the Pacific Islands. Compiled by Diane Dickson and Carol Dossor. Honolulu, University of Hawaii Press, 1970.

xii, 123 p. 22 cm. (Pacific monographs [no. 1])

OCEANOGRAPHY

Oregon. State University, Corvallis. Dept. of Oceanography.
Reference number listings and theses. [Corvallis] 1969.

[33] p. 28 cm. (Its Reference 69–33)

PHARMACY

American Association of Colleges of Pharmacy. *Committee on Academic Resources.*
Bibliography of theses and dissertations relevant to pharmacy administration. Edited by David A. Knapp. [Silver Spring, Md., American Association of Colleges of Pharmacy, 1970]

vii, 65 p. 28 cm.

Archimbaud, Jacques.
Catalogue des thèses de pharmacie soutenues devant les universités de province ... Clermont-Ferrand, Bibliothèque de médecine et de pharmacie, 1970–

v. 27 cm.

CONTENTS.—[1] 1960–1967.

PHILOLOGY

Chatham, James R 1931–
Dissertations in Hispanic languages and literatures; an index of dissertations completed in the United States and Canada, 1876–1966 [by] James R. Chatham & Enrique Ruiz-Fornells. With the collaboration of Sara Matthews Scales. [Lexington] University Press of Kentucky [1970]

xiv, 120 p. 29 cm.

Krishnacharya, 1917–
हिंदी के स्वीकृत प्रबंध. संपादक कृष्णाचार्य. [प्रथम संस्करण] कलकत्ता, आर्यावर्त प्रकाशन गृह [1964]

xxx, 137 p. 22 cm.

In Hindi.

London. University. *Institute of Germanic Studies.*
Theses in Germanic studies, 1962–67: a catalogue of theses and dissertations in the field of Germanic studies (excluding English) approved for higher degrees in the universities of Great Britain and Ireland between 1962 and 1967. Edited by S. S. Prawer and V. J. Riley. London, University of London, (Institute of Germanic Studies), 1968.

[5], 18 p. 23 cm. (*Its* Publications, 10)
Errata slip inserted.

Magner, Thomas F
Soviet dissertations for advanced degrees in Russian literature and Slavic linguistics, 1934–1962, compiled by Thomas F. Magner. University Park, Dept. of Slavic Languages, Pennsylvania State University, 1966.

iii, 100 p. facsims. 28 cm.

Varnhagen, Hermann, 1850–1924.
Systematisches Verzeichnis der Programmabhandlungen, Dissertationen und Habilitationsschriften aus dem Gebiete der romanischen und englischen Philologie, sowie der allgemeinen Sprach- und Litteraturwissenschaft und der Pädagogik und Methodik. 2. vollständig um gearb. Aufl., besorgt von Johannes Martin. New York, B. Franklin [1968]

xv, 296 p. 23 cm. (Essays in literature and criticism, 3)

Burt Franklin bibliography and references series, 248.
On spine: Romanische und englische Philologie.
Reprint of the edition published in Leipzig by G. A. Koch in 1893.

Editions previous to 1893 published under title: Systematisches Verzeichniss der auf die neueren Sprachen, hauptsächlich die französische und englische, sowie die Sprachwissenschaft überhaupt bezüglichen Programmabhandlungen, Dissertationen und Habilitationsschriften.

PHYSICS

North Carolina. University. *Dept. of Physics.*
Masters of science, masters of arts, and doctors of philosophy in the Physics Dept., University of North Carolina at Chapel Hill. Chapel Hill [1966]

22 l. 22 x 28 cm.

Records degrees from 1908 to 1966.

POLITICAL SCIENCE

Gautam, Brijendra Pratap, 1933–
Researches in political science in India; a detailed bibliography. Compiled by Brijendra Pratap Gautam, with a foreword by A. V. Rao. Kanpur, Oriental Pub. House [1965]

ii, v, 116 p. 23 cm.

POPULATION

Fuguitt, Glenn Victor, 1928–
Dissertations in demography. 1933–1963. Prepared by Glenn V. Fuguitt. Madison, Dept. of Rural Sociology, College of Agriculture, University of Wisconsin, 1964.

v, 72 p. 28 cm.

READING

Fay, Leo Charles, 1930–
Doctoral studies in reading, 1919 through 1960, by Leo C. Fay, Weldon G. Bradtmueller [and] Edward G. Summers. [Bloomington] Bureau of Educational Studies and Testing, School of Education, Indiana University, 1964.

vi, 80 p. 23 cm. (Bulletin of the School of Education, Indiana University, v. 40, no. 4)

REHABILITATION

Butler, Alfred James, 1923–
Wisconsin rehabilitation doctoral dissertations; abstracts of research completed for partial fulfillment of requirements of the Ph. D. in vocational rehabilitation at the University of Wisconsin, Madison. Compiled by Alfred J. Butler, and George N. Wright. Madison, University of Wisconsin, Rehabilitation Counseling, Psychology Program, 1970.

43 l. 28 cm.

SAN DIEGO, CALIFORNIA

Posner, Walter H
History of San Diego: San Diego State College theses; a bibliography, compiled by Walter H. Posner. [San Diego] Friends of the Library, San Diego State College, 1969.

6 p. 23 cm.

SCIENCE

Heertjes, Nicolaas.
Bibliografie van dissertaties, verdedigd aan de Technische Hogeschool Eindhoven in de jaren 1959–1974 [door N. Heertjes] Eindhoven, 1974.

ii, 370 p. 21 cm.

Indian Institute of Science, Bangalore.
Abstracts of theses.
Bangalore.

v. 24 cm.

Quebec (City) Université Laval. *Centre de documentation.*
Index des thèses de doctorat soutenues devant les universités françaises, 1959–1963. Sciences. Québec, 1967.

2 v. 21 x 27 cm.

Torossian, Araxie.
Catalogue des thèses de sciences physiques (mention: physique et chimie) soutenues devant la Faculté des sciences de l'Université de Paris de 1945 à 1960. Préf. de Germain Calmette. Paris, Person, 1964.

159 p. 21 cm.

At head of title: Bibliothèque de l'Université de Paris (Sorbonne)

SOCIAL SCIENCES

Akademie van Wetenschappen, *Amsterdam. Sociaal-Wetenschappelijke Raad.*
Dissertaties 1967–1968 in voorbereiding en in het afgelopen jaar verdedigd aan Nederlandse universiteiten en hogescholen. Sociale wetenschappen, sociale geneeskunde, rechtswetenschappen, economie, geschiedenis. Amsterdam, Noord-Hollandsche Uitg. Mij., 1968.

64 p. 24 cm.

Indian Council of Social Science Research.
Doctorates in social sciences awarded by Indian universities. 1968–
New Delhi.

v. 22 cm. annual. (Its Research Information series)

Lunday, G Albert.
Sociology dissertations in American universities, 1893–1966 [by] G. Albert Lunday. Commerce, East Texas State University, 1969.

x, 277 p. 23 cm.

Punjab, Pakistan (Province) University, *Lahore. Dept. of Sociology.*
Thesis index, 1957–1967. Compiled by Muhammad Fayyaz [and] Qaiyum Lodhi. Lahore, 1968.

v, 61 p. 25 cm. (*Its* Miscellaneous publication, no. 2)

SOCIAL SERVICE

Marín, Rosa Celeste.
Resúmenes de tesis (sometidas para optar a la maestría en trabajo social) ₁par₁ Rosa C. Marín, Carmen Fidelina Quinones Vda. Rodríguez ₁y₁ Belén Milagros Serra. Año lectivo 1966-1967. Río Piedras, Escuela de Trabajo Social, Facultad de Ciencias Sociales, Universidad de Puerto Rico ₁1968₁

73 l. 29 cm.

STEINBECK, JOHN

Hayashi, Tetsumaro.
John Steinbeck: a guide to the doctoral dissertations; a collection of dissertation abstracts (1946-1969) Muncie, Ind., Ball State University ₁1971₁

viii, 32 p. 22 cm. (Steinbeck monograph series, no. 1)

SUDAN

Hamza, Maymouna Mirghani.
Theses on the Sudan, and by Sudanese, accepted for higher degrees. Compiled by Maymouna Mirghani Hamza, assisted by the Library staff. Khartoum, University of Khartoum Library, 1966.

63 p. 21 cm. (₁Khartoum. University. Library. Publication₁ 2)

Khartum. University. Library.
Theses on the Sudan. 2d ed. Khartoum, 1971.

96 l. 29 cm.

Edition for 1966, by M. M. Hamza, published under title: Theses on the Sudan and by Sudanese accepted for higher degrees.

TAJIKISTAN

Kholdzhuraev, Khabibullo Kholdzhuraevich.
Диссертации историков по материалам Таджикистана. ₁Реферативный указатель₁. Под ред. акад. д-ра ист. наук, проф. М. И. Иркаева. ₁Душанбе, 1970.

281 p. 21 cm.

At head of title: Министерство народного образования Таджикской ССР. Таджикский государственный университет им. В. И. Ленина. Кафедра истории КПСС. Х. Холджураев.

Shevchenko, Zinaida Matveevna.
Каталог кандидатских и докторских диссертаций, защищенных на материалах Таджикской ССР. 1960-1965 гг. (Библиогр. указатель литературы). Отв. ред. д-р хим. наук К. Т. Порошин ₁и др.₁ Душанбе, "Дониш," 1970.

133 p. 20 cm.

At head of title: Академия наук Таджикской ССР. Центральная научная библиотека. З. М. Шевченко.

TECHNOLOGY

Becke, Elfriede.
Dissertationsverzeichnis der Technischen Hochschule in Graz 1901-1969. Graz ₁Technische Hochschule₁ 1972.

75, 11 l. 29 cm.

Georgia. Institute of Technology, Atlanta. Library.
Cumulative list of master's theses and doctoral dissertations accepted in partial fulfillment of the requirements for degrees granted by the Georgia Institute of Technology, 1925-1968. Atlanta, Price Gilbert Memorial Library, Georgia Institute of Technology, 1968.

iii, 163 p. 23 cm.

Indian Institute of Technology, Kharagpur, India.
Abstracts of the theses, approved for D. Sc., Ph. D.,

M. Tech. & M. Sc. degrees & post-graduate diplomas in the Indian Institute of Technology, Kharagpur, India. Kharagpur ₁1967–

v. 25 cm.

CONTENTS: v. 1. 1955-1966.

Lísková, Alena.
Technické disertace ve státních technických a státních vědeckých knihovnách 1972 : souborná bibliografie / ₁sest.₁ Alena Lísková. — 1. vyd. — Praha : ÚVTEI : St. techn. knihovna, 1974.

2. v. ; 21 cm. — (Prague. Státní technická knihovna : Bibliografie ; sv. 190-191)

CONTENTS: 1 č. Soupis disertací. — 2 č. Rejstříky.

Newark, N. J. College of Engineering.
Master of science theses. v. 1–
1950/64–
Newark.

v. 23 cm.

Prague. Státní technická knihovna.
Disertace ve Státní technické knihovně v Praze; souborná bibliografie. ₁Sest. Jitka Kostková₁ Praha, 1966.

265 p. 20 cm. (*Its* Bibliografie, sv. 91)

At head of title: Státní technická knihovna v Praze.

Saxena, Radhey Shyam, 1927–
Research publications and theses of Roorkee University, July 1960–July 1964: a classified and annotated bibliography, by R. S. Saxena & Shipra Gupta. Roorkee, Nem Chand, 1965.

xiv, 124 p. 22 cm.

Technische Hogeschool Delft.
Bibliografie van de dissertaties ter verkrijging van de titel van doctor in de technische wetenschappen en lijst van de promoties honoris causa 1905-1966. Uitg. ter gelegenheid van het 25. lustrum van de Technische Hogeschool. ₁Bibliography of doctoral dissertations and list of doctores honoris causa 1905-1966. Published on the occasion of the 125th anniversary of the university₁ 's-Gravenhage, Staatsdrukkerij- en Uitgeverijbedrijf, 1967.

vii, 245 p. with illus. 20 cm.

Vainio, Virpi.
Väitöskirjat, 1911-1968. Doktorsavhandlingar. Theses. ₁Kirj.₁ Virpi Vainio & Elin Törnudd. Otaniemi, Teknillinen Korkeakoulu, Tekniska högskolan, Finland's Institute of Technology, 1969.

24 p. 25 cm. (Teknillinen Korkeakoulu. Tieteellisiä tutkimuksia, no. 20)

Zürich. Eidgenössische Technische Hochschule.
Dissertationenverzeichnis 1909-1971. Répertoire des thèses 1909-1971. Zürich, 1972.

xv, 480 p. 21 cm. (Schriftenreihe der Bibliothek, Nr. 15)

Cover title.
Prefatory material in English, French, and German.

THEOLOGY

Corpus dissertationum theologicarum sive catalogus commentationum, programmatum allarumque scriptionum academicarum ab antiquissimo usque ad nostrum tempus editarum, ad exegeticam, dogmaticam, moralem ac reliquas disciplinas theologicas spectantium, quae in uberrima collectione Weigeliana Lipsiensi prostant. Praefatus est et indices tum locorum scripturae sacrae, tum rerum ac nominum conscripsit Otto Fiebig. ₍Herdr. van de uitg. Leipzig, 1847₎. Amsterdam, Grüner, 1971.

iv, 355 p. 23 cm.

Loidl, Franz.
Die Dissertationen der Katholisch-Theologischen Fakultät der Universität Wien 1831-1965. Alphabetisches Verzeichnis. Wien, Herder (1969).

106 p. 23 cm. (Wiener Beiträge zur Theologie, Bd. 25)

TOBACCO

Pohl, Emma W   1905–
Theses on the subject of tobacco written at North Carolina State University at Raleigh. Compiled by Emma W. Pohl. Raleigh, D. H. Hill Library, North Carolina State University, 1970.

17 l. 29 cm.

URUGUAY

Bustelo, Blanca Margarita.
Monografías y tesis universitarias sobre industrialización en el Uruguay, presentadas en la Facultad de Ciencias Económicas y de Administración, Universidad de la República, Montevideo, Uruguay (1937–1972). Montevideo, Comcorde, Secretaría Técnica ₍1973₎

40 p. 27 cm.

"Preparado por ... Blanca Margarita Bustelo de la Biblioteca de la Facultad de Ciencias Económicas para ser presentado en la 36° Conferencias y Congreso Internacional de la Federación Internacional de Documentación, Budapest, Hungría, 1972."

"Trabajos ... existentes en la Biblioteca de la Facultad de Ciencias Económicas."
"D.ST-3/973, 6 febrero 1973."

VETERINARY MEDICINE

Åkesson, Margareta, 1905–
Veterinärmedicinska avhandlingar 1938–1968, nr. 1–100. Förteckning. Doctoral dissertations in veterinary medicine. Stockholm. Kungl. Veterinärhögskolans bibliotek, 1968 ₍i. e. 1969₎

42 p. 24 cm.

Brünn.   Vysoká škola zemědělská a lesnická.   Fakulta veterinární.
Index dissertationum Facultatis (Academiae) Medicinae Veterinariae Brunensis, 1945–1965. ₍Sest. Rudolf Böhm₎ V Brně, 1965.

64–93, 218–377 p. 24 cm.

"Veterinární fakulta VŠZ v Brně předkládá seznanam vypracovaných a obhájenych diplomových a disertačnich prací. Seznam vyšel ve Sborníku VŠZ, řada B (Spisyveterinární) roč. 13 (34) 1965."

WATER

Deane, Mary, 1940–
Theses on water submitted to universities in California through June 1969. Berkeley, Water Resources Center Archives, University of California ₍1971₎

iii, 152 p. 28 cm. (University of California. Water Resources Center Archives. Archives series report no. 22)

Ferguson, Stanley.
Bibliography of water-related theses and dissertations written at the University of Texas at Austin, 1897–1970.

Austin, Center for Research in Water Resources, University of Texas, 1970.

v, 54 l. 28 cm. (Center for Research in Water Resources. University of Texas at Austin. CRWR–68)

McCann, James A
An annotated bibiography of the masters theses and doctoral dissertations on water resources and their uses, 1930–1970, University of Massachusetts, Amherst ₍by₎ James A. McCann and Gail G. Smith. Amherst, Massachusetts Water Resources Research Center, University of Massachusetts, 1971.

iii, 43 p. 28 cm. (Contribution of the Massachusetts Cooperative Fishery Unit, no. 22)

WILDLIFE CONSERVATION

Moore, Julie L   1941–
Bibliography of wildlife theses. Bibliographie des theses sauvage, 1900–1968 ₍by₎ Julie L. Moore. Los Angeles, Biological Information Service, 1970.

1 v. (various pagings) 28 cm.

WISCONSIN

Chiswick, Jeanne Hunnicutt.
A guide to theses on Wisconsin subjects, supplement ₍compiled and prepared by Jeanne Hunnicutt Chiswick₎ Madison, State Historical Society of Wisconsin, 1966–

v. 28 cm.

Supplements R. E. Wyman's A guide to theses on Wisconsin subjects.

3. Countries, States

AFRICA

Khartum.   University.   *Library*.
Theses accepted by the University of Khartoum to September 1966. Khartoum, 1966.

12 p. 21 cm. (*Its* Publication 1)

Makerere University.   Library.
Annotated list of theses submitted to University of East Africa, and held by Makerere University Library. Kampala, 1970.

vii l., 52 p. 25 cm. (Its Publications, no. 7)

Randse Afrikaanse Universiteit.
Opsommings van proefskrifte en verhandelinge. Abstracts of dissertations and theses. 1969/70–
Johannesburg.

v. 21 cm.

Afrikaans or English, with summaries in the other language.

Rhodes University, Grahamstown, South Africa.   Library. Publications Dept.
Rhodes University theses up to graduation 1971. Grahamstown, 1971.

36 l. 30 cm.

ARAB COUNTRIES

Jāmiʿat al-Kuwayt.   Qism al-Tawthīq.
(Dalīl al-risālāt al-ʿArabīyah)

دليل الرسالات العربية، درجات الدكتوراة والماجستير التى
منحتها الجامعات العربية منذ ١٩٣٠ حتى نهاية ١٩٧٠. ₍الكويت₎

جامعة الكويت ، مراقبة المكتبات ، قسم التوثيق ، 1972.

2 l., 510 p. 27 cm.

Added t. p.: Kuwait University. Libraries Department. Documentation Division. Arab dissertation index.

ARIZONA

Arizona. University. *Library.*
Checklist of theses and dissertations accepted for higher degrees at the University of Arizona through 1946. Compiled by Clinton E. Colby, Jr. Tucson, 1965.

52, 12 l. 28 cm.

ARKANSAS

Arkansas. University. *Graduate School.*
Abstracts of dissertations presented in partial fulfillment of requirements for the Ph. D. and Ed. D. degrees awarded at the University of Arkansas during the period from January 1959 through December 1965. Fayetteville [1966]

333 p. 23 cm.

Arkansas. University. Graduate School.
Abstracts of dissertations presented in partial fulfillment of requirements for the Ph.D. and Ed.D. degrees awarded at the University of Arkansas during the period from January 1966 through June 1970. Fayetteville [1971]

56 p. 23 cm.

AUSTRALIA

Australian National University, Canberra. Library.
Theses accepted for higher degrees, prepared by the University Library. Canberra, Australian National University, 1971.

75 p. 33 cm.

——— ———— Supplement 1 (1st July, 1970–30th June, 1971)
ii, 14 p. 30 cm.

Union list of higher degree theses in Australian university libraries: cumulative edition to 1965. [Edited by Enid Wylie] Hobart, University of Tasmania Library, 1967.

xxii, 568 p. 26 cm.

First compiled in 1959 by Mary J. Marshall.

AUSTRIA

Graz. Universität. *Bibliothek.*
Dissertationen-Verzeichnis der Universität Graz, 1872–1963. Hrsg. von Franz Kroller. Graz, 1964.

xi, 363 p. 23 cm.

"Dissertationen der Universität Graz, die während des Zeitraumes 1872–1963 approbiert und innerhalb des Universitätsbereiches noch wenigstens in einem Exemplar vorhanden sind."

——— ———— 1964–1965. Mit Nachträgen aus früheren Jahren. Wien, Verlag Notring, 1968.

47 p. 23 cm.

BELGIUM

Ghent. Rijksuniversiteit. Bibliotheek.
Doctorale proefschriften en hoger aggregatiewerken bewaard in de Centrale Bibliotheek, met abstracts 1973. Doctoral and inaugural dissertations preserved in the Central Library, with abstracts 1973. Gent, Centrale Bibliotheek van de Rijksuniversiteit, 1974.

vi, 80 l. 29 cm.

Louvain. Université catholique.
Bibliographie académique. Louvain, C. Peeters, 1880–[1972]

12 v. in 18. 20–25 cm.

Edited by J. Coppens and others.
Vols. 2–5 have title: Bibliographie; v. 7, pt. 8, and v. 11–12: Bibliographia academica.
Vol. 6, v. 7, pt. 1, 4, and v. 8–10 have title and explanatory material in French and Flemish.
Vols. 6–12 have imprint: Louvain, Bibliothèque de l'Université.
Vol. 7, pt. 3 and v. 11 issued together in 1 v.

Répertoire des thèses de doctorat. Reportorium van doctorale proefschriften. 1971/72–
Bruxelles, Ministère des affaires étrangères.

v. 22 cm. annual.

Flemish and French.

BULGARIA

Stanisheva, Lazarina.
Библиография на дисертациите, защитени в България, 1929–1964. (Ред. Тодор Боров и Искра Михайлова). София, Унив. библ., 1969.
xii, 593 p. 23 cm.
At head of title: Л. Станишева, С. Шопова.
Added title: Bibliography of dissertations, defended in Bulgaria, 1929–1964.
Introduction and table of contents also in English and Russian.
"Показалец на резюметата на чужди езици" (English, French, German, and Russian) : p. 482–582.

CANADA

L'Assomption, Que. Collège. *Bibliothèque.*
Bibliographie des œuvres des anciens du Collège de L'Assomption. Compilée par Réjean Olivier. L'Assomption [Québec] 1967.

52 p. 28 cm.

Mills, Judy.
University of Toronto doctoral theses, 1897–1967: a bibliography compiled by Judy Mills and Irene Dombra. [Toronto] Published for the University of Toronto Library by University of Toronto Press [°1968]

xi, 186 p. 24 cm.

Quebec (City). Université Laval. Centre de documentation.
Répertoire des thèses de doctorat soutenues devant les universités de langue française. v. 1–
1970–
[Québec]
v. 21 x 27 cm.
Vols. for 1970– issued with the Association des universités entièrement ou partiellement de langue française under a variant name: Association des universités partiellement ou entièrement de langue française.

Quebec (City) Université Laval. *École des gradués.*
Liste des thèses, 1940 à 1965. [Québec] 1965.

vi, 82 p. 23 cm.

Saskatchewan. University.
University of Saskatchewan postgraduate theses 1912–1966. Saskatoon, 1967.

iii, 93 p. 25 cm.

COLORADO

Colorado. State University, Fort Collins. Libraries.
A guide to theses, submitted in partial fulfillment of the

requirements for the master's and doctoral degrees at Colorado State University, 1920–1969, compiled by William F. Lindgren. 2d ed. Fort Collins, 1970.

102 p. 28 cm. (Its Publication no. 7)

CZECHOSLOVAK REPUBLIC

Okálová, Magda.
Bibliografia dizertačných a diplomových prác obhájených na Vysokej škole dopravnej. Sprac. Magda Okálová a Emil Rafaj. 1. vyd. Martin, Matica slovenská, 196

v. 29 cm. (Špeciálne bibliografie) (Na pomoc vede a výskumu)

CONTENTS: Zv. 1. Fakulta prevádzky a ekonomiky dopravy, 1954–1964.—Zv. 2. Fakulta strojnícka a elektrotechnická, 1957–1965.

DISTRICT OF COLUMBIA

Catholic University of America. Library.
Theses and dissertations; a bibliographical listing, keyword index, and author index. cumulation, 1961–1967. Prepared by the Catholic University of America libraries. Fred Blum, editor. Lloyd F. Wagner, director of libraries. Washington, Distributed by Catholic University of America Press, 1970.

548 p. 31 cm.

EGYPT

Markaz al-Wathā'iq wa-al-Buhūth al-Islāmīyah.
قائمة توثيق مكتبى للرسائل الجامعية التى أجيزت لنيل درجات الدراسات العليا بكليات أصول الدين، الشريعة، اللغة العربية. القاهرة، الهيئة العامة لشئون المطابع الأميرية، 1967.

22, 105 p. 24 cm.

At head of title: جامعة الازهر. امانة المكتبات والعلاقات الخارجية. مركز الوثائق والبحوث الاسلامية.

ESTONIA

Oissar, E
Tartu Ülikoolis kaitstud väitekirjad, 1802–1918 : bibliograafia / E. Oissar. — Tartu : Tartu Riiklik Ülikool, Teaduslik Raamatukogu, 1973.

180 p. ; 21 cm.

Added t. p.: Диссертации, защищенные в Тартуском университете, 1802–1918.
Estonian and Russian.

FLORIDA

Florida. University, *Gainesville. Research Council.*
University of Florida publications and theses. 1943/44–1963/65. Gainesville.

12 v. in 8. 23 cm. (1943/44: 26 cm.)

Annual, 1943/44–1952/53; biennial, 1953/55–1963/65.
Vols. for 1948/49–1951/52 published as the University record of the University of Florida.
Vols. for 1943/44–1949/50 not published.
Title varies: 1943/44–1949/50, Current research and publications.

FRANCE

Mourier, Athénaïs *i. e.* **Louis Athénaïs,** 1815–1889.
Notice sur le doctorat ès lettres, suivie du Catalogue et de l'analyse des thèses françaises et latines admises par les facultés des lettres depuis 1810, avec index et table alphabétique des docteurs, par Ath. Mourier et F. Deltour. 4. éd. corr. et considérablement augm. New York, B. Franklin [1969]

xii, 442 p. 23 cm. (Burt Franklin bibliography & reference series, 240)

"Originally published, Paris, 1880."

Paris. Université. *Faculté de droit et des sciences économiques. Centre de documentation africaine.*
Thèses et mémoires relatifs au Tiers monde (moins l'Afrique) soutenus et déposés, année 1967. [Paris,] Département de droit et économique des pays d'Afrique, 1968.

29 l. 27 cm.

Reiss, Françoise.
Theses en Sorbonne: 1963–1969 [par] Françoise Reiss ... Paris, Klincksieck, 1973.

515 p. 24 cm.

Université de Paris X: Nanterre.
Répertoire raisonné des sujets en cours des doctorats d'État, lettres et sciences humaines, inscrits en France, 1965–juillet 1970. [Établi par Hélène Falaise, collaboratrice technique, Université de Paris X-Nanterre, avec la collaboration du Centre de documentation des sciences humaines. Paris] Centre de documentation Sciences humaines, C. N. R. S. [1973?]

3 v. 30 cm.

GERMANY

Erman, Wilhelm, 1850–1932.
Verzeichnis der Berliner Universitätsschriften 1810–1885; nebst einem Anhang enthaltend die ausserordentlichen und Ehren-Promotionen. Hildesheim, New York, G. Olms, 1973.

848 p. 20 cm.

Reprint of the 1899 ed. published by W. Weber, Berlin.

Klussmann, Rudolf, 1846–1925.
Systematisches Verzeichnis der Abhandlungen, welche in den Schulschriften sämtlicher an dem Programmtausche teilnehmenden Lehranstalten vom Jahre 1876–1885 erschienen sind. New York, B. Franklin [1969]

viii, 315 p. 24 cm. (Burt Franklin bibliography & reference series, 247. Selected essays in literature & criticism, 21)

Reprint of the ed. published in Leipzig by B. G. Teubner in 1889 as v. 1 of a four-volume ed. which covered the years 1876–1900.

Kössler, Franz.
Katalog de Dissertationen und Habilitationsschriften der Universität Giessen von 1801 bis 1884. [Von] Franz Kössler. Die Promotions- und Habilitationsordnungen der Universität Giessen im 19. Jahrhundert. [Hrsg.:] H[ermann] Schüling. Giessen, Universitätsbibliothek, 1971.

vii, 138, 78 p. 23 cm. (Berichte und Arbeiten aus der Universitätsbibliothek Giessen, 22)

Lufer, Margarete.
Bibliographie der pädagogischen Dissertationen und Habilitationsschriften der Deutschen Demokratischen Republik, der Deutschen Bundesrepublik und Westberlins, 1945 bis 1965. Zusammengestellt und bearb. in der Abteilung Dokumentation und Information des Deutschen Pädagogischen Zentralinstituts. [Berlin, Volk und Wissen, 1966]

248 p. 21 cm.

Tübingen. Universität.
Sammlung aller Magister-Promotionen welche zu Tübingen von Anno 1477–1755 geschehen darinnen nebst dem Vor- und Zu-Namen das Vaterland, die Aemter, und andere Vergleichen Umstände der vorkommenden Personen aus vielen bewährten Urkunden zuverlässig angemercket werden. Amsterdam, Grüner, 1972.

1 v. (unpaged). 23 cm.

Reprint of the Stuttgart, 1756 ed.

GREAT BRITAIN

Exeter, Eng. University.
Index to theses accepted for higher degrees, 1955–1971. 3rd ed. Exeter, University of Exeter, 1972.

[3], 58 p. 21 cm.

Index to theses accepted for higher degrees by the universities of Great Britain and Ireland. v. 18– 1967/68–
London, Aslib.

v. 25 cm. annual.

Continues: Aslib. Index to theses accepted for higher degrees in the universities of Great Britain and Ireland.

Lancaster, Eng. University.
Theses and dissertations for higher degrees deposited in the University Library, 1965–1972. [Lancaster], University of Lancaster, 1972.

[2], 59 p. 21 cm.

Lancaster, Eng. University.
Theses and dissertations for higher degrees deposited in the University Library, 1965–1973. [Lancaster] University of Lancaster, 1973.

75 p. 21 cm.

Wales. University. University College, Swansea. Library.
University College of Swansea higher degree theses 1920–1970 [compiled by Frances Wood] [Swansea, 1971]

111 l. 26 cm.

ILLINOIS

Southern Illinois University. University Libraries.
Dissertations and theses presented for advanced degrees, 1949–1965. Carbondale, Central Publications, Southern Illinois University, 1966.

viii, 136 p. 28 cm. (*Its* Bibliographic contributions, no. 2)

INDIA

Aligarh, India. Muslim University.
List of theses approved for the D. Sc., Ph. D., M. Sc. & M. A. degrees in the Aligarh Muslim University, Aligarh, 1920–1969. Aligarh, Printed at the Aligarh Muslim University Press, 1969.

x, 68 p. 28 cm. (Maulana Azad Library. Reference and research publication, no. 1)

Indore, India (City). University. Library.
Catalogue of theses: 1966–1971. Indore, 1972.

ii, 38 p. 28 cm.

Inter-university Board of India and Ceylon.
A bibliography of doctoral dissertations accepted by Indian universities, 1857–1970. New Delhi, 1972–

v. 23 cm.

CONTENTS: [1] Education, library science, journalism.—[2] Psychology.—[3] Political science, law, public administration.—[4] Sociology.

Jayakar Library.
Catalogue of theses and dissertations (1950–1969). [Compiled by K. S. Hingwe. Poona, University of Poona, 1971.

xii, 249 p. illus. 25 cm.

Punjab, India (State) University. Extension Library, Ludhiana.
Panjab University doctoral dissertations, 1948–1964. [Compiled by Ramesh C. Sharma and Raj Kumar Puri. Edited by S. S. Lal.] Ludhiana, 1965.

22 p. 25 cm.

Punjab, India (State). University. Extension Library, Ludhiana.
Panjab University doctoral dissertations, 1965–1967. [Compiled by Raj Kumar Puri and M. S. Deogon; edited by S. S. Lal] Ludhiana, 1968.

15 p. 24 cm.

"Supplement 1."

Raza, Jafar.
Doctorate theses of the University of Allahabad: a bibliography from 1887 to 1967 of the recipients of doctorate degrees from the Faculties of Arts, Science, Commerce and Law of the University of Allahabad, with the years of award and the titles of their theses. Compiled by Jafar Raza. [Allahabad] University of Allahabad, 1969.

xii, 99 p. 25 cm. (University of Allahabad studies (new series) v. 1. nos. 1–6)

Udaipur, India (City). University. Central Library.
The catalogue of theses and dissertations available in the University Central Library. Udaipur, 1968.

8, 24, 15 l. 35 cm.

Introduction signed: V. B. Nanda, Deputy Librarian.

INDONESIA

Universitas Hasanuddin.
Skripsi-tesis, sampai dengan Agustus 1972. Udjung Pandang [1972]

66 l. 28 cm.

IOWA

Burlingame, Dwight.
Masters' theses presented in the College of Business Administration and the Graduate Program in Hospital and Health Administration at the University of Iowa, 1950–1966, compiled by Dwight Burlingame. Prelim. ed. [Iowa City] University of Iowa Libraries, 1967.

40 l. 28 cm.

"This list will update ... a previous compilation by Sarah Scott Edwards and Pauline Cook entitled Theses and dissertations presented in the Graduate College of the State University of Iowa, 1900–1950."

IRAQ

Bagdad. Jāmi'at Baghdād. al-Maktabah al-Markazīyah.
A list of theses and dissertations of Iraqis kept in the Central Library, University of Baghdad. [Compiled by Nazar M. A. Qassim, head, Reference and Circulation Dept.] Baghdad, Central Library, University of Baghdad, 1967.

163 l. 33 cm.

———————Supplement I. Compiled by Nazar M. A. Qassim, head, Reference and Circulation Dept. Baghdad, Central Library, University of Baghdad, 1969.

85 l. 33 cm.

ISRAEL

Tel-Aviv. University.
(To'ore Ph.D. ve-taktsirim shel 'avodot ha-meḥkar)
תארי Ph.D. ותקצירים של עבודות המחקר. 1970/72-
תל-אביב.

v. 23 cm.

Added title, 1970/72–   : Ph.D. degrees and abstracts.
English and Hebrew.

Tel-Aviv. University. *Library.*
List of theses ₁submitted by students of the Tel-Aviv
University₁ Tel Aviv, 1964.

7 l. 28 cm.

JAPAN

私立大学・短期大学紀要類論文題目索引 1967-
₁東京₁ 東京都私立短期大学協会

v. 25 cm. annual.

Supersedes 大学短期大学紀要論文題目索引
Vols. for 1967–   issued by 東京都私立短期大学協会図書
館研究委員会

KANSAS

Reed, Lawrence M   1942-
Bibliography of graduate theses: Fort Hays Kansas State College, 1930-1970 ₁by₁ Lawrence M. Reed and Robert D. Smith.
₁Hays, Fort Hays Kansas State College₁ 1971.

viii, 47 p. ports. 23 cm. (Fort Hays studies: New series. Bibliography
series, no. 4)

LEBANON

Jafet Memorial Library.
Masters' theses: 1909–70. Compiled by Nawal Mikdashi.
Beirut, 1971.

97, 13 l. 35 cm.

Text in English and Arabic.

LITHUANIA

Petrauskienė, Z
Lietuvos TSR mokslininkų disertacijos. 1945–1968. Bibliografija. Vilnius. 1971.

490 p. 22 cm.

At head of title: Lietuvos TSR Mokslų akademijos Centrinė biblioteka. Vilniaus Valstybinio V. Kapsuko universiteto Mokslinė biblioteka. Z. Petrauskienė ir P. Valentėlienė.
Added t. p. Dissertatsii uchenykh Litovskoi SSR.
Prefatory matter and table of contents also in Russian.

LOUISIANA

Dyson, Sam A   1928-
Master's theses accepted at Louisiana Polytechnic Insti-
tute, 1958–1968. Compiled and edited by Sam Dyson.
Ruston, Prescott Library Publications, 1968.

vi, 101 p. 28 cm.

Cover title: Master's theses; Louisiana Polytechnic Institute.

Hayward, Olga Hines.
Graduate theses of Southern University, 1959–1971, a
bibliography. Baton Rouge, La., Southern University,
1972-

v. 23 cm.

Louisiana. Northwestern State College of Louisiana,
Natchitoches.
Master's theses completed at Northwestern State College
of Louisiana, 1957–1968 ₁by₁ Donald N. MacKenzie.
Natchitoches, Louisiana Studies Institute, Northwestern
State College ₁1968₁

xi, 50 p. 23 cm. (Louisiana Studies Institute. Monograph series, no. 2)

Louisiana Tech University.
Abstracts of theses accepted by the Graduate School.
1968/69-
Ruston, La., Prescott Library Publications.

v. 28 cm. annual.

Report year ends June 30.
Vols. for 1968/69 issued by the university under its earlier name:
Louisiana Polytechnic Institute.
Editor: 1968/69–   S. A. Dyson.

Winder, Consuella P
Selected list of graduate theses and dissertations produced at
Louisiana colleges and universities (1959-1973) : (with a subject
index) / compiled by Consuella P. Winder. — ₁Baton Rouge₁ :
Louisiana State Dept. of Public Education, 1974.

vi leaves, 77 p. ; 28 cm. — (Bulletin - Louisiana State Department of Public
Education ; 1259)

MEXICO

Paley, Nicholas M
Tesis profesionales de la Universidad Interamericana
(1942–1969) ₁por₁ Nicholas M. Paley. Saltillo ₁Mexico₁
Ediciones Universitarias, 1969.

51 p. 23 cm.

MISSOURI

Pius XII Memorial Library.
Index to doctoral dissertations: St. Louis University, by
Linda Sloan ₁and others. St. Louis₁ 1971.

1 v. (unpaged) 29 cm.

MORAVIA

Olomouc, Moravia. Palackého universita. *Filosofická fa-*
kulta.
Bibliografie vědecké publikační činnosti pracovníků Filo-
sofické fakulty University Palackého v Olomouci v letech
1956–1965. ₁Sest. Eduard Petrů. Vyd. 1₁ Olomouc, 1966.

₁151 p. 21 cm.

NETHERLANDS

Akademie van Wetenschappen, *Amsterdam. Sociaal-Weten-*
schappelijke Raad.
Dissertaties 1968–1969 in voorbereiding en in het afgelopen jaar verdedigd aan Nederlandse universiteiten en
hogescholen. Sociale wetenschappen, sociale geneeskunde,
rechtswetenschappen, economische wetenschappen ₁en₁
geschiedwetenschappen. Amsterdam, Noord-Hollandsche
Uitg. Mij., 1969.

76 p. 24 cm.

OREGON

Brandt, Patricia.
O. S. U. theses and dissertations, 1960-1965. ₁Corvallis,
State University Press₁ 1967.

iv, 88 p. 23 cm. (Bibliographic series, no. 8)

"A departmental and author index of 1,388 masters theses and

doctoral dissertations accepted by the Graduate School, Oregon State University."
Supplement to Theses and dissertations, 1932-1959, by Rodney K. Waldron.

Guss, Margaret Basilia.
Theses and dissertations. 1966-1970, Oregon State University. Corvallis, Oregon State University Press ₁1973₁

79 p. 23 cm. (Bibliographic series no. 9)

Cover title: OSU theses and dissertations, 1966-1970.
"A departmental and author index of masters' theses and doctoral dissertations accepted by the Graduate School."
Continuation of O.S.U. theses and dissertations, 1960-1965 by P. Brandt.

PHILIPPINE ISLANDS

Manila. National Library. Filipiniana Division.
List of theses and dissertations available in the Filipiniana Division. ₁Manila, 1967?₁

54 l. 34 cm.

Philippines (*Republic*). *National Science Development Board.*
Compilation of graduate theses prepared in the Philippines, 1913-1960. Manila ₁1964 or 5₁

437 p. 21 cm.

Quezon, Philippines. University of the Philippines. *Library. Readers Services Division.*
U. P. theses and dissertations index, 1956-1968. Diliman, Rizal, Library, University of the Philippines, 1969.

397 l. 27 cm. (University of the Philippines. Library. Research guide no. 6)

Research abstracts; the Philippine Women's University, University Graduate School and its affiliates: the Philippine School of Graduate Studies, the Philippine School of Social Work, the Philippine College of Music and Fine Arts. ₁Manila, University Graduate School, Philippine Women's University, 1966?₁–

v. 23 cm.

"Abstracts of theses."
CONTENTS: v. 1. 1949-1958.—v. 2. 1959-1966.—v. 3. 1966-1970.

RUSSIA
Moscow. Universitet. *Biblioteka.*
Краткий указатель литературы по истории Московского университета за 50 лет Советской власти. ₁Составители: Э. А. Сендерович и М. Г. Степанова. Москва₁ Изд-во Московского университета, 1967.

39 p. 21 cm. 0.6

Cover title.
At head of title: Научная библиотека им. А. М. Горького.

Respublikanskaia mezhvuzovskaia nauchno-metodicheskaia konferentsiia po pedagogike i metodike prepodavaniia gumanitarnykh distsiplin, Grodno, 1969.
Тезисы докладов Республиканской межвузовской научно-методической конференции по педагогике и методике преподавания гуманитарных дисциплин. (18-19 дек. 1969 г.) Гродно, 1969.
178 p. 20 cm.
At head of title: Министерство высшего и среднего специального образования БССР. Гродненский государственный педагогический институт имени Янки Купалы.
Edited by B. M. Fikh.

SINGAPORE

Singapore (City). University. Library.
Academic exercises, theses, and dissertations submitted to the University of Singapore and deposited in the University of Singapore Library, 1947-1969. Singapore, 1969 ₁i. e. 1970₁

50, 12, 16 p. 33 cm.
Errata slip inserted.

SLOVENIA
Kokole, Jože.
Bibliografija doktorskih disertacij univerze in drugih visokošolskih in znanstvenih ustanov v Ljubljani 1920-1968. Ljubljana, ₁Univerza₁ 1969.

232 p. 24 cm.
Introduction, indexes and table of contents also in English.

SOUTH CAROLINA

Clemson University. *Graduate School.*
Abstracts of dissertations and theses, July 1, 1962–June 30, 1965. Clemson, S. C. ₁1966?₁

140 p. 23 cm.

TAIWAN
Chung yang t'u shu kuan, T'ai-pei.
(Chung-hua min kuo po shih shuo shih lun wên mu lu)

中華民國博士碩士論文目錄　國立中央圖書館主編　₁林愛芳等編輯　台北　中華叢書編審委員會　臺灣書店總經銷　民國59 i. e. 1970₁

2, 272 p. 21 cm. (國立中央圖書館目錄叢刊第3輯) (中華叢書)

Cover title.
本目著錄民國三十八年至五十七年間國內博士碩士論文及國軍派遣國外深造人員所撰學位論文(五十八年編輯時續收到該年部份資料故亦予著錄)

TEXAS

St. Mary's University, San Antonio. Graduate School.
Theses abstracts, June 1966–May 1971: master of arts in economics, English, history, political science, psychology, theology. Theses titles: 1971-1972. San Antonio ₁1972₁

xi, 90 p. 28 cm. (Its Selected papers, v. 10, no. 1)

St. Mary's University, San Antonio. Graduate School.
Theses abstracts, June 1966–May 1971, Master of Business Administration, Master of Science. ₁John C. Broadhurst, editor₁ San Antonio ₁1971₁

ix, 68 p. 28 cm. (Its Selected papers, v. 9, no. 1)

Texas Christian University, Forth Worth.
Theses and dissertations accepted by Texas Christian University: the Graduate School and Brite Divinity School, 1909-1972. Centennial ed. Fort Worth, 1973.

xiv, 166 p. 23 cm.

Texas. *Commission on Higher Education.*
Degrees awarded by program, by level, by subject area, 1959-60 to 1963-64; fifty-three colleges and universities in Texas. ₁Austin?₁ 1965.

141 p. 22 x 36 cm.

UNITED STATES

Albion College, *Albion, Mich. Library.*
Masters theses, honors theses, and other undergraduate research papers housed in Stockwell Memorial Library: 1890–1963 [by Max Langham, librarian. Albion, Mich., °1964]

1 v. (unpaged) 28 cm.

American doctoral dissertations. 1965/66–
[Ann Arbor, Mich.]

v. 29 cm. annual.

Vols. for 1965/66– issued by University Microfilms (vols. for 1965/66–1966/67, by its Library Service).
Compiled for the Association of Research Libraries.
Previously issued as the 13th no. in the vols. of Dissertation abstracts.

Li, Tze-chung, 1927–
A list of doctoral dissertations by Chinese students in the United States, 1961–1964. Chicago, Chinese-American Education Foundation, 1967.

viii, 84 p. 25 cm.

Continuation of A guide to doctoral dissertations by Chinese students in America, 1905–1960, compiled by Tung-li Yuan.

WISCONSIN

Wisconsin. University. *University-Industry Research Program.*
The University of Wisconsin directory of research in the humanities and social sciences. 1966–
[Madison]

v. 28 cm.

Wisconsin. University, *Milwaukee.*
Bibliography of research and creative activities. [Milwaukee] 1968.

viii, 171 p. 23 cm.

WYOMING

Wyoming. University. Graduate School.
Titles of masters' theses, August 1963–January 1972. Titles of doctoral theses, August 1965–August 1971. Laramie, 1972.
80 p. 26 cm. (University of Wyoming publications, v. 38, no. 1–2)
The list of masters' theses continues the list in v. 28, no. 3 (p. 23–173) of the series. The doctoral list, continuing the list in v. 31, no. 3 (p. 53–147), is the last to be published in this series; post-August 1971 theses are carried by International dissertation abstracts.

YUGOSLAVIA

Belgrad. Univerzitet.
Bibliografija doktorskih disertacija, 1951–1963. [Tekst pripremila i obradila: Milica Dodić. Beograd] Publikacija Rektorata Univerziteta, Odsek za nastavu i naučni rad, [predgovor 1964]

109 p. 24 cm.

At head of title: Beogradski univerzitet.

Belgrad. Univerzitet. *Biblioteka.*
Popis radova nastavnika i saradnika Beogradskog univerziteta u toku 1964. g. Beograd, Universzitet, 1966.

442, [2] p. 24 cm.

Belgrad. Univerzitet. *Biblioteka.*
Spisak prinova—rukopisne doktorske disertacije. Januar–decembar 1965. godine. [Beograd] Univerzitetska biblioteka "Svetozar Marković," [1966].

[3], 90 p. 21 cm.

Referativni bilten doktorskih disertacija, 1–
1966–
[Beograd]

no. in v. 30 cm.

No. 1– published by Savezna privredna komora and Institut za naučno-tehničku dokumentaciju i informacije (with Savezni fond za finansiranje naučnih delatnosti, no. 7–)

Savezni fond za finansiranje naučnih delatnosti.
Finansiranje naučnoistraživačke delatnosti. Dokumentalistička obrada radova finansiranih po programima 1960.–1964. godine. Beograd, Savezni fond za finansiranje naučnih delatnosti; Savezna privredna komora; Institut za naučno-tehničku dokumentaciju i informacije, 1967–

v. (loose-leaf) 30 cm.

Cover title.
CONTENTS: 1. Osnovne prirodne nauke.—2. Tehničke nauke.—3. Poljoprivredno šumarske i veterinarske nauke.—4. Medicinske nauke.

Skopje, Yugoslavia. Univerzitet.
Библиографија на докторските дисертации на Универзитетот во Скопје. Bibliography of the doctoral dissertations defended at the University of Skopje. Скопје, Издание на Универзитетот, 1969.

28 p. 24 cm.

DIVORCE
    see also Marriage

Israel, Stanley.
A bibliography on divorce, compiled and edited by Stan Israel. New York, Bloch Pub. Co. [1974]

xiv, 300 p. 22 cm.

Israel, Stanley, comp.
The complete bibliography on divorce. Compiled and edited by Stanley Israel. Foreword by Steven M. Greenberg. [n. p.] 1972.

1 v. (unpaged) 28 cm.

McKenney, Mary, 1946–
Divorce : a selected annotated bibliography / by Mary McKenney. — Metuchen, N. J. : Scarecrow Press, 1975.

vi, 157 p. ; 22 cm.

DJAKARTA

Surjomihardjo, Abdurrachman.
Sedjarah, masjarakat dan perkembangan kota Djakarta dalam bibliografi, 1900–1968. [Djakarta] 1970.

48 l. 28 cm. (Lembaga Research Kebudajaan Nasional. Terbitan tak berkala, seri no. II/3)

DJORDJEVIC, VLADAN see Đorđević, Vladan

DLABAČ, BOHUMÍR JAN

Křivský, Pavel.
Bohumír Jan Dlabač. (1758–1820). Lit. pozůstalost. Zprac. Pavel Křivský. Praha, Lit. archív Památníku nár. písemnictví, rozmn. Ruch, Liberec, 1971.

25, [1] p. 21 cm. (Edice inventářů, čís. 263)

DOBIE, JAMES FRANK

McVicker, Mary Louise.
The writings of J. Frank Dobie; a bibliography. Introd. by Harry H. Ransom. ₁1st ed.₁ Lawton ₁Okla.₁ Museum of the Great Plains ₁1968₁

xv, 258 p. facsims., ports. 24 cm.

DÖBLIN, ALFRED

Peitz, Wolfgang.
Alfred-Döblin-Bibliographie,1905–1966. Freiburg i. Br., Becksmann, 1968.

99 p. 21 cm. (Materialien zur deutschen Literatur, Bd. 1)

DOBRÉE FAMILY

Rouzeau, Léon.
Inventaire des papiers Dobrée, 1771–1896 ... Archives départementales de la Loire-Atlantique ... Nantes, Bibliothèque municipale, 1968.

90 p. geneal. table. 21 cm.

DOBROVSKÝ, JOSEF

Krbec, Miloslav.
Josef Dobrovský. Bibliographie der Veröffentlichungen von Josef Dobrovský. ₁Autoři:₁ Miloslav Krbec – Miroslav Laiske. Vorwort: Eduard Petrů. 1. vyd. Praha, Státní pedagogické nakladatelství, 1970–

v. port., facsims. 24 cm. (Series slavica, 1

DOBSON, AUSTIN

Dobson, Alban, 1885–   *comp.*
A bibliography of the first editions of published and privately printed books and pamphlets by Austin Dobson. With a pref. by Sir Edmund Gosse. New York, B. Franklin ₁1970₁

xii, 88 p. illus., facsims. 24 cm. (Essays in literature and criticism, no. 78)

Burt Franklin bibliography and reference series, no. 354.
Reprint of the 1925 ed.

Murray, Francis Edwin, *fl.* 1894–1900.
A bibliography of Austin Dobson. New York, B. Franklin ₁1968₁

xiii, 174 p. 24 cm. (Burt Franklin bibliography and reference series, 163)

Reprint of the 1900 ed.

DOCTORS see Physicians

DOCUMENTATION
see also Library science

Deutsche Gesellschaft für Dokumentation. *Bibliothek und Dokumentationsstelle.*
Deutschsprachiges Schrifttum zur Dokumentation. German language literature on documentation. Stand: 1. Aug. 1969. Frankfurt/M., Deutsche Gesellschaft f. Dokumentation, Bibliothek u. Dokumentationsstelle, 1969.

32 p. 30 cm.

Holzbauer, Herbert.
Mechanized bibliography of documentation and information sciences. Compiled by H. Holzbauer. Rev. ed. Washington, U. S. Dept. of the Interior, Dept. Library,

1967.

1, 157, ₁17₁ p. 27 cm.

Cover title.
"This bibliography represents a special collection maintained by the assistant director of the Department Library."

International Federation for Documentation.
75 years of FID publications: a bibliography, 1895–1970. The Hague, 1970.

70 p. 29 cm. (Its FID 469)

Rost, Gottfried.
Bibliothek und Dokumentation; eine bibliographische Grundlage für die Diskussion über ein einheitliches Informationssystem. Leipzig ₁Deutsche Bücherei₁ 1964.

34 p. 21 cm. (Bibliographischer Informationsdienst der Deutschen Bücherei, Nr. 5)

Verri, Gilda Maria Whitaker.
Normas para um serviço de documentação. Recife, Associação Pernambucana de Bibliotecários, 1968.

46 p. 24 cm. (Documentos da APEB, no. 1)

Issued also in Boletim, v. 4, n.° 1–2, 66/67 of Associação Pernambucana de Bibliotecários.

DODECANESE

Mavris, Nicholas G
Δωδεκανησιακὴ βιβλιογραφία, ὑπὸ Νικ. Γ. Μαυρῆ. Ἀθῆναι, 1965–

v. 26 cm. (Δωδεκανησιακὴ Ἱστορικὴ καὶ Λαογραφικὴ Ἑταιρεία. Δημοσίευμα ἀριθ. 1)

«Προσθῆκαι»: ₁2₁ p. inserted in v. 1.

CONTENTS.—τ. 1. Βιβλιογραφίαι, βιβλιοθῆκαι, γενικαὶ πραγματεῖαι, γεωλογία, χλωρίς, πανίς, ἐκκλησία, λαογραφία, γλωσσολογία, τοπωνυμία, ἐκπαίδευσις, ἰατρικά, νομικά, οἰκονομία.

DODGSON, CHARLES LUTWIDGE

Smith, Robert Dennis Hilton, 1903–
Alice one hundred; being a catalogue in celebration of the 100th birthday of Alice's adventures in Wonderland. ₁Compiled by R. D. Hilton Smith₁ Victoria, B. C., Adelphi Book Shop, 1966.

77 p. illus. 24 cm.

Annotated catalogue of books, pamphlets, leaflets and recordings, dating from 1858–1965, of works by and about C. L. Dodgson, purchased for the Library of the University of British Columbia by the graduating class of 1925.
"Bibliographies cited in catalogue notes": p. ₁6₁

Williams, Sidney Herbert.
The Lewis Carroll handbook, being a new version of a handbook of the literature of the Rev. C. L. Dodgson, by Sidney Herbert Williams and Falconer Madan. Rev., augm. and brought up to 1970 by Roger Lancelyn Green. Folkstone ₁Eng.₁ Dawsons of Pall Mall, 1970 ₁°1962₁

xv, 307 p. illus., facsims., ports. 23 cm.

Williams, Sidney Herbert.
The Lewis Carroll handbook; being a new version of A handbook of the literature of the Rev. C. L. Dodgson, by Sidney Herbert Williams and Falconer Madan. First published in 1931, now rev., augm., and brought up to 1970 by Roger Lancelyn Green. New York, Barnes & Noble, 1970 ₁°1962₁

xv, 307 p. illus., facsims., ports. 23 cm.

DOGS

Jones, E   Gwynne.
A bibliography of the dog: books published in the English language, 1570–1965 ₍by₎ E. Gwynne Jones. London, Library Association, 1971.

431 p. 26 cm.

Spiegler, Paul Eppley.
The greyhound: an annotated bibliography. Washington, Orford Press ₍1971₎

vii, 28 p. 29 cm.

DOLEZ FAMILY

Wellens, Robert.
Inventaire des archives de la famille Dolez. Bruxelles, Archives générales du Royaume, 1969.

xi, 21 p. tables. 24 cm.

At head of title: Ministère de l'éducation nationale. Archives générales du royaume et Archives de l'État dans les provinces. Archives de l'État à Mons.

DOLPHINS

Truitt, Deborah.
Dolphins and porpoises: a comprehensive, annotated bibliography of the smaller Cetacea. Detroit, Gale Research Co. ₍1974₎

xi, 582 p. 22 cm.

Whitfield, William K
An annotated bibliography of dolphin and porpoise families Delphinidae and Platanistidae ₍by₎ William K. Whitfield, Jr. St. Petersburg, Marine Research Laboratory, Florida Dept. of Natural Resources, 1971.

vii, 104 p. 28 cm. (₍Florida Dept. of Natural Resources, Marine Research Laboratory₎ Special scientific report no. 26)

DOMESTIC SCIENCE   see   Home economics

DOMINICAN REPUBLIC

Grabendorff, Wolf, 1940–
Bibliographie zu Politik und Gesellschaft der Dominikanischen Republik; neuere Studien 1961–1971. München, Weltforum Verlag ₍1973₎

103 p. 22 cm. (Materialien zu Entwicklung und Politik, 3)

Hitt, Deborah S
A selected bibliography of the Dominican Republic: a century after the restoration of independence, by Deborah S. Hitt ₍and₎ Larman C. Wilson. Washington, American University, Center for Research in Social Systems, 1968.

v, 142 p. map 28 cm.

Wiarda, Howard J   1939–
Materials for the study of politics and government in the Dominican Republic, 1930–1966. Compiled, annotated and with an introd., by Howard J. Wiarda. ₍Edición en inglés y español. Santiago de los Caballeros₎ UCMM ₍1968₎

142 p. 19 cm. (Universidad Católica Madre y Maestra. Colección estudios, 5)

Cover title: Política y gobierno en la Republica Dominicana, 1930–1966.

DOMINICANS

Ariza S   , Alberto E
Bibliografía de la provincia dominicana de Colombia ₍por₎ Alberto E. Ariza S. ₍Bogotá, 1967₎

119 p. illus. 23 cm.

A continuation of a work by P. Andrés Mesanza y Ozaeta published under the same title in Caracas, 1929.

Axters, Stephanus Gérard, 1901–
Bibliotheca Dominicana Neerlandica manuscripta. 1224–1500. Door Stephanus G. Axters. Louvain, Bureaux de la R. H. E., Bibliothèque de l'Université ₍&₎ Publications universitaires de Louvain, 1970.

383 p. 25 cm. (Bibliothèque de la Revue d'histoire ecclésiastique, fasc. 49)

Robles, Laureano.
Escritores dominicos de la Corona de Aragón (Siglos XIII–XV) ... Salamanca ₍Imp. Calatrava₎ 1972.

304 p. 24 cm.

Latin or Spanish.

DON JUAN   see   Juan, Don

DON VALLEY, RUSSIA

Brigadirov, Nikolaĭ Grigor'evich.
История Дона. Указатель литературы. В 2-х ч. Ростов н/Д., Кн. изд., 1968–

v. 21 cm.

DONELAITIS, KRISTIJONAS

Lebedienė, E
Kristijono Donelaičio bibliografija. Vilnius, Vaga, 1964.

381 p. 17 cm.

DONIZETTI, GAETANO

Museo donizettiano.
Il Museo donizettiano di Bergamo. Bergamo, Centro di studi donizettiani, 1970.

273 p. plates. 23 cm.

DONNE, JOHN

Keynes, Sir Geoffrey Langdon, 1887–
A bibliography of Dr. John Donne, by Geoffrey Keynes. 4th ed. Oxford, Clarendon Press, 1973.

x, 400 p. illus. 26 cm.

Pirie, Robert S
John Donne, 1572-1631; a catalogue of the anniversary exhibition of first and early editions of his works held at the Grolier Club, February 15 to April 12, 1972, compiled by Robert S. Pirie. New York, Grolier Club ₍c1972₎

xv, 41 p. illus. 24 cm.

Cover title: A catalogue of the four hundredth anniversary exhibition of first and early editions of the works of John Donne.
Title on spine: John Donne: an anniversary exhibition.

Roberts, John Richard.
John Donne; an annotated bibliography of modern criticism, 1912–1967 ₍by₎ John R. Roberts. Columbia, University of Missouri Press, 1973.

323 p. 25 cm. (University of Missouri studies, 60)

ĐORĐEVIĆ, VLADAN

Serbia (Federated Republic, 1945–). Arhiv.
Vladan Djordjević, lični fond; 1844–1930. Beograd,
Arhiv Srbije, 1969.

165 p. 30 cm. (Its Inventar)

At head of title: Arhiv Srbije. Smiljka Djurić.

DORDOGNE, FRANCE (DEPT.)

Dordogne, France (Dept.). Archives départementales.
Guide des Archives de la Dordogne ₍par₎ Noël Becquart,
directeur. Périgueux, 1970.

118 p. illus. 24 cm.

Dordogne, France (Dept.) Archives départementales.
Répertoire numérique de la série M, administration générale, personnel et économie, période 1800–1940, dressé par
Noël Becquart ... Périgueux, Archives départementales de
la Dordogne, 1971.

xxviii, 103 p. 32 cm.

Dordogne, France (Dept.). Archives départementales.
Répertoire numérique de la série N: administration et
comptabilité départementales, période 1800–1940, dressé par
Noël Becquart, directeur des services d'archives. Perigueux,
1974.

44 p. 32 cm.

Dordogne, France (Dept.). Archives départementales.
Répertoire numérique de la série Z, fonds des sous-pré-
fectures, période 1800–1940, dressé par Noël Becquart, directeur des Services d'archives. Périgueux. 1973.

52 p. map. 32 cm.

Dordogne, *France (Dept.). Archives départementales.*
Répertoire numérique des registres paroissiaux et de l'état
civil jusqu'à l'an XIII, archives départementales, sous-série
5 E et archives communales, dressé par Noël Becquart, directeur des Services d'archives. Périgueux, Archives de la
Dordogne, 1968.

236 p. 31 cm.

DORN, EDWARD

Streeter, David.
A bibliography of Ed Dorn. New York, Phoenix Bookshop, 1973 ₍c1974₎

ii, 64 p. 22 cm. (The Phoenix bibliographies)

DORTMUND

Bieber, Hedwig, 1915–
Dortmund, westfälische Grossstadt im Revier. Bücher
aus u. über Dortmund, Westfalen u. d. Ruhrrevier 1947–
1967. Bücher Dortmunder Autoren. (Ein Auswahlverz.
Bearb. von Hedwig Bieber und Fritz Hüser. 2., wesentl.
erw. Aufl.) Dortmund (Stadtbücherei) 1968.

40 p. 21 cm.

DOSTOEVSKIĬ, FEDOR MIKHAĬLOVICH

Ф. М. Достоевский. Библиогр. произведений Ф. М.
Достоевского и литературы о нем. 1917–1965. ₍Вступит.
статья В. Акопджановой и Г. Пономаревой₎. Москва,
"Книга," 1968.

407 p., port. 22 cm.

At head of title: Государственный литературный музей.
Музей-квартира Ф. М. Достоевского.
By V. V. Akopdzhanova and others.

Grossman, Leonid Petrovich, 1888–1965.
₍Seminariĭ po Dostoevskomu₎
Семинарий по Достоевскому. Seminar on Dostoevsky,
₍by₎ L. P. Grossman. Letchworth, Prideaux Press, 1972.

₍2₎, 119 p. 23 cm. (Russian titles for the specialist, no. 32)

Petrovskaíà, Valentina Ivanovna.
₍Fedor Mikhaĭlovich Dostoevskiĭ₎
Федор Михайлович Достоевский. (1821–1881). Метод. и библиогр. материалы для б-к к 150-летию со дня
рождения великого писателя. Москва, 1971.

54 p. 20 cm.

At head of title: Государственная библиотека СССР имени
В. И. Ленина.

DOUBLE-BASS MUSIC

Grodner, Murray.
Comprehensive catalog of available literature for the
double bass. 3d ed. ₍Bloomington, Ind., Lemur Musical
Research, 1974₎

xxx, 163 p. 22 x 28 cm.

DOVER, NEW HAMPSHIRE

Tapley, Priscilla M
A check list of Dover, New Hampshire, imprints from
1826 to 1847, with a historical introduction, by Priscilla
M. Tapley. Washington, 1968.

iv, 94 l. 29 cm.

"Part of a research project, called the American Imprints In-
ventory."
Thesis (M. S. L. S.)—Catholic University.
Typescript (carbon copy)

DOWN'S SYNDROME see Mongolism

DOYLE, SIR ARTHUR CONAN

Bergman, Ted.
Sherlock Holmes; a bibliography enumerating and de-
scribing some of the original and variant editions of the
Swedish translations of Dr. John H. Watson's Sherlock
Holmes stories. ₍Stockholm₎ Baker Street Cab Lantern;
₍distributed by Ted Bergman₎ 1964–

v. mounted illus. 18 cm.

"Edition ... limited to seventyfive ₍sic₎ copies."

CONTENTS.—1. 1891–1930—

DRAINAGE

U. S. *Agricultural Research Service. Soil and Water Conservation Research Division.*
Drainage of agricultural land; an annotated bibliography
of selected references, 1956–1964. Washington, National
Agricultural Library, U. S. Dept. of Agriculture, 1968.

iii, 524 p. 26 cm. (U. S. National Agricultural Library. Library
list, no. 91)

Cover title.
"Brings up-to-date 'Drainage of agricultural land, a bibliogra-
phy ...' by E. G. Davis and M. L. Gould, published in May 1956 as
U. S. Department of Agriculture Miscellaneous publication no. 713."

Vinogradova, O   N
Эксплуатация мелиоративных осушительных систем. Библиогр. указ. отеч. литературы и иностр. за 1960–1970 гг. Москва, 1971.

64 p. 20 cm.

At head of title: Всесоюзная академия с.-х. наук имени В. И. Ленина. Центральная научная сельскохозяйственная библиотека.

Vries, C   A   de.
Drainage of agricultural land; a bibliography, compiled by C. A. de Vries and B. C. P. H. van Baak. Wageningen, International Institute for Land Reclamation and Improvement, 1966.

28 p. 24 cm. (International Institute for Land Reclamation and Improvement. Bibliography, 5)

DRAKE, CARL JOHN

Ruhoff, Florence A
Bibliography and index to scientific contributions of Carl J. Drake for the years 1914–1967 [by] Florence A. Ruhoff. Washington, Smithsonian Institution Press; [for sale by the Supt. of Docs., U. S. Govt. Print. Off.] 1968.

viii, 81 p. 24 cm. (U. S. National Museum. Bulletin 267)

DRAMA; THEATER
   see also Amateur theatricals;
   Children's plays; Puppets and puppet-
   plays; Religious drama; and under
   Dissertations, Academic

Chicorel, Marietta.
Chicorel theater index to plays in collections, anthologies, periodicals, and discs in England, edited by Marietta Chicorel. 1st ed. New York, Chicorel Library Pub. Corp. [1972]

466 p. 26 cm. (Her Chicorel index series, v. 3)

Half title: Plays in print and on records published in England.

Chicorel, Marietta.
Chicorel theater index to plays in periodicals. 1st ed. New York, Chicorel Library Pub. Corp., 1973.

500 p. 26 cm. (Her Chicorel index series, v. 8)

Covers periodicals chiefly from 1900 to the present time.

Chicorel theater index to plays in anthologies, periodicals, discs, and tapes. v. 1–
New York, Chicorel Library Pub. Co. [1970–

v. 27 cm.

Cumulated Dramatic index, 1909–1949; a cumulation of the F. W. Faxon Company's Dramatic index, edited by Frederick Winthrop Faxon, Mary E. Bates [and] Anne C. Sutherland. Cumulated by G. K. Hall & Co. Boston, G. K. Hall, 1965.

2 v. 37 cm.

A composite photographic reproduction of the actual entries as they were originally printed in the 41 annual volumes of the Dramatic index, which first appeared as part II of Faxon's Annual magazine subject index.

Drury, Francis Keese Wynkoop, 1878–1954.
Drury's Guide to best plays, by James M. Salem. 2d ed. Metuchen, N. J., Scarecrow Press, 1969.

512 p. 22 cm.

Esquer Torres, Ramón.
La colección dramática "El Teatro moderno." Madrid, Consejo Superior de Investigaciones Científicas, 1969.

xviii, 365 p. 23 cm. (Anejos de la revista Segismundo, 2)

CONTENTS: Introducción, por P. García Díez y R. Esquer Torres.—Bibliografía descriptiva.—Indices analíticos.

Filippi, Joseph de.
Essai d'une bibliographie générale du théâtre; ou, Catalogue raisonné de la bibliothèque d'un amateur, complétant le catalogue Soleinne. New York, B. Franklin [1967]
vii, 223 p. 23 cm. (Burt Franklin bibliography and reference series, no. 83)
"Un simple aperçu de ce qui a été publié depuis la Renaissance sur les arts du théâtre chez les diverses nations de l'Europe."
Preface signed: J. D. F.
Title on spine: Collection Soleinne.
"Originally published Paris 1861. Reprinted 1967."

Firkins, Ina Ten Eyck, 1866–1937, comp.
Index to plays, 1800–1926. New York, H. W. Wilson Co., 1927. [New York, AMS Press, 1971]

307 p. 27 cm.

Hayman, Ronald, 1932–
One hundred years of drama: a selected list. London, National Book League, 1972.

21 p. 21 cm.

Hoblitzelle Theatre Arts Library.
A guide to the theatre and drama collections at the University of Texas. Compiled by Fredrick J. Hunter, curator. Austin, Humanities Research Center, University of Texas, 1967.

84 p. illus., facsims., ports. 26 cm.

Hunter, Frederick James, 1916–
Drama bibliography; a short-title guide to extended reading in dramatic art for the English-speaking audience and students in theatre. Compiled by Frederick J. Hunter. Boston, G. K. Hall, 1971.

x, 239 p. front. 24 cm.

Ireland, Norma (Olin) 1907–
Index to full length plays 1944 to 1964. Boston, F. W. Faxon Co., 1965.

xxxii, 296 p. 23 cm. (Useful reference series, no. 92)

Continuation of Index to full length plays, by Ruth Gibbons Thomson.

Keller, Dean H
Index to plays in periodicals, by Dean H. Keller. Metuchen, N. J., Scarecrow Press, 1971.

558 p. 22 cm.

Lacroix, Paul, 1806–1884.
Bibliothèque dramatique de Pont de Vesle. Formée avec les débris des bibliothèques de Saint-Ange, de Crozat, de Mme de Pompadour, etc., continuée par Mme de Montesson, possédée depuis par M. de Soleinne. Augm. et remise en ordre par le bibliophile Jacob (Paul Lacroix) New York, B. Franklin [1965]
279 p. 23 cm. (Burt Franklin bibliography and reference series, no. 83)
At head of title: Alliance des arts.
Title on spine: Collection Soleinne.
Reprint of the edition published in Paris, 1847.

Mersand, Joseph E   1907–
Index to plays, with suggestions for teaching, by Joseph

Mersand. New York, Scarecrow Press, 1966.

114 p. 22 cm.

Ottemiller, John Henry, 1916–
Index to plays in collections; an author and title index to plays appearing in collections published between 1900 and 1962. 4th ed., rev. and enl. New York, Scarecrow Press, 1964.

370 p. 22 cm.

Ottemiller, John Henry, 1916–1968.
Ottemiller's Index to plays in collections; an author and title index to plays appearing in collections published between 1900 and mid-1970, by John M. Connor and Billie M. Connor. 5th ed., rev. and enl. Metuchen, N. J., Scarecrow Press, 1971.

xiii, 452 p. 22 cm.

Poyraz, Türkân.
Tiyatro bibliyografyası, 1859–1928. Hazırlıyanlar: Türkân Poyraz [ve] Nurnisa Tuğrul. Ankara, Millî Kütüphane, 1967.

xiv, 288 p. plates (facsim., ports.) 24 cm. (Millî Kütüphane yayınları)

Slevin, Gerald.
Drama in education; selected by Gerald Slevin. London, National Book League, 1971.

29 p. 21 cm.

Stratman, Carl Joseph, 1917–1972.
Bibliography of medieval drama. 2d ed., rev. and enl. New York, F. Unger [1972]

2 v. (xv, 1035 p.) 25 cm.

BIBLIOGRAPHIES

Stratman, Carl Joseph, 1917–
Dramatic play lists, 1591–1963, by Carl J. Stratman. [New York] New York Public Library, 1966.

44 p. 26 cm.

"Reprinted from the Bulletin of the New York Public Library, February, March, 1966."

CATALOGS

Groningen. Openbare Bibliotheek.
Katalogus van de toneelbibliotheek. [Groningen, Kwinkenplein 8, 1968]

6 v. 14½ x 21 cm.

CONTENTS.—1. Nederlandse en Vlaamse toneelstukken, hoorspelen, televisiespelen.—2. Engelse en Amerikaanse toneelstukken, televisiespelen, filmscenario's.—3. Duitse, Skandinavische, Oost Europese toneelstukken, hoorspelen, filmscenario's.—4. Griekse, Latijnse, Franse, Italiaanse, Spaanse, Oosterse toneelstukken, hoorspelen, filmscenario's.—5. Toneelkunst, geschiedenis van het theater en de toneelliteratuur.—6. Toneelstukken voor het amateurtoneel.

Hertfordshire County Library.
A catalogue of play-reading sets. Hertford, Hertfordshire County Library, 1970.

viii, 506 p. 26 cm.

National Drama Library.
Basic catalogue of the National Drama Library and first supplement to March, 1966. Bloemfontein, Public Library, 1966.

xi, 289 p. 21 cm.

English and Afrikaans.

New York (City) Public Library. *Research Libraries.*
Catalog of the theatre and drama collections. Boston, G. K. Hall, 1967.

21 v. 37 cm.

CONTENTS.—pt. 1. [A] Drama collection: author listing. 6 v. [B] Drama collection: listing by cultural origin. 6 v.—pt. 2. Theatre Collection: books on the theatre. 9 v.

Teatralia Zámecké knihovny b Křimic. 1. díl. Bibliografický soupis. 2. díl. Rejstříky. Zprac. Jitka Šimáková a Eduarda Macháčková. 1. vyd. Praha, Divadelní ustav, rozmn. SČT, 1970.

2 v. (1007 p.) 6 p. of plates. 20 cm. (Prameny k dějinam českého divadla, sv. 4)

Introduction also in French and German.

Teatralia Zámecké knihovny z Radenína. Zprac. kolektiv pracovníků Oddělení zámeckých knihoven Knihovny Národního muzea v Praze za vedení Pravoslava Kneidla. Praha, Národní muzeum, 1962–70.
3 v. facsims. 21 cm. (Knihovna Národního muzea v Praze. Katalogy a inventáře, č. 5–6, 11)
Introduction also in German.
Includes bibliographies.
CONTENTS: 1. Radenínská zámecká knihovna a Filip Kolovrat Krakovský.—2. Bohemika Zámecké knihovny z Radenína.—3. Rejstříky. Jitka Šimáková, Eduarda Macháčková, Anežka Badurová.

United College, Hongkong. Library.
(Lien ho shu yüan t'u shu kuan kuan ts'ang Chung-kuo hsien tai hsi chü t'u shu mu lu)
聯合書院圖書館館藏中國現代戲劇圖書目錄
香港　香港中文大學聯合書院圖書館編印　1967.

ii, 109 p. 28 cm.

Cover title:中國現代戲劇圖書目錄

Worcestershire County Library.
Classified catalogue of the play set collection. Worcester (Loves Grove, Castle St., Worcester WR1 3BY), Worcestershire County Library, 1971.

(5), 103 p. 26 cm.

Cover title: Catalogue of play sets.

HISTORY AND CRITICISM

Adelman, Irving, *comp.*
Modern drama; a checklist of critical literature on 20th century plays, by Irving Adelman and Rita Dworkin. Metuchen, N. J., Scarecrow Press, 1967.

xvii, 370 p. 22 cm.

Baker, Blanch (Merritt) 1884–
Dramatic bibliography; an annotated list of books on the history and criticism of the drama and stage and on the allied arts of the theatre, compiled by Blanch M. Baker. New York, B. Blom, 1968.

xiv, 320 p. 26 cm.

Reprint of the 1933 ed.

Baker, Blanch (Merritt) 1884–
Theatre and allied arts; a guide to books dealing with the history, criticism, and technic of the drama and theatre and related arts and crafts, by Blanch M. Baker. New York, B. Blom [1967]

xiii, 536 p. 23 cm.

"First published 1952."
"Based on the author's ... Dramatic bibliography."

Breed, Paul Francis, 1916–
Dramatic criticism index; a bibliography of commentaries on playwrights from Ibsen to the avant-garde, compiled and edited by Paul F. Breed and Florence M. Sniderman. Detroit, Gale Research Co. ₁1972₎

1022 p. 23 cm.

Cheshire, David F.
Theatre: history, criticism, and reference. ₁Hamden, Conn.₎ Archon Books ₁1967₎

131 p. 23 cm. (The Readers guide series)

Cheshire, David F.
Theatre; history, criticism and reference ₁by₎ David Cheshire. London, Bingley, 1967.

131 p. 22½ cm. (The readers guide series)

Coleman, Arthur, 1926–
Drama criticism ₁by₎ Arthur Coleman and Gary R. Tyler. Denver, A. Swallow ₁1966–71₎

2 v. 23 cm.

Vol. 2 has imprint: Chicago, Swallow Press.
CONTENTS: v. 1. A checklist of interpretation since 1940 of English and American plays.—v. 2. A checklist of interpretation since 1940 of classical and continental plays.

Mikhail, E   H
Comedy and tragedy; a bibliography of critical studies, by E. H. Mikhail. Troy, N. Y., Whitston Pub. Co., 1972.

vi, 54 p. 22 cm.

Palmer, Helen H
European drama criticism, compiled by Helen H. Palmer and Anne Jane Dyson. Hamden, Conn., Shoe String Press, 1968.
460 p. 23 cm.
—— —— Supplement I–   ₁Hamden, Conn.₎ Shoe String Press, 1970–
v. 23 cm.

Salem, James M
A guide to critical reviews, by James M. Salem. New York, Scarecrow Press, 1966–

v.   21 cm.

Vol. 2–   have imprint: Metuchen, N.J., Scarecrow Press, 1967–
CONTENTS: pt. 1. American drama from O'Neill to Albee.—pt. 2. The musical from Rodgers and Hart to Lerner and Loewe.—pt. 3. British & continental drama from Ibsen to Pinter—pt. 4. The screenplay, from The jazz singer to Dr. Strangelove. 2 v.

Salem, James M
A guide to critical reviews, by James M. Salem. 2d ed. Metuchen, N. J., Scarecrow Press, 1973–

v. 22 cm.

CONTENTS: pt. 1. American drama, 1909–1969.

Samples, Gordon.
How to locate criticism and reviews of plays and films. ₁San Diego₎ San Diego State, Malcolm A. Love Library, 1971.

23 l. 28 cm.

PERIODICALS

Laiske, Miroslav.
Divadelní periodika v Čechách a na Moravě, 1772–1963. Praha, Divadelní ústav, 1967–

v. 21 cm.

Summary in German and French.

CONTENTS.—1. Divadelní časopisy a programy.

THEATRICAL PRODUCTION, ETC.

Angotti, Vincent L.
Source materials in the field of theatre: an annotated bibliography and subject index to the microfilm collection, by Vincent L. Angotti. Ann Arbor, Mich., XEROX, Education Division, University Microfilms Library Services ₁1967₎

ix, 73 p. 23 cm.

A complementary guide to the microfilm collection compiled by University Microfilms, Inc.

Biddulph, Helen R
Bibliography of books, pamphlets, and magazines relating to community theatre, compiled by Helen R. Biddulph and Julia H. Mailer for American Community Theatre Association, a Division of the American Educational Theatre Association. ₁Washington? 1966₎

21 p. 29 cm.

Dodrill, Charles W
Theatre management selected bibliography, by Charles W. Dodrill. ₁Westerville? Ohio, °1966₎

10 l. 28 cm.

"Prepared for Theatre Management Project, American Educational Theatre Association, Inc."

DuBois, William R
English and American stage productions: an annotated checklist of prompt books, 1800–1900, from the Nisbet-Snyder drama collection, Northern Illinois University Libraries. Compiled by William R. DuBois. Boston, G. K. Hall, 1973.

xiv, 524 p. 26 cm.

Leppla, Rupprecht, 1900–
Theater unserer Zeit im Schrifttum der Gegenwart. 2. verm. Ausg. ₁Bonn, Bund der Theatergemeinden₎ 1968.

60 l. 30 cm. (Arbeitspapier des Bundes der Theatergemeinden, 8)

"Die 1. Ausgabe erschien 1966 als Arbeitspapier zu den 'Frankfurter Theatergesprächen 1966,' einer Arbeitstagung des Bundes der Theatergemeinden e. V. zum Thema 'Das Theater in der Publizistik.'"

Library Association. *County Libraries Group.*
Readers' guide to books on stagecraft and the theatre. ₁New ed.₎ London, Library Association (County Libraries Group) 1965.

30 p. 18½ cm. (*Its* Readers' guides, new ser., no. 85)

"Compiled by D. F. Cheshire."

Lowe, Claudia Jean.
A guide to reference and bibliography for theatre research. ₁Columbus₎ Office of Educational Services, Ohio State University Libraries, 1971.

iii, 137 p. 28 cm.

Pence, James Harry.
The magazine and the drama; an index. New York, B. Franklin ₁1970₎

xiii, 190 p. 19 cm. (Burt Franklin research & source works series, 573) (Theatre & drama series, 12)

Reprint of the 1896 ed.

Queensland. Public Library, Brisbane. Country Extension Service.

The theater ₍prepared by the₎ Country Extension Service₍ State Library of Queensland. Brisbane, Country Extension Service, State Library of Queensland, 1972.

27 p. 28 cm.

Sumner, Mark Reese.

A selected bibliography on outdoor drama, by Mark R. Sumner. Chapel Hill, Institute of Outdoor Drama, University of North Carolina, 1965.

9, 4 l. 29 cm.

TRANSLATIONS

Horn-Monval, Madeleine.

Répertoire bibliographique des traductions et adaptations françaises du théâtre étranger du xv° siècle à nos jours. Préf. de Julien Cain. Paris, Centre national de la recherche scientifique, 1958-67.

8 v. 27 cm.

Cover title: Traductions et adaptations françaises du théâtre étranger.
Vol. 8 has title: Répertoire bibliographique des traductions et adaptations françaises du théâtre étranger du xv° siècle à nos jours conservées dans les bibliothèques et archives de Paris.
Contents.—t. 1. Théâtre grec antique.—t. 2. Théâtre latin antique. Théâtre latin médiéval et moderne.—t. 3. Théâtre italien. Opéras italiens (Livrets)—t. 4. Théâtre espagnol. Théâtre de l'Amérique latine. Théâtre portugais.—t. 5. Théâtre anglais. Théâtre américain.—t. 6. Théâtre allemand, autrichien, suisse.—t. 7. Théâtre scandinave. Théâtre flamand. Théâtre hollandais, pays nordiques.—t. 8. Théâtres des pays slaves et autres pays européens. Théâtres des pays d'Asie et d'Afrique. Addenda au Théâtre américain.

———— Index général des auteurs dramatiques étrangers traduits et cités dans les 8 tomes du Repertoire. Paris, Centre national de la recherche scientifique, 1967.

31 p. 27 cm.

Műsorajánlás a városi és falusi műkedvelő színjátszó csoportok számára. ₍București₎, 1973.

54 p. 21 cm.

At head of title: Szocialista Művelődési Tanács. A Népi Alkotások és a Művészeti Tömegmozgalom Irányító Központja.

Patterson, Charlotte A

Plays in periodicals; an index to English language scripts in twentieth century journals. Compiled by Charlotte A. Patterson. Boston, G. K. Hall, 1970.

ix, 240 p. 27 cm.

AFRICA

East, N   B

African theatre: a checklist of critical materials, edited by N. B. East. New York, Africana Pub. Corp. ₍1970₎

47 p. 26 cm.

McNeive, Kay.

African theatre bibliography. ₍Lawrence? Kan.₎ 1966.

11 l. 28 cm.

Caption title.

ARGENTINE REPUBLIC

La Crítica teatral argentina (1880–1962) Buenos Aires, Fondo Nacional de las Artes ₍1900₎

78 p. 28 cm. (Bibliografía argentina de artes y letras. Compilaciones especiales)

AUSTRALIA

Armidale, Australia. University of New England. Library.

Australian plays in manuscript; a check list of the Campbell Howard collection held in the University of New England Library. Edited by S. M. Apted. Pref. by A. C. M. Howard. Armidale, N. S. W., University of New England Library, 1968.

36 p. 21 cm. (Its Publication no. 1)

AUSTRIA

Schindler, Otto G

Theaterliteratur: Ein bibliographischer Behelf für das Studium der Theaterwissenschaft. Mit einem Anhang: Bibliographie zur österreichischen Theatergeschichte; zusammengestellt von Fritz Fuhrich. ₍2. Ausg.₎ Wien, 1972.

vi, 151 p. 29 cm.

BRAZIL

São Paulo, Brazil (City). Universidade. Departamento de Biblioteconomia e Documentação.

Bibliografia sobre teatro paulista. Edição preliminar. São Paulo, Universidade de São Paulo, Escola de Comunicações e Artes ₍Departamento de Jornalismo e Editoração₎ 1972.

103 l. 21 cm. (Série Biblioteconomia e documentação, 2)

CANADA

Dominion Drama Festival. *Canadian Plays Committee.*

Canadian full-length plays in English: a preliminary annotated catalogue, edited by W. S. Milne. ₍Ottawa₎ Dominion Drama Festival ₍1964₎

viii, 47 p. 25 cm.

———— Supplement. ₍Ottawa₎ Dominion Drama Festival, 1966.

vii, 89 p. 25 cm.

CHINA
see also under Poetry - China

Chou, Ming-t'ai, *ed.*

讀曲類稿 ₍周明泰編纂 再版 香港 龍門書店 1969₎

25, 141 p. 27 cm.

Hongkong. University. Centre of Asian Studies.

₍Yüeh chü chü pen mu lu₎

粵劇劇本目錄 黃兆漢₍著₎ A catalogue of Cantonese opera scripts, ₍by₎ Wong Shiu Hon. ₍Hong Kong₎ 1971.

xii, 59 p. 27 cm. (Centre of Asian Studies bibliographies and research guides, 3)

At head of title: 香港大學亞洲研究中心所藏
Text in Chinese, with prefatory matter also in English.

Huang, Wên-yang, b. 1736, ed.

(Ch'ü hai tsung mu t'i yao)

曲海總目提要 ₍46卷₎ 附索引 ₍黃文暘撰 董康纂輯 台北 新興書局 民國56 i. e. 1967₎

3 v. (2, 6, 3, 29, 2173 p.) 22 cm.

Reprint of 北京人民文學出版社 1959 ed.

Lo, Chin-t'ang, *ed.*

中國戲曲總目彙編　羅錦堂編著　香港　萬有圖書公司 1966.

368 p. 22 cm.

Added title on verso of t. p.: A comprehensive bibliography of Chinese drama.

CZECHOSLOVAK REPUBLIC

Boučková, Hana.

Paměti českých herců. Výběrová bibliografie. Praha, Měst. knihovna, rozmn., 1970.

11 p. 20 cm. (Metodické texty a bibliografie MK)

Repčák, Jozef.

Bibliografický príspevok k dejinám divadla v Prešove do r. 1918. Zost.: Jozef Repčák. Prešov, ŠVK, rozmn., 1971.

[2], 50, [1] l. 20 cm.

DENMARK

Danske dramatikeres forbund.

Danske dramatikeres forbund 1968. En fortegnelse over medlemmernes arbejder. [Ny udg.] København [1968]

199 p. 23 cm.

Earlier editions published under title: Danske dramatikere.

FRANCE

Léris, Antoine de, 1723-1795.

Dictionnaire portatif historique et littéraire des théâtres. (Réimpr. de l'éd. de Paris, 1763.) Genève, Slatkine Reprints, 1970.

iv, xxxiv, 732 p. 22 cm.

On spine: Dictionnaire des théâtres.

Maupoint, avocat.

Bibliotèque des théâtres, contenant le catalogue alphabétique des pièces dramatiques, opera, parodies et opera comiques, et le tems de leurs représentations avec des anecdotes sur la plûpart des pièces contenues en ce recüeil et sur la vie des auteurs, musiciens et acteurs. Paris, L.-F. Prault, 1733; Paris, l'Arche du livre, 1970.

373 p. illus. 21 cm.

Photo-offset reprint.

Petit de Julleville, Louis, 1841-1900.

Histoire du théâtre en France. Répertoire du théâtre comique en France au Moyen-Age [par] L. Petit de Julleville. Genève, Slatkine Reprints, 1967.

vi, 411 p. 24 cm.

"Réimpression de l'édition de Paris, 1886."

Rolland, Joachim, 1888-

Le théâtre comique en France avant le 15ᵉ siècle. ⟨Essai bibliographique.⟩ (Les origines latines du théâtre comique en France. Essai bibliographique.) Genève, Slatkine Reprints, 1972.

135, 219 p. 23 cm.

Reprint of the Paris 1926 and 1927 editions.

Soleinne, Martineau de, *d.* 1842.

Bibliothèque dramatique de Monsieur de Soleinne. Catalogue rédigé par P. L. Jacob, bibliophile (Paul Lacroix) New York, B. Franklin [1965]

6 v. in 5. 23 cm. (Burt Franklin bibliography and reference series, no. 83)

At head of title: Alliance des arts.

Title on spine: Collection Soleinne [sic]

Vol. 5 has only special title.

Reprint of the edition published in Paris, 1843-45.

Contents. — v. 1. Théâtre oriental. Théâtre grec et romain. Théâtre latin moderne. Ancien théâtre français. Théâtre français moderne depuis Jodelle jusqu'à Racine.—v. 2. Théâtre français depuis Racine jusqu'à Victor Hugo. Théâtre des provinces. Théâtre français à l'etranger. — v. 3. Suite du théâtre français. Recueils manuscrits. Recueils divers. Théâtre de la cour. Ballets. Répertoires des théâtres de Paris. Théâtre burlesque. Théâtres de société. Proverbes dramatiques. Théâtre d'éducation. Pièces satiriques. Pièces en patois. Dialogues.—v. 4. Théâtre italien. Théâtres espagnol et portugais. Théâtre allemand. Théâtre anglais. Théâtres suédois, flamand et hollandais, russe et polonais, turc, grec et valaque.—v. 5. Écrits relatifs au théâtre. Estampes et dessins. Appendice: Autographes. Livres doubles et livres omis. Corrections et additions.—v. 6. Table générale du catalogue de la Bibliothèque dramatique de M. de Soleinne, rédigée par Goizet. Prix des livres du premier volume de la Bibliothèque dramatique de M. de Soleinne.

—— Table des pièces de théâtre décrites dans le catalogue de la Bibliothèque de M. de Soleinne, par Charles Brunet. New York, B. Franklin [1965]

491 p. 23 cm. (Burt Franklin bibliography and reference series, no. 83)

Reprint of the edition published in Paris, 1914.

Thompson, Lawrence Sidney, 1916-

A bibliography of French plays on microcards, by Lawrence S. Thompson. Hamden, Conn., Shoe String Press, 1967.

vii, 689 p. 22 cm.

GERMANY

Binger, Norman.

A bibliography of German plays on microcards. Hamden, Conn., Shoe String Press, 1970.

224 p. 26 cm.

GREAT BRITAIN

Arnott, James Fullarton, 1914-

English theatrical literature, 1559-1900: a bibliography; incorporating Robert W. Lowe's 'A bibliographical account of English theatrical literature', published in 1888, by James Fullarton Arnott and John William Robinson. London, Society for Theatre Research, 1970.

xxii, 486 p. 26 cm.

"The inclusion of books and editions that have come to light since the publication of the original work, and the extension of the period covered to the end of the 19th century have so enlarged the work as to make it virtually a new compilation"—book jacket.

Baker, David Erskine, 1730-1767.

Biographia dramatica; or, A companion to the playhouse: containing historical and critical memoirs, and original anecdotes of British and Irish dramatic writers, from the commencement of our theatrical exhibitions ... Originally compiled, to the year 1764, by David Erskine Baker. Continued thence to 1782, by Isaac Reed, and brought down to the end of November 1811, with very considerable additions and improvements throughout, by Stephen Jones.

London, Printed for Longman, Hurst, Rees, Orme, and Brown [and others] 1812. New York, AMS Press, 1966.

3 v. 23 cm.

First published anonymously in 1764 under title: The companion to the playhouse.

Baker, David Erskine, 1730-1767.

Biographia dramatica. (Unveränderter Abdruck der 1812 in London erschienenen Ausg.) Graz, Akademische

Druck- und Verlagsanstalt, 1967.

3 v. in 4. 19 cm.

Original t. p. reads: Biographia dramatica; or, A companion to the playhouse. Continued ... to 1782 by Isaac Reed, and ... to ... 1811 ... by Stephen Jones.

Coleman, Edward Davidson, 1891–1939.
The Bible in English drama; an annotated list of plays including translations from other languages from the beginnings to 1931. New York, New York Public Library [1968]

xiii, 212 p. 24 cm.

Reprint of the 1931 ed., with A survey of recent major plays, 1968, by I. Sheffer.

Eldredge, H J *comp.*
"The Stage" cyclopædia; a bibliography of plays. An alphabetical list of plays and other stage pieces of which any record can be found since the commencement of the English stage, together with descriptions, authors' names, dates and places of production, and other useful information, comprising in all nearly 50,000 plays, and extending over a period of upwards of 500 years. Compiled by Reginald Clarence. New York, B. Franklin [1970]
503 p. 21 cm. (Theatre & drama series 13)
Burt Franklin bibliography & reference series 374.
Reprint of the 1909 ed.

Esher, Eng. Surrey County Library.
Plays in sets in the Surrey County Library: a classified list. Esher (Sy.), Surrey County Library, 1965 [i. e. 1966]

[vii], 303 p. tables. 21½ cm.

Greg, Sir Walter Wilson, 1875–1959.
A bibliography of the English printed drama to the Restoration, by W. W. Greg. London, Bibliographical Society, 1970.
4 v. (1752 p.) illus., facsims. 29 cm. (Bibliographical Society. Illustrated monographs, no. 24)
Reprint of 1st ed. published in 1939.
CONTENTS: v. 1. Stationers' records; plays to 1616: nos. 1–349.—v. 2. Plays; 1617–1689; nos. 350–836. Latin plays. Lost plays.—v. 3. Collections, appendix, reference lists.—v. 4. Introduction, additions, corrections, index of titles.

Greg, *Sir* **Walter Wilson,** 1875–1959.
A list of English plays written before 1643 and printed before 1700. New York, Haskell House, 1969.

xi, 158 p. 24 cm.

Reprint of the 1900 ed.

Greg, Sir Walter Wilson, 1875–1959.
A list of English plays written before 1643 and printed before 1700. St. Clair Shores, Mich., Scholarly Press, 1972.

xi, 158 p. 22 cm.

Reprint of the 1900 ed., which was issued as Publications 1899 of the Bibliographical Society, London.

Greg, *Sir* **Walter Wilson,** 1875–1959.
A list of masques, pageants, &c.; supplementary to A list of English plays. New York, Haskell House, 1969.

xi, 35, cxxxi p. 24 cm.

Reprint of the 1902 ed.

Halliwell-Phillips, James Orchard, 1820–1889.
A dictionary of old English plays, existing either in print or in manuscript, from the earliest times to the close of the seventeenth century; including also notices of Latin plays written by English authors during the same period. By James O. Halliwell. Naarden, [Turfpoortstraat 11] Anton W. van Bekhoven, 1968.

viii, 296 p. 23 cm.
Reprint of the London, 1860 ed.

Harbage, Alfred, 1901–
Annals of English drama, 975–1700; an analytical record of all plays, extant or lost, chronologically arranged and indexed by authors, titles, dramatic companies, &c. Rev. by S. Schoenbaum. London, Methuen [1964]

xvii, 321 p. 26 cm.

Hazlitt, William Carew, 1834–1913.
A manual for the collector and amateur of old English plays. Edited from the material formed by Kirkman, Langbaine, Downes, Oldys, and Halliwell-Phillipps, with extensive additions and corrections. New York, B. Franklin [1966]

viii, 284 p. 24 cm. (Burt Franklin bibliography and reference series, 109)

"Originally published London: 1892."

Hazlitt, William Carew, 1834–1913.
A manual for the collector and amateur of old English plays. Edited from the material formed by Kirkman [and others], with extensive additions and corrections, by W. Carew Hazlitt. New York, Johnson Reprint Corp. [1967]

viii, 284 p. 23 cm.

Title page includes original imprint: London, Pickering & Chatto, 1892.

Jacob, Giles, 1686–1744.
The poetical register: or, The lives and characters of the English dramatic poets. New York, Garland Pub., 1970.

vii, 433 (i. e. 334) p. ports. 22 cm.

Facsim. of the Yale University Library copy with imprint: London, Printed for E. Curll, in Fleetstreet, 1719.
Originally continued by An historical account of the lives and writings of our most considerable English poets ... first published in 1720.

Langbaine, Gerard, 1656–1692.
An account of the English dramatick poets (1691). Hildesheim, G. Olms, 1968.

556, [33] p. 18 cm. (Anglistica & Americana, 9)

Langbaine, Gerard, 1656–1692.
An account of the English dramatick poets; or, Some observations and remarks on the lives and writings of all those that have publish'd either comedies, tragedies, tragicomedies, pastorals, masques, interludes, farces, or opera's in the English tongue. New York, B. Franklin [1969?]

556 p. 24 cm. (Burt Franklin: bibliography and reference series, 91)

Langbaine, Gerard, 1656–1692.
Momus triumphans; or, The plagiaries of the English stage. Introd. by David Stuart Rodes. Los Angeles, William Andrews Clark Memorial Library, University of California, 1971.

xvii, 32 p. 22 cm. (Augustan reprint society. Publication no. 150)

Facsim. reprint of the ed. published in November 1687 under imprint: London: Printed for Nicholas Cox, and are to be sold by him in Oxford. MDCLXXXVIII.

Lowe, Robert William, 1853–1902.
A bibliographical account of English theatrical literature from the earliest times to the present day. London, J. C. Nimmo, 1888. Detroit, Republished by the Gale Research Co., 1966.

x, 384 p. 23 cm.

Sibley, Gertrude Marian, 1892–
The lost plays and masques 1500–1642. New York, Russell & Russell [1971]

xii, 205 p. 22 cm. (Cornell studies in English no. 19)

Reprint of the 1933 ed.

CONTENTS.—The lost plays and masques.—Lost masques with known titles.—English plays with known titles acted in Germany.

Stratman, Carl Joseph, 1917– *ed.*
Bibliography of English printed tragedy, 1565–1900, compiled and edited by Carl J. Stratman. Carbondale, Southern Illinois University Press [1966]

xx, 843 p. 24 cm.

Stratman, Carl Joseph, 1917–
Restoration and eighteenth century theatre research; a bibliographical guide, 1900–1968. Edited by Carl J. Stratman, David G. Spencer, and Mary Elizabeth Devine. Carbondale, Southern Illinois University Press [1971]

ix, 811 p. 24 cm.

Stratman, Carl Joseph, 1917–
Restoration and 18th century theatre research bibliography, 1961–1968. Edited by Carl J. Stratman. Compiled by Edmund A. Napieralski (1961–1968) & Jean E. Westbrook (1961–1966) Troy, N. Y., Whitston Pub. Co., 1969.

ii, 241 p. 23 cm.

Summers, Montague, 1880–1948.
A bibliography of the restoration drama. New York, Russell & Russell [1970]

143 p. 20 cm.

"First published in 1934."

Vinson, James, 1921–
Contemporary dramatists; with a preface by Ruby Cohn. London, St. James Press; New York, St. Martin's Press [1973]

xv, 926 p. 25 cm. (Contemporary writers of the English language, v. 3)

Washington (State). University. Drama Library.
Eighteenth- and nineteenth-century British acting editions: a catalogue of holdings in the University of Washington Drama Library. Compiled and edited by Richard L. Lorenzen. Seattle, University of Washington Press [1974]

2 sheets. 11 x 15 cm.
Microfiche (negative)

GREAT BRITAIN - HISTORY AND CRITICISM

Bergeron, David Moore.
Twentieth-century criticism of English masques, pageants, and entertainments: 1558–1642, by David M. Bergeron. With a supplement on the folk-play and related forms, by Harry B. Caldwell. San Antonio, Tex., Trinity University Press [c1972]

67 p. 24 cm. (Checklists in the humanities and education)

Caldwell, Harry B
English tragedy, 1370–1600: fifty years of criticism, compiled by Harry B. Caldwell and David L. Middleton. San Antonio, Trinity University Press [1971]

89 p. 24 cm. (Checklists in the humanities and education)

Ribner, Irving.
Tudor and Stuart drama. New York, Appleton-Century-Crofts [1966]

viii, 72 p. 24 cm. (Goldentree bibliographies)

GUYANA

Shepherd, Phyllis.
Guyanese plays and their location; a bibliography. Georgetown, Guyana, Public Library, 1967.

17 l. 27 cm.

"Grew out of the desire of the Libraries Co-operation Group to publish a bibliography on Guyana. This work ... is planned as part 2 of the bibliography and was compiled by Mrs. Phyllis Shepherd ... and edited by the staff of the Public Library."

HEBREW

International Theatre Institute. *Israeli Centre.*
Catalogue of Israeli plays, available in translation. [Tel-Aviv, Israeli Centre of the International Theatre Institute, 1968]

27 p. 21 cm.

International Theatre Institute. Israeli Centre.
Original Hebrew plays presented in Israel, 1948–1970. [Translated by M. Segal] Jerusalem, Centre for Public Libraries, 1971.

46 p. 22 cm.

"Appeared originally in Hebrew as an appendix to ... [ha-Maḥazeh ha-'ivri bemakor uve-tirgum] by E. Lahad."

Lahad, Ezra.
המחזה העברי במקור ובתרגום; ביבליוגרפיה [מאת] עזרא להד. ירושלים. מרכז ההדרכה לספריות ציבוריות. 730 [1970]

96 p. 24 cm.

"התוספות שלי לביבליוגרפיה של יערי ... עד תשכ"ח."

Raz, Avraham.
המחזה העברי בעשר השנים האחרונות (1957–67) ביבליוגרפיה (מבחר); חומר ביבליוגרפי לתרגילים של ג. שקד ואברהם רז. ערך אברהם רז. תל-אביב. אוניברסיטת תל-אביב, מפעל השכפול. 1967 or 8.

14 p. 24 cm.

INDIA

Krishnacharya, 1917–
हिंदी नाट्य साहित्य : ग्रंथपुटी, १८६३–१९६५. [लेखक] कृष्णाचार्य. [कलकत्ता] अनामिका [1966]

xv, 398 p. 22 cm. 20.00

In Hindi.

Mehta, Chandravadan Chimanlal, 1901–
Bibliography of stageable plays in Indian languages. Compiled by C. C. Mehta with the help of V. Raghavan [and others] and arranged in the alphabetical order of the languages. New Delhi, Published under the joint auspices of M. S. University of Baroda and Bharatiya Natya Sangha, 1963–65.

2 v. 25 cm.
Vol. 2: Published under the joint auspices of Bank of Baroda, ltd., Bharatiya Natya Sangha, New Delhi, and M. S. University of Baroda.
CONTENTS.—Pt. 1. Gujarati, Hindi, Kashmiri, Marathi, Punjabi, Sanskrit, Telugu, Urdu.—Pt. 2. Assamese, Bengali, Kannada, Malayalam, Oriya, Tamil.

Nāmī, 'Abdul 'Alīm.
بیلوگرافیا اردو ڈراما. [مصنف] عبدالعلیم نامی. [اشاعت 1.]
بمبئی، اورنئیل [sic] کالج بک ڈپو؛ [ملنے کا پته: مکتبه جامعه، 1966-]

(سلسله مطبوعات نهرو اكيدمى آف ليثرز، ۱ v. illus. 22 cm.

In Urdu.

IRELAND

French, Frances-Jane.
The Abbey Theatre series of plays; a bibliography. ₁Dublin₁ Dolmen Press ₁Distributed in the U. S. A. by Dufour Editions, Chester Springs, Pa., 1969₁

53 p. illus. 26 cm. (Abbey Theatre series)

Mikhail, E   H
A bibliography of modern Irish drama, 1899–1970 ₁by₁ E. H. Mikhail. With a foreword by William A. Armstrong. ₁London₁ Macmillan ₁1972₁

xi, 51 p. 22 cm.

Mikhail, E   H
A bibliography of modern Irish drama, 1899–1970 ₁by₁ E. H. Mikhail. With a foreword by William A. Armstrong. Seattle, University of Washington Press ₁1972₁

xi, 51 p. 23 cm.

ITALY

Allacci, Leone, 1586–1669.
Drammaturgia di Lione Allacci. Torino, Bottega d'Erasmo, 1966.

1016 columns. illus. 24 cm.

Facsim. of the Venice, 1755 ed.
Edited by Francesco Bernardelli.

Clubb, Louise George.
Italian plays (1500–1700) in the Folger Library; a bibliography with introduction. Firenze, Olschki, 1968.

xlviii, 267 p. 12 illus. 25 cm. (Biblioteca di bibliografia italiana, 52)

Herrick, Marvin Theodore, 1899–
Italian plays, 1500–1700, in the University of Illinois Library, compiled by Marvin T. Herrick. Urbana, University of Illinois Press, 1966.

92 p. 22 cm.

Mango, Achille.
La commedia in lingua nel Cinquecento; bibliografia critica. Introd. di Vito Pandolfi. ₁Milano₁ Lerici editori ₁1966₁

286 p. facsims. 25 cm.

JAPAN

Hankyū Gakuen Ikeda Bunko.
(Kabuki daihon mokuroku)
歌舞伎台本目録 阪急学園池田文庫所蔵 池田 阪急学園池田文庫 昭和45(1970)

59 p. illus. 26 cm.

日本演劇研究書目解題 河竹繁俊博士喜寿記念 出版刊行会編 ₁東京₁ 平凡社 ₁1966₁

353, 51, 68 p. 22 cm.

河竹繁俊博士著作・放送・講演目録 : p. 5–51 (2d group)

(Nihon gikyoku sōmokuroku)
日本戯曲総目録 横浜 日本アマチュア演劇連盟

昭和46–47(1971–72)

2 v. 22 cm.

編集責任者:加藤衛

Nippon Hōsō Kyōkai.
(Engeki gedai yōran)
演劇外題要覧 日本放送協会編 東京 日本放送出版協会 昭和46(1971)

544 p. 22 cm.

Ōsaka Shiritsu Chūō Toshokan.
大阪市立中央図書館
義太夫浄瑠璃本目録 鶴澤清六遺文庫・鶴澤 團造遺文庫・竹本彌太夫遺文庫
大阪 人形浄瑠璃因協会 昭和42(1967)

87 p. 図版共. 26 cm.

人形浄瑠璃因協会所蔵 大阪市立中央図書館寄託

Pronko, Leonard Cabell.
Guide to Japanese drama ₁by₁ Leonard C. Pronko. Boston, G. K. Hall, 1973.

125 p. 22 cm. (The Asian literature bibliography series)

Waseda Daigaku, Tokyo.   Engeki Hakubutsukan.
(Engeki Hakubutsukan shozō jōruribon mokuroku)
演劇博物館所蔵浄瑠璃本目録 東京 早稲田大学演劇博物館 昭和43(1968)

188 p. 26 cm.

On p. ₁4₁ of cover: Catalogue of jōruri texts of the Theatre Museum. Waseda University.

LATIN AMERICA

Hebblethwaite, Frank P
A bibliographical guide to the Spanish American theater, compiled by Frank P. Hebblethwaite. Washington, Pan American Union, 1969.

viii, 84 p. 28 cm. (₁Pan American Union. Division of Philosophy and Letters₁ Basic bibliographies, 6)

MEXICO

Igo, John N., 1927–
Los pastores; an annotated bibliography with an introd. by John Igo. ₁San Antonio, San Antonio College Library, 1967₁

xx, 85 p. 28 cm.

Monterde García Icazbalceta, Francisco, 1894–
Bibliografía del teatro en México ₁por₁ Francisco Monterde. New York, B. Franklin ₁1970₁

lxxx, 640 p. facsims. (1 fold.) 21 cm. (Theater & drama series, 11)

Burt Franklin bibliography & reference series, 369.
Reprint of the edition published in México, 1933.

PHILIPPINE ISLANDS

San Jose-Florentino, Eva Maria.
A directory of plays and playwrights. Compiled by Eva Maria San Jose-Florentino and Sonya Florentino. Manila, Philippines, A. S. Florentino, 1971.

xi, 34 l. 33 cm.

POLAND

Korotaj, Władysław, *ed.*
Dramat staropolski, od poczatków do powstania sceny narodowej: bibliografia. Opracował zespół: ₍Helena Bielak et al.₎ pod kierunkiem Władysława Korotaja. ₍Wyd. 1₎ Wrocław, Zakład Narodowy im. Ossolińskich, 1965–

v. 21 cm. (Książka w dawnej kulturze polskiej, 14)

On added title pages: Instytut Badań Literackich Polskiej Akademii Nauk, Biblioteka Narodowa.
Summary in French.

CONTENTS.—t. 1. Teksty dramatyczne, drukiem wydane do r. 1765.

Raszewski, Zbigniew.
Teatr polski XIX ₍i. e. dziewietnastego₎ wieku: Wystawa bibliofilska, maj–lipiec 1969; katalog. ₍Oprac. Zbigniew Raszewski. Warszawa, 1969₎

54 p., ₍10₎ p. of illus. 17 cm.

At head of title: Teatr Wielki w Warszawie. Muzeum Teatralne. Towarzystwo Przyjaciół Książki.

RUSSIA

История советского драматического театра. 50 лет. Рек. список литературы. Москва, 1967–

v. 19 cm.

At head of title, v. 1– : Министерство культуры СССР. Государственная центральная театральная библиотека.

CONTENTS.—ч. 1. Зерницкая, Э. И. Русский советский драматический театр.—ч. 2. Зерницкая, Э. И. Театр народов СССР.

Martínek, Karel.
Bibliografie základních materiálů k dějinám ruského sovětského činoherního divadla a dramatu 1917–1967. Praha. Divadelní ústav, rozmn. SČT, 1970.

2 v. 21 cm.

Vatatsy, Nina Barysaŭna.
Беларуская савецкая драматургія; бібліяграфія. Мінск, Кніжная палата БССР, 1966 ₍обл. 1967₎

276 p. 19 cm.

At head of title: Дзяржаўная бібліятэка БССР імя У. І. Леніна. Аддзел беларускай літаратуры і бібліяграфіі. Н. Б. Ватацы.

Zernitskaía, È   I
Молодежный театр в СССР. Библиогр. указатель литературы. ч. 1–   Москва, 1968–

v. 20 cm.

At head of title, v. 1– : Министерство культуры СССР. Государственная центральная театральная библиотека.
Vol. 1–   by È. I. Zernitskaía, E. D. Loïdina and N. V. Shashkova.
CONTENTS.— ч. 1. Комсомольский театр.

SPAIN

Ashcom, Benjamin Bowles, 1903–
A descriptive catalogue of the Spanish comedias sueltas in the Wayne State University Library and the private library of Professor B. B. Ashcom. By B. B. Ashcom. Detroit, Wayne State University Libraries, 1965.

103 p. facsim. 22 cm.

Esgueva Martínez, Manuel.
La colección teatral "La farsa"; ₍Bibliografía descriptiva₎. Madrid. Consejo Superior de Investigaciones Científicas ₍Instituto Miguel de Cervantes₎ 1971.

xvi. 511 p. 23 cm. (Anejos de la revista Segismundo, 3)

McCready, Warren T
Bibliografía temática de estudios sobre el teatro español antiguo, por Warren T. McCready. ₍Toronto₎ University of Toronto Press ₍1966₎

xix, 445 p. 26 cm.

North Carolina. University. *Library.*
A catalogue of comedias sueltas in the library of the University of North Carolina, by William A. McKnight, with the collaboration of Mabel Barrett Jones. Chapel Hill, 1965.

vii. 240 p. 23 cm. (North Carolina. University. Library studies, no. 4)

Regueiro. José M
Spanish drama of the golden age; a catalogue of the comedia collection in the University of Pennsylvania Libraries, by José M. Regueiro. ₍New Haven, Research Publications, c1971₎

x, 106 p. 29 cm.

"This catalogue is intended to serve mainly as an accompanying guide for the user of the comedia collection of the University of Pennsylvania Libraries, in its microfilm form available from Research Publications, Inc. Sufficient bibliographical information has been included, however, to provide the individual user, when the microfilm set is not available, with an accurate description of the contents of the collection."

Thompson, Lawrence Sidney, 1916–
A bibliography of Spanish plays on microcards, by Lawrence S. Thompson. Hamden, Conn., Shoe String Press, 1968.

490 p. 22 cm.

SWEDEN

Svensk litteraturhistorisk bibliografi. Teaterhistoria 1936–1960. Utarb. vid Litteraturhistoriska institutionen i Lund. Lund, Lundensiska litteratursällskapet; ₍Universitetsbiblioteket (distr.) 1966.

58, (1) l. 26 cm.

Based on yearly bibliographies which appeared in Samlaren 1938–1962.

Uppsala. Universitet. Litteraturvetenskapliga institutionen. Avdelningen för dramaforskning.
Dramatik tryckt på svenska 1914–1962. ₍Utg. av₎ Avdelningen för dramaforskning ₍vid Litteraturvetenskapliga institutionen i Uppsala₎. Uppsala, Utgivaren, 1970.

xi, 575 p. 30 cm.

Continuation of Svensk dramatisk litteratur under åren 1840–1913 by G. Wingren.

SWITZERLAND

Palmer, Peter.
Schweizer Bühnenwerke des 20. Jahrhunderts. Sachbearb.: Peter Palmer. (Zürich,) Zürcher Forum, (1972).

108 p. 19 cm.

UNITED STATES
*see also under Poetry - United States
(Brown)*

Brown University. *Library.*
Two hundred years of American plays, 1765–1964; ₍catalogue of₎ an exhibition arranged to celebrate the bicentennial of the publication of Thomas Godfrey's The Prince of Parthia. ₍Providence, 1965₎

1 v. (unpaged) 28 cm.

Cover title.

Exhibition, prepared by the Harris collection of American poetry and plays in Brown University Library, Providence, R. I., was held at the John D. Rockefeller, Jr. Library, April 19–May 15, 1965.

Hill, Frank Pierce, 1855–1941.
American plays printed 1714–1830; a bibliographical record. New York, B. Blom, 1968.

xi, 152 p. illus. 20 cm.

Reprint of the 1934 ed.

Hill, Frank Pierce, 1855–1941.
American plays printed 1714–1830; a bibliographical record. New York, B. Franklin ₁1970₎

xi, 152 p. illus., facsim. 19 cm. (Burt Franklin bibliography and reference, 387. Theatre and drama series, 17)

Reprint of the 1934 ed.

Long, Eugene Hudson, 1908–
American drama from its beginnings to the present, compiled by E. Hudson Long. New York, Appleton-Century-Crofts, Educational Division ₁1970₎

xi, 78 p. 24 cm. (Goldentree bibliographies in language and literature)

Moe, Albert F
American drama through 1830; a checklist. Compiled by Albert F. Moe and Margaret G. Moe. ₁Oakland, Calif., 1968₎

iii, ₁81₎ l. 30 cm.

Palmer, Helen H
American drama criticism; interpretations. 1890–1965 inclusive, of American drama since the first play produced in America. Compiled by Helen H. Palmer and Jane Anne Dyson. Hamden, Conn., Shoe String Press, 1967.

239 p. 23 cm.

———— Supplement 1ᴸ Hamden, Conn., Shoe String Press, 1970–
v. 23 cm.

Roden, Robert F 1874 or 5–1934.
Later American plays, 1831–1900; being a compilation of the titles of plays by American authors published and performed in America since 1831. New York, B. Franklin ₁1969₎

132 p. 23 cm. (Burt Franklin bibliography series, 76)

Reprint of the 1900 ed.
On spine: Early American plays, 1831–1900.

Ryan, Pat M
American drama bibliography; a checklist of publications in English, compiled by Pat M. Ryan. Fort Wayne, Ind., Fort Wayne Public Library, 1969.

240 p. 22 cm.

Stratman, Carl Joseph, 1917–
Bibliography of the American theatre, excluding New York City ₁by₎ Carl J. Stratman. ₁Chicago₎ Loyola University Press ₁1965₎

xv, 397 p. 24 cm.

Wegelin, Oscar, 1876–
Early American plays, 1714–1830; being a compilation of the titles of plays by American authors published and performed in America previous to 1830. Edited with an introd. by John Malone. New York, Haskell House Publishers, 1968.

xxvi, 113 p. illus. 23 cm.

Reprint of the 1900 ed.
"Haskell House catalogue item #256."

Wegelin, Oscar, 1876–1970.
Early American plays, 1714–1830; being a compilation of the titles of plays by American authors published and performed in America previous to 1830. Edited with an introd. by John Malone. New York, B. Franklin ₁1970₎

xxvi, 113 p. 19 cm. (Burt Franklin research and source works series, 573. Theatre and drama series, 12)

Reprint of the 1900 ed.

URUGUAY

Rela, Walter.
Reportorio bibliográfico del teatro uruguayo, 1816–1964. Montevideo, Editorial Síntesis, 1965.

85 p. facsim. 24 cm. (Colección Medusa)

WALES

Cardiganshire Joint Library.
Dramâu Cymraeg un act. Aberystwyth, Pwyllgor Addysg Ceredigion (Cardiganshire Education Committee), 1969.

191 p. 19 cm.

At head of title: Llyfrgelloedd Cymru.

DRAVIDIAN LANGUAGES

Andronov, Mikhail Sergeevich.
Materials for a bibliography of Dravidian linguistics ₁by₎ M. Andronov. Kuala Lumpur, Dept. of Indian Studies, University of Malaya ₁1966₎

52 p. 22 cm.

"International Association of Tamil Research series."

DREISER, THEODORE

Atkinson, Hugh C
The Merrill checklist of Theodore Dreiser, compiled by Hugh C. Atkinson. Columbus, Ohio, C. E. Merrill Pub. Co. ₁1969₎

iv, 43 p. 20 cm. (Charles E. Merrill program in American literature. Charles E. Merrill checklists)

Cover title: Checklist of Theodore Dreiser.

Atkinson, Hugh C
Theodore Dreiser; a checklist, by Hugh C. Atkinson. ₁1st ed. Kent, Ohio₎ Kent State University Press ₁1971₎

104 p. 23 cm. (The Serif series: bibliographies and checklists, no. 15)

McDonald, Edward David.
A bibliography of the writings of Theodore Dreiser, by Edward D. McDonald. With a foreword by Theodore Dreiser. New York, B. Franklin ₁1968₎

130 p. port. 23 cm. (Burt Franklin bibliography and reference series, no. 154)

Reprint of the 1928 ed.

Orton, Vrest, 1897–
Dreiserana; a book about his books. New York, Haskell House Publishers, 1973.

ix, 84 p. 23 cm.

A list of errata and addenda to E. D. McDonald's A bibliography of the writings of Theodore Dreiser, 1928.
Original ed. issued in series: The Chocorua bibliographies.

DRENTHE, NETHERLANDS

Ubink, Bertha R
Drents repertorium. Bibliografie van belangrijke boeken en tijdschriftartikelen betreffende de provincie Drenthe (afgesloten december 1964). Samengesteld voor het Drents Genootschap door Bertha R. Ubink. Met medewerking van G. A. Bontekoe. Woord vooraf van K. van Dijk. Assen, Van Gorcum, 1967–

v. 23 cm.

CONTENTS.—1. Plaatsen. fl 5.–

DREYFUS, ALFRED

Centre de documentation juive contemporaine. *Bibliothèque.*
La France de l'affaire Dreyfus à nos jours. Paris, 1964.

xii, 266 p. 22 cm. (*Its* Catalogue no 1)

Lipschutz, Léon.
Essai de bibliographie thématique et analytique de l'affaire Dreyfus; une bibliothèque dreyfusienne [par] Léon Lispschutz [sic] Paris, Fasquelle, 1970.

103 p. 22 cm.

DRILLING see Boring

DRINKS see Beverages

DRÔME, FRANCE (DEPT.)

Brun-Durand, Justin, 1836–
Dictionnaire biographique et biblio-iconographique de la Drôme ... [par] J. Brun-Durand. Geneve, Slatkine Reprints, 1970.

2 v. in 1. 23 cm.

"Réimpression de l'édition de Grenoble, 1900–1901."

DROPOUTS

Miller, Leonard Michael, 1896–
Dropouts: selected references, prepared by Leonard M. Miller. [Washington, U. S. Dept. of Health, Education, and Welfare, Office of Education; for sale by the Superintendent of Documents, U. S. Govt. Print. Off., 1964]

v. 32 p. 24 cm. (U. S. Office of Education. Bulletin 1965, no. 7)

"OE-20070."
"Revised version of a similar publication prepared in the Office in 1963 and lists many new items which have appeared in the interim."

DROSTE-HÜLSHOFF, ANNETTE ELISABETH, FREIIN VON

Thiekötter, Hans.
Annette von Droste-Hülshoff. Eine Auswahlbibliographie. (2., erw. Aufl.) Münster/Westf., Aschendorff (1968).

62 p. with facsim. 21 cm. (Schriften der Droste-Gesellschaft, 16)

DROUGHTS

Palmer, Wayne C
Drought bibliography [by] Wayne C. Palmer and Lyle

M. Denny. Silver Spring, Md., U. S. Environmental Data Service, 1971.

xi, 236 p. 27 cm. (NOAA technical memorandum EDS 20)

"A United States Department of Commerce publication."
Supt. of Docs. no.: C55.13/2 : EDS-20

DRUGS; DRUG ADDICTION

Ajami, Alfred M
Drugs: an annotated bibliography and guide to the literature, by Alfred M. Ajami, Jr., in collaboration with the Sanctuary, Cambridge, Mass. Boston, G. K. Hall, 1973.

xxiv, 205 p. 25 cm.

Alcoholism and Drug Addiction Research Foundation of Ontario. Documentation Dept.
Interaction of alcohol and other drugs: an annotated bibliography of the scientific literature on the interaction of ethanol and other chemical compounds normally absent in vivo, the influence of congeners in alcoholic beverages, conjunctive addiction to ethanol plus other drugs, and cross-tolerance between ethanol and other compounds. Compiled at the Addiction Research Foundation Documentation Dept. by E. Polacsek [and others] With a foreword by

xxii, 561 p. 29 cm. (Addiction Research Foundation bibliographic series, no. 3)

Bibliography on drug abuse: prevention, treatment, research. National Institute for Drug Programs, Center for Human Services. Washington, D. C., Human Service Press [1973]

v, 222 p. 27 cm.

Burg, Nan C
Forces against drug abuse: education, legislation, rehabilitation: a selected bibliography [by] Nan C. Burg. Mary Vance, editor. [Monticello, Ill., Available from Council of Planning Librarians] 1971.

11 l. 28 cm. (Council of Planning Librarians. Exchange bibliography, 231)

DACAS: Drug abuse current awareness system. v. 1–
July 3, 1972–
[Rockville, Md.] National Clearinghouse for Drug Abuse Information.

v. 27 cm. biweekly.

Drug dependence.
[Amsterdam, Excerpta Medica Foundation.]

v. 25 cm. monthly.

Began with Sept. 1972 issue. Cf. New serial titles.

Eastern Michigan University. Library.
A selected, annotated bibliography on drug use. Compiled by Jean Baardsen, Clare Beck [and] Walter Fishman. Ypsilanti, 1972.

10 l. 29 cm. (Its Bibliography series, no. 22)

"This bibliography represents recently acquired selections from the books, periodicals, documents, and audio visual materials available in the Eastern Michigan University library."

Gamage, James R
A comprehensive guide to the English-language literature on cannabis (marihuana) [by] J. R. Gamage & E. L. Zerkin. Beloit, Wis., STASH Press, 1969.

xi, 265 p. 30 cm. (STASH bibliographic series, no. 1)

Guide to selected resources for drug education. v. 1–
May 1972–
Sacramento, California State Dept. of Education.

v. 28 cm.

Vols. for 1972– prepared under the direction of the Drug Education Task Force.

Hirtz, Jean L
Le sort des médicaments dans l'organisme; bibliographie et tables analytiques préparées par un groupe de travail de la Société de technique pharmaceutique, sous la direction de J. Hirtz. Paris, Masson, 1970.

2 v. 25 cm.

Added t. p.: The fate of drugs in the organism.
CONTENTS: v. 1. Bibliographie.—v. 2. Tables.

Menditto, Joseph.
Drugs of addiction and non-addiction, their use and abuse; a comprehensive bibliography, 1960–1969. Troy, N. Y., Whitston Pub. Co., 1970.

315 p. 24 cm.

Mercer, G W
Non-alcoholic drugs and personality; a selected annotated bibliography, by G. W. Mercer. Toronto, Addiction Research Foundation, 1972.

77 p. 28 cm. (Addiction Research Foundation bibliographic series, no. 4)

Moore, Laurence A
Marijuana (*Cannabis*) bibliography, 1960–1968 [by] Laurence A. Moore, Jr. Los Angeles, Bruin Humanist Forum [1969]

[56] l. 28 cm.

National Clearinghouse for Drug Abuse Information.
Drug dependence and abuse: a selected bibliography. [Chevy Chase, Md.] For sale by the Supt. of Docs., U. S. Govt. Print. Off., Washington, 1971.

vi, 51 p. 26 cm.

National Clearinghouse for Drug Abuse Information.
Selected bibliography on the use of drugs by young people. [Chevy Chase, Md.] 1971.

4 p. 27 cm. (Its Selected reference series, ser. 1, no. 1)

New Jersey. *Bureau of Curriculum Services.*
Bibliography of drug education materials. Trenton [1970]

21 p. 28 cm.

New York (State). University.
A multimedia reference listing of materials on drug education. Albany, University of the State of New York, State Education Dept., 1971.

v, 149 p. 28 cm.

Ørnø, Inger.
A bibliography of research findings and opinions on narcotic addiction and drug abuse. By Anne Marie Orno. 2900 Hellerup, Amoforlaget, Eksp.: Ellehøj 4, 1972.

175 p. 30 cm.

Cover title: Narcotic addition : a bibliography.

The Question of cannabis; cannabis bibliography. [Geneva] 1965.

iii, 250 p. 28 cm. ([United Nations. Document] E/CN.7/479)

At head of title: United Nations. Economic and Social Council. Commission on Narcotic Drugs. Twentieth session. Item 8 of the provisional agenda.
"Entries originally written in English or French have not been translated; entries in other languages have been translated both into English and French."

Red Cross. Netherlands. Nederlandsche Roode Kruis. Bureau Druginformatie.
Algemene inleidende literatuur over drugs en druggebruik. [Den Haag, 1971?]

7 l. 30 cm.

Richardson, Winnifred.
A bibliography on drugs by subject and title [by] Winnifred Richardson [and] Bryan E. M. Cooke. Minneapolis, Burgess Pub. Co. [1972]

iv, 60 p. 27 cm.

Sandoz, inc. *Sandoz Pharmaceuticals.*
Bibliography on psychotomimetics, 1943–1966. [Washington] U. S. Dept. of Health, Education, and Welfare, National Institute of Mental Health [1968]

524 p. 31 cm.

Schmeiser, Gottfried.
Bibliographie Jugend und Rauschdrogen. [Bearb. von Gottfried Schmeiser, unter Mitwirkung von Gisela von Einem und Gwendolin Ropers-Maters. München, Deutsches Jugendinstitut, 1972]

vi, 227 p. 25 cm. (DJI-Dokumentation)

Sells, Helen F
A bibliography on drug dependence, compiled by Helen F. Sells. Fort Worth, Texas Christian University Press, 1967.

xiii, 137 p. 28 cm.

U. S. *National Clearinghouse for Mental Health Information.*
Bibliography on drug dependence and abuse, 1928–1966. [Chevy Chase, Md., 1969]

258 p. 27 cm.

U. S. *National Institute of Mental Health .*
Government publications on drug abuse. [Chevy Chase, Md., 1969]

16 p. 26 cm.

U. S. *National Institute of Mental Health.*
Selected bibliography on drugs of abuse. [Chevy Chase, Md., 1970?]

25 p. 26 cm.

Prepared in cooperation with the Bureau of Narcotics and Dangerous Drugs.

United States. National Library of Medicine. Toxicology Information Program.
Drug interactions; an annotated bibliography with selected excerpts. Bethesda, Md.; [For sale by the Supt. of Docs., U. S. Govt. Print. Off., Washington] 1972–

v. 31 cm. (DHEW publication no. (NIH) 73-322)

CONTENTS: v. 1. 1967–1970.

DRUGS ; DRUG ADDITION

Wells, Dorothy Pearl, 1910–
Drug education; a bibliography of available inexpensive materials, compiled by Dorothy P. Wells. Metuchen, N. J., Scarecrow Press, 1972.

111 p. 22 cm.

DRUGSTORES

Christensen, Edward L
Drug stores, by Edward L. Christensen. Rev. Washington, U. S. Small Business Administration, 1964.

8 p. 26 cm. (Small business bibliography, no. 33)

McEvilla, Joseph David.
Drugstores, by Joseph D. McEvilla. Washington, Small Business Administration ₁1970₎

7 p. 26 cm. (Small business bibliography no. 33)

DRY CLEANING see Cleaning

DRYDEN, HUGH LATIMER

Wells, Helen T
The publications of Dr. Hugh L. Dryden, compiled by Helen T. Wells. Comment ed. Washington, Historical Office, National Aeronautics and Space Administration, 1966.

15 l. 27 cm. (₁U. S. National Aeronautics and Space Administration. Historical Office₎ HHN–59)

DRYDEN, JOHN

Love, Harold, 1937–
John Dryden in Australian libraries: a checklist of pre-1800 holdings, by Harold Love, Mary Lord and contributing librarians. Melbourne, Monash University, English Dept., 1972.

31 l. 26 cm. (Monash University English Dept. Bibliographical checklists, no. 1)

Macdonald, Hugh, 1885–
John Dryden: a bibliography of early editions and of Drydeniana. ₁1st ed. reprinted₎. London, Dawsons, 1966 ₁i. e. 1967₎.

xlv, 358 p. port. 26 cm.

Facsimile reprint of 1st ed., London, Oxford U. P., 1939.

DUBLIN

Dix, Ernest Reginald McClintock, 1857–1936.
Catalogue of early Dublin-printed books, 1601 to 1700. Compiled by E. R. McC. Dix. With an historical introd. and bibliographical notes by C. Winston Dugan. New York, B. Franklin ₁1971₎
4 v. in 2 (386 p.) 26 cm. (Burt Franklin bibliography and reference series, 402. Essays in literature and criticism, 117)
On spine: Early Dublin-printed books, 1601 to 1700.
Each pt. also has special t. p.: pt. 1–2, List of books, tracts, &c. printed in Dublin from 1601 to 1700; pt. 3–4 & suppl., List of books, tracts, broadsides, &c., printed in Dublin from 1601 to 1700.
Reprint of the 1912 ed.
CONTENTS: pt. 1. 1626 to 1650 ₁i. e. 1601 to 1625₎—pt. 2. 1626 to 1650.—pt. 3. 1651 to 1675.—pt. 4. 1676 to 1700.—Supplement.

DUBOIS, WILLIAM EDWARD BURGHARDT

Kotei, S . I . A
Dr. W. E. B. Du Bois, 1868–1963; a bibliography, compiled by S. I. A. Kotei. Accra, 1964.

vi, 39 l. 26 cm. (Ghana Library Board. Padmore Research Library on African Affairs. Bibliography series. Special subject bibliography no. 4)

DUELING see Fencing

DUGÉS, ALFREDO see under Herpetology (Smith)

DULANEY, BLADEN

U. S. *Library of Congress. Manuscript Division.*
Bladen Dulany, Gustavus R. B. Horner, Daniel Todd Patterson: a register of their papers in the Library of Congress. Washington, Library of Congress, 1970.

4, 8, 4 l. 27 cm.

"Naval Historical Foundation collection."

DUMAS, ALEXANDRE

Nielsen, Aksel Jørgen, 1900–
Bibliographie d'Alexandre Dumas père en Danemark, Norvège et Suède; oeuvres traduites et, pour la plupart, imprimées, 1830–1963, avec une brève bibliographie des titres français et notes bibliographiqes ₁sic₎ de toutes ses œuvres, par Aksel J. Nielsen. Copenhague, 1964.

97 p. 18 cm.

"Il a été imprimé de cet oeuvre, seulement 200 exemplaires."

Slater, Ivan H   1899 or 1900–1968.
The Ivan H. Slater collection of the works of Alexandre Dumas. Auckland, B. A. Sturt ₁1968₎

106 p. 22 cm.

DUNANT, JEAN HENRY

Mercanton, Daisy Catherine.
Henry Dunant. Essai bio-bibliographique. ₁Genève,₎ Institut Henry-Dunant; ₁Lausanne,₎ Éditions l'Age d'homme, (1972).

xlv, 128 p. 12 plates. 23 cm. (Institut Henry-Dunant. Études et perspectives, v. 3)

At head of title: Daisy C. Mercanton.

DU PONT FAMILY

Eleutherian Mills Historical Library, *Greenville, Del.*
A guide to the manuscripts in the Eleutherian Mills Historical Library; accessions through the year 1965, by John Beverley Riggs. Greenville, Del., 1970.

xxii, 1205 p. 26 cm.

DUPRÉ, MARCEL

Marcel Dupré: Bibliothèque municipale, octobre-₁novembre₎ 1972, ville de Rouen. Rouen, Bibliothèque municipale, 1972.

18 p. 21 cm.

Cover title.
Exhibition catalog.

DÜRER, ALBRECHT

Berlin. Stadtbibliothek.
Albrecht Dürer. ₁Zusammengestellt anlässlich des 500.

Geburtstages von Albrecht Dürer am 21. Mai 1971 von einem Kollektiv unter Leitung von Friedegard Schaefer₁ Berlin, 1971.

42 p. port. 21 cm. (Bibliographische Kalenderblätter. Sonderblatt, 33)

Mende, Matthias.
Dürer-Bibliographie. Zur 500. Wiederkehr d. Geburtstages von Albrecht Dürer, 21. Mai 1971. (Federführend f. Hrsg. u. Red.: Elisabeth Rücker.) Wiesbaden, Harrassowitz, 1971.

xliv, 707 p., 24 p. of illus. 25 cm.

Ullrichová, Jana.
Albrecht Dürer. 21.5.1471–6.4.1528. Soupis literatury z fondu Universitní knihovny v Brně. V Brně, Universitní knihovna, 1971.

31 l. 21 cm. (Bibliografický leták, 170)

DURHAM, ENGLAND (CITY AND COUNTY)
see also under Baker Family

Benedikz, Phyllis Mary.
Durham topographical prints up to 1800: an annotated bibliography, by Phyllis M. Benedikz. Durham, University Library, 1968.

xii, 88 p. 4 plates. 22 cm. (Durham University Library. Publication no. 6)

Durham, Eng. University. *Durham Colleges. Dept. of Palaeography and Diplomatic.*
List of documents relating to the Manor of Chester Deanery, deposited in the Department of Palaeography and Diplomatic, South Road, Durham; ₁compiled by Dr. E. Peirce₁. Durham, University (Department of Paleography and Diplomatic), 1967.

₁4₁, 48 f. 33½ cm.

Durham, Eng. University. *Durham Colleges. Dept. of Palaeography and Diplomatic.*
The Weardale Chest: list of documents relating to the Forest of Weardale and Stanhope Park, deposited in the Department of Palaeography and Diplomatic, South Road, Durham; ₁compiled by Dr. E. Peirce₁. Durham, University (Department of Palaeography & Diplomatic), 1967.

₁3₁, 47 f. 33½ cm.

DÜRRENMATT, FRIEDRICH

Hansel, Johannes.
Friedrich Dürrenmatt Bibliographie. Bad Homburg v. d. H., Berlin, Zürich, (Dr.) Gehlen (1968).

87 p. 19 cm. (Bibliographien zum Studium der deutschen Sprache und Literatur, Bd. 3)

DUSHANBE. UNIVERSITET

Kadyrov, Abdusamad.
Исторический факультет к 50-летию Советской власти. (Справочник-каталог). Душанбе, 1968.

100 p. 20 cm.

At head of title: Министерство народного образования Таджикской ССР. Таджикский государственный университет им. В. И. Ленина. А. Кадыров, Ш. Джалилов.

DUST

Budapest. Építőanyagipari Központi Kutató Intézet. Dokumentációs Osztály.
Porártalom és porleküzdés; irodalmi tájékoztató és ajánló bibliográfia, összeállította: az ÉAKKI Dokumentációs Osztálya. Budapest, É. M. Építésügyi Dokumentációs Iroda, 1964.

68 p. 23 cm.

Ostrava, Czechoslovak Republic (City) Státní vědecká knihovna.
Zachycování elektrárenského popílku; výběrová bibliografie. ₁Sest. Marie Kurečkova₁ Ostrava, 1964.

36 p. 29 cm. (*Its* Publikace. Řada II, čís. 376)

DUTCH GUIANA see Surinam

DUTCH LANGUAGE AND LITERATURE
see also Flemish literature

Buuren, A   M   J   van.
Vermakelijk bibliografisch ganzenbord. Een eerste handleiding bij het systematisch-bibliografisch onderzoek op het gebied van de Nederlandse letterkunde. Samengesteld door A. M. J. van Buuren, W. P. Gerritsen en A. N. Paasman. 2e, herz. en vermeerderde uitg. Groningen, Wolters-Noordhoff, 1971.

viii, 91 p. 21 cm. (De Nieuwe taalgids cahiers, 1)

Delen, P   A   M
Forum, kritiek en essay. Bibliografie. Door P. A. M. Delen. Utrecht ₁St. Maartendreef 144, W. A. Hendriks₁ 1969.

16 p. 22 cm. (Bibliograafwerk 2)

Dortmund. Städtische Volksbüchereien.
Niederländische Literatur der Gegenwart; Bücher in niederländischer Sprache und deutschen Übersetzungen. Mit einem Beitrag von Pierre H. Dubois: Moderne Literatur in den Niederlanden. Dortmund, 1964.

71 p. 22 cm. (Völker im Spiegel der Literatur, F. 10)

Hendriks, Willem Antonius.
De neerlandistiek op dertig Nederlandse filologencongressen. Bibliografie. Door W. A. Hendriks. Utrecht, ₁St. Maartendreef 144, W. A. Hendriks₁, 1970.

20 p. 21 cm. (Bibliograafwerk, 3)

Kloeke, Gesinus Gerardus, 1887–1963.
Bibliografie en dagboekfragment. ₁Door₁ G. G. Kloeke. Verzorgd en toegelicht door M. J. Kloeke-van Lessen. Amsterdam, Noord-Hollandsche U. M., 1968 ₁1969₁

xii, 60 p. 24 cm. (Bijdragen en mededelingen der Dialectencommissie van de Koninklijke Nederlandse Akademie van Wetenschappen te Amsterdam, 35).

DUTCH LANGUAGE

Pepin, Jean Pierre.

Essai de bibliographie des traductions françaises des œuvres de la littérature néerlandaise depuis 50 ans; 1918–1968. Mémoire présenté aux cours provinciaux des sciences de la bibliothèque et de la documentation de la province de Brabant. Bruxelles, Commission belge de bibliographie, (r. des Tanneurs, 80–84), 1972.

xxi, 547 p. 21 cm. (Bibliographia Belgica, 115)

DUTCH PERIODICALS see Periodical publications - Netherlands

DWELLINGS see Houses

DYES AND DYEING

Moscow. TSentral'naĭa nauchno-tekhnicheskaĭa biblioteka legkoĭ promyshlennosti.

Высокотемпературное крашение тканей; список отече-
ственной и иностранной литературы, поступившей в библиотеку с 1957 по октябрь 1963 гг. ₁Составитель Г. С. Евстратова₁ Москва, 1964.

22 p. 22 cm. (В помощь инженерно-техническим и научным работникам)

At head of title: Государственный комитет по легкой промышленности при Госплане СССР.

DYKSTRA, WALING see Dijkstra, Waling Gerrits

DYSLEXIA

Evillen, Anna.

Books for dyslexic children: a parent's guide with teachers' supplement. Revised ₁ed.₁; additional list by Betty Root. Laleham, North Surrey Dyslexic Society, 1973.

19 p. 33 cm.

At head of title: North Surrey Dyslexic Society, Dyslexia Society.

E

EARTH

Akademiíà nauk SSSR. *Institut fiziki Zemli. Biblioteka.*
Кора и верхняя мантия Земли; библиографический
указатель, 1960–1964. ₍Составитель А. И. Павлова. Отв.
редакторы: Е. Н. Люстих, П. С. Вейцман₎ Москва,
Наука, 1967.

174 p. 22 cm.

At head of title: Академия наук СССР. Сектор сети специальных библиотек. Библиотека Института физики Земли им. О. Ю.
Шмидта.

\ **Akademiíà nauk SSSR. Institut fiziki Zemli. Biblioteka.**
₍Kora i verkhníàíà mantiíà Zemli₎
Кора и верхняя мантия Земли. Библиогр. указ. 1965–
1969. ₍Сост. Павлова А. И.₎ Москва, "Наука," 1972.

263 p. 21 cm.

On leaf preceding t. p.: Академия наук СССР. Сектор сети
специальных библиотек. Библиотека института физики Земли им.
О. Ю. Шмидта.

Kraskovskiĭ, Sergeĭ Aleksandrovich.
Тепловые потоки в Земле; библиография, 1865–1965.
Составили С. А. Красковский и Н. А. Никифоровская.
Ленинград, 1966.

73 p. 20 cm.

At head of title: Академия наук СССР. Библиотека Академии
наук СССР.

EARTH SCIENCES
    see also under Dissertations, Academic

Comité national francais des recherches antarctiques.
Catalogue of publications. ₍Paris₎ 1971.

21 p. 24 cm.

Abstracts of the first 29 publications in the Committee's CNFRA
series.

Geoscience documentation. v. 1–
July 1969–
London.

v. 30 cm. bimonthly.

Geotitles weekly. 1/1–
July 14, 1969–
London, Geoservices.

v. 30 cm.

"The current awareness service for geoscience."

Knížková, Jiřina.
Terminologické a jazykové slovníky v knihovně Ústředního ústavu geologického. Sest. Jiřina Knížková, Marie Le-
vínská. Praha, Ústř. ústav geolog., rozmn. Geofond, 1970.

67, ₍1₎ p. 20 cm. (Přehledy informativní literatury, 1)

Manser, W
Earth science abstracts, Papua New Guinea, to 1971 /
W. Manser. — Canberra : Published for the Bureau of Min-
eral Resources, Geology and Geophysics by the Australian

Govt. Pub. Service, 1974.
iv, 444 p. : 25 cm. — (Bulletin - Bureau of Mineral Resources,
Geology and Geophysics ; 143) (₍Report₎ PNG - Bureau of Mineral
Resources, Geology and Geophysics ; 6)

Morin, Philippe.
Bibliographie analytique des sciences de la terre: Tunisie
et régions limitrophes (depuis le début des recherches géologiques à 1971), par Philippe Morin. Documents an-
nexes et cartes par Lucia Memmi. Paris, Éditions du Centre de la recherche scientifique, 1972.

26, 644 p. 25 cm. (Centre de recherches sur les zones arides.
Série Géologie, no 13)

O'Callaghan, Timothy C
Bibliography on geophysical, geochemical, and geological
effects of nuclear events. T. C. O'Callaghan, ed. Alexandria, Va., General Pub. Services ₍1973₎

48 p. 24 cm. (Bibliographies in science series, no. 1)

Schmidt, Peter, Dr. rer. nat.
Zur Geschichte der Geologie. Geophysik. Mineralogie
und Paläontologie. Bibliographie u. Repertorium f. d.
DDR. Freiberg ⟨Sa.⟩ (Bibliothek d. Bergakademie
Freiberg), 1970.

134 p 21 cm. (Veröffentlichungen der Bibliothek der Bergakademie Freiberg, Nr. 40)

Walschot, L
Informatie en documentatie voor de aardewetenschappen.
₍Door₎ L. Walschot. Gent, Rijksuniversiteit, 1970.

₍11₎, 80 l. 30 cm.

At head of title: Rijksuniversiteit Gent. Laboratorium voor Fy-
sische Aardrijkskunde en Bodemkunde. Geologisch Museum.

Wood, David Norris.
Use of earth sciences literature. Editor: D. N. Wood.
₍Hamden, Conn.₎ Archon Books, 1973.

459 p. illus. 23 cm. (Information sources for research and development)

PERIODICALS

Indian National Scientific Documentation Centre, Delhi.
Union catalogue of serials in the Geological Survey of
India libraries. Delhi ₍1969?₎

ix, 536 p. 24 cm. (Its Union catalogue series, 11)

EARTHQUAKES see Seismology

EAST see Asia

EAST (NEAR EAST) see Middle East

EAST ANGLIA

Centre of East Anglian Studies.
East Anglian history and archaeology: work in progress
in Summer, 1970. Norwich, University of East Anglia
(Centre of East Anglian Studies) ₍1970₎

₍5₎, 28 p. 21 cm.

EAST INDIANS IN SOUTH AFRICA

Currie, Julia Clare.
A bibliography of material published during the period 1946–56 on the Indian question in South Africa. ₍Cape Town₎ University of Cape Town Libraries, 1969.

iv, 27 p. 23 cm. (University of Cape Town. School of Librarianship. Bibliographical series)

"Presented in partial fulfilment of the requirements for the Higher Certificate in Librarianship, 1957."

EASTERN CHURCHES

Arbanitēs, Athanasios K.
Βιβλιογραφία ἐλασσόνων ἐκκλησιῶν τῆς Ἀνατολῆς ₍ὑπὸ₎ Ἀθανασίου Κ. Ἀρβανίτη. Ἀθῆναι, 1967.

82 p. 24 cm.

CONTENTS.—Ἀρμενικὴ Ἐκκλησία.—Συριακὴ, Ἰακωβιτικὴ Ἐκκλησία.—Κοπτικὴ Ἐκκλησία.—Αἰθιοπικὴ Ἐκκλησία.—Συριακὴ Ἐκκλησία Μαλαμπὰρ Ἰνδιῶν.—Ἀσσυριακὴ, Νεστοριανικὴ Ἐκκλησία.

Meyer, Philipp, 1854–
Die theologische Literatur der griechischen Kirche im 16. Jahrhundert: mit e. allg. Einl./ Philipp Meyer. — Neudr. d. Ausg. Leipzig 1899. Aalen: Scientia-Verlag, 1972.

x, 179 p.; 21 cm.

Original ed. published by Dieterich and issued as v. 3, no. 6 of Studien zur Geschichte der Theologie und der Kirche.

EASTERN EUROPE see Europe, Eastern

EASTERN ORTHODOX CHURCH see Orthodox Eastern Church

ECCLESIASTICAL GEOGRAPHY

International Committee of Historical Sciences. *Commission internationale d'histoire ecclésiastique comparée.*
Bibliographie de cartographie ecclésiastique. **Leiden, E. J. Brill, 1968–**

v. 24 cm.

Text in German.

CONTENTS.—1. fasc. Allemagne-Autriche.

ECCLESIASTICAL HISTORY

Church history of a specific place is entered under the name of the place.

Chadwick, Owen.
The history of the Church: a select bibliography. 2nd ed. London, Historical Association, 1966.

52 p. 21½ cm. (Helps for students of history, no. 66)

Ghirardini, Lino Lionello.
Saggio di una bibliografia dell'età matildico-gregoriana. (1046–1122). Modena, Aedes Muratoriana, 1970.

xiii, 104 p. 24 cm. (Deputazione di storia patria per le antiche provincie modenesi. Biblioteca. nuova ser., n. 14)

Grundmann, Herbert, 1902–
Bibliographie zur Ketzergeschichte des Mittelalters ⟨1900–1966⟩. Roma, Edizioni di storia e letteratura, 1967.

93 p. 25 cm. (Sussidi eruditi, 20)

ECCLESIASTICAL LAW

Lariccia, Sergio.
Diritto ecclesiastico italiano : bibliografia, 1929–1972 / Sergio Lariccia. — Milano : A. Giuffrè, 1974.

vii, 331 p. ; 26 cm. — (Pubblicazioni della Facoltà di giurisprudenza. Università di Cagliari : serie 1 (Giuridica) ; v. 17) It 75–Jan

ECOLOGY

see also Conservation; Human ecology; and under Dissertations, Academic

Bibliography on the physical alteration of the aquatic habitat (channelization) and stream improvement ₍by₎ James R. Barton ₍and others₎ Provo, Utah, Brigham Young University Publications ₍c1972₎

30 p. 28 cm.

Brünn. Krajská lidová knihovna.
Na louce a v lese. Výběrová bibliografie. Brno, Knihovna Jiřího Mahena, rozmn., 1972.

47, ₍1₎ p. 21 cm. (Příroda kolem nás)

Deutsches Institut für Afrika-Forschung.
Umweltschutz und Ökologie in Afrika — ausgewählte neuere Literatur. (Bearbeiter: Ties Möller.) (Hamburg) Deutsches Institut f. Afrika-Forschung (1972).

76 l. 21 cm. (Dokumentationsdienst Afrika, 3)

"Dokumentations-Leitstelle im ADAF"

Hopkins, Sewell Hepburn, 1906–
Annotated bibliography on effects of salinity and salinity changes on life in coastal waters, by S. H. Hopkins. Vicksburg, Miss., U. S. Army Engineer Waterways Experiment Station, 1973.

ix, 411 p. 27 cm. (U. S. Army Engineer Waterways Experiment Station. Contract report H–73–2)

"Sponsored by Office, Chief of Engineers, U. S. Army. Conducted for U. S. Army Engineer Waterways Experiment Station, Vicksburg, Mississippi, under contract nos. DACW39–72–C–0002, DACW3–69–C–0043, and DACW73–70–C–0004, by Department of Biology, Research Foundation, Texas A & M University, College Station. Texas."

Ontario. Ministry of the Environment.
Bibliography, reference material and information sources on the environment. ₍Toronto, 1973₎

16 l. 28 cm.

Srnková, Marie.
Životní prostředí. Soupis literatury z inf. zdrojů ÚEK ₍Ústřední ekonomická knihovna₎. Sest. M. Srnková. Praha, St. knihovna ČSR–Ústř. ekon. knihovna, rozmn., 1972.

26 l. 20 cm.

Thurgood, Margaret Anne.
Mangrove swamp ecology of the Indo-West-Pacific region; a bibliography, compiled by M. A. Thurgood. ₍Johannesburg₎ University of the Witwatersrand, Dept. of Bibliography, Librarianship and Typography, 1968.

₍viii₎, 44 p. 30 cm.

Compiled in part fulfilment for the Diploma in Librarianship, University of the Witwatersrand.

Ulfstrand, Staffan, 1933–
Ecology in semi-arid East Africa: a selection of recent

ecological references. Stockholm, Swedish Natural Science Research Council ₁1971₁

62 p. 25 cm. (Ecological Research Committee. Bulletin no. 11)

Watkins, Jessie B
Ecology and environmental quality; a selected and annotated bibliography for biologists and earth scientists ₁by₁ Jessie B. Watkins. Syracuse, N. Y., Syracuse University Libraries, 1971.

127 l. 28 cm.

"Where have all the flowers gone?" A reference guide and sourcebook to ecological literature. Englewood, Colo., Arrow Co. ₁1970₁

iii, 121 p. 28 cm.

Winton, Harry N   M
Man and the environment: a bibliography of selected publications of the United Nations system, 1946–1971. Compiled and edited by Harry N. M. Winton. New York, Unipub, 1972.

xxi, 305 p. 24 cm.

ECONOMIC ASSISTANCE

Finegold, Donaldine S
International guide to directories on resources in international development: operational organizations and institutions, research and training institutes, expert personnel. Compiled by Donaldine S. Finegold. Washington, Society for International Development, 1965.

v, 26 p. 21 cm.

Finegold, Donaldine S
International guide to directories of resources in international development. ₁Compiled by Donaldine S. Finegold₁ 3d ed. Washington. Society for International Development, 1971.

v, 36 p. 21 cm.

Germany (*Federal Republic, 1949–   ) Bundestag. Wissenschaftliche Abteilung.*
Entwicklungshilfe—Entwicklungsländer. Auswahlbibliographie. Bonn (Deutscher Bundestag, Wissenschaftl. Abt.) 1969.

il, 63 p. 30 cm. (*Its* Bibliographien, Nr. 20)

Compiled by Günter Hindrichs and Inge Schlieper.

Gt. Brit. *Ministry of Overseas Development. Library.*
Select bibliography on British aid to developing countries. London, Ministry of Overseas Development, 1967.

₁3₁ 12 f. 32½ cm.

Gt. Brit. *Ministry of Overseas Development. Library.*
Select bibliography on British aid to developing countries. 2nd ed. London, Ministry of Overseas Development, 1969.

₁5₁, 20 p. 30 cm.

Great Britain. **Overseas Development Administration. Library.**
Select bibliography on British aid to developing countries. 3d rev. ed. London, Overseas Development Administration, 1971.

₁3, 23 p. 30 cm.

First–2d eds. published by the Library under its earlier name: Ministry of Overseas Development Library.

Lorch, Walter T
Entwicklungshilfe und ausländische Investititionen ₁sic₁ in Asien. Development aid and foreign investments in Asia. Zusammengestellt von Walter T. Lorch. Hamburg, Institut für Asienkunde, Dokumentations-Leitstelle, 1971–

v. 30 cm. (Documentatiao Asiae, Nr. 2

Preface in English and German.

Norsk utviklingshjelp.
Hvem vet hva om internasjonalt samarbeid og utviklingshjelp (NORAD) og Norsk samband for Forente nasjoner. Oslo. Utgiverne, 1970.

27 p. 21 cm.

Styrelsen för internationell utveckling.
U-landsproblem och biståndsprojekt. Litteraturförteckning utarb. av en arbetsgrupp inom SIDA. Lund, Bibliotekstjänst, 1967.

30 p. 21 cm. (Btj-serien, 4)

Tarr, Raïssa.
European recovery program (Marshall plan). Programme de relèvement européen ₁by R. Tarr.₁ Paris, Organisation for Economic Co-operation and Development, 1967.

v, 99 p. 27 cm. (Bibliographie spéciale analytique. Special annoted bibliography, 14)

United Nations. *Economic Commission for Asia and the Far East. Library.*
Regional economic cooperation; a select bibliography. Bangkok, 1968.

vi, 222 p. 28 cm. (*Its* Bibliographical bulletin no. 3)

United States. **Agency for International Development. Reference Center.**
A. I. D. memory documents. v. 1– Mar.–   1972– ₁Springfield, Va. National Technical Information Service₁

v. 28 cm. quarterly.

Willmington, S   Clay.
Complete handbook on the foreign aid policy of the United States; a complete manual and reference for high school debaters, and others interested in the subject, by S. Clay Willmington ₁and₁ Gale Sievers. Skokie, Ill., National Textbook Corp. ₁1966₁

239 p. illus. 28 cm.

ECONOMIC DEVELOPMENT
see also Underdeveloped areas

Andrić, Stanislava.
Bibliografija o infrastrukturi. Sastavile: Stanislava Andrić, Dubravka Kunštek, Marija Sever-Zebec. Zagreb, Ekonomski institut, 1971.

73 p. 22 cm.

Bremer Ausschuss für Wirtschaftsforschung.
Dokumente und Berichte über Entwicklungspläne; ein bibliographischer Nachweis. 3. völlig neu bearb. und erw. Ausg. ₁Bremen₁ 1965.

viii, 157 p. 22 cm.

Darchambeau, Valère, 1906–
Les théories et techniques du développement. Theories and techniques of development. Bruxelles, Centre international de documentation économique et sociale africaine, pl. Royale, 7, 1973.

xxii, 375 p. 23 cm. (Bibliographical enquiries, no 2)

Development: new approaches; a guide for educators with issues and resources. ₁New York, Center for War/Peace Studies of the New York Friends Group, 1972₁

68 p. 22 cm. (Intercom no. 69)

International Bank for Reconstructio and Development. Development Services Dept.
List of national development plans. 2d ed. ₁By H. J. Goris. Washington₁ 1968.

viii, 129 l. 28 cm.

Cover title.
First ed. published in 1965 as Appendix 3 of Development planning, by A. Waterston.

Капиталистическое "планирование"; теория и практика. Указатель книжной и журнальной лит-ры на русском и иностранных языках за 1946–1964 гг. ₁Составитель: А. Б. Бродская₁ Москва, 1967.

168 p. 20 cm.

At head of title: Фундаментальная библиотека общественных наук имени В. П. Волгина Академии наук СССР.

Katz, Saul M
Library research in economic and social development, by Saul M. Katz. ₁Pittsburgh₁ Graduate School of Public and International Affairs, University of Pittsburgh ₁1969₁

iii, 30 l. 29 cm.

Lawrence, Mary Margaret.
Decade of development: compendium of United States-sponsored CENTO economic publications, 1959–1969, compiled and edited by Mary Margaret Lawrence. ₁Ankara, Turkey, Office of United States Economic Coordinator for CENTO Affairs₁ 1970.

vi, 201 p. 26 cm.

Organization for Economic Cooperation and Development. Library.
Conférence des Nations Unies sur le commerce et le développement. United Nations Conference for Trade and Development. ₁Paris₁ 1965.

v, 58 p. 27 cm. (Its Bibliographie spéciale analytique, 5 (42))

Organization for Economic Co-operation and Development. Library.
Croissance économique. Economic growth. ₁Paris₁ Organization for Economic Co-operation and Development 1968–

v. 27 cm. (Its Special annotated bibliography, 17)

English or French

Organization for Economic Cooperation and Development. Library.
Planification économique. Economic planning. ₁Paris₁ 1964.

v, 57 p. 29 cm. (Its Bibliographie spéciale analytique, 3 (40))

Schumacher, August.
Development plans and planning; bibliographic and computer aids to research. London, New York, Seminar Press, 1973.

viii, 195 p. 24 cm. (International bibliographical and library series v. 3)

Spitz, Allan A
Developmental change; an annotated bibliography, by Allan A. Spitz. Lexington, University Press of Kentucky ₁1969₁

xi, 316 p. 29 cm.

Streumann, Charlotte, comp.
Economic regionalization. A bibliography of publications in the German language. A report prepared for the Commission on Methods of Economic Regionalization of the International Geographical Union at the Institut für Landeskunde in Bad Godesberg, compiled by Charlotte Streumann. Assisted by Georg Kluszka and Rolf Diedrich Schmidt. Bad Godesberg, Bundesforschungsanstalt für Landeskunde und Raumordnung, 1968.

380 p. 21 cm. (Berichte zur deutschen Landeskunde, Sonderheft 10)

United Nations. Dag Hammarskjold Library.
Economic and social development plans: Africa, Asia, and Latin America. New York, United Nations, 1964.

v, 25 p. 28 cm. (United Nations. ₁Document₁ ST/Lib/ser.B/9)

United Nations. Dag Hammarskjold Library.
Economic and social development plans: centrally-planned economies, developed market economies. New York, United Nations, 1966.

v, 59 p. 28 cm. (Its Bibliographical series, no. 11)

U. S. Information Agency.
Nation building and economic modernization. Washington, U. S. Information Agency, Information Center Service, 1968.

iv, 71 p. 27 cm. (Its Subject bibliography no. 8/68)

Vanderbilt University, Nashville. Graduate School.
Uma bibliografia sôbre desenvolvimento econômico, organizada pelo "Graduate Program in Economic Development" da Vanderbilt University. Manaus, CODEAMA, Setor de Publicações, 1967.

82 l. 28 cm. (Comissão de Desenvolvimento Econômico do Estado do Amazonas. Estudos específicos, ano 3, no. 22)

ECONOMIC FORECASTING

Brodskaĩa, A B
Экономическое прогнозирование в капиталистических странах. (Литература на рус. и иностр. яз. за 1946–1968 гг.) Москва, 1971.

116 p. 27 cm.

At head of title: Академия наук СССР. Институт научной информации и фундаментальная библиотека по общественным наукам.

Daniells, Lorna M
Business forecasting for the 1970's; a selected annotated bibliography. Lorna M. Daniells, compiler. ₁Boston₁ Baker Library, Graduate School of Business Administration, Harvard University, 1970.

48 p. 25 cm. (Harvard University. Graduate School of Business Administration. Baker Library. Reference list no. 26)

Moscow. Publichnaĩa biblioteka.
Научное предвидение и экономическое прогнозирование. Литература на рус., укр. и иностр. яз., преимущественно за 1967. ₁Сост. В. С. Шидловская₁. Москва, 1968.

98 p. 20 cm.

At head of title: Государственная ордена Ленина библиотека СССР имени В. И. Ленина.

New York (*State*). *Dept. of Commerce.*
   A bibliography of demographic and economic projections for New York State and areas. ₁Albany, 1969₁

   39 p. 28 cm. (*Its* Research bulletin no. 25)

Shidlovskaîa, V   S
   Научное предвидение и экономическое прогнозирование. Литература на рус. и иностр. яз. преимущественно за 1968 г. Москва, 1969.

   141 p. 20 cm.

   At head of title: Государственная ордена Ленина библиотека СССР имени В. И. Ленина.

Shidlovskaîa, V   S
   Научное предвидение и экономическое прогнозирование. Библиогр. указ. Литература на рус. и иностр. яз. преимуществ. за 1969 г. Москва, 1971.

   174 p. 20 cm.

   At head of title: Министерство культуры СССР. Государственная библиотека СССР имени В. И. Ленина.

Woy, James B
   Business trends and forecasting: information sources; an annotated guide to theoretical and technical publications, and to sources of data ₁by₁ James B. Woy. Detroit, Gale Research Co. ₁1966, °1965₁

   152 p. 23 cm. (Management information guide, 9)

ECONOMICS

   Bibliographies on the economic conditions, policy, etc., of a particular place are entered under the name of the place.

   see also under   Dissertations, Academic

Als, Georges.
   Introduction à la documentation économique ₁par Georges Als, avec la collaboration de Liliane Clement. 2. éd. Luxembourg₁ Grand-Duché de Luxembourg, Service central de la statistique et des études économiques ₁1968₁

   ii, 71 l. ports. 30 cm. (Collection "Définitions et méthodes," no 4)

Amano, Keitarō, 1901–
   Bibliography of the classical economics. Tokyo, Science Council of Japan, Division of Economics, Commerce & Business Administration, 1961–64.
   6 pts. in 5 v. 22 cm. (Science Council of Japan. Division of Economics, Commerce & Business Administration. Economic series, no. 27, 30–33)
   "Include₁s₁ all the world books and periodical articles published up to the end of 1960."
   CONTENTS.—₁v. 1₁ pt. 1. Adam Smith. pt. 2. Thomas Robert Malthus.—v. 2. pt. 3. David Ricardo.—v. 3. pt. 4. John Stuart Mill.—v. 4. pt. 5. Other British economists.—v. 5. pt. 6. General description of the classical economics.

Andreano, Ralph L   1929–
   The student economist's handbook: a guide to sources ₁by₁ Ralph L. Andreano, Evan Ira Farber ₁and₁ Sabron Reynolds. Cambridge, Mass., Schenkman Pub. Co. ₁1967₁

   x, 160 p. 21 cm.

Batson, Harold Edward, 1906–
   A select bibliography of modern economic theory, 1870–1929, compiled by Harold E. Batson; with an introduction by Lionel Robbins. ₁1st ed.₁ re-issued. London, Routledge & K. Paul, 1967 ₁i. e. 1968₁

   xii, 224 p. 22 cm. (Studies in economics and political science)

Batson, Harold Edward, 1906–
   A select bibliography of modern economic theory, 1870–1929, compiled by Harold E. Batson. With an introd. by Lionel Robbins. New York, A. M. Kelley, 1968.

   xii, 224 p. 23 cm. (Studies in economics and political science. Bibliographies, no. 6)

   Reprints of economic classics.
   Reprint of the 1930 ed.

Baude, Hans, 1922–
   Att söka ekonomisk litteratur. Stockholm, Studieförbundet Näringsliv och samhälle, 1967.

   199 p. 21 cm.

Bespalov, M   N
   Общеэкономическая библиография. Лекция для студентов отд-ния техн. б-к по курсу "Библиография соц. экон. литературы." Москва, 1968.

   34 p. 20 cm.

   At head of title: Министерство культуры РСФСР. Московский государственный институт культуры. М. Н. Беспалов.

BI: Ştiinţe economice. v. 8–
   1971–
   ₁Bucureşti₁ Centrul de Informare şi Documentare în Ştiinţele Sociale şi Politice.

   v. 24 cm. monthly.

   Continues: Academia Republicii Socialiste România.. Centrul de Documentare Ştiinţifică. Buletin de informare ştiinţifică: Ştiinţe economice.
   Cover title   : Ştiinţe economice; buletin de informare ştiinţifică.

A Bibliography for students of economics. London, Oxford U. P., 1968.

   63 p. 21 cm.

Bogardus, Janet, 1904–
   Outline for the course in business and economics literature (Library Service K8252y) Rev. ed. New York, School of Library Service, Columbia University, 1966.

   iv, 51 l. 29 cm.

Borchardt, Knut.
   Vademecum für den Volkswirt. Führer zu volkswirtschaftl. Literatur, Quellen u. Materialien. Stuttgart, G. Fischer, 1973.

   211 p. 19 cm. (Uni-Taschenbücher, 137)

Borovs'kyĭ, M
   Матеріяли до бібліографії господарської літератури, виданої в Галичині, на Волині, Закарпатті й Буковині, 1788–1944. Вінніпег, Накладом УВАН, 1968.
   82 p. 22 cm. (Slavistica, no. 61)
   At head of title: М. Боровський.
   Added t. p.: Selected bibliographical materials re Galicia, Volynia, Trans-Carpathian Ukraine, and Bukovina.

British Columbia. University. Library.
   Guide to reference materials in economics in the Library of the University of British Columbia; compiled by Marilyn Dutton. Vancouver, University of British Columbia, 1970.

   76 p. 23 cm. (Its Reference publication no. 32)

California. State College, *San Diego. Center of Economic Education.*
   Annotated bibliography of paperback library with supplement. ₁San Diego? 1969₁

   ii, 106 p. 22 cm.

Dahmash, Na'īm Husnī.

كتالوج المصادر العربية في العلوم التجارية، أعداد نعيم حسني دهمش لمؤتمر تطوير المكتبة العربية في موضوعات ادارة الاعمال والاقتصاد بفروعها المختلفة المنعقد في الجامعة الاردنية ــ عمان، نيسان ١٩٦٧. ﴿عمان؟﴾ 1967.

267, 3 l. 34 cm.

Added t. p.: Bibliography of materials available in Arabic for business administration and economics, compiled by Naim Husni Dahmash.
Introds. and contents in Arabic and English.

Dienes, Gedeonné.
Szakirodalmi forrásismeret: közgazdaságtudomány. Budapest, OSZK Könyvtártudományi és Módszertani Központ, 1968.

101 p. 22 cm. (A Könyvtárosképzés füzetei)

Doležalová, Magda.
Povinná a odporúčaná literatúra pre štúdium na Vysokej škole ekonomickej v Bratislave. Bratislava, Ústredná ekon. knižnica, rozmn., 1968.

105 p. 21 cm.

Economics Association.
Book list; compiled by J. R. French. Sutton (Surrey), Economics Association, 1968.

₁18₁ p. 21 cm.

(Ékonomicheskaia integratsiiā v kapitalizme)
Экономическая интеграция в капитализме; библиография. Отв. редакторы Ежи Бартосик, Здзислав Новак. Познань, Ин-тут Заходни, 1971.

68 p. 24 cm.

At head of title: Международная рабочая группа по проблемам экономической интеграции в капитализме.

Food and Agriculture Organization of the United Nations. Documentation Center.
Economic analysis: index, 1945–1966. Analyse économique: indice. Analisis economicos. ₁Rome, 1969₁

1 v. (various pagings) 28 cm.

"DC/Sp. 12 April 1969."
Introductory material in English, French and Spanish.

Gáliczky, Éva.
Könyvismeret, közgazdaságtan. Budapest, OSZK Könyvtártudományi és Módszertani Központ, 1963.

83 p. 20 cm. (A Könyvtárosképzés füzetei, középfok)

Germany (Federal Republic, 1949–   ). Bundestag. Wissenschaftliche Dienste.
Konvergenztheorie. Angleichung der ökonomischen, sozialen und politischen Systeme von Ost und West. Bibliographie mit Annotationen. Bonn, 1971.

38 p. 30 cm. (Its Bibliographien, Nr. 26)

"Die Bibliographie wurde im Referat Bibliothek von Bibliotheksrat Dr. rer. pol. Gerhard Hahn angefertigt."

ÍAkovleva, N   M
Хозяйственная реформа и экономика промышленного предприятия. Рек. указатель литературы. Москва, "Книга," 1968.

51 p. 20 cm.

At head of title: Государственная библиотека СССР им. В. И. Ленина.

Japanese annual bibliography of economics. v. 1– 1967–
Tokyo, Third Division, Japan Science Council.

v. 21 cm.

Supersedes: Japan. Nihon Gakujutsu Kaigi. Dai 3-bu. Economic series.

Keizai Dantai Rengōkai.
(Keizai dantai, kaisha tō kankōbutsu ichiran)
経済団体連合会
経済団体・会社等刊行物一覧
東京 昭和43（1968）
170p 21 cm

経済・経営図書総目録
₁東京₁ 法律書・経済書目録刊行会
v. 21 cm. annual.

Began with 1967 issue. Cf. Zen Nihon shuppanbutsu sōmokuroku, 1967.

(Keizai tosho sōmokuroku)
経済図書総目録
₁東京₁ 法律書・経済書・経営書目録刊行会
v. 21 cm. annual.

Began with 1971 issue. Cf. Shuppan nenkan, 1972.
Continues, in part, 経済・経営図書総目録

al-Khāzindār, Ibrāhīm Aḥmad.

بليوجرافية العلوم الاقتصادية والمالية بالجمهورية العربية المتحدة، المؤلفات والترجمات والمحاضرات، ١٩٢٦ ـ ١٩٦٥. اعداد ابراهيم احمد الخازندار، عبده سعد زهران، سمير محمد رضوان. اشراف محمد حلمي مراد. القاهرة، المجلس الاعلى لرعاية الفنون والاداب والعلوم الاجتماعية، لجنة الاقتصاد والمالية العامة، ١٩٦٧ـ.

v. 32 cm.

Kredietbank, N. V., Brussels.
Het boek ten dienste van de economie. Catalogus uitgegeven naar aanleiding van de beurs voor Nederlandstalige economische boeken, ingericht door de Kredietbank. (₁Brussel, Arenbergstr. 7₁) 1969.

63 p. 21 cm.

Library Association. *County Libraries Group.*
Readers' guide to books on economics. 2nd ed. London, Library Association (County Libraries Group), 1967.

47 p. 18½ cm. (*Its* Readers' guide, new ser., no. 97)

McGill University, Montreal. Library. Reference Dept.
Economics : a student's guide to reference resources / McGill University, McLennan Library, Reference Dept. — ₁Montreal₁ : McGill University, McLennan Library, Reference Dept., 1972.

11 p. ; 28 cm.

Maltby, Arthur.
Economics and commerce; the sources of information and their organisation. ₁Hamden, Conn.₁ Archon Books ₁1968₁

239 p. 23 cm.

Maltby, Arthur.
Economics and commerce: the sources of information and

their organisation. London, Bingley, 1968.

239 p. 23 cm.

Mannheim. Universität. Bibliothek.
Verzeichnis der in der Zentralbibliothek der Universität Mannheim vorhandenen Bibliographien aus dem Bereich der Wirtschaftswissenschaften und ihrer Randgebiete. Stand: 31. Juli 1971. 2., erw. Aufl. Mannheim, 1971.

47 p. 29 cm.

Melnyk, Peter.
Economics; bibliographic guide to reference books and information resources. Littleton, Colo., Libraries Unlimited, 1971.

263 p. 24 cm.

Memperkenalkan penerbitan' ekonomi baru. no. 1
Djan. 1969–
Djakarta, Lembaga Ekonomi dan Kemasjarakatan Nasional.

no. 24 cm.

Moscow. Publichnaîa biblioteka.
Основы политической экономии; рекомендательный указатель литературы. ₍Составитель Г. К. Донская. Редактор М. Н. Яковлева₎ Москва, Книга, 1965.

116 p. 22 cm.

Mossé, Robert, 1906–
Bibliographie d'économie politique, 1960–1961–1962 ₍par₎ Robert Mossé ... avec la collaboration de Michel Potier et des étudiants de 4ᵉ année de licence ès sciences économiques (Grenoble 1964–1965). Paris, Sirey, 1966.

61 p. 24 cm.

"Bibliographie des ouvrages français."

Mossé, Robert, 1906–
Bibliographie d'économie politique, 1963–1965 ... Grenoble, Centre régional de documentation pédagogique, 1967.

ii, 103 p. 25 cm.

Mossé, Robert, 1906–
Bibliographie d'économie politique, ouvrages français (1966–1968), par Robert Mossé et Nicole Clerc-Péchiné. Grenoble, Centre régional de documentation pédagogique, 1969.

224 p. 25 cm.

At head of title: Comité régional pour l'U. N. E. S. C. O. Académie de Grenoble.

Novinky literatury. Společenské vědy. Řada II: Bibliografie ekonomické literatury. roč. 4– 1964–
₍Praha₎

v. 21 cm. 12 no. a year.

Supersedes Bibliografie ekonomické literatury and continues its vol. numbering.
Issued jointly by Státní knihovna ČSSR, Ústřední ekonomická knihovna, Praha; and Ústredná ekonomická knižnica, Bratislava.
Vol. 4, no. 11 ("Zvláštní číslo") comprises Ekonomicka literatura ČSSR, 1962–1963.

Organization for Economic Cooperation and Development.
Library.
Bibliographie spéciale analytique. Special annotated bibliography. 1–
₍Paris₎ 1964–

v. 27 cm.

Supersedes its Bibliographie spéciale. Special bibliography.
No. 1–7 called also no. 38–44.

Ōta, Shigehiro.
(Tōkyō Daigaku Keizaigakubu shozō Meiji bunken mokuroku)
東京大学経済学部所蔵 明治文献目録 経済学とその周辺 太田重弘編 東京 東京大学経済学部 昭和44(1969)

237, 59 p. 25 cm. (和書主題別目録 5)

Pleskot, Jozef.
Zdroje a využívanie ekonomickej literatúry. ₍Vyd. 1.₎ Bratislava, Slovenské pedagogické nakl., 1964.

191 p. 29 cm. (Ústredná ekonomická knižnica. Ekonomické aktuality. Bibliografický zpravodaj, 1964 č. 8)

Pleskot, Jozef.
Zdroje a využívanie ekonomickej literatúry a informácií. ₍Vyd. 1₎ Bratislava, Slovenské pedagogické nakl., 1970.

378 p. 23 cm.

At head of title: Ústredná ekonomická knižnica, Bratislava.

Public Affairs Information Service.
Foreign language index. 1968/71–
New York.

v. 27 cm.

Rand Corporation.
Publications of the Economics Department. 1963/70–

Santa Monica, Calif.

v. 28 cm. (Its Rand report R–530)

Supersedes its Economics Department publications.
Compiled by H. Porch.

Reinhart, Bruce.
The vocational-technical library collection: a resource for practical education and occupational training. General editor: Bruce Reinhart. Williamsport, Pa., Bro-Dart Pub. Co., 1970.

xiv, 377 p. 29 cm.

Second ed. published in 1974 under title: Vocational-technical learning materials; books and manuals for schools and community colleges.

Union for Radical Political Economics.
Reading lists in radical political economics. ₍Ann Arbor, Mich.₎ 1971.

2 v. 28 cm.

Vacić, Aleksandar M
Pregled radova objavljenih u "Ekonomistu" u periodu 1948–1967. Glavni i odgovorni urednik Jakov Sirotković. Zagreb, "Ekonomist," organ Saveza ekonomista Jugoslavije, 1968.

147 p. 24 cm.

Cover title: Ekonomist 1948–1967.

Vacić, Aleksandar M
Pregled radova objavljenih u "Ekonomistu" u periodu 1968–1970. ⟨Beograd, Savez ekonomista Jugoslavije, 1971⟩.

38 p. 24 cm.

At head of title: Aleksandar M. Vacić.
Cover title: Ekonomist 1968–1970.

Vienna. Österreichisches Institut für Wirtschaftsforschung.
Publikationen, 1927–1967. (Wien) 1967.

72 p. 24 cm.

Warsaw. Szkoła Główna Planowania i Statystyki. *Biblioteka.*
Bibliografia publikacji pracowników naukowych Szkoły Głównej Planowania i Statystyki w okresie xx–lecia PRL. ₍Opracował zespół pracowników Biblioteki SGPiS pod kierunkiem Hanny Uniejewskiej₎ Warszawa, 1965.

2 v. 24 cm.

Yüan, K'un-hsiang, *comp.*
經濟 論文分類索引 袁坤祥 馬景賢編輯 A classified index to articles on economics (1945–65), compiled by Frank K. S. Yuan ₍and₎ Ma Ching-hsien. Taipei. ₍美國亞洲學會中文研究資料中心₎ 1967.

2 v. (ciii, 1742 p.) 27 cm. (中文研究資料中心 研究資料叢書 第2號 Chinese Materials and Research Aids Service Center. Research aids series, no. 2)

Text in Chinese, with English introduction by Robert L. Irick.

Zagreb. Ekonomski institut.
Bibliografija ekonomske literature. Zagreb, 1962–66.

4 v. 28 cm.

Vols. 2–4 compiled by Stanislava Andrić.

BIBLIOGRAPHIES

(Keizaigaku niji bunken sōmokuroku)
経済学二次文献総目録 経済資料協議会編 東京 有斐閣（発売） 昭和46(1971)

103 p. 22 cm.

EDUCATION

Bräuner, Vilém.
Ekonomická pedagogika. Výběr z knih, statí a článků. Sest. Vilém Bräuner. Brno, St. pedagog. knihovne, rozmn., 1970.

20 p. 20 cm. (Brünn. Státní pedagogická knihovna. Publikace, čís. 368)

Fowler, Peter Staniland.
An annotated bibliography of economics education, 1945–1971; compiled by P. S. Fowler, R. H. Ryba and R. Szreter. ₍Sutton₎, Economics Association, 1972.

39 p. 23 cm.

Kabsa, Fryderyk.
Przewodnik, do ćwiczeń z ekonomii politycznej. Gliwice, 1972.

44 p. 24 cm. (Politechnika Śląska im. W. Pstrowskiego. Skrypty uczelniane, nr. 374)

Platte, Hans Kaspar.
Wirtschafts- und Arbeitslehre. Eine wertende Bibliographie. ₍Von₎ Hans K₍aspar₎ Platte. Wuppertal, Ratingen, Düsseldorf, Henn ₍1970₎.

56 p. 21 cm. (Wirtschaft, Beruf, Gesellschaft)

Тематика контрольных работ по политической экономии для заочных высших учебных заведений, заочных факультетов и отделений вузов, по программе курса политической экономии на 100 и 140 часов. ₍Отв. редактор Г. В. Донской₎. Москва, Мысль, 1967.
46 p. 20 cm.

At head of title: Министерство высшего и среднего специального образования СССР. Отдел преподавания общественных наук.

Vangermain, Heinz, 1924–
Literatur zur Bildungsökonomie. ₍Berichtszeitraum 1961–1971₎ ⟨2. erw. u. erg. Aufl.⟩ (Bearbeiter: Heinz Vangermain ₍u.₎ Waltraud Matschewski). Berlin, Pädagogische Zentralbibliothek ₍bei d.₎ Akademie d. Pädagogischen Wissenschaften d. DDR, 1971.

52 p. 21 cm. (Auswahlbibliographie, Nr. 6/1971)

HISTORY

Brussels. Université libre. *Centre d'économie régionale.*
Bibliographie internationale d'économie régionale. ₍Bruxelles₎ Université libre de Bruxelles, Institut de sociologie ₍1964₎

757 p. 24 cm. (*Its* Études régionales)

"An English issue of this book was also published under the title: International bibliography on regional economy."

Keizai Dantai Rengōkai.
(Keizai dantai chōsa kikan tō kankōbutsu ichiran)
経済団体・調査機関等刊行物一覧 昭和42年8月–昭和45年7月 東京 経済団体連合会 昭和46 (1971)

215 p. 21 cm.

Ontario. Dept. of Trade and Development. Technical Information Centre.
International reference sources: a selected list of subject entries. ₍Toronto, 1969₎

126 p. 28 cm.

Polski Instytut Spraw Międzynarodowych, *Warsaw. Zakład Informacji Naukowej i Dokumentacji.*
Zeszyty bibliograficzne. Seria II: Sytuacja gospodarcza i społeczna państw imperialistycznych. r. 1–   1964– ₍Warszawa₎

v. 29 cm. 4 no. a year.

"Stany Zjednoczone, Wielka Brytania, Francja, NRF."
"Na prawach rękopisu."

United Nations. Library, Geneva.
League of Nations & United Nations monthly list of selected articles; cumulative, 1920–1970: economic questions. Edited by Norman S. Field, Associate Chief Librarian, United Nations Library, Geneva. Dobbs Ferry, N. Y., Oceana Publications, 1973–
v. 29 cm.
A compilation arranged by subject and country in chronological order from the card file used to issue the library's Liste mensuelle d'articles sélectionnés.
CONTENTS: v. 1. Economic conditions, 1920–1955.

JUVENILE LITERATURE

Nappi, Andrew T
Learning economics through children's stories ₍by₎ Andrew T. Nappi, R. Allen Moran and Mary Jo Berdan. ₍New York₎ Joint Council on Economic Education, 1973.

v, 55 p. 23 cm.

LIBRARY CATALOGS

Black, R   D   Collison.
A catalogue of pamphlets on economic subjects published between 1750 and 1900 and now housed in Irish libraries, by R. D. Collison Black. Belfast, Queen's University Bel-

fast, 1969.

xi, 632 p. 30 cm.

Black, R   D   Collison.
A catalogue of pamphlets on economic subjects published between 1750 and 1900 and now housed in Irish libraries, by R. D. Collison Black.   New York, A. M. Kelley, 1969.

ix, 632 p. 30 cm.

East Pakistan Small Industries Corporation. *Rural Industrial Service.*
Classified bibliographical catalogue.   Dacca [1965–

v. 34 cm.

CONTENTS.—pt. 1. Technical library.

Germany (*Federal Republic, 1949–   *). *Bundesministerium für Wirtschaft. Bibliothek.*
Verzeichnis der in der Bibliothek des Bundesministeriums für Wirtschaft vorhandenen Gutachten.   Mit einem Vorwort von Erich Richter.   Bonn, 1965.

vii, 142 p. 30 cm.

On spine: Gutachten-Verzeichnis.

Harvard University. *Graduate School of Business Administration. Baker Library. Kress Library of Business and Economics.*
Catalogue; with data upon cognate items in other Harvard libraries.   Boston, Baker Library, Harvard Graduate School of Business Administration [1940]–67.

5 v. 30 cm.

Arranged chronologically, with alphabetical index of authors and anonymous titles.

CONTENTS.—[v. 1.] Covering material published through 1776.—[v. 2.] Supplement, covering material through 1776.—[v. 3.] 1777–1817.—[v. 4.] 1818–1848.—[v. 5.] Supplement, 1473–1848.

Harvard University. *Library.*
Economics and economics periodicals.   Cambridge, Mass.; distributed by Harvard University Press, 1970.

2 v. 29 cm. (*Its* Widener Library shelflist, 23–24)

CONTENTS.—v. 1. Classification schedule, classified listing by call number, chronological listing.—v. 2. Author and title listing.

Hollander, Jacob Harry, 1871–1940.
The economic library of Jacob H. Hollander.   Compiled by Elsie A. G. Marsh.   Baltimore, 1937.   Detroit, Gale Research Co., 1966.

xi, 324 p. port. 23 cm.

Kiel. Universität. Institut für Weltwirtschaft. Bibliothek.
Personenkatalog.   Boston, G. K. Hall, 1966.

30 v. 37 cm.

Added t. p.: Bibliographical and biographical catalog of persons.

Kiel. Universität. *Institut für Weltwirtschaft. Bibliothek.*
Regionenkatalog.   Boston, G. K. Hall, 1967.

52 v. 36 cm.

Added t. p. in English.
Pref. in German and English.

Közgazdasági és Jogi Könyvkiadó.
A Közgazdasági és Jogi Könyvkiadó katalógusa, 1960–1966.   [Szerk. Bacsó Sándorné és Györki Mária]   Budapest, 1967.

269 p. 19 cm.

London.   University.   Goldsmiths' Company's Library of Economic Literature.
Catalogue of the Goldsmiths' Library of Economic Literature, compiled by Margaret Canney and David Knott; with an introduction by J. H. P. Pafford.   London, Cambridge University Press, 1970–

v. port. 31 cm.

CONTENTS.—v. 1. Printed books to 1800.

Nihon Ginkō.   Chōsakyoku.
(Tsuika tosho mokuroku, Wa-Kansho no bu)
追加図書目録　和漢書の部　[東京]　日本銀行調査局　[昭和47(1972)]

649 p. 26 cm.

昭和40年7月以降、同45年12月までの間に収集した図書を収録したもの

Senshū Daigaku.   Toshokan.
(Keizaigaku kankei tosho mokuroku; yōshohen)
経済学関係図書目録(洋書篇)　専修大学図書館編　東京　昭和42(1967)

457 p. 25 cm.

Smith, Adam, 1723–1790.
A catalogue of the library of Adam Smith, author of the "Moral sentiments" and "The wealth of nations." 2d ed., prepared for the Royal Economic Society by James Bonar, with an introd. and appendices.   New York, A. M. Kelley, 1966.

xxxiv, 218 p. illus., facsim., ports. 23 cm. (The Adam Smith library)

Reprints of economic classics.
Reprint of 1932 ed.

PERIODICALS

Bologna.   Università.   Facoltà di economia e commercio. Biblioteca.
Elenco dei periodici e atti accademici della Biblioteca della Facoltà di economia e commercio.   Bologna, Tip. Compositori, 1968.

104 p. 24 cm.

Edited by Gianfranco Franceschi.

Furtado, Dilma Ribeiro.
Indice de periódicos brasileiros de economia, Colaboração de Lygia de Lourdes Saide.   Introdução de Mário Ferreira da Luz.   Rio de Janeiro, Biblioteca Nacional, 1968.

266 p. 23 cm.

At head of title: Biblioteca Nacional, Divisão de Circulação, Seção de Referência Geral.

Grupo de Trabajo para la Integración de la Información.
Catálogo colectivo de publicaciones periódicas en desarrollo económico y social.   Lima, 1972.

xiii, 185 p. 29 cm.

Handbuch der wirtschaftswissenschaftlichen Information und Dokumentation in der DDR.   Berlin, Akademie-Verlag, 1967.

241 p. 24 cm.

At head of title: Deutsche Akademie der Wissenschaften zu Berlin. Institut für Wirtschaftswissenschaften. Zentralstelle für Wirtschaftswissenschaftliche Dokumentation und Information.

Hitotsubashi Daigaku, Tokyo. Sangyō Keiei Kenkyūjo. Shiryōshitsu.
(Zasshi sōmokuroku)

一橋大学.産業経営研究所資料室

雑誌総目録

〔東京 昭和45(1970)〕

84p 25 cm

Index of economic articles in collective volumes. v. –7A;

1964/65. Homewood, Ill., R. D. Irwin.

v. 2 cm.

Numbering adopted from "a companion volume": Index of economic journals.
Vols. for –1964/65 prepared under the auspices of the American Economic Association.
Superseded by Index of economic articles in journals and collective volumes.

Index of economic articles in journals and collective volumes. v. 8– 1966–
Homewood, Ill., R. D. Irwin.

v. 26 cm. annual.

Supersedes Index of economic journals, and Index of economic articles in collective volumes, and continues their numbering.
Vols. for 1967– prepared under the auspices of the American Economic Association.

Index to Indian economic journals. v. 1–
Jan./June 1966–
[Calcutta, Information Research Academy]

v. 24 cm. quarterly.

Organization for Economic Cooperation and Development. *Library.*
Catalogue des périodiques, 1966. Catalogue of periodicals. Paris, 1966.

3 v. 27 cm.

At head of title: Organisation de coopération et de développement économiques. Service d'information. Bibliothèque.
French and English.
CONTENTS.—1. Index alphabétique.—2. Index par pays ou organisations internationales, et par sujets.—3. Index alphabétique des sujets.

Organization for Economic Cooperation and Development. Library.
Catalogue of periodicals 1967–1968. Catalogue des périodiques. Paris, 1968.

353 p. 27 cm.

French and English.
Supersedes the Catalogue of periodicals 1966.

Organization for Economic Cooperation and Development. Library.
Catalogue of periodicals 1969–1970. Catalogue des périodiques. Paris, 1970.

vii, 485 p. 27 cm.

"INF/BIB(70)7"
English and French.

Oslo. Universitet. *Bibliotek.*
Løpende utenlandske periodika i norske biblioteker. Økonomi. Oslo, 1966.

24 l. 29 cm.

At head of title: Norsk samkatalog.

Rath, Vimal, 1929–
Index of Indian economic journals, 1916–1965. Poona, Gokhade Institute of Politics and Economics; Orient Longman [1971]

liv, 302 p. 25 cm. (Gokhale Institute studies, no. 57)

産業経済雑誌主要記事索引

〔東京〕日本図書館協会

v. 21-26 cm. annual.

Report year ends Mar. 31.
Began with 1964 issue.

Vols. for prepared by 日本開発銀行中央資料室

Vols. for published by 日本開発銀行中央資料室

Washington, D. C. Joint Library of the International Monetary Fund and the International Bank for Reconstruction and Development.
Economics and finance; index to periodical articles, 1947–1971, compiled by the staff of the Joint Bank-Fund Library for the International Monetary Fund and the World Bank Group. Boston, G. K. Hall, 1972.

4 v. 37 cm.

ECONOMICS, MATHEMATICAL

Akademiīa nauk SSSR. *Sibirskoe otdelenie. Institut matematiki.*
Математико-экономические методы и модели; применение математических методов и электронных вычислительных машин в технико-экономических вопросах. Библиографический указатель. [Составители: И. А. Лифшиц и др. Под ред. И. В. Романовского и К. И. Шафрановского] Ленинград, Наука [Ленинградское отдние] 1964.
170 p. 22 cm.
At head of title: Академия наук СССР. Институт математики Сибирского отделения АН СССР. Ленинградское отделение Математического института им. В. А. Стеклова АН СССР. Библиотека АН СССР.

Aleksandrova, K V
[Problemy optimal'nogo funktsionirovaniīa ekonomiki SSSR]
Проблемы оптимального функционирования экономики СССР. Описание материалов выставки. Сост. К. В. Александрова. Ленинград, 1972.
161 p. 20 cm.
At head of title: Библиотека Академии наук СССР. Справочно-библиографический отдел.
"Автоматизированные системы управления. Краткий перечень статей на русском и иностранных языках за 1969–1971 гг.": p. [79]–161.

Математико-экономические методы и модели. Применение матем. методов и электронных вычислит. машин в планировании и техн.-экон. задачах. Библиогр. указатель. Ленинград, "Наука," Ленингр. отд-ние, 1968.
314 p. 22 cm.
At head of title: Академия наук СССР. Ленинградское отделение математического института им. В. А. Стеклова. Библиотека Академии наук СССР.
By I. A. Lifshits and others.
"Июнь 1963 г.–декабрь 1966 г."

Pfersich, Hans Peter.
Wirtschaftskybernetik./ Hans Peter Pfersich. — Neuwied, Berlin: Luchterhand 1972.

xii, 90 p.; 21 cm. — (Bibliographie zum Fachgebiet Wirtschaftsführung, Kybernetik, Datenverarbeitung; Bd. 3)

Warsaw. Instytut Ekonomiki i Organizacji Przemysłu.
Ośrodek Informacji i Dokumentacji Naukowo-Technicznej.
Zastosowanie metod matematycznych do ekonomiki i organizacji przemysłu. ₍Opracowała J. Kasprzakowa. Warszawa₎ 1964.

112 p. 29 cm. (*Its* Tematyczne zestawienie dokumentacyjne, nr. 43)

ECUADOR
see also under Colombia *(Watson)*

Casa de la Cultura Ecuatoriana.
Catálogo general de publicaciones de la Casa de la Cultura Ecuatoriana, 1944–1965. Quito, 1965.

219 p. illus., facsims., ports. 21 cm.

Cover title: 20 años de labor, 1945–1965.

Ecuador. Junta Nacional de Planificación y Coordinación Económica. Sección Estudios Sociales.
Listado parcial de la bibliografía social, socio-económica y política del Ecuador: sección obras generales y sección histórica. Versión preliminar. ₍Quito, 1972₎

147 p. 28 cm.

Cover title: Bibliografía socio-económica y política del Ecuador. "Solo para circulación interna."

Mesa, Rosa Quintero.
Ecuador. Ann Arbor, Mich., Xerox University Microfilms, 1973.

xxxii, 142 p. 29 cm. (Latin American serial documents, v. 8)

Prepared under a grant from the Ford Foundation to the University of Florida Libraries.

LAW see Law - Ecuador

ECUMENICAL MOVEMENT

Buhler, Marine.
Les Unions chrétiennes de jeunes gens et le mouvement œcuménique. Bibliographie analytique et sélective. Genève, 1966.

41 l. 30 cm.

Crow, Paul A
The ecumenical movement in bibliographical outline, by Paul A. Crow, Jr. ₍1st ed.₎ New York, Dept. of Faith and Order, National Council of the Churches of Christ in the U. S. A., 1965.

viii, 80 p. 23 cm.

Delfs, Hermann.
Ökumenische Literaturkunde. Hrsg. von D. F. Siegmund-Schultze. Soest, Westfälische Verlagsbuchhandlung Mocker & Jahn, 1966.

xi, 579 p. 22 cm. (Schriften des Ökumenischen Archivs Soest, Bd. 3)

Soester Wissenschaftliche Beiträge, Bd. 29.

Lambeth Palace. *Library.*
Christian unity; the Anglican initiative; catalogue of an exhibition of books and manuscripts held in the library of Lambeth Palace. London, S. P. C. K., 1966.

₍23₎ p. 4 plates (incl. facsims.) 22 cm.

Lescrauwaet, Josephus Franciscus.
Critical bibliography of ecumenical literature ₍by₎ J. F. Lescrauwaet. ₍1st ed.₎ Nijmegen, Bestel Centrale V. S. K. B., 1965.

93 p. 24 cm. (Bibliographia ad usum seminariorum, v. 7)

World Council of Churches. Commission on Faith and Order.
An index to the doctrines, persons, events, etc. of the Faith and Order Commission, World Council of Churches, given in the English language editions, official, numbered publications, 1910–1948, and check list, Faith and Order Commission, official, numbered publications, series I, 1910–1948, series II, 1948–1970 ₍by₎ A. T. DeGroot, Honorary Archivist. Geneva, Faith and Order Commission, World Council of Churches, 1970.

258 p. 26 cm.

Previous ed. published in 1963 under title: Check list, Faith and Order Commission; official, numbered publications ...

World Council of Churches. Library.
Classified catalog of the ecumenical movement. Boston, G. K. Hall, 1972.

2 v. 37 cm.

EDE, NETHERLANDS

Ede, Netherlands. Archief.
Inventaris van de archieven der gemeente Ede tot 1 maart 1948, door J. Das. n. p., 1971.

93 p. 30 cm.

EDSCHMID, KASIMIR

Brammer, Ursula G
Kasimir Edschmid, Bibliographie. Zusammengestellt von Ursula G. Brammer. Mit einer Einführung von Fritz Usinger. Heidelberg, L. Schneider, 1970.

xv, 76 p. 24 cm. (Veröffentlichung der Deutschen Akademie für Sprache und Dichtung, Darmstadt, 43)

EDUCATION

Bibliographies on the teaching of specific subjects are entered under the appropriate subject headings.

see also Study, Method of; Teaching; and under Dissertations, Academic

AASL-TEPS Coordinating Committee for the Teachers' Library Project.
The teachers' library; how to organize it and what to include. ₍Washington, D. C.₎ National Education Association ₍1966₎

204 p. 23 cm.

AASL-TEPS Coordinating Committee for the Teachers' Library Project.
The teachers' library; how to organize it and what to include. ₍Rev. ed. Washington₎ National Education Association, 1968.

208 p. 23 cm.

Abdullah, Sayyid Mohammad.
اردو میں علمی اور سائنسی کتابوں کی فہرست؛ جو بسلسلہ نمائش

علمی یونیورسٹی ہال، لاہور میں رکھی گئی تھیں، یہ نمائش پاکستان
سائنٹفک سوسائٹی کی سالانہ کانفرنس ۱۹۶۶ کے سلسلے میں ہوئی
تھی۔ مرتبہ سید عبداللہ برائے مغربی پاکستان اردو اکیڈمی،
لاہور۔ الاہور، پاکستان اردو اکیڈمی، 1970.

124 p. 25 cm.
Cover title:
In Urdu.
اردو میں سائنسی اور علمی کتابیں

Alferov, IUriĭ Sergeevich.
Библиография по проблемам педагогического обра-
зования. (1960–1970 гг.) Сост. Алферов Ю. С. Ред.
Костяшкин Э. Г. Москва, 1970.

199 p. 20 cm.
Cover title.
At head of title: Научно-исследовательский институт общей
педагогики АПН СССР. Институт повышения квалификации пре-
подавателей педагогических дисциплин университетов и педвузов
АПН СССР.

Argentine Republic. *Centro Nacional de Documentación e Información Educativa.*
Conferencia de Ministros de Educación y Ministros En-
cargados del Planeamiento Económico en los Países de
América Latina y del Caribe, Buenos Aires, 20–30 de junio,
1966: referencias bibliográficas. Conference of Ministers
of Education and Ministers or Directors Responsible for
Economic Planning in Latin America and the Caribbean,
Buenos Aires, 20–30 June, 1966: bibliographical references.
[Buenos Aires, 1966]

xiii, 289 l. 28 cm.
Introductory matter in Spanish, French, and English.

Bernabei, Raymond.
Behavioral objectives; an annotated resource file. Compiled and produced by Raymond Bernabei. [Harrisburg,
Bureau of Curriculum Development and Evaluation, Commonwealth of Pennsylvania] 1969.

45 l. 29 cm.

ביבליוגרפיה [sic] למורים בבתי-מדרש למורים בתפוצות. ירושלים,
המחלקה לחינוך ולתרבות בגולה, 1966.

7 l. 28 cm.

Bjerstedt, Åke.
Pedagogisk dokumentation. Lund, Gleerup, 1973.

86 p. 21 cm. (Pedagogisk orientering och debatt, 42)

Bratislava. Slovenská pedagogická knižnica.
A Szlovák Pedagógiai Könyvtár legújabb magyar nyelvu
válogatoot könyveinek jegyzéke (1966–1968). Bratislava,
1968.

55 p. 21 cm.

Bräuner, Vilém.
Počáteční vyučování. Výběrový soupis domácích a zah-
raničních publikací 1961–1969. Sest. Vilém Bräuner. Brno,
St. pedagog. knihovna, rozmn., 1970.

65 p. 29 cm. (Publikace, č. 853)
At head of title: Státní vědecká knihovna.

CCM Information Corporation.
ERIC educational documents index, 1966-1969. New York,
1970.

2 v. 30 cm.
CONTENTS: v. 1. Major descriptors.—v. 2. Minor descriptors. Author index.

Classen, Johannes, 1940–
Bibliographie zur antiautoritären Erziehung. Heidelberg, Quelle & Meyer [c1971]

36 p. 19 cm.

Cooper, Lloyd G 1935–
The professional library in education collection. Lloyd
G. Cooper, editor. Newark, N. J., Bro-Dart Foundation,
1968.

xxii, 141 p. 29 cm.

Debl, Helmut.
Didaktische Bibliographie. Eine Einführung in das
Schrifttum der allgemeinen Didaktik. Geretsried, Schuster,
1968.

118 p. 21 cm. (Wissenschaftliche Bibliographien, Bd. 2)

Ealing, Eng. Libraries Dept.
Books on education: a list compiled by the Libraries Department of the London Borough of Ealing. London, London Borough of Ealing Libraries Department, [1972].

[6], 92 p. 21 cm.

Fediuk, Simon, 1910–
Bibliography on education. New York, New York State
Division of Human Rights, 1970.

60 p. 28 cm. ([New York (State). State Division of Human
Rights. Reference Library] Special collection no. 2)

Geisinger, Robert W
A selected bibliography project: evaluation, the affective
domain [by] Robert W. Geisinger. [Harrisburg] Bureau
of Research, Dept. of Education, Commonwealth of Pennsylvania, 1970.

15 l. 28 cm.

I Giovani nella letteratura inglese, francese e tedesca.
[Roma], Amministrazione per le attività assistenziali italiane e internazionali, 1970.

281 p. 24 cm. (Indagini e documentazioni sociali, 4)

Glaeser, Georg.
Zur Frage des bibliographischen Apparates an pädagogischen Bibliotheken; Besitznachweis. Dortmund, Pädagogische Zentralbücherei des Landes Nordrhein-Westfalen,
1965.

7 l. 30 cm.
Results of a survey of libraries, initiated at the yearly meeting,
1964, of the Arbeitsgemeinschaft Pädagogischer Bibliotheken.

**Gosudarstvennaĭa nauchnaĭa biblioteka po narodnomu ob-
razovaniĭu.**
Книжная выставка.

Москва.
v. 21 cm.
"Библиография новой педагогической литературы и план выставки."
Began with vol. for 1966/67.

Hall, Granville Stanley, 1844–1924.
Hints toward a select and descriptive bibliography of education. Arr. by topics, and indexed by authors, by G.
Stanley Hall and John M. Mansfield. And with a new foreword by Francesco Cordasco. Boston, Heath, 1886. De-

troit, Gale Research Co., 1973.

xv, 309, 110–135 p. 18 cm.

Hoell, Christel.
Verzeichnis von Recherche- und Informationsmitteln zur Pädagogik. Ein Bestandsnachweis. Berlin, Deutsches Pädagogisches Zentralinstitut, Abt. Dokumentation und Informaticn, Bibliothek, 1967.

87 p. 20 cm. (Sonderheft des Informations-Bulletins Pädagogik)

Horňák, Kamil.
Mravně narušená mládež; vyber literatury. Připravil Kamil Horňák. Brno, Státní pedagogická knihovna, 1967.

14 l. 21 cm. (Bibliografický leták, čís. 181)

Hoven, René.
Le livre scolaire au temps d'Érasme et des humanistes. Université de Liège, juin 1969. Catalogue rédigé par René Hoven et Jean Hoyoux. Préface de Léon-E. Halkin. Liège, Université de Liège, 1969.

vi, 58 p. 22 cm.

At head of title: Centre interuniversitaire d'histoire de l'humanisme. Exposition.

International Institute for Educational Planning.
Bibliographie de la planification de l'éducation. Paris, Institut international de planification de l'éducation, 1965.

x, 141 p. 27 cm.

International Seminar on the Prospective of Education, Madrid, 1971.
Elementos bibliográficos ... Madrid, 12 a 17 de abril de 1971. Madrid, Ministerio de Educación y Ciencia, Centro Nacional de Investigaciones para el Desarrollo de la Educación (1971)

51 p. 27 cm.

At head of title: Seminario Internacional sobre Prospectiva de la Educación.
Title and text in English, French, and Spanish. Title in English: Bibliographical elements.

Jerusalem. Hebrew University. *School of Education.*
ראשי - פרקים ורשימות - ביבליוגראפיה ללימודי החוג לחינוך. ירושלים, בית הספר לחינוך של האוניברסיטה העברית ושל משרד החינוך והתרבות. תשכ"ו. 1965/66.

110 p. 31 cm.

Jerusalem. Hebrew University. *School of Education.*
ראשי פרקים וביבליוגראפיה, ללימודי המחלקה להכשרת מורים לבתי-הספר העל-יסודיים. ירושלים, בית-הספר לחינוך של האוניברסיטה העברית. תשכ"ד. 1964.

31 p. 17 cm.

Job, Douglas E
Books and periodicals on liberal education: a bibliography; compiled by Douglas Job. Cambridge, Association for Liberal Education, 1972.

(2), ii, 58 p. 22 cm.

Job, Douglas E
Liberal education; (an annotated list) selected by Douglas E. Job. London, National Book League, 1971.

30 p. 21 cm.

At head of title: National Book League with the Association for Liberal Education.
"Distributed in the United States and Canada by Richard Abel & Co. Inc., Portland, Oregon."

Juif, Paul.
Manuel bibliographique des sciences de l'éducation, par Paul Juif ... et Fernand Dovero ... Paris, Presses universitaires de France, 1968.

319 p. 22 cm. (Bibliothèque scientifique internationale. Section pédagogie)

Kentucky. Dept. of Education. Curriculum Laboratory.
Resources for revision: materials available in the Curriculum Laboratory. (Frankfort) Office of Curriculum Development, 1967.

iv, 63 l. 28 cm.

Cover title: Curriculum materials on loan.

Kentucky. *Dept. of Education. Library.*
Archives report; a list of books in the Archives Room of the Kentucky State Department of Education. (Frankfort) Dept. of Education, 1967.

10, 14 l. 28 cm.

Kentucky. University. *Bureau of School Service.*
Publications of the Bureau of School Service, 1927–1964. Lexington (1964)

45 p. 22 cm.

Kleskeňová, Dagmar.
Zahraniční učebnice ve fondu SPK (Státní pedagogická knihovna) 1945–1967. Bibliografie. Zprac. Dagmar Kleskeňová a Dagmar Lišnovská. Brno, St. pedagog. knihovna, rozmn., 1968.

103 p. 29 cm. ((Brünn. Státní pedagogická knihovna) Publikace, č. 301)

Kokuritsu Kyōiku Kenkyūjo, Tokyo.
(Kokuritsu Kyōiku Kenkyūjo kankō kenkyū seika yōroku)
国立教育研究所刊行研究成果要録 (東京) 国立教育研究所 昭和45(1970)

160 p. 26 cm.

Library Association. *County Libraries Group.*
Readers' guide to books on education. 3rd ed. London, Library Association (County Libraries Group) 1966.

54 p. 18½ cm. (*Its* Reader's guide, new ser., no. 92)

Library Association. County Libraries Group.
Reader's guide to books on education. 4th ed. Newtown, Library Association (County Libraries Group), 1970.

80 p. 19 cm. (Its Readers' guides, new ser., no. 115)

Lišnovská, Dagmar.
Zahraniční učebnice pro učňovské školy. (Ve fondech St. pedagog. knihovny v Brně.) Sest. Dagmar Lišnovská. Brno, St. pedagog. knihovna, rozmn., 1968.

4 p. 20 cm. (Bibliografický leták, čís. 201)

Lowell, Mildred (Hawksworth)
Key word analytic subject index to the Library of education. New York, Center for Applied Research in Education (1967)

117 p. 24 cm.

Marks, Barbara S
The New York University list of books in education, compiled and edited by Barbara S. Marks. New York,

Citation Press, 1968.

527 p. 20 cm.

Michigan Association of School Librarians. *Committee on Professional Materials.*
Recommended materials for a professional library in the school. Helen Jean Healy, chairman. Rev. ed. Kalamazoo, Michigan Association of School Librarians, 1969.

viii, 188 p. 22 cm.

Monroe, Will Seymour, 1863–1939.
Bibliography of education, by Will S. Monroe. New York, D. Appleton, 1897. Detroit, Gale Research Co., 1968.

xxiv, 202 p. 20 cm.

Reprint of the 1897 ed. with a new introd. by F. Cordasco.

Natalis, Ernest.
Un quart de siècle de littérature pédagogique. Essai bibliographique 1945–1970. A quarter of a century of educational literature. Bibliographical essay 1945–1970. (Gembloux), Duculot, (1971).

766 p. 22 cm.

Naujokaitis, Pranas.
Pedagogika ir metodika. 1940–1965. Bibliografija. Kaunas, "Sviesa," 1968.

390 p. 21 cm.

Neal, Kenneth William.
A library guide to education ₍by₎ K. W. Neal. ₍Finchfield, Wolverhampton, Eng., 1965₎

24 p. 20 cm. (*His* Library guides)

New York (*City*) *Board of Education. Division of Curriculum Development.*
Improving the professional library in the school. New York ₍1965₎

v, 10 p. 22 cm.

New York (*State*) *University.*
Index to curriculum for teachers on microfiche, by grade, subject & accession number. St. Paul, Minnesota Mining and Manufacturing Co., 1968.

30 p. 28 cm.

Nordiske jordbrugsforskeres forening. Sektion X.
Pædagogisk litteratur. En oversigt udg. af Nordiske Jordbrugsforskeres Forenings sektion X og Landbrugets Informationskontor. København, Landbrugets Informationskontor ₍1968–

v. 21 cm.

Ontario. *Provincial Library Service.*
Teachers' reference library. ₍Toronto₎ 1967.

87 p. 28 cm.

Paulston, Rolland G
Non-formal education; an annotated international bibliography. Edited by Rolland G. Paulston. Foreword by Don Adams. New York, Praeger ₍1972₎

xxi, 332 p. 25 cm. (Praeger special studies in international economics and development)

Peciarová, Jana, comp.
Bibliografia článkov z časopisu Sovetskaja pedagogika;

výberová bibliografia z r. 1956–1966. ₍Zostavila: Jana Peciarová₎. Bratislava, Slovenská pedagogická knižnica, 1967.

206 p. 21 cm.

Педагогическая библиография. ₍Составители: В. А. Ильина. Отв. редактор Н. А. Сундуков₎ Москва, Просвещение, 1967–

v. 27 cm.

At head of title, v. 1– : Академия педагогических наук СССР. Государственная научная библиотека по народному образованию им. К. Д. Ушинского.

CONTENTS.—т. 1. 1924–1930.

Perkins, Ralph.
The new concept guide to reference in education; a quick answer to "Where can I find it." ₍Grand Forks? N. D., 1965₎

vii, 58 l. 28 cm.

Philosophy of education; an organization of topics and selected sources ₍by₎ Harry S. Broudy ₍and others₎ Urbana, University of Illinois Press, 1967.

xii, 287 p. 23 cm.

———— Supplement. 1969 ₍by₎ Christiana M. Smith ₍and₎ Harry S. Broudy. Urbana, University of Illinois Press ₍1969₎

139 p. 23 cm.

Powell, John Percival.
Philosophy of education: a select bibliography, compiled by John P. Powell. 2nd ed. Manchester, Manchester University Press, 1970.

xiii, 51 p. 22 cm.

Restrepo Posada, María Isabel.
Indice antioqueño de educación, 1871–1965. Medellín, Escuela Interamericana de Bibliotecología, 1967.

xv, 163 l. 27 cm. (Publicaciones de la E. I. B. Serie: Bibliografías, no. 24)

Tesis (licenciatura en bibliotecología)—Universidad de Antioquia.

Richmond, William Kenneth, 1910–
The literature of education: a critical bibliography, 1945–1970 ₍by₎ W. Kenneth Richmond. London, Methuen, 1972.

x, 206 p. 23 cm.

"Distributed in the U. S. A. by Barnes & Noble."

Rome (City). **Centro didattico nazionale per la scuola elementare e di completamento dell'obbligo scolastico.**
Orientamenti bibliografici per l'aggiornamento. 2. edizione riveduta e aggiornata. Roma, 1969.

173 p. 24 cm. (Archivio didattico. Serie 2: Scuola elementare e di completamento dell'obbligo scolastico)

Saskatchewan. Provincial Library, Regina. Bibliographic Services Division.
Education; a selected bibliography. Regina, 1973.

29 p. 28 cm.

Saskatchewan. Provincial Library, Regina. Bibliographic Services Division.
Education; a bibliography. Regina, 1973.

107 p. 28 cm.

Schaefer, James F

A bibliography of references used in the preparation of nine model teacher education programs. Prepared by James F. Schaefer, Jr. Washington, Printed and distributed by the ERIC Clearinghouse on Teacher Education, 1969.

95 l. 28 cm.

Schaefer, James F

Education and educational practices: a bibliography for teacher education; references used in the preparation of the nine model teacher education programs. Prepared by James F. Schaefer, Jr. Washington, Printed and distributed by the ERIC Clearinghouse on Teacher Education, 1969.

41 l. 28 cm.

Schmidt, Heiner.

Bibliographie zur allgemeinen Didaktik und Methodenlehre des Unterrichts. Zeitschriften-Nachweis 1947-1967. Zusammengestellt u. bearb. von Heiner Schmidt u. F[ranz] J[osef] Lützenkirchen. Weinheim, Berlin, Basel, Beltz (1969).

xvi, 331 p. 21 cm. (Erziehungswissenschaftliche Dokumentation. Reihe A: Der Inhalt neuerer pädagogischer Zeitschriften und Serien im deutschen Sprachgebiet, Bd. 6)

Schmidt, Heiner.

Materialien zur allgemeinen Didaktik und Methodenlehre des Unterrichts: Bücher, Bibliographien, Sammelwerke 1945-1971, 72/ zusammengestellt u. bearb. von Heiner Schmidt. Red. Mitarb. von Ellen Hantke [u. a.]. — Weinheim, Basel : Beltz, 1973.

xvii, 430 p.; 21 cm. — (Erziehungswissenschaftliche Dokumentation. Reihe B: Monographien, Hochschulschriften, selbständige und unselbständige Bibliographien, Beiträge aus Sammelwerken, Fachlexiken und Handbüchern der neueren Pädagogik im deutschen Sprachgebiet; Bd. 6)

Schmidt, Heiner.

Materialien zur Erziehungswirklichkeit und zur Theorie der Bildung: Bücher, Bibliographien, Sammelwerke 1915-1971/72/ zusammengestellt u. bearb. von Heiner Schmidt. Red. Mitarb. von Ellen Hantke [u. a.] — Weinheim, Basel : Beltz, 1973.

xvii, 585 p.; 22 cm. — (Erziehungswissenschaftliche Dokumentation. Reihe B: Monographien, Hochschulschriften, selbständige und unselbständige Bibliographien, Beiträge aus Sammelwerken, Fachlexiken und Handbüchern der neueren Pädagogik im deutschen Sprachgebiet; Bd. 3)

Schmidt, Heiner.

Materialien zur Schulorganisation und zur Reform des Bildungswesens; Bücher, Bibliographien, Sammelwerke 1945-1971/72, zusammengestellt und bearb. von Heiner Schmidt. Redaktionelle Mitarbeit von Ellen Hantke, Erwin Hanel und F. J. Lützenkirchen. Weinheim, Beltz [c1973]

xviii, 413 p. 22 cm. (Erziehungswissenschaftliche Dokumentation. Reihe B: Monographien, Hochschulschriften, selbständige und unselbständige Bibliographien, Beiträge aus Sammelwerken, Fachlexiken und Handbüchern der neueren Pädagogik im deutschen Sprachgebiet, Bd. 1)

Sedlák, Jiří.

Metodika cizojazyčného vyučování. Soupis knižních publ. z fondu St. pedagog. knihovny v Brně z let 1959-1970. Sest. Jiří Sedlák. Brno, St. věd. knihovna-St. pedagog. knihovna, rozmn., 1971.

108 p. 21 cm. (Brünn. Státní pedagogická knihovna. Publikace, č. 382)

Spieler, Josef, 1900-

Wirtschaft und Schule; eine Bibliographie zur wirtschaftskundlichen Bildung und Wirtschaftserziehung in Familie, Schule, Heim, Betriebs- und Erwachsenenbildung. Hrsg. im Auftrag des Deutschen Sparkassen- und Giroverbandes e. V. Bonn. Stuttgart, Deutscher Sparkassenverlag; Kommissionsverlag: Quelle & Meyer, Heidelberg, 1966.

227 p. 21 cm.

Tešič, Vladeta M

Библиографија 1952-1965. Саставио Владета М. Тешин. Београд, Педагошко друштво СР Србије, 1966.

96 p. 23 cm.

At head of title: Настава и васпитање (часопис за педагошка питања)

Tyler, Louise L

A selected guide to curriculum literature; an annotated bibliography [by] Louise L. Tyler. [Washington] National Education Association, Center for the Study of Instruction [1970]

v, 135 p. 23 cm. (Schools for the 70's. Auxiliary series)

United Nations Educational, Scientific and Cultural Organization.

International guide to educational documentation, 1960-1965. Guide international de la documentation pédagogique, 1960-1965. Guía internacional de la documentación pedagógica, 1960-1965. 2d ed. Paris, Unesco, 1971.

575 p. 27 cm. (Its [Document] ED.70/D.54/AFS)

Възпитанието на новия човек; библиография. [Съставители Павлина Едрева, Йота Данчева, Иван Цолов. Редактори Стефан Ангелов, Георги Младжов] София, 1966.

279 p. 20 cm.

At head of title: Народна библиотека "Кирил и Методий."

Yanes, Samuel, comp.

Big rock candy mountain; resources for our education, edited by Samuel Yanes & Cia Holdorf. [New York] Delacorte Press [1972, c1971]

188 p. illus. 37 cm.

Xochellis, Panagiotis.

Pädagogische Bibliographie. Eine Einführung in die pädagogische Fachliteratur, von P. Xochellis. Geretsried, Schuster, 1965.

102 p. 21 cm. (Bibliographien für Studierende, Heft 1)

Xochellis, Panagiotis.

Pädagogische Bibliographie. Eine Einführung in die pädagogische Fachliteratur. [Von] Panos Xochellis. 2., überarb. und erg. Aufl. Geretsried (b. München) Schuster, 1969.

193 p. 21 cm. (Wissenschaftliche Bibliographien, Bd. 1)

BIBLIOGRAPHIES

Beeler, Kent D

Bibliographies: helpful tools for research in higher education, for studies in language arts [by Kent D. Beeler, Leo C. Fay, and Ivan J. Quant] Bloomington, School of Education, Indiana University [1971]

vii, 182 p. 23 cm. (Viewpoints; bulletin of the School of Education, Indiana University, v. 47, no. 1)

CONTENTS: Source bibliographies in higher education: 1960-1970, by K. D. Beeler.—Doctoral research in reading and language arts at Indiana University, by L. C. Fay and I. J. Quant.

Besterman, Theodore, 1904–
Academic writings; a bibliography of bibliographies. Totowa, N. J., Rowman and Littlefield, 1971.

252 p. 20 cm. **(His The Besterman world bibliographies)**

Besterman, Theodore, 1904–
Education; a bibliography of bibliographies. Totowa, N. J., Rowman and Littlefield, 1971.

306 p. 20 cm. **(His The Besterman world bibliographies)**

DICTIONARIES

Kantor, Isaĭ Moiseevich.
Педагогическая лексикография и лексикология. Москва, "Просвещение," 1968.

200 p. 20 cm.

HISTORY

Cubberley, Ellwood Patterson, 1868–1941.
Syllabus of lectures on history of education; with selected bibliographies and suggested readings. With an introductory note by Francesco Cordasco. [2d ed.] Totowa. N. J., Rowman and Littlefield, 1971.

xv, 369 p. illus., maps, ports. 27 cm.

Reprint of the 1904 ed.

Higson, Constance Winifred Jane.
Sources for the history of education: a list of material (including school books) contained in the libraries of the institutes and schools of education, together with works from the libraries of the Universities of Nottingham and Reading, edited by Dr. C. W. J. Higson. London, Library Association, 1967.

x, 196 p. 31 cm.

Hillesheim, James W
A reader's guide to the history of educational thought [by] James W. Hillesheim. Anaheim, Calif., Yang-Yin Publishers [1967]

vii, 97 p. 28 cm.

Plancke, R   L
Documentatio paedagogica historica. 1968. [Door] R. L. Plancke en J. Souvage. Gand—Gent, Blandijnberg 2, 1968.

140 p. 24 cm.

"From volume VIII of the journal **Paedagogica historica** ..."

LAW see Educational legislation

LIBRARY CATALOGS

Columbia University. *Teachers College. Library.*
Dictionary catalog of the Teachers College Library. Boston, Mass., G. K. Hall, 1970.

36 v. 37 cm.

Harvard University. *Library.*
Education and education periodicals. Cambridge; Distributed by Harvard University Press, 1968.

2 v. 29 cm. **(Its Widener Library shelflist, 16–17)**

London. University. *Institute of Education.*
Catalogue of the collection of education in tropical areas. Boston, G. K. Hall, 1964.

3 v. 37 cm.

CONTENTS.—v. 1. Author catalogue.—v. 2. Regional catalogue.—v. 3. Subject catalogue.

London. University. Institute of Education. Library.
Catalogue of the comparative education library, University of London Institute of Education. Boston, Mass., G. K. Hall, 1971.

6 v. 37 cm.

CONTENTS: v. 1–2. Author catalogue. — v. 3–4. Subject catalogue.—v. 5–6. Regional catalogue.

Miller, Ingrid O
Edina Public Schools Professional Library catalog. Prepared by Ingrid O. Miller. Minneapolis, Josten's Library Services Division, 1973.

67, 55, 73 p. 28 cm.

Cover title: A catalog of books.
On spine: January '73 book catalog.

Pakistan. *Central Bureau of Education. Reference Library.*
Catalogue of books on education. Karachi, 1964.

131 p. 31 cm.

———————Supplement. 1965–
Karachi.

v. 30 cm.

PERIODICALS

Berdahl, Robert Oliver.
Comparative higher education: sources of information [by] Robert O. Berdahl and George Altomare. [New York, International Council for Educational Development, 1972]

115 p. 22 cm. **(International Council for Educational Development. Occasional paper no. 4)**

Camp, William L
Guide to periodicals in education, by William L. Camp. Metuchen, N. J., Scarecrow Press, 1968.

419 p. 22 cm.

Current index to journals in education. Annual cumulation.
v. 1–   1969–
New York, CCM Information Corp.

v. 29 cm.

Davis, Sheldon Emmor. 1876–
Educational periodicals during the nineteenth century. With a foreword by Francesco Cordasco. Metuchen, N. J., Scarecrow Reprint Corp., 1970.

125 p. map. 22 cm.

Reprint of the 1919 ed., with Cordasco's introd. added.

Diener, Thomas J
An annotated guide to periodical literature: higher education. Thomas J. Diener and David L. Trower, editors. Athens, Institute of Higher Education, University of Georgia, 1969.

iii, 35 p. 23 cm.

Hartung, A   Bruce.
A writer's guide to journals in education, by A. Bruce Hartung. [1st ed.] Dallas, N. C., Gaston College [1970]

115 p. 24 cm.

Title on spine: Writer's guide.

Henek, Tomáš.
Soupis českých a slovenských pedagogických časopisů do roku 1965. [Vyd. 1. Praha, Státní pedagogické nakl.,

1967)

177, xii p. facsims. 21 cm. (Edice Publikace státních vědeckých knihoven)

Kokuritsu Kyōiku Kenkyūjo, *Tokyo.*
国立教育研究所
明治前期文部省刊行雑誌総目録
東京 昭和43(1968)
205p 22cm (日本近代教育百年史編集資料 2)

Lins, Leon Joseph, 1918–
Scholars' guide to journals of education and educational psychology ₍by₎ L. Joseph Lins ₍and₎ Robert A. Rees. With a special section by Clarence A. Schoenfeld. ₍Madison, Wis., Dembar Educational Research Services₎ 1965.₋₎

150 p. 23 cm.

London. University. *Institute of Education. Library.*
Catalogue of periodicals in the library. London, University of London Institute of Education Library, 1968.

₍4₎ 112 p. 22 cm.

Mukerjee, A   K
Bibliography of periodicals; libraries of National Council of Educational Research and Training. Compiled by A. K. Mukerjee. ₍Rev. ed. Delhi₎ Central Institute of Education, National Council of Educational Research and Training ₍1964₎

118 p. 14 x 22 cm.

Näslund, Maja Lisa.
Tidskrifter för grundskolan. Ett kommenterat urval. Lund, Bibliotekstjänst, 1966.

20 p. 21 cm. (Bibliotekstjänsts bokurval, nr. 57)

Schmidt, Heiner.
Neuere pädagogische Zeitschriften und Serien in Bibliotheken des deutschen Sprachgebiets. Suppl. Bd. zur Erziehungswiss. Dokumentation. Weinheim, Berlin, Basel, Beltz (1970)

xii, 324 p. 22 cm. (Erziehungswissenschaftliche Dokumentation, Reihe A, Bd. 12)

AFRICA

African Bibliographic Center. Afriecon.
Educational development in Africa. Washington, African Bibliographic Center, 1973.

v, 93 p. 28 cm. (Current reading list series: v. 10, no. 2)

Hanson, John Wagner.
African education and development since 1960; a select and annotated bibliography ₍by₎ John W. Hanson ₍and₎ Geoffrey W. Gibson. East Lansing, Institute for International Studies in Education and African Studies Center, Michigan State University, 1966.

viii, 327 p. 26 cm. (Education in Africa series, 2)

Oshin, N   R   Olu.
Education in West Africa; a bibliography, compiled by N. R. Olu. Oshin. Yaba ₍Nigeria₎ West African Examinations Council, Test Development and Research Office, 1969.

v, 55 p. 21 cm. (West African Examinations Council. Test Development and Research Office. Library. Occasional publication no. 1)

Strowbridge, Nancy.
Education in East Africa, 1962–1968; a selected bibliography, compiled by Nancy Strowbridge for the National Institute of Education. ₍Kampala, Uganda₎ Makerere University College Library, 1969.

iii, 35 p. 23 cm. (Makerere Library publications no. 5)

AUSTRALIA

Brown, Cecily.
Bibliography of Australian education from colonial times to 1972. ₍Hawthorn₎ Australian Council for Educational Research ₍1973₎

169 p. 25 cm.

Roper, Thomas W
Bibliography on migration to Australia from non-English speaking countries with special reference to education, by T. W. Roper. ₍Melbourne, La Trobe University, School of Education, 1970?₎

15 l. 27 cm.

Prepared for the Centre for the Study of Urban Education, School of Education, La Trobe University.

Sanders, Colsell, 1904–
Educational writing and research in Australia, 1960–1965; a bibliographical review ₍by₎ C. Sanders. ₍Nedlands, W. A.₎ Faculty of Education, University of Western Australia, 1966.

iv, 69 l. 26 cm.

BRAZIL

Pernambuco, *Brazil (State) Conselho Estadual de Educação.*
Arquivos. 1–
out. 1964–
Recife.

no. in   v. 23 cm. quarterly.
Some no. issued in combined form.

Superintendência do Desenvolvimento da Região Sul. Divisão de Documentação.
Bibliografia de educação e assuntos correlatos; material bibliografico existente na Divisão de Documentação da SUDESUL. Pôrto Alegre, 1970.

₍36₎ l. 33 cm.

CANADA

Canada. *Bureau of Statistics.*
A bibliographical guide to Canadian education. Guide bibliographique de l'enseignement au Canada. ₍2d ed.₎ Ottawa, R. Duhamel, Queen's printer, 1964.

55 p. 28 cm.

At head of title: Dominion Bureau of Statistics. Education Division. Research Section.

Quebec (Province). Dept. of Education. Centre de renseignements.
Répertoire des publications du Ministère de l'éducation. ₍Québec₎ 1972.

viii, 231 l. 28 cm.

Quebec (Province). Dept. of Education. Centre de renseignements.
Répertoire des publications du Ministère de l'éducation. — Éd. revue et corr. — ₍Québec₎ : Le Centre, 1973.

325 leaves in various foliations ; 28 cm.

French or English.

CHINA

Fraser, Stewart E
Chinese education and society, a bibliographic guide; the cultural revolution and its aftermath ₍by₎ Stewart E. Fraser and Kuang-liang Hsu. White Plains, N. Y., International Arts and Sciences Press ₍1972₎

204 p. 24 cm.

Gregory, Peter B
China: education since the Cultural Revolution; a selected, partially annotated bibliography of English translations ₍by₎ Peter B. Gregory & Noele Krenkel. San Francisco, Evaluation and Research Analysts ₍1972₎

1 v. (various pagings) 28 cm. (Evaluation and Research Analysts. Document #100)

COMMONWEALTH OF NATIONS

Commonwealth Secretariat. Education Division.
Current research in education in some developing countries of the Commonwealth 1968; compiled by the Education Division. London, Commonwealth Secretariat ₍1968₎

53 p. 23 cm.

London. Commonwealth Institute.
Education in the Commonwealth. London, Commonwealth Institute, 1968.

23 p. 22 cm. (Selected reading lists for advanced study)

CZECHOSLOVAK REPUBLIC

Brünn. Státní pedagogická knihovna.
Vývoj učebních plánů a osnov na českých povinných školách, 1869–1963; bibliografie. Sest. Miloslav Vozdek. Hlavní redaktor Tomáš Henek. Brno, 1965.

31 p. 21 cm. (Its Publikace, čís. 209)

Hudobová, Darina.
Boj za jednotnú školu v zrkadle slovenskej periodickej tlače v období r. 1944–1948. Výberová bibliografia k 20. výr. Víťazného februára. Zost. D. Hudobová a E. Hurajová. Bratislava, Slov. pedag. knižnica, rozmn., 1968.

32, ₍2₎ p. 20 cm.

Hurajová, Emília.
Slovenská pedagogická tvorba v rokoch 1955–1965. Knižné publikácie a materiály. Registrujúca bibliografia. Zost. Emilia Hurajová a Darina Hudobová. Bratislava, SPK, rozmn., 1967.

165, ₍1₎ p. 20 cm.

Ostrava, Czechoslovak Republic (City) Státní vědecká knihovna.
Výchova dětí a mládeže; výběrová bibliografie. ₍Sest. Božena Legátová₎ Ostrava, 1965.

39 p. 21 cm. (Its Publikace. Řada II., čís. 389)
At head of title: Státní vědecká knihovna v Ostravě.

DENMARK

Denmark. Landsarkivet for Sjælland, Lolland, Falster og Bornholm.
Oversigt over skolehistorisk materiale i Landsarkivet for Sjælland m. m. Udg. af Landsarkivet for Sjælland m. m. og Institut for Dansk Skolehistorie. København, Intern, 1971.

2 v. 30 cm. (Its Foreløbige arkivregistraturer)

CONTENTS: 1. bd. De gejstlige arkiver. 2. bd. De verdslige arkiver. Med tillæg omfattende både gejstlige og verdslige arkiver.

EGYPT

Markaz al-Tawthīq al-Tarbawī.
(Qā'imah bibliyūjrāfīyah bi-intāj al-Markaz, 1956–1970)
قائمة ببليوجرافية بانتاج المركز ، ١٩٥٦ ــ ١٩٧٠ . القاهرة ، وزارة التربية والتعليم ، الإدارة العامة للوثائق التربوية ، مركز التوثيق التربوى ، ١٩٧٢.

88 p. 27 cm.

Limited distribution.

EUROPE

Apanasewicz, Nellie Mary, 1922–
Eastern Europe education: a bibliography of English-language materials ₍by₎ Nellie Apanasewicz, in collaboration with Seymour M. Rosen. ₍Washington₎ U. S. Dept. of Health, Education, and Welfare, Office of Education; ₍for sale by the Superintendent of Documents, U. S. Govt. Print. Off., 1966₎

vi, 35 p. 24 cm. (₍U. S. Office of Education₎ Bulletin 1966, no. 15)

Information Service of the European Communities.
L'enseignement dans les pays de la Communauté Européenne, document de travail. ₍Brussels?₎ Communautés Europeennes, Direction générale Presse et information, 1970.

ix., 223 p. 30 cm.

At head of title : Références bibliographiques.

FRANCE

Buisson, Ferdinand Édouard, 1841–1932.
Répertoire des ouvrages pédagogiques du XVIe siècle. (Bibliothèques de Paris et des départements). ₍Par₎ F. Buisson. ₍2nd reprint₎. Nieuwkoop, B. de Graaf, 1968.

xvi, 740 p. 23 cm.

"Original edition : Paris, 1886."

Marder, Joan V
Education in France: a union list of stock in institute and school of education libraries; edited by Joan V. Marder; with a foreword by W. D. Halls. 2nd ed. Southampton, Librarians of Institutes and Schools of Education, 1971.

₍2₎, xiii, 96 p. 30 cm.

At head of title : Librarians of Institutes and Schools of Education.

GERMANY

Germany (Democratic Republic, 1949–). Deutsches Pädagogisches Zentralinstitut. Bibliothek.
Lehrplanverzeichnis 1945–1969. Ein Bestandsverzeichnis bearb. von Ruth Fricke. Stand 31. 12. 1969. Berlin, Deutsches Pädagogisches Zentralinstitut, Zentralstelle für pädagogische Information und Dokumentation, 1970.

104 p. 21 cm. (Beilage zum Informations-Bulletin Pädagogik 5 (1970) 4)

Paulinyi, Emilia.
Wissenschaftlich-technische Revolution und Bildungswesen in der DDR: Auswahlbibliographie/ Emilia Paulinyi; Horst Messmer; Lothar Wenzel. — Marburg: Fachbereich Gesellschaftswiss. d. Philipps-Univ., Forschungsstelle f. Vergleichende Erziehungswiss., 1972.

vii, 79 p.; 21 cm. — (Texte, Dokumente, Berichte; zum Bildungswesen ausgewählter Industriestaaten; Heft 2)

Preissler, Gottfried, 1894–
Grundfragen der Pädagogik in westdeutschen Zeitschriften seit 1960. Darstellung, Analyse, Kritik. (2., wesent-
lich erw. Aufl.) Frankfurt a. M., Berlin, Bonn, München,
Diesterweg (1966).

152 p. 23 cm. (Diesterwegs rote Reihe)

Schmidt, Heiner.
Bibliographie zur besonderen Unterrichtslehre. Zeitschriften-Nachweis 1947–1967. Zusammengestellt und bearb.
von Heiner Schmidt und F. J. Lützenkirchen. Weinheim,
J. Beltz [1970–   v. 1, c1971]
v. 22 cm. (Erziehungswissenschaftliche Dokumentation.
Reihe A: Der Inhalt neuerer pädagogischer Zeitschriften und Serien
im deutschen Sprachgebiet, Bd. 7–

CONTENTS: T. 1. Deutsche Sprache, Literatur- und Fremdspra-
chenunterricht. — T. 2. Politische Bildung, Geschichte, Erdkunde,
Heimatkunde.

Schwarz, Karl, fl. 1968–
Bibliographie der deutschen Landerziehungsheime. Stuttgart, Klett (1970).

263 p. 22 cm. (Aus den deutschen Landerziehungsheimen, Heft
8)

GREAT BRITAIN

Argles, Michael.
British government publications concerning education; an
introductory guide [by] Michael Argles and J. E. Vaughan.
[New ed.] Liverpool, University of Liverpool Institute of
Education, 1966.

24 p. 24 cm.

Argles, Michael.
British government publications in education during the
19th century. Lancaster, History of Education Society,
1971.

[5], 20 p. 21 cm. (Guides to sources in the history of education,
no. 1)

Atkins, Sidney Hubert.
A select checklist of printed material on education published in English to 1800, [by] S. H. Atkins. Hull, University of Hull (Institute of Education), 1970.

76 p. 22 cm. (Aids to research in education, no. 1)

Baron, George.
A bibliographical guide to the English educational system. 3d ed. [London] University of London, Athlone Press,
1965.

124 p. 20 cm.

Bateman, Robin.
Yorkshire school history: a bibliography; publications
held by Yorkshire libraries, with locations; compiled for
the Yorkshire Branch of the Library Association by Robin
Bateman. London, Library Association, 1969.

[5], 81 p. 25 cm.

**Cambridgeshire and Isle of Ely, Eng. County Record
Office.**
Guide to education records in the County Record Office,
Cambridge; compiled by Angela Black. Cambridge, Cam-
bridgeshire and Isle of Ely County Council, 1972.

iii leaves, 85, [8] p. illus., facsims., plan. 30 cm.

Christophers, Ann.
An index to nineteenth century British educational biography. London, University (Institute of Education) 1965.

xii, 88 p. 20½ cm. (University of London. Institute of Education.
Education libraries bulletin. Supplement 10)

Librarians of Institutes of Education.
List of educational pamphlets of the Board of Education,
1904–1943, with locations in Institute of Education libraries. Revised ed. Newcastle, Librarians of Institutes of
Education, 1969.

[2], 8 p. 30 cm.

Vaughan, John Edmund.
Board of Education circulars: a finding list and index,
by J. E. Vaughan. Bailrigg, History of Education Society,
1972.

iv, 81, [22] p. 30 cm. index. (Guides to sources in the history
of education, no. 2)

Vaughan, John Edmund.
British government publications concerning education:
an introductory guide [by] J. E. Vaughan and Michael
Argles. 3rd ed. Liverpool, University of Liverpool School
of Education, 1969.

[1], 34 p. 24 cm.

Previous ed., 1963, by Michael Argles published as a short guide
to official (government) publications mainly educational.
In 1966 ed., authors' names appear in reverse order.

Wallis, Peter John.
Histories of old schools: a revised list for England and
Wales, by P. J. Wallis. Newcastle-upon-Tyne, University
(Department of Education) 1966.

98 p. 25 cm.

Watson, Foster, 1860–1929.
English writers on education, 1480–1603; a source book,
compiled by Foster Watson. A facsim. reproduction, with
an introd., by Robert D. Pepper. Gainesville, Fla.,
Scholars' Facsimiles & Reprints, 1967.

xiii, 153 p. 23 cm.

First published in the Annual reports of the U. S. Commissioner
of Education, 1902–06, under title: Notices of some early English
writers on education.

HUNGARY

Bárdi, Ilona.
Válogatott neveléstudományi bibliográfia; a Pecsi Tudományegyetem Állam- és Jogtudományi Kara oktatói számára. [A bibliográfia anyagát összegyűjtötte: Bárdi Ilona.
Válogatta és összeállította: Fényes Miklós] Pécs, 1970.

18 l. 29 cm.

ICELAND

Jósepsson, Bragi.
Icelandic culture and education; an annotated bibliography. Bowling Green, Ky., Western Kentucky University, Dept. of Sociology [c1968]
94 p. 28 cm. (Western Kentucky University. Dept. of Sociology. Research bulletin, 1)
Cover title.
Revision of the bibliography originally prepared for the author's
thesis Peabody College for Teachers, Nashville, entitled: Education
in Iceland; its rise and growth with respect to social, political and
economic determinants.

INDIA

Greaves, Monica Alice.
Education in British India 1698–1947: a bibliography and guide to the sources of information in London. London, London University Institute of Education, 1967.

xx, 182 p. maps. 21½ cm. (Education Libraries Bulletin. Supplement, 13)

India (*Republic*) *National Commission for Co-operation with UNESCO.*
Education for international understanding: a bibliography. ₁New Delhi₁ Indian National Commission for UNESCO ₁1964₁

195 p. 21 cm. (I. N. C. bibliography series, no. 1)

Indian educational material. v. 1–
Sept. 1966–
Delhi, Indian National Scientific Documentation Centre.

v. 25 cm. quarterly.

ISRAEL

Hofesh, Israel, 1905–
ספריה פדגוגית בקיבוץ; רשימת ספרים נבחרת. ערוך ע״י ישראל חופש. ₁תל־אביב₁ איחוד הקבוצות והקיבוצים. המחלקה לחינוך, 1966.

13 p. 24 cm.

מדריך ביבליוגרפי לספרות פדגוגית ₁לאמצעי עזר בהוראה. ירושלים ₁etc.₁₁ –1966 or 7₁ –727; –12

no. in v. 24 cm. irregular.

גליונות ביבליוגרפיים לבתי מדרש למורים
Supersedes
No. –9 issued by ha-Merkaziyah ha-pedagogit ha-artsit under its variant form of name: ha-Merkaziyah ha-pedagogit; no. 10–12 by ha-Mazkirut ha-pedagogit of the Misrad ha-ḥinukh veha-tarbut.
Merged with עלון ביבליוגרפי לספרות פדגוגית ₁לאמצעי עזר בהוראה
to form לקט תקצירי פירסומים בחינוך

JAPAN

Akita-ken Kyōiku Kenkyūjo.
(Kyōiku kenkyū shiryō kemmei mokuroku)
教育研究資料件名目録 ₁秋田₁ 秋田県教育研究所 昭和43– ₁1968–

v. 25 cm. ₁Its 研究 no. 105

Kanō, Masami.
(Kyōikugaku kankei sankō bunken sōran)
教育学関係参考文献総覧 加納正巳著 平塚益徳序 ₁東京₁ 帝国地方行政学会 ₁昭和46 i.e. 1971₁

7, 167 p. 27 cm.

Kokuritsu Kyōiku Kenkyūjo, *Tokyo.*
日本近代教育史文献目録 国立教育研究所 東京 昭和43– ₁1968–

v. 22 cm. (日本近代教育百年史編集資料 3)

Cover title.
On cover: Kokuritsu Kyōiku Kenkyūjo, Kyōiku Shiryō Sentā.

CONTENTS.—1. 総記・研究書

Passin, Herbert.
Japanese education: a bibliography of materials in the English language. New York, Teachers College Press ₁1970₁

xi, 135 p. 23 cm. (Publications of the Center for Education in Industrial Nations, Columbia University)

Teichler, Ulrich.
Bibliography on Japanese education : postwar publications in Western languages = Bibliographie zum japanischen Erziehungswesen / Ulrich Teichler, Friedrich Voss. — Pullach ₁Isartal₁ : Verlag Dokumentation, 1974.

294 p. ; 21 cm.

English and German.

KENYA

Court, David.
An inventory of research on education in Kenya. ₁Nairobi₁ Institute for Development Studies, University of Nairobi ₁1971₁

39 l. 30 cm. (Institute for Development Studies, University of Nairobi. Discussion paper no. 108)

Martin, L   A
Education in Kenya before independence; an annotated bibliography, by L. A. Martin. ₁Syracuse, N. Y., Syracuse University, Maxwell Graduate School of Citizenship and Public Affairs₁ 1969.

xiv, 196 l. 29 cm. (The Program of Eastern African Studies. Occasional bibliography, no. ₁15₁)

KOREA

Korea (Republic). Yunesŭk'o Han'guk Wiwŏnhoe.
Review of educational studies in Korea. ₁Seoul₁ Korean National Commission for UNESCO ₁1972–

v. 24 cm.

韓國教育目錄 Korean education index. 主題別著者綜合索引 編輯委貝徐英彩₁等₁ 專任·羅炳述 中央大學校₁文理科大學₁教育學科編 ₁시울 中央大學校教育學部出版局 1960–66₁

2 v. 22 cm.

Vol. 2 has subtitle: 主題別筆者綜合索引 編輯責任·金鍾喆 專任·崔昌均 中央大學校師範大學教育學科編 發行所·中央大學校出版局
In Korean.

CONTENTS.—v. 1. 1945–1959.—v. 2. 1960–1964.

LATIN AMERICA

Grenz, Wolfgang.
Das Bildungswesen in der Gesamtentwicklung Lateinamerikas. Ausgewählte, neuere Literatur. Hamburg, Institut für Iberoamerika-Kunde, 1966.

271 p. 21 cm. (Institut für Iberoamerika-Kunde. Reihe Bibliographie und Dokumentation, Heft 9)

Added t. p.: Educación y desarrollo en América Latina.

LEBANON

al-Majlis al-Ahlī lil-Ta'līm al-Thānawī.
(al-Ta'līm fī Lubnān)
التعليم فى لبنان ، دراسة ببليوغرافية للكتب والأبحاث المختارة التي تتعلق بالتعليم في لبنان . ₁اعد هذه الدراسة رمزي نجازي₁ بيروت ، المجلس الأهلي للتعليم الثانوي في لبنان ، 1967.

224 p. 24 cm.

MALAWI

Daube, Jonathan M
   Education in Malawi: a bibliography, by Jonathan M. Daube. 3d ed. Limbe ₍Malawi₎ Education Dept., Soche Hill College, 1970.

   15 p. 26 cm.

MALAYSIA

Wang, Hsiu Chin (Chen)
   Education in Malaysia: a bibliography. Compiled by Wang Chen Hsiu Chin. Singapore, 1964.

   35 p. 26 cm.

   At head of title: University of Singapore Library, Reference Dept.

NEW ZEALAND

Roth, Herbert Otto, 1917–
   A bibliography of New Zealand education. Wellington, New Zealand Council for Educational Research, 1964.

   234 p. 22 cm. (Educational research series, no. 41)

   Supplement (fold. leaf) in pocket has title: Outline of recurring education papers in the appendices to the Journals of the New Zealand House of Representatives (A. to J.)

NIGERIA

Ibadan, Nigeria. University. Institute of Education.
   Human ecology and education; a catalogue of environmental studies, 1957–1970, compiled and edited by J. W. Lieber. ₍Ibadan₎ 1970.

   v, 46 p. 22 cm. (Institute of Education, University of Ibadan. Occasional publication no. 10)

Oshin, N   R   Olu.
   Education in Nigeria; a bibliographical guide. Compiled by N. R. Olu Oshin and H. A. Odetoyinbo. ₍Yaba, Nigeria₎ 1972.

   xi, 452 p. 26 cm.

PAKISTAN

West Pakistan. Bureau of Education.
   Bibliography on education in Pakistan. Lahore, 1970.

   viii, 112 p. 25 cm.

PERU

Paulston, Rolland G
   Educación y el cambio dirigido de la comunidad; una bibliografía anotada con referencia especial al Perú, por Rolland G. Paulston. ₍Cambridge₎ Harvard University, Graduate School of Education, Center for Studies in Education and Development, 1969.

   ii, 190 p. 28 cm. (Occasional papers in education and development, no. 3)

   "Esta bibliografía fue realizada inicialmente durante los seis primeros meses de 1967 en Lima en conección con el programa de asistencia técnica que presta el Teachers College de Columbia University y la Agencia para el Desarrollo Internacional de los Estados Unidos al Ministerio de Educación Pública de Perú."

RUSSIA

Apanasewicz, Nellie Mary, 1922–
   Soviet education; a bibliography of English-language materials ₍by₎ Nellie Apanasewicz in collaboration with Seymour M. Rosen. ₍Washington₎ U. S. Dept. of Health, Education, and Welfare, Office of Education; ₍for sale by the Superintendent of Documents, U. S. Govt. Print. Off.,

1964₎
   vi, 42 p. 24 cm. (Studies in comparative education)
   ₍U. S. Office of Education₎ Bulletin 1964, no. 29.

Henek, Tomáš.
   Sovětská pedagogika a sovětské školství v naší knižní a časopisecké literatuře v letech 1918–1938; výběrová bibliografie. Připravili Tomáš Henek a Dagmar Kleskeňová. Brno, 1966.

   118 l. 20 cm.

   At head of title: Státní pedagogická knihovna v Brně.

Kalinin, Russia. Pedagogicheskiĭ institut.
   (Bibliograficheskiĭ ukazatel' nauchnykh rabot prepodavateleĭ Kalininskogo gosudarstvennogo pedagogicheskogo instituta im. M. I. Kalinina, opublikovannykh v "Uchenykh zapiskakh" i drugikh izdaniĭakh)
   Библиографический указатель научных работ преподавателей Калининского государственного педагогического института им. М. И. Калинина, опубликованных в "Ученых записках" и других изданиях. (1917–1967). Калинин, 1972.
   195 p. 20 cm.
   At head of title: Калининский государственный университет.
   By O. P. Fedorova and V. S. Lankova.

Khaslavskaii͡a, T   E
   ₍O novykh formakh i metodakh obuchenii͡a₎
   О новых формах и методах обучения. Библиогр. указ. литературы. ₍Москва₎, "Высш. школа," 1971.

   23 p. 20 cm.

   Cover title.
   At head of title: Государственный комитет Совета Министров СССР по профессионально-техническому образованию. Центральный учебно-методический кабинет профтехобразования.

Smolensk, Russia (City). Gosudarstvennyĭ pedagogicheskiĭ institut.
   Библиография научных трудов профессорско-преподавательского состава 1918–1968. Под общ. ред. проф. А. А. Кондрашенкова. Смоленск, 1970.
   263 p. 22 cm.
   At head of title: Министерство просвещения РСФСР. Смоленский государственный педагогический институт им. К. Маркса.

SCOTLAND

Craigie, James.
   A bibliography of Scottish education before 1872. ₍London₎ University of London Press ₍ᶜ1970₎

   255 p. 22 cm. (Publications of the Scottish Council for Research in Education, 60)

   Label mounted on t. p.: Distributed by Lawrence Verry, Mystic, Conn.

SLOVAKIA

Brünn. Státní pedagogická knihovna.
   Modernizace školy, vyučování a výchovy; bibliografie knižních publikací a časopiseckých článků. Sest. Kamil Horňák. Hlavní redaktor Tomáš Henek. V Brně, 1966.

   66 l. 20 cm. (*Its* Publikace, čís. 258)

   At head of title: Státní vědecká knihovna.

TANZANIA

Auger, George A
   Tanzania education since Uhuru: a bibliography, 1961–1971; incorporating a study of Tanzania today and yesterday and a guide to further sources of information on education in Tanzania, by George A. Auger. ₍Dar es Salaam₎ Institute of Education, University of Dar es Salaam, 1971.

iv, 269 p. maps. 25 cm.

"Pre-print of fifty copies for limited distribution."

TURKEY

Stone, Frank A
Çağdas Türk eğitim düşüncesine bibliyografik giriş. Modern Turkish educational thought: a bibliographic introduction. ₁Hazırlayan₁ Frank A. Stone. ₁Ankara, Hacettepe Üniversitesi, 1971₁

51 p. 25 cm. (Hacettepe Üniversitesi yayınları, D–12. Hacettepe University publications, D–12)

In Turkish and English.

UNITED STATES

Anderson, Frank J
Carlisle-Smith pamphlet collection, prepared by Frank J. Anderson and Elizabeth Sabin. Spartanburg ₁S. C.₁ Wofford Library Press, 1971.

34 l. 29 cm. (Wofford College Library. Special collection checklist. no. 5)

Fraser, Stewart E
British commentary on American education: a select and annotated bibliography, the nineteenth and twentieth centuries; by Stewart E. Fraser. London, University of London (Institute of Education Library), 1970.

vii, 140 p. 21 cm. (Education Libraries Bulletin, supplement 14)

Herbst, Jurgen.
The history of American education. Northbrook, Ill., AHM Pub. Corp. ₁1973₁

xv, 153 p. 23 cm. (Goldentree bibliographies in American history)

Maryland. *State Curriculum Center.*
Printed curriculum materials, 1955–1962. Baltimore, 1964.

97 p. 23 cm.

Park, Joe, *ed.*
The rise of American education; an annotated bibliography. Evanston, Northwestern University Press, 1965.

xi, 216 p. 24 cm.

U. S. Office of Education.
Bibliography of publications of the United States Office of Education, 1867–1959. With an introductory note by Francesco Cordasco. Totowa, N. J., Rowman and Littlefield, 1971.

xiv, 57, x, 158, v, 157 p. 25 cm. (Its Bulletin, 1910, no. 3; 1937, no. 22; 1960, no. 3)

Reprint of 3 publications originally published in 1910, 1937, and in 1960.

CONTENTS: List of publications of the United States Bureau of Education, 1867–1910.—List of publications of the Office of education, 1910–1936, including those of the former Federal Board for Vocational Education for 1917–1933.—Publications, Office of Education, 1937–1959.

WHITE RUSSIA

Nikolov, Asen Marinov.
(Za po-golîama efektivnost v uchebniîa protses)
За по-голяма ефективност в учебния процес. Препоръч. библиогр. София, Нар. библ. Кирил и Методий, 1972.

42 p. 20 cm.

At head of title: Народна библиотека "Кирил и Методий." Отдел "Препоръчителна библиография."

By A. Nikolov and R. Todorova.

EDUCATION, COMMUNIST see Communist education

EDUCATION, COMPARATIVE

Bristow, Thelma.
Comparative education through the literature; a bibliographic guide ₁by₁ Thelma Bristow and Brian Holmes. ₁Hamden, Conn.₁ Archon Books ₁1968₁

ix, 181 p. 22 cm.

Bristow, Thelma.
Comparative education through the literature: a bibliographic guide ₁by₁ Thelma Bristow and Brian Holmes. London, Butterworths, 1968.

ix, 181 p. 23 cm.

Kobayashi, Tetsuya, 1926–
Survey on current trends in comparative education, compiled by Tetsuya Kobayashi. Hamburg, UNESCO Institute for Education, 1971.

193 l. 30 cm. (Documents on educational research, 2)

Von Klemperer, Lily.
International education: a directory of resource materials on comparative education and study in another country. ₁Garrett Park, Md., c1973₁

202 p. 28 cm.

EDUCATION, ELEMENTARY

Abbott, Janet.
A selected bibliography of professional books for elementary schools. Tempe, Bureau of Educational Research and Services, College of Education, Arizona State University ₁1964₁

40 l. 28 cm. (Arizona State University. Bureau of Educational Research and Services. Educational services bulletin no. 11)

Hansen, Gynther, 1930–
Børnepsykologi og undervisningsmetodik. Et udvalg af hvad biblioteket kan tilbyde børnehavelærerinder og børnehaveseminarister, forsorgs- og fritidspædagoger, lærere og lærerstuderende. Redigeret af Gynther Hansen. Aabenraa, Det Sønderjydske Landsbibliotek, 1968.

32 p. 21 cm.

Oregon. *Division of Instruction.*
Bibliography for guide to elementary education in Oregon. Salem, State Dept. of Education, 1966.

52 p. 28 cm.

EDUCATION, HIGHER
see also Junior colleges

Altbach, Philip G
Higher education in developing countries: a select bibliography, by Philip G. Altbach, with the assistance of Bradley Nystrom. ₁Cambridge₁ Center for International Affairs, Harvard University, 1970.

118 p. 23 cm. (Occasional papers in international affairs, no. 24)

Bibliographie internationale de l'histoire des universités.
Genève, Droz, 1973–

v. 23 cm. (Études et documents publiés par la Section d'his-

toire de la Faculté des lettres de l'Université de Genève, 9
(Commission internationale pour l'histoire des universités. Études
et travaux, 2

"1ʳᵉ édition."
CONTENTS: 1. Gibert, R. et al. Espagne, Louvain, Copenhague,
Prague.

Bibliographische Materialien zur Hochschulforschung. Berlin, Institut für Bildungsforschung in der Max-Planck-Gesellschaft, 1967–

v. 30 cm. (Studien und Berichte, 9A–B

CONTENTS.—A. Hochschulökonomie und Bildungsplanung, von
K. Hüfner.—B. Sozialisationsprozesse und Einstellungsveränderungen
in der Hochschule am Beispiel USA, von S. Kleemann.

Bibliographische Materialien zur Hochschulforschung. 2., erw. Aufl. Berlin, Institut für Bildungsforschung in der Max-Planck-Gesellschaft, 1968–

v. 30 cm. (Studien und Berichte, 9A

CONTENTS. — A. Hochschulökonomie und Bildungsplanung, von
K. Hüfner.

Buenos Aires. Universidad. Departamento de Pedagogía y Metodología.
Catálogo del fichero centralizado de publicaciones sobre pedagogía universitaria. ₁Buenos Aires, 1966₁

112 p. 23 cm.

California. University. *Center for Higher Education.*
Bibliography of publications on higher education. Rev. Berkeley, 1965.

12 l. 28 cm.

Chambers, Merritt Madison, 1899–
A brief bibliography of higher education in the middle nineteen sixties, by M. M. Chambers. ₁Bloomington₁ Bureau of Educational Studies and Testing, School of Education, Indiana University ₁1966₁

vii, 52 p. 23 cm. (Bulletin of the School of Education, Indiana
University, v. 42, no. 5)

Dressel, Paul Leroy, 1910–
The world of higher education ₁by₁ Paul L. Dressel and Sally B. Pratt. ₁1st ed.₁ San Francisco, Jossey-Bass, 1971.

xv, 238 p. 24 cm. (The Jossey-Bass series in higher education)

"An annotated guide to the major literature."

Felsőoktatási szakirodalmi tájékoztató. A felsőoktatás általános kérdései. 1–   évf.; 1970–
₁Budapest₁ Tankönyvkiadó.

v. 24 cm.

Issued by Felsőoktatási Pedagógiai Kutatóközpont in cooperation
with other similar bodies.
Vols. for 1970–   carry also the same vol. numbering as
Felsőoktatási szakirodalmi tájékoztató, A sorozat and B sorozat,
v. 7–

Flaugher, Ronald L
Credit by examination for college-level studies; an annotated bibliography ₁by₁ Ronald L. Flaugher, Margaret H. Mahoney ₁and₁ Rita B. Messing. New York, College Entrance Examination Board, 1967.

233 p. 25 cm.

Guhde, Edgar.
Bibliographie zur Hochschuldidaktik. (Hamburg, Ar-

beitskreis f. Hochschuldidaktik) 1970.

156 p. 21 cm. (Hochschuldidaktische Materialien, Nr. 17)

Intercollegiate bibliography ₁of₁ cases in administration of higher education. 1966–   ₁Boston₁ Intercollegiate Case Clearing House.

v. 28 cm.

LaBeille, Daniel.
Bibliographic guide for advanced placement: French ₁by Daniel LaBeille and Kathleen Hollister₁ Albany, University of the State of New York, State Education Dept. ₁1965₁

16 p. 28 cm.

Mayhew, Lewis B
The literature of higher education 1971 ₁by₁ Lewis B. Mayhew. ₁1st ed.₁ San Francisco, Jossey-Bass, 1971.

xii, 162 p. 24 cm. (The Jossey-Bass series in higher education)

Mayhew, Lewis B
The literature of higher education 1972, by Lewis B. Mayhew. ₁1st ed.₁ San Francisco, Jossey-Bass, 1972.

xii, 184 p. 24 cm. (The Jossey-Bass series in higher education)

Meeth, Louis Richard.
Selected issues in higher education, an annotated bibliography, edited by L. Richard Meeth. ₁New York₁ Published for the Institute of Higher Education by Teachers College Press, Teachers College, Columbia University ₁1965₁

x, 212 p. 23 cm. (Publications of the Institute of Higher Education)

Научная организация учебного процесса в высшей школе.
Указатель русской и зарубежной литературы. 1966/68–

₁Москва₁ Изд-во Московского университета.

v. 22 cm.

Issued by Nauchnaíà biblioteka of Moskovskiĭ universitet.

Nitsch, Wolfgang.
Social science research on higher education and universities. By Wolfgang Nitsch and Walter Weller. Under the direction of Dietrich Goldschmidt. The Hague, Paris, Mouton, 1970–

v. 23 cm. (Confluence, 10)

Text in English; introduction to the series in English and French.
CONTENTS:
Pt. II. Annotated bibliography.

Powell, John Percival.
Universities and university education: a select bibliography, compiled by John P. Powell. Slough (Bucks.), National Foundation for Educational Research in England and Wales, 1966–

v. 25 cm. (v. 1: National Foundation for Educational Research in England and Wales. Occasional publication ₁series₁ no. 14

"Vol. 2: 1965–70 and supplement to vol. 1."

Retzlaff, Bernice R
Higher education administration: an annotated bibliography of research reports funded by the Cooperative research act, 1956–1970, by Bernice R. Retzlaff. ₁Washington₁ National Center for Educational Research and Development; ₁for sale by the Supt. of Docs., U. S. Govt. Print. Off., 1971₁

viii, 12 p. 26 cm.

Robinson, Lora H

Student participation in academic governance ₍by₎ Lora H. Robinson ₍and₎ Janet D. Shoenfeld. Washington, ERIC Clearinghouse on Higher Education ₍1970₎

i, 26 p. 28 cm. (₍ERIC Clearinghouse on Higher Education₎ Review 1)

Saint-Pierre, Henri.

Les formules pedagogiques de l'enseignement universitaire; bibliographie annotée ₍par₎ Henri Saint-Pierre et Roger Bédard. ₍Québec₎ Service de pédagogie universitaire, Université Laval, 1972.

2, 4, 84 l. 28 cm.

Schlaffke, Winfried. fl. 1967.

Höhere Schule und Wirtschaft. Eine Bibliographie. Köln (Dt. Industrieinst.) 1967.

iii, 73 p. 24 cm. (Materialien zu bildungs- und gesellschaftspolitischen Fragen, Folge 23)

Szekely, Kalman S

Higher education: its mission, goals, and problems; a selective bibliography, by Kalman S. Szekely and James L. Jones. Prelim. ed. Bowling Green, Ohio, Bowling Green State University Libraries, Bibliographic Research Center, 1969.

26 l. 28 cm.

Szymanowska, Teresa.

Bibliografia Międzyuczelnianego Zakładu Badań nad Szkolnictwem Wyższym, 1960–1967. ₍Wyd. 1.₎ Warszawa, Państwowe Wydawn. Naukowe ₍Oddz. w Łodzi₎ 1968.

55 p. 25 cm. (Międzyuczelniany Zakład Badań nad Szkolnictwem Wyższym. Bibliografie)

At head of title: Ministerstwo Oświaty i Szkolnictwa Wyższego. Międzyuczelniany Zakład Badań nad Szkolnictwem Wyższym. Ośrodek Dokumentacji i Biblioteka.

Szymanowska, Teresa.

Bibliografia Międzyuczelnianego Zakładu Badań nad Szkolnictwem Wyższym (1960–1970) Wyd. 2., popr. i uzup. Warszawa, Państwowe Wydawn. Naukowe, 1973.

87 p. 24 cm. (Seria Dokumenty, informacje, bibliografie)

At head of title: Ministerstwo Nauki, Szkolnictwa Wyższego i Techniki. Międzyuczelniany Zakład Badań nad Szkolnictwem Wyższym.

Tudományos Ismeretterjesztő Társulat. *Központi Könyvtár.*

Az iskolán kívüli felnőttoktatás, az ismeretterjesztés és a népművelés irodalma, 1953–1963; válogatott bibliográfia. Összeállította TIT Központi Könyvtára. ₍Szerk.: Sipos Aladárné₎ Budapest, 1965.

104 p. 21 cm.

Table of contents also in English, German, and Russian.

Universidad Nacional del Litoral (1969–). Servicios de Pedagogía Universitaria. Sección Información y Documentación.

Bibliografía analítica temática universitaria. ₍Elaboración bibliográfica a cargo de: Nelly Yvis Rossi Etchelouz₎ Santa Fe, República Argentina, 1971.

31 p. 21 cm. (Its Serie bibliográfica, no. 2)

Yokoo, Takehide, 1922–

(Daigaku ni kansuru Ōbun bunken sōgō mokuroku)
大学に関する欧文文献総合目録　横尾壮英　中
山茂共編　₍東京₎　学術書出版会　1970.

288 p. 26 cm.

Zygielbaum, Arta.

Academic assessment in higher education: an annotated bibliography, 1966–1972, compiled by Arta Zygielbaum and Susan Horwitz. Johannesburg, Dept. of Bibliography, Librarianship and Typography, University of the Witwatersrand, 1972.

vii, 56 p. 30 cm.

AUSTRALIA

Caiden, Naomi.

A bibliography for Australian universities. Canberra, Australian National University ₍1965₎

75 p. 21 cm.

First published in Vestes, Sept. 1964–March 1965.

BULGARIA

Topalova, Donka.

Библиографска справка за висшето образование в България 1968–1970. София, НИИ по образованието Акад. Т. Самодумов, 1971.

38 p. 22 cm.

At head of title: Научноизследователски институт по образованието "Т. Самодумов." Център за педагогическа документация и информация.

CANADA

Harris, Robin Sutton, 1919–

A bibliography of higher education in Canada ₍by₎ Robin S. Harris ₍and₎ Arthur Tremblay. ₍Toronto₎ University of Toronto Press ₍1960₎
xxv, 158 p. 24 cm. (Studies in higher education in Canada, no. 1)
Title page, introd., and captions in English and French.
————Supplement, 1965 ₍by₎ Robin S. Harris. ₍Toronto₎ University of Toronto Press ₍1965₎
xxxi, 170 p. 24 cm. (Studies in higher education in Canada, no. 3)
Title page, introd., and captions in English and French.
Includes publications for 1959–63.

Harris, Robin Sutton, 1919–

An index to the material bearing on higher education contained in J. G. Hodgins' Documentary history of education in Upper Canada (Ontario), compiled by Robin S. Harris, with the assistance of Constance Allen. ₍Toronto₎ Innis College, University of Toronto, 1966.

vi, 60 p. 25 cm.

Harris, Robin Sutton, 1919–

A list of reports to the Legislature of Ontario bearing on higher education in the province. Compiled by Robin S. Harris, with the assistance of Constance Allen and Mary Lewis. ₍Toronto₎ Innis College, University of Toronto, 1966.

v, 17 p. 25 cm.

CHILE

Cortés Pinto, Raúl.

Bibliografía anotada de educación superior. Valparaíso, Chile, Universidad Técnica Federico Santa María, 1967.

31 p. 27 cm.

GERMANY

Baum, Hanna.

20 ₍i. e. Zwanzig₎ Jahre Hochschulwesen in der Deutschen Demokratischen Republik 1949–1969. Auswahlbibliographie. Berlin, (Universitäts-Bibliothek) 1969.

89 p. 21 cm. (Schriftenreihe d. Universitäts-Bibliothek zu Berlin, Nr. 6)

Erman, Wilhelm, 1850–1932.

Bibliographie der deutschen Universitäten; systematisch geordnetes Verzeichnis der bis Ende 1899 gedruckten Bücher und Aufsätze über das deutsche Universitätswesen ₍von₎ Wilhelm Erman ₍und₎ Ewald Horn. Hildesheim, G. Olms, 1965.

3 v. 25 cm.
"Reprografischer Nachdruck der Ausgabe Leipzig 1904₍–65₎"
CONTENTS.—₍1₎ Allgemeiner Teil, unter Mitwirkung von E. Horn bearb. von W. Erman.—₍2₎ Besonderer Teil, unter Mitwirkung von W. Erman bearb. von E. Horn.—₍3₎ Dritter Teil, Register und Nachträge enthaltend, bearb. von W. Erman.

Hassinger, Erich.

Bibliographie zur Universitätsgeschichte; Verzeichnis der im Gebiet der Bundesrepublik Deutschland 1945–1971 veröffentlichten Literatur. Bearb. von Edwin Stark. Hrsg. von Erich Hassinger. Freiburg, K. Alber ₍c1974₎

316 p. 24 cm. (Freiburger Beiträge zur Wissenschafts- und Universitätsgeschichte, Bd. 1)

Rost, Gottfried.

Hochschulen des Volkes. Eine bibliographische Information über die Entwicklung des Hochschulwesens in der DDR nach dem 6. Parteitag der SED. Bearb. von Gottfried Rost. Leipzig (Deutsche Bücherei) 1967.

66 p. 21 cm. (Bibliographischer Informationsdienst der Deutschen Bücherei. Nr. 11)

GREAT BRITAIN

Jacobs, Phyllis M

Registers of the universities, colleges, and schools of Great Britain and Ireland; a list compiled by Phyllis M. Jacobs. ₍London₎ University of London, published for the Institute of Historical Research by the Athlone Press, 1964.

50 p. 25 cm.

Silver, Harold.

The history of British universities, 1800–1969, excluding Oxford and Cambridge: a bibliography, by Harold Silver and S. John Teague. London, Society for Research into Higher Edcuation, 1970.

xv, 264 p. 23 cm. Index. (Research into higher education monographs, 13)

HUNGARY

Déri, Miklósné.

A magyar felsőoktatás huszonöt éve (1945–1970); bibliográfia. Budapest, Felsőoktatási Pedagógiai Kutatóközpont, 1070.

vi, 230 p. 20 cm. (Felsőoktatástörténeti kiadványok, 2)

JAPAN

Higher education and the student problem. Tokyo, Kokusai Bunka Shinkokai, 1972.

x, 309 p. 24 cm. (Current social problems, 1)

At head of title: K. B. S. bibliography of standard reference books for Japanese studies, with descriptive notes.

Minshu Kyōiku Kyōkai.

(Daigaku gakusei mondai bunken mokuroku)
大学・学生問題文献目録　1965–1971. 改訂・増補　東京　民主教育協会　1971.

253 p. 26 cm.

Title also in English: A bibliography on higher education and students in Japan 1965–1971.

Minshu Kyōiku Kyōkai.

(Daigaku gakusei mondai bunken mokuroku)
民主教育協会
大学・学生問題文献目録　1968–1969
東京　1970
112p　26cm

Title also: A bibliography on higher education and students in Japan 1968–1969.
Text in Japanese.

RUSSIA

Milkova, Valentina Ivanovna.

₍Vysshee obrazovanie v SSSR i za rubezhom₎
Высшее образование в СССР и за рубежом. Библиогр. указ. книг и журн. статей. 1959–1969. Сост. В. И. Милкова. Москва, "Высш. школа," 1972.

462 p. 21 cm.

Moscow. Universitet. *Biblioteka.*

Университетское образование в СССР и за рубежом. Под ред. Г. Г. Кричевского и Э. А. Нерсесовой. ₍Москва₎ Изд-во Московского университета, 1966–

v. 27 cm.

At head of title: Московский государственный университет имени М. В. Ломоносова. Научная библиотека им. А. М. Горького. Научно-библиографический отдел.
Russian and English.

SWITZERLAND

Verband der Schweizerischen Studentenschaften. Nationale Bildungspolitik, Bibliographie 1965–1969. Politique universitaire nationale. Bern, Erlachstr. 9, Verband der Schweizerischen Studentenschaften, Informationsdienst, (1970).

iv p., 19 l. 30 cm. (Its Dokumentation VSS, 15)

Introduction in French and German.

UNITED STATES

Aptheker, Bettina.

Higher education and the student rebellion in the United States, 1960–1969; a bibliography. ₍New York, American Institute for Marxist Studies, 1969.

50 p. 29 cm. (₍American Institute for Marxist Studies₎ Bibliographical series, no. 6)

Crabbs, Richard F.

United States higher education and world affairs; a partially annotated bibliography ₍by₎ Richard F. Crabbs ₍and₎ Frank W. Holmquist. New York, Published in cooperation with the Indiana University Committee on International Affairs ₍by₎ F. A. Praeger ₍1967₎

xi, 207 p. 25 cm. (Praeger special studies in international politics and public affairs)

Newburn, Harry Kenneth, 1906–

Higher education in Arizona ₍by₎ H. K. Newburn and M. M. Chambers. Tempe, Bureau of Educational Research and Services, Arizona State University ₍1967₎

28 p. 23 cm. (Arizona State University. Bureau of Educational Research and Services. Educational services bulletin no. 20)

Powel, John H

An annotated bibliography of literature relating to the costs and benefits of graduate education, by John H. Powel, Jr., and Robert D. Lamson. Washington, Council of Graduate Schools, 1972.

vii, 59 p. 28 cm.

Pride, Cletis.
Securing support for higher education: a bibliographical handbook. New York, Praeger [1972]

ix, 403 p. 25 cm. (Praeger special studies in U. S. economic and social development)

"Published in cooperation with American College Public Relations Association."

Samples, Gordon.
College admission requirements: a source bibliography arranged by field of study. Rev. [San Diego] San Diego State College, Education Library, 1968.

26 l. 28 cm.

Stickler, William Hugh, 1910–
Higher education in America: a syllabus for En. C. U. 506 (Second revision) A basic course in the history, philosophy, policies, practices, and problems of America's junior colleges, senior colleges, and universities. [Tallahassee] Dept. of Higher Education, School of Education, Florida State University, 1964.

iv, 80 l. 29 cm.

Willingham, Warren W
The source book for higher education; a critical guide to literature and information on access to higher education, by Warren W. Willingham, in association with Elsie P. Begle [and others] New York, College Entrance Examination Board, 1973.

xxii, 481 p. 24 cm.

EDUCATION, INTERCULTURAL

New York (*State*) *University.*
Some suggested teacher references helpful in introducing intergroup relations information in the classroom. [Albany, 1964?]

12 p. 28 cm.

Reading ladders for human relations. Virginia M. Reid, editor, and the Committee on Reading Ladders for Human Relations of the National Council of Teachers of English. 5th ed. Washington, American Council on Education [1972]

xv, 346 p. 23 cm.

Fourth ed. edited by M. E. Crosby.

EDUCATION, PRESCHOOL
see also Kindergarten

Bernard van Leer Foundation.
Compensatory early childhood education; a selective working bibliography. The Hague [1971]

355 p. 21 cm.

Bibliographie zur Frühpädagogik/ beard. von Helga Kochan -Döderlein [u. a.]. Hrsg. vom Inst. f. Frühpädagogik, München. Pullach [Isartal]: Verlag Dokumentation, 1972.

328 p.; 21 cm.

Illinois. *Dept. of Educational Research.*
Early childhood and kindergarten education; a bibliography of ERIC materials. [Springfield, 1970]

39 p. 29 cm.

Kleskeňová, Dagmar.
Předškolní výchova podle jednotného výchovného sy-

stému. Výběr literatury připravila Dagmar Kleskeňová. Brno, Státní pedagogická knihovna, 1967.

6 l. 21 cm. (Bibliografický leták, čís. 282)

Project Head Start.
Bibliography on early childhood. [Washington] 1969.

16 p. 26 cm.

Russia (*1917–   R. S. F. S. R.*) *TSentral'nyĭ nauchno-metodicheskiĭ kabinet po doshkol'nomu vospitaniiū.*
Дошкольное воспитание; библиографический справочник. 2., доп. изд. [Ответственный редактор О. П. Соловьева] Москва, Просвещение, 1965.

128 p. 20 cm.

At head of title: Управление по дошкольному воспитанию. Центральный дошкольный методический кабинет Министерства просвещения РСФСР.

Sedlák, Jiří.
Předškolní výchova v zahraničí. Bibliogr. cizojaz. knih z let 1945–1970. Sest. Jiří Sedlák. Brno, St. pedagog. knihovna, rozmn., 1970.

34 p. 29 cm.

EDUCATION, RURAL

Chiva, I
Les études rurales en France: tendances et organisation de la recherche. Sous la direction de I. Chiva [et] P. Rambaud, avec la collaboration de C. Balland [et al.] Paris, Mouton [c1972]

367 p. 24 cm. (Maison des sciences de l'homme. Service d'échange d'informations scientifiques. Publications. Série B: Guides et répertoires, 3)

A **Educação** rural. [Tradução brasileira de Maria de Lourdes Borges Ribeiro] Rio de Janeiro, Instituto Brasileiro de Educação, Ciência e Cultura, 1965.

52 p. 22 cm. (Coleção Unesco, 3)

"Publicado pela Organização das Nações Unidas para a Educação, Ciência e Cultura, UNESCO."

Srivastava, L   R   N
An annotated bibliography on tribal education in India. Compiled and annotated by L. R. N. Srivastava; assisted by S. V. Gupta. New Delhi, Tribal Education Unit, Dept. of Adult Education, National Council of Educational Research & Training, 1967.

viii, 117 p. 22 cm. (Dept. of Adult Education. Publication no. 21)

Wurster, Stanley R
Rural education and small schools; a selected bibliography compiled by Stanley R. Wurster and James E. Heathman. Las Cruces, Educational Resources Information Center, Clearinghouse on Rural Education and Small Schools, New Mexico State University, 1969.

ii, 178 p. 28 cm.

EDUCATION, SECONDARY

Bunton, William James.
Comprehensive education: a select annotated bibliography; compiled by W. J. Bunton. Slough, National Foundation for Educational Research, 1971.

48 p. 21 cm.

Geneva. Université. Ecole de psychologie et des sciences de l'education.
Adolescence and the secondary school, prepared for the International Bureau of Education. Paris, Unesco. 1973.

81 p. 24 cm. (Educational documentation and information (Bulletin of the International Bureau of Education, no. 187)

Ibarrola Nicolín, María de.
La enseñanza media en México, 1900–1968; guía bibliográfica. [1. ed.] México, Instituto de Investigaciones Sociales, UNAM, 1970.

x, 266 p. 16 x 24 cm.

Laurence, Dee.
Writings on comprehensive education: 1,500 references with index. London, Campaign for Comprehensive Education, 1973.

115 p. 21 cm.

Marland, Michael.
Comprehensive school: organisation and responsibility: [catalogue of an exhibition] prepared for the Advisory Centre for Education Conference, 31 December 1972 to 3 January 1973; books selected and annotated by Michael Marland. London, National Book League, [1973].

[4], 17 p. 26 cm. (NBL book list)

Massachusetts. Dept. of Education.
Middle school bibliography. [Boston, 1971]

25 l. 29 cm.

Orlov, A   A
[Rukovodstvo sredneĭ obshcheobrazovatel'noĭ shkoloĭ]
Руководство средней общеобразовательной школой. (Библиография). Сост. Орлов А. А. Ред. Костяшкин Э. Г. Москва, 1971.

38 p. 20 cm.

At head of title: Институт повышения квалификации преподавателей педагогических дисциплин университетов и педвузов АПН СССР. НИИ общей педагогики АПН СССР.

Paulston, Rolland G
Folk schools in social change; a partisan guide to the international literature [by] Rolland G. Paulston. Pittsburgh, Pa., University Center for International Studies, University of Pittsburgh, 1974.

xi, 194 p. 23 cm.

Silvy, Auguste.
Essai d'une bibliographie historique de l'enseignement secondaire et supérieur en France avant la Révolution. (Réimpr. de l'éd. de Paris, 1894.) Genève, Slatkine Reprints, 1971.

iv, 150 p. 23 cm.

EDUCATION, UNIVERSITY AND COLLEGE see Education, Higher

EDUCATION, URBAN

Barr, Charles W
The school in the urban comprehensive plan: a partial bibliography [by] Charles W. Barr. Mary Vance, editor. Monticello, Ill., Council of Planning Librarians, 1972.

38 p. 28 cm. (Council of Planning Librarians. Exchange bibliography, 264)

Hunter College, *New York*. *Project TRUE*.
Urban education, an annotated bibliography [prepared by Helen Randolph] New York, Hunter College, City University of New York, 1963.

57 l. 28 cm.
Cover title.

————Supplement 1 [by] H. Helen Randolph. New York, Hunter College, City University of New York, 1964.
20 l. 28 cm.

Research Council of the Great Cities Program for School Improvement.
Creativity in urban education; a survey report of locally-developed materials, programs, and projects in sixteen cooperating great cities. [Chicago] 1968.

vi, 238 p. 28 cm.

EDUCATION, VOCATIONAL see Vocational guidance and training

EDUCATION IN LITERATURE

Campbell, Alasdair.
The school novel: a guide to fiction for adults with a background of school. London, Library Association (Branch and Mobile Libraries Group), 1970.

[11] p. 21 cm. (Fiction guides series, no. 2)

Tiedt, Iris M
Unrequired reading; an annotated bibliography for teachers and school administrators [by] Iris M. Tiedt and Sidney W. Tiedt. 2d ed. Corvallis, Oregon State University Press [1967]

vii, 127 p. 23 cm. ([Oregon. State University, Corvallis] Bibliographic series, no. 7)

EDUCATION OF ADULTS
see also under Dissertations, Academic - Education

Aker, George F   *comp.*
Adult education procedures, methods and techniques: a classified and annotated bibliography, 1953–1963. Compiled under the direction of George F. Aker for the University of Chicago Program of Studies and Training in Continuing Education. [Syracuse, N. Y.] The Library of Continuing Education at Syracuse University, 1965.

xi, 163 p. 24 cm.

Barnes, Robert F
Graded materials for teaching adult illiterates; a classified and annotated list of materials for teaching, reading, writing, and arithmetic to adults from the beginning level through eighth grade; plus a review of research in the field, by Robert F. Barnes and Andrew Hendrickson. Columbus, Center for Adult Education, School of Education, Ohio State University, 1965.

98 p. 28 cm.

Berdrow, John R
Bibliography [of] curriculum materials for adult basic education, prepared by John R. Berdrow. [Springfield, 1967]

ii l., 37 p. 28 cm. (Illinois. Dept. of Public Instruction. Circular series A–185)
Cover title.

————— ————Supplement A. ₍Urbana, 1967₎

7 l. 28 cm. (Illinois. Dept. of Public Instruction. Circular series A-185)

ERIC Clearinghouse on Adult Education.
Adult basic education. ₍Syracuse, N. Y.₎ 1970.

82 p. 28 cm. (Current information sources, no. 27)

ERIC Clearinghouse on Adult Education.
Continuing education in the professions. ₍Syracuse, N. Y.₎ 1969.

94 p. 28 cm. (Current information sources, no. 24)

Heleszta, Sándor.
Ajánló-bibliográfia a pedagógia népművelésre és felnőttképzésre vonatkozó szakirodalmából. Összeállította: Heleszta Sándor és Novák Irén. ₍Budapest₎ Népművelési Intézet, 1965.

94 p. 29 cm. (Népművelési Intézet. Bibliográfiák, 2)

Cover title: Pedagógia.

Jacobs, H   Lee.
Education for aging: a review of recent literature ₍by₎ H. Lee Jacobs. W. Dean Mason ₍and₎ Earl Kauffman. ₍Syracuse, N. Y.₎ ERIC Clearinghouse on Adult Education ₍1970₎

112 p. 28 cm.

Kalamazoo Library System. *Adult Reading Center.*
Adult basic education; a bibliography of materials. ₍Lansing, Mich.₎ Dept. of Education, Adult Education and Community Services Section ₍1967₎

ii, 164 p. 28 cm.

Kovačić, Aleksandar.
Bibliografija članaka objavljenih u časopisu "Andragogija" (ranije: "Narodno sveučilište," 1955–1958. i "Obrazovanje odraslih" 1959–1968) 1955–1971. Pripremio: Aleksandar Kovačić. Suradnici: pri izradi popisa članaka i indeksa autora surađivale su: Branka Hum, Jasminka Koren i Mira Rozman. Na klasifikaciji po UDK sistemu radila i Pogovor o načinu klasifikacije napisala Branka Hum. Kratki povijesni prikaz razvoja časopisa napisao Hodimir Sirotković. Zagreb, Andragoški centar Zajednice narodnih i radničkih sveučilišta ₍SR Hrvatske, 1972.

338, ₍1₎ p. 24 cm.

Michigan. *Dept. of Education.*
Adult basic education; a bibliography of materials. ₍Lansing₎ 1969.

165 p. 28 cm.

Cover title.
Issued in 1967 by the Adult Reading Center of the Kalamazoo Library System.

Neal, Kenneth William.
Teaching method in further education: a guide to the literature, by K. W. Neal. Manchester, College of Commerce (Department of Librarianship), 1968.

64 p. 22 cm.

Neal, Kenneth William.
Teaching method in further education: a bibliography, by K. W. Neal. 2nd ed. Wilmslow, K. W. Neal, 1972.

110 p. 23 cm.

Richard, Pierre.
L'Éducation permanente et ses concepts périphériques; recherches documentaires ₍par₎ Pierre Richard ₍et₎ Pierre Paquet ... Paris, Éditions Cujas, 1973.

viii, 448 p. 24 cm. (Communautés)

Smith, Edwin H
A selected annotated bibliography of instructional literacy materials for adult basic education ₍by₎ Edwin H. Smith and Weldon G. Bradtmueller. Tallahassee₎ Division of Vocational, Technical, and Adult Education, Adult and Veteran Education, 1968.

iv l., 47 p. 28 cm. (Florida. State Dept. of Education. Bulletin 71F-3)

Spencer, Marion D.
Bibliography of literacy materials, by Marion D. Spencer and Mary K. Chemerys. ₍3d ed. Kalamazoo, Mich.₎ Kalamazoo Library System, Adult Reading Center ₍1967₎

ii, 164 p. 28 cm.

Straka, Josef.
Výchova a vzdělávání dospělých. Bibliografie čes. a slov. literatury. Sest. Josef Straka ₍a₎ Eva Krátká. Praha, Osv. ústav, rozmn. Kraj. kult. středisko, Brno, 1968.

297, ₍5₎ p. 20 cm. (Ediční skup. 4, řada A—Bibliografie) unpriced

Taylor, Margot J
Self-education for adults, prepared by Margot J. Taylor. San Francisco ₍Pacific Air Forces₎ 1968.

iv, 40 p. 27 cm. (PACAF basic bibliographies for base libraries)

Thomas, Myra H
Books related to adult basic education and teaching English to speakers of other languages; a bibliography from the Educational Materials Center. Compiled by Myra H. Thomas. Thelma M. Knuths ₍and₎ Sidney E. Murphy. ₍Washington₎ National Center for Educational Communication; ₍for sale by the Supt. of Docs., U. S. Govt. Print. Off., 1970₎

iii, 18 p. 26 cm.

U. S. Office of Education. Adult Education Branch.
Bibliography: materials for the adult basic education student. Prepared by Adult Education Branch, Division of Adult Education, U. S. Office of Education, and National University Extention Association. ₍Washington₎ 1967.

iii, 129 p. 28 cm.

U. S. *Office of Education. Educational Materials Laboratory.*
Adult basic education; a bibliography from the Educational Materials Center, compiled by Lois B. Watt, chief ₍and₎ Sidney E. Murphy, library assistant. ₍Washington₎ U. S. Office of Education, Bureau of Research; ₍for sale by the Supt. of Docs., U. S. Govt. Print. Off.₎ 1968.

14 p. 26 cm.

Venables, Dorothy Rhoda, 1917–
Twenty years of adult education; a select general bibliography, 1945–1965, compiled by Rhoda Venables. ₍Auckland, Printed at the University of Auckland Bindery, 1968₎

39 p. 23 cm.

Vinter, Milica.
Permanentno obrazovanje. Izradila Milica Vinter. Beograd, Jugoslovenski zavod za proučavanje školskih i prosvetnih pitanja, 1972.

32 p. 21 cm. (Jugoslovenski zavod za proučavanje školskih i prosvetnih pitanja. Serija: Bibliografije. Tematske bibliografije, 5)

Whipple, James B
Community service and continuing education, a literature review, by James B. Whipple. [Syracuse, N. Y.] Syracuse University, 1970.

76 p. 23 cm. (Syracuse University. Publications in Continuing Education. Occasional papers, no. 21)

AFRICA

Bown, Lalage J
African adult education: a bibliography, by Lalage Bown. Lusaka, University of Zambia, 1966.

[77] p. 33 cm.

At head of title: The University of Zambia, Department of Extramural Studies.

AUSTRIA

Binder, Theodor Stephan.
Bibliographie der Erwachsenenbildung in Österreich, 1960–1972. Von Theodor Binder. Wien, FEB (Fachbibliothek für Erwachsenenbildung), 1972.

27 l. 30 cm.

Binder, Theodor Stephan.
Kleine Bibliographie der Erwachsenenbildung in Österreich. 1960–1971. Von Theodor Binder. Wien, FEB (Fachbibliothek f. Erwachsenenbildung), 1972.

15 l. 30 cm.

EUROPE

Kulich, Jindra.
Adult education in continental Europe; an annotated bibliography of English-language materials 1945–1969. Vancouver [Department of Adult Education, Ontario Institute for Studies in Education and Center for Continuing Education, University of British Columbia] 1971.

227 p. 28 cm.

Savický, Ivan.
European selective bibliography on adult education (1966–1971) compiled by I. Savický. Prague, European Centre for Leisure and Education, 1973.

107 p. 21 cm. (European Centre for Leisure and Education. Bibliographic series no. 6)

GERMANY

Keim, Helmut.
Bibliographie zur Volksbildung. 1933–1945. [Von] Helmut Keim [u.] Dietrich Urbach. Braunschweig, Westermann, 1970.

64 p. 23 cm. (Bibliographien zur Erwachsenenbildung)

Schadt, Armin L
Adult education in Germany; bibliography [by] Armin L. Schadt. Syracuse, N. Y., ERIC Clearinghouse on Adult Education [1969]

40 p. 28 cm.

Urbach, Dietrich.
Bibliographie zur Erwachsenenqualifizierung in der DDR. Braunschweig, Westermann, 1969.

102 p. 23 cm. (Bibliographien zur Erwachsenenbildung)

GREAT BRITAIN

Styler, William Edward, 1907–
A bibliographical guide to adult education in rural areas. 1918–1972 [by] W. E. Styler. Hull, University of Hull, Department of Adult Education, 1973.

50 p. 22 cm.

EDUCATION OF EXCEPTIONAL CHILDREN

Deschel, Erich.
Kleine Bibliographie zum Studium der Sonderpädagogik. 2. Bearbeitung. Dortmund, (Verband Deutscher Sonderschulen) 1967.

64 p. 21 cm. (Schriften zur Sonderpädagogik. Reihe B: Originalarbeiten, Heft 1)

Bibliographie der Sonderpädagogik und ihrer Grenzgebiete in der Deutschen Demokratischen Republik 1956–1966. Hrsg. von der Abt. Sonderschulen. Zusammengestellt von Adelbert Breitsprecher. Berlin, Volk und Wissen, 1968.

154 p. 25 cm.

Continues Heese, Gerhard. Bibliographie der Buch- und Zeitschriftenliteratur auf den Gebieten der Sonderschulpädagogik in der Deutschen Demokratischen Republik, 1947–1955.

Blatt, Burton, 1927– comp.
Selected media reviews: Exceptional children, 1970–1973. Burton Blatt, editor. Margery A. MacDonald, assistant editor. Reston, Va., Council for Exceptional Children [1973]

ix, 180 p. 26 cm.

Copenhagen. Statens pædagogiske studiesamling.
Katalog over bibliotekets litteratur vedrørende specialundervisning. København V, Statens Pædagogiske Studiesamling, 1969.

1 v. (various pagings) 30 cm.

Redigeret af Niels Skovgaard.

Council for Exceptional Children.
Physical environment & special education; selected abstracts. Washington, 1969.

ix, 14 p. 28 cm.

Exceptional child education abstracts. v. 1–
Apr. 1969–
[Washington, Council for Exceptional Children]

v. 28 cm. 4 no. a year.

Ferbitz, Gisela.
Sonderpädagogik. Auswahlverz. Potsdam, Wissenschaftliche Allgemeinbibliothek, 1970.

56 l. 30 cm.

Goldberg, Icchok Ignacy, 1916–
Selected bibliography of special education [by] I. Ignacy Goldberg. [New York, Teachers College, Columbia University, 1967]

vi, 126 p. 23 cm. (TC series in special education)

Jipson, Frederick J
Index of special education media, by Frederick J. Jipson. [n. p., 1970]

130 p. 28 cm.

Knežević, Mirjana.
Bibliografija časopisa "Specijalna škola" (1952–1972) Beograd, Savez društava defektologa Jugoslavije, 1973.

78 p. 24 cm.

At head of title: Mirjana Knežević, Borivoje Novčić.

McMurray, J   Grant, 1924–
The exceptional student of secondary school age : a bibliography for psychology and education, 1960–1970 / J. G. McMurray. — [London, Ont.] : J. G. McMurray, [1971]

viii, 138 leaves ; 28 cm.

Oslo. Universitet. Bibliotek. Norsk pedagogisk studie-samling.
Spesialpedagogikk. Spesialkatalog over bok- og tidsskriftlitteratur utkommet i tidsrommet 1967–1971. Oslo, 1972.

3, 71 l. 30 cm.

Research in special education. no. 1–
[Wallasey, Eng.] Association for Special Education, Research Committee, 1967–

no. 20 cm.

Sedlák, Jiří.
Speciální pedagogika (Defektologie) Sest. Jiří Sedlák. Brno, Státní pedagogická knihovna, 1971.

81 p. 21 cm. (Státní pedagogická knihovna v Brně. Publikace, čís. 376)

Thomas, D   J
A guide to the literature of special education [by] D. J. Thomas. Liverpool, University of Liverpool (School of Education) 1968.

87 p. 22 cm. (Education Library publication no. 2)

Trickett, Annie Sandifer.
Children with learning disabilities; a selected bibliography. [Shreveport? La., 1966]

29 l. 28 cm.

Watt, Lois Belfield.
Books related to compensatory education. Compiled by Lois B. Watt, Myra H. Thomas, and Eunice von Ende. [Washington] U. S. Office of Education, Bureau of Research; [for sale by the Supt. of Docs., U. S. Govt. Print. Off.] 1969.

v, 46 p. 26 cm.

Watt, Lois Belfield.
The education of disadvantaged children; a bibliography, compiled by Lois B. Watt, Myra H. Thomas [and] Harriet L. Horner. [Washington] Office of Education, U. S. Dept. of Health, Education, and Welfare, 1966.

32 p. 26 cm.

EDUCATION OF GIFTED CHILDREN

Gowan, John Curtis.
Annotated bibliography on creativity & giftedness. Northridge, Calif., San Fernando Valley State College Foundation, 1965.

iii, 197 p. 28 cm.

Cover title.
Continuation of the author's An annotated bibliography on the academically talented.
"Research reported herein was supported by the Cooperative Research Program of the Office of Education; U. S. Office of Education Cooperative research contract OE-S-061-64."

Start, Ann.
The gifted child: a select annotated bibliography; compiled by Ann Start. Windsor, National Foundation for Educational Research in England and Wales, 1972.

40 p. 22 cm.

U. S. *Office of Education. Talent Development Project.*
State and local provisions for talented students. an annotated bibliography. [Washington, 1966]

vi. 61 p. 24 cm. (U. S. Office of Education. Bulletin 1966, no. 5)

EDUCATION OF WOMEN

Argentine Republic. Centro Nacional de Documentación e Información Educativa.
Referencias bibliográficas. Buenos Aires, 1972.

[12] l. illus. 30 cm.

"Trabajo encomendado por el Ministerio de Cultura y Educación para la Conferencia Interamericana Especializada sobre Educación Integral de la Mujer, Buenos Aires, 21–25 de agosto de 1972."

South Africa. *Dept. of Education, Arts and Science. Library.*
Die vrou en dogter: gekeurde bibliografie. Saamgestel deur die Biblioteek, Departement van Onderwys, Kuns en Wetenskap. Pretoria, 1967.

21 p. 30 cm.

Westervelt, Esther Manning.
Women's higher and continuing education: an annotated bibliography with selected references on related aspects of women's lives [by] Esther Manning Westervelt [and] Deborah A. Fixter, with the assistance of Margaret Comstock. New York, College Entrance Examination Board, 1971.

vii, 67 p. 23 cm.

Wigney, Trevor.
The education of women and girls in a changing society; a selected bibliography with annotations. [Toronto] Dept. of Educational Research, Ontario College of Education, University of Toronto, 1965.

v, 76 p. 28 cm. (Dept. of Educational Research, Ontario College of Education, University of Toronto. Educational research series, no. 86)

EDUCATIONAL ADMINISTRATION

Anderson, Robert Henry, 1918–
Bibliography on organizational trends in schools [by] Robert H. Anderson. [Washington] Center for the Study of Instruction, National Education Association [1968?]

v, 33 p. 23 cm.

Bondarenko, L   I
[Voprosy shkolovedeniîa]
Вопросы школоведения. Краткий список литературы, 1964–1968 гг. Ленинград, 1969.

25 p. 21 cm.

At head of title: Фундаментальная библиотека Ленинградского государственного педагогического института им. Герцена. Справочно-библиографический отдел.

Delhi. National Institute of Education. Dept. of Educational Administration.
Annotated bibliography on inspection and supervision. ₁New Delhi, 1968₁

65 p. 22 cm.

Delhi. National Institute of Education. Dept. of Educational Administration.
Bibliography on inspection and supervision. ₁New Delhi, 1968₁

26 p. 22 cm.

Döring, Peter A
Der Schüler als Staatsbürger. Eine Bibliographie zu Schülermitverantwortung und Schülerpresse mit Rechtsvorschriften und Anschriften. ₁Von₁ Peter A. Döring ₁und₁ Sibylle Schneider. Frankfurt a. M., Dipa(-Verlag) 1967.

93 p. 24 cm.

ERIC Clearinghouse on Educational Administration.
Alternative organizational forms; analysis of literature and selected bibliography. Eugene, ERIC Clearinghouse on Educational Administration, University of Oregon, 1970.

18 p. 28 cm. (ERIC Clearinghouse on Educational Administration. Analysis and bibliography series, no. 2)

ERIC Clearinghouse on Educational Administration.
ERIC abstracts; a collection of ERIC document resumes on human relations in educational administration. ₁Washington, American Association of School Administrators₁ 1969.

vi, 13 p. 28 cm. (Its ERIC abstracts series, no. 2)

Georgiades, William.
Selected, annotated bibliography relating to new patterns of staff utilization, prepared by William Georgiades ₁and others. Salem₁ Division of Education Development, Oregon State Dept. of Education, 1965.

102 p. 28 cm.
Cover title: Selected bibliography relating to new patterns of staff utilization.
On cover: The Oregon program; a design for the improvement of education.

Gosden, P. H. J. H.
Educational administration in England and Wales: a bibliographical guide ₁by₁ P. H. J. H. Gosden. Leeds, University (Institute of Education) ₁1967₁

55 p. 23 cm. (University of Leeds. Institute of Education. Paper, no. 6)

Horňák, Kamil, comp.
Správa a řízení školy; výběr literatury. Připravil Kamil Horňák. Brno, 1965.

10 l. 21 cm. (Státní pedagogická knihovna v Brně. Bibliografický leták, č. 149)

Jones, Ione.
The department chairman; a bibliography. ₁Ann Arbor₁ Michigan Council of Teachers of English ₁1971₁

15 p. 22 cm.

McLoughlin, William P
The nongraded school; an annotated bibliography ₁by₁ William P. McLoughlin. Albany, University of the State of New York, State Education Dept., Office of Research and Evaluation, 1967.

32 p. 28 cm.

Moyer, Frank H
A comprehensive bibliography of open education and open space schools; a reader's guide, by Frank H. Moyer. ₁Plainfield, N. J.₁ 1972.

1 v. (various pagings) 28 cm.

National Education Association of the United States. *Dept. of Elementary School Principals.*
Selected references for elementary school principals. ₁Washington, °1965₁

32 p. 28 cm.

New Jersey. State Dept. of Education. Office of Program Development.
Annotated bibliography: extended school year materials, extended school year programs. Trenton, 1973.

47 p. 28 cm.

New York *(State). Bureau of School and Cultural Research.*
Elementary school organization; an annotated bibliography. ₁Albany₁ 1967.

28 p. 28 cm.

Ontario Institute for Studies in Education. Library Reference & Information Services.
Differentiated staffing; an annotated bibliography. ₁Toronto₁ 1971.

viii, 18 p. 28 cm. (Its Current bibliography no. 3)

Paulsen, Frank Robert.
Selected bibliographies for educational administrators, by F. Robert Paulsen. Storrs, School of Education, University of Connecticut, 1964.

46 l. 28 cm.

Ranney, James L
A bibliography of materials on the year-round school. Prepared by James L. Ranney in cooperation with Donald L. Beggs, Keith A. McNeil ₁and₁ Arthur R. Jones. ₁Springfield, Ill.₁ Office of the Supt. of Public Instruction ₁State of Illinois₁ 1970.

27 p. 29 cm.

Rideout, E   Brock.
City school district reorganization: an annotated bibliography: centralization and decentralization in the government of metropolitan areas with special emphasis on the organization, administration, and financing of large-city school systems ₁by₁ E. Brock Rideout and Sandra Najat. ₁Toronto₁ Ontario Institute for Studies in Education ₁°1967₁

v, 93 p. 28 cm. (Ontario Institute for Studies in Education. Educational research series, no. 1)

Schmidt, Heiner.
Bibliographie zur Schulorganisation und zur Reform des Bildungswesens. Zeitschriften-Nachweis 1947–1967. Zusammengestellt und bearb. von Heiner Schmidt und F₁ranz₁ J₁osef₁ Lützenkirchen. Weinheim(/Bergstr.) Berlin, Basel, Beltz (1969).

xvi, 392 p. 22 cm. (Erziehungswissenschaftliche Dokumentation. Reihe A: Der Inhalt neuerer pädagogischer Zeitschriften und Serien im deutschen Sprachgebiet, Bd. 1)

EDUCATIONAL DISCRIMINATION see
Discrimination in education

EDUCATIONAL EQUALIZATION

Cordasco, Francesco, 1920-
The equality of educational opportunity; a bibliography of selected references [by] Francesco Cordasco, with Maurie Hillson [and] Eugene Bucchioni. Totowa, N.J., Rowman and Littlefield [1973]

xiii, 139 p. 22 cm.

Cordasco, Francesco, 1920-
The equality of educational opportunity; a bibliography of selected references [by] Francesco Cordasco, with Maurie Hillson [and] Eugene Bucchioni. Totowa, N.J., Littlefield, Adams, 1973.

xiii, 139 p. 21 cm. (A Littlefield, Adams quality paperback no. 264)

EDUCATIONAL EXCHANGES

International educational materials exchange. no. 1–
Geneva, International Institute for Labour Studies, 1968–

no. 30 cm.

Spencer, Richard Edward, 1927–1970.
International educational exchange; a bibliography, by Richard E. Spencer and Ruth Awe. [New York, Institute of International Education, 1970]

v, 156 p. 23 cm.

EDUCATIONAL FINANCE

Andrić, Stanislava.
Bibliografija — Ekonomika obrazovanja. Sastavili: Stanislava Andrić. Dubravka Kunštek, Marija Sever-Zebec. Zagreb, Ekonomski institut, 1970.

[3], 56 l. 29 cm.

Blaug, Mark.
Economics of education; a selected annotated bibliography, by M. Blaug. [1st ed.] Oxford, New York, Pergamon Press [1966]

xiii, 190 p. 24 cm. (International series of monographs in library and information science, v. 3)

Blaug, Mark.
Economics of education; a selected annotated bibliography, by M. Blaug. 2d ed. Oxford, New York, Pergamon Press [1970]

xvi, 301 p. 24 cm. (International series of monographs in library and information science, v. 3)

Education Services Press, *St. Paul.*
Guide to support programs for education. St. Paul [1966]

160 p. 27 cm.

Kleskeňová, Dagmar.
Ekonomika vzdělání. Anotovaná bibliogr. knih a článků. Zprac. Dagmar Kleskenová. Brno, St. pedagog. knihovna, rozmn., 1969.

17 p. 29 cm. (Brünn. Státní pedagogická knihovna. Publikace, čís. 337)

Tompkins, Dorothy Louise (Campbell) Culver.
Local public schools: how to pay for them? Compiled by Dorothy Campbell Tompkins. Berkeley, Institute of Governmental Studies, University of California, 1972.

vii, 102 p. 23 cm. (Her Public policy bibliographies, 2)

EDUCATIONAL GUIDANCE

College Entrance Examination Board.
Educational information and guidance; a selected bibliography. [New York, 1966]

31 p. 20 cm.

Hechlik, John E
Small group work and group dynamics. Compiled by John E. Hechlik and James L. Lee. Ann Arbor, Counseling and Personnel Services Information Center, University of Michigan, 1968.

xiii, 89 p. 28 cm. (CAPS current resources series)

"The work ... was performed pursuant to a contract from the U. S. Office of Education, Department of Health, Education, and Welfare."

Kentucky. *Dept. of Education. Division of Guidance Services.*
Educational and occupational information; list of titles of educational and occupational information and other guidance materials which may be purchased by public secondary schools participating in guidance and counseling activities under Title V–A of the National defence education act. Rev. list. Frankfort, 1964.

39 p. 28 cm.

New York *(State). University. Bureau of Guidance.*
Elementary school guidance; an annotated bibliography. [Albany] 1966.

iv, 13 p. 28 cm.

Shane, June Grant.
Contemporary thought, with implications for counseling and guidance: a bibliography. [Bloomington] Bureau of Educational Studies and Testing, Indiana University; available at the Indiana University Bookstore [1967]

106 p. 23 cm. (Bulletin of the School of Education, Indiana University, v. 43, no. 4)

Stark, Matthew.
An annotated bibliography on residence counseling. [Ann Arbor, Mich.] Association of College and University Housing Officers, 1964.

ix, 90 p. 29 cm.

U. S. *Air Force Academy. Library.*
Guidance and counseling. [n. p., 1964?]

30 p. 21 cm. (*Its* Special bibliography series, no. 31)

Venezuela. Universidad Central, Caracas. Centro de Investigaciones Pedagógicas. Pre-Seminario Métodos de Investigación.
La orientación escolar y profesional en el plano nacional e internacional; síntesis de investigación documental. Caracas, 1968.

64 p. 28 cm. (Universidad Central de Venezuela. Centro de Investigaciones Pedagógicas. Monografías. Referencias bibliográficas e información documental, 1)

Walz. Garry Richard.
Pupil personnel services, compiled by Garry R. Walz and James L. Lee. Ann Arbor, Counseling and Personnel Services Information Center, University of Michigan, 1968.

xiv, 96 p. 28 cm. (CAPS current resources series)

"The work ... was performed persuant to a contract from the U. S. Office of Education, Department of Health, Education, and Welfare."

Zimpfer, David G

Group procedures in guidance; a bibliography [by] David G. Zimpfer. Albany, New York State Personnel and Guidance Association, 1969.

124 p. 28 cm.

PERIODICALS

Integrated personnel services index. v. 1–
June 1969–
Ann Arbor, Mich., ERIC Counseling and Personnel Services Information Center.

v. 28 cm. semiannual.

EDUCATIONAL INNOVATIONS

Havelock, Ronald G

Major works on change in education: an annotated bibliography with author and subject indices. Compiled by Ronald G. Havelock, Janet C. Huber [and] Shaindel Zimmerman. Ann Arbor, Center for Research on Utilization of Scientific Knowledge, University of Michigan, 1969.

60 p. 23 cm.

Skelton, Gail J

A selected and annotated bibliography: the change process in education [by] Gail J. Skelton [and] J. W. Hensel. Columbus, ERIC Clearinghouse on Vocational and Technical Education, 1970.

vii, 95 p. 28 cm. ([Ohio. State University, Columbus. Center for Vocational and Technical Education] Bibliography series, no. 5)
"Prepared pursuant to a contract with the [U. S.] Office of Education."

U. S. *Information Agency.*

Innovations in education. Washington, U. S. Information Agency, Information Center Service, 1968.

ii l., 25 p. 27 cm. (*Its* Subject bibliography no. 14/68)

EDUCATIONAL LEGISLATION

Argentine Republic. Congreso. Biblioteca.

Enseñanza universitaria; bibliografía y legislación comparada. Buenos Aires, 1966.

47 l. 34 cm.

Blackmon, C   Robert.

Education law : a comprehensive, annotated bibliography of books and pamphlets, with topical index / C. Robert Blackmon and S. A. Wilkins. — Baton Rouge : Bureau of Educational Materials and Research, College of Education, Louisiana State University, 1974.

ii, 44 p. ; 28 cm. — (Research report — Louisiana State University, Bureau of Educational Materials and Research ; v. 4, no. 8)

Roberts, Dayton Y

Legal issues in higher education, 1960-1970; a selected annotated bibliography. Edited by Dayton Y. Roberts. [Gainesville, Institute of Higher Education, University of Florida] 1971.

v, 36 p. 23 cm.

EDUCATIONAL PSYCHOLOGY

Bjerstedt, Åke.

Institutionens verksamhet läsåret 1965–66. Malmö, Lärarhögskolan, 1966.

42, (2) l. 30 cm. (Pedagogisk-psykologiska problem nr. 00)

Bücherei Nordertor.

Psychologie und Pädagogik. Bücherverzeichnis. (Neu-

aufl.) (Flensburg, Büchereizentrale [1966].)

98 p. 20 cm.

Byers, Joe L

A review of recent literature on verbal learning and concept learning, by Joe L. Byers. [East Lansing] Published for the Institute by Social Science Research Bureau, Michigan State University, 1968.

32 p. 23 cm. (Human Learning Research Institute, Michigan State University. Review series, v. 1)
Cover title: Verbal learning and concept learning.

Concept learning: a bibliography, 1950–1967 [by] Herbert J. Klausmeier [and others] Madison, Wisconsin Research and Development Center for Cognitive Learning, University of Wisconsin, 1969.

vii, 171 p. 28 cm. (Wisconsin Research and Development Center for Cognitive Learning. Technical report no. 82)
"Report from the project on situational variables and efficiency of concept learning. Herbert J. Klausmeier and Robert E. Davidson, principal investigators."
"U. S. Office of Education, Center no. C–03; contract OE 5–10–154."

——— A supplement to ... Concept learning: a bibliography, 1968– Madison, Wisconsin Research and Development Center for Cognitive Learning, University of Wisconsin, 1969–

v. 28 cm. (Wisconsin Research and Development Center for Cognitive Learning. Technical report no. 107, 120, 147
"U. S. Office of Education, Center no. C–03, contract OE 5–10–154."

Geisinger, Robert W

A selected bibliography project: evaluation—the cognitive domain [by] Robert W. Geisinger. [Harrisburg] Bureau of Research, Dept. of Education, Commonwealth of Pennsylvania, 1970.

16 l. 28 cm.

Osborn, Wayland Wayne, 1906–

Behavioral objectives; an annotated bibliography. [Prepared by Wayland W. Osborn and David C. Lidstrom] Des Moines, Iowa, Dept. of Public Instruction, 1971.

iv, 65 p. 29 cm.

Schaefer, James F

Educational psychology: a bibliography for teacher education; references used in the preparation of the nine model teacher education programs. Prepared by James F. Schaefer, Jr. Washington, Printed and distributed by the ERIC Clearinghouse on Teacher Education, 1969.

30 l. 28 cm.

Schmidt, Heiner.

Bibliographie zur pädagogischen Psychologie und zur Psychologie der Fehlentwicklungen. Zeitschriften-Nachweis 1947–1967. Zusammengestellt und bearb. von Heiner Schmidt und F[ranz] J[osef] Lützenkirchen. Weinheim(/ Bergstr.), Berlin, Basel, Beltz (1969).

xv, 341 p. 22 cm. (Erziehungswissenschaftliche Dokumentation. Reihe A: Der Inhalt neuerer pädagogischer Zeitschriften und Serien im deutschen Sprachgebiet, Bd. 4)

Schmidt, Heiner.

Bibliographie zur Pädagogischen Psychologie und zur Psychologie der Fehlentwicklungen : Zeitschriften-Nachweis 1947–1967 / zusammengestellt und bearb. von Heiner Schmidt und F. J. Lützenkirchen. — 2., verb. Aufl. — Weinheim : Beltz, 1974.

xv, 341 p. : 22 cm. — (Erziehungswissenschaftliche Dokumentation : Reihe A, Der Inhalt neuerer pädagogischer Zeitschriften und Serien im deutschen Sprachgebiet ; Bd. 4)

Schmidt, Heiner.

Materialien zur pädagogischen Psychologie und zur Psychologie der Fehlentwicklungen: Bücher, Bibliographien, Sammelwerke 1945-1971/72/ zusammengestellt u. bearb. von Heiner Schmidt. Red. Mitarb. von Ellen Hantke ₁u. a.₎. — Weinheim, Basel: Beltz, 1973.

xviii, 617 p.; 22 cm. — (Erziehungswissenschaftliche Dokumentation: Reihe B, Monographien, Hochschulschriften, selbständige und unselbständige Bibliographien, Beiträge aus Sammelwerken, Fachlexiken und Handbüchern der neueren Pädagogik im deutschen Sprachgebiet; Bd. 4)

Stern, Carolyn, 1915–

Problem solving and concept formation: an annotated bibliography. ₁Inglewood, Calif.₎ Southwest Regional Laboratory for Educational Research & Development, 1968₎

118 p. 28 cm.

Wisconsin Research and Development Center for Cognitive Learning.

Publications of the Wisconsin Research and Development Center for Cognitive Learning ₁by₎ Herbert J. Klausmeier, director. Madison, 1972.

vi, 141 p. 28 cm.

Cover title: Bibliography of publications, 1972-1973.

Wisconsin Research and Development Center for Cognitive Learning.

Publications of the Wisconsin Research and Development Center for Cognitive Learning, Richard A. Rossmiller, director. — Madison : The Center, 1973, 1974 printing.

vi, 185 p. ; 28 cm.

Cover title: 1973-1974 bibliography of publications, Wisconsin Research and Development Center for Cognitive Learning.
"Center contract no. NE-C-00-3-0065."

EDUCATIONAL RESEARCH

An Annotated bibliography of institutional research.

1st–   1966/67–
₁Athens, Ga., etc.₎ Association for Institutional Research.

v. 23 cm. annual.

Editor: 1966/67–   C. Fincher.

Bjerstedt, Åke.

Twelve years of educational and psychological research in Sweden. A bibliography of publications in English 1955-1966. Lund, Universitetet, Gleerup, 1968.

96 p. 24 cm. (Studia psychologica et paedagogica. Series altera : ₁Investigationes₎ 14)

Brüner, Karen.

International education resources; a summary of OE-funded research projects and reports available through the Educational Research Information Center, 1956-71, compiled by Karen Bruner, Kent Weeks, and Pat Kern. ₁Washington₎ U.S. Office of Education, Institute of International Studies; ₁for sale by the Supt. of Docs., U.S. Govt. Print. Off., 1972₎

vi, 486 p. 27 cm. (DHEW publication no. (OE) 72-195)

Coetzee, Johannes Christiaan, 1893–

Annotated bibliography of research in education ₁compiled by₎ J. Chr. Coetzee. Pretoria, Human Sciences Research Council, 1970–

v. in   30 cm.

Published also in Afrikaans.

Complete guide and index to ERIC reports: thru December 1969. Compiled by the Prentice-Hall editorial staff. Englewood Cliffs, N. J., Prentice-Hall ₁1970₎

1338 p. 24 cm.

Dublin. University College. *Library.*

List of research work in education and educational psychology presented at University College, Dublin, 1912-1968: a provisional list. Dublin, University College, 1969.

₁3₎, 201 l. 26 cm.

Education studies completed in Canadian universities. 1966/67–

Toronto, Canadian Education Association.

v. 29 cm.

Franke, Lydia.

Dokumentation Forschungsarbeiten Erziehungswissenschaft, Pädagogik, Bildungsforschung 1968/69. Hrsg. von Lydia Franke. Unter Mitarb. von Edelgard Friedrich. Weinheim, Berlin, Basel, Beltz, 1971.

488 p. 21 cm. (Pädagogisches Zentrum. Veröffentlichungen, Reihe A: Dokumentation, Bd. 13)

Frankfurt am Main. Deutsches Institut für Internationale Pädagogische Forschung.

Veröffentlichungen des Deutschen Instituts (1952-1963: Hochschule) für Internationale Pädagogische Forschung und seiner Mitarbeiter. Frankfurt am Main, 1967.

69 p. 21 cm.

On cover: Verzeichnis der Veröffentlichungen.

Manheim, Theodore, 1921–

Sources in educational research; a selected & annotated bibliography, by Theodore Manheim, Gloria L. Dardarian ₁and₎ Diane A. Satterthwaite. Detroit, Wayne State University Press, 1969–

v. 23 cm..

Research in education. v. ₁1₎–   Nov. 1966–
₁Washington₎

v. in   20-27 cm. monthly.

Issues for 1966-67 have no vol. numbering but constitute v. 1-2.
Issued by the Educational Resources Information Center (1966-July 1967 under an earlier name: Educational Research Information Center)
INDEXES:
Vols. 1-2, 1966-67. 1 v.

Testerman, Jack.

Institutional research: a comprehensive bibliography, by Jack Testerman, Robert Blackmon ₁and₎ Terry White. Lafayette. La., University of Southwestern Louisiana, Office of Institutional Research, 1972.

131 p. 29 cm. (Research series, no. 12)

Testerman, Jack.

Institutional research: a review of literature to 1972, by Jack Testerman, Robert Blackmon ₁and₎ John Mosier. ₁Lafayette. La., Office of Institutional Research, University of Southwestern Louisiana, 1972₎

29 l. 23 cm. (University of Southwestern Louisiana. Research series, no. 14)

U. S. *Educational Research Information Center.*

Office of Education research reports, 1956-65, ED 002 747-ED 003 960. ₁Washington, U. S. Govt. Print. Off..

1967₁

2 v. 20 x 27 cm.

U. S. *Office of Education.*
CRP: Cooperative research projects; a seven-year summary, July 1, 1956–June 30, 1963. ₁Washington, For sale by the Superintendent of Documents, U. S. Govt. Print. Off., 1964₁

iv, 75 p. 27 cm. (*Its* Circular no. 736)

EDUCATIONAL SOCIOLOGY

Bräuner, Vilém, *comp.*
Pedagogická sociologie; výběr z knižních publikací a časopiseckých článků. Sest, Vilém Bräuner. Odborný poradce Mojmír Hájek. V Brně, Státní Pedagogická knihovna, 1967.

20 l. 29 cm. (Státní pedagogická knihovna v Brně. Publikace, čís. 286)

At head of title: Státní vědecká knihovna.

Farrell, Joseph P
A selective annotated bibliography on education and social development ₁by₁ Joseph P. Farrell. ₁Syracuse, N. Y.₁ Center for Development Education, Syracuse University, 1966.

xi, 124 l. 28 cm.

EDUCATIONAL TECHNOLOGY

Berthold, Jeanne Saylor.
Educational technology and the teaching-learning process; a selected bibliography. Prepared by Jeanne Saylor Berthold ₁and₁ Mary Alice Curran. Arlington, Va., U. S. Dept. of Health, Education, and Welfare, National Institutes of Health. Bureau of Health Manpower, Division of Nursing ₁1968₁

v, 63 p. 26 cm.

Berthold, Jeanne Saylor.
Educational technology and the teaching-learning process; a selected bibliography. Prepared by Jeanne Saylor Berthold, Mary Alice Curran ₁and₁ Diana Y. Barhyte. Rev. Bethesda, Md., U. S. National Institutes of Health, Bureau of Health Professions Education and Manpower Training, Division of Nursing, 1969 ₁i. e. 1970₁

56 p. 26 cm.

Bjerstedt, Åke.
Recent trends in educational technology: notes from Munich, Nice, and Amsterdam ₁by₁ Å. Bjerstedt. Malmö, Sweden, Dept. of Educational and Psychological Research, School of Education, 1968.

9 l. 30 cm. (Didakometry no. 21) (Special topic bulletin from Dept. of Educational and Psychological Research, School of Education, Malmö, Sweden)

Cover title.
"A bibliography ... composed of selected papers from three international conferences: the Munich Symposium on Programmed Instruction and Teaching Machines (March 1968), the Nice Conference on Major Trends in Programmed Learning Research (May 1968) and the Amsterdam Congress of Applied Psychology (August 1968)."

Dechame, Alix.
Technologie de l'éducation, dynamique de groupe, non directivité, bibliographie analytique par Mᵐᵉ Alix Dechame, en collaboration avec Mˡˡᵉ Renée Capdupuy. Bordeaux, Centre régional de documentation pédagogique, 75, Cours d'Alsace et Lorraine, 1969.

i, 81, xiv l. 27 cm.

The Educational technology bibliography series. v. 1–
Englewood Cliffs, N. J., Educational Technology Publications ₁1971–

v. 23 cm.

Eraut, Michael.
An annotated select bibliography of educational technology; compiled by Michael Eraut and Geoffrey Squires. London, National Council for Educational Technology, 1971.

₁92₁ p. 30 cm.

Great Britain. British Council.
Educational technology: some relevant British organisations and their publications, together with a select annotated list of other relevant, currently available, books, bibliographies, catalogues, reports etc. and periodicals. London, British Council, 1973.

46 p. 23 cm.

EDUCATIONAL TESTS

Bräuner, Vilém.
Testování ve škole. Bibliogr. knižních publ. a čas. článků. Sest. Vilém Bräuner. Brno, St. věd. knihovna—St. pedagog. knihovna, rozmn., 1969.

46 p. 30 cm. (Brünn. Státní pedagogická knihovna. Publikace, čís. 329)

Samples, Gordon.
A bibliography of test study manuals. ₁n. p.₁ 1968.

30 p. 28 cm.

EDWARDS, JONATHAN

Johnson, Thomas Herbert.
The printed writings of Jonathan Edwards, 1703–1758; a bibliography, by Thomas H. Johnson. New York, B. Franklin ₁1970, ᶜ1940₁

xiii, 135 p. 23 cm. (Burt Franklin bibliography & reference series, 318. Philosophy monograph series, 27)

ÉFENDLEV, G. KH.

Safarova, IŪ V
Г. Х. Эфендиев. 1907–1967. Библиография. ₁Вступит. статья акад. М. А. Кашкая, с 11–37₁. Баку, Изд. АН АзССР, 1968.

93 p. 16 см. (Академия наук Азербайджанской ССР. Фундаментальная библиотека. Деятели науки и культуры Азербайджана)

Added t. p. in Azerbaijani.
By IŪ. V. Safarova and A. B. Magerramov.

EGGS

Faber, Frederic Lewis, 1914–
An inventory of market news reports for eggs ₁by₁ Fred L. Faber and Robert J. Van Houten. Washington₁ Economic Research Service and Consumer and Marketing Service, U. S. Dept. of Agriculture ₁1967₁

ii, 21 p. 26 cm. (ERS–332)

EGYPT

American University at Cairo. *Library.*
Guide to U. A. R. Government publications at the A. U. C.

Library. ₍Cairo₎ Periodicals and Documents Dept., American University in Cairo Library, 1965.

20, 41 p. 25 cm.

دليل بمقتنيات مكتبة الجامعة الأمريكية بالقاهرة من المطبوعات :.Added t. p

الحكومية ومطبوعات جامعة الدول العربية.

Includes titles in Arabic and Western languages.

Cairo. al-Maṭḥaf al-Miṣrī. *al-Maktabah.*
Catalogue de la Bibliothèque du Musée égyptien du Caire, 1927–1958, par Dia' Abou Ghazi et Abd el-Mohsen el-Khachab. Le Caire, Organisme général des imprimeries gouvernementales, 1966–

v. 24 cm.

At head of title: République arabe unie. Ministère du tourisme et des antiquités. Service des antiquités de l'Egypte.

CONTENTS.—₍1₎ A–C.

Jerusalem. Hebrew University. *Institute of Asian and African Studies.*
ביבליוגרפיה על מצרים. ירושלים, האוניברסיטה העברית, הפקולטה למדעי הרוח, המכון ללימודי אסיה ואפריקה, תשכ״ד
₍1963/64₎

28, 35 p. 27 cm.
Cover title.
Table of contents in Arabic and English.
״כוללת ספרים (בשפות אירופיות, בערבית ובעברית) ... הנמצאים בירושלים.״

Maunier, René, 1887–
Bibliographie économique, juridique, et sociale de l'Égypte moderne (1798–1916). New York, B. Franklin ₍1971₎

xxxii, 372 p. 22 cm. (Burt Franklin bibliography and reference series, 407. Selected essays in history, economics, and social science, 243)

Reprint of the edition published in Cairo, 1918.

Toren, Amnon.
(Bibliyografyah 'al Mitsrayim ha-natserit)
ביבליוגרפיה על מצרים הנאצרית, 1952–1970. ערך: אמנון תורן. ₍תל-אביב₎ מפעלים אוניברסיטאיים להוצאה לאור ₍1972₎

102 p. 24 cm. (מכון שילוח לחקר המזרח התיכון ואפריקה. סידרת עזרי הוראה ומחקר)

Added t. p.: A bibliography of books on Nasser's Egypt, 1952–1970.
Introd. also in English.

BIBLIOGRAPHIES

Geddes, Charles L
An analytical guide to the bibliographies on modern Egypt & the Sudan ₍by₎ C. L. Geddes. ₍Denver₎ American Institute of Islamic Studies ₍1972₎

78 p. 22 cm. (American Institute of Islamic Studies. (Bibliographic series, no. 2)

IMPRINTS

Nuṣayr, 'Āydah Ibrāhīm.
الكتب العربية التي نشرت في الجمهورية العربية المتحدة (مصر) بين عامي ١٩٢٦ – ١٩٤٠، دراسة وبيليوجرافيا. اعداد عايدة ابراهيم نصير. ₍القاهرة₎ 1966.

457, 6, 2 l. illus. 35 cm.

رسالة الماجستير — جامعة القاهرة
Introduction in English: l. 1–6 (2d group)

Nuṣayr, 'Āydah Ibrāhīm.
الكتب العربية التي نشرت في الجمهورية العربية المتحدة (مصر)

بين عامي ١٩٢٦/ ١٩٤٠. اعداد عايدة ابراهيم نصير. القاهرة، الجامعة الأمريكية، قسم النشر، 1969.

400, 2, 6 p. 35 cm.

Includes an introd. in English with caption title: Arabic books published in the U. A. R., "Egypt," between 1926 & 1940; a study & a bibliography.

EGYPTIAN INSCRIPTIONS see Inscriptions, Egyptian

EICHENDORFF, JOSEPH KARL BENEDIKT, FREIHERR VON

Döhn, Helga.
Der Nachlass Joseph von Eichendorff. Berlin, Deutsche Staatsbibliothek, 1971.

xiv, 59 p. illus. 21 cm. (Handschrifteninventare der Deutschen Staatsbibliothek, 2)

Krabiel, Klaus-Dieter.
Joseph von Eichendorff; kommentierte Studienbibliographie. ₍Frankfurt am Main₎ Athenäum Verlag ₍c1971₎

ix, 90 p. 21 cm.

EICHMANN, ADOLF

Braham, Randolph L
The Eichmann case: a source book, by Randolph L. Braham. New York, World Federation of Hungarian Jews, 1969.

xi, 186 p. 23 cm.

"The titles of items in languages other than French, German, Italian, and Spanish are also rendered in English translation."

EIGNER, LARRY

Wyatt, Andrea.
A bibliography of works by Larry Eigner, 1937–1969. Berkeley, Oyez, 1970.

82 p. 23 cm.

EINAUDI, LUIGI

Firpo, Luigi.
Bibliografia degli scritti di Luigi Einaudi. (Dal 1893 al 1970). A cura di Luigi Firpo. Pubblicazione promossa dalla Banca d'Italia. Torino, 1971.

900 p. illus., plates. 24½ cm.

At head of title: Fondazione Luigi Einaudi, Torino.

EISEN, CHARLES

Salomons, Vera Frances.
Charles Eisen, eighteenth century French book illustrator and engraver. An annotated bibliography of the best known books illustrated by Charles-Dominique-Joseph Eisen, 1720–1778, with descriptions of the plates and an index, preceded by a sketch of his life and art ₍by₎ Vera Salomons. Avec une préf. par Émile Bertaux. Amsterdam, Hissink, 1972.

315 p. illus. 23 cm. (Scripta artis monographia, 17)
"Reprint 1972 of the edition London 1914."

EISLER, HANNS

Tischmeyer, Margot.
Hanns Eisler. ₍Anlässlich des 75. Geburtstages von Hanns Eisler am 6. Juli 1973 zusammengestellt von Margot Tischmeyer und Achim Rohde unter Mitarbeit von Hans

-Joachim Kögel. Berlin, Berliner Stadtbibliothek, 1973.

80 p. 21 cm. (Bibliographische Kalenderblätter. Sonderblatt, 38)

EKELUND, ERIK RUNAR SELIM

Wiitanen, Svea.
Erik Ekelunds tryckta skrifter, 1917–1969; litteraturhistoria, litteratur- och teaterkritik, dikter. Åbo, ₁Åbo Akademi₁ 1970.

37 p. 25 cm. (Acta Academiae Aboensis. Ser. A: Humaniora, v. 38, nr. 4)

EL SALVADOR see Salvador

ELASTICITY

Smith, Denise Blakeley.
Elasto-plasticity; a selective bibliography. Johannesburg. University of the Witwatersrand, Department of Bibliography, Librarianship and Typography, 1967.

₁xii₁, 18 p. 28 cm.

"Compiled in part fulfilment for the Diploma in Librarianship, University of the Witwatersrand."

ELBLĄG, POLAND

Morcinek, Elżbieta.
Inwentarz zbioru "Rękopisy eiblĄskie." ₁Wyd. 1.₁ Warszawa, Naczelna Dyrekcja Archiwów Państwowych, 1967.

xxxviii, 272 p. 24 cm.

At head of title: Wojewódzkie Archiwum Państwowe w Gdańsku.

Wojewódzkie Archiwum Państwowe w Gdańsku.
Archiwum miasta Elbląga; przewodnik po zespołach, 1242–1945. Oprac.: Janina Czaplicka i Wanda Klesińska. ₁Wyd. 1.₁. Warszawa, Naczelna Dyrekcja Archiwów Państwowych ₁Łódź, Państwowe Wydawn. Naukowe; Oddział w Łodzi₁ 1970.

87 p. illus. 23 cm.

ELECTIONS

Agranoff, Robert.
Elections and electoral behavior: a bibliography. DeKalb, Center for Governmental Studies, Northern Illinois University ₁1972₁

30 l. 28 cm.

Germany (*Federal Republic, 1949–*) *Bundestag. Wissenschaftliche Abteilung.*
Wahlsystem und Wahlrecht der Bundesrepublik Deutschland; Auswahlbibliographie. Bonn, 1967.

98 p. 30 cm. (*Its* Bibliographien, Nr. 8)

"Das vorliegende Heft ... wurde im Referat Fachdokumentation von Herrn Diplom-Soziologen Peter Schindler bearbeitet."

Goodey, Brian R
The geography of elections, an introductory bibliography, by Brian R. Goodey. Grand Forks, Center for the Study of Cultural and Social Change, University of North Dakota ₁1968?₁

v, 04 p. 27 cm. (University of North Dakota. Center for the Study of Cultural and Social Change. Monograph 3)

Based on the author's thesis, Indiana University.

Kaid, Lynda Lee.
Political campaign communication: a bibliography and guide to the literature, by Lynda Lee Kaid, Keith R. Sanders ₁and₁ Robert O. Hirsch. Metuchen, N. J., Scarecrow Press, 1974.

v, 206 p. 22 cm.

Pagirienė, L
Tarybiniai rinkimai—liaudies valia; literatūros sąrašes. ₁Sudarė L. Pagirienė₁ Vilnius, 1965.

8 p. 20 cm.

Cover title.
At head of title: LTSR Valstybinė respublikinė biblioteka.

ELECTRIC ENGINEERING

Benedek, Pál.
Alumínium alkalmazása az elektronikában. Budapest, 1970.

41 cm. 20 cm. (A tudomány és technika újdonságai magyar nyelven; ajánló bibliográfia, 44. sz.)

Codlin, Ellen M *comp.*
Handlist of basic reference material for librarians and information officers in electrical and electronic engineering; compiled by Ellen M. Codlin. 4th issue revised. London, Aslib, 1967.

40 p. 25 cm. (Aslib. Electronics Group. Publication)

Codlin, Ellen M
Handlist of basic reference material in electrical and electronic engineering. 6th ed.; edited by Ellen M. Codlin. London, Aslib Electronics Group, 1973.

64 p. 21 cm.

Fourth ed. published in 1967 under title: Handlist of basic reference material for librarians and information officers in electrical and electronic engineering; 5th ed. published in 1969 under title: Handlist of basic references for librarians and information officers in electrical and electronic engineering.

Dobruská, Naděžda, comp.
Aplikace polovodičů v silnoproudé elektrotechnice. ₁Sest. Naděžda Dobruská. Vyd. 1.₁. Praha, Ústředí vědeckých, technických a ekonomických informaci, 1967.

64 p. 21 cm. (Statní technicka knihovna v Praze. Bibliografie, sv. 111)

At head of title: Ústředí vědeckých a ekonomických informaci.

Electrical safety abstracts. Edited by Alfred H. McKinney ₁and₁ Harry G. Conner. 4th ed. Pittsburgh, Instrument Society of America ₁1972₁

ii, 278 p. 29 cm

Eliseeva, N V
Электромонтажные работы. Библиогр. реферативный указатель за 1969 г. ₁Сост. инж. Н. В. Елисеева₁ Москва, 1970.

66 p. 20 cm.

At head of title: Министерство энергетики и электрификации СССР. Главтехстройпроект. Центр научно-технической информации по энергетике и электрификации. Информэнерго.

Gábor, František.
Elektrotechnická literatúra. Zost. a úvod ₁nap.₁ František Gábor. Košice, ŠVK, rotaprint, 1970–

v. diagrs. 20 cm. (Bibliografické správy ŠVK, Košice, čis. 2601/1070

At head of title, v. 1–: Štátna vedecká knižnica v Košiciach.
CONTENTS: 1. zv. Knihy.

Key to Turkish science: electrical & electronics abstracts.
v. 1–
Apr. 1969–
Yenişehir-Ankara, Türdok.

v. 24 cm.

At head of title: TBTAK. Scientific and Technical Research Council of Turkey.

Library Association. *County Libraries Group.*
Readers' guide to books on electrical engineering and electronics. 2d ed. ₁London₁ 1964.

44 p. 19 cm. (*Its* Readers' guide, new ser., no. 75)

Cover title: Electrical engineering.
"Compilation undertaken by the staff of the Staffordshire County Library."
First ed. published in 1955 under title: Readers' guide to books on electrical engineering.

Padua. Università. Istituto di elettrotecnica e di elettronica.
L'Istituto di elettrotecnica e di elettronica nel 1969. Padova, Università, Istituto di elettrotecnica e di elettronica, 1970.

10, ₁39₁ p. 29 cm. (Its UPee-70/01)

Svirina, E   V
₁Energeticheskoe khozīaĭstvo Belorusskoĭ SSR₁
Энергетическое хозяйство Белорусской ССР. Библиогр. указ. (1966–1970) Минск, 1971.

280 p. 21 cm.

At head of title: Академия наук БССР. Фундаментальная библиотека им. Я. Коласа.

Szilard, Paula.
Electrical engineering literature; a reference guide. ₁Honolulu₁ Thomas H. Hamilton Library, University of Hawaii, 1969.

69 l. 28 cm.

PERIODICALS

Current papers in electrical & electronics engineering. no. 1–
Aug. 1964–
₁London₁
no. 30–44 cm. monthly.
"An INSPEC publication."
Title varies: Aug. 1964–   Current papers for the professional electrical and electronics engineer. –
Dec. 1968, Current papers in electrotechnology.
₁Issues for 1964–   published by the Institution of Electrical Engineers (1969–   with the Institute of Electrical and Electronics Engineers).

ELECTRIC METAL-CUTTING AND WELDING

Boleszny, Ivan.
Electric discharge machining, compiled by I. Boleszny. Adelaide, Public Library of South Australia, 1966.

42 p. 27 cm. (Research Service bibliographies. Series 4, no. 78)

Machová, Elena, comp.
Oblúkové zváranie; výberový zoznam z domácej a zahraničnej literatúry. Zostavila: Elena Machová. Bratislava, Slovenská technická knižnica, 1968.

95 p. 21 cm. (Edícia II. Séria: B. Výberové bibliografie)

At head of title: Slovenská technická knižnica v Bratislave.

Прогрессивные методы обработки металлов с помощью пучка электронов, плазмы и светового луча; библиографи-

ческий указатель литературы. ₁Составитель И. В. Мельник₁ Москва, 1966.

51 p. 22 cm. (Актуальные проблемы техники)

At head of title: Государственный комитет Совета Министров СССР по науке и технике. Государственная публичная научно-техническая библиотека СССР.

Сварка порошковой проволокой. Библиогр. указатель отечеств. и зарубежной литературы за 1960–1968 гг. (ноябрь). Сост. канд. техн. наук Суптель А. М., Пшеничникова Д. С., Ительман С. А., Кутьянова О. М. Науч. ред. канд. техн. наук Суптель А. М. Киев, 1968.

65 p. 20 cm.

At head of title: Академия наук Украинской ССР. Ордена Ленина и ордена Трудового Красного Знамени институт электросварки им. Е. О. Патона. Научная библиотека.

ELECTRIC POWER
see also Rural electrification; Water-power electric plants

Belîaevskaîa, M   I
₁Edinaîa ėnergeticheskaîa sistema₁
Единая энергетическая система. ₁Рек. обзор литературы. Москва, "Книга," 1971₁.

15 p. 17 cm. (Новое в науке и технике)

At head of title: Государственная библиотека СССР им. В. И. Ленина. Центральная политехническая библиотека.

Bromberg, Erik.
An annotated bibliography of high voltage direct current transmission. 1963–1965. Compiled by Eric Bromberg. New York, Institute of Electrical and Electronics Engineers ₁1967₁

113 p. 28 cm.

Comisión de Integración Eléctrica Regional. Subcomité de Distribución de Energía Eléctrica.
Indice temático. Coordinador técnico: Angelo Innocenzi G. Lima ₁CIER, Secretaría General₁ 1972.

23 l. 28 cm.

Institute of Electrical and Electronics Engineers.
Bibliography on power system stability—1965–1969. ₁New York, 1971₁

68 p. 29 cm.

"Basic information ... compiled by Dr. E. W. Kimbark."
"Sponsored by the IEEE Working Group on Power System Stability."

Norwood, Douglas.
Bonneville Power Administration, a bibliography (1930–1963) by Douglas Norwood and James Burghardt. ₁Portland? Ore.₁ 1964.

107 p. 27 cm.

Cover title.
At head of title: The Library, U. S. Bonneville Power Administration, Portland, Ore.

Russia (1923–   U. S. S. R.). Gosudarstvennaîa inspektsiîa po énergeticheskomu nadzoru.
₁Pravila tekhnicheskoĭ ėkspluatatsiĭ ėlektroustanovok potrebiteleĭ₁
Правила технической эксплуатации электроустановок потребителей и Правила техники безопасности при эксплуатации электростановок потребителей. (Обязат. для потребителей электроэнергии всех м-в и ведомств). Утв. 12/IV 1969 г. ₁Вводятся в действие с 1/VII 1970 г.₁ Изд. 3-е. Днепропетровск, "Промінь," 1972.

352 p. with illus. 22 cm.

At head of title: Министерство энергетики и электрификации СССР.

Previous editions by Gosudarstvennaia inspektsiia po promyshlennoĭ énergetike i énergonadzoru, published under title: Правила технической эксплуатации и безопасности обслуживания электроустановок промышленных предприятий.

———— Дополнение. Днепропетровск, Изд-во Промінь, 1972.

49 p. 22 cm.

Svenska kraftverksföreningen.
Förteckning över Svenska kraftverksföreningens publikationer 1960–1969. Stockholm, föreningen, 1970.

30 p. 21 cm. (Its Publikationer, 1970:5)

Tagirov, M   A
Метод функций Ляпунова в энергетике. Библиогр. указатель 1935–1968 гг. Новосибирск, 1969.

33 p. 20 cm.

At head of title: Министерство энергетики и электрификации СССР. Сибирский научно-исследовательский институт энергетики. Отдел научно-технической информации.
By M. A. Tagirov and A. I. Kochergaeva.

Vinogradova, I   L
Теплоэнергетическое оборудование электростанций СССР. Библиогр. указатель отечеств. литературы за 1917–1966 (I пол.) гг. [В 6-ти ч. Сост.: Виноградова, И. Л.] Москва, 1968–
      v. 21 cm.

At head of title v. 6: Министерство тяжелого, энергетического и транспортного машиностроения. Центральная научно-техническая библиотека тяжелого машиностроения. Научно-исследовательский институт информации по тяжелому, энергетическому и транспортному машиностроению.
CONTENTS.—
ч. 6. Электрические станции.

ELECTRICITY; ELECTRIC APPARATUS; ETC.
see also Hall effect; Thermoelectricity

Alimina, N   F
Электрический разряд в газах. Библиогр. указатель. 1963–1965 (III квартал). Москва, 1968.

2 v. 20 cm.

At head of title: Министерство высшего и среднего специального образования СССР. Московский энергетический институт. Библиотека. Научно-библиографический отдел.
"Составитель Н. Ф. Алимина."
CONTENTS: ч. 1. Отечественная литература.—ч. 2. Литература на иностранных языках.

Bibliography and abstracts on electrical contacts, circuit breakers, and arc phenomena. 1965/69–
[New York]
      v. 28 cm. (IEEE)
Supersedes: American Society for Testing Materials. Bibliography and abstracts on electrical contacts.
Vols. for 1965/69– issued by the Electrical Contacts Technical Committee of the Institute of Electrical and Electronics Engineers, Holm Seminars on Electric Contact Phenomena, Illinois Institute of Technology, and IIT Research Institute.

Электротехника (аппараты низкого напряжения, смежные вопросы) [Составитель А. Г. Гессе]. Москва, Отд-ние ВНИИЭМ по научно-техн. информации, стандартизации и нормализации в электротехнике, 1966.

52 p. 22 cm. (Электротехническая промышленность за рубежом)

At head of title: Министерство электротехнической промышленности СССР.

Fiedlerová, Marie.
Světelná technika. Výběrová bibliogr. Zprac. Marie Fiedlerová. Předml.: Ladislav Monzer. Plzeň, St. věd. knihovna, rozmn., 1971.

51, [1] p. 21 cm. (Edice Bibliografie technické literatury, sv. 9)

(Kontakuto ni kansuru bunken sōgō mokuroku)
コンタクトに関する文献総合目録　武野国
太他編
東京　学術書出版会　啓学出版（発売）　昭和45(1970)
223p　27cm

Kunovjánková, Milena.
Spotřeba elektřiny jako činitel zvyšování životní úrovně obyvatelstva. Doporučující bibliogr. Sest. Milena Kunovjánková. Úvod: Blanka Podlešáková. 1. vyd. Praha, UVTEI-St. techn. knihovna, rozmn., 1968.

40, [1] p. 21 cm. (Prague. Státní technická knihovna. Bibliografie, sv. 125)

Machová, Elena.
Opravujeme elektrické spotřebiče. Výber. zoznam z domácej a zahran. lit. Zost. E. Machová. Bratislava, Slov. techn. knižnica, rozmn., 1970.

45, [2] p. 20 cm. (Bratislava. Slovenská technická knižnica. Edícia 2. Séria B: Výberové bibliografie)

Midwest Research Institute, Kansas City, Mo.
Bibliography on electromechanical transducers, with indexes. Material for this bibliography was selected by Applied Space Technology-Regional Advancement (ASTRA), Midwest Research Institute, Kansas City, Missouri. Washington, National Aeronautics and Space Administration; available from the Clearinghouse for Federal Scientific and Technical Information, Springfield, Va., 1966.

viii, 20, I–18 p. 27 cm. (U. S. National Aeronautics and Space Administration, Technology Utilization Division. Technology utilization bibliography)

Migdalski, Janusz.
Teoria niezawodności i jej zastosowania; bibliografia piśmiennictwa polskiego za lata 1957–1966. Warszawa, Instytut Automatyki Polskiej Akademii Nauk, 1967.

55 p. 24 cm. (Prace Instytutu Automatyki PAN, zesz. 65)

Новые источники энергии. Библиогр. указатель. Москва, 1970.

152 p. 22 cm. (Актуальные проблемы техники)

At head of title: Государственный комитет Совета Министров СССР по науке и технике. Государственная публичная научно-техническая библиотека СССР.
By L. I. Dmitrieva and others.

50 лет ленинского плана электрификации. Библиогр. указатель. Под общ. ред. В. Ю. Стеклова. Москва, 1970.

214 p. with illus. port. 21 cm.

At head of title: Министерство энергетики и электрификации СССР. Главтехстройпроект. Центр научно-технической информации по энергетике и электрификации Информэнерго.

Popova, N   M
Новые источники энергии. Библиогр. указатель. [1965–1967 гг. Сост. Н. М. Попова]. Москва, 1968.

146 p. 21 cm. (Актуальные проблемы техники)

At head of title: Государственный комитет Совета Министров СССР по науке и технике. Государственная публичная научно-техническая библиотека СССР.

Rejtharová, Alena.
Akumulátory. Zprác. Alena Rejtharová. Plzeň, St. věd. knihovna, rozmn., 1970–

v. 21 cm. (Bibliografie technické literatury, 4

CONTENTS: díl. 1. české a slovenské literární prameny.

Turner, H   W
Advances in electric fuses; a summary of published information. 1950–1965. Compiled by H. W. Turner and C. Turner. Leatherhead ₁Eng.₁ Electrical Research Association, 1967.

83 p. 26 cm. (ERA report no. 5228)

U. S. *Army. Electronic Parts and Materials Division.*
KWIC index of technical papers: Wire and cable symposia (1952–1966) Compiled by Electronic Parts & Materials Division, Electronic Components Laboratory, USAECOM, and Cooke Color and Chemical Co. Fort Monmouth, N. J., U. S. Army Electronics Command, 1967.

v, 53 p. 27 cm.

U. S. *Library of Congress. Aerospace Technology Division.*
Electrostatic and electromagnetic generators; annotated bibliography ₁by₁ Jordan V. Randjelovic. Washington₁ 1966.

iv, 18 l. 28 cm. (*Its* ATD report 66–10)

"Compiled from Soviet open sources published 1961–1964."

United States. Library of Congress. Aerospace Technology Division.
Materials for high-temperature energy converters: annotated bibliography ₁by₁ Michael Slesarenko. Washington₁ 1966.

iii, 35 l. 28 cm. (*Its* ATD report 66–20)

"Compiled from Soviet open sources published 1960–1965."

Vorob'ev, G   V
Настроенные электропередачи. Библиогр. указатель 1920–1967 г. Новосибирск, 1969.

47 p. 20 cm.

At head of title: Министерство энергетики и электрификации СССР. Сибирский научно-исследовательский институт энергетики. Отдел научно-технической информации.
By G. V. Vorob'ev and A. I. Kochergaeva.

Žilinský, Václav.
Vyhodnocování elektrických signálů při elektrickém měření tepelně technických veličin. Praha, Ústředí vědeckých, technických a ekonomických informací: Státní technická knihovna, 1970.

40 p. 20 cm. (Doporučující bibliografie knižní a časopisecké literatury. Bibliografie, sv. 151)

ELECTROENCEPHALOGRAPHY

Akademiîa nauk SSSR. *Sektor seti spetsial'nykh bibliotek.*
Библиография работ по электроэнцефалографии, 1875–1963 гг.; электрическая активность головного мозга животных и человека в норме. ₁Ответственный редактор А. М. Рябиновская. Составители: П. И. Гуляев, З. И. Плясова, С. Б. Аронова₁ Москва, Наука, 1965.

205 p. 20 cm.

On leaf preceding t. p.: Академия наук СССР. Сектор сети специальных библиотек. Всесоюзное физиологическое общество им. И. П. Павлова. Библиотека Института высшей нервной деятельности и нейрофизиологии.

Akademiîa nauk SSSR. *Sektor seti spetsial'nykh bibliotek.*
Электроэнцефалографические исследования в клинике; библиография работ по электроэнцефалографии, 1928–1963 гг. ₁Ответственный редактор А. М. Рябиновская. Составители: П. И. Гуляев, З. И. Плясова, С. Б. Аронова₁ Москва, Наука, 1966.

89 p. 22 cm.

At head of title: Академия наук СССР. Сектор сети специальных библиотек. Всесоюзное физиологическое общество им. И. П. Павлова. Библиотека Института высшей нервной деятельности и нейрофизиологии.

Barnes, Thomas Cunliffe, 1904–
Synopsis of electroencephalography; or, Guide to brain waves ₁by₁ Thomas C. Barnes. New York, Hafner Pub. Co., 1968.

177 p. 24 cm.

Bickford, Reginald G
A KWIC index of EEG literature (and society proceedings) Compiled by Reginald G. Bickford, James L. Jacobson, and David Langworthy. Amsterdam, New York, Elsevier Pub. Co., 1965.

viii, 581 p. 29 cm.

California. University. University at Los Angeles. Brain Information Service.
A KWIC index to E. E. G. and allied literature 1964–1966. Compiled by the staff of the UCLA Brain Information Service, NINDS Neurological Information Network. Edited by Margaret Wineburgh and Pat L. Walter. Amsterdam, New York, Elsevier Pub. Co., 1971.
392 p. 27 cm. (Electroencephalography and clinical neuro physiology. Supplement no. 30)

California. University. University at Los Angeles. Brain Information Service.
A KWIC index to E. E. G. and allied literature 1966–1969, compiled by the Staff of the UCLA Brain Information Service, NINDS Neurological Information Network. Edited by Pat L. Walter. Amsterdam, New York, Elsevier ₁1970₁

548 p. 27 cm. (Electroencephalography and clinical neurophysiology. Supplement no. 29)

ELECTROLYSIS see Electroplating

ELECTRONIC DATA PROCESSING
    see also Computers; Information
    storage and retrieval systems

Bibliography of current computing literature.

₁New York, Association for Computing Machinery₁
    v. 28 cm.

Cover title   : Computing reviews bibliography and subject index of current computing literature.
Editors: A. Finerman and L. Revens.

Canada. *Dept. of Labour. Economics and Research Branch.*
A selected bibliography on the social and economic implications of electronic data processing. ₁Prepared by Helen Traynor. Ottawa?₁ 1964.

75 l. 28 cm.

At head of title: Research program on the training of skilled manpower.
"Intended as a reference guide to material published between the years 1955 and 1963 inclusive, on office automation."

Duisburg. Stadtbücherei.
Datenverarbeitung; Auswahlverzeichnis. ₁Duisburg, 1968₁

23 p. 21 cm.

Bibliography compiled by G. Dittrich from the holdings of the library.

Evans, William Harold, 1902–
Small office automation, by W. H. Evans. Rev. by Elizabeth Janezeck. Washington, U. S. Small Business Administration, 1964 ₁i. e. 1965₁

8 p. 26 cm. (Small business bibliography, no. 58)

Florida. University, *Gainesville. Dept. of Accounting.*
Annotated bibliography of electronic data processing. Gainesville, Accounting Dept., College of Business Administration, University of Florida ₁1964₁

30 p 23 cm. (University of Florida. Accounting series no. 2)

Gotterer, Malcolm H 1924–
Kwic index; a bibliography of computer management ₁by₁ Malcolm H. Gotterer. Princeton, Brandon/Systems Press ₁1970₁

152 p. 26 cm.

Heise, Ole.
Bøger om elektronisk databehandling. Katalog. København, Gads Boghandel, ₁1967₁.

128 p. 22 cm.

Intercollegiate bibliography ₁of₁ cases in business administration.
Intercollegiate bibliography ₁of₁ cases in data processing. ₁Boston₁ Intercollegiate Case Clearing House, 1965.

32 p. 28 cm.

Selected and grouped from v. 1–9 of the Intercollegiate bibliography of cases in business administration, by Ruth C. Hetherston and others, and edited by Grace V. Lindfors.

Kubala, Pavel, comp.
Přenos a dálkové zpracování dat. ₁Sest. Pavel Kubala. Wyd. 1. Praha₁ Státní technická knihovna, 1967.

139 p. 21 cm. (Doporučující bibliografie knižní časopisecké literatury. Bibliografie, sv. 119)

Murphy, Janet.
Optical character recognition: a selected bibliography; compiled by J. Murphy. Hatfield, Hertis, 1970.

₁1₁, 28, viii p. 30 cm.

Oldham, Eng. Public Libraries. Technical Library Services.
Optical character recognition and optical page reading devices: a selected bibliography, 1961–1969. Oldham (Lancs.), Oldham Public Libraries (Technical Library Services), 1970.

₁28₁ leaves. 30 cm.

Pauw, Guy de, comp.
Bibliographie commentée du traitement électronique de l'information. G. de Pauw. ₁Bruxelles₁, Institut Administration-Université ₁rue de La Concorde, 53₁, ₁1972₁.

82 p. 21 cm.

At head of title: Seminarie voor produktiviteitsstudie en -onderzoek. Université de Gand.

Pîaskovskiĭ, Sergeĭ Vladimirovich.
(Bibliograficheskiĭ annotirovannyĭ ukazatel' literatury po mekhanizatsii i avtomatizatsii obrabotki ékonomicheskoĭ informatsii)
Библиографический аннотированный указатель литературы по механизации и автоматизации обработки экономической информации за 1968–1970 гг. ₁Сост. С. В. Пясковский₁. Москва, "Статистика," 1973.

200 p. 22 cm.

At head of title: ЦСУ СССР. Всесоюзный государственный проектно-технологический институт по механизации учета и вычислительных работ.
Cover title: Библиографический указатель литературы по механизации и автоматизации обработки экономической информации.

Pleskot, Jozef.
Využitie samočinných počítačov pre automatizáciu riadiacich prác. Zostavil Jozef Pleskot. Odborne spolupracoval Bohuslav Partyk. ₁Vyd. 1.₁ Bratislava, Slovenské pedagogické nakl., 1965.

15 l., ₁290₁ p. (in portfolio) 21 cm. (Ústredna ekonomická knižnica. Ekonomické aktuality. Bibliografický zpravodaj, 1964, č. 3)

Voshchennikova, L IA
Передача данных. Рек. библиогр. указатель литературы. ₁За 1960 г. по 1-е полугодие 1969 г.₁ Москва, 1969.

39 p. 22 cm.

At head of title: Центральный научно-исследовательский институт связи. Центральная научно-техническая библиотека.
By L. IA. Voshchennikova and A. G. Pankratov.

West Virginia. *Library Commission.*
Data processing; a bibliography of books and journals at the West Virginia Library Commission Annex. ₁Robert Willits, compiler₁ Charleston ₁1966₁

4 l. 28 cm.

Caption title.
At head of title: When books participate.

Zielke, Gerhard.
ALGOL-Katalog; Matrizenrechnung. Leipzig, B. G. Teubner, 1972.

148 p. 23 cm.

CARTOGRAPHY

Meine, Karl-Heinz.
Bibliographie zur Automation in der Kartographie. Bonn, Institut für Kartographie und Topographie der Universität, 1969.

vi, 47 l. 30 cm.

Taylor, David Ruxtan Fraser, 1937–
Bibliography on computer mapping ₁by₁ D. R. F. Taylor. Mary Vance, editor. Monticello, Ill., Council of Planning Librarians, 1972.

36 p. 28 cm. (Council of Planning Librarians. Exchange bibliography, 263)

EDUCATION

see also Programmed instruction

Aa, H J van der.
Computers and education; an international bibliography on computer education: education about computers as well as the use of computers in education. Editor: H. J. van der Aa a₁nd₁ o₁thers. New York, Science Associates/International, 1970₁

115 p. 30 cm.

"A special publication on occasion of the IFIP World Conference on Computer Education, prepared by the editors of new literature on automation, Netherlands Centre for Informatics, Amsterdam."

Batoff, Mitchell E

A source directory and bibliography on the background, present status, and future prospects of computer-assisted instruction, researched and compiled by Mitchell E. Batoff. ₁Jersey City ?₁ N. J. 1969.

11 l. 28 cm.
Cover title.

"Prepared for distribution at an all-day conference on CAI (computer-assisted instruction and elementary science), sponsored by the Science Department of Jersey City State College on 15 January 1969."

Organization for Economic Cooperation and Development.

Systems analysis for educational planning; selected annotated bibliography. Méthodes analytiques appliquées à la planification de l'enseignement; bibliographie choisie et annotée. ₁Paris₁ Organisation for Economic Co-operation and Development ₁1969₁

219 p. 24 cm.

Unwin, Derick.

The computer in education: a select bibliography, by Derick Unwin and Frank Atkinson; foreword by Basil Z. de Ferranti. London, Library Association, 1968.

74 p. 21 cm. (Library Association. Special subject list no. 50)

INDUSTRIAL APPLICATIONS

E(lektronische) D(aten-)V(erarbeitung) und Vertrieb.
₁Von₁ Carl W₁alter₁ Meyer ₁u. a.₁ Neuwied, Berlin ₁West₁, Luchterhand (1972).

v, 82 p. 21 cm. (Bibliographie zum Fachgebiet Wirtschaftsführung, Kybernetik, Datenverarbeitung, Bd. 6)

Hansen, Kjeld.

Bibliography on the application of digital computers in power stations 1962-1967. Risö, Danish Atomic Energy Commission. Research Establishment. Electronics Dept., 1968.

18 l. 29 cm. (Risö-M-725)

Kamenskaîa, A ÎA
₁Primenenie élektronno-vychislitel'noĭ tekhniki v derevoobrabatyvaĭushcheĭ promyshlennosti₁
Применение электронно-вычислительной техники в деревообрабатывающей промышленности. Библиогр. указ. отеч. и иностр. литературы за 1966–1970 гг. ₁Сост. А. Я. Каменская₁. Москва, 1971.

141 p. 21 cm.

At head of title: Всесоюзный научно-исследовательский и проектный институт экономики, организации управления производством и информации по лесной, целлюлозно-бумажной и деревообрабатывающей промышленности. Центральная научно-техническая библиотека лесной и бумажной промышленности.

Механизация обработки экономической информации. Библиогр. указатель литературы. (1924–1967 гг.) Науч. руководитель д-р экон. наук проф. М. А. Королев. Москва, "Статистика," 1969.
471 p. 22 cm.
At head of title: Московский экономико-статистический институт. Государственная библиотека СССР имени В. И. Ленина.
By N. V. Atriakhina, and others.

Nagel, Kurt,
Bibliographie zum Fachgebiet Revision und Kontrolle bei elektronischer Datenverarbeitung. (Neuvied, Berlin) Luchterhand (1970).

141 p. 21 cm.

Ostrava. Czechoslovak Republic (City) Státní vědecká knihovna.

Operační výzkum a použití samočinných počítačů v hornictví. ₁Zpracovatel: Jaroslava Lehká. Ostrava₁ 1964–

v. 29 cm. (*Its* Publikace. Řada ii, čís. 343

Cover title.

CONTENTS.—č. 1. Výběrová bibliografie.

Ostrava, Czechoslovak Republic (City) Státní vědecká knihovna.

Použití samočinných počítačů při výpočtech stavebních konstrukcí; výběrová bibliografie. ₁Sest. Božena Legátová₁ Ostrava, 1965.

36 p. 29 cm. (*Its* Publikace. Řada ii, č. 392)

Randall, C   R
A select bibliography on computer applications in commerce and industry, compiled by C. R. Randall. 2d ed. ₁Hatfield, Eng., Hertfordshire County Council Technical Library and Information Service₁ 1965.

64 p. illus. 21 cm.

Soboleva, N   A
₁Primenenie vychislitel'noĭ tekhniki v ugol'noĭ promyshlennosti₁
Применение вычислительной техники в угольной промышленности. Библиогр. указ. за 1970–1971 гг. ₁Сост. Соболева Н. А.₁ Москва, 1972.
118 p. 20 cm. (Справочно-информационный фонд угольной промышленности)
At head of title: Министерство угольной промышленности. Центральный научно-исследовательский институт экономики и научно-технической информации угольной промышленности. Центральная научно-техническая библиотека угольной промышленности.

Stannett, Annette.
Bibliography on the application of computers in the construction industry 1962–1967; prepared by Annette Stannett on behalf of the Committee on the Application of Computers in the Construction Industry. London, H. M. S. O., 1968.

vi, 87 p. 30 cm. (R & D bulletin)
At head of title: Ministry of Public Building and Works. Directorate of Research and Information.

——— ——— Supplement.
London, H. M. Stationery Off.
v. 30 cm. semiannual. (R & D bulletin)

Trondheim. Norges tekniske høgskole. *Biblioteket.*
EDB i byggefaget. En bibliografisk oversikt. Trondheim, 1966.

12 p. 29 cm. (*Its* Litteraturliste, 28)

Vanskaîa, G   P
Применение математических методов в управлении перевозочным процессом. Библиогр. указатель отечеств. и зарубежной литературы 1965–1969 гг. Москва, "Транспорт," 1970.
63 p. 20 cm.
At head of title: СССР. Министерство путей сообщения. Центральная научно-техническая библиотека.
"Составитель Ванская Г. П."

Warsaw. Instytut Ekonomiki i Organizacji Przemysłu.
Ośrodek Informacji i Dokumentacji Naukowo-Technicznej.
Projektowanie i funkcjonowanie systemów informacji techniczno-ekonomicznej w przedsiębiorstwie przemysłowym. ₁Opracował Jerzy Anacki. Warszawa₁ 1965.

77 p. 29 cm. (*Its* Tematyczne zestawienie dokumentacyjne, nr. 46)

MEDICINE

Allen, Ruth, 1911–

An annotated bibliography of biomedical computer applications. ₍Bethesda, Md., National Library of Medicine, 1969₎

216 p. 26 cm.

"Prepared by the Interuniversity Communications Council, Inc. (Educom), for the National Library of Medicine."

Dubois-Prieels, Anne Marie.

Automatisation et médecine, problèmes posés et résultats. Une bibliographie. ₍Bruxelles, Centre national de documentation scientifique et technique, Bibliothèque royale, 1967₎.

₍iv₎, 88 l. 30 cm.

Guiette-Limbourg, V

Automation in medicine; a bibliography ₍by₎ V. Guiette -Limbourg. Brussel, Nationaal Centrum voor Wetenschappelijke en Technische Documentatie, 1968₎

61 l. 29 cm.

Jena. Universität. Hochschulbereich Medizin. Verwaltungsdirektion.

Literaturzusammenstellung über die Anwendung von Computern in der Medizin. Berichtszeit: 1960–68. (Gesamtleitg.: Gertraud Wachowski.) Jena, Universitätsbibliothek. Informationsabt., 1969.

100 p. 30 cm. (Bibliographische Mitteilungen der Universitätsbibliothek Jena, Nr. 10)
"... Gemeinschaftsarbeit zwischen der Verwaltungsdirektion des Hochschulbereiches Medizin der Friedrich-Schiller-Universität und der Informationsabteilung der Universitätsbibliothek."

Olson, Nancy.

Medical information and computers; a bibliography ₍by₎ Nancy Olson and K. C. Tsien. ₍Brooklyn, Downstate Medical Center, State University of New York₎ 1972.

vi, 260 p. 28 cm.

Paichl, Přemysl.

Užití počítačů a kybernetiky v medicíně. Výběrová bibliografie. Zprac. Přemysl Paichl. Plzeň, St. věd. knihovna, rozmn., 1971.

36, ₍1₎ p. 20 cm. (Státní vědecká knihovna, Plzeň. Společenské, přírodní a užité vědy, 6)

Shahid, K   M

Involvement of computers in medical sciences. Abstracts of international literature. Compiled by K. M. Shahid, H. J. van der Aa and L. M. C. J. Sicking. Amsterdam, Swets & Zeitlinger, 1968.

235 p. 24 cm.

Wagner, Gustav, 1918–

Bibliography on mechanical and electronic medical record processing, compiled by G. Wagner. ₍Copenhagen₎ World Health Organization, Regional Office for Europe, 1968.

32 p. 28 cm.

"EURO 3092."
At head of title: Seminar on the Public Health Uses of Electronic Computers, London, 17–21 June 1968.

SOCIAL SCIENCES

Gardin, Natacha.

Applications des calculateurs aux sciences humaines, essai de présentation documentaire. Applications of computers in human sciences, essay of documentary presentation ... Paris. Maison des sciences de l'homme, Centre de calcul et service d'échange d' informations scientifiques, ₍1968?₎

1 v. (various pagings) 27 cm.

English or French.

Public Administration Service. *Public Automated Systems Service.*

Automation in the public service: an annotated bibliography, compiled by Public Automated Systems Service. Chicago, Public Administration Service ₍1966₎

70 p. 28 cm.

Public Administration Service. *Public Automated Systems Service.*

The computer in the public service: an annotated bibliography, 1966–1969. Chicago, Public Administration Service ₍1970₎

vi, 74 p. 28 cm.

This work is a supplement to the Service's Automation in the public service published in 1966.

Thannabauer, Vladimír.

Použití samočinných počítačů v nevýrobní sféře. Výběrová bibliografie. Sest. V. Thannabauer. 1. vyd. Praha, UVTEI-St. techn. knihovna, rozmn., 1969.

2 v. 21 cm. (₍Prague. Státní technická knihovna₎ Bibliografie, sv. 138–139)

MISCELLANEOUS APPLICATIONS

Chernova, L   V

Математические методы и электронно-вычислительная техника в сельском хозяйстве. Библиогр. указатель литературы за 1967–1968 гг. Москва, 1968.

119 p. 20 cm.

At head of title: Всесоюзная ордена Ленина Академия с.-х. наук имени В. И. Ленина. Центральная научная сельскохозяйственная библиотека. Справочно-библиографический отдел.

A Compilation of information on computer applications in nutrition and food service. John P. Casbergue, editor. Prepared by the Division of Medical Dietetics, School of Allied Medical Professions, the Ohio State University. Columbus, 1968.

86 p. illus. 28 cm.

Knight, Geoffrey.

Computer mathematics, series II, edited by Geoffrey Knight, Jr. Washington, Cambridge Communication Corp. ₍ᶜ1969₎

1 v. (various pagings) 29 cm.

"This collection is compiled from Computer & Information systems and is a continuation of ... Cumulative computer abstracts."

Lee, Kaiman.

Bibliography of the computer in environmental design. Boston, Center for Environmental Research, 1972–1973.

3 v. (loose leaf) 29 cm.

Pencheva, Denka.

Електронно-изчислителната техника в металургията. (Библиогр. указател). ⟨Литература 1967–1970 г.⟩. Изготвил ... ₍София₎ (МК—Кремиковци) 1970.

82 p. 22 cm.

On cover: Кремиковски металургичен комбинат. Бюро за производствена технико-икономическа информация.

Вычислительная техника и математические методы в инженерных изысканиях. Список рек. литературы. ₁Сост. О. А. Колесникова₁ Киев, 1968.

80 p. 20 cm.

At head of title: Госстрой УССР. Украинский государственный институт инженерно-технических изысканий "Укргиинтиз." Бюро научно-технической информации.

Žilinský, Václav.
Použití analogových a číslicových počítačů při řízení výrobních pochodů. Výběrová bibliografie. ₁Vyd. 1.₁ Praha ₁Ústředí vědeckých, technických a ekonomických informací; Státní technická knihovna₁ 1971.

110 p. 21 cm. (Prague. Státní technická knihovna. Bibliografie, sv. 157)

ELECTRONICS

Bulletin signalétique: Série télécommunications-informatique. no 73-94; jan.-déc. 1968. ₁Paris₁ Centre de documentation de l'armement, Antenne télécommunications-informatique.

22 no. 25 cm. semimonthly.

Supersedes in part Bulletin signalétique, issued 1965-67 by the Service de documentation scientifique et technique de l'armement, and continues its numbering.

Culver City, Calif. Electronic Properties Information Center.
Electronic properties of materials; a guide to the literature. 1965–
New York, Plenum Press.

v. in 29 cm. annual.

Vols. for 1965– also issued in a contract edition with title: Index to the collection.

Culver City, Calif. *Electronic Properties Information Center.*
Index to the collection. 1965–
₁Wright-Patterson Air Force Base, Ohio, Materials Information Center, Air Force Materials Laboratory₁
v. in 27 cm.
A contract version of its Electronic properties of materials; a guide to the literature.
Vols. for 1965– processed by the Clearinghouse for Federal Scientific and Technical Information, U. S. Dept. of Commerce, for the Defense Documentation Center, Defense Supply Agency.

Doroshkevich, I V
₁Nauchno-tekhnicheskiĭ progress v radioelektronike₁
Научно-технический прогресс в радиоэлектронике в свете решений XXIV съезда КПСС. (Указ. литературы). Москва, "Знание," 1971.

58 p. 20 cm.

At head of title: Всесоюзное общество "Знание." Центральная политехническая библиотека.
"Составители И. В. Дорошкевич, Л. Е. Воронкова."

Electron microscopy abstracts. v. 1–
July/Sept. 1972–
₁London₁ Science and Technology Agency.

v. 25 cm. quarterly.

IEEE Working Group on Transformer and Inductor Bibliography.
IEEE transformer and inductor bibliography, June 1967.
New York, Available from Order Dept., IEEE ₁1967₁

116 p. 28 cm.

"Sponsored by the Electronics Transformers Technical Committee of the IEEE Parts, Materials & Packaging Group."

Le Levier, Marie Geneviève.
Les Applications métallurgiques du bombardement électronique ... Gif-sur-Yvette, Service de documentation C. E. A., Centre d'études nucléaires de Saclay, 1966.

54 p. 27 cm. (Bibliographie CEA no 43)

Moore, Charles Kenneth, 1907–
Electronics: a bibliographical guide ₁by₁ C. K. Moore & K. J. Spencer. London, Macdonald ₁1961–65₁

2 v. 26 cm.

Vol. 2 issued in the series: The Macdonald bibliographical guides.

Moore, Charles Kenneth, 1907–
Electronics: a bibliographical guide ₁by₁ C. K. Moore & K. J. Spencer. New York, Macmillan, 1961–65.

2 v. 26 cm.

Vol. 2 has imprint: New York, Plenum Press Data Division; and on spine: Macdonald.
Vol. 2 in series: The Macdonald bibliographical guides.

Permuted index to IRE (IEEE) transactions on military electronics, 1957–1964; Winter Military Electronic Conferences, 1962–1964; National Military Electronic Conferences, 1957–1964. ₁North Hollywood, Calif., Western Periodicals Co., 1966?₁

12, 97, ₁76₁ p. 28 cm.

Randle, Gretchen R
Electronic industries, information sources ₁by₁ Gretchen R. Randle. Detroit, Gale Research Co. ₁1968₁

227 p. 23 cm. (Management information guide, 13)

Scott, C G
Bibliography on thick film print & fire technology, by C. G. Scott and A. Bennett. Stevenage, British Aircraft Corporation Ltd, Guided Weapons Division, 1972.

₁4₁, 45, ₁7₁ p. 30 cm. index. (British Aircraft Corporation. Guided Weapons Division. Library publication, no. 1)

Shiers, George.
Bibliography of the history of electronics, by George Shiers, assisted by May Shiers. Metuchen, N. J., Scarecrow Press, 1972.

xiii, 323 p. 22 cm.

Van Wyk, Jacobus Daniel.
Power- and machine-electronics 1914–1966; a selected bibliography and review on the electronic control of electrical machines, by J. D. van Wyk. Johannesburg, South African Institute of Electrical Engineers ₁197-₁

85 p. 28 cm.

Zil'bershteĭn, M M
Микроэлектроника. Рек. указ. литературы. Москва, "Знание," 1971.

23 p. 19 cm. (Решения XXIV съезда КПСС—в жизнь!) (В помощь лектору)

At head of title: Всесоюзное общество "Знание." Центральная политехническая библиотека.

ELECTROPHORESIS

Chandler, R   H
Advances in electrophoretic paint deposition, 1970; by R. H. Chandler. Braintree (P. O. Box 55, Braintree, CM7 6HD, Essex), R. H. Chandler Ltd., 1971.

58 p. 1 illus. 26 cm.

Cover title: Advances in electrophoretic painting.

Connaught Medical Research Laboratories.
Starch-gel electrophoresis; a bibliography of observations made using the technique of starch-gel electrophoresis. 2d ed. Willowdale, Ont., 1967.

58 p. 25 cm.

Haywood, B   J
Electrophoresis-technical application; a bibliography of abstracts, by B. J. Haywood. Ann Arbor, Ann Arbor-Humphrey Science Publishers [1969]

vii, 440 p. 24 cm.

Translation and Technical Information Services, *London.*
Electrocoating patents. Braintree (Ex.), Translation & Technical Information Services, 1967.

[1], 16 p. 28 cm. (Bibliographies in paint technology, no. 14)

ELECTROPLATING

Gringauz, I   M
Нанесение гальванопокрытий. (Указ. литературы 1968–1970 гг.) Москва, 1971.
54 p. 22 cm. (Библиографическая информация)

At head of title: Министерство местной промышленности РСФСР.
By I. M. Gringauz and O. L. Zheitonozhskaia.
Issued by the ministry's TSentral'noe biuro nauchno-tekhnicheskoĭ informatsii.

Herzlíková, Vlasta.
Katodické a chemické vylučování kovů. Seznam lit. Sest. Vlasta Herzlíková a Václav Čupr. Brno, St. věd. knihovna, t. G. 11, Dolní Kounice, 1969.

49, [1] p. 21 cm. (Brünn. Státní technická knihovna. Výběrový seznam, 2/1969)

Turner, *Mrs.* **Jacques de Beer,** *comp.*
Selected bibliography on electroplating, compiled by Mrs. J. Turner. Auckland, Auckland Industrial Development Division, 1968.

9 p. 26 cm.

ELECTROSTATICS

Аннотированный библиографический указатель; статическое электричество, предохранительные мембраны. [Составители: А. Н. Руденко и др.] Москва, Науч.-иссл. ин-т техн.-экон. исследований, 1968.

90 p. 26 cm.

At head of title: Всесоюзный научно-исследовательский институт техники безопасности в химической промышленности.

Electrostatics abstracts. v. 1–
Jan. 1971–
Leatherhead [Eng.] Electrical Research Association.

v. 30 cm. monthly.

Moulet, Élisée.
Électricité statique: formation, détection, mesure et prévention dans les ateliers. [Gif-sur-Yvette, Service central de documentation du C. E. A.] 1969.

31 p. 30 cm. (Bibliographie CEA-BIB-139)

At head of title: Centre d'études de Bruyères-le-Châtel.
Summaries in English and French.

ELEMENTARY SCHOOLS see Education, Elementary

ELEVATORS

Victoria, Australia. State Library, Melbourne. Research Dept.
Elevators; books and articles, 1960–1968. Melbourne, 1969.

7 p. 26 cm.

ELIOT, GEORGE, pseud.

Muir, Percival Horace, 1894–
A bibliography of the first editions of books by George Eliot (Mary Ann Evans) (1819–1880) Compiled by P. H. Muir. [Folcroft, Pa.] Folcroft Library Editions, 1973.
16 p. 26 cm.
Reprint of the 1927–28 ed. published in London as supplements to the Bookman's journal, 3d ser., v. 15, no. 4 and v. 16, no. 5.

Parrish, Morris Longstreth, 1867–1944.
Victorian lady novelists: George Eliot, Mrs. Gaskell, the Brontë sisters. 1st editions in the library at Dormy House, Pine Valley, N. J., described with notes. New York, Franklin [1969]

xii, 160 p. illus., facsims., ports. 26 cm. (Burt Franklin bibliography & reference series, 251)

ELIOT, THOMAS STEARNS

A Catalogue of English and American first editions of The waste land by T. S. Eliot, on the occasion of the publication of the facsimile of the "lost" manuscript-typescript of the poem along with appreciations of the poem by friends and critics of Mr. Eliot. Dubuque, Iowa, Wahlert Memorial Library [c1971]

27 p. facsims. 22 cm.

300 copies printed.

Gallup, Donald Clifford, 1913–
T. S. Eliot: a bibliography, by Donald Gallup. [New ed.]. London, Faber, 1969.

3–414 p. 23 cm.

A revision and extension of the author's bibliographical checklist of the writings of T. S. Eliot, published in 1947.

Gallup, Donald Clifford, 1913–
T. S. Eliot; a bibliography, by Donald Gallup. Rev. and extended ed. [1st American ed.] New York, Harcourt, Brace & World [1969]

414 p. 23 cm.

Published in 1947 as the author's A bibliographical checklist of the writings of T. S. Eliot.

Gunter, Bradley.
The Merrill checklist of T. S. Eliot. Columbus, Ohio, C. E. Merrill Pub. Co. [1970]

iv, 43 p. 20 cm. (Charles E. Merrill program in American literature)

Charles E. Merrill checklists.
Title on cover: Checklist of T. S. Eliot.

Martin, Mildred, 1904–
A half-century of Eliot criticism; an annotated bibliography of books and articles in English, 1916–1965. Lewisburg, Bucknell University Press [1972]

361 p. 24 cm.

ELK

Dalke, Paul David, 1901–
Bibliography of the elk in North America. Compiled by Paul D. Dalke. Moscow, Idaho Cooperative Wildlife Research Unit, University of Idaho, 1968.

87 p. 28 cm.

ELLICE ISLANDS

Krauss, Noel Louis Hilmer, 1910–
Bibliography of the Ellice Islands, Western Pacific, by N. L. H. Krauss. Honolulu, 1969.

13 p. 23 cm.

ELLING, CHRISTIAN

Jensen, Hannemarie Ragn.
Christian Elling bibliografi. Med indledning af Else Kai Sass. København, Gyldendal, [1970].

108 p. 7 plates. 28 cm.

ELLIOTT, EBENEZER

Brown, Simon.
Ebenezer Elliott: the Corn Law rhymer: a bibliography & list of letters, compiled by Simon Brown. Leicester (University Rd, Leicester) University of Leicester (Victorian Studies Centre) 1971.

23 l. 26 cm. (Victorian studies handlist, 8)

Cover title.

ELLISON, HARLAN

Swigart, Leslie Kay.
Harlan Ellison: a bibliographical checklist. Compiled by Leslie Kay Swigart. Dallas, Williams Pub. Co., 1973.

vi, 117 p. illus. 27 cm.

ELY, ENGLAND (DIOCESE)

Owen, Dorothy Mary.
Ely records: a handlist of the records of the Bishop and Archdeacon of Ely, by Dorothy M. Owen. [Chichester (c/o The County Archivist, West Sussex Record Office, County Hall, Chichester, Sussex)], Marc Fitch Fund, [1971]

xii, 89 p.; map. 26 cm.

EMBLEMS

Green, Henry, 1801–1873.
Andrea Alciati and his books of emblems; a biographical and bibliographical study. New York, B. Franklin [1965]

xvi, 344 p. illus., facsim., ports. 24 cm. (Burt Franklin bibliography & reference series, #131)

Reprint of the 1872 ed.
"A bibliographical catalogue of the various editions of the books of emblems of Andrea Alciati": p. [97]–279.

Landwehr, John.
Emblem books in the low countries 1554–1949; a bibliography. Utrecht, Haentjens Dekker & Gumbert, [1970].

xlvii, 151 p. 20 p. of photos. 27 cm. (Bibliotheca emblematica, 3)

Landwehr, John.
German emblem books 1531–1888. A bibliography. Utrecht, Haentjens Dekker & Gumbert; Leiden, Sijthoff. [1972].

vii, 184 p. 27 cm. (Bibliotheca emblematica, 5)

EMERSON, RALPH WALDO

Bryer, Jackson R
A checklist of Emerson criticism, 1951–1961, with a detailed index, by Jackson R. Bryer and Robert A. Rees. Hartford, Transcendental Books [1964]

53 l. illus., ports. 29 cm.

Cameron, Kenneth Walter, 1908–
Ralph Waldo Emerson's reading; a guide for source-hunters and scholars to the one thousand volumes which he withdrew from libraries, together with some unpublished letters and a list of Emerson's contemporaries, 1827–1850 ... also other Emerson materials and an introduction describing bibliographical resources in New England. New York, Haskell House, 1966.

144 p. 24 cm.

Reprint of the 1941 ed.

Cameron, Kenneth Walter, 1908–
Ralph Waldo Emerson's reading; a guide for source-hunters and scholars to the one thousand volumes which he withdrew from libraries, together with some unpublished letters and a list of Emerson's contemporaries, 1827-1850 ...; also other Emerson materials and an introduction describing bibliographical resources in New England. New York, Haskell House Publishers, 1973.

144 p. front. 23 cm.

Reprint of the 1941 ed.

Cooke, George Willis, 1848–1923.
A bibliography of Ralph Waldo Emerson. New York, Kraus Reprint Corp., 1966.

ix, 340 p. port. 24 cm.

Originally published in 1908.

Ferguson, Alfred Riggs.
The Merrill checklist of Ralph Waldo Emerson, compiled by Alfred R. Ferguson. Columbus, Ohio, Merrill [1970]

iv, 44 p. 19 cm. (Charles E. Merrill program in American literature. Charles E. Merrill checklists)

Sowder, William J
Emerson's reviewers and commentators; a biographical and bibliographical analysis of nineteenth-century periodical criticism with a detailed index, by William J. Sowder. Hartford, Transcendental Books [1968]

64 l. illus. 29 cm.

On cover: Emerson's commentators.

EMIGRATION AND IMMIGRATION

Centro studi emigrazione-Roma. Biblioteca.
Migrazioni. Catalogo della Biblioteca del Centro studi emigrazione. Roma ... Roma, Centro studi emigrazione, 1972.

xxxiv, 806 p. 21 cm. (Centro studi emigrazione-Roma. Sussidi e documentazione, 2)

At head of title: L. Bertelli, G. Corcagnani, G. F. Rosoli.
Title also in English.
Introduction in English, French, German, Italian, Portuguese, and Spanish.

Mangalam, J   J
Human migration; a guide to migration literature in English, 1955-1962 [by] J. J. Mangalam. With the assistance of Cornelia Morgan. Lexington, University of Kentucky Press, 1968.

194 p. 29 cm.

Welch, Ruth L
Migration research and migration in Britain: a selected bibliography [by] Ruth Welch. London, Research Publications, 1970.

vii, 69 p. 24 cm. Index. (University of Birmingham. Centre for Urban and Regional Studies. Occasional paper no. 14)

Żurek, Agnieszka, comp.
Bibliografia polskich prac o migracjach stałych, wewnętrznych ludności w Polsce, lata 1916-1969/70. Opracowała Agnieszka Żurek. Warszawa, 1971.

119 p. 21 cm. (Instytut Geografii Polskiej Akademii Nauk. Dokumentacja geograficzna, zesz. 1)

EMILIA-ROMAGNA

Tarozzi, Ermanno.
Elementi per una bibliografia sui temi dello sviluppo economico, sociale e territoriale con particolare riguardo all'Emilia Romagna. A cura di Ermanno Tarozzi, Francesco Bonazzi Del Poggetto. Presentazione dell'on. Rino Nanni. Bologna, STEB, 1969.

66 p. 2 maps. 28½ cm. (Collana di studi e monografie)

At head of title: Provincia di Bologna.

Toschi, Umberto, 1897-
Emilia-Romagna. A cura di Umberto Toschi, Dina Albani e Luigi Varani. Napoli, Tip. La buona stampa, 1967.

214 p. plate. 21 cm. (Collana di bibliografie geografiche delle regioni Italiane, v. 10)

At head of title: Consiglio nazionale delle ricerche. Comitato per le scienze storiche, filologiche e filosofiche.

EMINENT DOMAIN

Ferraz, Sérgio.
Desapropriação; indicações de doutrina e jurisprudência. [1. ed.] Rio [de Janeiro] Forense [1972]

164 p. 23 cm.

EMPLOYEE-MANAGEMENT RELATIONS

California. State Library, Sacramento. Law Library.
Public employee labor relations; a bibliography, prepared by Carleton W. Kenyon, law librarian. [Sacramento] 1968.

6 p. 28 cm.

Pegnetter, Richard.
Public employment bibliography. Ithaca, New York State School of Industrial and Labor Relations, Cornell University [1971]

ix, 49 p. 26 cm.

"The titles are primarily works which were published during the period from December 1966 to January 1970."

U. S. Civil Service Commission. Library.
Employee-management relations in the public service. Washington; [For sale by the Supt. of Docs., U. S. Govt. Print. Off.] 1970.

62 p. 27 cm. (Its Personnel bibliography series, no. 36)

Cover title.
"Covers material listed in Personnel literature from 1967-1969."

United States. Civil Service Commission. Library.
Labor management relations in the public service. Washington; [For sale by the Supt. of Docs., U. S. Govt. Print. Off.] 1972.

74 p. 27 cm. (Its Personnel bibliography series, no. 44)

U. S. Dept. of Labor. Library.
Employee-management relations in the public service, September 1967. [Washington, 1967]

43 p. 26 cm. (Its Current bibliographies, no. 1)

EMPLOYEES, TRAINING OF

Gol'dman, V   M
(Proizvodstvenno-tekhnicheskoe obuchenie rabochikh)
Производственно-техническое обучение рабочих. (Рек. указ. литературы). Москва, 1972.

226 p., 1 l. of diagrs. 20 cm.

At head of title: Министерство автомобильной промышленности. Центральная научно-техническая библиотека.
By V. M. Gol'dman and IU. A. Vlasova.

Mesics, Emil A
Education and training for effective manpower utilization; an annotated bibliography on education and training in work organizations, by Emil A. Mesics. [Ithaca, New York State School of Industrial and Labor Relations, Cornell University] 1969.

iv, 157 p. 23 cm. (Cornell University. New York State School of Industrial and Labor Relations. Bibliography series, no. 9)

Mesics, Emil A
Training and education for manpower development: business, industry, government, service organizations, educational institutions; an annotated bibliography on education and training in organizations, by Emil A. Mesics. [Ithaca, New York State School of Industrial and Labor Relations, Cornell University] 1964.

iv, 99 p. 23 cm. (Cornell University. New York State School of Industrial and Labor Relations. Bibliography series, no. 7)

National Book League, London.
Books for training officers, 1967. London, National Book League; British Association for Commercial and Industrial Education, 1967.

64 p. 22 cm.

National Book League, London.
Books for training officers. 2nd ed. London, National Book League; British Association for Commercial and Industrial Education, 1969.

58 p. 22 cm.

Stout, Ronald M
Local government in-service training; an annotated bibliography, edited by Ronald M. Stout. Albany, Graduate School of Public Affairs, State University of New York at Albany [1968]

xii, 79 p. 29 cm.

United States. Civil Service Commission. Library.
Planning, organizing, and evaluating training programs. Washington; [For sale by the Supt. of Docs., U. S. Govt. Print. Off.] 1971 [i. e. 1972]

140 p. 27 cm. (Its Personnel bibliography series no. 41)

EMPLOYEES' REPRESENTATION IN MANAGEMENT

Aćimović, Miroslav R.
Bibliografska grada o radničkom samoupravljanju u Jugoslaviji i oblicima učešća proizvođača u upravljanju preduzećima u drugim zemljama; prikazi i anotacije. ₁Saradnici: Erić Nevena et al.₁ Beograd, 1966.

xiv, 855 p. 22 cm.

At head of title: Institut društvenih nauka.

Andrić, Stanislava.
Bibliografija o učešću radnika u upravljanju poduzećima u Jugoslaviji. Bibliography on workers' participation in management in Yugoslavia. Sastavili: Stanislava Andrić, Marija Sever-Zebec. Zagreb, Ekonomski institut, 1969.

47 p. 21 cm.

————Dodatak bibliografiji o učešću radnika u upravljanju poduzećima u Jugoslaviji. Appendix to the bibliography on workers' participation in management in Yugoslavia. Zagreb, Ekonomski institut, 1970.

20 p. 22 cm.

Germany (Federal Republic, 1949–). Bundestag. Bibliothek.
Mitbestimmung in der Wirtschaft. 1962-1969. Auswahlbibliographie. (₁Von₁ Wilfried Skupnik bearb.) Bonn (Deutscher Bundestag, Wissenschaftliche Abt.) 1969.

ii, 3+ p. 30 cm. (Wissenschaftliche Abteilung des Deutschen Bundestages. Bibliographien, Nr. 21)

Pettman, B O
Industrial democracy in general & in Great Britain: a selected bibliography ₁by₁ B. O. Pettman. Bradford, Institute of Scientific Business Ltd., 1971.

₁1₁, 45 leaves. 28 cm. (Papers in management studies) (Bibliographical studies no. 4)

Tofft, Karin.
Om företagsdemokrati. En nordisk bibliografi efter första världskriget. ₁Sammanställd av Karin Tofft₁ ₁Utg. av₁ Utvecklingsrådet för samarbetsfrågor, SAF, LO, TCO. Stockholm, (box 16120, Stockholm 16) ₁1968₁

31 p. 21 cm.

Tofft, Karin.
Om företagsdemokrati. En nordisk bibliografi efter första världskriget. ₁Utg. av₁ Utvecklingsrådet för samarbetsfrågor, SAF, LO, TCO. 2., utökade uppl. Kompletteringen har utförts av Sylvia van Schaik. Stockholm, utgivaren, (box 16120, Stockholm 16). 1971.

50 p. 21 cm.

EMPLOYMENT   see   Labor

EMPLOYMENT FORECASTING

Keaveny, Timothy J
Manpower planning: a research bibliography. Prepared by Timothy J. Keaveny, with the assistance of Georgianna Herman. Minneapolis, Industrial Relations Center, University of Minnesota, 1966.

iii, 37 p. 23 cm. (Industrial Relations Center. University of Minnesota. Bulletin 45)

Sinha, Nageshwar P
Manpower planning: a research bibliography. Prepared by Nageshwar P. Sinha. with the assistance of Georgianna Herman. Including earlier work by Timothy J. Keaveny and Richard J. Snyder. Rev. ed. Minneapolis. Industrial Relations Center. University of Minnesota, 1970.

iv, 59 p. 23 cm. (University of Minnesota. Industrial Relations Center. Bulletin 52)

EMPLOYMENT OF WOMEN   see   Women – Employment

EMPLOYMENT TESTS

Wonderlic, E   F
A selected, annotated bibliography for the Wonderlic personnel test ₁by₁ E. F. Wonderlic. 1st ed. Northfield, Ill., E. F. Wonderlic & Associates, 1966.

104 p. 24 cm. (Cooperative research reports)

ENCEPHALITIS

Shabanova, I   P
Клещевой энцефалит на ₁Дальнем Востоке. Библиогр. указатель отечеств. литературы. (1935–1965). Сост. И. П. Шабанова, канд. мед. наук И. Е. Троп., канд. мед. наук Л. А. Верета. Хабаровск, 1969.

104 p. 20 cm.

At head of title: Хабаровский научно-исследовательский институт эпидемиологии и микробиологии. Хабаровская краевая научная библиотека.

ENCYCLOPEDIAS AND DICTIONARIES

Encyclopedias and dictionaries of a particular subject are entered under the subject

Akademiîa nauk SSSR. *Institut russkogo îazyka.*
Словари, изданные в СССР; библиографический указатель, 1918-1962. ₁Составители: М. Г. Ижевская и др. Редакторы: В. В. Веселитский, Н. П. Дебец₁ Москва, Наука, 1966.

231 p. 27 cm.

Collison, Robert Lewis.
Dictionaries of English and foreign languages; a bibliographical guide to both general and technical dictionaries with historical and explanatory notes and references, by Robert L. Collison. 2d ed. ₁New York₁ Hafner Pub. Co., 1971.

xvii, 303 p. 21 cm.

First ed. published in 1955 under title: Dictionaries of foreign languages.

Fachwörterbücher und Lexika. International bibliography of dictionaries. 5.–
Ausg.; 1972–
München, Verlag Dokumentation.

v. 22 cm. (Handbuch der technischen Dokumentation und Bibliographie, Bd. 4)

Continues Technik, Wissenschaft und Wirtschaft in fremden Sprachen. Techniques, science and economics in foreign languages.

Food and Agriculture Organization of the United Nations. *Terminology Reference Library.*
Dictionaries and vocabularies in the Terminology Reference Library. Dictionnaires et vocabulaires dans la Bibliothèque de terminologie et références. Diccionarios y vocabularios en la Biblioteca de Terminología y Referencia. Wörterbücher in der Terminologie-Bibliothek, 1966–1968. Compiled by Gertrude Stolp Nobile. Rome, 1968.

93 p. 28 cm.

Food and Agriculture Organization of the United Nations. Terminology Reference Library.
Dictionaries and vocabularies in the Terminology Reference Library, 1966–1970. Dictionnaires et vocabulaires disponibles à la Bibliothèque de terminologie et références. Diccionarios y vocabularios en la Biblioteca de Terminología y Referencia. Wörterbücher in der Terminologie-Bibliothek. Rome, 1970.

vii, 101 p. 28 cm.

Haensch, Günther.
Nachweis fremdsprachlicher Wörterbücher. ₍Bearbeitung: Günther Haensch und Edgar H. P. Meyer.₎ Köln, Bundesverband der Deutschen Industrie e. V. (1964).

73 l. 30 cm.

百科事典のしおり ₍東京₎ 平凡社 ₍1968?₎

60 p. 21 cm.

Informativní literatura: Slovníky.
₍Praha₎ Státní knihovna ČSR.

v. 21 cm. annual. (Novinky literatury: Přehledy informativní literatury)

Began with vol. for 1966.

International bibliography of dictionaries. Fachwörterbücher und Lexika; ein internationales Verzeichnis. 5th, rev. ed. ₍Editoral direction: Helga Lengenfelder₎ New York, R. R. Bowker Co., 1972.

xxvi, 511 p. 22 cm.

Janda, Bohumil.
Bibliografie encyklopedické literatury české a slovenské vydané v letech 1860 až 1967. ₋Uspoř. Bohumil Janda a Julie Dědičová. Praha, Encyklopedický institut ČSAV, t. ST 5, 1969.

24 p. 25 cm. (Československá akademie věd. Encyklopedický institut. Malá řada, sv. 3)

Müller, Karl-Heinz.
Bibliographie der Fachwörterbücher mit deutschen und russischen Äquivalenten. ₍Von₎ Karl-Heinz Müller. Unter Mitarbeit von Rita U. Müller und Elena Ternette. Hrsg. von der Deutschen Bücherei. Leipzig, Verlag für Buch- und Bibliothekswesen, 1966–

v. 23 cm. (Sonderbibliographien der Deutschen Bücherei, 43-

CONTENTS.—Bd. 1. Naturwissenschaften, Landwirtschaften, medizinische Wissenschaften.

National Book League, London.
Dictionaries and encyclopaedias. London, National Book League, 1966.

37 p. 21½ cm.

(Nihon no jiten sōmokuroku)
日本の辞(書)典総目録 1969–

₍東京₎ 日外敗

v. 19 cm. biennial.

Riedlová, Marie.
Encyklopedické a terminologické slovníky. Soupis publ. z fondů St. věd. knihovny v Olomouci. Sest. Marie Riedlová za spolupráce Svatavy Prečanové. Olomouc, St. věd. kni-

hovna, 1968.

156, ₍1₎ p. 29 cm. (Publikace Státní vědecké knihovny v Olomouci, čís. 6/1968)

Sa'diiev, Sh. M
Лүғөтлəрин библиографијасы. Бакы, "Елм," 1970.

55 p. 21 cm.
At head of title: Азəрбајчан ССР елмлəр Академијасы. Дилчилик институту.
Added t. p.: Библиография словарей.
"Тəртиб едəнлəр Ш. М. Сə²дијев вə Ш. Р. Пашајева."
Edited by B. T. Abdullaiev.

Shu, Austin C W
Lei shu: old Chinese reference works, and a checklist of cited titles available in Taiwan ₍by₎ Austin C. W. Shu. Taipei, 1973.

xvii, 36 p. 26 cm. (Chinese Materials and Research Aids Service Center. Bibliographical aid, no. 2)

Technical and multilingual dictionaries, a short list. Delhi, Indian National Scientific Documentation Centre, 1967.

86 p. 25 cm.

"Compilers: K. Ramaswami ₍and others₎"
"Brought out ... for the annual conference of the Indian Association of Special Libraries and Information Centres."

Tonelli, Giorgio.
A short-title list of subject dictionaries of the sixteenth, seventeenth and eighteenth centuries as aids to the history of ideas. London, Warburg Institute, 1971.

₍5₎, 64 p. 25 cm. Index. (Warburg Institute. Surveys, 4)

U. S. *Dept. of State. Office of External Research.*
List of Chinese dictionaries in all languages. Washington, 1967.

v, 44 p. 27 cm. (External research paper)

Walsh, James Patrick.
Anglo-American general encyclopedias; a historical bibliography, 1703–1967, by S. Padraig Walsh. New York, Bowker, 1968.

xix, 270 p. 23 cm.

Whittaker, Kenneth.
Dictionaries. London, Bingley, 1966.

88 p. 22½ cm.

Whittaker, Kenneth.
Dictionaries. ₍New York₎ Philosophical Library ₍1966₎

88 p. 23 cm.

Whittaker, Kenneth.
Dictionaries. Sydney, Bennett ₍1966₎

88 p. 23 cm. (The Readers guide series)

Wörterbücher und Lexika. Internationales bibliographisches Verzeichnis. München-Pullach und Berlin, Verlag Dokumentation, 1969–

v. 21 cm.

Cover title.

CONTENTS.—Berg- und Hüttenwesen, Geologie und Geographie.—Buch- und Bibliothekswesen, Publizistik und Abkürzungen.—Landwirtschaft und Nahrungsmittel, Veterinärmedizin.—Maschinenbau, Elektrotechnik und allgemeine Technik.—Medizin; Biologie, Gesundheitswesen, Pharmazie und Veterinärmedizin.—Physik und

Chemie, Astronomie und Geodäsie.—Rechts- und Staatswissenschaften; Politik, Recht; Soziologie und Abkürzungen.—Verkehrswesen; Luftfahrt, Transport und Fremdenverkehr.—Wehrwesen, Luftfahrt und Geodäsie.—Wirtschaftswissenschaften, Betriebs- und Volkswirtschaft, Werbung, Handel und Handwerk.—Geisteswissenschaften, Archäologie, Geographie, Pädagogik, Geschichte, Philosophie, Theologie und Sprachwissenschaft.

ENDOCRINOLOGY

Bibliography of gonadotropins. 1966–
Washington, For sale by the Supt. of Docs., U. S. Govt. Print. Off.

v. 26 cm. (U. S. National Institute of Child Health and Human Development. Reproduction Information Center. Report)

Vols. for 1966– prepared by the Reproduction Information Center of the National Institute of Child Health and Human Development for the institute's Center for Population Research.

Köves, Péter.
Az endokrinológia és az anyagcserebetegségek magyar bibliográfiája, 1945–1960. Budapest, Országos Orvostudományi Könyvtár és Dokumentációs Központ, 1965.

506 p. 23 cm.

ENDRIN   see under   Aldrin

ENERGY   see   Power

ENGELS, FRIEDRICH
see also under   Marx, Karl

Berlin. Stadtbibliothek.
Friedrich Engels. ₁Anlässlich des 150. Geburtstages von Friedrich Engels am 28. 11. 1970 zusammengestellt von Lieselotte Stöhr₁   Berlin, 1970.

72 p. 22 cm. (Bibliographische Kalenderblätter. Sonderblatt. 30)

Фридрих Енгелс. 1820–1970. Метод. и библиогр. материали по случай 150 г. от рождението. (Ред. Слави Рахнев и Велчо Ковачев). (София) Нар. библ. Кирил и Методий (1970).

138 p., 6 l. of illus. and facsims. 10 l. of ports. and facsims. inserted. 22 cm.

ENGINEERING
see also   Building; Technology; and Agricultural engineering, Civil engineering, and similar headings

Akademiia nauk URSR, *Kiev. Tsentral'na naukova biblioteka.*
Видання Академії наук УРСР, 1919–1967: фізико-технічні та математичні науки; бібліографічний покажчик. ₁Відп. редактор М. М. Онопрієнко₁   Київ, Наук. думка, 1970.
782 p. 23 cm.
Compiled by P. ÎU. Vysots'ka and others.

Akin, J   E
The finite element method; a bibliography of its theory and applications, by J. E. Akin, D. L. Fenton ₁and₁ W. C. T. Stoddart. ₁Knoxville, Dept. of Engineering Mechanics, University of Tennessee, 1972₁

1 v. (unpaged) 29 cm. (University of Tennessee. Dept. of Engineering Mechanics. Report EM72-1)

Bibliografia brasileira de engenharia. v. 1–
1970–
Rio de Janeiro, Instituto Brasileiro de Bibliografia e Documentação.

v. 28 cm.

Current index to conference papers in engineering. v. 1–
Sept. 1969–
₁New York₁ CCM Information Corp.

v. 26 cm. monthly.

Vols. for 1969– prepared by World Meetings Information Center.

Granskiĭ, Viktor Isidorovich.
Техника для всех. Рек. указатель науч.-попул. литературы. ₁С 1962–1968 гг.₁   Москва, "Книга," 1969.

172 p. with illus. 21 cm.

At head of title: Министерство культуры РСФСР. Государственная ордена Трудового Красного Знамени публичная библиотека им. М. Е. Салтыкова-Щедрина. В. И. Гранский и С. А. Крючковский.

Illinois. University. *Engineering Experiment Station.*
Catalog: a listing of engineering publications, 1904–1966. ₁Urbana, 1966₁

72 p. 28 cm. (University of Illinois bulletin, v. 63, no. 88)

Illinois. University. Engineering Experiment Station.
Catalog: a listing of engineering publications, 1904–1969. ₁Urbana₁ University of Illinois, College of Engineering ₁1969₁

80 p. 25 cm. (University of Illinois bulletin, v. 66, no. 76)

Institution of Engineers, Australia.
Author and subject index of publications 1920–1968. ₁Sydney, 1969₁

187 p. 23 cm.

Krause, Ruth.
Technische Statistik und Optimierung; Bibliographie deutschsprachiger Veröffentlichungen der Jahre 1963 und 1964. Berlin ₁Deutsche Staatsbibliothek₁ 1965.

59 p. 21 cm. (Deutsche Staatsbibliothek, Berlin. Bibliographische Mitteilungen, 21)

"Fortsetzung der 1963 erschienenen Bibliographie (Krause, R.: Technische Statistik (inbesondere statistische Qualitätskontrolle) und Optimierung. Bibliographische Mitteilungen, 20)"

Leningrad. Publichnaià biblioteka.
Математика для инженеров; рекомендательный указатель литературы. ₁Составители: М. Н. Васильева, В. И. Гранский, С. А. Крючковский₁   Москва, Книга, 1965.

157 p. 22 cm.

At head of title: Министерство культуры РСФСР. Государственная публичная библиотека имени М. Е. Салтыкова-Щедрина.

Li, Shu-t'ien, 1900–
Chronological bibliography on arctic engineering (a compilation embracing frost, permafrost, and snow-ice-glacier as related to arctic, subarctic, and cold-region constructions, and including artificial ground freezing, 1883 thru the turn of 1971/2) ₁Rapid City, S. D.₁ 1972.

vii, 36 l. 28 cm.

A Magyar épitésügyi szakirodalom bibliográfiája.
Budapest, Épitésügyi Tájékoztatási Központ.

v. 29 cm.

Society of Automotive Engineers.
SAE technical literature on microfiche.

New York.

v. 28 cm. annual.

Began with vol. for 1965.

Trondheim. Norges tekniske høgskole. *Biblioteket.*
Ingeniørgeologi ved anlegg i fjell. Utarb. av Randi
Gjersvik. Trondheim, NTH-trykk, 1968.

20 p. 30 cm. (Norges tekniske høgskoles biblioteker. Litteraturliste, 37)

LIBRARY CATALOGS

Belo Horizonte, Brazil. Universidade de Minas Gerais.
Escola de Engenharia. Biblioteca.
Catálogo geral, org. por Nominato Cançado. Belo Horizonte, Escola de Engenharia, 1965–68.

9 v. in 10. 23 cm.

Buenos Aires (Province). Dirección de Vialidad. Biblioteca Técnica.
Catálogo de la Biblioteca Técnica. La Plata, División
Publicaciones y Biblioteca, 1963 [i. e. 1964]

850 p. 27 cm. (Provincia de Buenos Aires. Dirección de Vialidad. Publicación no. 37)

PERIODICALS

Engineering index of India. v. 1–
Mar./June 1970–
Jaipur. Malaviya Regional Engineering College.

v. 24 cm. quarterly.

Global Engineering Documentation Services.
Directory of engineering document sources. Compiled by
D. P. Simonton. Newport Beach, Calif., Global Engineering Documentation Services [1972]

1 v. (unpaged) 28 cm.

Mason, Penelope C   R
A classified directory of Japanese periodicals—engineering and industrial chemistry; compiled by P. C. R. Mason.
London, Aslib, 1972.

[3], 160 p. 27 cm.

Distributed in the U. S. A. by Chicorel Library Pub. Corp., New
York.

ENGINES

Tiutcheva, F   M
Двигатели XX века. Рек. указатель литературы. Москва, "Книга," 1970.

65 p. with illus. 20 cm.

At head of title: Государственная ордена Ленина библиотека СССР имени В. И. Ленина.
By F. M. Tiutcheva and G. V. Uspenskaia.

ENGLAND   see   Great Britain

ENGLISH DRAMA   see Drama - Great Britain

ENGLISH FICTION   see   Fiction - Great
   Britain

ENGLISH IMPRINTS

British books available for sale in the U. S. A., listed by
title, author, subject and classification, with indexes to
British publishers and American agents. London, Whita-

ker, 1968.

54 p. 25 cm.

Kellaway, William.
Bibliography of historical works issued in the United
Kingdom, 1961–1965; compiled for the Eighth Anglo-American Conference of Historians, by William Kellaway. London, University Institute of Historical Research, 1967.

xv, 298 p. 25 cm.

Whitaker's books of the month & books to come. Jan. 1970–

London, J. Whitaker.

no. 25 cm. monthly.

Running title, 1970–   : Books of the month & books to come.

EARLY PRINTED BOOKS

Cambridge. University. Library.
Early English printed books in the University Library,
Cambridge (1475 to 1640). Cambridge, University Press,
1900–07. New York, Johnson Reprint Corp., 1971.

4 v. (1804, 462 p.) 23 cm.

"Compiled by Charles Edward Sayle."
CONTENTS: v. 1. Caxton to F. Kingston.—v. 2. E. Mattes to R. Marriot, and English provincial presses.—v. 3. Scottish, Irish, and foreign presses: with addenda.—v. 4. Indexes.

Cameron, William James.
Short title catalogue of books printed in the British
Isles, the British Colonies and the United States of America and of English books printed elsewhere, 1701–1800, held
in the libraries of the Australian Capital Territory, edited
by William J. Cameron and Diana J. Carroll. Canberra,
National Library of Australia, 1966–70.

3 v. facsims., port. 25 cm. (v. 3: 27 cm.)
Published as a contribution to the David Nichol Smith Memorial Seminars in Eighteenth Century Studies, Canberra, 15–19 August, 1966, 23–29 August, 1970.
CONTENTS: v. 1. Titles, and authors, A–C.—v. 2. Authors, D–Z.—v. 3. Supplement, edited by I. Page.

A Catalogue of such English Books. Amsterdam, Theatrum
Orbis Terrarum; New York, Da Capo Press, 1969.

[15] p. 22 cm. (The English experience, its record in early printed books published in facsimile, no. 190)

At head of title: William Iaggard.
Original t. p. reads: A catalogve of such English bookes, as lately haue bene, and now-are in printing for publication. From the ninth day of October, 1618. Vntill Easter terme, next ensuing. And from this forme of beginning ... to be continued for euery halfe yeare. London. Printed by W. Iaggard, 1618.
S. T. C. no. 14341.

Clavell, Robert, *d.* 1711.
The general catalogue of books printed in England since
the dreadful fire of London, 1666 to the end of Trinity term,
1680 ...; collected by R. Clavell. Farnborough (Hants,).
Gregg P. in association with the Archive P., 1965 [i. e. 1966]
[6], 191 p. 30½ cm. (English bibliographical sources, ser. 2: Catalogues of books in circulation, 5)

Facsimile reprint of 1680 ed.
The 3d edition of Clavell's summary catalogue, compiled from the Term catalogues.

Clavell, Robert, *d.* 1711.
The general catalogue of books printed in England since
the dreadful fire of London, 1666 to the end of Trinity
Term, 1674 ...; collected by Robert Clavel. Farnborough
(Hants.), Gregg P. in association with the Archive P. 1965
[1966]

[5], 120 p. table. 30½ cm. (English bibliographical sources.
Series 2: catalogues of books in circulation 4)

Facsimile reprint of 1675 ed.

Clough, Eric A
A short-title catalogue, arranged geographically, of books printed and distributed by printers, publishers and booksellers in the English provincial towns and in Scotland and Ireland up to and including the year 1700; compiled by E. A. Clough. London, Library Association, 1969.

[3], 119 p. 31 cm.

Early English books 1475–1640, selected from Pollard and Redgrave's short-title catalogue; cross index to reels. 1–
Ann Arbor, University Microfilms, 1972–
v. 23 cm.
Continues English books, 1475–1640. Consolidated cross index by STC number, issued by University Microfilms.

Erie Co., N. Y. Buffalo and Erie County Public Library.
Pollard and Redgrave titles; a checklist of items in the rare book room of the Buffalo & Erie County Public Library. Buffalo, 1968.

7 p. 23 cm.

Erie Co., N. Y. Buffalo and Erie County Public Library.
Wing titles; a checklist of items in the rare book room. Buffalo, 1968.

24 p. 23 cm.

Francis Bacon Foundation, *Pasadena, Calif. Library.*
Supplement to the Francis Bacon Library holdings in the short title catalogue of English books. Compiled by Elizabeth S. Wrigley. Claremont, Calif., 1967.

171 l. 29 cm.

Consists of accessions subsequent to the publication of Short title catalogue numbers [1475–1640] (1958), and Wing (Short title catalogue 1641–1700) numbers (1959).

Hasan, Masoodul.
Rare English books in India; a select bibliography. [1st ed.] Aligarh, Three Men Publications [1970]

vi, 216 p. 23 cm.

"List of English literary periodicals": p. [191]–203.

London. Guildhall Library.
A list of books printed in the British Isles and of English books printed abroad before 1701 in Guildhall Library. London, Corporation of London, 1966–67.

2 v. 27½ cm.

London, William, *bookseller, Newcastle-upon-Tyne.*
William London: A catalogue of the most vendible books in England (1657, 1658, 1660) [London, Gregg Press, 1965]

1 v. (unpaged) 25 cm. (English bibliographical sources. Series 2: Catalogues of books in circulation [no.] 2)

Includes the author's "A supplement of new books ... August the first 1657 till June the first 1628" [London, 1658] and his "A catalogue of new books ..." London, 1660.

Maunsell, Andrew, d. 1596.
The catalogue of English printed books, 1595. London, Printed by John Windet for Andrew Maunsell, 1595. [Farnborough (Hants.), Gregg, in association with Archive P., 1965 [i. e. 1966]]

[10], 123, [6], 27 p. 28 cm. (English bibliographical sources. Series 2: Catalogues of books in circulation, no. 1)

Facsimile of 1595 ed.

Mitchell Library, Glascow.
Catalogue of incunables and S. T. C. books in the Mitchell Library, Glasgow. [Glasgow] Glasgow Corp. Public Libraries, 1964.

131 p. 23 cm.

Compiled by A. G. Hepburn.

Pollard, Alfred William, 1859–1944.
A short-title catalogue of books printed in England, Scotland, & Ireland and of English books printed abroad 1475–1640. Compiled by A. W. Pollard & G. R. Redgrave with the help of G. F. Barwick [and others] London, Bibliographical Society, 1969.

xvi, 609 p. 25 cm.

"Reprinted photographically, by Scolar Press Limited, Menston."

Wing, Donald Goddard, 1904–
A gallery of ghosts; books published between 1641–1700 not found in the Short-title catalogue, by Donald Wing. [New York] Index Committee, Modern Language Association of America, 1967.

vi, 225 p. 28 cm.

Wing, Donald Goddard, 1904–
Short-title catalogue of books printed in England, Scotland, Ireland, Wales, and British America, and of English books printed in other countries, 1641–1700. Compiled by Donald Wing. 2d ed., rev. and enl. New York, Index Committee of the Modern Language Association of America, 1972–

v. 29 cm.

A continuation of A short-title catalogue of books printed in England, Scotland & Ireland and of English books printed abroad, 1475–1640, by A. W. Pollard and G. R. Redgrave, published in 1926.

ENGLISH LANGUAGE
see also under Dissertations, Academic

Alston, R   C
A bibliography of the English language from the invention of printing to the year 1800; a systematic record of writings on English, and on other languages in English, based on the collections of the principal libraries of the world. Compiled by R. C. Alston. Leeds [Eng.] Printed for the author by E. J. Arnold, 1965–

v. 28 cm.

Alston, R   C
A catalogue of books relating to the English language in Swedish libraries, by R. C. Alston. Leeds, R. C. Alston, 1965.

[1], vii, 29 p. 22 cm.

Alston, R   C
English grammars written in English and English grammars written in Latin by native speakers [by] R. C. Alston. Leeds [Eng.] Printed for the author by E. J. Arnold [1965]

xxvii, 118 p. 28 cm. (*His* A bibliography of the English language from the invention of printing to the year 1800, v. 1)

Bailey, Richard W
English stylistics; a bibliography [by] Richard W. Bailey and Dolores M. Burton. Cambridge, Mass., M. I. T. Press [1968]

xxii, 198 p. 24 cm.

Kohl, Norbert, 1939–
Bibliographie für das Studium der Anglistik. Bad Homburg v. d. H., Athenäum-Verl. (1970–

v. 19 cm. (Schwerpunkte Anglistik, 2)

CONTENTS: Bd. 1. Sprachwissenschaft.

Scheurweghs, Gustave, 1904–1965.
Analytical bibliography of writings on modern English morphology and syntax, 1877–1960, by G. Scheurweghs. Louvain, Nauwelaerts, 1963–68.

4 v. port. 25 cm. (Publications of the University of Louvain)

CONTENTS.—1. Periodical literature and miscellanies of the United States of America and Western and Northern Europe. With an appendix on Japanese publications, by H. Yamaguchi.—2. Studies in bookform, including dissertations and Programmabhandlungen, published in the United States of America and Western and Northern Europe. With appendixes on Japanese publications by H. Yamaguchi and on Czechoslovak publications by J. Simko.—3. Soviet research on English morphology and syntax, by G. G. Pocheptsov.

English studies in Bulgaria, Poland, Rumania, and Yugoslavia, by M. Mincoff and others.—4. Addenda and general indexes, by G. Scheurweghs, continued by E. Vorlat.

Šimko, Ján.
Analytical bibliography of Czechoslovak writings on modern English morphology and syntax, 1907–1960. (Vyd. 1.) Bratislava, Slovenské pedagogické nakl., 1965.

48 p. 29 cm. (Vysokoškolské učebné texty)

At head of title: Univerzita Komenského v Bratislave. Filozofická fakulta.

Stein, Gabriele.
English word-formation over two centuries; in honour of Hans Marchand on the occasion of his sixty-fifth birthday, 1 October 1972. Tübingen (Tübinger Beiträge zur Linguistik) 1973.

356 p. 21 cm. (Tübinger Beiträge zur Linguistik, Bd. 34)

DIALECTS AND SLANG

Alston, R   C
English dialects, Scottish dialects, cant and vulgar English (compiled by R. C. Alston. Menston, Scolar Press, 1971.

ii–xii, 178 p. facsims. 28 cm. index. (His A Bibliography of the English language from the invention of printing to the year 1800, v. 9)

Burke, William Jeremiah, 1902–
The literature of slang, by W. J. Burke. With an introductory note by Eric Partridge. New York, New York Public Library, 1939. Detroit, Gale Research Co., 1965.

vii, 180 p. 24 cm.

DICTIONARIES

Alston, R   C
The English dictionary (by) R. C. Alston. Leeds, Printed for the author by E. J. Arnold, °1966.

xxvi, 195 p. facsims. 28 cm. (His A bibliography of the English language from the invention of printing to the year 1800, v. 5)

Alston, R   C
Old English, Middle English, early modern English, miscellaneous works, vocabulary. (Compiled by R. C. Alston) Menston (Eng.), Printed for the author by Scolar Press, (1970–

v. facsims. 28 cm. (His A bibliography of the English language from the invention of printing to the year 1800, v. 3, pt. 1–

Alston, R   C
Polyglot dictionaries and grammars; treatises on English written for speakers of French, German, Dutch, Danish, Swedish, Portuguese, Spanish, Italian, Hungarian, Persian, Bengali and Russian. Bradford, printed for the author by Ernest Cummins (1967)

xx, 311 p. 151 (i. e. 150) facsims. 28 cm. (His A bibliography of the English language from the invention of printing to the year 1800, v. 2)

Mathews, Mitford McLeod, 1891–
A survey of English dictionaries, by M. M. Mathews. New York, Russell & Russell, 1966.

119 p. 20 cm.

"First published in 1933."

Walsh, James Patrick.
English language dictionaries in print; a comparative analysis, compiled by S. Padraig Walsh. Newark, Del., Reference Books Research Publications, 1965.

56 p. 22 cm.

STUDY AND TEACHING

Adams, Anthony.
Teaching English / selected and annotated by Anthony Adams. — London : National Book League, 1974.

40 p. : 21 cm.

Allen, Virginia French.
English as a second language; a comprehensive bibliography (by) Virginia F. Allen (and) Sidney Forman. New York, Teachers College Press (1967)

255 p. 23 cm.

Butler, Donna.
ERIC documents on the teaching of English, 1956–1968. Compiled by Donna Butler, Robert V. Denby, and the staffs of the ERIC clearinghouses on English. Champaign, Ill., National Council of Teachers of English (1969)

x, 66 p. 25 cm.

Butler, Donna.
A guide to available Project English materials, edited by Donna Butler (and) Bernard O'Donnell. Rev. ed. Champaign, Ill., Clearinghouse on the Teaching of English, 1969.

vii, 132 p. 28 cm.

California. Bureau of Adult Education.
A bibliography relative to teaching and learning English as a second language. (Sacramento, California State Dept. of Education, 1967)

iv, 13 p. 18 cm.

Clearinghouse on the Teaching of English.
Annotated list of recommended elementary and secondary curriculum guides in English.
Champaign, Ill.

v. 28 cm.

English for immigrant children. 2nd ed.; selected by Margaret Rogers (and others). London, National Book League, 1969.

44 p. 22 cm.

English-Teaching Information Centre, *London.*
English-teaching bibliography. London, British Council, English-Teaching Information Centre (1964)

1 v. (unpaged)   28 cm.

———— Supplement. London, British Council, English-Teaching Information Centre ₁1965–

pts.   27 cm.

Fox, Claudia.
T. E. L. L. in Wellington. *Teaching of Engish as a later language. Wellington, Dept. of Education's Correspondence School, 1966.

21 p.   21 cm.

Revision of bibliography begun at the New Zealand Library School, 1963.

Gefen, Raphael.
(Madrikh bibliyografi le-hora'at ha-Anglit)
מדריך ביבליוגראפי להוראת האנגלית. ליקט רפאל גפן.
וההעורך: אברהם ברטורא₁ מהד' 1.   ירושלים. 1970.

26 p.   24 cm.

Added t. p.: Annotated English-teaching bibliography.
At head of title: משרד החינוך והתרבות, המזכירות הפדגוגית לחינוך
יסודי ולהכשרת מורים; המזכירות הפדגוגית לחינוך העל-סודי.

Gt. Brit. *British Council.*
Audio-visual material for English language teaching: a catalogue. 2nd ed. London, published for the British Council, by Longmans, 1967 ₁i. e. 1968₁

102 p.   21 cm.

Gt. Brit. *Community Relations Commission.*
A bibliography for teachers of immigrants ₁compiled by June Derrick, Trevor Burgin and others₁. London, Community Relations Commission, 1967.

17 p.   21 cm.

Harris, Larry Allen, 1940–
For the reading teacher: an annotated index to Elementary English, 1924–1970. Compiled by Larry A. Harris and E. Marcia Kimmel. ₁Urbana, Ill.₁ National Council of Teachers of English ₁1972₁

73 p.   24 cm.

Majority of the annotations taken from W. J. Moore's Annotated Index to Elementary English: 1924–1967.

Jenkinson, Edward B
Books for teachers of English, an annotated bibliography, by Edward B. Jenkinson ₁and₁ Philip B. Daghlian. Bloomington, Indiana University Press ₁1968₁

xvi, 173 p.   22 cm.

Kreter, Herbert.
Bibliographie zur Didaktik der neueren Sprachen, besonders des Englischunterrichts. Deutsche Veröffentlichungen 1880 bis 1960 ⟨mit einer Auswahl neuerer österreichischer, englischer und amerikanischer Veröffentlichungen⟩ Frankfurt/M., Berlin, Bonn, München, Diesterweg (1965)

vii, 180 p.   21 cm. (Schule und Forschung, Heft 3)

La Borderie, Odette.
Documents pour l'angliciste ₁par₁ Odette La Borderie ... Alix Dechame ... Avec la collaboration de Simone Terrayre ... Bordeaux, Centre régional de documentation pédagogique, 75, cours d'Alsace-Lorraine, 1970.

ix, 79, 124 p.   27 cm.

Malkoç, Anna Maria.
A TESOL bibliography: abstracts of ERIC publications and research reports. Washington, Teachers of English to

Speakers of Other Languages ₁1971₁
ix, 310 p.   23 cm.
"A compilation of resumés of TESOL documents which have appeared in the monthly issues of the ERIC (Educational Resources Information Center) publication Research in education ... published during the period July 1967 through August 1970 ... ₁and₁ journal articles which have been listed from January 1969 through August 1970 in Current index to journals in education."

National Council of Teachers of English. *Committee on a Bibliography of College Teaching.*
An annotated bibliography on the college teaching of English, 1957–1963, by J. Carter Rowland, chairman, Lizette O. Van Gelder, associate chairman ₁and₁ John McKiernan, with Agnes V. Boner ₁and others. Champaign, Ill.₁ National Council of Teachers of English ₁1966₁

vi, 56 p.   25 cm.

National Council of Teachers of English. *Committee on a Bibliography of College Teaching.*
An annotated bibliography on the college teaching of English, 1963–1965 ₁by₁ J. Carter Rowland, chairman ₁and₁ Lizette O. Van Gelder, associate chairman, with Stanley Bank ₁and others. Champaign, Ill., 1968₁

v, 30 p.   25 cm.

Ohannessian, Sirarpi, *ed.*
Reference list of materials for English as a second language. Edited by Sirarpi Ohannessian, with the assistance of Carol J. Kreidler ₁and₁ Julia Sableski. Washington, Center for Applied Linguistics, 1964–69.
3 v.   23 cm.
Part 2 edited with the assistance of Carol J. Kreidler and Beryl Dwight; pt. 3 edited by Dorothy A. Pedtke, Bernarda Erwin, and Anna Maria Malkoç.
CONTENTS.—pt. 1. Texts, readers, dictionaries, tests.—pt. 2. Background materials, methodology.—₁pt. 3₁ Supplement, 1964–1968.

Shên, Yao, 1911–
Teaching English as a second language; a classified bibliography ₁by₁ Yao Shen and Ruth H. Crymes. Honolulu, East-West Center Press ₁1965₁

xiv, 110 p.   22 cm.

Sundermann, Karl Heinrich, 1909–
Zur Methodik und Didaktik des Englischunterrichts. Eine kritische Bibliographie in- und ausländischen Schrifttums. (Dortmund) Lensing (1966).

145 p.   22 cm. (Der neusprachliche Unterricht in Wissenschaft und Praxis, Bd. 12)

Visual Education National Information Service for Schools.
English as a second language: audio-visual teaching materials. 2d ed. London, Educational Foundation for Visual Aids, ₁1969₁.

24 p.   22 cm.

Cover title.
Previous ed. published as Audio-visual material for the teaching of English as a second language, 1966.

Watt, Lois Belfield.
Books related to English language and literature in elementary and secondary schools; a bibliography from the Educational Materials Center, compiled by Lois B. Watt, Delia Goetz, and Caroline Stanley. ₁Washington₁ U. S. National Center for Educational Research and Development: ₁for sale by the Supt. of Docs., U. S. Govt. Print. Off., 1970₁
24 p.   26 cm.

ENGLISH LANGUAGE IN AUSTRALIA

Eagleson, Robert D
Bibliography of writings on Australian English ₁by₁

Robert D. Eagleson. ₍Sydney₎ Australian Language Research Centre, University of Sydney, 1967.

19 p. 22 cm. (Sydney. University. Australian Language Research Centre. Occasional paper no. 11)

ENGLISH LANGUAGE IN CANADA

Avis, Walter Spencer, 1919–
A bibliography of writings on Canadian English (1857–1965) ₍by₎ Walter S. Avis. Toronto, W. J. Gage ₍°1965₎

17 p. 22 cm.

ENGLISH LANGUAGE IN HAWAII

Tsuzaki, Stanley M
English in Hawaii; an annotated bibliography ₍by₎ Stanley M. Tsuzaki and John E. Reinecke. ₍Honolulu, Pacific and Asian Linguistics Institute, University of Hawaii, 1966₎

ix, 61 p. 23 cm. (Oceanic linguistics special publications, no. 1)

ENGLISH LANGUAGE IN THE UNITED STATES

Brenni, Vito Joseph, 1923–
American English, a bibliography, compiled by Vito J. Brenni. Philadelphia, University of Pennsylvania Press ₍1964₎

221 p. 22 cm.

Leffall, Dolores C   1931–
Black English; an annotated bibliography. Compiled by Dolores C. Leffall and James P. Johnson. Washington, Minority Research Center ₍1973₎

75 p. 28 cm. (Minority group series)

Cover title: Focus on Black English.

McMillan, James B   1907–
Annotated bibliography of Southern American English, by James B. McMillan. Coral Gables, Fla., University of Miami Press ₍1971₎

173 p. 22 cm.

ENGLISH LITERATURE

For the English literature of countries other than Great Britain see African literature, Irish literature, etc.

see also American literature; English imprints; and under Dissertations, Academic - English language and literature

Bateson, Frederick Wilse, 1901–
A guide to English literature, by F. W. Bateson. Garden City, N. Y., Anchor Books, 1965.

xi, 259 p. 18 cm.

Bateson, Frederick Wilse, 1901–
A guide to English literature ₍by₎ F. W. Bateson. 2nd ed. London, Longmans, 1967.

xi, 260 p. 22 cm.

Bateson, Frederick Wilse, 1901–
A guide to English literature, by F. W. Bateson. Rev. ed. Chicago, Aldine Pub. Co. ₍1968₎

xi, 260 p. 22 cm.

Bateson, Frederick Wilse, 1901–
A guide to English literature, by F. W. Bateson. 2d ed. Garden City, N. Y., Anchor Books, 1968.

xi, 261 p. 18 cm.

Chandler, George, 1915–
How to find out about literature, by G. Chandler. ₍1st ed.₎ Oxford, New York, Pergamon Press ₍1968₎

xv, 224 p. facsims. 20 cm. (The Commonwealth and international library. Libraries and technical information division)

Dick, Aliki Lafkidou.
A student's guide to British literature; a selective bibliography of 4,128 title and reference sources from the Anglo-Saxon period to the present. Littleton, Colo., Libraries Unlimited, 1972 ₍c1971₎

285 p. 24 cm.

Gt. Brit. *British Council.*
English literature from the 16th century to the present: a select list of editions. Revised ed. London, Published for the British Council by Longmans, 1965.

viii, 164 p. 22 cm.

Hackett, Alice Payne, 1900–
70 years of best sellers, 1895–1965. New York, R. R. Bowker Co., 1967.

xi, 280 p. 24 cm.

First published in 1945 under title: Fifty years of best sellers. Published in 1956 under title: 60 years of best sellers.

Keats-Shelley journal.
Keats, Shelley, Byron, Hunt, and their circles; a bibliography: July 1, 1950–June 30, 1962. Edited by David Bonnell Green and Edwin Graves Wilson. Compiled by David Bonnell Green ₍and others₎ Lincoln, University of Nebraska Press ₍1964₎

ix, 323 p. 24 cm.

A collection of the first twelve annual bibliographies taken from Keats-Shelley journal.

Kirk, John Foster, 1824–1904.
A supplement to Allibone's critical dictionary of English literature and British and American authors. Detroit, Gale Research Co., 1965.

2 v. (x, 1562 p.) 24 cm.

Reproduced by photolithography from the 1891 ed.

Lowndes, William Thomas, 1798?–1843.
The bibliographer's manual of English literature, containing an account of rare, curious, and useful books, published in or relating to Great Britain and Ireland, from the invention of printing; with bibliographical and critical notices, collations of the rarer articles, and the prices at which they have been sold. New ed., rev., corr., and enl.; with an appendix relating to the books of literary and scientific societies, by Henry G. Bohn. With an essay on William T. Lowndes by Francesco Cordasco and An appreciation by Lowell Kerr. Detroit, Republished by Gale Research Co., 1967.

8 v. port. 23 cm.

Title page includes original imprint: London, H. G. Bohn, 1864. Vols. 1–7 paged continuously.

The New Cambridge bibliography of English literature, edited by George Watson. Cambridge ₍Eng.₎ University Press, 1969–

v. 26 cm.

1940 edition edited by F. W. Bateson under title: The Cambridge bibliography of English literature.
CONTENTS:
v. 2. 1660–1800.—v. 3. 1800–1900.—v. 4. 1900–1950.

Ogoshi, Kazuzō, 1917–
イギリス文学—案内と文献—御輿員三編　東京　研究社 ₍1968₎

xviii, 236 p. 19 cm.

The Reader's adviser: English literature. Edited by Winifred F. Courtney. New York, Barnes & Noble ₍1971, c1968₎

xvi, 317 p. 26 cm.

Selections from v. 1 (A guide to the best in literature) of the 11th ed. of the Reader's adviser, published by R. R. Bowker.

Schwartz, Jacob
1100 obscure points: the bibliographies of 25 English and 21 American authors. ₍1st ed., reprinted₎. Bristol, Chatford House Press, 1969.

xiii, 95 p. 2 plates. facsims. 26 cm.

"First published 1931."

Schwartz, Jacob.
1100 obscure points; the bibliographies of 25 English and 21 American authors. Folcroft, Pa., Folcroft Press ₍1969₎

xiii, 95 p. 26 cm.

Reprint of the 1931 ed.

**Watson, George, 1927–	ed.**
The concise Cambridge bibliography of English literature, 600–1950. 2d ed. Cambridge ₍Eng.₎ University Press, 1965.

xi, 269 p. 21 cm.

Watt, Robert, 1774–1819.
Bibliotheca Britannica; or, A general index to British and foreign literature. New York, B. Franklin ₍1965₎

4 v. 30 cm. (Burt Franklyn bibliography & reference series, 75)

Reprint of the 1824 ed.

CONTENTS.—v. 1.–2. Authors.—v. 3–4. Subjects.

Wright, Andrew H
A reader's guide to English & American literature ₍by₎ Andrew Wright. ₍Glenview, Ill.₎ Scott, Foresman ₍1970₎

xix, 166 p. 22 cm.

TO 1700

Bond, Donald Frederic, 1898–
The age of Dryden. Compiled by Donald F. Bond. New York, Appleton-Century-Crofts ₍1970₎

xii, 103 p. (p. 81–88 blank for "Notes") 24 cm. (Goldentree bibliographies in language and literature)

Booker, John Manning.
A Middle English bibliography: dates, dialects, and sources of the XII, XIII, and XIV century monuments and manuscripts exclusive of the works of Wyclif, Gower, and Chaucer, and the documents in the London dialect. ₍Folcroft, Pa.₎ Folcroft Library Editions, 1972.

76 p. 26 cm.

"Limited to 150 copies."
Reprint of the 1912 ed., which had its beginning in the author's dissertation, Heidelberg.

Donovan, Dennis G
Thomas Dekker, 1945–1965; Thomas Heywood, 1938–1965; Cyril Tourneur, 1945–1965, compiled by Dennis Donovan. London, Nether P., 1967.

56 p. 22 cm. (Elizabethan bibliographies supplements, no. 2)

Donovan, Dennis G
John Evelyn 1920–1968. Samuel Pepys 1933–1968, compiled by Dennis G. Donovan. London, Nether Press, 1970.

64 p. 22 cm. (Elizabethan bibliographies supplements, 18)

Donovan, Dennis G
Sir Thomas Browne 1924–1966; Robert Burton 1924–1966, compiled by Dennis G. Donovan. London, Nether Press, 1968.

50 p. 22 cm. (Elizabethan bibliographies supplements, 10)

Grolier Club, New York.
Catalogue of original and early editions of some of the poetical and prose works of English writers from Langland to Wither. With collations & notes, & 87 facsimiles of title-pages and frontispieces; being a contribution to the bibliography of English literature. New York, Imprinted for the Cooper Square Publishers, 1963.

xiii, 240 p. illus., facsims. 26 cm. (The Cooper Square library of bibliography)
First published in 1893.
Continued by "Catalogue of original and early editions of some of the poetical and prose works of English writers from Wither to Prior," first published by the Grolier Club in 1905.

Grolier Club, New York.
Catalogue of original and early editions of some of the poetical and prose works of English writers from Wither to Prior. With collations, notes, and more than 200 facsimiles of title-pages and frontispieces. New York, Imprinted for the Cooper Square Publishers, 1963.

3 v. illus., facsims. 26 cm. (The Cooper Square library of bibliography)
First published in 1905.
May be considered a continuation of "Catalogue of original and early editions of some of the poetical and prose works of English writers from Langland to Wither," first published by the Grolier Club in 1893.

Guffey, George Robert.
Robert Herrick, 1949–1965, Ben Jonson, 1947–1965, Thomas Randolph, 1949–1965, compiled by George Robert Guffey. London, Nether P., 1968.

53 p. 22 cm. (Elizabethan bibliographies supplements, 3)

Johnson, Robert Carl, 1938–
Robert Greene 1945–1965; Thomas Lodge 1939–1965; John Lyly 1939–1965; Thomas Nashe 1941–1965; George Peele 1939–1965, compiled by Robert C. Johnson. London, Nether P., 1967 ₍i. e. 1968₎

69 p. 22½ cm. (Elizabethan bibliographies supplements, 5)

Lievsay, John Leon.
The sixteenth century: Skelton through Hooker, compiled by John L. Lievsay. New York, Appleton-Century-Crofts ₍1968₎

xi, 132 p. 24 cm. (Goldentree bibliographies in language and literature)

Matthews, William, 1905–
Old and Middle English literature. New York, Appleton-Century-Crofts ₍1968₎

xvi, 112 p. 23 cm. (Goldentree bibliographies in language and literature)

Pennel, Charles A
Francis Beaumont, John Fletcher, Philip Massinger, 1937–1965; John Ford, 1940–1965; James Shirley, 1945–1965; compiled by Charles A. Pennel and William P. Williams. London, Nether P., 1968.

52 p. 22 cm. (Elizabethan bibliographies supplements, 8)

Robinson, Fred C
Old English literature; a select bibliography [by] Fred C. Robinson. [Toronto] University of Toronto Press [1970]

68 p. 22 cm. (Toronto medieval bibliographies, 2)

Simms, Norman Toby.
Ritual and rhetoric: intellectual and ceremonial backgrounds to Middle English literature; a critical survey of relevant scholarship. [Norwood, Pa.] Norwood Editions, 1973.

358 p. 24 cm.

Tucker, Lena Lucile.
A bibliography of fifteenth-century literature, with special reference to the history of English culture, by Lena Lucile Tucker and Allen Rogers Benham. New York, Lemma Pub. Corp., 1972.
162 p. 24 cm.
Reprint of the 1928 ed., which was issued as v. 2, no. 3 of University of Washington publications in language and literature.

18TH CENTURY

The British magazine.
The lists of books from the British Magazine, 1746–50; collected with annual indexes. Farnborough (Hants.), Gregg P. in association with the Archives P., 1965.

[177] p. 20½ cm. (English bibliographical sources. Series 1: Periodical lists of new publications, no. 8)

Ewen, Frederic, 1899–
Bibliography of eighteenth century English literature. New York, Haskell House Publishers, 1969 [°1935]

28 p. 24 cm.

Kimber, Edward, 1719–1769.
The Gentleman's magazine, 1731–51; the lists of books, collected with annual indexes and the index to the first twenty years, compiled by Edward Kimber (1752). London, Gregg P. in association with the Archive P., 1966 [i. e. 1967]

[446] p. 24 cm. (English bibliographical sources. Series 1: Periodical lists of new publications, no. 6)

Various paging. Facsimile reprint.

The Monthly catalogue: an exact register of all books, sermons, plays, poetry, and miscellaneous pamphlets, printed and published in London, or the universities [1723–1730], with a compleat index to the whole. London, Gregg P.; London, Archive P., 1964.

2 v. 29 cm. (English bibliographical sources, series 1, no. 2)

Facsimile reprints.

The Monthly catalogues from 'The London Magazine,' 1732–66: with the index for 1732–58 compiled by Edward Kimber. London, Gregg P.; Archive P., 1966 [i. e. 1967].

[740] p. 24 cm. (English bibliographical sources. Series 1: Periodical lists of new publications, 7)

Facsimile reprints. Various paging.

A Register of books, 1728–1732; extracted from the Monthly chronicle. [London] Gregg [Press] [1964]

1 v. (various pagings) 26 cm. (English bibliographical sources, series 1, no. 3)

Tobin, James Edward, 1905–
Eighteenth century English literature and its cultural background: a bibliography [by] James E. Tobin. New York, Biblo and Tannen, 1967.

vii, 190 p. 24 cm.

Reprint of the 1939 ed.

CONTENTS.—pt. 1. Cultural and critical background.—pt. 2. Bibliographies of individual authors.

Williams, Iolo Aneurin, 1890–1962.
Seven xviiith century bibliographies. New York, B. Franklin [1968]

244 p. 23 cm. (Burt Franklin bibliography and reference series, 108)

Reprint of the 1924 ed.

CONTENTS.—John Armstrong.—William Shenstone.—Mark Akenside. — William Collins. — Oliver Goldsmith. — Charles Churchill. — Richard Brinsley Butler Sheridan.

19TH - 20TH CENTURIES

Armstrong, Terence Ian Fytton, 1912–
Ten contemporaries; notes toward their definitive bibliography, by John Gawsworth. With a foreword by Viscount Esher. And original essays by Lascelles Abercrombie [and others. Folcroft, Pa., Folcroft Library Editions, 1972.

224 p. 22 cm.

"Limited to 150 copies."
Reprint of the 1932 ed.

Armstrong, Terence Ian Fytton, 1912–
Ten contemporaries; notes toward their definitive bibliography (second series) by John Gawsworth. With a prefatory word by P. H. Muir, and original essays by Dorothy M. Richardson [and others. Folcroft, Pa.] Folcroft Library Editions, 1972.

240 p. 23 cm.

Each essay is followed by a list of works of its author and blank pages for additional titles.
"Limited to 150 copies."
Reprint of the 1933 ed.

Bibliographies of modern authors. (Third series) George Eliot, Maurice Hewlett [and] A. A. R. Firbank, by P. H. Muir. Mark Rutherford, by S. Nowell Smith. Leigh Hunt, by A. Mitchell. [Folcroft, Pa.] Folcroft Library Editions, 1973.

58, 23, 73 p. illus. 26 cm.
Reprint of the 1931 ed. published by the Bookman's Journal, London.

Cutler, Bradley Dwyane, 1904– comp.
Modern British authors; their first editions. Compiled by B. D. Cutler and Villa Stiles. [Folcroft, Pa.] Folcroft Library Editions, 1973 [c1930]

xi, 171 p. 24 cm.

Danielson, Henry.
Bibliographies of modern authors. [First series] London, The Bookman's journal, 1921. [Folcroft, Pa.] Folcroft Library Editions, 1972.
xi, 211 p. 24 cm.
"Most of the material used in this volume originally appeared in the Bookman's journal."
CONTENTS: Max Beerbohm.—Rupert Brooke.—Hubert Crankanthorpe.—Walter De La Mare.—John Drinkwater.—Lord Dunsany.—James Elroy Flecker.—George Gissing.—Francis Ledwidge.—Compton Mackenzie.—John Masefield.—Leonard Merrick.—Richard Middleton.—Arthur Symons.—Hugh Walpole.

Ehrsam, Theodore George, comp.
Bibliographies of twelve Victorian authors. Compiled

by Theodore G. Ehrsam and Robert H. Deily under the direction of Robert M. Smith. New York, Octagon Books, 1968.

362 p. 26 cm.
Reprint of the 1936 ed.
CONTENTS. — Matthew Arnold. — Elizabeth Barrett Browning.— Arthur Hugh Clough.—Edward Fitzgerald.—Thomas Hardy.—Rudyard Kipling. — William Morris. — Christina Georgina Rossetti.— Dante Gabriel Rossetti.—Robert Louis Stevenson.—Algernon Charles Swinburne.—Alfred, Lord Tennyson.

Fogle, Richard Harter.
Romantic poets and prose writers. New York, Appleton-Century-Crofts [1967]

viii, 87 p. 24 cm. (Goldentree bibliographies)

Lauterbach, Edward S
The transitional age; British literature, 1880–1920, by Edward S. Lauterbach and W. Eugene Davis. Troy, N. Y., Whitston Pub. Co., 1973.

v, 323 p. 24 cm.

National Book League, *London.*
Fiction, drama & poetry from the Commonwealth. London, National Book League, 1966.

43 p. 21½ cm.

National Book League, *London.*
Imaginative literature from the Commonwealth. London, 1965.

42 p. 22 cm.

National Book League, *London.*
Literature and the arts in the Commonwealth. London, National Book League with the Commonwealth Institute, 1968.

43 p. 22 cm.

Sadleir, Michael. 1888–1957.
Excursions in Victorian bibliography. Folcroft, Pa., Folcroft Press [1969]

vii, 240 p. 24 cm.

Reprint of the 1922 ed.
CONTENTS: Anthony Trollope: essay and bibliography.—Frederick Marryat: essay and bibliography.—Benjamin Disraeli: essay and bibliography.—Wilkie Collins: essay and bibliography.—Charles Reade: note and bibliography.—G. J. Whyte-Melville: essay and bibliography.—Elizabeth Cleghorn Gaskell: bibliography.—Herman Melville: essay and bibliography.

Stonehill, Charles Archibald, 1900–
Bibliographies of modern authors. (Second series) Compiled and edited by C. A. and H. W. Stonehill. London, J. Castle. [Folcroft, Pa.] Folcroft Library Editions, 1972.

xiii, 162 p. 24 cm.

Reprint of the 1925 ed.
CONTENTS: John Davidson.—Ernest Dowson.—Katherine Mansfield.—Alice Meynell.—Walter Pater.—Francis Thompson.

Temple, Ruth (Zabriskie) *comp.*
Twentieth century British literature; a reference guide and bibliography, compiled and edited by Ruth Z. Temple, with the assistance for the author bibliographies of Martin Tucker. New York, F. Ungar Pub. Co. [1968]

x, 261 p. 24 cm.

BIBLIOGRAPHIES

Besterman, Theodore, 1904–
Literature. English & American; a bibliography of bibliographies. Totowa, N. J., Rowman and Littlefield, 1971.

457 p. 20 cm. (His The Besterman world bibliographies)

Cordasco, Francesco, 1920–
A register of 18th century bibliographies and references; a chronological quarter-century survey relating to English literature, booksellers, newspapers, periodicals, printing & publishing, aesthetics, art & music, economics, history & science; a preliminary contribution. Detroit, Gale Research Co., 1968 [°1950]

74 p. facsim. 22 cm.

Esdaile, Arundell James Kennedy, 1880–1956.
The sources of English literature; a guide for students. New York, B. Franklin [1969]

vii, 130 p. 19 cm. (Sandars lectures, 1926)

Burt Franklin bibliography and reference series, 293. Selected essays in literature and criticism, 34.
Reprint of the 1928 ed.

Howard-Hill, Trevor Howard.
Bibliography of British literary bibliographies [by] T. H. Howard-Hill. Oxford, Clarendon P., 1969.

xxv, 570 p. 24 cm. (Index to British literary bibliography, 1)

Mellown, Elgin W
A descriptive catalogue of the bibliographies of 20th century British writers, by Elgin W. Mellown. Troy, N. Y., Whitston Pub. Co., 1972.

xii, 446 p. 24 cm.

BIO-BIBLIOGRAPHY

Allibone, Samuel Austin, 1816–1889.
A critical dictionary of English literature and British and American authors, living and deceased, from the earliest accounts to the latter half of the nineteenth century, containing over forty-six thousand articles (authors), with forty indexes of subjects. Philadelphia, J. B. Lippincott, 1858–72. Detroit, Gale Research Co., 1965.

3 v. (3140 p.) 24 cm.

A Biographical dictionary of the living authors of Great Britain and Ireland; comprising literary memoirs and anecdotes of their lives and a chronological register of their publications, with the number of editions printed; including notices of some foreign writers whose works have been occasionally published in England. Illustrated by a variety of communications from persons of the first eminence in the world of letters. London, Printed for H. Colburn, 1816. Detroit, Gale Research Co., 1966.

viii, 449 p. 24 cm.

Reprint of a work first published in 1816.
Ascribed to John Watkins and Frederic Shoberl. cf. Brit. Mus. cat. and Halkett & Laing. Also attributed to William Upcott. cf. Halkett & Laing.

DeLaura, David J
Victorian prose; a guide to research. Edited by David J. DeLaura. New York, Modern Language Association of America, 1973.

xvi, 560 p. 25 cm.

"Designed to join two ... earlier volumes: Victorian fiction: a guide to research (1964), edited by Lionel Stevenson, and The Victorian poets: a guide to research (2nd ed., 1968), edited by Frederic E. Faverty."

Gillow, Joseph, 1850–1921.
A literary and biographical history; or Bibliographical dictionary of the English Catholics, from the breach with Rome, in 1534, to the present time. New York, B. Franklin

₁1968₁

5 v. 24 cm. (Burt Franklin bibliography and reference series, 25)

Reprint of the 1885–1902 ed.

CONTENTS.—v. 1. A–C—v. 2. D–Grad—v. 3. Gran–Kem—v. 4. Kem–Met—v. 5. Mey–Zoo.

Handley-Taylor, Geoffrey.

Cheshire, Derbyshire and Staffordshire authors today: being a checklist of authors born in these counties, together with brief particulars of authors born elsewhere who are currently working or residing in these counties—an assemblage of more than 460 authors together with their addresses and (where applicable) their pseudonyms; general editor Geoffrey Handley-Taylor. London, Eddison Press Ltd, 1972.

xiv, 70 p. 22 cm. (County authors today series)

Myers, Robin, fl. 1967–

A dictionary of literature in the English language, from Chaucer to 1940, compiled and edited by Robin Myers, for the National Book League. ₁1st ed.₁ Oxford, New York, Pergamon Press ₁1970₁

2 v. illus., facsim. 25 cm.

Phelps, Robert, 1922–

The literary life; a scrapbook almanac of the Anglo-American literary scene from 1900 to 1950, by Robert Phelps and Peter Deane. New York, Farrar, Straus and Giroux, 1968.

244 p. illus., ports. 29 cm.

Rivers, David.

Literary memoirs of living authors of Great Britain. New York, Garland Pub., 1970.

2 v. 21 cm.

"Facsimile ... made from a copy in the Yale University Library." Original t. p. reads: Literary memoirs of living authors of Great Britain, arranged according to an alphabetical catalogue of their names ... London, Printed for R. Faulder, New Bond Street. Sold also by T. Egerton, Whitehall, and W. Richardson, Royal Exchange, 1798.

₁**Robertson, Robert T**   ₁

Handbook to the study of British Commonwealth literature in English ₁by Robert T. Robertson. Blacksburg, Va., 1968₁

63 l. 29 cm.

Sadkowski, Wacław.

Wśród książek z literatury angielskiej i amerykańskiej; poradnik bibliograficzny. Warszawa, Biblioteka Narodowa, 1971.

153 p. 21 cm.

At head of title: Biblioteka Narodowa. Instytut Bibliograficzny.

Sharp, Robert Farquharson, 1864–1945.

A dictionary of English authors, biographical and bibliographical. Being a compendious account of the lives and writings of upwards of 800 British and American writers from the year 1400 to the present time. New ed., rev., with an appendix bringing the whole up to date and including a large amount of new matter. Boston, Milford House ₁1972₁

363 p. 22 cm.

Reprint of the new ed., rev., 1904.

Walpole, Horace, 4th Earl of Orford, 1717–1797.

A catalogue of the royal and noble authors of England, Scotland, and Ireland. ₁Enl. and continued to the present time, by Thomas Park₁ New York, AMS Press ₁1971₁

5 v. illus. 23 cm.

Reprint of the 1806 ed.

CATALOGS

Harvard University. Library.

English literature. Cambridge; Distributed by the Harvard University Press, 1971.

4 v. 29 cm. (Its Widener Library shelflist, 35–38)

CONTENTS: v. 1. Classification schedule. Classified listing by call number.—v. 2. Chronological listing.—v. 3. Author and title listing, A–L.—v. 4. Author and title listing, M–Z.

Keats-Shelley Memorial, *Rome.*

Catalog of books and manuscripts at the Keats-Shelley Memorial House in Rome. Boston, G. K. Hall, 1969.

ix, 667 p. 27 cm.

Krishnamurti, G

The eighteen-nineties; ₁catalogue of₁ a literary exhibition, September 4–21 1973, compiled by G. Krishnamurti ₁for₁ the National Book League ₁and the₁ Francis Thompson Society. London, National Book League, 1973.

₁1₁, 204, ₁8₁ p. illus., facsims. 22 cm.

Library Resources, inc.

The microbook library of English literature; author catalog and title catalog. Chicago, 1972–

v. 30 cm.

CONTENTS: pt. 1. Beginnings to 1660.

————— Shelf list. Chicago, 1972–

v. 28 cm.

Library Resources, inc.

The microbook library of English literature, basic collection: author catalog and title catalog. Chicago ₁1972₁

171, 65 p. 29 cm.

Magee, David Bickersteth, 1905–

Victoria R. I.: a collection of books, manuscripts, autograph letters, original drawings, etc., by the lady herself and her loyal subjects, produced during her long and illustrious reign. San Francisco ₁1969–70₁

3 v. illus. 29 cm.

CONTENTS: pt. 1. A–J, with a preface by G. N. Ray.—pt. 2. K–Z, with a preface by R. L. Wolff.—pt. 3. Mixed pickles, with a preface by R. F. Metzdorf.

Moll, June (Madison) 1917–

British heritage; an exhibition of books, manuscripts & iconography from the collections at the University of Texas at Austin. ₁Austin, University of Texas, 1967₁

50 p. illus., facsims. 26 cm.

Catalog of an exhibition held at Dallas Public Library Oct. 9–21, 1967.

New York (City). Public Library. Berg Collection.

Dictionary catalog of the Henry W. and Albert A. Berg Collection of English and American literature. Boston, G. K. Hall, 1969.

5 v. 37 cm.

Appendices (v. 4, p. 511–v. 5):—I. Correspondents, A–Z.—II. Provenance, A–Z.

New York. Public Library. *Berg Collection.*
New in the Berg Collection, 1959–1961; an exhibition, by John D. Gordan. New York, New York Public Library, 1964.

36 p. facsims. 26 cm.

"Reprinted from the December 1963, January and February 1964 Bulletin of the New York Public Library."

New York (City). Public Library. Berg Collection.
New in the Berg Collection, 1970–1972, by Lola L. Szladits. ₍New York₎ New York Public Library ₍1973₎

64 p. illus. 24 cm.

"Catalogue of an exhibition from the Henry W. and Albert A. Berg Collection of English and American literature."

Rovaniemen kaupunginkirjasto.
English books ₍Rovaniemen kaupunginkirjasto, Lapin maakuntakirjasto₎. Rovaniemi, Rovaniemen kaupunginkirjasto. 1970.

₍45₎ p. 21 cm.

Selections from the library of William E. Stockhausen.
New York, The Grolier Club ₍1966₎

14 p. 28 cm.

Catalog of the exhibition held December 14, 1966, to January 13, 1967, in the Grolier Club.

HISTORY AND CRITICISM

Altick, Richard Daniel, 1915–
Selective bibliography for the study of English and American literature, by Richard D. Altick and Andrew Wright. 3d ed. New York, Macmillan ₍1967₎

xii, 152 p. 21 cm.

Alternate pages blank (p. 11–115)

Altick, Richard Daniel, 1915–
Selective bibliography for the study of English and American literature, by Richard D. Altick and Andrew Wright. 4th ed. New York, Macmillan ₍1971₎

xii, 164 p. 22 cm.

Alternate pages blank (p. 13–127)

Bell, Inglis Freeman, 1917–
Reference books in English literature; an annotated list of basic books for undergraduates ₍by₎ Inglis F. Bell, Joan Selby ₍and₎ Elizabeth Vogel. 2d prelim. ed. Vancouver, Humanities Division, University of British Columbia Library, 1962.

85 p. 23 cm.

Bell, Inglis Freeman, 1917–
A reference guide to English, American and Canadian literature; an annotated checklist of bibliographical and other reference materials ₍by₎ Inglis F. Bell ₍and₎ Jennifer Gallup. Vancouver, University of British Columbia Press ₍1971₎

xii, 139 p. 24 cm.

Bibliographies of studies in Victorian literature for the thirteen years 1932–1944. Edited by William D. Templeman. Compiled by Samuel P. Chew ₍and others₎ Urbana, University of Illinois Press, 1945. New York, Johnson Reprint Corp., 1971.

ix, 450 p. 24 cm.

A collection of annual bibliographies originally published in Modern philology.

Buckley, Jerome Hamilton.
Victorian poets and prose writers. Compiled by Jerome

H. Buckley. New York, Appleton-Century-Crofts ₍1966₎

viii, 63 p. 24 cm. (Goldentree bibliographies)

Cordasco, Francesco, 1920–
Eighteenth century bibliographies; handlists of critical studies relating to Smollett, Richardson, Sterne, Fielding, Dibdin, 18th century medicine, the 18th century novel, Godwin, Gibbon, Young, and Burke. To which is added John P. Anderson's Bibliography of Smollett. Metuchen, N. J., Scarecrow Press, 1970.

230 p. 22 cm.

The handlists were first published, 1047–50, in the author's Eighteenth century bibliographical pamphlets series. The bibliography by John P. Anderson (p. 207–230) was first published in 1887 in the Life of Tobias George Smollett, by David Hannay.

Gabler, Hans Walter, 1938–
English Renaissance studies in German, 1945–1967. A check-list of German, Austrian, and Swiss academic theses, monographs, and book publications on English language and literature, c. 1500–1650. Compiled at the Shakespeare Bibliothek München. Edited, with an introduction, English title versions, and an index in English, by Hans Walter Gabler. Heidelberg, Quelle & Meyer, 1971 ₍i. e. 1970₎

77 p. 23 cm. (Schriftenreihe der Deutschen Shakespeare-Gesellschaft West, n. F., Bd. 11)

Kennedy, Arthur Garfield, 1880–1954.
A concise bibliography for students of English, by Arthur G. Kennedy and Donald B. Sands. Rev. by William E. Colburn. 5th ed. Stanford, Calif., Stanford University Press, 1972.

xvi, 300 p. 23 cm.

Ward, William Smith, 1907–
Literary reviews in British periodicals, 1798–1820; a bibliography with a supplementary list of general (non-review) articles on literary subjects, compiled by William S. Ward. New York, Garland Pub., 1972.

2 v. (xix, 633 p.) 22 cm.

TRANSLATIONS

Dortmund. Stadtbücherei.
Englische Literatur der Gegenwart. Prosa, Drama, Lyrik, Schauspiel, Hörspiel. Ein Auswahlverzeichnis bearb. von Sylvia Schütze. Mit einem Beitrag von A. Norman Jeffares: Die moderne englische Literatur. Dortmund, Stadtbücherei, 1969.

viii, 127 p. 21 cm. (Völker im Spiegel der Literatur, Folge 13)

Harris, William James.
The first printed translations into English of the great foreign classics; a supplement to text-books of English literature, by William J. Harris. New York, B. Franklin ₍1970₎

vii, 209 p. 19 cm. (Essays in literature and criticism, 64)

Burt Franklin bibliography and reference series, 332.
Reprint of the 1909 ed.

ENGLISH POETRY   see   Poetry - Great Britain

ENTLEBUCH (REGION)

Emmenegger, Emil, 1890–
Das Schrifttum zur Geschichte und Heimatkunde der Landschaft Entlebuch. Gesammelt und geordnet von Emil Emmenegger. Abgeschlossen Dezember 1971. Schüpfheim, Buchdruckerei Schüpfheim AG, 1972.

344 p. 23 cm.

ENTOMOLOGY
   see also   Medical entomology

Abstracts of entomology. v. 1–
Apr. 1970–
₍Philadelphia₎ BioSciences Information Service of Biological Abstracts.

v. 28 cm. monthly.

Barcia, Dorothy R
Bibliography on insects destructive to flowers, cones, and seeds of North American conifers, by Dorothy R. Barcia ₍and₎ Edward P. Merkel. ₍Asheville, N. C., Southeastern Forest Experiment Station₎ 1972.
80 p. 27 cm. (USDA Forest Service research paper SE–92)

Bibliography of family Bruchidae (Coleoptera) ₍by₎ G. L. Arora ₍and others. Chandigarh, Dept. of Zoology, Panjab University₎ 1969.

81 p. 25 cm.

Cover title.
"Supplement to Research bulletin of the Panjab University, vol. 20, 1969."

Chamberlin, Willard Joseph, 1890–
Entomological nomenclature and literature, by W. J. Chamberlin. 3d ed., rev. and enl. Westport, Conn., Greenwood Press ₍1970, °1952₎

vii, 141 p. 29 cm.

Entomology abstracts.
London, Information Retrieval Ltd.

no. 23 cm. monthly.

Began in 1969. Cf. Brit. union-cat. of periodicals, Mar. 1970.

Gressitt, J Linsley.
Bibliography of New Guinea entomology, by J. L. Gressitt and J. J. H. Szent-Ivany. Honolulu, Entomology Dept., Bernice P. Bishop Museum, 1968.

674 p. 26 cm. (Pacific insects monograph, 18)

Lima, Angelo Moreira da Costa, 1887–
Quarto catálogo dos insetos que vivem nas plantas do Brasil, seus parasitos e predadores ₍por₎ Aristóteles Godofredo d'Araujo e Silva ₍et alii,₎ Rio de Janeiro, 1967–68.
2 v. in 3. 23 cm.

At head of title: Ministério da Agricultura. Departamento de Defesa e Inspeção Agropecuária. Servico de Defesa Sanitária Vegetal. Laboratório Central de Patologia Vegetal.
"Edicão ampliada do 3.° Catálogo dos insetos que vivem nas plantas do Brasil, de autoria de Prof. A. M. da Costa Lima."
CONTENTS.—pt. 1. Bibliografia entomológica brasileira. 2 v.—pt. 2. Insetos, hospedeiros e inimigos naturais.

Mickel, Clarence Eugene, 1892–
Two hundred years of Mutillidae research (Hymenoptera): an annotated bibliography ₍by₎ Clarence E. Mickel. ₍St. Paul₎ Agricultural Experiment Station, University of Minnesota, 1970.

77 p. 28 cm. (University of Minnesota. Agricultural Experiment Station. Technical bulletin, 271) (Scientific journal series, paper no. 6812)

Rivard, Irénée.
Synopsis et bibliographie annotée sur la mouche de la pomme, *Rhagoletis pomonella* (Walsh), diptères: tephritidae. ₍Québec?₎ Société entomologique du Québec, 1968.

158 p. 25 cm. (Mémoires de la Société entomologique du Québec, no 2)

Slater, James Alexander.
A catalogue of the Lygaeidae of the world. ₍Storrs, University of Connecticut₎ 1964.

2 v. (xviii, 1668 p.) 23 cm.

Smetana, Oldřich.
Entomologická bibliografie Československa, 1951–1960. 1. vyd. Praha, Academia, 1969.

329, ₍1₎ p. 25 cm.

PERIODICALS

Brussels. Institut royal des sciences naturelles de Belgique. *Service de documentation.*
Liste de périodiques d'entomologie. Lijst van entomologische periodieken. Bruxelles, 1966.

1 v. (unpaged) 21 cm.

Compiled by P. Doyen and J. L. J. Hulselmans.
"La liste est clôturée au 31 décembre 1964."

ENVIRONMENT
see also Ecology; Landscape protection

Bennett, Gary F
Environmental literature; a bibliography ₍by₎ Gary F. Bennett ₍and₎ Judith C. Bennett. ₍3d ed.₎ Park Ridge, N. J., Noyes Data Corp., 1973.

viii, 134 p. 25 cm.

Edition for 1969 published under title: Bibliography of books on the environment.

Dee, Sandra R
A basic environmental collection ₍by₎ Sandra R. Dee. Monticello, Ill., Council of Planning Librarians, 1973.

15 p. 28 cm. (Council of Planning Librarians. Exchange bibliography 410)

Dee, Sandra R
Corporations and the environment: PR or propaganda? A bibliography ₍by₎ Sandra R. Dee. Monticello, Ill., Council of Planning Librarians, 1973.

10 p. 28 cm. (Council of Planning Librarians. Exchange bibliography 411)

Dinsmore, John.
International environmental policy: an annotated bibliography of selected articles, reports, books, documents, etc., which present discussions of or viewpoints on the formulation of international environmental policy, with special emphasis on U. S. thought preliminary to and focused upon the United Nations Conference on the Human Environment, Stockholm, June 1972. Compiled by John Dinsmore. ₍Green Bay₎ University of Wisconsin-Green Bay, 1972.

20 p. 28 cm. (UWGB Library occasional infocompilation no. 2)

Environmental periodicals: Indexed articles titles. v. 1–

Mar. 1972–
Santa Barbara, Calif., International Academy at Santa Barbara.

v. 28 cm. monthly.

Great Britain. Dept. of the Environment. Library Services.
DOE annual list of publications. 1971–
London.

v. 30 cm.

Juris, Gail.
From now on ... an environmental bibliography, compiled and edited by Gail Juris and Margaret Medling. ₍St. Louis₎ 1970.

46 p. 29 cm. (Pius XII Library. Publication no. 2)

Meshenberg, Michael J
Environmental planning: a selected annotated bibliog-

raphy, by Michael J. Meshenberg. ₍Chicago, American Society of Planning Officials, °1970₎

ii, 78 p. 28 cm.

Organization for Economic Cooperation and Development. Library.
Environnement et urbanisation. Environment and urbanisation. ₍Paris, OCDE₎ 1970–

v. 27 cm. (Its Bibliographie spéciale analytique. Special annotated bibliography, 29

"This bibliography has been selected and annotated by Mrs. R. Tarr."

Schildhauer, Carole.
Environmental information sources: engineering and industrial applications; a selected annotated bibliography. New York, Special Libraries Association, 1972.

45 p. 28 cm.

"Prepared for The environmental and ecological literature—where does it all come from? A continuing education seminar held during the 63rd annual conference of the Special Libraries Association, June 4–8, 1972, Boston, Mass."

Sumek, Lyle.
Environmental management and politics: a selected bibliography. ₍DeKalb₎ Center for Governmental Studies, Northern Illinois University, 1973.

iii, 74 l. 28 cm.

United States. Dept. of the Interior. Office of Library Services. Information Services Division.
Readings for the eco-activist; a bibliography of selected environmental publications of the Executive Branch of the Federal Government. 2d ed. Washington, 1972.

i, 41 p. 26 cm.

United States. Environmental Protection Agency. Office of Research and Monitoring.
Bibliography of R & M research reports, by Publications Branch, Research Information Division. Washington, 1973.

iii, 82 p. 27 cm. (Socioeconomic environmental studies series, EPA–R5–73–012)

ENZYMES

Fishman, Myer M 1918–
Hyaluronidase; an annotated bibliography ₍by₎ Myer M. Fishman. River Edge, N. J., Technical Service Laboratories ₍1965–66₎

2 v. 28 cm.

CONTENTS.—₍pt. 1.₎ 1940–1955.—pt. 2. 1955–1966.

Hoijer, Dorothy Jared, 1905–
A bibliographic guide to neuroenzyme literature. New York, IFI/Plenum, 1969.

xxiii, 306 p. 29 cm.

"A Brain Research Institute publication, University of California, Los Angeles."

EPIDEMIOLOGY

Würzburg. Universität. Bibliothek.
Katalog der Sammlung Schoenlein. Catalog of the Schonleiniana Collection. Boston, G. K. Hall, 1972.

v, 543 p. 27 cm.

EPIGRAPHY see Inscriptions

EPILEPSY

Penry, J   Kiffin, 1929–
Epilepsy bibliography, 1900–1950, with key-word and author indexes. Edited by J. Kiffin Penry and Richard L. Rapport II. ₍Bethesda, Md., National Institutes of Health₎; for sale by the Supt. of Docs., U. S. Govt. Print. Off., Washington, 1973.

v, 840 p. 27 cm. (DHEW publication no. (NIH) 73–476)

EPISCOPACY

Guitard, André.
Bibliographie sur l'épiscopat (janvier 1966–décembre 1968), compilée par André Guitard et Rolland Litalien. Montréal, Office national du clergé, 1969.

116 p. 28 cm. (His Bibliographie sur le sacerdoce, 2)

EQUATIONS see Functional equations

EQUITY

Hague. Palace of Peace. Library.
Le rôle de l'équité en droit international : bibliographie = The role of equity in international law : bibliography / préparée par la Bibliothèque du Palais de la paix. — La Haye : Académie de droit international, Centre d'étude et de recherche, 1972.

10, 2 p. : 34 cm.

ERASMUS, DESIDERIUS

Brussels. Bibliothèque royale de Belgique.
Erasmus en België. (Tentoonstelling georganiseerd ter gelegenheid van de vijhonderdste verjaardag van Erasmus' geboorte. Brussel, Koninklijke Bibliotheek Albert I, van 4 juni tot 13 juli 1969. Leuven, Stadsmuseum, van 17 november tot 15 december 1969). Brussel, Koninklijke Bibliotheek Albert I (Keizerslaan 4₎ 1969.

xi, 101 p. illus., facsims., music. 23 cm. (Its Catalogus. Reeks in octavo, nr. 1)

At head of title: Interuniversitair Centrum voor Geschiedenis van het Humanisme.
Catalog edited by Marie-Thérèse Lenger.

Brussels. Bibliothèque royale de Belgique.
Érasme et la Belgique. (Exposition organisée à l'occasion du cinq centième anniversaire de la naissance d'Érasme. Bruxelles, Bibliothèque royale Albert Iᵉʳ, du 4 juin au 13 juillet 1969. Louvain, Musée de la ville, du 17 novembre au 15 décembre 1969). Bruxelles, Bibliothèque royale Albert Iᵉʳ ₍bd de l'Empereur, 4₎, 1969.

xi, 97 p. illus.. facsims., music. 23 cm. (Its Catalogue. Série in -8°, no 1)
At head of title: Centre interuniversitaire d'histoire de l'humanisme.
Catalog edited by Marie-Thérèse Lenger.
Label mounted on t. p.: Supplied by Worldwide Books, New York.

Centre universitaire de l'État à Mons. *Bibliothèque centrale.*
Éditions anciennes d'Érasme. Exposition organisée dans les salons de l'Hôtel de ville, (Mons, du 26 au 29 octobre 1967), à l'occasion du cinquième centenaire de la naissance d'Érasme. Catalogue rédigé par Roland Crahay. Préface de Léon-E. Halkin. Mons, Centre universitaire de l'État, 1967.

71 p. facsims. 23 cm.

At head of title: Bibliothèque centrale universitaire de Mons.

Devereux, E   J
A checklist of English translations of Erasmus to 1700, by E. J. Devereux. Oxford, Oxford Bibliographical Society, 1968.

viii, 40 p. 25 cm. (₁Oxford Bibliographical Society₁ Occasional publication no. 8)

Erasme, l'Alsace, et son temps. Catalogue de l'exposition réalisée à la Bibliothèque nationale et universitaire de Strasbourg, et Communications de Jean-Claude Margolin, Otto Herding, et Jean Lebeau au colloque organisé par l'Université de Strasbourg (20 novembre 1970). Strasbourg, Palais de l'Université ₁1971₁

143 p. illus., fold. map. 24 cm. (Publications de la Société savante d'Alsace et des régions de l'Est. Collections Recherches et documents, t. 8)

"Exposition ... 21 novembre–18 décembre 1970."

Erasmus en Leuven. (In het kader van de Nederlandse Universitaire Week te Leuven ingericht door de Katholieke Universiteit te Leuven, in samenwerking met de Stad Leuven). Leuven, Stedelijk Museum, 17 nov.–15 dec. 1969. (Catalogus. Redactie: Jan Roegiers. Medewerkers: Antoon De Smet, Alfons De Witte, Edward De Maesschalck ₁e. a.₁). ₁Leuven, Stedelijk Museum, Savoyestraat 6₁, 1969.

456 p. ports., illus., facsims. 28 cm.

At head of title: Tentoonstelling.

Erasmus en zijn tijd. ₁Catalogus van de₁ tentoonstelling ₁in het₁ Museum Boymans-van Beuningen, Rotterdam, 3 oktober–23 november 1969 ingericht ter herdenking van de geboorte, 500 jaar geleden, van Erasmus te Rotterdam in de nacht van 27 op 28 oktober. ₁Samengesteld door J. Besse, N. van der Blom, C. J. du Ry van Beest Holle, J. C. M. van Geest, E. van Gulik, H. R. Hoetink, Josèphe Jacquiot, J. Kluiver, C. W. de Kruyter en C. Reedijk. Inleidingen van J. C. Ebbinge Wubben, René Maheu en S. Dresden. Rotterdam, Museum Boymans-van Beuningen (Mathenesserlaan 18–20), 1969₁.

2 v. with illus. 24 cm.

Gerlo, Aloïs. Répertoire des lettres traduites d'Érasme, par Aloïs Gerlo. Avec la collaboration de Frans De Raeve. Bruxelles, Presses universitaires de Bruxelles, (1969).

59 p. 24 cm. (Université libre de Bruxelles. Travaux de l'Institut pour l'étude de la Renaissance et de l'humanisme. Instrumenta humanistica, 2)

Gerlo, Aloïs. Répertoire des lettres traduites d'Érasme, par Aloïs Gerlo avec la collaboration de Frans de Raeve. Québec, Presses de l'Université Laval, 1969.

59 p. 24 cm.

Harvard University. *Library. Houghton Library.* Erasmus; on the 500th anniversary of his birth. Cambridge, Mass., 1969.

vii, 38 p. illus. 23 cm.

Machiels, Jérome. Erasmus. Tentoonstelling van Erasmusdrukken bewaard in de Universiteitsbibliotheek te Gent, ingericht ter gelegenheid van het Erasmusjaar 1969. Gent, 4–20 juni 1969. Gent ₁Rijksuniversiteit te Gent, Sint-Pietersnieuwstraat 25₁ 1969 ₁1970₁.

xiii, 108 p. 23 cm. (Werken uitg. door het Rectoraat van de Rijksuniversiteit Gent, no. 25)

Margolin, Jean Claude. Quatorze années de bibliographie érasmienne, 1936–1949 ... Paris, J. Vrin, 1969.

431 p. table. 25 cm. (De Pétrarque à Descartes, 21)

EREWANI PETAKAN HAMALSARAN

Erewani Petakan Hamalsaran. Gitakan Gradaran.
Երևանի Պետական Համալսարանի Հրատարակություն-

ների բիբլիոգրաֆիա, 1922–1963։ ₁Կազմող Լ. Ա. Գասպար-
յան₁ Երևան, Միտք Հրատկ., 1964։

293 p. 23 cm.

At head of title: Երևանի Պետական Համալսարան։ Գիտական Գրադարան։

Cover title: Բիբլիոգրաֆիա Երևանի Պետական Համալսարանի Հրատարակությունների

Added t. p.: Библиография издании Ереванского государственного университета, 1922–1963.

Armenian and Russian.

ERFURT, GERMANY

Rothe, Hans Werner, 1906–
Stadtkernforschung in Erfurt. Ein Literaturbericht. (Frankfurt a. M., Dr. Rothe, 1968.)

7 p. with illus. 21 cm.

ERIE, LAKE

Water Resources Scientific Information Center. Lake Erie, a bibliography. Washington ₁1972₁

iv, 240 p. 27 cm. (Its Bibliography series, WRSIC 72–209)

ERITREA

al-As'ad, Rashīd Jabr.
ثبت المصادر العربية عن القضية الارتيرية ₁sic₁ تأليف رشيد
جبر الاسعد. ₁الطبعة 1₁ بغداد، مطبعة الازهر، 1968.

30 p. 22 cm.

EROSION CONTROL see Soil conservation

EROTICA

see also Condemned books; Obscenity

Ashbee, Henry Spencer, 1834–1900.
A complete guide to forbidden books, by Henry Spencer Ashbee (Pisanus Fraxi) Edited by E. S. Sullivan. Introd. by Robert Kramer. North Hollywood, Calif., Brandon House ₁1966₁

447 p. 17 cm. (A Brandon House library edition, 2013)

Ashbee, Henry Spencer, 1834–1900.
Forbidden books of the Victorians: Henry Spencer Ashbee's bibliographies of erotica. ₁Abridged ed.₁; abridged and edited, with an introduction and notes, by Peter Fryer. London, Odyssey Press Ltd., 1970.

₁8₁, 239 p. 25 cm. Index.

Abridged edition of Index librorum prohibitorum.

Bonhomme, Jacques. L'Art érotique, voluptés sensuelles, livres, gravures, photographies obscènes ... Paris, l'Or du temps, ₁51, rue de l'Échiquier,₁ 1970.

99 p. 21 cm.

Damon, Gene. The lesbian in literature, a bibliography ₁by Gene Damon and Lee Stuart₁ San Francisco, Daughters of Bilitis ₁°1967₁

79 p. 22 cm.

Hayn, Hugo, 1843–1923.
Bibliotheca Germanorum erotica & curiosa; Verzeichnis der gesamten deutschen erotischen Literatur mit Einschluss der Übersetzungen, nebst Beifügung der Originale. Hrsg. von Hugo Hayn und Alfred N. Gotendorf. Hanau/M., Müller & Kiepenheuer ₁1968₁

9 v. 25 cm.

Vol. 9 edited by P. Englisch.

Reprint of 3d ed. published in Munich by G. Müller, 1912–29.
First–2d. ed. published under title: Bibliotheca Germanorum erotica.

Hayn, Hugo, 1843–1923.
Drei erotische Bibliographien. (Unveränd. fotomech. Nachdr. d. Orig.Ausg. 1886–1890.) ₁Leipzig₁ Zentralanti-quariat d. Deutschen Demokratischen Republik, 1972.

3 v. in 1. 21 cm.

CONTENTS: Bibliotheca Germanorum nuptalis. — Bibliotheca Germanorum gynaecologica et cosmetica. — Bibliotheca erotica et curiosa Monacensis.

Hayn, Hugo, 1843–1923.
Vier neue Curiositäten-Bibliographieen. Bayerischer Hiesel. Amazonen-Litteratur. Halsbandprozess und Cag-liostro. Bibliotheca selecta erotico-curiosa Dresdensis. Sämtliche zum ersten Male übersichtlich zusammengese-stellt. (Unveränderter fotomechanischer Nachdruck der Originalausgabe.) Jena, Schmidt, 1905. (Leipzig, Zentral-Antiquariat der DDR, 1967.)

88 p. 21 cm.

Hoffmann, Frank.
Analytical survey of Anglo-American traditional erotica. Bowling Green, Ohio, Bowling Green University Popular Press ₁1973₁

x, 309 p. 24 cm.

Saitō, Yozue, 1914–

斎藤　俊居

大正
昭和　艶本資料の探究

東京　芳賀書店　昭和44（1969）

382p　20 cm

Stern, Bernhard, 1867–1927.
Bibliotheca curiosa et erotica. ₁Von₁ Bernhard Stern-Szana. (Unveränderter photomechanischer Nachdruck nach der Privatdruck-Aufl. Wien 1921.) (₁Magstadt/Württ.₁ Bissinger ₁1967₁.)

247 p. with illus. 22 cm.

BIBLIOGRAPHIES

Deakin, Terence J
Catalogi librorum eroticorum; a critical bibliography of erotic bibliographies and book-catalogues, compiled by Terence J. Deakin. London, C. & A. Woolf, 1964.

xii, 28 p. 22 cm.

ESCHWEGE, GERMANY

Oppitz, Ulrich-Dieter.
Aufstellung von Eschwege—Stadt und Kreis—betreffender Literatur. Mit Angabe von Standorten. Ein Beginn. Stand: 15. 1. 1965. Eschwege, 1965.

102 l. 21 x 30 cm.

ESENIN, SERGEĬ ALEKSANDROVICH

Karpov, Evgeniĭ Leonidovich.
С. А. Есенин; библиографический справочник. Москва, Высшая школа, 1966.

160 p. 20 cm.

At head of title: Е. Л. Карпов.

Karpov, Evgenii Leonidovich.
(S. A. Esenin)
С. А. Есенин. Библиогр. справочник. Изд. _.е, доп. и испр. Москва, "Высш. школа," 1972.

239 p. 20 cm.

At head of title: Е. Л. Карпов.

ESKIMO NEWSPAPERS see Periodical publications - Greenland

ESKIMOS

Arora, Ved Parkash.
Eskimos; a bibliography ₁compiled by Ved P. Arora₁ Regina, Sask., Bibliographic Services Division, Provincial Library, 1972.

50 p. 22 cm.

Carney, R   J
A selected and annotated bibliography on the sociology of Eskimo education, prepared by R. J. Carney and W. O. Ferguson. With a foreword by B. Y. Card. Edmonton, Published ₁by₁ the Boreal Institute with the Dept. of Educational Foundations, University of Alberta, °1965.

v, 59 l. 28 cm. (University of Alberta. Boreal Institute. Occasional publication, no. 2)

Name of series changed from Occasional paper by mounted slip.

Hippler, Arthur E
Eskimo acculturation; a selected annotated bibliography of Alaskan and other Eskimo acculturation studies, by Arthur E. Hippler. College, Institute of Social, Economic and Government Research, University of Alaska, 1970.

vi, 200 p. 28 cm. (University of Alaska. ISEGR no. 28)

Title on spine: Alaskan and other Eskimo acculturation.

Ontario. *Education Dept.*
Multi-media resource list: Eskimos and Indians. ₁Toronto₁ 1969.

50 p. 28 cm.

VanStone, James W
An annotated ethnohistorical bibliography of the Nushagak River region, Alaska ₁by₁ James W. VanStone. ₁Chicago₁ Field Museum of Natural History, 1968.

149–189 p. 24 cm. (Fieldiana: Anthropology, v. 54, no. 2)

₁Field Museum of Natural History, Chicago₁ Publication 1040.

ESPERANTO

Nederlandse Esperantisten-Vereniging La Estonto Estas Nia.
Esperanto. Catalogus van de boekerij der Nederlandse Esperantisten-Vereniging "La Estonto estas Nia" en van de Esperanto-collectie in de Universiteitsbibliotheek. Amsterdam ₁Singel 423,₁ Universiteitsbibliotheek, 1969, ₁1970₁.
2 v. 24 cm. (Catalogi kunsttalen, no. 1–2) (Universiteitsbibliotheek van Amsterdam. Speciale catalogi, nieuwe series. no. 5)

CONTENTS: 1 deel ₁2326 boeknummers.₁—2. deel. Tijdschriften en serietitels.

Oslo. *Universitet. Bibliotek.*
Katalog over interlingvistisk litteratur i Universitetsbiblioteket i Oslo. Utarb. av Tom Arbo Høeg. Utg. av Studentenes Esperanto-forening. Oslo, 1973.

88 p. 23 cm.

Vienna. *Internacia Esperanto-Muzeo.*
Alfabeta a katalogo pri la kolektoj de Internacia Esperanto-Muzeo en Wien. Verkita de Hugo Steiner. Wein, 1969–

v. 29 cm.

CONTENTS: parto 1. Literoj A–L de la verkoj troveblaj en la biblioteko, escepte la gazetojn.

ESSEN, GERMANY

Essener Bibliographie. 1969–
Essen, Stadtbibliothek.

v. 22 cm. annual.

Vols. for 1969– published by the body under its variant form of name: Stadtbibliothek Essen.

ESSEX, ENGLAND

Emmison, Frederick George, 1907–
Guide to the Essex Record Office, by F. G. Emmison. 2nd ed. revised. Chelmsford, Essex County Council, 1969.

vii, 251 p. 26 cm. (Essex Record Office publications, no. 51)

ESSEX COUNTY, NEW JERSEY

Baldwin-Scarborough, Mayra.
Bicentennial bibliography, Essex County, New Jersey, 1973; basic history sources for boroughs, cities, towns, townships, and villages of Essex County, New Jersey, as selected by librarians from the public libraries. Mayra Baldwin-Scarborough, editor. ₍Nutley, N. J., American Revolution Bicentennial Committee, Special Libraries Association, N. J. Chapter, 1973₎

1 v. (unpaged) 30 cm.

"The Essex County ID & beyond ₍slide program₎ by Mayra Baldwin-Scarborough" inserted at end.

ESTONIA
see also under Livonia

Estonian S. S. R. *Riiklik Ajaloo Keskarhiiv.*
Центральный государственный исторический архив Эстонской ССР; путеводитель. ₍Под общей ред. Н. В. Бржостовской₎ Москва—Тарту, 1969.

387 p. 23 cm.

At head of title: Главное архивное управление при Совете Министров СССР. Центральный государственный исторический архив Эстонской ССР. Архивное управление при Совете Министров Эстонской ССР.

Palli, Heldur.
Eesti ajaloolise demograafia bibliograafia. ₍Koostanud H. Palli ja R. Pullat₎ Tallinn, 1969.
131 p. 20 cm. (Töid ajaloolise demograafia alalt)

At head of title: Eesti NSV Teaduste Akadeemia Ajaloo Instituut.
Added t. p.: Estonian historical demography bibliography. Библиография по исторической демографии Эстонии.
English, Estonian, and Russian.

Ränk, Aino.
A bibliography of works published by Estonian historians in exile 1945–1969; history, archaeology, history of art, music, the Church and law. Stockholm, Institutum Litterarum Estonicum, 1969.

56 p. 21 cm. (Institutum Litterarum Estonicum. Folia bibliographica, 2)

ESTONIAN IMPRINTS

Bibliograafianimestike loetelu 1965–1968. ₍Koostajad: L. Ploompuu, L. Vilmre ja V. Ennosaar₎ Tallinn, Eesti Raamat, 1971.
22 p. 22 cm.
At head of title: Eesti NSV Ministrite Nõukogu Riiklik Kirjastuskomitee. Eesti NSV Riiklik Raamatupalat.
Added t. p. in Russian: Указатель библиографических пособий 1965–1968.
"Jätkab ... Fr. R. Kreutzwaldi nimelise ENSV Riikliku Raamatukogu poolt 1961.–1964. aasta kohta väljaantud aastaraamatuid 'Bibliograafiliste nimestike bibliograafia.' "

Eerme, Karl.
Eesti raamatu aupäev. 6. dets. 1970 Torontos, Eesti

Majas; raamatute, trükiste ja eksliibriste näituse kataloog. ₍Koostanud K. Eerme. Toronto, Eesti Kultuurikogu Kanadas, 1970₎

20 p. 22 cm. (Eesti Kultuurikogu Kanadas väljaanne nr. 1)

Kangro, Bernard, 1910–
Eesti kirjandus vabas maailmas. Bibliograafiline ülevaade 1944–1965. Lund, Eesti kirjanike kooperativ, 1966.

32 p. 22 cm.

Kangro, Bernard, 1910–
Eesti raamat vabas maailmas. Bibliograafiline ülevaade 1944–1970. Lund, Eesti Kirjanike Kooperativ, 1971.

40 p. 22 cm.

Kuldkepp, E
Nõukogude Eesti raamat 1955–1965; koondnimestik. ₍Koostajad: E. Kuldkepp ja P. Toovere₎ Tallinn, Eesti Raamat, 1972.

1008 p. 22 cm.

Added t. p.: Книга советской Эстонии 1955–1965.
Estonian and Russian.
At head of title: Eesti NSV Ministrite Nõukogu, Riiklik Kirjastuskomittee; Eesti NSV Riiklik Raamatupalat.

Stockholm. Kungliga Biblioteket.
Estniska böcker utanför Estland. Arrangörer: Kungliga Biblioteket och Estniksa kultursamfundet. Stockholm, 1966.

46 p. illus. 23 cm. (*Its* Utställningskatalog nr. 41)

ESTONIAN LITERATURE

Kabur, Vaime.
Eesti kirjandus, kirjandusteadus ja kriitika, 1963–1966; bibliograafia. ₍Koostajad: V. Kabur ja O. Kivi₎ Tallinn, Eesti Raamat, 1968.

305 p. 21 cm.

Kangro, Bernard, 1910–
Den estniska boken i den fria världen. Bibliografisk översikt 1944–1965. ₍Utg. av₎ Estniska kultursamfundet. Stockholm, 1966.

32 p. 22 cm.

Translation of Eesti raamat vabas maailmas.

TRANSLATIONS

Kivi, O
Эстонская художественная литература, фольклор и критика на русском и других языках народов СССР 1956–1965. Библиография. Таллин, "Ээсти раамат," 1968.

519 p. 20 cm.

Püss, L
Nõukogude Eesti tõlkekirjandus 1940–1968; bibliograafiline nimestik ₍koostanud L. Püss₎ Tallinn, Eesti Raamat, 1970.

310 p. 23 cm.

Estonian and Russian.
Added t. p.: Переводная литература, изданная в Эстонской ССР.

ESTONIAN PHILOLOGY

Ränk, Aino.
A bibliography of works published by Estonian philologists in exile 1944–1970: linguistics, history of literature, theatre. Stockholm, 1971.

117 p. 21 cm. (Institutum Litterarum Estonicum. Folia bibliographica, 3)

ESZTERGOM, HUNGARY (ARCHDIOCESE)

Hungary. Országos Levéltár. Filmtár.
Az Esztergomi Római Katolikus Főegyházmegye anyakönyveinek mikrofilmjei az Országos Levéltár Filmtárában; tematikai konspektus. Készítette: Mandl Sándorné. Budapest, Művelődesügyi Minisztérium Levéltári Osztálya, 1964.

iii, 98 p. 28 cm. (Levéltári leltárak, 30)

Summary in French and Russian.

ETHICS see Business ethics; Communist ethics; Professional ethics

ETHIOPIA
see also under Italy *(Valley);*
Tunisia

Baylor, Jim.
Ethiopia, a list of works in English. ₁Berkeley? Calif.₁ 1966.

60, ₁5₁ l. 28 cm.

Baylor, Jim.
Ethiopia, a list of works in English. ₁2d ed. Berkeley? Calif.₁ 1967.

60, 10 l. 28 cm.

Bibliography of Ethiopia. With an introd. by H. E. Ato Ketema Yifru. Addis Ababa ₁Ministry of Foreign Affairs₁ 1968.

46 p. col. port. 19 cm.

Foreword signed: Press and Information Department, Ministry of Foreign Affairs.

Cohen, John M
A select bibliography on rural Ethiopia. Compiled by: John M. Cohen. Addis Ababa, Haile Sellassie I University Library, 1971.

82 p. 29 cm. (Ethiopian bibliographical series, no. 4)

Delaney, Annette.
Ethiopian survey; a selected bibliography. Washington, African Bibliographic Center ₁1964₁

12 l. 28 cm. (African Bibliographic Center. Special bibliographic series, v. 2, no. 1)

Fumagalli, Giuseppe, 1863–1939.
Bibliografia etiopica; catalogo descrittivo e ragionato degli scritti pubblicati dalla invenzione della stampa fino a tutto il 1891 intorno alla Etiopia e regioni limitrofe. Milano, Ulrico Hoepli, 1893. ₁Farnborough, Gregg, 1971₁

xi, 288 p. 23 cm.

Sequel: Bibliografia etiopica, by Silvio Zanutto.

Marcus, Harold G
The modern history of Ethiopia and the horn of Africa: a select and annotated bibliography, by Harold G. Marcus. Stanford, Calif., Hoover Institution Press ₁1972₁

xxii, 641 p. 29 cm. (Hoover Institution bibliographical series, 56)

Sergew Hable Selassie, 1929–
Bibliography of ancient and medieval Ethiopian history. Addis Ababa, Printed in Star Print. Press, 1969.

76 p. 25 cm.

Sommer, John W
A study guide for Ethiopia and the Horn of Africa, by John W. Sommer. ₁Boston, African Studies Center, Boston University₁ 1969.

iv, 94 p. 28 cm.

On cover: Development Program.

Vitale, Charles S
Bibliography on the climate of Ethiopia—includes the province of Eritrea, by Charles S. Vitale. Silver Spring, Md., U. S. Environmental Data Service; ₁available from the Clearinghouse for Federal Scientific and Technical Information, Springfield, Va.₁ 1968.

v, 98 p. map. 27 cm. (Environmental Data Service. WB/BC-100)

Wright, Stephen G
Ethiopian incunabula, compiled by Stephen Wright from the collections in the National Library of Ethiopia and the Haile Sellassie I University. ₁Addis Ababa, Commercial Print. Press₁ 1967.

107 p. 24 cm.

English and Amharic.

ETHNIC GROUPS see Minorities

ETHNIC PRESS

Wynar, Lubomyr Roman, 1932–
Encyclopedic directory of ethnic newspapers and periodicals in the United States ₁by₁ Lubomyr R. Wynar. Littleton, Colo., Libraries Unlimited, 1972.

260 p. 24 cm.

ETHNOLOGY see Anthropology

ETHNOMUSICOLOGY

Musikethnologische Jahresbibliographie Europas. Annual bibliography of European ethnomusicology. 1– 1966– Bratislava ₁Slovenské národné múzeum₁

v. 21 cm.

Nettl, Bruno, 1930–
Reference materials in ethnomusicology; a bibliographic essay. 2d ed., rev. Detroit, Information Coordinators, 1967.

xv, 40 p. 23 cm. (Detroit studies in music bibliography, no. 1)

ETIKHOVE, BELGIUM

Belgium. Archives de l'État, Renaix, Belgium.
Klapper op de minuten van staten van goed, rekeningen, verdelingen, verkavelingen, likwidaties van Etikhove, berustend op het Rijksarchief Ronse ₁door₁ P. van Butsele. Handzame, Familia et Patria, 1972.

281 p. 25 cm.

EUCALYPTUS

Marris, Bernice.
A bibliography of Australian references on eucalypts, 1956–June 1966. Canberra, Forestry and Timber Bureau, 1966.

x, 90 p. 21 cm.

Marris, Bernice.
A bibliography of Australian references to eucalypts, July 1966–1968. Compiled by Bernice Marris and the library staff, Division of Forest Products, C. S. I. R. O. Canberra. Dept. of National Development, Forestry and Timber Bureau, 1970.

40 p. 21 cm.

EUCLIDES

Duarte, Francisco José, 1883–
Bibliografía: Euclides, Arquímedes, Newton [por] F. J. Duarte. Caracas, 1967.

163 p. illus., facsims., ports. 23 cm. [Biblioteca de la Academia de Ciencias Físicas, Matemáticas y Naturales, v. 2]

EULER, LEONHARD

Леонард Эйлер; переписка. Аннотированный указатель. [Составители: Т. Н. Кладо и др. Под ред. В. И. Смирнова и А. П. Юшкевича] Ленинград, Наука; Ленинградское отд-ние, 1967.

390 p. 27 cm.

At head of title: Академия наук СССР. Институт истории естествознания и техники.
On verso of t. p.: Leonhard Eulers Briefwechsel.
Preface also in German.

EURASIANS

Van der Veur, Paul W
The Eurasians of Indonesia; a political-historical bibliography. Compiled by Paul W. van der Veur. Ithaca, N. Y., Modern Indonesia Project, Cornell University, 1971.

viii, 115 p. 28 cm. (Cornell University. Modern Indonesia Project. Bibliography series)

EURE, FRANCE (DEPT.)

L'Eure et l'invasion prussienne: 1870–1871, exposition documentaire, 7 novembre 1970–26 mars 1971. Archives départementales de l'Eure. Service éducatif. [Évreux. Catalogue par Marie-Thérèse Jouvin, le Dr Marc A. Dollfus et Georges Flamichaux; préfaces par Jeanne Albertini et Georges Merlier]. [Évreux]. Archives départementales de l'Eure. 1970.
xix, 30 p., [8] l. ill. 30 cm.

"Exposition organisée par: ... Ivan Cloulas ... Jeanne Albertini ... Georges Merlier."

EURE-ET-LOIR, FRANCE (DEPT.)

Merlet, Lucien Victor Claude, 1827–1898.
Bibliothèque chartraine antérieure au XIX⁶ siècle. Genève, Slatkine Reprints, 1971.

446 p. 22 cm.

"Réimpression de l'édition d'Orléans, 1882."

EUROPE

Blake, Judith.
Western European censuses, 1960; an English language guide [by] Judith Blake [and] Jerry J. Donovan. Berkeley, Institute of International Studies, University of California [1971]

v, 421 p. 24 cm. (Population monograph series, no. 8)

Boscaro, Adriana.
Sixteenth century European printed works on the first Japanese mission to Europe. A descriptive bibliography. Leiden, Brill, 1973.

xix, 196 p. with illus. 25 cm.

English and French, German or Latin.

Council of Europe. *Council for Cultural Co-operation.*
Bibliographie d'ouvrages sur l'Europe, à l'intention des enseignants. Strasbourg, Conseil de l'Europe, 1965.

68 p. 20 cm.

At head of title: Conseil de la coopération culturelle du Conseil de l'Europe.
Issued also under title: Books dealing with Europe.

Council of Europe. *Council for Cultural Co-operation.*
Books dealing with Europe; bibliography for teachers. Strasbourg, 1965.

67 p. 21 cm.

European Cultural Centre.
The European bibliography. Editors: Hjalmar Pehrsson and Hanna Wulf. Leyden, A. W. Sijthoff, 1965.

viii, 472 p. 25 cm.

French and English.

European demographic information bulletin. v. 1–1970–
The Hague, M. Nijhoff.

v. 24 cm.

Issued by European Centre for Population Studies.

Harvey, Joan M
Statistics Europe: sources for market research [by] Joan M. Harvey. Beckenham (eKnt), CBD Research Ltd., 1968.

[177] p. 30 cm.

Harvey, Joan M
Statistics Europe: sources for market research, [by] Joan M. Harvey. 2nd ed.; revised and enlarged. Beckenham (154 High St., Beckenham, Kent): C. B. D. Research Ltd, 1972.

255 p. 30 cm. (A CBD research publication)

Informationsquellen zur europäischen Wirtschaft = Sources of European economic information = Guide des sources d'information economique en Europe. — Frankfurt (a. M.), New York : Herder und Herder, 1974.

343 p. ; 31 cm.

English, French and German.

Inglezi, Raisa Markovna.
Мыслители и революционеры. Европа и Америка. XVII–XIX вв. Рек. указатель литературы. Москва, "Книга," 1970.

64 p. 20 cm. (Страницы биографий)

At head of title: Государственная публичная историческая библиотека РСФСР. Р. М. Инглези и Б. А. Каменецкий.

James Ford Bell Library.
A list of additions. 1965/69–
Minneapolis, University of Minnesota Press.

v. 26 cm.

Continues the James Ford Bell Collection, a list of additions issued by the library under its earlier name: Minnesota. University. Library. James Ford Bell Collection.

Lintonen, Raimo.
Bibliografia Euroopan turvallisuutta ja Euroopan turvallisuuskokousta käsittelevästä kirjallisuudesta ja artikkeleista. Bibliography of books and articles on European security and security conference. Kirj. Raimo Lintonen ja Riitta Suominen. [Helsinki, 1969–
v. 30 cm. (Info: Ulkopoliittisen Instituutin monistesarja, 1969:8)
English and Finnish.

Meyer, José Maria.
Official publications of European governments: an outline bibliography of serials and important monographs, including diplomatic documents, issued by European government offices and ministries: Albania, Austria, Belgium, Bulgaria, Czechoslovakia, Denmark, Esthonia, Finland, France. Compiled by José Meyer. New York, B. Franklin [1971]

vi, 255 p. 24 cm. (Burt Franklin research and source works series 444. Selected essays in history, economics and social science 67)

A revision of the mimeographed list of "Official publications of European governments" issued by the American Library in Paris, Reference Service on International Affairs, in 1926.

Reprint of the 1929 ed.

Mikulecká, Magda, *comp.*
Turistickí sprievodcovia Univerzitnej knižnice v Bratislave, 1963–1966; odporúčajúca bibliografia. Zostavila Magda Mikulecká. Bratislava, 1967.

101 p. 28 cm.

At head of title: Univerzitná knižnica v Bratislave.

Moscow. Publichnaia biblioteka.
Страны Европы; рекомендательный указатель литературы. ₁Н. А. Беспалова, С. М. Воякина. Под ред. А. М. Горбунова₁ Москва, Книга, 1965–

v. 22 cm.

At head of title, v. 1– : Государственная библиотека СССР имени В. И. Ленина.

Contents.—ч. 1. Социалистические страны.

Price, Glanville.
The present position of minority languages in Western Europe: a selective bibliography. Cardiff, University of Wales P., 1969.

81 p. 21 cm.

U. S. *Library of Congress. European Affairs Division.*
Introduction to Europe; a selective guide to background reading ₁Compiled by Helen F. Conover of the staff₁ New York, Greenwood Press ₁1968₁

v, 201 p. 27 cm.

Reprint of the 1950 ed.

Vienna. Hochschule für Welthandel. *Bibliothek.*
Zusammenstellung der von der Bibliothek erworbenen Literatur für Ost- und Südostwirtschaft. Vom 1. Jänner 1963–31. Dezember 1965. Wien ₁1966₁.

12 p. 30 cm.

ECONOMIC AND POLITICAL COOPERATION
see also European Economic Community;
European Free Trade Association

Bildungswerk Europäische Politik.
Bibliographie zur europäischen Integration. 2., revidierte und erweiterte Aufl. Auswahl und Kommentierung von Gerda Zellentin, unter Mitarbeit von Elisabeth Y. de Koster. ₁Köln, Europa-Union Verlag, 1965₁

209 p. 22 cm.

Bildungswerk Europäische Politik.
Bibliographie zur europäischen Integration. Begr. von Gerda Zellentin. (Hrsg. vom Bildungswerk Europ. Politik.) 3., rev. u. erw. Aufl. von Petra Buchrucker unter Mitarb. von Gunhild Holtmann. Köln, Europa-Union-Verl. (1970).

299 p. 21 cm.

Böttcher, Winfried.
Britische Europaideen, 1940–1970. Great Britain and Europe. La Grande Bretagne et l'Europe. Eine Bibliographie. Hrsg. von Winfried Böttcher. Mit einem Vorwort von Klaus Mehnert. Bearb. von Winfried Böttcher, Jürgen Jansen ₁und₁ Friedrich Welsch. Düsseldorf, Droste ₁c1971–

v. 23 cm.

CONTENTS: Bd. 1. Bücher und Broschüren.

California. State College, *San Diego. Library.*
Bibliography on European integration; list of the books, documents, and periodicals on European integration in San Diego State College Library. Compiled by Andrew Szabo and Walter H. Posner. San Diego, 1967.

62 p. 22 cm.

First published in 1965 under title: Bibliography on the economic and political integration of Europe.

California. State College, *San Diego. Library.*
Bibliography on the economic and political integration of Europe. Compiled by Andrew Szabo, social sciences librarian, and Walter H. Posner, assistant catalog librarian. San Diego, 1965.

47 p. 28 cm.

Chiti-Batelli, Andrea.
Les assemblées européennes. Bibliographie analitique ₁sic₁ ... Roma, Istituto affari internazionali, 1968.

liii, 153 p. 27½ cm. (Istituto affari internazionali. Documentazioni, n. 14. Problemi dell'Europa comunitaria)

Added t. p.: Vingt ans de parlementarisme continental. Bibliographie analytique des assemblées européennes. Précédée d'un essai sur la nature juridique et la signification politique de ces assemblées.

Commission of the European Communities.
Catalogue des publications, 1952–1971. Bruxelles, 1972–

v. 25 cm.

At head of title: Communautés européennes.
"Bulletin des Communautés européennes. Supplément hors série."

Commission of the European Communities.
List of the publications of the European Communities in English; supplement to the French edition of the Catalogue of publications of the European Communities, 1952–1971 (1972). ₁Brussels?₁ 1972.

127 p. 26 cm.

"Provisional edition."
"An extract from the French edition of the Catalogue of publications ₁of the European Communities₁ 1952–1971, vol. 1."

Commission of the European Communities.
List of the publications of the European Communities in English; supplement to the French edition of the "Catalogue of publications of the European Communities, 1952–1971" ₁1972₁. ₁Brussels₁ 1972.

135 p. 25 cm.

"Provisional edition."
"Extract from the French edition of the Catalogue of publications 1952–1971, vol. 1."

Cosgrove, Carol Ann.
A readers' guide to Britain and the European communities. London, P. E. P., 1970.

106 p. 22 cm. Index. (European series, no. 14)

Ekonomická integrace socialistických a kapitalistických zemí. čís. 32–
1. čtvrtletí 1971–
Praha, Státní knihovna ČSSR, Ústřední ekonomická knihovna.

no. 29 cm. quarterly.

"Výběrová bibliografie."
Continues Západoevropská ekonomická integrace.
"Rozmnoženo pro vnitřní potřebu."

Germany (*Federal Republic, 1949–) Bundestag. Wissenschaftliche Abteilung.*
Europäische Integration. Auswahlbibliographie. (Von ₁ünter₁ Hindrichs unter Mitarbeit von Anni Storbeck bearb.₁ Bonn₁ (Wissenschaftliche Abt. des Deutschen

Landestages) 1967.

76 p.   30 cm.   (Wissenschaftliche Abteilung des Deutschen Bundestages. Bibliographien, Nr. 10)

Information Service of the European Communities.

A guide to the study of the European Community. ₁Rev. ed.   Brussels₁ European Community Information Service ₁1965₁

19 p. 23 cm.

Medsker, Karen.

European international organizations and integration movements: reports and analyses. A selected bibliography of non-book materials appearing between 1965 and early 1970. Bloomington, Bureau of Public Discussion, Indiana University, 1970.

7 l. 28 cm.

Paklons, L   L

Bibliographie européenne. European bibliography ₁par₁ L. L. Paklons. Bruges, De Tempel, 1964.

217 p. 24 cm. (Cahiers de Bruges, n. s., 8)

On cover : Collège d'Europe.

Tarr, Raïssa.

Intégration régionale. Regional integration. Paris, O. C. D. E., 1969.

2 v. 27 cm. (O. E. C. D. Library. Bibliographie spécialisée analytique. Special annotated bibliography, 25, 26)
Cover title.
"This bibliography has been selected and annotated by Mrs. R. Tarr."

HISTORY

Bromley, John Selwyn.

A select list of works on Europe and Europe overseas, 1715–1815. Edited for the Oxford Eighteenth Century Group by J. S. Bromley and A. Goodwin. Westport, Conn., Greenwood Press ₁1974₁

xii, 132 p. 22 cm.

Reprint of the 1956 ed. published by Clarendon Press, Oxford, Eng.

Carter, Charles Howard.

The Western European powers, 1500–1700, by Charles Carter. Ithaca, N. Y., Cornell University Press ₁1971₁

347 p. 23 cm. (The Sources of history: studies in the uses of historical evidence)

Carter, Charles Howard.

The Western European powers, 1500–1700, by Charles H. Carter. London, Hodder and Stoughton ₁for₁ the Sources of History Ltd., 1971.

347 p. 23 cm. index. (The Sources of history: studies in the uses of historical evidence)

Davies, Alun Grier.

Modern European history, 1494–1788: a select bibliography, by Alun Davies. London, Historical Association, 1967.

39 p. 22 cm. (Helps for students of history, no. 68)

Davis, Ralph H   C

Medieval European history 395–1500: a select bibliography, by R. H. C. Davis. 2nd (revised) ed. London, Historical Association, 1968.

48 p. 22 cm. (Helps for students of history, no. 67)

France. *Ministère des affaires étrangères. Archives.*

Inventaire des mémoires et documents: Fonds France et fonds divers des pays d'Europe jusqu'en 1896. ₁Préparé par Mᵐᵉ Ozanam et Mᵐᵉ Helleu, conservateurs des Archives diplomatiques₁ Paris, Impr. nationale, 1964.

245 p. 23 cm.

On spine : Inventaire des Archives des affaires étrangères. Mémoires et documents: Fonds France et Europe.
Continuation of Inventaire sommaire des Archives du Département des affaires étrangères. Mémoires et documents (Paris, 1883–96).

Generallandesarchiv Karlsruhe.

Inventar der handgezeichneten Karten und Pläne zur europäischen Kriegsgeschichte des 16.–19. Jahrhunderts im Generallandesarchiv Karlsruhe. Bearb. von Alfons Schäfer unter Mitwirkung von Helmut Weber. Stuttgart, W. Kohlhammer, 1971.

xl, 307 p., 8 p. of illus. 24 cm. (Veröffentlichungen der Staatlichen Archivverwaltung Baden-Württemberg, Bd. 25)

Heler, Yosef, *ed.*

ביבליוגרפיה שימושית ללימוד התקופה: אירופה בין שתי מלחמות העולם; להרצאות ולסמינריונים של י׳ טלמון ₁וה׳ בן־ישראל. ערך וליקט: יוסף הלר. ירושלים, האוניברסיטה העברית, הפקולטה למדעי הרוח, החוג להסטוריה, תשכ״ה ₁1964₁

40 p. 28 cm.

Stanford University. *Hoover Institution on War, Revolution, and Peace.*

Western Europe; a survey of holdings at the Hoover Institution on War, Revolution and Peace, by Agnes F. Peterson. Stanford, Calif. ₁1970₁

iv, 60 p. 28 cm. (*Its* Collection survey)

LAW   see   Law - Europe

PERIODICALS

Centre international de formation européenne, *Paris.*

Répertoire des périodiques consacrés aux questions européennes. Paris, Presses d'Europe, 1967.

144 p. 23 cm.

Pemberton, John E

European materials in British university libraries: a bibliography and union catalogue, compiled and edited by John E. Pemberton; with a survey by William E. Paterson. London, University Association for Contemporary European Studies, 1973.

₁1₁, xl, 42 p. 30 cm.

EUROPE, EASTERN
see also Slavic peoples; and under Dissertations, Academic

Akademiiā nauk SSSR. *Fundamental'naiā biblioteka obshchestvennykh nauk.*

Развитие мировой социалистической системы хозяйства и экономическое сотрудничество европейских социалистических стран-участниц СЭВ; библиография. Книги и статьи 1957–1962 гг. ₁Ответственный редактор Е. М. Кан₁ Москва, 1964.

167 p. 22 cm.
On cover : Экономическое сотрудничество европейских социалистических стран-участниц СЭВ.

Berlin. Freie Universität. Osteuropa-Institut.

Veröffentlichungen 1951–1971. ₁Berlin-Dahlem, Osteuropa-Institut, 1971 ?₁

28 p. 21 x 10 cm.

Dorotich, Daniel.

A bibliography of Canadian Slavists, 1951–1971. Saskatoon, Sask., University of Saskatchewan Publications, 1972.

vi, 32 p. 23 cm.

At head of title: Canadian Association of Slavists.

Fischer, George, 1923-
Social structure and social change in Eastern Europe; guide to specialized studies published in the West since World War II in English, French, and German, by George Fischer and Walter Schenkel. New York, Foreign Area Materials Center, 1970.

xii, 100 p. 28 cm. (Foreign Area Materials Center. Occasional publication no. 15)

Hahn, Gerhard, Bibliotheksrat Dr. rer. pol.
Experimente sozialistischer Marktwirtschaft; jugoslawisches, tschechoslowakisches und ungarisches Modell. Auswahlbibliographie mit Annotationen [in der Bibliothek des Deutschen Bundestages von Gerhard Hahn zusammengestellt. Bonn, 1973]

xiv, 80 p. 30 cm. (Deutscher Bundestag. Wissenschaftliche Dienste. Bibliographien. Nr. 85)

Horecky, Paul Louis, 1913-
East Central Europe; a guide to basic publications. Paul L. Horecky, editor. Chicago, University of Chicago Press [1969]

xxv, 956 p. 25 cm.

Munich. Bayerische Staatsbibliothek.
Osteuropa Neuerwerbungen. Apr. 1972-

München.

v. 30 cm.

Supersedes its Slavica Neuerwerbungen.
At head of title, 1972- : Osteuropasammlung.

Новая литература по общим проблемам европейских социалистических стран. 1964-
Москва.

v. in 28 cm. 12 no a year (irregular)

Issued by Fundamental'naĭa biblioteka obshchestvennykh nauk of the Akademiĭa nauk SSSR and other libraries.

Pleskot, Jozef.
Ekonomická integrácia v socialistických krajinách. (Výberová bibliografia) Zost. a úvod [nap.] Jozef Pleskot. Odb. spolupráca Ján Přívara. 1. vyd. Bratislava, SPN, rozmn. Západoslov. tlač. 42, 1972.

123 p., [583] loose-leaves. 21 cm. (Ekonomické bibliografie)

At head of title: Ústredná ekonomická knižnica Bratislava.
Title also in Russian, English, German, and French; English title: Economic integration in the socialist countries.
Introduction also in Russian, English, German, and French.
In portfolio.

Prague. Výzkumný ústav obchodu.
Bibliografický přehled o mezinárodní spolupráci členských států RVHP [Rada vzájemné hospodářské pomoci] v oblasti obchodu. Sest. kol. Praha, Výzkumný ústav obchodu, t. Tiskopisy, 1973.

70, [1] p. 21 cm.

On cover: Středisko VTEI.

Prpic, George J
Eastern Europe and world communism; a selective annotated bibliography in English, by George J. Prpic. Cleveland, Institute for Soviet and East European Studies, John Carroll University, 1966.

iii l., 148 p. 28 cm.

Serbusová, Miroslava.
Komplexní socialistická ekonomická integrace. Výběrová bibliogr. Sest. Miroslava Serbusová. Hradec Králové, St. věd. knihovna, rozmn., 1972.

78 p. 21 cm. (Publikace SVK v Hradci Králové, č. 10/72)

U. S. Dept. of the Army.
Communist Eastern Europe; analytical survey of literature. Washington; [For sale by the Supt. of Docs., U. S. Govt. Print. Off.] 1971.

xi, 367 p. illus. (part col.), fold. col. maps. 26 cm.

Země střední a jihovýchodní Evropy v letech 1944–1949; výběrová bibliografie. Praha, Československá akademie věd, Ústav dějin východní Evropy, 1969.

492 p. 21 cm. (Bibliografické příručky ÚDVE. č. 6)

HISTORY

Akademiĭa nauk SSSR. *Fundamental'naĭa biblioteka obshchestvennykh nauk.*
Октябрь и революционное движение в странах Центральной и Юго-Восточной Европы. (1917–1923 гг.) Указатель литературы. 1945–1965. Москва, "Наука," 1968.
320 p. 22 cm.

At head of title: Фундаментальная библиотека общественных наук им. В. П. Волгина Академии наук СССР.
Compiled by T. V. Vladislavleva and others.

Meyer, Klaus, 1928-
Bibliographie der Arbeiten zur osteuropäischen Geschichte aus den deutschsprachigen Fachzeitschriften 1858–1964. Hrsg. von Werner Philipp. Berlin (Freie Universität, Osteuropa-Institut); Wiesbaden, Harrassowitz in Kommission, 1966.

314 p. 21 cm. (Bibliographische Mitteilungen des Osteuropa-Instituts an der Freien Universität Berlin, Heft 9)

Meyer, Klaus, 1928-
Bibliographie zur osteuropäischen Geschichte. Verzeichnis d. zwischen 1939 u. 1964 veröffentlichten Literatur in westeurop. Sprachen zur osteurop. Geschichte bis 1945 [von] Klaus Meyer. Unter Mitarb. von John H. L. Keep [u. a.] hrsg. v. Werner Philipp. Wiesbaden, Harrassowitz in Komm., 1972.

xlix, 649 p. 26 cm. (Bibliographische Mitteilungen des Osteuropa-Instituts an der Freien Universität Berlin, Heft 10)

LIBRARY CATALOGS

Birmingham, Eng. University. Library.
Russian and East European library materials at the University of Birmingham: a reader's guide. Birmingham, University of Birmingham Library, 1972.

31 p; forms, plan. 30 cm.

Gelsenkirchen. Stadtbücherei.
Nachbarn im Osten: Bulgarien, Polen, Rumänien, Tschechoslowakei, Ungarn; Auswahlsverzeichnis. [Bearbeitung: Gudrun Barten] Gelsenkirchen, 1970.

28 p. 20 cm. (Länder, Völker und Kulturen, Folge 15)

Johann Gottfried Herder-Institut, Marburg. Bibliothek.
Bibliothek des Johann Gottfried Herder-Instituts, Marburg/Lahn, Germany; alphabetischer Katalog. Boston, G. K. Hall, 1964.

5 v. 26 cm.

———————— Nachtrag. Boston, G. K. Hall, 1971.

2 v. 37 cm.

PERIODICALS

Birkos, Alexander S
East European and Slavic studies. Compiled and edited by Alexander S. Birkos and Lewis A. Tambs. [Kent? Ohio] Kent State University Press [1973]

572 p. 22 cm. (Academic writer's guide to periodicals, 2)

EUROPEAN ECONOMIC COMMUNITY

Drummond, Olive Frances.
The Common Market, sources of information; select list—addresses, directories, statistics; compiler O. F. Drummond, Assistant Librarian. Edinburgh, Edinburgh College of Commerce Library, 1972.
[5], 46 p. 22 cm. (Reading European)
Cover title.
At head of title: Edinburgh Corporation Education Department. Edinburgh College of Commerce.

Heymans, Frans.
De levensstandaard in de E. E. G.-landen. Analytische keurbibliografie. Documentatie verschenen van 1958 tot en met 1966. Brussel, Belgische Commissie voor Bibliografie, (Huidevetterstr. 80–84), 1970.
xiii, 481 p. 21 cm. (Bibliographia Belgica 110)

"Proefschrift voorgelegd aan de Provinciale Bibliotheekschool van Brabant ..."

Information Service of the European Communities.
Le Marché commun et la Turquie. Ortak Pazar ve Türkiye bibliyoğrafyası. Bruxelles, Communautés européennes, Service de presse et d'information [1967]
38 p. 30 cm. (Dossier bibliographique)
Cover title.
Caption title: Bibliographie sur le Marché commun et la Turquie.

Information Service of the European Communities.
La politique économique à moyen terme de la CEE. [Bruxelles, Communautés européennes, Service de presse et d'information, Division des publications, 1966]
22 p. 30 cm. (Dossier bibliographique)

Information Service of the European Communities.
Politique régionale des Communautés européennes. [Bruxelles, Communautés européennes, Service de Presse et d'information, Division des Publications, 1968]
35 p. illus. 30 cm. (Dossier bibliographique)

Information Service of the European Communities.
Rapports entre le droit communautaire et le droit national. Bruxelles, Service de presse et d'information des Communautés européennes, Division des publications, 1966.
32 p. 30 cm. (Its Dossier bibliographique)

Kaaber, Anna-Lise.
Et udvalg af litteratur om Danmark og Fællesmarkedet i perioden august 1965–november 1970. Et udvalg af litteratur om EFTA fra januar 1967–november 1970. Et udvalg af litteratur om Nordisk økonomisk samarbejde ⟨NORDEK⟩ fra januar 1968–november 1970. København, Udenrigspolitiske Selskab, (Det Danske Forlag), 1971.
31 p. 24 cm.

Karner, W   A
Österreich in der europäischen Integration; Bibliographie [von] W. A. Karner [und] H. M. Mayrzedt. Innsbruck, 1964.
vii, 180 p. 30 cm. (Akademische Vereinigung für Aussenpolitik, Universität Innsbruck. Schriftenreihe, Bd. 2)

Kitter, Audrey.
The U.S. and the EEC: American reaction to and involvement in the "Common Market." [Los Angeles] Center for the Study of Armament and Disarmament, California State University, Los Angeles [1973]
ix, 62 p. 22 cm. (Political issues series. v. 2, no. 7)

Ortak Pazar bibliyoğrafyası.
Ankara, Türkiye Ticaret Odaları, Sanayi Odaları ve Ticaret Borsaları Birliği Kütüphanesi.
no. in   v. 29–31 cm.
Began with Jan. 1969 issue. Cf. Türkiye bibliyografyası, 1969.

Oslo. Norske Nobelinstitutt. Biblioteket.
Sosialpolitikk i de Europeiske felleskap. Bibliografi. Utarb. av Elsa Skarprud. Oslo, 1971.
[2], 8 l. 30 cm.

Oslo. Universitet. Bibliotek.
Liste over litteratur om EF og EFTA, ved Universitetsbiblioteket i Oslo og Universitetsbibliotekets bibliotektjeneste ved det Samfunnsvitenskapelige fakultet, Blindern. Red. av Sabine Ameln og Harald Rønning. Oslo, 1972.
3 l., 59 p. 30 cm.
"Listen omfatter katalogiserte tidsskrifter og bøker ... i boksamlingene til Sosialøkonomisk institutt og Institutt for statsvitenskap i Fellesbiblioteket, Det samfunnsvitenskapelige fakultet, Blindern, og i Norske og Utenlandske avdeling ved Universitetsbiblioteket i Oslo."

Partington, Lena.
The European Communities : a guide to the literature and an indication of sources of information / compiled by Lena Partington. — London : Dept. of the Environment, Library, 1974.
iv, 101 p. ; 30 cm. — (Information series - Library, Dept. of the Environment)

Perumbulavil, Vilasini.
The European Economic Community and New Zealand, a checklist. Wellington, Library School, National Library Service, 1965.
v, 44 p. 21 cm. ([Wellington, N. Z. Library School] Bibliographical series, no. 8)

Tamuno, Olufunmilayo G
The E. E. C. and developing nations, 1958–1966; a bibliography. Compiled by Olufunmilayo G. Tamuno. Ibadan, Nigerian Institute of Social and Economic Research, 1967.
v l., 51 p. 26 cm.

EUROPEAN FREE TRADE ASSOCIATION

European Free Trade Association.
Selected publications on the European Free Trade Association and European integration. Rev. Washington, European Free Trade Association, Washington Information Office, 1963.
52 p. 28 cm.

———— Supplement. Washington, European Free Trade Association, Washington Information Office, 1964.
18 p. 28 cm.

European Free Trade Association. Washington Information Office.
Publications issued by the European Free Trade Association (1960–69). [Washington] 1969.
3 l. 27 cm.

Kaaber, Anna-Lise.
Et udvalg af litteratur om EFTA til slutningen af december 1966. A selective bibliography on EFTA up to the end of December 1966. København K, Det Udenrigspolitiske Selskab, Farvergade 4, 1967.
28 p. 24 cm.

EUROPEAN WAR   see   World War

EVAPORATION

Horton, Jerome S
Evapotranspiration and water[shed] research as related to riparian and phreatophyte management; an abstract bibliography, compiled by Jerome S. Horton. [Washington] Forest Service—U.S. Dept. of Agriculture; [for sale by the Supt. of Docs., U.S. Govt. Print. Off.] 1973.

iv, 192 p. 24 cm. ([United States. Dept. of Agriculture] Miscellaneous publication. no. 1234)

Water Resources Scientific Information Center.
Evaporation suppression : a bibliography. — Washington : Water Resources Scientific Information Center, Office of Water Resources Research, U. S. Dept. of the Interior ; Springfield, Va. : available from the National Technical Information Service, 1973.

iv, 478 p. : 26 cm. — (Bibliography series - Water Resources Scientific Information Center : WRSIC 73-216)

EVELYN, JOHN

Keynes, *Sir* **Geoffrey Langdon,** 1887–
John Evelyn: a study in bibliophily with a bibliography of his writings, by Geoffrey Keynes, Kt. 2nd ed. Oxford, London, Clarendon P., 1968.

xix, 313 p. 16 plates, illus., facsims. 26 cm.

EXCEPTIONAL CHILDREN see Education of exceptional children

EXECUTIVES

ERIC Clearinghouse on Adult Education.
Management and supervisory development. [Syracuse, N. Y.] 1969.

70 p. forms. 28 cm. (Current information sources, no. 26)
Cover title.

Contains abstracts of 210 documents, relating to the education and training of managers and supervisors, which have entered the ERIC Clearinghouse on Adult Education files from Sept. 1963–Nov. 1969.

United States. Civil Service Commission. Library.
Executive manpower. — Washington : U. S. Civil Service Commission, Library, 1973.

101 p. ; 26 cm. — (Personnel bibliography series ; no. 52)

Cover title.
Updates Personnel bibliography no. 40, Executive manpower management.

United States. Civil Service Commission. Library.
Executive manpower management. Washington; [For sale by the Supt. of Docs., U. S. Govt. Print. Off.] 1971 [i. e. 1972]

113 p. 27 cm. (Its Personnel bibliography series no. 40)

U. S. *Dept. of the Army.*
The executive: philosophy, problems, practices; a bibliographic survey. [Washington] Headquarters, Dept. of the Army [1966]

viii, 76 p. 26 cm.

EXERCISE

Brooke, John Dennis.
Cardiac output, circulatory mechanics and exercise; compiled by J. D. Brooke. Eccles (26 Grange Rd, Winton, Eccles, Lancs. M30 8JQ), Worthwhile Designs Ltd, 1971.

[23] l. 34 cm. (His Reference handbooks on human movement, no. 2)

Brooke, John Dennis.
Central nervous system modification of afferent impulses, pain and exercise; compiled by J. D. Brooke. Eccles (26 Grange Rd, Winton, Eccles, Lancs. M30 8JQ), Worthwhile Designs Ltd, 1971.

[10] l. 34 cm. (His Reference handbooks on human movement, no. 3)

Brooke, John Dennis.
Personality, perception and exercise tolerance; compiled by J. D. Brooke. Eccles (26 Grange Rd, Winton, Eccles, Lancs. M30 8JQ), Worthwhile Designs Ltd, 1971.

[14] l. 33 cm. (His Reference handbooks on human movement, no. 4)

Brooke, John Dennis.
Respiration and exercise; compiled by J. D. Brooke. Eccles (26 Grange Rd, Winton, Eccles, Lancs. M30 8JQ), Worthwhile Designs Ltd, 1971.

32[l. 33 cm. (His Reference handbooks on human movement, no. 1)

EXHIBITIONS

Lasnier, Albert.
Références sur les expositions, 1937–1964. [Références concernant livres, revues, diapositives, films. Compilation par Albert Lasnier. Québec, 1964]

220 l. 29 cm.

Ōsaka Furitsu Toshokan.
(Ōsaka Furitsu Toshokan zō bankoku hakurankai kankei shiryō mokuroku)
大阪府立図書館蔵万国博覧会関係資料目録　大阪　大阪府立図書館　昭和46(1971)

92 p. illus. 26 cm. (大阪府立図書館シリーズ　第29集)

Title also in English: A catalogue of the world's exposition collection in the Osaka Prefectural Library.

EXISTENTIALISM

Déri, Miklósné.
Az egzisztencializmus marxista bírálatának bibliográfiája, összeállította: Déri Miklósné és Pelle József. Budapest, 1967.

25 p. 24 cm. (A Budapesti Egyetemi Könyvtár kiadványai, 28)

Miller, Albert Jay.
A selective bibliography of existentialism in education and related topics. [1st ed.] New York, Exposition Press [1969]

39 p. 22 cm. (An Exposition-university book)

EXPERIMENTAL DESIGN

Federer, Walter Theodore, 1915–
Bibliography on experiment and treatment design, pre-1968, [by] Walter T. Federer and Leslie N. Balaam. Edinburgh, Oliver and Boyd for the International Statistical Institute, 1972.

[5], 769 p. 26 cm.

Federer, Walter Theodore, 1915–
Bibliography on experiment and treatment design, pre-1968 [by] Walter T. Federer and Leslie N. Balaam. New York, Hafner Pub. Co., 1973 [c1972]

767 p. 26 cm.

EXPLOSIVES

Bulletin signalétique: Série poudres. no 75–94; fév.–déc. 1968. ₁Paris₁ Centre de documentation de l'armement, Antenne poudres.

20 no. 25 cm. semimonthly.

Supersedes in part Bulletin signalétique, issued 1965–67 by the Service de documentation scientifique et technique de l'armement, and continues its numbering.

EXPORTING

Bromley, David William.
What to read on exporting ₁by₁ D. W. Bromley; foreword by Sir William McFadzean. 2nd ed. London, Library Association, 1965 ₁i. e. 1966₁

68 p. 22 cm. (Library Association. Special subject list, no. 42)

First published in 1963, with title: Exporting.

Bromley, David William.
What to read on exporting, by D. W. Bromley; foreword by Sir William McFadzean. 3rd ed. London, Library Association, 1970.

95 p. 22 cm. Index. (Library Association. Special subject list, no. 42)

First published in 1963 under title: Exporting.

Burgess, Norman.
How to find out about exporting. ₁1st ed.₁ Oxford, New York, Pergamon Press ₁1970₁

xii, 262 p. 20 cm. (The Commonwealth and international library. Libraries and technical information division)

Escuela de Administración de Negocios para Graduados. Biblioteca.
Promoción y gestión de exportaciones; guía bibliográfica, compilada por: Biblioteca "Alan B. Coleman" de la Escuela de Administración de Negocios para Graduados y Centro de Documentación del Comité de Exportadores de la Sociedad Nacional de Industrias. Lima ₁1972₁

xv, 191 p. 29 cm.

Cover title.
"A solicitud del Centro de Entrenamiento para Dirigentes de Exportación de E. S. A. N. su Biblioteca presenta una bibliografía básica."

Goldstucker, Jac L
International marketing, compiled and edited by Jac L. Goldstucker and Jose R. de la Torre, Jr. Chicago, American Marketing Association ₁1972₁

vi, 117 p. 23 cm. (₁American Marketing Association₁ Bibliography series, 19)

EXPOSITIONS see Exhibitions

EXPRESSIONISM

Chiarini, Paolo.
Caos e geometria. Per un regesto delle poetiche espressioniste ... Con la collaborazione di Franco Lo Re e Ida Porena. Firenze, La nuova Italia, 1969.

liv, 240 p. 21 cm. (Maestri e compagni, 27)

2d ed.

Perkins, G C
Expressionismus; eine Bibliographie zeitgenössischer Dokumente, 1910–1925 ₁von₁ G. C. Perkins. Zürich, Verlag für Bibliographie, 1971.

xix, 144 p. illus. 24 cm.

Raabe, Paul.
Index Expressionismus: Bibliographie der Beiträge in den Zeitschriften und Jahrbüchern des literarischen Expressionismus, 1910–1925. Im Auftrage des Seminars für Deutsche Philologie der Universität Göttingen und in Zusammenarbeit mit dem Deutschen Rechenzentrum Darmstadt hrsg. von Paul Raabe. Nedeln, Liechtenstein, Kraus-Thomson Organization, 1972.

18 v. 29 cm.

CONTENTS: Bd. 1–4. Serie A. Alphabetischer Index.—Bd. 5–9. Serie B. Systematischer Index.—Bd. 10–14. Serie C. Index nach Zeitschriften.—Bd. 15–16. Serie D. Titelregister.—Bd. 17–18. Serie E. Gattungsregister.

EYE see Ophthalmology

F

FABLES
see also under Aesop

Quinnam, Barbara.
Fables from incunabula to modern picture books; a selective bibliography, compiled by Barbara Quinnam, Children's Book Section. Washington, General Reference and Bibliography Division, Reference Dept., Library of Congress; ₁for sale by the Superintendent of Documents, U. S. Govt. Print. Off.₁ 1966.

viii, 85 p. illus., facsims. 24 cm.

Prepared in connection with an exhibition opened Apr. 17, 1966, at the Library of Congress.

FABRICS see Textile industry and fabrics

FACTORIES

(Novosti tekhnicheskoĭ literatury. Stroiteĺ'stvo i arkhitektura. Razdel A. Seriiă II: Promyshlennye kompleksy, zdaniiă i sooruzheniiă)

Новости технической литературы. Строительство и архитектура. Раздел А. Серия II: Промышленные комплексы, здания и сооружения.

Москва, Центр. ин-т науч. информации по строительству и архитектуре.

v. 22 cm. 12 no. a year.

"Библиографическая информация."

Title varies: –1972, Новости технической литературы. Строительство и архитектура. Раздел А. Серия II: Промышленное строительство.

Issues for   prepared by Informatsionno-bibliograficheskiĭ otdel of TSNTB po stroiteĺ'stvu i arkhitekture.

Pevzner, D   P
Культурно-бытовое обслуживание на промышленных предприятиях и в промышленных районах. (Отечеств. и иностр. литература за 1960–1966 гг.) Москва, 1967.
72 p. 25 cm.
At head of title: Госстрой СССР. Центральная научно-техническая библиотека по строительству и архитектуре.

Trondheim. Norges tekniske høgskole. *Biblioteket.*
Fabrikkplanlegging. Trondheim, 1968.

51 p. 30 cm. (*Its* Litteraturliste, 36)

FACULTÉS UNIVERSITAIRES SAINT-LOUIS

Paquet, Jacques, professeur.
Bibliographie académique. Corps académique et scientifique. 1960–1970. Publiée par Jacques Paquet et Gaston Braive. Bruxelles, Facultés universitaires Saint-Louis, bd du Jardin botanique, 43, 1971.

124 p. 25 cm.

FAIRY TALES

Ireland, Norma (Olin) 1907–
Index to fairy tales, 1949–1972; including folklore, legends, & myths, in cllections. Westwood, Mass., F. W. Faxon Co., 1973.

xxxviii, 741 p. 23 cm. (Useful reference series, no. 101)

Compiled to continue Index to fairy tales by Mary Huse Eastman.

Stockholm. Stadsbiblioteket.
Hur man hittar sagor; katalog över det svenska sagobeståndet 1910–1960. Lund, Bibliotekstjänst, 1963.

488 p. illus. 22 cm.

———— Supplement. 1961/65–
Lund, Bibliotekstjänst.

v. 22 cm.

FALCONRY see Hunting

FALK, SAWYER

Syracuse University. Archives.
Sawyer Falk: a register of his papers in the Syracuse University Library. Compiled by David C. Maslyn ₁and₁ Judy Woolcock. ₁Syracuse, N. Y.₁ 1965.

55 l. port. 28 cm. (Manuscript register series, register no. 8)

FALKLAND ISLANDS

Academia Nacional de la Historia, *Buenos Aires.*
Exposición histórica de las Islas Malvinas, Georgias del Sur y Sandwich del Sur. Organizada por Humberto F. Burzio. Salón Peuser, 24 de julio–7 de agosto de 1964. Buenos Aires, 1964.

89 p. illus., facsims, maps, port. 26 cm.

Fordham, Angela.
Falkland Islands; a bibliography of 50 examples of printed maps bearing specific reference to the Falkland Islands, by Angela Fordham. London, Map Collectors' Circle ₁1964₁

18 p. maps. 25 cm. (Map Collectors' Circle. Map collectors' series, no. 11)

On cover : Maps of the Falkland Islands.
Errata slip mounted at end.

FAMILY

Almeida, Maria Lêda Rodrigues de.
Família e desenvolvimento: uma análise bibliográfica (relatório final) ₁Rio de Janeiro₁ CLAPCS ₁i. e. Centro Latino-Americano de Pesquisas em Ciências Sociais₁ 1971.

28, 39 l. illus. 29 cm. (Centro Latino-Americano de Pesquisas em Ciências Sociais. Grupo de Eestudos sôbre Família. Documento no. 2)

American Home Economics Association.
Family relations and child development. 1966–
Washington.

v. 28 cm. (Home economics research abstracts, 6)

"Compiles abstracts of masters' theses and doctoral dissertations completed in graduate schools of home economics."

Glick, Ira D   1937–
Family therapy and research; an annotated bibliography of articles and books published 1950–1970 ₁by₁ Ira D. Glick ₁and₁ Jay Haley. New York, Grune & Stratton ₁1971₁

viii, 280 p. 26 cm.

Liggeri, Paolo, comp.
Indicazioni bibliografiche per la famiglia. 1969. Milano,

Istituto La casa, 1969.

229 p. 20½ cm.

McDonald, Michael, 1942–
Bibliography on the family from the fields of theology and philosophy. Ottawa, Vanier Institute of the Family, 1964.

vi, 95 l. 28 cm.

"Commissioned by the Canadian Conference on the Family, Ottawa, June 7–10, 1964."

May, Jean T
Family health indicators : annotated bibliography / by Jean T. May. — Rockville, Md. : National Institute of Mental Health ; Washington : for sale by the Supt. of Docs., U. S. Govt. Print. Off., 1974.
xi, 212 p. ; 26 cm. — (DHEW publication no. (ADM) 75–135)
"Compiled as a part of the Family Health Indicators Project, pursuant to contract HSM–42–72–189 with the National Institute of Mental Health."

Prokhorova, V   P
(Obshchestvo, sem'ia, lichnost')
Общество, семья, личность. Рек. указ. литературы. Москва, "Книга," 1972.

48 p. 20 cm.

At head of title: Государственная библиотека СССР имени В. И. Ленина. В. П. Прохорова, Н. В. Якимова.

Schlesinger, Benjamin.
The multi-problem family; a review and annotated bibliography. ₁Contributors: Beverly Ayres, and others₁ Editorial consultant. Florence Strakovsky. 2d ed. ₁Toronto₁ University of Toronto Press ₁ᵉ1965₁

xiv, 183 p. 24 cm.

Schlesinger, Benjamin.
The multi-problem family; a review and annotated bibliography. Editorial consultant: Florence Strakhovsky. 3d ed. ₁Toronto₁ University of Toronto Press ₁c1970₁

xii, 191 p. 24 cm.

Srećković, Olga R
Porodično vaspitanje. Bibliografska građa sa anotacijama. ₁Sastavila₁ Olga R. Srećković. ⟨Manojlo Bročić: Predgovor⟩. Beograd, "Radnička štampa"; Savet za vaspitanje i zaštitu dece Jugoslavije, 1969.

₁6₁, 156, ₁3₁ p. 20 cm.

U. S. *National Institute of Mental Health. Community Research and Services Branch.*
Family therapy; a selected annotated bibliography. Bethesda, Md., U. S. Dept. of Health, Education, and Welfare. Public Health Service, National Institutes of Health, 1965 ₁i. e. 1966₁

v, 30 p. 26 cm.

At head of title: National Clearinghouse for Mental Information.

Vanier Institute of the Family.
An inventory of family research and studies in Canada, 1963–1967. Un inventaire des recherches et études sur la famille, au Canada. Ottawa, 1967.

xiv, 161 p. 23 cm.

FAMILY HISTORY   see   Genealogy and
    names of individual families
FAMILY LIFE EDUCATION
    see also   Sex instruction

Centre régional de documentation pédagogique de Lyon.
Dossier documentaire: économie sociale familiale. 3. éd.

Lyon, C. R. D. P. ₁1970₁

174 p. 27 cm. (Annales du Centre régional de documentation pédagogique de Lyon)

Cover title.
"Le présent numéro constitue un dossier documentaire comportant la totalité des moyens que le Centre régional de documentation pédagogique de Lyon met à la disposition des professeurs."

ERIC Clearinghouse on Adult Education.
Parent, home, and family life education. ₁Syracuse, N. Y.₁ 1970.

82 p. 28 cm. (Current information sources no. 30)

Finch, Janette H   comp.
Guidance in family affairs; a selective list of books in the Public Library of South Australia. Adelaide, Public Library of South Australia, 1956 ₁i. e. 1965₁

13 p. 26 cm. (Research Service bibliographies, series 4, no. 42)

Library Association. County Libraries Group.
Bringing up the family. 2d ed. ₁London₁ 1970.

24 p. 18 cm. (Its Reader's guide, new series, no. 114)

Minnesota Council on Family Life.
Family life: literature and films; an annotated bibliography. ₁Minneapolis, 1964₁

74 p. illus. 28 cm.

Minnesota Council on Family Relations.
Family life: literature and films; an annotated bibliography. ₁Minneapolis₁ 1972.

vii, 353 p. 28 cm.

Cover title.
The 1964 ed. published by the body under its earlier name: Minnesota Council on Family Life.

Prince George Public Library.
Male and female. 2nd ed. ₁Prince George, B. C., 1970₁

45 p. 28 cm.

Cover title.
"List of books on family life education."

Watt, Lois Belfield.
Family life and sex education; a bibliography, compiled by Lois B. Watt, chief, ₁and₁ Myra H. Thomas, curriculum materials assistant, the Educational Materials Center. ₁Washington₁ Office of Education, U. S. Dept. of Health, Education, and Welfare ₁1967₁

7 p. 26 cm.

FANTASTIC FICTION   see Fiction - Science
fiction

FAR EAST   see   Asia

FARJEON, ELEANOR

Zeeman, Denise Avril.
Eleanor Farjeon; a bibliography. Johannesburg, University of the Witwatersrand, Department of Bibliography, Librarianship and Typography, 1970.

₁xii₁ 37 p. 30 cm.

FARM BUILDINGS
Agricultural Research Council.
A bibliography of farm buildings research, 1945–1958. ₁London₁ 1959–61.
7 v. in 2. 25 cm.

———— 1st supplement, 1958–1961. ₁London₁ 1962–

v. 25 cm.

———————— 2nd supplement, 1962–1964. ₁London₁ 196

v. 25 cm.

Estación Experimental Agropecuaria Pergamino.
Bibliografía sobre vivienda rural. Dirigló: Eduardo F.
Ferreira Sobral. (Pergamino₁ 1968–

v. 26 cm. (*Its* Serie bibliográfica, t. 83

Added t. p., v. 1– Bibliography on rural housing.
Vol. 1: Introd. in Spanish and English.

Wander, B
Bibliografie historisch boerderij-onderzoek, samengesteld
door B. Wander. Arnhem, Stichting Historisch Boerderij
-Onderzoek, 1971.

iv, 76 p. 25 cm.

Wander, B
Voorlopige bibliografie historisch boerderij-onderzoek,
1960–1963, samengesteld door B. Wander. Arnhem, Rijksmuseum voor Volkskunde "Het Nederlands Openlucht-
museum," 1965.

18 p. 25 cm.

FARM MANAGEMENT

Commonwealth Bureau of Agricultural Economics.
Companies, corporations and partnerships in farming:
an annotated bibliography, prepared by ₁the₁ Commonwealth Bureau of Agricultural Economics. Farnham
Royal, Commonwealth Agricultural Bureaux, 1971.

₁3₁, 5 p. 30 cm. (Its Annotated bibliography no. 8)

Includes supplement (1 p.)

Gorbatov, A   L
Научная организация труда (НОТ) в сельском хозяйстве. Библиогр. указатель отечеств. литературы за 1965–
1969 гг. и иностр. литературы за 1960–1968 гг. Москва,
1969.
83 p. 21 cm.
At head of title: Всесоюзная ордена Ленина академия с.-х. наук
имени В. И. Ленина. Центральная научная сельскохозяйственная библиотека. Справочно-библиографический отдел.
"Составитель А. Л. Горбатов."
Edited by I. G. Palilova.

Gorbatov, A   L
₁Nauchnaia organizatsiia upravleniia v sel'skom khoziaistve₁
Научная организация управления в сельском хозяйстве. Библиогр. указ. литературы за 1967–1972 гг.,
отеч. и иностр. Москва, 1973.

152 p. 19 cm.

At head of title: Всесоюзная академия сельскохозяйственных
наук имени В. И. Ленина. Центральная научная сельскохозяйственная библиотека.

Harrison, Virden L
Financial management research in farming in the United
States; an annotated bibliography of recent publications
and current work ₁by Virden L. Harrison. Washington₁
U. S. Dept. of Agriculture, Economic Research Service
₁1971₁
v. 78 p. 27 cm. (₁U. S. Dept. of Agriculture₁ Miscellaneous
publication no. 1222)

Todorova, Tamara.
₁Nauchna organizatsiia na upravlenieto v selskoto stopanstvo₁
Научна организация на управлението в селското
стопанство. ⟨Темат. справка⟩. София, ЦНТИИСГС,
1972.

24 p. 21 cm.

FARMERS' COOPERATIVES see Agriculture,
Cooperative

FARWELL, ARTHUR GEORGE

**A Guide to the music of Arthur Farwell and to the microfilm
collection of his work.** Prepared by his children. Price Farwell,
editor. Limited ed. Briarcliff Manor, N.Y., Issued by B. Farwell for the estate of Arthur Farwell, 1972.

iii, 138 p. illus. 28 cm.

FATHERS OF THE CHURCH see Patrology

FAULKNER, WILLIAM

Bassett, John, 1942–
William Faulkner: an annotated checklist of criticism.
₁1st ed.₁ New York, D. Lewis, 1972.

xii, 551 p. 24 cm.

Meriwether, James B
The literary career of William Faulkner; a bibliographical study, by James M. Meriwether. Columbia, University
of South Carolina Press ₁1971₁

xii, 192 p. illus., facsims. 25 cm.
"Authorized reissue."

Meriwether, James B
The Merrill checklist of William Faulkner. Compiled by
James B. Meriwether. Columbus, Ohio, C. E. Merrill Pub.
Co. ₁1970₁

37 p. 19 cm. (Charles E. Merrill checklists)

Charles E. Merrill program in American literature.
Cover title: Checklist of William Faulkner.
1957 ed. published under title: William Faulkner; a checklist.

Virginia. University. *Library.*
William Faulkner: "Man working," 1919–1962; a catalogue of the William Faulkner collections at the University
of Virginia. Compiled by Linton R. Massey. With an
introd. by John Cook Wyllie. Charlottesville, Bibliographical Society of the University of Virginia; distributed by the University Press of Virginia ₁1968₁

x, 250 p. facsims., ports. 27 cm.

FAUST

Engel, Carl Dietrich Leonhard, 1824–1913.
Bibliotheca Faustiana. Zusammenstellung der Faust-
Schriften vom 16. Jahrhundert bis Mitte 1884, ₁von₁ Karl
Dietrich Leonhard Engel. Hildesheim, New York, G.
Olms, 1970.

xii, 764 p. 22 cm.

"Zweiter reprografischer Nachdruck der Ausgabe Oldenburg 1885,
erschienen als 2. Auflage der Bibliotheca Faustiana unter dem
Titel Zusammenstellung der Faustschriften."

Henning, Hans, 1927–
Faust-Bibliographie. Berlin, Weimar, Aufbau-Verlag,
1966–

v. 25 cm. (Bibliographien, Kataloge und Bestandsverzeichnisse)

CONTENTS: T. 1. Allgemeines. Grundlagen. Gesamtdarstellungen. Das Faust-Thema vom 16. Jahrhundert bis 1790.—T. 2. Goethes
Faust. Bd. 1. Ausgaben und Übersetzungen. Bd. 2. Sekundärliteratur zu Goethes Faust. 2 v.

FEAST OF TABERNACLES see Sukkoth

FEDERAL GOVERNMENT
see also State government

Bachelder, Glen L
The literature of federalism; a selected bibliography. Compiled by Glen L. Bachelder and Paul C. Shaw. Rev. ed. [East Lansing] Institute for Community Development and Services, Michigan State University, 1966.

18 l. 28 cm. (Michigan State University. Institute for Community Development and Services. Bibliography no. 11)

Germany (*Federal Republic, 1949–*) *Bundestag. Wissenschaftliche Abteilung.*
Das Bund-Länder-Verhältnis in der Bundesrepublik Deutschland. Auswahlbibliographie. (Bearb. [von] Wolfgang Krengel) Bonn (Deutscher Bundestag, Wissenschaftliche Abt.) 1967.

96 p. 30 cm. (*Its* Bibliographien, Nr. 13)

"Die vorliegende Bibliographie ist eine erweiterte Neuauflage der Bibliographie Nr. 2 vom 1. Februar 1963."

Liboiron, Albert A
Federalism and intergovernmental relations in Australia, Canada, the United States and other countries; a bibliography, compiled by Albert A. Liboiron. Kingston, Ont., Institute of Intergovernmental Relations, Queen's University, 1967.

vi, 231 l. 28 cm.

Stenberg, Carl W
American intergovernmental relations: a selected bibliography [by] Carl W. Stenberg. [Monticello, Ill., Council of Planning Librarians, 1971]

37 l. 28 cm. (Council of Planning Librarians. Exchange bibliography, 227)

FEEDS AND FEEDING

Almeida, Norma Martins de.
Alimentação animal; uréia técnica. Cruz das Almas, 1968.

14 l. 28 cm. (Instituto de Pesquisas e Experimentação Agropecuárias do Leste. Lista bibliográfica no. 8)

Commonwealth Bureau of Agricultural Economics.
Computing least cost rations: an annotated bibliography, prepared by [the] Commonwealth Bureau of Agricultural Economics. Farnham Royal, Commonwealth Agricultural Bureaux, 1971.

[3], 5 p. 30 cm. (Its Annotated bibliography no. 9)

Gribanova, L A
Производство комбикормов. Библиогр. указатель науч.-техн. литературы. Москва, 1970.

40 p. 22 cm.

At head of title: Центральный научно-исследовательский институт информации и технико-экономических исследований Министерства заготовок СССР.
"Указатель подготовила ... Л. А. Грибанова."

Makarenko, G A
Химия в животноводстве; рекомендательный указатель литературы. [Составители: Г. А. Макаренко, В. Г. Григорьева. Редактор О. Н. Новосельцева]. Москва, Книга, 1964.

27 p. 17 cm. (За дальнейший подъем социалистического сельского хозяйства, вып. 2)
At head of title: Государственная ордена Ленина библиотека СССР имени В. И. Ленина. Центральная научная сельскохозяйственная библиотека.

Механизация и автоматизация раздачи кормов; библиографический список отечественной литературы в количестве 231 названия и иностранной литературы в количестве 282 названий за 1964–1965 гг. [Составитель Л. В. Чернова. Редактор И. Г. Палилова] Москва, 1966.
82 p. 21 cm.
At head of title: Всесоюзная академия сельскохозяйственных

наук имени В. И. Ленина. Центральная научная сельскохозяйственная библиотека. Справочно-библиографический отдел.

Moscow. TSentral'naia nauchnaia sel'skokhoziaistvennaia **biblioteka.** *Spravochno-bibliograficheskii otdel.*
Химическое консервирование кормов; библиографический список отечественной литературы [за 1961–1964 гг. Составила Е. А. Фалкина] Москва, 1964.

17 p. 21 cm.

At head of title: Всесоюзная академия с.-х. наук имени В. И. Ленина.

Sidorova, M V
Микроэлементы в кормлении сельскохозяйственных животных; [библиографический список отечественной литературы за 1960–1964 гг. Составила М. В. Сидорова] Москва, 1964.
20 p. 20 cm.
Cover title.
At head of title: Всесоюзная центральная научная сельскохозяйственная библиотека. Справочно-библиографический отдел.

Tarasova, K IA
(Problema kormovogo belka v sel'skom khoziaistve)
Проблема кормового белка в сельском хозяйстве. Библиогр. указатель отеч. литературы за 1966–1970 гг. и иностр. за 1968–1970 гг. [Сост. К. Л. Тарасова]. Москва, 1971.
144 p. 20 cm.
At head of title: Всесоюзная Академия сельскохозяйственных наук имени В. И. Ленина. Центральная научная сельскохозяйственная библиотека.

FELDSPAR

Waldbaum, David R 1937–
A bibliography of the feldspars, edited by D. R. Waldbaum. Ann Arbor, Mich., University Microfilms, 1969.

iii, 145 p. 24 cm.

"Published under the auspices of the Committee on Experimental Geology and Geophysics, Harvard University."

FENCING

Thimm, Carl Albert.
A complete bibliography of fencing & duelling [by] Carl A. Thimm. New York, B. Blom [1968]

xvi, 537 p. illus., facsims., ports. 20 cm.

Reprint of the 1896 ed.

FERGUSON, MICHAEL JOSEPH

Scollard, Robert Joseph.
The diaries and other papers of Michael Joseph Ferguson, C. S. B.; a bibliography, compiled by Robert J. Scollard. With an introd. by J. Stanley Murphy. Toronto, Basilian Press, 1970.

36 p. illus., port. 22 cm. (Basilian historical bulletin, 5)

FERNS

Jones, George Neville, 1904–
An annotated bibliography of Mexican ferns. Urbana, University of Illinois Press, 1966.

xxxiii, 297 p. 24 cm.

FERRARA, ITALY
Bonasera, Francesco.
Forma veteris urbis Ferrariæ; contributo allo studio delle antiche rappresentazioni cartografiche della citta di Ferrara. Firenze, L. S. Olschki, 1965.

105 p. maps, plans. 31 cm.

On cover: Comune di Ferrara. Centro di studi sul Rinascimento ferrarese.

FERROELECTRICITY

Connolly, T   F
Ferroelectric materials and ferroelectricity, compiled by
T. F. Connolly and Errett Turner. New York, IFI/
Plenum, 1970.

xi, 685 p. 29 cm. (Solid state physics literature guides, v. 1)

"Joint effort of the Research Materials Information Center ...
of the Solid State Division at Oak Ridge National Laboratory and
the Libraries and Information Systems Center at Bell Telephone
Laboratories."

Gridina, V   P
Сегнетоэлектрики. Библиогр. указатель. 1943–1965.
Москва, "Наука," 1967.

213 p. 27 cm.

At head of title: Академия наук СССР. Сектор сети специальных библиотек. Библиотека ордена Ленина физического института им. П. Н. Лебедева.

Сегнетоэлектрики; библиографический указатель, 1943–1965.
[Составители: В. П. Гридина, В. А. Рассушин. Отв. редактор Г. М. Коваленко] Москва, Наука, 1967.

210 p. 27 cm.

At head of title: Академия наук СССР. Сектор сети специальных библиотек. Библиотека ордена Ленина Физического института им. П. Н. Лебедева.

FERTILITY

United Nations. Economic Commission for Asia and the Far East.
Fertility studies in the ECAFE region; a bibliography
of books, papers, and reference materials. Bangkok, Thailand, United Nations, 1971.

v, 54 p. 28 cm. (Asian population studies series, no. 6) (United
Nations [Document] E/CN.11/992)

FERTILIZERS

Bystriakov, O   V
Мінеральні добрива Української РСР. Бібліографічний покажчик. 1918–1965. Київ, "Наукова думка," 1968.

2 v. 21 cm.

At head of title: Академія наук Української РСР. Центральна
наукова бібліотека.
By O. V. Bystriakov, Z. M. Vashchenko, and M. K. Zvyhlianych.

Chernova, L   V
[Izvestkovanie sel'skokhoziaistvennykh zemel']
Известкование сельскохозяйственных земель. Библиогр. указатель литературы за 1965–1969 гг., отечеств. в количестве 459 назв. и иностр. в количестве 210
назв. [Сост. Л. В. Чернова] Москва, 1970.

127 p. 20 cm.

At head of title: Всесоюзная Академия с.-х. наук имени В. И.
Ленина. Центральная научная сельскохозяйственная библиотека.
Справочно-библиографический отдел.

European Nitrogen Service Programme.
Nitrogen in Indian agriculture, 1961–70; a bibliography
of N, NP, NK, NPK, and other related factors. New Delhi
[1972]

xix, 466 p. 23 cm.

Title on spine: A bibliography on nitrogen in Indian agriculture,
1961–70.

"Compiled by Dr. H. L. S. Tandon, Senior Agronomist, as a part
of ENSP's research programme in India."

Fertilizer abstracts. v. 1–
Jan. 1968–
[Muscle Shoals, Ala., Technical Library, National Ferti-
lizer Development Center]

v. 28 cm. monthly.

Gladysheva, G   A
Производство сложных удобрений (нитрофоска и

нитроаммофоска) на основе азотнокислотного разло-
жения фосфатного сырья. Библиогр. указатель отечеств. и зарубежной литературы за 1960–1968 гг. Под
ред. канд. хим. наук Т. Ф. Абашкиной. Москва, 1970.

70 p. 22 cm.

Cover title: Библиографический указатель по минеральным
удобрениям и серной кислоте.

At head of title: Научно-исследовательский институт по удобрениям и инсектофунгицидам имени Я. В. Самойлова.

By G. A. Gladysheva and L. I. Antonova.

Issued by the Institute's Laboratoriia nauchno-tekhnicheskoĭ informatsii.

Moscow. TSentral'naia nauchnaia sel'skokhoziaistvennaia biblioteka.
Применение минеральных удобрений при орошении;
библиографический список. [Составила А. Я. Францева.
Редактор Т. И. Шейнина] Москва, 1964.

10 p. 20 cm.

At head of title: Всесоюзная академия сельскохозяйственных
наук имени В. И. Ленина.

FESTSCHRIFTEN

Berlin, Charles, 1936–
Index to festschriften in Jewish studies. Cambridge,
Harvard College Library, 1971.

xi, 319 p. 24 cm.

Danton, J   Periam, 1908–
Index to Festschriften in librarianship [by] J. Periam
Danton, with the assistance of Ottilia C. Anderson. New
York, R. R. Bowker Co., 1970.

xi, 461 p. 26 cm.

Dau, Helmut.
Bibliographie juristischer Festschriften und Festschriften-
beiträge. Deutschland, Schweiz, Österreich. 1962–1966.
Bielefeld, Runge in Kommission, 1967.

195 p. 23 cm.

Gerboth, Walter.
An index to musical festschriften and similar publications.
[1st ed.] New York, W. W. Norton [1969]

ix, 188 p. 24 cm.

Malmström, Rosa.
Svensk festskriftsbibliografi 1936–1960. Bibliography of
Swedish homage volumes 1936–1960. Göteborg, Universi-
tetsbiblioteket, 1967.

viii, (3), 390 p. 25 cm. (Acta Bibliothecae Universitatis Gothoburgensis, v. 10)

A continuation of Svensk festskriftsbibliografi åren 1891–1925 by
G. Taube.

Phillips University, Enid, Okla. Graduate Seminary. Library.
An index of Festschriften in religion in the Graduate
Seminary Library of Phillips University. Compiled by
John L. Sayre and Roberta Hamburger. Enid, Okla., Hay-
maker Press, 1970.

iv, 121 p. 28 cm.

———— ———— New titles, 1971–   Compiled by John L.
Sayre and Roberta Hamburger. Enid, Okla., Seminary
Press, 1973–

v. 28 cm.

Roberts, Lilly Melchior.
A bibliography of legal festschriften. The Hague, Nijhoff,
1972.

xii, 178 p. 24 cm.

Sawicka, Franciszka.
Bibliografia polskich wydawnictw pamiątkowych, 1801
–1914. Wrocław, Zakład Narodowy im. Ossolińskich, 1973.

499 p., 44 p. of facsims. 25 cm.

At head of title: Polska Akademia Nauk. Zakład Narodowy
imienia Ossolińskich. Biblioteka. Franciszka Sawicka, Jadwiga
Rupińska.

Schwickerath, Hildegard.
Inhaltsverzeichnis der Festschriften zur Ehrung und
Würdigung deutscher, österreichischer und schweizer Geo-
graphen sowie der Festschriften zu Jubiläen geographischer
Gesellschaften Deutschlands, Österreichs und der Schweiz.
Bearb. im Institut für Landeskunde, von Hildegard
Schwickerath und Rolf D. Schmidt. Bad Godesberg,
Bundesforschungsanstalt für Landeskunde und Raumord-
nung, 1969.

117 p. 21 cm. (Berichte zur deutschen Landeskunde, Sonderheft
11)

FICHTE, JOHANN GOTTLIEB

Baumgartner, Hans Michael.
J. G. Fichte: Bibliographie ₍von₎ Hans Michael Baumgartner ₍und₎ Wilhelm G. Jacobs. Stuttgart-Bad Cann-
statt, F. Frommann, 1968.

846 p. 28 cm.

FICTION

Büchereizentrale Flensburg.
Sozialkritische Romane. Auswahlverz. Flensburg,
Büchereizentrale Flensburg, 1972.

33 p. 15 x 21 cm.

Culpan, Norman.
Contemporary adult fiction, 1945–1965, for school and
college libraries: a list of books, with a short list of critical
works on the modern novel, chosen and annotated for the
use of Sixth-form and other students; compiled for the
School Library Association by Norman Culpan, assisted by
W. J. Messer. London, School Library Association, 1967.

viii, 66 p. 24 cm.

Day, Bradford M
Bibliography of adventure. Compiled and edited by
Bradford M. Day. Denver, N. Y., Science-Fiction & Fan-
tasy Publications, 1964.

125 p. 28 cm.

"Limited to 300 copies."

CONTENTS. — Talbot Mundy, a bibliography. — Sax Rohmer, a bibliography.—H. Rider Haggard, first editions.—Edgar Rice Burroughs,
a bibliography.

**Girault de Saint-Fargeau, Pierre Augustin Eusèbe, 1799–
1855.**
Revue des romans; recueil d'analyses raisonnées des productions remarquables des plus célèbres romanciers français
et étrangers. Genève, Slatkine Reprints, 1968.

2 v. in 1. 23 cm.

"Réimpression de l'édition de Paris, 1839."
"Essai de bibliographie spéciale des romans": t. 1, p. ₍ix₎–xv.

Griswold, William McCrillis, 1853–1899.
Descriptive lists of American, international, romantic and
British novels, compiled by W. M. Griswold. New York,
B. Franklin, 1968.

10, 617 p. 23 cm. (Burt Franklin bibliography & reference se-
ries, #135)
Reprint of the 1891 ed. of v. 1 (pts. 1–5) of the author's De-
scriptive lists of novels and tales.
On spine: i–v.
CONTENTS. — Descriptive list of novels and tales dealing with
American country life.—A descriptive list of novels and tales dealing

with American city life.—A descriptive list of international novels.—
Descriptive list of romantic novels.—A descriptive list of British
novels.

Griswold, William McCrillis, 1853–1899.
Descriptive lists of French, German, Italian, Russian, and
Norwegian tales and novels. New York, B. Franklin.
₍1970₎

10, 618–807 p. 23 cm. (Burt Franklin bibliography and reference
series, 135. Essays in literature and criticism, 101)

Reprint of the 1891 ed. of v. 2 (pts. 6–10) of the author's Descriptive lists of novels and tales.
On spine: Descriptive lists of tales-novels, vi–x.

CONTENTS.—A descriptive list of novels and tales dealing with
life in France.—A descriptive list of novels and tales dealing with
life in Germany.—A descriptive list of novels and tales dealing with
life in Italy.—A descriptive list of novels and tales dealing with
life in Russia.—A descriptive list of novels and tales dealing with
life in Norway.

Kerr, Elizabeth Margaret, 1905–
Bibliography of the sequence novel. New York, Octagon
Books, 1973 ₍c1950₎

v, 126 p. 29 cm.

Reprint of the ed. published by the University of Minnesota Press,
Minneapolis.

National Book League, London.
Chosen for teenagers, a selection of modern fiction. London ₍1970₎

18 p. 21 cm.

National Book League, *London.*
Have you read this? A wide range of books for parents,
teachers and librarians to read and consider suggesting to
teenagers. London, National Book League, 1967.

57 p. 21½ cm.

New Zealand Library Association. Fiction Committee.
Guide to authors of fiction, sixth report.

———— Supplement. Wellington, New Zealand Library
Association, 1969.

ii, 10 p. 26 cm.

Raabe, Juliette.
La bibliothèque idéale des littératures d'évasion ₍par₎
Juliette Raabe ₍et₎ Francis Lacassin. Paris, Éditions uni-
versitaires, 1969.

216 p. 20 cm. (La Bibliothèque idéale)

Romane und Erzählungen; ein Auswahlverzeichnis. ₍Bear-
beiter: Marianne Goltz, et al. Herausgeber: Zentralinstitut
für Bibliothekswesen, Berlin₎ Leipzig, Bibliographisches
Institut, 1965.

328 p. 22 cm.

"Auswahl von 1263 Werken ... die in mittleren und grösseren
allgemeinbildenden Bibliotheken unserer Republik vorhanden sind."
"Bearbeitete und ergänzte Neuaflage."
Previous ed. issued in 2 parts.

Romane und Erzählungen. Von 1900 bis zur Gegenwart.
Eine Auswahl. (Katalog zusammengestellt von Marga
Böhmer-Plitt ₍u. a.₎) (Hamburg) Hamburger Öffentliche
Bücherhallen, 1967.

160 p. 21 cm.

Sagehomme, Georges, 1862–1937.
Répertoire alphabétique de 16.700 auteurs, 70.000 romans
et pièces de théâtre cotés au point de vue moral ₍par₎ G.
Sagehomme ... 10ᵉ édition ... refondue par le chanoine A.
Donot. ₍Paris, Tournai₎ Casterman, 1966.

720 p. 18 cm.

Saskatchewan. Provincial Library, Regina. Bibliographic Services Division.
Fiction for young adults: a bibliography compiled by Bibliographic Services Division, Provincial Library. Regina, 1972.

37 p. 22 cm.

Sense and Sensibility Collective.
Women and literature : an annotated bibliography of women writers. — 2d ed., rev. and expanded / the Sense and Sensibility Collective. — ₍Cambridge, Mass. : The Collective, c1973₎

ii, 58 p. : ill. ; 24 cm.

Siemon, Frederick, 1935–
Ghost story index; an author-title index to more than 2,200 stories of ghosts, horrors, and the macabre appearing in 190 books and anthologies. San Jose, Calif., Library Research Associates, 1967.

141 p. 21 cm.

DETECTIVE STORIES

Barzun, Jacques, 1907–
A catalogue of crime ₍by₎ Jacques Barzun & Wendell Hertig Taylor. ₍1st ed.₎ New York, Harper & Row ₍1971₎

xxxi, 831 p. 22 cm.

Craigie, Dorothy.
Victorian detective fiction: a catalogue of the collection made by Dorothy Glover & Graham Greene, bibliographically arranged by Eric Osborne and introduced by John Carter, with a preface by Graham Greene. London, Sydney ₍etc.₎ Bodley Head, 1966.

xix, 151 p. 25½ cm.

Detective fiction: a century of crime; first and early editions. ₍Hastings, Eng., R. A. Brimmell, 1966?₎

45 p. (incl. cover) illus. 22 cm.

Friedland, Susan.
South African detective stories in English and Afrikaans from 1951–1971; a bibliography. Johannesburg, University of Witwatersrand, Dept. of Bibliography, Librarianship and Typography, 1972.

ii, 46 p. 30 cm.

English or Afrikaans.

Great Britain. British Council.
British crime fiction ₍by₎ the British Council and the National Book League. London, British Council; National Book League ₍1974₎

51 p. 21 cm.

Hagen, Ordean A
Who done it? A guide to detective, mystery, and suspense fiction, by Ordean A. Hagen. New York, Bowker, 1969.

xx, 834 p. 27 cm.

Hedman, Iwan, 1931–
Svensk deckare- & thrillerbibliografi. Strängnäs, författaren (Flodinsv. 5), 1972.

7, 524 p., 4 l. of plates. illus. 30 cm.

Indiana. University. Lilly Library.
The first hundred years of detective fiction, 1841-1941; by one hundred authors on the hundred thirtieth anniversary of the first publication in book form of Edgar Allan Poe's "The murders in the Rue Morgue", Philadelphia, 1843. ₍Bloomington, 1973₎

64 p. illus. 28 cm. (Lilly Library publication no. 18)

"An exhibition held at the Lilly Library, Indiana University, Bloomington, July-September, 1973."

Mundell, E   H
A checklist of detective short stories, by E. H. Mundell. Portage, Ind. 1968.

xii, 337 p. 19 cm.

Queen, Ellery, *pseud.*
The detective short story, a bibliography. With a new introd. by the author. New York, Biblo and Tannen, 1969.

146 p. 24 cm.

Queen, Ellery, *pseud.*
Queen's quorum; a history of the detective-crime short story as revealed in the 106 most important books published in this field since 1845. New York, Biblo and Tannen, 1969.

ix, 146 p. facsim. 24 cm.

Reprint of the 1951 ed., with supplements through 1967.

Rodríguez Joulia Saint-Cyr, Carlos.
La novela de intriga (Diccionario de autores, obras y personajes) Ediciones en castellano. Madrid, Asociación Nacional de Bibliotecarios, Archiveros y Arqueólogos (1972)

xii, 154 p. 24 cm. (Biblioteca profesional de Anaba. 2. Bibliografías, 2)

HISTORICAL FICTION
see also *Children's literature – Historical*

Baker, Ernest Albert, 1869–1941.
A guide to historical fiction. ₍New York₎ Argosy-Antiquarian, 1968.

xv, 565 p. 26 cm.

Reprint of the 1914 ed.

Baker, Ernest Albert, 1869–1941.
A guide to historical fiction. New York, B. Franklin ₍1969₎

xv, 565 p. 26 cm. (Burt Franklin bibliography & reference series, 253)

Reprint of the 1914 ed.

Berggren, Kerstin.
Historiska romaner. Ett kommenterat urval av Kerstin Berggren och Gösta Berggren. Lund, Bibliotekstjänst; ₍Solna, Seelig₎ 1968.

56 p. illus. 21 cm. (Btj-serien, 15)

Biblioteksentralen, A/l, *Oslo. Bibliografisk avdeling.*
Historiske romaner. Utarb. av Berit Lund og Emilie Bull. 2. utg. Oslo, 1969.

40 p. 21 cm. (Blant bøker, nr. 21)

California Library Association. Young Adult Librarians' Round Table.
A subject list of historical fiction for young adult reading. ₍n. p., 1964₎

iii, 40 p. 22 cm.

Irwin, Leonard Bertram, 1904–
A guide to historical fiction for the use of schools, libraries, and the general reader. Compiled by Leonard B. Irwin. 10th ed., new and rev. Brooklawn, N. J., McKinley Pub. Co., 1971.

vii, 255 p. 24 cm. (McKinley bibliographies, v. 1)

First-9th editions by H. Logasa, published under title: Historical fiction.

Jong, J   E   de.
Nederlandse klassiek-historische romans en verhalen (1800–1968). Proeve van een bibliografie. Door J. E. de Jong. ₁Werkstuk 2e cyclus Bibliotheek- en Documentatieschool, Amsterdam. Amsterdam, Bibliotheek- en Documentatieschool₁, 1969.

i, 54 l. 29 cm.

Kadečková, Marie.
Český historický román a povídka 1946–1967. Výběrová bibliografie. Sest. Marie Kadečková. Hradec Králové, Kraj. knihovna, rozmn., 1968.

50, ₁1₁ p. 29 cm.

Художественно-историческая литература по новой и новейшей истории; аннотированный указатель для учащихся средней школы. ₁Составители: Р. М. Абанина и др.₁ Москва, Книга, 1965.

206 p. illus., ports. 22 cm.

At head of title: Государственная публичная историческая библиотека.

LeDoux Library.
British historical fiction. ₁Eunice, La.₁ 1972.

₁9₁ l. 28 cm. (Its Bibliography 5)

Logasa, Hannah, 1879–
Historical fiction: guide for junior and senior high schools and colleges, also for general reader. 8th rev. and enl. ed. Philadelphia, McKinley Pub. Co., 1964.

368 p. 24 cm. (McKinley bibliographies, v. 1)

Logasa, Hannah, 1879–1967.
Historical fiction; guide for junior and senior high schools and colleges, also for general reader. 9th rev. and enl. ed. Brooklawn, N. J., McKinley Pub. Co., 1968.

383 p. 24 cm. (McKinley bibliographies, v. 1)

McGarry, Daniel D
World historical fiction guide: an annotated, chronological, geographical and topical list of selected historical novels, by Daniel D. McGarry and Sarah Harriman White. 2d ed. Metuchen, N. J., Scarecrow Press, 1973.

xxi, 629 p. 23 cm.

Edition for 1963 published under title: Historical fiction guide: annotated chronological, geographical, and topical list of five thousand selected historical novels.

Nield, Jonathan, 1863–
A guide to the best historical novels and tales. New York, B. Franklin ₁1968₁

xxvi, 424 p. 24 cm. (Burt Franklin Bibliography and reference series #228)

Reprint of the 5th ed., 1929.

Petra, Aune.
Historiallisia romaaneja ja ajankuvauksia. Helsinki, Suomen kirjastoseura, 1968.

70 p. 21 cm.

Rose, Leslae.
The Mohawk Valley in historical fiction; an annotated bilbiography ₁sic₁. New Berlin, N. Y., 1968.

iii, 21 l. 28 cm.

Thompson, William Bernard.
Classical novels; a catalogue of novels dealing with the people and events of Greece and Rome, with a prefatory essay ₁by₁ William B. Thompson. Leeds, Association for the Reform of Latin Teaching, 1966.

23 p. 22 cm.

Van Derhoof, Jack Warner.
A bibliography of novels related to American frontier and colonial history, by Jack VanDerhoof. Troy, N. Y., Whitston Pub. Co., 1971.

xii, 501 p. 24 cm.

Wilf, Michael.
הסיפורת העברית ההיסטורית; ביבליוגרפיה, אסף וערך מיכאל וילף. חיפה, מפעל השכפול, 728 ₁8 or 1967₁

69 l. 32 cm.

"רומנים וסיפורים היסטוריים מקוריים שיצאו לאור בסער ממאפו ער שנת תשכ"ו/כ"ז ... כולל מחזות שנרפסו בכתבי עת ובקבצים, וכן ... רשימות של דברי ביקורת."

HISTORY AND CRITICISM

Adelman, Irving.
The contemporary novel; a checklist of critical literature on the British and American novel since 1945, by Irving Adelman and Rita Dworkin. Metuchen, N. J., Scarecrow Press, 1972.

614 p. 22 cm.

Akademiia nauk SSSR. *Biblioteka.*
Советский роман, его теория и история; библиографический указатель. 1917–1964. Составила Н. А. Грознова. Ленинград, 1966.

256 p. 17 cm.

At head of title: Библиотека Академии наук СССР. Институт русской литературы (Пушкинский дом) Академии наук СССР.

Boyd, George N
Religion in contemporary fiction; criticism from 1945 to the present. Compiled by George N. Boyde and Lois A. Boyd. San Antonio, Tex., Trinity University Press ₁1973₁

viii, 99 p. 24 cm. (Checklists in the humanities and education)

Cotton, Gerald Brooks.
Fiction guides; general: British and American ₁by₁ Gerald B. Cotton & Hilda Mary McGill. ₁Hamden, Conn.₁ Archon Books ₁1967₁

126 p. 23 cm. (The Readers guide series)

Cotton, Gerald Brooks.
Fiction guides; general: British and American ₁by₁ Gerald B. Cotton & Hilda Mary McGill. London, Bingley, 1967.

126 p. 22½ cm. (Readers guides series)

Drescher, Horst W
The contemporary English novel; an annotated bibliography of secondary sources, by Horst W. Drescher and Bernd Kahrmann. ₁Frankfurt am Main₁ Athenäum-Verlag ₁1973₁

xvii, 204 p. 23 cm.

Gerstenberger, Donna Lorine.
The American novel; a checklist of twentieth-century criticism, by Donna Gerstenberger and George Hendrick. Denver, A. Swallow ₁1961–70₁

2 v. 23 cm.

Vol. 2 has subtitle: a checklist of twentieth century criticism on novels written since 1789.

CONTENTS.—₁1₁ 1789–1959.—v. 2. 1960–1968.

Hall, Susan Corwin.
Hawthorne to Hemingway; an annotated bibliography of books from 1945 to 1963 about nine American writers. Edited by Robert H. Woodward. New York, Garrett Pub.

Co., 1965.

iii, 70 p. 23 cm.

Holman, Clarence Hugh, 1914–   *comp.*
The American novel through Henry James, compiled by
C. Hugh Holman. New York, Appleton-Century-Crofts
[1966]

ix, 102 p. 24 cm. (Goldentree bibliographies)

Kearney, E   I
The continental novel; a checklist of criticism in Eng-
lish, 1900–1966, [by] E. I. Kearney and L. S. Fitzgerald.
Metuchen, N. J., Scarecrow Press, 1968.

xiv, 460 p. 22 cm.

Nevius, Blake.
The American novel: Sinclair Lewis to the present. New
York, Appleton-Century-Crofts [1970]

xii, 126 p. 24 cm. (Goldentree bibliographies in language and
literature)

Pages 109–114 blank for "Notes."

Palmer, Helen H
English novel explication: criticisms to 1972. Compiled
by Helen H. Palmer & Anne Jane Dyson. [Hamden,
Conn.] Shoe String Press, 1973.

vi, 329 p. 22 cm.

Pfeiffer, John R
Fantasy and science fiction: a critical guide, by John R.
Pfeiffer. Palmer Lake, Colo., Filter Press, 1971.

iv, 64 p. illus. 22 cm.

Ray, Gordon Norton, 1915–
Bibliographical resources for the study of nineteenth cen-
tury English fiction, by Gordon N. Ray. Los Angeles,
School of Library Service, University of California, 1964.

31 p. 23 cm.

Walker, Warren S
Twentieth-century short story explication; interpreta-
tions, 1900–1966, of short fiction since 1800. Compiled by
Warren S. Walker. 2d ed. [Hamden, Conn.] Shoe String
Press, 1967.

vi, 697 p. 22 cm.

———— Supplement I–   1967–
[Hamden, Conn.] Shoe String Press, 1970–
v. 23 cm.

Wiley, Paul L
The British novel: Conrad to the present. Compiled by
Paul L. Wiley. Northbrook, Ill., AHM Pub. Corp. [1973]

xii, 137 p. 23 cm. (Goldentree bibliographies in language and
literature)

LIBRARY AND EXHIBITION CATALOGS

Durham, Philip.
The West: from fact to myth [by] Philip Durham &
Everett L. Jones. Catalogue of an exhibit in the UCLA
Library, September 20–October 24, 1967. [Los Angeles?
1967]

19 p. illus., facsims. 24 cm.
Cover title.
"Prepared by the University of California Library, Los Angeles,
on the occasion of the International League of Antiquarian Book-
sellers meetings and the Second International Antiquarian Book Fair,
San Francisco and Los Angeles, September 1967."

Fales Library.
Fales Library checklist. Rev. and edited by Theodore
Grieder. New York, AMS Press [1970]

2 v. (ix, 1104 p.) 27 cm.

At head of title: New York University Libraries

Hain, Ulrich.
Katalog der Sammlung Trivialliteratur des 19. Jahrhun-
derts in der Univ. Bibl. Giessen [von] Ulrich Hain [und]
Jörg Schilling. Hrsg. von Hermann Schüling. Giessen,
Universitätsbibliothek, 1970.

3, 376 p. 23 cm. (Berichte und Arbeiten aus der Universitätsbibliothek Giessen, 20)

Hamilton, Alex.
A long look at the short story; a list of books, selected
by Alex Hamilton. London, National Book League [1972]

37 p. 21 cm.

National Book League exhibition, 10–24 July, 1972.

Liverpool. Public Libraries, Museums and Art Gallery.
Catalogue of fiction added to the lending libraries, 1958–
1966. Liverpool, Central Library, 1967.

[1], 227 p. 25 cm.

Ohio. State University, *Columbus. Libraries.*
The William Charvat American fiction collection. [Co-
lumbus, 1967–

v. facsims. 23 cm.

CONTENTS.—[1] An exhibition of selected works, 1787–1850, June
1 through July 15, 1967, Ohio State University Main Library.—2.
An exhibition of selected works, 1851–1875, November 15 through
December 31, 1967, Ohio State University Main Library.

Payne, John R
Modern British fiction; an exhibit of books, paintings
and manuscripts, November–December 1972. Catalog by
John R. Payne with introd. by Alan Friedman. [Austin]
Humanities Research Center, University of Texas at Austin
[c1972]

56 p. illus. 18 x 26 cm.
"Prepared for an exhibit to be displayed during a symposium ...
sponsored by the College of Humanities and the Department of English at the University of Texas at Austin."

PERIODICALS

McKinstry, Lohr.
The hero-pulp index, by McKinstry and Weinberg. [1st
ed. Hillside? N. J., 1970]

54 p. 28 cm.

SCIENCE FICTION

Clareson, Thomas D
Science fiction criticism; an annotated checklist, by
Thomas Clareson. [1st ed. Kent, Ohio] Kent State Uni-
versity Press [1972]

xiii, 225 p. 23 cm. (The Serif series: bibliographies and checklists, no. 23)

Cole, Walter R
A checklist of science-fiction anthologies, compiled by
W. R. Cole. [Brooklyn? 1964]

xvi, 374 p. 29 cm.

Cook, Frederick S   1929–
Fred Cook's index to the Wonder group, compiled and
arranged by Frederick S. Cook. [Grand Haven, Mich.,
1966]

239 p. 28 cm.

Indexes Air wonder stories, Science wonder quarterly, Wonder
stories quarterly, Science wonder stories, Wonder stories, Thrilling
wonder stories, Wonder stories annual, Startling stories, Captain
Future, Fantastic story quarterly, Fantastic story magazine, and
Space stories.

Day, Bradford M
The checklist of fantastic literature in paperbound books. Compiled by Bradford M. Day. Denver, N. Y., Science-Fiction & Fantasy Publications, 1965.

128 p. 29 cm.

Durie, A   J   L   comp.
An index to the British editions of the 'Magazine of fantasy and science fiction,' with a cross-reference to the original American edition, compiled and published by A. J. L. Durie. ₁Wisbech (Cambs.), Fantast, 1966₁

44 p. 25½ cm.

Houston, Tex. Public Library.
The future: science fiction book exhibit. Presented by Houston Public Library in connection with Houston Arts Festival, October 1968. ₁Houston, 1968₁

1 v. (unpaged) illus., facsims. 27 cm.

An Index to science fiction book reviews in Astounding/Analog 1949–1969, Fantasy and science fiction 1946–1969, Galaxy 1950–1969. Compiled by Barry McGhan ₁and others₁ Pref. by Damon Knight. College Station, Tex. ₁Science Fiction Research Association₁ 1973.

vii, 88 p. 28 cm. (SFRA miscellaneous publication no. 1)

Ishihara, Fujio.
(SF tosho kaisetsu sōmokuroku)

S F 図書解説総目録　昭和20年9月－昭和

43年8月

石原藤夫編

東京　シャンブロウ・プレス　昭和44(1969)

534p　26cm

Kerr, Stephen T
A bibliographical guide to Soviet fantasy and science fiction, 1957–1968. Compiled and with an introd. by Stephen T. Kerr. New York, 1969.

iv, 92 l. 29 cm.

Liapunov, Boris Valer'ianovich.
В мире мечты. Обзор науч.-фантаст. литературы. ₁Москва, "Книга," 1970₁.

213 p. with illus. 20 cm.

At head of title: Борис Ляпунов.

Lundwall, Sam J   1941–
Bibliografi över science fiction och fantasy ₁av₁ Sam J. Lundwall. ₁2. uppl.₁ Stockholm, Bokförlaget Fiktiva ₁1964₁

75 p. illus. 21 cm.

Saskatchewan. Provincial Library, Regina. Bibliographic Services Division.
Science fiction; a bibliography. Regina, Provincial Library, 1973.

33 p. 28 cm.

SF. 1968–
₁Lake Jackson, Tex.₁

v. 29 cm. annual.

Title varies: 1968, Science fiction.
Compiler: 1968–   J. Burger.

Siemon, Frederick, 1935–
Science fiction story index, 1950–1968. Chicago, American Library Association, 1971.

x, 274 p. 22 cm.

Slater, Kenneth F
A checklist of science fiction, fantasy and supernatural stories available in paperback in Britain, January 1966; compiled by Kenneth F. Slater. Wisbech (Cambs.) Fantast (Medway) ₁1966₁

₁3₁, 30 p. 34½ cm.

Stone, Graham Brice, 1926–
Australian science fiction index, 1925–1967, compiled by Graham Stone. Canberra, Australian Science Fiction Association ₁1968₁

158 p. 21 cm.

"This index is a revision of the Australian science fiction index, 1939–1962."

Viggiano, Michael, comp.
Science fiction title changes; a guide to the changing titles of science fiction and fantasy stories published in magazines and books. Compiled by Michael Viggiano & Donald Franson. 1st ed. ₁North Hollywood? Calif.₁ National Fantasy Fan Federation ₁1965₁

47 p. 22 cm.

SCIENCE FICTION – BIBLIOGRAPHIES

Briney, Robert E   1933–
SF bibliographies: an annotated bibliography of bibliographical works on science fiction and fantasy fiction, by Robert E. Briney and Edward Wood. ₁1st ed.₁ Chicago, Advent: Publishers, 1972.

ix, 49 p. 22 cm.

SCIENCE FICTION – PERIODICALS

Australian Science Fiction Association.
Index to British science fiction magazines, 1934–1953. Canberra ₁1968₁

2 v. 21 cm.

CONTENTS.—pt. 1. Scoops, tales of wonder, fantasy.—pt. 2. Astounding science fiction.

New England Science Fiction Association.
Index to the science fiction magazines, 1966–1970. ₁1st ed. Cambridge, Mass.₁ 1971.

ix, 82 p. 29 cm.

"Companion volume to the Index to the science fiction magazines, 1951–1965, compiled by Erwin S. Strauss."

New England Science Fiction Association.
The N. E. S. F. A. index ₁to₁ science fiction magazines: 1971–1972 and original anthologies: 1971–1972. 1st ed. Cambridge, Mass. ₁1973₁

iv, 42 p. 28 cm.

"Companion volume and supplement to the Index to the science fiction magazines, 1951–1965, published by Erwin S. Strauss, and the Index to the science fiction magazines, 1966–1970, published by the N. E. S. F. A."

Strauss, Erwin S
The MIT Science Fiction Society's index to the s-f magazines, 1951–1965. Compiled by Erwin S. Strauss. ₁Cambridge, Mass., MIT Science Fiction Society₁ c1966.

iii, 207 p. 29 cm.

Cover title.
Preceded by Index to the science-fiction magazines, 1926–1950, by D. B. Day.

TRANSLATIONS

Bibliothèque centrale de prêt de l'Eure.
Romans étrangers; catalogue. Évreux, 1967.

69 p. 31 cm.

At head of title: Ministère de l'éducation nationale. Conseil général de l'Eure. Bibliothèque centrale de prêt.

König, Gertrud.
Romane aus Amerika. Ein Auswahlverzeichnis. (Bearbeitung: Gertrud König [und] Otto Eckert). (Herausgeber: Stadtbücherei Bochum.) Dortmund, Stadtbücherei, 1966.

100 p. 21 cm.

May, Derwent, 1930–
European novels of the sixties; selected by Derwent May. London, National Book League, 1972.

36 p. 21 cm.

AFRICA

Astrinsky, Aviva.
A bibliography of South African English novels, 1930–1960. [Cape Town] University of Cape Town, School of Librarianship, 1965.

57 p. 23 cm. (University of Cape Town. School of Librarianship. Bibliographical series)

Astrinsky, Aviva.
A bibliography of South African English novels 1930–1960. Cape Town, University of Cape Town Libraries, 1970.

viii, 50 p. 23 cm. (University of Cape Town. School of Librarianship. Bibliographical series)

Presented in partial fulfilment of the requirements for the Higher Certificate in Librarianship, 1965.

Hobson, Mary Bonin.
A select bibliography of South African short stories in English, 1870–1950. Cape Town, University of Cape Town Libraries, 1972.

ii, 29 p. 23 cm. (University of Cape Town Libraries. Bibliographical series)

Miller, Anita.
Afrikaanse speurverhale uitgegee tot die einde van 1950. 'n Bibliografie saamgestel deur Anita Miller. Johannesburg, Universiteit van die Witwatersrand, 1967.

iv, 23 l. 30 cm.

"Saamgestel ter vervulling van 'n deel van die vereistes vir die Diploma in Biblioteekwese."

ARABIC

al-Nassāj, Sayyid Hāmid.
[Dalīl al-qiṣṣah al-Miṣrīyah al-qaṣīrah]
دليل القصة المصرية القصيرة، صحف ومجموعات ١٩١١ – ١٩٦١. اعداد سيد حامد النساج. [القاهرة] الهيئة المصرية العامة للكتاب، 1972.

224 p. 33 cm.

AUSTRALIA

Hubble, Gregory Valentine.
The Australian novel; a title checklist 1900–1970. Perth, Imperial Instant Printing, 1970.

1 v. (unpaged) 25 cm.

"Published in a limited edition of 400 numbered copies." No. 241.

BRAZIL

Gomes, Celuta Moreira.
Bibliografia do conto brasileiro, 1841–1967, por Celuta Moreira Gomes e Thereza da Silva Aguiar. Rio de Janeiro, Biblioteca Nacional, 1968–69.

2 v. 27 cm. (Anais da Biblioteca Nacional, v. 87)

CANADA

Hayne, David M
Bibliographie critique du roman canadien-français, 1837–1900 [par] David M. Hayne [et] Marcel Tirol. [Toronto] University of Toronto Press [°1968]

viii, 144 p. 24 cm.

Saskatchewan. Provincial Library, Regina. Bibliographic Services Division.
Canadian fiction; a bibliography. Regina, Sask., 1973.

31 p. 28 cm.

Cover title.
"Most of the material ... was collected by Andrea Hnatuk of the Bibliographic Services Division."

Wren, Sheila.
Short story index compiled from the Canadian periodical index, 1938–1947. Ottawa, Canadian Library Association, 1967.

46 p. 28 cm.

CHINA

Li, Tien-yi, 1915–
Chinese fiction; a bibliography of books and articles in Chinese and English. New Haven, Far Eastern Publications, Yale University, 1968.

xiv, 356 p. 24 cm.

Added t. p. in Chinese.

CZECHOSLOVAK REPUBLIC

Brünn. Krajská lidová knihovna.
Špionážní četba. Soupis knih vydaných v letech 1961–1971. Brno, Knihovna Jiřího Mahena, rozmn., 1972.

19, [1] p. 20 cm.

Kádnerová, Jiřina.
Poprvé k volebním urnám. Výběrová bibliogr. o životě mladých lidí. Sest. Jiřina Kádnerová. Kladno, Kraj. knihovna, rozmn., 1971.

44 p. 21 cm. (Edice Kk Kladno. Bibliografie. Malá řada, 18)

DENMARK

Møldrup, Anna Elise.
Romannøglen. 2. udg. [Gennemset af Kjeld Høyrup og Karen Wilson]. København, Bibliotekscentralen, 1968.

62 p. 20 cm.

FRANCE

Pigoreau, Alexandre Nicolas, 1765–1851.
Petite bibliographie biographico-romancière ou dictionnaire des romanciers [par] Alexandre Pigoreau. Genève, Slatkine reprints, 1968.

1 v. (various pagings) 23 cm.

"Réimpression de l'édition de Paris, 1821."

GERMANY

Dortmund. Stadtbücherei.
Romane und Erzählungen. Ein Auswahlverzeichnis. (Von Gisela Höngesberg und Edith Seyler.) Dortmund, Stadtbücherei, 1966.

292 p. 21 cm.

Germer, Helmut.
The German novel of education, 1792–1805; a complete

bibliography and analysis. ₍Berne₎ Herbert Lang, 1968.

₍xvl₎ 280 p. 23 cm. (German studies in America, no. 3)

GREAT BRITAIN

Baker, Ernest Albert, 1869–1941.
A guide to the best fiction, English and American, including translations from foreign languages, by Ernest A. Baker and James Packman. New and enlarged ed. reissued. London, Routledge & K. Paul, 1967.

viii, 634 p. 28½ cm.

First published 1903 as a Descriptive Guide to best fiction.

Baker, Ernest Albert, 1869–1941.
A guide to the best fiction, English and American, including translations from foreign languages, by Ernest A. Baker and James Packman. New York, Barnes & Noble ₍1967₎

viii, 634 p. 28 cm.

First published in 1903 under title: Descriptive guide to the best fiction.
Reprint of the new and enl. ed., 1932.

Beasley, Jerry C
A check list of prose fiction published in England, 1740–1749. Compiled by Jerry C. Beasley. Charlottesville, Published for the Bibliographical Society of the University of Virginia ₍by₎ the University Press of Virginia ₍1972₎

xiv, 213 p. 22 cm.

Block, Andrew, 1892–
The English novel, 1740–1850; a catalogue including prose romances, short stories, and translations of foreign fiction; with introductions by John Crow and Ernest A. Baker. London, Dawsons of Pall Mall; Dobbs Ferry, N. Y., Oceana, 1967.

349 p. 25 cm.

Bonheim, Helmut W   1930–
The English novel before Richardson; a checklist of texts and criticism to 1970, by Helmut Bonheim. Metuchen, N. J., Scarecrow Press, 1971.

vi, 145 p. 22 cm.

Bufkin, E   C
The twentieth-century novel in English; a checklist, by E. C. Bufkin. Athens, University of Georgia Press ₍1967₎

vi, 138 p. 23 cm.

Burgess, Moira.
The Glasgow novel, 1870–1970: a bibliography. Glasgow, Scottish Library Association, 1972.

59 p. 21 cm.

Crook, Arthur Charles William, 1912–
British and Commonwealth fiction since 1950; selected by Arthur Crook. London, published for National Library Week by the National Book League, 1966.

32 p. 22 cm.

Esdaile, Arundell James Kennedy, 1880–1956.
A list of English tales and prose romances printed before 1740. New York, B. Franklin ₍1971₎

xxxv, 329 p. 22 cm. (Burt Franklin bibliography and reference, 400. Essays in literature and criticism, 114)

Reprint of the 1912 ed.

Esdaile, Arundell James Kennedy, 1880–1956.
A list of English tales and prose romances printed before

1740. Norwood, Pa., Norwood Editions, 1973.

xxxv, 329 p. 26 cm.

Reprint of the 1912 ed. printed for the Bibliographical Society by Blades, East & Blades, London, which was originally issued in series: Bibliographical Society, London. Publications.

Gardner, Frank M.
Sequels, incorporating Aldred & Parker's 'Sequel stories,' compiled by Frank M. Gardner. 5th ed. London, Association of Assistant Librarians, 1967.

₍4₎ 214, vii–x, 215–291 p. 23½ cm.

Jenson, Florence L
Fiction men read, prepared by Florence L. Jenson. ₍San Francisco, Pacific Air Forces₎ 1967.

iv, 40 p. 27 cm. (PACAF basic bibliographies for base libraries)

McBurney, William Harlin, *comp.*
English prose fiction, 1700–1800, in the University of Illinois Library. Compiled by William H. McBurney, with the assistance of Charlene M. Taylor. Urbana, University of Illinois Press, 1965.

₍6₎ 162 p. 23 cm.

May, Derwent, 1930–
British and Commonwealth novels of the sixties; selected by Derwent May. London, National Book League, 1970.

27 p. 21 cm.

Sadleir, Michael, 1888–1957.
xix century fiction, a bibliographical record based on his own collection, by Michael Sadleir. New York, Cooper Square Publishers, 1969.

2 v. plates. 29 cm.

Summers, Montague, 1880–1948.
A gothic bibliography. New York, Russell & Russell, 1964.

xx, 620 p. illus., facsims. 22 cm.

"First published in 1941."

Summers, Montague, 1880–1948.
A Gothic bibliography. London, Fortune P. ₍1969₎

iii–xx, 621 p., 22 plates. illus., facsims. 22 cm.

Wright, Robert Glenn.
Chronological bibliography of English language fiction in the Library of Congress through 1950 / compiled by R. Glenn Wright, assisted by Barbara E. Rosenbaum. — Boston : G. K. Hall. 1974.

8 v. ; 37 cm.

"Bibliography of primary sources": v. 1, p. xvii–xxii; "Bibliography of secondary sources": v. 1, p. xxiii–xxiv.
CONTENTS: v. 1. Australia–United Kingdom, 1908.—v. 2. United Kingdom, 1909–United Kingdom, 1935.—v. 3. United Kingdom, 1936–71–United States, 1965.—v. 4. United States, 1866–United States, 1914.—v. 5. United States, 1915–United States, 1938.—v. 6. United States, 1939–United States, 1960.—v. 7. United States, 1961–72. Nationality unknown. Indexes.—v. 8. Index of translations. Index of translators.

Yorkshire Cobook Group of Libraries.
Some novels set in Yorkshire; illustrations by Marie Hartley. Nr. Leeds, Yorkshire Cobook Group of Libraries, 1967.

₍2₎ 21 p. illus. 22½ cm.

HUNGARY

Uray, Béla.
Regény-ciklusok jegyzéke. 2. bőv. és jav. kiad. Budapest,

OSZK Könyvtártudományi és Módszertani Központ, 1964.

36 p. 21 cm. (A Könyvtártudományi és Módszertani Központ kladványal, 2)

IRELAND

Brown, Stephen James Meredith, 1881–
Ireland in fiction; a guide to Irish novels, tales, romances, and folklore ₍by₎ Stephen J. Brown. Introd. by Desmond J. Clarke. ₍2d ed.₎ New York, Barnes & Noble ₍1969–ᶜ1968–

v. 23 cm.

Vol. 1 is a reprint of the 1919 ed.

Brown, Stephen James Meredith, 1881–
Ireland in fiction; a guide to Irish novels, tales, romances, and folk-lore, by Stephen J. Brown. New ed. New York, B. Franklin ₍1970₎

xx, 362 p. 24 cm. (Burt Franklin bibliography & reference series, 311)

Essays in literature & criticism 47.
Reprint of the 1919 ed.

JAPAN

Musashino, Jirō, 1921–
(Shun'yō bunko no sakkatachi)
春陽文庫の作家たち　武蔵野次郎₍著　新訂版
東京　春陽堂書店　1970₎

101 p. illus., ports. 15 cm.

Yokoyama, Shigeru, 1896–　　　ed.
(Monogatari sōshi mokuroku)
物語帖子目録　横山重　巨橋頼三編　東京　角
川書店　昭和46(1971)

518 p. 23 cm.

Photoreproduction of 1937 ed.
CONTENTS: 古ものかたり目録　山岡俊明著―物語書目備考　伴直方著―古物語類字鈔　黒川春村著―物語書名寄　岡本保孝著―古物語名寄類温　横山由清著―物語草紙解題　平出順益著―近古小説解題　平出鏗二郎著―室町時代小説集解題　平出鏗二郎著―後記　横山重著

KOREA

Skillend, W　　E
Kodae sosŏl: a survey of Korean traditional style popular novels ₍by₎ W. E. Skillend. London, School of Oriental and African Studies, 1969.

268 p. 25 cm.

English or Korean.

LATIN AMERICA

Ocampo de Gómez, Aurora Maura.
Novelistas iberoamericanos contemporáneos; obras y bibliografía crítica ₍por₎ Aurora M. Ocampo de Gómez. México, Universidad Nacional Autónoma de México, Centro de Estudios Literarios, 1971–

v. 23 cm. (Cuadernos del Centro de Estudios Literarios, 2

MEXICO

Iguíniz, Juan Bautista, 1881–
Bibliografía de novelistas mexicanos; ensayo biográfico, bibliográfico y crítico ₍por₎ Juan B. Iguíniz. New York, B. Franklin ₍1970₎

xxxv, 432 p. facsim. 19 cm. (Burt Franklin bibliography & reference series, 397. Essays in literature and criticism, 110)

Reprint of the edition published in Mexico in 1926.
"Indice de seudónimos": p. ₍405₎–406.

Rutherford, John David.
An annotated bibliography of the novels of the Mexican Revolution of 1910–1917. In English and Spanish. By John Rutherford. Troy, N. Y., Whitston Pub. Co., 1972.

180 p. 23 cm.

On spine: Novels of the Mexican Revolution.

NORWAY

Biblioteksentralen, A/l, *Oslo. Bibliografisk avdeling.*
Fortsettelser. Romaner og biografier. En katalog. Utarb. ved Tore Hernes og Emilie Bull. Oslo, 1966.

44 p. 21 cm. (Blant bøker, nr. 19)

Cover title.
First ed. published in 1961 under title: Forsettelsesromaner.

POLAND

Maciuszko, Jerzy J　　1913–
The Polish short story in English; a guide and critical bibliography, by Jerzy (George) J. Maciuszko. With a foreword by William J. Rose. Detroit, Wayne State University Press, 1968.

473 p. 24 cm.

A revision of the author's thesis—Case Western Reserve University.

Rudnicka, Jadwiga.
Bibliografia powieści polskiej 1601–1800. ₍Wyd. 1.₎ Wrocław, Zakład Narodowy im. Ossolińskich, 1964.

336 p. facsims. 26 cm. (Książka w dawnej kulturze polskiej, 13)

On added t. p.: Instytut Badań Literackich Polskiej Akademii Nauk. Biblioteka Narodowa.
Summary in French.

SPAIN

Palomo, María del Pilar.
La novela española en 1961 y 1962. Madrid, C. S. I. C., 1964.

69 p. 26 cm. (Cuadernos bibliográficos, 13)

Issued in portfolio.

SWEDEN

Bibliotekstjänst.
Fortsättningsarbeten. En förteckning över ett urval svenska och översatta romaner. 4. omarb. uppl. Lund, Bibliotekstjänst, 1967.

32 p. 21 cm. (Btj-serien, 1)

First-2d ed., by C. T. Fries, published under title: Förteckning över fortsättningsarbeten bland svenska och översatta romaner; 3d ed., by C. T. Fries, published under title: Förteckning över fortsättningsarbeten.

UNITED STATES
Bibliographies which include both American and English fiction are entered under Fiction - Great Britain

Boger, Lorise C
The southern mountaineer in literature, an annotated bibliography ₍by₎ Lorise C. Boger. Morgantown, West Virginia University Library, 1964.

ix, 105 p. illus. 24 cm.

Bragin, Charles.
Dime novels, 1860–1964: bibliography. 1st ed. Brooklyn, N. Y., 1964.

[20] p. port., facsims. 23 cm. (Dime Novel Club. Fac-simile reprints, no. 63)

Coan, Otis Welton.
America in fiction; an annotated list of novels that interpret aspects of life in the United States, Canada, and Mexico [by] Otis W. Coan [and] Richard G. Lillard. 5th ed. Palo Alto, Calif., Pacific Books, 1967.

viii, 232 p. 24 cm.

Deodene, Frank.
Black American fiction since 1952; a preliminary checklist, by Frank Deodene and William P. French. Chatham, N. J., Chatham Bookseller, 1970.

25 p. 22 cm.

Duncan, Jeffrey.
American novels of the sixties; selected by Jeffrey Duncan. London, National Book League, 1971.

20 p. 21 cm.

Distributed in the United States and Canada by Richard Abel & Co. Inc., Portland, Ore.

Eichelberger, Clayton L   1925–
A guide to critical reviews of United States fiction, 1870–1910, compiled by Clayton L. Eichelberger. Assisted by Karen L. Bickley [and others] Metuchen, N. J., Scarecrow Press, 1971.

v. 22 cm.

Hannigan, Francis James, 1880–   comp.
The standard index of short stories, 1900–1914, compiled by Francis J. Hannigan. Boston, Gregg Press, 1972 [c1918]

334 p. 27 cm. (The Library reference series. Basic reference sources)

Reprint of the ed. published by Small, Maynard, Boston.

Johnson, James Gibson, 1871–1957.
Southern fiction prior to 1860: an attempt at a first-hand bibliography. New York, Phaeton Press, 1968.

vii, 126 p. 24 cm.

Reprint of 1909 ed.

LeDoux Library.
America in fiction. Compiled by Shih Yang. [Eunice, La.] 1972.

[14] l. 28 cm. (Its Bibliography 4)

Lost Cause Press, Louisville, Ky.
Lyle H. Wright: American fiction, 1774–1900. Louisville, 1970.

41 p. 23 cm.

Cover title.
At head of title: Lost Cause Press microcard/microfiche collection.
"The bibliographical work for this collection was done by Lawrence S. Thompson."
Does not list titles in Wright's American fiction, 1876–1900.

Wright, Lyle Henry, 1903–
American fiction, 1774–1850: a contribution toward a bibliography by Lyle H. Wright. 2d rev. ed. San Marino, Calif., Huntington Library, 1969.

xviii, 411 p. 24 cm. (Huntington Library publications)

Wright, Lyle Henry, 1903–
American fiction, 1851–1875; a contribution toward a bibliography, by Lyle H. Wright. San Marino, Calif., Huntington Library, 1965.

xviii, 438 p. front. 24 cm. (Huntington Library publications)

Wright, Lyle Henry, 1903–
American fiction, 1876–1900; a contribution toward a bibliography, by Lyle H. Wright. San Marino, Calif., Huntington Library, 1966.

xix, 683 p. 24 cm. (Huntington Library publications)

URUGUAY

Englekirk, John Eugene, 1905–
La narrativa uruguaya; estudio crítico-bibliográfico by John E. Englekirk and Margaret M. Ramos. Berkeley, University of California Press, 1967.

338 p. 24 cm. (University of California publications in modern philology, v. 80)

FIESOLE, ITALY

Raspini, Giuseppe.
Gli archivi parrocchiali della diocesi di Fiesole : inventario / Giuseppe Raspini. — Roma : Il centro di ricerca, 1974.

lxvii, 415 p. ; 24 cm. — (Fonti e studi di storia, legislazione e tecnica degli archivi moderni ; 9)

FIGUERES FERRER, JOSÉ

Kantor, Harry.
Bibliography of Jose Figueres. Tempe, Center for Latin American Studies, Arizona State University, 1972.

50 p. 23 cm.

FIGULI, MARGITA

Fischerová-Šebestová, Anna.
Margita Figuli. Sprac. Anna Fischerová-Šebestová. Martin, Matica slovenská, rozmn. Esopress, Bratislava, 1970.

89, [2] p. illus., facsim. 26 cm.

FIGUŠ-BYSTRÝ, VILIAM

Muntág, Emanuel.
Viliam Figuš—Bystrý. Život a dielo [1875–1937] Tematický katalog hud. tvorby a bibliografia o živote a diele slov. skladateľa. Noty kreslili M. Belorid a J. Soukup. Martin, Matica slovenská, t. T[lač.] SNP, 1973.

326, [1] p. tables, ports., music (also on lining paper) 25 cm. (Edícia: Personálne bibliografie, r. 1973, č. 1)

Summary in Russian and German.

FIJI ISLANDS

Baksh, S
Serial publications of the Government of Fiji. Compiled by S. Baksh. Suva, Central Archives of Fiji and the Western Pacific High Commission, 1967.

13 l. 33 cm. (Central Archives of Fiji and W. P. H. C. Reference Library. Serial publications catalogue no. 1)

Baksh, S
Serial publications of the Government of Fiji. Compiled by S. Baksh. Rev. and enl. by L. S. Qalo. Suva, Central Archives of Fiji and the Western Pacific High Commission, 1970.

16 l. 33 cm. (Central Archives of Fiji and W. P. H. C. Reference Library. Serial publications catalogue, no. 2)

Central Archives of Fiji and W. P. H. C.
Catalogue of microfilm. Rev. and enl. Suva, Central

Archives of Fiji and the Western Pacific High Commission, 1970.

2 v. in 1 (various pagings) 29 cm.

Photocopy of transcript.
CONTENTS: [1] Archives series.—[2] Library series.

National Archives of Fiji.
Catalogue of microfilm. Suva, 1971.

2 v. in 1. 33 cm.

Edition for 1970 prepared by the Archives under its earlier name: Central Archives of Fiji and W. P. H. C.
CONTENTS: [1] Archives series.—[2] Library series, rev. and enl.

Snow, Philip A
A bibliography of Fiji, Tonga and Rotuma [by] Philip A. Snow. Preliminary working ed. Canberra, Australian National University Press [1969]

xliii, 418 p. maps. 25 cm.

Snow, Philip A
A bibliography of Fiji, Tonga, and Rotuma [by] Philip A. Snow. Preliminary working ed. Coral Gables, Fla., University of Miami Press, 1969.

xliii, 418 p. map. 26 cm.

FILBERT

Çakman, Akif.
Fındık bibliyografyası; ziraat, ticaret, endüstri, 1945–1972. Bibliography of filbert; agriculture, trade, industry. Editör: S. Günsel Korul. [Ankara] Türdok [1973]

vi (i. e. ix), 47 p. 24 cm. (Ziraat yayınları serisi, 1) (Türdok bibliyografya serisi, 12)

At head of title: Türkiye Bilimsel ve Teknik Araştırma Kurumu. In Turkish and English.
Errata slip inserted.

FILICALES see Ferns

FILIPPO NERI, SAINT see under Oratorians

FINANCE
see also Banking; Capital; Investment

Archivio finanziario. Annali degli studi tributari a cura dell'Istituto di finanza dell'Università di Ferrara diretto da Emanuele Morselli. Tavole ventennali (1948–1967). Padova, CEDAM, 1968.

103 p. 25 cm.

Banco de México (*Founded 1925*) *Biblioteca.*
Bibliografía fiscal de México, 1940–1967. México, 1968.

56 p. 21 cm. (*Its* Serie de bibliografías especiales, no. 9)

Banco de México (Founded 1925). Biblioteca.
Bibliografía monetaria y bancaria de México (1943–1958). México, 1965.

64 p. 21 cm. (Its Serie de bibliografías especiales, no. 6)

Bogart, Ernest Ludlow, 1870–1958.
Trial bibliography and outline of lectures on the financial history of the United States, by Ernest L. Bogart and William A. Rawles. New York, Greenwood Press [1969]

49 l. 22 cm.

On spine: Outline of lectures on the financial history of the U. S.
Reprint of the 1901 ed., which was issued as Bulletin no. 5 of the Oberlin College Library.

Bourke, Margaret M
Bibliography of Australian finance, 1900–1968 [by] Margaret M. Bourke. Sydney, Reserve Bank of Australia, 1971.

104 p. 29 cm. (Reserve Bank of Australia. Occasional paper no. 5)

Brealey, Richard A
A bibliography of finance and investment. Compiled by Richard A. Brealey and Connie Pyle. Cambridge, Mass., MIT Press [1973]

361 p. 25 cm.

Финансы, деньги и кредит СССР; библиографический указатель, 1946–1966. [Составители: З. Е. Дремина и др. Отв. редактор В. В. Лавров] Москва, Финансы, 1967.

478 p. 21 cm.

At head of title: Научная библиотека Министерства финансов СССР.

Germany (*Federal Republic, 1949–*) *Bundestag. Wissenschaftliche Abteilung.*
Bundesfinanzreform, Gemeindefinanzreform; Auswahlbibliographie. Bonn, 1968.

59 p. 30 cm. (*Its* Bibliographien, Nr. 17)

"Die Bibliographie Nr. 17 wurde im Referat Fachdokumentation von Herrn Dipl.-Volksw. Walter Greiner bearbeitet."

Germany (*Federal Republic, 1949–*) *Bundestag. Wissenschaftliche Abteilung.*
Mehrjährige Finanzplanung; Auswahlbibliographie. Bonn, 1967.

18 p. 30 cm. (*Its* Bibliographien, Nr. 11)

"Die Bibliographie wurde im Referat Fachdokumentation von Herrn ... Greiner zusammengestellt."

Information Research Associates.
Evidence and bibliography; 1969–1970 national collegiate debate topic. [n. p., 1969]

[70] l. 29 cm.

On cover: Revenue sharing with the States.

Kállay, István.
Az abszolutizmuskori pénzügyigazgatási levéltár; repertórium. Budapest, Magyar Országos Levéltár, 1970.

133 p. 29 cm. (Levéltári leltárak, 50)

Summary in Russian, German, and French.

Knox, Vera H
Public finance: information sources [by] Vera H. Knox. Pref. by C. Lowell Harriss. Detroit, Gale Research Co. [1964]

142 p. 23 cm. (Management information guide, 3)

López Yepes, José, 1946–
Bibliografía del ahorro, cajas de ahorros y montes de piedad. Madrid, Confederación Española de Cajas de Ahorros [1969]

2 v. (774 p.) 23 cm. (Publicaciones del Fondo para la Investigación Económico y Social de la Confederación Española de Cajas de Ahorros, 3)
"Ampliación de la Memoria de Licenciatura ... presentado bajo el título 'Montes de piedad y cajas de ahorros, ensayo bibliográfico' ante un Tribunal de la madrileña Facultad de Filosofía y Letras, el 18 de octubre de 1968."

Masui, Mitsuzo, 1885–
A bibliography of finance. New York, B. Franklin [1969]

3 v. 26 cm. (Burt Franklin bibliography and reference series, 221)

Reprint of the 1935 ed.

CONTENTS.—v. 1. British books and articles. Ouvrages françaises.—v. 2. Deutsche literatur.—v. 3. American books and articles.

Nihon Keizai Kenkyū Sentā. Shiryōbu.
(En kiriage bunken mokuroku)

円切り上げ文献目録　〔東京〕　日本経済研究セ
ンター資料部　1971.

78 p.　25 cm.

Cover title.
At head of title: 部内資料
収録対象: 日本経済研究センター資料部所蔵の雑誌、単行書、資料および日本経済新聞
収録対象期間: 1969年1月1日-1971年8月15日

Novotný, Jan Maria, 1898–
A library of public finance and economics. New York,
Available from B. Franklin, 1953 [i. e. 1972]

xii, 383 p.　27 cm.

Reprint of the 1953 ed.

Sewell, John Willard, 1940–
Financing State and local government in Oregon; a
bibliography. Prepared in cooperation with the Bureau of
Governmental Research and Service, University of Oregon,
and the Oregon Council on Economic Education. [Eugene?
Or., 1970]

52 p.　28 cm.

Soetbeer, Adolf, 1814–1892.
Litteraturnachweis über Geld- und Münzwesen, insbesondere über den Währungsstreit, 1871–1891. Mit geschichtlichen und statistischen Erläuterungen. New York, B.
Franklin [1972]

iv, 322 p.　24 cm. (Burt Franklin research & source works series.
Selected studies in history, economics, & social science, n. s. 9.
(c) Modern European studies)

Reprint of the 1892 ed.

Stourm, René, 1837–1917.
Bibliographie historique des finances de la France au dix-
huitième siècle. New York, B. Franklin [1968]

iii, 341 p.　23 cm. (Selected essays in history, economics, and
social science, 66)

Burt Franklin bibliography and reference series, 114.
On spine: Bibliographie des finances de la France.
"Originally published, 1895."

U. S. *Advisory Commission on Intergovernmental Relations.*
Catalogs and other information sources on Federal and
State aid programs; a selected bibliography. Rev. ed.
[Washington] 1968.

32 l.　27 cm.

**U. S. Library of Congress. Legislative Reference Serv-
ice.**
Bibliography of Federal grants-in-aid to State and local
governments, 1964–1969. Prepared for the Subcommittee
on Intergovernmental Relations (pursuant to S. Res. 310,
91st Cong.) of the Committee on Government Operations,
United States Senate. Washington, U. S. Govt. Print. Off.,
1970.
vii, 456 p.　24 cm.
At head of title: 91st Congress, 2d session. Committee print.

U. S. *National Archives.*
Preliminary inventory of the records of the Solicitor of
the Treasury (Record group 206) Compiled by George S.
Ulibarri. Washington, 1968.

vii, 35 p.　27 cm. (*Its* Publication no. 69–5. Preliminary inventories, no. 171)

Yüan, K'un-hsiang, *comp.*
財政論文分類索引　袁坤祥　馬景賢編輯　A
classified index to articles on fiscal policy (1945–65), compiled by Frank K. S. Yuan [and] Ma Ching-hsien. Tai-

pei, [美國亞洲學會中文研究資料中心] 1967.

xxxvi, 303 p.　27 cm.　中文研究資料中心研究資料叢書第
1 號　Chinese Materials and Research Aids Service Center. Research aids series, no. 1)

Text in Chinese, with English introduction by Robert L. Irick.

FINANCE, INTERNATIONAL

Argentine Republic. *Consejo Nacional de Desarrollo. Biblioteca.*
Bibliografía sobre problemas actuales del sistema mo-
netario internacional. [Buenos Aires] 1969.

[36] l.　30 cm.

Brazil. *Congresso. Câmara dos Deputados. Biblioteca.
Seção de Referência e Circulação.*
Reforma monetária internacional; bibliografia. Brasília,
1967.

98 p.　21 cm.

Burgard, H
Literaturhinweise zur Koordinierung der Währungspoli-
tik im Gemeinsamen Markt [von] H. Burgard. Bibliographie concernant la coordination des politiques monétaires
dans Le Marché commun. [Brüssel? 1968]
44 p.　30 cm.
At head of title: Kommission der Europäischen Gemeinschaften.
Generaldirektion Wirtschaft und Finanzen.

**Grupo de Trabalho Permanente para a Documentação e
Informação Económico-Social.**
Bibliografia sinalética sobre financiamento e investimento.
[Lisboa, 1972]

82 p.　30 cm.

Cover title: Investimento e fianciamento; bibliografia sinalética.

International Monetary Fund.
Catalogue of publications, 1946–71. Washington, 1972.

viii, 104 p.　22 cm.

Organization for Economic Co-operation and Development.
Library.
International monetary system. Système monétaire international. [Paris] Organisation for Economic Co-operation and Development, 1967.

130 p.　27 cm. (*Its* Special annotated bibliography, 16)

English or French.

Organization for Economic Cooperation and Development.
Library.
Payements internationaux. International payments.
[Paris] 1964.

v, 51 p.　29 cm. (*Its* Bibliographie spéciale analytique 4 (41))

Oslo. Norske Nobelinstitutt. Biblioteket.
Penge- og valutapolitikken i de europeiske fellesskap.
Bibliografi. Utarb. av Elsa Skarprud. Oslo, 1971.

6 l.　30 cm.

FINE ARTS　see　Art

FINISTÈRE, FRANCE (DEPT.)

Finistère, France (Dept.). Archives départementales.
Guide des Archives du Finistère [par] Jacques Charpy,
directeur des Services d'archives du Finistère. Quimper,
1973.

516 p. 24 cm.

Finistère, *France (Dept.)* *Archives départementales.*
Répertoire numérique de la série V : cultes, 1800—1907—
(1930) par Jacques Charpy, directeur des services d'archives
du Finistère. Quimper, 1965.

153 p. 32 cm.

Finistère, France (Dept.). Archives départementales.
Répertoire numérique de la sous-série 1Q, domaines nationaux, par Jacques Charpy. Quimper, 1971.

182 p. map. 32 cm.

On spine: Répertoire des domaines nationaux.

Finistère, France (Dept.). Archives départementales.
Répertoire numérique de la sous-série 100 J : archives de
Kernuz, et de la sous-série 9 J (supplément au fonds
Guezno) par Jacques Charpy. Quimper, 1970.

xi, 171 p. 24 cm.

FINITE GROUPS
Davis, Constance.
A bibliographical survey of simple groups of finite order,
1900–1965. ₁New York₁ Courant Institute of Mathematical
Sciences ₁1969₁

xxi, 200 p. 27 cm.

FINK, EUGEN
Herrmann, Friedrich-Wilhelm von.
Bibliographie Eugen Fink. Den Haag, Nijhoff, 1970.

47 p. 24 cm.

FINKE, FIDELIO F.
Hofmeyer, Günter.
Vorläufiges Verzeichnis der Kompositionen von Fidelio
F. Finke. (Stand 1. August 1966.) Berlin, Deutsche Aka-
demie der Künste (Sektion Musik) 1966.

75 l. 29 cm.

FINLAND
Aarnio, Marja-Leena.
Suomen liiketaloustieteellinen kirjallisuus 1945–1970.
Business literature in Finland 1945–1970. Helsinki, Kaup-
pakorkeakoulun Kirjasto. 1972.

57 p. 30 cm. (Kauppakorkeakoulun kirjaston julkaisuja, 1)

English and Finnish.

Finland. Merikarttaosasto.
Merikarttaluettelo. Katalog över finska sjökort. Catalogue of Finnish charts. Helsinki, 1967.

16 p. maps. 30 cm.

Finnish, Swedish, and English.

Grönroos, Henrik.
Suomen bibliografisen kirjallisuuden opas. Helsinki,
Suomalaisen Kirjallisuuden Seura, 1965.

210 p. illus. 19 cm. (Tietolipas n:o 42)

Table of contents and pref. also in French.

Hartonen, Irma.
Elintaso; valikoima kotimaista ja ulkomaista kirjallisuutta. Standard of living. Helsinki, Kauppakorkeakoulun kirjasto, 1972.

58 p. 21 cm. (Kauppakorkeakoulun kirjaston julkaisuja, 5)

Harvard University. Library.
Finnish and Baltic history and literatures. Cambridge;

Distributed by the Harvard University Press, 1972.

250 p. 29 cm. (Its Widener Library shelflist, 40)

Holm, Tor W
Bibliography of Finnish sociology, 1945–1959 ₁by₁ Tor
W. Holm and Erkki J. Immonen. With an introd. by
Erik Allardt. ₁Åbo, printed by Åbo Tidnings och Tryckeri,
1966₁

179 p. 25 cm.

"Dr. Immonen made the first draft, which since then has been
supplemented by Mr. Holm." The draft was issued in 1960? under
title: Suomen sosiologinen bibliografia, 1945–1959.

Hovi, Kalervo.
Bibliografia yleistä historiaa koskevista laudatur- ja
lisensiaattitöistä Suomessa vv. 1914–1968. Bibliography of
master's and lic. phil. theses concerning general history in
Finland. Toimittanut Kalervo Hovi. Turku, 1968.

xvi, 143 l. 29 cm. (Turun yliopisto. Yleisen historian laitos.
Monistejulkaisusarja, 1/1968)

English and Finnish.

Itkonen, Martti.
Kunnallisen viranomaisen arkistonhoito. Helsinki, Maa-
laiskuntien liitto, 1968.

272 p. illus. 21 cm. (Kunnallistietoa)

Julkunen, Martti.
A select list of books and articles in English, French, and
German on Finnish politics in the 19th and 20th century.
Compiled by Martti Julkunen and Anja Lehikoinen. Turku,
Institute of Political History, University of Turku, 1967.

125 p. 19 cm. (Institute of Political History, University of Turku.
₁Publication₁ B : 1)

On spine: Finnish politics in the 19th and 20th century.

Lehikoinen, Anja.
Bibliografisk översikt över böcker, artiklar och andra
publikationer på svenska, om finländsk politik på 1800–
och 1900–talet. A list of books, articles and other publications in Swedish on Finnish politics in the 19th and 20th
century. Red. av/Compiled by Anja Lehikoinen. Åbo,
Institutionen för politisk historia, 1970.

208 p. 19 cm. (Institutionen för politisk historia, Åbo universitet.
₁Publikation₁ B : 2)

On spine: Finländsk politik på 1800– och 1900–talet.

Maakunta-arkistojen yleisluettelo. Helsinki, 1971.

3 v. 30 cm. (Valtionarkiston monistesarja 2 : 1–2 : 3)

Cover title.

CONTENTS: 1. Esipuhe, johdanto, sisällys. Hämeenlinnan maakunta-arkisto. Jyväskylän maakunta-arkisto. Oulun maakunta-arkisto. — 2. Savo-Karjalan maakunta-arkisto. — 3. Turun maakunta
-arkisto. Vaasan maakunta-arkisto. Valtionarkisto. Lakkautet-
tujen seurakuntien keskusarkisto. Ortodoksinen kirkkollishallitus.
Liitteet: hakemistot, arkistoja koskevia säädöksiä, ohjeita ja kirjallisuutta.

Paikallishistoriallinen Toimisto.
Paikallishistoriallinen bibliografia. Helsinki, 1965–67.

6 v. (1186 l.) 30 cm.

CONTENTS: 1. Ahlainen-Impilahti.—2. Impilahti-Kuolemajärvi.—
3. Kuopio-Oulu.—4. Oulujoki-Suolahti.—5. Suomenniemi-Töysä.—6.
Ullava-Öja.

Sota-arkisto.
Sota-arkiston opas. — Helsinki : ₁Sota-arkisto₁, 1974.

42 p. : ill. ; 25 cm. — (Valtionarkiston julkaisuja ; 5)

Valtionarkisto.
Suomen kirkonarkistojen mikrofilmien luettelo. Förteckning över mikrofilmer av kyrkoarkiv i Finland. Summary
inventory of microfilms on parish records in Finland. Helsinki, 1973.

153 p. 25 cm. (Its Julkaisuja, 4) (Its Publikationer, 4)

English, Finnish, and Swedish.

Viikki, Raimo.
Maakunta-arkistojen opas. Helsinki, 1972.

64 p. 25 cm. (Valtionarkiston julkaisuja, 2)

Wolfsburg, Ger. Stadtbücherei.
Finnland stellt sich vor durch Finnland-Bücher.
(Zusammengestellt von Aino Rauhaniemi.) Wolfsburg,
Stadtbücherei, 1966.

27 p. 21 x 10 cm. (Kataloge der Stadtbücherei Wolfsburg, 28)

PERIODICALS

Screen, J E O
A union list of periodicals relating to Finland (in arts
subjects) in British libraries, compiled by J. E. O. Screen.
London, Finland Research Seminar, 1972–

v. 33 cm.

Photocopy of the original work.
CONTENTS: pt. 1. General arts, archaeology, ethnography, folklore, genealogy, geography, history, language, law, literature and
war studies.

FINNESBURH see under Beowulf

FINNISH IMPRINTS

Aarhus, Denmark. Statsbibliotek.
Litteratur på finsk. (Udarb. af Otto Larsen) Århus,
Statsbiblioteket i Århus, 1971.

65 p. 21 cm.

Books from Finland. v. 1–
1967–
Helsinki, Publishers' Association of Finland.

v. illus., ports. 24 cm. quarterly.

Kotiranta, Kaarina.
Amerikansuomalaisen kirjallisuuden yhteisluettelo. Helsinki, 1970.

108 l. 30 cm. (Helsingin Yliopiston Kirjaston monistesarja, 3
Helsingfors universitetsbiblioteks stencilserie, 3)

Preface in English, Finnish, and Swedish.

Otava, Kustannusosakeyhtiö.
Kustannusosakeyhtiö Otavan kustannustuotteet, 1890–
1960; bibliografinen luettelo, julkaistu Otavan juhlavuonna
1965. (Helsinki) Otava (1965)

xii, 843 p. 25 cm.

Suomen kirjallisuus; vuosiluettelo. Finlands litteratur;
årskatalog. The Finnish national bibliography; annual
volume. 1972
(Helsinki) Helsingin Yliopiston Kirjasto.

v. 25 cm.

Based on the material contained in the monthly catalogs and, in
addition, includes maps and printed music.

Varastoluettelo 1971. (Helsinki) Kirjavälitys (1970)

543, 224 p. 30 cm.

FINNISH LITERATURE

Finskspråkiga böcker i urval för bibliotek i Sverige. (Helsingfors, Skolstyrelsens biblioteksbyrå, 19

v. 30 cm.

CONTENTS.—

4. Urval av Vuokko Blinnikka. Förteckningen innehåller böcker
utkomna 1963–sept. 1966 samt romaner under hösten 1966. gratis
(S 67-25/26)

Pipping, Fredrik Wilhelm, 1783–1868.
Förteckning öfver i tryck utgifna skrifter på finska, äf-
vensom öfver några andra arbeten, innehållande någon upp-
sats på detta språk, eller annars ledande till dess kännedom.
Luettelo suomeski präntätyistä kirjoista, kuin myös muu-
tamista muista teoksista, joissa löytyy joku kirjoitus suomen
kielellä, tahi joku johdatus sitä tuntemaan. Helsingfors,
Finska litteratur-sällskapets tryckeri, 1856–57. (Helsinki,
W. Söderström, 1967)

xiv, 756, xii p. 23 cm. (Suomalaisen Kirjallisuuden Seuran toimi-
tuksia, 20. osa)

In Finnish; introduction in Swedish.
"Jäljennöspainos, jonka Suomalaisen Kirjallisuuden Seuran til-
auksesta valmisti Werner Söderstrom Osakeyhtiö ... Porvoossa vu-
onna 1967."

TRANSLATIONS

Manninen, Kerttu.
Suomennettua kaumokirjallisuutta. Valikoiman laatinut
Kerttu Manninen. (Helsinki) Suomen Kirjastoseura, 1966.

232 p. 21 cm.

FINNO-UGRIAN PHILOLOGY

Suomalais-ugrilainen Seura.
Julkaisut. Publications de la Société finno-ougrienne.
Veröffentlichungen der Finnisch-Ugrischen Gesellschaft.
Publications of the Finno-Ugrian Society. Helsinki, 1968.

54 p. 25 cm.

FIRBANK, ARTHUR ANNESLEY RONALD

Muir, Percival Horace, 1894–
A bibliography of the first editions of books by Arthur
Annesley Ronald Firbank (1886–1926) Compiled by
P. H. Muir. (Folcroft, Pa.) Folcroft Library Editions,
1973.

8 p. 26 cm.

Reprint of the 1927 ed. published in London as a supplement to
the Bookman's journal, 3d ser., v. 15, no. 1.

FIRE
see also Forest fires

Fire Prevention Information and Publications Centre.
Fire booklist 1969–1970: a guide to major publications on
fire including those from Her Majesty's Stationery Office
and the British Standards Institution. London, Fire Protection Association, 1969.

44 p. 21 cm.

Institution of Fire Engineers, London.
Index to technical subjects in the quarterly, annual reports, and collected papers of the Institution of Fire Engineers. (London, 1967)

(72) p. 22 cm.

Knoth, Günter.
Brandschutz; eine Literaturzusammenstellung für die
Angehörigen aller Brandschutzorgane in der Deutschen
Demokratischen Republik. Leipzig (Deutsche Bücherei)
1964.

52 p. 21 cm. (Bibliographischer Informationsdienst der Deutschen Bücherei, Nr. 7)

U. S. *Clearinghouse for Federal Scientific and Technical
Information.*
Fire incidence & inhibition, a report bibliography.
(Washington) 1965.

1 v. (unpaged) 27 cm.

West, Clarence Jay, 1886–1953.
Flameproofing (by) Clarence J. West (and others)

Introd. by Betty John. Appleton, Wis., 1959.

244 p. 28 cm. (Appleton, Wis. Institute of Paper Chemistry. Bibliographic series, no. 185)

————————[Supplement. By] Jack Weiner and Jerry Byrne. Appleton, Wis., Institute of Paper Chemistry, 1965–

v. 28 cm. (Appleton, Wis. Institute of paper chemistry. Bibliographic series, no. 185, Suppl. 1–
Suppl. 2 by J. Weiner and L. Roth.

FIREARMS

Hughes, Marija Matich.

Bibliography on gun legislation. Prepared by Marija M. Hughes. Sacramento, California State Library, Law Library [1969]

10 p. 28 cm.

Lord, G. M.

A Colt bibliography; articles and books of interest to the Colt collector, shooter, gunsmith, and historian, by G. M. Lord. [n. p., 1966]

32 l. 28 cm.

FISCHER, ADOLF

Křivský, Pavel.

Adolf Fischer (1782–1857). Lit. pozůstalost. Zprac. Pavel Křivský. Praha, Lit. archív Památníku nár. písemnictví, rozmn., 1972.

23, [1] p. 21 cm. (Edice Inventářů, čís. 237)

FISH; FISHERIES
see also specific fish, e.g. Crabs, Goldfish, Tuna; and under Dissertations, Academic

Atz, James W

The pituitary gland and its relation to the reproduction of fishes in nature and in captivity; an annotated bibliography for the years 1956–1963. Compiled by James W. Atz [and] Grace E. Pickford. Rome, Food and Agriculture Organization of the United Nations, 1964.

iii, 61 p. 28 cm. (FAO fisheries technical paper, no. 37)

"FB/T37."
Added titles and prefatory material in French and Spanish.

Berka, Rudolf.

Bibliografie 1922–1953. Sest. Rudolf Berka—Jiřina Chocholová. Předml.: František Chytra. Vodňany, Výzkum. ústav rybářský, rozmn., 1968.

128 p. 20 cm.

British Columbia. University. Institute of Fisheries.

Library bulletin. v. 1–
1967–
Vancouver.

v. 28 cm. 10 no. a year.

Editor, 1967– H. Verwey.
Continued by: Newfoundland. Memorial University, St. John's. Library bulletin.

Carter, Neal M

Index and list of titles, Fisheries Research Board of Canada and associated publications, 1900–1964, by Neal M. Carter. Ottawa [Queen's Printer] 1968.

xviii, 649 p. 25 cm. (Canada. Fisheries Research Board. Bulletin no. 164)

Carter, Neal M

Index and list of titles, Fisheries Research Board of Canada and associated publications, 1965–1972, [by] Neal M. Carter. Ottawa, Fisheries Research Board of Canada, 1973.

vi, 588 p. 26 cm. (Fisheries Research Board of Canada. Miscellaneous special publication, no. 18)

Dean bibliography of fishes. 1968–
New York, American Museum of Natural History.

v. 26 cm.

Vols. for 1968– published from the Dean Memorial Library.
Compiler: 1968– J. W. Atz.

Food and Agriculture Organization of the United Nations.

FAO Department of Fisheries: list of publications and documents 1948-1969. Département des pêches de la FAO; liste des publications et documents 1948-1969. Departamento de Pesca de la FAO: lista de publicaciones y documentos 1948-1969. Rome, 1969.

1 v. (various pagings) 28 cm. (Its FAO fisheries circular no. 100, rev. 1)

Food and Agriculture Organization of the United Nations. Documentation Center.

Fisheries; FAO publications and documents. Pêches; publications et documents de la FAO. Pesca; publicaciones y documentos de la FAO, 1945–1969. [Rome] 1969.

2 v. 28 cm.

"PU: DC/Sp. 14"
CONTENTS: v. 1. Annotated bibliography.—v. 2. Author and subject index.

Food and Agriculture Organization of the United Nations. *Documentation Center.*

Index, índice, 1945–1966: fisheries, pêches, pescas. [Rome?] 1967.

iii, 29, 154, 18, 231 p. 28 cm.

Food and Agriculture Organization of the United Nations. Fishery Resources and Exploitation Division. Biological Data Section.

North Atlantic bibliography and citation index; an index of the publications of the International Council for the Exploration of the Sea and the International Commission for the Northwest Atlantic Fisheries. Rome, Food and Agriculture Organization of the United Nations, 1968.

1 v. (various pagings) 28 cm. (FAO fisheries technical paper no. 54)

————————Subject index — physical oceanography, prepared by L. Otto. Rome, Food and Agriculture Organization of the United Nations, 1968.

[8] p. 28 cm. (FAO fisheries technical paper no. 54, suppl. 1)

Food and Agriculture Organization of the United Nations. Terminology and Reference Section.

Dictionaries and encyclopaedias in the field of fisheries. Dictionnaires et encyclopédies intéressant la pêche. Diccionarios y enciclopedias de pesca, 1945–1973. [Rome] 1973.

20 p. 28 cm. (Its Terminology notes, GIP: Blb/5)

Cover title: Fisheries: dictionaries and encyclopedias, 1945–1973.

George Washington University, *Washington, D. C.*

Fishery publication index, 1955–64; publications of the Fish and Wildlife Service by series, authors, and subjects. Washington [U. S. Bureau of Commercial Fisheries]; for sale by the Supt. of Docs., U. S. Govt. Print. Off., 1969.

ii, 240 p. 27 cm. (U. S. Fish and Wildlife Service. Circular 296)

Hunn, Joseph B

Bibliography on the blood chemistry of fishes [by] Joseph B. Hunn. [Washington, Bureau of Sport Fisheries and Wildlife; for sale by the Supt. of Docs., U. S. Govt. Print. Off., 1967]

32 p. 26 cm. (U. S. Bureau of Sport Fisheries and Wildlife. Research report 72)

Kanakasabapathi, K comp.

Bibliography of contributions from Central Marine

Fisheries Research Institute, 1947–1969. Compiled by K. Kanakasabapathi. Mandapam Camp, Central Marine Fisheries Research Institute, 1970.

73 p. 28 cm. (Bulletin of the Central Marine Fisheries Research Institute, no. 19)

Landberg, Leif C   W

A bibliography for the anthropological study of fishing industries and maritime communities, compiled by Leif C. W. Landberg. ₍Kingston₎ University of Rhode Island, 1973.

xiii, 572 p. 29 cm.

Marchant, C   J

Feeding and feedstuffs in fish culture, complied by C. J. Marchant. Adelaide, Public Library of South Australia, 1966.

9 p. 27 cm. (Research service bibliographies, series 4, no. 63)

Margolis, L

A bibliography of parasites and diseases of fishes of Canada: 1879–1969 ₍by₎ L. Margolis. Nanaimo, B. C., Fisheries Research Board of Canada, Biological Station, 1970.

38 p. 28 cm. (Fisheries Research Board of Canada. Technical report no. 185)

Oren, O   H

Artificial reefs; a short review and appeal, by O. H. Oren. Rome, Food and Agriculture Organization of the United Nations, 1968.

ii, 6 p. 28 cm. (FAO fisheries circular no. FRs/C305)

Schwartz, Frank Joseph, 1929–

World literature to fish hybrids, with an analysis by family, species, and hybrid, by Frank J. Schwartz. ₍Ocean Springs, Miss., Gulf Coast Research Laboratory, 1972₎

328 p. 23 cm. (Publications of the Gulf Coast Research Laboratory Museum, 3)

Selected references to literature on marine expeditions, 1700–1960. ₍An index in the₎ Fisheries-Oceanography Library, University of Washington. Boston, G. K. Hall, 1972.

iv, 517 p. 27 cm.

"The University of Washington does not have all of the publications cited in the index."

Topp, Robert W

Annotated list of post-1950 literature pertaining to distribution of Gulf of Mexico fishes ₍by₎ Robert W. Topp and Robert M. Ingle. St. Petersburg, Fla., Marine Research Laboratory, 1972.

17 p. map. 29 cm. (Marine Research Laboratory. St. Petersburg, Fla. Special scientific report no. 33)

PERIODICALS

Food and Agriculture Organization of the United Nations. Dept. of Fisheries. Fishery Resources Division. Inland Fishery Resources Branch.

A list of scientific and semi-popular periodicals on inland fisheries and aquaculture, prepared by Inland Fishery Resources Branch, Fishery Resources Division, Dept. of Fisheries. Rome, Food and Agriculture Organization of the United Nations, 1970.

4 p. (FAO fisheries circular no. 311)

Paul, Adriana.

Catálogo de publicaciones periódicas ₍por₎ Adriana Paul ₍y₎ Luisa Viveros. Santiago, Chile, Instituto de Fomento Pesquero, 1970.

viii, 61 p. 27 cm. (Instituto de Fomento Pesquero. Publicación

no. 46)

Introd. in Spanish and English.

AFRICA

Matthes, Hubert.

A bibliography of African freshwater fish. Bibliographie des poissons d'eau douce de l'Afrique. Prepared by H. Matthes. Rome, Food and Agriculture Organization of the United Nations, 1973.

x, 299 p. illus., col. map. 28 cm.

English, French, or German.

ASIA

Romanov, N   S

Annotated bibliography on Far Eastern aquatic fauna, flora and fisheries. (Ukazatel' literatury po rybnomu khozyaistvu Dal'nego Vostoka za 1923–1956gg.) ₍by₎ N. S. Romanov. Translated from Russian ₍by₎ B. Hershkovitz and R. M. Ettinger₎ Jerusalem, Israel Program for Scientific Translations; ₍available from the U. S. Dept. of Commerce, Clearinghouse for Federal Scientific and Technical Information, Springfield, Va.₎ 1966.

391 p. 24 cm.

At head of title: Academy of Sciences of the U. S. S. R., Department of Biological Sciences. Ichthyological Commission.

AUSTRALIA

Australia. *Commonwealth Scientific and Industrial Research Organization. Division of Fisheries and Oceanography. Library.*

Selected bibliography of Australian fisheries. ₍Canberra₎ Dept. of Primary Industry, Fisheries Branch, 1967.

₍28₎ l. 26 cm. (Australia. Fisheries Branch. Fisheries paper no. 3)

BOHEMIA

Lohniský, Karel.

Kruhoústí a ryby povodí Labe a Stěnavy v severovýchodních Čechách. (Vertebrata: Cyclostomata et Teleostei). Hradec Králové, Kraj. muzeum, t. MTZ 416, Trutnov, 1968.

66, ₍6₎ p. 20 cm. (Fontes Musei Reginaehradecensis, 6)

Summary also in German.

NORWAY

Ålesund, Norway. Folkebiblioteket.

Litteratur om fiske- og fangst på Sunnmøre. Ålesund, 1969.

31 l. 21 cm.

RUSSIA

Moscow.   Vsesoíuznyĭ nauchno-issledovatel'skiĭ institut morskogo rybnogo khozíaĭstva i okeanografii.

Библиографический указатель отечественной литературы по рыбному хозяйству и рыбной промышленности за второе полугодие 1968 года. Сост. б-кой ВНИРО. Москва, 1969–

v. 20 cm.

At head of title, v. 1– : Всесоюзный научно-исследовательский институт морского и рыбного хозяйства и океанографии (ВНИРО) Отдел научно-технической информации.

Romanov, N   S

Annotated bibliography on fisheries of the Southern Basins of the U. S. S. R., 1918–1953; fish resources and replenishment of commercial fish stocks. Ukazatel' literatury po rybnomu khozyaistvu yuzhnykh basseinov SSSR za 1918–1953 gg. ₍By₎ N. S. Romanov. Translated from Russian ₍and edited by IPST staff₎ Jerusalem, Israel Program for Scientific Translations ₍available from the U. S. Dept. of Commerce, Clearinghouse for Scientific and Technical Information, Springfield, Va., 1968.

400 p. 24 cm.

At head of title: Academy of Sciences of the USSR. Department of Biological Sciences. Ichthyological Commission.

Romanov, N

Annotated bibliography on population dynamics, behavior and distribution of fish, marine mammals, commercial invertebrates and algae (covering publications of 1956). (Annotirovannyi ukazatel' opublkovannykh v 1956 godu rabot po probleme "Zakonomernosti dinamiki chislennosti, povedeniya i raspredeleniya ryb, morskikh mlekopitayushchikh, promyslovikh bespozvonochnykh i vodoroslei v svyazi s usloviyami ikh sushchestvovaniya"). ₁By₁ N. S. Romanov. Initiated by E. N. Pavlovskii and G. V. Nikol'skii. E. N. Pavovskii, chief editor. Translated from Russian ₁by₁ B. Shenkman. Edited by IPST staff₁ Jerusalem, Israel Program for Scientific Translations ₁available from the U. S. Dept. of Commerce, Clearinghouse for Federal Scientific and Technical Information, Springfield, Va.₁ 1967.

168 p. 24 cm.

At head of title: Academy of Sciences of the U. S. S. R. Department of Biological Sciences. Ichthyological Commission.

Shekhter, R   B

Библиографический указатель по гидробиологии, ихтиологии и рыбному хозяйству водоемов южной зоны СССР. (1917–1963 гг.) Кн. 1–2. Кишинев, 1967–

v. 21 cm.

At head of title, v. 1– : Академия наук Молдавской ССР. Центральная научная библиотека.

FISH PROTEIN CONCENTRATE

Shkol'nikova, Sima Solomonovna.

(Annotirovannyi bibliograficheskii ukazatel' inostrannoi literatury po ispol'zovaniiu rybnogo belkovogo kontsentrata)

Аннотированный библиографический указатель иностранной литературы по использованию рыбного белкового концентрата. Сост. С. С. Школьникова. Москва, Отд. науч.-техн. информации, 1971.

63 p. 20 cm.

At head of title: Всесоюзный научно-исследовательский институт морского и рыбного хозяйства и океанографии.

U. S. *Library of Congress. Science and Technology Division. Special Bibliographies Section.*

Fish protein concentrate; a comprehensive bibliography. Compiled for the National Center for Fish Protein Concentrate, Bureau of Commercial Fisheries, Fish and Wildlife Service, U. S. Dept. of the Interior. Washington, Library of Congress; ₁available from the Clearinghouse for Federal Scientific and Technical Information, Springfield, Va.₁ 1970.

v, 77 p. 27 cm.
Based on literature published from 1940 through 1969.

FISHER, IRVING

Fisher, Irving Norton, 1900–

A bibliography of the writings of Irving Fisher. New Haven, Yale University Library, 1961.

xii, 543 p. 23 cm.

———————Supplement. New Haven, Yale University Library, 1972.

v. 22 p. 22 cm.

FISHING

British Columbia. University. Library.

The contemplative man's recreation; a bibliography of books on angling and game fish in the Library of the Uni-

versity of British Columbia, compiled by Susan B. Starkman and Stanley E. Read. With a chronological appendix indicating landmarks in the evolution of angling literature and some prefatory matters pertaining to the history of the Harry Hawthorn Foundation for the Inculcation and Propagation of the Principles and Ethics of Fly-Fishing, including an informal foreword by N. A. M. Mackenzie and a tribute to the memory of Tom Brayshaw by Roderick L. Haig-Brown. Vancouver, 1970.

138 p. illus. 24 cm.

British Columbia. University. Library.

More recreation for the contemplative man : a supplemental bibliography of books on angling and game fish in the Library of the University of British Columbia / compiled by Laurenda Daniells and Stanley E. Read. — Vancouver : Library of the University of British Columba, 1971.

33 p., ₁1₁ leaf of plates ; 24 cm.
Supplement to The contemplative man's recreation; a bibliography of books on angling and game fish in the Library of the University of British Columbia.

Library Association. *County Libraries Group.*

Readers' guide to books on fishing & angling. 2d ed. ₁London, 1965?₁

22 p. 19 cm. (*Its* Readers' guide, new ser., no. 79)

"Compilation undertaken by the Librarian and staff of Stirlingshire County Library."

Library Association. County Libraries Group.

Readers' guide to books on fishing and angling. 3d ed. ₁London₁ Library Association, County Libraries Group, 1971.

22 p. 19 cm. (Library Association. County Libraries Group. Readers' guide no. 117)

PERIODICALS

Hogan, Austin S

American sporting periodicals of angling interest; a selected check list and guide ₁by₁ Austin S. Hogan. Manchester, Vt., Museum of American Fly Fishing, 1973.

xiv, 128 p. 28 cm.

FITZGERALD, FRANCIS SCOTT KEY

Bruccoli, Matthew Joseph, 1931–

F. Scott Fitzgerald; collector's handlist. ₁Columbus, Ohio, Fitzgerald newsletter, 1964₁

₁11₁ p. 23 x 11 cm.

Bruccoli, Matthew Joseph, 1931–

F. Scott Fitzgerald; a descriptive bibliography ₁by₁ Matthew J. Bruccoli. ₁Pittsburgh₁ University of Pittsburgh Press, 1972.

xxiii, 369 p. illus. 25 cm. (Pittsburgh series in bibliography)

Bruccoli, Matthew Joseph, 1931–

The Merrill checklist of F. Scott Fitzgerald. Compiled by Matthew J. Bruccoli. Columbus, Ohio, Merrill ₁1970₁

iv, 39 p. 19 cm. (Charles E. Merrill checklists)

Charles E. Merrill program in American literature.
Cover title: Checklist of F. Scott Fitzgerald.

Bryer, Jackson R.

The critical reputation of F. Scott Fitzgerald; a bibliographical study, by Jackson R. Bryer. ₁Hamden, Conn.₁ Archon Books, 1967.

xvii, 434 p. 22 cm.

FITZGERALD, ROBERT DAVID

Van Wageningen, Jennifer Marjorie, 1944–
R. D. Fitzgerald: a bibliography. Adelaide, Libraries Board of South Australia, 1970.

72 p. port. 22 cm. (Bibliographies of Australian writers)

Compiled in the Research Service of the State Library of South Australia by J. M. Van Wageningen and P. A. O'Brien.

FIUME see Rijeka, Croatia (City)

FLAGS

Baron, Louis.
Bibliographie, la Symbolique militaire en France, drapeaux et étendards, par le chef de bataillon Baron, Louis ... ₍Paris (7ᵉ), "Revue historique de l'armée," 231 bd Saint-Germain, 1970?₎

79 l. 26 cm.

At head of title: Service historique de l'armée.

Smith, Whitney.
The bibliography of flags of foreign nations. Compiled and annotated by Whitney Smith. Flag Research Center, Winchester, Mass. Boston, G. K. Hall, 1965.

viii, 169 p. 27 cm.

FLAMENCO see Dance

FLANDERS

Belgium. Archives de l'État, Courtrai.
Inventaris van de parochieregisters, door E. Warlop en N. Maddens. Brussel, Algemeen Rijksarchief, 1973.

117 p. map. 30 cm.

Belgium. Archives de l'État, Renaix.
Inventarissen van archieven van kerkfabrieken (Oud Regiem) ₍op het₎ Rijksaarchief te Ronse. Brussel ₍Gedrukt op offset bij het Algemeen Rijksarchief te Brussel₎ 1971–

v. illus. 30 cm.

Provinciale Bibliotheek en Cultuurarchief te Brugge.
Westflandrica. Keuze uit de onderwerpscatalogus van de Provinciale Bibliotheek en Cultuurarchief te Brugge. Samengesteld door Luc Schepens. Brugge, Provincie West-Vlaanderen, Provinciale Dienst voor cultuur (Burg 3), 1972.

456 p. 28 cm.

FLANDERS, RALPH EDWARD

Applegate, Howard L
Ralph E. Flanders: a register of his papers in the Syracuse University Library. Prepared by: Howard L. Applegate, Paul McCarthy ₍and₎ Fran Stalsonberg. ₍Syracuse, N. Y.₎ Manuscript Collections, Syracuse University Library, 1964.

56 l. 28 cm. (Manuscript Register Series. Register no. 4)

FLAXMAN, JOHN

Bentley, Gerald Eades, 1930–
The early engravings of Flaxman's classical designs; a bibliographical study, by G. E. Bentley, Jr. With a note on the duplicating of engravings by Richard J. Wolfe. New York, New York Public Library, 1964.

63 p. illus. 26 cm.

"Reprinted from the Bulletin of the New York Public Library, May, June, 1964."

FLEMISH LITERATURE

Nauwelaerts, René.
Bibliografie over de Vlaamse letterkundigen. Naslagwerk, over werk en leven van onze Vlaamse romanciers, dichters, toneelschrijvers, essayisten en critici, verspreid in kritische bundels en monografieën. (₍Duffel₎), Openbare Biblioteek van Duffel, (₍Kapelstraat 14₎), (1969).

₍v₎, 438 l. 27 cm.

Tiendaagse van de Vlaamse naoorlogse literatuur: 1945–1967. Georganiseerd door de Vriendenkring der Oud-Atheneumstudenten, met de medewerking van het Stadsbestuur van Sint-Niklaas, in het kader van de viering van het 750-jarig bestaan van de stad, 17–26 april 1967. Catalogus van de tentoonstelling, met inleiding door Bernard Kemp ₍pseudoniem van Bernard-Frans van Vlierden₎ en proeve van bibliografie gewijd aan de Vlaamse naoorlogse literatuur (1945–1967). ₍Sint-Niklaas, Vriendenkring der Oud-Atheneumstudenten, Stationsstraat 45₎ 1967.

40 p. ports. 24 cm.

FLEMISH PERIODICALS see Periodical publications - Belgium

FLIGHT see Aeronautics

FLOODS

(Kōzui bunken shū)
洪水文献集 ₍東京₎ 科学技術庁資源調査所 昭和43(1968)

143 p. 26 cm. （資源調査所資料 第1号）

Cover title.
編集: 資源調査会水資源部会洪水文献集編纂作業グループ

Shigen Chōsajo.
Bibliography of floods and their computation, Japan. ₍Tokyo₎ 1968.

304 p. 1 col. fold. map. 26 cm

Tennessee Valley Authority. *Library.*
Flood damage prevention; an indexed bibliography. 4th ed. Knoxville, Tenn., 1966.

37 p. illus. 22 cm.

At head of title: Tennessee Valley Authority. Technical Library.

Tennessee Valley Authority. Library.
Flood damage prevention; an indexed bibliography. 5th ed. Knoxville, Tennessee Valley Authority, Technical Library, 1967.

39 p. 21 cm.

Tennessee Valley Authority. Library.
Flood damage prevention; an indexed bibliography. 7th ed. Knoxville, Tennessee Valley Authority, Technical Library, 1973.

56 p. 21 cm.

Vlasov, Andreĭ IŪr'evich.
Селевые явления на территории СССР и меры борьбы с ними. Указатель литературы, изд. в 1850–1967 гг. Науч. ред. д-р техн. наук Флейшман С. М. Москва, Изд. Моск. ун-та, 1969.

216 p. 22 cm.

At head of title: Московский государственный университет имени М. В. Ломоносова. Географический факультет. Проблемная лаборатория снежных лавин и селей. А. Ю. Власов, Н. В. Крашенинникова.

FLORA see Botany

FLORENCE, ITALY

Bigazzi, Pasquale Augusto.
Firenze e contorni. Manuale bibliografico e bibliobiogra-

fico delle principali opere e scritture sulla storia, i monumenti, le arti, le istituzioni, le famiglie, gli uomini illustri, ec., della città e contorni. Bologna, Forni, 1969.

300 p. 24 cm.

At head of title: Pasq. Aug. Bigazzi.
Reproduction of the Florence 1893 ed.

Negri, Giulio, 1648–1720.
Istoria degli scrittori fiorentini ... ₁of₁ Giulio Negri Ferrarese ... Farnborough, Gregg, 1969.

₁12₁, 558 p. 33 cm.

Facsimile reprint of 1st ed., Ferrara: Per Bernadino Pomatelli Stampatore Vescovale, 1722.

Piazzo, Marcello del.
Il protocollo del carteggio della signoria di Firenze, 1459–1468. Roma, 1969.

273 p. 24 cm. (Quaderni della rassegna degli archivi ai Stato, 39)

In Latin; preface in Italian.

FLORICULTURE see Horticulture

FLORIDA

Florida. Atlantic University, *Boca Raton. Library.*
A keyword-in-context index to Florida public documents in the Florida Atlantic University. Edited by Nancy P. Sanders. Tallahassee, Dept. of State, Florida State Library ₁1969?₁

4, 163 p. 22 x 28 cm.

Florida index. 1966–
Gainesville, Bates-Belknap.

v. 23 cm. annual.

Compiler: 1966– S. Y. Belknap.

Florida public documents. 1968–
Tallahassee.

v. 28 cm.

Vols. for 1968–69 published by the Florida State Library; 1970– by the Library under its later name: Division of State Library Services.

Harris, Michael H
Florida history: a bibliography, compiled by Michael H. Harris. Metuchen, N. J., Scarecrow Press, 1972.

257 p. 22 cm.

FLORIDA TECHNOLOGICAL UNIVERSITY

Florida Technological University. Reference Dept.
A bibliography of faculty and staff publications. Orlando ₁Florida Technological University₁ 1970.

41 p. 23 cm. (Florida Technological University. University publications series, no. 1)

FLORISTS
see also Horticulture

Kiplinger, Donald Carl, 1915–
Retail florist ₁by₁ D. C. Kiplinger. Washington, Small Business Administration, 1964.

8 p. 26 cm. (Small business bibliography no. 74)

FLOUNDER

Topp, Robert W
An annotated bibliography of the winter flounder, *Pseudopleuronectes americanus* (Walbaum) ₁by₁ Robert W. Topp. Boston, Massachusetts Division of Marine Fisheries, Dept. of Natural Resources, 1965.

30 p. 28 cm.

FLOUR-MILLS

Gribanova, L   A
Мукомольно-крупяное производство. Библиогр. указатель науч.-техн. литературы. Москва, 1970.

55 p. 21 cm.

At head of title: Центральный научно-исследовательский институт информации и технико-экономических исследованний Министерства заготовок СССР.

FLOW OF LIQUIDS see Hydraulics

FLUIDIC DEVICES

Brock, Thomas Ephraim.
Fluidics applications: analysis of the literature and bibliography ₁by₁ T. E. Brock. Bedford, British Hydromechanics Research Association, 1968.

₁5₁, 131 p. 16 illus. 31 cm.

Cadig Liaison Centre. *Reference Library.*
Fluidics: a bibliography. Coventry, Cadig Liaison Centre, 1968.

₁3₁, 16 l. 30 cm.

König, Gerhard,
Bibliographie über Strahlelemente. ⟨Literaturzusammenstellung zum Forschungsbericht "Strahlelemente."⟩ Stand vom Dez. 1965. Dresden, Institut für Regelungs- und Steuerungstechnik ₁der₁ Deutsche₁n₁ Akademie der Wissenschaften, (1967).

95 p. 21 cm.

Michałowicz, Stanisław K   comp.
Technika strumieniowa; bibliografia, 1959–1969. Warszawa, Instytut Automatyki, Polskiej Akademii Nauk, 1971.

205 p. 24 cm. (Prace Instytutu Automatyki, PAN, zesz. 99)

FLUORESCENCE

Passwater, Richard A
Guide to fluorescence literature ₁by₁ Richard A. Passwater with the assistance of Jarratt G. Bennett and Barbara G. Passwater. New York, Plenum Press Data Division, 1967–

v. 26 cm.

FLUORINE

Cincinnati. University. *Kettering Laboratory.*
The occurrence and biological effects of fluorine compounds; annotated bibliography. Cincinnati, 1958–

v. in   28 cm.

CONTENTS.—v. 1. The inorganic compounds. 2 v.

—— Fluoride abstracts, 1963–1965. Supplement. Cincinnati ₁1965₁

v. 28 cm.

Prepared by Irene R. Campbell and Irene P. Kukainis.

FLUTE MUSIC

Wilkins, Wayne.
The index of flute music including the index of baroque trio sonatas. Magnolia, Ark., Music Register ₁1974₁.

131 p. 22 cm.

FLYING SAUCERS

Brennan, Norman.
Flying saucer books and pamphlets in English; a bibliographical checklist. ₁Buffalo? 1971?₁

vi, 94 p. 28 cm.

Catoe, Lynn E
UFOs and related subjects: an annotated bibliography

[by] Lynn E. Catoe. Prepared by the Library of Congress, Science and Technology Division, for the Air Force Office of Scientific Research, Office of Aerospace Research, USAF. [Washington, For sale by the Supt. of Docs., U. S. Govt. Print. Off., 1969]

xi, 401 p. illus. 26 cm.

Jain, Sushil Kumar.
Twenty years of flying saucers: a select list of interesting books and periodical articles published during 1947–1966; compiled by Sushil Kumar Jain & Christine Horswell. Tenderden (Kent.), Sushil Jain Publications, 1967–

v. 28 cm.

CONTENTS.—
pt. 2. Periodical articles.

Page, Henrietta M
Flying saucers; a bibliography, by H. M. Page. Foxboro, Mass. [1968]

i, 17 l. 28 cm.

Sable, Martin Howard.
UFO guide: 1947–1967; containing international lists of books and magazine article[s] on UFO's, flying saucers, and about life on other planets; world-wide directories of flying saucer organizations, professional groups and research centers concerned with space research and astronautics, a partial list of sightings, and an international directory of flying saucer magazines, by Martin H. Sable. 1st ed. Beverly Hills, Calif., Rainbow Press Co., 1967.

100 p. 23 cm.

Wegner, Willy.
Ufonauter. København F., Fufos (Frederiksberg UFO Studiekreds), Eksp.: Jul. Valentinersvej 15/5, 1970.

28 p. 22 cm.

FLYNN, JOHN THOMAS
Oregon. University. Library.
Inventory of the papers of John T. Flynn. Eugene, 1966.

32 l. 28 cm. (Its Occasional paper no. 3)

"Prepared by Martin Schmitt, curator of special collections."

FOCKEMA ANDREAE, SYBRANDUS JOHANNES
Westenberg, J
Bibliografie van de werken Mr. S. J. Fockema Andreae. Samengesteld door J. Westenberg. Met een inleiding door J. Th. de Smidt. 's-Gravenhage, Algemeen Rijksarchief (Bleyenburg 7), 1968, [1969].

vii, 57 p. port. 29 cm.

FODOR, JÓZSEF
Vasvári, István.
Fodor József. Budapest, Fővárosi Szabó Ervin Könyvtár, 1970.

26 p. 20 cm. (Mai magyar költők, 1)

FOGARTY, JOHN EDWARD
Providence. College. Library.
John E. Fogarty: an inventory of his papers in the archives and manuscripts collections of the Library of Providence College. Compiled by Matthew J. Smith. Providence, R. I., Providence College, 1970.

iv, 187 p. port. 28 cm.

FOLIO SOCIETY
Folio Society, ltd., *London.*
Folio 21: a bibliography of the Folio Society 1947–1967; with an appraisal by Sir Francis Meynell. London, Folio

P., 1968.

208 p. illus. (some col.), facsims. 29 cm.

FOLK-LORE
Bell and Howell Company. *Micro Photo Division.*
Out-of-print books from the John G. White Folklore Collection at the Cleveland Public Library, reproduced by the duopage process by Micro Photo Division, Bell & Howell Co. Cleveland, 1966.

321 p. 35 cm.

Reproduced from library catalog cards.

Cleveland. Public Library. *John G. White Dept.*
Catalog of folklore and folk songs. Boston, G. K. Hall, 1964.

2 v. 37 cm.

Ramsey, Eloise.
Folklore for children and young people : a critical and descriptive bibliography for use in the elementary and intermediate school / compiled and annotated by Eloise Ramsey, in collaboration with Dorothy Mills Howard. — New York : Kraus Reprint Co., 1970.

xii, 110 p. ; 24 cm.
Reprint of the 1952 ed. published by American Folklore Society, Philadelphia, which was issued in Publications of the American Folklore Society, Bibliographical series, v. 3.

Seijō Daigaku.
柳田文庫蔵書目録 [東京] 成城大学 1967.

222, 30 p. 27 cm.

Thomas, Northcote Whitridge, 1868–
Bibliography of folk-lore, 1905, compiled by N. W. Thomas. Nendeln/Liechtenstein, Kraus Reprint, 1967.

xxxvi, lxxii, lxxiv p. 23 cm. (Publications of the Folk-Lore Society, 57)

Ullom, Judith C
Folklore of the North American Indians; an annotated bibliography. Compiled by Judith C. Ullom, Children's Book Section. Washington, Library of Congress; [for sale by the Supt. of Docs., U. S. Govt. Print. Off., 1969.

x, 126 p. illus., map, port. 24 cm.

Ziegler, Elsie B
Folklore: an annotated bibliography and index to single editions, by Elsie B. Ziegler. Westwood, Mass., F. W. Faxon Co., 1973.

x, 203 p. 23 cm.

AFRICA
Delancey, Virginia.
A bibliography of Cameroun folklore [by] Virginia and Mark Delancey. [Waltham, Mass., African Studies Association, 1972]

iii, 69 p. 22 cm. (An occasional publication of the Literature Committee of the African Studies Association, no. 1)

Scheub, Harold.
Bibliography of African oral narratives. Madison [African Studies Program, University of Wisconsin] 1971.

160 p. 28 cm. (University of Wisconsin. African Studies Program. Occasional paper no. 3)

ASIA
Kirkland, Edwin Capers.
A bibliography of South Asian folklore. [Bloomington] Indiana University Research Center in Anthropology, Folklore, and Linguistics [1966]

xxiv, 201 p. 28 cm. (Asian folklore studies monographs, no. 4)

Indiana University folklore series, no. 21.

Nha-Trang Công-Huyê'n-Tôn-Nü'.

Vietnamese folklore; an introductory and annotated bibliography. Berkeley, Center for South and Southeast Asia Studies, University of California, 1970.

xxi, 33 l. 28 cm. (Center for South and Southeast Asia Studies, University of California. Occasional paper no. 7)

FINLAND

Orava, Ritva.

Suomalaisia kansatieteellisiä tutkimuksia ja kirjoituksia sisältäviä bibliografioita, aikakausjulkaisuja ja julkaisusarjoja. ₁Jyväskylä₁ Jyväskylän yliopiston kirjasto. 1970.

9 l. 30 cm.

Cover title.
"Luettelo ... pohjautuu Jyväskylän yliopiston kirjaston ja etnologian laitoksen kokoelmiin."

HUNGARY

Sándor, István.

A magyar néprajztudomány bibliográfiája. Budapest, Akadémiai Kiadó, 1965–

v. 25 cm.

CONTENTS: ₁1₁ 1945–1954.—₁2₁ 1955–1960.

INDIA

Islam, Mazharul.

A history of folktale collections in India and Pakistan ₁by₁ Mazharul Islam. Dacca, Bengali Academy ₁1970₁

336 p. 22 cm.

Modified version of author's dissertation which was accepted by the faculty of the Graduate School, Indiana University, U. S. A. in partial fulfilment of the requirement for the degree of Doctor of Philosophy in folklore in Sept. 1968.

Jain, Sushil Kumar.

Folklore of India & Pakistan; a complete catalogue of publications in English language, compiled from uptodate sources, with short notes and annotations. Regina, Regina Campus Library, Univ. of Saskatchewan ₁1965₁

36 l. 29 cm.

Nahta, Agarchand, 1911–

राजस्थानी लोकसाहित्य सम्बन्धी प्रकाशन सूची. ₁संपादक₁ अगरचन्द नाहटा. जोधपुर, राजस्थानी-शोध-संस्थान ₁between 1964 and 1969₁

26 p. 24 cm. (राजस्थानी प्रकीर्णक प्रकाशन, पुष्प 1)

Prasad, Harishchandra.

A bibliography of folklore of Bihar; books, articles, reports, and monographs in English and Hindi. Compiled by Harishchandra Prasad and Gita Sen Gupta. Calcutta, Indian Publications, 1971.

96 p. 25 cm. (Indian Publications folklore series, no. 17)

"The first draft of the bibliography ... appeared in four consequitive ₁sic₁ issues of 'Folklore' Calcutta, from July to October, 1970."

Sen Gupta, Sankar.

A bibliography of Indian folklore and related subjects, by Sankar Sen Gupta with Shyam Parmar. Calcutta, Indian Publications, 1967.

196 p. 25 cm. (Indian folklore series, no. 11)

ITALY

Biblioteca trivulziana.

Stampe popolari della Biblioteca trivulziana; ₁mostra₁ Catalogo a cura di Caterina Santoro. Presentazione di Lamberto Donati. Milano, Castello sforzesco, 1964. ₁Milano, 1964₁

xix, 168 p. illus. 21 cm.

Del Monte Tàmmaro, Cosimo.

Indice delle fiabe abruzzesi. Firenze, L. S. Olschki, 1971.

xxix, 278 p. 21 cm. (Biblioteca di "Lares," v. 34)

JAVA

Danandjaja, James.

An annotated bibliography of Javanese folklore. Berkeley, Center for South and Southeast Asia Studies, University of California, 1972.

xxx, 162 p. maps. 28 cm. (University of California. Center for South and Southeast Asia Studies. Occasional paper no. 9)

Originally presented as the author's thesis (M.A.), University of California at Berkeley.

JEWS

Noy, Dov.

חקר הסיפור העממי בישראל ובעמים; מבחר ביבליוגראפי לתלמידי התרגילים והסמינריונים באנדה ובספרות עממית ₁מאת₁ דב נוי. ירושלים, אקדמון, 729 ₁1968₁

89 l. 24 cm.

KAZAKHSTAN

Sidel'nikov, Viktor Mikhaĭlovich.

Устное поэтическое творчество казахского народа. Библиогр. указатель. 1771–1966 гг. Алма-Ата, "Наука," 1969.

174 p. 21 cm.

At head of title: Академия наук Казахской ССР. Институт литературы и искусства им. М. О. Ауэзова. В. М. Сидельников.

LATIN AMERICA

Bibliografía del folklore argentino. Buenos Aires, Fondo Nacional de las Artes ₁1965–66₁

2 v. (271 p.) 23 cm. (Bibliografía argentina de artes y letras. Compilaciones especiales)

Vol. 1: "Correspondiente al no. 21/22;" v. 2: "Correspondiente al no. 25/26."
CONTENTS: 1. Libros.—2. Artículos de revistas.

Boggs, Ralph Steele, 1901–

Bibliography of Latin American folklore: tales, festivals, customs, arts, magic, music. New York, H. W. Wilson Co., 1940. Detroit, B. Ethridge-Books, 1971.

x, 109 p. 22 cm. (Inter-American Bibliographical and Library Association. Publications, ser. 1, v. 5)

Dannemann Rothstein, Manuel.

Bibliografía del folklore chileno, 1952–1965. Austin Center for Intercultural Studies in Folklore and Oral History, University of Texas, 1970.

xvi, 60 p. 23 cm. (Latin American folklore series, no. 2)

"Con la contribución compiladora del Centro de Estudios 'Rodolfo Lenz' de la Agrupación Folklórica Chilena."

LATVIA

Greble, Vilma, 1906–

Latviešu vēstītājas folkloras un folkloristikas bibliogrāfija. Rīgā, Zinātne, 1971–

v. 20 cm.

At head of title, v. 1– : Latvijas PSR Zinatņu akadēmija. Valodas un literatūras institūts. V. Grebe.

MOLDAVIA

Béeshu, N M

Фолклор Молдовенеск. Библиографие (1924–1967). Кишинэу, "Картя Молдовеняскэ," 1968.

122 p. 20 cm.

At head of title: Академия де штиинце дин PCC Молдовеняскэ. Институтул де лимбэ ши литературэ.
Moldavian and Russian.

NETHERLANDS

Herman, Rik.
Zuidnederlandse toeristische tijdschriften. 1895–1960. Door R. Herman. Antwerpen, Centrum voor Studie en Documentatie, ₁Tentoonstellingslaan, 37₁, 1972.

xxviii, 285 p. tables. 24 cm. (Nederlandse volkskundige bibliografie, deel 14)

Nederlandse volkskundige bibliografie; systematische registers op tijdschriften, reekswerken en gelegenheidsuitgaven, onder leiding van K. C. Peeters. Antwerpen, Centrum voor Studie en Documentatie, 1964–
v. 25 cm.

Published under the auspices of the Volkskunde-Commissie van de Koninklijke Nederlandse Academie van Wetenschappen te Amsterdam and the Koninklijke Belgische Commissie voor Volkskunde (Vlaamse Sectie) te Brussel.
CONTENTS.—deel. 1. Volkskunde, 1888–1938.—deel. 2. Volkskunde, 1939–1960.—deel. 3. Rond den Heerd.—deel. 4. Grootmoederken, 1842. Wodana, 1843. Tijdschriften met "museum" in de titel.

PHILIPPINE ISLANDS

Bernardo, Gabriel Adriano, 1891–1963.
A critical and annotated bibliography of Philippine, Indonesian and other Malayan folk-lore. Edited by Francisco Demetrio Y Radaza. Cagayan de Oro City ₁Philippines₁ Xavier University, 1972.

xviii, 150 p. illus. 27 cm. (A museum and archives publication no. 5) (Ateneo de Manila University. Dept. of History. Occasional papers, bibliographical series no. 3)

RUSSIA

Andreeva, M   N
(Fol'klor Nizhegorodskogo kraîa)
Фольклор Нижегородского края. Библиогр. указ. ₁с 40-х г. XIX в. по 1969 г.₁ Горький, 1971.

145 p. 19 cm.

At head of title: MB и CCO РСФСР. Горьковский государственный университет им. Н. И. Лобачевского.
By M. N. Andreeva, A. N. Donin, and K. E. Korepova.

Pavlova, V   A   comp.
Фольклор Воронежского края; библиографический указатель. Составила В. А. Павлова. Под ред. В. А. Тонкова. Библиографическая ред. Э. Я. Брун. Воронеж, Изд-во Воронежского университета, 1965.

106 p. 20 cm.

At head of title: Министерство высшего и среднего специального образования РСФСР. Воронежский государственный университет. Фундаментальная библиотека.

TURKEY

Türk folklor ve etnografya bibliyografyası. 1–
1971–
₁Ankara₁ Millî Folklor Enstitüsü Müdürlüğü.

v. 24 cm. (₁Millî Folklor Enstitüsü₁ Millî Folklor Enstitüsü yayınları)

Issued by Millî Folklor Enstitüsü.

UKRAINE

Klymasz, Robert Bogdan, 1936–
A bibliography of Ukrainian folklore in Canada, 1902–64, compiled by Robert B. Klymasz. ₁Ottawa, Queen's Printer₁ 1969.

vi, 53 p. 25 cm. (National Museum of Canada, Ottawa. Anthropology papers no. 21)

UNITED STATES

Bratcher, James T   1934–
Analytical index to Publications of the Texas Folklore Society, volumes 1–36 ₁by₁ James T. Bratcher. Dallas, Southern Methodist University Press, 1973.

xxi, 322 p. illus. 24 cm.

Corgan (D. Leonard) Library.
A description of the George Korson folklore archive. Compiled by Judith Tierney, special collections librarian. Wilkes-Barre, Pa., King's College Press, 1973.

vii, 46 p. 23 cm. (Wyoming Valley series, no. 1) (Publications of the D. Leonard Corgan Library)

Ferris, William R
Mississippi Black folklore; a research bibliography and discography ₁by₁ William R. Ferris, Jr. Hattiesburg, University and College Press of Mississippi ₁1971₁

v, 61 p. illus. 22 cm. (The University & College Press of Mississippi series—humanities)

Randolph, Vance, 1892–
Ozark folklore; a bibliography. Bloomington, Indiana University Research Center for the Language Sciences ₁1972₁

572 p. 26 cm. (Indiana. University. Folklore Institute. Monograph series, v. 24)

YUGOSLAVIA

Bogavac, Mirjana.
Bibliografija radova o narodnoj književnosti. Sarajevo, Akademija nauka i umjetnosti Bosne i Hercegovine, 1972.
226, ₁2₁ p. 24 cm. (Akademija nauka i umjetnosti Bosne i Hercegovine. Posebna izdanja, knj. 18) (Odjeljenje za književnost i umjetnost, knj. 1)
At head of title: Mirjana Bogavac, Vojislav Maksimović, Luka Šekara.
Added t. p. in French.

FOLK-LORE OF WOMEN

Folklore feminists' communication. no. 1–
fall 1973–
Austin, Tex.

no. 28 cm.

FOLK-SONGS, MUSIC AND DANCE
see also Ballads

Arseven, Veysel.
Açıklamalı Türk halk müziği kitap ve makaleler bibliyografyası. İstanbul, M. E. B. Devlet Kitapları, 1969.

210 p. 24 cm. (Millî Folklor Enstitüsü yayınları, 1)

Clark, Keith.
Folk song and dance; a list of books selected by Keith Clark. London, National Book League; English Folk Dance and Song Society, 1972.

48 p. illus. 21 cm.

Davis, Arthur Kyle, 1897–
Folk-songs of Virginia; a descriptive index and classification of material collected under the auspices of the Virginia Folklore Society. New York, AMS Press ₁1965, c1949₁

lxiii, 389 p. 24 cm.

Deutsch, Walter.
Die Volksmusiksammlung der Gesellschaft der Musikfreunde in Wien 〈Sonnleithner-Sammlung〉. Bearb. v. Walter Deutsch u. Gerlinde Hofer mit einem Beitrag v. Leopold Schmidt (Zur Bedeutung d. österr. Volkslied-

sammlung v. 1819.) ₍Mit Faks. u. Noten.₎ Wien, Schendl (1969)–

v. 23 cm. (Schriften zur Volksmusik, Bd. 2

Klusen, Ernst, *comp.*

Rheinische Volkslieder in mehrstimmigen Sätzen. Eine Zusammenstellung von Volksliedbearbeitungen. ₍Von₎ Ernst Klusen ₍u.₎ Klaus Weiler. Köln, Rhein, Heimatbund, 1969.

40 p. 24 cm. (Schriftenreihe des Rheinischen Heimatbundes, Heft 30)

MacDougall, John.

Scottish country dances; a listing index of 900 dances, with reference sources. Memorial ed. ₍Boston₎ Boston Branch of the Royal Scottish Country Dance Society ₍1968₎

64 p. 25 cm.

Cover title: Index book of Scottish country dances. Pages 63–64 blank for notes.

Raccolta Barbi di canti popolari italiani; esperimento di elaborazione elettronica E1/RB. Pisa ₍C. N. U. C. E.₎ 1967.

2 v. 27–30 cm.

CONTENTS: ₍1₎. Fotocopia dei cento testi manoscritti utilizzati per l'esperimento E1/RB.—₍2₎ I tabulati.

United States. Library of Congress. Music Division.

Bibliography of Latin American folk music. Compiled by Gilbert Chase. New York, AMS Press ₍1972₎

ix, 141 p. 26 cm.

Reprint of the 1942 ed.

Vaughan Williams Memorial Library.

The Vaughan Williams Memorial Library catalogue of the English Folk Dance and Song Society; acquisitions to the Library of books, pamphlets, periodicals, sheet music and manuscripts, from its inception to 1971. ₍London₎ Mansell, 1973.

xiv, 769 p. 28 cm.

Veen, Meliena van der.

Bibliografie van de Nederlandse volksdansen. ₍Amsterdam₎ 1969.

15 l. 28 cm.

Cover title.
"Werkstuk 2e cyclus Bibliotheek- en Documentatieschool, Amsterdam."

Vetterl, Karel, *comp.*

A select bibliography of European folk music. Editor-in-chief: Karel Vetterl. Co-editors: Erik Dal, Laurence Picken ₍and₎ Erich Stockmann. Prague, 1966.

vii, 144 p. 24 cm.

At head of title: Institute for Ethnography and Folklore of the Czechoslovak Academy of Sciences in co-operation with the International Folk Music Council.

Virginia. University. *Library.*

The folksongs of Virginia; a checklist of the WPA holdings, Alderman Library University of Virginia ₍by₎ Bruce A. Rosenberg. Charlottesville, University Press of Virginia ₍1969₎

xx, 145 p. 21 cm.

Vorarlberger Volksliedarchiv.

Der Liederschatz der Vorarlberger; Liedkatalog der Bestände des Vorarlberger Volksliedarchives in Bregenz am Ende des Jahres 1968. Erstellt von Josef Bitsche. ₍Lustenau, Buchdrukerei Lustenau, 1969₎

ix, 139 p. 21 x 30 cm.

Vuyst, Julien de.

Het Nederlandse volkslied. Bibliografie. 1800–1965. Brussel, Belgische Commissie voor Bibliografie ₍Huidevetterstraat 80–84₎ 1967.

2 v. 21 cm. (Bibliographia Belgica, 98)

Proefschrift—Provinciale Bibliotheekschool van Brabant.

FOLMANIS, ŽANIS

Deglava, Aina.

Žanis Griva. Biobibliogrāfija. Жан Грива. Биобиблиография. Rīgā, 1970.

88 p. 19 cm.

At head of title: Vīla Lača Latvijas PSR Valsts bibliotēka.

FOOD

see also Cookery; Nutrition

Drake, Birger.

Sensory evaluation of food; annotated bibliography, by Birger Drake and Birgit Johansson. Göteborg ₍Sweden₎ Svenska Institutet för Konserveringsforskning ₍1969₎

2 v. 30 cm. (SIK-rapport 1969, no. 255)

Food and Agriculture Organization of the United Nations. Documentation Center.

Food and nutrition. Alimentation et nutrition. Alimentación y nutrición. Annotated bibliography. Author and subject index. ₍Rome₎ Food and Agriculture Organization of the United Nations ₍1973₎

₍588₎ p. 28 cm.

Goff, Michael.

Food and wine; an annotated list; selected by Michael Goff and Anthony Berry. London, National Book League, 1972.

40 p. 21 cm.

Leung, Woot-tsuen (Wu) 1915–

A selected bibliography on 1. African foods and nutrition; 2. African botanical nomenclature. Bethesda, Md., Nutrition Section, Office of International Research, National Institutes of Health, 1966.

130, 11 p. 27 cm.

Leung, Woot-tseun (Wu), 1915–

A selected bibliography on East-Asian foods and nutrition arranged according to subject matter and area, by Woot-tseun Wu Leung, and Ritva Rauanheimo Butrum and Flora Huang Chang. ₍Bethesda, Md., U. S. National Institutes of Health, 1973₎

vii, 296 p. 27 cm. (DHEW publication no. (NIH) 73–466)

Neumannová, Jarmila.

Bibliografie fyzikálních vlastností potravin. Uspoř. Jarmila Neumannová, Daniela Fryšová. Předml.: Miloslav Adam. Praha, Čes. akademie zeměd.-Výzkum. ústav potrav. průmyslu, rozmn. ₍1970₎.

13, 375 p. 21 cm.

Title also in English: Bibliography of physical properties of foodstuffs.

Moscow. TSentral'naía nauchno-tekhnicheskaía biblioteka pishchevoĭ promyshlennosti.

Технохимический и микробиологический контроль в пищевой промышленности. (Аннот. библиогр. указатель отечеств. и зарубежной литературы за 1962–1967 (I кв.) гг.) Москва, 1967 ₍вып. дан. 1968₎.

148 p. 26 cm.

At head of title: Министерство пищевой промышленности СССР. Центральная научно-техническая библиотека пищевой промышленности.

Moscow. TSentral'naia nauchno-tekhnicheskaia biblioteka pishchevoĭ promyshlennosti. Nauchno-bibliograficheskiĭ otdel.

Современные способы сушки пищевых продуктов. Аннот. библиогр. указатель отечеств. и зарубежной литературы за 1965–1968 гг. Москва, 1969.

201 p. 20 cm. 0.00rub
At head of title: Министерство пищевой промышленности СССР. Центральная научно-техническая библиотека пищевой промышленности.
"Составлен Научно-библиографическим отделом Центральной научно-технической библиотеки пищевой промышленности."

Radoĭkov, Vladimir.

Прогнози за развитието на хранително-вкусовата промишленост. ⟨Темат. библиогр. справка⟩. Състав. Вл. Радойков, М. Кирова. ЦНТИИСГС, 1971.

48 p. 22 cm.

At head of title: Академия на селскостопанските науки. Център за научно-техническа и икономическа информация по селско и горско стопанство.

LIBRARY CATALOGS

United States. National Agricultural Library. Food and Nutrition Information and Educational Materials Center.
Catalog. ₁Beltsville, Md., 1973₁

ix, 286 p. 28 cm.

United States. National Agricultural Library. Food and Nutrition Information and Educational Materials Center.
Catalog. Supplement. 1974–

₁Beltsville, Md.₁

v. 28 cm.

Vols. for 1974– include cumulative index.

PERIODICALS

Mann, E J

Evaluation of the world food literature: results of an international survey, by E. J. Mann. Farnham Royal (Bucks.), Commonwealth Agricultural Bureaux, 1967.

₁4₁, viii, 181 p. tables, diagr. 23½ cm.

FOOD AND AGRICULTURE ORGANIZATION see under United Nations

FOOD INDUSTRY AND TRADE

Автоматическое управление и регулирование на пищевых предприятиях; библиографический аннотированный указатель отечественной и зарубежной литературы за 1960–1966 гг., январь–май. Москва, 1966.

23 p. 26 cm.

At head of title: Министерство пищевой промышленности. Центральная научно-техническая библиотека пищевой промышленности.

Centre de documentation internationale des industries utilisatrices de produits agricoles.
Bulletin bibliographique. v. 6–
jan. 1972–
₁Paris₁ Association pour la promotion industrie-agriculture.

v. 27 cm. monthly.

Continues a publication with the same title issued under the earlier name of the center: Centre de documentation des industries utilisatrices de produits agricoles.
At head of title, 1972– : Commission internationale des industries agricoles et alimentaires.

European food market research sources 1970. Zug, Switzerland, Noyes Data S. A.; Park Ridge, N. J., Noyes Data Corp. ₁1970₁

111 p. 28 cm.

Food and Agriculture Organization of the United Nations. Documentation Center.

Food and agricultural industries, annotated bibliography, author and subject index. Industries alimentaires et agricoles, bibliographie annotée, index par auteurs et par sujets. Industrias de la agricultura y la alimentación, bibliografía anotada, indice por autores y temas. ₁Rome, 1970₁

1 v. (various pagings) 28 cm.

Goldblith, Samuel A

An annotated bibliography on microwaves: their properties, production, and applications to food processing ₁by₁ Samuel A. Goldblith and Robert V. Decareau. Cambridge, Mass., MIT Press ₁1973₁

xi, 356 p. 26 cm.

Institute of Food Distribution.

A bibliography of the wholesale and retail distributive trades. London, I. F. D., 1970.

₁4₁, 51 p. 30 cm.

Комплексное использование отходов пищевой промышленности; аннотированный библиографический указатель отечественной и зарубежной литературы за 1960–1965 гг. Москва, 1965.

29 p.
At head of title: Государственный комитет по пищевой промышленности при Госплане СССР. Центральная научно-техническая библиотека пищевой промышленности.
Microfilm. 1 reel. 35 mm.

Margolina, Z G
(Avtomaticheskoe upravlenie i regulirovanie na pishchevykh predpriiatiiakh)

Автоматическое управление и регулирование на пищевых предприятиях. Аннот. библиогр. указ. отеч. и зарубеж. литературы за 1966–1971 гг. ₁В 2-х ч.₁ Москва, ₁1972₁

2 v. 20 cm.
At head of title: Министерство пищевой промышленности СССР. Центральная научно-техническая библиотека пищевой промышленности.
"Составители: З. Г. Марголина, С. М. Кауфман."

Moscow. TSentral'naia nauchno-tekhnicheskaia biblioteka pishchevoĭ promyshlennosti.

Экономико-математические методы планирования, учета и управления в пищевой промышленности. (Аннот. указатель рус. и иностр. литературы за 1965–1968 (янв.-апр. гг.)) Москва, 1968.

19 p. 26 cm.

Mysore (City). Central Food Technological Research Institute.
Abstracts of CFTRI papers. ₁Mysore, 1966₁

15 v. in 1. 25 cm.

CONTENTS.—1. Infestation control and shelf-life of food materials.—2. Refrigeration and preservation of perishables.—3. Fruit and vegetable technology.—4. Meat and fish technology.—5. Infant and weaning foods.—6. Biochemistry, nutrition, and dietetics.—7. Substitute and supplementary foods.—8. Biscuits, bakery, and confectionery.—9. Oils and fats.—10. Coffee and tea technology.—11. Spices and condiments.—12. Food additives.—13. Microbiology and sanitation.—14. Packaging and containers.—15. Miscellany.

Samoĭlova, N V
(Khimiia v pishchevoĭ promyshlennosti)

Химия в пищевой промышленности. Аннот. библиогр. указ. отеч. и зарубеж. литературы за 1965–1968 гг. ₁Сост. Н. В. Самойлова₁ Москва, 1972.

232 p. 25 cm.

At head of title: Министерство пищевой промышленности СССР. Центральная научно-техническая библиотека пищевой промышленности.

Vara, Albert C

Food and beverage industries: a bibliography and guidebook ₁by₁ Albert C. Vara. Detroit, Gale Research Co.

[1970]

215 p. 22 cm. (Management Information guide, 16)

FOOD SUPPLY

Contracting Parties to the General Agreement on Tariffs and Trade. *International Trade Centre.*
Répertoire bibliographique: Sélection de statistiques des produits. Genève, 1967.

vi, 243 p. 28 cm.

At head of title: GATT. Centre du commerce International.

Henderson, Elizabeth Wilhelm, 1912–
Ayuda alimentaria: selección bibliográfica anotada sobre la utilización de los productos alimentarios para el desarrollo económico, preparada para el Programa Mundial de Alimentos por Elizabeth Henderson. Roma, Naciones Unidas. 1965.

vii, 233 p. 23 cm.

Translation of Food aid.

Henderson, Elizabeth (Wilhelm) 1912–
Food aid: a selective annotated bibliography on food utilization for economic development. Prepared for the World Food Program by Elizabeth Henderson. Rome, United Nations [and] Food and Agriculture Organization of the United Nations, 1964.

vii, 203 p. 23 cm.

Lundeen, Glen, 1922–
World food problems bibliography, by Glen Lundeen and Barbara Lundeen. [Fresno, Calif., Food Science Research Center] 1969.

iv, 46 l. 28 cm.

Pusat Dokumentasi Ilmiah Nasional.
Food in Indonesia, 1952–1967; a bibliography. [Djakarta] Indonesian National Scientific Documentation Center [1968]

x, 104 p. 24 cm.

Prepared for the United States National Academy of Sciences and the Indonesian Institute of Sciences "Workshop on Food" held at Djakarta, May–June, 1968.

U. S. *Air Force Academy. Library.*
The Malthusian spectre: the challenges of food and population [by Ottie K. Sutton, senior reference librarian. Colorado Springs, 1969]

33 p. 21 cm. (*Its* Special bibliography series, no. 42)

FOOT-AND-MOUTH DISEASE

Balassa, Béla, 1899–
Bibliography of foot-and-mouth disease in man, 1695–1965, compiled by B. Balassa. Greenport, N. Y., U. S. Dept. of Agriculture, Agricultural Research Service, Animal Disease & Parasite Research Division, Plum Island Animal Disease Laboratory [1966?]

29 l. 27 cm.

Ящур; библиографический указатель иностранной литературы. [Составитель А. А. Дороговцев. Редакторы П. В. Малярец, Л. С. Авраамова] Москва, 1967–

v. 20 cm.

At head of title, v. 1–: Всесоюзный научно-исследовательский ящурный институт. Центральная научная сельскохозяйственная библиотека ВАСХНИЛ.

FORAGE see Grass

FORD, JESSE HILL

White, Helen, 1914–
Jesse Hill Ford: an annotated check list of his published works and of his papers / by Helen White. — Memphis : Memphis State University, 1974.

55 p., [5] leaves of plates : ill. ; 25 cm. — (MVC bulletin ; no. 7)

FORECASTING
see also Economic forecasting; Employment forecasting

Czechoslovak Republic. Ministerstvo kultury. Oddělení dlouhodobého výhledu.
Výběrová bibliografie z oblasti prognostiky a dlouhodobého plánování. Vyprac. [kol.] Praha, Min. kultury ČSR, rozmn, 1969.

60 l. 30 cm.

Germany (Federal Republic, 1949–) Bundestag. Wissenschaftliche Dienste.
Zukunftsforschung (Futurologie). Bonn, 1971.

101 p. 30 cm. (Its Bibliographien, Nr. 25)

"Die vorliegende Bibliographie wurde Im Referat Zeitgeschichte und Allgemeine Politik von Herrn Oberregierungsrat Dr. Kessel unter Mitarbeit von Frau Dalades erstellt."

Krejčí, Emil.
Prognostika v kultuře. Výběrová bibliografie z prognostické lit.—společenskovědní oblast. [Autoři:] Emil Krejčí—Ladislav Pištora. 1. vyd. Praha, Scénografický ústav, rozmn., 1971.

196, [1] p. 29 cm. (Knihovna divadelního prostoru, sv. 105, č. 2) (Bibliografická řada o scénografii a divadelní technice, č. 2)

Padbury, Peter.
The future: a bibliography of issues and forecasting techniques. Prepared by: Peter Padbury, with the assistance of: Diane Wilkins. [Monticello, Ill., Council of Planning Librarians, 1972]

102 p. 29 cm. (Council of Planning Librarians. Exchange bibliography 279)

FOREIGN AID see Economic assistance; Technical assistance

FOREIGN RELATIONS see International law and relations

FOREIGN STUDENTS see Students, Foreign

FOREL, AUGUSTE HENRI

Vaud. *Bibliothèque cantonale et universitaire, Lausanne. Département des manuscrits.*
Inventaire des archives Auguste Forel, 1848–1931 (IS 1925 et 3765) par Siegried Unterfichter et Olivier Pavillon. Lausanne, Bibliothèque cantonale et universitaire, 1969.

91, III l. 30 cm. (Its Inventaires des fonds manuscrits, 5)

FOREST FIRES
Cushwa, Charles T
Fire: a summary of literature in the United States from the mid-1920's to 1966, by Charles T. Cushwa. [Asheville, N. C., U. S. Southeastern Forest Experiment Station, 1968]

ii, 117 p. 27 cm.

Forest Fire Research Institute. Information Centre.
Document list. Ottawa, Forest Fire Research Institute, Dept. of Fisheries and Forestry, 1969–

1 v. (loose-leaf) 28 cm.

Hostetter, Anita, 1938–

Annotated bibliography of publications by U. S. Forest Service forest fire research staff, their colleagues, and co-operators in California, 1962–1965. Berkeley, Pacific Southwest Forest and Range Experiment Station, Forest Service, U. S. Dept. of Agriculture, 1966.

24 p. 27 cm.

Ramsey, G   S

Bibliography of departmental forest fire research literature, by G. S. Ramsey. Ottawa, Forest Fire Research Institute, Dept. of Forestry & Rural Development, 1966.

1 v. (various paging) 28 cm. (Forest Fire Research Institute. Information report FF–X–2)

FORESTER, FRANK   see   Herbert, H. W.

FORESTS AND FORESTRY

see also   Trees and shrubs; and under Dissertations, Academic

Adams, R   D

Index of selected articles from Canadian journals pertaining to the forest products industries, 1965–1967, by R. D. Adams, M. L. El-Osta, and R. W. Wellwood. Vancouver, Faculty of Forestry, University of British Columbia, 1968.

iv, 22 l. 28 cm.

Bogdanov, I   IA

(Orositel'nye sistemy na prosadochnykh lessovykh gruntakh)

Оросительные системы на просадочных лессовых грунтах. Инж.-геол. исследования. Библиогр. указ. отеч. литературы за 1930–1970 гг. Москва, 1972.

242 p. 20 cm.

At head of title: Министерство мелиорации и водного хозяйства СССР. Главное управление науки. Центральное бюро научно-технической информации.

Dempsey, Gilbert P

Forest cooperatives; a bibliography. Compiled by Gilbert P. Dempsey. Upper Darby, Pa., Northeastern Forest Experiment Station, 1967.

53 p. 23 cm. (U. S. Forest Service research paper NE–82)

Droste zu Hülshoff, Bernd, Freiherr von.

Bibliographie der Erholungsfunktion des Waldes. Hrsg. von B. Freiherr von Droste zu Hülshoff. ₁München, Forstliche Forschungsanstalt, 1972?₁

17, 295, 465 l. 29 cm.

"Abteilung für Forstpolitik und Forstgeschichte der Forstlichen Forschungsanstalt in München, in Zusammenarbeit mit der Dokumentationszentrale der Bundesforschungsanstalt für Forst- und Holzwirtschaft in Reinbek."

Food and Agriculture Organization of the United Nations.
Documentation Center.

Forestry index 1945–1966. Forêts index. Montes índice. ₁Rome, 1967₁

1 v. (various paging) 28 cm.

Text in English, French, and Spanish.

Food and Agriculture Organization of the United Nations.
Terminology Reference Library.

Dictionaries and vocabularies in the field of forestry. Dictionnaires et vocabulaires intéressant la foresterie. Diccionarios y vocabularios en materia de montes, 1945–1972. Paris, Food and Agriculture Organization of the United Nations, 1972.

viii, 38 p. 27 cm.

At head of title: Terminology and Reference Section, Translation Service, Publications Division.

Gatterer, Christoph Wilhelm Jakob.

Allgemeines Repertorium der forstwissenschaftlichen Literatur; nebst beygefügten kritischen Bemerkungen über den Werth der einzelnen Schriften. Amsterdam, B. R. Grüner, 1972.

2 v. in 1. 23 cm.

Reprint of the Ulm, 1796 ed.

Grossová, Ivana.

Fyziológia, higiena a bezpečnosť práce v lesnej výrobe. Sociálne opatrenia. Výber, zozn. čas. a kniž. lit z fondov ŠVK Zvolen. Zost. Ivana Grossová. Zvolen, ŠVK, 1969.

20, ₁2₁ l. 20 cm.

Grossová, Ivana.

Spôsoby pestovania lesov. Výberová anot, bibl. Zost.: Ivana Grossová. Zvolen, ŠVK, rozmn., 1970.

₁2₁, 40 l. 20 cm.

At head of title: Štátna vedecká knižnica vo Zvolene.

Hemmings, Ernest Frederick.

Basic library list for forestry; edited by E. F. Hemmings. 4th ed. Oxford, The Library, Commonwealth Forestry Institute, University of Oxford, 1967.

60 p. 25 cm.

Hiller, István.

Egyetemi oktatók és tudományos dolgozók irodalmi munkássága, 1955–1965; bibliográfia. Sopron, 1966.

138 p. 29 cm.

At head of title: Erdészeti és Faipari Egyetem, Központi Könyvtár.

Hiller, István.

Értekezések, utibeszámolók, diplomatervek és tudományos diákköri dolgozatok, 1957–1966; bibliográfia. Sopron, Erdészeti és Faipari Egyetem Központi Könyvtára, 1966.

205 p. 29 cm.

Hosley, Neil Wetmore, 1901–

A selected bibliography of forest management-wildlife management for southeast Alaska, by N. W. Hosley. Carbondale, School of Agriculture, Southern Illinois University, 1969.

19 p. 28 cm. (Department of Forestry publication no. 3)

"Outgrowth of a cooperative study by Southern Illinois University and the Institute of Northern Forestry, U. S. Forest Service, Juneau, Alaska."

Klock, Glen O

Forest and range soils research in Oregon and Washington; a bibliography with abstracts from 1964 through 1968, compiled by Glen O. Klock. Portland, Or., Pacific Northwest Forest and Range Experiment Station, 1969.

28 p. 28 cm. (USDA Forest Service research paper PNW–90)

Supplements previous bibliography: Forest soils research in Oregon and Washington; a bibliography with abstracts through 1963, compiled by R. F. Tarrant.

Macková, Anna.

Mechanizačné prostriedky pre nakladanie dreva na dopravné prostriedky. Výber. zoznam odb. kniž. a čas. lit. z fondov. ŠVK Zvolen. Zost.: Anna Macková. Zvolen, ŠVK, rozmn, 1969.

₁1₁, 25, ₁2₁ l. 20 cm.

Mitchell, Adair A

Utilization of wood residues; an annotated bibliography ₁by Adair A. Mitchell₁ Washington, U. S. Dept. of Commerce, Business and Defense Services Administration; for sale by the Supt. of Docs., U. S. Govt. Print. Off., 1968.

46 p. 24 cm.

Orlova, E   N

Рубки ухода. Библиогр. указатель отечеств. и иностр. литературы за 1959–1969 гг. Москва, 1970.

39 p. 22 cm.

At head of title: Государственный комитет лесного хозяйства Совета Министров СССР. Центральное бюро научно-технической информации.
By E. N. Orlova, M. N. Alfámovskaîa, and V. M. Zubarev.

Pank, Larry F

A bibliography on seed-eating mammals and birds that affect forest regeneration, by Larry F. Pank. Washington, Bureau of Sport Fisheries and Wildlife; [for sale by the Supt. of Docs., U. S. Govt. Print. Off.] 1974.

28 p. 26 cm. (Special scientific report—wildlife, no. 174)

Rudolf, Paul Otto, 1906–

Forest genetics and related research at the Lake States Forest Experiment Station; an annotated bibliography, 1924–1965, compiled by Paul O. Rudolf. [St. Paul] North Central Forest Experiment Station, Forest Service, U. S. Dept. of Agriculture, 1966.

35 p. 27 cm. (U. S. Forest Service research paper NC–5)
Cover title.
Updates a list in Proceedings of 1st (1953) Lake States Forest Genetics Conference, issued as: U. S. Lake States Forest Experiment Station. Miscellaneous report no. 22.

Saari, Eino, 1894–

Bibliographia universalis silviculturae Suomi-Finlandia usque ad annum 1933. Ediderunt Eino Saari & Arvo Seppälä. Helsinki, Suomen metsätieteellinen seura, 1970–

v. 26 cm.

Finnish and German.
CONTENTS:
Pars 2. Alphabetica.

Toda, Ryookiti, 1918–

Abstracts of Japanese literature in forest genetics and related fields. Tokyo, Govt. Forest Experiment Station, 1970–

v. 26 cm.

U. S. *Forest Service.*

Forest recreation research: bibliography of Forest Service outdoor recreation research publications, 1942 through 1966. [Washington, 1967]

16 p. 27 cm.

U. S. *Pacific Northwest Forest and Range Experiment Station, Portland, Or.*

Publications of the Pacific Northwest Forest and Range Experiment Station, compiled by Mildred I. Hoyt and Edith P. Tomkins. Portland, Or., 1965.

67 p. 27 cm.

U. S. Southeastern Forest Experiment Station, Asheville, N. C.

Recent publications. Jan./June 1966–

[Asheville, N. C.]

v. 27 cm. semiannual.

At head of title, July/Dec. 1966–   : Research information digest.
Supersedes the station's Publications.

Viçosa, Brazil. Universidade Federal. Biblioteca Central.

Bibliografia de ciências florestais. Compilado por Maria Dias Bicalho e Maria das Graças Moreira Ferreira. Viçosa, Seção de Bibliografia e Documentação, 1973.

iv, 188 p. 23 cm. (Its Série Bibliografias especializadas, 2)

Weiner, Jack, 1910–

Forest fertilization [by] Jack Weiner and Kathleen

Mirkes. Appleton, Wis., Institute of Paper Chemistry, 1972.

xvii–xix, 261 p. 28 cm. (Institute of Paper Chemistry. Bibliographic series, no. 258)

PERIODICALS

New York. College of Forestry, *Syracuse. Moon Memorial Library.*

List of serials in the library, October 1964. Syracuse [1964?]

55 p. 28 cm. (Its Bibliographic series, publication no. 2)

Oxford. University. *Commonwealth Forestry Institute. Library.*

List of periodicals and serials in the Forestry Library, University of Oxford. 3rd ed., revised and edited by J. S. Howse. Oxford, (The Library), Commonwealth Forestry Institute, University of Oxford, 1968.

[1], xvii, 187 p. 34 cm.

AFRICA

Verhaegen, Paul T   1926–

Exploitation, utilisation et potentiel économique locaux des bois d'Afrique intertropicale: aspects juridiques, sociaux, économiques et techniques, par P. Verhaegen. Bruxelles, Centre de documentation économique et sociale africaine, 1964.

3 v. (630 p.) 22 cm. (Centre de documentation économique et sociale africaine. Enquêtes bibliographiques, 11)

BRAZIL

Coimbra Filho, Adelmar Faria.

Bibliografia florestal brasileira, 1. contribuição [por] Adelmar Faria Coimbra Filho [e] Alceo Magnanini. [Manaus] Conselho Nacional de Pesquisas, Instituto Nacional de Pesquisas da Amazônia, 1964.

93 p. 23 cm. (Instituto Nacional de Pesquisas de Amazônia. Botânica. Publicação, no. 20)

BULGARIA

Sakareva, Bistra Khr.

Указател на статиите в сп. „Горскостопанска наука." 1 ⟨1964⟩ — 5 ⟨1968⟩. София, АСН, 1970.

51 p. 22 cm.

At head of title: Академия на селскостопанските науки. Централа библиотека. Институт за гората—София. Бистра Хр. Сакарева.
Added t. p.: Index of the articles published in the periodical "Gorskostopanska nauka."
Introduction and table of contents also in English.

CANADA

Montreal. Pulp and Paper Research Institute of Canada.

List of Woodlands Research Department publications. Pointe Claire, P. Q., 1968.

14 p. 28 cm. (Its Woodlands Research Index no. 36)

Walters, John, 1921–

An annotated bibliography of reports, theses, and publications pertaining to the Campus and Research Forests of the University of British Columbia. Vancouver, Faculty of Forestry, University of British Columbia, 1968.

viii, 71 p. 29 cm.

CZECHOSLOVAK REPUBLIC

Zbraslav, Czechoslovak Republic (City). Výzkumný ústav lesního hospodářství a myslivosti.

50 [i. e. Padesát] let lesnického výzkumu. Výzkumný ústav lesního hospodářství a myslivosti. Bibliografie 1921–1969. Zprac. [kol.] pod ved. Zikmunda Želtvaye. [Předml.:] Jan Jindra. [Zbraslav-Strnady, nákl. vl., t. Mír] 1971.

192, ₁1₁ p. 24 cm.

Zvolen, Czechoslovak Republic (City) Vysoká škola lesnícka a drevárska. *Lesnícka fakulta.*
Bibliografia Lesníckej fakulty, 1952–1966. Bibliography of the Faculty of Forestry. ₁Zostavil Štefan Šmelko. Vyd. 1.₁ Vo Zvolene, Vysoká škola lesnícka a drevárska ₁1967₁

132 p. 24 cm.

Preface and table of contents also in English, Russia, and German.

Zvolen, Czechoslovak Republic (City). Vysoká škola lesnícka a drevárska. Lesnícka fakulta.
Bibliografia lesníckej fakulty, 1952–1971 = Bibliography of the Faculty of Forestry, 1952–1971. — Zvolen : Vysoká škola lesnícka a drevárska, 1971.

220 p. ; 24 cm.
Cover title.
Introduction and table of contents also in English, Russian, and German.

GERMANY

Mantel, Kurt, 1905–
Deutsche forstliche Bibliographie. 1560–1965. Hrsg. von K. Mantel. (Hrsg. anlässlich des 75jährigen Jubiläums des Internationalen Verbandes Forstlicher Forschungsanstalten und seines 14. Kongresses in München 1967.) Freiburg i. Br. (Universität, Forstgeschichtliches Institut; Hannover: Schaper in Kommission) 1967–72.
3 v. 24 cm. (Mitteilung des Forstgeschichtlichen Instituts der Universität Freiburg i. Br.)

GREAT BRITAIN

Edlin, Herbert Leeson.
Check list of Forestry Commission publications, 1919–65, by H. L. Edlin. London, H. M. S. O. ₁1966₁

36 p. 20½ cm. (₁Gt. Brit.₁ Forestry Commission. Forest record no. 58)

"Compiled by Miss L. M. Starling."

JAPAN

Kurata, Satoru, 1922–
A bibliography of forest botany in Japan, 1940–1963, edited by S. Kurata. With the collaboration of K. Aoshima ₁and others₁ Tokyo, University of Tokyo Press ₁ᶜ1966₁

xiii, 146 p. port. 27 cm.

NETHERLANDS

Brouwer, W D
Bibliografie van de Nederlandse bosbouwgeschiedenis. ₁Door₁ W. D. Brouwer. Wageningen, Landbouwhogeschool, 1967.

88 p. 25 cm.

NORTH AMERICA

Wheeland, Hoyt A
Bibliography of timber products harvesting in Eastern United States and Canada, by Hoyt A. Wheeland. ₁Columbus, Ohio, U. S. Dept. of Agriculture. Forest Service, Central States Forest Experiment Station₁ 1964.

27 p. 27 cm.

RUSSIA

Краткий обзор и аннотированный указатель литературы по экономике лесного хозяйства и лесной промышленности за 1966–1969 гг. Москва, 1970.

84 p. 21 cm.

At head of title: Госплан СССР. Совет по изучению производительных сил. Сектор лесных ресурсов.

Manushina, A D
(Bibliograficheskiĭ ukazatel' stateĭ, pomeshchennykh v izdanifakh TSBNTIleskhoza za tysfacha devfat'sot sem'desfatyĭ god)
Библиографический указатель статей, помещенных в изданиях ЦБНТИлесхоза за 1970 год. ₁Составители А. Д. Манушина и О. Н. Ганшина₁ Москва, 1972.
48 p. 21 cm.
At head of title: Государственный комитет лесного хозяйства Совета Министров СССР. Центральное бюро научно-технической информации.

UNITED STATES

Bruce, David, 1916–
Literature on timber measurement problems in the Douglas-fir region, a bibliography. Portland, Or., Pacific Northwest Forest and Range Experiment Station, 1968.

28 p. 27 cm. (U. S. D. A. Forest Service research paper PNW-67)

New York (State). College of Forestry, Syracuse.
An annotated bibliography on the timber resources and primary wood-using industries of New York State. Prepared for the Office of Planning Coordination. Albany, 1969.

148 p. 28 cm.

Smith, David Clayton, 1914–
Lumbering and the Maine woods: a bibliographical guide ₁compiled by David C. Smith. Portland, Maine Historical Society, 1971₁

34 p. 26 cm.

U. S. *National Archives.*
Preliminary inventory of the cartographic records of the Forest Service (Record group 95) Compiled by Charlotte M. Ashby. Washington, 1967.

vii, 71 p. 26 cm. (*Its* Publication no. 67-5. Preliminary inventories, no. 167)

U. S. *National Archives.*
Preliminary inventory of the records of the Forest Service (record group 95) Compiled by Harold T. Pinkett. Rev. by Terry W. Good. Washington, 1969.

vii, 23 p. 26 cm. (*Its* Preliminary inventories no. 18 (rev.))

National Archives publication no. 69-10.

FORÊTS, FRANCE

Belgium. *Archives de l'État, Arlon.*
Inventaire des archives de l'Administration du département des Forêts. Par Marcel Bourguignon, chef de travaux. Bruxelles, Archives générales du Royaume, 1969.

419 p. 25 cm.

At head of title: Ministère de l'éducation nationale. Archives générales du Royaume et Archives de l'État dans les provinces. Archives de l'État à Arlon.

FORLIMPOPOLI, ITALY

Aramini, Alberto.
Di Forlimpopoli. Contributo ad una bibliografia. Forlimpopoli, Cassa rurale e artigiana di Forlimpopoli, 1969.

110 p. illus., plates. 24½ cm.

At head of title: A. Aramini, R. Martelli.

FORMOSA see Taiwan

FORMSMA, WIEBE JANNES

Lijst van geschriften van Dr. W. J. Formsma. Aangeboden bij zijn afscheid als rijksarchivaris in de provincie Groningen. 's-Gravenhage, 1968.

14 l. port. 29 cm.

FORSTER, EDWARD MORGAN

Borrello, Alfred.
E. M. Forster: an annotated bibliography of secondary materials. Metuchen, N. J., Scarecrow Press, 1973.

xiii, 188 p. 22 cm. (The Scarecrow author bibliographies, no. 11)

Kirkpatrick, Brownlee Jean.
A bibliography of E. M. Forster ₍by₎ B. J. Kirkpatrick. With a foreword by E. M. Forster. London, R. Hart-Davis, 1965.

200 p. facsim., port. 23 cm. (The Soho bibliographies, 19)

FORSTER, GEORG

Fiedler, Horst.
Georg-Forster-Bibliographie 1767 bis 1970. ₍Hrsg.:₎ Dt. Akad. d. Wiss. zu Berlin; Zentralinst. f. Literaturgeschichte. Berlin, Akademie-Verl., 1971.

208 p. 25 cm.

FORT, PAUL

Châlons-sur-Marne, France. Bibliothèque municipale.
Centenaire de la naissance de Paul Fort: 1872–1972, exposition, 23 novembre–23 décembre 1972. Bibliothèque municipale de Châlons-sur-Marne. ₍Catalogue par Jean-Marie Arnoult; préface par François Veillerette₎. Châlons-sur-Marne. Bibliothèque municipale, 1972.

14 p. 22 cm.

FOSCOLO, UGO

Mazzolà, Maria.
Catalogo della raccolta foscoliana donata alla Biblioteca comunale di Treviso. Edizione fuori commercio. Treviso, Editrice trevigiana, 1971.

xiv, 248 p. plate. 24 cm.

At head of title: Maria Calzavara in Mazzolà.

FOSSILS   see Paleontology

FOSTER, STEPHEN COLLINS

U. S. Library of Congress. Music Division.
Catalogue of first editions of Stephen C. Foster (1826–1864) by Walter R. Whittlesey and O. G. Sonneck. New York, Da Capo Press, 1971.

79 p. 24 cm. (Da Capo Press music reprint series)

Reprint of the 1915 ed.

FOUNDATIONS, BENEVOLENT

Russell, Henry G
Guide to foundation annual reports on film. 1970. Compiled by Henry G. Russell. ₍New York₎ Foundation Center ₍1972₎

24 p. 28 cm.

FOUNDING

Barskaîa, R   I
Применение циркония в литейном производстве; библиографическая справка: Отечественная и иностранная литература за 1953–1964 гг., 58 назв. ₍Составитель Р. И. Барская₎. Москва, 1965.

11 l. 30 cm. (Технология машиностроения, № 483/65)

At head of title: Государственный комитет автотракторного и сельскохозяйственного машиностроения при Госплане СССР. Центральная научно-техническая библиотека тракторного и сельскохозяйственного машиностроения.

Demidova, N   N
Литейное производство. (Аннот. указатель литерату-

ры). Киев, "Техніка," 1969.

32 p. 20 cm.

At head of title: Министерство культуры УССР. Харьковская государственная научная библиотека имени В. Г. Короленко.

Indian National Scientific Documentation Centre, *Delhi.*
Bibliography on foundry practice ₍compiled by R. N. Neogi and others₎ New Delhi, 1966.

91, ₍6₎ p. 29 cm.

"Brought out by INSDOC on the occasion of the 33rd International Foundry Congress being held in New Delhi from 5 to 10 December, 1966."
"List of periodicals cited in the bibliography": p. ₍93₎–₍97₎

Indian National Scientific Documentation Centre, Delhi.
Technical books exhibition: catalogue of exhibits. ₍New Delhi, 1966₎

54 p. 28 cm.

At head of title: 33rd International Foundry Congress, New Delhi, India, 5–9 December 1966.
"Organised by Indian National Scientific Documentation Centre, New Delhi and National Metallurgical Laboratory, Jamshedpur."

Indian Standards Institution, Delhi.
Bibliography of standards on foundry practice ₍compiled by V. P. Vij and D. N. Kulkarni₎ New Delhi, Indian Standards Institution ₍and₎ Indian National Scientific Documentation Centre, 1966.

33 p. 28 cm.

Thomson, Robert, 1902–
An indexed list of references on continuous casting ₍by₎ R. Thomson. Ottawa, Dept. of Energy, Mines and Resources, Mines Branch, 1970.

iii, 68 p. 28 cm. (Mines Branch. Information circular IC253)

Cover title.
Summary in French.

FOWLDS, SIR GEORGE

Auckland, N. Z. University. *Library.*
The Fowlds papers; an inventory of the Sir George Fowlds collection, by Frank Rogers. ₍Auckland, N. Z.₎ 1964.

vi, 34 p. 22 cm. (University of Auckland Library. Bibliographical bulletin 2)

FRACTURES

Elliott, Robert B
A key bibliography of implant fixation of shaft fractures of the long bones, by Robert B. Elliott. ₍n. p.₎ 1964.

1 v. (unpaged) illus. 28 cm.

Cover title.
"Prepared for ASTM Committee F–4 on Surgical Implants, Subcommittee III on Performance."

FRANCE
see also under Dissertations, Academic

Association des documentalistes et bibliothécaires ·spécialisés. *Sous-groupe Économie régionale.*
Répertoire des périodiques économiques régionaux. ₍Paris (8ᵉ), Bibliothèque de la Chambre de commerce de Paris, 27, av. Friedland,₎ 1970.
iv, 51, vi, v l. 21 x 27 cm.

Bibliographie italo-française, 1948–1958. Paris, Maison du livre italien ₍1962–73₎

2 v. 25 cm.

CONTENTS: 1. ptie. 1948–1954.—2. ptie. 1955–1958.

Changements dans la société française contemporaine, panorama bibliographique (1947–1967), document collectif. ₍Sous la direction de Andrée Collot et Michel Morin.₎ Nancy, Institut national pour la formation des adultes, rue de Saurupt, 1971.

68 p. 26 cm. (Les Documents de l'INFA)

Claval, Paul.
Région et régionalisation dans la géographie française et dans d'autres sciences sociales, bibliographie analytique présentée par Paul Claval ... Étienne Juillard ... Paris, Dalloz, 1967.

99 p. 21 cm. (Cahiers de l'Institut d'études politiques de l'Université de Strasbourg, 3)

Demangeon, Albert, 1872–1940.
Les sources de la géographie de la France aux archives nationales. New York, B. Franklin ₍1970₎

120 p. 22 cm. (Burt Franklin research & source works series, 594. Selected essays in history, economics & social science, 197)

Reprint of the 1905 ed.

France. Comité des travaux historiques et scientifiques.
Catalogue des ouvrages en vente. ₍Nouvelle édition.₎ Paris, Bibliothèque nationale, 1969.

116 p. 21 cm.

At head of title: Ministère de l'éducation nationale. Direction des bibliothèques et de la lecture publique.

John Crerar Library, *Chicago.*
A catalogue of French economic documents from the sixteenth, seventeenth, and eighteenth centuries. New York, B. Franklin ₍1969₎

6, 104 p. 26 cm. (Selected essays in history, economics and social science, 74)

Burt Franklin bibliography and reference series, 222.
Title on spine: French economic documents.
Reprint of the 1918 ed.

Lille. Bibliothèque municipale.
Livres du Grand siècle, Bibliothèque municipale de Lille, 2 mai–30 juin 1968. ₍Catalogue par Madeleine Chardonneau et Brigitte Duthoit. Préface par Étienne Dennery.₎ Lille, Bibliothèque municipale, 1968.

xvi, 148 p. plates. 21 cm.
At head of title: Tricentenaire du rattachement de Lille à la France.

Lindsay, Robert O
French political pamphlets, 1547–1648; a catalog of major collections in American libraries. Compiled by Robert O. Lindsay and John Neu. Madison, University of Wisconsin Press, 1969.

xii, 510 p. 24 cm.

The **Maps** of south-west France with special reference to Cognac; being the catalogue of a collection. London, Map Collectors' Circle, 1966.

14 p. 24 maps. 25 cm. (Map Collectors' Circle. Map collectors' series, no. 26)

Maps from the collection of Richelieu et Cie of Cognac.

Pemberton, John E
How to find out about France; a guide to sources of information, by John E. Pemberton. ₍1st ed.₎ Oxford, New York, Pergamon Press ₍1966₎

xvi, 199 p. illus. (part fold. col.) fold. col. maps. 20 cm. (The Commonwealth and international library. Library and technical information division)

Préfecture de la région Rhône-Alpes. Bureau de la documentation.
Liste indicative des ouvrages, études et principaux articles

de caractère économique et social ... ₍Lyon,₎ la Préfecture, 1968.

₍ii₎, 74 l. 27 cm.
At head of title. Préfecture de la région Rhône-Alpes. Préfecture du Rhône. Mission régionale. Documentation.

Saffroy, Gaston.
Bibliographie généalogique, héraldique et nobiliaire de la France, des origines à nos jours, imprimés et manuscrits. Préface de Michel Fleury ... Paris, G. Saffroy, 1968–

v. illus., col. plates. 27 cm.

Illustrated cover.

CONTENTS.— t. 1. Généralités: Nos 1–16008.

Touring-Club de France. *Groupe d'archéologie antique.*
Bibliographie. Nouvelle édition ... Paris, Touring-Club de France, 1965.

28 p. illus. 27 cm. (Groupe d'archéologie antique du Touring club de France. Notice technique no 1)

BIO-BIBLIOGRAPHY

Ersch, Johann Samuel, 1766–1828.
La France littéraire, contenant les auteurs français de 1771 à 1796. Genève, Slatkine Reprints, 1971.

5 v. 22 cm.

"Réimpression de l'édition de Hambourg, 1797–1806."

FOREIGN RELATIONS

Rollet, Henry.
Liste des engagements bilatéraux au 30 juin 1969; accords et traités souscrits par la France. Paris, A. Pedone, 1970.

206 p. 24 cm.

Rollet, Henry.
Liste des engagements bilatéraux et multilatéraux au 30 juin 1972; accords et traités souscrits par la France. Avec une table méthodique. Paris, A. Pedone, 1973.

571 p. 24 cm.

"Ce recueil regroupe en un seul volume et met à jour ... les deux volumes parus, le premier en 1970 (Liste des engagements bilatéraux au 30 juin 1969), le deuxième en 1971 (Liste des engagements multilatéraux au 30 juin 1969 avec une table méthodique)."

GOVERNMENT PUBLICATIONS

Catalogue des publications éditées ou diffusées par La Documentation française. 1971–
₍Paris₎

v. 24 cm.

Continues the Index général of the agency.

Commission de coordination de la documentation administrative.
Répertoire des publications périodiques et de série de l'administration française. ₍Paris, Documentation française, 1973₎

xiii, 368 p. 21 cm.

France. *Direction de la documentation.*
Cinquantième congrès de l'Association des maires de France, 21–25 novembre 1966. ₍Catalogue₎ Paris, Éditions de la Documentation française ₍1966?₎

24 p. 21 cm.

Cover title.
"La Documentation française a sélectionné, à l'intention des maires de France, quelques uns des titres de son catalogue."

HISTORY

France. Archives nationales.
Archives privées: état des fonds de la série AP, par

Chantal de Tourtier-Bonazzi [et] Suzanne d'Huart, conservateurs. Avant-propos par Jacques Monicat. Paris, S. E. V. P. E. N., 1973–

v. 24 cm. (Its Inventaires et documents)

France. Archives nationales.
Inventaire de la série AJ³⁷ ... Paris, S. E. V. P. E. N., 1971–

v. illus., plates (part fold.) 24 cm.

At head of title: Ministère d'État chargé des affaires culturelles. Direction des archives de France. Archives nationales, Paris. Élisabeth Dunan, conservateur aux Archives nationales.

France. Archives nationales.
Inventaire général de la série AF, sous-série AFiv (Secrétairerie d'État impériale) ... Paris, Impr. nationale, 1968–

v. in 25 cm. (Its Inventaires et documents)

CONTENTS: t. 1, fasc. 1. Du Verdier, P., Favier, J., et Mathieu, R. AFiv 1 à 1089ᴮ.

France. Ministère des affaires étrangères. Archives.
État numérique des fonds de la correspondance politique et commerciale, 1897 à 1918 [par M. V. Duval et F. Péquin, conservateurs] Paris, Impr. nationale, 1973.

xi, 282 p. 30 cm.

At head of title: Archives du Ministère des affaires étrangères.

France. Ministère des affaires étrangères. Archives.
Inventaire des mémoires et documents France; mémoires et documents France, volumes 588 à 647 et 1891, 1892 (Fonds "Bourbons"). Paris, Impr. nationale, 1960.

viii, 243 p. 24 cm.

"Le présent inventaire ... a été préparé et imprimé par les soins de: M. Robert de Grandsaignes d'Hauterive, conseiller-maître à la Cour des comptes, et Mlle Françoise Demanche, conservateur des Archives diplomatiques."

Gadille, Jacques.
Guide des archives diocésaines françaises. Lyon (7ᵉ), Centre d'histoire du catholicisme, 74, rue Pasteur, 1971.

167 p. maps. 24 cm. (Collection du Centre d'histoire du catholicisme, Université de Lyon II, 3)

Heinz, Grete.
The French Fifth Republic, establishment and consolidation (1958–1965); an annotated bibliography of the holdings at the Hoover Institution, by Grete Heinz and Agnes F. Peterson. Stanford, Calif., Hoover Institution Press [1970]

xiii, 170 p. 29 cm. (Hoover Institution bibliographical series, 44)

Joughin, Jean T
France in the nineteenth century, 1815–1914; selected studies in English since 1956, by Jean T. Joughin. Washington, Service Center for Teachers of History [1968]

35 p. 23 cm. (Service Center for Teachers of History. Publication no. 72)

Lasteyrie du Saillant, Robert Charles, comte de, 1849–1921.
Bibliographie générale des travaux historiques et archéologiques publiés par les sociétés savantes de la France, dressée sous les auspices du Ministère de l'instruction publique. New York, B. Franklin [1972]

6 v. 27 cm. (Burt Franklin bibliography and reference series, 452. Selected studies in history, economics & social science, n. s. 5. (c) Modern European studies)

Title on spine: Bibliographie générale des sociétés savantes de la France.
Reprint of the 1888–1918 ed.

Vol. 1, by R. de Lasteyrie and E. Lefèvre-Pontalis: v. 2, by R. de Lasteyrie with the collaboration of E. Lefèvre-Pontalis and E. S. Bougenot; v. 3, by R. de Lasteyrie; v. 4–6, by R. de Lasteyrie with the collaboration of A. Vidier.

Covers the literature published up to 1900. Supplemented by Bibliographie annuelle des travaux historiques et archéologiques publiés par les sociétés savantes de la France, covering literature published 1901–10, and continued by R. Gandilhon's Bibliographie générale des travaux historiques et archéologiques publiés par les sociétés savantes de la France, période 1910–1940.

CONTENTS: t. 1. Ain-Gironde.—t. 2. Hérault-Haute-Savoie.—t. 3. Seine: Paris, 1. ptie.—t. 4. Seine: Paris (suite). Seine-et-Marne -Yonne. Colonies. Instituts français à l'étranger.—t. 5. [Supplément, 1886–1900] Ain-Savoie. — t. 6. Supplément, 1886–1900: Seine -Yonne. Colonies. Instituts français à l'étranger.

Molinier, Auguste Émile Louis Marie, 1851–1904.
Les sources de l'histoire de France des origines aux guerres d'Italie (1494) New York, B. Franklin [1964]

6 v. 24 cm. (Burt Franklin bibliography and reference series, no. 80)

Reprint of the edition published in Paris, 1901–06.

CONTENTS.—v. 1. Époque primitive. Mérovingiens et Carolingiens.—v. 2. Époque féodale. Les Capétiens jusqu'en 1180.—v. 3. Les Capétiens, 1180–1328.—v. 4. Les Valois, 1328–1467.—v. 5. Introduction générale. Les Valois (suite). Louis XI et Charles VIII (1461–1494).—v. 6. Table générale, par L. Polain.

Monod. Gabriel Jacques Jean, 1844–1912.
Bibliographie de l'histoire de France. Catalogue méthodique et chronologique des sources et des ouvrages relatifs à l'histoire de France depuis les origines jusqu'en 1789. Par G. Monod. Bruxelles, Culture et civilisation, 1968.

xi, 420 p. 23 cm.

Reprint of Paris ed., 1888. "Impression anastaltique."

Paris. Bibliothèque nationale. Département des imprimés.
Catalogue de l'histoire de France. Reproduction de l'édition publiée de 1855 à 1895 ... Paris, Bibliothèque nationale. 1968–69.

16 v. 27 cm.
Caption title: Histoire de France et des Français.
The first and most important of a series of classed catalogs, begun under Taschereau's administration (1852–1874). Ed. by J. A. Schmit.
Minutely classified under 15 main and 904 subclasses.
CONTENTS.—t. 1. Préliminaires et généralités. Histoire par époques. Histoire par règnes [jusqu'a Louis XIII]—t. 2. Louis XIV-Louis XVI.—t. 3. 1792–1848.—t. 4. 1848–1856. Journaux et publications périodiques.—t. 5. Histoire religieuse.—t. 6. Histoire constitutionnelle.—t. 7. Histoire constitutionnelle (suite). Histoire administrative, diplomatique, militaire. Mœurs et coutumes. Archéologie.—t. 8. Histoire locale.—t. 9. Histoire locale (suite). Histoire des classes. Histoire généalogique. Biographie. — t. 10. Biographie (suite). Supplément: Préliminaires et généralités. Histoire par époques. Histoire par règnes [jusqu'à 1792]—t. 11. Supplément (suite): 1792–1870. Journaux et publications périodiques.—t. 12. Table des auteurs.—t. 13. Supplément (suite): Histoire constitutionnelle.—t. 14.—Supplément (suite): Histoire militaire. Mœurs et coutumes. Archéologie.—t. 15. Supplément (suite): Histoire locale.—t. 16. Supplément (suite): Histoire généalogique. Biographie.

Répertoire bibliographique de l'histoire de France. t. 1–

1920/21–
[Darmstadt] Scientia Verlag Aalen, 1972–

v. 25 cm.

Reprint of a biennial publication issued in Paris by the Société française de bibliographie.

Société de l'histoire du protestantisme français.
Les réformés à la fin du XVIᵉ siècle: relevés de documents dans les fonds d'archives. Paris. 1972.

140 p. 24 cm.

Les sources de l'histoire de France des origines à la fin du XVᵉ siècle. Refonte de l'ouvrage d'Auguste Molinier, entreprise sous la direction de Robert Fawtier. [Paris, Éditions A. et J. Picard, 1971–

v. in 25 cm.

Tulard, Jean.
Bibliographie critique des mémoires sur le Consulat et l'Empire, écrits ou traduits en français. Genève, (Paris,) Droz, 1971.

xiv, 184 p. 25 cm. (Hautes études médiévales et modernes, 13)

At head of title: Centre de recherches d'histoire et de philologie de la IVᵉ section de l'École pratique des hautes études, 5.

HISTORY - REVOLUTION

Boissonnade, Prosper, 1862–1935.
Les études relatives à l'histoire économique de la Révolution française, ar ₍i. e. par₎ P. Boissonnade. New York, B. Franklin ₍1967₎

168 p. 24 cm. (Burt Franklin research and source works series, 130)

Bibliographical footnotes.
Reprint of the Paris, 1906 ed.

Florida. University, Gainesville. Libraries.
French revolutionary pamphlets at the University of Florida; a list compiled by Laura V. Monti. Gainesville, 1971.

166 p. front. 25 cm.

Gavrilichev, Valentin Andreevich.
Великая Французская буржуазная революция конца XVIII века в советской историографии, 1917–1960 гг.; библиографический указатель. Казань, 1961.

255 p.

At head of title: Казанский государственный университет имени В. И. Ульянова Ленина. Кафедра всеобщей истории. В. А. Гаврилычев.
Microfilm. 1 reel. 35 mm.

Gliozzo, Charles A
A bibliography of ecclesiastical history of the French Revolution. ₍Compiled by Charles A. Gliozzo, Pittsburgh, Clifford E. Barbour Library ₍c1972₎

98 p. 28 cm. (Bibliographia tripotamopolitana, no. 6)

Horward, Donald D
The French Revolution and Napoleon collection at Florida State University: a bibliographical guide, by Donald D. Horward. ₍Tallahassee₎ Friends of the Florida State University Library, 1973.

xvii, 462 p. 24 cm.

Pennsylvania. University. *Library.*
The Maclure collection of French revolutionary materials. Edited by James D. Hardy, Jr., John H. Jensen, and Martin Wolfe. Philadelphia, University of Pennsylvania Press ₍1966₎

xxix, 456 p. 32 cm.

HISTORY, MILITARY

France. *Archives nationales.*
Inventaire des archives de la marine. Sous-série D²: Travaux hydrauliques et bâtiments, déposée aux Archives nationales. Par Paul Lecacheux, révisé et mis au point par Thérèse Tour et Agathe Bellas. Paris, Impr. nationale, 1965.

136 p. 24 cm. (*Its* Inventaires et documents)

France. Armée. État-Major. Service historique.
Guide bibliographique sommaire d'histoire militaire et coloniale française. ₍Sous la direction de René Couret₎ Paris, Impr. nationale, 1969.

522 p. 25 cm.

At head of title: Ministère des armées. État-Major de l'Armée de terre. Service historique.

Michaux, Monique.
Iconographie militaire française, bibliographie. Monique Michaux ... 94 Vincennes, Château de Vincennes, ₍1971–

v. 30 cm.

At head of title: Ministè re d'État chargé de la défense nationale. État-major de l'armée de terre. Service historique.

IMPRINTS see French imprints

LAW see Law - France

FRANCE, ANATOLE see under Balzac, Honoré de

FRANCESCO D'ASSISI, SAINT see under Dante Alighieri *(Felice da Mareto)*

FRANCHE-COMTÉ

Dantès, Alfred Langue, 1830–1891.
La Franche-Comté; littéraire, scientifique, artistique. Recueil de notices sur les hommes les plus remarquables du Jura, du Doubs et de la Haute-Saône. Genève, Slatkine Reprints, 1971.

vi, 379 p. 19 cm.

"Réimpression de l'édition de Paris, 1879."

FRANCISCANS

Castro y Castro, Manuel.
Manuscritos franciscanos de la Biblioteca Nacional de Madrid ₍por₎ Manuel de Castro. ₍Madrid, Servicio de Publicaciones del Ministerio de Educación y Ciencia, 1973₎

844 p. 25 cm.

Naples. Biblioteca nazionale.
Manoscritti francescani della Biblioteca nazionale di Napoli. Quaracchi/Florentiae, Typographia Collegii S. Bonaventurae; ₍poi₎ Grottaferrata, Editiones Collegii S. Bonaventurae ad Claras Aquas, 1971.

2 v. (1197 p.) 24½ cm. (Spicilegium Bonaventurianum, 7–8)

Name of editor, Cesare Cenci, at head of title.

San Antonio, Juan de, *18th cent.*
Bibliotheca universa Franciscana, concinnata ar. P. Fr. Joanne a s. Antonio, Salmantino. Farnborough (Hants.), Gregg P., 1966 ₍i. e. 1967₎.

3 v. plate (facsim.). 28 cm.

Facsimile reprint of 1732 ed.

Soto Pérez, José Luis.
Un siglo de historia literaria, 1862–1962 : noticia bio-bibliográfica sobre los religiosos hijos del Colegio de Misioneros Franciscanos para Tierra Santa y Marruecos establecido en Santiago de Compostela / José Luis Soto Pérez. — ₍s. l. : s. n.₎, 1963 i. e. 1969 (Santiago de Compostela : Imp. El Eco Franciscano)

750 p. : facsims., ports. ; 25 cm.

Troeyer, Benjamin de, 1913–
Bio-bibliographia franciscana neerlandica ante saeculum XVI. Nieuwkoop, B. de Graaf, 1974.

2 v. illus. 25 cm.

Foreword and pref. of v. 2 also in English.
Includes bibliographical references.
CONTENTS: 1. Troeyer, B. de. Pars biographica: auctores editionum qui scripserunt ante saeculum XVI.—2. Mees, L. Pars bibliographica: incunabula.

Wadding, Luke, 1588–1657.
Scriptores ordinis minorum. Quibus accessit syllabus illorum, qui ex eodem ordine pro fide Christi fortiter oc-

cubuerunt. Recensuit Fr. Lucas Waddingus. Frankfurt/
M., Minerva, 1967.

1 v. (various pagings) 22 cm.

Facsimile reprint of Rome ed., 1650.

FRANCK, HANS

Schwerin. Stadtarchiv. Aussenstelle Hans-Franck-Archiv.
Hans-Franck-Bibliographie. Bearb. von Heidemarie
Sobotha. Hrsg. durch Hans Heinrich Leopoldi. Schwerin,
Stadtarchiv, Aussenstelle Hans-Franck-Archiv, 1969.

83 p. 21 cm. (Veröffentlichungen des Stadtarchivs Schwerin.
N. F., Bd. 6)

FRANCKE, AUGUST HERMANN

Halle. Universitäts- und Landesbibliothek Sachsen-Anhalt.
Katalog der in der Universitäts- und Landesbibliothek
Sachsen-Anhalt zu Halle (Saale) vorhandenen handschrift-
lichen und gedruckten Predigten August Hermann
Franckes. In Verbindung mit Friedrich de Boor bearb.
von Erhard Peschke — Halle (Saale): Universitäts- und
Landesbibliothek Sachsen-Anhalt, 1972.

135 p. 21 cm. (Schriften zum Bibliotheks- und Büchereiwesen in
Sachsen-Anhalt; 36)
Cover title: Katalog der Predigten August Hermann Franckes.

FRANCONIA

Fränkische Bibliographie. Schrifttumsnachweis zur histori-
schen Landeskunde Frankens bis zum Jahre 1945. Im
Auftrag der Gesellschaft für Frankische Geschichte unter
Mitwirkung zahlreicher Bearbeiter hrsg. von Gerhard
Pfeiffer. Würzburg, Schöningh [in Kommission] 1965–

v. 25 cm. (Veröffentlichungen der Gesellschaft für Fränkische Geschichte. Reihe 11, 3

FRANK, LEONHARD

Zhitomirskaia, Zinaida Viktorovna.
Леонгард Франк; биобиблиографический указатель.
[Составитель З. В. Житомирская. Отв. редактор Н. М.
Эйшискина] Москва, Книга, 1967.

66 p. port. 22 cm. (Писатели зарубежных стран)

At head of title: Всесоюзная государственная библиотека
иностранной литературы.

FRANKFURTER, FELIX

Harvard University. Law School. Library.
Felix Frankfurter: an inventory of his papers in the
Harvard Law School Library. Prepared by Erika Chad-
bourn. [Cambridge, Mass.] Manuscript Division, Harvard
Law School Library, 1970.

iv, 135 l. 28 cm.

Photocopy of typescript.

U. S. Library of Congress. Manuscript Division.
Felix Frankfurter: a register of his papers in the Library
of Congress. Washington, Library of Congress, 1971.

70 p. 26 cm.

FRANKLIN, BENJAMIN

Ford, Paul Leicester, 1865–1902.
Franklin bibliography; a list of books written by, or relating to Benjamin Franklin. New York, B. Franklin
[1968]

lxxi, 467 p. 24 cm. (Burt Franklin bibliography and reference
series, 160)
Reprint of the 1886 ed.

Ford, Paul Leicester, 1865–1902.
Franklin bibliography; a list of books written by or relating to Benjamin Franklin. Boston, Milford House
[1972]

1 v. (various pagings) 22 cm.
Reprint of the 1889 ed.

Miller, Clarence William, 1914–
Benjamin Franklin's Philadelphia printing. 1728–1766:
a descriptive bibliography, by C. William Miller. Philadelphia, American Philosophical Society, 1974.

lxxxv, 583 p. illus. 30 cm. (Memoirs of the American Philosophical Society, v. 102)

United States. Library of Congress. Manuscript Division.
Benjamin Franklin: a register and index of his papers
in the Library of Congress. Washington, Library of Congress, 1973.

iii, 27 p. 29 cm.

FRANKLIN COUNTY, PENNSYLVANIA

Weiser, Frederick Sheely, 1935–
Parochial registers for Lutheran congregations in Frank-
lin County and Fulton County, Pennsylvania, 1790–1970.
Compiled by Frederick S. Weiser. Gettysburg, Pa., 1971.

10 l. 28 cm. (His Guide to central Pennsylvania Lutheran
Church records, no. 8)

"A guide to genealogical resources in the parish records of bap-
tisms, marriages and burials, as well as to translations and copies
in print and in public institutions."

FRANKO, IVAN

Moroz, Myroslav Oleksandrovych.
Іван Франко; бібліографія творів 1874–1964. Склав
М. О. Мороз. Київ, Наукова думка, 1966.

445 p. 22 cm.

At head of title: Львівська державна наукова бібліотека. Інститут літератури ім. Т. Г. Шевченка АН УРСР.

Sokolyszyn, Aleksander.
Іван Франко—шевченкознавець; бібліографічна розвід-
ка. В Лондоні, Укр. видавнича спілка, 1967.

20 p. 24 cm.

At head of title: Олександер Соколишин.

FRANZ, ROBERT

Boonin, Joseph M
An index to the solo songs of Robert Franz, by Joseph M.
Boonin. Hackensack, N.J., J. Boonin [1970]

v, 19 p. 28 cm. (Music indexes and bibliographies no. 4)

FRANZ FERDINAND, ARCHDUKE OF AUSTRIA

Trišić, Nikola Đ., d. 1957.
Sarajevski atentat u svjetlu bibliografskih podataka. [2.
izd.] Dopune, 1954–1964, Branko Čulić. Redaktor: Todor
Kruševac. Sarajevo, 1964.

527 p. 24 cm.

At head of title: Muzej grada Sarajeva.
Summaries in German and French.

FREDERIC, HAROLD

O'Donnell, Thomas Francis, 1915–
The Merrill checklist of Harold Frederic, compiled by
Thomas F. O'Donnell. Columbus, Ohio, C. E. Merrill Pub.
Co. [1969]

iv, 34 p. 19 cm. (Charles E. Merrill program in American literature)

Charles E. Merrill checklists.

FREE THOUGHT

Becker, Karl, 1907–

Freigeistige Bibliographie; ein Verzeichnis freigeistiger, humanistischer und religionskritischer Literatur. Stuttgart, Verlag der Freireligiösen Landesgemeinde Württemberg ₁1973?₁

170 p. 24 cm.

FREEDOM OF INFORMATION

Boston. Public Library.

The public interest and the right to know: access to government information and the role of the press; a selective bibliographic guide. ₁Boston₁ 1971.

iii, 59 p. 23 cm.

FREEDOM OF SPEECH

Schroeder, Theodore Albert, 1864–1953.

Free speech bibliography; including every discovered attitude toward the problem covering every method of transmitting ideas and of abridging their promulgation upon every subject-matter. New York, B. Franklin ₁1969₁

247 p. 27 cm. (Burt Franklin bibliography & reference series, 278)

Reprint of the 1922 ed.

FREEDOM OF THE PRESS

McCoy, Ralph Edward, 1915–

Freedom of the press; an annotated bibliography, by Ralph E. McCoy. With a foreword by Robert B. Downs. Carbondale, Southern Illinois University Press ₁1968₁

₁526₁, ix p. 32 cm.

São Paulo, Brazil (City). Universidade. Departamento de Biblioteconomia e Documentação. Disciplina Referência e Bibliografia.

Bibliografia sôbre censura e liberdade de imprensa para a II Semana de Estudos de Jornalismo, do Departamento de Jornalismo e Editoração da Escola de Comunicações e Artes da USP. Compilada pela Disciplina Referência e Bibliografia do Departamento de Biblioteconomia e Documentação. São Paulo, Universidade de São Paulo, Departamento de Jornalismo e Editoração ₁Editoria de Textos₁ 1970.

10 l. 32 cm. (Série Biblioteconomia e documentação, 1)

Silver, Louise.

Restrictions on freedom of publication in South Africa, 1948 to 1968; a select and annotated bibliography. Johannesburg, University of the Witwatersrand, Dept. of Librarianship, Bibliography and Typography, 1972.

vii, 54 p. 30 cm.

FREEMASONS

Buryshkin, Pavel Afanas'evich, 1887–1953.

Bibliographie sur la franc-maçonnerie en Russie ₁par₁ Paul Bourychkine. Complétée et mise au point par Tatiana Bakounine ... Paris, La Haye, Mouton et C¹ᵉ, 1967.

179 p. 24 cm. (Études sur l'histoire, l'économie et la sociologie des pays slaves, 11)

Freemasons and freemasonry: an extract from The National union catalog, pre-1956 imprints, volume 184; representing holdings of North American libraries reported to the National Union Catalog in the Library of Congress. ₁London₁ Mansell, 1973.

195 p. 35 cm.

Hungary. Országos Levéltár.

A szabadkőműves szervezetek levéltára; repertórium. Összeállította: Pataky Lajosné. Budapest, Művelődésügyi Minisztérium Levéltári Osztálya, 1967.

208 p. 29 cm. (Levéltári leltárak, 39)

Summary in Russian, German, and French.

Kloss, Georg Franz Burkhard, 1787–1854.

Bibliographie der Freimaurerei, ₁von₁ Georg Kloss. Graz, Akademische Druck- u. Verlagsanstalt, 1970.

xiv, 430 p. 20 cm.

Reprint of the 1844 edition, Frankfurt am Main.

Taute, Reinhold.

Maurerische Bücherkunde. Ein Wegweiser durch die Literatur d. Freimaurerei (mit literarisch-kritischen Notizen u. zugleich ein Supplement zu Kloss' Bibliographie). (Unveränd. Nachdr. d. 1886 in Leipzig ersch. Ausg. Photomechan. Nachdr.) Graz, Akad. Druck- u. Verlagsanst., 1971.

viii, 268 p. 20 cm.

Critical annotated catalog of the combined libraries of the Loge Karl zu den 3 Ulmen in Ulm and of J. G. Findel.

FRENCH-CANADIAN LITERATURE   see Canadian literature - French

FRENCH DRAMA   see   Drama - France

FRENCH GUIANA

Saint Jacques Fauquenoy, Marguerite.

Bibliographie sur les Guyanes et les territoires avoisinants ... Paris, O. R. S. T. O. M., 1966.

iv, 127 p. 27 cm.

FRENCH IMPRINTS

Le Catalogue de l'édition française. 1.–   éd.; 1970–

₁Paris₁ VPC livres, S. A.; ₁Port Washington, N. Y.₁ Paris Publications, Inc.

v. in   29 cm.   annual.

Vols. for 1970–   issued in 4 pts.

Catalogue des livres disponibles. Littérature et sciences humaines. Paris, Cercle de la librairie, 1969.

iv, 973 p. 27 cm.

Krauss, Werner, 1900–

Französische Drucke des 18. Jahrhunderts in den Bibliotheken der Deutschen Demokratischen Republik. Eingeleitet und hrsg. von Werner Krauss und Martin Fontius. Berlin, Akademie-Verlag, 1970.

2 v. (801 p.) 24 cm. (Deutsche Akademie der Wissenschaften zu Berlin. Schriften des Instituts für Romanische Sprachen und Kultur, Bd. 1)

CONTENTS.—₁1₁ Bibliographie.—₁2₁ Register.

Livres français d'érudition de 1965 à 1970. Paris, S. P. E. L. D. ₁1971₁

x, 229 p. 21 cm.

Répertoire des livres de langue française disponibles. 1972–

₁Paris₁ France-Expansion.

v. 21 cm.

Cover title, 1972–   : Répertoire des livres disponibles. Each edition issued in 2 vols.; Auteurs, and Titres.

Vicaire, Georges, 1853–1921.

Manuel de l'amateur de livres du XIXᵉ siècle, 1801–1893. Éditions originales.—Ouvrages et périodiques illustrés.—Romantiques.—Réimpressions critiques de textes anciens ou classiques.—Bibliothèques et collections diverses.—Publications des sociétés de bibliophiles de Paris et des départements.—Curiosités bibliographiques, etc., etc. Préf. de Maurice Tourneux. New York, B. Franklin ₁1973₎

8 v. 23 cm. (Burt Franklin bibliography and references series, 474)

Vol. 8 without subtitle.
Vol. 8: Table des ouvrages cités.
Reprint of the 1894–1920 ed. published by A. Rouquette, Paris.

EARLY PRINTED BOOKS

British Museum. *Dept. of Printed Books.*
Short-title catalogue of books printed in France and of French books printed in other countries from 1470 to 1600 in the British Museum. 1st ed. reprinted. London, British Museum ₁1966₎

viii, 491 p. 22½ cm.

Prepared by Henry Thomas, assisted by A. F. Johnson and A. G. Macfarlane.

British Museum. Dept. of Printed Books.
A short title catalogue of French books, 1601–1700, in the Library of the British Museum, by V. F. Goldsmith. Folkestone ₁Eng.₎ Dawsons, 1973.

x, 690 p. 29 cm.

"First published in seven fascicules 1969–1973."

Conlon, Pierre M
Prélude au siècle des lumières en France. Répertoire chronologique de 1680 à 1715. ₁Par₎ Pierre M. Conlon. Genève, Droz, 1970–

v. 23 cm. (Histoire des idées et critique littéraire, v. 104

CONTENTS.—t. 1. 1680–1691.

Répertoire bibliographique des livres imprimés en France au seizième siècle ... Baden-Baden, Heitz, 1968–

v. 25 cm. (Bibliotheca bibliographica Aureliana, 25, 27

Issued in parts.

Sorel, Charles, 1602?–1674.
La bibliothèque françoise. 2ᵉ éd. rev. et augm. (Réimpr. de l'éd. de Paris, 1667.) Genève, Slatkine Reprints, 1970.

124 p. 31 cm.

FRENCH INDOCHINA   see   Indochina
FRENCH LANGUAGE
   see also under   Dissertations,
   Academic - French studies

Centre d'étude du français moderne et contemporain.
Bibliographie des chroniques de langage publiées dans la presse française ... Paris, Didier, 1970–

v. 26 cm. (Its Études et documents, v. 1)

CONTENTS: 1. 1950–1965, sous la direction de B. Quemada.

Centre régional de documentation pédagogique, Dijon.
Français, documentation disponible au C. R. D. P. Dijon, Centre régional de documentation pédagogique, bd Gabriel, 1969.

₁iv₎, 135 p. 27 cm.

Centre régional de documentation pédagogique d'Orléans. *Bibliothèque pédagogique.*
Linguistique, langue française, littérature ... Bibliothèque pédagogique du C. R. D. P. ... Orléans, Centre régional de documentation pédagogique, 1968.

55 p. 27 cm. (Annales du Centre régional de documentation pédagogique d'Orléans)

Centre régional de documentation pédagogique, Poitiers.
La Documentation du professeur de lettres. Poitiers, C. R. D. P., ₁6, rue Sainte-Catherine,₎ 1970.

237 p. 27 cm. (Annales un Centre régional de documentation pédagogique de Poitiers. Documentation pédagogique)

Docking, J
Text books for French: an annotated bibliography ₁by₎ J. Docking. ₁Sydney₎ Macquarie University, 1970.

45 p. 25 cm. (Monographs for teachers of French, v. 3, no. 2)

Littérature et langue françaises. ₁Documentation recueillie sous la direction de Maurice Crouslé.₎ ₁Paris,₎ Hachette, 1967.

vii, 709 p. 23 cm.

Ohio. State University, *Columbus. Libraries.*
French language dictionaries in the Ohio State University libraries; a bibliographic guide, by Ana R. Llorens and Rosemary L. Walker. Columbus, Office of Educational Services, Ohio State University Libraries, 1970.

iv, 56 p. 23 cm.

"A project of the Foreign Languages Graduate Library."

Olivieri, Jean.
Bibliographie commentée, enseignement du français et linguistique / J. Olivieri, B. Ricatto. — Nice : C. R. D. P., ₁1974₎

211 leaves ; 30 cm. — (Annales du Centre régional de documentation pédagogique de Nice)

Osburn, Charles B
Research and reference guide to French studies, by Charles B. Osburn. Metuchen, N. J., Scarecrow Press, 1968.

517 p. 22 cm.

Pelz, Manfred.
Kritische Bibliographie zur Didaktik und Sprachwissenschaft des Französischen/ Manfred Pelz; Heidrun Pelz. — Freiburg (i. Br.): Becksmann, 1972.

vi, 212 p.: 21 cm. (Arbeitsmittel für den Unterricht. Reihe A: Kritische Bibliographien; Bd. 1)

Ronge, Peter.
Studienbibliographie Französisch; Beiträge zur bibliographischen Erschliessung der französischen Philologie. ₁Frankfurt (M)₎ Athenäum Verlag ₁c1971–

v. 19 cm. (Schwerpunkte Romanistik, 5,

Spaziani, Marcello.
Introduzione bibliografica alla lingua e alla letteratura francese. Palermo, U. Manfredi, 1969.

199 p. 16½ cm.

Stengel, Edmund, 1845–1935.
Chronologisches Verzeichnis französischer Grammatiken vom Ende des 14. bis zum Ausgange des 18. Jahrhunderts, nebst Angabe der bisher ermittelten Fundorte derselben. Voraufgeschickt ist ein auf dem dritten Neuphilologentage gehaltener Vortrag: Zur Abfassung einer Geschichte der französischen Grammatik besonders in Deutschland. Amsterdam, Grüner, 1970.

vii, 152 p. 23 cm.
Reprint of the Oppeln, 1890 ed.

Telle, Julien Aimable, *b.* 1807.
Les grammairiens français depuis l'origine de la grammaire en France jusqu'aux dernières œuvres connues; ouvrage servant d'introduction à l'étude générale des langues ₁par₎ J. Tell. Genève, Slatkine Reprints, 1967.

DIALECTS AND SLANG

Behrens, Dietrich, 1859–1929.
Bibliographie des patois gallo-romans. 2ᵉ éd. revue et augmentée par l'auteur, traduite en français par Eugène Rabiet. Bruxelles, Éditions Libro-sciences, 1967.

viii, 255 p. 24 cm. (Französische Studien, n. F., Heft 1)

Facsim. reproduction of the 1893 ed., Berlin, W. Gronau, which was rev. and edited from Rabiet's mss. by Paul Lejay.

Page, Louis.
La patois fribourgeois et ses écrivains. Romont, Éditions La Colline. [Louis Page, prof.], 1971.

viii, 89 p. 21 cm.

Wartburg, Walther von, 1888–
Bibliographie des dictionnaires patois galloromans (1550–1967) [par] Walther von Wartburg, Hans-Erich Keller [et] Robert Geuljans. Nouv. éd. entièrement revue et mise à jour. Genève, Droz, 1969.

376 p. 25 cm. (Publications romanes et françaises, 103)

First ed., 1934, has title: Bibliographie des dictionnaires patois.

Yve-Plessis, Robert.
Bibliographie raisonnée de l'argot et de la langue verte en France du xvᵉ au xxᵉ siècle. Préf. de Gaston-Esnault. Genève, Slatkine Reprints, 1968.

173 p. illus. 24 cm.

"Réimpression de l'édition de Paris, 1901."

OLD FRENCH

Rebok, Mirra Vladimirovna.
Памятники французского и провансальского языков IX–XV века; списки материалов, имеющихся в Государственной ордена Трудового красного знамени публичной библиотеке имени М. Е. Салтыкова-Щедрина. Составила М. В. Ребок. Минск, 1967.

141 p. 20 cm.
At head of title: Министерство высшего и среднего специального образования БССР. Минский государственный педагогический институт иностранных языков.

FRENCH LITERATURE

For the French literature of countries other than France see African literature, Canadian literature, Swiss literature, etc.

Cioranescu, Alexandre.
Bibliographie de la littérature française du dix-huitième siècle ... Paris, Éditions du Centre national de la recherche scientifique, 1969.

3 v. (x, 2137 p.) 28 cm.

CONTENTS.—t. 1. Généralités. A–D.—t. 2. E–Q.—t. 3. R–Z et index.

Cioranescu, Alexandre.
Bibliographie de la littérature française du dix-septième siècle. Paris, Éditions du Centre national de la recherche scientifique, 1965–66.

3 v. (2233 p.) 28 cm.

Langlois, Pierre, *of Paris.*
Guide bibliographique des études littéraires [par] Pierre Langlois ... André Mareuil ... 3ᵉ édition revue ... Paris, Hachette, 1965.

206, xxxv p. 20 cm.

Le Petit, Jules, 1845–1915.
Bibliographie des principales éditions originales d'écrivains français du XVᵉ au XVIIIᵉ siècle. Ouvrage contenant

environ 300 fac-similés de titres des livres décrits. Amsterdam, J. C. Gieben, 1969.

vii, 383 (i. e. 583) p. illus. 24 cm.

On spine: Les éditions originales.

Le Petit, Jules, 1845–1915.
Bibliographie des principales éditions originales d'écrivains français du XVᵉ au XVIIIᵉ siècle. Hildesheim, New York, G. Olms, 1969.

vii, 583 p. illus. 24 cm.

"Reprografischer Nachdruck der Ausgabe Paris 1888."

Quérard, Joseph Marie, 1797–1865.
La littérature française contemporaine. XIXᵉ siècle. Le tout accompagné de notes biographiques et littéraires. Paris, G.-P. Maisonneuve & Larose [1965]
6 v. 23 cm.
Vols. 2–3 have subtitle: 1827–1844; v. 4–6: 1827–1849; added t. p., v. 4 has subtitle: 1827–1844.
Begun by Quérard; from v. 2, p. 282, by C. Louandre, F. Bourquelot, and F. A. Maury.
A continuation of Quérard's La France littéraire.
Reproduced from the original ed. published in Paris, 1840–48, by Daguin, 1854–57, by Delaroque aîné. Cf. Biblio 1965; FBF 1965: 9512.

BIO-BIBLIOGRAPHY

La France littéraire. Genève, Slatkine Reprints, 1968.

4 v. in 1 (625 p.) 31 cm.

At head of title: Jacques Hébrail, Joseph de la Porte.
"Réimpression de l'édition de Paris, 1769–1784. 4 vol."
Each page reproduces 4 p. of the original text.

Longeon, Claude, 1941–
Les Écrivains foréziens du XVIᵉ siècle, répertoire bio-bibliographique. [Saint-Étienne,] Centre d'études foréziennes, [2, rue Tréfilerie,] 1970.

456 p. map. 24 cm. ([Collection Thèses et mémoires publiée par le Centre d'études foréziennes, 1])

Malignon, Jean, 1906–
Dictionnaire des écrivains français. [Paris] Éditions du Seuil [1971]

552 p. illus. 22 cm.

Monselet, Charles, 1825–1888.
Le lorgnette littéraire. Augmenté du complément Dictionnaire des grands et des petits auteurs de mon temps. Genève, Slatkine Reprints, 1971.

xviii, 240 p. 20 cm.

"Réimpression des éditions de Paris, 1857–1870."

HISTORY AND CRITICISM

French XX bibliography. v. 5–
(no. 21–
New York, French Institute, 1969–

v. 23 cm.

"Critical and biographical references for the study of French literature since 1885."
Continues French VII bibliography; critical and biographical references for the study of contemporary French literature.

Trousson, Raymond.
Encyclopédie de la philologie romane. Partie littéraire: Répertoire bibliographique. Par R. Trousson. 1ᵉʳᵉ éd. (Bruxelles, Presses universitaires de Bruxelles), 1968.

23 l. 27 cm.

LIBRARY AND EXHIBITION CATALOGS

Bordeaux. Bibliothèque municipale.
Une Génération dans l'orage, exposition organisée par la Bibliothèque municipale et consacrée aux écrivains de Bor-

deaux et de l'Aquitaine du début du siècle, à l'occasion du 50° anniversaire de l'armistice du 11 novembre 1918. Catalogue par Louis Desgraves et Michel Suffran ... Bordeaux, Bibliothèque municipale, 1968.

101 p. facsims. 24 cm.

Illustrated cover.

Charleroi. Palais des beaux-arts.
Trois cents ans de littérature française et dialectale au pays de Charleroi. ₍Charleroi, Palais des beaux-arts₎, 1966.

1 v. (unpaged) illus., ports. 22 cm.

On cover: Charleroi 1666-1966. Palais des beaux-arts. Exposition littéraire, du 13 mai au 10 juillet.

Harvard University. Library.
French literature. Cambridge, Mass.; distributed by Harvard University Press, 1973.

2 v. 29 cm. (Its Widener Library shelflist, 37-38)

CONTENTS: v. 1. Classification schedule, classified listing by call number, chronological listing.—v. 2. Author and title listing.

TRANSLATIONS

Broukalová, Zdeňka.
La littérature française en Tchécoslovaquie de 1945 à janvier 1964. ₍Bibliographie établie, par Zdenka Broukalová et Saša Mouchová₎ Prague, P. E. N. Club tchécoslovaque, 1964.

107 p. illus. 21 cm.

Literatura francuska; przewodnik bibliograficzny. Warszawa, 1971.

213 p. 25 cm. (Biblioteka Publiczna m. st. Warszawy. Materiały metodyczne i bibliograficzne)

Séguin, J A R
French works in English translation (1731-1799); a bibliographical catalogue, compiled and edited by J. A. R. Séguin. Jersey City, R. Paxton, 1965-70 ₍v. 1, 1970₎

8 v. 25 cm.

CONTENTS.—v. 1. A general index of authors, translators & subjects, with an introduction & additions.—₍2₎ 1731-1740.—₍3₎ 1741-1750.—₍4₎ 1751-1760.—₍5₎ 1761-1770.—₍6₎ 1771-1780.—₍7₎ 1781-1790.—₍8₎ 1790-1799.

FRENCH POETRY see Poetry - France

FRENCH PROTESTANT CHURCH OF LONDON

French Protestant Church of London.
The archives of the French Protestant Church of London; a handlist compiled by Raymond Smith. London, 1972.

104 p. 27 cm. (Huguenot Society of London. ₍Publications₎ Quarto series, v. 50)

FRENCH SOMALILAND see Somaliland

FRENEAU, PHILIP

Marsh, Philip Merrill, 1893-
Freneau's published prose: a bibliography, by Philip Marsh. Metuchen, N. J., Scarecrow Press, 1970.

167 p. 22 cm.

Paltsits, Victor Hugo, 1867-1952.
A bibliography of the separate and collected works of Philip Freneau, together with an account of his newspapers. New York, B. Franklin ₍1968₎

xv, 96 p. facsims. 23 cm. (Burt Franklin: bibliography and reference series #185)

Paltsits, Victor Hugo, 1867-1952.
A bibliography of the separate & collected works of Philip Freneau, together with an account of his newspapers. ₍Folcroft, Pa.₎ Folcroft Press ₍1969₎

xv, 96 p. illus. 23 cm.

Reprint of the 1903 ed.

FREUD, SIGMUND

Dufresne, Roger.
Bibliographie des écrits de Freud, en français, allemand et anglais. Paris, Payot, 1973.

268 p. 23 cm. (Collection Science de l'homme)

Jerusalem. Hebrew University. Jewish National and University Library.
Freudiana from the collections of the Jewish National and University Library. Exhibited in the Berman Hall of the library, March 28-April 13th, 1973. ₍Compiled and edited by Reuben Klingsberg₎ Jerusalem, 1973.

xxi, 19 p. illus. 23 cm.

Added t. p.: פרוידיאנה מאוספי בית-חספרים הלאומי והאוניברסיטאי
Cover title: Sigmund Freud.
Added cover title: זיגמונד פרויד
Catalog of the exhibition.
English and Hebrew.

FREWEN FAMILY

Warne, Heather M
A catalogue of the Frewen archives / by Heather M. Warne. — Lewes (Pelham House, Lewes, Sussex) : East Sussex County Council, 1972.

₍2₎, 44 p., fold. leaf : geneal. table ; 21 cm. — (Handbook - East Sussex Record Office ; no. 5)

FREYER, HANS

Willers, Dietrich.
Verzeichnis der Schriften von Hans Freyer. Darmstadt, Wissenschaftliche Buchgesellschaft, 1966.

10 p. 22 cm.

FRICTION see Tribology

FRIEDLÄNDER, LUDWIG

Franz, Eckhart G
Nachlass Ludwig Friedländer, 1824-1909. Bearb. von Eckhart G₍ötz₎ Franz. Marburg, Historische Kommission für Hessen Waldeck, 1971.

52 l. 30 cm. (Repertorien des Hess. Staatsarchivs Marburg, Bestand 340: Familienarchive und Nachlässe. Depositum Dehio, T. A.)

FRIENDS, SOCIETY OF

Goodbody, Olive C
Guide to Irish Quaker records, 1654-1860, by Olive C. Goodbody. With contribution on Northern Ireland records by B. G. Hutton. Dublin, Stationery Office for the Irish Manuscripts Commission, 1967.

237 p. 25 cm.

At head of title: Coimisiún Láimhscríbhinní na hÉireann.

Smith, Joseph, *bookseller*.
Bibliotheca anti-Quakeriana; or, A catalogue of books adverse to the Society of Friends. Alphabetically arranged; with biographical notices of the authors ... London, 1873. New York, Kraus Reprint Co., 1968.

474, 32 p. 23 cm.

Bound with the author's Bibliotheca Quakeristica. London, 1883. New York, Kraus Reprint Co., 1968.

Smith, Joseph, *bookseller*.
Bibliotheca Quakeristica, a bibliography of miscellaneous

literature relating to the Friends (Quakers), chiefly written by persons not members of their society; also of publications by authors in some way connected; and biographical notices. London, 1883. ₍New York, Kraus Reprint Co., 1968₎

32 p. 23 cm.

Bound with the author's Bibliotheca anti-Quakeriana. London, 1873. New York, Kraus Reprint Co., 1968.

Tasmania. University, Hobart. Library.

The Quaker collection of the Morris Miller Library, University of Tasmania; a preliminary checklist compiled by F. M. Dunn. Hobart, 1973.

72 p. 30 cm.

FRIESLAND

Fockema Andreae, Sybrandus Johannes, 1904–

Index op de besluiten van het departementaal bestuur van de Eems, voor zoveel Friesland betreft, 1799–1802. ₍Door₎ S. J. Fockema Andreae. Ljouwert, Fryske Akademy, 1968.

41 p. 20½ cm. (Monumenta Frisica. nr. 12) (Fryske Akademy. ₍Utjeften₎ nr. 321)

Fockema Andreae, Sybrandus Johannes, 1904–1968.

Index op de besluiten van het Departementaal Bestuur van Friesland onder Koning Lodewijk, 1 juli 1806–31 maart 1807. Ljouwert, (Leeuwarden), Fryske Akademy (Doelestrjitte 8), 1970.

31 p. 21 cm. (Monumenta Frisica, nr. 18) (Fryske Akademy. ₍Utjeften₎ nr. 389)

Fockema Andreae, Sybrandus Johannes, 1904–1968.

Index op de besluiten van het Departementaal Bestuur van Friesland uit de tijd van de Raadpensionaris Schimmelpenninck, 1805–1806. Ljouwert ₍Leeuwarden₎, Fryske Akademy (Coulonhuis), 1970.

32 p. 20 cm. (Monumenta Frisica, nr. 17) (Fryske Akademy. ₍Utjeften₎ nr. 388)

Fockema Andreae, Sybrandus Johannes, 1904–1968.

Index op het verbaal van de landdrost van Friesland van 16 mei 1807–eind 1810. Ljouwert ₍Leeuwarden₎, Fryske Akademy (Coulonhuis), 1971.

77 p. 20 cm. (Monumenta Frisica, nr. 19) (Fryske Akademy. ₍Utjeften₎ nr. 390)

Netherlands (Kingdom, 1815–   ). Rijksarchief in Friesland, Leeuwarden.

Register op de openbare werken in de provincie Friesland in de jaren 1803–1813. Door C. B. Menalda. ₍Voorwoord door M. Eerdmans₎. Ljouwert (Leeuwarden), Fryske Akademy, (Doelestrjitte 8), 1969.

100 p. 21 cm. (Monumenta Frysica, nr. 16) (Fryske Akademy. ₍Utjeften₎ nr. 357)

Werf, A   van der.

Gids voor de toerist in Friesland; een selectieve bibliografie van reisgidsen en enige reisbeschrijvingen, samengesteld door A. van der Werf. ₍n. p.₎ 1969.

80 l. 29 cm.

"Werkstuk 2e cyclus Bibliotheek- en Documentatieschool Amsterdam."

FRIIS, AAGE

Simon, Georg.

Bibliografi over trykte arbejder af historikeren, professor, dr. phil. Aage Friis. I anledning af hundredeårsdagen for hans fødsel den 16. august 1870. ₍Red. af Georg Simon i samerbejde med Henry Bruun₎. København, Rigsarkivet, 1970.

63 p. port. 30 cm.

FRIULI

Valentinelli, Giuseppe, 1805–1874.

Bibliografia del Friuli. Bologna, Forni, 1969.

viii, 540 p. 24½ cm.

Reproduction of the Venice 1861 ed.

FRIULI-VENEZIA GIULIA

Valussi, Giorgio.

Friuli-Venezia Giulia. A cura di Giorgio Valussi. Napoli, Tip. La buona stampa, 1967.

276 p. plate. 21 cm. (Collana di bibliografie geografiche delle regioni italiane, v. 9)

At head of title: Consiglio nazionale delle ricerche, Comitato per le scienze storiche filologiche e filosofiche.

FRÖBEL, FRIEDRICH WILHELM AUGUST

Heiland, Helmut.

Literatur und Trends in der Fröbelforschung. Ein krit. Literaturbericht über Quellen u. Sekundärliteratur v. d. Anfängen bis zur Gegenwart. Mit vollst. Bibliographie d. Fröbelliteratur. Weinheim, Beltz, 1972.

280 p. 21 cm. (Literatur und Forschungsberichte zur Pädagogik, Bd. 1) (Beltz-Monographien)

FROMENTIN, EUGENE

Wright, Barbara.

Eugène Fromentin — a bibliography / ₍by₎ Barbara Wright. — London, Grant and Cutler, 1973.

63 p. ; 21 cm. — (Research bibliographies and checklists : 8)

FRONTIER AND PIONEER LIFE

Vail, Robert William Glenroie, 1890–1966.

The voice of the old frontier. New York, Octagon Books, 1970 ₍c1949₎

xii, 492 p. 24 cm.

Half title: The A. S. W. Rosenbach Fellowship in Bibliography. "Three lectures ... delivered at the University ₍of Pennsylvania₎ in the fall of 1945, supplemented by a bibliographical appendix ₍p. 84–466₎"

FROST, ROBERT

Greiner, Donald J

The Merrill checklist of Robert Frost, compiled by Donald J. Greiner. Columbus, Ohio, C. E. Merrill ₍1969₎

iv, 42 p. 19 cm. (Charles E. Merrill checklists)

Charles E. Merrill program in American literature.
Cover title: Checklist of Robert Frost.

FRUIT

Bashlakova, V   V

₍Bibliograficheskiĭ ukazatel' rabot sotrudnikov MNIISViV₎

Библиографический указатель работ сотрудников МНИИСВиВ. (1957–1970 гг.) Кишинев, "Штиинца," 1973.

251 p. 21 cm.

At head of title: Министерство сельского хозяйства МССР. Молдавский научно-исследовательский институт садоводства, виноградарства и виноделия.

Eliseev, Ivan Petrovich.

₍Sadovodstvo Volgo-Viatskoĭ zony₎

Садоводство Волго-Вятской зоны. (Горьк., Киров. обл., Мордов., Марийск., Чуваш. АССР). Библиогр. список литературы за 1943–1967 гг. Горький, 1971.

23 p. 21 cm.

At head of title: МСХ СССР. Горьковский сельхозинститут. Кафедра плодоовощеводства. Библиотека.
By I. P. Eliseev, A. V. Zvereva, and E. A. Michurina.

Klosep, L   G
  ₁Khranenie i pervichnaîa pererabotka plodov i ovoshcheĭ.₁
  Хранение и первичная переработка плодов и овощей.
  Библиогр. указ. отеч. литературы за 1966–1970 гг. и
  иностр. литературы за 1968–1969 гг. ₁Сост. Л. Г. Кло-
  сеп₁. Москва, 1971.
    140 p. 20 cm.
    At head of title: Всесоюзная академия сельскохозяйственных
  наук имени В. И. Ленина. Центральная научная сельскохозяйственная библиотека.

Knight, Robert L   1907–
  Abstract bibliography of fruit breeding and genetics,
  1956–1969. Rubus and Ribes; by R. L. Knight, Jill H.
  Parker, and Elizabeth Keep. Slough, Commonwealth Agricultural Bureau, 1972.
    ix, 449 p. 23 cm. Index. (Commonwealth Bureau of Horticul-
  ture and Plantation Crops. Technical communication no. 32)

Morris, Leonard Leland, 1914–
  Modified atmospheres; an indexed reference list through
  1969, with emphasis on horticultural commodities ₁by₁ L. L.
  Morris, L. L. Claypool ₁and₁ D. P. Murr. ₁Berkeley, University of California, Division of Agricultural Sciences,
  1971.
    115 p. 26 cm.

Sépunaru, A   D
  Физиология плодовых культур. Библиогр. указатель
  литературы. (1955–1966 гг.) Кишинев, 1968.
    315 p. 21 cm.
    At head of title: Академия наук Молдавской ССР. Центральная
  научная библиотека.

Spain. *Dirección General de Archivos y Bibliotecas.*
  El naranjo; exposición bibliográfica conmemorativa de la
  inauguración de la Casa de la Cultura de Castellón de la
  Plana, 1967. ₁Madrid, 1967₁
    1 v. (unpaged) illus., facsim. 21 cm. (Serie Casas de la Cultura)

Stoy, F   A
  The citrus fruit industry in South Africa, 1951–1963; a
  bibliography, by F. A. Stoy. ₁Rondebosch₁ University of
  Cape Town, School of Librarianship, 1964.
    90 p. 23 cm. (University of Cape Town, School of Librarianship.
  Bibliographical series)
    Compiled as a continuation of the bibliography by R. G. Webb pub-
  lished in 1951.
    Thesis (Higher certificate in librarianship)—Cape Town.

FRYE, NORTHROP

Denham, Robert D
  Northrop Frye; an enumerative bibliography. Compiled
  and annotated by Robert D. Denham. Metuchen, N. J.,
  Scarecrow Press, 1974.
    vii, 142 p. 22 cm. (Scarecrow author bibliographies, no. 14)

FUEL
  see also Coal; Peat

Jiālgāra, India. Central Fuel Research Institute.
  Classified list of publications, 1947–1966. ₁Ranchi, 1968?₁
    83, 5 p. 25 cm.

Kozlova, K   P
  Наукові праці співробітників Інституту геології і
  геохімії горючих копалин АН УРСР, 1951–1966; бібліографічний покажчик. Укладач К. П. Козлова. Львів,
  1968.
    255 p. 22 cm.
    At head of title: Академія наук Української РСР. Інститут
  геології і геохімії горючих копалин. Наукова бібліотека.
    Added t. p. in Russian.

Králová, Anna.
  Práce Ústavu pro výzkum a využití paliv o spalování a
  analytice paliv. Naps. A. Králová, H. Hotová, Z. Wittochová. Běchovice, Ústav pro výzkum a využití paliv,
  rozmn., 1970.
    111, ₁1₁ p. 21 cm. (Monografie ÚVP, čis. 17)
    Title also in Russian and English: Труды Научно-исследователь-
  ского института топлив по сжиганию и аналитике топлив. Reports of the Fuel Research Institute on combustion and analyses of
  fuels.
    Text in Czech, Russian, and English.

Nahodilová, Aza.
  Práce Ústavu pro výzkum a využití paliv o využití tu-
  hých paliv. Naps. A. Nahodilová, M. Starý. Běchovice,
  Ústav pro výzkum a využití paliv, rozmn., 1970.
    66, ₁1₁ p. 21 cm. (Monografie ÚVP, čis. 19)
    Title also in Russian and English: Труды научно-исследователь-
  ского института топлив об использовании твердых топлив. Reports of the Fuel Research Institute on solid fuels utilization.
    Czech, Russian, and English.

Práce Ústavu pro výzkum a využití paliv o výzkumu uhlí.
  Bibliogr. prací publikovaných v letech 1950–1967. Běchovice, ₁nákl. vl.₁, rozmn. SČT 18, ₁P₁, 1968.
    111, ₁1₁ p. 21 cm. (Monografie ÚVP, čis. 5)
    Czech, Russian, German, English, and French.

Wittochová, Zdeňka.
  Seznam vybraných výzkumných zpráv vypracovných
  v Ústavu pro výzkum a využití paliv v letech 1967 až 1971.
  Zprac. a angl. překlad: Z. Wittochová. Rus. překlad: A.
  Nahodilová. Běchovice, ₁nákl. vl.₁, rozmn., 1971.
    100, ₁1₁ p. 21 cm. (Monografie ÚVP, čis. 24)
    Title also in Russian and English: Перечень избранных исследо-
  вательских отчетов разработанных в научно-исследовательском
  институте топлив в 1967–1971 годах. List of selected research
  reports worked out at the Fuel Research Institute in 1967 to 1971.

FUEL CELLS
U. S. *Aeronautical Center, Oklahoma City.   Library
Branch.*
  Fuel cells; selected references. Oklahoma City, Federal
  Aviation Agency, Aeronautical Center, 1964.
    93 p. 27 cm. (*Its* Bibliographic list no. 2)

FÜHMANN, FRANZ

Weise, Hilde.
  Franz Fühmann. ₁Anlässl. des 50. Geburtstages von
  Franz Fühmann am 15. 1. 1972 zusammengestellt von Hilde
  Weise und Ewald Birr. Berlin₁ Berliner Stadtbibliothek,
  1972.
    26 p. 21 cm. (Bibliographische Kalenderblätter. Sonderblatt,
  34)

FUKUZAWA, YUKICHI

Maruyama, Makoto, 1929–
  (Fukuzawa Yukichi to sono monka shoshi)
  福沢諭吉とその門下書誌　丸山信編著
  東京　慶応通信　昭和45(1970)
  247p 図版 22cm （慶応義塾関係者文献シリーズ
  第1集）
  監修者：富田正文
    Title also: A bibliography of the books, the essays and other
  writings by and on Yukichi Fukuzawa and his contemporaries at
  Keio University, 1858–1901.
    Text in Japanese.

FULLAM, WILLIAM FREELAND see under
  Chester, C. M.

FULTON COUNTY, PENNSYLVANIA   see under
  Franklin County

FUNCTIONAL ANALYSIS

São José dos Campos, Brazil. Centro Técnico de Aeronáutica. *Biblioteca Central.*
  Bibliografia, análise funcional, equações diferenciais parciais. São José dos Campos, Instituto Tecnológico de Aeronáutica, 1967.

  146 l. 27 cm. (*Its* Série bibliográfica, no. 2)

FUNCTIONAL EQUATIONS

Targonski, György I
  A bibliography on functional equations [by] György I. Targonski. [Brussels, European Office of Aerospace Research, 1964]

  iv, 96, [15] l. 28 cm.

  "Annual summary report nr. 2, April 1964, contract nr. AF 61 (052)–602."
  "Research ... sponsored by the Office of Scientific Research, OAR, through the European Office, Aerospace Research, United States Air Force."

FUND RAISING

Taft Products.
  The Taft guide to fund raising literature: an annotated bibliography. [Washington] 1973.

  21 p. 26 cm.

FUNDULUS

Huver, Charles W
  A bibliography of the genus Fundulus, compiled by Charles W. Huver. Boston, G. K. Hall, 1973.

  v, 138 p. 24 cm.

FUNERAL MUSIC

Snell, Frederick A.
  Music for church funerals and memorial services, by Frederick A. Snell. Philadelphia, Fortress Press [°1966]

  52 p. 23 x 11 cm.

  Cover title: Funeral music.

FUNGI see Mycology

FUR FARMING

Řidká, Bohuslava.
  Chov králíků a jiných kožešinových zvířat. Sest. Bohuslava Řidká. Brno, Univ. knihovna, rozmn., 1969.

  10, [1] p. 20 cm. ([Brünn. Universita. Knihovna] Výběrový seznam, č. 142)

FURER, JULIUS AUGUSTUS   see under
  Bloch, C. C.

FURNITURE

Hladíková, Jana.
  Nábytok a umelecké stolárstvo. Výberová anot. bibl. Zost.: Jana Hladíková. Zvolen, ŠVK, rozmn., 1970.

  [2], 49 l. 20 cm.

Viaux, Jacqueline.
  Bibliographie du meuble (mobilier civil français) Paris, Société des amis de la Bibliothèque Forney, 1966.

  589 p. 24 cm.

FÜRST, LUDVÍK

Literární činnost Ludvíka Fürsta v letech 1924–1971.
  Březnice, Měst. muzeum, rozmn., 1971.

  25 p. 30 cm.

  "K 60. narozeninám Ludvíka Fürsta"

FUSSELL, GEORGE EDWIN

Reading, Eng. University. *Museum of English Rural Life.*
  G. E. Fussell: a bibliography of his writings on agricultural history. Reading (Berks.), University of Reading (Museum of English Rural Life), 1967.

  vii, 34 p. 24½ cm.

FUTUNA see Wallis and Futuna Islands

FYEN, DENMARK

Denmark. Landsarkivet for Fyn.
  Landsarkivet for Fyn og hjælpemidlerne til dets benyttelse. En oversigt. Af Anne Riising. Odense, Landsarkivet for Fyn, Eksp.: Jernbanegade, 1970.

  179 p., 4 p. of plates. 24 cm.

Denmark. Landsarkivet for Fyn.
  Magistratsarkiver indtil 1868 i Landsarkivet for Fyn. — Odense : Landsarkivet for Fyn, eksp., Jernbanegade 36, 1973.

  348 p. ; 22 cm. — (Its Arkivregistratur)

Denmark. Landsarkivet for Fyn.
  3. [i. e. Tredie] udskrivningskreds' arkiv, 1788–1956. Med indledning af Knud J. V. Jespersen. Odense, 1970.

  64 l. 29 cm. (Its Arkivregistratur)

G

GABALDÓN MÁRQUEZ, JOAQUÍN

Venezuela. Universidad Central, *Caracas. Escuela de Biblioteconomía y Archivos.*
Joaquín Gabaldón Márquez; ₍compilación por Marisa Vannini de Gerulewicz₎ Caracas, 1964.

75 p. 17 cm. (*Its* Serie bibliográfica, 2)

GAELIC LITERATURE

Aberdeen, Scot. University. *Library.*
Scottish-Gaelic holdings: classified list. Aberdeen, University Library, 1966.

₍9₎, 100 p. 27 cm.

Compiled by Donald John MacLeod.

Reid, John, 1808–1841?
Bibliotheca Scoto-Celtica; or, an account of all the books which have been printed in the Gaelic language. With bibliographical and biographical notices. Naarden, Anton W. van Bekhoven, 1968.

lxxii, 180 p. 23 cm.

"Reprint of the 1832 Glasgow edition."

GAFUROV, BABADZHAN GAFUROVICH

Shevchenko, Zinaida Matveevna.
Бободжан Гафурович Гафуров. Вступит. статья И. С. Брагинского ₍с. 4–22₎. Библиогр. сост. З. М. Шевченко. Душанбе, "Дониш," 1969.

93 p., port. 16 cm. (Академия наук Таджикской ССР. Центральная научная библиотека. Материалы к библиографии ученых Таджикистана, вып. 18)

GAGARIN, ĪURIĬ ALEKSEEVICH

Bobtšova, L   M
Советский летчик-космонавт Ю. А. Гагарин. (Краткий список литературы). Москва, 1971.

16 p. 20 cm.

At head of title: Государственная библиотека СССР имени В. И. Ленина. Военный отдел.
By L. M. Bobtšov and G. M. Ignatova.

GAINSBOROUGH, ENGLAND

Gainsborough, Eng. Public Library.
Gainsborough local studies: a handlist of books and pamphlets, articles, illustrations, and maps, relating to the town and its past, based on the local and Brace collections of the Gainsborough Public Library. Gainsborough (Lincs.), Gainsborough Public Library, 1965.

₍4₎, 25 p. 25½ cm.

GAŁCZYŃSKI, KONSTANTY ILDEFONS

Stradecki, Janusz.
Konstanty Ildefons Gałczyński, 1905–1953; poradnik bibliograficzny. Warszawa, Biblioteka Narodowe, 1970.

45 p. 21 cm.

At head of title: Biblioteka Narodowa. Instytut Bibliograficzny.
"Twórczość K. I. Gałczyńskiego," p. ₍21₎–45.

GALE FAMILY

West Sussex, *Eng. County Record Office.*
The Lytton Manuscripts: a catalogue; edited by Noel H. Osborne. Chichester, West Sussex County Council, 1967.

ix. 79 p. 4 plates (incl. ports.), diagr. 25½ cm.

GALICIA, SPAIN

Archivo Histórico del Reino de Galicia.
Archivo Histórico del Reino de Galicia; guía del investigador, por Antonio Gil Merino, director del Archivo, en colaboración con Elvira Dugnol Villasonte, funcionaria del mismo. Prólogo del Ilmo. Sr. D. Antonio Matilla Tascón. La Coruña, 1968.

129 p. illus. 22 cm.

GALLEGOS, RÓMULO

Caracas. Universidad Católica Andrés Bello. Seminario de Literatura Venezolana.
Contribución a la bibliografía de Rómulo Gallegos, 1884–1969. ₍Caracas, Gobernación del Distrito Federal, 1969₎

405 p. port. 21 cm. (Colección Bibliografías, 1)

Cover title: Bibliografía Rómulo Gallegos.
"Trabajo de investigación realizados ₍sic₎ durante los años académicos 1965–66, 1966–67 y 1968–69 por los siguientes alumnos: María Eugenia Viquez Viquez ₍et al.₎ bajo la dirección del profesor Efraín Subero."

GALLETTI, ALFREDO

Mensi, Pino.
L'opera di Alfredo Galletti. Saggio di bibliografia. Cremona, Athenaeum Cremonense, 1967.

259 p. port. 25 cm. (Annali della Biblioteca governativa e Libreria civica di Cremona, v. 18, fasc. 2)

GALSWORTHY, JOHN

Birmingham, Eng. University. *Library.*
John Galsworthy: catalogue of the collection. Birmingham, University, 1967.

₍4₎, 88 p. front. (facsim.). 25½ cm.

Fabes, Gilbert Henry, 1894–
John Galsworthy, his first editions: points and values, by Gilbert H. Fabes. ₍Folcroft, Pa.₎ Folcroft Library Editions, 1973.

xxiv, 64 p. (p. 60–64 blank for "Notes") 23 cm.

Reprint of the 1932 ed. published by W. and G. Foyle, London, as no. 1 of First editions and their values.

Marrot, Harold Vincent.
A bibliography of the works of John Galsworthy, by H. V. Marrot. New York, B. Franklin ₍1968₎

xii, 252 p. illus., facsims., port. 23 cm. (Burt Franklin: bibliography and reference series, no. 184)

Reprint of the 1928 ed.

Marrot, Harold Vincent.
A bibliography of the works of John Galsworthy, by H. V. Marrot. ₍Folcroft, Pa.₎ Folcroft Library Editions, 1973.

xii, 252 p. illus. 24 cm.

Reprint of the 1028 ed. published by E. Mathews & Marrot, London.

Mikhail, E   H

John Galsworthy the dramatist: a bibliography of criticism. Compiled by E. H. Mikhail. Troy, N. Y., Whitston Pub. Co., 1971.

v, 91 p.   23 cm.

GALVANIZING

ZDA/LDA Joint Library.

Heating of galvanizing baths: bibliography. London, Z. D. A./L. D. A. Joint Library ₁1968₁.

₁10₁ p.   30 cm.

Cover title.
"This bibliography covers articles published from 1950 to approximately the end of 1967. Later articles are abstracted in the monthly journal Zinc abstracts."

GÁLVEZ, MANUEL

Kisnerman, Natalio.

Bibliografía de Manuel Gálvez. Buenos Aires, Fondo Nacional de las Artes ₁1964₁

75 p.   facsim., port.   23 cm.   (Bibliografía argentina de artes y letras. Compilaciones especiales)

"Correspondiente al no. 17."

GAMBIA

Gamble, David P

Bibliography of the Gambia, by David P. Gamble. ₁Bathurst, Gambia, Govt. printer, 1967₁

153 p.   33 cm.

"Revised and enlarged version."

GAMBLING

Bibliographies of works on playing cards and gaming; a reprint of A bibliography of works in English on playing cards and gaming, by Frederic Jessel and A bibliography of card-games and of the history of playing-cards, by Norton T. Horr. Montclair, N. J., Patterson Smith, 1972.

xii, 311, 79 p.   23 cm.   (Patterson Smith reprint series in criminology, law enforcement, and social problems. Publication no. 132)

Reprints of the 1905 and 1892 editions, respectively.

Nevada. University. Library.

A gambling bibliography based on the collection, University of Nevada, Las Vegas, by Stephen Powell. Las Vegas, 1972.

vi, 166 p.   24 cm.

GAME PROTECTION

Irkutsk, Siberia. Universitet. *Biblioteka.*

Библиография Иркутской области: охота и рыболовство. ₁Составлена Л. Е. Зубашевой. Под ред. В. Н. Скаловна. Иркутск₁ Восточно-Сибирское книжное изд-во, 1966.

178 p.   21 см.   (Иркутский государственный универтитет им. А. А. Жданова. Труды Научной библиотеки, вып. 17)

Speight, A   M

Game reserves and game protection in Africa (with special reference to South Africa): a bibliography, compiled by Ann-Marie Speight. 2nd impression. Cape Town, University of Cape Town Libraries, 1972.

₁5₁, v, 32 p.   23 cm.   (University of Cape Town Libraries. Bibliographical series)
Presented in partial fulfilment of the requirements for the Higher Certificate in Librarianship, 1950.

GAME THEORY

Duke, Richard D

Operational gaming and simulation in urban research: an annotated bibliography, by Richard D. Duke and Allen H. Schmidt. ₁East Lansing₁ Institute for Community Development and Services, Continuing Education Service, Michigan State University, 1965.

33 p.   28 cm.   (Michigan State University. Institute for Community Development. Bibliography no. 14)

Shubik, Martin.

The literature of gaming, simulation, and model-building: index and critical abstracts ₁by₁ M. Shubik, G. Brewer, and E. Savage. Santa Monica, Rand, 1972.
xvi, 121 p.   28 cm.   (Rand Corporation. ₁Rand report₁ R–620–ARPA)
"ARPA order no.: 189–1."
A report prepared for Advanced Research Projects Agency under contract no. DAHC15 67 C 0141.

GAMES

see also   Sports

Belch, Jean.

Contemporary games; a directory and bibliography covering games and play situations or simulations used for instruction and training by schools, colleges and universities, government, business, and management. Detroit, Gale Research Co. ₁1973–

v.   29 cm.

CONTENTS: v. 1. Directory.

GANDHI, MAHATMA KARAMCHAND

Dharma Vir, 1919–

Gandhi bibliography ₁by₁ Dharma Vir. With a foreword by Zakir Husain. ₁1st ed.₁ Chandigarh, Gandhi Smarak Nidhi, Punjab, Haryana & Himachal Pradesh ₁1967₁

xxiv, 575 p.   port.   23 cm.

Kovalsky, Susan Joan.

Mahatma Gandhi and his political influence in South Africa, 1893–1914, a selective bibliography. Johannesburg, University of the Witwatersrand, Dept. of Bibliography, Librarianship and Typography, 1971.

iii, 27 p.   30 cm.

"Compiled in part fulfilment for the requirements of the Diploma in Librarianship, University of Witwatersrand."

Sharma, Jagdish Saran, 1924–

Mahatma Gandhi; a descriptive bibliography. ₁2d ed.₁ Delhi, S. Chand ₁1968₁

xxxvii, 650 p.   port.   25 cm.   (National bibliography, no. 1)

Originally issued as thesis, University of Michigan.

GANGS

Tompkins, Dorothy Louise (Campbell) Culver.

Bibliography on juvenile gangs in the United States since World War II, compiled by Dorothy Campbell Tompkins. ₁Los Angeles₁ Delinquency Prevention Training Project, 1965.

28 l.   29 cm.   (Training series for social agencies) (₁Delinquency Prevention Training Project₁ Bibliographic series)

Tompkins, Dorothy Louise (Campbell) Culver.

Juvenile gangs and street groups; a bibliography, compiled by Dorothy Campbell Tompkins. Berkeley, Institute of Governmental Studies, University of California, 1966.

viii, 88 p.   23 cm.

"A revision of a manuscript prepared for the Youth Studies Center of the University of Southern California in February, 1965."

GANIEV, M. K.

М. К. Ганиев; библиография. [Составители: Р. А. Айрапетова, Э. А. Алиева] Баку, Изд-во Академии наук Азербайджанской ССР, 1967.

125 p. 16 cm. (Деятели науки и культуры Азербайджана)

At head of title: Академия наук Азербайджанской ССР. Фундаментальная библиотека.
Added t. p. in Azerbaijani.

GARCÍA LORCA, FEDERICO

Braginskaia, Ella Vladimirovna.

Федерико Гарсиа Лорка. [1898–1936]. Биобиблиогр. указ. [Вступит. статья канд. филол. наук З. И. Плавскина]. Москва, "Книга," 1971.

87 p. 21 cm. (Писатели зарубежных стран)

At head of title: Всесоюзная государственная библиотека иностранной литературы."
"Составитель: Э. В. Брагинская."

Laurenti, Joseph L

Federico García Lorca y su mundo: ensayo de una bibliografía general. The world of Federico García Lorca: a general bibliographic survey, by Joseph L. Laurenti and Joseph Siracusa. With a pref. by Alberto Porqueras Mayo. Metuchen, N.J., Scarecrow Press, 1974.

viii, 282 p. front. 22 cm. (The Scarecrow author bibliographies, no. 15)
Introd. and chronology in Spanish and English.

GARD, FRANCE (DEPT.)

Gard, *France (Dept.). Archives départementales.*

Répertoire numérique de la série v; cultes: 1800–1910 (1941) rédigé par Marcel Baccou, sous la direction de Jean Sablou. Nîmes, 1969.

59 p. 31 cm.

Gard, France (Dept.). Archives départementales.

Répertoire numérique de la sous-série 3 E: communautés et consulats. Suivi d'un état des compoix conservés aux Archives du Gard. Par Y. Chassin Du Guerny. Avant-propos de Jean Sablou. Nîmes, Archives départementales, 1970.

43 p. 31 cm.

GARDENING see Horticulture

GARDNER, ERLE STANLEY

Moore, Ruth.

Bibliography of Erle Stanley Gardner. Compiled by Ruth Moore. [n. p., 1970]

115 l. 28 cm.

Mundell, E   H

Erle Stanley Gardner; a checklist, by E. H. Mundell. [Kent, Ohio] Kent State University Press [°1968]

91 p. 20 cm. (The Serif series: bibliographies and checklists, no. 6)

GARIBALDI, GIUSEPPE

Campanella, Anthony P

Giuseppe Garibaldi e la tradizione garibaldina. Una bibliografia dal 1807 al 1970. Raccolta con introduzione e annotazioni da Anthony P. Campanella. Ginevra, Gran Saconnex, Comitato dell'Istituto internazionale di studi Garibaldini, 1971.

2 v. (xxxiv, 1312 p.) ports. 25 cm.

Introduction also in English.

GARIN, EUGENIO

Bibliografia degli scritti di Eugenio Garin. Bari, G. Laterza, 1969.

207 p. 21½ cm.

GARLAND, HAMLIN

Bryer, Jackson R

Hamlin Garland and the critics; an annotated bibliography, by Jackson R. Bryer and Eugene Harding, with the assistance of Robert A. Rees. Troy, N. Y., Whitston Pub. Co.. 1973.

v, 282 p. 24 cm.

GARRETT, GEORGE

George Palmer Garrett; a bibliography and index of his published works and criticism of them. Potsdam, N. Y., Frederick W. Crumb Memorial Library, 1968.

[5] l. 28 cm. ([Frederick W. Crumb Memorial Library] Pub[ica-tion] 3)

GAS ENGINEERING AND INDUSTRY
see also   Petroleum

Akademiia nauk URSR, *Kiev. Instytut vykorystannia hazu.*

Библиография печатных трудов сотрудников Института газа АН УССР, опубликованных в 1963–1965 годах. Киев, Наук. думка, 1966.

18 p. 20 cm.

At head of title: Академия наук Украинской ССР. Институт газа.

Verner, Vladimír, Ing.

Práce Ústavu pro výzkum a využití paliv o výrobě, čistění a distribuci plynu, odpadních vodách, protikorozní ochraně a čistotě ovzduší. [Bibliografie.] Zprac. V. Verner. [Souběž.] překlad do angl.: V. Verner, do ruš.: A Nahodilová. Běchovice, Ústav pro výzkum a vyuzití paliv, rozmn., 1971.

122, [1] p. 21 cm. (Monografie ÚVP. čis. 21)
Cover title.
Title also in Russian and English: Труды Научно-исследовательского института топлив о производстве, очистке и распределении газа, сточных водах, антикоррозионной защите и чистоте атмосферы. Reports of the Fuel Research Institute on the manufacture, purification and distribution of gaz, waste waters, corrosion prevention and air pollution.
Czech, Russian, and English.

GASCONY

Samaran, Charles Maxime Donatien, 1879–

La Gascogne dans les registres du trésor des chartes, par Charles Samaran ... avec la collaboration de Pierre Rouleau ... Paris, Bibliothèque nationale, 1966.

xvi, 308 p. 24 cm. (Collection de documents inédits sur l'histoire de France. Série in-8°, v. 4)

GASES

Ruch, Walter E   ed.

Chemical detection of gaseous pollutants, an annotated bibliography. Edited and rev. by Walter E. Ruch. Ann Arbor, Mich., Ann Arbor Science Publishers, 1966.

iv, 180 p. 29 cm.

"Credit for the original work is due the Los Alamos Scientific Laboratory."
"Originally published by the Office of Technical Services, U. S. Department of Commerce, in two volumes."

GASKELL, ELIZABETH CLEGHORN STEVENSON
see under Eliot, George

GASPÉ DISTRICT, QUEBEC

Saint-Denis, *Sister.*
Gaspésiana. Avant-propos de l'abbé Claude Allard.
Préf. du docteur Guy Fortier. Montréal, Fides ₍°1965₎

xix, 180 p. illus., maps. 21 cm.

Issued also as thesis, Université Laval.

GASTROENTEROLOGY

Gastroenterology abstracts and citations. v. 1–
Jan. 1966–
₍Bethesda, Md.₎ U. S. Dept. of Health, Education, and Welfare, Public Health Service, National Institutes of Health;
₍for sale by the Superintendent of Documents, U. S. Govt.
Print. Off., Washington₎

v. 26 cm. monthly.

Issues for Jan. 1966–   prepared for the National Institute of Arthritis and Metabolic Diseases by Medical Literature, Inc.

GASTRONOMY   see   Cookery; Food

GASYMZADĂ, FEĬZULLA SÁMÁD OGHLU

Zŭlalova, H   A
Ф. С. Гасымзадэ; библиографија. ₍Тэртиб едэни Һ. Ә.
Зулалова₎ Бакы, Азэрбаіҹан ССР Елмлэр Академијасы
Нэшријіаты, 1968.

66 p.   17 cm.   (Азэрбајҹанын елм вэ мэдэнијјэт хадимләри)

At head of title: Азэрбајҹан ССР елмлэр академијасы. Әсаслы китабхана.

GATESHEAD, ENGLAND

Gateshead, *Eng. Public Libraries.*
Gateshead archives: a guide; compiled by F. W. D.
Manders. Gateshead (Co. Durham), Gateshead Public
Libraries, 1968.

30 p.   22 cm.

Gateshead, *Eng. Public Libraries.*
Historic Gateshead: a select bibliography. ₍Compiled by
F. W. D. Manders, librarian in charge of Local History
and Archives₎. Gateshead, Gateshead Public Libraries,
1967.

₍1₎, 33 p.   22 cm.

GAULLE, CHARLES DE

Krommenacker, Raymond J
Le gaullisme: état des recherches et guide bibliographique
₍par₎ Raymond J. Krommenacker. Préf. de François
Georges Dreyfus. Paris, Dalloz, 1971.

127 p.   22 cm.   (Cahiers de l'Institut d'études politiques. Université des sciences juridiques, politiques et sociales, 7)

Staffordshire County Library.
Charles de Gaulle, 1890–1970. ₍Stafford, Eng., 1970₎

7 p.   21 cm.

GAVIDIA, FRANCISCO ANTONIO

San Salvador. Biblioteca Nacional.
Francisco Gavidia; bibliografía compilada por la Biblioteca Nacional. San Salvador, Administración de Bibliotecas
y Archivo₍s₎ Nacionales ₍1970₎

269 p.   25 cm.

"Anaqueles, número extraordinario."

GDAŃSKIE TOWARZYSTWO NAUKOWE

Gdańskie Towarzystwo Naukowe.
Wydawnictwa Gdańskiego Towarzystwa Naukowego,
dawniej, Towarzystwa Przyjaciół Nauki i Sztuki w Gdańsku za lata 1947–1965; katalog. ₍Opracowała i przygotowała do druku Alina Szafranowa. Wyd. 1.₎ Gdańsk,
1965.

55 p.   24 cm.   (*Its* Publikacje)

Errata slip inserted.

GEIGER, WILLI

Schneider, Franz, 1932–
Bibliographie der Veröffentlichungen von Willi Geiger.
Mit einem Geleitwort von Gerhard Leibholz. Tübingen,
Mohr ⟨Siebeck⟩ 1969.

24 p.   24 cm.

GELDERLAND

Netherlands (*Kingdom, 1815–   ) Rijksarchief in Gelderland, Arnhem.*
Het archief van de kelnarij van Putten.
————————Supplement. Door R. Wartena. Rijswijk,
Ministerie van Cultuur, Recreatie en Maatschappelijk
Werk, 1968.

38 p.   24 cm.

GENALA, FRANCESCO

Cipelletti, Giuditta.
Francesco Genala. Bibliografia delle sue opere e degli
scritti su di lui. A cura di Giuditta Cipelletti. ₍1972?₎

1 v. (various pagings)   port.   21 cm.

GENEALOGY

*Genealogies of specific places are
entered under the place names*

see also   Heraldry; and names of
individual families

Corbin, John Boyd, *comp.*
Catalog of genealogical materials in Texas libraries, compiled by John B. Corbin. ₍Austin, Tex., State Library and
Historical Commission. 1965–

v. 28 cm. (Texas. State Library ₍Austin₎ Monograph no. 2

CONTENTS.—pt. 1. Virginia.

Rubincam, Milton, 1909–
Genealogy; a selected bibliography. Prepared for the
Institute of Genealogy, Samford University. Birmingham,
Ala., Banner Press ₍1967₎

18 p.   26 cm.

St. Louis. Public Library.
Genealogical material and local histories in the St. Louis
Public Library. Rev. ed. by Georgia Gambrill, Reference
Dept. ₍St. Louis₎ 1965 ₍cover 1966₎

356 p.   28 cm.

Wellauer, Maralyn A
A guide to foreign genealogical research; a selected bibliography of printed material with addresses. Compiled by
Maralyn A. Wellauer. Milwaukee, Wis. ₍1973₎

vi, 78 p.   28 cm.

BIBLIOGRAPHIES

Besterman, Theodore, 1904–
Family history; a bibliography of bibliographies. To-

towa, N. J., Rowman and Littlefield, 1971.

149 p. 20 cm. (The Besterman world bibliographies)

Compiled by the publisher from the 4th ed. of the author's A world bibliography of bibliographies and of bibliographical catalogues, calendars, abstracts, digests, indexes, and the like.

GENETICS

Brünn. Universita. *Knihovna.*
Soupis genetické zahraniční literatury nově získané Universitní knihovnou v Brně a Genetickým oddělením Moravského musea v Brně. Sest. Milan Jakubíček. V Brně, 1965.

13 l. 20 cm. (*Its* Výběrový seznam, 113)

Muller, Hermann Joseph, 1890–1967.
List of works by H. J. Muller. [n. p., 1967?]

25 l. 28 cm.

Sorenson, James R
Social and psychological aspects of applied human genetics: a bibliography, by James R. Sorenson. Bethesda, Md., Fogarty International Center, National Institutes of Health; for sale by the Supt. of Docs., U. S. Govt. Print. Off., Washington [1972?]

iv, 98 p. 26 cm. (DHEW publication no. (NIH) 73-412)

GENEVA

Chaix, Paul.
Les livres imprimés à Genève de 1550 à 1600 [par] Paul Chaix, Alain Dufour et Gustave Moeckli. Nouv. éd., revue et augm. par Gustave Moeckli. Genève, Droz, 1966.

176 p. 25 cm. (Travaux d'humanisme et Renaissance, 86)

Geisendorf, Paul Frédéric.
Bibliographie raisonnée de l'histoire de Genève des origines à 1798 [par] Paul-F. Geisendorf. Genève, Jullien, 1966.

xvi, 635 p. 24 cm. (Mémoires et documents publiés par la Société d'histoire et d'archéologie de Genève, t. 43)

GENNEP, ARNOLD VAN

Gennep, Ketty van, *comp.*
Bibliographie des œuvres d'Arnold van Gennep, publiée par les soins de K. van Gennep. Préf. de G.-H. Rivière. Paris, A. & J. Picard, 1964.

91 p. port. 22 cm.

GENZMER, HARALD

Interpreten über Harald Genzmer. Werkverzeichnis zum 60. Geburtstag, 9. Febr. 1969. (Frankfurt, C. F. Peters, 1969.)

39 p. 21 cm.

GEOCHEMISTRY

Billings, Gale K
Chemical geology: an annotated bibliography, by Gale K. Billings. Washington, Council on Education in the Geological Sciences [1973]

40 p. 28 cm. (CEGS programs publication no. 11)

Геохимические методы поисков рудных месторождений; библиографический указатель литературы, 1925–1963 гг. [Составитель Л. В. Бугельская. Отв. редактор А. И. Перельман] Москва, Наука, 1966–

v. 22 cm.

At head of title, v. 1– : Академия наук СССР. Сектор сети спецбиблиотек. Библиотека Отделения наук о Земле.

Contents.—вып. 1. Общие вопросы, литохимические поиски.

Tompkins, Dorothy Louise (Campbell) Culver.
Power from the earth: geothermal energy. Compiled by Dorothy Campbell Tompkins. Berkeley, Institute of Governmental Studies, University of California, 1972.

vii, 34 p. 23 cm. (Her Public policy bibliographies: 3)

GEODESY

Belikov, Evgenii Fedorovich.
Библиографический указатель геодезической литературы с начала книгопечатания до 1917 г. Сост. доц. Е. Ф. Беликов и инж. Л. П. Соловьев. Под ред. проф. Л. С. Хренова. Москва, "Недра," 1971.

272 p. 22 cm.

Bendefy, László, *ed.*
Magyar geodéziai irodalom, 1498–1960; bibliográfia. Budapest, Műszaki Könyvkiadó, 1964.

396 p. 25 cm.

Added t. p.: Bibliography of the Hungarian geodesian literature. Tables of contents and introductory matter in English, French, German, Hungarian, Russian, and Spanish.

Bibliografia publikacji z dziedziny obliczeń geodezyjnych, 1967–1970; przedstawicna na XV Zgromadzeniu Ogólnym Międzynarodowej Asocjacji Geodezji Międzynarodowej (Moskwa, 28 VII–14 VIII 1971) przez Instytut Geodezji Akademii Górnoczo-Hutniczej w Krakowie i Specjalną Grupę Studiów 1.21 MAG-MUGG. [Oprac.: L. Halama et al. Wyd. 1.] Kraków, 1971.

81 p. 24 cm. (Zeszyty naukowe Akademii Górniczo-Hutniczej im. Stanisława Staszica, nr. 320. Zeszyt specjalny, 23) zł5.00
Added t. p.: Bibliography of publications on the field of geodetical calculations.

Potsdam. Geodätisches Institut.
Bibliographie der Mitarbeiter des Geodätischen Instituts 1861–1967, von Lothar Lerbs, Ingeborg Sass [und] Annerose Stange. Potsdam, 1968.

148 p. 30 cm. (Arbeiten aus dem Geodätischen Institut Potsdam, Nr. 22)

Summary in German, English, French, and Russian.

Rżewski, Kazimierz.
Bibliografia wydawnictw geodezyjnych Państwowego Przedsiębiorstwa Wydawnictw Kartograficznych (1945–1965). Warszawa, Państwowe Przedsiębiorstwo Wydawnictw Kartograficznych, 1969.

81 p. 24 cm.

GEOGRAPHY
see also under Dissertations, Academic and Festschriften

Akademiiā nauk SSSR. *Sibirskoe otdelenie. Institut geografii Sibiri i Dal'nego Vostoka.*
Каталог изданий Института географии Сибири и Дальнего Востока. (1959–1968 гг.) Иркутск, 1968.

20 p. 20 cm.

At head of title: Академия наук СССР. Сибирское отделение. Институт географии Сибири и Дальнего Востока. "Составитель К. С. Курбатова."

Anderson, Frank J
Geography and travels, compiled and edited by Frank J. Anderson. Spartanburg [S. C.] Wofford Library Press, 1970.

54 l. 28 cm. (Wofford College Library. Special collections checklist no. 2)

Arena, Gabriella.
Il pensiero geografico in Italia. [Bibliografia tematica). Roma, 1973.

38 p. 24 cm. (Università di Roma. Facoltà di lettere e filosofia. Pubblicazioni dell'Istituto di geografia. Serie C: Miscellanea, 4)

Arnim, Helmuth.
Bibliographie der geographischen Literatur in deutscher Sprache. [1. Aufl.] Baden-Baden, Librairie Heitz, 1970.

177 p. 24 cm. (Bibliotheca bibliographica Aureliana, 21)

Atkinson, Geoffroy, 1892–1960.
La littérature géographique française de la Renaissance; répertoire bibliographique. (Avec 300 reproductions photographiques) Description de 524 impressions d'ouvrages publiés en français avant 1610, et traitant des pays et des peuples non européens, que l'on trouve dans les principales bibliothèques de France et de l'Europe occidentale. New York, B. Franklin [1968]

563, 87 p. facsims. 26 cm. (Burt Franklin Bibliography and reference series, 213)

"Originally published Paris, 1927[–30] Reprinted 1968."

Reprint includes the author's "Supplément au répertoire bibliographique se rapportant à La littérature géographique française de la Renaissance" issued separately in 1936.

Bogatova, Galina Petrovna.
(Geografiía na novykh rubezhakh)
География на новых рубежах : рек. обзор литературы. / сост., Г. П. Богатова. — Москва : "Книга," 1973.

14 p. ; 16 cm. — (Новое в науке и технике)

Caption title.
At head of title: Государственная библиотека СССР имени В. И. Ленина.

Brewer, James Gordon.
The literature of geography; a guide to its organisation and use [by] J. Gordon Brewer. [Hamden, Conn.] Linnet Books [1973]

208 p. illus. 23 cm.

Church, Martha.
A basic geographical library; a selected and annotated book list for American colleges, compiled and edited by Martha Church, Robert E. Huke [and] Wilbur Zelinsky. Washington, Association of American Geographers [1966]

xi, 153 p. 23 cm. (Association of American Geographers. Commission on College Geography. Publication no. 2)

Costa Rica. Instituto Geográfico Nacional.
Publicaciones del Instituto Geográfico Nacional: XV aniversario (1954–1969), indice bibliográfico. Preparado por Eduardo Protti Martinelli. [San José, Costa Rica] 1970.

16 p. 25 cm.

Cover title.
Caption title: Indice bibliográfico del Instituto Geográfico Nacional.

Costa Rica. Instituto Geográfico Nacional.
Publicaciones del Instituto Geográfico Nacional (1954–1972), índice bibliografico. San José, 1973.

24 p. 25 cm.

Cucu, Vasile.
Bibliografie geografică, 1944–1964, Romînia [de] Vasile Cucu [şi Alexandru Roşu. Bucureşti, Editura de Stat pentru Imprimate şi Publicaţii, 1964.

154 p. 20 cm. (Biblioteca geografulul, nr. 1)

At head of title: Societatea de Ştiinţe Naturale şi Geografie din R. P. R.

Ealing Technical College.
Concise guide to the literature of geography [edited by Jack Burkett and prepared by students of the school of Librarianship, Ealing Technical College]. London, Ealing Technical College, 1967.

[1], 47 p. 28 cm. (Ealing Technical College. Occasional papers, 1)

Engelmann, Wilhelm, 1808–1878.
Bibliotheca geographica; Verzeichniss der seit der Mitte des 18. Jahrhunderts bis zu Ende des Jahres 1856 in Deutschland erschienenen Werke Über Geographie und Reisen. Hrsg. von Wilhelm Engelmann. Amsterdam, Meridian Pub. Co., 1965.

2 v. (1225 p.) 24 cm.

Reprint of the 1857 ed.

Greer-Wootten, Bryn.
A bibliography of statistical applications in geography. Washington, Association of American Geographers, Commission on College Geography [1972]

91 p. 23 cm. (Association of American Geographers. Commission on College Geography. Technical paper no. 9)

Hancock, John Charles.
The geographer's vademecum of sources and materials; compiled by J. C. Hancock and P. F. Whiteley. London, G. Philip, 1971.

[4], 124 p. 22 cm.

Helff, Bernice.
Understanding peoples of the non-Western World through books for boys and girls; an annotated bibliography. Rev [Cedar Falls? Iowa] 1968.

vi, 82, 8 p. 28 cm.

"A study made under the joint auspices of the Ford Foundation and the teaching department of the University of Northern Iowa."

Íakovlev, Aleksandr Aleksandrovich.
Внеклассное чтение по географии в старших классах средней школы. Москва, Просвещение, 1964.

206 p. 20 cm. (Педагогическая библиотека учителя)

At head of title: Академия педагогических наук РСФСР. Институт общего и политехнического образования. А. А. Яковлев.

Isida, Ryuziro, 1904–   comp.
(Chirigaku kenkyū no tame no bunken to kaidai)
地理学研究のための文献と解題　石田龍次郎編著　東京　古今書院　昭和44(1969)

364 p. 22 cm.

Revision of articles originally published in Chiri under title: Bunken ni yoru chirigaku annai, Jan. 1966–Dec. 1967.

Kaufman, Isaak Mikhaĭlovich.
Географические словари; библиография. Москва, Книга, 1964.

76 p. 22 cm.

At head of title: И. М. Кауфман.

Kinauer, Rudolf.
Lexikon geographischer Bildbände. Wien, Brüder Hollinek [1966]

xi, 463 p. 20 cm.

CONTENTS.—Kosmos und Erde.—Kontinente und Länder.—Mensch, Tiere, Pflanzen.

Leipziger Kommissions- und Grossbuchhandel. Abteilung Importbuch.
Geographie, Völkerkunde, Karten, Atlanten. (Leipzig, 1966)

47 p. 20 cm. (Its Fremdsprachige Importliteratur)

Lewthwaite, Gordon Rowland, 1925–
A geographical bibliography for American college libraries. A revision of A basic geographical library; a

selected and annotated book list for American colleges. Original ed. compiled and edited by Martha Church, Robert E. Huke ₍and₎ Harold A. Winters. Rev. ed. compiled and edited by Gordon R. Lewthwaite, Edward T. Price, Jr. ₍and₎ Harold A. Winters. Washington, Association of American Geographers, Commission on College Geography, ₍1970₎

xi, 214 p. 23 cm. (Association of American Geographers. Commission on College Geography. Pubblication no. 9)

Library Association. County Libraries Group.
Readers' guide to books on geography ₍compiled by Valerie Bonham₎ 2d ed. ₍London₎ 1973.

52 p. 19 cm. (**Its** New series no. 129)

Lock, Clara Beatrice Muriel, 1914–
Geography; a reference handbook ₍by₎ C. B. Muriel Lock. ₍Hamden, Conn.₎ Archon Books ₍1968₎

179 p. 23 cm.

Lock, Clara Beatrice Muriel, 1914-
Geography: a reference handbook ₍by₎ C. B. Muriel Lock. 2nd ed., revised and enlarged. London, Bingley, 1972.

529 p. 23 cm.

Mandulova, Mirîana Ilieva.
Какво да четат учениците от V до VIII клас по география; препоръчителен списък. София, Нар. просвета, 1965.

42 p. 17 cm.

At head of title: Министерство на народната просвета. Дом на детската книга. М. Мандулова, Хр. Шаллиева.

Mérő, Józsefné.
Földrajz; ajánló bibliográfia az 5–8. osztályos tanulók számára. Budapest, Tankönyvkiadó, 1967.

99 p. illus. 20 cm. (Tantárgyi bibliográfiák, általános iskolai sorozat, 4)

Minto, Charles Sinclair.
How to find out in geography; a guide to current books in English, by C. S. Minto. ₍1st ed.₎ Oxford, New York, Pergamon Press ₍1966₎

xiii, 99 p. illus., maps. 20 cm. (The Commonwealth and international library. Libraries and technical information division)

Piasecka, Janina Ewa, comp.
Bibliografia geografii polskiej, 1918–1927. Opracowała Janina Piasecka przy współudziale Pracowni Bibliografii IG PAN. Warszawa, Nakł. Polskiego Towarzystwa Geograficznego, 1971.

446 p. 24 cm.

At head of title: Instytut Geografii PAN.
Added t. p.: Библиография польской географии. Bibliography of Polish geography.
Preface also in Russian and English.

Riva, Ambrogio.
Una piccola biblioteca, una piccola battaglia per la geografia. Milano-Varese, Istituto editoriale cisalpino, 1970.

215 p. 24 cm. (Università di Parma. Facoltà di magistero. Istituto di scienze geografiche. ₍Pubblicazioni₎ 2)

CONTENTS: Recensioni.—Note su tesi di laurea.—Articoli divulgativi.

Sabottke, Siegfried.
Ausgewählte Kapitel aus der geographischen Bibliographie. Potsdam, Pädagogische Hochschule 1966.

73 p. 23 cm. (Lehrbriefe für das Fernstudium der Lehrer. Geographie)

"Herausgegeben im Auftrage des Ministeriums für Volksbildung der Deutschen Demokratischen Republik von der Pädagogischen Hochschule Potsdam, Hauptabteilung Fernstudium."

A Selected list of basic guides and readings for graduate students in geography. Compiled by the students of Geog. 498, bibliography and library methods. ₍Boulder₎ University of Colorado, 1967.

30 l. 28 cm.

Sociedad Geográfica de Colombia.
Boletín bibliográfico. no. 1/8–
mayo 1963/enero/jun. 1968–
Bogota.

no. in v. 24 cm.

Tolchinskaîa, L   I
Географическая литература. 1962–1969. Каталог. Москва, "Мысль," 1971.

152 p. 20 cm.

"Автор-составитель Л. И. Толчинская."

Tuszyńska-Rekawek, Halina.
Bibliografia geografii polskiej, 1969–1970 / Halina Tuszyńska-Rękawek, Barbara Kawecka-Endrukajtis, Jadwiga Sielużycka. — Warszawa : Nakł. Polskiego Tow. Geograficznego, 1973.
359 p. ; 24 cm.
At head of title: Instytut Geografii PAN.
Preface also in Russian and English.
Added t. p.: Bibliografiîa polskoî geografiî. Bibliography of Polish geography.

Vinge, Clarence L.
U. S. Government publications for research and teaching in geography, and related social and natural sciences ₍by₎ C. L. Vinge ₍and₎ A. G. Vinge. Totowa, N. J., Littlefield, Adams, 1967.

xiv, 360 p. 21 cm. (Littlefield quality paperbacks, no. 225)

Published in 1962 under title: U. S. Government publications for teaching and research in geography.

Wright, John Kirtland, 1891–1969.
Aids to geographical research; bibliographies, periodicals, atlases, gazetteers, and other reference books, by John Kirtland Wright and Elizabeth T. Platt. 2d ed., completely rev. Westport, Conn., Greenwood Press ₍1971, ᶜ1947₎

xii, 331 p. 23 cm.

BIBLIOGRAPHIES
see also under History - Bibliographies

Harris, Chauncy Dennison, 1914–
Bibliographies and reference works for research in geography ₍by₎ Chauncy D. Harris. Chicago, Dept. of Geography, University of Chicago, 1967.

v, 89 l. 29 cm.

A supplement to Aids to geographical research: bibliographies, periodicals, atlases, gazetteers and other reference books, by J. K. Wright and E. T. Platt. 2d ed. 1947. Entries in Wright and Platt generally are not repeated in this bibliography.

Josuweit, Werner.
Studienbibliographie Geographie: Bibliographien u. Nachschlagewerke/ Werner Josuweit. — Wiesbaden: Steiner, 1973.

xx, 122 p.: ill.; 23 cm. — (Wissenschaftliche Paperbacks; Studienbibliographien)

Errata slip inserted.
Based on the author's class work at the Bibliothekar-Lehrinstitut des Landes Nordrhein-Westfalen in Cologne.

Morehouse, Ward, 1929–
Survey of bibliographies and reference works on Asia,

Africa, Latin America, Russia, and East Europe; and compilation of bibliographies on East Asia, South Asia, and Africa south of the Sahara, for undergraduate libraries. New York, University of the State of New York, Foreign Area Materials Center, 1967.

7 l, 4, 5 p. 28 cm.
"Final report on phase one, project no. 50931, contract no. OEC1-6-050931-1278."
Includes the report of a conference on the place of non-European language materials in undergraduate libraries, held Nov. 17, 1967 in Chicago.

Quebec (City). Université Laval. Bibliothèque.
Introduction aux ouvrages de référence en géographie; choix d'ouvrages de la collection de la Bibliothèque de l'Université Laval, préparé par Louise Dion. Québec, Bibliothèque de l'Université Laval, 1970.

108 l. 28 cm. (Guides bibliographiques, 4)

EDUCATION

Ball, John M
A bibliography for geographic education, by John M. Ball. Athens, Ga., 1968.

vii, 92 l. 28 cm. (Geography curriculum project, publication no. 2)

"A publication of the Geography curriculum project, Research and Development Center in Educational Stimulation, University of Georgia."

Ball, John M
A bibliography for geographic education, by John M. Ball. Athens, University of Georgia, 1969 ¡i. e. 1970¡

vii, 109 p. 28 cm. (Geography Curriculum Project, University of Georgia. Revised publication no. 2)

Horňák, Kamil, *comp.*
Metodika zeměpisu; bibliografie knižních publikací a časopiseckých článků. Sest. Kamil Horňák. Hlavní redaktor Vilém Bräuner. V Brně, Státní pedagogická knihovna, 1967.

44 l. 29 cm.

At head of title: Státní vědecká knihovna.

Kent, *Eng. Education Committee.*
Catalogue of recommended books and publications, for secondary schools: geography. Maidstone (Kent), County Education Offices, 1967.

48 p. 25 cm.

Lukehurst, Clare Therese, 1935–
Geography in education: a bibliography of British sources, 1870–1970; compiled and edited by Clare T. Lukehurst and N. J. Graves. Sheffield, Geographical Association, 1972.

86 p. 25 cm. Index.

Thomas, C   E
The geography teacher's sourcebook ¡by C. F. Thomas¡ Toronto, Holt, Rinehart and Winston of Canada ¡1967¡

77 p. illus. 28 cm.

Tikhomirov, Georgiĭ Sergeevich.
Библиографический очерк истории географии в России XVIII века. Москва, "Наука," 1968.

135 p. with illus. 21 cm.

At head of title: Академия наук СССР. Библиотека Академии наук СССР. Г. С. Тихомиров.

LIBRARY AND EXHIBITION CATALOGS

Blois, France. Bibliothèque centrale de prêt de Loir-et-Cher.
Catalogue: Géographie. Blois, 1966.

iii, 133 p. 27 cm.

Kazan, Russia (City). Universitet. Biblioteka.
Географические рукописи, карты и планы. ¡Сост. А. Н. Варламова¡. Казань, Изд. Казан. ун-та, 1969.

76 p. 22 cm. (Its Описание рукописей, вып. 14)

Polska Akademia Nauk. *Instytut Geografii. Biblioteka.*
Catalogue of literature on the history of geography at the exposition "The historical development of Polish geography and of Polish literature in the field of the history of geography" on the occasion of the xith International Congress of the History of Science, Warsaw, August 24–September 4, 1965 ¡by H. Poznańska and J. Kunicka¡ Warsaw, 1965.

viii, 54 p. 25 cm.

At head of title: Institute of Geography, Polish Academy of Sciences, Library ¡and¡ Geographical Institute, Warsaw University, Library.
Added t. p., in Polish.
Introductory matter in English and Polish. Titles of Polish-language publications are given also in English when a parallel title in French or German is not printed.

PERIODICALS

Documentatio geographica; Jahresband. 1966–
Bonn-Bad Godesberg, Bundesanstalt für Landeskunde und Raumforschung.

v. in   31 cm.

Issued by Institut für Landeskunde.
Issued in parts.

Harris, Chauncy Dennison, 1914–
Annotated list of selected current geographical serials of the Americas and the Iberian Peninsula; Lista selectiva y anotada de revistas geográficas corrientes de las Américas y la Península Ibérica, by Chauncy D. Harris. Rev. Chicago, Center for International Studies, University of Chicago, 1967.

16 p. 23 cm.
"Revised from Revista geográfica (Instituto Panamericano de Geografia e Historia. Comissão de Geografia), no. 64 (junho de 1966), pp. 156–167."

Harris, Chauncy Dennison, 1914–
Annotated world list of selected current geographical serials in English, French, and German: including serials in other languages with supplementary use of English or other international languages, by Chauncy D. Harris. 3d ed., expanded and rev. ¡Chicago, Dept. of Geography, University of Chicago¡ 1971.

77 p. maps (on lining paper) 23 cm. (University of Chicago. Dept. of Geography. Research paper no. 137)

Harris, Chauncy Dennison, 1914–
International list of geographical serials. Compiled by Chauncy D. Harris and Jerome D. Fellman. With the assistance of Jack A. Licate. 2d ed., rev., expanded, and updated. ¡Chicago¡ University of Chicago, Dept. of Geography, 1971.
xxvi. 267 p. 23 cm. (University of Chicago. Dept. of Geography. Research paper no. 138)
First published in 1949 under title: A comprehensive checklist of serials of geographic value. Part 1.

Lake Macquarie Shire. Library. Information Service.
A guide to the labyrinth: geography; a bibliography for students. Speers Point ¡N. S. W.¡ 1971.

viii, 32 p. 25 cm.

Répertoire des principaux périodiques d'intérêt géographique cités dans la "Bibliographie géographique internationale." Paris, Éditions du Centre national de la recherche scientifique, 1966.

75 p. 24 cm.

Snipe, Ronald H

A guide to geographic periodicals: Annals of the Association of American Geographers, Economic geography, Geographic[al] review, volumes ı–present. [By] Ronald H. Snipe. [Manitou Springs, Colo., 1969]

347, a–l p. 29 cm.

Snipe, Ronald H

A guide to geographic periodicals: Annals of the Association of American Geographers, Economic geography, Geographical review, issues 1 through 1970 [by Ronald H. Snipe] 2d ed. Manitou Springs, Colo., R. H. Snipe Publications [1972]

iv, 366 p. 29 cm.

Snipe, Ronald H

A tri-index to geography periodicals: Canadian geographer, Professional geographer [and] Soviet geography: review and translation; issues one through 1970 [by Ronald H. Snipe] Manitou Springs, Colo., R. H. Snipe Publications [1971]

iv, 187 p. 29 cm.

GEOLOGY
see also Mineralogy; Paleontology; and under Zoology (*Agassiz*) and Dissertations, Academic

Aistov, L   N

Аннотированный библиографический указатель основной советской и зарубежной литературы по геологическому дешифрированию, 1959-1964 гг. Москва, 1965.

120 p. 20 cm.

At head of title: Министерство геологии СССР. Всесоюзный научно-исследовательский институт экономики минерального сырья и геологоразведочных работ. Отдел научно-технической информации. Л. Н. Аистов, В. Н. Брюханов, В. В. Козлов.

Bogatova, Galina Petrovna.

Геологи ведут поиск. Рек. обзор литературы. [Москва, "Книга," 1968].

17 p. 17 cm. (Государственная ордена Ленина библиотека СССР имени В. И. Ленина. Новое в науке и технике, вып. 20)

At head of title: Государственная ордена Трудового Красного Знамени публичная библиотека имени М. Е. Салтыкова-Щедрина. Prepared by G. P. Bogatova.

Bulletin signalétique 216: Sciences de la terre ıı—géologie, paléontologie. v. 30–   1969–
Paris, Centre de documentation du C. N. R. S.

v. 28 cm. monthly.

Supersedes in part Bulletin signalétique 11: Sciences de la terre ıı—physique du globe, géologie, paléontologie, and continues its vol. numbering.

Bulletin signalétique 221: Gîtologie, économie minière.
v. 33–
1972–
Paris, Centre national de la recherche scientifique. Centre de documentation.

v. 30 cm. monthly.

"Bibliographie des sciences de la terre. Cahier B."
Formerly issued as a section of Bulletin signalétique 214, and continues its numbering.
Vols. for 1972–   issued with the Bureau de recherches géologiques et minières.

Absorbed Bibliographie des sciences de la terre. Cahier B: Gîtologie et économie minière. 1972.

Bulletin signalétique 224: Stratigraphie, géologie régionale, géologie générale. v. 33–

1972–
Paris, Centre national de la recherche scientifique, Centre de documentation.

v. 30 cm. monthly.
"Bibliographie des sciences de la terre. Cahier E."
Formerly issued as a section of Bulletin signalétique 216, and continues its numbering.
Vols. for 1972–   issued with the Bureau de recherches géologiques et minières.
Absorbed Bibliographie des sciences de la terre. Cahier E: Stratigraphie et géologie régionale, 1972.

Charlesworth, L   J

Physical modeling in the geological sciences: an annotated bibliography, by L. J. Charlesworth, Jr. [and] R. N. Passero. Edited by Jackson E. Lewis. Washington, Council on Education in the Geological Sciences [1973]

ix, 85 p. 28 cm. (CEGS programs publication no. 16)

Commission for the Geological Map of the World.
Selected geologic bibliography. Paris, 1964–

v. 28 cm.

On cover: Regional descriptions and maps.
CONTENTS: 1. Africa.
3. South America.—4. Middle East.

Corbin, John Boyd, *comp.*

An index of state geological survey publications issued in series. Compiled by John B. Corbin. New York, Scarecrow Press, 1965.

xi, 667 p. 22 cm.

Companion volume to Museum publications, by J. Clapp.

Dudkin, K   N

Геология и разведка месторождений полезных ископаемых. Москва, 1967 [вып. дан. 1968].

80 p. 21 cm. (Указатель учебной литературы)

At head of title: Университет дружбы народов имени Патриса Лумумбы. Научная библиотека.
By K. N. Dudkin and V. A. Aleksandrov.

Fircks, Barbara von.

Fachwörterbuch-Bibliographie. Geowissenschaften. Ein- u. mehrsprachige Wörterbücher u. Lexika d. Geowissenschaften von 1700–1968. Bearb. vom Barbara von Fircks. Freiberg, Bergakad., Bibliothek, Abt. Information, 1968.

40 p. 23 cm. (Veröffentlichungen der Bibliothek der Bergakademie Freiberg, Nr. 27)

Geological Society of America.
Catalog of works in print. 1969/70–
Boulder, Colo.

v. 28 cm.

Gromin, Vadim Ivanovich.
[Eksperimental'naîa tektonika]
Экспериментальная тектоника. Библиография. (1812–1970 гг.) [Вступит. статья И. В. Лучицкого и В. И. Громина]. Новосибирск, 1971.
132 p. 20 cm.
At head of title: Академия наук СССР. Сибирское отделение. Институт геологии и геофизики. В. И. Громин, А. А. Запорожченко.
Added t. p. in English: Experimental tectonics.
Table of contents also in English.

Heath, Jo Ann, 1923–
Bibiography of reports resulting from U. S. Geological Survey participation in the United States technical assistance program, 1940–65. Washington, U. S. Govt. Print. Off., 1965.

vi, 51 p. 24 cm. (Geological Survey bulletin 1193)

Prepared under the auspices of the Agency for International Development of the U. S. Dept. of State.

Heath, Jo Ann, 1923–
Bibliography of reports resulting from U. S. Geological Survey participation in the United States technical assistance program, 1940–67, by Jo Ann Heath and Nancy B. Tabacchi. Washington ₁U. S. Dept. of the Interior, Geological Survey; for sale by the Supt. of Docs.₁ U. S. Govt. Print. Off., 1968.

vi. 68 p. 24 cm. (U. S. Geological Survey. Bulletin 1263)

Revision of the author's publication issued by the U. S. Geological Survey in 1965 as Bulletin 1193.
Prepared under the auspices of the Agency for International Development of the U. S. Dept. of State.

Howard, James Campbell, 1940–
Bibliography of statistical applications in geology ₁compiled by James C. Howard₁ Washington, Council on Education in the Geological Sciences, American Geological Institute ₁1968₁

vii, 24 p. 28 cm. (CEGS programs publication no. 2)

Informacja bibliograficzna: Geologia, ekonomika i technika prac geologicznych. rocz. 1–
lip. 1971–
Warszawa, Branżowy Ośrodek Informacji Naukowo-Technicznej i Ekonomicznej.

v. 21 cm. monthly (irregular).

Inter-documentation Company, *Zug.*
Geology, mineralogy, palaeozoology, palaeobotany. Zug, Switzerland, 1967.

7 p. 21 cm. (Basic collections in microedition)

Kasbeer, Tina.
Bibliography of continental drift and plate tectonics. ₁Boulder, Colo.₁ Geological Society of America ₁1973, c1972₁

xi, 96 p. 24 cm. (Geological Society of America. Special paper 142)

Kelley, Robert W
Sources of geological information in Michigan, by R. W. Kelley and E. A. Kirkby. Lansing, 1967.

iv, 24 p. map. 22 cm. (Geological Survey. Circular 5)

Kristal'nyĭ, Boris Vladimirovich.
₁Pervichnye dokumental'nye istochniki opublikovannoĭ geologicheskoĭ informatsii₁
Первичные документальные источники опубликованной геологической информации. Москва, 1971.

107 p. with diagrs. 20 cm. (Серия: Научно-техническая информация в геологии)
At head of title: Министерство геологии СССР. Всесоюзный научно-исследовательский институт экономики минерального сырья и геологоразведочных работ. Всесоюзный институт научной и технической информации. Б. В. Кристальный, З. С. Устинова.

Library Association. *County Libraries Group.*
Readers' guide to books on geology. 2nd ed. London, Library Association (County Libraries Group), 1967.

20 p. 18½ cm. (Its Readers' guide, new ser., no. 93)

Mackay, John Watson.
Sources of information for the literature of geology: an introductory guide ₁by₁ John W. Mackay. London, Geological Society of London, 1973.

iv, 61 p. 1 illus. 30 cm.

Математическая геология. Реферативный системат. указатель. основой литературы по 1968 г. Под ред. ₁и со вступит. статьей₁ А. Б. Вистелиуса. Ленинград, 1969.

246 p. 21 cm.
At head of title: Ордена Трудового Красного Знамени библиотека Академии наук СССР. Всесоюзная геологическая библиотека Министерства геологии СССР. Лаборатория математической геологии Ленинградского отделения Математического института им. В. А. Стеклова АН СССР.

Matorina, N I
Что читать юным геологам и краеведам. ₁3-е изд.₁ Ленинград, Изд. Ленингр. ун-та, 1968.

84 p. with illus. 14 cm.
On leaf preceding t. p.: Ленинградский ордена Ленина государственный университет имени А. А. Жданова. Научная библиотека имени А. М. Горького. Ленинградский дворец пионеров имени А. А. Жданова. Клуб юных геологов имени акад. В. А. Обручева.

Natsional'nyĭ komitet geologov Sovetskogo Soĭuza.
(Karty geologicheskogo soderzhaniĭa Soĭuza Sovetskikh Sotsialisticheskikh Respublik na Georame–72)
Карты геологического содержания Союза Советских Социалистических Республик на Геораме–72. ₁Составитель каталога: Е. П. Миронюк₁ Москва, 1972.

34 p. 17 cm.
At head of title: Национальный комитет геологов СССР.
Cover title: Maps of USSR.
Added t. p.: Maps of geological contents of the Union of Soviet Socialist Republics at Georama–72.
Russian and English.

Northrop, Stuart Alvord, 1904–
University of New Mexico contributions in geology, 1898–1964, by Stuart A. Northrop. Albuquerque, University of New Mexico Press, 1966.

152 p. ports. 23 cm. (University of New Mexico publications in geology, no. 7)

Novikov, Énergiĭ Alekseevich.
Путеводитель по геологической литературе мира. ₁Справочник₁. Ленинград, "Недра," Ленингр. отд-ние, 1971.

167 p. 21 cm.

Novinky literatury: Geologie, geografie. 1973–
Praha ₁Státní knihovna ČSR₁

v. 20 cm. 4 no. a year.

Continues Novinky literatury. Přírodní vědy. Řada geologicko-geograficka.

Ostrava, Czechoslovak Republic (City) Státní vědecka knihovna.
Geologie pro technickou praxi; výběrová bibliografie. ₁Zpracovatel: Jaroslava Lehká₁ Ostrava, 1965.

67 p. 20 cm. (Its Publikace. Řada II, čís. 396)

Prawirasumantri, Kosasih.
Petunjuk literatur mengenai geologi, disusun oleh Kosasih Prawirasumantri ₁dan₁ Hernandono. Jakarta, Pusat Dokumentasi Ilmiah Nasional ₁1972₁

63 p. 28 cm.

Richards, Horace Gardiner, 1906–
Annotated bibliography of Quaternary shorelines, 1945–1964 ₁by₁ Horace G. Richards ₁and₁ Rhodes W. Fairbridge. Philadelphia, Academy of Natural Sciences, 1965.

vii, 280 p. 25 cm. (Academy of Natural Sciences, Philadelphia. Special publication 6)
"Prepared for the VII International Congress of International Association for Quaternary Research (INQUA) meeting at Boulder, Colo., August 30–September 5, 1965."

———————Supplement 1965–1969. Philadelphia, Academy of Natural Sciences, 1970.

240 p. 24 cm. (Academy of Natural Sciences, Philadelphia, Special publication 10)

"Prepared for the VIII International Congress of International Union for Quaternary Research (INQUA) meeting at Paris, France, August 30–September 5, 1969."

Tkachenko, V T
₁Glubinnye razlomy₁
Глубинные разломы. Библиогр. указ. литературы. 1950–1970 гг. Москва, "Наука," 1972.

154 p. 22 cm.

On leaf preceding t. p.: Академия наук СССР. Сектор сети спецбиблиотек. Геологический институт. Библиотека геологической литературы при Секции наук о Земле.

Ward, Dederick C.
Geologic reference sources, by Dederick C. Ward. Boulder, University of Colorado Press, 1967.

xii, 114 p. 26 cm. (University of Colorado studies. Series in earth sciences, no. 5)

Ward, Dederick C
Geologic reference sources; a subject and regional bibliography to publications and maps in the geological sciences, by Dederick C. Ward and Marjorie W. Wheeler. With a section on geologic maps, by Mark W. Pangborn, Jr. Metuchen, N. J., Scarecrow Press, 1972.

453 p. 22 cm.

BIBLIOGRAPHIES

Margerie, Emmanuel de, 1862–1953.
Catalogue des bibliographies géologiques. Amsterdam, Meridian Pub. Co., 1966.

2 v. (xx, 733 p.) 23 cm.

Prepared with the assistance of members of the Commission internationale de bibliographie géologique, established by the International Geological Congress, 5th session, 1891, and edited by the Secretary of the Commission.
"Édition originale 1896."

LIBRARY CATALOGS

U. S. *Geological Survey. Library.*
Catalog of the United States Geological Survey Library. Boston, G. K. Hall, 1964.

25 v. 37 cm.

PERIODICALS

Soupis geologických periodik a zkratky jejich názvů.
[Zprac. kol.] 1. vyd. Praha, Ústř. ústav geologický, 1971.

256 p. 21 cm.

At head of title: Marie Levinská [et al.]

Soupis zahraničních geologických periodik odebíraných knihovnou ÚÚG-Ústřední ústav geologický a dalšími geologickými knihovnami v ČSSR. Sest. Marie Levinská, Alena Huková, Jiřína Knížková a kol. Praha, Geofond, rozmn., 1971.

140, [1] p. 20 cm. (Přehledy informativní literatury, 2)

AFGHANISTAN

Kästner, Hermann.
Bibliographie zur Geologie Afghanistans und unmittelbar angrenzender Gebiete (Stand Ende 1970) Hannover, Bundesanstalt für Bodenforschung, 1971.

43 p. 24 cm. (Belhefte zum Geologischen Jahrbuch, Heft 114)

Introduction in English, French, German, and Russian.

Kästner, Hermann.
Bibliography on the geology of Afghanistan and the immediately adjacent areas (as at the end of 1970). Kabul, 1971.

43 p. 24 cm. (Bulletin of the Afghan Geological and Mineral Survey, no. 6)

AFRICA

South Africa. Geological Survey.
Bibliography of South African geology, 1936–1956: index of authors. Pretoria, Govt. Printer, 1972.

72 p. 30 cm.

ALASKA

Fritts, Crawford Ellsworth, 1927–
Bibliography of Alaskan geology, compiled by Crawford E. Fritts and Mildred E. Brown. College, Alaska, Division of Geological Survey, 1971–

v. 28 cm.

CONTENTS: [1] 1831–1918. — [2] 1919–1949. — [3] 1950–1959. — [4] 1960–1964.—[5] 1965–1968, by C. E. Fritts and E. J. Tuell.—[6] 1969–1971, by C. E. Fritts and others.

Kelley, J   S
Geological literature on the Alaska peninsula and adjacent areas, by J. S. Kelley and J. M. Denman. [Juneau, Alaska, Dept. of Natural Resources, Division of Geological and Geophysical Surveys, 1972]

64 p. illus. 29 cm.

Maher, John Charles, 1914–
Geological literature on the gulf and southeastern coastal regions of Alaska, by J. C. Maher and W. M. Trollman. [Juneau] State of Alaska, Dept. of Natural Resources [1971]

136 p. maps. 28 cm.

Cover title.
Includes the literature published prior to July 1, 1970.

Maher, John Charles, 1914–
Geological literature on the North slope of Alaska. Compiled by J. C. Maher and W. M. Trollman. Tulsa, Okla., American Association of Petroleum Geologists, 1970.

133 columns. maps. 22 x 29 cm.

"This compilation has been prepared by the U. S. Geological Survey in cooperation with the U. S. Department of the Navy, Office of Naval Petroleum and Oil Shale Reserves."

ALGERIA

Merabet, Omar.
Bibliographie de l'Algérie du sud (Sahara) et des régions limitrophes. Alger, Service géologique de l'Algérie, 1968.

196 p. 28 cm. (Service géologique. Bulletin, nouv. sér., no 37)

ARGENTINE REPUBLIC

Buenos Aires (*Province*). *Comisión de Investigación Científica.*
Indice bibliográfico de estratigrafía argentina. Editado bajo la dirección de Angel V. Borrello. La Plata, 1965 [i. e. 1966]

v, 638 p. 27 cm.

Stamped on t. p.: Exclusive distributors: Librart, Buenos Aires.

Peña, Hugo A
Bibliografía geológica de Tucumán, por H. A. Peña. Tucumán, Fundación e Instituto Miguel Lillo, 1971.

35 p. 22 cm. (Fundación e Instituto Miguel Lillo. Miscelánea, no. 38)

"Comprende la nómina de todos o casi todos los trabajos de carácter geológico realizados hasta mayo de 1970, en el territorio tucumano y algunas zonas limítrofes."
Errata slip inserted.

AUSTRALIA

Australia. Commonwealth Scientific and Industrial Research Organization. Division of Applied Geomechanics.
Abstracts of published papers. no. 1–
1972–
[Mount Waverley]

no. 24 cm.

Bridge, Peter J
Combined index to the publications of the Geological

Survey of Western Australia 1910–1970 ₍by₎ Peter J. Bridge. ₍2d ed.₎ Mt. Lawley, W. A., Hesperian Press ₍1972₎

x, 341 p. 35 cm.

BOTSWANA

Bennett, John Dixon.
Annotated bibliography and index of the geology of Botswana, 1967–1970. Compiled by J. D. Bennett. ₍Lobatse, Botswana₎ Geological Survey and Mines Dept. ₍1971₎

70 p. 25 cm.

Errata slip inserted.
Supplement to the work by C. A. Laughton published in 1967 under title: Annotated bibliography and index of the geology of Botswana to 1966.

Laughton, C   A
Annotated bibliography and index of the geology of Botswana to 1966. Compiled by C. A. Laughton. ₍Gaberones, Govt. Printer, 1967?₎

v, 172 p. 26 cm.

At head of cover title: Republic of Botswana. Ministry of Commerce, Industry, and Water Affairs. Geological Survey Dept.

BRAZIL

Bibliografia e índice da geologia da Amazônia legal brasileira, 1641–1964 ₍por₎ Pedro Loewenstein ₍et al.₎ Normalização bibliográfica: Léa Diniz. Belém, Museu Paraense Emílio Goeldi, 1969.

291 p. 28 cm. (Museu Paraense Emílio Goeldi. Publicações avulsas, no. 11)

Iglesias, Dolores.
Bibliografia e índice da geologia do Brasil: 1966–1967 ₍por₎ Dolores Iglesias e Maria de Lourdes Meneghezzi. Rio de Janeiro, 1972.

187 p. 23 cm. (República Federativa do Brasil. Divisão de Geologia e Mineralogia. Boletim no. 256)

Mahrholz, Wolfgang W
Bibliografia suplementar da literatura geológica do Estado da Bahia, Brasil, de 1923–1966 ₍por₎ Wolfgang W. Mahrholz. ₍Salvador, Fundação Comissão de Planejamento Econômico do Estado da Bahia₎ 1967.

15 l. 29 cm.

Mezzalira, Sérgio.
Bibliografia e índice da geologia do Estado de São Paulo, 1959–1962. ₍São Paulo, Secretaria da Agricultura, Instituto Geográfico e Geológico, 1964₎

53 p. 24 cm. (Instituto Geográfico e Geológico. Boletim no. 40)

BRITISH GUIANA

Dixon, Cyril George, 1910–
Bibliography of the geology and mining of British Guiana, by C. G. Dixon & H. K. George. ₍Georgetown, Govt. Printery, 1964₎

iv, 87 p. 28 cm. (British Guiana. Geological Survey. Bulletin 32)

CANADA

Canada. Geological Survey.
Index of publications of the Geological Survey of Canada, 1970–1971. ₍Ottawa₎ Dept. of Energy, Mines and Resources ₍1971₎

66 p. 25 cm. (Its Paper 71–3)

Lists Geological Survey publications issued from 1 April 1970 to 31 March 1971, and includes a supplement covering the period January 1, 1970 to March 31, 1970.

Canada. Geological Survey.
Index to reports of Geological Survey of Canada from 1951–59. Compiled by J. F. Wright. ₍Ottawa₎ Dept. of Mines and Technical Surveys, 1965.

xii, 379 p. 25 cm.

Christie, Robert Loring, 1926–
Publications on the geology of the Arctic Islands by the Geological Survey of Canada, compiled by R. L. Christie. Rev. ₍Ottawa₎ Dept. of Energy, Mines and Resources ₍1971₎

iii, 21 p. maps. 25 cm. (Geological Survey of Canada. Paper 71–10)

Kupsch, Walter Oscar, 1919–
Annotated bibliography of Saskatchewan geology (1823–1965 incl.) by W. O. Kupsch and Michael D. Wright. ₍Rev. ed.₎ Regina ₍Dept. of Mineral Resources, Geological Sciences Branch₎ 1967.

296 p. 26 cm. (Saskatchewan. Dept. of Mineral Resources. Report no. 9)

New Brunswick Research and Productivity Council.
Bibliography of New Brunswick geology. D. Abbott, editor. Fredericton, 1965.

iv, 79 p. 29 cm. (Its Record 2, pt. C)

Quebec (*Province*). *Dept. of Natural Resources.*
Catalogue des publications depuis 1883. Québec, Direction de l'information, 1968–

1 v. (loose-leaf) 28 cm.

"Index des cartes géologiques publiées": fold. col. map inserted in pocket.
Issued also in English under title: Catalogue of publications since 1883.

Quebec (Province) *Dept. of Natural Resources.*
Catalogue of publications since 1883. Quebec, 1968–

1 v. (looseleaf) 28 cm.

Index of published geological maps: fold. col. map in pocket. English or French.

Research Council of Alberta.
List of publications, 1968. ₍Edmonton, 1968₎

32 p. 26 cm.

Rice, Harington Molesworth Anthony, 1900–
1964 index of publications of the Geological Survey of Canada ₍by₎ H. M. A. Rice. ₍Ottawa₎ Dept. of Energy, Mines and Resources ₍1969₎

vi, 110 p. 25 cm. (Geological Survey of Canada. Paper 65–3)

CZECHOSLOVAK REPUBLIC

Prague. Ústřední ústav geologický.
Katalog knižních a mapových publikací Ústředního ústavu geologického. Каталог печатных трудов и карт Центрального геологического института ЧССР. Catalogue of the publications and maps of the Geological Survey of the ČSSR. Catalogue de publications et cartes du Service géologique de la ČSSR. Schriften und Kartenkatalog der Geologischen Zentralanstalt der ČSSR. ₍1. vyd.₎ Praha, Ústřední ústav geologický, 1971.

210 p. illus. 22 cm.

Rejtharová, Alena.
Geologie a mineralogie západních Čech. Zprac. Alena Rejtharová. Plzeň, 1968.

92 p. 22 cm. (Na pomoc čtenářům a knihovníkům, 180)

Cover title.
At head of title: Státní vědecká knihovna v Plzni.

Skutil, Josef.
Bibliografie moravského pleistocénu, 1850–1950. Brno, 1965.

xiii, 316 p. 30 cm.

At head of title: BMP 1850–1950 (Bibliografie mor. pleist. 1850–1950) ČSAV-Archeologický ústav, Pobočka Brno.
Summary in German.

Tvrzník, Břetislav.
Mineralogicko-geologická bibliografie Českých zemí od roku 1919 do r. 1927. ₍Autor:₎ Břetislav Tvrzník a kol. 1. vyd. Praha, Academia, t. Jihočes. tisk. 7, Blatná, 1970.

159, ₍1₎ p. 21 cm.

Title also in Russian, French, and English: Mineralogical and geological bibliography of Bohemia, Moravia and Silesia from 1919 to 1927.

Tvrzník, Břetislav.
Mineralogicko-geologická bibliografie Českých zemí od roku 1919 do r. 1927. Mineralogical and geological bibliography of Bohemia, Moravia and Silesia from 1919 to 1927. ₍Vědecký redaktor Jan Kořan. Vyd. 1.₎ Praha, Ústřední ústav geologický, 1970.
159 p. 21 cm.
At head of title: Břetislav Tvrzník a kolektiv.
Title also in Russian and French.

DENMARK

Denmark. Geologiske undersøgelse.
Fortegnelse over skrifter 1890–1971. København, (C. A. Reitzel), 1971.

32 p. illus. 22 cm.

Title also in English: List of publications 1890–1971.
"Price-list": ₍5₎ p. in pocket.

EGYPT

United Arab Republic. Maṣlaḥat al-Abḥāth al-Jiyūlūjiyah wa-al-Taʻdīnīyah.
List of publications up to the end of 1964. Cairo, General Organisation for Govt. Print. Offices, 1964.

10 p. 27 cm.

At head of title: United Arab Republic. Ministry of Mining and Petroleum. Geological Survey and Mineral Research Dept.
"This list was prepared and checked by Abdel Aziz A. Huzaiyin."

FIJI ISLANDS

Duberal, R   F
Bibliography of the geology of Fiji, including published and unpublished references up to November, 1968, by R. F. Dubernal & P. Rodda. ₍Suva₎ Govt. of Fiji, Dept. of Geological Surveys ₍1968?₎

81 p. fold. map. 24 cm.

GREAT BRITAIN

Bassett, Douglas Anthony.
A source-book of geological, geomorphological and soil maps for Wales and the Welsh Borders (1800–1966), ₍by₎ Douglas A. Bassett. ₍Cardiff₎, Amgueddfa Genedlaethol Cymru, 1967.

x. 239 p. 25½ cm.

Thorpe, Jan A
North and west Lancashire and the Isle of Man—a bibliography of the geology and physical geography; compiled by Jan Thorpe. Lancaster, University of Lancaster Library, 1972.

iv, 81 p. map. 30 cm. index. (University of Lancaster. Library. Occasional papers, no. 5)

Hungary. Földtani Intézet.
A Magyar Állami Földtani Intézet kiadványainak bibliográfiája, 1869–1969-ig. Bibliography of the publications of the Hungarian Geological Institute, ₍Szerk. Gergelyffy Lászlóné, ₍Budapest, 1969₎

46 p. 24 cm.

Pref. in Hungarian, English, and Russian.

ISRAEL

Israel. ha-Makhon ha-geʻologi.
Reports and publications of the Geological Survey staff, 1969–1973 / Geological Survey of Israel. — Jerusalem : The Survey, 1974.

59 p. ; 27 cm.

ITALY

Nicosia, Maria Luisa.
Bibliografia del paleozoico italiano. A cura di Maria Luisa Nicosia. Roma, Tip. Olimpica, ₍1971?₎

211 p. 24 cm.

At head of title: Consiglio nazionale delle ricerche. Comitato per la geografia, geologia e mineralogia.

JAPAN

Chishitsu Chōsajo.
(Chishitsu Chōsajo shuppanbutsu mokuroku)
地質調査所出版物目錄
川崎 昭和44 1969
251p 地図 26cm
明治12年－昭和43年8月

Added cover title: List of publications of the Geological Survey of Japan, 1879–1968.

KENYA

Dosaj, N   P
Bibliography of the geology of Kenya, 1859–1968, by N. P. Dosaj and J. Walsh. ₍Nairobi, Geological Survey of Kenya, 1970₎

65 p. 25 cm. (₍Kenya. Geological Survey₎ Bulletin no. 10) 10/-

LATIN AMERICA

Bischoff, Gerhard, 1925–
Wirtschaftsgeologische Literatur über Iberoamerika. Eine Übersicht über das neuere deutsch- und fremdsprachige Schrifttum. Bearb. von Gerhard Bischoff und Friedrich Renger. Hamburg (Institut für Iberoamerika-Kunde) 1966.

276 p. 21 cm. (Institut für Iberoamerika-Kunde. Reihe Bibliographie und Dokumentation, Heft 7)

LEVANT

Avnimelech, Moshe A   1899–
Bibliography of Levant geology, including Cyprus, Hatay, Israel, Jordania, Lebanon, Sinai and Syria. Compiled and arranged by M. A. Avnimelech. Jerusalem, Israel Program for Scientific Translations, 1965.

x, 192 p. map. 28 cm.

Label mounted on t. p.: Published in the U. S. A. by D. Davey, New York.

NEW ZEALAND

Adkin, G   Leslie.
A bibliography of New Zealand geology to 1950, by G. L.

Adkin and B. W. Collins. ₍Wellington₎ Scientific and Industrial Research, 1967.

> xx, 243 p. 28 cm. (New Zealand. Geological Survey. Bulletin n. s. 65)

NEWFOUNDLAND

Butler, J
Bibliography of the geology of Newfoundland and Labrador, 1814 through 1968, by J. Butler and G. Bartlett. St. John's Newfoundland, Dept. of Mines, Agriculture and Resources, Mineral Resources Division, 1969.

> 273 p. 25 cm. (Newfoundland and Labrador. Dept. of Mines, Agriculture and Resources. Mineral Resources Division. Bulletin 38)

NORTH AMERICA

Abstracts of North American geology. Jan. 1966–

Washington, U. S. Geological Survey; ₍for sale by the Superintendent of Documents₎ U. S. Govt. Print. Off.

> v. 24 cm. monthly.

Bannatyne, Barry B
Annotated bibliography of the Quaternary in Manitoba and the adjacent Lake Agassiz region (including Archaeology of Manitoba), B. B. Bannatyne, S. C. Zoltai and M. J. Tamplin. Winnipeg, Province of Manitoba, Dept. of Mines and Natural Resources, Geological Division, 1970.

> vi, 142 p. 25 cm. (Manitoba. Dept. of Mines and Natural Resources. Mines Branch. Geological paper 2/70)

Geoscience Information Society. Guidebook and Ephemeral Materials Committee.
Geologic field trip guidebooks of North America; a union list incorporating monographic titles. Houston, Tex., P. Wilson Pub. Co., 1971.

> x, 152 p. 28 cm.

PAKISTAN

Offield, Terry W
Preliminary bibliography and index of the geology of Pakistan, by Terry W. Offield. ₍Karachi₎ Director General, Geological Survey of Pakistan, 1965.

> vi, 54 p. 28 cm. (Records of the Geological Survey of Pakistan, v. 12, pt. 1)

Pakistan National Scientific and Technical Documentation Centre (Dacca)
Publications on the geology of East Pakistan. Compiled & published by PANSDOC. Dacca, 1968.

> 10 p. 28 cm. (Its Bibliography no. 51)

PHILIPPINE ISLANDS

Aquino, Benigna T
Bibliography on Philippine geology, mining and mineral resources, 1953–1965, by Benigna T. Aquino and Leticia G. Santos. Manila, Bureau of Mines, 1971.

> vi, 163, 108 p. 28 cm. (₍Philippines (Republic). Bureau of Mines. Bibliography₎ series 2)

POLAND

Biuletyn informacyjny: Geologia, ekonomika i technika prac geologicznych. rocz. 1–
1972–
Warszawa, Branżowy Ośrodek Informacji Naukowo-Technicznej i Ekonomicznej.

> v. 21 cm.

Warsaw. Instytut Geologiczny.
List of publications, 1945–1971. Warsaw ₍Wydawnictwa

Geologiczne₎ 1972.

> 127 p. map. 17 cm.

POLAR REGIONS

McLeod, I   R
Bibliography of reports on geology, geomorphology and glacial geology resulting from Australian work in Antarctica, by I. R. McLeod. Canberra, Bureau of Mineral Resources, Geology and Geophysics, 1970.

> 9 p. 25 cm. (Australia. Dept. of National Development. Bureau of Mineral Resources, Geology and Geophysics, report no. 146)

Проспект книг по геологии Советской Арктики. Ленинград, 1969.

> 37 p. 20 cm.
>
> Cover title.
> At head of title: Научно-исследовательский институт геологии Арктики Министерства геологии СССР.

PUERTO RICO

Hooker, Marjorie, 1908–
Bibliography and index of the geology of Puerto Rico and vicinity, 1866–1968. San Juan, Geological Society of Puerto Rico, 1969.

> 53 p. 25 cm.

RUSSIA

(Armi͡anskai͡a SSR)
Армянская ССР; период 1956–1960. Ереван, Изд-во Академии наук Армянской ССР, 1968–

> v. 27 cm. (Геологическая изученность СССР, т. 48
>
> At head of title, v. 1–   : Академия наук Армянской ССР. Институт геологических наук. Управление геологии Армянской ССР. Added t. p.: Հայկական UU2. 1956–1960 ևամահատզրման։
> CONTENTS: вып. 1. Опубликованные работы.

(Bashkirskai͡a ASSR i Orenburgskai͡a oblast′)
Башкирская АССР и Оренбургская область. Период 1946–1950. Уфа, 1973–

> v. 27 cm. (Геологическая изученность СССР, т. 15
>
> At head of title, v. 1–   : Академия наук СССР. Башкирский филиал. Институт геологии.
> CONTENTS: вып. 1. Опубликованные работы.

(Dagestanskai͡a ASSR)
Дагестанская АССР. Период IX (1961–1965 гг.). ₍Авт. Тихомиров И. А., Галин В. Л., Ракушева Ф. А. и др. Сост. А. И. Войтусенок, Н. Я. Рогозин, И. А. Тихомиров, Л. М. Ярчук₎. Махачкала, ₍Даг. кн. изд-во₎, 1972–

> v. 27 cm. (Геологическая изученность СССР, т. 13)
>
> At head of title, v. 1–   : Министерство геологии РСФСР. Северо-Кавказское геологическое управление.
> CONTENTS: вып. 1. Опубликованные работы.

(Éstonskai͡a SSR. Period 1918–1940)
Эстонская ССР. Период 1918–1940. ₍Сост. Р. М. Мянниль₎. Таллин, "Валгус," 1972–

> v. 27 cm. (Геологическая изученность СССР, т. 50
>
> At head of title: Академия наук Эстонской ССР.
> CONTENTS: вып. 1. Опубликованные работы.

Эстонская ССР. Период 1941–1960. ₍Обзорные главы, аннот. и библиогр. справки₎ Таллин, "Валгус," 1968–

> v. 27 cm. (Геологическая изученность СССР, т. 50
>
> At head of title, v. 1–   : Академия наук Эстонской ССР.
> Added t. p. in Estonian.
> Edited by S. S. Baukov, and others.
> CONTENTS: вып. 1. Опубликованные работы.

(Éstonskaĭa SSR. Period 1961–1965)
Эстонская ССР. Период 1961–1965. Таллин, "Валгус,"
1973–

    v. 27 cm. (Геологическая изученность СССР. т. 50)

At head of title, v. 1– : Академия наук Эстонской ССР.
Added t. p. in Estonian.
Edited by S. S. Baukov and others.
CONTENTS : вып. 1. Опубликованные работы.

Грузинская ССР. Период 1946–1955. Тбилиси, "Мецниереба," 1967–

    v. 27 cm. (Геологическая изученность СССР, т. 41)

At head of title, v.   – : Академия наук Грузинской ССР.
Геологический институт. Управление геологии при Совете Ми-
нистров Грузинской ССР.
Added t. p. in Georgian.
CONTENTS : вып. 1. Опубликованные работы.

Kaliningradskaia oblast' RSFSR.
Калининградская область РСФСР; период 1946–1960.
Вильнюс, Минтис, 1966–

    v. map. 27 cm. (Геологическая изученность СССР, т. 6

At head of title: v. 1– : Министерство геологии СССР. Институт геологии (Вильнюс).
CONTENTS : вып. 1. Печатные работы.

Kenzina, V   L
Инженерная геология Сибири и Дальнего Востока.
Библиогр. указатель. Иркутск, 1970.

    196 p. 26 cm.

At head of title: Академия наук СССР. Сибирское отделение.
Научная библиотека Восточно-Сибирского филиали. Институт
земной коры.
By V. L. Kenzina and IU. B. Trzhtsinskiĭ.

Khriukova, Galina Mikhaĭlovna.
(Geologi Kolymy i Chukotki)
Геологи Колымы и Чукотки. Биобиблиогр. спра-
вочник. Магадан, Кн. изд., 1969.

    126 p. with ports. 20 cm. ("Помни их имена," вып. 2)

At head of title: Магаданская областная библиотека им. А. С.
Пушкина. Г. М. Хрюкова.

(Kirgizskaĭa SSR)
Киргизская ССР; период 1946–1950. Фрунзе. Илим, 1966–

    v. 27 cm. (Геологическая изученность СССР, т. 46

At head of title, v. 1– : Академия наук Киргизской ССР. Ин-
ститут геологии. Управление геологии Киргизской ССР.
Added t. p. in Kirghiz.
CONTENTS : вып. 1. Опубликованные работы.

Коми АССР. Период 1941–1945. Ленинград, "Наука,"
Ленингр. отд-ние, 1969–

    v. 27 cm. (Геологическая изученность СССР. т. 5)

At head of title, v. : Академия наук СССР. Коми филиал.
Институт геологии.
CONTENTS : вып. 1. Опубликованные работы.

Коми АССР. Период 1946–1955. Москва, "Наука," 1968–

    v. 27 cm. (Геологическая изученность, т. 5

At head of title, v. 1– : Академия наук СССР. Коми филиал.
Институт геологии.
Edited by V. P. Abramov and others.

Kuprienko, M   G
Библиографический указатель отечественной литературы к III Международному симпозиуму по границе
силур-девон 1950–1967 г. г. [Составитель М. Г. Куприен-
ко]. Ленинград, 1968.

    [159], 27 p. 20 cm.

At head of title: Министерство геологии СССР. Всесоюзная
геологическая библиотека.

Мурманская область; период 1929–1940 гг. Ленинград,
Наука, Ленингр. отд-ние, 1968–

    v. 27 cm. (Геологическая изученность СССР, т. 1)

At head of title, v.   : Академия наук СССР. Ордена Ленина
Кольский филиал им. С. М. Кирова. Геологический институт.
Северо-Западное геологическое управление.
CONTENTS : вып. 1. Опубликованные работы.

(Murmanskaĭa oblast')
Мурманская область; период 1941–1950. Ленинград,
Наука; Ленинградское отд-ние, 1967–

    v. 27 cm. (Геологическая изученность СССР, т. 1

At head of title, v. 1– : Академия наук СССР. Кольский
филиал им. С. М. Кирова. Геологический институт. Северо
-Западное геологическое управление.
CONTENTS : вып. 1. Опубликованные работы.

(Murmanskaĭa oblast')
Мурманская область; период 1956–1960. Москва, Наука,
1966–

    v. 27 cm. (Геологическая изученность СССР, т. 1

At head of title, v. 1– : Академия наук СССР. Кольский
филиал им. С. М. Кирова. Геологический институт. Северо
-Западное геологическое управление Министерства геологии
РСФСР.
CONTENTS : вып. 1. Опубликованные работы.

РСФСР. Алтайский край, Кемеровская область. Период
1946–1950. Москва. "Наука," 1969–

    v. 27 cm. (Геологическая изученность СССР, т. 19)

At head of title, v. 1– : Академия наук СССР. Сибирское
отделение. Институт геологии и геофизики.
Edited by S. G. Belrom, and others.

(RSFSR. (Belgorodskaĭa, Briânskaĭa, Voronezhskaĭa, Kur-
skaĭa, Lipetskaĭa, Orlovskaĭa i Tambovskaĭa oblasti))
РСФСР. (Белгородская, Брянская, Воронежская, Курская, Липецкая, Орловская и Тамбовская области).
Период 1800–1917. [Обзорные главы, реф., аннот., библиогр. справки. Москва; Калуа, Приок. кн. изд-во,
Калуж. отд-ние, 1973]–

    v. 27 cm. (Геологическая изученность СССР, т. 9)

At head of title, v. 1– : Министерство геологии РСФСР. Тер-
риториальное геологическое управление центральных районов
РСФСР.
"Редакторы выпуска: Л. В. Полякова, А. В. Симонов (отве-
ственный)."
CONTENTS : вып. 1. Опубликованные работы.

(RSFSR. Belgorodskaĭa, Briânskaĭa, Voronezhskaĭa ... i
Tambovskaĭa oblasti)
РСФСР. (Белгородская, Брянская, Воронежская, Кур-
ская, Липецкая, Орловская и Тамбовская области):
Период 1929–1950. [Обзорные главы, рефераты, аннот.
и библиогр. справки]. Москва, 1971–

    v. 27 cm. (Геологическая изученность СССР, т. 9, вып. 1–

At head of title, v. 1– : Министерство геологии РСФСР. Тер-
риториальное геологическое управление центральных районов
РСФСР.
By L. M. Krasnopevtseva and others.
CONTENTS : вып. 1. Опубликованные работы.

**RSFSR. (Belgorodskaĭa, Briânskaĭa, Voronezhskaĭa, ... i
Tambovskaĭa oblasti).**
РСФСР. (Белгородская, Брянская, Воронежская,
Курская, Липецкая, Орловская и Тамбовская области).
Период 1956–1960. [Обзорные главы, реф., аннот. и
библиогр. справки] Москва, 1971–

    v. 26 cm. (Геологическая изученность СССР, т. 9

At head of title, v. 1– : Министерство геологии РСФСР. Гео-
логическое управление центральных районов РСФСР.
Edited by I. N. Leonenko and others.
CONTENTS : вып. 1. Опубликованные работы.

(RSFSR. (Belgorodskaia, Brianskaia, Voronezhskaia, Kurskaia, Lipetskaia, Orlovskaia i Tambovskaia oblasti))
РСФСР. (Белгородская, Брянская, Воронежская, Курская, Липецкая, Орловская и Тамбовская области). Период 1961–1965. ₍Обзорные главы реф., аннот., библиогр. справки₎ Москва, 1974–
  v. 27 cm. (Геологическая изученность СССР, т.

At head of title, v. 1– : Министерство геологии РСФСР. Территориальное геологическое управление центральных районов.
CONTENTS : вып. 1. Опубликованные работы.

РСФСР. Бурятская АССР. Период 1956–1960. ₍Сост. В. Г. Канакин, С. А. Гурулев, К. Б. Булнаев и др.₎ Улан-Удэ, 1971–
  v. 27 cm. (Геологическая изученность СССР, т. 26)

At head of title, v. 1– : Академия наук СССР. Сибирское отделение. Бурятский филиал. Бурятский институт естественных наук.
On page facing t. p.: Академия наук СССР. Министерство геологии СССР. Комиссия по геологической изученности СССР.
Added t. p. in Burlat.
CONTENTS : вып. 1. Опубликованные работы.

(RSFSR: Irkutskaia oblast')
РСФСР: Иркутская область; период 1951–1955. Москва, Наука, 1965–
  v. 27 cm. (Геологическая изученность СССР, т. 24
At head of title, v. 1– : Академия наук СССР. Государственный геологический комитет СССР. Иркутское геологическое управление. Комиссия по геологической изученности.
Includes bibliographies.
CONTENTS : вып. 1. Опубликованные работы.

РСФСР. Иркутская область. Период 1956–1960. Москва, "Наука," 1971–
  v. 26 cm. (Геологическая изученность СССР, т. 24)

At head of title, v. 1– : Академия наук СССР. Сибирское отделение. Институт земной коры. Научная библиотека Восточно-сибирского филиала.

CONTENTS : вып. 1. Опубликованные работы. Сост. В. Л. Кензина, Л. Н. Иваньев.

РСФСР. Хабаровский край, Амурская область. Период 1956–1960. Москва, "Наука," 1969–
  v. 27 cm. (Геологическая изученность, т. 28

At head of ttile, v. 1– : Академия наук Союза ССР. Сибирское отделение. Дальневосточный филиал им. В. Л. Комарова. Дальневосточный геологический институт. Министерство геологии РСФСР. Дальневосточное геологическое управление.
Edited by I. I. Bersenev and others.

RSFSR: Krasnoiarskii krai.
РСФСР: Красноярский край (территория края южнее Полярного круга и Норильский район); период 1951–1955. Москва, Наука, 1966–
  v. 27 cm. (Геологическая изученность СССР, т. 20
At head of title, v. 1– : Академия наук СССР. Сибирское отделение. Институт геологии и геофизики.
CONTENTS : вып. 1. Опубликованные работы.

(RSFSR: Sakhalin)
РСФСР: Сахалин; период 1941–1960. Москва, Наука, 1968–
  v. 27 cm. (Геологическая изученность СССР, т. 30

At head of title, v. 1– : Академия наук СССР. Сибирское отделение. Сахалинский комплексный научно-исследовательский институт.
CONTENTS : вып. 1. Опубликованные работы.

РСФСР. Средний Урал. Период 1941–1945. ₍Авт. М. П. Жуйкова, Г. Н. Папулов, Б. И. Чувашов и др. Сост. М. П. Жуйкова₎. Москва, "Наука," 1971–
  v. 27 cm. (Геологическая изученность СССР, т. 14)

At head of title, v. 1– : Академия наук СССР. Уральский филиал. Институт геологии и геохимии. Министерство геологии РСФСР. Уральское территориальное геологическое управление.
CONTENTS : вып. 1. Опубликованные работы.

РСФСР. Средний Урал. Период 1946–1950. Москва. "Наука," 1969–
  v. 27 cm. (Геологическая изученность СССР, т. 14)

At head of title, v. 1– : Академия наук СССР. Уральский филиал. Институт геологии и геохимии. Министерство геологии РСФСР. Уральское территориальное геологическое управление.
Edited by N. I. Arkhangel'skii, and others.

РСФСР. Томская, Омская и Новосибирская области. Период 1941–1955. Москва, "Наука," 1969–
  v. 27 cm. (Геологическая изученность, т. 18

At head of title, v. 1– : Академия наук СССР. Сибирское отделение. Институт геологии и геофизики.
Edited by S. G. Belrom and others.

Sitnikaitė, A
  Lietuvos geologijos bibliografija. 1800–1965. Vilnius, 1970.

  276 p. 22 cm.

At head of title: Lietuvos TSR Mokslu akademijos Centrinė biblioteka. Lietuvos geologijos institutas. A. Sitnikaitė.
Added t. p.: Библиография геологии Литвы.
Prefatory matter and table of contents also in Russian.

(Srednee Povolzh'e)
Среднее Поволжье. Куйбышев., Сарат., Ульян. и Пенз. обл. VIII период. 1956–1960. Саратов, 1971–
  v. 27 cm. (Геологическая изученность СССР, т. 10)

At head of title, v. 1– : Министерство геологии РСФСР. Средне-Волжское геологическое управление. Куйбышевская геологоразведочная экспедиция.
Errata slip inserted.
CONTENTS : вып. 1. Опубликованные работы.

Центральная часть Советской Арктики. IX. период 1961–1965. Ленинград, 1970–
  v. 29 cm. (Геологическая изученность СССР, т. 16)

At head of title, v. 1– : Научно-исследовательский институт геологии Арктики Министерства геологии СССР.
CONTENTS : вып. 1. Рефераты опубликованных работ и обзорные главы.

(Turkmenskaia SSR)
Туркменская ССР. Периоды I–IV. 1800–1940 гг. Ашхабад, 1973–
  v. 27 cm. (Геологическая изученность СССР, т. 49

At head of title, v. 1– : Управление геологии Совета Министров ТССР. Туркменская геологическая экспедиция.
Added t. p. in Turkoman.
CONTENTS : вып. 1. Опубликованные работы.

Tuvinskaia ASSR.
  Тувинская АССР; период 1941–1955. Москва, Наука, 1967–
  v. 27 cm. (Геологическая изученность СССР, т. 25

At head of title, v. 1– : Академия наук СССР. Сибирское отделение. Институт геологии и геофизики.
CONTENTS : вып. 1. Опубликованные работы.

(Ukrainskaia SSR: Krymskaia oblast')
Украинская ССР: Крымская область. Период 1918–1950. Киев, "Наук. думка," 1972–
  v. 26 cm. (Геологическая изученность СССР, т. 83)

At head of title, v. 1– : Министерство геологии УССР. Институт минеральных ресурсов.
Added t. p.: Українська РСР: Кримська область.
CONTENTS : вып. 1. Опубликованные работы.

(Ukrainskaia SSR: Krymskaia oblast')
Украинская ССР. Крымская область. Период 1956–1960. Москва, "Недра," 1973–
  v. 26 cm. (Геологическая изученность СССР, т. 33

At head of title, v. 1– : Министерство геологии СССР. Институт минеральных ресурсов.
Added t. p.: Українська РСР. Кримська область.
CONTENTS : вып. 1. Опубликованные работы.

Украпнская ССР. (Западные области). Период 1956–1960. Киев, "Наукова думка," 1970–

v. 27 cm. (Геологическая изученность СССР, т. 31)

At head of title, v. : Академия наук Украинской ССР. Институт геологии и геохимии горючих ископаемых. Министерство геологии УССР.
Added t. p. in Ukrainian.
CONTENTS: вып. 1. Опубликованные работы.

(Uzbekskaĭa SSR. Vos'moĭ period, 1956–1960)
Узбекская ССР. VIII период, 1956–1960. [Сост. О. Н. Халецкая, Г. Ф. Тетюхин, Л. Н. Лордкипанидзе и др.] Ташкент, "Фан," 1971–

v. 27 cm. (Геологическая изученность СССР, т. 35)

At head of title, v. 1– : Академия наук Узбекской ССР. Институт геологии и геофизики им. Х. М. Абдуллаева. Министерство геологии УзССР. Институт гидрогеологии и инженерной геологии. Институт геологии и разведки нефтяных и газовых месторождений.
CONTENTS: вып. 1. Опубликованные работы и обзорные главы.

SAXONY

Prescher, Hans, 1926–
Die geologische Literatur über Sachsen. 1966–70. (Dresden, Th. Steinkopff, 1971.)

123 p. 30 cm. (Abhandlungen des Staatlichen Museums für Mineralogie und Geologie zu Dresden, Bd. 18)

SPAIN

Donat Zopo, José.
Repertorio de bibliografía geológica espeleológica valenciana. Valencia, Grupo Espeleológico "Vilanova y Piera," Diputación Provincial, 1971–

v. 24 cm.

Hernando de Luna, R
Bibliografía geológico-minera de la Provincia de Córdoba [por R. Hernando de Luna] Madrid, 1970.

268 p. 24 cm. (Memoria del Instituto Geológico y Minero de España, t. 74)

"Memoria redactada como contribución a las Jornadas Geológico-Mineras en homenaje a D. Antonio Carbonell y Trillo-Figueroa, celebradas en Córdoba del 9 al 11 de octubre de 1968."

Spain. Instituto Geológico y Minero. Departamento de Publicaciones.
Boletín informativo. no. 1– 1. cuatrimes-tre 1970– Madrid.

no. 25 cm.

SWEDEN

Larsson, Walter.
Swedish geological literature. 1958–1963. Edited by Walter Larsson. Stockholm, Sv. reproduktions AB (distr.) 1968.

546 p. 24 cm. (Sveriges geologiska undersökning. Ser. C. Avhandlingar och uppsatser, 630. Årsbok 62; nr. 1)

TANZANIA

Taylor, Barbara Mary, 1942–
Catalogue of early German material relating to Tanzania in the Library of the Mineral Resources Division, Dodoma, by Barbara M. Taylor. Dodoma, 1968.

26 p. 33 cm.

UNITED STATES

Bibliography and index of Illinois geology through 1965; a contribution to the Illinois sesquicentennial year [by] H. B. Willman [and others] Urbana, Illinois State Geological Survey, 1968.

373 p. 26 cm. (Illinois State Geological Survey. Bulletin 92)

Billings Geological Society.
Selected bibliography of stratigraphy in Montana and adjacent areas. Compiled under a cooperative agreement with the Montana Bureau of Mines and Geology. Contributors: Howard L. Garrett [and others] Ernest H. Gilmour. editor. Butte, Montana College of Mineral Science and Technology, 1966.

iv, 61 p. 28 cm. (Montana. Bureau of Mines and Geology. Special publication 38)

Bovee, Gladys G
Bibliography and index of Wyoming geology, 1823–1916, by Gladys G. Bovee. Cheyenne, Wyo., S. A. Bristol Co., 1918. Cheyenne, Frontier Print. and Mailing Co., 1969.

[317]–446 p. 23 cm. (The State of Wyoming. Geologist's Office. Bulletin 17)

Chelini, J M
Index of unpublished geologic studies in Montana, by J. M. Chelini. Butte, Montana College of Mineral Science and Technology, 1965.

iii, 88 p. maps (fold. col. in pocket) 28 cm. (Montana. Bureau of Mines and Geology. Special publication 34)

Cramer, Howard Ross.
Annotated bibliography of Georgia geology through 1959, by Howard Ross Cramer, Arthur Thomas Allen, Jr. and James George Lester. Atlanta, Georgia Dept. of Mines, Mining and Geology, 1967.

vi, 368 p. map. 23 cm. (Geological Survey. Bulletin no. 79)

Cramer, Howard Ross.
Annotated bibliography of Georgia geology from 1960 through 1964. Atlanta, Georgia Dept. of Mines, Mining and Geology, 1972.

vi, 110 p. illus. 23 cm. (The Geological Survey. Bulletin no. 84)

Cramer, Howard Ross.
Annotated bibliography of Pennsylvania geology to 1949. [Harrisburg] Dept. of Internal Affairs, Topographic and Geology Survey, 1961.

453 p. map. 23 cm. ([Pennsylvania. Topographic and Geologic Survey. Bulletin G34)

At head of title: Pennsylvania Geological Survey, fourth series.

————— Supplement to 1959. Harrisburg, Dept. of Internal Affairs, Bureau of Topographic and Geologic Survey; [for sale by the Division of Documents, Bureau of Publications] 1965.

237 p. map. 24 cm. ([Pennsylvania. Topographic and Geologic Survey] Bulletin G42)

"Pennsylvania Geological Survey fourth series."

————— Supplement to 1969. Harrisburg, Dept. of Environmental Resources, Bureau of Topographic and Geologic Survey; [for sale by the Division of Documents, Bureau of Publications] 1972.

ii, 345 p. maps. 24 cm. ([Pennsylvania. Topographic and Geologic Survey] Bulletin G61)
"Pennsylvania Geological Survey fourth series."

Geological Society of America.
Abstracts with programs. 1969– Boulder, Colo.

no. 22 cm.

Vols. for 1970– called v. 2–
Supersedes its Abstracts.
Vols. for 1969– issued in 7 parts.

Gillespie, William H
West Virginia geology, archeology, and pedology: a bibliography and index [by] William H. Gillespie and John A. Clendening. Archeological references compiled by Edward V. McMichael. Soils references compiled by Willem A. van Eck. Morgantown, West Virginia University Library, 1964.

xi, 241 p. 24 cm. (West Virginia University bulletin)

Hoffer, Frank B
Bibliography of Virginia geology and mineral resources—1950-1959 [by] F. B. Hoffer. Charlottesville, Commonwealth of Virginia, Division of Mineral Resources, 1972.

103 p. 23 cm. (Virginia. Division of Mineral Resources. Information circular 19)

Horick, Paul J
Bibliography of the geology of Iowa, 1960–1964, compiled and edited by Paul J. Horick, Jean C. Prior [and] Eugene E. Hinman. Iowa City, State of Iowa, 1967.

49 p. 23 cm.

Cover title.
Sponsored by the Geological Society of Iowa.

Koehn, Marsha A
Bibliography of New Mexico geology and mineral technology, 1966 through 1970, by Marsha A. Koehn and Henry H. Koehn. [Socorro] New Mexico State Bureau of Mines and Mineral Resources, 1973.

viii, 288 p. 23 cm. (New Mexico State Bureau of Mines and Mineral Resources. Bulletin 99)

Landers, Ronald A
Bibliography of environmental geology in West Virginia, by Ronald A. Landers and Peter Lessing. [Morgantown] West Virginia Geological and Economic Survey, 1973.

v, 33 p. 28 cm. (Environmental geology bulletin no. 8)

Love, Jane M
Bibliography of Wyoming geology, 1945–1949, by Jane M. Love. Laramie, Geological Survey of Wyoming, 1973.

103 p. 23 cm. (Geological Survey of Wyoming. Bulletin 57)

Michigan. Geological Survey Division.
Geologic map index of Michigan, 1843–1962, by Edward A. Kirkby. Lansing, 1970.

viii, 56 p. map. 23 cm. (Its Circular) $0.25

Montana. *State Bureau of Mines and Geology*.
Publications of Montana Bureau of Mines and Geology, 1919–1968. Butte, Montana College of Mineral Science and Technology [1968]

ii, 21 p. 22 cm.

Moore, Elizabeth T
Bibliography and index of Texas geology, 1951–1960, by Elizabeth T. Moore and Margaret D. Brown. Austin, Bureau of Economic Geology, University of Texas at Austin, 1972.

575 p. 28 cm.

Moore, Richard T
Bibliography of the geology and mineral resources of Arizona, 1818-1964, by Richard T. Moore and Eldred D. Wilson. Tucson, University of Arizona Press [1965]

321 p. 23 cm. (Arizona. Bureau of Mines. Bulletin 173)

Mullens, Marjorie C
Bibliography of the geology of the Green River Forma-

tion. Colorado, Utah, and Wyoming, to March 1, 1973, by Marjorie C. Mullens. Washington [U. S. Geological Survey] 1973.

iii, 20 p. 26 cm. (Geological survey circular 675)

Muller, Ernest Hathaway, 1923–
Bibliography of New York quaternary geology, by Ernest H. Muller. With historical note on studies of New York quaternary geology, by Ernest H. Muller and William A. Garrabrant. Albany, University of the State of New York, 1965.

vi, 116 p. illus. 23 cm. (New York State Museum and Science Service. Bulletin no. 398)

National Association of Geology Teachers. East-Central Section. Education Committee.
A bibliography of geological field trip guidebooks and related publications for Indiana, Kentucky, Michigan, and Ohio, 1950–1972. [Kalamazoo, Dept. of Geology. Western Michigan University] 1972.

i, 25 p. maps. 28 cm.

North Carolina. *Division of Mineral Resources*.
A summary of current geologic research in North Carolina. Raleigh, 1965.

11 p. 28 cm.

Pestana, Harold R
Bibliography of congressional geology, by Harold R. Pestana. New York, Hafner Pub. Co., 1972.

285 p. 24 cm.

"Includes and indexes all of the geologic documents published from 1818 to 1907 in the congressional documents set."

Ray, Teri.
Bibliography of New Mexico geology and mineral technology, 1961–1965. Socorro, State Bureau of Mines and Mineral Resources, New Mexico Institute of Mining & Technology, 1966.

124 p. 23 cm. (State Bureau of Mines and Mineral Resources. Bulletin 90)

Schmeckebier, Laurence Frederick, 1877–1959.
Catalogue and index of the publications of the Hayden, King, Powell, and Wheeler surveys. New York, Da Capo Press, 1971.

208 p. 23 cm.

Half title: Publications of the Hayden, King, Powell, and Wheeler surveys.
Reprint of the 1904 ed., which was issued as Bulletin no. 222 of the U. S. Geological Survey.

Scott, Mary Woods.
Annotated bibliography of the geology of North Dakota, 1806–1959. [Grand Forks, North Dakota Geological Survey] 1972.

i, 132 p. 26 cm. (North Dakota Geological Survey. Miscellaneous series, no. 49)

Smyth, Pauline.
Bibliography of Ohio geology, 1961–1965. Columbus, State of Ohio, Division of Geological Survey, 1969.

46 p. map. 28 cm. ([Ohio. Division of Geological Survey] Information circular no. 36)

Smyth, Pauline.
Bibliography of Ohio geology, 1966-1970. Columbus, State of Ohio, Division of Geological Survey, 1972.

52 p. map. 28 cm. (Ohio. Division of Geological Survey. Information circular no. 37)

South Carolina. Division of Geology.
Catalog of geologic publications. 1st– ed.;

1971/72–
Columbia.

v. 23 cm (Its Circular)

Strand, Rudolph G

Index to geologic maps of California to December 31, 1956, by R. G. Strand, J. B. Koenig, and C. W. Jennings. San Francisco, 1958.

128 p. maps. 28 cm. (California. Division of Mines. Special report 52)

———— Index to geological maps of California, 1957–1960, by James B. Koenig. San Francisco, 1962.

60 p. maps. 28 cm. (California. Division of Mines. Special report 52A)

———— Index to geologic maps of California, 1961–1964, by James B. Koenig and Edmund W. Kiessling. San Francisco, 1968.

72 p. (p. 7–53 maps) 28 cm. (California Division of Mines and Geology. Special report 52B)

Tipton, Merlin J

Bibliography of reports containing maps on South Dakota geology published before January 1, 1959, by Merlin J. Tipton, Cleo M. Christensen, and Allen F. Agnew. Vermillion, Science Center, University of South Dakota, 1966.

71 p. illus. 27 cm. (South Dakota State Geological Survey. Circular no. 33)

U. S. *Geological Survey.*

Publications of the Geological Survey, 1879–1961. [Washington, U. S. Govt. Print. Off., 1964]

vi, 457 p. 24 cm.

"Permanent catalog of books, maps, and charts. Later publications will be listed in supplementary catalogs."
Newly issued publications to be reported monthly in "New publications of the Geological Survey."

———— 1962– [Supplement] Washington, U. S. Govt. Print. Off., 1963–

v. 24 cm.

U. S. Geological Survey. Special Projects Branch.

Bibliography of reports by Special Projects Branch personnel, May 16, 1958 to July 31, 1967. [Washington, 1968?]

iv, 117 l. 27 cm.

U. S. *Superintendent of Documents.*

Reports of explorations printed in the documents of the United States government; a contribution toward a bibliography. Compiled by Adelaide R. Hasse. New York, B. Franklin [1969]

90 p. 24 cm. (Burt Franklin bibliography and reference series 284)

Reprint of the 1899 ed.

Vineyard, Jerry D

Bibliography of the geology of Missouri, 1955–1965 [by] Jerry D. Vineyard, John W. Koenig [and] Bonnie L. Happel. Rolla, 1967.
229 p. 27 cm. (Missouri. Division of Geological Survey and Water Resources. [Reports] 2d ser., v. 42.)

Incorporates all of the entries of Bibliography of the geology of Missouri, 1955–1960 and all of the annual bibliographies since 1960.
Supplements and expands the cumulative bibliographies published in 1945 and 1956 with the same title.

Vineyard, Jerry D

Bibliography of the geology of Missouri, 1968, by Jerry D. Vineyard. Rolla, Missouri Geological Survey and Water Resources, 1969.

iv, 48 p. 28 cm. (Missouri Geological Survey and Water Resources. Information circular no. 21)

Vineyard, Jerry D

Bibliography of the geology of Missouri, 1971, by Jerry D. Vineyard. Rolla, Missouri Geological Survey and Water Resources, 1972.

vi, 38 p. 28 cm. (Missouri Geological Survey and Water Resources. Information circular no. 25)

Webb, Harry W

Bibliography of published measured sections west of the Blue Ridge in Virginia [by] Harry W. Webb, Jr. [and] W. Edward Nunan. Charlottesville, Virginia Division of Mineral Resources, 1972.

219 p. maps. 23 cm. (Virginia. Division of Mineral Resources. Information circular 18)

GEOMETRY

Sommerville, Duncan M'Laren Young, 1879–1934.

Bibliography of non-Euclidean geometry. [2d ed.] New York, Chelsea Pub. Co. [1970]

xii, 410 p. 21 cm.

GEOMORPHOLOGY see Physical geography

GEOPHYSICS

Avco Corporation. Space Science Dept. Geophysics Section.

Chronological list of scientific publications with abstracts and symposium papers. Wilmington, Mass., Avco Corporation, Research and Advanced Development Division, 1965.

iii, 141 p. 24 cm.

Bibliography and index [of the Annals of the International Geophysical Year] Editor: W. J. G. Beynon. [1st ed.] Oxford, New York, Pergamon Press [1970]

ix, 180 p. ports. 25 cm. (Annals of the International Geophysical Year, v. 48)

Bogatova, Galina Petrovna.

Земля—родной дом человечества. Рек. указатель литературы для молодежи. Москва, "Книга," 1970.

80 p. 20 cm.

At head of title: Государственная ордена Ленина библиотека СССР имени В. И. Ленина.

Cooperative investigation of the Caribbean and adjacent regions, CICAR. Rockville, Md., U. S. National Oceanographic Data Center, 1970–

v. 34 cm.

(K'o chi wên hsien so yin. T'ê chung wên hsien pu fên: Ti ch'iu wu li hsüeh, t'ien wên hsüeh)

科技文献索引 (特种文献部份) 地球物理学·天文学·

总第 1– 期 1964 年 1 月–

[北京] 中国科学技术情报研究所

no. 27 cm. quarterly.

K'o hsüeh chi shu wen hsien so yin: Ti ch'iu wu li hsüeh, t'ien wen hsüeh.

科学技术文献索引 地球物理学 天文学

Kexue jishu wenxian suoyin. 总第 74– 期 1965 年 1 月–

[重庆 etc.] 中国科学技术情报研究所重庆分所 [etc.]

no. 27 cm. monthly.

Continues 科学技术文献索引 (期刊部分) 地球物理学 天文学 and 科学技术文献索引 (特种文献部分) 地球物理学 天文学

Leningrad. Glavnaīa geofizicheskaīa observatoriīa. Biblioteka.
Библиографический указатель работ Главной геофизической обсерватории за период 1918–1967 г. г. Сост. Е. Л. Андроникова, Э. А. Слободская и Г. А. Циммер. Под общ. ред. М. Е. Швеца. Ленинград, 1967–

v. 26 cm.

At head of title, v. 1– : Главное управление гидрометеорологической службы при СМ СССР. Ордена Трудового Красного Знамени Главная геофизическая обсерватория им. А. И. Воейкова. Библиотека.
CONTENTS : вып. 1. 1918–1945 г. г.

PERIODICALS see under Astronomy – Periodicals

GEORGE, DAVID LLOYD, EARL GEORGE see Lloyd George, David

GEORGIA

Georgia. State Engineering Experiment Station, Atlanta. Basic Data Branch.
Bibliography of Georgia business and economic periodicals. Rev. ed. ₁Atlanta₁ Industrial Development Division, Engineering Experiment Station, Georgia Institute of Technology, 1967.

9 p. 29 cm. (₁Georgia. State Engineering Experiment Station, Atlanta₁ Bibliographical series, no. 2.)

Rowland, Arthur Ray, 1930–
A bibliography of the writings on Georgia history. ₁Hamden, Conn.₁ Archon Books, 1966.

xii, 289 p. 20 cm.

Turnbull, Augustus Bacon, 1940–
Selected bibliography on Georgia government. Augustus B. Turnbull III ₁and₁ Ruth Spence, editors. ₁Athens₁ Institute of Government, University of Georgia, 1968.

98 l. 28 cm.

Warren, Mary Bondurant.
Georgia genealogical bibliography, 1968. Danielsville, Ga., Heritage Papers ₁1969₁

₁31₁ p. 21 cm.

Caption title.
Cover title: Georgia bibliography, 1968.

GEORGIA (TRANSCAUCASIA)

(Bibliografiīā literatury i trudov v oblasti istoricheskikh nauk)
Библиография литературы и трудов в области исторических наук.
1970–
Тбилиси, Мецниереба.
v. 20 cm. (Серия исторических наук)
Issued by Sektor nauchnoĭ informatsii po obshchestvennym naukam of Akademiīā nauk Gruzinskoĭ SSR.

Oxford. University. Bodleian Library.
Catalogue of the Wardrop Collection and of other Georgian books and manuscripts in the Bodleian Library ₁by₁ David Barrett. ₁Oxford₁ Published for the Marjory Wardrop Fund by Oxford University Press, 1973.

354 p. 26 cm.

GEORGIAN LANGUAGE

Imnaĭshvili, Grigoriĭ Moĭseevich.
Библиография литературы по грузинской диалектологии. Сост. Г. М. Имнайшвили. Тбилиси, "Мецниереба," 1969.

217 p. 22 cm.

On leaf preceding t. p.: Академия наук Грузинской ССР. Институт языкознания.
Russian and Georgian.

GEOSCIENCE see Earth sciences; Geology

GÉRARD DE NERVAL see Nerval, Gérard de

GERBENZON, PIETER

Wrotterslean. Bibliografie van de geschriften van Prof. Mr. P. Gerbenzon. Verzorgd door C. J. van Heel, A. L. Hempenius, B. S. Hempenius-Van Dijk e. a. Leeuwarden, A. L. Hempenius ₁1971?₁

27 p. illus. 30 cm.

"Oplage van 147 genummerde exemplaren ... Dit is nummer: 130."

GERIATRICS see Gerontology

GERMAN DRAMA see Drama - Germany

GERMAN IMPRINTS

Berlin. Stadtbibliothek.
Die Deutsche Demokratische Republik im 15. Jahr nach ihrer Gründung; eine Auswahlbibliographie zum 15. Jahrestag der Gründung der Deutschen Demokratischen Republik. ₁Berlin₁ 1964.

77 p. 21 cm.

At head of title: Berliner Stadtbibliothek.

Börsenverein des Deutschen Buchhandels.
Knjige iz Savezne Republike Nemačke. 1967. Katalog izložbe knjiga u Jugoslaviji. Bücher aus der Bundesrepublik Deutschland. Katalog der Buchausstellung in Jugoslawien. ₁Austellungskatalog₁ (Frankfurt a. M., Börsenverein des Deutschen Buchhandels, Ausstellungsund Messe-GmbH) 1967.
179 p. 20 cm.
Dodatak. Nachtrag (ix p.) inserted.

Bücher aus der DDR. 1972/73–

Leipzig, Deutscher Buch-Export und -Import G. m. b. H.

v. in 21 cm.

Continues Leipziger Bücherkatalog.
Issued in parts.

Deutsche Bibliographie. Wöchentliches Verzeichnis. ₁Reihe₁ A: Erscheinungen des Buchhandels. März 1947–
Frankfurt am Main, Buchhändler-Vereinigung.

v. in 21–25 cm.

Frequency varies 1947–49.
Title varies: 1947–52. Bibliographie.—1953–64; Deutsche Bibliographie. Wöchentliches Verzeichnis.
"Bearbeitet von der Deutschen Bibliothek Frankfurt a. M."
"Im amtlichen Auftrage des Bundesministers des Inneren und des Hessischen Kultusministers herausgegeben," 1964–
Issued with monthly and quarterly cumulative indexes (called "Sondernummer"). indexing also österreichische Bibliographie and Das Schweizer Buch (Serie A).
—— Beilage. ₁Reihe₁ B: Erscheinungen ausserhalb des Buchhandels. 14. Jan. 1965–
Frankfurt am Main, Buchhändler-Vereinigung.
v. in 21–25 cm. monthly.
Issued by Deutsche Bibliothek, Frankfurt am Main.
Issued with annual indexes, called "Sondernummer."
—— Beilage. ₁Reihe₁ C: Karten. 11. Feb. 1965–
Frankfurt am Main, Buchhändler-Vereinigung.
v. in 21–25 cm. bimonthly.
Issued by Deutsche Bibliothek, Frankfurt am Main.
Issued with annual indexes, indexing also österreichische Bibliographie and Das Schweizer Buch.

Exposición del nuevo libro alemán en Chile, 1969. ₁Catálogo de obras. Frankfurt am Main, Ausstellungs und

Messe-GmbH des Börsenvereins des Deutschen Buchhandels, 1969?]

xxix, 218 p. 2 fold. maps. 20 cm.

On cover: Deutsche Buchausstellung: El nuevo libro alemán.
Added t. p.: Deutsche Buchausstellung in Chile 1969.
Introductions and captions also in German.

Fuchs, Hermann, 1896–
Systematisches Verzeichnis der Veröffentlichungen der westdeutschen Akademien in Göttingen, Heidelberg, Mainz und München 1945–1964. Mainz, Verlag der Akademie der Wissenschaften und der Literatur; Wiesbaden, F. Steiner in Kommission (1966)

viii, 168 p. 24 cm.

Heinsius, Wilhelm, 1768–1817.
Alphabetisches Verzeichnis der von 1700 bis zu Ende 1810 erschienenen Romane und Schauspiele, welche in Deutschland und in den durch Sprache und Literatur damit verwandten Ländern gedruckt worden sind. Leipzig, Zentralantiquariat der Deutschen Demokratischen Republik, 1972.

376 columns. 27 cm.
Reprint of the ed. published in 1813.
Supplement to the author's Allgemeines Bücher-Lexikon.
"Ausgabe für Verlag Dokumentation München-Pullach."

Die Neue Barke. 1–   1971–
[Hamburg, Lesen Verlag]

no. illus. 24 cm. 4 no. a year.

Supersedes Die Barke.

Das Neue deutsche Buch. Eine Ausstellung von 3000 Büchern und Zeitschriften in Tel Aviv, Jerusalem und Haifa 1968. (Auswahl: Clemens Köttelwesch [u. a.]) Frankfurt a. M., Ausstellungs- und Messe-GmbH des Börsenvereins des Deutschen Buchhandels (1968).

266 p. 20 cm.

Added t. p.: ‏הספר הגרמני החדש‏
Introd. and captions also in Hebrew.

Ostwald, Renate.
Nachdruckverzeichnis von Einzelwerken, Serien und Zeitschriften aus allen Wissensgebieten (Reprints). Wiesbaden, G. Nobis, 1965–

v. 25 cm.

Saskatchewan. Provincial Library, Regina. Bibliographic Services Division.
German books. Deutsche Bücher. Regina, Sask., 1972.

31 p. 22 cm.

Cover title.
Introduction in English and German.

Thomas, Hans.
Des Volkes Riesenschritte. Material für die sozialist. Fest- u. Feiergestaltung. Hrsg. anlässl. d. 20 Jahrestages der DDR. Leipzig, Zentralhaus f. Kulturarbeit der DDR, 1969.

488 p. 21 cm.

Verzeichnis lieferbarer Bücher. 1971/72–

Frankfurt am Main, Verlag der Buchhändler-Vereinigung GmbH.

v. in 31 cm.
Issued by Börsenverein der Deutschen Buchhändler.
Vols. for 1971/72–   issued in parts.
——— Nachtrag.
[Frankfurt am Main]
v. 30 cm.

Bibliographie der deutschen Bibliographien. Jahrg. 1–
Apr. 1966–
[Leipzig, Verlag für Buch- und Bibliothekswesen]

v. 21 cm. monthly.

Supersedes Bulletin wichtiger Literatur-Zusammenstellungen.
"Bearbeitet von der Deutschen Bücherei."

EARLY PRINTED BOOKS

Bruckner, J
A bibliographical catalogue of seventeenth-century German books published in Holland. [By] J. Bruckner. The Hague, Mouton, 1971.

xxxviii, 552 p., 18 p. of photos. 22 cm. (Anglica germanica; British studies in Germanic languages and literatures, 13)

Deutsche Gesellschaft zur Erforschung vaterländischer Sprache und Altertümer, Leipzig.
Katalog der Büchersammlung der Deutschen Gesellschaft in Leipzig. Nach dem von Ernst Kroker bearb. handschriftlichen Bestandsverzeichnis der Universitätsbibliothek Leipzig hrsg. vom Zentralantiquariat der DDR in Leipzig. Mit Vorwort von Dietmar Debes. München, Kösel-Verlag [1971]

2 v. (xlv, 778 p.) 20 cm. (Bibliographie zur Barockliteratur)

At head of title: Bibliotheca societatis Teutonicae saeculi XVI–XVIII.

Fletcher, John Edward.
Short-title catalogue of German imprints in Australia from 1501–1800, compiled by J. E. Fletcher. [Melbourne] Dept. of German, Monash University, 1970.

229 p. 28 cm.

Leeds, Eng. University. Brotherton Library.
German literature printed in the seventeenth & eighteenth centuries: a catalogue of the Library's collection. Leeds, Brotherton Library, 1973.

82 p. 24 cm.

GERMAN LANGUAGE

Bibliographie Deutschunterricht; ein Auswahlverzeichnis, zusammengestellt von Dietrich Boueke [et al.] Paderborn, F. Schöningh [c1973]

222 p. 19 cm. (Uni-Taschenbücher, 230. Germanistik)

Fletcher, John Edward.
German language books in the libraries of Canberra, Melbourne and New South Wales, edited by John Fletcher and Marlene Norst. North Ryde, N. S. W., Macquarie University, School of Modern Languages, German Section, 1972.

iv, 417 p. 20 x 33 cm.

Goethe-Institut, *Munich. Wissenschaftliche Arbeitsstelle.*
Arbeitsmittel für den Deutschunterricht an Ausländer. 5. Aufl. [München] 1967.

43 p. 24 cm.

Hansel, Johannes.
Bücherkunde für Germanisten. Studienausg. 3., erweiterte Aufl. [Berlin] E. Schmidt [1965]

156 p. 21 cm.

Hansel, Johannes.
Bücherkunde für Germanisten. Studienausg. 4., verm. Aufl. (Berlin) E. Schmidt (1967)

163 p. 21 cm.

Hansel, Johannes.
Bücherkunde für Germanisten. Studienausg. 5., verm.

Aufl. (Berlin) E. Schmidt (1968).

166 p. 21 cm.

Hansel, Johannes.
Bücherkunde für Germanisten; Studienausgabe von Johannes Hansel, bearb. von Lydia Tschakert. 6., verm. Aufl. ₍Berlin₎ E. Schmidt ₍1972, c1961₎

197 p. 21 cm.

Herfurth, Gisela.
Topographie der Germanistik; Standortbestimmungen 1966–1971. Eine Bibliographie von Gisela Herfurth, Jörg Hennig ₍und₎ Lutz Huth. Mit einem Vorwort von Wolfgang Bachofer. ₍Berlin₎ E. Schmidt ₍c1971₎

143 p. 21 cm.

Lemmer, Manfred.
Deutscher Wortschatz. Bibliographie zur deutschen Lexikologie. Halle ⟨Saale⟩, Niemeyer, 1967.

123 p. 22 cm.

London. University. *Institute of Germanic Studies*.
German language and literature: select bibliography ₍compiled by L. M. Newman₎ London, Institute of Germanic Studies, 1966.

₍3₎, 59 p. 24 cm.

Otto Harrassowitz (Firm)
German series publications in the fields of Germanic language & literature, German history. An itemized list presented by Otto Harrassowitz. Wiesbaden, 1967–69.

2 v. 22 cm.

Schindler, Frank.
Bibliographie zur Phonetik und Phonologie des Deutschen. Bearb. von Frank Schindler u. Eike Thürmann unter Mitw. von Christine Riek. Hrsg. von Inst. f. Phonetik d. Univ. zu Köln. Tübingen, Niemeyer, 1971.

xiii, 156 p. 24 cm. (Bibliographische Arbeitsmaterialien)

Toronto. University. Library. Humanities and Social Sciences Division.
German reference aids in the University of Toronto Library, Humanities & Social Sciences Division, prepared by S. Sampson Elisha. Toronto, Reference Dept., University of Toronto Library, 1968.

iii, 72 l. 28 cm. (Reference series, no. 12)

Walden, Barbara.
Guide to reference materials in German language and literature in the Library of the University of British Columbia. Vancouver, University of British Columbia Library, 1969.

29 p. 23 cm. (University of British Columbia Library. Reference publication no. 28)

DIALECTS

Althaus, Hans Peter.
Ergebnisse der Dialektologie. Bibliographie d. Aufsätze in d. dt. Zeitschriften f. Mundartforschung. 1854–1968. Wiesbaden, F. Steiner, 1970.

xi, 240 p. 25 cm. (Zeitschrift für Dialektologie und Linguistik. Beihefte, n. F., 7)

Mentz, Ferdinand, 1864–
Bibliographie der deutschen Mundartforschung für die Zeit vom Beginn des 18. Jahrhunderts bis zum Ende des Jahres 1889. ₍Walluf bei Wiesbaden₎ M. Sändig ₍1972₎

xx, 181 p. 21 cm.

Reprint of the 1892 ed. which was issued as Bd. 2 of Sammlung kurzer Grammatiken deutscher Mundarten.

Wiechmann, Carl Michael, 1828–1883.
Meklenburgs altniedersächsische Literatur. Ein bibliographisches Repertorium. ⟨Ende des 15. Jahrhunderts—1625⟩. ₍Von₎ C. M. Wiechmann. 2. unveränderte Aufl. Nieuwkoop, B. de Graaf, 1968.

3 v. in 1. 22 cm.

Facsim. of the Schwerin ed., 1864–85.

GERMAN LITERATURE

see also Austrian literature; Swiss literature

Ahnert, Heinz Jörg.
Deutsches Titelbuch 2. Ein Hilfsmittel zum Nachweis von Verfassern deutscher Literaturwerke 1915–1965 mit Nachträgen und Berichtigungen zum Deutschen Titelbuch I für die Zeit von 1900 bis 1914 (von Max Schneider) Berlin, Haude & Spenersche Verlagsbuchhandlung (1966)

xii, 636 p. 22 cm.

Albrecht, Günter.
Internationale Bibliographie zur Geschichte der deutschen Literatur von den Anfängen bis zur Gegenwart, erarbeitet von deutschen, sowjetischen, bulgarischen, jugoslawischen, polnischen, rumänischen, tschechoslowakischen und ungarischen Wissenschaftlern unter Leitung und Gesamtredaktion von Günter Albrecht und Günther Dahlke. ₍1. Aufl.₎ Berlin, Volk und Wissen, 1969–

v. 25 cm.

"Gleichzeitig als Ergänzung der 11bändigen ... 'Geschichte der deutschen Literatur von den Anfängen bis zur Gegenwart.'"

Arnold, Robert Franz, 1872–1938.
Allgemeine Bücherkunde zur neueren deutschen Literaturgeschichte. 4. Aufl. Neu bearb. von Herbert Jacob. Berlin, De Gruyter, 1966.

xiii, 395 p. 25 cm.

Berlin. Amerika-Gedenkbibliothek.
Junge Literatur der DDS; eine Auswahlliste der Amerika-Gedenkbibliothek, Berliner Zentralbibliothek. ₍Zusammengestellt von Hans-Ulrich Mehner und Günther Wulff₎. Berlin, 1972.

39 p. 21 cm.

Original ed. published in 1967 under title: Von Bitterfeld bis Oobliadooh.

Berlin. Amerika-Gedenkbibliothek.
Von Bitterfeld bis Oobliadooh. Die andere deutsche Literatur. Ein Bücherverzeichnis der Amerika-Gedenkbibliothek. (Zusammengestellt von Hans-Ulrich Mehner und Günther Wulff.) Berlin, Amerika-Gedenkbibliothek, 1967.

39 p. 21 cm.

Revised ed. published in 1972 under title: Junge Literatur der DDR.

Bibliographie der deutschen Sprach- und Literaturwissenschaft. Bd. 9–   1969–
Frankfurt am Main, V. Klostermann.

v. 23 cm. annual.

Continues Bibliographie der deutschen Literaturwissenschaft.

Cowen, Roy C   1930–
Neunzehntes Jahrhundert ⟨1830–1880⟩. ₍Von₎ Roy C. Cowen. Bern, München, Francke, (1970).

216 p. 24 cm. (Handbuch der deutschen Literaturgeschichte. Abt. 2: Bibliographien, Bd. 9)

Deutsche Akademie der Künste, *Berlin. Sektion Dichtkunst und Sprachpflege.*

Veröffentlichungen deutscher sozialistischer Schriftsteller in der revolutionären und demokratischen Presse, 1918–1945. Bibliographie. (Bearbeitung: Edith Zenker) Berlin u. Weimar, Aufbau-Verlag, 1966.

xi, 657 p. 22 cm.

Based on Katalog der Zeitschriften- und Zeitungsbeiträge deutscher sozialistischer Schriftsteller which was compiled by the Abteilung Geschichte der Sozialistischen Literatur of the Sektion Dichtung und Sprachpflege.

Deutsche Akademie der Künste, *Berlin. Sektion Dichtkunst und Sprachpflege.*

Veröffentlichungen deutscher sozialistischer Schriftsteller in der revolutionären und demokratischen Presse 1918–1945. Bibliographie. (Bearb.: Edith Zenker. 2., durchges. Aufl.) Berlin, Weimar, Aufbau-Verl., 1969.

xvi, 657 p. 22 cm.

Based on Katalog der Zeitschriften- und Zeitungsbeiträge deutscher sozialistischer Schriftsteller which was compiled by the Abteilung Geschichte der Sozialistischen Literatur of the Sektion Dichtung und Sprachpflege.

Glenn, Jerry.

Deutsches Schrifttum der Gegenwart ⟨ab 1945⟩. Bern, München, Francke, (1971).

128 p. 24 cm. (Handbuch der deutschen Literaturgeschichte. Abt. 2: Bibliographien, Bd. 12)

Goff, Penrith.

Wilhelminisches Zeitalter. Bern, München, Francke, (1970).

216 p. 24 cm. (Handbuch der deutschen Literaturgeschichte. Abt. 2: Bibliographien, Bd. 10)

Hirschberg, Leopold, 1867–1929.

Der Taschengoedeke. Bibliographie deutscher Erstausgaben. (Verb. Ausg. nach d. von Elisabeth Friedrichs durchges. u. erg. Neudruck). (München) Deutscher Taschenbuch-Verl. (1970).

2 v. (611 p.) 18 cm. (Dtv[-Taschenbücher] Wissenschaftliche Reihe, 4030–4031)

Internationale Bibliographie zur deutschen Klassik 1750–1850. Folge 11/12– 1964/65–

Weimar, Nationale Forschungs- und Gedenkstätten der Klassischen Deutschen Literatur in Weimar.

v. 24 cm. annual. (Bibliographien Kataloge Bestandsverzeichnisse)

Issues 1–10 published in Weimarer Beiträge.

Jungbauer, Fritz.

Kleine Kunde der Interpretationen und Deutungen von Werken der deutschen Literatur. Wien, Brüder Hollinek (1966)

142 p. 20 cm.

Literatur aus der D[eutschen] D[emokratischen] R[epublik]. (Bücherverzeichnis.) [Flensburg, Büchereizentrale, 1966.]

12 p. 21 cm.

Osborne, John.

Romantik. Bern, München, Francke, (1971).

166 p. 24 cm. (Handbuch der deutschen Literaturgeschichte. Abt. 2: Bibliographien, Bd. 8)

Raabe, Paul.

Die Zeitschriften und Sammlungen des literarischen Expressionismus; Repertorium der Zeitschriften, Jahrbücher, Anthologien, Sammelwerke, Schriftenreihen und Almanache, 1910–1921. Stuttgart, J. B. Metzler [1964]

xiv, 263 p. illus. 24 cm. (Repertorien zur deutschen Literaturgeschichte, Bd. 1)

Rudnitskii, M　　**L**

Художественная литература ГДР в 1962–1969 гг. Библиогр. обзор. Москва, 1970.

128 p. 20 cm. (В помощь работникам библиотек)

At head of title: Всесоюзная государственная библиотека иностранной литературы.

Schlawe, Fritz.

Die Briefsammlungen des 19. [Neunzehnten] Jahrhunderts. Bibliographie der Briefausgaben und Gesamtregister der Briefschreiber und Briefempfänger 1815–1915. Stuttgart, Metzler, 1969–

v. 24 cm. (Repertorien zur Deutschen Literaturgeschichte, Bd. 4)

Bibliographien und Verzeichnisse im Forschungsunternehmen der Fritz Thyssen Stiftung "Neunzehntes Jahrhundert," Bd. 1.

Soffke, Günther.

Deutsches Schrifttum im Exil ⟨1933–1950⟩ Ein Bestandsverzeichnis. Bonn, Bouvier, 1965.

64 p. 23 cm. (Bonner Beiträge zur Bibliotheks- und Bücherkunde, Bd. 11)

Veröffentlichungen aus den Beständen der Universitätsbibliothek Bonn, 2.

Stadtbücherei Wilhelmshaven.

Zum Thema: Literatur in der DDR. Auswahlkatalog. Wilhelmshaven, Stadtbücherei (1970).

27 p. 30 cm.

Wilpert, Gero von.

Erstausgaben deutscher Dichtung. Eine Bibliographie zur deutschen Literatur 1600–1960. [Von] Gero von Wilpert und Adolf Gühring. Stuttgart, Kröner (1967).

ix, 1468 p. 18 cm.

TO 1700

Batts, Michael S

Hohes Mittelalter. Bern, München, Francke, (1969).

112 p. 24 cm. (Handbuch der deutschen Literaturgeschichte. Abt. 2: Bibliographien, Bd. 2)

Engel, James E

Renaissance, Humanismus, Reformation. [Von] James E. Engel. Bern, München, Francke, (1969).

80 p. 24 cm. (Handbuch der deutschen Literaturgeschichte. Abt. 2: Bibliographien, Bd. 4)

On cover: Zeitalter der Renaissance, des Humanismus und der Reformation.

Heyse, Karl Wilhelm Ludwig, 1797–1855.

Bücherschatz der deutschen Nationalliteratur des XVI. und XVII. Jahrhunderts. Systematisch geordnetes Verzeichnis einer reichhaltigen Sammlung deutscher Bücher aus dem Zeitraume vom XV. bis um die Mitte des XVIII. Jahrhunderts. Ein bibliographischer Beitrag zur deutschen Literaturgeschichte. [Von] K. W. L. Heyse. (Reprografischer Nachdruck der Ausg. Berlin, 1854.) Hildesheim, Gg. Olms, 1967.

viii, 186 p. 22 cm.

Jones, George Fenwick, 1916–

Spätes Mittelalter ⟨1300–1450⟩. [Von] George F. Jones. Bern, München, Francke, (1971).

124 p. 24 cm. (Handbuch der deutschen Literaturgeschichte. Abt. 2: Bibliographien, Bd. 3)

Merkel, Ingrid.

Barock. Bern, München, Francke, (1971).

113 p. 24 cm. (Handbuch der deutschen Literaturgeschichte. Abt. 2: Bibliographien, Bd. 5)

Otto Harrassowitz (*Firm*)
German literature of the 17th century: baroque; a list of books available. Deutsche Literatur des 17. Jahrhunderts: Barock; ein Verzeichnis lieferbarer Bücher. Wiesbaden, 1968.

109 p. 22 cm.

Cover title: Baroque: German literature of the 17th century.

BIBLIOGRAPHIES

Fleischhack, Kurt.
Bibliographisches Grundwissen, von Curt Fleischhack. 5., veränderte Aufl. Leipzig, Bibliographisches Institut ₁1964₁

104 p. illus. 22 cm.

Fleischhack, Kurt.
Bibliographisches Grundwissen. Von Curt Fleischhack. Bearb. von Gottfried Rost. 6., veränderte Aufl. Leipzig, Bibliographisches Institut (1968).

107 p. 22 cm.

Hansel, Johannes.
Personalbibliographie zur deutschen Literaturgeschichte. Studienausg. (Berlin) E. Schmidt (1967).

175 p. 21 cm.

Hansel, Johannes.
Personalbibliographie zur deutschen Literaturgeschichte; Studienausgabe von Johannes Hansel. Neubearbeitung und Fortführung von 1966 bis auf den jüngsten Stand von Carl Paschek. 2., neubearb. und erg. Aufl. ₁Berlin₁ E. Schmidt ₁1974, c1967₁

258 p. 21 cm.

Wiesner, Herbert.
Bibliographie der Personalbibliographien zur deutschen Gegenwartsliteratur. ₁Von₁ Herbert Wiesner, Irena Živsa ₁u.₁ Christoph Stoll. (Rund 1500 Personalbibliographien, Forschungsberichte, Nachlassverz. zu über 500 deutschsprachigen Autoren d. 20. Jahrhunderts.) München, Nymphenburger Verlagshandl., 1970.

858 p. 19 cm.

BIO-BIBLIOGRAPHY

Albrecht, Günter.
Lexikon deutschsprachiger Schriftsteller von den Anfängen bis zur Gegenwart ₁von₁ Günter Albrecht ₁et al. 2., überarb. Aufl.₁ Leipzig, Bibliographisches Institut, 1972–74.

2 v. 24 cm.

First ed. published in 1960 under title: Deutsches Schriftstellerlexikon.

Aufbau-Verlag, Berlin.
56 ₁i. e. Sechsundfünfzig₁ Autoren. Photos, Karikaturen, Faksimiles. (Almanach, 25 J. Aufbau-Verl.) Biographie, Bibliographie. 1945/1970. (Zsstellg u. Red.: Lektorat Zeitgenöss. Dt. Literatur. 2., veränd. Aufl. Berlin, Weimar, Aufbau-Verl. (1970).

401 p. illus., facsims. 20 cm.

Bortenschlager, Wilhelm.
Deutsche Dichtung im 20. ₁zwanzigsten₁ Jahrhundert. Strömungen—Dichter—Werke. Eine Bestandsaufnahme. Wunsiedel, Wels, Zürich, Leitner ₁1966₁.

492 p. 20 cm. (Leitners Studienhelfer für Schule und Leben)

Hamberger, Georg Christoph, 1726–1773.
Das gelehrte Teutschland oder Lexikon der jetzt lebenden teutschen Schriftsteller. Angefangen von Georg Christoph Hamberger, fortgeführt von Johann Georg Meusel. (Re-

prografischer Nachdruck der 5. Aufl., Lemgo 1796–98.) Hildesheim, Gg. Olms, 1965–

v. 18 cm.

Jördens, Karl Heinrich, 1757–1835.
Lexikon deutscher Dichter und Prosaisten, hrsg. von Karl Heinrich Jördens. Hildesheim, New York, G. Olms, 1970.

6 v. 22 cm.

Reprint of the Leipzig ed., 1806–1811.
Vol. 6: Supplemente.

Lexikon sozialistischer deutscher Literatur, von den Anfängen bis 1945; monographisch-biographische Darstellungen. ₁Redaktionskollegium: Inge Diersen, et al. 2. Aufl.₁ Leipzig, Bibliographisches Institut, 1964.

592 p. 22 cm.

"Dieses Handbuch entstand in Rahmen eines Forschungsauftrages des Germanistischen Instituts der Humboldt-Universität zu Berlin.

Mały słownik pisarzy niemieckich, austriackich i szwajcarskich. Pod red. Jana Chodery, Mieczysława Urbanowicza. ₁Wyd. 1.₁ Warszawa, Wiedza Powszechna, 1973.

407 p. ports. 21 cm.

Meusel, Johann Georg, 1743–1820.
Lexikon der vom Jahr 1750 bis 1800 verstorbenen teutschen Schriftsteller. Mit einem Geleitwort von Paul Raabe. (Reprografischer Nachdruck der Ausg. Leipzig 1802–1816. Hildesheim, G. Olms, 1967–

v. 17 cm.

Mitteldeutscher Verlag, *Halle.*
Situation 66 ₁sechsundsechzig₁ 20 Jahre Mitteldeutscher Verlag Halle ⟨Saale⟩, Verlag für neue deutsche Literatur. (Halle, ⟨Saale⟩ Mitteldeutscher Verlag) 1966.

255 p. with illus. 19 cm.

P. E. N. Zentrum Deutschsprachiger Autoren im Ausland.
Autobiographien. (Ausg. 1968.) London, (Zentrum Deutschsprachiger Autoren im Ausland) 1968.

108 p. 30 cm.

Cover title.
"Zusammengestellt von Gabriele Tergit."
Original ed. published in 1959 under title: Autobiographien und Bibliographien.

Pataky, Sophie, 1860–
Lexikon deutscher Frauen der Feder; eine Zusammenstellung der seit dem Jahre 1840 erschienenen Werke weiblicher Autoren, nebst Biographieen der lebenden und einem Verzeichnis der Pseudonyme. Hrsg. von Sophie Pataky. Bern, H. Lang, 1971.

2 v. 19 cm.

Reprint of the ed. published in Berlin by C. Pataky in 1898.

Quistorf, Hermann, 1884–
Niederdeutsches Autorenbuch ₁von₁ Hermann Quistorf ₁und₁ Johannes Sass. Hamburg, Verlag der Fehrs-Gilde, 1959.

252 p. ports. 21 cm.
Errata slip inserted.

————— Nachtrag. Hamburg, Verlag der Fehrs-Gilde, 1966.

77 p. ports. 21 cm.

Schaumann, Lore.
Düsseldorf schreibt: 44 Autorenporträts / Lore Schaumann. — Düsseldorf : Triltsch, 1974.

210 p. : ill. ; 20 cm.

Originally published in Düsseldorfer Hefte, 1973–1975.

Schmidt, Valentin Heinrich, 1756–1838.

Neuestes gelehrtes Berlin; oder literarische Nachrichten von jetzlebenden Berlinischen Schriftstellern und Schriftstellerinnen. Gesammlet und hrsg. von Valentin Heinrich Schmidt ⌊und⌋ Daniel Gottlieb Gebhard Mehring. Berlin, F. Maurer, 1795 ⌊Leipzig, Zentralantiquariat der Deutschen Demokratischen Republik, 1973⌋

2 v. 21 cm.

Continued by J. E. Hitzig's Verzeichniss im Jahre 1825 in Berlin lebender Schriftsteller und ihrer Werke, and by W. D. Koner's Gelehrtes Berlin im Jahre 1845.

Sternfeld, Wilhelm, 1888–

Deutsche Exil-Literatur 1933–1945; eine Bio-Bibliographie ⌊von⌋ Wilhelm Sternfeld ⌊und⌋ Eva Tiedemann. 2., verb. und stark erw. Aufl. Mit einem Vorwort von Hanns W. Eppelsheimer. Heidelberg, L. Schneider, 1970.

606 p. 24 cm. (Veröffentlichung der Deutschen Akademie für Sprache und Dichtung, Darmstadt ⌊29a⌋)

Wissenschaftliche Allgemeinbibliothek des Bezirkes Schwerin.

Schriftsteller des Bezirkes Schwerin. (Bibliographie) Bearb.: Heinke Bernitt, Regina Buch ⌊und⌋ Peter Tille. (Schwerin): Wissenschaftliche Allgemeinbibliothek d. Bezirkes Schwerin, 1971.

48 p. illus. 18 cm.

HISTORY AND CRITICISM

Friedrich, Wolfgang, 1926–

Einführung in die Bibliographie zur deutschen Literaturwissenschaft. Halle ⟨S.⟩ Niemeyer (1967).

115 p. 22 cm.

Istituto italiano di studi germanici, *Rome*.

Repertorio bibliografico della letteratura tedesca in Italia (1900–1965) A cura dell'Istituto italiano di studi germanici in Roma. Roma, Edizioni di Storia e letteratura, 1966–68.

2 v. 25 cm. (Sussidi eruditi, 18, 21)

Raabe, Paul.

Einführung in die Bücherkunde zur deutschen Literaturwissenschaft. Mit 13 Tabellen im Anhang. 5., verb. Aufl. Stuttgart, Metzler, 1966.

viii, 91 p. 2 inserts (in pocket) 19 cm. (Sammlung Metzler, 1. Realienbücher für Germanisten, Abt. B: Literaturwissenschaftliche Methodenlehre)

Raabe, Paul.

Einführung in die Bücherkunde zur deutschen Literaturwissenschaft. Mit 13 Tabellen im Anhang. 6., überarb. Aufl. Stuttgart, Metzler, 1969.

viii, 90 p. 2 inserts (in pocket) 19 cm. (Sammlung Metzler, 1. Realienbücher für Germanisten, Abt. B: Literaturwissenschaftliche Methodenlehre)

Raabe, Paul.

Einführung in die Bücherkunde zur deutschen Literaturwissenschaft. Mit 13 Tab. im Anh. 7., durchges. Aufl. Stuttgart, Metzler, 1971.

viii, 92 p., 2 l. (in pocket) 19 cm. (Sammlung Metzler, Bd. 1. Abt. B: Literaturwissenschaftliche Methodenlehre)

Raabe, Paul.

Einführung in die Quellenkunde zur neueren deutschen Literaturgeschichte. 2., umgearb. Aufl. des darstellenden Teils der Quellenkunde zur neueren deutschen Literaturgeschichte. Stuttgart, Metzler, 1966.

viii, 94 p. 19 cm. (Sammlung Metzler, Realienbücher für Germanisten, 21a. Abt. B: Literaturwissenschaftliche Methodenlehre) DM

Raabe, Paul.

Quellenrepertorium zur neueren deutschen Literaturgeschichte. 2., umgearb. Aufl. des quellenkundlichen Teils der Quellenkunde zur neueren deutschen Literaturgeschichte. Stuttgart, Metzler, 1966.

112 p. 19 cm. (Sammlung Metzler, Realienbücher für Germanisten, 21b; Abt. B: Literaturwissenschaftliche Methodenlehre)

Schmitt, Franz Anselm.

Stoff- und Motivgeschichte der deutschen Literatur; eine Bibliographie. Begründet von Kurt Bauerhorst. 2. neubearb. und stark erweiterte Aufl. ⌊Berlin⌋ De Gruyter, 1965.

xvi, 332 p. 25 cm.

First published in 1959, superseding the 1932 Bibliographie der Stoff und Motivgeschichte der deutschen Literatur, by K. Bauerhorst.

Winter, Jutta.

Tausend Titel zur deutschen Literaturgeschichte. Aus der Stadtbibliothek Hannover. (Zusammenstellung: Jutta Winter und Ingrid Hecht. Redaktion: Herta Dürr) (Hannover, Stadtbibliothek, 1965)

86 p. 24 cm.

LIBRARY AND EXHIBITION CATALOGS.

Brussels. Deutsche Bibliothek.

Deutsche Literatur. Littérature allemande. Duitse literatuur. Katalog. Brüssel, Deutsche Bibliothek, Goethe-Institut, r. Belliard, 58, (1970).

xvii, 188 p. 30 cm.

Introductory matter in Dutch, French and German.

Frankfurt am Main. Deutsche Bibliothek.

Exil-Literatur, 1933–1945. Ausstellung, Mai bis August 1965. ⌊Ausstellung und Katalog: Werner Berthold; Mitarbeiterin: Christa Wilhelmi. Frankfurt am Main, 1965⌋

324 p. illus., facsims., ports. 21 cm. (*Its* Sonderveröffentlichungen, Nr. 1)

"Aus den Beständen ... der Sondersammlung Deutsche Exil-Literatur 1933–1945."

Frankfurt am Main. Deutsche Bibliothek.

Exil-Literatur 1933–1945 ⌊neunzehnhundertdreiunddreissig bis neunzehnhundertfünfundvierzig⌋ Eine Ausstellung aus Beständen der Deutschen Bibliothek. Frankfurt a. M. ⟨Sammlung Exil-Literatur⟩. (Katalog: Werner Berthold. Mitarbeiterin: Christa Wilhelmi. 2. Aufl. ⌊Ausstellungskatalog.⌋) (Frankfurt A. M., Buchhändler-Vereinigung in Kommission, 1966.)

324 p., illus. 21 cm. (Sonderveröffentlichungen der Deutschen Bibliothek, Nr. 1.)

"Ausstellung vom 7. Mai bis 2. Juni 1966, Rijksmuseum Meermanno-Westreenianum/Museum van het Boek, 's-Gravenhage.

Frankfurt am Main. Deutsche Bibliothek.

Exil-Literatur 1933–1945 ⌊neunzehnhundertdreiunddreissig bis neunzehnhundertfünfundvierzig⌋. Eine Ausstellung aus Beständen der Deutschen Bibliothek, Frankfurt am Main ⟨Sammlung Exil-Literatur.⟩ (Katalog: Werner Berthold. Mitarbeiterinnen: Christa Wilhelmi und Gudrun Anschütz. 3., erw. und verb. Aufl. ⌊Ausstellungskatalog.⌋) (⌊Frankfurt a. M., Verlag der Buchhändler-Vereinigung in Kommission⌋ 1967.)

352 p., 40 p. of illus. 22 cm. (Sonderveröffentlichungen der Deutschen Bibliothek, Nr. 1)

Leeds, Eng. University. *Brotherton Library.*

Catalogue of an exhibition of German books and periodicals from the Library's collections, by E. Langstadt. Leeds, University of Leeds, 1968.

54 p. 26 cm.

Marbach, Ger. Schiller-Nationalmuseum. Deutsches Literaturarchiv.

Gestalten und Begegnungen; deutsche Literatur seit dem Ausgang des 19. Jahrhunderts. ₍Ausstellung und Katalog: Bernhard Zeller in Zusammenarbeit mit den Archivaren und Bibliothekaren des Deutschen Literaturarchivs. Stuttgart, Druck: Turmhaus-Druckerei, 1964₎

199 p. illus., facsims., ports. 21 cm. (Sonderausstellungen des Schiller-Nationalmuseums, Katalog Nr. 13)

Marbach, Ger. Schiller-Nationalmuseum. Handschriftenabteilung.

Nachlässe und Sammlungen in der Handschriftenabteilung des Schiller-Nationalmuseums und des Deutschen Literaturarchivs. Ein Verz. Marbach a. Neckar (Deutsches Literaturarchiv; ₍zu beziehen: Marbach a. Neckar, Deutsche Schillergesellschaft₎) 1972.

93 p. 21 cm. (Deutsches Literaturarchiv. Verzeichnisse, Berichte, Informationen, 1)

Stern, Desider.

Bücher von Autoren jüdischer Herkunft in deutscher Sprache. Eine Ausstellung der B'nai B'rith Wien, 5.–14. März 1967 im Künstlerhaus, Wien. (Ausstellungsleitung und Katalog: Desider Stern. Arbeitsausschuss: Leopold Ehrlich-Hichler ₍u. a.₎ Ausstellungsgestaltung: Ernst Toch. Herausgeber: B'nai B'rith. Wien, 1967)

247 p. 17 cm.

Stern, Desider.

Werke von Autoren jüdischer Herkunft in deutscher Sprache. Eine Bio-Bibliographie. (Eine Ausstellung d. B'nai B'rith, 27. April—14. Mai 1969 in d. Universitätsbibliothek Frankfurt/M. 2., rev. u. bedeutend erw. Aufl.) (₍München₎ B'nai B'rith ₍Zentralbüro₎ Frankfurt a. M., Frankfurter Bücherstube Schumann u. Cobet in Komm.₎ 1969.)

407 p. 20 cm.
Cover title: Werke jüdischer Autoren deutscher Sprache.
First ed. published in 1967 under title: Bücher von Autoren jüdischer Herkunft in deutscher Sprache.

Stern, Desider.

Werke von Autoren jüdischer Herkunft in deutscher Sprache. (Eine Bio-Bibliographie.) Sonderausg. d. 3. Aufl. 1970 f. B'nai B'rith Loge Wien. Enthält zusätzlich … einen Bericht über die B'nai B'rith-Buchausstellung Wien, Künstlerhaus, 5. bis 14. Mai 1967. ₍A–1010₎ Wien, Wollzeile 20, Stern (1970).

8 l., 455 p. 20 cm.

First ed. published in 1967 under title: Bücher von Autoren jüdischer Herkunft in deutscher Sprache.

Yale University. *Library. Yale Collection of German Literature.*

German Baroque literature; a catalogue of the collection in the Yale University Library by Curt von Faber du Faur, curator of the German Literature Collection. New Haven, Yale University Press, 1958–69.

2 v. illus., facsims. 26 cm. (Bibliographical series from the Yale University Library collections)

PERIODICALS

Marbach, Ger. Schiller-Nationalmuseum. Deutsches Literaturarchiv.

Literarische Zeitschriften und Jahrbücher: 1880–1970. Verz. d. im Dt. Literaturarchiv erschlossenen Periodica/ ₍bearb. von Dagmar Laakmann u. Reinhard Tgahrt. Hrsg. vom Dt. Literaturarchiv₎. — Marbach (am Neckar): Dt. Literaturarchiv, 1972.

227 p.; 21 cm. — (Its Verzeichnisse, Berichte, Informationen, 2)

TRANSLATIONS

Morgan, Bayard Quincy, 1883–

A critical bibliography of German literature in English translation, 1481–1927. 2d ed., completely rev. and greatly augm. New York, Scarecrow Press, 1965 ₍°1938₎

690 p. 23 cm.
First published in 1922 under title: A bibliography of German literature in English translation.

———— ———— Supplement embracing the years 1928–1955. New York, Scarecrow Press, 1965.

vii, 601 p. 22 cm.

Smith, Murray F 1931–

A selected bibliography of German literature in English translation, 1956–1960, by Murray F. Smith. Metuchen, N. J., Scarecrow Press, 1972.

v, 398 p. 22 cm.
A second supplement to Bayard Quincy Morgan's A critical bibliography of German literature in English translation, first published in 1922 under title: A bibliography of German literature in English translation.
Originally presented as the author's thesis, University of Southern California, 1968.

Wrzeciono, Maria.

Literatura niemiecka w Polsce; bibliografia, 1945–1958. Opracowała Maria Wrzeciono. Poznań, 1966.

219 p. 30 cm. (Uniwersytet im Adama Mickiewicza w Poznaniu. Prace Wydziału Filologicznego. Seriafilologia germańska, nr. 2)
Added t. p.: Deutsche Literatur in Polen; Bibliographie, 1945–1958.
Prefatory matter and table of contents also in German.

GERMAN PERIODICALS see Periodical publications - Germany

GERMAN POETRY see Poetry - Germany

GERMANIC PHILOLOGY

Diesch, Carl Hermann, 1880–1957.

Bibliographie der germanistischen Zeitschriften. Neudr. ₍d. Ausg.₎ ⟨1927⟩. Stuttgart, Hiersemann, 1970.

xi, 441 p. 28 cm. (Bibliographical Publications. Germanic section, Modern Language Association of America, v. 1)

Seymour, Richard K

A bibliography of word formation in the Germanic languages ₍by₎ Richard K. Seymour. Durham, N. C., Duke University Press, 1968.

xv, 158 p. 24 cm.

GERMANIC TRIBES

Berlin. Universität. *Institut für Ur- und Frühgeschichte.*

Bibliographie zur archäologischen Germanenforschung. Deutschsprachige Literatur 1941–1955. Hrsg. vom Institut für Ur- und Frühgeschichte der Humboldt-Universität zu Berlin. Berlin, VEB Deutscher Verlag der Wissenschaften, 1966.

220 p. 24 cm.

GERMANS IN FOREIGN COUNTRIES

Colóquio de Estudos Teuto-Brasileiros, *2d, Recife, 1968.*

Catálogo da Exposição Bibliográfica do II Colóquio de Estudos Teuto-Brasileiro, realizada no Recife, de 4 a 10 de abril de 1968. Recife, Universidade Federal de Pernambuco, 1968.

4 l. 32 cm.

Kräenbring, Artur.

Bibliographie über das Bessarabiendeutschtum. Hannover, Hilfskomitee d. Ev.-Luth. Kirche aus Bessarabien, 1970.

48 p. 21 cm. (Hilfskomitee der ev.-luth. Kirche aus Bessarabien

e. V. Schriftenreihe des Referates Film und Bild und des Referates Presse, Bd. 3)

Kuhn, Dorothea.
Auch ich in Arcadien. Kunstreisen nach Italien 1600–1900. (Eine Ausstellung im Schiller-Nationalmuseum, Marbach a. N. vom 14. Mai–31. Okt. 1966. Katalog: Dorothea Kuhn unter Mitarbeit von Anneliese Hofmann und Anneliese Kunz. Ausstellungskatalog. 2. Aufl.) (Marbach a N., Schiller-Nationalmuseum, 1966.)

288 p. with illus. 21 cm. (Sonderausstellung des Schiller-Nationalmuseums. Katalog Nr. 16.)

Meynen, Emil, 1902–
Bibliographie des Deutschtums der Kolonialzeitlichen Einwanderung in Nordamerika, insbesondere der Pennsylvanien-Deutschen und ihrer nachkommen, 1683–1933. Zusammengestellt und hrsg. von Emil Meynen. Leipzig, O. Harrassowitz, 1937. ₁Detroit, Republished by Gale Research Co., 1966₁

xxxvi, 636 p. 24 cm.

Added t. p.: Bibliography on German settlements in colonial North America, especially on the Pennsylvania Germans and their descendants, 1683–1933.

Stumpp, Karl.
Das Schrifttum über das Deutschtum in Russland. Eine Bibliographie. 3., erneut erw. Aufl. Tübingen, Autenriethstr. 16, Selbstverlag, 1971.

viii, 77 p. 24 cm.

Südmährischer Landschaftsrat.
Vollständiges Verzeichnis der Büchereien des Südmähr. Landschaftrates und des Kreises Znaim. Zusammengestellt von Emmy Kreuss. Stand vom 31. März 1968. Geislingen/Steige, Verlag des Südmähr. Landschaftsrates ₁1968?₁

90 p. 21 cm.

GERMANY
see also Communism - Germany

Bibliographie fremdsprachiger Germanica. Jahrg. 1–1972–
Leipzig, Verlag für Buch- und Bibliothekswesen.

v. 21 cm. quarterly.

Issued by Deutsche Bücherei.

La Civilisation allemande, guide bibliographique et pratique. Hans Manfred Bock ... Gilbert Krebs ... Jean-François Tournadre ... Bernd Witte ... Paris, A. Colin, 1971.

384 p. 17 cm. (Collection U2, 178. Série Études allemandes) (Synthèses)

Deutsche Gesellschaft für Auswärtige Politik. *Forschungsinstitut.*
Schrifttum über Deutschland, 1918–1963; ausgewählte Bibliographie zur Politik und Zeitgeschichte. Bearb. vom Forschungsinstitut der Deutschen Gesellschaft für Auswärtige Politik für Inter Nationes. 2. erweiterte Aufl. Bonn ₁1964₁

292 p. 21 cm.

Previous ed. prepared by Inter Nationes and published under title: Schrifttum über Deutschland, 1918–1962.

Deutschlandstudien. ₁Bonn-Bad Godesberg₁ Deutscher Akademischer Austauschdienst ₁1972?₁–

v. 24 cm.

English, 1948–1964. 2d rev. ed. Göttingen, Vandenhoeck & Ruprecht, 1968.

500 p. 24 cm. (Translations from the German, no. 1)

Germany (*Federal Republic, 1949–*) *Bundestag. Wissenschaftliche Abteilung.*
Die internationale Vertretung Deutschlands nach 1945; Auswahlbibliographie. Bonn, 1967.

52 p. 30 cm. (*Its* Bibliographien, Nr. 9)

"Die Bibliographie wurde in Referat Fachdokumentation von Herrn Diplom-Volkwirt Günter Hindrichs ... zusammengestellt."

Inter Nationes.
Dokumentationen über Deutschland: Auswahl amtlicher und von amtlicher Seite geförderter Publikationen. Bearb. von Inter Nationes, Bonn. ₁Verantwortlich für den Inhalt: Helmut Arntz₁ 2., neu bearb. Aufl. ₁Bonn, 1964₁

198 p. 21 cm.

"Von ... Edith Teige ... in der Sektion Dokumentation von Inter Nationes erstellt worden."
The 1st ed. was included in the agency's Schrifttum über Deutschland, 1918–1962, published in 1962.

Radvansky, Susan.
German culture in the libraries of Melbourne: the State Library of Victoria; Baillieu Library, University of Melbourne; German Dept. Library, University of Melbourne; Monash University Library ₁by₁ Susan Radvansky and Leslie Bodi. ₁Melbourne₁ German Section, Dept. of Modern Languages, Monash University, 1967.

vii, 536 p. 25 x 29 cm.

Richter, Paul Emil, 1844–1918.
Bibliotheca geographica Germaniae: Litteratur der Landes- und Volkskunde des Deutschen Reichs. Bearb. im Auftrage der Zentral-Kommission für Wissenschaftliche Landeskunde von Deutschland. New York, B. Franklin ₁1969₁

x, 841 p. 24 cm. (Burt Franklin: bibliography and reference series, 88)

Reprint of the ed. published in Leipzig by W. Engelmann in 1896.

Sarkowski, Heinz, 1925–
Der Insel-Verlag. Eine Bibliographie, 1899–1969. Bearb. und hrsg. von Heinz Sarkowski. (Mit 231, teils farb. Abb.) (Frankfurt a. M.) Insel-Verl. (1970).

x, 677 p. illus. 21 cm.

Slass, Adam.
Pionierbibliographie. (München, Pionierschule, Fachbibliothek) 1966.

xii, 426 p. 30 cm.

At head of title: Pionierschule München, Fachbibliothek.

Translations from the German; a series of bibliographies edited by Richard Mönnig. Göttingen, Vandenhoeck & Ruprecht, 1968–

v. 24 cm.

BIBLIOGRAPHIES

Schüling, Hermann.
Bibliographischer Wegweiser zu dem in Deutschland erschienenen Schrifttum des 17. Jahrhunderts. Giessen, Universitätsbibliothek, 1964.

vi, 176 p. 23 cm. (Berichte und Arbeiten aus der Universitätsbibliothek Giessen, 4)

FOREIGN RELATIONS

Carlson, Andrew R
German foreign policy, 1890–1914, and colonial policy to 1914; a handbook and annotated bibliography, by Andrew R. Carlson. Metuchen, N. J., Scarecrow Press ₁1970₁

vii, 333 p. maps. 22 cm.

Jäger, Eckhard.
Die deutsch-französischen Beziehungen im Spiegel der DDR-Literatur. Les relations franco-allemandes dans la littérature de la RDA. Eine Bibliographie. Zusammengestellt und eingeleitet von Eckhard Jäger. Lüneburg (Ost-Akademie) 1968.

60 p. 18 cm. (Deutsche Studien. Schirften der Ost-Akademie Lüneburg)

Introductory matter in French and German.

Riesser, Hans Eduard, 1887–
Aussenpolitische Memoiren, Aufzeichnungen und Briefe deutscher Staatsoberhäupter, Reichs-, Bundeskanzler, Aussenminister und Angehöriger des Auswärtigen Amtes. Eine Bibliographie als Beitrag zur Geschichte des Auswärtigen Amtes und der auswärtigen Politik von Bismarck bis Adenauer. 4. (verb. und erw.) Fassung. (Von) Hans E. Riesser. Bonn, Bouvier in Kommission, 1966.

15 p. 21 cm.

GENEALOGY

Stammfolgen-Verzeichnisse für das Genealogische Handbuch des Adels, Bände 1–35, und das Deutsche Geschlechterbuch, alte Reihe Bände 1–19, neue Reihe Bände 120–140. Limburg/Lahn, C. A. Starke (1966)

xx, 224 p. (p. 216–224 advertisements) 17 cm.

HISTORY

Baumgart, Winfried.
Bücherverzeichnis zur deutschen Geschichte. Hilfsmittel, Handbücher, Quellen. (Frankfurt/M., Berlin, Wien, Ullstein, 1971.)

195 p. 18 cm. (Deutsche Geschichte, 14) (Ullstein-Bücher. Nr. 3856)

Based on the author's Bibliographie zum Studium der neueren Geschichte.

Conway, John S
German historical source material in United States universities, by J. S. Conway. Pittsburgh, Pa., Council for European Studies, 1973.

ii, 23 p. 28 cm. (Council for European Studies. Occasional papers series)

Devoto, Andrea.
Bibliografia dell'oppressione nazista fino al 1962. Firenze, L. S. Olschki, 1964.

ix, 149 p. 21 cm.

Germany (Federal Republic, 1949–   ). Bundesarchiv.
Findbücher zu Beständen des Bundesarchivs. Koblenz, 1970–

v. 24 cm.

Germany (*Federal Republic, 1949–   ) Bundesministerium für Gesamtdeutsche Fragen.*
Literatur zur deutschen Frage. Bibliographische Hinweise auf neuere Veröffentlichungen aus dem In- und Auslande. (Bearb. im Büro Bonner Berichte von Günter Fischbach. 4. überarb. und erw. Aufl. Bonn, Deutscher Bundes-Verlag (in Kommission) 1966)

323 p. 21 cm.

Hochmuth, Ursel, 1931–
Faschismus und Widerstand 1933–1945; ein Verzeichnis deutschsprachiger Literatur. Bearb. von Ursel Hochmuth. Frankfurt/Main, Röderberg (c1973)

107 p. 21 cm. (Bibliothek des Widerstandes)

Ménudier, Henri.
L'Allemagne après 1945. Paris, A. Colin (1972)

225 p. 19 cm. (Bibliographies françaises de sciences sociales. Guides de recherches, 4)

Neufforge, Ernst Ferdinand, Baron von.
Über den Versuch einer deutschen Bibliothek als Spiegel deutscher Kulturentwicklung, von Ferdinand Baron von Neufforge. (Niederwalluf bei Wiesbaden) M. Sändig (1970)

612 p. 22 cm.

Reprint of the Berlin ed. published by G. Lüttke in 1940.

Oberschelp, Reinhard.
Die Bibliographien zur deutschen Landesgeschichte und Landeskunde im 19. und 20. Jahrhundert. Frankfurt a. M., Klostermann (1967)

102 p. 24 cm. (Zeitschrift für Bibliothekswesen und Bibliographie. Sonderheft 7)

Picht, Robert.
Kommentierte Bibliographie — Deutschland nach 1945, zusammengestellt von Robert Picht. (Bonn-Bad Godesberg) Deutscher Akademischer Austauschdienst (1972?)

259 p. 24 cm. (Deutschlandstudien, 1)

Rich, Norman.
Germany, 1815–1914. Washington, Service Center for Teachers of History (1968)

43 p. 23 cm. (Service Center for Teachers of History. Publication no. 73)

Rohlach, Peter P
Novemberrevolution 1918 (i. e. neunzehnhundertachtzehn). Zum 50. Jahrestag am 9. Nov. (Zusammengestellt von Peter P. Rohlach u. Ewald Birr.) (Berlin) Berliner Stadtbibliothek, 1968.

82 p. 21 cm. (Bibliographische Kalenderblätter. Sonderblatt 23)

Stokes, Lawrence D
Medieval and Reformation Germany (to 1648): a select bibliography, by Lawrence D. Stokes. London, Historical Association, 1972.

(1), 67 p. 22 cm. Index. (Helps for students of history, no. 84)

Walther, Philipp Alexander Ferdinand, 1812–1887.
Systematisches Repertorium über die Schriften sämmtlicher historischer Gesellschaften Deutschlands. Auf veranlassung des Historischen Vereins für das Grossherzogthum Hessen bearb. von Ph. A. F. Walther. New York, B. Franklin (1969)

xxix, 649 p. 23 cm. (Burt Franklin bibliography & reference series, 245)

Reprint of the ed. published in Darmstadt by G. Jonghaus in 1845.

Wentzcke, Paul, 1879–1960.
Kritische Bibliographie der Flugschriften zur deutschen Verfassungsfrage 1848–1851. (Reprografischer Nachdruck der Ausg. Halle 1911.) Hildesheim, Gg. Olms, 1967.

xxi, 313 p. 22 cm.

Wiener Library, *London.*
From Weimar to Hitler: Germany, 1918–1933. 2d, rev. and enl. ed. London, Published for the Wiener Library by Vallentine, Mitchell, 1964.

x, 268 p. 23 cm. (*Its* Catalogue series, no. 2)

IMPRINTS see German imprints
LAW see Law – Germany
MAPS

Klaus, Wolfram.
Grossmassstäbliche Karten vom Gebiet der DDR ⟨1599–

1945.⟩ Berlin, Deutsche Staatsbibliothek, 1972.

x, 139 p. 21 cm. (Kartographische Bestandsverzeichnisse der Deutschen Staatsbibliothek, 1)

Stopp, Klaus.
Maps of Germany with marginal town views, by K. Stopp. London, Map Collectors' Circle, 1967.

21 p. 22 maps. 25 cm. (Map collectors' series, no. 35)

GERMANY, EAST

Blos, Gisela.
Befreiung vom Faschismus. ₍Zum 25. Jahrestag der Befreiung des deutschen Volkes vom Faschismus am 8. Mai 1970 erarbeitet von Gisela Blos, Horst Kaiser und Peter P. Rohrlach₎ ₍Berlin₎ Berliner Stadtbibliothek, 1970.

106 p. 22 cm. (Bibliographische Kalenderblätter. Sonderblatt, 27)

Bibliographie zu den Thesen "20 Jahre Deutsche Demokratische Republik." (Berlin) Berliner Stadtbibliothek, 1969.

121 p. 21 cm. (Bibliographische Kalenderblätter. Sonderblatt 25)

Bonn. Archiv für Gesamtdeutsche Fragen.
Zusammenstellung der von der "Deutschen Demokratischen Republik" seit deren Gründung ⟨7. Oktober 1949⟩ abgeschlossenen internationalen Verträge und Vereinbarungen. Zusammengestellt von Lothar Kapsa. (5. Aufl. Stand: November 1967.) Bonn ₍1967₎

vii, 232 p. 21 cm.

—— ——Ergänzungsheft zur 5. Aufl. (Dezember 1967

Stand: 31.12.1970–
Als Ms. vervielf. Hrsg. vom Gesamtdt. Inst., Bundesanst.

f. Gesamtdt. Aufgaben. ₍Bonn-Bad Godesberg: Gesamtdt. Inst., Bundesanst. f. Gesamtdt. Aufgaben, 1971–

v. 21 cm.

Germany (Democratic Republic, 1949–). Staatliche Archivverwaltung.
Taschenbuch Archivwesen der D₍eutschen₎ D₍emokratischen₎ R₍epublik₎. Hrsg. v. d. Staatl. Archivverwaltung d. Ministeriums d. Innern d. DDR. (Verantw. Red.: Eberhard Schetelich.) Berlin, Staatsverl. d. Deutschen Demokratischen Republik, 1971.

304 p., 16 l. of illus. 22 cm.

Hanover. Niedersächsische Landesbibliothek.
Katalog des Schrifttums über den deutschen Osten. Hannover, 1956–68 ₍v. 1, 1958₎

5 v. 30 cm.

Contents.—1. Ostpreussen und Westpreussen. Stand vom 31. 12. 1957.—2. Schlesien. Stand vom 1. 4. 1956.—3. Verzeichnis der Schriften über Pommern. Stand vom 31.12.1963.—4. Verzeichnis der Schriften über Ostbrandenburg und die Grenzmark Posen-Westpreussen. Stand vom 31.12.1965.—5. Register zu Band 1 bis 4.

Knauthe, Erhart.
Verzeichnis ausgewählter laufender Literatur über die Volkswirtschaft der Deutschen Demokratischen Republik. Compiled by Erhart Knauthe, edited by Karl W. Roskamp. Detroit, Dept. of Economics, Wayne State University, 1967.

13 l. 29 cm.

Kučerová, Božena.
Hospodářská reforma v NDR. Výběr literatury. Sest. B. Kučerová. Praha, St. knihovna ČSR-Ústř. ekon. knihovna, rozmn., 1972.

₍2₎, 147, ₍1₎ l. 20 cm.

Leipzig. Stadt- und Bezirksbibliothek.
Unser Staat, unser Stolz. (Auswahlbibliographie. Erarb. von einer Arbeitsgruppe unter Leitg. von Christa Wolff und Gisela Piater.) Leipzig, 1969.

2 v. 21 cm.

Price, Arnold Hereward, 1912–
East Germany, a selected bibliography, compiled by Arnold H. Price, Slavic and Central European Division, Reference Dept. Washington, Library of Congress; ₍for sale by the Supt. of Docs., U. S. Govt. Print. Off.₎ 1967.

viii, 133 p. 26 cm.

GERMANY, WEST

Bermbach, Udo.
Hamburger Bibliographie zum parlamentarischen System der Bundesrepublik Deutschland 1945–1970. Hrsg. v. Udo Bermbach. Wiss. Red.: Falk Esche ₍u. a.₎ Opladen, Westdeutscher Verl., 1973.

viii, 629 p. 24 cm.

Deutscher Industrie- und Handelstag.
DIHT-Meinung 1971; eine Auswahl aus den DIHT-Nachrichten und DIHT-Informationen im Jahre 1971. ₍Bonn₎ Deutscher Industrie- und Handelstag ₍1971₎

80 p. 21 cm. (DIHT Schriftenreihe, Heft 128)

Germany (Federal Republic, 1949–). Bundesstelle für Aussenhandelsinformation.
Publikationsspiegel. Köln ₍1971₎

40 p. 30 cm.

Germany (Federal Republic, 1949–). Bundestag. Wissenschaftliche Abteilung.
Gesetze zur Änderung des Grundgesetzes (Nr. 1 bis 26) Bonn, 1970.

14 p. 30 cm. (Its Materialien, Nr. 15)

Lohse, Eva-Maria.
Planung in Politik und Verwaltung in der Bundesrepublik Deutschland. Bonn, 1972.

i, 96, 2 p. 30 cm. (Deutscher Bundestag. Wissenschaftliche Dienste. Bibliographien, Nr. 30)

Price, Arnold Hereward, 1912–
The Federal Republic of Germany; a selected bibliography of English-language publications, with emphasis on the social sciences, compiled by Arnold H. Price, Slavic and Central European Division. Washington, Library of Congress; ₍for sale by the Supt. of Docs., U. S. Govt. Print. Off.₎ 1972.

ix, 63 p. 26 cm.

Richter, Erich.
Alphabetisches Verzeichnis der vom Bundesministerium für Wirtschaft herausgegebenen laufenden Veröffentlichungen. Bonn ₍Bibliothek des Bundesministeriums für Wirtschaft₎ 1967.

x, 46 p. 25 cm.

Schindler, Peter, 1938–
Der Deutsche Bundestag; Auswahlbibliographie. Bonn, Wissenschaftliche Abteilung des Deutschen Bundestages, 1966.

132 p. 30 cm. (Wissenschaftliche Abteilung des Deutschen Bundestages. Bibliographien, Nr. 6)

Wolfsburg, Ger. Stadtbücherei.
Westdeutschland, ein Reiseland; Buchverzeichnis. Zusammengestellt von Brigitte Herborg. ₍Wolfsburg₎ 1965.

50 p. 21 cm. (Kataloge der Stadtbücherei Wolfsburg, Nr. 29)

GERONTOLOGY
see also Aged

Akademie van Wetenschappen, Amsterdam. Sociaal-Weten-schappelijke Raad.
Register van sociaal-gerontologisch onderzoek 1945–1964. Amsterdam, Noord-Hollandsche U. M., 1966.

xxix, 202 p. 24 cm.

Balkema, John B
A general bibliography on aging, compiled by John B. Balkema. Washington, National Council on the Aging, 1972.

52 p. 28 cm.

"Covers the years 1967–1972."

Beregi, Edit.
A gerontologia és geriatria válogatott bibliográfiája. Budapest, Országos Orvostudományi Könyvtár és Dokumentációs Központ, 1967.

83 p. 29 cm.

Brown, Myrtle Irene.
Nursing care of the aged; an annotated bibliography for nurses. Arlington, Va., U. S. Dept. of Health, Education, and Welfare, Adult Health Protection and Aging Branch; [for sale by the Supt. of Docs., U. S. Govt. Print. Off., 1967]

ix, 131 p. 26 cm. (Public Health Service publication no. 1603)

Authors: Myrtle Irene Brown, Priscilla Holmes Basson, and Dorothy Ellen Burchett.

Canada. Parliament. Library.
Canadian books, pamphlets, and documents on gerontology in the Library of Parliament, compiled by the reference staff. Articles on aging indexed in Canadian periodical index, 1948–1965, excerpted by Joan O'Rourke. Ottawa, Canadian Library Association, 1966.

46, 10 p. 28 cm. (Canadian Library Association. Occasional paper no. 64)

Ciompi, Luc.
Geronto-psychiatric literature in the postwar period; a review of the literature to January 1, 1965, by L. Ciompi. Chevy Chase, Md., U. S. National Institute of Mental Health; [for sale by the Supt. of Docs., U. S. Govt. Print. Off., Washington, 1969]

vi, 97 p. 27 cm. (Public Health Service publication no. 1811)

"Translated from Fortschritte der Neurologie, Psychiatrie und Ihrer Grenzgebiete (Stüttgart), 34(2): 40–159, 1966."

Kellam, Constance E
A literary bibliography on aging, by Constance E. Kellam. New York, Council on Social Work Education [c1968]

viii, 49 p. 23 cm.

Müller, Christian, 1921–
Bibliographia gerontopsychiatrica. Bibliography of geriatric psychiatry. Geronto-psychiatrische Bibliographie. Bibliographie géronto-psychiatrique. Ed.: C. Müller. Bern, H. Huber [c1973]

448 p. 23 cm.

Introduction in English, French, and German.

Ontario. Office on Aging.
Bibliography on aging and religion and aging. Prepared for the Conference on Aging and Its Implications for Theological Colleges and Training Schools. Toronto, 1968.

26 l. 29 cm.

United States. Dept. of Health, Education, and Welfare. Library.
Words on aging: a bibliography of selected annotated references, compiled for the Administration on Aging. Washington, U. S. Administration on Aging; [for sale by the Supt. of Docs., U. S. Govt. Print. Off., 1970]

vi, 190 p. 24 cm. (AoA publication no. 216–A)

—— More words on aging. Supplement. Washington, U. S. Administration on Aging, 1971.

vi, 107 p. 24 cm. (AoA publication no. 216–S)

U. S. Office of Aging.
Selected references on aging. no. 1–8; Sept. 1962–May 1965. [Washington, U. S. Govt. Print. Off.]

8 no. 27 cm.

No. for Aug. published as its OA.
Issues for Apr.–Nov. 1963 not numbered.
Some no. also in rev. editions.
No. for Sept.–Nov. 1962 issued by the office under its earlier name: Special Staff on Aging, Dept. of Health, Education, and Welfare.

GERSON, JOANNES

Gerz-von Büren, Veronika.
La Tradition de l'œuvre de Jean Gerson chez les chartreux: la chartreuse de Bâle [par] Veronika Gerz-von Büren. Paris, Éditions du C. N. R. S., 1973.

149 p. and table of contents (1 l.) 31 cm. (Institut de recherche et d'histoire des textes. Bibliographies, colloques, travaux préparatoires)

GEYL, PIETER

Hees, P van.
Bibliografie van P. Geyl. Samengesteld door P. van Hees. Groningen, Wolters-Noordhoff, 1972.

128 p. 24 cm. (Historische studies, 28)

Errata slip inserted.

GFELLER, SIMON

Grandjean-Wyder, Christine.
Bibliographie der gedruckten Werke von Simon Gfeller. Diplomarbeit der Vereinigung schweizerischer Bibliothekare. [Bern] 1972.

ii, xii, 49 l. 30 cm.

GHĀLIB

Qaiṣar, Ibn Ḥasan, 1909–

غالب لما؛ يعني، مرزا اسداللہ خان غالب ہر ۱۹۳۴ء سے
۱۹۶۸ء تک پاکستان رسائل و جراند میں شائع شدہ مضامین کا
وضاحتی اشاریہ۔ مرتبہ سید ابن حسن قیصر۔ کراچی، ادارۂ یادگار
غالب، ۱۹۶۹۔

8, 148 p. 22 cm.

In Urdu.

"اشاعت کی تقریب—غالب کی صد سالہ برسی۔"

GHANA
see also under Dissertations, Academic

Adams, Cynthia, 1939–
A study guide for Ghana; [a bibliography] [Boston, Boston University, African Studies Center, Development Program] 1967.

iii l., 95 p. 28 cm.

Aguolu, Christian Chukwunedu, 1940–
Ghana in the humanities and social sciences, 1900–1971: a bibliography. Metuchen, N. J., Scarecrow Press, 1973.

xi, 469 p. 22 cm.

Amedekey, E   Y
The culture of Ghana; a bibliography ₍by₎ E. Y. Amedekey. Accra, Published for the University of Ghana by Ghana Universities Press, 1970.

xii, 215 p. 25 cm.

"Part of this bibliography which was entitled 'The cultural history of the Akans' was accepted by the University of London in part fulfilment of the requirements for the diploma in librarianship."

Cardinall, Allan Wolsey, 1887–
A bibliography of the Gold Coast, by A. W. Cardinall. Westport, Conn., Negro Universities Press ₍1970₎

xix, 384 p. 23 cm.

Reprint of the 1932 ed. issued as a companion vol. to the census report of 1931.

Ghana. ₍n. p., 1968₎

28 l. 29 cm.

Ghana. Bureau of Ghana Languages.
Bibliography of works in Ghana languages. ₍Accra₎ 1967.

iii, 161 p. 32 cm.

Ghana national bibliography. 1965–
Accra, Ghana Library Board.

v. 22 cm. annual.

Compiled at the Research Library on African Affairs of the Ghana Library Board.

Ghana Publishing Corporation.
Government publications price list, 1969. Accra ₍1970₎

23 p. 19 cm.

Johnson, Albert Frederick.
A bibliography of Ghana, 1930–1961, compiled by A. F. Johnson. ₍Accra₎ Published for the Ghana Library Board by Longmans, 1964.

xiii, 210 p. 23 cm.

Johnson, Albert Frederick.
A bibliography of Ghana, 1930–1961, compiled by A. F. Johnson. ₍Evanston, Ill.₎ Published for the Ghana Library Board by Northwestern University Press, 1964.

xiii, 210 p. 23 cm.

Kotei, S   I   A
Selected annotated bibliography of Ghana. Compiled by: S. I. A. Kotei. Accra, Padmore Research Library on African Affairs, 1965.

46 p. 34 cm. (Bibliography series) (Special subject bibliography no. 5)

Caption title.

Witherell, Julian W
Ghana; a guide to official publications, 1872–1968. Compiled by Julian W. Witherell and Sharon B. Lockwood, African Section. Washington, General Reference and Bibliography Division, Library of Congress; ₍for sale by the Supt. of Docs., U. S. Govt. Print. Off.₎ 1969.

xi, 110 p. 26 cm.

GHENT

Archives communales de Gand.
Bedrijfsarchieven op het Stadsarchief van Gent; inventaris van de fondsen De Hemptinne en Voortman ₍door₎ H. Coppejans-Desmedt. Leuven, Nauwelaerts, 1971.

52 p. 25 cm. (Interuniversitair Centrum voor Hedendaagse Geschiedenis. Bijdragen, 67)

GHICA, ION

Biblioteca Municipală Tîrgoviște.
Ion Ghica. (1816–1897). Biobiografie. ₍Coperta colecției: Emil Florin Grama₎. Tîrgoviște, 1972.

28 p. 21 cm. (Personalități ale culturii dimboviței)

At head of title: Comitetul de Cultură și Educație Socialistă Dimbovița. Biblioteca Municipală Tîrgoviște.
"Întocmirea bibliografiei: Rachila Trandafir, Stela Marin."

GHOSE, AUROBINDO

Kaul, Hari Krishen, 1941–
Sri Aurobindo; a descriptive bibliography, by H. K. Kaul. With a foreword by C. D. Deshmukh. New Delhi, Munshiram Manoharlal ₍1972₎

xxvii, 222 p. 23 cm.

GIBBON, EDWARD

Norton, Jane Elizabeth, 1893–
A bibliography of the works of Edward Gibbon, by J. E. Norton. New York, B. Franklin ₍1970₎

xvi, 256 p. 23 cm. (Selected essays in history, economics, & social science, 130)

Burt Franklin bibliography & reference series, 330.
Reprint of the 1940 ed.

GIDE, ANDRÉ PAUL GUILLAUME

Archives et musée de la littérature.
Présence d'André Gide. (Exposition organisée à l'occasion du centenaire de la naissance de l'écrivain par les Archives et musée de la littérature, avec le concours de la Bibliothèque littéraire Jacques Doucet à Paris. Bruxelles, Bibliothèque royale Albert Ier. du 4 juillet au 22 août 1970). Catalogue rédigé par Jean Warmoes. Avant-propos de Carlo Bronne. Bruxelles, Bibliothèque royale Alber Ier, ₍bd de l'Empereur, 4₎, 1970.
xvi, 151 p. ports., facsims. 22 cm.
Label mounted on t. p.: Supplied by Worldwide Books, Boston.

Bibliothèque littéraire Jacques Doucet.
Catalogue de fonds spéciaux de la Bibliothèque littéraire Jacques Doucet, Paris. Lettres à André Gide. Boston, G. K. Hall, 1972.

vii, 507 p. 38 cm.

Added t. p.: Catalog of special collections of the Jacques Doucet Literary Library, Paris. Letters to André Gide.

Fongaro, Antoine.
Bibliographie d'André Gide en Italie. Firenze, Sansoni; Paris, M. Didier, 1966.

199 p. 26 cm. (Publications de l'Institut français de Florence. 2. sér. Collection d'études bibliographiques, no 9)

Naville, Arnold.
Bibliographie des écrits de André Gide. Préf. de Maurice Bedel. New York, B. Franklin ₍1971₎

223, ₍14₎ p. 22 cm. (Burt Franklin bibliography & reference series, 203. Essays in literature and criticism, 56)

Title on spine: Bibliographie de André Gide.
Reprint of the 1962 ed.

Paris. Bibliothèque nationale.
André Gide. Paris, 1970.

xxiv, 216 p. illus., ports. 21 cm.

Exhibition catalog by F. Callu and S. Gravereau.

GIDEONSE, HARRY DAVID

Preminger, Alexander S
Urban educator: Harry D. Gideonse, Brooklyn College

and the City University of New York; an annotated bibliography, by Alexander S. Preminger, Antoinette Ciolli [and] Lillian Lester. New York, Twayne Publishers [1970]

xiii, 304 p. 22 cm.

GIESSEN. UNIVERSITÄT

Giessen. Universität. Universitätsarchiv.
Bestandsverzeichnis. Zusammengestellt von Erwin Schmidt. Giessen, Universitätsbibliothek, 1969.

xiv, 177 p. 23 cm. (Berichte und Arbeiten aus der Universitätsbibliothek Giessen, 15)

GIFT-BOOKS (ANNUALS, ETC.)

Boyle, Andrew.
An index to the annuals. Worcester, A. Boyle, 1967–

v. 22 cm.

CONTENTS.—v. 1. The authors, 1820–1850.

Faxon, Frederick Winthrop, 1866–1936.
Literary annuals and gift books : a bibliography, 1823–1903 / [by] Frederick W. Faxon. — [1st ed.] reprinted ; with supplementary essays by Eleanore Jamieson & Iain Bain. — Pinner (Ravelston, Southview Rd., Pinner, Middx) : Private Libraries Association, 1973.

352 p. in various pagings ; ill., facsims. ; 23 cm.

Reprint of 1912 ed. published by Boston Book Co., Boston, Mass.

GIFT OF TONGUES see Glossolalia

GIFTED CHILDREN see Education of gifted children

GILDS
see also under Great Britain - History, Local *(Gross)*

Blanc, Hippolyte, *b.* 1820.
Bibliographie des corporations ouvrières avant 1789. New York, B. Franklin [1968]

102 p. 24 cm. (Burt Franklin bibliography and reference series, no. 201)

"Originally published Paris: 1885."

GILL, ERIC

Gill, Evan R
Bibliography of Eric Gill [by] Evan R. Gill. Foreword by Walter Shewring. Totowa, N. J., Rowman and Littlefield, 1973.

xv, 223 p. illus. 26 cm.

Reprint of the 1953 ed. published by Cassell, London.

Gill, Evan R *comp.*
The inscriptional work of Eric Gill; an inventory [by] Evan R. Gill. London, Cassell [1964]

xvii, 140 p. illus., facsims. 26 cm.

West Sussex, *Eng. County Record Office.*
The Eric Gill Memorial Collection: a catalogue, edited by Noel H. Osborne. Chichester (Sx.), West Sussex County Council, 1967.

[1] iv, 26 p. 4 plates. 25 cm. (The Chichester papers, no. 51)

GINSBERG, ALLEN
Dowden, George.
A bibliography of works by Allen Ginsberg, October, 1943 to July 1, 1967. With a chronology and index by Laurence McGilvery and a foreword by Allen Ginsberg. [San Francisco] City Lights Books [1971]

xvi, 343 p. illus. 24 cm.

GIPSIES

Black. George Fraser, 1866–1948.
A gypsy bibliography. Ann Arbor, Mich., Gryphon Books, 1971.

vii, 226 p. 22 cm. (Gypsy Lore Society. Monographs, no. 1)

Reprint of the 1914 ed.

Bräuner, Vilém.
Výchova cikánských dětí. Bibliogr. leták. Uspoř. Vilém Bräuner. Brno, St. pedagog. knihovna, rozmn., 1968.

6, [1] p. 21 cm. (Bibliografický leták, čís. 198)

GIRGAL, OTTO

Mourková, Jarmila.
Otto Girgal (1886–1958). Literární pozůstalost. Zprac. Jarmila Mourková. Praha, Literární archív Památníku nár. písemnictví, rozmn., 1969.

13, [1] p. 20 cm. (Edice inventářů čís. 196)

GIRONDE, FRANCE (DEPT.)

Gironde, France (Dept.). Archives.
Guide des Archives de la Gironde [par] A. Betgé-Brezetz, conservateur en chef honoraire. Bordeaux, 1973.

202 p. illus. 24 cm.

GISSING, GEORGE ROBERT

Spiers, John.
The rediscovery of George Gissing: [an exhibition at the National Book League, 23 June to 7 July, 1971] : a reader's guide, by John Spiers and Pierre Coustillas. London, National Book League, 1971.

[7], 163 p. 22 cm.

GLACIERS

Skretteberg, Liv.
Breer i Norge 1868–1968. En bibliografi. Oslo (Den Norske turistforening) 1968.

48 l. 31 cm.

Issued in portfolio.

GLADKOV, FEDOR VASIL'EVICH

GLADSTONE, WILLIAM EWART

St. Deiniol's Library, *Hawarden.*
Materials for the study of the Rt. Hon. W. E. Gladstone and his times at St. Deiniol's Library, Hawarden. Hawarden, Chester, St. Deiniol's Library [1969]

[8] p. 2 illus., 2 col. facsims. 21 cm.

Akademiía nauk SSSR. *Fundamental'naía biblioteka obshchestvennykh nauk.*
Библиография текстов Ф. В. Гладкова, 1900–1964. [Составитель: А. М. Гуткина] Москва, 1965.

100 p. 21 cm.

At head of title: Академия наук СССР. Фундаментальная библиотека общественных наук им. В. П. Волгина. Библиотека Института мировой литературы им. А. М. Горького.

GLASENAPP, HELMUTH VON

Károlyi, Zoltán.
Helmuth von Glasenapp: Bibliographie. Wiesbaden, F. Steiner, 1968.

xiii, 100 p. 23 cm. (Glasenapp-Stiftung. [Veröffentlichungen] Bd. 2)

GLASGOW, ELLEN ANDERSON GHOLSON

Kelly, William W
Ellen Glasgow, a bibliography, by William W. Kelly. Charlottesville, Published for the Bibliographical Society of Virginia [by the] University Press of Virginia [1964]

xi, 330 p. port. 22 cm.

GLASS

Calcutta. Central Glass and Ceramic Research Institute. *Documentation Unit.*
CGCRI documentation list. v. 1–
1966–
Calcutta.

v. 32 cm. monthly.

International Commission on Glass. *Sub-Committee A11.*
The chemical durability of glass; a bibliographic review of literature. [Charleroi, Belgium, 1965]

76 p. 23 cm.

Prefatory matter in English, French, and German.

International Commission on Glass. Sub-Committee A II.
The chemical durability of glass. A bibliographic review of literature. Compiled by Sub-Committee A II of the International Commission on Glass, under the supervision of V. Gottardi. Ed. by the Secretariat of Sub-Committee A I and the Secretariat of Sub-Committee A XII [Charleroi, I. C. G., (bd. Defontaine, 10)], 1972.

211 p. 21 cm.

Prefatory matter in English, French and German.

International Commission on Glass. *Sub-committee A vi.*
Bibliography of physical properties of glass. Strength, hardness, elasticity. Compiled by Sub-Committee A vi of the International Commission on glass. Charleroi, Secretariat of Sub-Committee A1, (International Commission on glass). Institut national du verre, [bd. Defontaine, 10] 1967.

108 p. 21 cm.

"Addendum" (96a–96l p.) inserted.

International Commission on Glass. Sub-committee AIX.
Electrical properties of glass and glass-ceramics. A bibliography covering the period 1957–1968. Compiled by Sub-Committee AIX of the International Commission on Glass, under the supervision of J. D. Mackenzie. Edited by the Secretariat of Sub-Committee AI and the Secretariat of Sub-Committee AXII. ([Charleroi], International Commission on Glass, I. C. G., [bd Defontaine, 10]), 1969.

222 p. 21 cm.

Klaarenbeek, Friederich Wilhelm.
Bibliography of glass literature. Under the aegis of the International Commission on Glass, edited by F. W. Klaarenbeek and J. M. Stevels, with the collaboration of F. Newby [and others. Bussum, Holland, Printed by Grafisch Bedrijf T. Hamers, 1964?]

116 p. 23 cm.

Robredo, Jaime.
L'analyse thermique différentielle en verrerie. Differential thermal analysis in glass. Par J. Robredo. [Charleroi]; Commission internationale du verre, [bd. Defontaine, 10]; (1968).

480 p. diagrs., tables. 22 cm.

GLEAVES, ALBERT

U. S. *Library of Congress. Manuscript Division.*
Albert Gleaves; a register of his papers in the Library of Congress. Washington, Library of Congress, 1968.

12 l. 27 cm.

"Naval Historical Foundation collection."

GLOBES

Yonge, Ena L   1895–
A catalogue of early globes, made prior to 1850 and conserved in the United States; a preliminary listing, by Ena L. Yonge. New York, American Geographical Society, 1968.

118 p. illus., maps. 24 cm. (American Geographical Society library series, no. 6)

GLOSSOLALIA

Martin, Ira Jay, 1911–
Glossolalia, the gift of tongues; a bibliography [by] Ira J. Martin, III. [Cleveland, Tenn.] Pathway Press [1970]

72 p. 21 cm.

GLOUCESTER, ENGLAND (DIOCESE)

Gloucester, *Eng. (Diocese)*
A catalogue of the records of the Bishop and Archdeacons; compiled by Isabel M. Kirby, with a foreword by the Rt. Rev. the Lord Bishop of Gloucester. Gloucester, Gloucester City Corporation, 1968.

ii–xxiv, 208 p. coat of arms. 26 cm. (Records of the Diocese of Gloucester, v. 1)

Gloucester, *Eng. (Diocese)*
A catalogue of the records of the Dean and Chapter including the former St Peter's Abbey; compiled by Isabel M. Kirby, with a foreword by the Very Reverend the Dean of Gloucester. Gloucester, Gloucester County Council, 1967.

ii–xv, 200 p. 25 cm. (Records of the Diocese of Gloucester, v. 2)

Gloucester Cathedral. Library.
A catalogue of Gloucester Cathedral library; compiled by Suzanne Mary Eward; with a foreword by the Dean of Gloucester and additions by Neil Ker, H. M. Nixon [and] R. A. May. [Gloucester], Dean and Chapter of Gloucester Cathedral. 1972.

xx, 250, [3] p. 3 illus. 24 cm.

GLOWACKI, ALEKSANDER

Melkowski, Stefan.
Bolesław Prus, 1847–1912; poradnik bibliograficzny. Warszawa, 1964.

39 p. port. 21 cm.

At head of title: Biblioteka Narodowa. Instytut Bibliograficzny.

GLUCK, CHRISTOPH WILLIBALD, RITTER VON

Wortsmann, Stephan, 1891–
Die deutsche Gluck-Literatur; (Christoph Willibald Ritter v. Gluck, 1714–1787) [Walluf bei Wiesbaden] M. Sändig [1973]

viii, 121, [1] p. 22 cm.

Reprint of the Leipzig, 1914 ed.
Originally presented as the author's thesis, Leipzig, 1914.
Vita: p. [122]

GLÜCKSTADT, GERMANY

Köhn, Gerhard.
Repertorium der glückstädtischen Akten: ein Register d. Glückstadt betreffenden Akten in d. Archiven Glückstadts, d. Kreises Steinburg, d. Landes Schleswig-Holstein u. Dänemarks; mit e. Bibliographie z. Geschichte d. Stadt Glück-

stadt/ zusammengestellt von Gerhard Köhn. Glückstadt: Stadtarchiv, 1970.

lx, 379 l.; 20 cm.

"Auflage: 50 Exemplare."

GLUE see Adhesives

GLYNDE, ENGLAND

Dell, Richard F
The Glynde Place archives; a catalogue. Edited by Richard F. Dell. Lewes, East Sussex County Council, 1964.

xxviii, 312 p. illus. 25 cm.

GNOSTICISM

Scholer, David M
Nag Hammadi bibliography 1948–1969. By David M. Scholer. Leiden, Brill, 1971.

xvi, 201 p. 25 cm. (Nag Hammadi studies, 1)

GOA

Costa, Aleixo Manuel da, 1909–
Literatura goesa; apontamentos bio-bibliográficos para a sua história. Lisboa, Agência-Geral do Ultramar ₍cover 1967₎

476 p. 23 cm.

GOBIND SINGH, GURU see Govinda Siṃha, 10th guru of the Sikhs

GODWIN, WILLIAM

Pollin, Burton Ralph.
Godwin criticism; a synoptic bibliography ₍by₎ Burton R. Pollin. ₍Toronto₎ University of Toronto Press ₍1967₎

xlvi, 659 p. 24 cm.

GOES FAMILY

Netherlands (Kingdom, 1815–   ). Rijksarchief, The Hague.
Inventaris van het familiearchief Van der Goes van Dirxland, 1419–1928, door J. A. Jaeger. ₍'s-Gravenhage, Algemeen Rijksarchief₎ 1965.

64 l. geneal. table, port. 30 cm.

GOETHE, JOHANN WOLFGANG VON
see also under Faust

Avanzi, Giannetto, 1892–1956.
Bibliografia italiana su Goethe (1779–1965). Firenze, L. S. Olschki, 1972.

vii, 255 p. 25 cm. (Università di Genova. Facoltà di lettere e filosofia. Pubblicazioni dell'Istituto di lingua e letteratura tedesca e di filologia germanica, 2)

At head of title: Giannetto Avanzi, Giorgio Sichel.

Baldensperger, Fernand, 1871–1958.
Bibliographie critique de Goethe en France. New York, B. Franklin ₍1972₎

ix, 251 p. 23 cm. (Burt Franklin bibliography & reference series, 455. Selected essays and texts in literature and criticism, 177)

Reprint of the 1907 ed.

Hagen, Waltraud.
Die Drucke von Goethes Werken. Bearbeiter: Waltraud Hagen. ₍Hrsg. von der Deutschen Akademie der Wissenschaften zu Berlin₎ Berlin, Akademie-Verlag, 1971.

xxi, 382 p. 25 cm.

First-2d editions published in 1956 under title: Die Gesamt- und Einzeldrucke von Goethes Werken.

Hagen, Waltraud.
Quellen und Zeugnisse zur Druckgeschichte von Goethes Werken. Bearbeiter des Bandes: Waltraud Hagen. Unter Mitarbeit von Edith Nahler. Berlin, Akademie-Verlag, 1966–

v. 25 cm. (Werke Goethes. Ergänzungs- bd. 2, T. 1

CONTENTS.—T. 1. Gesamtausgaben bis 1822.

Merensky Library.
Goethe; bibl₍i₎ografie van die Goethe-versameling in die Merensky-Biblioteek, Universiteit van Pretoria, saamgestel deur die personeel van die Merensky-Biblioteek. Bibliotekaris: A. J. van den Bergh. Onder-bibliotekaris: A. J. Pienaar. Pretoria, 1965.

xiii, 130 p. port. 26 cm.

Nihon Gēte Kyōkai.
(Nihon ni okeru "Fausuto" bunken mokuroku)

日本ゲーテ協会

日本における「ファウスト」文献目録

〔東京〕 1968

40p 21cm

「ゲーテ年鑑」復刊第10巻「ファウスト」研究特集付録

Zhitomirskaïa, Zinaida Viktorovna.
(Iogann Vol'fgang Gete)₎
Иоганн Вольфганг Гете. Библиогр. указ. рус. пер. и критич. литературы на рус. яз. 1780–1971. ₍Вступит. статья Л. Е. Генина, с. 7–38₎. Москва, "Книга," 1972.

615 p. 22 cm.

At head of title: Всесоюзная государственная библиотека иностранной литературы. З. В. Житомирская.

GOEVERNEUR, JOHAN JACOB ANTONIE

Gideonse, Cornelia L   T
J. J. A. Goeverneur. Proeve van een bibliografie. ₍Door₎ Corn.a L. T. Gideonse. ₍Amsterdam, Bibliotheek- en Documentatieschool₎, 1969.

49 l. 27 cm.

GOFMAN, E. T. A. see Hoffmann, E. T. A.

GOGOL', NIKOLAĬ VASIL'EVICH

Akademiīa nauk SSSR. *Biblioteka.*
Письма к Н. В. Гоголю; библиография. ₍Составители: Л. П. Архипова, А. Н. Степанов. Отв. редактор Н. А. Никифоровская₎ Ленинград, 1965.

78 p. 17 cm.

Prague. Městská knihovna. Divadelní a filmové oddělení.
Nikolaj Vasiljevič Gogol (1809–1852). Praha, ₍Městská knihovna₎ 1972.

9 l. 29 cm. (Bibliografický leták MK. Č. 11/72)

GOIANA, BRAZIL (PERNAMBUCO)

Silva, Genny da Costa e.
Bibliografia sôbre Goiana; aspectos históricos e geográficos ₍por₎ Genny da Costa e Silva ₍e₎ Maria do Carmo Rodrigues. Recife, Comissão Organizadora e Executiva das Comemorações do IV Centenário do Povoamento de Goiana, 1972.

421 p. 23 cm.

GOIÁS, BRAZIL (STATE)

Catálogo bibliográfico de Goiás. ₍Organizado por Francisco Balduino Santa Cruz, et al.₎ Goiânia, Estante do Escritor Goiano, Serviço Social do Comércio, Departamento Regional, 1966.

108 p. 23 cm.

Cover title.
"Waldir Castro Quinta : Letras e literatos, de ontem e de hoje ; com anotações adicionais do autor" : p. ₍91₎–108.

GÖKALP, ZIYA

Binark, İsmet.

Doğumunun 95. ₍i. e. doksan beşinci₎ yıldönümü münasebetiyle Ziya Gökalp bibliyografyası ; kitap, makale. ₍Hazırlayanlar₎ İsmet Binark ₍ve₎ Nejat Sefercioğlu. Ankara, Türk Kültürünü Araştırma Enstitüsü, 1971.

xxviii, 200 p. 24 cm. (Türk Kültürünü Araştırma Enstitüsü yayınları, 88. Seri X, sayı A1)

GOLD

Cooper, Margaret, 1913–

Selected annotated bibliography on the geochemistry of gold. Washington, U.S. Govt. Print. Off., 1971.

iii, 63 p. 24 cm. (Geological Survey bulletin 1337)

Rabinovich, S   I

Золото. Горноразведочные и эксплуатационные работы на месторождениях золота. Библиогр. указатель отечеств. и иностр. литературы за 1960–1967 гг. Москва, ВИЭМС ₍ОНТИ₎, 1970.

157 p. 28 cm. (Библиографическая информация)

At head of title : Министерство геологии СССР.

Sinclair, Dorothy Mary.

The Orange Free State goldfields : a bibliography. Cape Town, University of Cape Town, School of Librarianship, 1967.

₍xii₎, 51 p. 23 cm. (University of Cape Town. School of Librarianship. Bibliographical series)

Zaletkina, M   IU

Золото. Обогащение золотосодержащих руд и песков и методы их анализа. Библиогр. указатель отечеств. и иностр. литературы за 1960–1967 гг. Москва, ₍ОНТИ₎, ВИЭМС, 1970.

130 p. 29 cm. (Библиографическая информация)

At head of title : Министерство геологии СССР.
"Указатель составлен Центральным научно-исследовательским горноразведочным институтом цветных, редких и благородных металлов ... Составитель—Залеткина М. Ю."

GOLD COAST (COLONY) see Ghana

GOLDFISH

Clemens, Howard T

A goldfish bibliography ₍compiled by Howard T. Clemens₎ Norristown, Pa., Aquarium Pub. Co. ₍1965₎

i, 41 p. illus. 26 cm.

GOLDSZMIT, HENRYK

Elkoshi, Gedaliah, 1910–

₍Yanush Korts'ak be-'Ivrit₎

יאנוש קורצ׳אק בעברית; ביבליאוגראפיה מוערת בצירוף מבוא
₍מאת₎ גדליה אלקושי. ₍לוחמי הגיטאות₎ בית לוחמי הגיטאות
ע״ש יצחק קצנלסון, 732 ₍1972₎

257 p. port. 22 cm.

Added t. p.: Janusz Korczak in Hebrew ; his works and the writings about him ₍by₎ Gedalyah Elkoshi.

GOLF

Murdoch, Joseph S   F

The library of golf, 1743–1966 ; a bibliography of golf books, indexed alphabetically, chronologically, & by subject matter. Compiled and annotated by Joseph S. F. Murdoch. Detroit, Gale Research Co., 1968.

viii, 314 p. illus. 24 cm.

GOLLEROVÁ, ELSA

Hellmuth-Brauner, Vladimír.

Elsa Gollerová. (1868–1955.) Literární pozůstalost. Zprac. Vladimír Hellmuth Brauner. Praha, Literární archív Památníku nár. písemnictví, t. Ruch, Liberec, 1971.

7, ₍1₎ p. 20 cm. (Edice inventářů. čís. 221)

GOLLWITZER, HELMUT

Marquardt, Friedrich-Wilhelm.

Bibliographie Helmut Gollwitzer, 1934–1969. ₍München₎ C. Kaiser ₍1969₎

37 p. 23 cm.

GONCHAROV, IVAN ALEKSANDROVICH

Alekseev, Anatolii Dmitrievich.

Библиография И. А. Гончарова. Гончаров в печати. Печать о Гончарове. (1832–1964). Ленинград, "Наука," Ленингр. отд-ние, 1968.

232 p. 22 cm.

At head of title: Академия наук СССР. Институт русской литературы (Пушкинский дом) А. Д. Алексеев.

GONZÁLEZ DEL VALLE Y RAMÍREZ, FRANCISCO

Peraza Sarausa, Fermín, 1907–

Bibliografía de Francisco González del Valle. 2. ed. Gainesville, Fla., 1964.

15 l. 28 cm. (Biblioteca del bibliotecario, 4)

GOOR, NETHERLANDS

Wit, J   A   de.

Bibliografie van Goor. Samengesteld door J. A. de Wit. ₍Werkstuk 2e cyclus Bibliotheek- en Documentatieschool, Amsterdam. Amsterdam, Bibliotheek- en Documentatieschool₎ 1969.

35 l. 29 cm.

GORDIMER, NADINE

Nell, Racilia Jilian.

Nadine Gordimer, novelist and short story writer ; a bibliography of her works and selected literary criticism. Johannesburg, University of the Witwatersrand, Dept. of Bibliography, Librarianship and Typography, 1964.

ix, 33 l. 30 cm.

Thesis (Dip. Lib.)—University of the Witwatersrand.

GORDON, THOMAS
see also under Trenchard, J.

Séguin, J   A   R

A bibliography of Thomas Gordon, ca. 1692–1750. Compiled and edited by J. A. R. Séguin partially as a contribution to the history of xviiith-century deism and freethought. Jersey City ₍N. J.₎ R. Paxton, 1965.

71 p. 25 cm.

GORKI, RUSSIA (PROVINCE)

Наш край; указатель основной литературы о Горьковской области. ₍Составители: И. А. Ефремова и др. Горький₎ Волго-Вятское книжное изд-во, 1967.

142 p. 17 cm.

At head of title: Горьковская областная библиотека им. В. И. Ленина. Отдел библиографии.

GOR'KIĬ, MAKSIM

Birr, Ewald.

Maxim Gorki. Zum 100. Geburtstag am 28. März. (Zusammengestellt von Ewald Birr. Red. Bearb.: Adolf Wesser u. Hilde Weise.) Berlin, Berliner Stadtbibliothek, 1968.

61 p. 21 cm. (Bibliographische Kalenderblätter. Sonderblatt 20)

Brodskaia, Sof'ia Iakovlevna.

Публикации текстов А. М. Горького в СССР, 1959–1963; библиографический указатель. Москва, Наука, 1967.

252 p. 22 cm.

At head of title: Академия наук СССР. Фундаментальная библиотека общественных наук им. В. П. Волгина. С. Я. Бродская.

Budapest. Állami Gorkij Könyvtár.

Gorkij bibliográfia; a könyvtár állományában lévő válogatott időszaki kiadványok Gorkijra vonatkozó címanyaga. ₍Szerk.: Fodor Magdolna₎ Budapest, 1969.

220 p. port. 20 cm.

Czikowsky, E

Maxim Gorki in Deutschland: Bibliographie 1899 bis 1965. Zusammengestellt und annotiert von E. Czikowsky, I. Idzikowski und G. Schwarz. Berlin, Akademie-Verlag, 1968.

380 p. 24 cm. (Deutsche Akademie der Wissenschaften zu Berlin. Veröffentlichungen des Instituts für Slawistik. Sonderreihe Bibliographie, Nr. 2)

Ebin, F   E

А. М. Горький. 1868–1936. Список библиогр. указателей и справочных пособий. ₍Составитель: Ф. Е. Эбин.₎ Москва, 1968.

21 p. 20 cm.

At head of title: Государственная ордена Ленина библиотека СССР имени В. И. Ленина.
Cover title.
"Библиография подготовлена Отделом справочно-библиографической работы и научно-информационной библиографии."

Havana. Biblioteca Nacional José Martí. *Servicio de Información.*

Bibliografía de Máximo Gorki, con motivo del centenario de su nacimiento. ₍Havana, 1968₎

24 p. 28 cm.

Khaev, S   A

М. Горький в Нижегородской-Горьковской печати; 1893–1958; библиографический указатель. ₍Составители: С. А. Хаев, А. Д. Зайдман, В. Е. Успенская₎ Горький, 1960.

412 p.
At head of title: Горьковская областная библиотека им. В. И. Ленина. Отдел библиографии.
Microfilm. 1 reel. 35 mm.

Lūkina, Velta.

Maksims Gorkijs Latvijā un latviešu presē. Bibliogrāfija, 1899–1967. Rīgā, "Zinātne," 1968.

330 p. 20 cm.

At head of title: Latvijas PSR Zinātņu akadēmija. Fundamentālā bibliotēka. V. Lūkina un O. Saldone.

Added t. p.: Максим Горький в Латвии и латышской печати.
Latvian and Russian.

Lukirskaia, Kseniia Petrovna.

Литература о М. Горьком; библиография 1955–1960. Под ред. К. Д. Муратовой. Ленинград, Наука ₍Ленинградское отд-ние₎ 1965.

404 p. 22 cm.

At head of title: Академия наук СССР. Библиотека АН СССР. Институт русской литературы (Пушкинский дом) К. П. Лукирская, А. С. Морщихина.

Lukirskaia, Kseniia Petrovna.

Литература о М. Горьком. Библиография 1961–1965. Сост. К. П. Лукирская, О. В. Миллер, А. С. Морщихина. Под ред. К. Д. Муратовой. Ленинград, 1970.

291 p. 21 cm.

At head of title: Академия наук СССР. Ордена Трудового Красного Знамени Библиотека Академии наук СССР. Институт русской литературы (Пушкинский дом)

Martínková, Hana.

Dílo Maxima Gorkého v českém jazyce. Bibliografie. Zprac. Hana Martínková. ₍Předml.:₎ Vladimír Pek. Ústí nad Labem, Kraj. knihovna Maxima Gorkého, rozmn., 1969.

63, ₍1₎ p. 20 cm. (Ústí nad Labem, Czechoslovak Republic. Krajská knihovna Maxima Gorkého. Edice "Bibliografie", roč. 1969, č. 14)

Pérus, Jean.

Gorki en France, bibliographie des œuvres de Gorki traduites en français, des études et articles sur Gorki publiés en France, en français, de 1899 à 1939, établie sous la direction de Jean Pérus ₍par I. Sokologorsky, M. Beyssac, A. Stratonovitch et R. Collas₎ ... Paris, Presses universitaires de France, 1968.

315 p. 25 cm. (Faculté des lettres et sciences humaines de l'Université de Clermont-Ferrand. ₍Publications₎ 2. sér., fasc. 26)

Zernitskaia, É   I

Горький и театр. Рек. указатель литературы. Москва, 1968.

101 p. 20 cm.

At head of title: Министерство культуры СССР. Государственная центральная театральная библиотека.
By É. I. Zernitskaia, E. D. Loidina and N. V. Shashkova.

GOSUDARSTVENNYĬ UNIVERSITET see Samarkand (City) Gosudarstvennyĭ Universitet

GOTHENBURG, SWEDEN. LÄRARHÖGSKOLAN

Gothenburg, Sweden. Lärarhögskolan. Pedagogiska institutionen.

Förteckning över tryckta skrifter författade av medlemmar av pedagogiska institutionen vid Lärarhögskolan i Göteborg under tiden 1 januari–30 juni 1969. Göteborg, Lärarhögskolan i Göteborg, Pedagogiska institutionen, 1969.

₍1₎, 16 l. 30 cm.

Gothenburg, Sweden. Lärarhögskolan. Pedagogiska institutionen.

Förteckning över tryckta skrifter författade av medlemmar av pedagogiska institutionen vid Lärarhögskolan i Göteborg under tiden 1 juli 1969–31 december 1970. Göteborg, Pedagogiska institutionen, Lärarhögskolan i Göteborg, 1971.

8 l. 30 cm.

GOTHENBURG AND BOHUS, SWEDEN

Gothenburg, Sweden. Universitet. Biblioteket.

Förteckning över mikrofilmade kyrkoarkivalier för Göteborgs och Bohus län.   Göteborg. Universitetsbiblioteket, 1972.

1, xii, 348 l. 30 cm.

GOTHIC ART   see   Art, Gothic

GOTTFRIED VON STRASSBURG

Steinhoff, Hans-Hugo.
Bibliographie zu Gottfried von Strassburg. ₍Berlin₎ E. Schmidt ₍1971₎

110 p. 21 cm. **(Bibliographien zur deutschen Literatur des Mittelalters, Heft 5)**

GOTTHELF, JEREMIAS, pseud. see   Bitzius, Albert

GÖTTINGEN

Göttinger Stadtarchiv.
Das Göttinger Stadtarchiv. Seine Geschichte u. seine Bestände. Von Walter Nissen. Göttingen, Vandenhoeck u. Ruprecht (1969).

108 p., 10 l. of illus. 25 cm.

GOTTSCHALK, LOUIS MOREAU

Offergeld, Robert.
The centennial catalogue of the published and unpublished compositions of Louis Moreau Gottschalk. Prepared for Stereo review by Robert Offergeld. New York, 1970.

34 p. illus., facsims., ports. 29 cm.

GOVERNMENT   see   Political science

GOVERNMENT BUSINESS ENTERPRISES

Indian Institute of Public Administration.
A bibliography on public enterprises in India. ₍New ed.₎ New Delhi, 1968.

135 p. 27 cm.

Marsden, R   P
Bibliography of public enterprise: with special reference to the developing countries; based on the collections of A. H. Hanson, by R. P. Marsden. Leeds, University of Leeds, 1973.

x, 97 p. 25 cm.

Smith, Hadley E
Public enterprise and economic development: an international bibliography. Hadley E. Smith, compiler. ₍Los Angeles₎ International Public Administration Center, School of Public Administration, University of Southern California, 1964.

55 l. 28 cm. (International public administration series, no. 3)

GOVERNMENT OWNERSHIP

Akademiîa nauk SSSR. *Fundamental'naîa biblioteka obshchestvennykh nauk.*
Национализация и проблемы национализированных отраслей в Великобритании в послевоенный период; библиографический указатель книг и журнальных статей за 1946–1963 г. г. ₍Составители: В. А. Архангельская, Т. Л. Виленкина, отв. ред. Л. Ф. Вольфсон₎ Москва, 1964.
137 p. 22 cm.

GOVERNMENT PUBLICATIONS

List of the serial publications of foreign governments, 1815–1931, edited by Winifred Gregory for the: American Council of Learned Societies, American Library Association, National Research Council. New York, H. W. Wilson Co., 1932. Millwood, N. Y., Kraus Reprint Co., 1973.

720 p. 32 cm.

Nigeria. *National Archives. Library.*
A handlist of foreign official publications in the National Archives Library, Ibadan. Compiled by L. C. Gwam. Ibadan, National Archives Headquarters. 1964.

v, 200 l. 30 cm.

Staatsbibliothek der Stiftung Preussischer Kulturbesitz. Abteilung Internationaler Amtlicher Schriftentausch.
Bestands-Verzeichnis laufend erscheinender ausländischer Amtsdruckschriften. Berlin, 1967.

2 v. (ii, 329 p.) 30 cm.

———————— Nachtrag. Berlin, 1969–

v. 30 cm.

BIBLIOGRAPHIES

Childs, James Bennett, 1896–
Current bibliographies of national official publications ₍by₎ James B. Childs. Washington, 1966.

9 p. 28 cm.

Cover title.
"Reprint from the Herald of library science, vol. 5, no. 1, January 1966, p. 10–27."

GOVERNMENT SPENDING POLICY

Hampshire Technical Research Industrial Commercial Service.
A bibliography of cost-benefit analysis. Southampton, Hampshire Technical Research Industrial Commercial Service, 1967.

₍2₎, v, 20 p. 22 cm.

Research for Better Schools, inc.
An annotated bibliography of benefits and costs in the public sector. Philadelphia ₍1968₎

xi, 242 p. 27 cm.

GOVINDA SIMHA, 10TH GURU OF THE SIKHS

Ramdev, Jogindar Singh, 1930–
Guru Gobind Singh; a descriptive bibliography, by Jagindar Singh Ramdev. With a foreword by M. S. Randhawa. ₍1st ed.₎ Chandigarh, Panjab University ₍1967₎

xvi, 260 p. illus., geneal. table. 23 cm.

GOYAZ, BRAZIL   see   Goiás, Brazil

GRAAFF-REINET, SOUTH AFRICA

Shaw, R   C
Graaff-Reinet, a bibliography compiled by R. C. Shaw. ₍Cape Town₎ University of Cape Town School of Librarianship, 1964.

vii, 44 p. 23 cm. (University of Cape Town. School of Librarianship. Bibliographical series)

GRABBE, CHRISTIAN DIETRICH

Bergmann, Alfred, 1887–
Grabbe Bibliographie von Alfred Bergman. Amsterdam, Rodopi, 1973.

xix, 520 p. 22 cm. (Amsterdamer Publikationen zur Sprache und Literatur, Bd. 3)

GRADMANN, ROBERT
Linnenberg, Friedrich.
Bibliographie Robert Gradmann. Erlangen, Fränkische Geographische Gesellschaft, Palm & Enke in Kommission, 1965.

19–42 p. front. 24 cm.

Cover title:
"Sonderdruck aus den Mitteilungen der Fränkischen Geographischen Gesellschaft, Bd. 11/12 für 1964/65."

GRADNIK, ALOJZ

Brecelj, Marijan, 1931–
Gradnikova bibliografija. Nova Gorica, Goriška knjižnica, 1964.

66 p. 17 cm. (Publikacije Goriške knjižnice, 2)

Summary in Italian.

GRAFTIO, GENRIKH OSIPOVICH

IAkovleva, N   G
[Akademik Genrikh Osipovich Graftio]
Академик Генрих Осипович Графтио. 1869–1949. Библиография трудов и литературы о жизни и деятельности. Сост. И. Г. Яковлева. Ленинград, 1971.

24 p. port. 20 cm.

At head of title: Министерство энергетики и электрификации СССР, and other organizations.

GRAIN

Commonwealth Bureau of Agricultural Economics.
The green revolution: annotated bibliography, prepared by [the] Commonwealth Bureau of Agricultural Economics. Farnham Royal, Commonwealth Agricultural Bureaux, 1971.

[3], i, 19 p. 30 cm. (Its Annotated bibliography no. 1)

Klosep, L   G
Удобрение зерновых культур. Библиогр. указатель отечеств. литературы за 1968–1970 гг. [Сост. Л. Г. Клосеп]. Москва, 1970.

111 p. 20 cm.

At head of title: Всесоюзная ордена Ленина Академия с.-х. наук имени В. И. Ленина. Центральная научная сельскохозяйственная библиотека. Справочно-библиографический отдел.

Naletova, N   B
Зерновое хозяйство нечерноземной зоны РСФСР; библиографический указатель отечественной литературы за 1961–1966 гг. в количестве 272 названий. [Составитель Н. Б. Налетова]. Москва, 1967.

32 p. 22 cm.
At head of title: Всесоюзная академия сельскохозяйственных наук имени В. И. Ленина. Центральная научная сельскохозяйственная библиотека. Справочно-библиографический отдел.

Strebelev, E   E
Селекция высокоурожайных озимых сортов пшеницы, ржи и ячменя. Библиогр. указатель отечеств. литературы и иностр. за 1958–1967 гг. Москва, 1968.

96 p. 20 cm.

At head of title: Всесоюзная ордена Ленина Академия сельскохозяйственных наук имени В. И. Ленина. Центральная научная сельскохозяйственная библиотека.

GRAMMAR   see   Language

GRANADA, SPAIN

Granada (City) Catedral. Archivo.
Archivo Catedral: inventario general [por] Manuel Casares Hervás. Granada, 1965.

xx, 629 p. 25 cm. (Publicaciones Archivo diocesano, 2)

GRANDVOIR, BELGIUM

Hannick, Pierre.
Inventaire des archives du château de Grandvoir. [Par] P. Hannick. Neufchâteau, Cercle "Terre de Neufchâteau," [Hôtel de ville], (1969).

[22] p. ports., illus., table, facsim. 24 cm. (Cercle "Terre de Neufchâteau." Publication no 8)

Pages numbered 103–124.
"Extrait du Bulletin de l'Institut archéologique du Luxembourg, Arlon, no 4, 1968."

GRANOVSKIĬ, TIMOFEĬ NIKOLAEVICH

Грановский Тимофей Николаевич. Библиография. (1828–1967). Под ред. С. С. Дмитриева. Вступит. очерки С. С. Дмитриева и Е. В. Гутновой. Москва, Изд. Моск. ун-та, 1969.

238 p. with illus. port. 21 cm.

By E. E. Blank and others.

GRANULAR MATERIALS

New York. Engineering Societies Library.
Bibliography on flow of granular materials from bins, bunkers, and silos. New York [1967]

34 p. 26 cm. (Its ESL bibliography no. 16)

"Updates and revises the Bibliography on flow of bulk materials from storage" published in 1962.

GRAPES   see   Wine

GRAPH THEORY

Ho, Yong Song.
Theory of graphs; a bibliography. Singapore, Lee Kong Chian Institute of Mathematics, Nanyang University, 1969.

242 p. 19 cm.

GRAPHIC ARTS
see also   Printing

Gerber, Jack.
A selected bibliography of the graphic arts. Pittsburgh, Graphic Arts Technical Foundation [1967]

84 p. 22 cm.

Halpern, George Martin, 1919–
Bibliography for graphic arts and advertising technology, by George M. Halpern. [New Hyde Park, N. Y., Nonpareil Associates]; distributed exclusively by Bee-Hive Campus Store [1965]

60 l. 28 cm.

Halpern, George Martin, 1919–
Bibliography for graphic arts and advertising technology. Compiled by George M. Halpern. [Rev. ed. New Hyde Park, N. Y., Nonpareil Associates, 1968]

65 p. 28 cm.

GRAPHOLOGY

International Graphoanalysis Society. Research Dept.
An annotated bibliography of studies in handwriting analysis research. Prepared by the IGAS Research Department. Chicago, International Graphoanalysis Society [1970]

30 p. 23 cm.

Kimball, Thomas D
An index of major articles appearing in the Journal of graphoanalysis from February, 1962 through December, 1969, inclusive. Compiled by Thomas D. Kimball. [n. p., 1970]

14 l. 28 cm.

Müller, Alfred Eugen.
Weltgeschichte graphologisch gesehen; internationales Quellenverzeichnis der Schriftanalysen berühmter Persönlichkeiten des 13. bis 20. Jahrhunderts, von Alfred Eugen Müller, unter Mitarbeit von Gert Krausp und Wolfgang

Fischer. Geleitwort von Max Simoneit. Köln, Bücherstube am Dom, H. Meyer, 1965.

211 p., 24 l. facsims. 30 cm.

Pref. in German, English, and French.

GRASS

Almeida, Norma Martins de.
Forragem; bibliografia das publicações que se encontram na Biblioteca dêste Instituto. Cruz das Almas, Instituto de Pesquisas e Experimentação Agropecuárias do Leste, 1967.

111 l. 32 cm. (Instituto de Pesquisas e Experimentação Agropecuárias do Leste. Lista bibliográfica no. 8)

Almeida, Norma Martins de.
Pasto elefante (*Pennisetum purpureum*); bibliografia das publicações que se encontram na Biblioteca dêste Instituto. Cruz das Almas, 1968.

8 l. 33 cm. (Instituto de Pesquisas e Experimentação Agropecuárias do Leste. Lista bibliográfica no. 10)

Bibliografía forrajera. fasc. 1–
1967–
[Oliveros] Estación Experimental Agropecuaria Oliveros.

no. 28 cm. annual.

Casaravilla, N   A
Gramíneas, correspondiente al material classificado durante el año 1969/70 [por] N. A. Casaravilla [y] J. P. R. Giacone. [Oliveros, República Argentina, Estación Experimental Agropecuaria Oliveros, 1970?]

163 l. 28 cm. (Bibliografía forrajera, fascículo 4)

Casaravilla, N   A
Gramíneas y misceláneas, correspondiente al material clasificado durante el año 1968 [por] N. A. Casaravilla [y] J. P. R. Giacone. [Oliveros, República Argentina, Estación Experimental Agropecuaria Oliveros, 1969?]

114 l. 28 cm. (Bibliografía forrajera, fascículo 3)

George Washington University, *Washington, D. C. Biological Sciences Communication Project.*
The millets; a bibliography of the world literature covering the years 1930–1963. Metuchen, N. J., Scarecrow Press, 1967.

xviii, 154 p. 22 cm.

Kabis, Ernst.
Bibliographie der Grünland-Literatur in der DDR. 1945–1965. (Als Manuskript gedruckt.) Brieselang, Institut für Ausbildung und Qualifizierung beim Landwirtschaftsrat der DDR (1966).

101 p. 21 cm.

Knobloch, Irving William, 1907–
A check list of crosses in the Gramineae [by] Irving W. Knobloch. [E. Lansing?] 1968.

170 p. 23 cm.

Rachie, Kenneth O
The millets and minor cereals; a bibliography of the world literature on millets, pre-1930 and 1964–69, and of all literature on other minor cereals, by Kenneth O. Rachie. Metuchen, N. J., Scarecrow Press, 1974.

xxiii, 202 p. 22 cm.

"The present work supplements The millets: a bibliography of the world literature covering the years 1930–1963, published ... in 1967."

Улучшение лугов и пастбищ; библиографический список отечественной литературы за 1964–1966 гг. в количестве

376 названий. [Составитель Н. Б. Налетова. Редактор Т. П. Шейнина] Москва, 1966.

36 p. 20 cm.

At head of title: Всесоюзная академия сельскохозяйственных наук имени В. И. Ленина. Центральная научная сельскохозяйственная библиотека. Справочно-библиографический отдел.

Victoria, Australia. Dept. of Agriculture. Division of Animal Industry.
Some references to research and extension publications on pastures in Victoria, 1903–June 1970. Collated by S. C. Powell. [Melbourne, 1970]

42 l. 33 cm.

GRAU, REINHOLD

Bibliographie der wissenschaftlichen Veröffentlichungen 1922 bis 1967 von Reinhold Grau. Zusammengestellt aus Anlass des 70. Geburtstages von Reinhold Grau am 22.2.1968. Alzey, Verlag der Rheinhessischen Druckwerkstätte Dietl (1968).

28 p., front. 21 cm.

GRAULS, JAN

Roemans, Robert, 1904–
Jan Grauls' bibliografie. Door Rob Roemans en Hilda van Assche. Met een woord vooraf door Jozef Droogmans. Hasselt [Dr. Willemsstraat, 23, Provinciebestuur van Limburg] 1967.

119 p. port. 24 cm. (Werken uitgegeven onder de auspiciën van de Bestendige Deputatie van de Provincie Limburg, nr. 8)

GRAUNT, JOHN see under Petty, Sir William

GRAVES, ROBERT

Higginson, Fred H
A bibliography of the works of Robert Graves, by Fred H. Higginson. Hamden, Conn., Archon Books, 1966.

328 p. illus., port. 23 cm.

Higginson, Fred H
A bibliography of the works of Robert Graves, by Fred H. Higginson. London, N. Vane, 1966.

320 p. illus., facsims., port. 23 cm.

GRAVITY

Canada. Earth Physics Branch. Gravity Division.
Index of publications, 1948–1970. Ottawa, Dept. of Energy, Mines and Resources, Earth Physics Branch, 1971.

15 p. maps (2 fold.) 25 cm.

GRAY, THOMAS

Northup, Clark Sutherland, 1872–1952.
A bibliography of Thomas Gray. New York, Russell & Russell [1970, ᶜ1917]

xiii, 296 p. 23 cm. (Cornell studies in English, 1)

GRAZ. UNIVERSITÄT

Grazer Universitätsprofessoren publizieren. (Bibliographie. Mitarbeiter: Helga Lurger [u. a.]) [Mit Portr.] (Graz, Österreichische Hochschülerschaft an der Universität Graz, 1966.)

483 p. 21 x 25 cm.

GREAT BRITAIN
see also Commonwealth of Nations

Abbey, John Roland, 1896–1969.
Life in England in aquatint and lithography, 1770–1860;

architecture, drawing books, art collections, magazines, navy and army, panoramas, etc., from the library of J. R. Abbey; a bibliographical catalogue. Folkestone, Dawsons of Pall Mall, 1972.

xxi, 427 p. illus. 32 cm.

Reprint of the 1953 ed.

Abbey, John Roland, 1896–1969.
Scenery of Great Britain and Ireland in aquatint and lithography, 1770–1860, from the library of J. R. Abbey; a bibliographical catalogue. Folkestone, Dawsons of Pall Mall, 1972.

xx, 399 p. illus. 32 cm.

Reprint of the 1952 ed.

Anderson, John Parker, 1841–
The book of British topography; a classified catalogue of the topographical works in the Library of the British Museum relating to Great Britain and Ireland, by John P. Anderson. Baltimore, Genealogical Pub. Co., 1970.

xvi, 472 p. 23 cm.

Reprint of the 1881 ed.

Bell, Peter.
Social reform and social structure in Victorian England: a handlist of university theses; compiled by Peter Bell. [Leicester], University of Leicester, Victorian Studies Centre, 1972.

16 leaves. 30 cm. (Victorian studies handlist 5)

Canberra, Australia. National Library.
The Kashnor collection; the catalogue of a collection relating chiefly to the political economy of Great Britain and Ireland from the 17th to the 19th centuries. Canberra, 1969.

2 v. 29 cm.

"This list ... is that made by Kashnor ... and does not represent a full bibliographical description of the items."

Johnson, Richard Hugh.
A geographical bibliography of Northwest England; editors: R. H. Johnson and L. Wharfe. Salford, Geographical Association (Manchester Branch), 1969.

vii, 68 p. 21 cm.

London. Guildhall Library.
A handlist of poll books and registers of electors in Guildhall Library. [London] Corporation of London, 1970.

87 p. 22 cm.

Upcott, William, 1779–1845.
A bibliographical account of the principal works relating to English topography. New York, B. Franklin [1968]

3 v. fronts. 23 cm. (Burt Franklin bibliography and reference series 225)

Reprint of the 1818 ed.
On spine: Bibliography of English topography.

BIOGRAPHY

Hepworth, Philip.
Select biographical sources: the Library Association manuscripts survey, edited by Philip Hepworth. London, Library Association, 1971.

154 p., plate. 2 illus. 30 cm. (Library Association. Research publication, no. 5)

Matthews, William, 1905–
British autobiographies; an annotated bibliography of British autobiographies published or written before 1951.

[Hamden, Conn.] Archon Books, 1968 [°1955]

xiv, 376 p. 23 cm.

Stauffer, Donald Alfred, 1902–1952.
The art of biography in eighteenth century England. New York, Russell & Russell [1970, °1941]

xiv, 572 p. 23 cm.

Includes bibliographical references.

—— —— Bibliographical supplement. New York, Russell & Russell [1970, °1941]

viii, 293 p. 23 cm

CHURCH HISTORY

Lambeth Palace. Library.
Catalogue of ecclesiastical records of the Commonwealth 1643–1660 in the Lambeth Palace Library, by Jane Houston. Farnborough, Gregg, 1968.

vii, 338 p. 25 cm.

Lambeth Palace. *Library.*
A catalogue of Lambeth manuscripts 889 to 901 (carte antique et miscellanée): charters in Lambeth Palace Library, by Dorothy M. Owen. London, Lambeth Palace Library, 1968.

[7], 213 p. 2 plates, facsims. 26 cm. (Charters in Lambeth Palace Library)

On spine: Lambeth charters.

Owen, Dorothy Mary.
The records of the Established Church in England, excluding parochial records [by] Dorothy M. Owen. London, British Records Association, 1970.

64 p. 25 cm. Index. (Archives and the user no. 1)

COLONIES

Flint, John E
Books on the British Empire and Commonwealth: a guide for students, by John E. Flint. London, published on behalf of the Royal Commonwealth Society by Oxford U. P., 1968.

vi, 66 p. 19 cm. 12/6

Gt. Brit. Colonial Office. Library.
Catalogue of the Colonial Office Library, London. Boston, G. K. Hall, 1964.

15 v. 37 cm.

—— —— First– supplement. Boston, G. K. Hall, 1967–

v. 37 cm.

CONTENTS: [1] 1963–1967.

Gt. Brit. *Public Record Office.*
List of Colonial Office confidential print to 1916. London, H. M. Stationery Off., 1965.

179 p. 25 cm. (*Its* Handbooks, no. 8)

Parker, John, 1923–
Books to build an empire; a bibliographical history of English overseas interests to 1620. Amsterdam, N. Israel, 1965.

viii, 290 p. 25 cm.

On label mounted on t. p.: W. S. Heinman, New York.

Royal Commonwealth Society. *Library.*
Subject catalogue of the Library of the Royal Empire Society, by Evans Lewin; with a new introduction by Donald H. Simpson. [1st ed. reprinted]. London, Dawsons

for the Royal Commonwealth Society, 1967.

4 v. 28½ cm.

CONTENTS.—v. 1. The British Empire generally and Africa.—v. 2. The Commonwealth of Australia, the Dominion of New Zealand, the South Pacific, general voyages and travels, and Artic and Antarctic regions.—v. 3. The Dominion of Canada and its provinces, the Dominion of New Foundland, the West Indies and Colonial America.—v. 4. The Mediterranean colonies, The Middle East, Indian Empire, Burma, Ceylon, British Malaya, East Indian Islands, and the Far East.—

Royal Commonwealth Society. Library.
Subject catalogue of the Royal Commonwealth Society, London. Boston, Mass., G. K. Hall, 1971.

7 v. 37 cm.

Supplements the Subject catalogue of the Library of the Royal Empire Society and the Biography catalogue of the Library of the Royal Commonwealth Society.
CONTENTS: v. 1. British Commonwealth and Europe. Asia: in general, Mideast, India.—v. 2. Asia: other Asian areas. Africa: Africa in general. North Africa.—v. 3. Africa: West Africa, East Africa.—v. 4. Africa: noncommonwealth Africa, including former foreign colonies, Republic of South Africa, other southern African countries.—v. 5. The Americas.—v. 6. Australia, New Zealand, Pacific.—v. 7. Biography. Voyages and travels. World War I. World War II.

FOREIGN RELATIONS

Gt. Brit. *Foreign Office.*
Foreign Office confidential papers relating to China and her neighbouring countries, 1840–1914; with an Additional list 1915–1937, [compiled by] Lo Hui-Min. [Maison des sciences de l'homme] The Hague, Paris, Mouton, 1969.

280 p. 22 cm. (Matériaux pour l'étude de l'Extrême-Orient moderne et contemporain. Travaux, 4)

Great Britain. Public Record Office.
The records of the Foreign Office 1782-1939. London, H.M. Stationery Off., 1969.

viii, 180 p. facsims., port. 25 cm. (Its Handbooks, no. 13)

Distributed in the U.S.A. by Sales Section, British Information Services, New York.

Temperley, Harold William Vazeille, 1879–1939, *ed.*
A century of diplomatic blue books, 1814–1914; lists edited, with historical introductions by Harold Temperley and Lillian M. Penson. London, Cass, 1966.

xviii, 600 p. 24½ cm.

Temperley, Harold William Vazeille, 1879–1939, *ed.*
A century of diplomatic blue books, 1814–1914; lists, edited with historical introductions by Harold Temperley and Lillian M. Penson. New York, Barnes & Noble [1966]

xvi, 600 p. 24 cm.

"First edition 1938."

GENEALOGY
see also under United States - Genealogy (U. S. Library of Congress)

Bridger, Charles, 1825 or 6–1879.
An index to printed pedigrees contained in county and local histories, the Heralds' visitations, and in the more important genealogical collections. Baltimore Genealogical Pub. Co., 1969.

iv, 384 p. 23 cm.

Reprint of the 1867 ed.

Higgs, Audrey Hamsher, *comp.*
West Midland genealogy: a survey of the local genealogical material available in the public libraries of Herefordshire, Shropshire. Staffordshire, Warwickshire and Wor-

cestershire, compiled by Audrey H. Higgs and Donald Wright. London, Library Association (West Midlands Branch), 1966.

vii, 101, ix–xiii p. 25 cm.

Kaminkow, Marion J
Genealogical manuscripts in British libraries; a descriptive guide, by Marion J. Kaminkow. With a foreword by Sir Anthony Wagner. Baltimore, Magna Charta Book Co., 1967.

x, 140 p. 24 cm.

Kaminkow, Marion J
A new bibliography of British genealogy with notes, by Marion J. Kaminkow. With a foreword by Sir Anthony Wagner. Baltimore, Magna Charta Book Co., 1965.

xvii, 170 p. 24 cm.

Marshall, George William, 1839–1905.
The genealogist's guide, by George W. Marshall. Reprinted from the last ed. of 1903 [i. e., 4th] with a new introd. by Anthony J. Camp. Baltimore, Genealogical Pub. Co., 1967.

xiii, 880 p. 23 cm.

Moule, Thomas, 1784–1851.
Bibliotheca heraldica Magnæ Britanniæ; an analytical catalogue of books on genealogy, heraldry, nobility, knighthood & ceremonies, with a list of provincial visitations, pedigrees, collections of arms, and other manuscripts, and a supplement enumerating the principal foreign genealogical works. London, Heraldry Today [1966]

xvi, 668 p. illus., port. 23 cm.

"Reproduced from the original edition of 1822."

Sims, Richard, 1816–1898.
An index to the pedigrees and arms contained in the heralds' visitations, and other genealogical manuscripts in the British Museum. Baltimore, Genealogical Pub. Co., 1970.

vi, 330 p. 24 cm.

Reprint of the 1849 ed.

Society of Genealogists.
A catalogue of parish register copies in the possession of the Society of Genealogists. Revised enlarged ed. London, Society of Genealogists [1969].

[2], 78 leaves. 26 cm.

Society of Genealogists.
Parish register copies. 3rd ed. Chichester, Phillimore, 1970–

v. 21 cm.

Previous ed. published in 1 vol. under title: A catalogue of parish register copies in the possession of the Society of Genealogists. 1969.
CONTENTS: pt. 1. Society of Genealogists collection.

Steel, Donald John.
National index of parish registers [edited] by D. J. Steel and Mrs. A. E. F. Steel. London, Society of Genealogists, 1966– [v. 1, 1968]
v. 24 cm.
Volume 5 has subtitle: A guide to Anglican, Roman Catholic, and Nonconformist registers before 1837, together with information on marriage licenses, bishop's transcripts and modern copies.
Stamped on t. p. of v. 5: Magna Carta Book Co., Baltimore, Md.
CONTENTS.—v. 1. Sources of births, marriages, and deaths before 1837 (I).—

v. 5. South Midlands and Welsh Border comprising the Counties of Gloucestershire, Herefordshire, Oxfordshire, Shropshire, Warwickshire, and Worcestershire.

—— ——Another issue. London, Society of Genealogists; Baltimore, Magna Carta Book Co., 1967–   ₍°1968–

GOVERNMENT PUBLICATIONS

British Museum. State Paper Room.
Check list of British official serial publications. 1967–

₍London₎

v. 30 cm. annual.

Vols. for 1967–   called also Provisional issue.
Title varies slightly.

Colchester, Eng. University of Essex. *Library.*
British government publications. Colchester (Essex), University of Essex (Library), 1968.

₍3₎, 7 p. 21 cm. (*Its:* Reference leaflet no. 1)

Di Roma, Edward, 1919–
A numerical finding list of British command papers published 1833–1961/62, compiled by Edward Di Roma and Joseph A. Rosenthal. ₍New York₎ New York Public Library, 1967.

148 p. 26 cm.

"Numerical lists, bound with the annual alphabetical indexes to the Sessional papers, have been the source of the present compilation."

Di Roma, Edward, 1919–
A Numerical finding list of British command papers published 1833–1961/62. Compiled by Edward Di Roma and Joseph A. Rosenthal. New York, New York Public Library ₍1971, °1967₎
148 p. 24 cm.
On spine: British command papers: finding list, 1833–1962.
"Numerical lists, bound with the annual alphabetical indexes to the Sessional papers, have been the source of the present compilation."

Irish University Press.
Checklist of British parliamentary papers in the Irish University Press 1000-volume series, 1801–1899. Shannon, Ireland ₍1972₎

xii, 218 p. 35 cm.

"IUP series of British parliamentary papers."

Irish University Press series of British parliamentary papers. ₍General₎ index. Shannon, Irish University Press ₍1968₎

8 v. 35 cm. (IUP library of fundamental source books)

Title on spine: British parliamentary papers.
On spine of v. 1: "Index."
CONTENTS: 1. 1696–1834. Hansard's Catalogue.—2. 1801–1852. Reports of select committees.—3. 1801–1852. Accounts and papers.—4. 1852–1869. Bills, reports, estimates, accounts, and papers.—5. 1801–1852. Bills, printed by order of the House of Commons.—6. 1870–1879. Bills, reports, estimates, accounts, and papers.—7. 1880–1889. Bills, reports, estimates, accounts, and papers.—8. 1890–1899. Bills, reports, estimates, accounts, and papers.

King (P. S.) & Son, ltd., London.
Catalogue of parliamentary papers, 1801–1920. ₍New York, B. Franklin, 1972₎
vii, 317, 81, 58 p. 23 cm. (Burt Franklin bibliography & reference series, 404) (Selected studies in history, economics & social science, n. s. 22 (c) Modern European studies)
Reprint of the 3-volume work published 1904–22.
Annotated subject index to "the more important papers, diplomatic correspondence, the reports of commissions and select committee ... an amalgamation of a number of separate catalogues, dealing with special subjects, which have been issued by our firm during the last fifty years."—Publishers' note.
CONTENTS: 1801–1900, with a few of earlier date.—1901–1910.—1911–1920.

Marshallsay, Diana.
British government publications; a (mainly) alphabetical guide to what they are, what the Library has and how to find them. ₍Southampton, Eng.₎ University of Southampton, c1970.

14 p. 29 cm. (Southampton University Library. Occasional paper no. 2)

Morgan, Annie Mary.
British Government publications: an index to chairmen and authors, 1941–1966. Edited by A. Mary Morgan. London, Library Association, Reference, Special and Information Section in association with Birmingham Public Libraries, 1969.

₍3₎, 193 p. 24 cm.

"Distributed in the U. S. A. by Gale Research Company."

Morgan, Annie Mary.
British government publications: an index to chairmen and authors, 1941–1966; edited by A. Mary Morgan. Corrected reprint; incorporating Amendment one. London, Library Association, Reference, Special and Information Section, 1973.

₍3₎, 198 p. 24 cm.

"This index is based on one compiled by the staff of the periodicals section of the Birmingham Reference Library."

Ollé, James Gordon Herbert.
An introduction to British government publications, by James G. Olle. London, Association of Assistant Librarians, 1965.

128 p. 22 cm.

Pemberton, John E
British official publications, by John E. Pemberton. ₍1st ed.₎ Oxford, New York, Pergamon Press ₍1971₎

xiii, 315 p. 22 cm. (The Commonwealth and international library. Library and technical information division)

Rodgers, Frank, 1927–
Serial publications in the British Parliamentary papers, 1900–1968; a bibliography. Chicago, American Library Association, 1971.

xix, 146 p. 25 cm.

Rodgers, Frank, 1927–
Serial publications in the British parliamentary papers, 1900–1968; a bibliography. London, Library Association, 1971.

xix, 146 p. 23 cm.

HISTORY

Elton, Geoffrey Rudolph.
Modern historians on British history, 1485–1945: a critical bibliography, 1945–1969, by G. R. Elton. London, Methuen, 1970.

viii, 239 p. 22 cm.

Distributed in the U. S. A. by Barnes & Noble.

Elton, Geoffrey Rudolph.
Modern historians on British history, 1485–1945; a critical bibliography, 1945–1969 ₍by₎ G. R. Elton. Ithaca, N. Y., Cornell University Press ₍1971, °1970₎

viii, 239 p. 22 cm.

Great Britain. Historical Manuscripts Commission.
Guide to the reports of the Royal Commission on Historical Manuscripts, 1911-1957. London, H.M.S.O., 1966–

v. 25.5 cm.

A continuation of Guide to the reports of the Royal Commission on Historical Manuscripts 1870-1911, published as pt. 2 of A guide to the reports on collections of manuscripts of private families, corporations and institutions in Great Britain and Ireland issued by the Royal Commissioners for Historical Manu-

scripts.
CONTENTS:
—pt. 2. Index of persons, edited by A. C. S. Hall.

Gt. Brit. *Public Record Office.*
Gifts and deposits. London, Swift, 1966–

> v. facsims. 34 cm. (List & Index Society [Publications] v. 10

Gt. Brit. *Public Record Office.*
State papers supplementary. London, Swift, 1966–

> v. 33½ cm. (List & Index Society. [Publications] v. 9)

CONTENTS.—pt. 1. General papers to 1603.

Gross, Charles, 1857–1909.
The sources and literature of English history from the earliest times to about 1485. 2d ed. New York, A. M. Kelley, 1970.

> xxiii, 820 p. 23 cm.
> Reprint of the 1915 ed.

Hardy, *Sir* **Thomas Duffus,** 1804–1878.
Descriptive catalogue of materials relating to the history of Great Britain and Ireland, to the end of the reign of Henry VII. New York, B. Franklin [1964?]

> 3 v. in 4. 26 cm. (Burt Franklin bibliographical and reference series, no. 45)
> (L. C. lacks v. 1, pt. 1 and v. 2)
> Reprint of the 1862 ed.
> CONTENTS.—v. 1. From the Roman period to the Norman invasion. 2. v.—v. 2. From A. D. 1066 to A. D. 1200.—v. 3. From A. D. 1200 to A. D. 1327.

Historical Association, *London. Local History Committee.*
English local history handlist: a short bibliography and list of sources for the study of local history and antiquities; edited for the Local History Committee of the Historical Association by F. W. Kuhlicke and F. G. Emmison. 3rd ed. completely revised and rewritten. London, Historical Association, 1965.

> 73 p. 22 cm. (Helps for students of history, no. 69)

Historical Association, *London. Local History Committee.*
English local history handlist: a select bibliography and list of sources for the study of local history and antiquities; edited for the Local History Committee of the Historical Association by F. W. Kuhlicke & F. G. Emmison. 4th edition by F. G. Emmison. London, Historical Association, 1969.

> 84 p. 22 cm. (Helps for students of history, no. 69)

Humphrey, Elizabeth.
Periodicals and sets relating to British history in Norfolk and Suffolk libraries: a finding list; [compiled by Elizabeth Humphrey]. Norwich (University Plain, Norwich NOR 88C), University of East Anglia (Library); Centre of East Anglian Studies, 1971.

> [1], vi, 143 p. 21 cm.

Library Association. *County Libraries Group.*
Readers' guide to books on Hanoverian Britain. 2nd ed. London, Library Association (County Libraries Group), 1968.

> 40 p. 19 cm. (*Its* Readers' guides, new ser., no. 100)
> Cover title: Hanoverian Britain.

Macray, William Dunn, 1826–1916.
A manual of British historians to A. D. 1600. Containing a chronological account of the early chroniclers and monkish writers, their printed works and unpublished MSS. Naar-

den, Anton W. van Bekhoven, 1967.

> xxiii, 113 p. 21 cm.
> Reprint of the 1845 London ed.

Mullins, Edward Lindsay Carson.
A guide to the historical and archaeological publications of societies in England and Wales, 1901–1933; compiled for the Institute of Historical Research [by] E. L. C. Mullins. London, Athlone P., 1968.

> xiii, 850 p. 26 cm.

Royal Historical Society, *London.*
Writings on British history 1901–1933: a bibliography of books and articles on the history of Great Britain from about 400 A. D. to 1914, published during the years 1901–1933 inclusive, with an appendix containing a select list of publications in these years on British history since 1914. London, Cape, 1968–

> v. 24 cm.
> CONTENTS.—v. 1. Auxiliary Sciences and general works.

Shaw, William Arthur, 1865–1943.
A bibliography of the historical works of Dr. Creighton, Dr. Stubbs, Dr. S. R. Gardiner and the late Lord Acton. Edited for the Royal Historical Society by W. A. Shaw. New York, B. Franklin [1969]

> 63 p. 23 cm. (Burt Franklin: bibliography and reference series, 286)
> Reprint of the 1903 ed.

TO 1485

Altschul, Michael.
Anglo-Norman England, 1066–1154. London, Cambridge U. P. for the Conference on British Studies, 1969.

> xii, 83 p. 23 cm. (Conference on British Studies. Bibliographical handbooks)

Bonser, Wilfrid, 1887–
A Romano-British bibliography, 55 B. C.–A. D. 449, by Wilfrid Bonser. Oxford, B. Blackwell, 1964 [i. e. 1965]

> 2 v. 26 cm.
> Vol. [2]: Indexes.
> "Includes material published to the end of 1959."

Hastings Public Library.
The Norman conquest; a ninth centenary booklist, 1966. [Hastings, Eng., 1966]

> 28 p. 22 cm.

Library Association. *County Libraries Group.*
Readers' guide to books on medieval Britain. 2d ed. [London] 1964.

> 23 p. 19 cm. (*Its* Readers' guide, new ser., no. 82)
> Cover title: Medieval Britain.
> "Compiled by the Librarian and staff of the Somerset County Library."

Moore, Margaret Findlay.
Two select bibliographies of mediæval historical study, by Margaret F. Moore. With a pref. by Hubert Hall. New York, B. Franklin [1967?]

> 185 p. 24 cm. (Burt Franklin bibliography & reference series, no. 124)
> Reprint of the 1912 ed.
> CONTENTS.—Account of the classes in mediæval history at the London School of Economics.—Bibliography of palæography & diplomatic.—Bibliography of manorial and agrarian history.

National Book League, *London.*
Life at the time of the Conquest, with a foreword by Hope Muntz. London, National Book League, 1966.

37 p. 21½ cm. 3/-

Platt, Colin.
Medieval archaeology in England: a guide to the historical sources. Isle of Wight, Pinhorns, 1969.

[3], 32 p. 21 cm. (Pinhorns handbooks, 5)

1485 - 1800

Crawford, James Ludovic Lindsay, *26th Earl of,* 1847–1913.
A bibliography of royal proclamations of the Tudor and Stuart sovereigns and of others published under authority, 1485–1714. With an historical essay on their origin and use, by Robert Steele. New York, B. Franklin [1967]

4 v. in 3. coats of arms. 32 cm. (Burt Franklin: Bibliography and reference series, #128)

On spine: A bibliography of proclamations, 1485–1910.
Half title v. 1–3: Tudor and Stuart proclamations.
Vol. 4 has title: Handlist of proclamations issued by royal and other constitutional authorities, 1714–1910, George I to Edward VII, together with an index of names and places.
"First published as Bibliotheca Lindesiana v–[VI, VIII], 1910–[13]"

"The bibliography of proclamations": v. 1, p. [xxxiii]–xlviii. "Authorities consulted": v. 1, p. [cliii]–clvi.

CONTENTS.—v. 1. England and Wales.—v. 2. Ireland. v. 3. Scotland. 2 v. in 1.—v. 4. George I to Edward VII.

Davies, Godfrey, 1892–1957, ed.
Bibliography of British history, Stuart period, 1603–1714. Issued under the direction of the American Historical Association and the Royal Historical Society of Great Britain. 2nd ed. [edited by] Mary Frear Keeler. Oxford, Clarendon Press, 1970.

xxxv, 734 p. 24 cm.

Gt. Brit. *Public Record Office.*
Public Record Office gifts and deposits, Chatham papers. London, Swift, 1966.

[2] p. 212 f. 33 cm. (List & Index Society. [Publications] v. 8)

Grose, Clyde Leclare, 1889–1942.
A select bibliography of British history, 1660–1760. New York, Octagon Books, 1967 [c1939]

xxv, 507 p. 24 cm.

Levine, Mortimer.
Tudor England 1485–1603. London, Cambridge U. P. for the Conference on British Studies, 1968.

xii, 115 p. 22 cm. (Conference on British Studies. Bibliographical handbooks)

Library Association. County Libraries Group.
Readers' guide to books on Tudor & Stuart Britain. 2d ed. Newtown, Library Association (County Libraries Group), 1970.

45 p. 19 cm. (Its Readers' guides, new series no. 113)

Miller, Helen.
Early modern British history, 1485–1760: a select bibliography, by Helen Miller and Aubrey Newman. London, Historical Association, 1970.

42 p. 22 cm. Index. (Helps for students of history no. 79)

Morgan, William Thomas, 1883–1946.
A bibliography of British history (1700–1715) with special reference to the reign of Queen Anne. New York, B. Franklin [1973–   c1934–

v. 27 cm. (Burt Franklin bibliography & reference series, 463. Selected studies in history, economics & social science, n. s. 24. (c) Modern European studies)
Original ed. issued as v. 18–19, 23–26, no. 94–95, 114–124 of Indiana University studies.
Vols. 2–3 and 5 by W. T. Morgan and C. S. Morgan.

Sachse, William Lewis, 1912–
Restoration England, 1660–1689 [by] William L. Sachse. Cambridge [Eng., Published] for the Conference on British Studies at the University Press, 1971.

ix, 114 p. 22 cm. (Conference on British Studies. Bibliographical handbooks)

19TH - 20TH CENTURIES

Altholz, Josef Lewis, 1933–
Victorian England 1837–1901 [by] Josef L. Altholz. Cambridge [Eng.] for the Conference on British Studies at the University Press, 1970.

xi, 100 p. 22 cm. (Conference on British studies. Bibliographical handbooks [3])

Brighton, Eng. Public Library, Museums, and Fine Art Galleries.
Regency England: a booklist. Brighton. Brighton Public Libraries, 1971.

vii, 36 p., 4 plates. illus., port. 21 cm.

Canberra, Australia. National Library.
Oxford and Cambridge University Club's pamphlet collection acquired in 1968 by the National Library of Australia; contents list. Canberra, 1971.

236 p. 25 cm.

Collection comprises 1300 pamphlets published in Britain between 1829 and 1882.

Christie, Ian R
British history since 1760: a select bibliography, by Ian R. Christie. London, Historical Association, 1970.

56 p. 22 cm. index. (Helps for students of history, no. 81)

Great Britain. Public Record Office.
Records of interest to social scientists 1919–1939: introduction. [By] Brenda Swann [and] Maureen Turnbull. London, H. M. Stationery Off., 1971.

viii, 280, [2] p. 25 cm. (Its Handbooks, no. 14)

Library Association. *County Libraries Group.*
Readers' guide to books on Victorian Britain. 2d ed. [London] 1965.

38 p. 19 cm. (*Its* Readers' guide, new ser., no. 84)

Cover title: Victorian Britain.
"Compiled by the Librarian and staff of Surrey County Library."

Madden, Lionel.
How to find out about the Victorian period; a guide to sources of information. [1st ed.] Oxford, New York, Pergamon Press [1970]

xiv, 173 p. 20 cm. (The Commonwealth and international library. Libraries and technical information division)

Mowat, Charles Loch, 1911–1970.
Great Britain since 1914. Ithaca, N. Y., Cornell University Press [1971]

224 p. 23 cm. (The Sources of history: studies in the uses of historical evidence)

Mowat, Charles Loch, 1911–1970.
Great Britain since 1914, by C. L. Mowat. London, Hodder and Stoughton [for] the Sources of History Ltd, 1971.

224 p. 23 cm. index. (The sources of history: studies in the uses of historical evidence)

[Standen, John].
The Victorian age. London, National Book League, 1967.

86 p. 22 cm.

Webb, Robert Kiefer.

English history, 1815–1914, by R. K. Webb. Washington, Service Center for Teachers of History ₍1967₎

32 p. 23 cm. (Service Center for Teachers of History. Publication no. 64)

Winkler, Henry Ralph, 1916–

Great Britain in the twentieth century, by Henry R. Winkler. 2d ed. Washington, Service Center for Teachers of History ₍1966, °1960₎

36 p. 23 cm. (Service Center for Teachers of History. Publication no. 28)

HISTORY, LOCAL

Dillon's University Bookshop, *London.*

British local history; a selected bibliography. ₍Compiled by Peter Stockham. London, 1964₎

80 p. 22 cm.

Caption title.

Emmison, Frederick George, 1907–

County records (quarter sessions, petty sessions, Clerk of the Peace and Lieutenancy), by F. G. Emmison and Irvine Gray. ₍Revised ed.₎ reprinted (appendices revised). London, Historical Association, 1967.

₍1₎, 32 p. 22 cm. (Helps for students of history, no. 62)

Gross, Charles, 1857–1909.

A bibliography of British municipal history, including gilds and Parliamentary representation. 2nd ed., with a preface by G. H. Martin. Leicester, Leicester U. P., 1966.

vi, xvi, vii–xxxiv, 461 p. 22½ cm.

Gross, Charles, 1857–1909.

A bibliography of British municipal history, including gilds and parliamentary representation. New York, B. Franklin ₍1971?₎

xxxiv, 461 p. 24 cm. (Burt Franklin bibliography and reference series, no. 64)

Reprint of the 1897 ed., which was issued as v. 5 of the Harvard historical studies.

Humphreys, Darlow Willis.

Local history for students; material compiled by D. W. Humphreys, and F. G. Emmison. London, published for the Standing Conference for Local History by the National Council of Social Service ₍1966₎

24 p. 21½ cm.

Lancashire and Cheshire Antiquarian Society, *Manchester, Eng. Library.*

Author catalogue of the Lancashire and Cheshire Antiquarian Society Library in the Manchester Central Library ₍the catalogue has been compiled by the Book Services Department of the Manchester Public Libraries and edited by N. K. Firby₎ Manchester, Lancashire and Cheshire Antiquarian Society, 1968.

₍87₎ p. 26 cm.

Library Association. County Libraries Group.

Readers' guide to books on sources of local history, ₍by the₎ Library Association, County Libraries Group. 4th ed. Newtown (c/o Hon Publications Officer, County Libraries Group. Montgomeryshire County Library, Park La., Newtown, Montgomeryshire SY16 1EJ), Library Association (County Libraries Group), 1971.

34 p. 19 cm. (Its Readers' guide, new series, no. 122)

Martin, Geoffrey Haward.

A bibliography of British and Irish municipal history,

₍by₎ G. H. Martin and Sylvia MacIntyre. Leicester, Leicester University Press, 1972–

v. 23 cm.

CONTENTS: v. 1. General works.—

Stephens, W   B

Sources for English local history ₍by₎ W. B. Stephens. Manchester, Manchester University Press, 1973.

x, 260 p. 23 cm.

Distributed in the USA by Rowman and Littlefield, Totowa, N. J.

Youings, Joyce A

Local record sources in print and in progress 1971–72. Compiled for the Local History Committee of the Historical Association, by Joyce Youings. ₍London₎ Historical Association, 1972.

24 p. 22 cm. (Helps for students of history, no. 85)

HISTORY, MILITARY AND NAVAL

Higham, Robin D   S

A guide to the sources of British military history. Edited by Robin Higham. Berkeley, University of California Press, 1971.

xxi, 630 p. 25 cm.

Manwaring, George Ernest, 1882–1939.

A bibliography of British Naval history; a biographical and historical guide to printed and manuscript sources, by G. E. Manwaring. ₍London₎ Conway Maritime Press, 1970.

xxii, 163 p. 23 cm.

Distributed in U. S. A. by Antheil Booksellers, No. Bellmore, N. Y. First published in 1930.

National Book League, *London.*

Story of the Royal Air Force: a selected list ₍compiled by₎ the National Book League in association with the Air Historical Branch (R. A. F.). London, National Book League, 1968.

28 p. 22 cm.

White, Arthur Sharpin.

A bibliography of regimental histories of the British Army, compiled by Arthur S. White. With a foreword by Sir Gerald W. R. Templer. ₍London₎ Society for Army Historical Research, 1965.

viii, 265 p. 26 cm.

IMPRINTS see English imprints

LAW see Law - Great Britain

MAPS

Campbell, Tony.

Catalogue 6 maps; outline of the British Isles: printed maps 1482–1887. ₍Compiled by Tony Campbell. London, Printed by R. Stockwell, 1970₎

107 p. maps, coats of arms. 21 cm.

At head of title: Weinreb and Douwma Ltd.

Fordham, Angela, *comp.*

Town plans of the British Isles; series appearing in atlases from 1580–1850. London, Map Collectors' Circle, 1965.

17, ₍30₎ p. maps. 25 cm. (Map collectors' series, no. 22)

Newcastle-upon-Tyne. *University. Library.*

An exhibition of old maps of North East England, 1600–1865; September–October 1967. Newcastle-upon-Tyne, University of Newcastle-upon-Tyne ₍1969₎

₍3₎, 8 l. 30 cm. (Its Publications. Extra series, no. 7)

Oxford. University. Bodleian Library.
The large scale county maps of the British Isles, 1596–1850: a union list; compiled by Elizabeth M. Rodger. 2nd, revised ed. Oxford, Bodleian Library, 1972.

xx, 56 p. 24 cm.

Skelton, Raleigh Ashlin.
County atlases of the British Isles, 1579–1850; a bibliography compiled by R. A. Skelton in collaboration with members of the staff of the Map Room, British Museum. London, Map Collectors' Circle, 1964–

v. facsim. 25 cm. (Map Collectors' Circle. Map collectors' series, no. 9, 14
Issued in parts.
Supersedes Thomas Chubb's The printed maps in the atlases of Great Britain and Ireland; a bibliography, 1579–1870.

Skelton, Raleigh Ashlin.
County atlases of the British Isles, 1579–1850: a bibliography; compiled by R. A. Skelton. London, Carta Press, 1970–

v. illus., facsims., maps, ports. 26 cm

Supersedes Thomas Chubb's The printed maps in the atlases of Great Britain and Ireland: a bibliography, 1579–1870.
Vols also issued in parts in the Map Collectors series of the Map Collectors Circle.
CONTENTS: v. 1. 1579–1703.

RACE QUESTION

Gt. Brit. *Community Relations Commission.*
Race relations in Britain: selected bibliography with emphasis on Commonwealth immigrants. London, Community Relations Commission, 1969.

[14] p. 23 cm.

"Based on the Reading list on race relations produced by the Institute of Race Relations in 1966."

Institute of Race Relations.
Coloured immigrants in Britain; a select bibliography based on the holdings of the library of the Institute of Race Relations. [London] 1965.

18 p. 27 cm.

Sivanandan, Ambalavaner.
Coloured immigrants in Britain: a select bibliography; compiled by A. Sivanandan. 2nd ed. London, Institute of Race Relations, 1967.

vi, 82 p. 21 cm.

First ed., 1965, prepared by the Institute of Race Relations.

Sivanandan, Ambalavaner.
Register of research on Commonwealth immigrants in Britain. 3rd ed., compiled by A. Sivanandan and Sheila Bagley. London, Institute of Race Relations; distributed by Research Publications, 1968.

[4], 30 p. 21 cm.

Sivanandan, Ambalavaner.
Register of research on Commonwealth immigrants in Britain. 4th ed., compiled by A. Sivanandan and Jane Marix Evans. London, Institute of Race Relations; distributed by Research Publications, 1969.

[3], 37 p. 21 cm.

STATISTICS

Colchester, Eng. University of Essex. Library.
British statistics: a select list of sources. (Colchester), University of Essex Library, 1972.

[1], xii, 60 p. 21 cm. index. (Its Reference leaflet no. 3)

Great Britain. Central Statistical Office.
List of principal statistical series and publications. London, H. M. Stationery Off., 1972.

v, 41 p. 30 cm. (Its Studies in official statistics, no. 20)

Joint Working Party of Librarians and Economic Statisticians.
Recommended basic statistical sources for community use. London, Library Association, 1969.

16 p. 20 cm.

A Union list of statistical serials in British libraries. Committee of Librarians and Statisticians [of the] Library Association and Royal Statistical Society. London, Library Association, 1972.

86 p. 30 cm. index. (LA-RSS resources in economic statistics, 3)

GREAT BRITAIN. ADMIRALTY

Gt. Brit. *Public Record Office.*
List of Admiralty records (to 1913). New York, Kraus Reprint Corp., 1966–67.

2 v. 32 cm. (Its Lists and indexes. Supplementary series, no. 6)

CONTENTS. — V. 1. Accounting departments — dockyard records. — v. 2. Greenwich Hospital—Transport Department.

GREAT BRITAIN. BOARD OF TRADE

Gt. Brit. *Public Record Office.*
List of Board of Trade records to 1913. New York, Kraus Reprint Corp., 1964.

ii, 266 p. 32 cm. (Its Lists and indexes. Supplementary series, no. 11)

GREAT BRITAIN. HOME DEPARTMENT

Gt. Brit. Home Dept.
Home Office registered papers. London, Swift, 1967.

2, 259 l. 33 cm. (List & Index Society. [Publications] v. 30)

GREAT BRITAIN. INDIA OFFICE

Lancaster, Joan Cadogan.
A guide to lists and catalogues of the India Office records [by] Joan C. Lancaster. London, Commonwealth Office, 1966.

iii, 26 p. 21½ cm.

GREAT BRITAIN. PARLIAMENT

Bond, Maurice Francis.
Guide to the records of Parliament [by] Maurice F. Bond. London, H. M. Stationery Off., 1971.

x, 352 p. 26 cm.

At head of title: House of Lords Record Office.

Gt. Brit. *Parliament. House of Commons.*
List of House of Commons sessional papers, 1701–1750; edited by Sheila Lambert. London, Swift (P. & D.) Ltd., 1968.

155 l. 33 cm. (List & Index Society. Special series, v. 1)

Palmer, John, 1930–
Government and Parliament in Britain: a bibliography. 2d ed., rev. and enl. London, Hansard Society for Parliamentary Government, 1964.

51 p. 22 cm.

GREAT BRITAIN. PRIVY COUNCIL

Adair, Edward Robert, 1888-1965.
The sources for the history of the Council in the sixteenth &

seventeenth centuries. Port Washington, N.Y., Kennikat Press [1971]

96 p. 21 cm.

Reprint of the 1924 ed.

GREAT LAKES REGION

Hacia, Henry.
A selected annotated bibliography of the climate of the Great Lakes. Silver Spring. Md., U. S. Environmental Data Service, 1972.

iv, 70 p. 27 cm. (NOAA technical memorandum EDS BS-7)

Towle, Edward L
Bibliography on the economic history and geography of the Great Lakes-St. Lawrence drainage basin; preliminary draft, by Edward L. Towle. Rochester, N. Y. [1964]
41 l. 29 cm.
Cover title.
———— Supplementary list #1, by Edward L. Towle. Rochester, N. Y., 1964.

34 l. 29 cm.

GREECE
see also under Rome

Belin de Ballu, Eugène.
L'histoire de colonies grecques du littoral nord de la mer Noire; bibliographie annotée des ouvrages et articles publiés en U. R. S. S. de 1940 à 1962, par E. Belin de Ballu. [2d éd.] Leiden, E. J. Brill, 1965.

xxv, 209 p. maps. 25 cm.

Cinq ans de bibliographie historique en Grèce (1965–1969) avec un supplément pour les années 1950–1964. Athènes, Comité national hellénique de l'association internationale des études du sud-est européen, 1970.

viii, 133 p. 24 cm.

"Offert à l'occasion du deuxième congrès international des études du sud-est européen."

Dimaras, C   Th   1904–
Modern Greek culture; a selected bibliography, in English, French, German, Italian [by] C. Th. Dimaras, C. Koumarianou [and] L. Droulia. [Enl. ed.] Thessaloniki, Institute for Balkan Studies, 1968.
viii, 137 p. 25 cm. ('Εταιρεία Μακεδονικῶν Σπουδῶν. Ἵδρυμα Μελετῶν Χερσονήσου τοῦ Αἵμου. [Ἐκδόσεις] 103)
"First appeared [in 1966] as a supplement to the French edition of ... [the author's] History of modern Greek literature."

National Book League, *London.*
Greece: an annotated list of current books. London, National Book League in association with the Anglo-Hellenic League, 1968.

34 p. 22 cm.

Vlachos, Evan.
Modern Greek society: continuity and change; an annotated classification of selected sources. [Fort Collins, Dept. of Sociology and Anthropology, Colorado State University, 1969]

177 l. 28 cm. (Colorado State University. Dept. of Sociology and Anthropology. Special monograph series, no. 1)

LIBRARY CATALOGS

American School of Classical Studies at Athens. *Gennadius Library.*
Catalogue. Boston, G. K. Hall, 1968.

7 v. 37 cm.

GREEK CHURCH   see   Orthodox Eastern Church

GREEK IMPRINTS
La Stampa greca a Venezia nei secoli xv e xvi. Catalogo di mostra a cura di Marcello Finazzi. Venezia, Libreria vecchia del Sansovino, 31 maggio–30 settembre 1968. Venezia, Centro arti e mestieri, Fondazione Giorgio Cini, 1968.

vii, 67 p. 26 plates. 24½ cm.

At head of title: Biblioteca nazionale marciana, Venezia, v centenario della fondazione, 1468–1968.

Vienna. Ethnikē Hellēnikē Scholē. Bibliothēkē.
Κατάλογος. Ἐν Βιέννῃ, Ἐκ τῆς τυπογραφίας 'Α. Μπέγκου, 1846. [Ἀθῆναι, Βιβλιοπωλεῖον Ν. Καραβία, 1967]

82 p. 27 cm. (Βιβλιοθήκη ἱστορικῶν μελετῶν, 24)

GREEK INSCRIPTIONS   see   Inscriptions, Greek

GREEK LANGUAGE, BIBLICAL

Tov, 'Imanu'el.
מחקרים דקדוקיים ולכסיקוגרפיים על לשון תרגום השבעים; לקט בבליוגרפי. בעריכת עמנואל טוב. ירושלים, אקדמון, [1970]

16 p. 27 cm.

GREEK LAW   see   Law, Greek

GREEK LITERATURE
see also   Classical literature

Fabricius, Johann Albert, 1668–1736.
Bibliotheca Graeca. Hildesheim, G. Olms, 1966–

v. 23 cm.

Facsimile reprint of Hamburg ed., 1790–

GREEK LITERATURE, MODERN

Ladas, Geōrgios Geōrg.
   (Hellēnikē vivliogarphia)
Ἑλληνικὴ βιβλιογραφία· συμβολὴ στὸ δέκατο ὄγδοο αἰώνα [ὑπὸ] Γεωργίου Γ. Λαδᾶ καὶ 'Αθανασίου Δ. Χατζηδήμου. Προσθῆκες, διορθώσεις καὶ συμπληρώσεις στὴν Ἑλληνικὴ βιβλιογραφία τῶν Émile Legrand, Louis Petit καὶ Hubert Pernot. 'Αθήνα, 1964.

31, 282 p. facsims. 29 cm. (Ἐκδόσεις τοῦ περιοδικοῦ "Συλλέκτης," ἀρ. 1)

On spine: Συμβολὴ στὴν Ἑλληνικὴ βιβλιογραφία τῶν E. Legrand, L. Petit [καὶ] H. Pernot. XVIIIος αἰώνας.

Later ed. published under title: Ἑλληνικὴ βιβλιογραφία τῶν ἐτῶν 1791–1795.

Ladas, Geōrgios Geōrg
   (Hellēnikē vivliographia tōn etōn 1791–1795)
Ἑλληνικὴ βιβλιογραφία τῶν ἐτῶν 1791–1795 [ὑπὸ] Γεωργίου Γ. Λαδᾶ καὶ 'Αθανασίου Δ. Χατζηδήμου. 'Αθήνα, 1970.

431 p. facsims. 25 cm.

Previous ed. published under title: Ἑλληνικὴ βιβλιογραφία.

Mpoumpoulidēs, Phaidōn K
Βιβλιογραφία Νεοελληνικῆς φιλολογίας τοῦ ἔτους 1966 [ὑπὸ] Φαίδωνος Κ. Μπουμπουλίδου. 'Αθῆναι, 1969.

62 p. 26 cm.

Reprinted from the Ἐπιστημονικὴ ἐπετηρὶς τῆς Φιλοσοφικῆς Σχολῆς τοῦ Πανεπιστημίου 'Αθηνῶν, v. 19 (1968–69)

Raste, B   E
Ἑλληνικὴ βιβλιογραφία (συμβολὴ στὴ δεκατετία 1791–1799) [ὑπὸ] Β. Ε. Ράστε. 'Αθῆναι, Βιβλιοπωλεῖον Ν. Καραβία, 1969.

11, 69 p. 26 cm. (Βιβλιοθήκη ἱστορικῶν μελετῶν, 28)

Sathas, Kōnstantinos N   1842–1914.
Νεοελληνικὴ φιλολογία· βιογραφίαι τῶν ἐν τοῖς γράμμασι διαλαμψάντων Ἑλλήνων, ἀπὸ τῆς καταλύσεως τῆς Βυζαντινῆς Αὐτοκρατορίας μέχρι τῆς Ἑλληνικῆς ἐθνεγερσίας (1453–1821). Ἐν 'Αθήναις, Ἐκ τῆς τυπογραφίας τῶν τέκνων 'Α. Κορομηλᾶ,

1868· ₍'Αθῆναι, 'I. Χιωτέλη, 196–₎
3, 761 p. 24 cm.

—————— Νεοελληνικῆς φιλολογίας παράρτημα· ἱστορία τοῦ ζητή-
ματος τῆς νεολληνικῆς γλώσσης. Ἐν 'Αθήναις, 'Ἐκ τῆς τυπο-
γραφ. τῶν τέκνων 'Α. Κορομηλᾶ, 1870· ₍'Αθῆναι, 'I. Χιωτέλη,
1969₎
338 p. 25 cm.

Søholm, Ejgil, comp.
Nygræsk litteratur. Århus, Statsbiblioteket, 1966.

83 p. 21 cm.

GREEK PHILOLOGY

Amerongen, R   van.
Beknopte bibliographie voor de studie der Griekse taal-
en letterkunde. Bewerkt door W. J. Verdenius. 4. herz.
druk. Uitg. onder auspiciën van de Wetenschappelijke
Sectie van het Nederlands Klassiek Verbond. Amsterdam,
A. M. Hakkert, 1967.

96 p. 21½ cm.

Bonaria, Mario.
Commento ai programmi di greco. Milano, Marzorati,
₍1969₎.

246 p. 19 cm.

Corte, Francesco della.
Avviamento allo studio delle lettere greche. Genova, M.
Bozzi, 1969.

151 p. 23½ cm.

GREEKS IN FOREIGN COUNTRIES

Cutsumbis, Michael N   1935–
A bibliographic guide on Greeks in the United States,
1890–1968 ₍by₎ Michael N. Cutsumbis. Staten Island, N. Y.,
Center for Migration Studies ₍1970₎

100 p. 23 cm.

Cutsumbis, Michael N   1935–
Selective bibliography for the sociological study of Greek-
Americans ₍by₎ M. N. Cutsumbis. ₍Lancaster? Pa., 1967₎

₍9₎ l. 28 cm.

Vlachos, Evan.
An annotated bibliography on Greek migration ₍by₎
Evangelos Vlachos. Athens, Social Sciences Centre, 1966.

viii, 127 l. 28 cm. (Research monographs on migration, 1)

GREEN, JULIEN
Hoy, Peter C
Julien Green; essai de bibliographie des études en langue
française consacrées à Julien Green (1923–1967), par Peter
C. Hoy. 1. livr. Paris, Lettres modernes, 1970.

1 v. (unpaged) 18 cm. (Calepins de bibliographie, no 3)
(Lettres modernes)

"Chaque livraison annule et remplace la précédente."

GREENE, GRAHAM
Vann, Jerry Don.
Graham Greene; a checklist of criticism, by J. Don Vann.
₍1st ed. Kent, Ohio₎ Kent State University Press ₍1970₎

vii, 69 p. (p. 67–68 advertisements) 23 cm. (Serif series: bibliographies and checklists, no. 14)

GREENE, ROBERT
Hayashi, Tetsumaro.
Robert Greene criticism: a comprehensive bibliography.
With an introd. by Louis Marder. Metuchen, N. J., Scare-
crow Press, 1971.·

146 p. 22 cm. (The Scarecrow author bibliographies series, no.
6)

GREENIDGE, CHARLES WILTON WOOD
Oxford. University. Rhodes House Library.
Papers of Charles Wilton Wood Greenidge; Mss Brit.
Emp. s 285. ₍Prepared by J. C. Williams. Oxford?, 1969?₎

227 l. 26 cm.

At head of title: Oxford University colonial records project.

GREGOR-TAJOVSKÝ, JOZEF
Maruniaková, Anna, comp.
Jozef Gregor-Tajovský, 1874–1940, Hana Gregorová,
1885–1958. Spracovala Anna Maruniaková. V Martine,
Matica slovenská, 1968.

96 p. illus. 20 cm. (Rukopisné fondy Literárneho archívu Matice slovenskej v Martine, 37)

GREGORIAN CHANT see Chants (Plain,
Gregorian, etc.)

GREGORIUS, SAINT, BP. OF NYSSA
Bergadá, María Mercedes.
Contribución bibliográfica para el estudio de Gregorio de
Nyssa. ₍Buenos Aires₎ Instituto de Filosofía, Universidad
de Buenos Aires, 1970.

63 p. 23 cm. (Centro de Estudios de Filosofía Medieval. Serie
C, no. 1)

GREGOROVA, HANA see under Gregor-
Tajovský, Jozef

GRÉGR, EDUARD
Křivský, Pavel.
Eduard Grégr. (1827–1907.) Literární pozůstalost.
Zprac. Pavel Křivský. Praha, Literární archív Památníku
nár. písemnictví, t. Ruch, Liberec, 1971.

6, ₍1₎ p. 20 cm. (Edice inventářů. čís. 205)

GRÉGR, JULIUS
Křivský, Pavel.
Julius Grégr. (1831–1896). Literární pozůstalost.
Zprac. Pavel Křivský. Praha, Literární archív Památníku
nár. písemnictví, t. Ruch, Liberec, 1971.

6, ₍1₎ p. 20 cm. (Edice inventářů. čís. 224)

GRENOBLE see under Dauphiné *(Nigay)*
GRIECO, AGRIPPINO
Rio de Janeiro. Biblioteca Nacional.
Agripino Grieco, 1888–1968, exposição comemorativa do
80° aniversário de nascimento. Rio de Janeiro, 1968.

39 p. port. 23 cm.

GRIER, SIR SELWYN MACGREGOR
Oxford. University. Rhodes House Library.
Papers of Sir Selwyn Grier; Mss Afr. s 1379. ₍Prepared
by S. C. Willson-Pepper. Oxford?, 1970?₎

7 l. 26 cm.

At head of title: Oxford University colonial records project.

GRIEVE, CHRISTOPHER MURRAY
Scotland. National Library, *Edinburgh.*
Hugh MacDiarmid. Edinburgh, 1967.

39 p. illus., facsims. 25 cm. (*Its* Catalogue no. 7)

GRILLPARZER, FRANZ
Vienna. Nationalbibliothek. Theatersammlung.
Franz Grillparzer. Zum 100. Todestag. Ausstellung im
Prunksaal d. Österr. Nationalbibliothek (vom 2. Juni bis

14. Okt. 1972). Katalog. (Leitung d. Ausstellung u. Red. des Katalogs: Karl Gladt ₍und₎ Josef Mayerhöfer. Bearb. des Katalog: Rüdiger Schiferer.) Wien (Österr. Nationalbibliothek) 1972.

120 p. 4 l. of illus. 21 cm.

On cover: Grillparzer Ausstellung.

GRIMM, JAKOB LUDWIG KARL and WILHELM KARL

Wegehaupt, Heinz.
150 ₍i. e. Hundertfünfzig₎ Jahre "Kinder- und Hausmärchen" der Brüder Grimm; Bibliographie und Materialien zu einer Ausstellung der Deutschen Staatsbibliothek. ₍Bearb. von Heinz Wegehaupt und Renate Riepert₎. Berlin, Deutsche Staatsbibliothek, 1964.

111 p. illus., col. plates, ports. 24 cm.

GRISONS

Bornatico, Remo, 1913–
Bibliografia grigionitaliana, ⟨dagli inizi al 1969⟩. Coira, Biblioteca cantonale dei Grigioni, 1969/70.

153 p. 25 cm.

GRIVA, ŽANIS, pseud. see Folmanis, Zanis

GRONINGEN (PROVINCE)

Noordhoff, L   J
Archieven van de ambtenaren van de waterstaat die binnen het gebied der tegenwoordige provincie Groningen en soms mede daarbuiten gefungeerd hebben in de eerste helft der 19e eeuw. Door L. J. Noordhoff. Groningen, Rijksarchief, 1967.

100 p. 29 cm.

GRÖNLOH, J. H. F.

Aandacht voor Nescio; een bibliografie van de reacties op het werk en de figuur van J. H. F. Grönloh, met een bloemlezing uit die reacties en een toegift. Amsterdam, Instituut voor Neerlandistiek, Universiteit, 1972.

ix, 121 p. illus. 21 cm.

GROSS, VILLEM

Villem Gross: bibliograafiline nimestik. Koostanud M. Gross. Autobiograafia: V. Gross. Tallinn, 1971.

61 p. 20 cm.

At head of title: Eesti NSV Kultuuriministeerium. Fr. R. Kreutzwaldi nim. Eesti NSV Riiklik Raamatukogu.
"Villem Grossi 50. sünnipäevaks."

GROTIUS, HUGO

Institut néerlandais, *Paris.*
La vie et l'œuvre de Grotius (1583–1645). Exposition, Institut néerlandais, Paris, 15 mars–15 avril, 1965. ₍Paris, Presses artistiques, 1965₎

69 p., 46 p. of illus. (facsims., ports.) 23 cm.

GROULX, LIONEL ADOLPHE

Barbeau, Victor, 1896–   *ed.*
L'œuvre du chanoine Lionel Groulx: témoignages, biobibliographie. ₍Conçu et réalisé par Victor Barbeau. La bibliographie est l'oeuvre de Juliette Rémillard et de Madeleine Dionne₎ Montréal, Académie canadienne-française ₍1964₎

197 p. port. 26 cm.

GROUND-NUTS see Peanuts
GROUPS, THEORY OF

Davis, Constance.
A bibliographical survey of groups with two generators

and their relations. ₍New York₎ Courant Institute of Mathematical Sciences, 1972.

viii, 353 p. 28 cm.

GUADALAJARA, MEXICO

Medina, José Toribio, 1852–1930.
La imprenta en Guadalajara de Mexico: 1793–1831. Amsterdam, N. Israel, 1966.

104 p. 22 cm. (Reprint series of José Toribio Medina's bibliographical works, 20)

Reprint of the 1904 ed.

GUARDA, PORTUGAL (DISTRICT)

Gomes, Jesué Pinharanda, 1939–
Subsídios para a bibliografia do Distrito da Guarda. Lisboa, Junta Distrital da Guarda, 1970.

111 p. 21 cm.

GUATEMALA

Guatemala (City) Biblioteca Nacional.
Indice bibliográfico de los discursos pronunciados en Guatemala, durante las fiestas de la Independencia, desde el 15 de septiembre de 1821, hasta 1964. Guatemala, 1965.

88 p. 26 cm.

Guatemala (City). Museo del Libro Antiguo.
Catálogo del Museo del Libro Antiguo: impresos guatemaltecos de la época colonial ₍por₎ Manuel Reyes Hernández. ₍Guatemala₎ Editorial José de Pineda Ibarra, 1971.

165 p. illus. 21 cm.

Lines, Jorge A   1891–
Anthropological bibliography of aboriginal Guatemala, British Honduras; Bibliografía antropológica aborigen de Guatemala. Belice ₍by₎ Jorge A. Lines. Provisional ed. San José, Costa Rica, Tropical Science Center, 1967.
xiv, 309 p. 22 cm. (Tropical Science Center. Occasional paper no. 6. Estudio ocasional no. 6)
"The author prepared this bibliography while serving as a resident and rotating staff member with the Associated Colleges of the Midwest Central American Field Program, from July 1965 to April 1967."

Medina, José Toribio, 1852–1930.
La imprenta en Guatemala, 1660–1821. Amsterdam, N. Israel, 1964.

lxxxv, 696 p. facsims., ports. 23 cm. (Reprint series of José Toribio Medina's bibliographical works, 2)

Original ed. published in Santiago de Chile, 1910.

Mulet de Cerezo, María Luisa.
Bibliografía analítica de la revolución del 20 de octubre de 1944. Guatemala, 1967.

136 p. 23 cm.

Tesis (licenciatura en bibliotecología)—Universidad de San Carlos de Guatemala.

Reyes Monroy, José Luis.
Bibliografía de la imprenta en Guatemala. (Adiciones de 1769 a 1900) ₍1. ed. Guatemala₎ Editorial "José de Pineda Ibarra" ₍Ministerio de Educación₎ 1969.

143 p. 27 cm.

Valenzuela Reyna, Gilberto.
Bibliografía guatemalteca y catálogo general de libros, folletos, periódicos, revistas, etc., 1941–1950 (una década) ₍1. ed.₎ Guatemala ₍Tip. Nacional₎ 1963 ₍i. e. 1964₎

383 p. port. 27 cm. (Colección bibliográfica del tercer centenario de la fundación de la primera imprenta en Centro América, t. 9)

Valenzuela Reyna, Gilberto.
Bibliografía guatemalteca, y catálogo general de libros,

folletos, periódicos, revistas, etc., 1951–1960 (una década), ₁1. ed.₎ Guatemala ₁Tip. Nacional₎ 1964.

573 p. ports. 27 cm. (Colección bibliográfica del tercer centenario de la fundación de la primera imprenta en Centro América, t. 10)

GUATEMALA (CITY) UNIVERSIDAD DE SAN CARLOS

Bendfeldt Rojas, Lourdes.
Reseña bibliográfica de las publicaciones periódicas de la Facultad de Humanidades. ₁Guatemala₎ Universidad de San Carlos de Guatemala, Departamento de Publicaciones, 1968.

40 p. 23 cm.

Bendfeldt Rojas, Lourdes.
Reseña bibliográfica de las publicaciones periódicas de la Facultad de Humanidades. ₁Guatemala₎ Universidad de San Carlos de Guatemala, Departamento de Publicaciones, 1971.

76 p. 23 cm.

"Fuentes": p. ₁69₎–70.

GUBKIN, IVAN MIKHAĬLOVICH

Samsonova, N   N
₁Ivan Mikhaĭlovich Gubkin₎
Иван Михайлович Губкин. ₁1871–1939₎. Библиогр. аннот. указ. ₁отеч. и иностр. книжной, журн. и газ. литературы за 1923–1970 гг.₎ Москва, 1971.

20 p. 20 cm.
At head of title: Научно-техническое общество нефтяной и газовой промышленности. Центральная научно-техническая библиотека нефтяной промышленности.
On cover: Министерство газовой промышленности.

GUERRILLA WARFARE

Cuban guerrilla training centers and Radio Havana; a selected bibliography, by Jon D. Cozean ₁and others₎ Washington, American University, Center for Research in Social Systems, 1968.

iv, 36 p. 28 cm.

Harsányi, János.
Az antifasiszta ellenállási és partizánharcok válogatott irodalmának bibliográfiája. ₁Összeállította és szerk. a Magyar Partizán Szövetség bibliográfiai munkaközössége: Harsányi János, Tiszay Andor és Vágó Ernő₎ Budapest, Tankönyvkiadó, 1968.

53 p. 20 cm.

U. S. *Air Force Academy. Library.*
Unconventional warfare. ₁n. p.₎ 1962–₁64₎

4 pts. diagr. 21 cm. (*Its* Special bibliography series, no. 21–23, 30)

GUIANA see French Guiana; Guyana; Surinam

GUIDANCE see Educational guidance; Vocational guidance

GUILDS see Gilds

GUILLÉN, NICOLÁS

Moscow.   Vsesoĭuznaĭa gosudarstvennaĭa biblioteka inostrannoĭ literatury.
Николас Гильен; биобиблиографический указатель. ₁Составитель Л. А. Шур. Ответственный редактор и автор вступ. статьи З. И. Плавскин₎ Москва, Книга, 1964.

99 p. port. 21 cm. (Писатели зарубежных стран)

GUILLOT, RENÉ

Ludwin, Vivien Rose.
Children's books by René Guillot; a bibliography. Johannesburg, University of the Witwatersrand, Dept. of Bibliography, Librarianship and Typography, 1970.

vi, 48 p. 30 cm.

"Compiled in part fulfilment for the requirements of the Diploma in Librarianship, University of the Witwatersrand."

GUIMARD, HECTOR

Culpepper, Ralph.
Bibliographie d'Hector Guimard. Paris (4e), Société des amis de la Bibliothèque Forney, 1971.

iii, 94 p. 27 cm.
Cover title.
Label mounted on verso of t. p.₁ 2. 6d.

GUINEA

Organization for Economic Cooperation and Development. Development Centre.
Bibliographie sur la Guinée. Bibliography on Guinea. Paris ₁1965₎

iii, 46 l. 29 cm. (*Its* CD/D/Bibl./2)

GUITAR AND GUITAR MUSIC

Exeter City Library.
Music for guitar and lute, compiled by David Lindsey Clark. Exeter, Exeter City Library, 1972.

₁36₎ p. 21 cm.

Maslen, J
Guitars and guitar playing; a list of selected references and music, compiled by J. Maslen. Melbourne, State Library of Victoria, 1966.

43 p. 26 cm. (Victoria. State Library. Research service bibliographies, 1966, no. 4)

GULIK, ROBERT HANS VAN

Bibliography of Dr. R. H. van Gulik (D. Litt.) ₁Boston, Boston University, 1968?₎

82 p. 22 cm.

"Compiled for the benefit of the Boston University Libraries—Mugar Memorial Library 'Robert van Gulik collection' Boston University."
"Notes written by Dr. R. H. van Gulik to Mr. H. B. Gotlieb, chief of special collections": p. 64–82.

GUMMA, JAPAN (PREFECTURE)

Gumma-ken Toshokan Kyōkai.
(Gumma-ken kyōdo shiryō sōgō mokuroku)
群馬県郷土資料総合目録　前橋　群馬県立図書館　昭和44–46(1969–71)

2 v. 26 cm.

編集: 群馬県図書館協会
Errata slip inserted.
CONTENTS: ₁1₎ 昭和40年3月現在—₁2₎ 追録 昭和41年4月–昭和45年3月

GUNDOLF, FRIEDRICH

Neutjens, Clem.
Friedrich Gundolf; ein biobibliographischer Apparat ₁von₎ Clemens Neutjens. Bonn, H. Bouvier, 1969.

195 p. 23 cm. (Bonner Beiträge zur Bibliotheks- und Bücherkunde, Bd. 20)

GUNS see Firearms

GÜNTEKIN, REŞAT NURI

Moscow. Vsesoíûznaíà gosudarstvennaíà biblioteka inostrannoi literatury.
Решад Нури Гюнтекин; биобиблиографический указатель. ₍Составитель и автор вступ. статьи И. Л. Тучинская₎ Москва, Книга, 1965.

36 p. 21 cm. (Писатели зарубежных стран)

GÜNTHER, JOHANN CHRISTIAN

Hoffmann, Adalbert, 1859–
Johann Christian Günther-Bibliographie. Hrsg. von Adalbert Hoffmann. Anhang: Eine zum ersten Mal veröffentlichte Satire gegen Günther mit deren Vorspiel. (Reprografischer Nachdruck der Ausg. Breslau 1929) Hildesheim, G. Olms, 1965.

94 p. 22 cm.

GUSEĬNOV, ASHRAF ISKENDER

Babaev, A A
А. И. Гусейнов. Библиография. ₍Вступит. статья д-ров физ.-мат. наук проф. Д. Э. Аллахвердиева и А. А. Бабаева₎. Баку, "Элм," 1969 ₍вып. дан. 1970₎.
51 p. 16 cm. (Деятели науки и культуры Азербайджана)

At head of title: Академия наук Азербайджанской ССР. Фундаментальная библиотека.
Added t. p. in Azerbaijani.
"Составители: А. А. Бабаев, А. И. Газарова."

GUSEĬNOV, DZHALIL ÍÛ.

Gamidova, A M
Д. Ю. Гусейнов; библиография. ₍Составитель А. М. Гамидова₎ Баку, Изд-во Академии наук Азербайджанской ССР, 1966.

86 p. 17 cm. (Деятели науки и культуры Азербайджана)

At head of title: Академия наук Азербайджанской ССР. Фундаментальная библиотека.
Added t. p. in Azerbaijani.

GUTENBERG, JOHANN see under Incunabula
(*Stillwell*) ; Printing - Exhibitions

GUYANA

Georgetown, Guyana. Public Library. Reference Dept.
A select bibliography of the works of Guyanese and on Guyana. ₍Georgetown, 1967₎

51 p. 21 cm.

On the occasion of Guyana Week, Feb. 19–25, 1967.

University of Guyana. Library.
A selection of documents on Guyana in the Library. ₍Georgetown, 1969?₎

17 l. 35 cm.

Caption title.
"Prepared as a token contribution to the Conference on Sharing Caribbean Resources for Study and Research."

GYMNASTICS see Physical education and training

GYNECOLOGY AND OBSTETRICS

Dellenbach, Pierre.
Titres et travaux scientifiques ₍du₎ Dʳ Pierre Dellenbach. 67 Woerth, Éditions de Woerth, 1969.

80 p. illus. 27 cm.

Indice de la bibliografía mexicana en ginecología y obstetricia, 1901–1965, ₍por₎ Fernando Herrera Lasso A. ₍et al.₎ México, Hospital de Gineco-Obste₍t₎ricia Núm. Uno, 1966.

506 p. 24 cm.

London. Royal College of Obstetricians and Gynaecologists. *Library.*
Short-title catalogue of books printed before 1851 in the library of the Royal College of Obstetricians and Gynaecologists. 2nd ed. London, Royal College of Obstetricians and Gynaecologists, 1968.

₍6₎, 85 p. 16 plates, illus., facsims. 23 cm.

Permutiertes Register zum Schrifttum soziale Gynäkologie; Auswahl der von 1946 bis 1970 in medizinischen Fachzeitschriften der DDR erschienenen Beiträge. Ausgearbeitet von einem Mitarbeiterkollektiv unter Leitung von W. Hübner und J. Rothe. Berlin, Verlag Volk und Gesundheit ₍c1972₎

1 v. (various pagings) 30 cm. (Schriftenreihe der Akademie für Ärztliche Fortbildung der DDR, 43)

GYPSIES see Gipsies

H

HAAKSBERGEN, NETHERLANDS

Meijerink, Th   J
Haaksbergen; bibliografie van boeken, boekfragmenten, brochures en tijdschriften, samengesteld door Th. J. Meijerink. ₁n. p.₎ 1969.

33 l. maps. (1 col.) 29 cm.

"Werkstuk 2e. cyclus Bibliotheek- en Documentatieschool, Amsterdam."

HAARHOFF, THEODORE JOHANNES

McCleery, Colleen Shirley.
Professor Theodore Johannes Haarhoff; a bibliography of his works. Johannesburg, University of the Witwatersrand, Department of Bibliography, Librarianship and Typography, 1968.

₁xiv₎ 69 p. 30 cm.

Compiled in part fulfilment for the Diploma in Librarianship.

HAARLEM

Ratelband, Ga
Bijdrage tot een bibliografie van Haarlem 1876–1960. ⟨Waarin opgenomen aanvullingen op C. Ekama, Catalogus van boeken, pamfletten enz. over de geschiedenis van Haarlem, enz., 1188–1875⟩ Haarlem ₁Prinsenhof 7₎ Stadsbibliotheek, 1968.

xii, 136 p. 30 cm.

HAGADAH

Ben-Menahem, Naftali, 1911–
ההגדה של פסח בצפון-אפריקה; רשימה ביבליוגראפית. מאת נפתלי בן-מנחם. ירושלים, ועד העדה המערבית, הוג דובבי שפתי ישנים, 729 ₁1969₎

105 p. facsims. 17 cm.

Added t. p.: La Haggada de Pessah en Afrique du Nord; bibliographie. Introd. par André Chouraqui.

Hirschhorn, Harry J
Mah nishtana; a selection of one hundred & eleven Passover Hagadot. ₁An exhibition at Kol Ami Museum₎ Highland Park, Kol Ami Museum, 1964.

ix, 115 p. facsims. (incl. maps) 28 cm.

Title in Hebrew precedes English title.
"Keren Hahagadot, a bibliography by Harry J. Hirschhorn: 118 addenda to Yaari's bibliography": p. 53–115.

HAGIOGRAPHY   see   Saints

HAGUE.   INTERNATIONAL COURT OF JUSTICE see   International Court of Justice

HAIDUKS

Fermandzhiev, Nikola.
Български хайдути. Препоръч. биобиблиогр. ₁Ред. Йорданка Първанова). (София, Нар. библ. Кирил и Методий, 1969).

184 p. 21 cm.

By N. Fermandzhiev and D. Dmitrov.

Знаеш ли, горо, помниш ли ... 100 години в прослава на хайдутството; методично-библиографски материал. Бур-

гас, Окръжна библиотека, 1968.

29 p. illus., port. 20 cm.

HAITI

Lowenthal, Ira P
Catalogue de la collection Mangonès, Pétionville, Haïti / Ira P. Lowenthal and Drexel G. Woodson, rédacteurs. — New Haven, Conn. : Antilles Research Program, Yale University, ₁1974₎

xii, 377 p. ; 22 cm. — (ARP occasional papers ; 2)

HAKEN, JOSEF

Ptačník, František.
Josef Haken-člověk, učitel, politik. (Publicistická činnost.) 1. vyd. Hradec Králové, Kruh, t. Východočes. tisk. 02, 1971.

91, ₁2₎ p. ₁16₎ p. of plates. 21 cm.

HALBERTSMA, JUSTUS HIDDES and EELTSJE

Kalma, J   J
Halbertsma-bibliografy. Hwat der sa foar en nei oer de bruorren Halbertsma skreaun is. ₁Fan₎ J. J. Kalma. Ljouwert, Fryske Akademy, 1968.

76 p. 20½ cm. (Minsken en boeken, nr. 8)

Fryske Akademy. ₁Utjeften₎ nr. 324.

HALDEN, NORWAY

Halden bibliotek.
Halden slekter. Et utvalg. ₁Halden₎, Halden bibliotek, ₁1972₎.

28 l. 30 cm.

HALÉVY, ELIE   see under   History (Wurgaft)

HALEY, JAMES EVETTS

Robinson, Chandler A
J. Evetts Haley, cowman-historian, by Chandler A. Robinson. El Paso, Tex., C. Hertzog, 1967.

viii, 75 p. facsims, port. 24 cm.

On spine: Haley bibliography.

HALL, GERMANY

Stadtarchiv Schwäbisch Hall.
Die Urkunden des Archivs der Reichsstadt Schwäbisch Hall, bearb. von Friedrich Pietsch. Stuttgart, W. Kohlhammer, 1967–

v. illus. 24 cm. (Veröffentlichungen der Staatlichen Archivverwaltung Baden-Württemberg, Bd. 21,

Includes bibliographical references.
CONTENTS: Bd. 1. 1156–1399.

Uhland, Robert.
Das Haalarchiv in Schwäbisch Hall. Inventar der Urkunden, Akten und Bände. Bearb. von Robert Uhland. Hrsg. von der Archivdirektion Stuttgart. Karlsruhe, Braun, 1965.

40 p., 151 p. with illus. 25 cm. (Inventare der nichtstaatlichen Archive in Baden-Württemberg, Heft 10)

HALL EFFECT

Glybach, E   D
(Primenenie Affekta Kholla)
Применение эффекта Холла. Библиография. (1898–1969). Кишинев, 1972.

333 p. 19 cm.

At head of title: Кишиневский государственный университет имени В. И. Ленина. Научная библиотека. Кафедра физики полупроводников.
By E. D. Glybach and G. V. Bulat.

Schober, Christa.
Internationale Bibliographie zu Hall-Effekt. 1963–1968. Bearb. von Christa Schober, Barbara Resasadeh ¡und¡ Gunda Herrmann. Dresden. (Techn. Univ., Bibliothek) 1970.

xviii, 165 p. 21 cm. (Bibliothek der Technischen Universität Dresden. Bibliographische Arbeiten, Nr. 6)

HALLE, GERMANY

Höhne, Horst, 1896–
Bibliographie zur Geschichte der Stadt Halle und des Saalkreises. Halle ⟨Saale⟩, Universitäts- und Landesbibliothek, 1968–

v. 30 cm. (Arbeiten aus der Universitäts- und Landesbibliothek in Halle an der Saale, Bd. 8)

CONTENTS.—Bd. 1. Von den Anfängen bis 1648.

HALLE, GERMANY.   UNIVERSITÄT

Halle. Universität.
Bericht 1951–1966. Gesamtregister der Jahrgänge I–XV: Wissenschaftliche Zeitschrift der Martin-Luther-Universität Halle-Wittenberg. Halle (Saale), 1969.

540 p. 24 cm.

Includes listings from the Wissenschaftliche Beiträge of the University.

HALLSTEIN, WALTER

Gestel, M   B   van.
Walter Hallstein; Bibliographie seiner Veröffentlichungen. Zusammengestellt von M.-B. van Gestel. Leuven, J. Reekmans, 1965.

52 p. 22 cm.

HAMBURG, GERMANY

Hamburg. Staats- und Universitäts-Bibliothek.
Hamburger Bücher 1491–1850. Aus der Hamburgensien-Sammlung der Staats- und Universitätsbibliothek Hamburg. Hrsg. von Werner Kayser. Hamburg, E. Hauswedell, 1973.

162 p. illus. 30 cm. (Mitteilungen aus der Staats- und Universitätsbibliothek Hamburg, Bd. 7)
Introduction in English, French, and German.

Hamburger Öffentliche Bücherhallen.
Hamburg in Vergangenheit und Gegenwart; ein Auswahlverzeichnis der Hamburger Öffentlichen Bücherhallen. ¡Bearbeitung: Barbara Hahn et al. Hamburg¡ 1970.

215 p. illus. 20 x 21 cm.

HAMELIN, LOUIS EDMOND

Publications de Louis-Edmond Hamelin, professeur de géographie et directeur du Centre d'études nordiques. Québec, Université Laval, 1969.

1 v. (various pagings) 29 cm.

HAMILTON, ALEXANDER

Ford, Paul Leicester, 1865–1902.
Bibliotheca Hamiltoniana; a list of books written by, or

relating to Alexander Hamilton. New York, Printed for the author ¡by¡ the Knickerbocker Press, 1886. ¡New York, AMS Press, 1972¡

vi, 159 p. 24 cm.

Pt. I was issued also the same year under title: A list of editions of "The Federalist."
Pt. II was issued also separately with same date under title: A list of Treasury reports and circulars issued by Alexander Hamilton, 1789–1795.

Ford, Paul Leicester, 1865–1902.
A list of Treasury reports and circulars, issued by Alexander Hamilton, 1789–1795. New York, B. Franklin ¡1970¡

47 p. 23 cm. (Burt Franklin bibliography and reference, 390. American classics in history and social science, 105)

Alternate pages blank.
Reprint of pt. 2 of the author's Bibliotheca Hamiltoniana, 1886 (p. 109–153) with addition of t. p.
Reprint of the 1886 ed.

HAMILTON, CHARLES

The Magnet companion: a collective biography, index and directory. London, Howard Baker, 1971.

3–120 p.; illus. 16 x 28 cm.

HAMMETT, DASHIELL

Mundell, E   H
A list of the original appearances of Dashiell Hammett's magazine work. Assembled by E. H. Mundell. ¡Kent, Ohio¡ Kent State University Press ¡°1968¡

52 p. 20 cm. (The Serif series: bibliographies and checklists, no. 13)

Half-title: Dashiell Hammett.
On spine: Dashiell Hammett's magazine work.

Mundell, E   H
A list of the original appearances of Dashiell Hammett's magazine work. Assembled by E. H. Mundell. Portage, Ind., 1968.

52 p. 21 cm.

HAMSUN, KNUT

Østby, Arvid.
Knut Hamsun. En bibliografi. Oslo, Gyldendal, 1972.

xviii, 316 p. 22 cm.

Foreword in English, German, and Norwegian.

HÄNDEL, GEORG FRIEDRICH

Bell, A   Craig.
Chronological catalogue of Handel's works, by A. Craig Bell. Greenock (Renfrewshire), Grain-Aig P., 1969.

¡2¡, ix, 68 p. 23 cm.

Bell, A   Craig.
Handel; chronological thematic catalogue by A. Craig Bell. Darley, Eng., Grian-Aig Press, 1972.

xii, 452 p. music. 22 cm.

Leipzig. Musikbibliothek.
Handschriften und ältere Drucke der Werke Georg Friedrich Händels in der Musikbibliothek der Stadt Leipzig. ¡Leipzig¡ Bibliographische Veröffentlichungen der Musikbibliothek der Stadt Leipzig, 1966.

44 p. 24 cm.

Manchester, Eng. Public Libraries. Henry Watson Music Library.
George Frideric Handel—the Newman Flower Collection in the Henry Watson Music Library: a catalogue; compiled by Arthur D. Walker; with a foreword by Winton Dean. ¡Manchester¡, Manchester Public Libraries, 1972.

xiii, 134 p. 22 cm.

Smith, William Charles.
Handel; a descriptive catalogue of the early editions, by William C. Smith, assisted by Charles Humphries. 2d ed. with supplement. New York, Barnes & Noble, 1970 [°1960]

xxiii, 378 p. facsim., music. 26 cm.

Smith, William Charles.
Handel; a descriptive catalogue of the early editions, by William C. Smith, assisted by Charles Humphries. 2d ed. with suppl. Oxford [Eng.] B. Blackwell, 1970.

xxiii, 378 p. facsim., music. 26 cm.

HANDICAPPED
see also Mentally handicapped

Berggren, Gösta.
Handikapp och rehabilitering. En förteckning över böcker och tidskriftsartiklar. Lund, Bibliotekstjänst; [Solna, Seelig] 1968.

105 p. 22 cm. (Btj-serien, 9)

Lovett, B   H
Building for the disabled, compiled by B. H. Lovett. Adelaide Public Library of South Australia, 1966.

18 p. 26 cm. (Research Service bibliographies, Series 4, no. 79)

Riley, Lawrence E
Disability and rehabilitation: a selected bibliography. Edited by Lawrence E. Riley, Elmer A. Spreitzer [and] Saad Z. Nagi. Columbus, Ohio, Forum Associates, 1971.

xx, 178 p. 22 cm.

HANDICAPPED CHILDREN
see also Education of exceptional children; Socially handicapped children

American Academy of Pediatrics. *Committee on Handicapped Child.*
Selected references on handicapped children, an annotated bibliography. 2d ed. [Evanston, Ill., 1968]

22 p. 22 cm. ([American Academy of Pediatrics] Bibliographic series)

Pilling, Doria.
The child with cerebral palsy—social, emotional and educational adjustment: an annotated bibliography. Windsor, National Foundation for Educational Research, 1973.

61 p. 22 cm. index. (National Children's Bureau. Report)

Winchell, Carol Ann.
The hyperkinetic child : a bibliography of medical, educational, and behavioral studies / Carol Ann Winchell. — Westport, Conn. : Greenwood Press, 1975.

xiv, 182 p. ; 23 cm.

HANDICRAFTS

Brodmeier, Beate.
Literaturführer durch das Handwerksschrifttum 1900–1945, mit erläuternden Hinweisen. Münster, Westfalen [Handwerkswissenschaftliches Institut] 1965.

163 p. 22 cm. (Forschungsberichte aus dem Handwerk, Bd. 12)

On spine: Literaturführer Handwerk.

Council for Small Industries in Rural Areas.
Select list of books and information sources on trades, crafts, and small industries in rural areas. London, Council for Small Industries in Rural Areas (Advisory Services Section), 1968.

[5], 70 p. 21 cm. ([Its] Publication no. 79)

Jewell, Andrew.
Crafts, trades, and industries; a book list for local historians. London, Published for the Standing Conference for Local History by the National Council of Social Service [1964]

24 p. 22 cm.

Jewell, Andrew.
Crafts, trades and industries: a book list for local historians. London, published for the Standing Conference for Local History, by the National Council of Social Service, 1968.

24 p. 22 cm.

Library Association. *County Libraries Group.*
Readers' guide to books on handicrafts. 4th ed. London, Library Association (County Libraries Group), 1969.

38 p. 19 cm. (Readers' guide, new ser., no. 108)

Logan, William Boyd.
Handicrafts and home businesses, by William B. Logan and George Traicoff, Jr. Washington, Small Business Administration, 1964.

12 p. 26 cm. (Small business bibliography no. 1)

National Book League, *London.*
Junior arts and crafts, selected with the advice and assistance of the staff of Jordanhill College, Glasgow, and local authority advisers in art. London, National Book League, 1970.

18 p. 21 cm.

Nueckel, Susan.
Selected guide to make-it, fix-it, do-it-yourself books. New York, Fleet Press Corp. [1973]

213 p. 24 cm.

Rice, John Wade.
Handicrafts and home businesses. Rev. by J. Wade Rice. Washington, Small Business Administration, 1966.

19 p. 26 cm. (Small business bibliography no. 1)

Caption title.
Earlier editions by W. B. Logan and G. Traicoff, Jr.

Rice, John Wade.
Handicrafts and home businesses. Rev. by J. Wade Rice. Washington, Small Business Administration, 1970.

19 p. 27 cm. (Small business bibliography, 1)

Caption title.
Earlier editions by W. B. Logan and G. Traicoff, Jr.

HANDWRITING   see   Graphology

HANSEN, HANS PETER

Hansen, Vagn Lindebo.
Bibliografi over H. P. Hansens trykte arbejder. [Af Vagn Lindebo Hansen og Hanne Arent]. Herning, Herning Museum, Museumsgade, 1970.

75 p. illus. 21 cm.

HANUS, LADISLAV

Brünn. Státní pedagogická knihovna.
Ladislav Hanus, 1890–1943. Bibliografii prací připravil Kamil Horňák. [V Brně, 1965]

99 l. 20 cm. (*Its Život a dílo čs. pedagogů, č. 3*)

HARBURG-WILHELMSBURG, GERMANY

Dodegge, Werner R
Katalog der Bibliothek des Verein für Heimatkunde in Wilhelmsburg e. V. im Museum der Elbinsel Wilhelmsburg/

Werner R. Dodegge. Hrsg.: Verein f. Heimatkunde in Wilhelmsburg e. V. Hamburg: Verein f. Heimatkunde in Wilhelmsburg, 1972.

A–E, 52 ₁i. e. 53₁ l.; 30 cm.

HARDBOARD

Kamenskaĭa, A   ĪA
₁Proizvodstvo drevesnykh plit₁
Производство древесных плит. Библиогр. указ. отеч. и иностр. литературы за 1966–1968 гг. Ч. 1–2. Москва, 1971.

2 v. 21 cm.
At head of title: Всесоюзный научно-исследовательский и проектный институт экономики, организации управления производством и информации по лесной, целлюлозно-бумажной и деревообрабатывающей промышленности. Центральная научно-техническая библиотека лесной и бумажной промышленности.

Weiner, Jack, 1910–
Hardboards ₁by₁ Jack Weiner and Jerry Byrne. Appleton, Wis., Institute of Paper Chemistry, 1964.

3 v. 28 cm. (Appleton, Wis. Institute of Paper Chemistry. Bibliographic series, no. 209–211)

Includes Supplement 1–   ₁by₁ Jack Weiner and Vera Pollock, to each number of the series.
CONTENTS: 1. Fiberboards.—2. Particle board.—3. Inorganic and miscellaneous boards.

HARDENBERG, FRIEDRICH, FREIHERR VON

Novalis (Friedrich Freiherr von Hardenberg) 2.5.1772– 25.3.1801; der handschriftliche Nachlass des Dichters. Zur Geschichte des Nachlasses von Novalis, von Richard Samuel. Hildesheim, H. A. Gerstenberg, 1973.

45, 117 p. facsims. 25 cm.

Reprint of the 1930 ed. published by Meyer & Ernst, Berlin.

HARDY, THOMAS

Dorset County Library.
Thomas Hardy catalogue: a list of the books by and about Thomas Hardy, O. M., (1840–1928) in Dorset County Library; compiled by Kenneth Carter, County Librarian. ₁Dorchester (Dorset)₁, Dorset County Council (Library Committee), 1968.

₁2₁ 37 p. 2 plates, 1 illus., port. 26 cm.

Gerber, Helmut E   1920–
Thomas Hardy: an annotated bibliography of writings about him. Compiled and edited by Helmut E. Gerber and W. Eugene Davis. Contributors: Richard C. Carpenter ₁and others₁ De Kalb, Northern Illinois University Press ₁1973₁

x, 841 p. 25 cm. (An Annotated secondary bibliography series on English literature in transition, 1880–1920)

Purdy, Richard Little, 1904–
Thomas Hardy: a bibliographical study. ₁1st ed.₁ reprinted. Oxford, Clarendon P., 1968.

xiii, 388 p. 7 plates, 7 facsims. 23 cm.

Webb, A   P
A bibliography of the works of Thomas Hardy, 1865– 1915, by A. P. Webb. New York, B. Franklin ₁1968₁

xiii, 127 p. facsims., port. 23 cm. (Burt Franklin bibliography & reference series, 110)

"Originally published 1916."

Weber, Carl Jefferson, 1894–
The first hundred years of Thomas Hardy, 1840–1940; a centenary bibliography of Hardiana, compiled by Carl J. Weber. New York, Russell & Russell, 1965 ₁°1942₁

276 p. 22 cm.

Weber, Carl Jefferson, 1894–1966.
Thomas Hardy's correspondence at Max Gate; a descriptive check list. Compiled by Carl J. Weber and Clara Carter Weber. Waterville, Me., Colby College Press, 1968.

238 p. 24 cm.

Yamamoto, Bunnosuke, 1896–
(Tōmasu Hādi no shoshi)

山本　文之助

トマス・ハーディの書誌　完本版

東京　千城書房　昭和46(1971)

630p　図　肖像　22cm

Text also in English, with added t. p.: Bibliography of Thomas Hardy in Japan, with reference books in England and America, outlines of his principal works.

HARKAVI, ZVI

Harkavi, Zvi.
(Avtobibliografiyah)
אבטוביבליאוגראפיה, כל הפירסומים כ1200 ערכים, ספרים,
קונטרסים, מחקרים ומאמרים, מהדורות, תרגומים ועריכה
בעברית, בידיש, בלאדינו ובלעז ... תרצ״ט–תש״ל ₁מאת₁ צבי
הרכבי. ₁מהד׳ מצומצמת־ביבליאופילית. ירושלים, הוצאת
הספרים הארץ־ישראלית, 5730 ₁1970₁

49 l. port. 25 cm.

HARMON FAMILY

Harmon, Robert Bartlett, 1932–
A preliminary checklist of materials of Harman-Harmon genealogy, by Robert B. Harmon. San Jose, Calif., Dibco Press, 1964.

ili. 4 l. 30 cm.

HARMONY SOCIETY

Reibel, Daniel B
Bibliography of items related to the Harmony Society with special reference to old Economy, and many works on communities and utopias which also discuss the Harmony Society. Compiled by Daniel B. Reibel. Ambridge, Pa., Pennsylvania Historical and Museum Commission, 1969.

16 p. 28 cm.

HARP MUSIC

Zingel, Hans Joachim, 1904–
Harfenmusik. Harp music. Musique de la harpe. Harp muziek. Musica per arpa. Verzeichnis der gedruckten und zur Zeit greifbaren Literatur für Pedalharfe. Hofheim am Taunus, Hofmeister (1965)

35 p. 21 cm.

HARPSICHORD MUSIC
see also under Organ *(Alker)*

Bedford, Frances.
Twentieth-century harpsichord music; a classified catalog, by Frances Bedford and Robert Conant. Hackensack, N. J., J. Boonin ₁1974₁

xxi, 95 p. 28 cm. (Music indexes and bibliographies, no. 8)

HARRINGTON, BERNARD JAMES

McGill University, Montreal. Archives.
A preliminary calendar of the papers of Bernard J. Harrington, accession 1010, by Susan W. Osler. With a foreword by John C. L. Andreassen. Montreal, 1971.

iii, 40 p. 28 cm.

HARRISBURG, PENNSYLVANIA

Baxtresser, Betty B
A preliminary check list of imprints, Harrisburg, Pennsylvania, 1841–1858, with a historical introduction, by Betty B. Baxtresser. Washington, 1964.

iii, 72 l. 28 cm.

Typescript (carbon copy)
Thesis (M. s.)—Catholic University of America.

HARTE, BRET

Gaer, Joseph, 1897–   *ed.*
Bret Harte; bibliography and biographical data. New York, B. Franklin [1968]

189 p. 24 cm. (Burt Franklin bibliography and reference series, #102)

Reprint of the 1935 ed.

HARTFORD, CONNECTICUT

Cale, William E.
A checklist of Hartford, Connecticut, imprints from 1826–1828, with a historical introduction, by William E. Cale. Washington, 1966.

iv, 127 l. 29 cm.

Typescript (carbon copy)
Thesis (M. A.)—Catholic University of America.

Dion, Dora E
A check list of Hartford, Connecticut imprints from 1828–1829, with a historical introduction [by] Dora E. Dion. Washington, 1966.

ii, 86 l. 28 cm.

Typescript (carbon copy)
Thesis (M. A.)—Catholic University of America.

HARTMANN VON AUE

Klemt, Ingrid.
Hartmann von Aue. Eine Zusammenstellung der über ihn und sein Werk von 1927 bis 1965 erschienenen Literatur. Köln, Greven, 1968.

60 p. 21 cm. (Bibliographische Hefte, 5)

HARVESTING   see Agriculture

HASDEŬ, BOGDAN PETRICEĬCU

Kiriiak, Vladimir.
Богдан Петричейку Хашдеу. (1838–1907). Индиче биобиблиографик. Кишинэу, "Картя молдовеняскэ," 1968.

28 p. with port. 17 cm. (Класичий литературий молдовенешть)

At head of title: Библиотека републиканэ де Стат а РССМ "Н. К. Крупская."

HASIDISM

[Bodek, Menahem Mendel] d. 1874.
סדר הדורות מתלמידי הבעש"ט ... שמות הצדיקים מימות הבעש"ט ותלמידיו עד היום הזה ... עפ"י סדר דורותיהם גם קצת ... ממעשיהם ... ודברי מוסרם ... ונלוה ... שמות כל הספרים מהצדיקים ... אחר זמן הבעש"ט. ירושלים, תשכ"ה [1964/65]

88 p. 22 cm.
Running title: סדר הדורות חחדש
Photo-offset.
For authorship cf. B. Friedberg. Bet 'eked sefarim.

Kenig, Natan Tsevi.
ספר נוה צדיקים; סיפור תולדות חייו של רבי נחמן מברסלב, בצירוף פרקים מובחרים על ספריו וספרי תלמידיו, חובר ע"י נתן צבי קעניג. בני־ברק, [להשיג: כולל ברסלב] 729 [1968 or 9]

228 p. 22 cm.

HASSALL, CHRISTOPHER VERNON   see under Brooke, Rupert

HASSELT, BELGIUM

Hasselt, Belgium. Provinciale Bibliotheek.
De zevenjaarlijkse Virga-Jessefeesten in woord en beeld. Een keuze [uit] boeken en artikelen uit tijdschriften en dagbladen van 1660 tot op heden. Hasselt, Begijnhof [1968]

14 l. 28 cm.

HAUER, JOSEF MATTHIAS

Josef Matthias Hauer. [Katalog. 9. Sonderschau. 23. Mai–15. Juni 1966. Redaktion: Walter Szmolyan. Für den Inhalt verantwortlich: Heino Seitler. Wien, Verein zur Erhaltung und Förderung des Josefstädter Heimatmuseums] 1966.

91–121 p. ports. 21 cm. (Das Josefstädter Heimatmuseum, Heft 45)

HAUG, HANS

Vaud. Bibliothèque cantonale et universitaire, Lausanne. Département de la musique.
Catalogue de l'œuvre de Hans Haug, par Jean-Louis Matthey et Louis-Daniel Perret. Lausanne, Bibliothèque cantonale et universitaire, 1971.

ii, 83 p. port. 21 cm. (Its Inventaire des fonds manuscrits, 1)

HAUGLID, ROAR

Pharo, Alf Lowum.
Roar Hauglid 60 år. 26.12.1970. Bibliografi 1935–1970. Oslo [1971]

40 p., 2 l. ports. 22 cm.

HAUPTMANN, GERHART JOHANN ROBERT

Reichart, Walter Albert, 1903–
Gerhart-Hauptmann-Bibliographie. Von Walter A[lbert] Reichart. Mit e. Geleitw. von Johannes Hansel. Bad Homburg v. d. H., Berlin, Zürich, Gehlen (1969).

96 p. 19 cm. (Bibliographien zum Studium der deutschen Sprache und Literatur, 5)

Tschörtner, Heinz Dieter.
Gerhart-Hauptmann-Bibliographie. Bearb. von H[einz] D[ieter] Tschörtner. Berlin (Deutsche Staatsbibliothek) 1971.

196 p. 21 cm. (Deutsche Staatsbibliothek. Bibliographische Mitteilungen, 24)

HAVANA

Medina, José Toribio, 1852–1930.
La imprenta en La Habana, 1707–1810. Amsterdam, N. Israel, 1964.

xxxii, 199 p. 23 cm. (Reprint series of José Toribio Medina's bibliographical works, 13)
Original ed. published in Santiago de Chile, 1904.

HAVAS NEWS AGENCY   see Agence Havas

HAVET, JULIEN PIERRE EUGÈNE

Mélanges Julien Havet; recueil de travaux d'érudition dédiés à la mémoire de Julien Havet (1853–1893). Genève, Slatkine Reprints, 1972.

xvi, 780 p. illus. 23 cm.

French or Latin.
"Réimpression de l'édition de Paris, 1895."

פרקים בחיי אדמו"ר הגנגמ"ח.—ספרי אדמו"ר הגנגמ"ח.—ספרי CONTENTS.— אדמו"ר ר' נתן.—ספרי תלמידי אדמו"ר.—ספרי תלמידי אדמו"ר ר' נתן.— ספרי ר' נחמן גאלדשטיין.—ספרי גדולי אנ"ש.—ספרי ר' משה יהושע בזשילנסקי והר"ר שמשון בארסקי.—ספרי אנ"ש ארץ־ישראל—פולין.

499

HAWAII

Hawaii. *Dept of Planning and Economic Development.*
Hawaii State research inventory, 1961–1966. Honolulu, 1967.

ii, 199 l. 28 cm.

Hawaii register of historic places: bibliography of Hawaiiana, by T. Stell Newman ₁and others₁ Honolulu, Division of State Parks, 1970 or 71₁

vi, 94 p. 28 cm. (Hawaii State archaeological journal 70–3)

Hawaii State Library.
The James Tice Phillips collection. Presented to the Hawaii State Library historical collection by the Friends of the Library of Hawaii. Honolulu, Office of Library Services. State of Hawaii, 1968.

50 p. 23 cm.

A listing of 1705 books, pamphlets, and manuscripts about Hawaii.

Murdoch, Clare G
Basic Hawaiiana, selected and annotated by Clare G. Murdoch and Masae Gotanda. ₁Honolulu₁ Hawaii State Library, 1969.

34 p. 28 cm.

Rubano, Judith.
Culture and behavior in Hawaii; an annotated bibliography. Honolulu, Social Science Research Institute, University of Hawaii ₁1971₁

xii, 147 p. 28 cm. (Hawaii series, no. 3)

HAWTHORNE, NATHANIEL

Browne, Nina Eliza.
A bibliography of Nathaniel Hawthorne, compiled by Nina E. Browne. New York, B. Franklin ₁1968₁

ix, 215 p. port. 23 cm. (Burt Franklin bibliography and reference series, 197)

Reprint of the 1908 ed.

Clark, C   E   Frazer, comp.
Hawthorne at auction, 1894–1971. Edited by C. E. Frazer Clark, Jr. With an appendix by Matthew J. Bruccoli. Detroit, Gale Research Co. ₁1972₁

xx, 419 p. illus. 26 cm.

Auction sales catalogues.
"A Bruccoli-Clark book."

Clark, C   E   Frazer.
The Merrill checklist of Nathaniel Hawthorne, compiled by C. E. Frazer Clark, Jr. Columbus, Ohio, C. E. Merrill Pub. Co. ₁1970₁

45 p. 20 cm. (Charles E. Merrill program in American literature)

Charles E. Merrill checklists.
Title on cover: Checklist of Nathaniel Hawthorne.

Gross, Theodore L
Hawthorne, Melville, Stephen Crane; a critical bibliography, by Theodore L. Gross, and Stanley Wertheim. New York, Free Press ₁1971₁

viii, 301 p. 24 cm.

CONTENTS.—Nathaniel Hawthorne, by T. L. Gross.—Herman Melville, by T. L. Gross.—Stephen Crane, by S. Wertheim.

Jones, Buford.
A checklist of Hawthorne criticism, 1951–1966. Hartford, Transcendental Books ₁1967₁

91 l. illus., ports. 29 cm.

Ricks, Beatrice.
Nathaniel Hawthorne: a reference bibliography, 1900–

1971; with selected nineteenth century materials. ₁Compiled by Beatrice Ricks, Joseph D. Adams ₁and₁ Jack O. Hazlerig₁ Boston, G. K. Hall, 1972.

v, 337 p. 24 cm.

HAZLITT, WILLIAM

Ireland, Alexander, 1810–1894.
List of the writings of William Hazlitt and Leigh Hunt, chronologically arranged with notes, descriptive, critical, and explanatory, and a selection of opinions regarding their genius and characteristics by distinguished contemporaries and friends as well as by subsequent critics, preceded by a review of, and extracts from, Barry Cornwall's "Memorials of Charles Lamb," with a few words on William Hazlitt and his writings, and a chronological list of the works of Charles Lamb. New York, B. Franklin ₁1970₁

xxiii, 233 p. 23 cm. (Burt Franklin bibliography and reference series, 299. Essays in literature and criticism, 76)

Reprint of the 1868 ed.

HEALTH   see   Hygiene; Public health

HEALTH CARE   see   Medical care

HEALTH EDUCATION

Alaska. *Dept. of Health and Welfare. Health Education Library.*
Pamphlet catalog. Juneau, Dept. of Health and Welfare, Health Education, 1964.

5 l. 28 cm.

Canadian Health Education Specialists Society. *School Health Committee.*
Annotated guide to health instruction materials in Canada. ₁Editor: Michael E. Palko₁ 2d ed. Ottawa, 1967.

105 p. 24 cm.

A **Directory** of selected references and resources for health instruction. 1966–
Minneapolis, Burgess Pub. Co.

v. 26 cm. biennial.

Compilers: 1966–   M. K. Beyrer, A. E. Nolte, and M. K. Solleder.

Maryland. *State Dept. of Health.*
A guide book describing pamphlets, posters, films on health and disease: an annotated reference to free and inexpensive health information materials selected for general use. 2d ed. ₁Baltimore. Order from: Office of Public Health Education. Maryland State Dept. of Health, 1964₁

150 p. 23 cm.

Maryland. *State Dept. of Health.*
A guide book describing pamphlets, posters, films on health and disease; an annotated reference to free and inexpensive health information materials selected for general use. 3d ed. ₁Baltimore₁ 1967.

xiii, 172 p. 23 cm.

Solleder, Marian K
Evaluation instruments in health education. ₁An annotated bibliography₁ compiled by Marian K. Solleder. Rev. ed. Washington, American Association for Health, Physical Education, and Recreation, 1969.

23 p. 23 cm.

HEALTH RESORTS, WATERING-PLACES, ETC.

Jordan, Herbert, *comp.*
Zwölf Jahre balneologische und balneobioklimatologische Forschung der DDR im Referat. ⟨1950–1961⟩ ₁Von₁ H. Jordan. Bad Elster. (Forschungsinstitut für Balneologie und Kurortwissenschaft) 1965.

146 p.   21 cm.

Teodosieva, Elena.
Курортното дело и физикалната терапия в България, 1835–1965; анотирана библиография. София, Изд-во на Българската академия на науките, 1968.

423 p.   25 cm.

HEARN, LAFCADIO

Perkins, Percival Densmore, 1897–
Lafcadio Hearn; a bibliography of his writings, by P. D. and Ione Perkins. With an introd. by Sanki Ichikawa. New York, B. Franklin [1968]

xvii, 444 p.   6 facsims.   24 cm.   (Burt Franklin: bibliography and reference series, 187)

Originally published 1934.

HEART   see   Cardiovascular system

HEAT; HEATING
see also under   Plumbing

Bayley, Frederick John.
Bibliography of heat-transfer instrumentation, by F. J. Bayley and A. B. Turner. London, H. M. S. O., 1968.

[1], 59 p.   28 cm.   (Aeronautical Research Council. Reports & memoranda, no. 3512)

(Bibliografiiā po teplo- i massoobmenu)
Библиография по тепло- и массообмену.   1967–1969. [В 3-х т.] Минск, 1971–73.

3 v.   21 cm.

At head of title: Институт тепло-и массообмена Академии наук БССР. Филиал Фундаментальной библиотеки АН БССР при ИТМО.
By R. A. Dolinskaiā and others.

Boleszny, Ivan.
Solar heating, compiled by I. Boleszny.   Adelaide, State Library of South Australia, 1967.

34 p.   26 cm.   (Research Service bibliographies.   Series 4, no. 88)

Dobruská, Naděžda.
O problematice teplárenství a rozvodu tepla; doporučující bibliografie knižni a časopisecké literatury. [Sest. Naděžda Dobruská] Praha, UVTEI, Státní technická knihovna, 1969.

60 p.   21 cm.   (Státní technická knihovna v Praze. Bibliografie, sv. 140)

Dolinskaiā, R   A
Библиография по тепло- и массообмену.   (1964–1966). Т. 1–2. Минск, 1968.

2 v. (974 p.)   20 cm.

At head of title   : Филиал Фундаментальной библиотеки АН БССР. Институт тепло- и массообмена АН БССР.
By R. A. Dolinskaiā and V. M. Murashko.

Heat pipe technology.
Albuquerque.

v.   28 cm.   (New Mexico. University. Technology Application Center. TAC bibliographic series)

"A bibliography with abstracts."
Vols. for   compiled by the Heat Pipe Information Office, University of New Mexico.

Julian, Donald V
Bibliography of natural convection heat transfer from a vertical flat plate [by] D. V. Julian and R. G. Akins. [Manhattan, Kansas Engineering Experiment Station] 1957 [i. e. 1967]

ii, 27 l.   28 cm.   (Kansas Engineering Experiment Station. Special report no. 77)

Kansas State University bulletin, v. 51, no. 6.

Kramárová, A
Moderné vykurovanie rodinných domčekov.   Výberový zoznam z domácej a zahraničnej literatúry.   Zost. Alžbeta Kramárová.   Bratislava, Slov. techn. knižnica, cyklostyl, 1969–

v.   20 cm.   (Bratislava. Slovenská technická knižnica. Edícia 2.   Séria B: Výberové bibliografie

Kramárová, A
Vetranie a klimatizácia občianskych budov.   Výberový zoznam z domácej a zahraničnej literatúry ku kurzu organizovanému SR ČSVTS v Bratislave. Zost.: A. Kramárová. 2. dopl. vyd. Bratislava, Slov. techn. knižnica, cyklostyl, 1970.

[1], 144, [2] p.   21 cm.   (Bratislava. Slovenská technická knižnica. Edícia 2. Séria B: Výberové bibliografie)

Lehká, Jaroslava.
Efektivnost centralizovaného zásobování teplem v nové ekonomické soustavě.   Výberová bibliogr. pro účastníky celost. konf. v Ostravě ve dnech 4.–6. června 1968.   Sest. Jaroslava Lehká. Ostrava, St. věd. knihovna, 1968.

42 p.   29 cm.   (Státní vědecká knihovna v Ostravě.   Publikace, řada 2, čis. 429)

Makarova, E   A
Пути экономии тепла и топлива.   Библиогр. указатель. Москва, 1969.

89 p.   22 cm.   (Актуальные проблемы техники)

At head of title: Государственный комитет Совета Министров СССР по науке и технике. Государственная публичная научно-техническая биолиотека.

São José dos Campos, Brazil.   Centro Técnico de Aeronáutica. *Biblioteca Central.*
Bibliografia: transferência de calor.   São José dos Campos, Instituto Tecnológico de Aeronáutica, 1967.

148 l.   27 cm.   (*Its* Série bibliográfica, 1)

"Contribução ao 1.º Simpósio Brasileiro de Transferência de Calor e Mecânica dos Fluidos, realizado de 8 a 10 de dezembro de 1966, em São José dos Campos."

Valatkevičiene, L
Darbai šilumos mainu srityje.   1950–1970.   Bibliografija. Red. A. Žukauskas. Kaunas, 1971.

78 p.   20 cm.

At head of title: Lietuvos TSR Mokslu akademija.   Fizikiniu -techniniu energetikos problemu institutas. L. Valatkevičiene, J. Žiugžda.
Added t. p.: Работы в области теплообмена.
Lithuanian and Russian.

HEBBEL, FRIEDRICH

Gerlach, Ulrich Henry, 1938–
Hebbel-Bibliographie 1910–1970/ U. Henry Gerlach. — Heidelberg: Winter, 1973.

529 p.;   25 cm.

HEBREW IMPRINTS
see also   Ladino imprints

Akademiiā nauk SSSR. *Institut vostokovedeniiā.*
קהלת משה אריה ליב פרידלאנד; רשימת כל הספרים העברים. נדפסים וכתבי-יד, הנמצאים באספת-פרידלאנד באוצר מוזיאום האזיאטי של האקאדעמיא למדעים בס״ט פטרבורג. ערוכה בסדר א״ב בהוצאות המאפף ובפקודת הדירעקטור של המוזיאום. תחת השגחת דניאל חוואלואן, מאת שמואל וויגער. [אות א–ל] פטרבורג, 653 [1936]–1893. ירושלים, 729 [1968 or 9]

1 v. in 2 (iv, 680 p.)   25 cm.
At head of title: Bibliotheca Friedlandiana.
No more published.

Bamberger & Wahrmann, *Jerusalem.*

קטלוגים: רשימות ספרים ורשימות מחירים של ספרים עברים
נדירים. ירושלים. 728 [8 or 1967[

7 v. in 2. port. 25 cm. (ספרית מקורות)

Cover title: קטלוגים ורשימות ספרים עבריים עתיקים.

"נדפס במהדורה בת 200 עותקים."

Each v. has imprint of original ed., Jerusalem, 1915–57; v. 3 and 5 without t. p.

Original ed. except for v. 1 published under title: רשימה (romanized: Reshimah)

CONTENTS.—רשימה 3.—Karaitica 3 מס' רשימה.2—.1 מס' רשימה.
41 מס' רשימה.6—.40 מס' רשימה.5—.25 מס' רשימה.4—.27 מס'
דיינארד.—[7], עתיקות יהודה; רשימת הספרים העבריים היקרים, מאת אפרים Judaica.

Bartolocci, Giulio, 1613–1687.

קרית ספר והוא הבזר גדול שבו נכתבו כל ספרי היהודים, הברו
ויסדו יוליוס ברטולוקי.

Bibliotheca magna rabbinica de scriptoribus, et scriptis Hebraicis, ordine alphabetico Hebraicè et Latinè digestis. Auctore D. Iulio Bartoloccio de Celleno. [Farborough, Gregg, 1965–

v. 34 cm.

Facsimile reprint of Rome ed., 1675–94.

Hebrew and Latin.

CONTENTS.—Pars 1. Tres primas Alphabeti literas complectens, א', ב' ג'. (B 68–09613)

Otto Harrassowitz (Firm)

Bibliotheca Judaica-Hebraica-Rabbinica. Pinczower -Porges. (Neudr. [d. Ausg.] Leipzig, Harrassowitz, 1931–1932.) Mit e. Einl. von Felix Daniel Pinczower. (Niederwalluf b. Wiesbaden) M. Sändig (1971).

xxx, 759 p. 22 cm.

Reissue in 1 vol. of catalogues no. 431–436, with the addition of collective t. p., "Inhaltsverzeichnis," and "Register der hebräischen Büchertitel."

(Patent: pirsumim tekhnologiyim she-nitkablu ba-Tekhniyon)

פטנ"ט: פרסומים טכנולוגיים שנתקבלו בטכניון.
כרך 1– מאי/יוני 1971–
חיפה, ספרית אלישר, המחלקה לספרות עברית.

v. 25 cm. bimonthly.

Added title, 1971–   : Technical publications received by Technion libraries.

Prijs, Joseph, d. 1956.

Die Basler hebräischen Drucke, 1492–1866. Im Auftrag der Öffentlichen Bibliothek der Universität Basel bearb. von Joseph Prijs. Ergänzt und hrsg. von Bernhard Prijs. Olten, Urs Graf-Verlag, 1964 [1965]

lxiii, 583 p. facsim. 32 cm.

Rosenthal, Eliezer, 1794–1868.

Catalog der Hebraica und Judaica aus der L. Rosenthal'-schen Bibliothek. Bearb. von M. Roest. Amsterdam, B. M. Israël, 1966.

2 v. 22 cm.

"Unchanged reprint of the edition, Amsterdam 1875."

Sulzberger, Mayer, 1843–1923.
(Or Me'ir)

אור מאיר : כולל רשימת ספרי ישראל. כתבי יד ונדפסים,
הנמצאים בבית אוצר ספרים הגדול של מאיר זולצבערגער =
Or Mayer : catalogue of the old Hebrew manuscripts and printed books of the liberary [sic] of M. Sulzberger of Philadelphia, Pa. ; מאת אפרים ... העברות, מאמרים ושירים
דיינארד. — ירושלים : הוצאת קדם, 1973.

100 p. ; 19 cm.
In Hebrew.
Reprint of the 1896 ed. printed by J. Aronson, New York.

Yaari, Abraham, 1899–1966.

הדפוס העברי בקושטא; תולדות הדפוס העברי בקושטא
מראשיתו עד פרוץ מלחמת־העולם השניה ורשימת הספרים שנדפסו

בה. מאת אברהם יערי. ירושלים, הוצאת ספרים ע"ש י. ל. מאגנס,
האוניברסיטה העברית. 727 [1967[

303 p. facsims. 25 cm.

Added t. p.: Hebrew printing at Constantinople; its history and bibliography.

"Supplement to Kirjath sepher, vol. 42."

LIBRARY CATALOGS

British Museum. *Dept. of Oriental Printed Books and Manuscripts.*

Catalogue of the Hebrew books in the library of the British Museum. [Compiled by Joseph Zedner. London] Printed by order of the Trustees, 1867. [London, c1964]

xiv, 891 p. 26 cm.

Harvard University. Library.

Catalogue of Hebrew books. Cambridge; Distributed by the Harvard University Press, 1968.

6 v. 32 cm.

CONTENTS: v. 1–4. Authors and subjects.—v. 5–6. Titles.

———— Supplement I. Cambridge; Distributed by the Harvard University Press, 1972.

3 v. 32 cm.

CONTENTS: v. 1. Classified listing. Appendix: Judaica in the Houghton Library.—v. 2. Authors and selected subjects.—v. 3. Titles.

Isaacson, Isaac.

Check-list of Hebraica and Judaica in the library of the University of the Witwatersrand, compiled by I. Isaacson. Johannesburg. The Library. University of the Witwatersrand, 1967–

v. 30 cm.

English and Hebrew.

Johannesburg. University of the Witwatersrand. Library.

Catalogue of Hebrew printed books in the J. L. Landau collection. Johannesburg, University of the Witwatersrand, 1974.

vii, 188, 26 p. 34 cm.

English or Hebrew.

HEBREW LANGUAGE

ha-Mo'atsah le-hanḥalat ha-lashon.

עלון. –1; –1968.
ירושלים.

no. in   v. 21 cm.

Added t. p.: Bulletin.

Steinschneider, Moritz, 1816–1907.

Christliche Hebraisten: Nachrichten über mehr als 400 Gelehrte, welche über nachbibl. Hebräisch geschrieben haben/ Moritz Steinschneider. — Reprograph. Nachdr. d. Ausg. Berlin, Frankfurt/Main, 1896–1901. — Hildesheim: Gerstenberg, 1973.

92 p.; 22 cm.

"Sonderabdruck aus Zeitschrift für hebräische Bibliographie, Jg. I, II, III, IV and V."

HEBREW LITERATURE
see also   Yiddish literature

Ben-Menahem, Naftali, 1911–

בשערי ספר, מאת נפתלי בן־מנחם. ירושלים, מוסד הרב קוק
[1967[727.

280 p. illus., facsims., port. 22 cm.

Benjacob, Isaac, 1801–1863.

אוצר הספרים, ספר ערוך לתכונת ספרי ישראל נדפסים וכתבי
יד. ווילנא, בדפוס האלמנה והאחים ראם, 1880.

3 v. in 1 (xxxii, 678 p.) 26 cm.

Added t. p.: Ozar ha-sepharim, thesaurus librorum hebraicorum tam impressorum quam manu scriptorum. Ozar ha-sepharim (Bücherschatz) Bibliographie der gesammten hebraelschen Literatur mit Einschluss der Handschriften.
Added t. p. also in Russian.

———————— Photo-offset ‏ניו יארק, הוצאת ירושלים‎ ‏1943/44‎

xxxii, 678 p. 26 cm.

Partially covered by label: ‏בית האצר של ספרים עתיקים ונחצים‎

——————— ‏חלק שני: כולל העדות. תקונים. הוספות ומפתחה שמות‎
‏המהברים ... מאת מנחם מענדל זלאטקין. ירושלים ‏קרית ספר‏‎
‏דפוס סיון, תשב"ה‎ ‏1965‎

481 p. 24 cm.

Chicago. University. Library.
Hebraica at the University of Chicago. ‏Chicago?‏ 1965‏

22 p. illus., facsims. 23 cm.

Catalog of an exhibition which honors the 175th meeting of the American Oriental Society and which consists of books in the collections of the University of Chicago Library.

Hagiti, Hayim.
‏Reshimat sifre yesod ve-shimush le-sifriyot tsiburiyot‏
‏רשימת ספרי יסוד ושמוש לספריות ציבוריות. ערוכה על ידי‎
‏חיים הגיתי בהדרכתו של י. דלigדיש. ירושלים, משרד החינוך‎
‏והתרבות. היהידה לתרבות. המדור לספריות.‎
1965-.

v. 32 cm.

Hagiti, Hayim.
‏Reshimat sifre yesod ve-shimush le-sifriyot tsiburiyot‏
‏רשימת ספרי יסוד ושמוש לספריות ציבוריות. ערוכה על ידי‎
‏חיים הגיתי בהדרכתו של י. דלigדיש. מהד' ב. ירושלים, משרד‎
‏החינוך והתרבות. המדור לספריות.‎ 1969-.

v. 32 cm.

Hebräische Bibliographie; Blätter für neuere und ältere Literatur des Judenthums. Redigirt von Moritz Steinschneider. Hildesheim, New York, G. Olms, 1972.

21 v. in 4. 22 cm.

Original t. p.: ha-Mazkir.
Vols. 2–4 ed. by M. Steinschneider and J. Benzian.
Reprint of the vols. published in Berlin, 1858–82.

Institutum Iudaicum.
Bibliographie sélective au profit de l'étude du Targum, Mishna et Tosephta, Talmud et Midrash. Selectieve bibliografie ten behoeve van de studie van Targoen, Misjna en Tosefta, Talmoed en Midrasj. Bruxelles, Institutum iudaicum, drève de Nivelles, 95, ‏1972‏.

‏lii‏, 46 l. tables. 21 x 30 cm.

Cover title.
Introductory matter in English, French and Flemish.

Kasher, Menachem Mendel, 1895–
‏שרי האלף; רשימת הספרים שבדפוס ומחבריהם מזמן החתימת‎
‏התלמוד. שנת ד"א ר"ס. עד שנת ה"א ר"ס. תקופת השלהן ערוך.‎
‏בתוספת רשימת כל ספרי התנאים והאמוראים והמיוחסים להם.‎
‏ערוך ומסודר על ידי מנחם מ. כשר ויעקב דב מנדלבוים. ניו יורק,‎
‏מכון "תורה שלמה," 719‏ ‏1959‏

15, 455 p. 24 cm.

Added t. p.: Sarei ha-elef; a millenium of Hebrew authors, 500–1500 CE.

——————— ‏ספרי ראשונים; ספרי הלכה ... שראו אור לראשונה‎
‏בשנים תשי"ט-תשכ"ז. רשימה ביבליוגרפית. תיכנה: ישראל‎
‏תא-שמע. ירושלים, הספריה שע"י הישיבה המרכזית לישראל‎
‏"מרכז הרב." 727‏ ‏1967‏

30 p. illus. 24 cm.

‏"ספרים שהוצאו ... מכ"י, או שהוצאו מחדש במהדורות מדעיות או עם"י‎
‏ב"י חדשים."‎ p. 25–30.
‏"ש. ז. חבלין: על המהדורות התחרשות של ספרי הקדמונים"‎
‏"נדפס ב 400 מפסים בלבד."‎

Rossi, Giovanni Bernardo de, 1742–1831.
Historisches Wörterbuch der jüdischen Schriftsteller und

ihrer Werke ‏von‏ Joh. Bern. de Rossi. Aus dem Italienischen von C. H. Hamberger. Mit ausführliches ‏sic‏ Sach und Namenregister von H. Jolowicz. Amsterdam, Philo Press, 1967.

xvi, 336, 32 p. 22 cm. (Bibliotheca Rossiana, v. 3)

"Neudruck 1967 der Ausgaben Leipzig 1839 und 1846."

‏תנים.‎ -1.
‏בני ברק, המרכז לספריות תורניות.‎ -729 ‏ ‏1969‏

v. 24 cm.

Summaries in English, v. 1–
‏"קובץ ביבליוגרפיה תורני-מדעי."‎

Tel-Aviv. University. *Dept. of Hebrew Literature.*
‏הדרכה בבליוגרפית; דפים לעבודה עצמית במסגרת שעורי‎
‏הקריאה המודרכת. תל-אביב, האוניברסיטה של תל-אביב, החוג‎
‏לספרות עברית. מדור ספרות ימי חביניים. תשכ"ו. 1966.‎

23 l. 21 cm.

Walden, Aaron, *b. ca.* 1835.
‏שם הגדולים החדש, בו נקבצו ובאו שמות גאוני וגדולי ישראל‎
‏... משפחות סופרים ומחברי ספרים, חכמי אשכנז ופולין, רוסיא‎
‏וספרד, אשר היו מזמן הרב חיים יוסף דוד אזולאי ... ומכמה‎
‏דורות שלפניו. ערכתי וסדרתי ... ‏אהרן ואלדען‏ עם הוספות‎
‏ותקונים רבים ... ע"י יוסף אריה ליב. ירושלים, תשכ"ה‎
‏1964/65‏

2 v. in 1. 24 cm.
Photo-offset of Warsaw, 1879/80 ed.
CONTENTS.—‏חלק 1. מערכת גדולים.—חלק 2. מערכת ספרים.‎

Werses, Samuel, 1915–
‏הדרכה ביבליוגראפית בספרות העברית; ילקוט אמונים. ערך‎
‏ש. ורסס. מהד' ב. מורחבת. ירושלים, האוניברסיטה העברית,‎
‏הפקולטה למדעי הרוח, החוג לספרות עברית, תשכ"ד‎ ‏1963/64‏

232 p. 24 cm.

Cover title.
Pages 229–232 blank for ‏"תוספות ותיקונים"‎

HISTORY AND CRITICISM

Jerusalem. Hebrew University. Dept. of Hebrew Literature.
‏רשימות ביבליוגראפיות לשנת תשל"ב. ירושלים, האוניברסיטה‎
‏העברית, הפקולטה למדעי-הרוה, המכון למדעי היהדות, החוג‎
‏לספרות עברית. 732‏ ‏1971‏

163 p. 27 cm.

Shaked, Gershon.
‏בעיות ברומאן העברי במאה ה-20; חומר ביבליוגראפי לסמינר‎
‏של ג. שקד. ערך י. האפרתי. ירושלים, האוניברסיטה העברית.‎
‏הפקולטה למדעי הרוח, החוג לספרות עברית. 727‏ ‏1966‏

17 l. 28 cm.

Shaked, Gershon.
‏מבחר ביבליוגרפי לשעורו של ג. שקד: "הספרות העברית בדורו‎
‏של ביאליק." ירושלים, האוניברסיטה העברית, הפקולטה למדעי‎
‏הרוח החוג לספרות העברית. תשכ"ז‎ ‏1966‏

12 p. 24 cm.

TRANSLATIONS

Goell, Yohai.
Bibliography of modern Hebrew literature in English translation. Jerusalem, Executive of the World Zionist Organization, Youth and Hechalutz Dept; Jerusalem, New York, Israel Universities Press, 1968.

vii, 110, 22 p. 28 cm.

"Based ... almost solely upon the holdings of the Jewish National and University Library in Jerusalem."
On cover: Ktav Publishing House ‏New York‏
Includes alphabetical author index in Hebrew.

Israel. *Misrad ha-ḥuts.*

ספרות עברית מתורגמת לצרפתית; רשימה ביבליוגרפית
1940–1965. ‏הוכנה על ידי רות טרוניק וטניה מנצור‏ ירושלים,
משרד החוץ‏, המחלקה לקשרי תרבות. 1966.

17, il l. 34 cm.
Cover title.
Added cover title: Bibliographie d'ouvrages hébraïques traduits en français, 1940–1965.
Introduction and index also in French.

HEBREW UNIVERSITY, JERUSALEM

סקרון. .1968–

‏ירושלים‏ המחלקה לחסברה ויחסי־צבור, האוניברסיטה העברית.

v. 23 cm. annual.

Added title, 1968– : Sikron.
‏"סקירת ספרים ... האוניברסיטה העברית בירושלים."

HEDENVIND-ERIKSSON, GUSTAV

Svensson, Conny.
Gustav Hedenvind-Eriksson. En bibliografi. Uppsala, Litteraturvetenskapliga institutionen, ‏Lundequistska bokh. (distr.)‏, 1973.

51 p. 21 cm. (Meddelanden utgivna av Avdelningen för litteratursociologi vid Litteraturvetenskapliga institutionen i Uppsala, nr. 6)

HEEGER, VIKTOR EMANUEL

König, Josef Walter.
Viktor-Heeger-Bibliographie. Wolfratshausen, Gödel, 1966.

30 p., 8 l. of illus. 21 cm.

HEGEL, GEORG WILHELM FRIEDRICH

Nuremberg. Stadtbibliothek.
Georg Wilhelm Friedrich Hegel ⟨1770–1831⟩ in Nürnberg 1808–1816. Ausstellung. Eröffnet am 15. Sept. 1966. (Einrichtung der Ausstellung und Katalog: Franz Xaver Pröll) Nürnberg, Stadtbibliothek (1966)

10 l. 17 cm. (Ausstellungs-Katalog der Stadtbibliothek Nürnberg, 51)

HEIBERG, JOHAN LUDVIG

Spang-Hanssen, Esbern, 1884–
Filologen J. L. Heiberg, 1854–1928. Bibliografi. Ved E. Spang-Hanssen. 2 udg. 1219 København K, Det Kongelige Bibliotek, Christians Brygge 8, 1969.

141 p. 24 cm. (Det Kongelige Bibliotek. Nationalbibliografisk afdelings publikationer)

HEIDEGGER, MARTIN

Sass, Hans Martin.
Heidegger-Bibliographie. Meisenheim am Glan, A. Hain, 1968.

181 p. 24 cm.

HEILIGGEIST-BRUDERSCHAFT see Order of the Holy Ghost

HEINE, HEINRICH

Hamburg. Öffentliche Bücherhalle. Musikbücherei.
Dichterliebe: Heinrich Heine im Lied; ein Verzeichnis der Vertonungen von Gedichten Heinrich Heines zusammengestellt zum 175. Geburtstag des Dichters, 13. Dezember 1972. ‏Bearbeitung des Kataloges: Annemarie Eckhoff. Hamburg, 1972‏

87 p. illus. 19 cm.

Owen, Claude R
Heine im spanischen Sprachgebiet; eine kritische Bibliographie, von Claude R. Owen. Münster, Westfalen, Aschendorff ‏1968‏

xlviii, 336 p. 27 cm. (Spanische Forschungen der Görresgesellschaft. 2. Reihe, Bd. 12)

Seifert, Siegfried.
Heine-Bibliographie, 1954–1964. ‏1. Aufl.‏ Berlin, Aufbau-Verlag, 1968.

xiii, 395 p. 25 cm. (Bibliographien, Kataloge und Bestandsverzeichnisse)

Continuation of Heine Bibliographie by Gottfried Wilhelm.

HEINRIC EN MARGRIETE VAN LIMBORCH

Vijfvinkel, Elly.
Bibliographie zu dem Lymburgroman / von Elly Vijvinkel. — Amsterdam : Rodopi, 1974.

90 p. : ill. ; 23 cm. — (Beschreibende Bibliographien ; 6. Heft)

HELGASON, JÓN

Loth, Agnete.
Jón Helgason. Bibliografi 1919–1969. København, Rosenkilde og Bagger, 1969.

58 p., 7 l. port. 24 cm.

HELIADE-RĂDULESCU, ION

Biblioteca Municipală Tîrgoviște.
Ion Heliade Rădulescu. (1802–1872). Biobibliografie. ‏Cuvînt înainte de prof. Ion Gavrilă. Coperta colecției: Emil Florin Grama‏. Tîrgoviște, 1972.

47 p. 21 cm.

At head of title: Comitetul de Cultură și Educație Socialistă Dimbovița. Biblioteca Municipală Tîrgoviște.
"Intocmirea bibliografiei: Rachila Trandafir, Stela Marin."

HELIUM

Tully, Philip C   1923–
Helium: bibliography of technical and scientific literature, 1962 including papers on alpha-particles, by Philip C. Tully and Lowell Stroud. ‏Washington‏ U. S. Bureau of Mines; ‏for sale by Supt. of Docs., U. S. Govt. Print. Off., 1969‏

vi, 367 p. 26 cm. (U. S. Bureau of Mines. Information circular 8398)

Wheeler, Henry P
Helium: bibliography of technical and scientific literature from its discovery (1868) to January 1, 1947, by Henry P. Wheeler, Jr., and Louise B. Swenarton. Washington, U. S. Govt. Print. Off., 1952.

xii, 76 p. 26 cm. (U. S. Bureau of Mines. Bulletin 484)

———— A supplement, January 1, 1947 to January 1, 1962, compiled by Harold W. Lipper and Carla W. Cherry. ‏Washington, U. S. Dept. of the Interior, Bureau of Mines; ‏for sale by the Supt. of Docs., U. S. Govt. Print. Off., 1968‏

iii, 525 p. 26 cm. (U. S. Bureau of Mines. Information circular 8373)

HELLMAN, LILLIAN

Texas. University. *Library.*
The Lillian Hellman collection at the University of Texas. Compiled by Manfred Triesch. Austin ‏Humanities Research Center‏ University of Texas; ‏distributed by University of Texas Press, 1968, °1966‏

167 p. illus., ports. 26 cm.
A descriptive catalog of the manuscript material, various drafts of L. Hellman's dramas, correspondence, etc.
Appendix (p. 102–160) contains character descriptions and plot outlines from various versions of her dramas with scenes reproduced verbatim.

HELMINTHOLOGY

Helminthological abstracts. Series A: Animal and human helminthology. v. 39– Mar. 1970–
₍Farnham Royal, Commonwealth Agricultural Bureaux₎

v. 25 cm. quarterly.

Supersedes, in part, Helminthological abstracts, and continues its vol. numbering.

Kurashvili, Boris Epifanovich.
Библиография по гельминтам и гельминтозам человека, животных и сельскохозяйственных растений в Грузии. (За период с 1865 г. по 1967 г.) Тбилиси, "Мецниереба," 1968.

100 p. 21 cm.

At head of title: Б. Е. Курашвили, Н. Г. Кямалов, И. Я. Элиава. On leaf preceding t. p.: Академия наук Грузинской ССР. Институт зоологии.
Added t. p. in Georgian and English: Bibliography of the helminths and helminthoses of man, of animals and of agricultural plants in Georgia.

Rossouw, S. F.
Radioisotopes and radiation in helminthology: a bibliography compiled by S. F. Rossouw. Pelindaba, Atomic Energy Board, 1966.

29 l. 29 cm.

Threlfall, William.
The helminth parasites of the herring gull (*Larus argentatus* Pontopp.) Farnham Royal (Bucks.) Commonwealth Agricultural Bureaux, 1966.

₍2₎, 23 p. 24 cm. (Commonwealth Bureau of Helminthology, St. Albans, Eng. Technical communications no. 37)

HEMATOLOGY see Blood

HEMINGWAY, ERNEST

Bruccoli, Matthew Joseph, 1931–
Hemingway at auction, 1930–1973. Compiled by Matthew J. Bruccoli ₍and₎ C. E. Frazer Clark, Jr. Introd. by Charles W. Mann. Detroit, Gale Research Co. ₍1973₎

xx, 286 p. illus. 26 cm.

"A Bruccoli-Clark book."

Cohn, Louis Henry.
A bibliography of the works of Ernest Hemingway. New York, Haskell House Publishers, 1973.

116 p. illus. 23 cm.

Reprint of the 1931 ed. published by Random House, New York.

Hanneman, Audre, *comp.*
Ernest Hemingway, a comprehensive bibliography. Princeton, N. J., Princeton University Press, 1967.

xi, 568 p. facsims. 25 cm.

Levidova, Inna Mikhaĭlovna.
(Ernest Kheminguĕĭ)
Эрнест Хемингуэй. Биобиблиогр. указатель. ₍Вступит. статья И. М. Левидовой, с. 5–23₎. Москва, "Книга," 1970.

144 p. 21 cm. (Писатели зарубежных стран)

At head of title: Всесоюзная государственная библиотека иностранной литературы.

White, William, 1910–
The Merrill checklist of Ernest Hemingway. Columbus, Ohio, Merrill ₍1970₎

45 p. 19 cm. (Charles E. Merrill program in American literature. Charles E. Merrill checklists)

Young, Philip, 1918–
The Hemingway manuscripts; an inventory ₍by₎ Philip Young and Charles W. Mann. University Park, Pennsylvania State University Press ₍1969₎

xiii, 138 p. facsims. 21 cm.

HEMP

Corkern, Ray.
Kenaf; a bibliography, 1950–1962. ₍Washington₎ U. S. Dept. of Agriculture, Economic Research Service, Marketing Economics Division ₍1964₎

16 p. 26 cm. (₍U. S. Dept. of Agriculture. Economic Research Service₎ ERS–153)

HENDRICKSON, ROBERT C.

George Arents Research Library. Manuscripts Dept.
Robert C. Hendrickson: inventory of his papers, Syracuse University Libraries. Compiled by John Janitz. Syracuse, N. Y., Syracuse University Libraries, 1971.

41 l. port. 28 cm. (Syracuse University. Libraries. Manuscripts Dept. Manuscript inventory series, inventory no. 14)

HENGELO, NETHERLANDS

Egmond, R J van.
Hengelo. Bibliografie. Samengesteld door R. J. van Egmond. ₍Werkstuk 2. cyclus Bibliotheek- en Documentatieschool, Amsterdam. Amsterdam, Bibliotheek- en Documentatieschool₎ 1969.

l, 33 l. 29 cm.

HENSEL, FANNY

Staatsbibliothek Preussischer Kulturbesitz. Mendelssohn-Archiv.
Fanny Hensel, geb. Mendelssohn Bartholdy, 14. Nov. 1805–14. Mai 1847 : Dokumente ihres Lebens : Ausstellung z. 125. Todestag im Mendelssohn-Archiv d. Staatsbibliothek Preuss. Kulturbesitz vom 3.–31. Mai 1972, Berlin-Dahlem / ₍bearb. von Rudolf Elvers₎. — Berlin : Staatsbibliothek Preuss. Kulturbesitz, 1972.

₍12₎ p. ; 21 cm. — (Ausstellungskataloge - Staatsbibliothek Preussischer Kulturbesitz ; 2)

HENTY, GEORGE ALFRED

Dartt, Robert L
G. A. Henty, a bibliography ₍by₎ Robert L. Dartt. Cedar Grove, N. J., Dar-Web ₍1971₎

xvii, 184 p. illus. 23 cm.

HERACLITUS, OF EMPHESUS

Roussos, Euangelos N 1931–
Heraklit-Bibliographie. ₍Von₎ Evangelos N. Roussos. Darmstadt, Wissenschaftliche Buchges., 1971.

xx, 164 p. 20 cm.

HERALDRY
see also Genealogy

Achen, Sven Tito.
Bibliografi over heraldisk litteratur i Danmark og om Danmark 1589–1969. ₍Af₎ Sven Tito Achen og Ole Rostock. København, Dansk Historisk Fællesforening, 1971.

102 p. illus. 24 cm.

Cover title: Dansk heraldisk bibliografi 1589–1969.

Bern. Schweizerische landesbibliothek.
Armoriaux et recueils d'armoiries familiales suisses, 19° et 20° siècles. Essai bibliographique. Schweizerische Wappenbücher und Familienwappensammlungen ... (Rédacteurs: Régis de Courten, Bernard de Vevey.) Berne, 1967.

iii, 25 p. 29 cm.

At head of title: Bibliothèque nationale suisse. Service d'information bibliographique. Schweizerische Landesbibliothek. Bibliographische Auskunftsstelle.

Gatfield, George.
Guide to printed books and manuscripts relating to English and foreign heraldry and genealogy, being a classified catalogue of works of those branches of literature. Detroit, Gale Research Co., 1966.

646 p. 24 cm.

Reprint of the 1892 ed.

Heraldry Society.
Library and slide collection catalogue. London, Heraldry Society, 1967.

[3], 68 p. 22 cm.

Hohlfeld, Johannes, 1888–1950, *comp.*
Wappen- und Siegelkunde. Bibliographie 1938–1945. Bearb. von Johannes Hohlfeld und Ottfried Neubecker. Neustadt an der Aisch, Degener, 1967.

p. 772–840. 24 cm.

Cover title.
"Sonderdruck aus 'Familiengeschichtliche Bibliographie,' [Bd. 7], hrsg. von der Stiftung Zentralstelle für Personen- und Familiengeschichte zu Berlin, bei diesem Abschnitt 'Wappen- und Siegelkunde in Zusammenarbeit mit dem Herold, Verein für Heraldik, Genealogie und verwandte Wissenschaften zu Berlin."

Pennsylvania. State Library, *Harrisburg.*
Heraldry; a bibliography of books in the Pennsylvania State Library. Compiled by Carol Carlson, reference librarian. Harrisburg, General Library Bureau, Pennsylvania State Library, 1970.

18 p. 29 cm.

HÉRAULT, FRANCE (DEPT.)

Hérault, France (Dept.). Archives départementales.
Répertoire numérique des Archives départementales antérieures à 1790, Hérault. Archives ecclésiastiques. Série G, clergé séculier. Rédigé par Marcel Gouron, conservateur en chef, directeur des Services d'archives du département. Montpellier, 1970.
iv, 268 p. 31 cm.
Half title: Répertoire numérique détaillé des archives départementales antérieures à 1790.
On spine: Répertoire numérique des archives de l'Herault.

HERBART, JOHANN FRIEDRICH

Schmitz, Josef Nikolaus.
Herbart-Bibliographie, 1842–1963 [von] Josef N. Schmitz. Weinheim, J. Beltz [1964]

63 p. 21 cm.

HERBERT, HENRY WILLIAM

Van Winkle, William Mitchell, 1885–
Henry William Herbert (Frank Forester) a bibliography of his writings, 1832–1858. Compiled by William Mitchell Van Winkle, with the bibliographical assistance of David A. Randall. New York, B. Franklin [1971]

xviii, 189 p. illus. 23 cm. (Burt Franklin bibliography & reference series, 403. Essays in literature and criticism, 120)

Reprint of the 1936 ed.

HERBICIDES

Bibliotheca Bogoriensis.
Bibliografi mengenai ekologi rumput dan herbisida di Indonesia. (Bibliography on the ecology of weeds and herbicides in Indonesia). Bogor [1969]

ii, 9 l. 33 cm. (Seri bibliografi, no. 15)

Condon, Patricia Aten, 1935–
The toxicity of herbicides to mammals, aquatic life, soil microorganisms, beneficial insects and cultivated plants, 1950–65: a list of selected references [compiled by Patricia A. Condon] Washington, National Agricultural Library, U. S. Dept. of Agriculture, 1968.

iii, 161 p. 26 cm. (Library list no. 87)

Štěpánek, Dušan, comp.
Herbicidy; [soupis literatury] Sest. Dušan Štěpánek. V Brně, 1966.

11 p. 21 cm. (Universitní knihovna v Brně. Výběrový seznam, 114)

HERCULANEUM see under Pompeii

HERDER, JOHANN GOTTFRIED VON

Tronchon, Henri, d. 1941.
La fortune intellectuelle de Herder en France. Bibliographie critique. (Réimpr. de l'éd. de Paris, 1920). Genève, Slatkine Reprints, 1971.

73 p. 23 cm.

HEREDIA, JOSÉ MARÍA

Fernández Robaina, Tomás.
Bibliografía sobre José María Heredia [compilado por Tomás F. Robaina. La Habana] Biblioteca Nacional José Martí [1970]

xiii, 111 p. 24 cm.

HEREDITY

McKusick, Victor A
Mendelian inheritance in man; catalogs of autosomal dominant, autosomal recessive, and X-linked phenotypes [by] Victor A. McKusick. Baltimore, Johns Hopkins Press [1966]

xvii, 344 p. 25 cm.

McKusick, Victor A
Mendelian inheritance in man; catalogs of autosomal dominant, autosomal recessive, and X-linked phenotypes [by] Victor A. McKusick. 2d ed. Baltimore, Johns Hopkins Press [1968]

xix, 521 p. 25 cm.

McKusick, Victor A
Mendelian inheritance in man; catalogs of autosomal dominant, autosomal recessive, and X-linked phenotypes [by] Victor A. McKusick. 3d ed. Baltimore, Johns Hopkins Press [1971]

xlv, 738 p. 25 cm.

HERESIES AND HERETICS

Kulcsár, Zsuzsánna.
Eretnekmozgalmak a xi–xiv. században. Budapest, Tankönyvkiadó, 1964.

335 p. 20 cm. (A Budapesti Egyetemi Könyvtár kiadványai, 22)
Introd. and chapter headings also in French and Russian.

HERMAN, LEON M.

Whelan, Joseph G
Leon M. Herman: a bibliography of published works, compiled by Joseph G. Whelan, and others. [Washington?] 1969.

12 l. 29 cm.

Reprinted from the Aste bulletin, v. 11, no. 2, fall, 1969.

HERMANS, WILLEM FREDERIK

Janssen, Frans Anton.
Bibliografie van de verspreide publicaties van Willem Frederik Hermans. Samengesteld door Frans A. Janssen en Rob Delvigne. Amsterdam, Rap, ₁1972₁.

xiv, 80 p. 23 cm.

HERPETOLOGY

Gilboa, I
A bibliography on the chromosomes of amphibians and reptiles: 1891–1971 ₁by I. Gilboa and H. G. Dowling₁ New York, Herpetological Information Search Systems, 1972.

33 p. 29 cm. (Publications in herpetology, 4)

Gilboa, I
A bibliography on the longevity of amphibians and reptiles: 1882–1971 ₁by I. Gilboa and H. G. Dowling₁ New York, Herpetological Information Search Systems, 1972.

9 p. 29 cm. (Publications in herpetology, 3)

Gilboa, I
A bibliography on the reproductive system of reptiles, 1822–1972: a bibliographic service ₁by I. Gilboa, H. G. Dowling, & T. C. Majupuria₁ New York, Herpetological Information Search Systems, 1973.

34 p. 28 cm. (Publ herpetol 5)

Herpetological Information Search Systems.
HISS titles and reviews. v. 1–
Feb. 1973–
₁New York₁

v. 28 cm. 5 no. a year.

Smith, Hobart Muir, 1912–
Analysis of the literature exclusive of the Mexican axolotl, by Hobart M. Smith and Rozella B. Smith. Augusta, W. Va., E. Lundberg, 1973.

xxxiii, 367 p. 24 cm. (Synopsis of the herpetofauna of Mexico, v. 2)

Smith, Hobart Muir, 1912–
Analysis of the literature on the Mexican axolotl, by Hobart M. Smith and Rozella B. Smith. Augusta, W. Va., E. Lundberg, 1971.

xxvii, 245 p. 24 cm. (Synopsis of the herpetofauna of Mexico, v. 1)

Smith, Hobart Muir, 1912–
Early foundations of Mexican herpetology; an annotated and indexed bibliography of the herpetological publications of Alfredo Dugès, 1826–1910, by Hobart M. Smith and Rozella B. Smith. Urbana, University of Illinois Press, 1969.

85 p. illus., facsims., ports. 24 cm.

HERRIGEL, HERMANN

Schulz, Ursula.
Hermann Herrigel, der Denker und die deutsche Erwachsenenbildung. Eine Bibliographie seiner Schriften z. 80. Geburtstag. Mit e. Einl. von Günter Schulz. (Bremen) Bremer Volkshochschule, 1969.

53 p. with port. 24 cm. (Bremer Beiträge zur freien Volksbildung, Heft 12)

Bibliographien zur Zeit- und Kulturgeschichte, Heft 4.

HERTFORDSHIRE, ENGLAND

Hertfordshire, *Eng. Record Office.*
A catalogue of manuscript maps in the Hertfordshire Record Office; compiled by₁ Peter Walne, County Archivist. Hertford. Hertfordshire County Record Office. 1969.

₁3₁, ii, 156 p. 21 cm.

At head of title: Hertfordshire County Council.

Hodson, Donald.
The printed maps of Hertfordshire, 1577–1900, by D. Hodson. London, Map Collectors' Circle, 1969–

v. maps. 25 cm. (Map collectors' series, no. 53, 59, 75, 83)

CONTENTS: pt. 1: 1577–1784.—pt. 2: 1785–1820.

pt. 4: 1861–1885.—pt. 5: 1886–1900, and Supplement.

HESSE

Hesse. Staatsarchiv, Darmstadt.
Abteilung Handschriften ⟨C 1⟩. ⟨Kopialbücher, Lager- u. Zinsbücher, Statuten, Chroniken, Protokolle, Nekrologe, Kalendarien, Anniversarien, Matrikel, Kirchenbücher, Heraldica, Sphragistica, Genealogica, Familien- u. Stammbücher, Kollegnachschriften, etc.⟩ Bearb. von Albrecht Eckhardt. Darmstadt, Marburg (Hess. Staatsarchiv) 1970.

vi, 166 l. 30 cm. (Its Repertorien)

Hesse (Landgraviate). Kanzlei.
Das Schriftgut der Landgräflich Hessischen Kanzlei im Mittelalter ⟨vor 1517⟩. Verzeichnis d. Bestände. Bearb. von K. E. Demandt. Marburg (Hess. Staatsarchiv) 1969–

v. 30 cm. (Repertorien des Hess₁ischen₁ Staatsarchivs Marburg)

CONTENTS.—
T. 2. Rechnungen und Rechnungsbelege.

Hessisches Hauptstaatsarchiv Wiesbaden.
Übersicht über die Bestände des Hessischen Hauptstaatsarchivs Wiesbaden. Wiesbaden, Hess. Hauptstaatsarchiv, 1970.

xxix, 388 p. with 9 illus. 25 cm.

Leist, Winfried.
Schrifttum zur Geschichte und geschichtlichen Landeskunde von Hessen, 1965–1967. Marburg, N. G. Elwert 1973.
xx, 341 p. 24 cm. (Veröffentlichungen der Historischen Kommission für Hessen, 31/1)
Continues K. E. Demandt's work of the same title published 1965–68.

Sieburg, Armin.
Landgräflich Hessische Regierung Kassel. Mit Unterstützung der Historischen Kommission für Hessen. Marburg/Lahn ₁Hessisches Staatsarchiv₁ 1974–

v. 21 cm. (Repertorien des Hessischen Staatsarchivs Marburg, Bestand 17e: Ortsreposituren (1518–1821))

CONTENTS: Bd. 1. A D.

HESSE, HERMANN

Bareiss, Otto.
Hermann Hesse; eine Bibliographie der Werke über Hermann Hesse. Mit einem Geleitwort von Bernhard Zeller. Basel ₁K. Maier-Bader₁ 1962–64.

2 v. ports. 24 cm.

On spine: Hesse-Bibliographie.
Vol. 1: Neudruck 1964.
Vol. 2 has title: Zeitschriften- und Zeitungsaufsätze.

Bentz, Hans Willi.
Hermann Hesse in Übersetzungen ₍von₎ Hans W. Bentz. Hermann Hesse translated. Hermann Hesse traduit. Frankfurt a. M. ₍1965₎

38, 5 p. facsim. 30 cm. (Weltliteratur in Übersetzungen. Reihe 1: Deutschsprachige Autoren, Bd. 3)

"Nach Manuskriptabschluss noch ermittelte Hesse-Übersetzungen": leaf inserted.

Pfeifer, Martin.
Hermann-Hesse-Bibliographie; Primär- und Sekundärschrifttum in Auswahl. ₍Berlin₎ E. Schmidt ₍c1973₎

104 p. 21 cm.

Unseld, Siegfried.
Hermann Hesse; eine Werkgeschichte. ₍Frankfurt am Main₎ Suhrkamp ₍1973₎

319 p. illus. 18 cm. (Suhrkamp Taschenbuch, 143)

Greatly enl. ed. of Unseld's Das Werk von Hermann Hesse, containing chiefly commentary and interpretation with excerpts from Hesse's correspondence.

HETZEL, PIERRE JULES

Paris. Bibliothèque nationale.
P.-J. Hetzel, Paris, 1966. ₍Catalogue par Marie Cordroc'h avec la collaboration de Marie-Laure Chastang et Roger Pierrot. Préface par Étienne Dennery₎ Paris, Bibliothèque nationale, 1966.

xx, 92 p. plates. 20 cm.

Illustrated cover.
At head of title: De Balzac à Jules Verne, un grand éditeur du xixᵉ siècle.

Paris. Bibliothèque nationale.
Pierre Jules Hetzel. Un grande editore del xix secolo. Da Balzac a Giulio Verne. Biblioteca nazionale Braidense, Milano, 1967. Milano, Tip. U. Allegretti di Campi, 1967.

110 p. 9 plates. 21½ cm.

Translation of P.-J. Hetzel.
"Catalogo ... compilato da Mme. Marie Cordroc'h ... Tradottto da Giannina Alloisio."

HEUSCHELE, OTTO

Otto Heuschele: Bibliographie. Schwäbisch Gmünd, Lempp (1972).

24 p. 21 cm.

Limited ed. of 220 copies.

HEVES MEGYE, HUNGARY

Szecskó, Károly.
Heves megye uj- és legujabbkori történetének irodalma, 1790–1970. Eger ₍Szakszervezetek Heves Megyei Elnöksége₎ 1971.

52 p. 21 cm.

HEWLETT, MAURICE HENRY

Muir, Percival Horace, 1894–
A bibliography of the first editions of books by Maurice Henry Hewlett (1861–1923) Compiled by P. H. Muir. ₍Folcroft, Pa.₎ Folcroft Library Editions, 1973.

30 p. 26 cm.

Reprint of the 1927 ed. issued as a supplement to the Bookman's Journal, London.

HEYDUK, ADOLF

Krulichová. Marie.
Adolf Heyduk. (1835–1923.) Literární pozůstalost. Zprac. Marie Krulichová. Praha, Literární archív Památníku nár. písemnictví. t. Ruch, Liberec, 1970.

87. 1 p. 20 cm. (Edice inventářů, čís. 215)

HEYNICKE, KURT

Heynicke, Kurt, 1891–
Kurt Heynicke. Mit Beiträgen von Kurt Heynicke, Bruno Berger und einer Kurt-Heynicke-Bibliographie von Hedwig Bieber. Dortmund, Stadtbücherei, 1966.

48 p. 21 cm. (Dichter und Denker unserer Zeit, Folge 36)

HICKS, GRANVILLE

Bicker, Robert J
Granville Hicks: an annotated bibliography, February, 1927 to June 1967 with a supplement to June 1968, by Robert J. Bicker. Emporia, Graduate Division, Kansas State Teachers College, 1968.

100 p. 23 cm. (The Emporia State research studies, v. 17, no. 2)

Originally submitted as the author's thesis (M. s.) Kansas State Teachers College.

HIERONYMUS, SAINT

Lambert, Bernard.
Bibliotheca Hieronymiana manuscripta. La tradition manuscrite des œuvres de Saint Jérôme. Steenbrugis, in abbatia S. Petri ₍'s-Gravenhage, Martinus Nijhoff₎ 1969-72.

4 v. in 7. 25 cm. (Instrumenta patristica, 4)

Imprint on t. p. of v. 2. (1959) corrected by label: 1969.

HIERONYMUS VON PRAG see under Hus, Jan

HIGGINS, HENRY BOURNES

Canberra, Australia. National Library.
Henry Bournes Higgins: a guide to his papers and those of the Higgins family in the National Library of Australia. Canberra, Manuscript Branch, Reference Division, National Library of Australia, 1965.

17 l. 25 cm.

HIGH PRESSURE (TECHNOLOGY)

Richardson, Christine A
Jet cutting technology: a bibliography, by Christine A. Richardson ₍and₎ Wendy A. Thornton. Bedford, BHRA Fluid Engineering, 1973.

₍3₎ 75 p. 30 cm.

Zeitlin, Alexander.
Annotated bibliography on high-pressure technology. New York, American Society of Mechanical Engineers ₍1964₎

₍a₎-m, 290 p. 29 cm.

"A report of the ASME Research Committee on Pressure Technology ... presented by title as one of the papers of the Symposium on High-Pressure Measurement ... 1962."

HIGH SCHOOLS see Education, Secondary

HIGHER EDUCATION see Education, Higher

HIGHWAY SAFETY see Traffic safety

HIGHWAY RESEARCH BOARD see National Research Council. Highway Research Board

HIGHWAYS see Roads

HIKING

Barkauskas, Mary Ellen.
Hiking and hiking trails; a trails and trail-based activities bibliography. Washington, U. S. Dept. of the Interior, Office of the Secretary, 1970.

11 l., 57 p. 27 cm. (Office of Library Services. Bibliography series, no. 20)

Deutscher Alpenverein (Founded 1874) Alpenvereinsbücherei, Munich.
Kataloge der Alpenvereins Bücherei, München; Sachkatalog. Boston, G. K. Hall, 1970.

3 v. 37 cm.

Added t. p.: Catalogs of the Alpine Association Library, Munich; subject catalog.

Heaston, Michael D
Trails of Kansas, a bibliography, compiled by Michael D. Heaston under the direction of Ross McL. Taylor, Henry H. Malone, and Cultural Heritage and Arts Center. Dodge City? Kan., ₁1969₁

63 p. maps. 21 cm.

HILDEGARDIS, SAINT

Lauter, Werner.
Hildegard-Bibliographie. Wegweiser zur Hildegard-Literatur. Alzey, Verl. d. Rheinischen Druckwerkstätte ₁1970₁

83 p. 24 cm. (Alzeyer Geschichtsblätter, Sonderheft 4)

HILLEBRECHT, RUDOLF

Hillebrecht, Rudolf.
Verzeichnis der Veröffentlichungen. (₁Hannover, Büro R. Hillebrecht₁ 1967–

1 v. (loose-leaf) 30 cm.

Caption title.
Kept up to date by loose-leaf supplements.

HILLER, KURT

Müller, Horst H W 1941–
Kurt Hiller, von Horst H. W. Müller. Mit Beiträgen von Ernst Buchholz und Alfred Kerr. ₁Hamburg₁ H. Christians ₁1969₁

98 p. facsim., port. 22 cm. (Hamburger Bibliographien, Bd. 6)

HILLERS, SOLOMONS

Peile, Eiženija.
Akadēmiķis Solomons Hillers; biobibliogrāfija. ₁Sastādītāji: E. Peile un I. Reinis. Biogrāfisko apcerējumu sarakstījuši G. Vanags, M. Šimanska un J. Stradiņš₁ Rīgā, Zinātne, 1967.

126 p. port. 21 cm. (Padomju Latvijas zinātnieki)
At head of title: Latvijas PSR Zinātņu akadēmija. Fundamentālā bibliotēka.
Added t. p. in Russian.
Latvian and Russian.

HIMALAYA REGION

Yakushi, Yoshimi.
(Himaraya kankei tosho mokuroku)
ヒマラヤ関係図書目録　薬師義美編　長岡京
薬師義美　1972.

343 p. 26 cm.

Title also in English: Catalogue of the Himalayan literature.

HINCE, KENNETH

Canberra, Australia. National Library. Manuscript Section.
Kenneth Hince; a guide to his papers in the National Library of Australia. Canberra, 1971.

35 p. 26 cm.

HINDEMITH, PAUL

Rösner, Helmut.
Paul Hindemith; Katalog seiner Werke, Diskographie, Bibliographie, Einführung in das Schaffen. ₁Bearbeitung und Redaktion: Helmut Rösner₁ Frankfurt am Main, Städtische Musikbibliothek ₁1970₁

60 p. 21 cm.

HINDI DRAMA see Drama - India

HINDI LITERATURE

Asiatic Society, Calcutta. Library.
A catalogue of printed Hindi books in the library of the Asiatic Society. Compiled by Girijanath Bhattacharya. Calcutta, 1967.

xvii, 50 p. 25 cm.

वृहद् हिन्दी ग्रन्थ विवरणिका; हिन्दी में प्रकाशित तथा प्राप्य समस्त हिन्दी पुस्तकों की सम्पूर्ण सूची. ₁1. संस्करण₁ जबलपुर, सुपमा साहित्य मंदिर ₁1965₁

1 v. (various pagings) 27 x 11 cm.

In Hindi.

Mahajan, Yash Pal, 1932–
हिंदी साहित्य: आलोचना ग्रंथ-सूची, १९४७-१९७१; हिंदी साहित्य पर आलोचना तथा भाषाविज्ञान-संबंधी पुस्तकों की विस्तृत सूची. संपादक यशपाल महाजन. ₁1. संस्करण₁ दिल्ली, भारतीय ग्रंथ निकेतन ₁1971₁

₁8₁, 336 p. (p. 335-336 blank for notes) 25 cm.

In Hindi.

Roadarmel, Gordon C 1932–
A bibliography of English source materials for the study of modern Hindi literature, by Gordon C. Roadarmel. Berkeley, Center for South and Southeast Asia Studies, University of California, 1969.

vii, 96 l. 28 cm. (Center for South and Southeast Asia Studies, University of California. Occasional paper no. 4)

HINDI PHILOLOGY see under Dissertations, Academic - Philology

HINDI POETRY see Poetry - India

HINDU LAW

Sternbach, Ludwik.
Bibliography on dharma and artha in Ancient and Mediaeval India. Wiesbaden, Harrassowitz, 1973.

xiv, 152 p. 24 cm.

Additions to the bibliography to be published periodically in the Revue historique du droit français et étranger.

HINDUISM

अद्वैत ग्रन्थ कोश:. Advaita grantha kośa. Prepared by a disciple of Ista Siddhindra Saraswati Swami of the Upanisad Brahmendra Mutt, Kancheepuram. ₁Calcutta, Deva Vani Parisad, 1964?₁

ii, lvii, 12, 37, 151, ix, ₁l₁ p. col. illus., ports. 20 x 28 cm.

English and Sanskrit.

HIRAYAMA FAMILY
Saitama Kenritsu Toshokan.
(Musashi no kuni Iruma-gun Hirayama-mura Hirayama-ke monjo mokuroku)
武蔵国入間郡平山村　平山家文書目録　₁浦和₁

埼玉県立図書館　昭和43(1968)

410 p.　25 cm.　(近世史料所在調査報告　3)

HIROSAKI, JAPAN

Kuzunishi, Keizō.

(Hirosaki Toshokan zō kyōdoshi bunken kaidai)

弘前図書館蔵郷土史文献解題　弘前　弘前図書館　昭和45(1970)

100 p.　21 cm.

HIROSHIMA, JAPAN

Gembaku Shiryō Hozonkai.

(Gembaku Kinen Bunko shozō gembaku kankei bunken mokuroku)

原爆記念文庫所蔵原爆関係文献目録　昭和40年8月31日調　原爆資料保存会編　［横田工著　広島　1965］

64 p.　22 cm.

Hiroshima Shiritsu Asano Toshokan.

浅野図書館（広島市）

広島市立浅野図書館蔵郷土資料目録

広島　昭和44(1969)

138, 41p　22cm

昭和44年2月現在

Toyo, Motokuni.

(Hiroshima-ken kodai shi bunken sōmokuroku)

広島県古代史文献総目録　豊元国　吉岡郁夫編　新市町（広島県）　豊元国　昭和45(1970)

64 p.　22 cm.

Toyoda, Seishi, 1921–

(Gembaku bunken shi)

原爆文献誌　豊田清史著　流山　崙書房　東京　郁文社（発売）　1971.

222 p.　22 cm.

HIRSCH, EMANUEL

Schütte, Hans-Walter.
Bibliographie Emanuel Hirsch. ［Berlin］ Verlag Die Spur ［c1972］

85 p.　19 x 21 cm.

HISPANIC ... see Spain; Spanish ...

HISPANIC AMERICA see Latin America

HISPANIC CIVILIZATION see Civilization, Hispanic

HISPANOS see Mexican-Americans

HISTORICAL FICTION see Fiction - Historical

HISTORICAL RECORDS SURVEY

Child, Sargent Burrage, 1900–
Check list of Historical Records Survey publications; bibliography of research projects reports. Prepared by Sargent B. Child and Dorothy P. Holmes. Baltimore, Genealogical Pub. Co., 1969.

vi, 110 p.　27 cm.　(W. P. A. Technical series. Research and records bibliography no. 7)

Reprint of the 1943 ed.

HISTORY

see also Middle Ages; and under Dissertations, Academic

Bindoff, Stanley Thomas.
Research in progress in English and historical studies in the universities of the British Isles; edited by S. T. Bindoff and James T. Boulton. London, Chicago, St James Press, 1971.

viii, 109 p.　22 cm.

Buchholz, Ursula.
Von Alexander bis Adenauer. Biographien von Persönlichkeiten des geschichtlichen und politischen Lebens. (Zusammengestellt von Ursula Buchholz und Ursula Knoche.) Wolfsburg, Stadtbücherei (1966).

52 p.　21 cm.　(Kataloge der Stadtbücherei Wolfsburg, Nr. 32)

Centre régional de documentation pédagogique de Lyon.
Dossier documentaire sur l'enseignement de l'histoire en classes terminales ... Lyon (4°), C. R. D. P., 47–49, rue Philippe-de-Lassalle, 1968.

150 p.　27 cm.　(Its Annales (Collection Dossiers documentaires)

Clausen, Hans Peter, *comp.*
Et udvalg af historiemetodisk litteratur. Ved H. P. Clausen, Poul Enemark og Otto Larsen. ［Århus］ Statsbiblioteket i Århus, 1966.

15 p.　24 cm.

Reprint of Historie, Jyske samlinger, ny række, bind VII, p. 77–91.

Faissler, Margareta, 1902–
Key to the past; some history books for pre-college readers. 3d ed. Washington, Service Center for Teachers of History, American Historical Association ［c1965］

iv, 84 p.　23 cm.　(Service Center for Teachers of History. Publication no. 1)

Forssell, Helge, 1909–
Vi söker själva i historia. 4. uppl. Stockholm, Almqvist & Wiksell, 1965.

107, (1) p.　19 cm.　(Vi söker själva)

Frewer, Louis Benson.
Bibliography of historical writings published in Great Britain and the Empire, 1940–1945, by Louis B. Frewer. Edited for the British National Committee of the International Committee of Historical Sciences. Westport, Conn., Greenwood Press ［1974］

xx, 346 p.　23 cm.

Reprint of the 1947 ed. published by B. Blackwell, Oxford.

Gwyn, Julian.
Reference works for historians; a list of reference works of interest to historians in the libraries of the University of Ottawa, by Julian Gwyn. ［Ottawa］ Central Library, University of Ottawa, 1971.

iv, 131 l.　28 cm.

History. v. 1–
Oct. 1972–
［Washington, D. C., HELDREF Publications.

v. 28 cm. 10 no. a year.

Reviews of new books.
Issued by Helen Dwight Reid Educational Foundation.

Introduktion til historie. Bibliografi over fagets hjælpemidler med en vejledning i litteratursøgning. Red. af Bent Jørgensen ［m. fl.］ København, Akademisk Forlag, (D. B. K.), 1970.

23, 361 p.　24 cm.

Irwin, Leonard Bertram, 1904–
A guide to historical reading: non-fiction; for the use of schools, libraries and the general reader. Compiled by Leonard B. Irwin. 9th rev. ed. Brooklawn, N. J., Mc-Kinley Pub. Co., 1970.

vii, 276 p. 24 cm. (McKinley bibliographies, v. 2)

Originally included in H. Logasa's Historical fiction, 1st–6th editions. Beginning with the 7th ed. the non-fiction titles were published separately. The 7th–8th editions, compiled by H. Logasa, were published under title: Historical non-fiction.

Kellaway, William.
Bibliography of historical works issued in the United Kingdom, 1957–1960; compiled for the Seventh Anglo-American Conference of Historians. ₁1st ed.₁ reprinted. London, Dawsons for University of London (Institute of Historical Research), 1969.

xvii, 236 p. 24 cm.

Label mounted on t. p.: Humanities Press, New York.

Kellaway, William.
Bibliography of historical works issued in the United Kingdom, 1966–1970; compiled for the Ninth Anglo-American Conference of Historians by William Kellaway. London, University of London Institute for Historical Research, 1972.

xv, 322 p. 25 cm.

Kienast, Walther, 1896–
Literaturberichte über Neuerscheinungen zur ausserdeutschen Geschichte / hrsg. v. Walther Kienast. — München : Oldenburg, 1973.

720 p. : 23 cm. — (Historische Zeitschrift. Sonderheft ; 5)

Koner, Wilhelm David, 1817–1887.
Repertorium über die vom Jahre 1800 bis zum Jahre 1850 in akademischen Abhandlungen, Gesellschaftsschriften und wissenschaftlichen Journalen auf dem Gebiete der Geschichte und ihrer Hülfswissenschaften erschienenen Aufsätze. Von W. Koner. (Unveränderter Nachdruck der 1852–56 in Berlin erschienenen Ausg. Photomechanischer Nachdruck.) Graz, Akademische Druck- u. Verlagsanstalt, 1968.

2 v. 19 cm.

CONTENTS.—1. Bd. Geschichte.—2. Bd. Hülfswissenschaften der Geschichte.

Kraĭneva, N IA
Труды Института истории Академии наук СССР, 1936–1965 гг.; библиография. Москва, 1968.

4 v. 22 cm.

At head of title: Академия наук СССР. Институт истории. Н. Я. Крайнева и И. В. Пронина. CONTENTS: ₁вып.₁ 1. 1936–1954 гг.—₁вып.₁ 2. 1955–1960 гг.—₁вып.₁ 3. 1961–1965 гг.—₁вып.₁ 4. Указатели.

Leipziger Kommissions- und Grossbuchhandel. Abteilung Importbuch.
Marxismus-Leninismus, Philosophie, Geschichte. ₁Leipzig, 1966₁

144 p. 20 cm. (Its Fremdsprachige Importliteratur)

Linder, A
ביבליוגרפיה להיסטוריה, בעריכת א. לינדר. ירושלים, האוניברסיטה העברית, הפקולטה למדעי הרוח, החוג להיסטוריה. תשכ״ד–₁1964–

v. 27 cm.

Cover title.

CONTENTS.—חלק 1. ספרי שימוש עזר ומקור.—חלק 2. ספרי למוד.

Literaturkatalog; Klassiker des Marxismus-Leninismus, Philosophie, Geschichte.

₁Leipzig, Leipziger Kommissions- und Grossbuchhandel₁

v. 21 cm.

Began with vol. for 1964.

Logasa, Hannah, 1879–
Historical non-fiction; an organized, annotated, supplementary reference book for the use of schools, libraries, general reader. Compiled by Hannah Logasa. 8th rev. and enl. ed. Brooklawn, N. J., McKinley Pub. Co., 1964.

328 p. 24 cm. (McKinley bibliographies, v. 2)

Formerly included in the author's Historical fiction, 1st–6th editions; 7th ed. published separately.

Monfort, Gérard.
Bibliotheca historica; ou, Index des livres d'histoire, disponibles chez les éditeurs français. ₁Brionne, Le Portulan, Manoir de₁ St. Pierre de Salerne, 1969.

83 p. 24 cm.

Nielsen, Erland Kolding.
Kompendium i historisk litteratursøgning og søgeteknik. København, Danmarks Biblioteksskole, ₁1971–

v. 30 cm.

Novinky historické literatúry. 1971–
₁Praha₁ Státní knihovna ČSR.

v. 21 cm. 4 no. a year.

Continues Novinky literatury. Společenské vědy. Řada IV: Historie.
Issued by Státní knihovna ČSR, Ústřední bibliografické středisko.

Novinky literatury: Historie. 1972–
₁Praha₁ Státní knihovna ČSR.

v. 21 cm. 4 no. a year.

Continues Novinky historické literatury.
Issued by Ústřední bibliografické středisko.

Novodobé dějiny v československé historiografii.

₁Praha₁
v. 23 cm. annual.
"Bibliografie."
Began with vol. for 1965.
Vols. for   issued by Knihovna of Ústav dějin socialismu;
                   by Knihovna of Ústav marxismu-leninismu ÚV KSČ.
Compiler: K. Gavalierová (with K. Sosna
        M. Měšťánek   )
Vols. for   issued as supplement to Revue dějin socialismu.

Oesterley, Hermann, 1834–1891.
Wegweiser durch die Literatur der Urkundensammlungen. (Reprograf. Nachdr. d. Ausg. Berlin, Reimer, 1885–86.) Hildesheim, New York, G. Olms, 1969.

2 v. 23 cm.

Pleticha, Heinrich, ed.
Unterrichtshilfen für den Geschichtslehrer, hrsg. von Heinrich Pleticha und Erhard Reichert. ₁München₁ Bayerischer Schulbuch-Verlag ₁1965₁

xxxix, 220 p. 23 cm.

Poulton, Helen J
The historian's handbook; a descriptive guide to reference works, by Helen J. Poulton, with the assistance of Marguerite S. Howland. Foreword by Wilbur S. Shepperson. ₁1st ed.₁ Norman, University of Oklahoma Press ₁1972₁

xi, 304 p. 24 cm.

Recent trends in Japanese historiography; bibliographical essays. Japan at the XIIIth International Congress of Historical Sciences in Moscow. Tokyo, Japan Society for the Promotion of Science, 1970.

2 v. 27 cm.

Edited by the Japanese National Committee of Historical Sciences.
CONTENTS: 1. Text.—2. Bibliographical references and index.

Romein, Jan Marius, 1893–1962.
Apparaat voor de studie der geschiedenis. Nieuwe uitg.
door J. Haak met medewerking van W. H. Roobol. Groningen, J. B. Wolters, 1964.

176 p. 24 cm.

Schippers, Donald J
A bibliography on oral history, by Donald J. Schippers
and Adelaide Tusler. Rev. ed. Los Angeles, Oral History
Association, c1968.

18 p. 28 cm. (Oral History Association. Miscellaneous publications, no. 1)

Tooze, Ruth.
Literature and music as resources for social studies [by]
Ruth Tooze and Beatrice Perham Krone. Westport, Conn.,
Greenwood Press [1974, c1955]

x, 457 p. illus. 23 cm.

Includes unacc. melodies with words.
Reprint of the ed. published by Prentice-Hall, Englewood Cliffs,
N. J.

Wagar, W   Warren.
Books in world history; a guide for teachers and students
[by] W. Warren Wagar. Bloomington, Indiana University
Press [1973]

x, 182 p. 21 cm.

Warsaw. Uniwersytet. Instytut Historyczny.
Bibliografia publikacji pracowników. zesz. 1–
1945/66–
Warszawa.

v. 24 cm.

Compilers: 1945/66, I. Klarner and others.—1967/68–
Z. Totjew.

Witschi-Bernz, Astrid.
Bibliography of works in the philosophy of history, 1500–
1800. Compiled by Astrid Witschi-Bernz. [Middletown,
Conn.] Wesleyan University Press [c1972]

90 p. 26 cm. (History and theory; studies in the philosophy of
history. Beiheft 12)

CONTENTS: Introductory note.—Bibliography of works in the
philosophy of history, 1500–1800.—Main trends in historical-method
literature: sixteenth to eighteenth centuries.

Wurgaft, Lewis D
Bibliography of works in the philosophy of history, 1962–
1965, compiled by Lewis D. Wurgaft; bibliography of
signed works by Elie Halévy, compiled by Melvin Richter.
[Middletown, Conn.] Wesleyan University Press [c1967]

71 p. 26 cm. (History and theory; studies in the philosophy of
history. Beiheft 7)

—— Bibliography of works in the philosophy of history,
1966–1968. 1965: addenda; [a supplement to Bibliography
of works in the philosophy of history, 1962–1965. Middletown, Conn.] Wesleyan University Press [1971]

52 p. 25 cm. (History and theory: studies in the philosophy of
history, Beiheft 10)

BIBLIOGRAPHIES

Berkowitz, David Sandler, 1913–
Bibliographies for historical researchers. Trial ed.
Waltham, Mass., 1969.

421 l. 29 cm.

Photocopy of typescript.

Besterman, Theodore, 1904–
History and geography; a bibliography of bibliographies.
Totowa, N. J., Rowman and Littlefield, 1972 [c1971]

4 v. (1587 p.) 20 cm. (His The Besterman world bibliographies)

Coulter, Edith Margaret, 1880–
Historical bibliographies; a systematic and annotated
guide [by] Edith M. Coulter [and] Melanie Gerstenfeld.
With a foreword by Herbert Eugene Bolton. New York,
Russell & Russell, 1965 [c1935]

xii, 206 p. 22 cm.

First published in 1935; reissued, 1965.

Gerlach, Gudrun.
Verzeichnis vor- und frühgeschichtlicher Bibliographien,
von Gudrun Gerlach und Rolf Hachmann. Berlin, De
Gruyter, 1971.

269 p. maps. 27 cm.

Beiheft zum 50. Bericht der Römisch-Germanischen Kommission
1969.

Kandel', Boris L'vovich.
История зарубежных стран; библиография русских
библиографий, опубликованных с 1857 по 1965 год. Москва, Книга, 1966.

255 p. 23 cm.

At head of title: Государственная публичная библиотека имени
М. Е. Салтыкова-Щедрина. Б. Л. Кандель.

Langlois, Charles Victor, 1863–1929.
Manuel de bibliographie historique. (Lizenzausg. der
1901–1904 in 2 Teilen in Paris erschienenen Ausg. Photomechanischer Nachdruck) Graz, Akademische Druck- und
Verlagsanstalt, 1968.

623 p. 19 cm.

CONTENTS.—1. ptie. Instruments bibliographiques.—2. ptie. Histoire et organisation des études historiques.

Pochepko, Galina Pavlovna.
История зарубежных стран: Европа, Америка, Австралия; библиография иностранных библиографий.
Под ред. О. Л. Вайнштейна. Москва, Книга, 1967.

411 p. 23 cm.

At head of title: Государственная публичная библиотека им.
М. Е. Салтыкова-Щедрина. Г. П. Почепко, И. И. Фролова.

Simon, Konstantin Romanovich.
Библиографические обзоры: История и экономика.
Москва, Наука, 1965.
82 p. 20 cm.
At head of title: Академия наук СССР. Фундаментальная библиотека общественных наук имени В. П. Волгина.
Bibliographical footnotes.
CONTENTS.—Симон, К. Р. Зарубежные исторические библиографии послевоенных лет.—Бродская, А. Б. Национальный институт
статистики и экономических исследований Франции и его публикации в 1946–1962 гг.

CATALOGS

Centre régional de documentation pédagogique, *Dijon.*
Guide des ressources pédagogiques, histoire ... Dijon,
C. R. D. P. [1966?]–

v. map. 21 cm. (Annales du Centre régional de documentation pédagogique de Dijon) unpriced (v. 1)

CONTENTS.—t. 1. Répertoire des musées de l'Académie, bibliothèques archives, sociétés savantes, revues régionales.

Centre régional de documentation pédagogique d'Orléans.
Bibliothèque pédagogique.
Catalogue des ouvrages d'histoire. Bibliothèque pédagogique du C. R. D. P. ... Orléans, Centre régional de
documentation pédagogique, 1968.

52 p. 27 cm. (Annales du Centre régional de documentation
pédagogique d'Orléans)

Guru Nanak University. Library.
Classified catalogue of books on History available in the
library. Amritsar, 1972.

xii, 108 p. 27 cm.

Harvard University. Library.
General European and world history; classification schedule, classified listing by call number, chronological listing, author and title listing. Cambridge, Mass.; distributed by the Harvard University Press, 1970.

959 p. 29 cm. (Its Widener Library shelflist, 32)

Institut für Zeitgeschichte, Munich. Bibliothek.
Länderkatalog. Boston, G. K. Hall, 1967.

2 v. 37 cm.

Added t. p. has title: Regional catalog.

Katalogabteilung der Firmen Koehler & Volckmar und Koch, Neff & Oetinger & Co.
Geschichte. ₁Köln, Koehler & Volckmar, 1964–66₁

3 v. 22 cm. (Koehler & Volckmar-Fachbibliographien)

CONTENTS.—1. Allgemeines. Geschichte der Geschichtsschreibung und Geschichtswissenschaft. Geschichtsphilosophie. Geschichtsunterricht. Historische Hilfswissenschaften. Gesamtdarstellungen der Weltgeschichte und europäischen Geschichte. Sonderprobleme und Grenzgebiete.—2. Vorgeschichte und Geschichte des Altertums.—3. Deutsche Geschichte. Weltgeschichte des Mittelalters und der Neuzeit.

Prague. Francouzská knihovna.
Dějiny. Praha, ₁nákl. vl.₁, rozmn., ₁1968₁

122 p. 29 cm. (Seznamy příručních knihoven, 2)

Caption title.
At head of title: Státní knihovna ČSSR. Francouzská knihovna.

Stuttgart. Bibliothek für Zeitgeschichte.
Bibliothek für Zeitgeschichte—Weltkriegsbücherei, Stuttgart; systematischer Katalog. Boston, G. K. Hall, 1968.

20 v. 36 cm.

Added t. p.: Library for Contemporary History—World War Library, Stuttgart: classified catalog.
CONTENTS: Bd. 1. A: Allgemeine Werke–E: Staat/Aussenpolitik.—Bd. 2. E: Staat/Aussenpolitische Beziehungen–F: Wehrwesen.—Bd. 3. F: Wehrtechnik–G: Wirtschaft.—Bd. 4. H: Gesellschaft–J: Geistesleben.—Bd. 5. K: Weltgeschichte–Weltkrieg 1914–18/Sozialgeschichte.—Bd. 6. K: Weltkrieg 1914/18/Geistesgeschichte–Geschichte 1919–39.—Bd. 7. K: Weltkrieg 1939–45/Allgemeines.—Bd. 8. K: Weltkrieg 1939–45/Kriegsschauplätze: Europa. — Bd. 9. K: Weltkrieg 1939–45/Kriegsschauplätze: Mittlemeerraum, Ostasien — Geschichte nach 1945.—Bd. 10. L: Mehrere Erdteile–Europa/Deutschland: Land und Volk. — Bd. 11. L: Europa/Deutschland: Staat–Wehrwesen/Heer.—Bd. 12. L: Europa/Deutschland: Militaria–Kirche und Religion. — Bd. 13. L: Europa/Deutschland: Geschichte—Deutsche Länder.—Bd. 14. L: Europa/Estland–Grossbritannien.—Bd. 15. L: Europa/Irland–Norwegen. — Bd. 16. L: Europa/Österreich–Rumänien.—Bd. 17. L: Europa/Russland (Sowjetunion).—Bd. 18. L: Europa/San Marino–Vatikan–Afrika–Asien/Israel. — Bd. 19. L: Asien/Japan–Amerika/Venezuela.—Bd. 20. L: Amerika/Vereinigte Staaten–Ozeanien–Physikalische Geographie.

JUVENILE LITERATURE

Barton, Malcolm.
A junior history book list, by M. Barton and K. Davies. London, Historical Association, 1968.

₁2₁, 23 p. 22 cm. (Teaching of history pamphlet, no. 27)

Metzner, Seymour.
World history in juvenile books: a geographical and chronological guide. New York, H. W. Wilson Co., 1973.

xvi, 357 p. 20 cm.

Sutherland, Zena.
History in children's books; an annotated bibliography for schools and libraries, compiled by Zena Sutherland. Brooklawn, N. J., McKinley Pub. Co., 1967.

248 p. 24 cm. (McKinley bibliographies, v. 5)

PERIODICALS

American Bibliographical Center.
List of periodicals: America, history and life and Historical abstracts. 2d ed. Santa Barbara, Calif., 1967.

16 p. 28 cm. (Bibliography and references series, no. 3)

Periodicals covered as of Jan. 1967.

American Bibliographical Center.
List of periodicals: ABC POL SCI; America: history and life, and Historical abstracts. ₁3d ed. Santa Barbara, Calif., 1969₁

28 p. 28 cm. (Bibliography and reference series, no. 3)

Cover title.
Second ed. published in 1967 under title: List of periodicals: America, history and life, and Historical abstracts.
Periodicals covered as of June 1969.

Association européenne d'histoire contemporaine.
Guide de la recherche en histoire contemporaine. ₁Paris, Ophrys₁ 1970–

v. 25 cm.

Includes the Association's bylaws.

BI: Istorie-arheologie. v. 8–1971–
₁Bucureşti₁ Centrul de Informare şi Documentare în Ştiinţele Sociale şi Politice.

v. 24 cm. bimonthly.

Supersedes in part: Academia Republicii Socialiste România. Centrul de Documentare Ştiinţifică. Buletin de informare ştiinţifică: Istorie, etnografie, and continues its numbering.
Cover title, 1971– : Istorie-arheologie; buletin de informare ştiinţifică.

Dunedin, N. Z. University of Otago. Dept. of Classics.
Check-list of classical periodicals in New Zealand libraries. ₁Rev. ed.₁ ₁Dunedin₁ 1967.

14 l. 27 cm.

Frankfurt am Main. Universität. Seminar für Alte Geschichte.
Frankfurter Zeitschriftenverzeichnis zur Vor- und Frühgeschichte und zum Altertum. Stand Jan. 1969. Frankfurt a. M., Johann Wolfgang Goethe Univ., Seminar für Alte Geschichte, ₁1969₁

ii, 146 p. 21 cm.

Kirby, John Lavan.
A guide to historical periodicals in the English language, by J. L. Kirby. ₁London₁ Historical Association, 1970.

48 p. 22 cm. (Helps for students of history, no. 80)

Novinky literatury. Společenské vědy. Řada IV: Historie. 1964–
₁Praha₁ Státní knihovna ČSSR, Bibliografické středisko společenských věd.

v. 21 cm. 12 no. a year.

Previously (1962–63) issued as a section of Novinky literatury. Společenské vědy. Řada I.

Paulhart, Herbert.
Historische Zeitschriften im Historischen Institut, im Institut für Sozial- und Wirtschaftsgeschichte und im Institut für Österreichische Geschichtsforschung in Wien. Wien (Thiel) 1967.

40 p. 30 cm.

STUDY AND TEACHING

Fines, John.
A select bibliography of the teaching of history in the United Kingdom. London, Historical Association, 1969.

56 p. 1 illus. 22 cm. Index. (Helps for students of history, no. 77)

Horňák, Kamil, *comp.*
Metodika dějepisu; bibliografie knižních publikací a časopiseckých článků. Sest. Kamil Hornak. Hlavní redaktor Vilém Bräuner. V Brne, Státní pedagogická knihovna, 1967.

50 l. 29 cm. (Státní pedagogická knihovna v Brně. Publikace, čís. 281)

At head of title: Státní vědecká knihovna.

HISTORY, ANCIENT

Bengtson, Hermann, 1909–
Einführung in die alte Geschichte. 5., durchgesehene Aufl. München, Beck, 1965.

viii, 205 p. 23 cm.

Bengtson, Hermann, 1909–
Einführung in die alte Geschichte. 6., überarb. Aufl. München, Beck, 1969.

viii, 217 p. 23 cm.

Bengtson, Hermann, 1909–
Introduction to ancient history. Translated from the 6th ed. by R. I. Frank and Frank D. Gilliard. Berkeley, University of California Press, 1970.

viii, 213 p. 25 cm.

Translation of Einführung in die alte Geschichte.

Brockmeyer, Norbert.
Literatur zur Einführung in die alte Geschichte. Zusammengestellt von N[orbert] Brockmeyer u. E[rnst]-F[riedrich] Schultheiss. 2., überarb. u. erw. Aufl. Bochum, Brockmeyer, 1969.

98 p. 21 cm.

Brockmeyer, Norbert.
Studienbibliographie Alte Geschichte/ Norbert Brockmeyer; Ernst Friedrich Schultheiss. — Wiesbaden: Steiner, 1973.

xi, 148 p.; 23 cm. — (Wissenschaftliche Paperbacks Studienbibliographien)

Kohns, Hans Peter.
Anleitung für Teilnehmer althistorischer Proseminare. Von Hans-Peter Kohns u. Karl-Heinz Schwarte. Paderborn, Schöningh (1971).

31 p. 24 cm.

Petit, Paul.
Guide de l'étudiant en histoire ancienne (antiquité classique) ... [3ᵉ édition.] Paris, Presses universitaires de France, 1969.

239 p. 18 cm.

Popov, Andreĭ Nikolaevich, 1841–1881.
Обзоръ хронографовъ русской редакціи Андрея Попова. [Москва, Тип. Лазаревскаго инст., 1866–69]; Osnabrück, Otto Zeller, 1968.

2 v. in 1. 23 cm.

HISTORY, MODERN

Baumgart, Winfried.
Bibliographie zum Studium der neueren Geschichte. Mit e. Geleitw. v. Konrad Repgen. Bonn, Rheinische Friedrich-Wilhelms-Universität, Historisches Seminar. (Vertrieb: L. Röhrscheid) 1969.

xiii, 312 p. 21 cm.

Brunet, Jean Paul.
Introduction à l'histoire contemporaine [par] Jean-Paul Brunet et Alain Plessis. Paris, A. Colin [1972]

325 p. 17 cm.. (Collection U/U2, 211. Histoire contemporaine)

Gérin, Paul.
Initiation à la documentation écrite de la période contemporaine, fin du xviiie siècle à nos jours. Liège, Librairie F. Gothier, 1970.

xvi, 233 p. 18 cm.

Guiral, Pierre.
Guide de l'étudiant en histoire moderne et contemporaine, par Pierre Guiral, René Pillorget et Maurice Agulhon. Paris, Presse universitaires de France, 1971.

330 p. 18 cm.

Halstead, John P
Modern European imperialism; a bibliography of books and articles, 1815-1972 [by] John P. Halstead and Serafino Porcari. Boston, G. K. Hall, 1974.

2 v. 29 cm.

CONTENTS: v. 1. General and British Empire.—v. 2. French and other empires. Regions.

Krikler, Bernard.
A reader's guide to contemporary history. Edited by Bernard Krikler and Walter Laqueur. [1st American ed.] Chicago, Quadrangle Books [c1972]

259 p. 23 cm.

Krikler, Bernard.
A reader's guide to contemporary history, edited by Bernard Krikler and Walter Laqueur. London, Weidenfeld & Nicolson [1972]

259 p. 23 cm.

Michigan. Central Michigan University, Mount Pleasant. Library.
Guide to the Dag Hammarskjöld collection on developing nations; a selected bibliography. Mount Pleasant, Central Michigan University Press, 1968.

vi, 157 p. 23 cm.

———————Supplement no. 1–   Mount Pleasant, Central Michigan University Press, 1970–

v. 23 cm.

Moscow. Gosudarstvennaia publichnaia istoricheskaia biblioteka.
Новая история; аннотированный указатель литературы для учителей средней школы. Под ред. И. С. Галкина. [Составители: Б. Я. Галина. Е. А. Гутерман и М. А. Николаевский] Москва, Книга, 1965.

210 p. 22 cm.

Munby, Lionel M.
Marxism and history: a bibliography of English language works; edited by Lionel Munby and Ernst Wangermann. London, Lawrence & Wishart, 1967.

[7], 62 p. 25 cm.

National Book League, *London.*
Today's world. London, National Book League with the British Society for International Understanding, 1967.

32 p. 22 cm.

Roach, John Peter Charles.
A bibliography of modern history; edited by John Roach. London, Cambridge U. P., 1968.

xxiv, 388 p. 24 cm.

'... a one volume bibliography to supplement the "New Cambridge modern history".'

Tolnai, György.
Az újkori világtörténet magyarnyelvű irodalmának bib-

liográfiája. Szerk. és a bevezetést írta Tolnai György. Budapest, Fővárosi Szabó Ervin Könyvtár, 1966.

200 p. 24 cm.

Universal Reference System.
Current events and problems of modern society; an annotated and intensively indexed compilation of significant books, pamphlets, and articles, selected and processed by the Universal Reference System. Prepared under the direction of Alfred de Grazia, general editor, Carl E. Martinson, managing editor, and John B. Simeone, consultant. Princeton, N. J., Princeton Research Pub. Co. ₁1969₁

xx, 935 p. illus. 28 cm. (*Its* Political science, government & public policy series, v. 5)

HLAVÁČ, BEDŘICH

Vaculík, Lubomír.
Bedřich Hlaváč. (1868–1936.) Literární pozůstalost. Zprac. Lubomír Vaculík. Praha, Památník nár. písemnictví, rozmn., 1970.

6. ₁1₁ p. 20 cm. (Edice inventářů, čís. 214)

At head of title: Literární archív Památníku národního písemnictví v Praze.

HOCART, ARTHUR MAURICE

Needham, Rodney.
A bibliography of Arthur Maurice Hocart (1883–1939); with a foreword by E. E. Evans-Pritchard. Oxford, Blackwell for the Institute of Social Anthropology (University of Oxford), 1967.

57 p. front. (port.). 18½ cm.

HOCKEY

Saskatchewan. Provincial Library, Regina. Bibliographic Services Division.
Hockey; a bibliography. Regina, 1973.

21 p. 21 cm.

HODGSON, MARGARET LIVINGSTONE see Ballinger, M. L.

HØFFDING, FINN

Bruhns, Svend.
Finn Høffdings kompositioner. En fortegnelse ved Svend Bruhns og Dan Fog. ₁Udg. af₁ Samfundet til Udgivelse af Dansk Musik. København, Dan Fog, 1969.

49 p. 22 cm.

HOFFMAN, DANIEL

Lowe, Michael.
Daniel Hoffman; a comprehensive bibliography. Norwood, Pa., Norwood Editions, 1973.

64 l. port. 24 cm.

HOFFMANN, ERNST THEODOR AMADEUS

Moscow. Vsesoíûznaíã gosudarstvennaíã biblioteka inostrannoĭ literatury.
Э. Т. А. Гофман; библиография русских переводов и критической литературы. ₁Составитель З. В. Житомирская. Ответственный редактор Л. З. Копелев₁ Москва, Книга, 1964.

130 p. port. 21 cm.

Voerster, Jürgen.
160 ₁Hundertsechzig₁ Jahre E. T. A. Hoffmann-Forschung 1805–1965. Eine Bibliographie mit Inhaltserfassung und Erläuterungen. Stuttgart, Eggert, 1967.

227 p. front. 25 cm. (Bibliographien des Antiquariats Fritz Eggert, Bd. 3)

HOFFMANN VON FALLERSLEBEN, AUGUST HEINRICH

Nelde, Peter H
Hoffmann von Fallersleben und die Niederlande ₁von₁ Peter H. Nelde. Amsterdam, Rodopi, 1972.

93 p. illus. 23 cm. (Beschreibende Bibliographien, Heft 3)

HOFMANNSTHAL, HUGO VON

Vienna. Nationalbibliothek.
Hugo von Hofmannsthal. Katalog d. Ausstellung im Prunksaal d. Österr. Nationalbibliothek, 11. Juni bis 16. Okt. 1971. Bearb. v. Franz Hadamowsky. Wien, Österr. Nationalbibliothek, 1972.

viii, 55 p. illus. 21 cm. (Biblos-Schriften, Bd. 65)

On spine: Hofmannsthal in der Österreichischen Nationalbibliothek.
Originally a part of Hugo von Hofmannsthal in der Österreichischen Nationalbibliothek, published in 1971.
Limited ed. of 250 copies.

Vienna. Nationalbibliothek.
Hugo von Hofmannsthal. Verzeichnis des gedruckten Oeuvre u. seines literarischen Echos in den Beständen d. Österr. Nationalbibliothek. Bearb. v. Walter Ritzer. Wien, Österr. Nationalbibliothek, 1972.

vii, 202 p. 21 cm. (Biblos-Schriften, Bd. 66)

On spine: Hofmannsthal in der Österreichischen Nationalbibliothek.
Originally a part of Hugo von Hofmannsthal in der Österreichischen Nationalbibliothek, published in 1971.

Vienna. Nationalbibliothek.
Hugo von Hofmannsthal in der Österreichischen Nationalbibliothek. Katalog d. Ausstellung, Prunksaal, 11. Juni bis 16. Okt. 1971. Verzeichnis des gedruckten Oeuvre u. seines literarischen Echos in den Beständen d. Bibliothek. (Bearb. d. Katalogs: Franz Hadamowsky. Bearb. des Verzeichnisses: Walter Ritzer) Wien, Österr. Nationalbibliothek, 1971.

xii p., xiii–xv p. of facsims., xvi p., 55 p., 16 p. of illus., 194 p. 21 cm.

Weber, Horst, fl. 1966–
Hugo von Hofmannsthal. Bibliographie des Schrifttums 1892–1963. Berlin, De Gruyter, 1966.

xii, 254 p. 24 cm.

Weber, Horst, fl. 1966–
Hugo von Hofmannsthal. Bibliographie. Werke, Briefe, Gespräche, Übers., Vertonungen. Bearb. von Horst Weber. Berlin, New York, de Gruyter, 1972.

xvi, 775 p. 25 cm.

Continuation of Hugo von Hofmannsthal. Bibliographie des Schrifttums 1892–1963.

HOFRÉN, MANNE

Zweigbergk, Brita von, 1905–
Manne Hofréns tryckta skrifter under femtio år. En bibliografi upprättad till 70-årsdagen. Kalmar, Statsbiblioteket (distr.) 1966.

87 p. (1) plate. 19 cm.

HOKKAIDO

(Hokkaidō kankō shiryō mokuroku)
北海道刊行資料目錄

₁札幌₁ 北海道総務部
no. 26 cm. annual.

Began with 1966 issue. Cf. Zen Nihon shuppanbutsu sōmokuroku, 1968.

Vols. for 19 –67 prepared by 北海道総務部文書課; 1968– by 北海道総務部行政資料室

Matsui, Masato.
Research resources on Hokkaido, Sakhalin, and the Kuriles at the East West Center Library. 北海道文献目録 [By] Masato Matsui [and] Katsumi Shimanaka. Honolulu, East West Center Library, 1967.

vii, 266 p. 22 cm. ([Honolulu. East West Center Library] Occasional paper no. 9)

Takakura, Shin'ichirō, 1902–
北海道史の歴史—主要文献とその著者たち—高倉新一郎著 改訂版 [札幌] みやま書房 [1964]

115 p. ports. 21 cm.

HOLBACH, PAUL HENRI THIRY, BARON D'

Vercruysse, Jerôme.
Bibliographie descriptive des écrits du baron d'Holbach [par] Jeroom Vercruysse. Paris, Lettres modernes, 1971.

1 v. (various pagings) illus. 23 cm. (Bibliothèque, nº 2)

HOLBEIN, HANS, THE YOUNGER see under Huberinus, Caspar

HOLBERG, LUDVIG, BARON

Cherniâvskiĭ, E   M
Людвиг Хольберг. Биобиблиогр. указатель. [Сост. и авт. вступит. статьи Е. М. Чернявский]. Москва, "Книга," 1970.

35 p. 22 cm. (Писатели зарубежных стран)

At head of title: Всесоюзная государственная библиотека иностранной литературы.

HOLINESS CHURCHES

Dayton, Donald W
The American Holiness movement; a bibliographic introduction, by Donald W. Dayton. Wilmore, Ky., B. L. Fisher Library, Asbury Theological Seminary, 1971.

59 p. 22 cm. (Occasional bibliographic papers of the B. L. Fisher Library)

"Originally published in the 1971 'Proceedings' of the American Theological Library Association."

Jones, Charles Edwin, 1932-
A guide to the study of the holiness movement. Metuchen, N.J., Scarecrow Press, 1974.

xxviii, 918 p. 22 cm. (ATLA bibliography series, no. 1)

On spine: The Holiness Movement.

HOLLAND see Netherlands

HOLLAND, SOUTH (PROVINCE)

Balen-Chavannes, A   E   van.
Bibliografie van de geschiedenis van Zuid-Holland tot 1966, samengesteld door A. E. van Balen-Chavannes. Met indices van J. H. Rombach en J. E. H. Rombach-de Kievid. Delft, Culturele Raad van Zuid-Holland, 1972.

310 p. 25 cm.

HOLLANDER, WALTHER VON

Kayser, Werner.
Walther von Hollander./ Von Werner Kayser. Eingel. von Günter Schab. — Hamburg: Christians 1971.

75 p.: illus.; 22 cm. (Hamburger Bibliographien; Bd. 14)

HOLMBERG, ARNE

Wallgren, Anita, 1898–
Arne Holmbergs tryckta skrifter 1913 [i. e. nittonhundratretton]–1964 [i. e. nittonhundrasextiofyra]; bibliografisk förteckning. A bibliography of Dr. Arne Holmberg, former librarian of the Royal Swedish Academy of Science. Stockholm, Almqvist & Wiksell [1964]

32 p. port. 23 cm. (Bidrag till Kungl. Svenska vetenskapsakademiens historia, 4)

HOLMES, OLIVER WENDELL

Currier, Thomas Franklin, 1873–1946.
A bibliography of Oliver Wendell Holmes. Edited by Eleanor M. Tilton for the Bibliographical Society of America. New York, Russell & Russell [1971, °1953]

xiii, 707 p. illus., facsims., ports. 25 cm.

Ives, George Burnham, 1856–1930.
A bibliography of Oliver Wendell Holmes. [Folcroft, Pa.] Folcroft Press [1969]

xi, 322 p. port. 23 cm.

Reprint of the 1907 ed.

HOLOCAUST, JEWISH (1939-1945)

Bass, David.
(Bibliografye fun yidishe bikher vegn ḥurbn un gvure)
ביבליאָגראַפיע פון ייִדישע ביכער וועגן חורבן און גבורה. רעדאַקטירט פון דוד באַס. ניו-יאָרק, ייִוואָ. 1970.

54 p. 27 cm. [יד ושם, אינסטיטוטאָ צו פאָראיַביקן דעם חורבן און די גבורה. ייִדישער וויסנשאַפטלעכער אינסטיטוט — ייִוואָ. בשותפותדיקער דאָקומענטאַציע-פּראיַעקטן, ביבליאָגראפישע סעריע, נומ' 11]

Added t. p.: Bibliography of Yiddish books on the catastrophe and heroism.
Added t. p. in Hebrew.
ביבליאָגראפיע פון ייִדישע ביכער וועגן חורבן
Supplements J. Gar's און גבורה.

Piekarz, Mendel.
(ha-Sho'ah u-sefiḥeha ba-sefarim ha-'ivriyim she-yats'u la-or ba-shanim 1933–1972)
השואה וספיחיה בספרים העבריים שיצאו לאור בשנים 1972–1933 : ביבליוגראפיה / מאת מנדל פיקאַז'. — ירושלים : יד ושם, [1974]

2 v. (11, 920, vii p.) ; 28 cm. — [סידרת ביבלי וגראפית משוחפת ; 14–13]
Added t. p.: The Holocaust and its aftermath.

Robinson, Jacob, 1889–   ed.
Guide to the unpublished materials of the holocaust period; specimen pages. Edited by Jacob Robinson and Shaul Esh. Jerusalem, Hebrew University and "Yad Vashem," Institute for the Study of the European Jewish Catastrophe, 1965.

48, 14, 13, 6 p. 24 cm.
Added t. p.: מורה דרך למקורות ארכיוניים לתקופת השואה; חוברת לדוגמא.
Introd. also in Hebrew.

Robinson, Jacob, 1889–   ed.
Guide to unpublished materials of the holocaust period. Edited by Jacob Robinson and Yehuda Bauer. Jerusalem, Hebrew University, Institute of Contemporary Jewry, 1970–

v. 25 cm.

HOLOGRAPHY

Atkins, John Leslie.
Holography: a bibliography, edited by J. L. Atkins. Coventry (Warwickshire), Cadig Liaison Centre, Reference Library, 1969.

[4], 52 l. 30 cm.

Jena. Universität. Bibliothek. Informationsabteilung.
Zusammenstellung in- und ausländischer Patentschriften
auf dem Gebiet der Holographie. Berichtszeit: 1948–1970.
(Gesamtleitung: Konrad Marwinski.) Jena, Universitätsbibliothek, Informationsabt., 1971.

x, 115 p. 21 cm. (Its Bibliographische Mitteilungen, Nr. 12)

HOLST, WILHELM

Bibliografi med prekoordinert indeks til dr. techn. Wilhelm
Holsts produksjon: 1931–1968. Utg. i anledning 25
-årsjubileet for Studieselskapet for norsk industri 5. mai
1969. Oslo, SNI, 1969.

24 l. 30 cm.

HOLT, HAMILTON

Mills Memorial Library.
Register: Hamilton Holt papers. Processed by Peter E.
Robinson. Winter Park, Fla., 1964.

119 p. 28 cm.

HOLY GHOST, ORDER OF THE see Order of
the Holy Ghost

HOLZBACH, ANTONÍN

Hlaváček, Antonín.
Antonín Holzbach. 1874–1959. Výstřižkový archív.
Zprac. Antonín Hlaváček. Praha, Lit. archív Památníku
nár. písemnictví, 1968.

18, [1] p. 20 cm.

HOMAGE VOLUMES see Festschriften

HOME AND SCHOOL

Sharrock, Anne Nola.
Home and school: a select annotated bibliography; compiled by Anne Sharrock. Slough, National Foundation
for Educational Research in England and Wales, 1971.

[2], 31 p. 21 cm.

HOME ECONOMICS
see also under Dissertations, Academic

American Home Economics Association. Family Eco-
nomics-Home Management Section.
Selected bibliography of theses and research in family
economics and home management, by Sarah L. Manning and
Marilyn Dunsing. Washington, American Home Economics Association [1965]

54 p. 28 cm.

Bibliographie der Zeitschriftenliteratur aus dem Bereich
Hauswirtschaft, Bauen, Wohnen und Haushaltstechnik.
1960–1968. Stuttgart-Hohenheim, Bundesforschungsanstalt
für Hauswirtschaft, Abteilung Dokumentation, 1969.

x, 183 p. 21 cm.

Danielsson, Katarina, 1923–
Köksstudier. Referenslista. Stockholm, Statens institut
för konsumentfrågor, 1969.

64, (1) p. 17 x 25 cm. (Konsumentinstitutet meddelar, 22)

Dyer, Annie Isabel Robertson, 1889–
Guide to literature of home and family life; a classified
bibliography for home economics, with use and content
annotations, by Annie Isabel Robertson. Ann Arbor, Mich.,
Gryphon Books, 1971.

xv, 284 p. illus. 22 cm.

"Facsimile reprint of the 1924 edition."

Great Britain. British Council.
Home economics & domestic science: a select annotated
list. [London], British Council, 1973.

[7], 43 p. 21 cm.

(Kaseigaku tosho mokuroku)
家政学図書目録　1968 年版　東京　家政学図書出版
会　昭和 43 (1968)

61 p. 21 cm.

Krassa, Lucie G
Research on time spent in homemaking; an annotated list
of references. [Compiled by Lucie G. Krassa and Emma
G. Holmes. Washington] Agricultural Research Service,
U. S. Dept. of Agriculture, 1967.

16 p. 20 cm. ([U. S. Agricultural Research Service] ARS
62–15)

Library Association. County Libraries Group.
Readers' guide to books on house and home. 2d ed.
[London] 1973.

102 p. 19 cm. (Its Readers' guide, new ser., no. 130)

Martinaitienė, R
Buities kultūra; rekomenduojamos literatūros rodyklė.
[Sudarytojai R. Martinaitienė ir V. Venslovaitė] Vilnius,
1971.

65 p. illus. 20 cm.

At head of title: Lietuvos TSR Valstybinė respublikinė biblioteka.

Pattison, Mattie.
Annotated bibliography of research related to home science in India. Compiled by Mattie Pattison with assistance from Shakti Chhaya. Baroda, Faculty of Home Science, Maharaja Sayajirao University of Baroda, 1967.

xx, 262 p. 25 cm.

"Home Science Project, Baroda University, Iowa State University,
Ford Foundation in India."

Poser und Gross-Naedlitz, Ingeborg von.
Bibliographie des Schrifttums zur Wirtschaftslehre des
Haushalts. Stuttgart-Hohenheim, Bundesforschungsanst.
f. Hauswirtschaft, Abt. Wirtschaftslehre d. Haushalts,
1969.

xxviii, 477 p. 21 cm.

Rudolph, G   A
Kansas State University receipt book and household
manual, compiled by G. A. Rudolph. Manhattan, Kansas
State University Library, 1968.

v. 230 p. 28 cm. (Kansas State University Library. Bibliography
series, no. 4)

Tōkyō Kasei Gakuin Daigaku. Toshokan.
東京家政学院大学図書館蔵　大江文庫本目録
田中初夫校閲　吉井婧子編述 [東京 1967–

v. 25 cm. (東京家政学院大学図書館叢刊 第2

Vilna. Lietuvos TSR valstybinė respublikinė biblioteka.
Buities kultūra; rekomenduojamosios literatūros sąrašas.
Vilnius, 1965.

25 p. 21 cm.

EDUCATION

Florida. State Dept. of Education.
Teaching aids for home economics; a source list. Tallahassee, 1966.

2 l., 41 p. 28 cm. (Its Bulletin 75F-6)

Gorman, Anna Marguriette, 1923–
Bibliography of research on consumer and homemaking education ₁by₁ Anna M. Gorman ₁and₁ Joel H. Magisos. Columbus, ERIC Clearinghouse on Vocational and Technical Education, Ohio State University, 1970.

v, 71 p. 28 cm. (Center for Vocational and Technical Education, Ohio State University. Bibliography series, no. 6)

HOME LABOR   see   Handicrafts

HOMILETICS

Toohey, William.
Recent homiletical thought; a bibliography, 1935–1965, edited by William Toohey and William D. Thompson. Nashville, Abingdon Press ₁1967₁

303 p. 23 cm.

HOMOSEXUALITY

Meek, Oscar.
A new selected bibliography on homosexuality; including listings of publishers, per₁i₁odical articles, and other informational sources. ₁1st ed.₁ Santa Fe ₁New Mexico Research Library of the Southwest₁ 1969.

34 p. 22 cm.

Millett, Antony Percival Upton.
Homosexuality; a bibliography of literature published since 1959 and available in New Zealand ₁by₁ A. P. U. Millett. Wellington, New Zealand Library School, 1967 ₁i. e. 1968₁

vii, 55 p. 21 cm. (Bibliographical series no. 9)

Parker, William.
Homosexuality; selected abstracts and bibliography. San Francisco, Society for Individual Rights, 1966.

107 p. 28 cm.

Cover title.
Printing limited to 200 copies.

Parker, William.
Homosexuality: a selective bibliography of over 3,000 items. Metuchen, N. J., Scarecrow Press, 1971.

viii, 323 p. 22 cm.

Sharma, Umesh D
Homosexuality: a select bibliography, compiled by Umesh D. Sharma and Wilfrid C. Rudy. Waterloo, Ont., 1970.

114 p. 28 cm.

Weinberg, Martin S
Homosexuality; an annotated bibliography. Edited by Martin S. Weinberg and Alan P. Bell. ₁1st ed.₁ New York, Harper & Row ₁1972₁

xiii, 550 p. 24 cm.

HONDURAS
    see also   British Honduras

García, Miguel Angel, director de la Biblioteca Nacional de Honduras.
Bibliografía hondureña, por Miguel A. García. ₁Tegucigalpa₁ Banco Central de Honduras ₁1971–

v. 25 cm.

CONTENTS: v. 1. 1620–1930.

Pan American Institute of Geography and History. *Commission on History.*
Honduras; guía de los documentos microfotografiados por la Unidad Móvil de Microfilm de la UNESCO. México, Instituto Panamericano de Geografía e Historia, Comisión de Historia, 1967.

iii, 245 p. 27 cm. (*Its* ₁Publicación₁ 120. Guías, 3)
Instituto Panamericano de Geografía e Historia. Publicación no. 307.

HONGKONG

Berkowitz, Morris I
Hongkong studies: a bibliography. Compiled by M. I. Berkowitz ₁and₁ Eddie K. K. Poon. ₁1st ed. Hong Kong₁ Dept. of Extramural Studies, Chinese University of Hong Kong, 1969.

xvi, 137 p. map (on lining paper) 19 cm.

Braga, José Maria.
A Hong Kong bibliography, 1965 ₁by J. M. Braga₁ Hong Kong, Govt. Press ₁1965₁

17 p. 24 cm.

HOOGHE, ROMEIN DE

Landwehr, John.
Romeyn de Hooghe (1645–1708) as book illustrator; a bibliography. Amsterdam, VanGendt; New York, A. Schram, 1970.

247 p. illus., port. 28 cm.

HOOGHEEMRAADSCHAP VAN RIJNLAND

Hoogheemraadschap van Rijnland.
Inventaris van het archief van de Buurterpolder onder Alkemade, 1876–1960. ₁Leiden, 1969 or 70₁

10 l. 29 cm. (Archieven van Rijnland, volgnr., 176)

Hoogheemraadschap van Rijnland.
Inventaris van het archief van de polder Vrouwgeest onder Alphen a/d Rijn, 1755–1959. ₁Leiden? 1969?₁

16 l. 29 cm.

At head of title: Archieven van Rijnland.
"Volgnummer 131."
Introd. signed: G. E. Nederhorst.

HOOKER, RICHARD

Grislis, Egil.
Richard Hooker: a selected bibliography. Compiled by Egil Grislis and W. Speed Hill. Pittsburgh, Clifford E. Barbour Library, Pittsburgh Theological Seminary ₁1971₁

58 p. front. 28 cm. (Bibliographia tripotamopalitana, no. 4)

Hill, William Speed, 1935–
Richard Hooker, a descriptive bibliography of the early editions: 1593–1724 ₁by₁ W. Speed Hill. Cleveland, Press of Case Western Reserve University, 1970.

xiii, 140 p. 28 cm.

HOOKWORMS

World Health Organisation.
Bibliography of hookworm disease (ancylostomiasis), 1920–1962. Geneva, W. H. O. ₁London, H. M. S. O.₁ 1965.

251 p. 24½ cm.

Title-page and text in English and French.

HOOPER, STANFORD CALDWELL   see under Casey, Silas

HOPE, ALEC DERWENT

O'Brien, Patricia Anne, 1945–
A. D. Hope; a bibliography. Adelaide, South Australia. Libraries Board, 1968.

48 p. 22 cm. (Bibliographies of Australian writers)

"Compiled in the Research Service of the State Library of South Australia by Miss Patricia O'Brien."

HOPKINS, GERARD MANLEY

Cohen, Edward H
Works and criticism of Gerard Manley Hopkins; a comprehensive bibliography, by Edward H. Cohen. Washington, Catholic University of America Press, 1969.

xv, 217 p. 24 cm.

Seelhammer, Ruth.
Hopkins collected at Gonzaga. Chicago, Loyola University Press [1970]

xiv, 272 p. illus., facsim., plates, group port. 24 cm.

HORAN, WALTER FRANKLIN

Washington (State) State University, *Pullman. Library.*
Walt Horan; a register of his papers, 1943–1965, in the Washington State University Library. Pullman, Manuscripts-Archives Division, Washington State University Library, 1965.

20 p. 27 cm.

HORATIUS FLACCUS, QUINTUS

Büchner, Karl, 1910–
Horaz. (Bericht über d. Schrifttum d. Jahre 1929–1936. 2. Aufl. Unveränd. reprograf. Nachdr.) Darmstadt, Wissenschaftliche Buchges., 1969.

179 p. 23 cm. (Jahresbericht über die Fortschritte der klassischen Altertumswissenschaft, Bd. 267)

HORN MUSIC

Brüchle, Bernhard.
Horn Bibliographie. Wilhelmshaven, Heinrichshofen [°1970]

272 p. illus., [7] l. of plates. 21 cm.

HORNER, GUSTAVUS R. B.   see under
Dulaney, Bladen

HORNSEY, ENGLAND

Haringey. Libraries, Museum and Arts Dept. Archives.
Deposited parish records, (All Hallows, Tottenham, and St. Mary's, Hornsey). [London], London Borough of Haringey, Libraries, Museum and Arts Dept. [1972].

[1], 64 p. 30 cm. index. (Its Handlist, no. 1)

HOROLOGY
    see also Clocks and watches

Hotta, Ryōhei.
時計文献藏書目録 List of books and booklets on horological subjects. [改訂版] **Tokyo,** 堀田両平 1967.

110, 128 p. 25 cm.

Hotta, Ryōhei.
(Tokei no bunken mokuroku)
時計の文献目録 堀田両平著 東京 昭和46 (1971)

252 p. 25 cm.

On cover: List of books and booklets on horological subject.

HORSES

Jones, William Elvin.
A descriptive bibliography of 1001 horse books. Edited by William E. Jones. East Lansing, Mich., Caballus Publishers [1972]

103 p. 22 cm.

HORTICULTURE
    see also Florists

Australia. *Commonwealth Scientific and Industrial Research Organization. Division of Horticultural Research.*
Publications list, 1962–1969. [Merbein, Vic., 1969]

17 p. 25 cm.

Cannon, Thomas F
The nursery business, by Thomas F. Cannon. Revision. Washington, Small Business Administration, 1964.

8 p. 26 cm. (Small business bibliography no. 14)

Caption title.
"Originally issued as Small business bulletin no. 14."

Cannon, Thomas F
The nursery business, by Thomas F. Cannon. Revision. Washington, Small Business Administration, 1966.

6 p. 26 cm. (Small business bibliography no. 14)

Dochnahl, Friedrich Jacob, 1820–1904.
Bibliotheca hortensis. Vollständige Garten-Bibliothek; oder, Alphabetisches Verzeichniss aller Bücher, welche über Gärtnerei, Blumen- und Gemüsezucht, Obst- und Weinbau, Gartenbotanik und bildende Gartenkunst von 1750 bis 1860 in Deutschland erschienen sind. Mit einem chronologischen Sachregister. Hrsg. von Friedrich Jacob Dochnahl. Hildesheim, New York, G. Olms, 1970.

lx, 179 p. 22 cm.

Reprint of the ed. published in Nuremberg by W. Schmid in 1861.

Eley, Cleveland P
Annotated bibliography of floriculture and ornamental horticulture; marketing and other economic information. [Compiled by Cleveland P. Eley. Washington] U. S. Dept. of Agriculture. Economic Research Service [1967]

41 p. 26 cm. ([U. S. Dept. of Agriculture. Economic Research Service] ERS–337)

Supersedes Bibliography of marketing and other economic information for floriculture and ornamental horticulture, by A. Z. Macomber, issued as U. S. Agricultural Marketing Service, AMS–136.

Evans, Mary, 1882–
Garden books, old and new: selected, classified, and with annotations. [Philadelphia] Pennsylvania Horticultural Society, 1926. Ann Arbor, Mich., Gryphon Books, 1971.

86 p. 22 cm.

Hazlitt, William Carew, 1834–1913.
Gleanings in old garden literature. London, E. Stock, 1887. Detroit, Gale Research Co., 1968.

vii, 263 p. 19 cm.

Library Association. *County Libraries Group.*
Readers' guide to books on gardening. 3rd ed. London, Library Association (County Libraries Group), 1967.

43 p. 18½ cm. (*Its* Readers' guide, new ser., no. 96)

Michigan. State Library, *Lansing.*
Roots and references, a selected bibliography for the retail florists and growers of Michigan. Lansing [1964?]

36 p. 28 cm.

Moscow. TSentral'naia nauchnaia sel'skokhoziaĭstvennaia biblioteka. *Spravochno-bibliograficheskiĭ otdel.*
Использование гетерозиса в овощеводстве и бахчеводстве; библиографический список отечественной литературы в количестве 182 названий за 1959–1964 гг. [Составил Е. Е. Стребелев] Москва, 1965.

23 p. 27 cm.

At head of title: Всесоюзная академия с.-х. наук имени В. И. Ленина. Центральная научная сельскохозяйственная библиотека. Справочно-библиографический отдел.

Naftalin, Mortimer L   1921–
Historic books and manuscripts concerning horticulture and forestry in the collection of the National Agricultural

Library ₍compiled by Mortimer L. Naftalin₎ Washington, National Agricultural Library, U. S. Dept. of Agriculture, 1968.

106 p. 26 cm. (U. S. National Agricultural Library. Library list no. 90)

LIBRARY CATALOGS

Massachusetts Horticultural Society. Library.
Dictionary catalog of the library of the Massachusetts Horticultural Society. Boston, G. K. Hall, 1962.

3 v. 27 cm.
1854 ed. published under title: Catalogue of books in the library of the Massachusetts Horticultural Society. 1867, 1873, and 1918–20 editions published under title: A catalogue of the library of the Massachusetts Horticultural Society.

—— First supplement. Boston, G. K. Hall, 1972.
iii, 441 p. 27 cm.

HOSPITALS

Detloff, Virginia.
Utilization of health facilities and services, 1950–63; an annotated selected bibliography, by Virginia Detloff, Daniel L. Drosness, and Nancy Ribak. ₍Sacramento?₎ Hospital Utilization Research Project, Bureau of Hospitals, State of California. Dept. of Public Health ₍1964₎

72 p. 28 cm.

Le Rocco, August.
Planning for hospital discharge; a bibliography with abstracts and research reviews. ₍Washington₎ National Center for Health Services Research and Development, 1970.

ix, 85 p. 26 cm.

Riedel, Donald C
Utilization review; a selected bibliography, 1933–1967. ₍Prepared by Donald C. Riedel₎ Arlington, Va., U. S. Division of Medical Care Administration, 1968.

iv, 20 p. 26 cm.

U. S. *Public Health Service. Division of Hospital and Medical Facilities.*
Publication. ₍Rev.₎ Washington ₍For sale by the Superintendent of Documents. U. S. Govt. Print. Off., 1965₎

viii, 15 p. 28 cm. (Public Health Service publication no. 930–G–3)

"Supersedes ... Hill-Burton publications: an annotated bibliography, Public Health Service publication no. 930–G–3."

U. S. *Public Health Service. Division of Hospital and Medical Facilities.*
Publications: Hill-Burton program, health professions education, facilities for the mentally retarded, mental health facilities. ₍Rev.₎ Washington ₍For sale by the Supt. of Docs., U. S. Govt. Print. Off., 1966₎

viii, 18 p. 28 cm. (Public Health Service publication no. 930–G–3)

HÖSSLINSÜLZ, GERMANY

Cordes, Günter, 1937–
Findbuch des Archivs der früheren Gemeinde Hösslinsülz/ Bearb.: Günter Cordes. Reinschrift: Gotelind Cordes. ₍Landratsamt Heilbronn₎. — ₍Heilbronn: Landratsamt₎ 1971.

xii, 83 l.; 30 cm.

HOTELS
Bootle, Valerie.
A bibliography of hotel and catering operation, compiled by Valerie Bootle and Philip Nailon. London, New University Education, 1970.

252 p. 23 cm. index. (Hotel & catering management)

Borsenik, Frank D
Literature of the lodging market; an annotated bibliography, by Frank D. Borsenik. East Lansing, Bureau of Business and Economic Research, Division of Research, Graduate School of Business Administration, Michigan State University, 1966.

xxii, 213 p. 25 cm. (Bureau of Business and Economic Research, Michigan State University. Occasional paper)

Markos, Béla.
Vendéglátóipari szakbibliográfia; 600 válogatott cim könyvtáraink állományából. Budapest ₍Belkereskedelmi Kutató Intézet₎ 1965.

85 p. 27 cm. (Szakbibliográfiai kiadványok. 6)

Morgan, Howard Edwin, 1913–
Motels. Revision. Washington, Small Business Administration, 1964.

8 p. 26 cm. (Small business bibliography, no. 66)

Pleskot, Jozef.
Hotelníctvo a spoločné stravovanie. Zost. Jozef Pleskot. Odborne spoluprac. Gustáv Sládek. 1. vyd. Bratislava, Slovenské pedagogické nakladateľstvo, ÚEK, rozmn. Západoslov. tlač., 42, 1971.

48 p., 183 loose l. 20 cm. (Ekonomické aktuality. Bibliografický zpravodaj, 1970, č. 5)

In portfolio.
Introductory matter also in Russian, English, German, and French.

HOURS, BOOKS OF

Milan. Biblioteca ambrosiana.
I libri d'ore della Biblioteca Ambrosiana. A cura di mons. Carlo Marcora. Milano, L'ariete, 1973.

194 p., incl. plates. illus. 26 cm.

Edition of 600 copies.

HOUSE PAINTING
Rice, John Wade.
Painting and wall decorating ₍by J. Wade Rice₎ Washington, Small Business Administration, 1967 ₍i. e. 1968₎

8 p. 27 cm. (Small business bibliography no. 60)

HOUSEFLY
West, Luther Shirley, 1899–
An annotated bibliography of Musca domestica Linnaeus, by Luther S. West and Oneita Beth Peters, with the technical assistance of Jan Elizabeth Phillips. Folkestone, Dawsons; Marquette, Mich., Northern Michigan University, 1973.

xiii, 743 p., leaf. 1 illus. 26 cm.

HOUSEHOLD APPLIANCES
Flewellen, William Crawford, 1918–
Selling and servicing household appliances and radio-TV, by William C. Flewellen, Jr. Washington, Small Business Administration, 1966.

11 p. 17 cm. (Small business bibliography no. 57)

HOUSES
Alonso, William.
Information on and evaluations of innovations in housing design and construction techniques as applied to low-cost housing. Prepared for Kaiser Engineers by William Alonso, Sami Hassid ₍and₎ Wallace F. Smith. Berkeley, Calif., 1969.

202 l. 28 cm.

"A collateral literature survey in connection with phase II of the

In-cities experimental housing research and development project, performed by Kaiser Engineers for the Department of Housing and Urban Development under prime contract no. H–1011."
Report no. 69–8–R–1.

Fiedlerová, Marie.
Bytová výstavba-hromadná a individuální. Doporučující bibliogr. Zprac. Marie Fiedlerová. Plzeň, St. věd. knihovna, rozmn., 1971.

59, [1] p. 20 cm. (Bibliografie technické literatury, 11)

Gábor, František.
Vykurovanie obytných budov tekutými palivami. [Výberová bibliografia] Zost. František Gábor. Košice, ŠVK, cyklostyl, 1969.

84, [1] p. 20 cm. (Bibliografické správy ŠVK Košice, č. 3/1969)

Pevzner, D   P
Жилые дома (малоэтажные и многоэтажные) в условиях жаркого климата. (Отечеств. и иностр. литература за 1965–1970 гг.) [Библиогр. указатель.] Москва, 1970.

45 p. 26 cm.

At head of title: Госстрой СССР. Центральная научно-техническая библиотека по строительству и архитектуре.

Schipf, Robert G
Home repair and improvement [by] Robert G. Schipf. Littleton, Colo., Libraries Unlimited, 1974.

75 p. 24 cm. (Spare time guides: information sources for hobbies and recreation, no. 3)

HOUSING
    see also   Discrimination in housing

California. Dept. of Housing and Community Development.
Bibliography of surveys and studies relating to housing, building, and community development. [Sacramento] 1968.

24 l. 28 cm.

Central Mortgage and Housing Corporation. Library.
Condominiums; bibliography. [Ottawa] 1969.

4 l. 28 cm.

Daniel, Robert E
Local residential mobility, a selected and annotated bibliography, by Robert E. Daniel. [Monticello, Ill., Council of Planning Librarians, 1969]

14 l. 29 cm. (Council of Planning Librarians. Exchange bibliography 104)

Caption title.
Condensation thesis, University of Illinois.

Epstein, Lisa.
Condominiums: financial and legal aspects, an annotated bibliography, 1967-1972. Sacramento, California State Library, Law Library, 1972.

14 p. 28 cm.

Fediuk, Simon, 1910–
Bibliography on housing and urban renewal. New York, New York State Division of Human Rights, 1970.

92 p. 28 cm. ([New York (State). State Division of Human Rights. Reference Library] Special collection no. 1)

National Association of Housing and Redevelopment Officials.
Housing management bibliography. Washington, 1971.

27 p. 28 cm.

"NAHRO publication no. N552."

Housing and planning references. new ser. no. 1–
July/Aug. 1965–
[Washington, U. S. Govt. Print. Off.,]

no. in   v.   21 x 28 cm.   bimonthly.
No. 1–3 issued by U. S. Housing and Home Finance Agency Library; no. 4   by U. S. Dept. of Housing and Urban Development.
INDEXES:
    Author index.
    No. 16–24, Jan./Feb. 1968–May/June 1969, with no. 24.

National Association of Housing and Redevelopment Officials.
Housing code; bibliography. Washington, 1972.

39 p. 28 cm.

Pevzner, D   P
Проблемы жилища будущего. Отечеств. и иностр. литература за 1959–1968 гг. (I–IV). Москва, 1968.

110 p. 26 cm.

At head of title: Госстрой СССР. Центральная научно-техническая библиотека по строительству и архитектуре.

Social aspects of housing and urban development. A bibliography. Compiled and publ. in agreement with the United Nations Centre for Housing, Building and Planning, Department of Economic and Social Affairs, New York. Stockholm, Svensk byggtjänst (distr.), [1969].

173 p. 30 cm. (National Swedish building research. Document no. 3:1969)

United Nations. Centre for Housing, Building, and Planning. Research, Training and Information Section.
Cumulative list of United Nations documents and publications related to the field of housing, building, and planning. [New York, 1968]

49 p. 28 cm.

United States. Dept. of Housing and Urban Development. Homeownership Counseling Branch.
Homeownership and resident counseling; a selected bibliography. Washington, 1972.

i, 65 p. 26 cm.

U. S. *Dept. of Housing and Urban Development. Library.*
Bibliography on housing, building and planning for use of overseas missions of the United States Agency for International Development. Prepared by the Library for the Dept. of Housing and Urban Development, Office of International Affairs. Rev. Washington; [For sale by the Supt. of Docs., U. S. Govt. Print. Off.] 1969.

iii, 43 p. 27 cm.

U. S. *Dept. of Housing and Urban Development. Library.*
Housing markets; selected references. Washington [1968]

40 p. 26 cm. ([U. S. Dept. of Housing and Urban Development] MP–49)

U. S. *Dept. of Housing and Urban Development. Library.*
Operation breakthrough; mass produced and industrialized housing; a bibliography. Washington; For sale by the Supt. of Docs., U. S .Govt. Print. Off., [1970]

iii, 72 p. 26 cm.

United States. Dept. of Housing and Urban Development. Library and Information Division.
Condominium and cooperative housing, 1960–1971; a bibliography of economic, financial and legal factors. [Washington]; For sale by the Supt. of Docs., U. S. Govt. Print. Off., 1972.

v, 32 p. 26 cm.

United States. Dept. of Housing and Urban Development. Library and Information Division.
Information sources in housing and community development. Washington, U. S. Dept. of Housing and Urban Development; for sale by the Supt. of Docs., U. S. Govt. Print. Off., 1972.

iii, 44 p. 27 cm.

Wellar, Barry S
Introduction and selected bibliography on the quality of housing and its environment ₁by₁ Barry S. Wellar and Thomas O. Graff. ₁Monticello, Ill., Council of Planning Librarians₁ 1972.

35 p. 29 cm. (Council of Planning Librarians. Exchange bibliography, 270)

LIBRARY CATALOGS

United States. Dept. of Housing and Urban Development. Library and Information Division.
The dictionary catalog of the United States Department of Housing and Urban Development, Library and Information Division, Washington, D. C. Boston, G. K. Hall, 1972.

19 v. 37 cm.

ISRAEL

Association of Engineers and Architects in Israel. *Building Centre, Haifa. Documentation Dept.*

ביבליוגרפיה על שיכונים.
Bibliography on housing, 1960–1964.

חיפה, אגודת האינג׳נרים והארכיטקטים בישראל, מרכז הבניה,
1965.

56 p. 25 cm.

"Prepared ... at the request of the Ministry of Housing."

LATIN AMERICA

Porzecanski, Leopoldo.
A selected bibliography on urban housing in Latin America. Monticello, Ill. Council of Planning Librarians, 1973.

31 p. 29 cm. (Council of Planning Librarians. Exchange bibliography 412)

POLAND

Bibliografia zagadnień mieszkaniowych za lata 1945–1967. ₁Oprac. redakcyjne; Ł. Rozumowa i J. Witkowska₁. Warszawa, Instytut Gospodarki Mieszkaniowej, 1969.

256 p. 25 cm.

Table of contents also in English, French, and Russian.

Dąbrowska, Stanisława.
Bibliografia wydawnictw CZSBM, lata 1956–1968. Warszawa, ZW CRS, 1969.

56 p. 21 cm.

At head of title: Centralny Związek Spółdzielni Budownictwa Mieszkaniowego.

SCANDINAVIA

Københavns almindelige boligselskab.
Alfabetisk forfatter-index over litteratur om boligforhold, boligundersøgelser m. m. i Skandinavien. Samt appendix over del af øvrigt forefindende litteratur på danske biblioteker for Vest-europa og Nordamerika. København V., Eksp., Vester Voldgt. 17, 1971.

41, (6) l. 30 cm.

HOUSING, RURAL

Bogotá. Inter-American Housing and Planning Center.
Bibliografía de la vivienda rural para América Latina. Bogotá, 1967.

19 l. 28 cm.

De Rocchi Storai, Tina.
Bibliografia degli studi sulla casa rurale italiana. Firenze, L. S. Olschki, 1968 ₁i. e. 1969₁.

130 p. 25½ cm. (Ricerche sulle dimore rurali in Italia, v. 25)

HOUSMAN, LAURENCE
Somerset County Library. *Street Branch Library.*
Laurence Housman 1865–1959: a brief catalogue of the collection of books, manuscripts and drawings presented to the Street Library by the family of Roger and Sarah Bancroft Clark to mark the centenary of Laurence Housman's birth, 1965, by Ivor Kemp. Street (Som.), Somerset County Library (Street Branch), 1967.

₁1₁, 17 p. plate, 2 facsims. (1 col.), port. 22 cm.

HOWARD FAMILY
Durham, Eng. University. *Durham Colleges. Dept. of Palaeography and Diplomatic.*
List of the Howard family documents relating to Northumberland, formerly at Naworth Castle, now deposited in the Department of Palaeography and Diplomatic, South Road, Durham; ₁compiled by C. R. Hudleston₁. Durham, Durham University (Department of Palaeography & Diplomatic), 1967.

₁2₁, 143 f. 33½ cm.

HOWELL, ARTHUR HOLMES
Jackson, Hartley Harrad Thompson, 1881–
Published writings of Arthur Holmes Howell (1872–1940) by Hartley H. T. Jackson. ₁Lawrence₁ Museum of Natural History, University of Kansas ₁1967₁

15 p. 23 cm. (University of Kansas. Museum of Natural History. Miscellaneous publication no. 47)

Includes the text of Howell's radio broadcast of April 25, 1928, "The relations of wildlife to the forest."

HOWELLS, WILLIAM DEAN
Brenni, Vito Joseph, 1923–
William Dean Howells: a bibliography. Compiled by Vito J. Brenni. Metuchen, N. J., Scarecrow Press, 1973.

212 p. 22 cm. (The Scarecrow author bibliographies, no. 9)

Gibson, William Merriam, 1912–
A bibliography of William Dean Howells, by William M. Gibson and George Arms. New York, New York Public Library ₁1971₁

184 p. illus. 24 cm.

Reprint of the 1948 ed. with an additional note by the compilers.

HOZDECKÝ, JOSEF
Wagner, Jan, fl. 1966–
Josef Hozdecký. (1851–1929.) Literární pozůstalost. ₁Fragment.₁ Zprac. Jan Wagner. Praha, Památník nár. písemnictví, rozmn., 1970.

6, ₁1₁ p. 20 cm. (Edice inventářů, čís. 205)

At head of title: Literární archív Památníku národního písemnictví v Praze.

HRABÁK, JOSEF
Veselý, Jan.
Bibliografie díla Josefa Hrabáka (do roku 1971) Universitní knihovna v Brně. ₁Vyd. 1. V Praze, Státní pedagogické nakl., 1972₁

184 p. 21 cm. (Edice státních vědeckých knihoven)

HRABOVS'KYĬ, PAVLO ARSENOVYCH
Akademiia nauk URSR, Kiev. *Instytut literatury.*
Павло Грабовський; бібліографічний покажчик. ₁Склав М. О. Мороз. Відповідальний редактор М. С. Сиваченко₁ Київ ₁Наукова думка₁ 1964.

78 p. 20 cm.

HRADEC KRÁLOVÉ, CZECHOSLOVAK REPUBLIC

Koudelková, Lia.
Bibliografie města a okresu Hradec Králivé. [Autoři:] Lia Koudelková, František Vích. [1. vyd.] Hradec Králové, Kruh, rozmn., [1970]

2 v. 20 cm. (Knihy a knihovny, 5)

HREJSOVÁ, BOŽENA

Sedlák, Jiří.
Božena Hrejsová, 1870–1945. Bibliogr. prací připr. Jiří Sedlák. Brno, St. pedagog. knihovna, rozmn., 1971.

13 p. 20 cm. (Brünn. Státní pedagogická knihovna. Publikace, č. 375) (Život a dílo čs. pedagogů, č. 9)

HUBERINUS, CASPAR

Franz, Gunther, 1942–
Huberinus, Rhegius, Holbein. Bibliographische und druckgeschichtliche Untersuchung der verbreitesten Trost- und Erbauungsschriften des 16. Jahrhunderts. Nieuwkoop, De Graaf, 1973.

viii, 353 p. with illus. 25 cm. (Bibliotheca humanistica & reformatorica, v. 7)

Summary in English.

HUDSON, WILLIAM HENRY

Wilson, George Francis.
A bibliography of the writings of W. H. Hudson, by G. F. Wilson. Port Washington, N. Y., Kennikat Press [1968]

79 p. facsims. 22 cm.

Reprint of the 1922 ed.

Wilson, George Francis.
A bibliography of the writings of W. H. Hudson, by G. F. Wilson. New York, Haskell House Publishers, 1972.

79 p. 23 cm.

Reprint of the 1922 ed.

HUGHES, LANGSTON

Moscow. Vsesoíuznaía gosudarstvennaía biblioteka inostrannoí literatury.
Ленгстон Хьюз; биобиблиографический указатель. [Составитель Б. М. Парчевская. Автор вступ. статьи И. М. Левидова] Москва, Книга, 1964.

90 p. port. 21 cm. (Писатели зарубежных стран)

HUGO, VICTOR MARIE, COMTE

Dubois, Pierre, abbé.
Bio-bibliographie de Victor Hugo, de 1802 à 1825. New York, B. Franklin [1971]

xiv, 240 p. 27 cm. (Burt Franklin bibliography and reference series, 408. Essays in literature and criticism, 124)

Reprint of the 1913 ed.

Grant, Elliott Mansfield, 1895–
Victor Hugo: a select and critical bibliography, by Elliott M. Grant. Chapel Hill, University of North Carolina Press [1967]

94 p. 23 cm. (University of North Carolina studies in the Romance languages and literatures, no. 67)

HUGUENOTS

Huguenot Society of America. Library.
Catalogue or bibliography of the Library of the Huguenot Society of America. Compiled by Julia P. M. Morand. 2d ed. Baltimore, Genealogical Pub. Co., 1971.

xi, 351 p. port. 24 cm.

Reprint of the 1920 ed.

Verner, Beryl Anne.
Huguenots in South Africa; a bibliography. Cape Town, University, School of Librarianship, 1967.

vi, 44 p. 23 cm. (University of Cape Town. School of Librarianship. Bibliographical series)

"Presented in partial fulfilment of the requirements for the Higher Certificate in Librarianship, University of Cape Town, 1966."

HULL, ENGLAND

Hull, Eng. City Libraries.
A select list of books on Hull and district: a guide to the collections in the Local History Library; compiled by R. F. Drewery. Kingston upon Hull (Yorks.), City Libraries, 1968.

vi, 32 p. 19 cm.

HUMAN ECOLOGY
see also Population

Aroro, Ved Parkash.
Man and the environment [compiled by Ved P. Arora] Regina, Bibliographic Services Division, Provincial Library, 1973.

57 p. 22 cm.

Cover title: Man and his environment.

Durrenberger, Robert W
Environment and man; a bibliography [by] Robert W. Durrenberger. Palo Alto, Calif., National Press Books [1970]

x, 118 p. 22 cm.

Fadeeva, G   P
(Chelovek i sreda)
Человек и среда. (Экология города). Библиогр. указ. отеч. и иностр. информ. материалов. Москва, 1972.
137 p. 22 cm.
At head of title: Центр научно-технической информации по гражданскому строительству и архитектуре. Отдел справочно-информационного обслуживания.

Sciences humaines et environnement, orientations bibliographiques, recherche effectuée à l'Institut de l'environnement. Paris (5ᵉ), Institut de l'environnement, 14–20, rue Érasme [1971].

[iv], 150 p. 21 cm.

At head of title: Christian Gaillard [et al.]

Woodrow Wilson International Center for Scholars.
The human environment. Washington, 1972.

2 v. 28 cm. (Environment series 201)

CONTENTS: v. 1. A selective annotated bibliography of reports and documents on international environmental problems.—v. 2. Summaries of national reports.

HUMAN ENGINEERING

Azerskaía, N   ÍA
Инженерная психология. Рек. указатель литературы. Москва, "Знание," 1968.

20 p. 20 cm. (В помощь лектору)

At head of title: Всесоюзное общество "Знание." Центральная политехническая библиотека.

Goovaerts, Jeanine.
Bibliographie internationale de l'ergonomie, 1954–1963. Mémoire présenté à l'École provinciale de bibliothécaires du Brabant. Bruxelles, Commission belge de bibliographie, 1966.

2 v. (xxxiv, 626 p.) 21 cm. (Bibliographia Belgica, 95)

Legátová, Božena.
Ergonomie; výběrová bibliografie. ₁Vypracovala: Božena Legátová₁. Ostrava, 1970.

vi, 238 p. 21 cm. (Státní vědecká knihovna v Ostravě. Publikace. Rada 2., čís. 450)

Recla, Josef.
Die Biomechanik der Leibesübungen in der Literatur der Gegenwart; eine Literaturstudie. Eine Gemeinschaftsarbeit von Helga und Otto Fleiss, Karl Ringli und Peter Rümmele. Hrsg. von Josef Recla. (Graz, Institut für Leibeserziehung, Karl-Franzens-Universität Graz; Liége. Internationales Büro für Dokumentation und Information, Kommission Bibliographie, Generalsekretariat Liége) 1967.

109 p. 30 cm.

Stevenage, Eng. Warren Spring Laboratory.
Ergonomics. ₁Stevenage, Eng.₁ 1964.

iv, 128 p. 33 cm. (Human sciences in industry; annotated bibliography, pt. 1)

HUMAN FERTILITY see Fertility

HUMAN GENETICS see Genetics

HUMAN INTELLIGENCE see Intellect

HUMAN MECHANICS

Brown, John R   1919–
Manual lifting & related fields: an annotated bibliography ₁by₁ John R. Brown. ₁Toronto, Labour Safety Council of Ontario, Ontario Ministry of Labour, 1972₁

iii, 583 p. 23 cm.

HUMAN PERFORMANCE

Man, his job, and the environment: a review and annotated bibliography of selected recent research on human performance ₁by₁ William G. Mather, III ₁and others₁. Gaithersburg, Md.₁ National Bureau of Standards; for sale by the Supt. of Docs., U. S. Govt. Print. Off., ₁Washington₁ 1970.

vi, 101 p. 26 cm. (National Bureau of Standards special publication 319)

HUMAN RIGHTS see Civil rights

HUMANISM
  see also Renaissance

Cosenza, Mario Emilio, 1880–
Biographical and bibliographical dictionary of the Italian humanists and of the world of classical scholarship in Italy, 1300–1800. ₁2d ed., rev. and enl. Boston, G. K. Hall, 1962₁–67.

6 v. 37 cm.

Photocopy of the author's MS. card file.
"First edition was printed in microfilm form by the Renaissance Society of America in 1954."
Vol. 6, Supplement A–Z, has half title: Dictionary of the Italian humanists.

Gerlo, Aloïs.
Bibliographie de l'humanisme belge, précédée d'une bibliographie générale concernant l'humanisme européen, par Aloïs Gerlo, avec la collaboration d'Émile Lauf. Bruxelles, Presses universitaires de Bruxelles ₁1965₁

248 p. 24 cm. (Instrumenta humanistica, 1)

Université libre de Bruxelles. Travaux de l'Institut pour l'étude de la Renaissance et de l'humanisme.

Gerlo, Aloïs.
Bibliographie de l'humanisme des anciens Pays-Bas. Avec un répertoire bibliographique des humanistes et poètes néo-latins. Par Aloïs Gerlo et Hendrik D. L. Vervliet. Bruxelles, Presses universitaires de Bruxelles, 1972.

546 p. 24 cm. (Université libre de Bruxelles. Institut pour l'étude de la Renaissance et de l'humanisme. Instrumenta humanistica, 3)

Katushkina, L   G
₁Ot Dante do Tasso₁
От Данте до Тассо. Каталог писем и сочинений итал. гуманистов в собрании ЛОИИ СССР. Сcставитель Л. Г. Катушкина. ₁Авт. предисл. В. Рутенбург₁. Ленинград, "Наука," Ленингр. отд-ние, 1972.

107 p. 20 cm.

At head of title: Академия наук СССР. Ленинградское отделение Института истории СССР.

Lovett, B   H
Humanism: a book list, compiled by B. H. Lovett. Adelaide, State Library of South Australia, 1967.

10 p. 26 cm. (State Library (Research Service bibliographies. Series 4, no. 91)

Oxford. University. Bodleian Library.
Duke Humfrey and English humanism in the fifteenth century: catalogue of an exhibition held in the Bodleian Library, Oxford ₁compiled by Tilly de la Mare and Richard Hunt, Keeper of Western Manuscripts₁. Oxford, Bodleian Library, 1970.

₁10₁, 77 p., 24 plates. coats of arms, facsims. 22 cm.

HUMANITIES

Chung yang t'u shu kuan, T'ai-pei.
(Chung-hua min kuo T'ai-wan ch'ü kung ts'ang Chung wên jên wên shê hui k'o hsüeh ch'i k'an) 中華民國臺灣區公藏中文人文社會科學期刊聯合目錄 ₁臺北₁ 國立中央圖書館編印 ₁民國 59 i. e. 1970₁

2, 271, 9 p. 22 cm.

Martens, Johanne.
Håndbok over norsk bibliografi; bibliografisk litteratur i utvalg, de humanistiske fag ₁av₁ Johanne Martens og Gerhard Munthe. Med forord av Harald L. Tveterås. ₁Oslo₁ Universitetsforlaget ₁c1965₁

61 p. 21 cm.

Needles, burrs, and bibliographies; study resources in technological change, human values, and the humanities. Maxwell H. Goldberg, general editor. ₁University Park₁ Center for Continuing Liberal Education, Pennsylvania State University ₁1969₁

v, 200 l. 29 cm.

"Developed largely from the CCLE–IBM humanities project on technological change."

Rogers, A   Robert, 1927–
The humanities; a selective guide to information sources ₁by₁ A. Robert Rogers. Littleton, Colo., Libraries Unlimited, 1974.

400 p. 24 cm. (Library science text series)

BIBLIOGRAPHIES

Fialová, Božena.
Soupis rešerší z humanitních oborů vypracovaných za roky 1961–1970. Sest. Božena Kyjovská. Brno, Univ. knihovna, rozmn., 1971.

45, ₁1₁ l. 20 cm. (Výběrový seznam, č. 169)

HUMBOLDT, ALEXANDER, FREIHERR VON

Humboldt, Alexander, *Freiherr von,* 1769–1859.
The Humboldt Library; a catalogue of the library of Alexander von Humboldt; with a bibliographical and biographical memoir by Henry Stevens. London, Henry Stevens, American Agency, 1863. ₁Leipzig, Zentral-Antiquariat, 1967₁

9, 791 p. 22 cm.

Instituto Geofísico de los Andes Colombianos. Biblioteca.
Las obras de Alejandro von Humboldt en la Biblioteca del Instituto Geofísico de los Andes Colombianos ₍por₎ Jesús Emilio Ramírez. Bogotá, 1969.

15 p. 24 cm. (Publicación del Instituto Geofísico de los Andes Colombianos. Serie C: Geología, no. 11)

Lange, Fritz G
Alexander von Humboldt; eine Bibliographie der in der Deutschen Demokratischen Republik erschienenen Literatur. Mit einer Übersicht über die Eigentümer von Humboldt-Handschriften in der DDR. Zusammengestellt von Fritz G. Lange. Berlin, Akademie-Verlag, 1974.

98 p. 24 cm. (Beiträge zur Alexander-von-Humboldt-Forschung, 3)

Schmidmaier, Dieter.
Alexander von Humboldt. 14. 9. 1769–6. 5. 1859. Eine Ausw. aus d. Bestand d. Bibliothek d. Bergakad. zur 200. Wiederkehr d. Geburtstages v. Alexander von Humboldt. (Freiberg, Bibliothek d. Bergakademie Freiberg) 1969.

12 p. 23 cm. (Veröffentlichungen d. Bibliothek d. Bergakademie Freiberg, Nr. 32)

HUME, DAVID

Hall, Roland.
A Hume bibliography, from 1930. York, Roland Hall, -1971.

₍4₎, 80 p. 21 cm.

Jessop, Thomas Edmund, 1896–
A bibliography of David Hume and of Scottish philosophy from Francis Hutcheson to Lord Balfour, by T. E. Jessop. New York, Russell & Russell, 1966.

xiv, 201 p. 23 cm.

First published in 1938.
"The Gifford lectures": p. 185–189.

HUMMEL, JOHANN NEPOMUK and CARL

Goethe-Museum, Düsseldorf.
Johann Nepomuk Hummel, Komponist der Goethe-Zeit, und sein Sohn Carl, Landschaftsmaler des späten Weimar. Ausstellg. 27. Aug.–31. Okt. 1971. Katalog. ₍Von₎ Christina Kröll u. Hartmut Schmidt. In Zsarb. mit Inge Kähmer, Irmgard Kräupl, Ruth Pink. Hrsg. v. Jörn Göres. Düsseldorf, Goethe-Museum, Anton- u. -Katharina -Kippenberg-Stiftung (1971).

81 p. 16 l. of illus. 21 cm.

HUMOR see Wit and humor

HUMPHREY, HERBERT ALFRED

Pingree, Jeanne.
Herbert Alfred Humphrey: list of his papers in the Imperial College Archives; compiled by Jeanne Pingree and Denis Smith. London, Imperial College of Science and Technology, 1971.

₍4₎, iii, 37 p., plate. port. 30 cm.

Cover title: List of the papers of H. A. Humphrey in the Imperial College Archives.

HUNEDOARA, ROMANIA

Romania. Arhivele Statului. Filiala Județului Hunedoara.
Îndrumător în Arhivele Statului județul Hunedoara. ₍Întocmită de: Ion Frățilă, Nicolae Wardegger, Mihai Cerghedean, ...₎ București, 1972.

251 p. with figs. and facsims. 24 cm.

At head of title: Direcția Generală a Arhivelor Statului din Republica Socialistă România.

Summary in French.

HUNGARIAN IMPRINTS

Büky, Béla.
A Jankovich Miklós-féle katalógusgyűjtemény, mint ismeretlen, 1712 előtti régi magyar könyv- és variánsadatok forrása. Székesfehérvár, Vörösmarty Mihály Megyei Könyvtár, 1966.

28 p. illus. 25 cm. (A Vörösmarty Mihály Megyei Könyvtár kiadványai. B. sorozat. Tanulmányok, 1)
Summary in German.

Hungarian book review. v. 14–
Jan./Mar. 1972–
₍Budapest, Hungarian Publishers' and Booksellers' Association; distributed by Kultura₎

v. illus. 24 cm. quarterly.

Continues Books from Hungary.

Könyvkiadók és Terjesztők Tájékoztató Központja.
A magyarországi könyvkiadók tématerve, 1964. ₍Budapest₎ 1964.

217 p. 20 cm.

Magyar könyvészet. 1712/1860–
Budapest ₍Országos Széchényi Könyvtár, 1968–

v. in 24 cm.

Reprint of the bibliography with new preface in English and Hungarian.
Title varies: 1712/1860, Magyarország bibliographiája.
Vols. for 1712/1860 have added t. p.: Bibliographia Hungariae.
Editors: 1712/1860– G. Petrik—1911/20–
S. Kozocsa.

Magyar Tudományos Akadémia, Budapest.
Régi magyarországi nyomtatványok, 1473–1600. ₍Az Akadémia könyvtörténeti munkabizottságának irányítása alatt Borsa Gedeon, et al. munkája₎ Budapest, Akadémiai Kiadó, 1971.

928 p. facsims., map. 25 cm.
At head of title: Magyar Tudományos Akadémia. Országos Széchényi Könyvtár.
Added t. p.: Res litteraria Hungariae vetus operum impressorum.
Pref. also in Latin and English.

HUNGARIAN LANGUAGE

Fialová, Božena.
Učíme se maďarsky. Soupis literatury. Sest. Božena Kyjovská. Brno, Univ. knihovna, t. G 07, Blansko, 1968.

₍7₎ p. 21 cm. (Brünn. Universita. Knihovna. Bibliografický leták, č. 151)

Halasz de Beky, I L
Bibliography of Hungarian dictionaries, 1410–1963, compiled by I. L. Halasz de Beky. Toronto, University of Toronto Press ₍1966₎

xiv, 148 p. 26 cm.

"Published under the auspices of the Hungarian Rákóczi Association."

Pálinkás, László.
Avviamento allo studio della lingua e letteratura ungherese. Bibliografia italiana a cura di László Pálinkás ... Napoli, Cymba, 1970.

vii, 138 p. 24 cm. (Enchiridion, 2)

HUNGARIAN LITERATURE

Höhl, Martha.
Ungarische Literatur des 20. Jahrhunderts. Ein Auswahlverz. Mit e. Beitr. v. Miklós Béládi. Dortmund, Stadtbücherei, 1971.

62 p. 21 cm. (Völker im Spiegel der Literatur, Folge 14)

Magyar irodalom ajánló bibliográfia az 5–8. osztályos tanulók számára. ₍Szerk. Károlyi Zsigmondné. Összeállította:

Aszódi Lászlóné, et al.] Budapest, Tankönyvkiadó, 1967.

109 p. illus. 20 cm. (Tantárgyi bibliográfiák. Általános iskolai sorozat, 2)

Az Országos Pedagógiai Könyvtár kiadványa.

A magyar irodalomtörténet bibliográfiája. [Szerk: Vargha Kálmán és V. Windisch Éva. Készült a Magyar Tudományos Akadémia Irodalomtudományi Intézetében] Budapest, Akadémiai Kiadó, 1972–

v. 25 cm.

CONTENTS: 1. Stoll, B., Varga, I. és Kovács, S. V. A magyar irodalomtörténet bibliográfiája 1772–ig.

Pomogáts, Béla.
Huszonöt év magyar prózája, 1945–1969; bibliográfia. Budapest, Fővárosi Szabó Ervin Könyvtár, 1970.

185 p. 20 cm.

Slovník spisovatelů. Maďarsko, Za ved. Petra Rákoso zprac. [kol.] Úv. studii naps., chronologický přehl. sest. P. Rákos. 1. vyd. Praha, Odeon, t. Rudé právo, 1971.

386, [22] p. 20 cm.

Szabó, Károly, 1824–1890.
Régi magyar könyvtár ... Kiadja a M. Tud. Akadémia. Budapest, A M. Tud. Akadémia Könyvkiadó Hivatala, 1879–98.

3 v. in 4. 26 cm.

CONTENTS.—[1. köt.] Az 1531–1711 megjelent magyar nyomtatványok könyvészeti kézikönyve, írta Szabó K.—2. köt. Az 1473-tól 1711-ig megjelent nem magyar nyelvű hazai nyomtatványok könyvészeti kézikönyve, írta Szabó K.—3. köt. Magyar szerzőktől külföldön 1480-tól 1711-ig megjelent nem magyar nyelvű nyomtatványoknak könyvészeti kézikönyve, írták Szabó K. és Hellebrant Á.

————— Adalékok Szabó Károly Régi magyar könyvtár c. munkájának I–II kötetéhez. Pótlások és igazítások 1472–177, egybeállitotta Sztripszky Hiador. [Az 1912. évi kiad. uj kiadása] Budapest, Országos Széchényi Könyvtár] 1967.

xix, 621 p. 23 cm.
"Bibliographia Hungariae, series editionum stereotyparum. Magyarországi könyvészet, hasonmáskiadások sorozata, 1472–1711."

Tezla, Albert.
Hungarian authors; a bibliographical handbook. Cambridge, Mass., Belknap Press of Harvard University Press, 1970

xxviii, 792 p. 25 cm.

Extension of the author's An introductory bibliography to the study of Hungarian literature (1964), and is to be used in conjunction with that work.

Tezla, Albert.
An introductory bibliography to the study of Hungarian literature. Cambridge, Harvard University Press, 1964.

xxvi, 290 p. 22 cm.

TRANSLATIONS

Czigány, Magda, 1935–
Hungarian literature in English translation published in Great Britain, 1830–1968; a bibliography. London, Szepsi Csombor Literary Circle, 1969.

117 p. 21 cm. (Szepsi Csombor Literary Society. English series, 2)

"A first version of this bibliography was accepted in part requirement for University of London Diploma in Librarianship, 1964."

Idegen nyelven megjelent magyar szépirodalmi művek listája 1962–1967 között. Liste des ouvrages littéraires édités an langue étrangère entre 1962 et 1967. [Budapest]

Magyar Irók Szövetsége, 1968.

60 p. 24 cm.

Cover title: Magyar szépirodalom idegen nyelven.

Vančová, Tatiana.
Bibliografia slovenských prekladov maďarskej literatúry, 1945–1972 / zost. [a úvod nap.] Tatiana Vančová. — 1. vyd. — Bratislava : Alfa, 1974.

161 p. ; 24 cm. — (Bibliografie prekladov zahraničnej literatúry)

HUNGARIANS IN FOREIGN COUNTRIES

Pražák, Richard.
Bibliografie československé hungaristiky za léta 1966–1968. Sest., red. a k vyd. připravil Richard Pražák. Určeno pro podl. filosof. fak. 1. vyd. Brno, Univ. J. E. Purkyně, rozmn., 1971.

98, [1] p. 28 cm. (Učební texty vysokých škol) (Materiály k dějinám a kultuře střední a jihovýchodní Evropy, sv. 2)

At head of title: Universita J. E. Purkyně v Brně. Fakulta filosofická.

United States. Library of Congress.
Hungarians in Rumania and Transylvania: a bibliographical list of publications in Hungarian and West European languages, compiled from the holdings of the Library of Congress, by Elemer Bako and William Sólyom-Fekete. With a pref. by Edward J. Patten. Washington, U. S. Govt. Print. Off., 1969.

vii, 192 p. 24 cm. (91st Congress, 1st session. House document no. 91–134)

HUNGARY

Abstracts of Hungarian economic literature. v. 1–
1971–
[Budapest] Hungarian Scientific Council for World Economy, Scientific Information Service.

v. 25 cm. bimonthly.

Bako, Elemer.
Guide to Hungarian studies. Stanford, Calif., Hoover Institution Press [1973]

2 v. (xv, 1218 p.) illus. 29 cm. (Hoover Institution bibliographical series, 52)

Banner, János, 1888–
A Közép-Dunamedence régészeti bibliográfiája, 1954–1959. Összeállította Jakabffy Imre. Budapest, Akadémiai Kiadó, 1961–68.

2 v. 25 cm.

At head of title: Banner—Jakabffy.
Added titles: Archäologische Bibliographie des Mittel-Donau-Beckens, 1954–1959; Bibliographie archéologique du bassin danubien, 1954–1959.
Title, introd. and table of contents also in French, German, and Russian.

Czigany, Lóránt György.
The Béla Iványi-Grünwald collection of Hungarica: a catalogue; edited with a short biographical notice and with a bibliography of his writings, by Lóránt Czigány. London, Szepsi Csombor Literary Circle, 1967.

159 p. front. (port.). 21½ cm. (Szepsi Csombor Literary Society. Publications. English series)

Cover title: Hungarica; catalogue of the Béla Iványi-Grünwald collection.

Czigány, Lóránt György.
Hungarica: English books, prints, maps, periodicals, etc. relating to Hungary, collected by Béla Iványi-Grünwald; catalogue compiled by Lóránt Czigány; introduction by Gregory Macdonald, foreword by G. H. Bolsover. Alphamstone. Mrs. Jocelyn Iványi, 1967.

159 p. port. 21 cm.

Also published under title: The Béla Iványi-Grünwald collection of Hungarica. London, Szepsi Csombor Literary Circle, 1967.
Cover title: Hungarica; catalogue of the Béla Iványi-Grünwald collection.

Halle. Universitäts- und Landesbibliothek Sachsen-Anhalt.
Ungarische Bibliothek.
Bibliographische Seltenheiten der Hallenser Ungarischen Bibliothek. Zusammengestellt und eingeleitet von Miklós Pálfy. Halle ⟨Saale⟩ Niemeyer, 1967.

124 p. 25 cm. (Arbeiten aus der Universitäts- und Landesbibliothek Sachsen-Anhalt in Halle a. d. Saale, Bd. 6)

Added t. p. and introd. in Hungarian.

Hungarica külföldi folyóiratszemle. 1.-
évf.; 1971–
Budapest, Országos Széchényi Könyvtár.

v. 29 cm. quarterly.

"A Magyar folyóiratok repertóriuma negyedéves melléklete."

Hungary. *Központi Statisztikai Hivatal. Könyvtár. Bibliográfiai Osztály.*
Statisztikai adatforrások; bibliográfia, 1867–1967. ₁Összeállitotta a Könyvtár Bibliográfiai Osztálya₁ Источники статистических данных; библиография. Sources of statistical data; bibliography. Statistische Datenquellen; Bibliographie. Budapest, 1967.

xiv, 344 p. 20 cm.

Hungarian, Russian, English, and German.

Hungary. Országos Levéltár.
Magyar Országos Levéltár P szekció kisebb családi és személyi fondok. Áttekintő raktári jegyzék. Összeállitották: Bakács István és Dávid Lászlóné Művelodésügyi Minisztérium Levéltári igazgatósága megbizásából. Budapest, 1968–

v. 29 cm. (Levéltári leltárak, 44)

Summary in Russian and French.
CONTENTS: 1. köt. 1–144. törzsalapszámok.

Kőhalmi, Béla.
A tudományos tájékoztatás fejlődése hazánkban, 1945–1965. Budapest, ₁Népművelési Propaganda Iroda₁ 1967.

574 p. 24 cm. (Az Országos Könyvtárügyi és Dokumentációs Tanács, 25. sz. kiadványa)

Magyar Tudományos Akadémia, Budapest. Közgazdaságtudományi Intézet. Könyvtár.
Selected bibliography on the reform of the system of economic control and management in Hungary. ₁Edited by Tamás Földi₁ Budapest, 1968.

40 p. 24 cm.

Nikolaenko, K   A
Новая система планового руководства народным хозяйством Венгрии. Библиография книг и статей за 1966–1968 гг. ₁Сост. К. А. Николаенко. Предисл. Р. Н. Евстигнеева₁. Москва, 1970.

xiv, 163, 11 p. 20 cm.

HISTORY

Bibliográfia Magyarország legujabbkori történetéhez; Magyarország legujabbkori történetére vonatkozó, 1954–1962 között megjelent fontosabb könyvek, tanulmányok, cikkek jegyzeke. Kézirat 4. változatlan utánnyomás. ₁Összeállitotta: Siklós András₁ Budapest, Tankönyvkiadó, 1964.

107 p. 24 cm.

At head of title: Eötvös Loránd Tudományegyetem, Bölcsészettudományi Kar.

Ecsedy, Andorné.
Forradalmak kora; a magyar polgári demokratikus forradalom a KMP megalakulása és a Tanácsköztársaság irodalmának válogatott jegyzéke. ₁Összeállitotta Ecsedy Andorné és Gáliczky Éva₁ Budapest, Fővárosi Szabó Ervin Könyvtár, 1968.

39 p. 19 cm.

Hungary. Országos Levéltár.
Az 1848–1849 ₁i. e. ezernyolcszáznegyvennyolc-ezernyolcszáznegyvenkilenc₁-i minisztériumi levéltár; repertorium. Készítette: Fábián Istvánné. Művelődésügyi Minisztérium Levéltári Igazgatósága megbízásából. Budapest, 1969.

189 p. 29 cm. (Levéltári leltárak, 45)

Summary in Russian, German, and French.

Hungary. *Országos Levéltár.*
Polgári kori és tanácsköztársasági központi kormányhatóságok levéltárai; kiegészités a repertóriumokhoz, fond- és állagjegyzék. Összeállitotta: Bekény István. Budapest, Művelődésügyi Minisztérium Levéltári Osztálya, 1964.

221 p. 28 cm. (Levéltári leltárak, 27)

Summary in French and Russian.

Hungary. Országos Levéltár. Filmtár.
Ausztriai levéltári anyagról készült mikrofilmek (1969. január 1-én): repertórium. Összeállitotta: Borsa Iván. Budapest, Magyar Országos Levéltár, 1969.

200 p. 29 cm. (Levéltári leltárak, 46)

Summary in Russian and German.

Kárász, József.
Éljen a köztársaság, éljen a proletárdiktatúra; az 1918–1919-es forradalmak hódmezővásárhelyi sajtójának repertóriuma. Hódmezővásárhely ₁Csongrád Megyei Könyvtár₁ 1970.

58 p. 24 cm.

Lakos, Katalin.
25 ₁i. e. Huszonöt₁ éve történt; ajánló bibliográfia Magyarország felszabadulásának negyedszázados jubileumára. Budapest, Fővárosi Szabó Ervin Könyvtár, 1969.

49 p. 20 cm.

Magyar Tudományos Akadémia, Budapest. Történettudományi Intézet.
A magyar történettudomány válogatott bibliográfiája, 1945–1968. Budapest, Akadémiai Kiadó, 1971.

855 p. 25 cm.

Papp, László, 1903–
Bibliográfiai bevezető: történelem. Budapest, Tankönyvkiadó, 1970.

432 p. 24 cm.

At head of title: Bölcsészettudományi Karok.

Szeplaki, Joseph.
Selected bibliography on Hungary with special reference to the Hungarian Revolution, 1956, available in the Ohio University Library. ₁Athens? Ohio, 1971?₁

12 l. 20 cm.

Caption title.
At head of title: 15th Anniversary of the Hungarian Revolution, 1956–1971.

Történelmi emlékeztető; felszabadulásunk évfordulójára ajánlott könyvek. ₁Szerk. Lakos Katalin₁ Budapest, Fővárosi Szabó Ervin Könyvtár, 1969.

47 p. 30 cm.

United States. National Archives.
Guide to the collection of Hungarian political and military records, 1909-45. Washington, 1972.

vi. 20 p. 21 x 36 cm.

Útmutató a felszabadulási ünnepségekhez. ₍Összeállították: Bánszky Pál, et al. Szerk.: Dombrády Loránd, Felejtei Tibor és Rácz Zoltán₎ Budapest, Népművelési Propaganda Iroda, 1969.

303 p. illus., maps. 21 cm.

Vas megye a Tanácsköztársaság idején a korabeli sajtó tükrében (1919. március 21-augusztus 3); repertórium. ₍Szerk.: Bánó Zsuzsa₎ Szombathely, 1969.

121 p. 21 cm.

Cover title: Vasi sajtó.

Völgyes, Iván, 1936–
The Hungarian Soviet Republic, 1919; an evaluation and a bibliography. Stanford, Calif., Hoover Institution Press ₍1970₎

ix, 90 p. 29 cm. (Hoover Institution bibliographical series, 43)

LAW see LAW - HUNGARY

HUNT, LEIGH
see also under Hazlitt, William

Brewer, Luther Albertus, 1858-1933.
My Leigh Hunt library. Collected and described by Luther A. Brewer. New York, B. Franklin ₍1970₎

xliv, 301 p. facsims., ports. 24 cm. (Burt Franklin bibliography & reference series 326)

Essays in literature & criticism, 58.
Reprint of the 1932 volume.

CONTENTS.—The first editions.

Mitchell, Alexander.
A bibliography of the writings of Leigh Hunt with critical notes. ₍Folcroft, Pa.₎ Folcroft Library Editions, 1973.

65 p. 26 cm.

Reprint of the 1930-31 ed. published in London as supplements to the Bookman's journal, 3d ser., v. 18, no. 15 and no. 16.

HUNTER VALLEY

Coffey, W   G
A bibliography of the Hunter Valley region, New South Wales, by W. G. Coffey. Maryville, Newcastle, New South Wales, Research Centre, 1964.

84 l. 26 cm. (Hunter Valley Research Foundation Monograph no. 19)

HUNTING

Ceresoli, Adriano.
Bibliografia delle opere italiane, latine e greche su la caccia, la pesca e la cinologia, con aggiunte di mammologia, ornitologia, ittiologia ed erpetologia ₍di₎ A. Ceresoli. Bologna, Forni, 1969.

x, 569 p. facsims. 33 cm.

Olendorff, Richard R
An extensive bibliography on falconry, eagles, hawks, falcons, and other diurnal birds of prey, by Richard R. Olendorff and Sharon E. Olendorff. ₍Fort Collins, Colo., 1968₎–

pt. illus. 28 cm.

CONTENTS.—pt. 1. Falconry and eagles.

Saskatchewan. Provincial Library, Regina. Bibliographic Services Division.
Hunting & fishing; a bibliography. Regina, 1973.

22 p. 21 cm.

Souhart, Roger François.
Bibliographie générale des ouvrages sur la chasse, la vénerie et la fauconnerie. Publiés ou composés depuis le 15e siècle jusqu'à ce jour en français, latin, allemand, anglais. espagnol, italien, etc. Avec des notes critiques et l'indication de leur prix et de leur valeur dans les différentes ventes. Par R. Souhart. (Unveränderter Nachdruck ₍der Ausg.₎) Paris, Rouquette, 1886. ₍Leipzig, Zentralantiquariat der Deutschen Demokratischen Republik, 1968.₎

vii p., 750 columns. 23 cm.

On spine: Bibliographie la chasse la vénerie.

HURON, LAKE

Water Resources Scientific Information Center.
Lake Huron, a bibliography. Washington ₍1972₎

iv, 95 p. 27 cm. (Its Bibliography series, WRSIC 72-210)

HUS, JAN

Bartoš, František Michálek, 1889–
Soupis pramenů k literární činnosti M. Jana Husa a M. Jeronýma Pražského. Redigoval Ant. Škarka. Praha, Historický ústav ČSAV, 1965.

369 p. 21 cm.

At head of title: F. M. Bartoš, P. Spunar.
Added t. p.: Catalogus fontium M. Iohannis Hus et M. Hieronymi Pragensis opera exhibentium.
Preface also in Latin.

HUSÉN, TORSTEN

Kullman, Siv-Aino, 1921–
Torsten Husén. Tryckta skrifter 1940-1965. Av Siv-Aino Kullman och Erik Degerman. ₍Stockholm, T. Husén₎ 1966.

59, (2) p. 24 cm.

Kullman, Siv-Aino, 1921–
Torsten Husén. Tryckta skrifter, 1940-1970. ₍Av Siv-Aino Kullmann och Anna Greta Schaffer. Stockholm, T. Husén₎, 1972.

69, (2) p. 24 cm.

HUSLYSTYĬ, KOST' H.

Skokan, Kateryna Ieronimivna.
(Kost' Hryhorovych Huslystyĭ)
Кость Григорович Гуслистий. Вступ. стаття Є. С. Шабліовського. Бібліогр. склад. К. І. Скокан. Київ, "Наук. думка," 1972.

55 p. port. 17 cm. (Біобібліографія вчених Української РСР)

HUTTERITE BRETHREN

Riley, Marvin P
The Hutterite Brethren; an annotated bibliography with special reference to South Dakota Hutterite colonies ₍by Marvin P. Riley₎ Brookings, Sociology Dept., Agricultural Experiment Station, South Dakota State University, 1965.

188 p. map. 23 cm. (South Dakota. Agricultural Experiment Station, Brookings. Bulletin 529)

HUXLEY, ALDOUS LEONARD

California. University. *University at Los Angeles. Library.*
Aldous Huxley at UCLA; a catalogue of the manuscripts in the Aldous Huxley collection, with the texts of three unpublished letters. Edited with an introd. by George Wickes. Los Angeles, University of California Library, 1964.

36 p. facsims., ports. 25 cm.

Duval, Hanson Rawlings.
Aldous Huxley; a bibliography, by Hanson R. Duval. ₍Folcroft, Pa.₎ Folcroft Library Editions, 1972 ₍c1939₎

205 p. 26 cm.

Milne Library.

By and about Aldous Huxley; a bibliography of the Aldous Huxley collection at Milne Library. Compiled by Barry Lash, with a foreward [sic] by Donald Watt. [Geneseo, N. Y.] 1973.

[34] p. illus. 22 cm.

HUXLEY, ELSPETH JOSCELINE GRANT

Oxford. University. Rhodes House Library.

Papers of Elspeth Josceline Huxley, MSS Afr. s 782 kept in Rhodes House Library, Oxford. [Prepared by P. A. Empson. Oxford, introd. 1966]

26 l. 26 cm.

At head of title: Oxford colonial project.

HUXLEY, THOMAS HENRY

Pingree, Jeanne.

Thomas Henry Huxley: a list of his scientific notebooks, drawings and other papers, preserved in the College archives. London, Imperial College of Science and Technology, 1968.

x, 94 p. plate, port. 30 cm.

HYDRAULICS; HYDRAULIC ENGINEERING

Barskova, N A
[In"ektsionnye suspenzii, rastvory i betony]

Инъекционные суспензии, растворы и бетоны с добавками полимерных материалов в гидротехническом строительстве. Аннот. библиогр. указатель зарубежной литературы за 1965–1969 гг. [Сост. Н. А. Барскова]. Ленинград, "Энергия," Ленингр. отд-ние, 1970.

80 p. 20 cm.

At head of title: Министерство энергетики и электрификации СССР. Главтехстройпроект. Всесоюзный научно-исследовательский институт гидротехники имени Б. Е. Веденеева. Отдел патентов и научно-технической информации. Лаборатория цементации оснований гидротехнических сооружений.

Dowden, Ruth Rosemary.

Fluid flow measurement: a bibliography [by] R. Rosemary Dowden. Cranfield, British Hydromechanics Research Association, 1972.

[8], 234 p. 31 cm.

Épshtein, V S
[Vozdeĭstvie voln na gidrotekhnicheskie sooruzheniîa]

Воздействие волн на гидротехнические сооружения и берега морей и водохранилищ. Аннот. библиогр. указатель за 1960–1968 гг. Ленинград, 1970.

80 p. 20 cm.

At head of title: Министерство энергетики и электрификации СССР. Главтехстройпроект. Всесоюзный научно-исследовательский институт гидротехники имени Б. Е. Веденеева. Отдел патентов и научно-технической информации.

Gouse, S William.

An index to the two-phase gas-liquid flow literature [by] S. William Gouse, Jr. Cambridge, Mass., M. I. T. Press [1966]

viii, 867 p. 24 cm. (M. I. T. report no. 9)

Originally published in 3 parts from May 1963 to Jan. 1966.

International Association for Hydraulic Research.

List of papers. Index to the papers presented at the various General Meetings and Symposia of the I. A. H. R., held during the period from 1959 up to and including 1966. Delft, Raam 61, 1967.

68 p. 20½ cm.

Jrayin Problemneri ew Hidrotekhnikayi Gitahetazotakan Instiṭowt. *Otdel nauchno-tekhnicheskoĭ informatsii.*

Библиография работ, выполненных в Армянском научно-исследовательском институте водных проблем и гидротехники в 1944–1967 гг. Ереван, "Айастан," 1969.

120 p. 21 cm.

At head of title: Министерство мелиорации и водного хозяйства Армянской ССР. Научно-исследовательский институт водных проблем и гидротехники. Отдел научно-технической информации.

Kaminarova, R I

Гидравлика стратифицированных потоков. (Библиогр. зарубежной литературы за период 1950–1966 гг.) Ленинград, "Энергия," Ленингр. отд-ние, 1968.

219 p. 21 cm.

At head of title: Министерство энергетики и электрификации СССР. Главтехстройпроект. Всесоюзный научно-исследовательский институт гидротехники имени Б. Е. Веденеева. Отдел научно-технической информации. Отдел технического водоснабжения и охладителей тепловых электростанций.

Kaminarova, R I

Неустановившееся движение жидкости в открытых руслах. Расчет на ЭЦВМ. Информ. справка. (Отечеств. и зарубежная литература 1960–1967 гг.) Ленинград, "Энергия," Ленингр. отд-ние, 1968.

40 p. 20 cm.

At head of title: Министерство энергетики и электрификации СССР. Главтехстройпроект. Всесоюзный научно-исследовательский институт гидротехники имени Б. Е. Веденеева. Отдел научно-технической информации. Лаборатория речной гидравлики.

Kormushina, D A

Перемещение наносов и русловые переформирования в бъефах гидроузлов. Информация по материалам отечеств. и зарубежной литературы за период 1931–1966 г. Ленинград, "Энергия," Ленингр. отд-ние, 1968.

96 p. 20 cm.

At head of title: Министерство энергетики и электрификации СССР. Главтехстройпроект. Всесоюзный научно-исследовательский институт гидротехники имени Б. Е. Веденеева. Отдел научно-технической информации. Лаборатория речной гидравлики.

Kormushina, D A
[Vodopronitsaemost' gruntov]

Водопроницаемость грунтов оснований гидротехнических сооружений. Трещиноватость и фильтрац. прочность скальных пород. Информ. справка отечеств. и зарубежной литературы за 1963–1967 гг. Ленинград, "Энергия," Ленингр. отд-ние, 1968.

41 p. 20 cm.

At head of title: Министерство энергетики и электрификации СССР. Главтехстройпроект. Всесоюзный научно-исследовательский институт гидротехники имени Б. Е. Веденеева. Отдел научно-технической информации. Лаборатория фильтрационных исследований.

Mielczarski, Aleksander, *comp.*

Piśmiennictwo polskie z zakresu hydrotechniki morskiej w okresie od 1945 do 1964 roku. Poznań, Państwowe Wydawn. Naukowe, 1967.

184 p. 24 cm.

At head of title: Instytut Budownictwa Wodnego Polskiej Akademii Nauk w Gdańsku. Aleksander Mielczarski, Zbigniew Szopowski.

Minina, E IA
[Gidrodinamicheskie nagruzki na gidrotekhnicheskie sooruzheniîa]

Гидродинамические нагрузки на гидротехнические сооружения. Аннот. библиогр. указ. зарубежной литературы ... Ленинград, 1971.

32 p. 20 cm.

At head of title: Министерство энергетики и электрификации СССР. Центр научно-технической информации по энергетике и электрификации-ИНФОРМЭНЕРГО. Всесоюзный научно-исследовательский институт гидротехники имени Б. Е. Веденеева. Отдел патентов и научно-технической информации. Лаборатория динамики бетонных и железобетонных сооружений.

Naumchik, L I

Бурные потоки. Аннот. библиогр. указатель отечеств. и зарубежной литературы за 1967–1969 гг. Ленинград, "Энергия," Ленингр. отд-ние, 1970.

64 p. 20 cm.

At head of title: Министерство энергетики и электрификации СССР. Главтехстройпроект. Всесоюзный научно-исследовательский институт гидротехники имени Б. Е. Веденеева. Отдел патентов и научно-технической информации.

Naumchik, L   I

Гидравлические лабораторные исследования. (Гидравл. лаборатории, моделирование и измерит. техника). Аннот. библиогр. указатель отечеств. и зарубежной литературы за 1965–1969 (I пол.) гг. [Сост. Наумчик Л. И.] Ленинград, "Энергия," Ленингр. отд-ние, 1970.

172 p. 20 cm.

At head of title: Министерство энергетики и электрификации СССР. Главтехстройпроект. Всесоюзный научно-исследовательский институт гидротехники имени Б. Е. Веденеева. Отдел патентов и научно-технической информации.

Nencetti, Gianfranco.

Flusso bifase gas-liquido in equicorrente. Rassegna degli studi svolti sulla fluodinamica del sistema. [Di] G. F. Nencetti [e] S. Zanelli. Pisa, Editrice tecnico scientifica, 1967.

xiii, 63, 4 p. 33 cm.

At head of title: Università degli studi di Pisa. Istituto di chimica industriale e applicata, Facoltà di ingegneria.

(Novosti tekhnicheskoĭ literatury. Stroitel'stvo i arkhitektura. Razdel A. Serifa VII: Vodokhozĭaĭstvennoe stroitel'stvo)

Новости технической литературы. Строительство и архитектура. Раздел А. Серия VII: Водохозяйственное строительство.

Москва, Центр. ин-т науч. информации по строительству и архитектуре.

v. 22 cm. 12 no. a year.

"Библиографическая информация."

Issues for   prepared by Informafsionno-bibliograficheskiĭ otdel of TSNTB po stroitel'stvu i arkhitekture.

Perovskaĭa, Elena Pavlovna.

Противодавление воды в бетоне гидротехнических сооружений. Исследования и методика расчета. Информация по материалам отечеств. и зарубежной литературы. Ленинград, "Энергия," Ленингр. отд-ние, 1968.

88 p. 20 cm.

At head of title: Министерство энергетики и электрификации СССР. Главтехстройпроект. Всесоюзный научно-исследовательский институт гидротехники имени Б. Е. Веденеева. Отдел научно-технической информации. Отдел бетонных и железобетонных конструкций гидросооружений.

Round, George Frederick, 1932–

Solid-liquid flow abstracts. Compiled by G. F. Round. New York, Gordon and Breach [1969]

3 v. (1046 p.) 23 cm.

A collection of abstracts of works published between 1885 and 1965.

Contents.—v. 1. A.–J.—v. 2. K–Z.—v. 3. Indexes and supplements.

Shufertova, N   N

Пульсация гидродинамических нагрузок, действующих на элементы проточной части гидроблоков ГЭС. Информ. справка. Отечеств. и зарубежная литература ... Ленинград, "Энергия," Ленингр. отд-ние, 1967.

25 p. 20 cm.

At head of title: Министерство энергетики и электрификации СССР. Главтехстройпроект. Всесоюзный научно-исследовательский институт гидротехники имени Б. Е. Веденеева. Отдел научно-технической информации.

Thornton, Wendy A

The hydraulic transport of solids in pipes: a bibliography [by] Wendy A. Thornton. Cranfield (Bedford), British Hydromechanics Research Association, 1970.

[10], 137 p. illus. 31 cm.

Volovik, M   S

Динамическая гидроупругость элементов гидросооружений. Информ. материалы за 1963–1966 гг. [Сост. Воловик М. С.] [Москва], "Энергия," [1968].

29 p. 20 cm.

At head of title: Министерство энергетики и электрификации. Главтехстройпроект. Всесоюзный научно-исследовательский институт гидротехники им. Б. Е. Веденеева. Отдел научно-технической информации.

Voronkova, É   M

(Ekspluatatsiĭa gidrotekhnicheskikh sooruzhenii v zimnikh usloviĭakh)

Эксплуатация гидротехнических сооружений в зимних условиях. Библиогр. указ. отеч. и зарубеж. литературы за 1967–1971 гг. [Сост. Э. М. Воронкова]. Ленинград, 1972.

108 p. 20 cm.

At head of title: Министерство энергетики и электрификации СССР. Главниипроект. Всесоюзный научно-исследовательский институт гидротехники имени Б. Е. Веденеева. Отдел патентов и научно-технической информации.

Zrínyi, József.

A vízgazdálkodási tudományos kutatás 15 éve; a Vízgazdálkodási Tudományos Kutató Intézet 1952–1966 évek alatt végzett kutatásainak jegyzéke. Összeállította: Zrínyi József. A feldolgozásban résztvettek: Bolgár László [et al.] Budapest [Vízgazdálkodási Tudományos Kutató Intézet] 1968.

203 p. 29 cm.

HYDRO-ELECTRIC PLANTS   see   Water-power electric plants

HYDROLOGY

see also   Meteorology; Water

Bhabha Atomic Research Centre. Desalination and Effluent Engineering Division.

A bibliography on hydrological considerations in i) water resources for agriculture ii) ground disposal of radioactive wastes. Bombay, 1971.

xi, 329, xxxi p. 29 cm.

At head of title: Govt. of India, Atomic Energy Commission.

Bulletin signalétique 226: Hydrologie, géologie de l'ingénieur, formations superficielles. v. 33–
1972–
Paris, Centre national de la recherche scientifique, Centre de documentation.

v. 30 cm. monthly.

"Bibliographie des sciences de la terre. Cahier G."

Formerly issued as sections of Bulletin signalétique 214, and Bulletin signalétique 216, and continues their numbering.

Vols. for 1972–   issued with the Bureau de recherches géologiques et minières.

Absorbed Bibliographie des sciences de la terre. Cahier G: Hydrogéologie et géologie de l'ingénieur, 1972.

Henning, Ingrid.

Bibliographie hydrologischer Karten von Deutschland. Zusammengestellt im Auftrage der Arbeitsgruppe "Hydrologische Karten" des Deutschen Ausschusses für die Internationale Hydrologische Dekade. Bearb. von Ingrid Henning. Mit einem Vorwort von R. Keller. Bad Godesberg, Bundesforschungsanstalt für Landeskunde und Raumordnung, 1969.

135 p. 28 cm. (Bibliotheca cartographica. Sonderheft 3)

Minnesota. University. Water Resources Research Center.

Publications related to Water Resources Research Center projects, 1965–71; abstract—index. Minneapolis, 1971.

59 p. 23 cm. (WRRC bulletin 32)

National Research Council, Canada. Subcommittee on Hydrology.
Selected bibliography of hydrology for the years 1962 to 1964, annotated. Ottawa, 1966.

viii, 77 p. 21 cm.

At head of title: International Council of Scientific Unions, International Union of Geodesy and Geophysics, International Association of Scientific Hydrology.

Schlunz, Thomas P
An annotated bibliography of observations on Illinois water resources. 1673–1850 ₍by₎ Thomas P. Schlunz, Robert M. Sutton ₍and₎ George W. White. Urbana, University of Illinois. Water Resources Center, 1967.

xiv, 77 l. 29 cm. (WRC research report no. 12)
"Final report; project no. A-017-Ill: Evaluation of water resources development in Illinois, February 1, 1966–August 31, 1967."

Sharpe, Jane.
Bibliography of Murray Valley hydrology, 1946–1967. ₍Melbourne?₎ Commonwealth Scientific and Industrial Research Organization, 1969.

117 p. 30 cm.

Stasseyns-Vastiau, Maria.
De hydrologie van België. L'hydrologie de la Belgique. Brussel, Belgische Commissie voor Bibliografie, 1964.

2 v. (xxxiv, 776 p.) 21 cm. (Bibliographia Belgica, 81)

United States. Geological Survey.
Bibliography of U. S. Geological Survey water-resources reports for Arizona, May 1965 through June 1971. Phoenix, 1972.

iii, 60 p. 28 cm. (Arizona. Water Commission. Bulletin 2)

Walton, William Clarence.
Lists of references and selected books bearing on water resources in Minnesota. Prepared by William C. Walton, director. Rev. Minneapolis, Water Resources Research Center, University of Minnesota, 1972.

ii, 75 p. 23 cm. (University of Minnesota. Water Resources Research Center. WRRC bulletin 4)

Warsaw. Państwowy Instytut Hydrologiczno-Meteorologiczny.
Katalog publikacji PIHM, 1946–1968. ₍Wyd. 1.₎ Warszawa, Wydawnictwa Komunikacji i Łączności, 1969.

46 p. 20 cm.

Water Resources Scientific Information Center.
Aerial remote sensing; a bibliography. Edited by Donald B. Stafford. Washington; ₍available from the National Technical Information Service, Springfield, Va.₎ 1973.

iv, 482 p. 27 cm. (Its Bibliography series, WRSIC 73-211)

PERIODICALS

Österreichischer Wasserwirtschaftsverband. *Bücherei.*
Verzeichnis der Zeitschriften und Schriftenreihen der Bücherei des Österreichischen Wasserwirtschaftsverbandes. ⟨Stand vom Dez. 1965.⟩ ₍Wien, Österreichischer Wasserwirtschaftsverband, 1966.₎

2 l. 21 cm.

HYDROMETALLURGY

Nagy, Gusztáv.
Baktériumok a hidrometallurgiában (biometallurgia); annotált bibliográfia. Miskolc, 1971.

70 p. 21 cm. (A Nehézipari Müszaki Egyetem Központi Könyvtárának kiadványai, 13)

HYGIENE
see also Mental health; Public health

Fox, Gertrude W
Design of clean rooms, a classified list of selected references, 1955–1964. Compiled by Gertrude W. Fox. Bethesda, Md., U. S. Dept. of Health, Education, and Welfare. Public Health Service, National Institutes of Health, Division Research Services; ₍for sale by the Superintendent of Documents, U. S. Govt. Print. Off.₎ 1964.

v, 15 p. 24 cm. (Public Health Service publication no. 1219. Public health bibliography series, no. 54)

Kiel. Universität. *Hygiene-Institut.*
Arbeiten aus dem Hygiene-Institut der Christian-Albrechts-Universität in Kiel, 1957–1967. Kiel (Univ., Hygiene-Inst.) 1968.

49 p. 21 cm.

Moscow. Publichnaîa biblioteka.
Происхождение человека. Жизнь человеческого организма. Указатель научно-популярной лит-ры. ₍Составитель Г. Н. Белавенцева₎ Москва, Книга, 1967.

37 p. illus. 17 cm.

At head of title: Государственная библиотека СССР имени В. И. Ленина. Государственная центральная научная медицинская библиотека Минздрава СССР.

New Zealand. *Education Dept.*
Health resource list: a bibliography to accompany Health: suggestions for health education in primary schools. Wellington, Dept. of Education, 1969.

32 p. 21 cm.

STUDY AND TEACHING see Health education

HYMA, ALBERT

DeMolen, Richard L
Albert Hyma; bibliography and biographical sketch, by Richard L. DeMolen and Kenneth A. Strand. Ann Arbor, Mich., Ann Arbor Publishers ₍1964₎

40 p. port. 22 cm.

"Adapted and revised from the foreword, appendix B, and the supplement to appendix B in The dawn of modern civilization; studies in Renaissance, Reformation and other topics presented to honor Albert Hyma ₍2d ed., 1964₎"

HYMNS

Becker, Carl Ferdinand, 1804–1877.
Die Choralsammlungen der verschiedenen christlichen Kirchen. Hildesheim, H. A. Gerstenberg, 1972.

vi, 220 p. 22 cm.

Reprint of the Leipzig, 1845 ed.

Revitt, Paul Joseph, 1922–
The George Pullen Jackson collection of southern hymnody, a bibliography. Compiled, with an introd. by Paul J. Revitt. Los Angeles, University of California Library, 1964.

26 p. 28 cm. (UCLA Library occasional papers, no. 13)

Shaw, John MacKay.
The poetry of sacred song; a short-title list supplementing Childhood in poetry—a catalogue. Tallahassee, Friends of the Library, Florida State University, 1972.

18 l. 29 cm.

Additions to the Shaw Childhood in Poetry Collection in the Library of the Florida State University.

Warrington, James.
Short titles of books, relating to or illustrating the history and practice of psalmody in the United States, 1620–

1820. Theodore M. Finney, editor. Philadelphia, Priv. print., 1898. Pittsburgh, Clifford E. Barbour Library ₁1970₁

96 p. 23 cm. (Bibliographia tripotamopolitana, no. 1)

Title on cover and spine: Psalmody short titles.

Warrington, James.
Short titles of books relating to or illustrating the history and practice of psalmody in the United States, 1620–1820. New York, B. Franklin ₁1971₁

96 p. 23 cm. (Burt Franklin bibliography and reference series, 438) (American classics in history and social science, 218)

Reprint of the 1898 ed.

Wofford College, Spartanburg, S. C. Library.
Hymns & hymnody. Compiled and edited by Frank J. Anderson. Spartanburg, Wofford Library Press, 1970.

25 l. 28 cm. (Wofford College Library. Special collections checklists, no. 1)

BIO-BIBLIOGRAPHY

Fischer, Albert Friedrich Wilhelm, 1829–1896.
Kirchenliederlexikon. Hymnologisch-literarische Nachweisungen über ca. 4500 der wichtigsten und verbreitetsten Kirchenlieder aller Zeiten in alphabetischer Folge nebst einer Übersicht der Liederdichter ₁von₁ A. F. W. Fischer. (Reprografischer Nachdruck der Ausg. Gotha 1878.) Hildesheim, Gg Olms, 1967.

2 v. in 1. 25 cm.

Richter, Gottfried Lebrecht, d. 1813.
Allgemeines biographisches Lexikon alter und neuer geistlicher Liederdichter. Leipzig: Martini 1804. (Unveränd. fotomech. Nachdr.) (Leipzig, Zentralantiquariat der Deutschen Demokratischen Republik, 1970.)

viii, 487 p. 21 cm.

HYMNS, LATIN

Blume, Clemens, 1862–1932.
Repertorium repertorii; kritischer Wegweiser durch Ulysse Chevaliers Repertorium hymnologicum. Alphabetisches Register falscher, mangelhafter oder irreleitender Hymnenanfänge und Nachweise mit Erörterung über Plan und Methode des Repertoriums. Hrsg. von Clemens Blume. Hildesheim, New York, G. Olms, 1971.

315 p. 22 cm.

Reprint of the Leipzig, 1901 ed., which was issued as Bd. 2 of Hymnologische Beiträge; Quellen und Forschungen zur Geschichte der lateinischen Hymnendichtung.

Mearns, James.
Early Latin hymnaries; an index of hymns in hymnaries before 1100. With an appendix from later sources. Hildesheim, New York, G. Olms, 1970.

xx, 107 p. facsim. 22 cm.

Reprint of Cambridge University Press, 1913 ed.

I

ÎACHEVSKIĬ, ARTUR ARTUROVICH

Akademiîâ nauk SSSR.
Артур Артурович Ячевский. Вступ. статья Л. С. Гитман и М. В. Горленко. Библиография составлена Л. С. Гитман. Москва, Наука, 1964.

118 p. port. 17 cm. (Материалы к биобиблиографии ученых СССР. Серия биологических наук: Ботаника, вып. 7)

ÎAKIR, IONA ÉMMANUILOVICH

Kozhukhar', P   M
Иона Эммануилович Якир, 1896–1937; биобиблиографический указатель. Составитель П. М. Кожухарь. Под ред. А. С. Есауленко. Кишинев, Картя молдовеняскэ, 1967.

50 p. 17 cm.
At head of title: Государственная республиканская библиотека МССР им. Н. К. Крупской.
Added t. p. in Moldavian.
Moldavian and Russian.

ÎAKOVLEV, NIKOLAĬ NIKOLAEVICH

Arendt, Ĭûriĭ Andreevich.
Николай Николаевич Яковлев, 1870–1966. Вступ. статья Ю. А. Арендта. Библиография составлена Ю. А. Арендтом и Р. И. Горячевой. Москва, Наука, 1967.

90 p. port. 17 cm. (Материалы к биобиблиографии ученых СССР. Серия биологических наук: Палеонтология, вып. 2) 0.20 (pbk.)
At head of title: Академия наук СССР.

ÎAKUBOV, AKHAD ALEKPER OGLY

Alieva, É   A
А. А. Якубов. Библиография. Баку, Изд. АН АзССР, 1968.

86 p. 16 cm. (Академия наук Азербайджанской ССР. Фундаментальная библиотека. Деятели науки и культуры Азербайджана)

Added t. p. in Azerbaijani.

IANOVICI, VIRGIL

Virgil Ianovici. Bio-bibliografie. București, 1971.

xvii, 75 p. 21 cm.

At head of title: Biblioteca Centrală Universitară București.
"Lucrare executată în cadrul Sectorului de Documentare Universitară."

ÎANSHIN, ALEKSANDR LEONIDOVICH

Garetskiĭ, Radim Gavrilovich.
[Aleksandr Leonidovich Îanshin]
Александр Леонидович Яншин. Вступит. статья Р. Г. Гарецкого. Библиогр. сост. Р. Г. Гарецким и Г. Н. Финашиной. Москва, "Наука," 1972.

88 p. port. 16 cm. (Материалы к библиографии ученых СССР. Серия геологических наук, вып. 23)

At head of title: Академия наук СССР.

IAȘI, ROMANIA

Biblioteca Municipală Gheorghe Asachi.
Dezvoltarea economiei județului Iași. 1944–1969. [Cuvînt înainte de prof. dr. Mihai Todosia]. Iași, 1970.

347 p. 24 cm. (Contribuții la bibliografia județului Iași) lei

ÎATSIMIRSKIĬ, ALEKSANDR IVANOVICH

Kidel', A   S
Александр Иванович Яцимирский; биобиблиография. [Составител. А. С. Кидель] Кишинев, Редакционно-издательский отдел Академии наук Молдавской ССР, 1967.

39, [1] p. 21 cm.
At head of title: Академия наук Молдавской ССР. Центральная научная библиотека.

IBN AL-JAWZĪ, ABŪ AL-FARAJ 'ABD AL-RAḤMĀN IBN 'ALĪ

al-'Alwajī, 'Abd al-Ḥamīd.
مؤلفات ابن الجوزى، تأليف عبد الحميد العلوجى، بغداد،
دار الجمهورية للنشر والطبع، 1965.

290 p. 23 cm.

(وزارة الثقافة والارشاد. مديرية الثقافة العامة. سلسلة الكتب الحديثة 9)

IBSEN, HENRIK

Firkins, Ina Ten Eyck, 1866–1937.
Henrik Ibsen; a bibliography of criticism and biography, with an index to characters. [Folcroft, Pa.] Folcroft Library Editions, 1972.

80 p. 23 cm.

Reprint of the 1921 ed., issued in series: Practical bibliographies.
"Limited to 150 copies."

ICE
see also Glaciers

Bolsenga, S   J
River ice jams; a literature review, by S. J. Bolsenga. [Detroit] Great Lakes Research Center, U. S. Lake Survey, 1968.

iii, 568 p. illus. 27 cm. (U. S. Lake Survey. Research report 5–5)

Cavan, Bruce P
A literature review of dusting technology in deicing, by Bruce P. Cavan. [Detroit] Great Lakes Research Center, 1969.

15, 6, 23 p. illus., maps (1 fold.) 27 cm. (U. S. Lake Survey. Research report 5–7)

ICE CREAM INDUSTRY

U. S. Small Business Administration.
Soft frozen dessert stands. [Rev. 1970] Washington [1971]

11 p. 27 cm. (Its Small business bibliography no. 47)

ICELAND

Mindegave om Carl Christian Rafn fra Landsbókasafn Íslands til Odense universitetsbibliotek i anledning af Landsbókasafns 150 års jubilæum den 28. august 1968.
Reykjavík; (Odense. Odense universitetsbibliotek) 1968.

19 p. 26 cm.

ICELANDIC AND OLD NORSE STUDIES

Bekker-Nielsen, Hans.
Old Norse-Icelandic studies; a select bibliography, com-

piled by Hans Bekker-Nielsen ₍Toronto₎ University of Toronto Press ₍1967₎

94 p. 21½ cm.

ICONOGRAPHY

Petzoldt, Leander.
Bibliographie zur Ikonographie und materiellen Kultur des Wallfahrtswesens ₍von₎ Leander Petzoldt unter Mitarbeit von Heinz Plempe. Freiburg i. Br., 1972.

viii, 88 p. 21 cm.

IDAHO

Idaho. State Library, *Boise.*
Idaho, the Gem State: a bibliography of books about Idaho and by Idaho authors. Selected by Mildred Selby and Rose Coventry. Boise, 1966.

'30 p. 28 cm.

Bibliography of books found in the State Library.

Weatherby, James Benjamin.
Selected bibliography on politics and government in Idaho, by James B. Weatherby. ₍Moscow₎ Bureau of Public Affairs Research, University of Idaho, 1972.

v, 24 p. 28 cm.

IEPER see Ypres

IEVIŅŠ, ALFRĒDS

Allena, Veronika.
Akadēmiķis Alfrēds Ieviņš; biobibliogrāfija. ₍Sastādītājas: V. Allena un V. Lūkina. Biogrāfisko apcerējumu sarakstījusi J. Švarce₎ Rīgā, Zinātne, 1967.

88 p. port. 21 cm. (Padomju Latvijas zinātnieki)

At head of title: Latvijas PSR Zinātņu akadēmija. Fundamentālā bibliotēka.
Added t. p. in Russian.
Latvian and Russian.

IFUGAO, PHILIPPINE ISLANDS

Conklin, Harold C
Ifugao bibliography ₍by₎ Harold C. Conklin. ₍New Haven, Dept. of Anthropology and the Council on Southeast Asia Studies, Yale University 1968₎

vi, 75 p. 23 cm. (Southeast Asia Studies, Yale University. Bibliography series, no. 11)

ILLEGITIMACY

Minnesota. *Division of Child Welfare.*
Bibliography: unmarried parenthood. Prepared by: Division of Child Welfare and Dept. of Public Welfare Library. St. Paul, Minnesota Dept. of Public Welfare, 1969.

14 l. 28 cm.

ILLINOIS

Buck, Solon Justus, 1884-1962.
Travel and description, 1765-1865, together with a list of county histories, atlases, and biographical collections and a list of territorial and State laws. New York, B. Franklin ₍1971₎

xi, 514 p. port. 22 cm. (American classics in history and social science, 207) (Burt Franklin research and source works series, 827)

Reprint of the 1914 ed., issued in series: Collections of the Illinois State Historical Library, v. 9. Bibliographical series, v. 2.

Byrd, Cecil K
A bibliography of Illinois imprints, 1814-58, by Cecil K. Byrd. Chicago, University of Chicago Press ₍1966₎

xxv, 601 p. 26 cm.

Hinman, Dorothy.
Reading for boys and girls: Illinois; a subject index and annotated bibliography ₍by₎ Dorothy Hinman and Ruth Zimmerman, for the Illinois State Library. Chicago, American Library Association, 1970.

vi, 128 p. 21 cm.

Illinois documents list. Mar. 15, 1971–

Springfield, Illinois State Library, Documents Unit.

v. 28 cm. semimonthly.

Supersedes Illinois state documents shipping list.

Illinois State documents shipping list.

–Feb. 28, 1971. Springfield, Illinois State Library, Documents Unit.

v. 28 cm. semimonthly.

Superseded by Illinois documents list.

Stillwell, Charlotte B
The constitution of Illinois: a selective bibliography. Compiled by Charlotte B. Stillwell and Stanley E. Adams. Springfield, Illinois State Library, 1970.

171 p. 28 cm.

Tolva, Donald E
Bibliography; a basic bibliography for study of the Illinois Constitution. Springfield, 1966.

37 l. 28 cm.

At head of title: State of Illinois, Constitution Study Commission. (Created by House bill no. 1011, Seventy-fourth General Assembly, approved August 17, 1965)

U. S. *Library of Congress.*
Illinois: the sesquicentennial of statehood; an exhibition in the Library of Congress, Washington, D. C., December 3, 1968, to October 31, 1969. Washington; ₍For sale by the Supt. of Docs., U. S. Govt. Print. Off.₎ 1968.

viii, 58 p. illus., facsims., maps, ports. 26 cm. (*Its* ₍State exhibition catalogs₎ 23)

ILLITERACY see Education of adults

ILLUMINATED BOOKS AND MANUSCRIPTS

LIBRARY AND EXHIBITION CATALOGS

Alexander, Jonathan James Graham.
English illuminated manuscripts 700–1500; catalogue by J. J. G. Alexander and C. M. Kauffmann. Bruxelles, Bibliothèque Royale Albert Ier; supplied by Worldwide Books, Boston, 1973.

120 p. facsims. 26 cm.

Catalog of an exhibition held 29 Sept.–10 Nov., 1973 at the Bibliotheque Royale Albert Ier, Brussels.

Binney, Edwin.
Turkish miniature paintings and manuscripts from the collection of Edwin Binney, 3rd, by Edwin Binney, 3rd. ₍New York₎ The Metropolitan Museum of Art ₍1973₎

139 p. illus. 22 cm.

Catalog of an exhibition held in the Metropolitan Museum of Art, New York and the Los Angeles County Museum of Art.

Binyon, Laurence, 1869-1943.
Persian miniature painting, including a critical and descriptive catalogue of the miniatures exhibited at Burlington House, January-March, 1931, by Laurence Binyon, J. V. S. Wilkinson and Basil Gray. New York, Dover Publications ₍1971₎

xiv, 212 p. 225 illus. (part col.) 24 cm.

Reprint of the 1933 ed.

Brounts, Albert.

La miniature hollandaise. Le grand siècle de l'enluminure du livre dans les Pays-Bas septentrionaux. (Exposition organisée dans le cadre du festival Europalia 71 et à l'occasion du vingt-cinquième anniversaire de l'accord culturel belgo-néerlandais. Bruxelles, Bibliothèque royale Albert Ier, 18 septembre–15 octobre 1971). Catalogue (rédigé par Albert Brounts). (Traduit en français par Cl[audine] Lemaire). Bruxelles, Bibliothèque royale Albert Ier, [bd de l'Empereur, 4], 1971.

vii, 93 p. illus., facsims. 26 cm. (Catalogues des expositions organisées à la Bibliothèque royale Albert Ier à Bruxelles)

"Table des ektachromes exposés": [2] p. inserted.
Translation of Noordnederlandse miniaturen.

Brounts, Albert.

Noordnederlandse miniaturen. De gouden eeuw der boekverluchting in de Noordelijke Nederlanden. (Tentoonstelling georganiseerd in het kader van Europalia '71 en van de viering van het 25-jarig bestaan van het Belgisch-Nederlands cultureel akkord. Brussel, Koninklijke Bibliotheek Albert I, 18 september–16 oktober 1971). Catalogus [samengesteld door] Albert Brounts). Brussel, Koninklijke Bibliotheek Albert I, [Keizerslaan 4] 1971.

vii, 97 p. illus., facsims. 26 cm.
"Lijst van tentoongestelde ektachromen": [2] p. inserted.
Issued also under title: La miniature hollandaise.

Brussels. Bibliothèque royale de Belgique.

La librairie de Philippe le Bon. Exposition organisée à l'occasion du 500e anniversaire de la mort du duc. (Bibliothèque Albert Ier, Bruxelles, 9 septembre–12 novembre 1967). Catalogue rédigé par Georges Dogaer et Marguerite Debae. Bruxelles, [Bibliothèque royale de Belgique], 1967.

vi, 167 p. illus., facsims. 26 cm. (Its Catalogues des expositions organisées à la Bibliothèque Albert Ier à Bruxelles. Catalogue no 26)

Brussels. Bibliothèque royale de Belgique. Section des manuscrits.

La librairie de Bourgogne et quelques acquisitions récentes de la Bibliothèque royale Albert Ier. (Introduction: Léon Gilissen. Notices rédigées par Marguerite Debae, Marianne Dewèvre, Anne Rouzet). Cinquante miniatures. (Bruxelles), Cultura, (bd de l'Empereur, 4), (1970).

52 p. of text and 50 plates (illus., facsims.) 31 cm. (L'Art en Belgique, 10)

Caleca, Antonino.

Miniatura in Umbria ... Firenze, Marchi & Bertolli, 1969–

v. plates. 24 cm. (Raccolta pisana di saggi e studi, 27)

CONTENTS.—1. La Biblioteca capitolare di Perugia.

Chanashian, Mesrop.

Armenian miniature paintings of the Monastic Library at San Lazzaro [by Mesrop Janashian. English version of the text by Bernard Grebanier] Venice [Casa editrice armena, 1966–

v. col. plates. 45 cm.
At head of title: Oriental art.
Foreword, by Sirarpie Der Nersessian: v. 1, p. 1–4.
Vol. 1 covers 13 mss, dating from the 9th to the 13th century.

Daneu Lattanzi, Angela.

Italiaanse miniaturen van de 10de tot de 16de eeuw. (Tentoonstelling ingericht in het kader van het Europalia-Festival 1969 ... met medewerking van het Italiaans Ministerie van Openbaar Onderwijs. Brussel, Koninklijke Bibliotheek Albert I, 16 september–19 oktober 1969). Catalogus door Angela Daneu Lattanzi en Marguerite Debae. Inleiding door Mario Salmi. Brussel, Koninklijke Bibliotheek Albert I [Keizerslaan 4] 1969.

viii, 93 p. illus., facsims. 26 cm. (Catalogi van tentoonstellingen gehouden in de Koninklijke Bibliotheek Albert I te Brussel. Reeks A, nr. 38)

Issued also under title: La miniature italienne du xe au xvie siècle.

Daneu Lattanzi, Angela.

La miniature italienne du Xe au XVIe siècle. (Exposition organisée dans le cadre du festival "Europalia 69" ... avec la colaboration du Ministère de l'Instruction publique d'Italie. Due 16 septembre au 19 octobre 1969). Catalogue par Angela Daneu Lattanzi et Marguerite Debae. Introduction de Mario Salmi. Bruxelles, Bibliothèque royale Albert Ier, [bd de l'Empereur, 4], 1969.

viii, 93 p. facsims. 25 cm. ([Catalogues des expositions organisées à la Bibliothèque Albert Ier à Bruxelles] Série A, catalogue no 38)

Dartmouth College. Library.

Illuminated manuscripts in the Dartmouth College Library. Compiled by Georgia G. Cook [and others] Edited by Robert L. McGrath. Hanover, N. H., 1972.

85 p. illus. 29 cm.

Der Nersessian, Sirarpie.

Armenian manuscripts in the Walters Art Gallery. Baltimore, The Trustees, 1973.

x, 111 p., 243 p. of illus. 8 col. plates. 39 cm.

Erlangen. Universität. Bibliothek.

Die Bilderhandschriften der Universitätsbibliothek Erlangen. Beschrieben von Eberhard Lutze. Neubearb. Unveränd. Nachdr. [d. Ausg.] Erlangen, Universitätsbibliothek, 1936. (Mit 166 Abb. u. 16 Taf.) Wiesbaden, Harrassowitz, 1971.

xx, 285 p., 16 p. of illus. 25 cm. (Katalog der Handschriften der Universitätsbibliothek Erlangen, Bd. 6, [T. 1])

Illuminated Greek manuscripts from American collections; an exhibition in honor of Kurt Weitzmann. Edited by Gary Vikan. [Princeton, N.J.] Art Museum, Princeton University; distributed by Princeton University Press [1973]

231 p. illus. (part col.) 27 cm.
Catalog of an exhibition held at the Princeton University Art Museum Apr. 14-May 20, 1973.

Istanbul. Topkapı Sarayı Müzesi. Minyatür Bölümü.

XII.-XVII. [i. e. On ikinci-on yedinci] yüzyıllar arasında minyatür sanatından örnekler; Topkapı Sarayı Minyatür Bölümü rehberi. [Yazan: Filiz Öğütmen. Ankara, Güzel Sanatlar Matbaası, 1966]

48 p. col. illus. 17 cm.

Levi d'Ancona, Mirella.

The Wildenstein Collection of illuminations. The Lombard school. With a preface by Bernard Berenson. Firenze, L. S. Olschki, 1970.

xii, 179 p. illus., 28 plates. 29 cm. (Storia della miniatura. Studi e documenti, 4)

Milan. Biblioteca Ambrosiana.

Inventario dei codici decorati e miniati (secc. VII–XIII) della Biblioteca Ambrosiana. [A cura di] Maria Luisa Gengaro [e] Gemma Villa Guglielmetti. Firenze, L. S. Olschki, 1968.

xvi, 147 p. 42 plates (1 mounted) 29 cm. (Storia della miniatura. Studi e documenti, 3)

Miniatures arméniennes. Bibliothèques des Pères mékhitharistes de Saint-Lazare. Venise, impr. Arménienne, 1966–

v. col. plates. 45 cm.
At head of title: Art oriental.

Oxford. University. Bodleian Library.
Anglo-Saxon illumination in Oxford libraries. Oxford, Bodleian Library, 1970.

16, [36] p. illus., facsims. 24 cm. (Bodleian picture books. Special series, no. 1)

Paris. Bibliothèque nationale.
La Librairie de Charles v, Paris, [octobre-décembre] 1968. [Catalogue par François Avril et Jean Lafaurie. Préface par Étienne Dennery. L'Enluminure parisienne à l'époque de Charles v, par Marcel Thomas.] Paris, Bibliothèque nationale, 1968.

xxii, 135 p. geneal. table, plates (part col.) 24 cm.

Paris. Bibliothèque nationale.
Du manuscrit carolingien au livre d'aujourd'hui, Nice, Galerie des Ponchettes, 1969. [Catalogue par Erwana Brin, Jacqueline Guilbaud et François Avril.] Paris, Bibliothèque nationale, 1969.

133 p. plates (part col.) 20 cm.

Pierpont Morgan Library, New York.
Mediaeval & Renaissance manuscripts. New York [1974]

xvi, 106 p. facsims. 30 cm. (Its Major acquisitions, 1924–1974)
Errata slip inserted.

Prague. Národní muzeum. Knihovna.
Iluminované nejkrásnější rukopisy Knihovny Národního muzea v Praze. [Katalog připravili Miloslav Bohatec et al. V Praze, 1965]

[72] p. illus. (part col.) 21 cm.

Robinson, Basil William.
The Persian art of the book: catalogue of an exhibition held at the Bodleian Library to mark the sixth International Congress of Iranian Art and Archaeology; compiled by B. W. Robinson and Basil Gray. Oxford, Bodleian Library, 1972.

35, [25] p. illus. (incl. 1 col.). 24 cm. index.

Sotheby, *firm, auctioneers, London.*
The Chester Beatty western manuscripts ... which will be sold by auction by Messrs. Sotheby & Co. [London, Messrs. Sotheby & Co.] 1968–

v. illus., plates (part col.), port. 29 cm.

CONTENTS.—pt. 1. Catalogue of thirty-seven illuminated manuscripts of the 9th to the 16th century.

Staatsbibliothek der Stiftung Preussischer Kulturbesitz.
Illuminierte islamische Handschriften. Beschrieben von Ivan Stchoukine [et al.] Wiesbaden, F. Steiner, 1971.

vii, 340 p. 54 plates (part col.) 29 cm. (Verzeichnis der orientalischen Handschriften in Deutschland, Bd. 16)

Le Tétraévangile de la Laurentienne, Florence, Laur. VI. 23 [par] Tania Velmans. Préf. par André Grabar. Paris, Klincksieck, 1971.

51, [09] p. plates. 82 cm. (Bibliothèque des cahiers archéologiques, 6)

ILLUMINATION see Lighting

ILLUSTRATED BOOKS
see also Illuminated books and manuscripts

Alderson, Brian W
Edward Ardizzone, a preliminary hand-list of his illustrated books, 1929–1970 [by] Brian Alderson. Pinner, Private Libraries Association, 1972.

[1], 64 p. illus. 22 cm.

Atanasov, Petŭr.
25 години Българска илюстрация на книгата. 1944–1969. Библиогр. (София) Нар. библ. Кирил и Методий (1970).

228 p. 20 cm.

Javůrek, Josef.
Československé nejkrásnější knihy 1965; [soutěž]. Самые красивые книги Чехословакии. Les plus beaux livres de la Tchécoslovaquie. The most beautiful books of Czechoslovakia. Die tschechoslowakischen schönsten Bücher. [Sest. a redigoval Josef Javůrek. Úvod napsal Pravoslav Kneidl. Praha, Československé ústředí knižní kultury, 1966]

46 p. illus. (part col.) 21 cm.
Summary in English, French, German, and Russian.

Lecuire, Pierre, 1922–
Livres de Pierre Lecuire; catalogue. [Paris, Éditions des livres de Pierre Lecuire, 1969]

20 p. 33 cm.

"This catalogue ... will be brought up to date regularly."

Lewine, J
Bibliography of eighteenth century art and illustrated books. Being a guide to collectors of illustrated works in English and French of the period. [By] J. Lewine. Amsterdam, G. W. Hissink, 1969.

615 p. with photos. 23 cm.
Photomechanical reprint of the London, 1898 ed.

Muther, Richard, 1860-1909.
German book illustration of the Gothic period and the early Renaissance (1460-1530). Translated by Ralph R. Shaw. Metuchen, N.J., Scarecrow Press, 1972.

xxii, 566 p. facsims. 28 cm.
Translation of Die deutsche Bücherillustration der Gothik und Frührenaissance (1460-1530).

Rava, Carlo Enrico.
Supplément à Max Sander, Le livre à figures italien de la Renaissance. Milan, U. Hoepli, 1969.

xxxiii, 314 p., incl. 60 plates. 31¼ cm.

Tooley, Ronald Vere, 1898–
English books with coloured plates, 1790 to 1860; a bibliographical account of the most important books illustrated by English artist in colour aquatint and colour lithography. [by] R. V. Tooley. Folkestone, Dawsons, 1973.

vii, 424 p. 26 cm.

Distributed in U. S. A. by Harper & Row Publishers, Barnes & Noble Import Division.
First ed. published in 1935 under title: Some English books with coloured plates.

LIBRARY AND EXHIBITION CATALOGS

Baltimore. Museum of Art.
French illustrated books of the 19th and 20th century: [exhibition] the Baltimore Museum of Art, October 15 through January 14. Baltimore [1967?]

[24] p. illus. 22 cm.

Bienále ilustrácií, 3d, Bratislava, 1971.
Bienále ilustrácií, Bratislava 1971; Dom umenia Bratislava. september-október. La Biennale d'illustrations, Bratislava 1971; La Maison de la culture Bratislava, septembre-octobre. [Príprava a redakcia katalógu: Anna Urblíková, Eva Trojanová. Bratislava, Slovenská národna galéria] 1971.

1 v. (unpaged) 204 plates. 22 x 24 cm.
Slovak and French.

Biennale of Graphic Design, 5th, Brünn, 1972.
Mezinárodní výstava ilustrace a knižní grafiky; Moravská galerie v Brně. Exposition internationale de l'illustration et du graphisme du livre. ₍Katalog zprac. redakční kolektiv, vedouci ₍K. Holešovský. V Brně, Moravská galerie, 1972₎

326 p. illus. (part col.) 21 cm.
At head of title: Bienále užité grafiky Brno 1972.
Label mounted on jacket: Supplied by Worldwide Books, Inc., Boston, Mass.

Brooklyn Institute of Arts and Sciences. Museum.
A century of American illustration. ₍Brooklyn₎ Brooklyn Museum ₍1972₎

155 p. illus. 23 cm.

Catalog of the exhibition held Mar. 22-May 14, 1972 in the Brooklyn Museum.

Buch und Bild. Buchgrafik d. 20. Jahrhunderts. (Ausstellung, Kunstmuseum Düsseldorf, 28.2-19.4.1970. Katalogbearb.: Dieter Graf ₍u.₎ Friedrich W. Heckmanns. Vorw.: Wend von Kalnein. Einl.: Friedrich W. Heckmanns. ₍Ausstellungskatalog.₎) (Düsseldorf, Kunstmuseum, 1970.)

82 p. with illus. 20 x 21 cm.

Civica biblioteca di storia dell'arte L. Poletti.
Scelta di cinquecentine illustrate dalle raccolte della Biblioteca d'arte Luigi Poletti. A cura di Enrichetta Cecchi. Modena, Palazzo dei Musei, Sala Poletti, 19 febbraio-19 marzo 1972. Modena, Cooptip, ₍1972₎

₍30₎ l. illus. 24 cm.
At head of title: Comune di Modena. Civica biblioteca di storia dell'arte Luigi Poletti.

Cognac, France. Musée municipal.
Le Livre illustré, XVIᵉ-XXᵉ siècle. 17 janvier-9 mars 1970. ₍Catalogue par Pauline Reverchon.₎ Cognac, Musée municipal, 1970.

19 l. 30 cm.

Delaware Art Museum.
The golden age of American illustration, 1880-1914. ₍Catalog of the exhibition₎ September 14-October 15, 1972. ₍Wilmington, 1972₎

67 p. illus. 22 x 28 cm.

Deusch, Werner Richard, 1903–
Das Buch als Kunstwerk. Französische illustrierte. Bücher des 18. Jahrhunderts aus der Bibliothek Hans Fürstenberg. Ausstellung im Schloss Ludwigsburg, 15. Mai-20. Sept., 1965. (Katalog₍-Bearb.₎: Werner R. Deusch. 1.-3. Tsd. ₍Ausstellungskatalog.₎) (Stuttgart, Württembergische Landesbibliothek, Staatsgalerie, Deutsch-Französisches Institut, 1965.)

xv, 161 p. with 144 illus. and frontis. 24 cm.

Douai. Bibliothèque municipale.
Le Livre illustré, manuscrit et imprimé: du 8ᵉ au 20ᵉ siècle, exposition organisée à l'occasion de l'Année internationale du livre, 13 avril-24 juin 1972, Bibliothèque municipale de Douai. Douai (Nord), Bibliothèque municipale, 1972.

22 p. illus. 30 cm.

The Francis Williams bequest. an exhibition of illustrated books, 1967-1971. Selected by John Harthan ₍and others₎ London, National Book League ₍1972₎

51 p. illus. 21 cm.

"National Book League with the Victoria & Albert Museum, 111 March 9-April 23, 1972."

Garvey, Eleanor M
The turn of a century, 1885-1910; art nouveau-Jugendstil books. ₍Catalogue by Eleanor M. Garvey, Anne B. Smith, and Peter A. Wick. Cambridge₎ Dept. of Printing and Graphic Arts, Harvard University, 1970.

124 p. illus., facsims. 24 cm.

Exhibition held at Houghton Library.

Grenoble. Bibliothèque municipale.
Le Livre contemporain illustré par les peintres de l'École de Paris, exposition, Bibliothèque de Grenoble, novembre-décembre 1971, catalogue par P. ₍Pierre₎ Vaillant, ... Grenoble, Bibliothèque de Grenoble, 1971.

2, ₍6₎ p. 24 cm.

Henry Clay Frick Fine Arts Library.
An informal catalogue for an exhibition of eighty-six books selected from the Henry Clay Frick Fine Arts Library and held in memory of John Gabbert Bowman, 1879-1963 ₍i. e. 1877-1962₎, chancellor of the University of Pittsburgh, 1921-1945. Spring 1964. Pittsburgh, University of Pittsburgh ₍1964₎

52 p. illus., port. 28 cm.
On cover: None can see the limits of its reach. John Gabbert Bowman.
Introd. signed: Walter Read Hovey.

Illustrateurs des modes et manières en 1925. ₍Paris, Galerie du Luxembourg, 1972₎

75 p. illus. 25 cm.

Catalog of an exhibition held Oct. 25, 1972-Jan. 15, 1973.

John and Mable Ringling Museum of Art, Sarasota, Fla.
Twentieth century illustrated books; a selection of important contemporary illustrated books from a Sarasota private collection. ₍Exhibition₎ Ringling Museum of Art, October 2-22, 1967. ₍Sarasota, 1967₎

24 p. illus. 18 x 26 cm.

Lecuire, Pierre, 1922–
Livres de Pierre Lecuire. ₍Catalogue₎ Édité ... à l'occasion de l'exposition Livres de Pierre Lecuire au Centre national d'art contemporain ... du 26 janvier au 12 mars 1973. ₍Paris, Centre national d'art contemporain, 1973₎

80 p. illus. (part col.) 22 cm. (Archives de l'art contemporain, 22)

New York (City). Public Library. Spencer Collection.
Dictionary catalog and shelf list of the Spencer Collection of illustrated books and manuscripts and fine bindings. Boston, G. K. Hall, 1971.

2 v. 37 cm.

At head of title: The New York Public Library, Astor, Lenox & Tilden Foundations. The Research Libraries.

Princeton University. *Library.*
Early American book illustrators and wood engravers, 1670-1870; a catalogue of a collection of American books, illustrated for the most part with woodcuts and wood engravings, in the Princeton Library. With an introductory sketch of the development of early American book illustration by Sinclair Hamilton. With a foreword by Frank Weitenkampf. Princeton, N. J., Princeton University Press, 1968.

2 v. illus., facsims. (1 fold.) 29 cm.
Vol. 1 is a reprint of the 1958 ed.
CONTENTS.—v. 1. Main catalogue.—v. 2. Supplement.

ILLYRIA

Stipčević, Aleksandar.
Bibliographia illyrica. Urednik: Alojz Benac. Sarajevo, Akademija nauka i umjetnosti Bosne i Hercegovine, 1967.

420, ₂₁ p. 24 cm. (Akademija nauka i umjetnosti Bosne i Hercegovine. Posebna izdanja, knj. 6. Centar za balkanološka ispiti-
vanja, knj. 3)

Added t. p. in French.
Foreword also in German.

IMBAULT, JEAN JÉRÔME

Imbault, Jean Jérôme
Catalogue thématique des ouvrages de musique. Avec un
index des compositeurs cités. (Réimpr. de l'éd. de Paris,
ca. 1792.) Genève, Minkoff Reprint, 1972.

288 p. 23 cm.

IMITATIO CHRISTI

Backer, Augustin de, 1809–1873.
Essai bibliographique sur le livre De imitatione Christi.
Amsterdam, P. Schippers, 1966.

viii, 257 p. 23 cm.

Facsim. reproduction of the ed. published in Liège, 1864.

IMMIGRANT WORKERS   see   Alien labor

IMMIGRATION   see   Emigration and immigration

IMMUNOLOGY
see also Microbiology

Библиография болгарских трудов по иммунологии
размножения ⟨1948–1971⟩. ₁По случай II междунар.
симпозиум по имунология на размножаването, състоял
се на 13–16 септ. 1971 г.—Варна₁. ₁София, ЦНТИИСГС,
1971₁.
34 p. 21 cm.
At head of title: Второй международный симпозиум по иммy-
нологии размножения.

Dausset, Jean.
Titres et travaux scientifiques du Dʳ Jean Dausset ...
22 Châtelaudren, Impr. de Châtelaudren, 1968.

148 p. illus. 27 cm.

Gerber, Klaus.
Bibliographie der Arbeiten aus dem Robert Koch-Insti-
tut, 1891–1965. ₁Stuttgart, G. Fischer, 1966₁

274 p. 23 cm.

At head of title: Aus dem Bundesgesundheitsamt. Robert Koch-
Institut, Berlin. Leiter: Vizepräsident Direktor Prof. Dr. G. Henne-
berg.
"Sonderdruck aus 'Zentralblatt für Bakteriologie, Parasitenkunde,
Infektionskrankheiten und Hygiene, I. Abteilung Referate' Band 203."

IMSHENETSKIĬ, ALEKSANDR ALEKSANDROVICH

Zavarzin, G   A
Александр Александрович Имшенецкий. Вступ. статья
Г. А. Заварзина. Библиография составлена Л. М. Жуко-
вой. Москва, Наука, 1967.

82 p. port. 17 cm. (Материалы к биобиблиографии ученых
СССР. Серия биологических наук: Микробиология, вып. 3)

IN-SERVICE TRAINING   see   Employees, Training of

INCOME see Wealth

INCOME TAX

Owens, Elisabeth A
Bibliography on taxation of foreign operations and
foreigners, compiled by Elisabeth A. Owens. Cambridge,
Law School of Harvard University, 1968.

xx, 92 p. 23 cm.

On cover: Harvard Law School. International Tax Program.

Washington (State) State Library, *Olympia.*
State & local income taxation: a selective, annotated
bibliography with a separate section on Washington State.
₁Olympia, 1967₁

10 l. 28 cm.

White, Anthony G
Municipal income taxes: a selected bibliography ₁by₁
Anthony G. White. Monticello, Ill., Council of Planning
Librarians, 1973.

9 p. 29 cm. (Council of Planning Librarians. Exchange bibliography 434)

INCUNABULA
see also Bibliography - Early printed
books; Bibliography - Rare books

Clarke, Adam, 1760?–1832.
A bibliographical dictionary; plus, The bibliographical
miscellany (a supplement to the dictionary) With a foreword by Francesco Cordasco. Metuchen, N. J., Mini-Print
Corp., 1971.

1 v. (unpaged) 31 cm.

Reprint of the 1802-04 and 1806 ed.

Falk, Franz, 1840–1909.
Die deutschen Sterbebüchlein von der ältesten Zeit des
Buchdruckes bis zum Jahre 1520. Amsterdam, Rodopi,
1969.

vi, 83 p. facsim. 23 cm.

Photomechanical reprint of the Köln, 1890 ed.

Falk, Franz, 1840–1909.
Die deutschen Sterbebüchlein von der ältesten Zeit des
Buchdruckes bis zum Jahr 1520. Köln, J. P. Bachem, 1890
₁Heidelberg, H. Tenner, 1969₁

₁iv₁, 83 p. facsims. 23 cm. (Beiträge zur Geschichte des Buch-
und Kunstantiquariats, Heft 4)

Flodr, Miroslav.
Incunabula classicorum. Wiegendrucke der griechischen
und römischen Literatur. Amsterdam, Adolf H. Hakkert,
1973.

xv, 530 p. 30 cm.

Gesamtkatalog der Wiegendrucke. Hrsg. von der Kommission für den Gesamtkatalog der Wiegendrucke. 2. Aufl.,
durchgesehener Neudruck der 1. Aufl. Stuttgart, A. Hiersemann; New York, H. P. Kraus, 1968–
v. 31 cm.
Vorwort signed by Erich v. Rath.
Reprint of v. 1-7 (1925-38), including all supplements. Does not
include v. 8, pt. 1 (Eike von Repgow-Federicis), the last part issued
before World War II interrupted the work.
CONTENTS. — Bd. 1. Abano-Alexius. — Bd. 2. Alfarabius-Arznei. —
Bd. 3. Ascher-Bernardus Claravallensis.—Bd. 4. Bernardus de Cra-
covia-Brentius.—Bd. 5. Breviaire-Byenboeck.—Bd. 6. Caballus-Con-
fessione.—Bd. 7. Coniuratio-Eigenschaften.

Goldschmidt (E. P.) and Company, ltd., *London.*
Books from early German presses. London ₁1968₁

107 p. illus. 22 cm. (*Its* Catalogue 138)

Kaufmann, Hans.
Verzeichnis schweizerischer Inkunabeln und Frühdrucke.
Von Hans Kaufmann und Peter Nabholz. Zürich, (H. Kaufmann Forchstrasse 163), 1968–
v. 21 cm.

CONTENTS.—Faszikel 1. Die Inkunabeln von Beromünster, Burgdorf,
Zürich, Rougemont, Promentoux, Lausanne, Sursee, Genf.

Rossi, Giovanni Bernardo de, 1742–1831.
Annales Hebraeo-typographici seculi xv et ab anno 1501 ad 1540. Descripsit et instruxit fuso commentario notisque historicis-criticis illustravit cum indicibus alphabeticis auctorum et operum. Amsterdam, Philo Press, 1969.

xxix, 184, 64, 4 p. 29 cm. (Bibliotheca Rossiana, v. 2)

At head of title: Joh. Bern. de Rossi.
"Reprint 1969 of the edition Parma 1795–1799."

Stillwell, Margaret Bingham, 1887–
The beginning of the world of books, 1450 to 1470; a chronological survey of the texts chosen for printing during the first twenty years of the printing art, with a synopsis of the Gutenberg documents. New York, Bibliographical Society of America, 1972.

xxviii, 112 p. 26 cm.

Appendixes (p. [73]–106): A. The Gutenberg documents: notes on the manuscript records, 1420–1468. The Gutenberg tradition as stated in the printed books of the fifteenth century, 1468–1499.—B. Undated imprints assigned to the Netherlands.

An Unusual selection of fine incunabula and other books prior to 1501 : a special publication / from the editors of Chapter & verse ; introd. by Frederick Richmond Goff. — Bristol, R. I. : Current Co., [1974]

48 p. : ill. (some col.) ; 25 cm.

Zapf, Georg Wilhelm, 1747–1810.
Augsburgs Buchdruckergeschichte. Nebst den Jahrbüchern derselben. Verfasset, hrsg. und mit literarischen Anmerkungen erläutert. (Unveränderter fotomechanischer Nachdruck [der Ausg.] Augsburg 1786–1791. Leipzig, Zentralantiquariat der Deutschen Demokratischen Republik, 1968.)

2 v. illus. 25 cm.
Includes bibliographical footnotes.
CONTENTS.—1. T. Vom Jahre 1468 bis auf das Jahr 1500.—2. T. Vom Jahre 1501 bis auf das Jahr 1530.

BIBLIOGRAPHIES

Berkowitz, David Sandler, 1913–
Bibliotheca bibliographica incunabula; a manual of bibliographical guides to inventories of printing, of holdings, and of reference aids. With an appendix of useful information on place-names and dating, collected and classified for the use of researchers in incunabulistics. Waltham, Mass., 1967.

vi, 336 l. 29 cm.

Peddie, Robert Alexander, 1869–1951.
Fifteenth-century books: a guide to their identification. With a list of the Latin names of towns and an extensive bibliography of the subject. New York, B. Franklin [1969]

89 p. 20 cm. (Burt Franklin bibliography and reference series, 294)

"Originally published: 1913."

EXHIBITION CATALOGS

Grolier Club, New York.
Fifty-five books printed before 1525 representing the works of England's first printers; an exhibition from the collection of Paul Mellon, January 17–March 3, 1968. [New York] 1968.

xiii, 62, [10] p. illus. 26 cm.

Wahlert Memorial Library.
Printed books, 1471–1500; an exhibition commemorating the UNESCO International Book Year. Dubuque, Iowa [1972]

viii, 71 p. illus. 22 cm.

Wolfenbüttel. Herzog-August-Bibliothek.
Incunabula incunabulorum. Früheste Werke d. Buchdruckkunst Mainz, Bamberg, Strassburg, 1454–1469. Ausstellg im Renaissancesaal d. Wolfenbütteler Schlosses 1972. (Katalog. [Von] Wolfgang Milde.) (Wolfenbüttel, Herzog August Bibliothek, 1972.)

71 p. 26 cm. (Its Ausstellungskataloge, Nr. 4)

LIBRARY CATALOGS

Aberdeen, Scot. University. *Library.*
Catalogue of the incunabula in Aberdeen University Library; compiled by William Smith Mitchell. [Rev. ed.] Edinburgh, London, Published for the University of Aberdeen [by] Oliver & Boyd, 1968.

xi, 107 p. 8 plates, 4 illus., 5 facsims. 24 cm. (Aberdeen University studies no. 150)

First ed. published in 1925 under title: A list of fifteenth century books in the University library of Aberdeen.

Bath Municipal Libraries.
Printed books 1476–1640 [in] Bath Municipal Libraries: catalogue [compiled by V. J. Kite, Reference Librarian] Bath (Somerset), Bath Municipal Libraries, 1968.

[3], 93 p. 20 cm.

Córdoba, Argentine Republic. Universidad Nacional. Biblioteca Mayor.
Los incunables de la Biblioteca Mayor de la Universidad Nacional de Córdoba [por] Graciela Bringas Aguiar. Córdoba, 1973.

56 l. illus. 29 cm.

Originally presented as the author's thesis (bibliotecario), Universidad Nacional de Córdoba, 1972.

Desguine, André.
Inventaire des incunables du fonds Caticantus. Saint-Étienne, Dumas, 1965.

84 p. facsims. 18 cm.

Dokoupil, Vladislav.
Soupis prvotisků z fondů Universitní knihovny v Brně. Sest. Vladislav Dokoupil. 1. vyd. Praha, SPN, Tisk 1, Brno, 1970.

407, [3] p. 32 p. of plates. 25 cm.

Illustrated t. p.
Introduction and title also in German: Katalog der Inkunabeln aus den Beständen der Universitätsbibliothek in Brünn.

Dublin. University. *Library.*
Catalogue of fifteenth-century books in the Library of Trinity College, Dublin, and in Marsh's Library, Dublin, with a few from other collections (with illustrations) by T. K. Abbott. New York, B. Franklin [1970]

vi, 225 p. illus., facsims. 24 cm. (Burt Franklin bibliography and reference series, 360)

Reprint of the 1905 ed.

Finger, Frances L
Catalogue of the incunabula in the Elmer Belt Library of Vinciana, by Frances L. Finger. Los Angeles, Friends of the UCLA Library, 1971.

xvii, 80 p. facsim. 27 cm.

Giessen. Universität. *Bibliothek.*
Die Inkunabeln der Universitätsbibliothek Giessen [von] H. Schüling. Giessen, Universitätsbibliothek, 1966.

vii, 273 p. 1 illus. 23 cm. (Berichte und Arbeiten aus der Universitätsbibliothek Giessen, 8)

Goff, Frederick Richmond, 1916-   ed.

Incunabula in American libraries; a third census of fifteenth-century books recorded in North American collections. Reproduced from the annotated copy maintained by Frederick R. Goff, compiler and editor.   Millwood, N.Y., Kraus Reprint Co., 1973 ₍c1964₎

lxiii, 798 p. 29 cm.

Reprint of the ed. published by the Bibliographical Society of America, New York; annotated and corrected, with new introd. and list of dealers.

Greece. Boulē. Bibliothēkē.
₍Archetypa kai ekdoseis₎
'Αρχέτυπα καὶ ἐκδόσεις ιε' & ις' αἰῶνος. 'Αθῆναι, Βιβλιοθήκη τῆς Βουλῆς τῶν 'Ελλήνων, 1971–

v. facsims. 32 cm.

Hellwig, Barbara.

Inkunabelkatalog des Germanischen Nationalmuseums Nürnberg. Bearb. nach einem Verzeichnis von Walter Matthey. Wiesbaden, Harrassowitz, 1970.

xxiv, 331 p. illus. 27 cm. (Kataloge des Germanischen Nationalmuseums Nürnberg)

Inkunabelkataloge bayerischer Bibliotheken.

Hispanic Society of America.

Printed books, 1468-1700, in the Hispanic Society of America: a listing by Clara Louisa Penney. New York, 1965.

xlii, 614 p. illus., ports. 26 cm. (Hispanic notes & monographs; essays, studies, and brief biographies. Catalogue series)

Hubay, Ilona.

Incunabula aus der Staatlichen Bibliothek Neuburg/Donau ₍und₎ in der Benediktinerabtei Ottobeuren. Wiesbaden, O. Harrassowitz, 1970.

xx, 271 p. plates (part col.) 28 cm. (Inkunabelkataloge bayerischer Bibliotheken)

Hubay, Ilona.

Incunabula der Universitätsbibliothek Würzburg. Wiesbaden, Harrassowitz, 1966.

xvi, 516 p. illus. 28 cm. (Inkunabelkataloge bayerischer Bibliotheken)

Hubay, Ilona.

Incunabula Eichstätter Bibliotheken. Wiesbaden, O. Harrassowitz, 1968.

xviii, ₍1₎, 260 p. illus. (part col.), coats of arms, facsims. (part col.) 28 cm. (Inkunabelkataloge bayerischer Bibliotheken)

Illibato, Antonio.

Gli incunabuli della Biblioteca del Seminario arcivescovile di Napoli. Napoli, Laurenziana, 1973.

21 p. plates. 24 cm.

Incunaboli in biblioteche calabresi. Napoli, 1967.

30 p. 24 cm. (Pubblicazioni della Soprintendenza bibliografica per la Campania e la Calabria, n. 12)

Edited by Maria Vicenzo Romano.

Institut grand-ducal de Luxembourg. *Section historique. Bibliothèque.*

Die Drucke des 15. ₍i. e. fünfzehnten₎ und 16. Jahrhunderts in der Bibliothek der Historischen Sektion des Grossherzoglichen Institutes von Luxemburg ₍von₎ Emil van der Vekene. Luxemburg, 1968.

58 p. facsims., map, plan. 26 cm. (In Institut grand-ducal de Luxembourg. Section historique. Publications. Luxembourg. v. 84 (1968))

Pages also numbered 112-166.

Johannesburg. University of the Witwatersrand. Library.

Fifteenth century printed books in the library of the University of the Witwatersrand, Johannesburg; a hand list. Johannesburg, University of the Witwatersrand, 1972.

₍16₎ p. illus. 30 cm.

Kazan, Russia (City). Universitet. Biblioteka.
(Katalog inkunabulov Nauchnoĭ biblioteki imeni N. I. Lobachevskogo)

Каталог инкунабулов Научной библиотеки имени Н. И. Лобачевского. Сост. Л. Н. Копосова. Казань, Изд-во Казан. ун-та, 1973.

18, ₍10₎ p. with illus. 21 cm.

At head of title: Казанский государственный университет имени В. И. Ульянова-Ленина. Научная библиотека имени Н. И. Лобачевского.

Kotvan, Imrich.

Inkunábuly archívov, múzeí a niektorých historických knižníc na Slovensku. Martin ₍Matica slovenská₎ 1964.

192 p. illus., facsims. 24 cm.

Added t. p.: Incunabula archivorum, museorum, nonnullarumque bibliothecarum historicarum Slovaciae.
Preface also in Russian and German.

Leningrad. Universitet. *Biblioteka.*

Каталог инкунабулов. Сост. ₍и авт. вступит. статьи₎ А. Х. Горфункель. Ленинград, Изд. Ленингр. ун-та, 1967₎.

43 p. with illus., 10 l. of illus. 23 cm.

On leaf preceding t. p.: Ленинградский ордена Ленина Государственный университет имени А. А. Жданова. Научная библиотека имени М. Горького.

Leopold-Sophien-Bibliothek.

Überlinger Inkunabel-Katalog; Katalog der Inkunabeln der Leopold-Sophien-Bibliothek, Überlingen. Bearb. von D. H. Stolz. Konstanz, Seekreis-Verlag ₍1970₎

xii, 144 p. illus. (part col.) 25 cm.

Loches, France. Bibliothèque municipale.

Catalogue des incunables. Loches, 1967.

21 l. 27 cm.

London. University. *Library.*

Incunabula in the libraries of the University of London; a hand-list. ₍London₎ University of London, 1963 ₍i. e. 1964₎

iii, 40 p. 25 cm.

Madrid. Universidad. Biblioteca.

58 ₍i. e. Cincuenta y ocho₎ incunables de medicina en la Universidad de Madrid ... ₍IV Aniversario de Noticias Médicas₎ Madrid 16 febrero de 1971. ₍Texto, Rafaela Castrillo₎ Madrid ₍Publicaciones Controladas, 1971₎

125 p., plates (part col.) 24 cm.

Milan. Biblioteca ambrosiana.

Gli incunaboli dell'ambrosiana. A cura di Felice Valsecchi. 121 illustrazioni in nero ... Vicenza, N. Pozza, 1972–

v. plates. 30 cm. (Fontes ambrosiani in lucem editi cura et studio Bibliothecae ambrosianae, 48)

Milan. Convento dei servi in San Carlo. Biblioteca.

Catalogo degli incunaboli del fondo "Giacinto Amati" della Biblioteca dei servi di Milano ₍di₎ Giuseppe M. Besutti, con una notizia preliminare di Davide M. Montagna. Milano, Convento dei servi in S. Carlo, 1964.

159 p. illus., 7 plates. 24 cm. (Biblioth₍h₎eca Servorum Mediolanensis. Sussidi, 1)

Milan. Università. Facoltà di giurisprudenza. Biblioteca.

Libri a stampa dei secoli XV e XVI, a cura di Giuliana Sapori. ₍Milano, 1967₎

64 p. illus. 25 cm.

At head of title: Università degli studi di Milano. Biblioteche delle Facoltà di giurisprudenza, lettere e filosofia.

Ohly, Kurt, 1892–

Inkunabelkatalog der Stadt- und Universitätsbibliothek und anderer öffentlicher Sammlungen in Frankfurt am Main. Bearb. von Kurt Ohly und Vera Sack. Frankfurt a. M., Klostermann (1966–

v. 29 cm. (Kataloge der Stadt- und Universitätsbibliothek Frankfurt am Main)

Palermo. Biblioteca nazionale.

Catalogo degli incunabuli della Biblioteca nazionale di Palermo. Palermo, 1971.

190 p. 25 cm. (Centro di studi filologici e linguistici siciliani. Supplementi al Bollettino, 2)

Name of editor, Anna Maria Dotto, at head of title.

Parguez, Guy.

Supplément au "Catalogue des incunables," nᵒˢ 637–1066 ... Paris, Bibliothèque nationale, 1967.

108 l. 26 cm. (Recensement des livres anciens des bibliothèques françaises. Travaux préparatoires, 1)

At head of title: Bibliothèque de la ville de Lyon.

Paris. Université. Bibliothèque.

Catalogue des incunables de la Bibliothèque de l'Université de Paris, par Émile Chatelain. New York, B. Franklin ₍1971₎

152, 26 p. facsims. 23 cm. (Burt Franklin bibliography and reference series, 427)

Reprint of the 1902–05 ed.
"Supplément": p. ₍3₎–26 (2d group)

Pellechet, Marie Léontine Catherine, 1840–1900.

Catalogue général des incunables des bibliothèques publiques de France, par M. Pellechet. Avec une introd. écrite pour la réimpression par Frederick R. Goff. Nendeln, Liechtenstein, Kraus-Thomson Organization Ltd., 1970.

26 v. 28 cm.
At head of title, v. 1–3: Ministère de l'instruction publique et des beaux-arts.
Vols. 4–26, "par Louis Polain."
Vols. 1–3, "Reprint of Louis Polain's working copy, with his numerous amendments and corrections."
Vols. 1–3: reprint of the 3 volumes published in Paris, 1897–1909; v. 4–26: Photoreproduction of the manuscript of later volumes never published, largely in the hand of Louis Polain.

Pierpont Morgan Library, New York.

Early printed books. New York ₍1974₎

xvi, ₍105₎ p. facsims. 30 cm. (Its Major acquisitions, 1924-1974)

Errata slip inserted.

Saint-Étienne, France (Loire). Bibliothèque municipale.

Catalogue des incunables et des ouvrages imprimés au XVIᵉ siècle conservés à la Bibliothèque municipale de Saint-Étienne. Saint-Étienne, 1973.

78 p. 22 cm.

Sajó, Géza.

Catalogus incunabulorum quae in bibliothecis publicis Hungariae asservantur. Ediderunt Géza Sajó et Erzsébet Soltész. In colligenda materia et identificandis incunabulis socii fuerunt Csaba Csapodi et Miklós Vértesy. Budapestini, In aedibus Academiae Scientiarum Hungaricae, 1970.

2 v. (lxxix, 1444 p.) 78 facsims. 21 cm.
Introd. in English.

Seville. Universidad. *Biblioteca.*

Catálogo de incunables de la Biblioteca universitaria. Publicado por Juan Tamayo y Francisco ₍y₎ Julia Ysasi-Ysasmendi. Sevilla, Universidad de Sevilla, 1967.

xiii, 106 p. 30 facsims. 24 cm.

Sydney. Public Library of New South Wales.

A first census of incunabula in Australia and New Zealand, compiled by H. G. Kaplan. Sydney, Trustees of the Public Library of New South Wales, 1966.

vi, 52 p. 25 cm.

Trieste. Biblioteca civica.

Catalogo degli incunabuli della Biblioteca civica di Trieste. ₍Di₎ Sauro Pesante. Firenze, L. S. Olschki, 1968.

xv, 81 p. 25 cm. (Biblioteca di bibliografia italiana, 54)

Uppsala. . Universitet. *Bibliotek.*

Katalog der Inkunabeln der Kgl. ₍i. e. Königlichen₎ Universitätsbibliothek zu Uppsala; Neuerwerbungen der Jahre 1954–1964, nebst Kurztitelverzeichnis sämtlicher Inkunabeln in der Universitätsbibliothek, von Hans Sallander. Uppsala, Almqvist & Wiksells boktr. ₍1965₎

221 p. 25 cm. (Bibliotheca Ekmaniana, 68)

Zdanevych, Borys Ivanovych.

(Каталог₍ інкунабул)

Каталог інкунабул. Уклав ₍і передмову написав₎ Б. Зданевич. ₍Упорядник Г. І. Ломонос-Рівна₎. Київ, "Наук. думка," 1974.

250 p. with illus. 25 cm.

At head of title: Академія наук Української РСР. Центральна наукова бібліотека.
Summary in Russian and English.

INDEX NUMBERS (ECONOMICS)

Bibliography of index numbers: an international team project. ₍2nd ed.₎ edited by W. F. Maunder. London, Athlone P., 1970.

xxviii, 215 p. illus. 22 cm.

"Published for the International Statistical Institute."

Davenport, Donald Hills, 1896–

An index to business indices, by Donald H. Davenport and Frances V. Scott. Ann Arbor, Mich., Gryphon Books, 1971.

viii, 187 p. 22 cm.

"Facsimile reprint of the 1937 edition published in Chicago by Business Publications, inc."
Pages 182–187, forms "for additional indexes."

INDEXES

American Library Association. Junior Members Round Table.

Local indexes in American libraries; a union list of unpublished indexes. Edited by Norma Olin Ireland and National Editorial Committee of Junior Members. Boston, Gregg Press, 1972 ₍c1947₎

xxxiv, 221 p. 23 cm. (The Library reference series. Basic reference sources)

Reprint of the ed. published by F. W. Faxon, Boston, which was issued as no. 73 of Useful reference series.

Hampshire Technical Research Industrial Commercial Service.

Abstracting and indexing services held by Hatrics members. Southampton, Hatrics, 1968.

₍3₎ p., v leaves, 113 p. 22 cm.

Ireland, Norma (Olin) 1907–

An index to indexes; a subject bibliography of published indexes. Boston, Gregg Press, 1972 ₍c1942₎

xvi, 107 p. 23 cm. (The Library reference series. Basic reference sources)

Reprint of the ed. published by F. W. Faxon, Boston, which was issued as no. 67 of the Useful reference series.

Lancaster, Eng. University. Library.
Abstracts and indexes ₍compiled by I. M. Stuart₎ Lancaster, University of Lancaster Library, 1974.

₍4₎, xii, 53 p. 21 cm. (Its Bibliographic guide no. 2)

INDIA

Akademiia nauk SSSR. *Institut narodov Azii.*
Библиография Индии; дореволюционная и советская литература на русском языке и языках народов СССР, оригинальная и переводная. ₍Ответственный редактор Г. Г. Котовский₎ Москва, Наука; Глав. ред. восточной лит-ры, 1965.

607 p. 22 cm.
On leaf preceding t. p.: Академия наук СССР. Институт народов Азии. Фундаментальная библиотека общественных наук им. В. П. Волгина. Академия наук УзбССР. Институт востоковедения им. Абу Райхана Бируни.

Books on India. 1969–
Jaipur, Rajasthan University Library.

v. 20 cm.

Guha, Chitta Ranjan.
Basic bibliography on foreign trade. ₍Prepared by C. R. Guha.₎ New Delhi, Indian Institute of Foreign Trade ₍1970₎

39 l. 27 cm.

At head of title: Sources of information.

Gupta, Giriraj Prasad, 1922–
Economic investigations in India; a bibliography of researches in commerce and economics approved by Indian universities, with supplement, 1966, by G. P. Gupta. Agra, Ram Prasad, 1966.

iv, 170 p. 25 cm.

"Prepared under the auspices of Department of Commerce, Madhav College, Vikram University, Ujjain."

Index India, a quarterly documentation list of selected articles, editorials, notes and letters etc. from periodicals and newspapers published in English language all over the world. v. 1–
Jan./Mar. 1967–
Jaipur, Rajasthan University Library.

v. in 33 cm.

India International Centre, Delhi.
Early writings on India; a catalogue of books on India in English language published before 1900: an exhibition organised by the India International Centre, New Delhi, December 19–25, 1968. ₍Delhi, Exclusively distributed by Munshiram Manoharlal, 1969₎

124, xxxiv p. facsim. 24 cm.

India (Republic). Office of the Registrar General.
Bibliography on scheduled castes, scheduled tribes, and selected marginal communities of India. Compilation H. L. Harit; assistance: Charan Singh, K. R. Kapoor ₍and₎ Ram Gopal. Supervision and editing: B. K. Roy Burman. New Delhi ₍1966₎
7 v. 29–35 cm.
At head of title: Census of India, 1961.
Includes bibliographies.
CONTENTS.—1. A series.—₍2₎ B series.—₍3₎ C–F series.—₍4₎ G–J series.—₍5₎ K series.—₍6₎ L–N series.—₍7₎ O–Z series.

Indian Council for Cultural Relations.
Aspects of Indian culture; select bibliographies. Editors: H. S. Patil ₍and₎ R. N. Sar. ₍New Delhi₎ sole distributors; Bhatkal Books International ₍Bombay, 1966–

v. 22 cm.

CONTENTS.—1. The arts.

Jain, Sushil Kumar.
A bibliography of Indian autobiographies, including journals, diaries, reminiscences, and letters, etc. Regina, Sask., Regina Campus Library, Univ. of Saskatchewan ₍1965₎

39 l. 28 cm.

Jaipur, India (Rajasthan) University of Rajasthan. *Library.*
A select bibliography on panchayati raj, planning and democracy. Jaipur, 1964.

v, 70 p. 25 cm.

At head of title: Seminar on Panchayati Raj, Planning and Democracy, December 6–11, 1964.
"Prepared in connection with a seminar ... organised under the auspices of the Economics and Public Administration Department ..."

Kapadia, K
India : a select list of books in the State Library of South Australia, compiled by K. Kapadia and K. Worsfold. Adelaide, State Library of South Australia, 1967.

8 p. 26 cm. (Research Service bibliographies, ser. 4, no. 87)

Mahar, J Michael.
India; a critical bibliography, by J. Michael Mahar. Tucson, University of Arizona Press ₍1964₎

119 p. 28 cm.

Pareek, Udai Narain, 1925–
Foreign behavioural research on India. Editor: Udai Pareek. Delhi, Ācharan Sahkār, 1970.

159 p. 25 cm.

"A directory of research and researchers."—jacket.

Sakharov, I V
(India)
Индия : рек. указ. литературы / И. В. Сахаров ; науч. ред. Г. Г. Котовский. — Москва : Книга, 1974.

143 p. ; 20 cm. — (Страны и народы мира)

At head of title: Государственная публичная библиотека им. М. Е. Салтыкова-Щедрина. Географическое общество СССР. Общество советско-индийских культурных связей.

Samuel, C M *comp.*
India treaty manual, 1966, giving citations to the text of over 1000 treaties binding India in 1966; arranged chronologically with a numerical part giving their register numbers in the League and UN records. Compiled from non-official sources by C. M. Samuel. ₍Kozhikode, 1967₎

viii, 232 p. 22 cm.

Bibliographical references included in "guide to abbreviations": p. ₍v₎

Samuel, C. M
India treaty manual, 1972; containing information about 1600 treaties and related documents concerning India. Compiled by C. M. Samuel. ₍Mysore City, P. M. Kuruvilla at the Wesley Press, 1972₎

xii, 307 p. 22 cm.

A reissue of India treaty manual, 1966, with addendum and treaties, 1967–71.

Scholberg, Henry.
The district gazetteers of British India. A bibliography. Zug, ₍Poststr. 4,₎ Inter Documentation, (1970).

vi, xii, 131 p. map. 21 cm. (Bibliotheca Asiatica, 3)

Sengupta, Benoyendra, 1910–
Indiana; a select list of reference & representative

books on all aspects of Indian life & culture. Calcutta, World Press [1966]

xiv, 125 p. 22 cm.

Sharma, Hari Dev, 1928–
Indian reference sources; an annotated guide to Indian reference books [by] H. D. Sharma, S. P. Mukherji [and] L. M. P. Singh. Varanasi, Indian Bibliographic Centre [1972]

vii, 313 p. 25 cm.

Sparks, Stanley V
Bibliography on development administration, India and Pakistan [by] Stanley Sparks, Arun Shourie [and] Jay B. Westcott. [Syracuse] Center for Overseas Operations and Research, Maxwell Graduate School of Citizenship and Public Affairs, Syracuse University, 1964.

51 p. 28 cm. (Maxwell Graduate School of Citizenship and Public Affairs, Syracuse University. Publication no. 11)

Styrelsen för internationell utveckling.
Indien och Pakistan. Litteraturförteckning utarb. av en arbetsgrupp inom SIDA. Lund, Bibliotekstjänst, 1967.

54 p. 21 cm. (Btj-serien, 6)

BIBLIOGRAPHIES

Jain, Sushil K
A bibliography of Indian bibliographies relating to the history & polites [sic] of India; being a part of author's Bibliography of Indian bibliographies [by] Sushil K. Jain. Regina, Sask., 1966.

21 l. 28 cm.

Skagen, Kiki.
Bibliographical resources about India; an annotated list of English-language reference works published in India, 1965–70. Compiled by Kiki Skagen. [Washington] U. S. Dept. of Health, Education, and Welfare; [for sale by the Supt. of Docs., U. S. Govt. Print. Off., 1972]

v, 28 p. 24 cm. (DHEW publication no. (OE) 72–190)

GOVERNMENT PUBLICATIONS

Datta, Rajeshwari.
Union catalogue of the Central Government of India publications held by libraries in London, Oxford and Cambridge. London, Mansell, 1970.

[6] p., 471 columns. 26 cm.

At head of title: Centre of South Asian Studies, University of Cambridge.

India (Republic) Government of India Publication Branch.
Catalogue of Government of India civil publications; subject-wise arranged, corr. up to 31st Dec., 1959. Delhi, Manager of Publications, 1966.

xxi, 761 p. 26 cm.

India (Republic). Government of India Publication Branch.
List of official publications not included in the general catalogue of Government of India publications, issued during the period 1-1-1940 to 31-12-1960. Delhi, Manager of Publications, 1967.

95 p. 24 cm.

Indian Documentation Service.
Indian Government publications in print: subject list. Corr. up to 31st December, 1959. Naisubzimandi, 1971]

442 p. 23 cm.

Macdonald, Teresa.
Union catalogue of the serial publications of the Indian

government 1858–1947 held in libraries in Britain. [London] Mansell, 1973.

154 p. 26 cm.

At head of title: Centre of South Asian Studies, University of Cambridge.

Singh, Mohinder
Government publications of India; a survey of their nature, bibliographical control and distribution systems, including over 1500 titles. Assisted by J. F. Pandya; foreword by S. R. Ranganathan. [1st ed.] Delhi, Metropolitan Book Co. [1967]

iv, ii, ii, 270 p. 23 cm.

HISTORY
see also Mogul Empire

Aziz, Khursheed Kamal.
The historical background of Pakistan, 1857–1947; an annotated digest of source material [by] K. K. Aziz. [1st ed.] Karachi, Pakistan Institute of International Affairs [1970]

xi, 626 p. 25 cm.

Diehl, Katharine Smith.
Carey library pamphlets: secular series; a catalogue. Prepared by Katharine Smith Diehl. Serampore, Council of Serampore College, 1968.

xiii, 106 p. 25 cm.

India (Republic). National Archives.
National register of private records. [New Delhi, 1971–]

v. 29 cm.

Issued in parts.
CONTENTS: v. 1, pt. 1. Descriptive list of documents in the Kapad Dwara collection, Jaipur.

Irish University Press series of British parliamentary papers. Special index 1. Shannon, Irish University Press [1968]

xlvii, 194 p. 35 cm. (IUP library of fundamental source books)

Title on spine: British parliamentary papers.
"Annual lists and general index of the parliamentary papers relating to the East Indies, 1801–1907."

Ladendorf, Janice M
The revolt in India 1857–58. An annotated bibliography of English language materials. [By] Janice M. Ladendorf. Zug, Inter Documentation Company, (1966).

vi, 191 p. 21 cm. (Bibliotheca Indica, no. 1)

Saran, Parmatma.
Descriptive catalogue of non-Persian sources of medieval Indian history, covering Rajasthan and adjacent regions. Compiled by P. Saran. New York, Asia Pub. House [1965]

xi, 234 p. 30 cm.

IMPRINTS

Bibliography of selected Indian books. 1970/71–

New Delhi, Navrang.

v. 22 cm.

Diehl, Katharine Smith.
Early Indian imprints [by] Katharine Smith Diehl, assisted in the oriental languages by Hemendra Kumar Sircar. New York, Scarecrow Press, 1964.

533 p. 22 cm.

"Based on the William Carey Historical Library of Serampore College."

India (Republic). Office of the Registrar General.
Bibliography of publications in tribal languages. Compilation: S. P. Bhatnagar. Compilation & supervision: N. K. Banerjee. Editing: B. K. Roy Burman. New Delhi [1969]

iv, 96 l. 29 cm.

At head of title: Census of India 1961.

Indian books. v. 1–
Jan. 1968–
Calcutta, Mukherji Book House.

v. 25 cm. monthly.

Indian books. 1969–
Varanasi, Indian Bibliographic Centre.

v. 25 cm. annual.

Indian books; an annual bibliography. 1971–

Delhi, Researchco Reprints.

v. 25 cm.

Sher Singh, 1934–
Indian books in print, 1955–67; a select bibliography of English books published in India. Compiled by Sher Singh and S. N. Sadhu, assisted by Vimla Sadhu. Delhi, Indian Bureau of Bibliographies [1969]

1116 p. 29 cm.

Sher Singh, 1934–
Indian books in print, 1972; a bibliography of Indian books published up to December 1971, in English language. Compiled by Sher Singh and S. N. Sadhu. [2d ed.] Delhi, Indian Bureau of Bibliographies [1972–

v. 28 cm.

First ed., 1969, has title: Indian books in print, 1955–67.
CONTENTS: v. 1. Authors. v. 2. Title.

U. S. *Library of Congress. American Libraries Book Procurement Center, Delhi.*
Accessions list, India. v. 1–
July 1962–
New Delhi.
v. 28 cm. monthly.
At head of title: The Library of Congress Public Law 480 Project.
———— Annual supplement: cumulative list of serials.
1969–
New Delhi.
v. 28 cm.
Earlier lists issued as pt. 2 of the July number of the main work.

LAW see Law - India

LIBRARY AND EXHIBITION CATALOGS

Colgate University, Hamilton, N. Y. Library.
India and Indians: a bibliography; holdings of the Colgate University Library. Edited by Ravindra N. Sharma. Hamilton, N. Y., 1974.

2 v. (ix, 278 p.) illus. 28 cm.

Guyana Group for Social Studies.
India, catalogue of a book exhibition, February 5–10, 1968. [Georgetown?] 1968.

41, 11, 6 p., xxxvi l. 28 cm.

Cover title.
Exhibition held at Georgetown Public Free Library.

India Office Library.
Catalogue of European printed books. Boston, G. K.

Hall, 1964.

10 v. 37 cm.

CONTENTS: v. 1–2. Sheaf catalogue.—v. 3–6. Author catalogue.—v. 7–9. Subject catalogue.—v. 10. Catalogue of periodicals.

POLITICS AND GOVERNMENT

Jaipur, India (Rajasthan) University of Rajasthan. *Library.*
A select bibliography on electoral and party behaviour in India. Jaipur, 1966.

iv, 159 l. 28 cm.
At head of title: Institute on the Study of Electoral and Party Behaviour in India, December 1–10, 1966.
"Specially prepared ... [for the Institute] ... organized by the Department of Political Science of this university in 1966."

Jaipur, India (Rajasthan) University of Rajasthan. *Library.*
A select bibliography on Indian government and politics. Jaipur, 1965.

vii, 196 l. 27 cm.
At head of title: Seminar on State Politics in India, December 6–15, 1965.
"Prepared in connection with a seminar ... organised under the auspices of the University Department of Political Science ... 1965."

Wadhwa, O   P
Centre state and inter state relations in India, 1919–1970; a bibliography [by] O. P. Wadhwa. Delhi, Vidya Mandal; [sole distributors: Kapoor Book Service, 1973]

148 p. 22 cm.

INDIAN LANGUAGES AND LITERATURE (EAST INDIAN)

Calcutta. National Library.
A bibliography of dictionaries and encyclopaedias in Indian languages. Calcutta, 1964.

x, 165 p. 24 cm.

Central Institute of English and Foreign Languages.
A bibliography of Indian English. Prepared by Central Institute of English and Foreign Languages. Hyderabad, India, 1972.

2 v. in 1. 26 cm.

"Issued on the occasion of Indian English Seminar, 29th July 1972."
CONTENTS: pt. 1. Indian English literature.—pt. 2. Indian English.

Jain, Sushil Kumar.
Indian literature in English: a bibliography, being a checklist of works of poetry, drama, fiction, autobiography, and letters written by Indians in English, or translated from modern Indian languages into English. Regina, Regina Campus Library, Univ. of Saskatchewan, 1965–

v. 28 cm.

CONTENTS.— pt. 3. Fiction.

Jain, Sushil Kumar.
Indian literature in English; a bibliography. Windsor, Ont., Univ. of Windsor Library [c1965, 1972]

62 p. 22 cm.

Cover title.
Consists of previously published material.

Long, James, 1814–1887.
বাংলা গ্রন্থের তালিকা, ১৮৬৭. [সংকলক] জেমস লঙ. ঢাকা [বাংলা বিভাগ, ঢাকা বিশ্ববিদ্যালয়] 1964.

143 p. 24 cm.

"প্যারিস আন্তর্জাতিক প্রদর্শনীতে প্রেরণের জন্য ভারত সরকারের আদেশে সংকলিত।"

Includes facsim. t. p. of original 1867 ed. : Descriptive catalogue of vernacular books & pamphlets forwarded by the Govt. of India to the Paris Universal Exhibition of 1867.

In Bengali.
Bibliography of James Long's writings : p. 33–42.

Navlani, K
Dictionaries in Indian languages; a bibliography. Compiled & edited by K. Navalani & N. N. Gidwani. Jaipur, Saraswati Publications ₍1972₎

370 p. 21 cm.

Summer Institute of Linguistics.
A bibliographical index of the lesser known languages and dialects of India and Nepal. Editor: Richard D. Hugoniot. ₍Kathmandu₎ 1970.

2, 312 p. 29 cm.

INDIANA

Franklin College, *Franklin, Ind. Library.*
Catalog of the David Demaree Banta Indiana collection, edited by Robert Y. Coward and Hester H. Coward. 2d ed. ₍Franklin? Ind.₎ 1965.

xiii, 212 p. port. 22 cm.

Means, Eloise R
Hoosier ancestors index. ₍Compiled by Eloise R. Means. Indianapolis? 1969–70₎

2 v. 29 cm.

Caption title.
Indexes the column: Hoosier ancestors, by Pearl Brenton, which appears weekly in the Indianapolis star.

CONTENTS.—[1] June 23, 1963–Dec. 26, 1965.—2. Jan. 2, 1966–June 30, 1968.

INDIANS, AMERICAN see American Indians

INDIANS, EAST see East Indians

INDIC INSCRIPTIONS see Inscriptions, Indic

INDIC LANGUAGES AND LITERATURE see Indian languages and literature (East Indian)

INDO-EUROPEANS see Aryans

INDOCHINA

Auvade, Robert.
Bibliographie critique des œuvres parues sur l'Indochine française, un siècle d'histoire et d'enseignement. Paris, G.-P. Maisonneuve & Larose ₍1965₎

153 p. 21 cm.

Brébion, Antoine.
Bibliographie des voyages dans l'Indochine française du IXe au XIXe siècle. New York, B. Franklin ₍1970₎

v, 299, xliv p. 23 cm. (Burt Franklin bibliography & reference series, 395. Geography and discovery, 8)

Reprint of the 1910 ed.

Brébion, Antoine.
Livre d'or du Cambodge, de la Cochinchine, et de l'Annam, 1625–1910 (biographie) et bibliographie. New York, B. Franklin ₍1971₎

79 p. 24 cm. (Burt Franklin research & source works series, 665. Essays in literature & criticism, 118)

Reprint of the 1910 ed.

Désiré, Michel.
La Campagne d'Indochine, (1945–1954), bibliographie. Commandant Michel Désiré. 94 Vincennes, État-major de l'armée de terre, Service historique, 1971–

v. 30 cm.

U. S. *Library of Congress. Reference Dept.*
Indochina; a bibliography of the land and people, compiled by Cecil C. Hobbs ₍and others₎ New York, Greenwood Press ₍1969₎

xii, 367 p. 27 cm.

Reprint of the 1950 ed.

INDONESIA
see also under Dissertations, Academic

A Bibliography on Indonesian material for the humanities & social sciences, 1960–1970. Editorial staff: W. W. Wanny Supit ₍et al.₎ Djakarta, Lembaga Ilmu Pengetahuan Indonesia, 1972–

v. 33 cm. (Lembaga Research Kebudajaan Nasional. Seri bibliografi, no. 1–

Djakarta. Lembaga Ekonomi dan Kemasjarakatan Nasional. Perpustakaan.
Bibliografi-indeks: beberapa buku² dan artikel² dalam lapangan ekonomi dan kemasjarakatan, termasuk politik, diterbitkan Djuli 1964 s/d Agustus 1965, termasuk djuga perdagangan umum dan management. ₍Djakarta, 1965?₎

20 p. 33 cm.

Excerpta Indonesica. 1– Jan. 1970–
₍Leyden, Centre for Documentation of Modern Indonesia, Royal Institute of Linguistics and Anthropology₎

no. 30 cm.

Hicks, George L
The Indonesian economy, 1950–1965: a bibliography ₍by₎ George L. Hicks ₍and₎ Geoffrey McNicoll. ₍New Haven₎ Southeast Asia Studies, Yale University; ₍distributor: The Cellar Book Shop, Detroit, 1967₎

248 p. 23 cm. (Yale University Southeast Asia Studies. Bibliography series, no. 9)

—— —— 1950–1967; bibliographic supplement. ₍New Haven₎ Southeast Asia Studies, Yale University; distributor: The Cellar Book Shop, Detroit, 1967₎

iii, 211 p. 23 cm. (Yale University. Southeast Asia Studies. Bibliography series, no. 10)

Indonesia. Angkatan Bersenjata. Pusat Sedjarah.
Bibliografi sedjarah Hankam/ABRI dan masalah² Hankam. Ed. 2. ₍Djakarta₎ 1971.

97 l. 33 cm.

First ed. published by Lembaga Sedjarah HANKAM.

Indonesia. Biro Pusat Statistik.
Daftar penerbitan2. (List of publications issued by C. B. S.) Jakarta, 1973.

20 p. 34 cm.

McNicoll, Geoffrey.
Research in Indonesian demography; a bibliographic essay. ₍Honolulu, East-West Center₎ 1970.

50 p. 28 cm. (Working papers of the East-West Population Institute, paper no. 6)

Perskaía, Ivetta íUr'evna.
(Istochniki po istorii Indonezii s drevnеĭshikh vremen po tysiacha deviat'sot semnadtsatyĭ g.)
Источники по истории Индонезии с древнейших времен по 1917 г. : библиогр. публикаций по фондам

б-к Москвы и Ленинграда / И. Ю. Перская. — Москва : Наука, 1974–

v. ; 22 cm.
At head of title, v. 1: Академия наук СССР. Институт научной информации по общественным наукам. Институт востоковедения.

Singarimbun, Masri.
The population of Indonesia, 1930–1968; a bibliography. ₁Canberra? International Planned Parenthood Federation, 1969₁

56 p. 30 cm.

Published by the I. P. P. F. for distribution at their Regional Conference, Bandung, June 1–7, 1969.

Sjahrial-Pamuntjak, Rusina.
Daftar penerbitan Pemerintah Republik Indonesia; suatu usaha pertjobaan. Djakarta, Perpustakaan Sedjarah Politik dan Sosial, 1964.

56 p. 33 cm.

Surjomihardjo, Abdurrachman.
Sumber-sumber sejarah Budi Utomo. ₁Jakarta, 1973₁

15, ₁3₁ l. 21 cm.

Errata slip inserted.
"Diterbitkan khusus untuk Pameran Dokumen Sejarah dalam Rangka Menyambut Peringatan 65 Tahun Pergerakan Nasional di gedung Museum Pusat, Jakarta, 15 s/d 26 Mei 1973."

The, Liang Gie.
Bibliografi ilmu administrasi dalam bahasa Indonesia. Jogjakarta, Balai Pembinaan Administrasi, Universitas Gadjah Mada, 1968.

220 p. 19 cm.

Van Niel, Robert.
A survey of historical source materials in Java and Manila. ₁Honolulu₁ University of Hawaii Press, 1970.

255 p. 23 cm. (Asian studies at Hawaii, no. 5)

IMPRINTS

Echols, John M
Preliminary checklist of Indonesian imprints, 1945–1949, with Cornell University holdings ₁by₁ John M. Echols. Ithaca, N. Y., Modern Indonesia Project, Southeast Asia Program, Dept. of Asian Studies, Cornell University, 1965.

vi, 186 p. 28 cm. (Cornell University. Modern Indonesia Project. Bibliography series)

Ikatan Penerbit Indonesia.
Daftar buku 20 ₁i. e. duapuluh₁ tahun penerbitan Indonesia, 1945–1965. Djakarta, IKAPI ₁1966₁

xii, 416 p. 23 cm.

Continued by Penerbitan Indonesia, 1966–1967, compiled by Ikatan Penerbit Indonesia, Seksi Bibliografi.

Ikatan Penerbit Indonesia. Seksi Bibliografi.
Penerbitan Indonesia, 1966–1967. Djakarta ₁1968₁

iv, 86 p. 33 cm.

Cover title.
Continuation of Daftar buku 20 tahun penerbitan Indonesia, 1945–1965, compiled by Ikatan Penerbit Indonesia.

U. S. Library of Congress. Library of Congress Office, Djakarta.
Accessions list, Indonesia, Malaysia, Singapore, and Brunei. v. 1–
July 1964–
Djakarta.

v. 28 cm.

Frequency varies.
At head of title, 1964–May/June 1969: The Library of Congress

Public Law 480 Project; July/Aug. 1969– The Library of Congress National Program for Acquisitions and Cataloging.
Title varies: July 1964–July/Aug. 1970, Accessions list, Indonesia.

Vols. for 1964–May/June 1969 issued by the office under its earlier name: American Libraries Book Procurement Center, Djakarta.
——————Cumulative list of serials. Jan. 1964/Sept. 1966–

Djakarta.
v. 28 cm. annual.
At head of title, Jan. 1964/Sept. 1966–1964/68: The Library of Congress Public Law 480 Project.
Vols. for June 1964/Sept. 1966–1964/68 issued by the office under its earlier name: American Libraries Book Procurement Center, Djakarta.

Kept up to date by supplements.

LAW see Law - Indonesia

INDONESIAN LANGUAGE AND LITERATURE

Amran, Ali.
Karya sastra Indonesia, 1945–1967. Djakarta, Ikatan Penerbit Indonesia ₁1968₁

20 p. 21 cm.

Daftar buku kesusastraan Indonesia. Disusun oleh Urusan Pameran Buku Musjawarah Kesenian Nasional. Front Kebudajaan Revolusioner. ₁Penjusun daftar buku: Lukman Ali, et al.₁ Djakarta, 1966.

17 p. 34 cm.

Lembaga Bahasa dan Kesusastraan.
Daftar pustaka bahasa dan kesusastraan Indonesia, termasuk bahasa² dan kesusastraan Nusantara. ₁Koordinator penjusunan Soelastri Soerjoatmodjo₁ Djakarta, Lembaga Bahasa dan Kesusastraan, Direktorat Djenderal Kebudajaan, Departemen P. dan K., 1966.

iv, 116 p. 31 cm.

Lembaga Bahasa dan Kesusastraan.
Daftar pustaka bahasa dan kesusastraan Indonesia, termasuk bahasa-bahasa dan kesusastraan Nusantara. Cetakan 2. Jakarta, 1968.

xx, 223 p. 34 cm. 500.00

Lembaga Bahasa Nasional.
Almanak sastra Indonesia. Djakarta, 1972–

16– v. 33 cm. (Bahasa dan kesusastraan. Seri chusus, no.)

CONTENTS: 1. Daftar pustaka.

INDRE-ET-LOIRE, FRANCE (DEPT.)

Cordier, Gérard, fl. 1963–
L'Indre-et-Loire préhistorique et proto-historique, répertoire topo-bibliographique ... Rennes, Faculté, des sciences, Laboratoire d'anthropologie préhistorique, 1967.

136 l. maps. 27 cm. (Travaux du Laboratoire d'anthropologie préhistorique, Faculté des sciences, Rennes)

INDUSTRIAL ARTS see Technology

INDUSTRIAL DESIGN

Gibson, Carl.
A bibliography for industrial designers. ₁New York, Industrial Designers Society of America, 1967₁

16 p. 28 cm.

Kostková, Jitka.
Průmyslové výtvarnictví (průmyslový design). Výběrová bibliografie knižní a čas. lit. Sest. Jitka Kostková. Úvod: Bohumil Chotěborský. 1. vyd. Praha, UVTEISt. techn. knihovna, rozmn. 1968.

135 p. 21 cm. (₁Prague. Státní technická knihovna₁ Bibliografie, sv. 34)

INDUSTRIAL EDUCATION see Technical education

INDUSTRIAL HEALTH AND SAFETY

Besser, Carl.
Arbeitsschutzbibliographie. Bearb. von Carl Besser und Siegfried Hartung. Berlin, Verlag Tribüne, 1967.

231 p. 20 cm. (Schriftenreihe des Zentralinstituts für Arbeitsschutz Dresden, Heft 25)

Bibliography of papers published in the years 1952–1971.
Introduction: L. Rosival. 1. vyd. Bratislava, Research Institute of Industrial Hygiene and Occupational Medicine -Obzor, rozmn. Nitrianske tlač., Nitra, 1973.

170, [1] p. 24 cm.

Boleszny, Ivan.
Control of noise in industry, compiled by I. Boleszny. Adelaide, State Library of South Australia, 1967.

32 p. 26 cm. (Research Service bibliographies. Series 4, no. 85)

Bundesarbeitsgemeinschaft für Arbeitssicherheit. Arbeitsgruppe Ausländische Mitarbeiter.
Deutsches Arbeitsschutzmaterial in Fremdsprachen. Koblenz, Bundesinstitut für Arbeitsschutz, 1971.

1 v. (unpaged) 21 cm.

Canada. Dept. of Labour. Accident Prevention and Compensation Branch.
Occupational safety and health; a bibliography. Sécurité et hygiène professionelles; bibliographie [Ottawa, 1974]

ix, 139 p. 23 cm.
Cover title.
English or French.
A continuing project of the Accident Prevention Division; prepared by Celia Bookman.

Czechoslovak bibliography on industrial hygiene and occupational diseases. v. 16–
1971–
Prague.

v. 21 cm. annual.
Continues Scientific reports on industrial hygiene and occupational diseases in Czechoslovakia issued by the Ústav hygieny práce a chorob z povolání in Prague.
Vols. for 1971– issued by the Institute of Hygiene and Epidemiology, Prague and Research Institute of Industrial Hygiene and Occupational Diseases, Bratislava.

Deutsches Zentralinstitut für Arbeitsmedizin.
Arbeiten aus dem Deutschen Zentralinstitut für Arbeitsmedizin. 1948–1967. (Bearb.: Rudolf Gorisch [und] Werner Schüttmann.) Berlin (Dt. Zentralinst. f. Arbeitsmedizin) 1969.

190 p. 21 cm.

Deutsches Zentralinstitut für Arbeitsmedizin.
25 [i. e. Fünfundzwanzig] Jahre Deutsches Zentralinstitut für Arbeitsmedizin; Arbeiten aus dem Deutschen Zentralinstitut für Arbeitsmedizin 1968–1972. [Bearbeiter: R. Gorisch und E. Wegwerth] Berlin, 1973.

iv, 96 p. 20 cm.

Dzięgielewski, Tadeusz.
Bibliografia pomieszczeń socjalnych w zakladach przemysłowych. Opracowali: Tadeusz Dzięgielewski, Klara Hermelińska. Warszawa, 1966.

59 p. 29 cm. (Istytut Urbanistyki i Architektury. Seria prac własnych, zesz. 131).

At head of title: Instytut Urbanistyki i Architektury.

Germany (Federal Republic, 1949–). Bundesinstitut für Arbeitsschutz. Bibliothek und Dokumentationsstelle.
Arbeitsschutz; Bücher und Zeitschriften. 4. neu bearb. und erw. Aufl. Koblenz, 1971.

xi, 308 p. 21 cm.

International Labor Office.
Publications on occupational safety and health. Geneva, 1972.

22 p. 24 cm.

International Labor Office. International Occupational Safety and Health Information Centre.
The cost of occupational accidents and diseases. The economics of safety and health. Geneva [1968?]

12 p. 24 cm. (CIS bibliography 7)

Jugoslavenska akademija znanosti i umjetnosti. Institut za medicinska istraživanja i medicinu rada.
Publikacije. List of publications. 1948–1967. Zagreb, Institut za medicinska istraživanja i medicinu rada Jugoslavenske akademije znanosti i umjetnosti, 1968.

62 p. 24 cm.

Leningrad. Nauchno-issledovatel'skiĭ institut gigieny truda i professional'nykh zabolevaniĭ.
Научные работы института, опубликованные в период 1959–1963 годов; библиографический указатель. Ленинград, 1964.

105 p. 20 cm.
At head of title: РСФСР. Министерство здравоохранения. Государственный научно-исследовательский институт гигиены труда и профзаболеваний. З. Э. Григорьев.

National League for Nursing. *Council on Occupational Health Nursing.*
Bibliography on occupational health nursing. [New York, 1965?]

15 p. 23 cm.
Cover title.
Supplements the League's Bibliographies on nursing, v. 12, Occupational health nursing.

Pakhomov, A V comp.
Библиографический указатель статей по охране труда, 1958–1963 гг.: по изданиям Всесоюзного центрального научно-исследовательского института охраны труда ВЦСПС. [Указатель подготовлен А. В. Пахомовым и А. В. Ушковой] Москва, 1964.

23 p. 22 cm.
At head of title: Всесоюзный центральный научно-исследовательский институт охраны труда ВЦСПС. Отдел научно-технической информации.

Tarrants, William Eugene.
A selected bibliography of reference materials in safety engineering and related fields. Editor: William E. Tarrants. [1st ed.] Chicago, American Society of Safety Engineers [1968, ©1967]

152 p. 22 cm.

Vsesoiuznyĭ nauchno-issledovatel'skiĭ institut okhrany truda. *Otdel nauchno-tekhnicheskoĭ informatsii i propagandy.*
Охрана труда; библиографический указатель трудов института, 1925–1965 гг. [Составитель М. А. Курамшина] Москва, 1966.

97 p. 22 cm.
At head of title: ВЦСПС. Всесоюзный центральный научно-исследовательский институт охраны труда. Отдел научно-технической информации и пропаганды.

White Plains, N. Y. *Center for Occupational Mental Health.*
A selected bibliography on occupational mental health. Bethesda, Md., U. S. Dept. of Health, Education, and Welfare, Public Health Service, National Institutes of Health, National Institute of Mental Health [1965]

vii, 170 p. 24 cm. (Public Health Service publication no. 1338)

"Prepared under contract for the National Clearinghouse for Mental Health Information."

PERIODICALS

International Labor Office. *International Occupational Safety and Health Information Centre.*
List of periodicals abstracted. Liste des périodiques dépouillés. Verzeichnis der erfassten Zeitschriften. Genève, 1965.

52 p. 29 cm.

Preface in English, French, and German.
"Lists all those periodicals from which at least one article has been abstracted by the CIS or its national centres since 1960."

INDUSTRIAL LOCATION

Boykin, James H   1936–
Industrial real estate: an annotated bibliography, by James H. Boykin. Washington, Society of Industrial Realtors, 1969.

v, 78 p. 28 cm.

"Prepared for the Society of Industrial Realtors through the Homer Hoyt Institute, the American University."

Pakshong, Jean Sylvia.
Industrial property; a bibliography. [Johannesburg] University of the Witwatersrand, Dept. of Bibliography, Librarianship and Typography, 1966.

v, 38 l. 30 cm.

Schiavo-Campo, Salvatore.
Industrial location and regional development; an annotated bibliography [by S. Schiavo-Campo] New York, United Nations, 1970.

165 p. 30 cm. ([United Nations. Document] ID/43)

"United Nations publication. Sales no.: E.70.II.B.15."
At head of title: United Nations Industrial Development Organization, Vienna.

Stevens, Benjamin H
Industrial location; a review and annotated bibliography of theoretical, empirical and case studies [by] Benjamin H. Stevens [and] Carolyn A. Brackett. Philadelphia, Regional Science Research Institute [*c*1967]

v, 199 p. 22 cm. (Regional Science Research Institute. Bibliography series, no. 3)

Townroe, P   M
Industrial location and regional economic policy: a selected bibliography [by] P. M. Townroe. Birmingham, University of Birmingham (Centre for Urban & Regional Studies), 1968.

vii, 43 p. Index. 24 cm. (University of Birmingham. Centre for Urban and Regional Studies. Occasional paper no. 2)

U. S. *Area Redevelopment Administration.*
Information sources for locating industrial prospects. [Washington] 1964.

23 p. 24 cm.

INDUSTRIAL MANAGEMENT
see also Business

American Management Association. Research and Information Service.
Ten-year index of AMA publications, 1954–1963. [Compiled by Bernardine H. Thomas and Vera Kohn] New York, American Management Association [1964]

187 p. 23 cm.

American Management Association. *Research and Information Service.*
Ten-year index of AMA publications, 1957–1966. [Compiled by Jo Ann Sperling] New York, American Manage-

ment Association [1967]

xii, 186 p. 23 cm.

Association for Systems Management.
An annotated bibliography for the systems professional. [2d ed.] Cleveland [1970]

183 p. 28 cm.

Prepared with the assistance of Maurice F. Ronayne and others. First ed., edited by M. F. Ronayne, with assistance from A. R. DeLuca, N. L. Senensieb, and R. W. Reynolds, published under the same title in 1962.

Bakewell, K. G. B.
How to find out: management and productivity; a guide to sources of information arranged according to the Universal decimal classification, by K. G. B. Bakewell. [1st ed.] Oxford, New York, Pergamon Press [1966]

x, 354 p. facsims. 20 cm. (The Commonwealth and international library. Libraries and technical information division)

Includes bibliographical references.

Bakewell, K   G   B
How to find out: management and productivity; a guide to sources of information arranged according to the Universal decimal classification, by K. G. B. Bakewell. 2d ed. Oxford, New York, Pergamon Press [1970]

x, 389 p. facsims. 20 cm. (The Commonwealth and international library. Libraries and technical information division)

Includes bibliographical references.

Bergen, Norway. Norges handelshøgskole. Biblioteket.
Bedriftsøkonomisk langtidsplanlegging. Litteratur utgitt i tiden 1965–1972 i NHHB. Utarb. av Torill Steien. Bergen, 1972.

4, 18 l. 31 cm.

Branch, Melville Campbell, 1913–
Selected references for corporate planning; annotated, with a partial list of companies in the United States and Canada with corporate or divisional planning actually or potentially comprehensive in nature, by Melville C. Branch, with the assistance of Amos R. L. Deacon, Jr. [New York] American Management Association [1966]

191 p. 21 cm.

British Institute of Management.
Basic library of management. [New ed.] London, British Institute of Management, 1967.

[4] 39, v p. 31 cm.

British Institute of Management.
A basic library of management. New ed. London, British Institute of Management [1969].

[1], 17 p. 30 cm.

Bulletin signalétique. Série III: Économie, organisation, commandement. no 95–   jan. 1969–

[Paris] Centre de documentation de l'armement.

no. 25 cm. semimonthly.

Supersedes (with series 1–2, 4) the 7 series issued in 1968 by the Centre de documentation de l'armement and its sections, and continues their numbering.
Issued in cooperation with the Institut européen d'administration des affaires.

Cannons, Harry George Turner.
Bibliography of industrial efficiency and factory management (books, magazine articles, etc.) With many annotations and indexes of authors and of subjects, by H. G. T. Cannons. Easton [Pa.] Hive Pub. Co., 1973.

viii, 167 p. 26 cm. ([Hive management history series, no. 18])

Facsim. reprint of the 1920 ed., issued in series: Efficiency books.

Damljanović, Božidar, *comp.*

Upravljanje poslovnim sistemom. Bibliografija. Materijale prikupili i obradili: Božidar Damljanović, Vesna Marsenić [i] Desanka Stamatović. ⟨Beograd⟩, Institut za naučnotehničku dokumentaciju i informacije, ⟨1968⟩.

312 p. 21 cm.

Dothan, Joseph, 1914–

A bibliography of articles on management & efficiency written by Joseph Dothan. [Tel-Aviv, 1965]

13, [2] l. 28 cm.

Added t. p.: ביבליוגרפיה מקצועית בנושאי המינהול והייעול
First ed. published in 1963 under title: מאמריו של יוסף דותן

Eksperymenty ekonomiczne w przemyśle krajów socjalistycznych. [Opracował J. Kasprzakowa. Warszawa] 1966.

24 p. 29 cm. (Tematyczne zestawienie dokumentacyjne, nr. 50)

On cover: Instytut Ekonomiki i Organizacji Przemysłu. Ośrodek Informacji Naukowej.

Evgeniev, Georgi.

Научна организация на труда. Избрана библиогр. София, М-во на труда и соц. грижи, 1969.

154 p. 22 cm.

At head of title: Г. Евгениев, В. Кунчев.
On cover: Национална изложба НОТ 69.

Franken, Wilhelm Gerd.

Leasing. Eine neue Form der Anlagenfinanzierung. Eine Bibliographie zusammengestellt von Wilhelm G. Franken. Hamburg, Verlag Weltarchiv, 1966.

130 p. 21 cm. (Veröffentlichungen des Hamburgischen Welt-Wirtschafts-Archivs)

Le Guide de l'information et du perfectionnement des dirigeants et cadres d'entreprises. [Sous la direction de Patrick Fauconnier.] [Paris (7°),] Études et promotion, [58, rue de Babylone,] 1971.

1 v. (various pagings) illus. 32 cm.

On cover: Le Gip.
"Cet ouvrage constitute la réédition et l'élargissement du Répertoire du marketing et du management paru en 1968/69 sous la direction de Michel de Chollet ... avec le concours de Patrick Fauconnier."

Instituto Nacional del Libro Español.

Libros de organización y administración de empresas. Barcelona, 1970.

89 p. 24 cm.

Intercollegiate Case Clearing House, Boston.

Case bibliography and index, management of organizations, Europe. Jean Burleson, editor. Boston, 1973.

xxiv, 1157 p. 28 cm.

On spine: Case bibliography and index—Europe 1973.

Joschke, Heinz Karl, 1916–

Betriebswirtschaftliche Organisation [von] Heinz K. Joschke. [Neuwied] Luchterhand [1972]

216 p. 21 cm. (Bibliographie zum Fachgebiet Wirtschaftsführung, Kybernetik, Datenverarbeitung, Bd. 5)

Kullstedt, Mats, 1945–

Chefer på administrativ mellannivå. En litteraturstudie. [Av] Mats Kullstedt och Henrik Wallén. Stockholm, PArådet, 1969.

(5), 304 p. 30 cm. (Rapport från Personaladministration rådet, 0021)

Library Association. County Libraries Group.

Readers' guide to books on management [compiled by B. B. Smith] Newtown [County Library, Park La., New-town, Montgomeryshire 5Y16 1EJ]: Library Association, County Libraries Group, 1971.

73 p. 19 cm. (Its Readers guide, new series, no. 116)

Liège. Université. *Institut de sociologie.*

Bibliographie de l'entreprise. Une sélection d'ouvrages commentés par l'Institut de sociologie de l'Université de Liège. 2° éd. entièrement revue. (Liège, Institut de sociologie de la Faculté de droit de Liège, 1968?)

99 p. 21 cm. (*Its* Sciences sociales et administration des affaires, no 13)

Norsk produktivitetsinstitutt. *Biblioteket.*

Produktivitetslitteratur. Ledelse, rasjonalisering, organisasjon, samarbeidsspørsmål, personaladministrasjon, opplæring, markedsføring, finansiering m. v. (Katalog) Oslo, 1966.

146 p. 21 cm.

Организация рабочих мест. (Рек. указ. литературы). Москва, 1971.

27 p. 22 cm. (Библиографическая информация. Серия 9)

At head of title: Министерство местной промышленности РСФСР.
Issued by TSBNTI of Ministerstvo mestnoĭ promyshlennosti RSFSR.

Peterson, Richard B

Bibliography [sic] on comparative (international) management [by] Richard B. Peterson. Seattle, Office of Faculty Publications, Graduate School of Business Administration, University of Washington [1969?]

20 l. 28 cm. (Washington (State) University. Graduate School of Business Administration. Occasional paper, 21)

Rauscherová, Marie.

Organizace a řízení výroby; výběrová bibliografie. Sest.: M. Rauscherová, za odborné spolupráce E. Hüttlové z katedry Organizace a řízení průmyslu VŠE. Praha, 1967.

74 p. 21 cm.

At head of title: Státní knihovna ČSSR. Ústřední ekonomická knihovna.

Rozantseva, E   M

[Sovershenstvovanie organizatsii i upravleniia proizvodstvom]

Совершенствование организации и управления производством. Библиогр. указ. Отеч. и иностр. литература ... Москва, Центр. науч-исслед. ин-т информации и техн.-экон. исследований по тракт. и с.-х. машиностроению, 1971.

73 p. 21 cm.
At head of title: Министерство тракторного и сельскохозяйственного машиностроения. Центральная научно-техническая библиотека тракторного и сельскохозяйственного машиностроения.

Shkliar, V   I

Научная организация труда. Библиогр. указатель литературы. [1967–1969 гг. Сост. В. И. Шкляр] Москва, "Знание," 1970.

32 p. 20 cm. (В помощь лектору)

At head of title: Всесоюзное общество Знание. Центральная политехническая библиотека.

Stichting Studiecentrum voor Administratieve Automatisering. Bibliotheek en Documentatiedienst.

Nederlandse boeken over automatisering. Bibliografie van niet-periodieke Nederlandstalige literatuur over automatisering, moderne wetenschap en administratie. [Voorwoord door L. M. C. J. Sicking] Amsterdam, 1967 [1968]

iv, 51 l. 29½ cm.

U. S. *Business and Defense Services Administration.*
Aids to modernization, a bibliography. ₍Washington, 1964₎

9 p. 26 cm.

U. S. Regional Technical Aids Center, Mexico.
Catalogo de libros y folletos en Español del Centro Regional de Ayuda Técnica—Agencia para el Desarrollo Internacional. Catalog of books and pamphlets in Spanish: Regional Technical Aids Center—Agency for International Development. Mexico, 1966.

xlv, 321 p. 14 x 22 cm.

English and Spanish.

Warsaw. Instytut Ekonomiki i Organizacji Przemysłu.
Ośrodek Informacji i Dokumentacji Naukowo-Technicznej.
Analiza i mierniki oceny działalności gospodarczej przedsiębiorstw in branż przemysłowych. ₍Opracowała K. Tubiańska. Warszawa₎ 1965.

68 p. 29 cm. (*Its* Tematyczne zestawienie dokumentacyjne, nr. 48)

Warsaw. Instytut Ekonomiki i Organizacji Przemysłu.
Ośrodek Informacji i Dokumentacji Naukowo-Technicznej.
Koncentracja, specjalizacja i kooperacja produkcji przemysłowej. ₍Opracowała Janina Kasprzakowa₎ Warszawa, 1965.

74 p. 29 cm. (*Its* Tematyczne zestawienie dokumentacyjne, nr. 45)

Warsaw. Instytut Ekonomiki i Organizacji Przemysłu.
Ośrodek Informacji i Dokumentacji Naukowo-Technicznej.
Zarządzanie przemysłem; eksperymenty ekonomiczne w przemyśle krajów socjalistycznych. ₍Opracowała K. Tubiańska₎ Warszawa, 1964.

30 p. 29 cm. (*Its* Tematyczne zestawienie dokumentacyjne, nr. 40)

Warsaw. Instytut Ekonomiki i Organizacji Przemysłu.
Ośrodek Informacji i Dokumentacji Naukowo-Technicznej.
Zrzeszenia przedsiębiorstw przemysłowych. ₍Opracowała K. Miłodrowska i J. Kasprzakowa₎ Warszawa, 1964.

60 p. 29 cm. (*Its* Tematyczne zestawienie dokumentacyjne, nr. 42)

Warsaw. Instyut Ekonomiki i Organizacji Przemysłu.
Ośrodek Informacji Naukowej.
Rentowność i deficytowość finanasowa w przemyśle oraz ich analiza. ₍Opracował Jerzy Anacki. Warszawa, 1966₎

49 p. 29 cm. (Tematyczne zestawienie dokumentacyjne, nr. 51)

Waterloo, Ont. University. *Engineering, Mathematics & Science Library.*
Reference list: management science. Ontario, 1967.

11 p. 22 cm.

Die Wissenschaft von der Leitung und Führung des Staates. Spezialbibliographie zu Fragen der Verwaltungs- und Leitungswissenschaft in den sozialistischen und bürgerlichen Ländern. (Zusammengestellt von einem Kollektiv der Abteilung Wissenschaftliche Dokumentation und der Bibliothek der Deutschen Akademie für Staats- und Rechtswissenschaft "Walter Ulbricht," unter Leitung von Heinz Engelbert) Potsdam-Babelsberg, (Deutsche Akademie für Staats- und Rechtswissenschaft "Walter Ulbricht," Institut für Staats- und Rechtswissenschaftliche Forschung, Zentralstelle für Staats- und Rechtswissenschaftliche Information und Dokumentation) 1966.

88 p. 21 cm. (Spezialbibliographien zu Fragen des Staates und des Rechts, Heft 3)

Wybrane problemy dotyczące programowania rekonstrukcji branż i gałęzi przemysłu. ₍Opracowała K. Tubiańska₎

Warszawa, 1966.

60 p. 29 cm. (Tematyczne zestawienie dokumentacyjne, nr. 49/66)

On cover: Instytut Ekonomiki i Organizacji Przemysłu. Ośrodek Informacji Naukowej.

AFRICA

Halbach, Axel Jonas.
Aspekte der Industrialisierung in Tropisch-Afrika; eine kommentierte Aufsatz-Bibliographie, von Axel J. Halbach. München, IFO-Institut für Wirtschaftsforschung, Afrika-Studienstelle, 1971.

292 p. 30 cm.

CZECHOSLOVAK REPUBLIC

Literatura o řízení; výběrový přehled. 1–
Praha, UTEIN, 1966–

v. 21 cm.

"Pro potřebu ústředních úřadů, výzkumných ústavů, podniků socialistického sektoru, vysokých a odborných škol."

Prague. Městská lidová knihovna.
Nová soustava řízení. ₍Autor: Olga Jirečková₎ Praha, 1965–

v. 29 cm. (*Its* Metodické texty a bibliografie)

CONTENTS.—1– seš. Výběrová bibliografie článků z českých novin a časopisů.

Rauscherová, Marie.
Úloha a význam sféry nevýrobních základních fondů v rozvoji ekonomiky. Výběr literatury. Sest. M. Rauscherová. Praha, St. knihovna ČSR-Ústř. ekon. knihovna, rozmn., 1969.

37, ₍1₎ l. 20 cm.

Řízení ekonomiky v socialistických zemích.

Praha.
v. 21 cm. monthly.
Begar. in 1966.
Issues for 1966–68, Jan. 1970, lack vol. statement but constitute v. 1–3, v. 5.
Title varies: 1966–69, Nová soustava řízení.
Czech or Slovak.
Issued by Československá tisková kancelář, Redakce hospodářských informací and Institut řízení.

FINLAND

Vaisto, Erkki.
Organisaatio-opin ja yrityksen hallinnon kirjallisuus Suomessa vuosilta 1945–1970. Bibliography of organization and administration in Finland 1945–1970. Helsinki, Kauppakorkeakoulu; Jakelu: Kyriiri, 1972.

180 (1) p. 21 cm. (Kauppakorkeakoulun julkaisuja. Sarja C II : 12)

INDIA

Pandya, Jayendra Farsuram, 1932–
Studies in Indian management: a survey of literature, 1970 ₍by₎ J. F. Pandya, M. C. Shah ₍and₎ G. J. Trivedi. Foreword: Ravi J. Matthai. Pref.: N. H. Atthreya. ₍1st ed.₎ Bombay, Indian Centre for Encouraging Excellence ₍1972₎

128 p. 23 cm.

Sethi, Narendra Kumar.
A bibliography of Indian management; with reference to the economic, industrial, international, labor, marketing, organizational, productivity and the public administration perspectives. Compiled by Narendra K. Sethi. Bombay, Popular Prakashan ₍1967₎

xvi, 116 p. 23 cm.

Tremblay, Louis Marie, 1932–
Bibliographie des relations du travail au Canada, 1940–1967, par Louis-Marie Tremblay, avec la collaboration de Francine Panet-Raymond. Montréal, Presses de l'Université de Montréal, 1969.

ix, 242 p. 26 cm.

On cover: Faculté des sciences sociales. Département de relations industrielles.

INDUSTRIAL RESEARCH

Goslin, Lewis N
A selected annotated bibliography on R&D management, by Lewis N. Goslin. [Bloomington] Bureau of Business Research, Graduate School of Business, Indiana University [1966]

xiv, 204 p. 23 cm. (Indiana business information bulletin, no. 56)

Hauzner, Ivan.
Technická tvůrčí práce. Doporučující bibliografie. Praha [Ústředí vědeckých, technických a ekonomických informací, Státní technická knihovna] 1971.

52 p. 21 cm. (Prague. Státní technická knihovna. Bibliografie, sv. 163)

Schmidt, Gerhard, 1930–
Forschung und Industrie. Bibliographische Hinweise zu Problemen der Industrieforschung in der Deutschen Demokratischen Republik. Leipzig (Deutsche Bücherei) 1968.

52 p. 21 cm. (Bibliographischer Informationsdienst der Deutschen Bücherei, Nr. 13)

INDUSTRIAL SECURITY

Davis, L
Security against burglary and theft; a list of selected references, compiled by L. Davis. Melbourne, State Library of Victoria, 1966.

17 p. 26 cm. (Victoria. State Library. Research Service bibliographies, 1966, no. 8)

INDUSTRIAL SOCIOLOGY

Hodáková, Lýdia.
Sociológia práce. Sociology of work. Zost. Lýdia Hodáková. Odborne spoluprac. Sigfríd Milly. 1. vyd. Bratislava, SPN, rozmn. Západoslov. tlač. 42, 1968.

71 p., [456] l. (in portfolio) 20 cm. ([Bratislava] Ústredná ekonomická knižnica. Ekonomické aktuality. Bibliografický spravodaj, 1967, č. 5)

Cover title.
Introduction and table of contents also in Russian, German, English and French.

Legátová, Božena.
Sociologie prace a průmyslu; výběrová bibliografie. [Sest. Božena Legátová] Ostrava, 1965.

32 p. 29 cm. (Státní vědecká knihovna v Ostravě. Publikace. Rada II, čís. 397)

Legátová, Božena.
Sociologie práce v průmyslu. [Soupis lit.] Časové rozmezí: 1965–1968. Sest. Božena Legátová. Ostrava, St. věd. knihovna, rozmn., 1968.

50 p. 29 cm. (Státní vědecká knihovna v Ostravě. Publikace. Rada 2, čís, 430)

Materiały do studiowania socjologii pracy; wybór tekstów. [Wybór dokonali: J. Balcerek et al. Wyd. 1.]. Warszawa, Szkoła Główna Planowania i Statystyki, 1970.

199 p. 25 cm.

Parker, Stanley Robert.
A bibliography of industrial sociology (including the sociology of occupations), compiled by S. R. Parker. London, Polytechnic, 1965.

[1], 15 p. 20½ cm.

Tomíška, František.
Ekonomická sociologie a psychologie. Pokračovací a doplňující výběr z lit. za 2. pololetí 1970 a r. 1971. Sest. František Tomíška. Praha, St. knihovna ČSR-Ústř. ekon. knihovna, rozmn., 1972.

78, [1] l. 20 cm.

INDUSTRY

Ahn, Michael.
Industrial bibliography / by Michael Ahn. — Washington : Urban Land Institute, [1974]

90 p. ; 28 cm. — (ULI research report ; 22)

Deutscher Industrie- und Handelstag.
Bibliographie Kammerpublikationen. Veröffentlichungen der Industrie- und Handelskammern, der Deutschen Auslandshandelskammern und des Deutschen Industrie- und Handelstages. (Bonn) Deutscher Industrie- und Handelstag (1967)

[173 p. 21 cm. (Its Schriftenreihe, Heft 102)

Hitotsubashi Daigaku, Tokyo. Keizai Kenkyūjo. Nihon Keizai Tōkei Bunken Sentā.
(Fuken kangyō nempō shozai mokuroku)
府県勧業年報所在目録　昭和41年(1966) 3 月現在調　[東京]　一橋大学経済研究所日本経済統計文献センター　[1966]

96 p. 25 cm. (Its 特殊文献目録シリーズ　2)

On p. [4] of cover: Union catalogue of fukenkangyonenpo.
本目録の編集は八巻滋が担当した

John Crerar Library, *Chicago.*
A list of books on the history of industry and industrial arts, January, 1915. Prepared by Aksel G. S. Josephson. Detroit, Gale Research Co., 1966.

9, 486 p. 24 cm.

Title page includes original imprint: Chicago, Printed by order of the Board of Directors, 1915.
Reprint of the 1915 ed.

Organization for Economic Cooperation and Development. *Library.*
Politique industrielle. Industrial policy. [Paris] 1968.

v, 118 p. 27 cm. (Its Bibliographie spéciale analytique. Special annotated bibliography, 20)

Pusat Dokumentasi Ilmiah Nasional.
Daftar buku & madjalah mengenai industri [di] Pusat Dokumentasi Ilmiah Nasional, Lembaga Ilmu Pengetahuan Indonesia. Djakarta [1971]

59 l. 28 cm.

Sentralinstitutt for industriell forskning.
Registrering av informasjonskilder vedrørende industriell forhold. 2. utg. Oslo, 1966.

49 l. 30 cm.

United Nations. *Economic Commission for Africa.*
Selected subject bibliography: model schemes of small scale industries. [New York] 1969.

iii, 69 p. 26 cm. ([United Nations. Document] E/CN.14/LIB/ser. C/5)

INFLATION (FINANCE)

Organization for Economic Cooperation and Development.
Library.
Inflation. [Paris] 1965.

v, 84 p. 27 cm. (*Its* Bibliographie spéciale analytique, 6 (43))

Introductory matter in French and English; annotations in French or English.

Organization for Economic Cooperation and Development. Library.
L'inflation. Inflation. Paris, O. C. D. E., 1972.

2 v. 27 cm. (Its Bibliographie spécialisée analytique. Special annotated bibliography, 32–33)

At head of title: Service de l'information. Information service.
"Bibliography ... selected by Mrs. R. Tarr."
Vol. 2: "INF/BIB (72)12"
French or English.

INFORMATION SCIENCE
see also   Documentation; Library science

Bibliografía sobre documentación e información, compilada por Romalinda Ambruster [et al.] alumnos del curso sobre técnica de la documentación de la Facultad de Humanidades, Escuela de Letras y de Arte, Departamento de Bibliotecología y Documentación, Universidad de La Habana. La Habana, Departamento de Publicaciones, Biblioteca Nacional José Martí, 1970.
v, 85 l. 27 cm. (Biblioteca Nacional José Martí. Folletos de divulgación técnica y científica, 83)
Cover title: Bibliografía sobre documentación.

Neeland, Frances.
A bibliography on information science and technology. Santa Monica, Calif., System Development Corp., 1965–66.

4 v. 28 cm. (System Development Corporation. Tech memo. TM–2625/001/00–TM–2625/004/00)

Produced in performance of contract ADI 65–1 for the American Documentation Institute.

Neeland, Frances.
A bibliography on information science and technology for 1967. Santa Monica, Calif., System Development Corp., 1967–

v. 28 cm. (System Development Corporation, Santa Monica, Calif. Technical memorandum; TM series)

"TM–(L) 3553/001/00."
"Supported by contract 68–1 for the American Documentation Institute, and SDC."

Neeland, Frances.
A bibliography on information science and technology for 1968, by Frances Neeland and Eileen Sever. Santa Monica, Calif., System Development Corp. 1968–1969.

4 v. 28 cm. (Technical memorandum; TM series)

"TM(L)–3951/001/00"–"TM(L)–3951/004/00."
"Supported by contract 68–1 for the American Society for Information Science and SDC."

Neeland, Frances.
Bibliography on information science and technology. Detroit, American Data Processing [1969]

287 p. 28 cm. (Information technology series)

Общее науковедение и документалистика; библиографический указатель. [Составлен сотрудниками Отдела машинных методов переработки историко-научной информации Сектора истории техники и естествознания Института истории АН УССР А. И. Гринкруг, В. Н. Клименюком и Е. И. Левшиным] Под ред. Г. М. Доброва. Киев, Наук. думка, 1966.
130 p. 21 cm.

At head of title: Академия наук УССР. Сектор истории техники и естествознания Института истории АН УССР.

Olsen, Harold Anker.
The economics of information: bibliography and commentary on the literature. Washington, ERIC Clearinghouse on Library and Information Sciences, 1971.

vii, 30 p. 29 cm.

Prepared in cooperation with the Special Interest Group on Costs, Budgeting & Economics, American Society for Information Science.

Роль библиотек в системе информации. вып. 2–
1968/1969–
Москва, Центр. науч. с.-х. библиотека.

no. 20 cm.

"Библиографический указатель отечественной литературы."
Continues Роль библиотек в научной информации.

Šimová, Viera.
Informatika v publikáciách štátnych vedeckých knižníc na Slovensku. Súpis za roky 1961–1970. Sprac.: Viera Šimová, Štefan Hanakovič. Bratislava, Slov. techn. knižnica, rozmn., 1971.

165, [2] p. 20 cm. (Edícia: Metodické pomôcky SITK. Séria B: Bibliografie, č. 12)

Summary also in Russian, German, and English.

Šimová, Viera.
Slovníky a terminologické normy z informatiky. Sprac. a úvod [nap.] Viera Šimová. Bratislava, Slov. techn. knižnica, rozmn., 1973.

92, [2] p. table. 21 cm. (Edícia: Metodické pomôcky SITK. Séria B: bibliografie, č. 15)

Summary also in Russian, German, and French.

Zegarac, Elizabeth N
Information systems: annotated bibliography of related literature [by] Elizabeth N. Zegarac, Jeffrey L. Holzem [and] Raymond C. Manion. Kansas City, Mo., Mid-continent Regional Educational Laboratory, 1971.

iii, 33 l. 28 cm.

INFORMATION STORAGE AND RETRIEVAL SYSTEMS
see also   Computers; Electronic data processing; Management information systems; Punched card systems

Balz, Charles F
Literature on information retrieval and machine translation. Compiled and edited by Charles F. Balz and Richard H Stanwood. 2d ed. [Gaithersburg, Md.] International Business Machines Corp., 1966.

x, 168 p. 28 cm.

Jaeger, Herman de.
Information storage and retrieval: the coordinate indexing principle, terminal digit and feature card systems; a preliminary report. A study undertaken at the request of the Fondation industrie-Université, Brussels. Brussels, National Centre for Scientific and Technical Documentation [1968]
vi, 49 l. 29 cm.
Abstract in English, Dutch, French, German, and Russian.

Ügyvitelgépesítés. [Szerk.: Szabó Bendegúz] Budapest, Országos Műszaki Könyvtár és Dokumentációs Központ, 1970–

v. 21 cm. (A Tudomány és technika újdonságai magyar nyelven; ajánló bibliografia, 45.–46., 57.– sz.)

Western Reserve University, *Cleveland. Center for Documentation and Communication Research.*
A selected bibliography of documentation & information retrieval. ₍Rev.₎ Cleveland, 1964.

10 l. 28 cm.

Cover title.
Published in 1962 under title: Documentation & information retrieval.

Zell, Hans M
An international bibliography of non-periodical literature on documentation & information, compiled & edited by Hans Zell & Robert Machesney. Oxford, R. Maxwell ₍1965₎

vi, 294 p. 25 cm.

GEOLOGY

Burk, C   F
Computer-based storage and retrieval of geoscience information: bibliography 1970–72 ₍by₎ C. F. Burk, Jr. Prepared for International Union of Geological Sciences, COGEODATA. W. W. Hutchinson, Chairman; Committee on Geological Documentation, L. Delbos, Chairman. ₍Ottawa₎ Dept. of Energy, Mines and Resources ₍1973₎
iii, 38 p. 25 cm. (Geological Survey of Canada. Paper 73–14)

At head of title: Canadian Centre for Geoscience Data.
Previous ed. by J. Hruška and C. F. Burk.

Hruška, J
Computer-based storage and retrieval of geoscience information: bibliography 1946–69 ₍by₎ J. Hruška ₍and₎ C. F. Burk. Prepared for International Union of Geological Sciences, COGEODATA, S. C. Robinson, Chairman; Committee on Geological Documentation, L. Delbos, Chairman. ₍Ottawa₎ Dept. of Energy, Mines and Resources ₍1971₎
v, 52 p. 25 cm. (Geological Survey of Canada. Paper 71–40)

Lorettov, Vadim Vladimirovich.
Аннотированный указатель литературы по вопросам применения перфокарт в геологии. ₍Составили: В. В. Лореттов, В. И. Кленов₎. Москва, ОНТИ ВИЭМС, 1968.
16 p.
At head of title: Министерство геологии СССР. Всесоюзный научно-исследовательский институт экономики минерального сырья и геологоразведочных работ.
Microfilm. 1 reel. 35 mm.

LAW

Bigelow, Robert Pratt, 1927–
Automation and law; a bibliography ₍by₎ Robert P. Bigelow. 3d ed., Nov. 1965. Boston ₍1965₎

37 p. 28 cm.

Caption title.

Kenyon, Carleton W
Computers in law practice; a bibliography. Sacramento, California State Library, Law Library, 1966.

11 p. 28 cm.

"The bibliography section of an article published by the compiler entitled Requiem for the digest."

National College of the State Judiciary. Court Studies Division.
Computers and courts: a selected and annotated bibliography. ₍Reno, Nev. ₍1972₎

11 l. 28 cm.

Schubert, Wolfram.
JUDAC; Recht, Datenverarbeitung, Kybernetik. Jurisprudence, data processing, cybernetics. Internationale Bibliographie, English, Deutsch, Francais, Russkii, hrsg.

von Wolfram Schubert ₍und₎ Wilhelm Steinmüller, unter Mitarbeit von Erwin Arldt ₍et al.₎ München, Beck ₍°1971₎

xv, 299 p. 29 cm.

Vandersypen, Karla M
Computer applications and quantitative techniques in law enforcement and criminal justice; selected references. Compiled by Karla M. Vandersypen. ₍Evanston, Ill., Traffic Institute, Northwestern University₎ 1972.

19 p. 28 cm.

"Produced at the Criminal Justice Library Unit, Transportation Center Library, Northwestern University, a project supported by the Illinois Law Enforcement Commission."

MUSIC

Kostka, Stefan M
A bibliography of computer applications in music, by Stefan M. Kostka. Hackensack, N. J., J. Boonin ₍1974₎

iii, 58 p. 28 cm. (Music indexes and bibliographies, no. 7)

INGERSOLL, ROBERT GREEN

Stein, Gordon.
Robert G. Ingersoll; a checklist, by Gordon Stein. ₍1st ed. Kent, Ohio?₎ Kent State University Press ₍1969₎

xxx, 128 p. 23 cm. (Serif series: bibliographies and checklists, no. 9)

INJURIES   see   Wounds

INLAND WATERWAYS

Cincinnati. Public Library. Rare Book Dept.
Catalog of the Inland Rivers Library, with a foreword by Frederick Way, Jr. Compiled by Clyde N. Bowden, curator. ₍Cincinnati₎ Public Library of Cincinnati and Hamilton County, 1968.

156 p. 28 cm.

"Based on the collection of the Sons and Daughters of Pioneer Rivermen."

Harvard University. *Graduate School of Business Administration. Baker Library.*
Inland waterways transportation; a bibliography and guide to information sources. Compiled by Mary Chatfield ₍reference librarian. Cambridge₎ 1966.

x, 42 p. port. 25 cm.

At head of title: A memorial to John Oliver Innes.

Sartorius, Françis.
La navigation intérieure en Belgique. 1880–1962. Extraits de périodiques en cours de publication au 31 décembre 1962. Mémoire présenté à l'École provinciale le bibliothécaires du Brabant, session 1963. Bruxelles, Commission belge de bibliographie, 1965.

xxviii, 354 p. 21 cm. (Bibliographia Belgica, 87)

Vos, Alex de.
Bibliografie van de Belgische binnenscheepvaart. Gent, Belgisch Studiecentrum voor Binnenscheepvaart, (Tolhuislaan, 44), 1972–74.

2 v. 19 cm.

CONTENTS: deel 1. 1830–1950.—deel 2. 1951–1970.

INNS   see   Hotels

INNSBRUCK

Eppacher, Wilhelm.
Bibliographie zur Stadtkunde von Innsbruck. Innsbruck (Selbstverl. des Stadtmagistrates) 1971.

8 l., 339 p. 25 cm. (Veröffentlichungen des Innsbrucker Stadtarchivs, n. F., Bd. 1/2)

INPUT-OUTPUT ANALYSIS

Bourque, Philip John, 1922–
An inventory of regional input-output studies in the United States, by Philip J. Bourque and Gerald Hansen. Seattle, Graduate School of Business Administration, University of Washington, 1967.

21 p. 28 cm. (Graduate School of Business Administration, University of Washington. Occasional paper 17)

Bourque, Philip John, 1922–
An inventory of regional input—output studies in the United States ₍by₎ Philip J. Bourque and Millicent Cox. Seattle, Graduate School of Business Administration, University of Washington ₍1970₎

38 l. 28 cm. (University of Washington. Graduate School of Business Administration. Occasional paper no. 22)

Revision of occasional paper no. 17.

Hungary. Központi Statisztikai Hivatal. Könyvtár.
A bibliography of the Hungarian literature on input-output tables. ₍Compiled by Rácz Albert. Rev. by András Bródy and Tamás Földi. Edited by Dezsö Dányi₎ Budapest, 1967.

90 p. 28 cm.

At head of title: Institute of Planning, National Planning Office. Library of the Central Statistical Office. Library of the Institute of Economics, Hungarian Academy of Sciences.

INSCRIPTIONS, CHINESE

Li, Yü-sun.
(Chin shih hsüeh lu)
金石學錄 ₍4 卷₎ 李遇孫輯 ₍臺北₎ 臺灣商務印書館 ₍民國 59 i. e. 1970₎

2, 1, 15, 56 p. 18 cm. (人人文庫 1438) NT$8.00

Lin, Chün.
(Shih lu chin shih shu chih)
石廬金石書志 ₍22 卷 林鈞編輯 臺北₎ 文史哲出版社 ₍民國 60 i. e. 1971₎

3 v. (1802 p.) 21 cm. (中國文史哲資料叢刊 7)

Reprint of 南昌寶偁閣刊本

INSCRIPTIONS, CUNEIFORM

Borger, Riekele, 1929–
Handbuch der Keilschriftliteratur. Berlin, de Gruyter, 1967–

v. 23 cm.

CONTENTS.—Bd. 1. Repertorium der sumerischen und akkadischen Texte.

British Museum. *Dept. of Western Asiatic Antiquities.*
A bibliography of the cuneiform tablets of the Kuyunjik collection in the British Museum, by Erle Leichty. London, Trustees of the British Museum, 1964.

xiii, 289 p. 29 cm.

INSCRIPTIONS, EGYPTIAN

Schenkel, Wolfgang.
Memphis, Herakleopolis, Theben. Die epigraphischen Zeugnisse der 7.–11. Dynastie Ägyptens. Wiesbaden, Harrassowitz, 1965.

xi, 306 p. 30 cm. (Ägyptologische Abhandlungen, Bd. 12)

INSCRIPTIONS, GREEK

Grumach, Ernst.
Bibliographie der kretisch-mykenischen Epigraphik;

nach dem Stande vom 31. Dezember 1961. München, Beck, 1963.

xxxii, 256 p. 24 cm.

At head of title: Kommission für Alte Geschichte und Epigraphik.

———— Supplement. München, Beck, 1967–
v. 23 cm.

At head of title: Kommission für Alte Geschichte und Epigraphik.
CONTENTS.—1. 1962–1965.

Pfohl, Gerhard.
Bibliographie der griechischen Vers-Inschriften. Hildesheim, G. Olms, 1964.

62 p. 21 cm.

INSCRIPTIONS, INDIC

Chaudhuri, Sibadas, *comp.*
Bibliography of studies in Indian epigraphy, 1926–50. Edited with an introd. ₍1st ed.₎ Baroda, Oriental Institute, 1966.

x, 113 p. 25 cm. (M. S. University oriental series, no. 6)

"Reprinted from the Journal of the Oriental Institute."

INSECTICIDES

Boleszny, Ivan.
Pyrethrins and pyrethrum insecticides: author index to Research Service bibliographies no. 13 and no. 65, compiled by I. Boleszny. Adelaide, Public Library of South Australia, 1966.

24 p. 26 cm. (Public Library of South Australia. Research Service bibliographies. Series 4, no. 67)

INSECTS see Entomology

INSTITUT PASTEUR D'ALGÉRIE

Sergent, Edmond, 1876–
Les travaux scientifiques de l'Institut Pasteur en Algérie de 1900 à 1902. ₍1. éd.₎ Paris, Presses universitaires de France, 1964.

548 p. illus. (part col.), maps. 25 cm.

INSTRUCTIONAL MATERIALS see Teaching - Aids and devices

INSURANCE

American Bar Association. Section of Insurance, Negligence and Compensation Law. Fidelity and Surety Law Committee.
Fidelity & surety law bibliography 1946-1971. ₍Chicago₎ Section of Insurance, Negligence and Compensation Law, American Bar Association ₍1972₎

ix, 98 p. 23 cm.

Prepared by a joint committee of the Fidelity and Surety Law Committee of the American Bar Association's Section of Insurance, Negligence and Compensation Law, the Federation of Insurance Counsel, and the International Association of Insurance Counsel.
Revision of the bibliography on fidelity and insurance law published in 1967 by the Defense Research Institute.

Bayerische Rückversicherung, A. G., Munich.
I. B. R.; Internationale Bibliographie der Rückversicherung. International Bibliography of Reinsurance. 2. Aufl. Stand vom 31. Dez. 1968. Listing Books and Articles published up to the 31st Dec. 1968. München, Bayerische Rückversicherung AG ₍1970–

xx, 251 p. (loose leaf) 23 cm.

California. State Library, *Sacramento. Law Library.*
Automobile insurance and the State; a bibliography. Sacramento, 1966.

17 p. 28 cm.

Hart, Carole S
Sourcebook on international insurance and employee benefit management ₍by₎ Carole S. Hart. ₍New York₎ American Management Association ₍1967–68₎

2 v. 28 cm. (AMA research study 80, 88)

Vol. 2, by Robert Wells, has title: Sourcebook on international corporate insurance and employee benefit management.
Includes bibliographies.
CONTENTS.—v. 1. Europe.—v. 2. Selected countries of the world.

International Credit Insurance Association.
Bibliography of credit insurance. Zurich, 1970.

13 v. 30 cm.

At head of title: International Credit Insurance Association, Union d'assurerus des credits internationaux, Berne.
CONTENTS: ₍1₎ Australia.—₍2₎ Belgium.—₍3₎ Canada.—₍4₎ Denmark.—₍5₎ Finland.—₍6₎ India.—₍7₎ Italy.—₍8₎ Netherlands.—₍9₎ Norway.—₍10₎ Republic of South Africa.—₍11₎ Sweden.—₍12₎ United Kingdom.—₍13₎ United States of America.

Nelli, Humbert O   1900–   comp.
A bibliography of insurance history, prepared by Humbert O. Nelli. Compiled from the Insurance History Collection, the Center for Insurance Research at Dept. of Insurance, School of Business Administration, Georgia State University. Atlanta, Bureau of Business and Economic Research, Georgia State University; for Educational Foundation, inc. ₍1971₎

71 p. 28 cm.

Pendleton, Oswald William, 1902–
How to find out about insurance; a guide to sources of information, by O. W. Pendleton. ₍1st ed.₎ Oxford, New York, Pergamon Press ₍1967₎

x, 196 p. facsims. 20 cm. (The Commonwealth and international library. Libraries and technical information division)

Thomas, Roy Edwin, comp.
Insurance information sources. Detroit, Mich., Gale Research Co. ₍1971₎

332 p. 23 cm. (Management information guide, 24)

Wiktor, Christian L
Automobile insurance publications ₍by₎ Christian L. Wiktor. Halifax, Dalhousie University, Faculty of Law, 1973.

xii, 220 p. 22 cm.

INSURANCE, SOCIAL

Bortz, Abe.
Social security sources in Federal records, 1934–1950. ₍Washington₎ U. S. Social Security Administration, Office of Research and Statistics; ₍for sale by the Supt. of Docs., U. S. Govt. Print. Off., 1969₎

viii, 118 p. 24 cm. (U. S. Social Security Administration. Office of Research and Statistics. Research report no. 30)

Chile. Superintendencia de Seguridad Social.
Bibliografía de la seguridad social chilena. ₍Santiago, ca. 1970₎

226 p. 26 cm.

Hitotsubashi Daigaku, Tokyo. Keizai Kenkyūjo. Nihon Keizai Tōkei Bunken Sentā.
(Shakai hoshō)
社 会 保 障 (1945–1967) 国 立 一 橋 大 学 経 済 研 究所日本経済統計文献センター₍編集.発行₎ 昭 和43 (1968)

186 p. 26 cm. (日本経済文献目録シリーズ no. 1)

Inter-American Conference on Social Security. *General Secretariat.*
Bibliografía de seguridad social. México, Conferencia Interamericana de Seguridad Social, Secretaría General, 1966.

133 p. 23 cm.

International Social Security Association.
Aspects économiques de la sécurité sociale. Recherche en matière de sécurité sociale. Bibliographie. Economic aspects of social security. Research on social security. Aspectos economicos de la seguridad social. Investigaciones en la seguridad social. Wirtschaftliche Aspekte der sozialen Sicherheit. Forschung auf dem Gebiet der sozialen Sicherheit. (Genève, Secrétariat général de l'Association ...) 1971.

156 p. 30 cm. (Association internationale de la sécurité sociale. Recueil documentaire. Documentation series, no. 4)

French, English, Spanish, and German.

Jantz, Kurt.
Studienwerk der Sozialversicherung, Sozialhilfe und Versorgung; Bibliographie. Herausgeber: Kurt Jantz ₍und₎ Eberhart Finke. Wiesbaden, Betriebswirtschaftlicher Verlag Dr. Th. Gabler ₍1968₎

60 p. 24 cm.

Prague. Výzkumný ústav sociálního zabezpečení.
10 ₍i. e. Deset₎ let Výzkumného ústavu sociálního zabezpečení. Praha, Vydalo Oddělení tiskové a literární služby Ministerstva práce a sociálních věci, 1968.

150 h (i. e. 174) p. 21 cm. (Its Sborník prací, č. 27)

"Soupis výzkumných a větších studijných prací" (in Czech, English, and Russian), p. 40–150h.

U. S. *Dept. of Health, Education, and Welfare. Library.*
Basic readings in social security; 25th anniversary of the social security act, 1935–1960. Compiled for the Social Security Administration by the Library of the U. S. Dept. of Health, Education, and Welfare. New York, Greenwood Press ₍1968₎

vi, 221 p. 27 cm.

Reprint of the 1960 issue of Basic readings in social security.

Vaisto, Erkki.
Sosiaaliturvan kirjallisuus Suomessa 1965–1971. Litteratur i socialskydd i Finland. Literature on social security in Finland. ₍Helsinki₎ Sosiaaliturvan keskusliitto, 1973.

336 p. 25 cm.

English, Finnish, and Swedish.

PERIODICALS

Hänel, Wolfgang.
Bibliographie des periodischen Schrifttums in der sozialen Sicherheit. Mit 58 Abbildungen. (2. Aufl.) Bad Godesberg, Asgard-Verlag, 1969.

272 p. 21 cm. (Fortbildung und Praxis, 58)

First ed. has title: Bibliographie des periodischen Schrifttums der Sozialversicherung.

International Social Security Association. *Documentation Service.*
Liste universelle des périodiques de la sécurité sociale. World list of social security periodicals. ₍2. éd. Genève, Secrétariat général, Association internationale de la sécurité sociale, General Secretariat, International Social Security Association₎ 1966.

59 p. 29 cm. (Its Recueil documentaire. Documentation series, no. 3)

English, French, German and Spanish.

INSURANCE, UNEMPLOYMENT

Brinkman, Robert E
Selected bibliography of unemployment insurance program research studies, 1951–1966, [prepared by Robert E. Brinkman with the principal assistance of Evelyn E. Ekert] Washington, U. S. Bureau of Employment Security, 1967.

ix, 132 p. 26 cm.

"BES no. U–257."
"This bibliography includes studies listed in, and updates, the publication Selected bibliography of unemployment research benefit studies and related topics 1951–1956."

INTELLECT

Wright, Logan, 1933–
Bibliography on human intelligence: National Clearinghouse for Mental Health Information; an extensive bibliography. [Chevy Chase, Md.] U. S. National Clearinghouse for Mental Health Information; [for sale by the Supt. of Docs., U. S. Govt. Print. Off., Washington, 1969]

viii, 222 p. 26 cm. (Public Health Service publication no. 1839)

INTELLIGENCE SERVICE

Gunzenhäuser, Max.
Geschichte des geheimen Nachrichtendienstes (Spionage, Sabotage und Abwehr); Literaturbericht und Bibliographie. Frankfurt am Main, Bernard & Graefe, 1968.

vii, 434 p. 21 cm. (Schriften der Bibliothek für Zietgeschichte, Weltkriegsbücherei Stuttgart; neue Folge der Bibliographien der Weltkriegsbücherei, Heft 7)

Harris, William Robert, 1941–
Intelligence and national security; a bibliography with selected annotations, by William R. Harris. [Cambridge? Mass., 1968]

3 v. (xcii, 838 l.) 30 cm.

United States. Library of Congress. Congressional Research Service.
Soviet intelligence and security services, 1964–70; a selected bibliography of Soviet publications, with some additional titles from other sources. Prepared at the request of and based on materials provided by the Subcommittee to Investigate the Administration of the Internal Security Act and Other Internal Security Laws of the Committee on the Judiciary, United States Senate. Washington, U. S. Govt. Print. Off., 1972.

v, 289 p. 24 cm.

At head of title: 92d Congress, 1st session. Committee print.

INTERIOR DECORATION

Jelley, Herbert M
Interior decorating, by Herbert M. Jelley. 1965 revision. Washington, Small Business Administration, 1970.

7 p. 26 cm. (Small business bibliography no. 54)

INTERNAL MEDICINE see Medicine, Internal

INTERNAL SECURITY

U. S. *Congress. Senate. Committee on the Judiciary.*
Cumulative index to published hearings and reports of the Subcommittee to Investigate the Administration of the Internal Security Act and Other Internal Security Laws of the Committee on the Judiciary, 1951–1955. Washington, U. S. Govt. Print. Off., 1957.

ii, 844 p. 24 cm.

———— Second supplement (1961–1966) Washington,

U. S. Govt. Print. Off., 1967.
ii, 355 p. 24 cm.

INTERNATIONAL BUSINESS ENTERPRISES

Lindfors, Grace V
Bibliography: cases and other materials for the teaching of multinational business. Grace V. Lindfors, editor. Boston, Harvard University, Graduate School of business Administration, 1964.

xi, 283 p. 28 cm.

Nehrt, Lee Charles.
International business research; past, present, & future [by] Lee C. Nehrt, J. Frederick Truitt [and] Richard W. Wright. [Bloomington] Bureau of Business Research, Indiana University [1970]

vi, 362 p. illus. 23 cm. (International business research series, no. 2)

Stewart, Charles F
A bibliography of international business, compiled by Charles F. Stewart and George B. Simmons. New York, Columbia University Press, 1964.

xiii, 603 p. 23 cm.

Wheeler, Lora Jeanne, 1923–
International business and foreign trade; information sources. Detroit, Gale Research Co. [1968]

221 p. 23 cm. (Management information guide, 14)

Windsor, Ont. University. International Business Studies Research Unit.
An international business library bibliography, compiled by International Business Studies Research Unit, Faculty of Business Administration, University of Windsor. 4th ed. Windsor, Ont., 1972.

34 p. 28 cm.

Windsor, Ont. University. International Business Studies Research Unit.
An international business library bibliography. 5th ed. [Windsor, Ont.] 1973.

36 l. 28 cm.

INTERNATIONAL CHILDREN'S CENTRE, PARIS

Falkner, Frank Tardrew, 1918–
Publications of the Centre international de l'enfance coordinated growth studies, 1951–1968, compiled by Frank Falkner. [Washington] U. S. Maternal and Child Health Service, 1969.

22 p. 27 cm.

INTERNATIONAL COURT OF JUSTICE

Hague. International Court of Justice.
Publications of the International Court of Justice; catalogue. Hague, distributed in the United States by the United Nations Sales Section, New York, 1967.

25 cm. 23 cm.

Hague. International Court of Justice.
Publications of the International Court of Justice; catalogue. Hague, 1972.

23 p. 23 cm.

INTERNATIONAL ECONOMIC ASSISTANCE see Economic assistance

INTERNATIONAL FINANCE see Finance, International

INTERNATIONAL LABOR ORGANIZATION
see also under United Nations (Cairo)

Olesen, Lili.
Et udvalg af litteratur på skandinaviske sprog vedrørende ILO ⟨International Labour Organisation⟩ i perioden 1945–1968. København, Arbejds- og Socialministerierne, Bibliotek, 1969.

(3), 19 l. 30 cm.

"Udarbejdet i anledning af Den internationale arbejdsorganisations 50 år jubilaeum i 1969."

INTERNATIONAL LAW AND RELATIONS
see also Peace; Treaties; United
Nations

Bespalova, N   A
Империализм перед судом народов. Рек. указатель литературы. Москва, "Книга," 1971.

110 p. 20 cm.

At head of title: Государственная библиотека СССР имени В. И. Ленина. Н. Беспалова, И. Свиридова.

Carnegie Endowment for International Peace.
Publications of the Carnegie Endowment for International Peace, 1910–1967, including International conciliation, 1924–1967. Compiled by Jane A. Hannigan. New York, 1971.

229 p. 24 cm.

Egorov, Valeriĭ Nikolaevich.
Краткий библиографический справочник, 1964–1966. Составитель В. Н. Егоров. Москва, Международные отношения, 1967.

47 p. 17 cm. (Лектору-международнику, пропагандисту, агитатору)

European and Atlantic affairs. London, National Book League with the European-Atlantic Movement, 1968.

24 p. 22 cm.

The Foreign affairs 50-year bibliography; new evaluations of significant books on international relations 1920–1970. Byron Dexter, editor. assisted by Elizabeth H. Bryant and Janice L. Murray. New York, Published for the Council on Foreign Relations by R. R. Bowker Co., 1972.

xxviii, 936 p. 26 cm.

Gascard, Johannes Rainer.
Bibliographie des deutschen Schrifttums ⟨BRD⟩ zum Völkerrecht 1965–1971. Bearb. von Johannes R₍ainer₎ Gascard. Hamburg, Hansischer Gildenverl., 1972.

xliv, 414 p. 24 cm. (Institut für Internationales Recht an der Universität Kiel. Bibliographien, Bd. 3)

Continuation of Bibliographie des deutschen Schrifttums zum Völkerrecht 1945–1964, by D. Rauschning.

Gould, Wesley L
Social science literature; a bibliography for international law, by Wesley L. Gould and Michael Barkun. Princeton, N. J., Published for the American Society of International Law ₍by₎ Princeton University Press ₍1972₎

xiii, 641 p. 25 cm.

Hamburg. Universität. *Forschungsstelle für Völkerrecht und Ausländisches Öffentliches Recht.*
Sämtliche Veröffentlichungen. 1948–1965. Hamburg, 1965.

28 p. 24 cm.

"Nachtrag zum Veröffentlichungsverzeichnis 1948–1965. Stand: 1. Juni 1967." (₍3₎ l.) inserted.

Ibler, Vladimir.
Bibliographie des jugoslawischen Schrifttums zum Völkerrecht 1945–1968. Hamburg, Hansischer Gildenverlag, 1970.

xix, 380 p. 24 cm. (Institut für Internationales Recht an der Universität Kiel. Bibliographien, Bd. 2)

Kenworthy, Leonard Stout, 1912–
Free and inexpensive materials on world affairs ₍by₎ Leonard S. Kenworthy. 2d ed. ₍New York₎ Bureau of Publications, Teachers College, Columbia University, 1965.

69 p. 23 cm. (*His* World affairs guides)

First published in 1949 under title: Free and inexpensive materials on world affairs for teachers.

Kenworthy, Leonard Stout, 1912–
Free and inexpensive materials on world affairs ₍by₎ Leonard S. Kenworthy and Richard A. Birdie. 3d ed. ₍New York₎ Teachers College Press, Columbia University ₍1968, ᶜ1969₎

65 p. illus. 23 cm. (*His* World affairs guides)

First published in 1949 under title: Free and inexpensive materials on world affairs for teachers.

Kenworthy, Leonard Stout, 1912–
Studying the world; selected resources ₍by₎ Leonard S. Kenworthy. 2d ed. ₍New York₎ Bureau of Publications, Teachers College, Columbia University, 1965.

71 p. 23 cm. (*His* World affairs guides)

First ed. published in 1962 with title: Selected resources for studying the world.

Kuhn, Jean.
An annotated bibliography of selected unclassified materials published during 1966 on problems of development and internal defense. ₍Washington, Foreign Service Institute, 1967₎

v, 113 p. 27 cm.

On cover: National Interdepartmental Seminar: Problems of development and internal defense.

Medling, Margaret.
The eagle and the dove; selected titles on war and peace. ₍St. Louis₎ Pius XII Library, St. Louis University, 1971.

41 p. 28 cm.

Moussa, Farag.
Diplomatie contemporaine; guide bibliographique. 2. éd. Genève, Centre européen de la Dotation Carnegie pour la paix internationale, 1965 ₍ᶜ1964₎

201 p. 25 cm.

Pindić, Dimitrije.
Bibliografija odabranih članaka iz medunarodnog javnog prava objavljenih u domaćim i inostranim periodičnim publikacijama u periodu od 1955–1965. Bibliography of the selected articles on international public law published in Yugoslav and foreign periodicals covering the period 1955–1965. ₍Sastavili₎ Dimitrije Pindić, Tomislav Mitrović ₍i₎ Prvoslav Davinić. Beograd, Institut za medunarodnu politiku i privredu, Odeljenje za medunarodno pravo, 1968.

xxi, 243 p. 30 cm.
Serbo-Croatian and English.

Polski Instytut Spraw Międzynarodowych, Warsaw. Zakład Informacji Naukowej i Dokumentacji.
Sytuacja polityczna i polityka zagraniczna państw imperialistycznych: Stany Zjednoczone, Wielka Brytania, Francja, NRF, NATO. ₍Opracowanie redakcyjne: Józef Chudek. Warszawa₎ 1964.

60 p. 29 cm. (Its Zeszyty bibliograficzne. Seria I, r. 1, zesz. 2)

"Na prawach rękopisu."

Polski Instytut Spraw Międzynarodowych, Warsaw. Zakład Informacji Naukowej i Dokumentacji.

Sytuacja polityczna i polityka zagraniczna państw imperialistycznych: Stany Zjednoczone, Wielka Brytania, Francja, NRF, NATO. ₁Opracowanie redakcyjne Jozef Chudek. Warszawa, 1965₁

71 p. 29 cm. (Its Zeszyty bibliograficzne. Seria I, r. 1, 1964, zesz. 3)

Rauschning, Dietrich.

Bibliographie des deutschen Schrifttums zum Völkerrecht 1945–1964. ₁Hrsg.:₁ Institut für Internationales Recht an der Universität Kiel. Hamburg, Hansischer Gildenverlag, 1966.

xii, 569 p. 24 cm.

Robinson, Jacob, 1889–

International law and organization. General sources of information. Leiden, A. W. Sijthoff, 1967.

560 p. 24 cm.

Satō, Kazuo, 1927–

国際法現代文献解説 佐藤和男著 ₁東京₁ 新生社 ₁1967₁

4, 441 p. 22 cm.

Schutter, Bart de.

Bibliography on international criminal law. By Bart de Schutter. With the collaboration of Christian Eliaerts. With a foreword by Hans-Heinrich Jescheck. Leiden, Sijthoff, 1972.

li, 423 p. 23 cm.

United Nations. Library, Geneva.

International Law Commission; a guide to the documents, 1949–1969. Geneva, 1970.

iii, 55 p. 28 cm. (Reference lists, no. 2) (ST/GENEVA/LIB./ser.B/ref.2)

United Nations. Library, Geneva.

League of Nations & United Nations monthly list of selected articles; cumulative, 1920–1970: political questions. Edited by Norman S. Field, Associate Chief Librarian, United Nations Library, Geneva. Dobbs Ferry, N. Y., Oceana Publications, 1971–73.

6 v. 29 cm.

A compilation arranged by subject and country in chronological order from the card file used to issue the library's Liste mensuelle d'articles sélectionnés.
CONTENTS: v. 1. 1920–1928.—v. 2. 1929–1945.—v. 3. 1946–1960.—v. 4. 1961–1970.—v. 5. Special problems, 1920–1970.—v. 6. Security and international peace, 1920–1970.

U. S. *Foreign Service Institute. National Interdepartmental Seminar.*

An annotated bibliography of selected unclassified materials published during 1965 on problems of development and internal defense. ₁Washington, 1967?₁

iv l., 115 p. 27 cm.

On cover: Problems of development and internal defense.

U. S. *Information Agency.*

International relations. Washington, U. S. Information Agency, Information Center Service, 1969.

ii l., 45 p. 27 cm. (Its Subject bibliography no. 6/69)

U. S. *Library of Congress. General Reference and Bibliography Division.*

A guide to bibliographic tools for research in foreign affairs, compiled by Helen F. Conover. 2d ed. with suppl. Westport, Conn., Greenwood Press ₁1970₁

145, 15 p. 24 cm.

Universal Reference System.

International affairs; an annotated and intensively indexed compilation of significant books, pamphlets, and articles, selected and processed by the Universal Reference System, a computerized information retrieval service in the social and behavioral sciences. Prepared under the direction of Alfred de Grazia. New York ₁1965₁

xxxii, 1205 p. illus. 29 cm. (Political science, government & public policy series, v. 1)

Universal Reference System.

International affairs; an annotated and intensively indexed compilation of significant books, pamphlets, and articles, selected and processed by the Universal Reference System. Prepared under the direction of Alfred De Grazia, general editor, Carl E. Martinson, managing editor, and John B. Simeone, consultant. ₁2d ed.₁ Princeton, N. J., Princeton Research Pub. Co. ₁1969₁

xx, 1206 p. 28 cm. (Its Political science, government & public policy series, v. 1)

Zawodny, Janusz Kazimierz.

Guide to the study of international relations ₁by₁ J. K. Zawodny. San Francisco, Chandler Pub. Co. ₁1965, °1966₁

xii, 151 p. 22 cm. (Chandler publications in political science)

LIBRARY CATALOGS

Foreign Relations Library.

Catalog of the Foreign Relations Library. Boston, G. K. Hall, 1969.

9 v. 37 cm.

At head of title: The Council on Foreign Relations, inc., New York.

Great Britain. Foreign Office. Library.

Catalogue of the Foreign Office Library, 1926–1968. Boston, G. K. Hall, 1972.

8 v. 37 cm.

"₁Lists₁ the holdings of that part of the Foreign Office Library which was known as the Printed Library."
Pre-1926 accessions are included in the Catalogue of printed books in the library of the Foreign Office. Accessions to the library subsequent to the merger of the Foreign Office and the Commonwealth Office in 1968 are included in the supplements to the Catalogue of the Colonial Office Library, beginning with the 2d, 1972.
CONTENTS: v. 1–2. Author catalogue.—v. 3–4. Subject catalogue.—v. 5–6. Title catalogue.—v. 7–8. Classified catalogue.

Harvard University. *Law School. Library.*

Catalog of international law and relations. Edited by Margaret Moody. Cambridge, Mass., 1965–

v. 29 cm.

Kokuritsu Kokkai Toshokan, Tokyo. Sankō Shoshibu.

(Kokuritsu Kokkai Toshokan shozō Kokusai Remmei Kokusai Rengō kanko shiryō mokuroku)

国立国会図書館所蔵国際連盟・国際連合刊行資料目録 国立国会図書館参考書誌部編 東京 国立国会図書館 昭和46– (1971–

v. 26 cm.

Cover title.
Added t. p.: Catalogue of the League of Nations and the United Nations publications for the period of 1920–1968 in the National Diet Library.
CONTENTS: 第1巻 国際連盟・国際連合(除: 専門機関)

Squire Law Library.

Catalogue of international law. Compiled by M. A. Lekner, under the direction of W. A. F. P. Steiner. Dobbs Ferry, N. Y., Oceana Publications, 1972.

4 v. (xv, 1449 p.) 27 cm.

INTERNATIONAL ORGANIZATIONS
see also   United Nations, and the names
of other international organizations

Dimitrov, Théodore Delchev.
Documentation of the United Nations and other intergovernmental organizations: information and functional purposes, processing and utilization; a bibliography, prepared by Theodore D. Dimitrov. Geneva, 1972.

111 p. 28 cm.
"UNITAR/EUR/SEM.1/WP.III/15"
At head of title: International Symposium on Documentation of the United Nations and Other Intergovernmental Organizations, 21–23 August, Geneva, 1972.

Dimitrov, Théodore Delchev.
Documents of international organisations: a bibliographic handbook covering the United Nations and other intergovernmental organisations. Compiled and edited by Th. D. Dimitrov. London, International University Publications; Chicago, American Library Association, 1973.

xv, 301 p. 26 cm.

Die **Internationalen** Wirtschaftsorganisationen im Schrifttum. Kiel ₍Bibliothek des Instituts für Weltwirtschaft₎ 1969-

v. 24 cm. (Kieler Schrifttumskunden- zu Wirtschaft und Gesellschaft, 5

CONTENTS.—T. 1. Allgemeines Schrifttum, Atlantik-Charta, Vereinte Nationen, von A. Wittkowski.

Johnson, Harold S
International organization; a classified bibliography, by Harold S. Johnson and Baljit Singh. East Lansing, Asian Studies Center, Michigan State University, 1969.

261 p. 28 cm. (South Asia series, no. 11)

国連資料年鑑 1965/66-
₍京都₎ 京都国連寄託図書館

v. 26 cm.

McGill University, Montreal. Library. Reference Dept.
A guide to information on conferences, meetings, symposia and the publications of international organizations / McLennan Library, Reference Department, McGill Library ₍i. e. University₎. — ₍Montreal₎ : McLennan Library, Reference Dept., McGill Library ₍i. e. University₎, 1973.

5 p. : 28 cm.

Speeckaert, Georges Patrick.
Bibliographie selective sur l'organisation internationale. 1885–1964. Select bibliography on international organization. Bruxelles, Union des associations internationales, 1965.
x, 150 p. 21 cm. (Publication FID no. 361)
Publication UAI no. 191.
At head of title: G. P. Speeckaert.
First published in 1956 in English under title: International Institutions and international organization, a select bibliography; and in French under title: Les organismes internationaux et l'organisation internationale, bibliographie sélective.

INTERNATIONAL SECURITY

Williams, Stillman P
Toward a genuine world security system; an annotated bibliography for layman and scholar, by Stillman P. Williams. ₍Washington₎ United World Federalists ₍1964₎

v, 65 p. 23 cm.

INVENTIONS
see also   Patents

Bratislava. Slovenská technická knižnica.
Technické myslenie a tvorivá práca, vynálezectvo, zlepšovateľstvo; výberový zoznam literatúry. Technical suppose, creative work, invention, the work of innovators; select list of books and articles. V spolupráci s Domom techniky pri Slov. rade ČsVTS. Zostavil Ľudovít Kohutiar. Zodpovedný redaktor: Jozef Hajdušek. ₍V Bratislave₎ 1964.
43 p. 20 cm.
Title also in Russian and German; pref. also in Russian, German, and English.

INVENTORIES

Mulvihill, Donald Ferguson.
Inventory management, by Donald F. Mulvihill. Washington, Small Business Administration, 1969 ₍i. e. 1970₎

8 p. 26 cm. (Small business bibliography no. 75)

Sherman, Kenneth Nathaniel.
Inventory control. Washington, Small Business Administration, 1964.

12 p. 26 cm. (Small business bibliography no. 75)

INVESTMENT
see also   Stock-exchange

Banco de México (*Founded 1925*) *Biblioteca.*
Inversiones extranjeras en México, 1940–1967. México, 1968.

28 p. 22 cm. (Serie de bibliografías especiales, no. 7)

Gáspár, István.
Beruházások és gazdaságosság; témabibliográfia, 1966–1970. Budapest, Országos Műszaki Könyvtár és Dokumentációs Központ, 1971.

115 p. 29 cm.

Society of Investment Analysts.
A bibliography for investment and economic analysis. London, Society of Investment Analyst, 1965 ₍i. e. 1966₎

₍105₎ p. 28½ cm.

低開発諸国における外国資本 ₍藤井正夫編   東京₎
アジア経済研究所 ₍1966-67₎

2 v. 21 cm. (文献解題シリーズ   第12, 14集)

アジア経済研究所出版物   通巻第558, 641号

Woy, James B
Investment information: a detailed guide to selected sources ₍by₎ James B. Woy. Detroit, Gale Research Co. ₍1970₎

231 p. 23 cm. (Management Information guide, 19)

Woy, James B
Investment methods; a bibliographic guide ₍by₎ James B. Woy. New York, R. R. Bowker, 1973.

viii, 220 p. 24 cm.

IONIAN ISLANDS

Legrand, Émile Louis Jean, 1841–1903.
Bibliography ionienne; description raisonnée des ouvrages pub. par les Grecs des Sept-Iles ou concernant ces iles du quinzième siècle à l'année 1900, par Émile Legrand. Oeuvre posthume complétée et pub. par Hubert Pernot ... Paris, E. Leroux, 1910.

2 v. 28 cm. (Publications de l'École des langues orientales vivantes, 5. sér., v. 6–7)

Paged continuously.
"Émile Legrand Oeuvres posthumes nº 3 ₍–4₎"

—— —— Suppléments ₍par₎ Nakis Pierris. Athènes, 1966.

xiv, 293 p. port. 28 cm.

Moschonas, Emmanouël I

῎Αγνωστα καὶ σπάνια μονόφυλλα συλλογῆς Ν. Καραβία· βιβλιογραφικὴ παρουσίαση ₍ὑπὸ₎ ᾿Εμμ. ᾿Ι. Μοσχονᾶ. ᾿Αθῆναι, Βιβλιοπωλεῖον Ν. Καραβία, 1966–67.

2 v. in 1. 25 cm. (᾿Αρχεῖον ἱστορικῶν μελετῶν, 11, 22)

IONS

Harllee, F   N

A bibliography on ion-molecule reactions, January 1900 to March 1966. Compiled by the Mass Spectrometric Data Center: F. N. Harllee, H. M. Rosenstock, and J. T. Herron. Washington. Physical Chemistry Division, Institute for Basic Standards, National Bureau of Standards; for sale by the Supt. of Docs., U. S. Govt. Print. Off., 1966.

iii, 38 p. 26 cm. (NBS technical note 291)

Ионообменные мембраны, их свойства и применение; библиография, 1950–1965. ₍Составители: Н. И. Скурихина и др. Отв. редактор Т. М. Сосипатров₎ Новосибирск, 1967 ₍cover 1968₎

840 p. 22 cm.

At head of title: Государственная публичная научно-техническая библиотека Сибирского отделения Академии наук СССР. Отдел научной библиографии.

IOWA

Iowa. State Historical Society.

Guide to manuscripts. Compiled by Katherine Harris. ₍Iowa City₎ 1973.

iv, 332 p. 28 cm.

IRAN

Afshār, Īraj.

فهرست مقالات فارسی ، فهرست موضوعـی تحقیقـات و مطالعات ایرانشناسی بزبان فارسی که در نشریات ادواری چاپ ایران و ممالك دیگـر تا پایان سال ۱۳۳۸ شمسی چاپ شده است . بکوشش ایرج افشار . ₍تهران ، کتابهای جیبی₎ ، با همکاری مؤسسه انتشارات فرانکلین ۱۹۷۰ .i. e ₍1348–

v. 25 cm.

CONTENTS :   ش ۱۳۲۸ – ق ۱۳۲۸ .۱ جلد

Bartsch, William H

The economy of Iran, 1940–1970: a bibliography ₍by₎ William H. Bartsch & Julian Bharier. Durham, University of Durham, 1971.

₍6₎, 114 p. 24 cm. Index. (University of Durham. Centre for Middle Eastern and Islamic Studies. Publication no. 2)

Handley-Taylor, Geoffrey, comp.

Bibliography of Iran; compiled by Geoffrey Handley-Taylor, with a memoir of His Imperial Majesty Mohammad Reza Shah Pahlavi Shahanshah of Iran by His Excellency Ardeshir Zahedi. Coronation edition, revised and enlarged. London, Bibliography of Iran, 1967.

₍2₎, xviii, 34 p. front. 19 cm.

Handley-Taylor, Geoffrey.

Bibliography of Iran. Compiled by Geoffrey Handley Taylor, with a memoir of His Imperial Majesty Mohammad Reza Pahlavi Aryamehr Shahanshah of Iran by Ardeshir Zahedi. ₍5th ed.₎ Chicago, St. James Press, 1969.

xviii, 150 p. port. 24 cm.

Nawabi, Y   M

A bibliography of Iran; a catalogue of books and articles on Iranian subjects, mainly in European languages, by Y. M. Nawabi. ₍Tehran, Printed at Khajeh Press, 1969–

v. 25 cm. (Iranian Culture Foundation, 53   )

CONTENTS: v. 1. Studies on Avesta, Mani & Manichaeism, Old Persian, Pahlavi (Parsik & Parthian), Parsis of India and Zoroaster & Zoroastrianism.

Shifā, Shujāʻ al-Dīn.
(Jahān-i Īran'shināsī)

جهان ایرانشناسی ₍از₎ شجاع الدین شفا . ₍تهران ، کتابخانه پهلوی و دبیرخانـه مرکزی اتحادیه جهانـی ایران شناسان ۱۹۶۹؟ .i. e   –₍1348؟

v. 25 cm.

Cover title.
CONTENTS : الاتحاد جماهیر · الارش · آلمان · آلبانی · آروانتین .۱ جلد
— شوروی

Sverchevskaià, A   K

Библиография Ирана. Литература на рус. яз. (1917–1965 гг.) Сост. А. К. Сверчевская. Под ред. Н. А. Кузнецовой. Москва, "Наука," 1967.

391 p. 22 cm.

At head of title: Академия наук СССР. Институт народов Азии.

Teheran.   Dānishgāh.   Gurūh-i Bar'rasī-i Madārik va Asnād.
₍Fihrist-i maqālāt-i marbūṭ bih ʻulūm-i ijtimāʻī₎

فهرست مقالات مربوط به علوم اجتماعـی . ₍تهران ، گروه بررسی مدارك و اسناد ، مؤسسه مطالعات و تحقیقات اجتماعی ۱۳۴۷– ₍1968 or 9–

v. 24 cm.

CONTENTS :   شماره ، اجتماعی تحقیقات و مطالعات مؤسسه انتشارات₎
(62
آمار · جمعیت شناسی ، جامعه شناسی .۱ جلد

U. S. Library of Congress. General Reference and Bibliography Division.

Iran: a selected and annotated bibliography. Compiled by Hafez F. Farman. New York, Greenwood Press ₍1968₎

viii, 100 p. 29 cm.

Reprint of the 1951 ed.

IMPRINTS
see also *Persian imprints*

Mushār, Khānbābā, 1900 or 1901–

فهرست کتابهای چاپی عربی · ایران ، از آغاز چاپ تا اکنون · سایر کشورها ، بیشتر از سال ۱۳۴۰ هـ ببعد · تألیف خانبابا مشار · ₍تهران ₎۱۳۴۴ ₍1965₎

20 p., 1014 columns, 108 p. 24 cm.

IRAQ

ʻAwwād, Kūrkīs.

معجم المؤلفين العراقیین فی القرنین التاسع عشر والعشرین ، ۱۸۰۰ – ۱۹۶۹ · تألیـف کورکیس عواد · بغداد ، مطبـعة الارشاد ، ₍1969–

Bagdad. Jāmiʻat Baghdād. al-Maktabah al-Markazīyah. Qism al-Maṭbūʻāt al-Ḥukūmīyah.

فهرس موضوعی بالمطبوعات الحکومیة فی المکتبة المرکزیه لجامعة بغداد · بغداد ، المکتبة المرکزیة لجامعة بغداد ، 1969 .

53, 14, 8, 14 l. 33 cm.

At head of title: الکومیة المطبوعات قسم · بغداد لجامعة المرکزیة الکتبة
Added t. p.: Classified catalog of government publications available in the Central Library, Baghdad University.

Cairo. Dār al-Kutub al-Miṣrīyah.

قائمة بالکتب والمراجع عن العراق · الطبعة ۲. القاهرة ₍ مطبعة دار الکتب ، 1964 .

172, 87 p. 24 cm.

(۵ ، العربی بالعالم للتعریف والمراجع الکتب قوائم سلسلة)

At head of title: الجمهورية العربية المتحدة. وزارة الثقافة والارشاد.
القومي. دار الكتب.

Added t. p.: A bibliographical list of works about Iraq.
Includes publications in Arabic and Western languages.

IRELAND

see also Northern Ireland; and under
Dissertations, Academic and Great
Britain - History, Local

Brown, Stephen James Meredith, 1881–   ed.
A guide to books on Ireland. Part 1: Prose literature,
poetry, music, and plays. Edited by Stephen J. M. Brown.
New York, Lemma Pub. Corp., 1970.

xvii, 371 p. 23 cm.

No more published.
Reprint of the 1912 ed.
"Irish plays," by Joseph Holloway: p. ₁159₁–324.

Clare, Wallace.
A simple guide to Irish genealogy; first compiled by the
Rev. Wallace Clare. 3rd ed. revised by Rosemary Ffolliott.
London, Irish Genealogical Research Society, 1966.

45 p. 22 cm.

Ireland (*Eire*). *Ordnance Survey.*
Catalogue of the large-scale maps with dates of survey
and latest revision shown on the indexes to each county.
₁Dublin₁ Stationery Off., 1964.

1 v. (chiefly maps) 33 cm.

Library Association. *County Libraries Group.*
Readers' guide to books on face of Ireland. 2nd. ed.
London, L. A. (County libraries group), 1968.

39 p. 19 cm. (*Its* Readers' guides, new series, no. 105)

Cover title: Face of Ireland.

Oslo. Norske Nobelinstitutt. Biblioteket.
Irland 1949–1972. Litteratur i Nobelinstituttets bibliotek. Av Anne Kjelling. Oslo, 1972.

5 l. 30 cm.

Peel, Sir Robert, bart., 1788–1850.
Bibliotheca Hibernicana, or; A descriptive catalogue of a
select Irish library collected for the Right Hon Robert Peel.
With an essay by Norman D. Palmer. Shannon, Irish University Press ₁1970₁

101–113, v. 51 p. facsims. 23 cm.

Compiled by W. S. Mason.
"Photolithographic facsimile of the first edition ₁1823₁"
"Essay by Norman D. Palmer first published in Irish historical
studies, vol. VI, no. 22, September 1948."

Wagner, Henry Raup, 1862–1957.
Irish economics, 1700–1783; a bibliography with notes.
New York, A. M. Kelley, 1969.

94 p. 23 cm. (Reprints of economic classics)

Reprint of the 1907 ed.

BIBLIOGRAPHIES

Eager, Alan R
A guide to Irish bibliographical material, being a bibliography of Irish bibliographies and some sources of information, by Alan R. Eager. London, Library Association,
1964.

xiii, 392 p. 23 cm.

HISTORY

**Asplin, P   W   A   ** 1939–
Medieval Ireland, c. 1170–1495; a bibliography of sec-

ondary works, by P. W. A. Asplin. Dublin, Royal Irish
Academy, 1971.

xv, 139 p. 25 cm. (A New history of Ireland. Ancillary publications, no. 1)

Dublin. National Library of Ireland.
Manuscript sources for the history of Irish civilisation.
Edited by Richard J. Hayes. Boston, G. K. Hall, 1965.

11 v. 37 cm.

**Hayes, Richard J   ** 1902–
Sources for the history of Irish civilisation; articles in
Irish periodicals, edited by Richard J. Hayes. Boston,
G. K. Hall, 1970.

9 v. 37 cm.

CONTENTS.—v. 1–5. Persons.—v. 6–8. Subjects.—v. 9. Places-
Dates.

Johnston, Edith Mary.
Irish history: a select bibliography, by Edith M. Johnston.
London, Historical Association, 1969.

63 p. 22 cm. (Helps for students of history, no. 73)

Johnston, Edith Mary.
Irish history: a select bibliography, by Edith M. Johnston. Rev. ₁ed.₁ London, Historical Association, 1972.

76 p. 22 cm. (Helps for students of history, no. 73)

London. Imperial War Museum. Library.
Ireland 1914–1921; a selected list of references. ₁London₁ Imperial War Museum ₁1966₁

11 l. 34 cm. (₁London. Imperial War Museum₁. Bibliography
no. PH. 851)

Moody, Theodore William, 1907–   comp.
Irish historiography, 1936–70. Edited by T. W. Moody.
Dublin, Irish Committee of Historical Sciences, 1971.

viii, 155 p. 24 cm.

"Presented by the Irish Committee of Historical Sciences to the
Bureau of the Comité International des Sciences Historiques to
mark the occasion of the Bureau's first meeting in Ireland, 16–18
July 1971."

Northern Ireland. Public Record Office.
Eighteenth century Irish official papers in Great Britain.
Belfast, H. M. Stationery Off., 1973–

v. 30 cm.

CONTENTS: v. 1. Private collections.

IMPRINTS

Irish publishing record. 1967–
₁Dublin₁ School of Librarianship, University College Dublin.

v. 26 cm. annual.

LAW see Law - Ireland

IRIAN BARAT, INDONESIA

Bibliotheca Bogoriensis.
Irian Barat. Bogor ₁1967?₁

9 p. 32 cm. (Its Seri bibliografi, no. 4)

—— Bibliografi mengenai Irian Barat; suplemen. Bibliography on Irian Barat; supplement. Bogor ₁1968?₁

8 p. 33 cm. (Its Seri bibliografi, no. 12)

IRIS (PLANT)

Cook, Tressie, 1903–
Louisiana irises, a bibliography. Rev. ed. Lafayette,
Society for Louisiana Irises, ₁1972₁

28 p. illus. 22 cm.

Page 28 blank for "Notes."

IRISH IN THE UNITED STATES

Rose, Walter R   1937–
A bibliography of the Irish in the United States, by Walter R. Rose. Afton, N. Y., Tristram Shanty Publications, 1969.

18 l. 30 cm. 25.00

IRISH LANGUAGE AND LITERATURE
see also Celtic literature

Arbois de Jubainville, Henry d', 1827–1910.
Essai d'un catalogue de la littérature épique de l'Irlande; précédé d'une étude sur les manuscrits en langue irlandaise conservés dans les Iles britanniques et sur le continent. Nieuwkoop, B. de Graaf, 1969.

clv, 282 p. 22 cm.

"Réimpression de l'édition Paris, 1883."

Arbois de Jubainville, Henry d', 1827–1910.
Essai d'un catalogue de la littérature épique de l'Irlande. Précédé d'une étude sur les manuscrits en langue irlandaise conservés dans les Iles britanniques et sur le continent. Par H. d'Arbois de Jubainville. Réimpression de l'éd. 1883. Osnabrück, Zeller, 1969.

clv, 282 p. 22 cm.

Dublin. *National Library of Ireland.*
Bibliography of Irish philology and of printed Irish literature. New York, Johnson Reprint Corp. [1970]

xii, 307 p. 24 cm.

Reprint of the 1913 ed.

Harmon, Maurice.
Modern Irish literature, 1800–1967; a reader's guide. [Chester Springs, Pa.] Dufour Editions [1968]

71 p. 21 cm.

Keaney, Marian.
Westmeath authors: a bibliographical and biographical study. Mulligar, Longford-Westmeath Joint Library Committee, 1969.

xv, 230 p. 23 cm.

Kocztur, Gizella.
Irish literature in Hungarian translation. Budapest, Hungarian P. E. N. Club, 1971.

65 p. 20 cm.

"A bibliography compiled and published for the Golden Jubilee Congress of International P. E. N. to be held in Dublin in September 1971."

IRKUTSK, SIBERIA

Иркутск. Библиогр. указ. [Вступит. статья Г. А. Вендриха и Н. Ф. Салацкого, с. 3–65]. Иркутск, 1971.

249 p. 20 cm. 1.67rub

At head of title: Исполнительный комитет Иркутского городского Совета депутатов трудящихся. Научная библиотека Иркутского государственного университета имени А. А. Жданова. By G. A. Vendrikh and others.

Irkutsk, Siberia. Oblastnaía biblioteka. *Spravochno-bibliograficheskiĭ otdel.*
Земля Иркутская. (Аннот. рек. указатель литературы об Иркут. обл.) Иркутск, 1968.

132 p. 20 cm.

At head of title: Иркутская областная библиотека им. И. И.

Молчанова-Сибирского. Справочно-библиографический отдел. Prepared by P. P. Borovskiĭ and others.

IRON AND STEEL
see also Cast-iron

Iron and Steel Institute.
Ironmaking in the blast furnace. London, Iron & Steel Institute, 1966.

[188] p. 30 cm. (Bibliography no. 23a)

Legátová, Božena, *comp.*
Vědecké řízení práce v hutním průmyslu; výběrova bibliografie. [Zprac. Legátová Božena] Ostrava, 1964.

66 p. 20 cm. (Státní vědecká knihovna v Ostravě. Publikace. Řada II, čís. 381)

Sedlář, Oldřich, *comp.*
Aglomerace železných rud; výběrová bibliografie. [Zpracovatel: Oldřich Sedlář] Ostrava, 1966.

136 p. 29 cm. (Státní vědecká knihovna v Ostravě. Publikace. Řada II, čís. 402)

Sklíanchenkova, A   A
[Kislorodno-konverternoe proizvodstvo stali]
Кислородно-конверторное производство стали. Отеч. и иностр. литература за 1969–1971 (I кв.) гг. [Сост. А. А. Склянченкова]. Библиогр. справка. Москва, 1971.
35 p. 22 cm.
At head of title: Научно-исследовательский институт информации по тяжелому, энергетическому и транспортному машиностроению. Центральная научно-техническая библиотека тяжелого машиностроения.

Wainwright, Eric John.
Bibliography on the brittle fracture of iron and steel at cryogenic to room temperatures, compiled by E. J. Wainwright. Guildford (Surrey), University of Surrey (Library), 1969.

[1], 122 l. 30 cm. (Library bibliography GUSL/BIB/L)

White, D
How to find out in iron and steel, by D. White. [1st ed.] Oxford, New York, Pergamon Press [1970]

v, 184 p. 20 cm. (Commonwealth and international library. Libraries and technical information division)

IRON ORE

Earney, Fillmore C   F
Researcher's guide to iron ore : an annotated bibliography on the economic geography of iron ore / Fillmore C. F. Earney. — Littleton, Colo. : Libraries Unlimited, 1974.

595 p. ; 24 cm.

IROQUOIS INDIANS

Weinman, Paul L
A bibliography of the Iroquoian literature, partially annotated, by Paul L. Weinman. Albany, University of the State of New York, 1969.

ix, 254 p. 22 cm. (New York State Museum and Science Service. Bulletin no. 411)

IRRIGATION

Boleszny, Ivan.
Overhead irrigation, compiled by I. Boleszny. Adelaide, State Library of South Australia, 1970–

v. 27 cm. (State Library of South Australia. Research service bibliographies, series 4, no. 129

Casey, Hugh E
Salinity problems in arid lands irrigation: a literature review and selected bibliography, by Hugh E. Casey. Tucson, University of Arizona, Office of Arid Lands Studies,

1972.

iv, 300 p. 27 cm. (Arid lands resource information paper no. 1)

Floss, Ludmilla.
Sprinkler irrigation; a bibliography selected from foreign literature, 1964–1969. Washington, U. S. Dept. of the Interior. Office of the Secretary, 1970.

54 p. 27 cm. (Office of Library Services. Bibliography series, no. 15)

Moscow. TSentral'naiã nauchnaiã sel'skokhoziãĭstvennaiã biblioteka. *Spravochno-bibliograficheskiĭ otdel.*
Ирригация—важнейший резерв интенсификации сельскохозяйственного производства. ₍Библиограф А. Л. Горбатов₎ Москва, 1964.

26 p. 20 cm.
At head of title: Всесоюзная академия с.-х. наук имени В. И. Ленина. Центральная научная сельскохозяйственная библиотека. Справочно-библиографический отдел.

Освоение орошаемых земель; библиографический указатель отечественной литературы в количестве 508 названий за 1960–1966 гг. и иностранной литературы в количестве 112 названий за 1964–1966 гг. ₍Составитель Л. В. Чернова. Редактор И. Г. Палилова₎ Москва, 1967.

98 p. 20 cm.
At head of title: Всесоюзная ордена Ленина академия с.-х. наук имени Ленина. Центральная научная сельскохозяйственная библиотека. Справочно-библиографический отдел.

Raadsma, S
Annotated bibliography on surface irrigation methods, compiled by S. Raadsma and G. Schrale. Wageningen, the Netherlands, International Institute for Land Reclamation and Improvement, 1971.

72 p. 24 cm. (International Institute for Land Reclamation and Improvement. Bibliography 9)

Selected irrigation return flow quality abstracts. 1st–
1968/69–
Washington. Office of Research and Monitoring, U. S. Environmental Protection Agency; For sale by the Supt. of Docs., U. S. Govt. Print. Off.

v. 27 cm. annual (Environmental protection technology series)

Tîrgul-Mureş, Romania. Biblioteca Municipală. Serviciul de Informare Bibliografică.
Programul naţional privind gospodărirea raţională a resurselor de apă, extinderea lucrărilor de irigaţii, îndiguiri, desecări şi de combatere a eroziunii solului în R. S. R. în anii 1971–1975 şi prevederile generale de perspectivă pînă în 1985. Bibliografie de recomandare. ₍Tîrgu-Mureş₎, 1970.

11 l. 30 cm.
At head of title: Biblioteca Municipală Tîrgu-Mureş. Direcţia Agricolă Jud. Tîrgu-Mureş.

Tyrsina, T   I
Библиография публикаций ЮжНИИГиМА (1921–1969 гг.) Новочеркасск, 1970 ₍вып. дан. 1971₎.

126 p. 20 cm. 0.43rub
At head of title: Министерство мелиорации и водного хозяйства РСФСР. Южный научно-исследовательский институт гидротехники и мелиорации.
"Составители: Т. И. Тырсина, Л. В. Озолзарс и В. Е. Чернохлебова."

Water Resources Scientific Information Center.
Irrigation efficiency; a bibliography. Washington; ₍available from the National Technical Information Service, Springfield, Va.₎ 1973.

iii, 418 p. 26 cm. (Its Bibliography series, WRSIC 73–214)

Water Resources Scientific Information Center.
Use of naturally impaired water; a bibliography. Wash-

ington; ₍Available from the National Technical Information Service, Springfield, Va., 1973₎

iv, 364 p. 27 cm. (Its Bibliography series, WRSIC 73–217)

Зрошення та обводнення на півдні Української РСР. Бібліогр. покажчик. 1952–1965 рр. Київ, "Наукова думка," 1968.

220 p. 22 cm.
At head of title: Академія наук Української РСР. Центральна наукова бібліотека.
By O. V. Bystriãkov, and others.
Edited by S. M. Alpat'ev.

IRVING, WASHINGTON

Langfeld, William Robert, 1882–
Washington Irving; a bibliography complied by William R. Langfeld, with the bibliographic assistance of Philip C. Blackburn. Folcroft, Pa., Folcroft Press ₍1969₎

vii, 90 p. illus. 29 cm.

Reprint of the 1933 ed.

Langfeld, William Robert, 1882–
Washington Irving; a bibliography, compiled by William R. Langfeld, with the bibliographic assistance of Philip C. Blackburn, and A census of Washington Irving manuscripts, by H. L. Kleinfield. Port Washington, N. Y., Kennikat Press ₍1968₎

vii, 90, 13–32 p. illus., facsims., port. 23 cm.
The bibliography is a reprint of the 1933 ed.; the census is reprinted from the Bulletin of the New York Public Library, v. 68, no. 1, Jan. 1964.

Williams, Stanley Thomas, 1888–1956, comp.
A bibliography of the writings of Washington Irving; a check list. Compiled by Stanley T. Williams and Mary Allen Edge. Folcroft, Pa., Folcroft Press ₍1969₎

xix, 200 p. 26 cm.

Reprint of the 1936 ed.

Williams, Stanley Thomas, 1888–1956, *comp.*
A bibliography of the writing of Washington Irving; a check list, compiled by Stanley T. Williams and Mary Allen Edge. New York, B. Franklin ₍1970₎

xix, 200 p. 24 cm. (Essays in literature & criticism, 70)

Burt Franklin bibliogrgaphy and reference series, 844.
Reprint of the 1936 ed.

IQBAL, SIR MUHAMMAD

Waheed, K   Abdul.
A bibliography of Iqbal, by K. A. Waheed. ₍1st ed.₎ Karachi, Iqbal Academy ₍1965₎

iii, 224 p. 23 cm.

ISAACS, JORGE

McGrady, Donald.
Bibliografía sobre Jorge Isaacs. Bogotá, 1971.

75 p. 23 cm. (Publicaciones del Instituto Caro y Cuervo. Serie bibliográfica, 8)

ISAKOVSKIĬ, MIKHAIL VASIL'EVICH

Михаил Васильевич Исаковский. (К 70-летию со дня рождения). Рек. указатель литературы. ₍Предисл. Ю. Пашкова₎. Смоленск, ₍"Моск. рабочий"₎, 1969.

55 p. 20 cm.

At head of title: Смоленское областное управление культуры. Смоленская областная библиотека им. В. И. Ленина.
By L. S. Dobrokhotova, and others.

ISHERWOOD, CHRISTOPHER

Westby, Selmer.
Christopher Isherwood; a bibliography, 1923–1967, by

Selmer Westby and Clayton M. Brown. Los Angeles, Published by the California State College at Los Angeles Foundation for the John F. Kennedy Memorial Library, California State College at Los Angeles, 1968.

51 p. illus. 22 cm.

ISIDORUS, SAINT, BP. OF SEVILLE

Fernández Caton, José María.
Las etimologías en la tradición manuscrita medieval estudiada por el Prof. Dr. Anspach. Prólogo del Dr. Manuel C. Díaz y Díaz. León, Centro de Estudios e Investigaciones Científicas "San Isidro," Consejo Superior de Investigaciones Científicas, 1966.

291 p. port. 25 cm.

Half title: Las etimologías de San Isidro.

ISIS

Leclant, Jean.
Inventaire bibliographique des Isiaca (Ibis). Répertoire analytique des travaux relatifs à la diffusion des cultes isiaques 1940-1969. Avec la collaboration de Gisèle Clerc. Leiden, Brill, 1972–

v. photos. 25 cm. (Études préliminaires aux religions orientales dans l'Empire romain, t. 18

ISLAM; ISLAMIC COUNTRIES

American Institute of Islamic Studies.
Bibliographic series. no. 1–
Denver, °1969–

no. 21 cm.

Hamburg. Deutsches Orient-Institut. Dokumentationsleitstelle Moderner Orient.
Bibliographie zum Erziehungs- und Bildungswesen in den Ländern des muslimischen Orients. Hamburg, 1967.

vi, 52 p. 30 cm. (Hamburg. Deutsches Orient-Institut. Schriften. Reihe Bibliographien)

At head of title: Deutsches Orient-Institut (Deutsche Orient-Stiftung)

Hampson, Ruth M
Islam in South Africa, a bibliography compiled by Ruth M. Hampson. Cape Town University of Cape Town, School of Librarianship, 1964.

iii, 55 p. 23 cm. (University of Cape Town. School of Librarianship. Bibliographical series)

Husaini, Imdādu.
(Sindhu ji dini adaba jo ka' talāgu)

سنڌ جي ديني ادب جو ڪٽلاگ. تيار ڪندڙ امداد حسيني ۾ سحر بلوچ. نگران اعليٰ غلام مصطفيٰ قاسمي. نگران خواجه غلام علي الانا. حيدرآباد، سنڌ، انسٽيٽيوٽ آف سنڌالاجي،
1971

40, 22 p. 28 cm.

''انسٽيٽيوٽ آف سنڌالاجي'' جي ريسرج سيل ۾ تيار ٿيو.''
In Sindhi.

Islam in paperback. 1969–
Denver, American Institute of Islamic Studies.

v. 21 cm. annual. (American Institute of Islamic Studies. Bibliographic series)

London. University. School of Oriental and African Studies. Library.
Index Islamicus, 1906-1955; a catalogue of articles on Islamic subjects in periodicals and other collective publications, compiled by J. D. Pearson, Librarian, with the assistance of Julia F. Ashton. London Mansell 1972, c1958

xxxvi, 897 p. 26 cm.

McGill University, Montreal. Institute of Islamic Studies. Library.
Periodica Islamica; a check-list of serials available at McGill Islamics Library, compiled by Muzaffar Ali. Montreal, McGill University, Institute of Islamic Studies, 1973.

28 p. 28 cm.

Motzkin, A   L   1934–
מבוא ללימודי האסלם; הדרכה ביבליוגרפית מאת, א. ל. מוצקין. ערכו לפי הרצאות חנה עמית ו,שלמה אלון. ירושלים, אקדמון, 727 1967,

4, 60 p. 24 cm.

Paris. École pratique des hautes études. *Centre russe.*
Catalogue des microfilms du Centre russe de l'École pratique des hautes études: ouvrages et périodiques concernant l'islam en Russie et le socialisme au Moyen Orient. (Supplément 1964) Paris? 1964?

75 l. 28 cm.

Cover title.
Supplements the center's Catalogue des microfilms des ouvrages intéressant les musulmans de l'U. R. S. S. et la politique musulmane du Gouvernement soviétique and its Catalogue des microfilms des périodiques publiés en Russie et des périodiques publiés à l'étranger par des musulmans russes émigrés, avant 1920.

Sauvaget, Jean, 1901-1950.
Introduction to the history of the Muslim East: a bibliographical guide. Based on the 2d ed. as recast by Claude Cahen. Berkeley, University of California Press, 1965.

xxi, 252 p. 25 cm.

BIBLIOGRAPHIES

Geddes, Charles L
An analytical guide to the bibliographies on Islam, Muhammad, and the Qur'an by C. L. Geddes. Denver American Institute of Islamic Studies 1973,

102 p. 22 cm. (American Institute of Islamic Studies. Bibliographic series, no. 8)

ISLAM, KAZI NAZRUL

Islam, Rafiqul.
নজরুল নির্দেশিকা. লেখক রফিকুল ইসলাম. ঢাকা, বাংলা একাডেমী 1969,

11, 379 p. 22 cm.

In Bengali.

Razia Sultana.
নজরুল-অন্বেষা; নজরুলের রচিত কাব্য, কবিতা, গান, প্রবন্ধ, নাটক, ছোটগল্প, উপন্যাস, ও চরিত্রের বর্ণানুক্রমিক পরিচিতি ও আলোচনা. লেখিকা, রাজিয়া সুলতানা. সৈয়দ আলী আহ্সান লিখিত ভূমিকাসহ. 1. সংস্করণ, ঢাকা, মখদুমী অ্যাণ্ড আহ্সানউল্লাহ্ লাইব্রেরী 1969–
v. 22 cm.

"নজরুল গ্রন্থপঞ্জী": v. 1, p. 185-187.

ISLANDS OF THE PACIFIC   see   Oceania
ISOTOPES
    see also   Radioisotopes

Moulet, Elisée.
Les Isotopes de l'hydrogène, réactions nucléaires, par Elisée Moulet, Denise Gondal. Saclay, Centre d'études nucléaires, Service de documentation, 1967.

ii, 167 p. 27 cm. (Bibliographie CEA no 82)

Summary in English and French.
Errata slip inserted.

Moulet, Elisée.
Les isotopes du béryllium: réactions nucléaires. Gif-sur-

Yvette, Service de documentation du C. E. A., Centre d'études nucléaires de Saclay, 1965.

151 p. 27 cm. (France. Commissariat à l'énergie atomique, Série "Bibliographies," no 32)

Philippine Atomic Energy Commission.
Iodine isotopes 131; a literature search. Manila, 1971.

ii, 334 l. 27 cm.

Philippine Atomic Energy Commission.
Iron-59 (Fe^{59}); a literature search. [Manila] 1967.

ii, 76 l. 28 cm.

Philippine Atomic Energy Commission.
Plutonium isotopes 239; a literature search. [Manila] 1970.

iii, 177 l. 28 cm.

Philippine Atomic Energy Commission. Classification and Information Branch.
Chromium isotopes-Cr 51; a literature search. Manila, 1971.

120 l. 28 cm.

Philippine Atomic Energy Commission. Classification and Information Branch.
Cobalt-60; a literature search. Manila, Philippine Atomic Energy Commission, 1972.

241 l. 28 cm.

Weber, Jon Noel Earl, 1935–
Bibliography—geochemistry of the stable isotopes of carbon and oxygen [by] Jon N. Weber. [University Park, Mineral Industries Experiment Station, College of Mineral Industries, Pennsylvania State University] 1964.

80 l. 28 cm. (Pennsylvania. State University. Mineral Industries Experiment Station. Circular 67)

ISRAEL
see also Palestine

Alexander, Yonah.
Israel; selected, annotated, and illustrated bibliography. [1st ed.] Gilbertsville, N. Y., V. Buday, 1968.

116 p. illus., maps. 23 cm.

Basin, Giyora.
(ha-Noflim be-madim)
הנופלים במדים; רשימת פרסומים לזכרם ועזבונם של הנופלים במערכות ישראל, ערך גיורא בסין. [תל-אביב, ההוצאה לאור של משרד הבטחון] 1973.

193 p. 22 cm.

Educational Research Council of America.
Jews in Israel and in other lands abroad. [Cleveland, Ohio, 1972]

iv, 17 p. illus. 26 cm. (A Graded, annotated bibliography for grades 7–12, pt. 3)

"A collaborative project of the Educational Research Council of America of Cleveland, Ohio and the American Association for Jewish Education of New York, New York."

Gat, Z
Rural development in Israel; a list of publications in languages other than Hebrew. Prepared by Z. Gat and S. T. Marton. Tel Aviv, 1966.
69 p. 28 cm.
At head of title: Ministry of Agriculture, Department for Agricultural Cooperation with Developing Countries, Centre for Comparative Studies on Agricultural Development.

Hagiti, Ḥayim.
רשימה של פרסומים למתן אינפורמציה, ערוכה ע"י חיים הגיתי

בהדרכתו של י. דלינדיש. ירושלים, משרד החינוך והתרבות, היחידה לתרבות, המדור לספריות, 1967.

11 l. 33 cm.

Israel. *Maḥleket ha-medidot.*
קטלוג מפות. תל-אביב, מחלקת המדידות, משרד העבודה, 1964.

26, iii p. maps (part col.) 25 cm.

Cover title: Catalogue of maps.
Preface also in English.

Kutten, A
(Bibliyografyah shel sifre ketovot u-madrikhim be-Yisrael)
בבליוגרפיה של ספרי כתבות ומדריכים בישראל, מאת אהרן קוטין. [מהד' חדשה] תל-אביב, הסתדרות הפקידים, עובדי המינהל והשירותים, המחלקה להשכלה ולחינוך מקצועי, 1970.

34, [35], 3 p. 23 cm. (ספרית הפקיד)

Added t. p.: Bibliography of guides and directories in Israel.
Hebrew and English.

המבנה החברתי של ישראל; לקט ביבליוגרפי. השתתפו בעריכה: כהנא ר. [ואחרים] ירושלים, האוניברסיטה העברית בירושלים, המרכז לתעוד ולמחקר המבנה החברתי של ישראל, [1968] 729.

5, 173 p. 27 cm.

Neuberg, Assia.
מדינת ישראל תש"ח–תשכ"ח; ביבליוגרפיה מוערת, מאת אסיה נויברג. ירושלים, בית הספר לספרנות ע"י האוניברסיטה העברית, [1970] 730.

12, 254, xlv p. 28 cm.

Added t. p.: The state of Israel 1948–1968; an annotated bibliography.
Prefatory material and index also in English.

Pickering, Peter E
A brief bibliography of reference works containing data on the land of Israel, past and present, compiled by Peter E. Pickering. Melbourne, Alphega Publications, 1969.

21 l. 26 cm.

Reich, Bernard.
Israel in paperback. Prepared for the Middle East Studies Association. [New York, Middle East Studies Association of North America, c1971]

a-b, 26, ix p. 23 cm. (Middle East Studies Association of North America. Bibliographic series, 2)

Shelah, Elana.
The social structure of Israel; a bibliography. Edited by Ilana Shelach, Hana Harlap [and] Shifra Weiss. Jerusalem, Hebrew University of Jerusalem, 1971.

146 p. 27 cm.

"Every listing ... appeared during the years 1948–1968."

U. S. *Library of Congress. American Libraries Book Procurement Center, Tel-Aviv.*
Accessions list, Israel. v. 1–
Apr. 1964–
Tel-Aviv.

v. 28 cm. monthly.

At head of title: The Library of Congress Public Law 480 Project.

LAW see Law – Israel

ISTRIA

Combi, Carlo A 1827–1884.
Saggio di bibliografia istriana. Pubblicato a spese di una società patria. Bologna, Forni, 1967.

vii, 484 p. 25 cm.

Reprint of the Capodistria, 1864 ed.

ISTVÁN, SAINT, KING OF HUNGARY

Horvath, Michael Joseph.
An annotated bibliography of Stephen I, King of Hungary: his reign and his era. College Park, Md., University of Maryland Library, 1969.

28 p. illus. 23 cm.

Prepared for an exhibit held at the University of Maryland Library.

ITALIAN IMPRINTS

Associazione italiana editori.
Catalogo dei libri italiani in commercio. Milano, Associazione italiana editori, 1970–

v. 29 cm.

Dizionario bibliografico. 1967–
[Bologna] Società editrice Il Mulino.

v. 25 cm. annual.

At head of title, 1967–   : Consorzio provinciale per la pubblica lettura, Bologna.
Editor: 1967–   P. Petrucci.

Florence. Biblioteca nazionale centrale.
Catalogo cumulativo 1886–1957 del Bollettino delle pubblicazioni italiane ricevute per diritto di stampa dalla Biblioteca nazionale centrale di Firenze. Nendeln, Liechtenstein, Kraus Reprint, 1968–69.

41 v. 34 cm.

At head of title: Centro nazionale per il catalogo unico delle biblioteche italiane e per le informazioni bibliografiche, Roma.
"Il CUBI (così sarà indicato brevemente questo catalogo) è il risultato della fusione in unica sequenza alfabetica ... delle schede contenute nelle settantadue annate del Bollettino delle pubblicazioni italiane ricevute per diritto di stampa, edito dalla Biblioteca nazionale centrale di Firenze dal 1886 al 1957."

On spine: CUBI
Vol. 40: Indice degli autori secondari; v. 41: Indice degli autori secondari. Aggiunte.

Lievsay, John León.
The Englishman's Italian books, 1550–1700, by John L. Lievsay. Philadelphia, University of Pennsylvania Press [1969]

ix, 104 p. facsims., ports. 24 cm.

"Publications of the A. S. W. Rosenbach Fellowship in Bibliography."

Michel, Suzanne P
Répertoire des ouvrages imprimés en langue italienne au XVII⁰ siècle [par] Suzanne et Paul-Henri Michel ... Firenze, L. S. Olschki, 1970–

v. plates. 25 cm. (Biblioteca di bibliografia italiana, 59

Introd. in French and Italian.

Michel, Suzanne P
Répertoire des ouvrages imprimés en langue italienne au XVII⁰ siècle conservés dans les bibliothèques de France [par] Suzanne P. Michel ... Paul-Henri Michel ... Paris, Éditions du Centre national de la recherche scientifique, 1967–

v. 27 cm.

"Publié sur la recommendation du Conseil international de la philosophie et des sciences humaines."

Rome (City) Mostra Cinque secoli del libro italiano, *1965.*
Cinque secoli del libro italiano; mostra storica sotto gli auspici del Ministero della pubblica istruzione. Roma,

Palazzo Braschi, 20 maggio–30 giugno 1965. Catalogo. Roma, De Luca, 1965.

ix, 190 p. facsims. (part col.) plates. 25 cm.

At head of title: Comitato per la celebrazione del v centenario dell'arte tipografica in Italia.

Short-title catalog of books printed in Italy and of books in Italian printed abroad, 1501–1600, held in selected North American libraries. [Robert G. Marshall, editor] Boston, G. K. Hall, 1970.

3 v. 27 cm.

CONTENTS.—v. 1. A–F.—v. 2. G–P.—v. 3. Q–Z. Index of printers and publishers.

ITALIAN LANGUAGE

Accademia della Crusca, Florence. Opera del vocabolario.
Indice dei testi sottoposti a spoglio lessicale fino al 30 settembre 1972. Firenze, 1972.

xv, 133 l. 28 cm.

Hall, Robert Anderson, 1911–
Bibliografia della linguistica italiana. 2. ed. riv. e aggiornata. Firenze, Sansoni, 1958.

3 v. 26 cm. (Biblioteca bibliografica italica, 13–15)
1st ed. published in English.

———— Supplemento decennale. Firenze, Sansoni, 1969–

v. 26 cm. (Biblioteca bibliografica italica, 35
CONTENTS.—1. 1956–1966.

Mazzoni, Guido, 1859–
Avviamento allo studio critico delle lettere italiane. 4. edizione riveduta e aggiornata per cura di Carmine Jannaco. Con prefazione di Francesco Maggini e appendici di Pio Rajna e Ernesto Giacomo Parodi. Firenze, G. C. Sansoni, 1971.

xlv, 238 p. 20½ cm. (Manuali di filologia e storia. Ser. 2, v. 3)

Muljačić, Žarko.
Introduzione allo studio della lingua italiana. Torino, G. Einaudi, 1971.

388 p. 18 cm. (Piccola biblioteca Einaudi, 159)

Prantauer, Alois, *comp.*
Deutsche Bibliographie des italienischen Sprachbuches der Gegenwart. Zusammengestellt anlässlich der Tagung von Italienischlehrern an Technischen, Gewerblichen und Frauenberuflichen Lehranstalten im Peter-Rosegger-Heim in Krieglach vom 16. bis 19. Sept. 1957. (Salzburg, [1957])

20 l. 29 cm.

———— Zusatzblätter mit Ergänzungen und Berichtigungen unter besonderer Berücksichtigung des fachlichen Italienisch. Zusammengestellt anlässlich des Pflichtseminars für Italienischlehrer an Berufsbildenden Mittleren und Höheren Schulen vom 16. bis 18. Feb. 1966 im Peter-Rosegger-Heim in Krieglach. Salzburg, 1966.

7 l. 30 cm.

ITALIAN LITERATURE

Doni, Anton Francesco, 1513–1574.
La libraria ... A cura di Vanni Bramanti. Otto tavole. Milano, Longanesi, 1972.

498 p. 8 plates. 18 cm. (I Cento libri, v. 33)

Olschki, *firm, Florence.*
Lettere italiche. Firenze, [1967].

128 p. illus. 24 cm. (*Its* Catalogo, 143)

Cover title: Lettere di diversi nobilissimi hvomini, et eccellentissimi ingegni, scritte in diuerse materie.

Repertorio bibliografico della letteratura italiana. A cura della Facoltà di magistero di Roma, sotto la direzione di Umberto Bosco. 1943–1947. Firenze, Sansoni, 1969.

xii, 138 p. 27 cm.

Continues Prezzolini's Repertorio bibliografico della storia e della critica della letteratura italiana, and is continued by Bosco's Repertorio bibliografico della letteratura italiana.

De Storkøbenhavnske folkebibliotekers samarbejdsudvalg.
Italiensk skønlitteratur i de storkøbenhavnske folkebiblioteker og i Statsbiblioteket. Red. af Ane Marie Bonde. København; (Bibliotekscentralen) 1969.

79 p. 20 cm.

BIO-BIBLIOGRAPHY

Dizionario critico della letteratura italiana. Diretto da Vittore Branca. Redattori Armando Balduino, Manlio Pastore Stocchi, Marco Pecoraro. Torino, Unione tipografico editrice torinese, [1974?].

3 v. plates. 26 cm.

Dizionario degli scrittori italiani d'oggi. **Cosenza, Pellegrini, 1969.**

269 p. plates. 24¼ cm.

Dizionario generale degli autori italiani contemporanei ... Firenze, Vallecchi, 1974.

2 v. (xliv, 1551 p.) illus. 23 cm.

"Coordinamento Enzo Ronconi."
CONTENTS: 1. Movimenti letterari, Abba-Luzzatto Fegiz. — 2. Maccari-Zumbini, Influenze e corrispondenze.

Slovník spisovatelů: Itálie — Vatikánské Město — San Marino—Švýcarsko (Ticino, Grigioni). Zprac. kol. za ved. Josefa Bukáčka, [který také] naps. úv. studii. 1. vyd. Praha, Odeon, 1968.

426, [33] p. 19 cm.

Triggiani, Domenico, 1929–
Per la storia della letteratura italiana contemporanea. [Bari, Grafiche Levante, 1967]

297 p. 22 cm.

HISTORY AND CRITICISM

Binni, Walter, 1913–
Introduzione ai problemi critici della letteratura italiana [di] Walter Binni [e] Riccardo Scrivano. Messina-Firenze, G. D'Anna, 1967.

415 p. 22 cm.

Esposito, Enzo.
Critica letteraria; rassegna degli studi sulla letteratura italiana apparsi nei periodici del 1962. Milano, Marzorati [1964]

327 p. 21 cm.

TRANSLATIONS

Scott, Mary Augusta, 1851–1918.
Elizabethan translations from the Italian. New York, B. Franklin [1969]

lxxxi, 558 p. 23 cm. (Vassar semi-centennial series)

Burt Franklin bibliography & reference series, 280.
Essays in literature & criticism, 32.
Reprint of the 1916 ed.

ITALIANS IN THE UNITED STATES

Cordasco, Francesco, 1920–
Italians in the United States; a bibliography of reports, texts, critical studies and related materials [by] Francesco Cordasco [and] Salvatore LaGumina. New York, Oriole Editions, 1972.

xvi, 137 p. illus. 27 cm.

ITALY

see also Communism - Italy; and under France *(Bibliographie)* and Dissertations, Academic

Ancona, Alessandro d', 1835–1914.
Saggio di una bibliografia ragionata dei viaggi e delle descrizioni d'Italia e dei costumi italiani in lingue straniere. A cura della libreria Tonini. Ravenna, Libreria antiquaria Tonini, [1971?]

142 p. 25 cm.

From His L'Italia alla fine del secolo XVI. Giornale del viaggio di Michele Di Montaigne in Italia nel 1580 e 1581. "400 esemplari numerati."

Biblioteca Giustino Fortunato.
Catalogo della Biblioteca G. Fortunato. 1970. Riprodotto con il contributo del Centro di formazione e studi per il Mezzogiorno ... Roma, 1970.

2 v. (1753 p.) 30 cm.

At head of title: Associazione nazionale per gli interessi del Mezzogiorno d'Italia.

Camera di commercio, industria, artigianato e agricoltura, Foggia. Biblioteca.
Catalogo biblioteca ed emeroteca. 2. ed. Foggia, Stamperia Multilith, 1970.

1043 p. 24¼ cm.

Esposito, Enzo.
La cultura italiana; rassegna bibliografica. Roma, Centro editoriale internazionale [1964]

472 p. 30 cm.

Falconer, Margaret.
Italian reference aids in the University of Toronto Library, Humanities and Social Sciences Division. Toronto, Reference Dept., University of Toronto Library, 1967.

48 l. 28 cm. (Reference series, no. 11)

Gheno, Antonio.
Contributo alla bibliografia genealogica italiana. Bologna, Forni, 1971.

297 p. 24 cm.

"Ristampa anastatica dell'edizione di Roma, 1924."

Italy. Direzione generale degli archivi di Stato.
Le pubblicazioni degli archivi di Stato, 1951–71. [Spoleto, Arti grafiche Panetto & Petrelli, 1972]

111 p. 24 cm.

Pine-Coffin, R   S
Bibliography of British and American travel in Italy to 1860 / R. S. Pine-Coffin. — Firenze : L. S. Olschki, 1974.

371 p., [13] leaves of plates ; 25 cm. — (Biblioteca di bibliografia italiana ; 76)

Stych, Franklin Samuel, 1916–
How to find out about Italy, by F. S. Stych. [1st ed.] Oxford, New York, Pergamon Press [1970]

xiii, 320 p. illus., facsims., maps. 20 cm. (Commonwealth and international library; library and information science)

Toesca, Pietro Maria, 1927–
I grandi libri del Risorgimento.   Torino, ERI, 1967.

142 p. 18 cm. (Classe unica, 112)

United States. National Archives.
Guide to records of the Italian armed forces.   Washington, 1967.

3 v. 21 x 36 cm.

An inventory of seized World War II records presently in the care of the National Archives.

Varley, Douglas Harold.
A bibliography of Italian colonisation in Africa with a section on Abyssinia compiled by Douglas H. Varley. 1st ed. reprinted; with new introduction. Folkestone, Dawsons, 1970.

[1], 92 p. 22 cm.

"First published in 1936."

Vianello, Nereo.
La raccolta di Angiolo Tursi nella Biblioteca Marciana. Venezia, Stamperia di Venezia, 1968.

22 p. 23 cm.

Zazo, Alfredo.
Dizionario bio-bibliografico del Sannio. Con 10 illustrazioni fuori testo. Napoli, F. Fiorentino, 1973.

7, 397 p. illus., 10 plates. 24 cm.

HISTORY

Archivio centrale dello Stato.
Gli archivi del IV [i. e. quarto] corpo d'esercito e di Roma capitale. Inventario. A cura di Raoul Guêze e Antonio Papa. Roma, (Spoleto, Panetto & Petrelli), 1970.

xxiv, 277 p. 23½ cm. (Ministero dell'Interno. Pubblicazioni degli archivi di Stato, 71) [Roma capitale: Documenti 1870, v. 1.]

Bibliografia deli'età del Risorgimento. In onore di Alberto M. Ghisalberti. Firenze, L. S. Olschki, 1971–

v. port. 24 cm. (Biblioteca di bibliografia italiana, 63)

British Museum. Dept. of Printed Books.
Risorgimento collection: accessions to the general catalogue of printed books. London, British Museum, 1971.

[3], 78 columns. 32 cm.

Delzell, Charles F
Italy in modern times: an introduction to the historical literature in English, by Charles F. Delzell. Washington, Service Center for Teachers of History [°1964]

85 p. 23 cm. (Service Center for Teachers of History. Publication no. 60)

"A publication of the American Historical Association."

IVES, CHARLES EDWARD

De Lerma, Dominique-René
Charles Edward Ives, 1874–1954: a bibliography of his music. [1st ed. Kent, Ohio] Kent State University Press [1970]

xi, 212 p. 23 cm.

IVORY COAST

Bibliographie de la Côte d'Ivoire.
[Abidjan] Bibliothèque nationale.

v. 22 cm. annual.

At head of title   : Ministère de l'Éducation nationale.
Began with vol. for 1969.

Janvier, Geneviève.
Bibliographie de la Côte-d'Ivoire. [Abidjan] Université d'Abidjan, 1972–

v. 24 cm.

"Annales de l'Université d'Abidjan, 1972, volume hors série."
CONTENTS: v. 1. Sciences de la vie.—

Organization for Economic Cooperation and Development.
Development Centre.
Essai d'une bibliographie sur la Côte d'Ivoire. Paris, Centre de développement de l'OCDE, 1964.

iv, 122 l. 30 cm. (*Its* CD/D/Bibl./1)

Schwartz, A
Études de sciences humaines en Côte d'Ivoire; essai de bibliographie, par A. Schwartz. Paris, 1964.

47 l. 27 cm.

At head of title: Office de la recherche scientifique et technique outre-mer. Sciences humaines.

IWAKURA, TOMOMI

Naikaku Bunko, Tokyo.
(Naikaku Bunko shozō Iwakura Tomomi kankei monjo mokuroku)

内 閣 文 庫

内閣文庫所蔵 岩倉具視関係文書目録

東京 昭和43 (1968)

72p 21 cm

J

JACKSON, ANDREW

Wise, W. Harvey, Jr.
A bibliography of Andrew Jackson and Martin Van Buren, compiled by W. Harvey Wise, Jr. and John W. Cronin. New York, B. Franklin [1970]

72 p. 27 cm. (Burt Franklin bibliography & reference series, 342. American classics in history & social science, 131)

Pages 67–72 blank.

JACOB OF SERUG

Vööbus, Arthur.
Handschriftliche Überlieferung der Mēmrē-Dichtung des Ja'qōb von Serūg. Louvain, Secrétariat du Corpus SCO, 1973.

2 v. 25 cm. (Corpus scriptorum christianorum orientalium. v. 344–345. Subsidia. t. 39–40)

CONTENTS: 1. Sammlungen: Die Handschriften.—2. Sammlungen Der Bestand.

JACOBITE REBELLIONS

Scotland. National Library, Edinburgh.
Shelf-catalogue of the Blaikie Collection of Jacobite pamphlets, broadsides, and proclamations. Boston, G. K. Hall, 1964.

v, 42 l. 27 cm.

JACOBSEN, JOSEPHINE

Adler, Betty, 1918–
Josephine Jacobsen; a bibliography. Compiled by Betty Adler. Rev. and edited by Judith L. Richelieu. [Washington, General Reference and Bibliography Division, Library of Congress, 1971]

28 p. 27 cm.

JACOBSON, DAN

Yudelman, Myra.
Dan Jacobson: a bibliography. Johannesburg, University of the Witwatersrand, Department of Bibliography, Librarianship and Typography, 1967.

iv, 27 p. 29 cm.

JAENIG, KAREL

Křivský, Pavel.
Karel Jaenig (1835–1914). Lit. pozůstalost. Zprac. Pavel Křivský. Praha, Lit. archív Památníku nár. písemnictví, rozmn. Ruch, Liberec, 1971.

26, [1] p. 21 cm. (Edice inventářů. čís. 238)

JAGATAIC LITERATURE

Hofman, H   F
Turkish literature. A biobibliographical survey. Section III. Moslim Central Asian Turkish literature being in the main a list of Chaghatayan authors and works in Chaghatay as registered in Professor M. F. Köprülü's article: Çagatay edebiyati, İA. vol. III (270–) (with some additions Navā'-iāna, however excepted) By H. F. Hofman. (Utrecht, published by the University of Utrecht under the auspices of the Royal Asiatic Society of Great Britain and Ireland, 1969–

v. in   24 cm.
CONTENTS: pt. 1. Authors.

JAHNN, HANS HENNY

Meyer, Jochen, 1941–
Verzeichnis der Schriften von und über Hans Henny Jahnn. (Neuwied a. Rh. u. Berlin) Luchterhand (1967).

184 p. 21 cm. (Die Mainzer Reihe, Bd. 21)

JAIPUR, INDIA (STATE)

Rajasthan, India. State Archives.
A descriptive list of the vakil reports addressed to the rulers of Jaipur. Bikaner, 1967–

v. 25 cm.

CONTENTS: v. 1–2. Persian.

JAKOBSON, ROMAN

Roman Jakobson: a bibliography of his writings. With a foreword by C. H. van Schooneveld. The Hague, Mouton, 1971.

63 p. port. 23 cm. (Janua linguarum. Series minor, 134)

JĂLAL, MIR

Teĭmurova, N   M
Мир Чэлал: библиографија. [Тэртиб едэни Н. М. Тејмурова]. Бакы, Азэрбајчан ССР Елмлэр Академијасы Нэшријјаты, 1968.

139 p. 16 cm. (Азэрбајчанын елм ве мэдэнијјэт хадимлэри)

At head of title: Азэрбајчан ССР Елмлэр академијасы. Өсаслы китабхана.
Added t. p. in Russian.

JAMAICA

Institute of Jamaica, Kingston. Library.
Bibiographia Jamaicensis; a list of Jamaica books and pamphlets, magazine articles, newspapers, and maps, most of which are in the Library of the Institute of Jamaica, by Frank Cundall. New York, B. Franklin [1971]

83 p. 22 cm. (Burt Franklin bibliography and reference series, 433. American classics in history and social science, 206)

Reprint of the 1902 ed.

Institute of Jamaica, *Kingston. West India Reference Library.*
A guide to Jamaican reference material in the West India Reference Library, by Rae Delattre. Kingston, Institute of Jamaica, 1965.

76 p. 22 cm.

Institute of Jamaica, *Kingston. West India Reference Library.*
Jamaican accessions. 1964–
Kingston.

v. 21 cm. annual.

Kapp, Kit S
The printed maps of Jamaica up to 1825, by Kit S. Kapp. London, Map Collectors' Circle, 1968.

36 p., 33 maps. 25 cm. (Map collectors' series, vol. 5, no. 42)

JAMĀLZĀDAH, MUḤAMMAD 'ALĪ

Dorri, Dzhakhangir Khabibulovich.
(Dzhamal'-zade)

Джамаль-заде. Биобиблиогр. указ. ₍Авт. вступит. статьи и отв. ред. канд. филол. наук Д. Дорри₎. Москва, "Книга," 1972.

93 p. 20 cm. (Писатели зарубежных стран)

At head of title: Всесоюзная государственная библиотека иностранной литературы.
By D. Kh. Dorri and N. H. Safarova.

JAMES, HENRY

Phillips, Le Roy, 1870–
A bibliography of the writings of Henry James, by Le Roy Phillips. New York, B. Franklin ₍1968₎

xviii, 285 p. facsims. 23 cm. (Burt Franklin bibliography and reference series #189)

Reprint of the 1930 ed.

JAMES, WILLIAM

Perry, Ralph Barton, 1876–1957.
Annotated bibliography of the writings of William James. ₍Folcroft, Pa.₎ Folcroft Library Editions, 1973 ₍c1920₎

69 p. 24 cm.

Reprint of the ed. published by Longmans, Green, New York.

JĀMĪ

Akademiiā nauk Uzbekskoĭ SSR, *Tashkend. Institut vostokovedeniiā.*
Рукописи произведений Абдаррахмана Джами в собрании Института востоковедения Академии наук Узбекской ССР; ₍аннотированный список₎ Составители: А. Урунбаев и Л. М. Епифанова. Ташкент, Наука, 1965.

99 p. illus., facsims. 22 cm.

Added t. p. in Uzbek.

al-Ṭirāzī, Naṣr Allāh Mubashshir.
نور الدين عبد الرحمن الجامي، فهرس بمؤلفاته المخطوطة والمطبوعة التي تقتنيها الدار. اعداد نصر الله مبشر الطرازى. القاهرة، مطبعة دار الكتب، 1964.

10, 78 p. 24 cm.

At head of title: الجمهورية العربية المتحدة وزارة الثقافة والارشاد القومى. دار الكتب.

JĀMIʿAT AL-KUWAYT

Jāmiʿat al-Kuwayt.
(al-Āthār al-ʿilmīyah li-aʿḍāʾ hayʾat al-tadrīs bi-Jāmiʿat al-Kuwayt)
الآثار العلمية لأعضاء هيئة التدريس بجامعة الكويت. ₍الكويت، جامعة الكويت، 1969/70.

270 p. 24 cm.

JANÁČEK, JAROSLAV

Křivský, Pavel.
Jaroslav Janáček. (1878–1963.) Literární pozůstalost. Zprac. Pavel Křivský. Praha, Literární archiv Památníku nár. písemnictví, rozmn.. 1970.

S. l. p. 20 cm. (Edice inventářů, čís. 218)

JANONIS, JULIUS
Žukas, Vladas.
Julius Janonis; bibliografinė rodyklė. Vilnius, 1965.

214 p. 20 cm.

At head of title: Lietuvos TSR Valstybinė respublikinė biblioteka.
A. Žukas.

JAPAN
see also under China (*Kolylinski*) and Dissertations, Academic

Akademiiā nauk SSSR. *Institut narodov Azii.*
Библиография Японии: литература, изданная в России с 1734 по 1917 г. ₍Составители: В. С. Гривнин, Н. Ф. Лещенко, М. В. Сутягина. Ответственные редакторы: М. И. Лукьянова, Х. Т. Эйдус, А. Е. Глускина. Москва; Наука, Глав. ред. восточной лит-ры, 1965.

378 p. 22 cm.

On leaf preceding t. p.: Академия наук СССР. Институт народов Азии. Министерство культуры СССР. Всесоюзная государственная библиотека иностранной литературы.

Cordier, Henri, 1849–1925.
Bibliotheca Japonica. Dictionnaire bibliographique des ouvrages relatifs à l'empire Japonais rangés par ordre chronologique jusqu'à 1870. (Reprografischer Nachdruck der Ausg. Paris 1912.) Hildesheim, G. Olms, 1969.

xii p., 762 columns. 25 cm.

Forms with the author's Bibliotheca Sinica and Bibliotheca Indosinica a Bibliographie des pays d'Extrême-Orient.

Dōshisha Daigaku, Kyoto.
(Dōshisha Daigaku shozō tōkei shiryō nenkan mokuroku)
同志社大学. 人文科学研究所
同志社大学所蔵統計資料・年鑑目録 −付.
統計資料二次文献一覧−
京都 昭和44(1969)
223p 26cm.

Fukuda, Naomi.
Union catalog of books on Japan in western languages. Reprint edition. Edited by Naomi Fukuda. ₍Tokyo₎ International House Library, 1968.

iii, 543 p. 26 cm.

Hall, Robert Burnett, 1896–
Japanese geography: a guide to Japanese reference and research materials, by Robert B. Hall and Toshio Noh. Rev. ed. Ann Arbor, University of Michigan Press, 1970.

iv, 233 p. 28 cm. (University of Michigan. Center for Japanese Studies. Bibliographical series, no. 6)

Hanabusa, Nagamichi, 1902–
日本外交史關係文献目錄 英修道編 東京 慶應義塾大學法學研究會 昭和36 ₍1961₎

3, 485 p. 22 cm. (慶應義塾大學法學研究會叢書 9)

In colophon: 發行所 慶應通信

――――追補篇 ₍東京₎ 慶應義塾大学法学研究會 ₍慶應通信発売 昭和43− i. e. 1968−

v. 22 cm. (慶應義塾大学法学研究會叢書 9)

Japan-Bibliographie. Hamburg, Düsseldorf, Deutsch-Japanisches Wirtschaftsbüro (1968).

42 p. 25 cm.

Cover title: Bibliographie–Japan.

Japan. Gaimushō. Jōhō Bunkakyoku.
Introducing Japan through books, a selected bibliography. ₍Tokyo₎ Public Information Bureau, Ministry of Foreign Affairs, 1968.

57 p. illus. 21 cm. (Japan reference series, 1968, no. 1)

Kanagawa Kenritsu Kawasaki Toshokan.
本館所蔵・産業史関係図書目録 川崎 神奈川県立川崎図書館 1968.

v, 328, 53 p. 22 cm.

Kokuritsu Kokkai Toshokan, Tokyo.
(Gikai kaisetsu hachijūnen kinen gikai seiji tenjikai mokuroku)
議会開設八十年記念議会政治展示会目録　主催
国立国会図書館　期日　昭和45年12月1日-7日
場所　国立国会図書館展示室　〔東京　昭和45
(1970)序〕
iv. 29 p.　illus.　21 cm.

Kokuritsu Kokkai Toshokan, *Tokyo. Sankō Shoshibu.*
日本旧外地関係統計資料目録　〔東京〕　国立国
会図書館参考書誌部 1964.
14, 101 p.　21 cm.

Matsuda, Kiichi, 1921–
近世初期日本関係南蛮史料の研究　松田毅一著
〔東京〕　風間書房〔1967〕
60, 1286, 73 p.　facsims.　22 cm.

Matsuda, Kiichi, 1921–
在南欧日本関係文書探訪録　Catalogo dos documentos sobre o japão existentes na europa meridional.　松
田毅一著　天理　養徳社　昭和39〔1964〕
viii, 437 p.　illus.　22 cm.

Nihon no Sankō Tosho Henshū Iinkai.
Guide to Japanese reference books.　日本の参考図書
Chicago, American Library Association, 1966.
303 p.　28 cm.

Includes Sino-Japanese characters, their romanization, and English translation of each title.
Based on the revised Japanese edition edited by the Compilation Committee (Nihon no Sankō Tosho Henshū Iinkai) in the Library of the International House of Japan.

Nihon Shiryō Kenkyūkai.
日本年鑑類総目録　昭和39年3月末現在　日本
資料研究会編　〔改訂増補〕　東京　清和堂出版部
昭和39〔1964〕
236 p.　25 cm.

First ed. published in 1968 under title: 戦後日本年鑑類総目録

Shuppan Kagaku Kenkyūjo.
(Kankyō akarui "tabi no hon")
環境明るい"旅の本"　〔東京〕　出版科学研究所
〔昭和44　i.e.　1969〕
25p.　26 cm.　(*Its* 解説シリーズ　103)

Tōyōgaku Informēshon Sentā, *Tokyo.*
A selected list of books on Japan in Western languages (1945–1960)　〔Tokyo〕 Information Centre of Asian Studies, 1964.
vi, 74 p.　26 cm.　(Studies on Asia abroad, 1)

Intended as a continuation of A selected list of books and articles on Japan in English, French, and German, edited by Hugh Borton and others.
"Some ... publications before 1945 and after 1960 are also included."

Webb, Herschel.
Research in Japanese sources, a guide 〔by〕 Herschel Webb, with the assistance of Marleigh Ryan.　New York, Published for the East Asian Institute, Columbia University, by Columbia University Press, 1965.
xiii, 170 p.　23 cm.

Yamaguchi, Ichirō, 1915–
山口　一郎
近代中国の対日観
東京　アジア経済研究所　（発売）アジア経済出版会
昭和44(1969)
152p　26cm　（アジア・アフリカ文献解題 4）

Ajia Keizai Kenkyūjo shuppanbutsu, tsūkan dai 879-gō.

HISTORY

Atsusaka, Rintarō, 1936–
(Chihōshi bunken sōgō mokuroku)
地方史文献総合目録　阿津坂林太郎編　東京
巌南堂書店　昭和45-　(1970-
v.　26 cm.
Contents.—1. 戦前編

Atsusaka, Rintarō, 1936–
(Sengo shichōson shi sōgō mokuroku)
戦後市町村史総合目録　〔編集・横浜市立大学事
務局学生課　横浜〕　横浜市立大学　1967.
194, 22 p.　21 cm.　（都市問題講座文献シリーズ　1）
阿津坂林太郎・村田基安の両氏に依嘱して編さんしたもの

(Chihōshi kenkyū no genjō)
地方史研究の現状
日本歴史学会編
東京　吉川弘文館　昭和44(1969)
3冊　23cm
内容
第1.　北海道・東北・関東編
第2　中部・近畿編
第3　中国・四国・九州・沖縄編

Endō, Motoo, 1908–　*ed.*
國史文献解説　遠藤元男・下村冨士男編　東京
朝倉書店　昭和32〔1957〕-1965.
2 v.　22 cm.

(Kinsei komonjo mokuroku)
近世古文書目録　編集：山中清孝　東京　山中清孝
昭和47(1972)
48 p.　26 cm.
Cover title.
Photoreproduction of MS. copy.

明治百年展出品目録　昭和43年4月5日-5月31日—
午前9時-午後5時　会場　湊川神社宝物館　主催
湊川神社・神戸新聞社・デイリースポーツ社　〔神戸
1968〕
12 p.　26 cm.
Cover title.
At head of title: 湊川神社創祀御沙汰百年・神戸新聞社創刊
七十周年・神戸高速鉄道開通記念

Minami, Kazuo, 1927–
(Kyū Bakufu hikitsugisho kaisetsu)
旧幕府引継書解説　南和男著　東京　日本マイ
クロ写真　昭和45-　(1970-
v.　21 cm.
CONTENTS:　〔1〕　第1・4集解説

(Nihon senryō bunken mokuroku)

日本占領文献目録 ₍東京₎ 日本学術振興会₍編集・
発行 昭和47 i.e. 1972₎

    xxiv, 349 p. 27 cm.

    Colophon inserted.
関係者リスト published as suppl. (24 p.) and inserted at end.

Ōsaka Furitsu Toshokan.

大阪府立図書館所蔵 地方史誌目録 昭和38
年 3 月31 日現在 ₍大阪₎ 1964.

    vi, 130, 45 p. 26 cm. (大阪府立図書館シリーズ 9)

Takahashi, Bonsen, 1904–

高橋 梵仙

日本地方史誌目録・索引 高橋梵仙編

    東京 大東文化大学東洋研究所 昭和44 1969
    571. 126p 22cm 大東文化大學東洋研究所叢刊
    第 2

Ward, Robert Edward.

The Allied occupation of Japan, 1945-1952: an annotated bibliography of Western-language materials. Compiled and edited for the Joint Committee on Japanese Studies of the Social Science Research Council—American Council of Learned Societies and the Center for Japanese Studies of the University of Michigan by Robert E. Ward and Frank J. Shulman, with the assistance of Masashi Nishihara and Mary Tobin Espey. Chicago, American Library Association, 1974.

    xx, 867 p. 26 cm.

Yagyū, Shirō.

幕末 研究雑誌目次集覧 柳生四郎、朝倉治彦編
明治

    東京 日本古書通信社 昭和43(1968)

    265p 22cm

    Added title in colophon: Contents of journals for the study of late Tokugawa and Meiji periods.

GOVERNMENT PUBLICATIONS

Kokuritsu Kokkai Toshokan, *Tokyo. Renrakubu.*

国(中央官庁・公共企業体・政府関係機関・政府関係
団体)が編集・監修し、政府関係団体・出版社が発行し
た刊行物一覧 List of the publications compiled by or under supervision of the government of Japan (central government agencies; public corporations and extra-departmental organizations) and published by extra-departmental organizations (gaikaku-dantai) or commercial publishers. 未定稿 (preliminary edition) ₍調査作成・国立国会図書館連絡部₎ Tokyo. 1969.

    175 l. 25 x 36 cm.

    In Japanese.

Kokuritsu Kokkai Toshokan, Tokyo. Renrakubu.

(Kuni no kankōbutsu)
国の刊行物 解説目録 国立国会図書館連絡部
編 東京 国立国会図書館 昭和46(1971)

    808 p. 21 cm.

Kuroki, Tsutomu, 1935–

₍Seifu kankōbutsu gaisetsu₎
政府刊行物概説 黒木努著 東京 帝国地方行
政学会 昭和47(1972)

    216 p. 22 cm.

LAW see Law - Japan

LIBRARY CATALOGS

Japan. Sōrifu. Tōkeikyoku.

(Sōrifu Tōkeikyoku kankō shiryō sōmokuroku)
総理府統計局刊行資料総目録 Bureau of Statistics catalog. 1966–
₍東京₎

    v. 26 cm.

    Supersedes its 総理府統計局主要統計解題および刊行統計資料目録
    In Japanese.

Kokuritsu Kokkai Toshokan, *Tokyo.*

Catalog of materials on Japan in Western languages in the National Diet Library, April 1948–December 1962. Prelim. ed. Tokyo, National Diet Library, 1963.

    306, 74 p. 21 cm.

Kokuritsu Kokkai Toshokan, Tokyo. Sankō Shoshibu.

(Nihon chihō shishi mokuroku sōran)
日本地方史誌目録総覧 国立国会図書館参考書
誌部編 ₍東京₎ 国立国会図書館 昭和46(1971)

    162 p. 21 cm.

Kokusai Bunka Shinkōkai. *Toshoshitsu.*

A classified list of books in western languages relating to Japan. Tokyo, University of Tokyo Press ₍°1965₎

    ix, 316, 124 p. 26 cm.

    1937 ed. published under title: Catalogue of the K. B. S. Library.

Kokusai Kirisutokyō Daigaku, Tokyo. Toshokan.

Books on Japan in western languages. ₍Tokyo₎ International Christian University Library, 1971.

    139 p. 26 cm.

Kyōto Gaikokugo Daigaku. Toshokan.

Nipponalia; books on Japan in European languages in the Library of Kyoto University of Foreign Studies. ₍Kyoto₎ Kyoto University of Foreign Studies, 1972.

    xlvi, 320 p. 26 cm.

Tōkyō Joshi Daigaku. Hikaku Bunka Kenkyūjo.

(Hikaku Bunka Kenkyūjo zōsho mokuroku)
比較文化研究所蔵書目録 東京 東京女子大学
比較文化研究所 昭和46- (1971-

    v. 26 cm.

    Cover title.
    CONTENTS: 1. 今井宏 欧米語による日本および東洋研究
    Books on Japan and Asia.

MAPS

Campbell, Tony.

Japan: European printed maps to 1800. London, Map Collectors' Circle, 1967.

    22 p. 25 cm. (Map collectors' series, no. 36)

Hasegawa, Izumi, 1927–

(Chizu kankei bunken mokuroku)
地図関係文献目録 明治・大正・昭和 長谷川和
泉編 東京 地図協会 主婦の友出版サービスセ
ンター(制作) 昭和46(1971)

    277 p. 22 cm.

Nihon Kokusai Chizu Gakkai.

(Meiji ikō hompō chizu mokuroku)

日本国際地図学会

明治以降本邦地図目録

東京　昭和44(1969)

181p　26cm　（日本国際地図学会刊行物　第1号）

Added title on cover: Catalogue of maps & charts in Japan issued mainly since the Meiji era.

SOCIAL AND ECONOMIC CONDITIONS

Australia. Dept. of Trade and Industry. Central Library.
Japan: a select reading list of material held in the Central Library. Canberra, 1972.

18 l. 30 cm.

Beardsley, Richard King, 1918–
Japanese sociology and social anthropology: a guide to Japanese reference and research materials. Compiled by Richard K. Beardsley [and] Nakano Takashi. Ann Arbor, University of Michigan Press, 1970.

viii, 276 p. 28 cm. (University of Michigan. Center for Japanese Studies. Bibliographical series, no. 10)

Kokuritsu Kokkai Toshokan, Tokyo. Sankō Shoshibu.
(Maeda Masana kankei monjo mokuroku)
前田正名関係文書目録　国立国会図書館参考書誌部編　[東京]　国立国会図書館　1969.

35 p. 21 cm. （憲政資料目録　第7）

Komiya, Ryūtarō, 1928–
A bibliography of studies in English on the Japanese economy. Tokyo, University of Tokyo Press, 1966.

52 p. 22 cm. (Research Institute for the Japanese Economy. Faculty of Economics, University of Tokyo. Research materials series, no. 3)

Nihon Bōeki Shinkōkai.
Publications on Japanese market. [Tokyo, Japan External Trade Organization, 1972]

15 p. 21 cm. (Its JETRO marketing series, 3)

Nihon keizai bunseki bunken sakuin.
日本経済分析文献索引　Index of analytical literature on the Japanese economy.

Tokyo, 一橋大学経済研究所日本経済統計文献センター　Documentation Center for Japanese Economic Statistics, Institute of Economic Research, Hitotsubashi University.

no. 25 cm.

Began in 1968. Cf. Zen Nihon shuppanbutsu sōmokuroku, 1968. No. -2 have title only in characters.

Nihon Keizai Kenkyū Sentā.
List of Japanese economic and business periodicals in English, 1969. [Rev. ed.] Tokyo, Japan Economic Research Center [1969]

ix, 56 p. 21 cm.

Shiga Daigaku, *Hikone, Japan. Keizaigakubu. Shiryōkan.*
滋賀大学経済学部附属史料館所蔵史料目録　第1-　集
[彦根]　昭和41-　[1966-

no. 22 cm.

Title varies slightly.

Simonis, Heide.
Japan; Bibliographie ausgewählter ökonomischer und sozialer Studien. Bearb. von Heide Simonis [und] Udo Ernst Simonis. Kiel, 1974.

iv, 197 p. 24 cm. (Kieler Schrifttumskunden zu Wirtschaft und Gesellschaft, 19)

Tsurutani, Taketsugu.
Rural development in Japan, Korea, and the Philippines; a bibliographical aid. Cambridge, Mass., Center for Rural Development, 1969.

xvi, 101 p. 28 cm.

JAPANESE DRAMA see Drama - Japan

JAPANESE IMPRINTS

Asakura, Haruhiko, 1924–　comp.
(Meiji shoki santo shinkoku shomoku)
明治初期三都新刻書目　朝倉治彦　佐久間信子編　[東京]　日本古書通信社　[昭和46 i.e. 1971]

418 p. 22 cm.

CONTENTS: 戊辰以来新刻書目便覧（太田勘右衛門著・明治7年板の複製）—御維新以来京都新刻書目便覧（村上勘兵衛著・明治7年板の複製）—戊辰以来新刻書目一覧（松田正助著・明治7年板の複製）

Japan. Naimushō. Toshokyoku.
[Shuppan shomoku geppō]
出版書目月報　第1-114號　明治11年1月-明治20年6月　[1878-87. 東京]　明治文献　[昭和46-47 i.e. 1971-72]

114 no. in 3 v. 31 cm. （明治前期書目集成　第1-3分冊）

Photoreproduction of a periodical issued by 内務省図書局 (May-Nov. 1885 by 内務省總務局; Dec. 1885-1887 by 内務省總務局圖書課)

Keiō Gijuku Daigaku, *Tokyo. Shidō Bunko.*
江戸時代書林出版書籍目録集成　慶應義塾大學附属研究所斯道文庫編　東京　井上書房　昭和37-39 [1962-64]

4 v. 31 cm. （斯道文庫書誌叢刊之1）

本書影印の底本となった[ものは]慶応義塾図書館蔵本[で、その]不備は、横山氏赤木文庫・京都大学附属図書館・大東急記念文庫本を以て補った。

(Kokusho sōmokuroku)
国書総目録　東京　岩波書店　昭和38-47 [1963-72]

8 v. 26 cm.

(Meiji zenki shomoku shūsei)
明治前期書目集成　明治文献資料刊行会編　東京　明治文献　昭和46- (1971-

v. 30 cm.

Yajima, Genryō.
(Hampan ichiran kō)
藩版一覧稿　[矢島玄亮編　仙台]　東北大学附属図書館　昭和41 [1966]

145 p. 26 cm. （[東北大学附属図書館]　参考資料　第72号）
Cover title.
Colophon inserted.
右部砕板

Yajima, Genryō.
矢島　玄亮

徳川時代出版者出版物集覧 準備版 矢島玄亮編
仙台 東北大学附属図書館 昭和43(1968)
843p 25cm (参考資料 第75号)

LIBRARY AND EXHIBITION CATALOGS
see also under Chinese imprints -
Library catalogs

Chicago. University. Library. Far Eastern Library.
Author-title catalog of the Japanese collection. Boston,
G. K. Hall, 1973.

4 v. 37 cm.

At head of title: Catalogs of the Far Eastern Library, University
of Chicago, Chicago, Illinois.

Japan. Naimushō. Toshokyoku.

(Toshokyoku shomoku)

図書局書目 [東京] 内務省図書局 [明治16
i. e. 1883. 東京] 明治文献 [昭和47 i. e. 1972]

5 v. in 1. 30 cm. (明治前期書目集成 第4分冊)

Kokuritsu Kokkai Toshokan, Tokyo.

(Meiji kaika no hon tenjikai mokuroku)

明治開化の本 展示会目録 とき・昭和46年5月
26日-31日 ところ・国立国会図書館講堂 [東京]
国立国会図書館 [編集・発行 昭和46 i. e. 1971]

44 p. illus. 26 cm.

At head of title:「国立国会図書館所蔵明治期刊行図書目録」発刊記念

Kukhoe Tosŏgwan, *Seoul, Korea.*

藏書目錄 (장서목록) 日本語圖書篇 The
classified catalogue of books in Japanese. 서울 大韓民
國國會圖書館 National Assembly Library, Korea, 1966–

v.

In colophon: 發行及編輯人 大韓民國國會圖書館司書局
CONTENTS.—1. 1966年1月31日現在

Nagano Toshokan.

(Kenritsu Nagano Toshokan zōsho mokuroku)

県立長野図書館蔵書目録 長野 長野県立長野
図書館 昭和47- (1972-

v. 27 cm.

Subtitle: 昭和46年3月末現在
CONTENTS: 第1巻 総記・哲学・歴史—第2巻 社会科学

Stanford University. *Hoover Institution on War, Revolution, and Peace.*
The library catalogs of the Hoover Institution on War,
Revolution, and Peace, Stanford University: catalog of
the Japanese collection. Boston, G. K. Hall, 1969.

7 v. 37 cm.

JAPANESE IN HAWAII
Matsuda, Mitsugu.
The Japanese in Hawaii, 1868–1967: a bibliography of
the first hundred years. Honolulu, Social Science Research
Institute, University of Hawaii, 1968.

xi, 222 p. 28 cm. (Hawaii series, no. 1)

JAPANESE LITERATURE
Jō, Ichirō.

(Shohanbon)

初版本 現代文学書百科 城市郎著 東京 桃

源社 昭和46(1971)

365 p. illus. 19 cm. (桃源選書)

Kanagawa Kenritsu Toshokan Ongakudō, Yokohama.

(Bungakushōten shutchin mokuroku)

文学賞展出陳目録 神奈川県にゆかりの作家と
作品 神奈川県立図書館編 横浜 昭和43(1968)

17 p. 26 cm.

Cover title.
Catalog of the exhibition held at Yūrindō Shoten Gararī, Oct. 19-24,
1968.

Kanagawa Kenritsu Toshokan Ongakudō, *Yokohama.*

(Nihon no bungakushō)

日本の文学賞 神奈川県立図書館[音楽堂]編
横浜 昭和43(1968)

99p 26cm

Ōsaka Shiritsu Chūō Toshokan.

鶴澤清六遺文庫・鶴澤綱造遺文庫・竹本彌太夫遺
文庫義太夫浄瑠璃本目録 [編集 大阪市立中央
図書館 大阪] 人形浄瑠璃因協会 [昭和42 i. e.
1967]

87 p. illus. 26 cm.

At head of title:人形浄瑠璃因協会所蔵 大阪市立中央
図書館寄託

Takasaki, Ryūji, 1925–

(Sensō bungaku bunken mokuroku)

戦争文学文献目録 高崎隆治編 [横浜 戦争
文学研究会 昭和46 i. e. 1971]

34 p. 21 cm.

Yamanashi Daigaku, *Kōfu, Japan.* *Toshokan.*

山梨大学. 附属図書館
近代文学文庫目録

甲府 1968
106p 26cm

PERIODICALS

近代文学雑誌事典 付・収載雑誌の市価一覧と有利な
売り方買い方 執筆者・青木美智子[等 長谷川泉
編 東京] 至文堂 [1966]

270 p. illus. 23 cm.

Errata slip inserted.

Nihon Kindai Bungakukan, Tokyo. **Tosho Shiryō
Iinkai.**

(Nihon Kindai Bungakukan shozō zasshi mokuroku kō)

日本近代文学館所蔵雑誌目録稿 昭和46年12月
末現在 東京 日本近代文学館 昭和47(1972)

130 p. 26 cm.

In colophon: 編集人 日本近代文学館図書資料委員会 委員長 稲垣
達郎

TRANSLATIONS

Inada, Hide Ikehara.
Bibliography of translations from the Japanese into
Western languages from the 16th century to 1912. Tokyo,
Sophia University [c1971]

viii, 112 p. 26 cm. (A Monumenta Nipponica monograph)

Kokusai Bunka Kaikan, Tokyo. Toshokan.
Modern Japanese literature in western translations; a bibliography. Tokyo, International House of Japan Library, 1972.

190 p. 27 cm.

JAPANESE MATHEMATICS see Mathematics, Japanese

JAŠÍK, RUDOLF

Lipová, Irena.
Pozostalosť Rudolfa Jašíka. Sprac.: Irena Lipová. Martin, Matica slovenská, rozmn., 1970.

10, [2] p. [7] p. of plates, port. 21 cm. (Rukopisné fondy Literárneho archívu Matice slovenskej, 49)

Cover title: Rudolf Jašík.

JAWĀHIR-LĀL NEHRŪ see Nehru, Jawaharlal

JAZZ MUSIC

Bogaert, Karel, 1944–
Blues lexicon. Blues, cajun, boogie woogie, gospel. [Antwerpen,] Standaard, [1972].

480 p., 12 p. of photos. 19 cm.

Introduction in English.

Carl Gregor, *Duke of Mecklenburg.*
International jazz bibliography; jazz books from 1919 to 1968 [by] Carl Gregor Herzog zu Mecklenburg. Strasbourg [France] P. H. Heitz, 1969.

xx, 198 p. 23 cm. (Sammlung musikwissenschaftlicher Abhandlungen, Bd. 49)

Haselgrove, J   R
Readers' guide to books on jazz [compiled by J. R. Haselgrove and D. Kennington]. 2d ed. London, Library Association (County Libraries Section), 1965 [i. e. 1966]

16 p. 18½ cm. (Readers' guides, new ser., no. 83)

Kennington, Donald.
The literature of jazz: a critical guide. London, Library Association, 1970.

xv, 142 p. 22 cm.

Kennington, Donald.
The literature of jazz; a critical guide. Chicago, American Library Association, 1971 [c1970]

xiv, 142 p. 23 cm.

Markewich, Reese, 1936–
Bibliography of jazz and pop tunes sharing the chord progressions of other compositions. [Riverdale, N. Y., 1970]

58 l. 29 cm.

Markewich, Reese, 1936–
The new expanded bibliography of jazz compositions based on the chord progressions of standard tunes / Reese Markewich. — New York : Markewich, [1974]

45 leaves ; 28 cm.

1970 ed. published under title: Bibliography of jazz and pop tunes sharing the chord progressions of other compositions.

Merriam, Alan P   1923–
A bibliography of jazz, by Alan P. Merriam. With the assistance of Robert J. Benford. New York, Da Capo Press, 1970.

xiii, 145 p. 24 cm. (Da Capo Press music reprint series)

Reprint of the 1954 ed.

Merriam, Alan P   1923–
A bibliography of jazz, by Alan P. Merriam. With the assistance of Robert J. Benford. Philadelphia. American Folklore Society. 1954. New York, Krause Reprint Co., 1970.

xiii, 145 p. 24 cm.

Original ed. issued as v. 4 of Publications of the American Folklore Society, Bibliographical series.

BIO-BIBLIOGRAPHY

Bohländer, Carlo, 1919–
Reclams Jazzführer. Von Carlo Bohländer und Karl Heinz Holler. (Zeichn.: Peter Anselm Riedl.) Mit 32 Taf., 12 Abb. im Text u. zahlr. Notenbeisp. Stuttgart, Reclam (1970).

991 p. music, plates. 16 cm. (Universal-Bibliothek, Nr. 10185–98)

Chilton, John, 1931 or 2-
Who's who of jazz: Storyville to Swing Street. London, The Bloomsbury Book Shop, 1970.

[8], 447 p. ports. 22 cm.

Chilton, John, 1931 or 2-
Who's who of jazz! Storyville to Swing Street. Foreword by Johnny Simmen. [1st American ed.] Philadelphia, Chilton Book Co. [1972]

419 p. illus. 24 cm.

DISCOGRAPHIES

Moon, Pete.
A bibliography of jazz discographies published since 1960 / compiled by Pete Moon ; edited by Barry Witherden. — 2d ed. — South Harrow [Eng.] : British Institute of Jazz Studies, 1972.

[32] p. ; 28 cm.

At head of title: A British Institute of Jazz Studies project.

———— Supplement. [South Harrow, Eng.] : British Institute of Jazz Studies, 1972–

v. 28 cm.

JEANNE D'ARC, SAINT

Lanéry d'Arc, Pierre, 1861–
Le livre d'or de Jeanne d'Arc. Bibliographie raisonnée et analytique des ouvrages relatifs à Jeanne d'Arc; catalogue méthodique, descriptif, et critique des principales études historiques, littéraires, et artistiques, consacrées à la pucelle d'Orléans depuis le XV° siècle jusqu'à nos jours. Amsterdam, B. R. Grüner, 1970.

xx, 1007 p. illus., ports. 24 cm.

Cover title: Bibliographie Jeanne d'Arc.
Reprint of the Paris 1894 ed.

JEBAVÝ, VÁCLAV

Kubíček, Jaromír.
Otokar Březina. Soupis literatury o jeho životě a díle. V Brně, Universitní knihovna, 1971.

109 p. 21 cm. (Výběrový seznam, č. 159)

Papírník, Miloš.
Knižní dílo Otokara Březiny. Soupis. Zprac. Miloš Papírník za spolupráce Anny Zykmundové. Brno, Univ. knihovna, t. G, 1969.

45, [1] p. 21 cm. (Brünn. Universita. Knihovna. Výběrový seznam, č. 137)

JEFFERS, ROBINSON

Alberts, Sydney Seymour.
A bibliography of the works of Robinson Jeffers [by] S. S. Alberts. Rye, N. Y., Cultural History Research, 1966,

ₑ1933₎

xvi, 262 p. facsims., port. 25 cm.

"Poetry and prose not previously printed in book form ₍by Robinson Jeffers₎": p. ₍115₎-156.

Alberts, Sydney Seymour.
A bibliography of the works of Robinson Jeffers ₍by₎ S. S. Alberts. New York, B. Franklin ₍1968₎

xvi, 262 p. facsims., port. 24 cm. (Burt Franklin: Bibliography and reference series, no. 173)

Reprint of the 1933 ed.
"Poetry and prose not previously printed in book form ₍by Robinson Jeffers₎": p. ₍115₎-156.

Nolte, William Henry, 1928–
The Merrill checklist of Robinson Jeffers. Compiled by William H. Nolte. Columbus, Ohio, C. E. Merrill Pub. Co. ₍1970₎

iv, 25 p. 19 cm. (Charles E. Merrill checklists)

Charles E. Merrill program in American literature.
Cover title: Checklist of Robinson Jeffers.

Vardamis, Alex A 1934–
The critical reputation of Robinson Jeffers; a bibliographical study ₍by₎ Alex A. Vardamis. ₍Hamden, Conn.₎ Archon Books, 1972.

317 p. 22 cm.

JEFFERSON, THOMAS

Jefferson, Thomas, *Pres. U. S.*, 1743–1826.
Calendar of the correspondence of Thomas Jefferson. New York, B. Franklin ₍1970₎

3 v. 24 cm. (Burt Franklin bibliography & reference series, 310)

Reprint of the 1894–1903 ed.

CONTENTS.—pt. 1. Letters from Jefferson.—pt. 2. Letters to Jefferson.—pt. 3. Supplementary.

Virginia. University. Library.
The Jefferson papers of the University of Virginia. Part I: A calendar compiled by Constance E. Thurlow and Francis L. Berkeley, Jr., of manuscripts acquired through 1950. Part II: A supplementary calendar compiled by John Casteen and Anne Freudenberg of manuscripts acquired 1950–1970. With a combined index. Charlottesville, Published for the University of Virginia Library ₍by₎ the University Press of Virginia ₍1973₎

xvi, 496 p. 26 cm.

Part I was originally published in 1950.

JEFFERSON COUNTY, KENTUCKY

Jillson, Willard Rouse, 1890–
A bibliography of Jefferson County, Kentucky; citations of printed and manuscript sources touching upon its history, cartography, geology, paleontology, oil and gas, 1751–1960, with annotations. Frankfort, Ky., Roberts Print. Co., 1964.

85 p. 23 cm.

JEFFREYS, MERVYN DAVID WALDGRAVE

Stone, David Allan.
Doctor Mervyn David Waldgrave Jeffreys; a bibliography of his works, 1928–1971. Johannesburg, University of the Witwatersrand, Dept. of Bibliography, Librarianship and Typography, 1972.

xvii, 161 p. 30 cm.

"Compiled in part fulfilment for the requirements of the Diploma in Librarianship, University of the Witwatersrand, Johannesburg."

JELEN, JIŘÍ

Křivský, Pavel.
Jiří Jelen. (1906–1961.) Literární pozůstalost. Zprac.

Pavel Křivský. Praha, Literární archív Památníku nár. písemnictví, t. Ruch, Liberec, 1971.

17, ₍1₎ p. 20 cm. (Edice inventářů. čís. 226)

JERUSALEM

Eibeshutz, Jehoshua, 1916–
ירושלים הנצחית; ילקוט ביבליוגרפי על ירושלים מראשיתה עד ימינו. בעריכת יהושע אייבשיץ. ירושלים. משרד החינוך והתרבות. היחידה לתרבות, המדור לספריות, 1970.

122, 8 p. 32 cm.

ירושלים; ביבליוגרפיה ₍ערך חגי בן־יהושע₎. ירושלים ₍הספריה העירונית ע"ש פרופ' יוסף קלוזנר₎ 1967–

v. 28 cm.

At head of title: המחלקה לחינוך ולתרבות. עירית ירושלים.
"מכילה חומר שהתפרסם בשפה העברית בלבד."

JERUSALEM. HEBREW UNIVERSITY see Hebrew University

JESUITS

Belgium. Archives de l'État, Mons.
Inventaire des archives des jésuites de Mons, par Robert Wellens, premier assistant. Bruxelles, Archives générales du Royaume, 1971.

vi, 14 p. 29 cm.

At head of title: Ministère de l'éducation nationale et de la culture française et Ministère de l'éducation nationale et de la culture néerlandaise. Archives générales du Royaume et Archives de l'État dans les provinces. Archives de l'État à Mons.
Includes bibliographical references.

Guglieri Navarro, Araceli.
Documentos de la Compañía de Jesús en el Archivo Histórico Nacional. Inventario por Araceli Guglieri Navarro. Introd. de Francisco Mateos. Madrid, Editorial Razón y Fe; exclusiva: Ediciones FAX ₍1967, c1966₎

lxxxviii, 486 p. 25 cm.

McCoy, James Comly, 1862–1934.
Jesuit relations of Canada, 1632–1673; a bibliography. With an introd. by Lawrence C. Wroth. New York, B. Franklin ₍1972₎

xv, 310 p. illus. 24 cm. (Burt Franklin: philosophy & religious history monographs, 109) (Bibliography & reference series, 456)

Reprint of the 1937 ed.

Polgár, László.
Bibliography of the history of the Society of Jesus ... Rome, Jesuit historical institute; St. Louis, Mo., St. Louis University (Romae, Typis Pontificiae Universitatis Gregorianae), 1967.

207 p. 24 cm. (Sources and studies for the history of the Jesuits v. 1)

Rey, José del, S. J.
Bio-bibliografía de los Jesuitas en la Venezuela colonial / José del Rey Fajardo. — Caracas : Universidad Católica Andrés Bello, Instituto de Investigaciones Históricas, 1974.

590 p. ; 23 cm.

Rivadeneira, Pedro de, 1527–1611.
Bibliotheca scriptorum Societatis Iesu: a Petro Ribadeneira, Philippo Alegambe, Nathanaele Sotvello. ₍1st ed. reprinted₎: with a new introduction by A. F. Allison. Farnborough, Gregg, 1969.

₍4₎, xxxvi, 984 p. 33 cm.

Photolithographic facsim. of the 1676 ed.

JEWELRY TRADE

Wienslaw, Arthur E
Jewelry retailing, by Arthur E. Wienslaw. Revision. Washington, Small Business Administration, 1965.

12 p. 26 cm. (Small business bibliography no. 36)

Wienslaw, Arthur E
Jewelry retailing, by Arthur E. Wienslaw. Revision. Washington, Small Business Administration, 1965 ₁i. e. 1968₁

8 p. 26 cm. (Small business bibliography no. 36)

JEWETT, GEORGE FREDERICK

Idaho. University, Library.
Descriptive inventory of the papers of George Frederick Jewett, Sr. Moscow, 1969.

45 p. 28 cm. (Its Publication no. 5)

Prepared by Barbara Richards.

JEWISH-ARAB RELATIONS

Shahrabani, Naim.
(ha-Sikhsukh ha-'arvi-Yisre'eli)

הסכסוך הערבי ישראלי; ביבליוגרפיה של ספרים ופרסומים בערבית. ליקט וערך נעים שהרבני. ירושלים ₁מרכז הר הצופים לחקר ערבי ארץ-ישראל ויחסי ישראל-ערב₁ 1973.

301 p. 24 cm. (מרכז הר הצופים לחקר ערבי ארץ-ישראל ויחסי ישראל ־ערב. סקרים ועזרי מחקר, מס' 1)

At head of title: המכון ללימודי אסיה ואפריקה, חמכון למחקר ע"ש הרי טרומן.

On verso of t. p.: النزاع العربي الاسرائيلي
Added t. p.: The Arab Israeli conflict.

JEWISH ART   see Art, Jewish

JEWISH CHRISTIANS

Cohen, Adèle Naomi.
The Judean Church up to A. D. 70; an annotated bibliography. Johannesburg, University of the Witwatersrand, Dept. of Bibliography, Librarianship and Typography, 1972.

vii, 96 p. 29 cm.

JEWISH HOLOCAUST   see Holocaust

JEWISH LANGUAGE   see Hebrew language

JEWISH LAW

Cohen, Boaz, 1899–1968.
קונטרס התשובות; מפתח וביבליוגרפיה של ספרות הש"ת מתקופת הגאונים ועד ימינו, מאת בועז כהן ... ירושלים, מקור,
730 ₁1969 or 70₁

226 p. 25 cm.

Reprint of Budapest, 1930 ed.

Falk, Ze'ev Wilhelm, 1923–
Current bibliography of Hebrew law. no. 1–
Feb. 1966–
₁Tel-Aviv₁

no. in   v. 21 cm. semiannual.

Title varies slightly.
Beginning with no. 8 continued as a section in דיני ישראל

מאיר עינים. ₁–1,   .727–   ₁1967–68₁
בני ברק, המרכז לספריות תורניות.

v. 24 cm. annual.

Added t. p., 1967– : Meir einayim.

Paul, Shalom M
₁Homer bibliyografi le-mivhar nos'im ba-hukah ha-yisre'elit veha mesopotamit₁

חומר ביבליוגרפי למבחר נושאים בחוקה הישראלית

והמסופוטמית ₁מאת₁ שלום מ. פאול. ירושלים, האוניברסיטה העברית. הפקולטה למדעי הרוח. החוג למקרא, 730 ₁1969₁

b, 13 l. 28 cm.

JEWISH LITERATURE   see Hebrew literature; Yiddish literature

JEWISH PERIODICALS   see   Periodical publications - Jewish

JEWS; JUDAISM
see also Hasidism; and under Dissertations, Academic - Jewish studies and Festschriften

עלון ביבליוגרפי לתפוצות. גל' 4–
–May 1969.
ירושלים, המרכזיה הפדגוגית, מיסודה של המועצה העולמית לחינוך יהודי ₁הלשכה הישראלית₁

no. in   v. 23 cm.

Added title: Bibliographic bulletin for the Diaspora.
No more published?

Arnon, Johanan.
אברהם בן אברהם; ביבליוגרפיה מקיפה על גרים וגיור מן המאה ה-ט ועד ימינו ₁מאת₁ יוחנן ארנון. תל אביב, 729 ₁1969₁

15, 15 p. 25 cm.

Cover title.
Added cover title: Abraham ben Abraham; a comprehensive bibliography on proselytes and proselytism from the 9th century up to our times.
Pref. also in English and German.

Barzilai, Jehoshua.
השלח, תרנ"ז–תרפ"ז; ₁ביבליוגרפיה₁ ₁מאת₁ יהושע ברזלי ₁פולמן₁ תל-אביב, ההסתדרות הכללית של העובדים העברים בארץ-ישראל, הועד הפועל, המרכז לתרבות ולחינוך, המדור לספרות, תשכ"ד ₁1964₁

6, 161 p. ports. 27 cm.

Added t. p.: Ha'Shiloah, 1896–1927 (Bibliography)

Ben-Menahem, Naftali, 1911–
ספרי מוסד הרב קוק שיצאו לאור בשנים תרצ"ז–תש"ל. נרשמו על-ידי נפתלי בן-מנחם. ירושלים, מוסד הרב קוק ₁1970₁

11, 329, ix p. illus., ports. 22 cm.

Added t. p.: Books of Mossad ha-Rav Kook, published during the years 1937–1970.
Introd. also in English.

ביבליוגרפיה למורים במוסדות לימוד יהודיים בתפוצות להקניית מקצועות הלימוד היהודיים בבתי-ספר יסודיים ועל יסודיים. ירושלים, המחלקה לחינוך ולתרבות בגולה, 1966.

36 l. 28 cm.

Celnik, Max.
A bibliography on Judaism & Jewish-Christian relations; a selected annotated listing of works on Jewish faith and life, and the Jewish-Christian encounter. Compiled by Max Celnik, and Isaac Celnik. New York, Anti-defamation League of B'nai B'rith, 5725 ₁1965₁

68 p. 23 cm.

Deligdish, Y
₁Mekorot li-rekhishat pirsumim₁
מקורות לרכישת פרסומים, בעריכת י' דליגדיש. ירושלים, 1966.

5 l. 28 cm.

Cover title.
At head of title: משרד החינוך והתרבות, היחידה לתרבות/המדור לספריות, בשיתוף עם בית הספר לספרנות ליד האוניברסיטה העברית, ירושלים.

Educational Research Council of America.
World Jewish history, religion, and culture. [Cleveland, Ohio, 1972]

vii, 24 p. illus. 26 cm. (A Graded, annotated bibliography for grades 7–12, pt. 1)

"A collaborative project of the Educational Research Council of America of Cleveland, Ohio and the American Association for Jewish Education of New York, New York."

Eppler, Elizabeth E
Jewish humour through the ages: a bibliography and catalogue prepared on the occasion of Jewish Book Week, 1967, for an exhibition of Jewish books [by Elizabeth E. Eppler] London, World Jewish Congress [1967].

15 p 22 cm.

"Held at the Adolph Tuck Hall, Woburn House, Upper Woburn Place, W. C. 1 from March 20th–23rd, 1967 under the auspices of the Jewish Book Council."

Harkavi, Zvi.
השלמות ל״מפתח המפתחות״ לש. שונמי, מהד׳ ב׳ תשכ״ה; ודפוסי שאנגהאיי, השלמות למאמרי ב״הספר״ ט׳ [מאת צבי הרכבי. הדפס ב׳ מתוקן ... ירושלים, הוצאת הספרים הארץ ישראלית, 728 [1967 or 8]

7 p. 25 cm.

Jackson, Herbert C
Judaism, Jewish-Christian relations, and the Christian mission to the Jew; a selected bibliography. Herbert C. Jackson, editor. New York, Missionary Research Library [1966]

v, 69 p. 28 cm.

Jerusalem. Hebrew University. *Institute of Jewish Studies.*
רשימת הפרסומים המדעיים של חברי המכון למדעי היהדות, תשי״ז–תשכ״ח. ירושלים, המכון למדעי היהדות, האוניברסיטה העברית, 729 [1969]

111 p. 24 cm. N. T.
Added t. p.: Bibliographical list of scholarly books and articles by the members of the Institute of Jewish Studies, 1957–1968.
Pref. also in English.
"באה להמשיך את ... 'רשימת הפרסומים המדעיים של העובדים האקדימיים במדעי הרוח, משפטים, מתומטיקה ומדעי הטבע ותקלאות' לשנות תש״ו–תשי״ב ... והרשימה של פרסומי חברי המכון ... שהיתה כלולה בחוברת 'מדעי היהדות,' תשכ״א."

Joel, Issachar, 1900–
.1966– ;1–
רשימת מאמרים במדעי היהדות. חוב׳ ירושלים. הוצאת ספרים ע״ש י״ל מאגנס.

v. 24 cm. annual.

Added t. p., 1966– : Index of articles on Jewish studies.
"יו״ל מטעם מערכת קרית ספר."

Judaica book news. v. 1–　　　　fall 1970–
[New York, Book News, inc.]

v. illus., ports. 28 cm. semiannual.

Menorah Book Service.
MBS reference catalogue of books of Jewish interest published in Great Britain, Israel & United States and available in print. Summer 1970. London [1970]

103 p. 23 cm.

"A companion volume to the Reference catalogue, Autumn, 1968."

Oppenheim, Micha Falk.
A guide to the study and practice of Judaism; a selected list. New York, Yavneh, 1972.

14 p. 22 cm.

Petri, Sigurd, 1922–
Israels land och folk. Ett urval böcker om Bibelns land, judarnas religion och kultur samt sionismen och det moderna

Israel. 2. revid. och utökade uppl. Stockholm, Israels ambassad, Informationsavdelningen, 1967.

15, (1) p. 21 cm.

Rothenberg, Joshua.
Judaica reference materials; a selective annotated bibliography. Compiled and annotated by Joshua Rothenberg. Preliminary ed. Waltham, Brandeis University Library, 1971.

v, 87 l. 28 cm.

Guide to the Jewish studies reference materials in the Brandeis Library.

Schmelz, Oskar.
Jewish health statistics; world bibliography, edited by O. Schmelz, assisted by F. Keidanski. Jerusalem, 1966.
xxii, 348, 33 p. 24 cm.
Added t. p.: סטטיסטיקה בריאותית של היהודים בעולם; ביבליוגרפיה
English and Hebrew.
At head of title: The Hebrew University of Jerusalem, Institute of Contemporary Jewry, Department of Medical Ecology.
"First draft, not for publication or sale."

Schwab, Moïse, 1839–1918.
Index of articles relative to Jewish history and literature published in periodicals, from 1665 to 1900. Augmented ed., with an introd. and edited list of abbreviations, by Zosa Szajkowski. New York, Ktav Pub. House [1971], i. e. 1972]

xvi, 539, 409–613 p. 24 cm.

Pages 409–613 (3d group) continue the paging of the 1900 ed.
1914–23 ed. published under title: Répertoire des articles relatifs à la littérature juives parus dans les périodiques, de 1665 à 1900.
Includes the combined printed ed. of 1914–23; a reproduction of subjects and Hebrew words in the 1900 ed., pts. 2–3, and List of errata, by B. Wachstein.

Wunder, Meir.
רשימת הספרים על שביעית [מאת] מאיר וונדר. ירושלים, [המעין] 726 [1965]

56 p. 23 cm.

"תדפים מ,המעין' מבת תשכ״ו עם מפתחות."
"מלואים ותקונים" (p. 71–72) inserted.

BIBLIOGRAPHIES

Brisman, Shimeon.
Jewish research literature: history and guide. Experimental ed. Jerusalem [Printed by Polypress] 1973–

v. 33 cm. (Sources of Jewish information, 1)

Shunami, Shlomo.
Bibliography of Jewish bibliographies. 2d ed. enl. Jerusalem, Magnes Press, Hebrew University, 1965.

xxiv, 997, xxiii p. 25 cm.

Added t. p.: מפתח המפתחות; ביבליוגרפיה של ביבליוגרפיות כל־ישראליות
Prefatory material also in Hebrew.
"Corrections": p. 993–997.

HISTORY

Bibliographie zur jüdisch-hellenistischen und intertestamentarischen Literatur. 1900–1965. In Verbindung mit Gerhard Zachhuber und Heinz Berthold hrsg. von Gerhard Delling. Berlin, Akademie-Verl., 1969.

xxvii, 128 p. 24 cm. (Texte und Untersuchungen zur Geschichte der altchristlichen Literatur, Bd. 106)

Eliav, Mordecai.
תולדות עם ישראל בדורות האחרונים; ביבליוגרפיה מבוארת. ערוכה בידי מרדכי אליאב. [ירושלים, משרד החינוך והתרבות, אגף החינוך הדתי, 727 [1966 or 7]
59 p. 21 cm.

Jerusalem. Hebrew University. *ha-Ḥug le-historyah shel 'am Yisrael.*
חיבורים שקריאתם חובה על תלמידי התואר הראשון הנבחנים

בהיסטוריה של עם ישראל. ירושלים, האוניברסיטה העברית,
הפקולטה למדעי הרוח, החוג להיסטוריה של עם ישראל, תשכ״ה
1965]

19 1. 24 cm.

Jerusalem. Hebrew University. *ha-Ḥug le-historyah shel
'am Yisrael.*

חיבורים שקריאתם חובה למסיימי התואר הראשון. ירושלים,
האוניברסיטה העברית, הפקולטה למדעי הרוח, החוג להיסטוריה
של עם ישראל, 727 [1967]

25 1. 24 cm.

Malamat, Abraham.

מדריך ביבליוגרפי לתולדות ישראל בתקופת המקרא. ערכו:
א. מלמט [ו]ח. רביב. מהדורת תשכ״ד. ירושלים, האוניברסיטה
העברית, הפקולטה למדעי הרוח, החוג להיסטוריה של עם ישראל,
626 [1966]

11. 40 p. 27 cm.
Cover title.
Added cover title: A bibliography of the Biblical period (with
emphasis on publications in modern Hebrew)

Malamat, Abraham.

מדריך ביבליוגרפי לתולדות ישראל בתקופת המקרא. ערכו:
א. מלמט [ו]ח. רביב. מהדורת תשכ״ט. ירושלים, האוניברסיטה
העברית, הפקולטה למדעי הרוח, החוג להיסטוריה של עם ישראל,
730 [1969]

46 p. 27 cm.
Cover title.
Added cover title: A bibliography of the Biblical period (with
emphasis on publications in modern Hebrew) selected and classified by A. Malamat & H. Reviv.

Rappaport, Uriel, 1935–

ביבליוגרפיה נבחרת לתולדות ישראל בתקופת הבית השני,
כינסה וסודרה בידי א. רפפורט. הדפסה 2. עם תוספות. [חיפה]
המכון האוניברסיטאי של חיפה, החוג לתולדות ישראל, 1969.

xi, 84 p., 9 1. 28 cm.
Cover title.
Added cover title: A selected bibliography of Jewish history in
the period of the second Temple.

JUVENILE LITERATURE

Saretsky, Augusta.

A guide to Jewish juvenile literature. Prepared by Augusta Saretsky [and] Elias Schulman. New York, Jewish
Education Committee Press [°1964]

1 v. (unpaged) 25 cm.

Saretsky, Augusta.

A guide to Jewish juvenile literature. Prepared by Augusta Saretsky [and] Elias Schulman. [Rev. New York]
Jewish Education Committee [Press [1968]

70 p. 24 cm.

LIBRARY CATALOGS

Frankfurt am Main. Stadtbibliothek.

Katalog der Judaica und Hebraica [von] Aron Freimann.
Vorwort zur Neuaufl.: Annie Fraenkel. (Um ein Vorwort
verm. Nachdruck der 1932 in Frankfurt am Main erschienenen Ausg. Photomechanischer Nachdruck) Bd. Judaica.
Graz, Akademische Druck- u. Verlagsanstalt, 1968.

vi, xii, 646 p. 25 cm.

Harvard University. Library.

Judaica; classification schedule, classified listing by call
number, chronological listing, author and title listing.
Cambridge; Distributed by the Harvard University Press,
1971.

302 p. 29 cm. (Its Widener Library shelflist. 39)

Hebrew Union College-Jewish Institute of Religion. *Library.*

Dictionary catalog of the Klau Library, Cincinnati. Boston, G. K. Hall, 1964.

32 v. 37 cm.

Jerusalem. Hebrew University. *Oral History Division.*

קאטאלוג 1.–
ירושלים. –725 [1965–]

no. 21 cm.

Issued also in English.

Rosenberger, Ludwig, 1894–

Judaica; a short-title catalogue of the books, pamphlets,
and manuscripts relating to the political, social, and cultural history of the Jews and to the Jewish question in the
library of Ludwig Rosenberger, Chicago, Illinois. Cincinnati, Hebrew Union College Press, 1971.

495 p. illus., facsims. 29 cm. (Bibliographica Judaica 2)

JEWS IN AFRICA

Attal, Robert.

(Yahadut tsefon Afrikah)

יהדות צפון־אפריקה : ביבליוגרפיה / מאת אברהם הטל. –
ירושלים : מכון בן־צבי של יד יצהק בן־צבי והאוניברסיטה
העברית, 733 [1973]

12, 248, xxxiv p. ; 25 cm.

Added t. p.: Les juifs d'Afrique du nord.
Preface also in French.
Includes indexes in French and Hebrew.

Stern, Maureen Joan.

South African Jewish biography, 1900–1966: a bibliography. Cape Town, University of Cape Town Libraries,
1972.

[9], 28 p. 23 cm. (University of Cape Town Libraries. Bibliographical series)

JEWS IN CANADA see under Jews in the United States (*Lifschutz*)

JEWS IN FRANCE

Blumenkranz, Bernhard.

Bibliographie des Juifs en France [par] Bernhard Blumenkranz en collaboration avec Monique Lévy. [Paris] E.
Privat [1974]

viii, 349 p. 24 cm. (Collection Franco-judaïca)

Centre de documentation juive contemporaine. *Bibliothèque.*

La France, le Troisième Reich, Israël. Paris, C. D. J. C.,
1968.

xii, 255 p. 22 cm. (Bibliothèque du Centre de documentation
juive contemporaine, Paris. Catalogue no 2)

Centre de documentation juive contemporaine. Publications, 40.

Schwarzfuchs, Simon.

Supplément bibliographique, additions et corrections à
l'ouvrage de Henri Gross: Gallia judaica; dictionnaire géographique de la France d'après les sources rabbiniques.
Amsterdam, Philo Press, 1969.

37 p. 23 cm.

JEWS IN GERMANY

Leo Baeck Institute of Jews from Germany.

Katalog. Hrsg. von Max Kreutzberger unter Mitarbeit
von Irmgard Foerg. Tübingen, Mohr, 1970–

v. plates. 24 cm. (Schriftenreihe wissenschaftlicher Abhandlungen des Leo Baeck Instituts, 22,

CONTENTS.—Bd. 1. Deutschsprachige jüdische Gemeinden, Zeitungen, Zeitschriften, Jahrbücher, Almanache und Kalender. Unveröffentliche Memoiren und Erinnerungsschriften.

JEWS IN GREAT BRITAIN

Calisch, Edward Nathaniel, 1865–1946.
The Jew in English literature, as author and as subject. Port Washington, N. Y., Kennikat Press ₁1969₎

277 p. 21 cm.

Reprint of the 1909 ed.

Coleman, Edward Davidson, 1891–1939.
The Jew in English drama; an annotated bibliography. With a pref. by Joshua Bloch. The Jew in Western drama: an essay and a check list (1968), by Edgar Rosenberg. New York, New York Public Library ₁1970₎

50, ₇₇, 265 p. 24 cm.

Reprint of the 1943 ed., with Rosenberg's contribution added from the Sept. 1968 Bulletin of the New York Public Library.

Lehmann, Ruth Pauline.
Anglo-Jewish bibliography, 1937–1970, by Ruth P. Lehmann. London, Jewish Historical Society of England, 1973.

xi, 364 p. 26 cm.

JEWS IN ITALY

Milano, Attilio, 1907–
Bibliotheca historica italo-judaica. Firenze, Sansoni, 1954.

209 p. 26 cm. (Contributi alla Biblioteca bibliografica italica, 6)

———— Supplemento 1954–1963. Firenze, Sansoni, 1964.

82 p. 26 cm. (Contributi alla Biblioteca bibliografica italica, 26)

JEWS IN LATIN AMERICA

Jerusalem. Hebrew University. Jewish National and University Library.
₁Ta'arukhah₎
תערוכה: יהודים בארצות אמריקה הלטינית, תולדות ותרבות; קטלוג. בית הספרים הלאומי והאוניברסיטאי, אולם ברמן, ירושלים, תשל"ב. ₁התערוכה והקטלוג נערכו על-ידי יהיאל שיינטוך₎. ירושלים, 1972.

9, 55 p. illus. 24 cm.
Cover title: Exhibition: Latin-American Jewry, history, and culture: catalogue.
At head of title: בית הספרים הלאומי והאוניברסיטאי, שבוע יהדות אמל"מ, הוועדה המארגנת בשיתוף עם הקונגרס היהודי העולמי

JEWS IN RUSSIA

Eibeshutz, Jehoshua, 1916–
יהדות הדממה; יהדות ברית-המועצות, תולדותיה, סבלותיה ומאבקה על ערכי היהדות וכמיההתה ₁sic₎ לעליה לארץ-ישראל. ילקוט ביבליוגרפי ערוך בידי יהושע אייבשיץ. קרית-אתא, 731 ₁1971₎

60 l. 33 cm.

Cover title.
At head of title: עירית קרית-אתא. המחלקה לחינוך ולתרבות, משרד החינוך והתרבות. היחידה לתרבות. המדור לספריות.

Pinkus, B
Russian publications on Jews and Judaism in the Soviet Union, 1917–1967; a bibliography, compiled by B. Pinkus and A. A. Greenbaum with an introd. by M. Altshuler. Edited by Mordechai Altshuler. Jerusalem, Society for Research on Jewish Communities, 1970.

xvi, 273, 113 p. 22 cm.

"פרסומים רוסיים בברית-המועצות על יהודים ויהדות, 1917–1967" (p. ₁5₎–98, 3d group) has special t. p.
"Continuation of Jewish publications in the Soviet Union, 1917–1960; bibliographies compiled and arranged by Y. Y. Cohen."

Rosenberg, Louise Renée.
Jews in the Soviet Union; an annotated bibliography, 1967–1971. New York, American Jewish Committee, Institute of Human Relations ₁1971₎

59 p. 28 cm.

Rothenberg, Joshua.
An annotated bibliography of writings on Judaism published in the Soviet Union, 1960–1965. Foreword by Erich Goldhagen. Waltham, Mass., Institute of East European Jewish Studies, Brandeis University ₁1969₎

x, 66 p. 28 cm.

JEWS IN SPAIN

Kayserling, Meyer, 1829–1905.
Biblioteca española-portugueza-judaica and other studies in Ibero-Jewish bibliography by the author, and by J. S. da Silva Rosa; with a bibliography of Kayserling's publications by M. Weisz. Selected with a prolegomenon by Yosef Hayim Yerushalmi. ₁Augm. ed.₎ New York, Ktav Pub. House, 1971.

xxxii, 272 p. 24 cm. (Studia Sephardica)

JEWS IN THE NETHERLANDS

Neut, E M van der.
Het lot der Joden in Nederland tijdens de Tweede Wereldoorlog; bibliografie, samengesteld door E. M. van der Neut. ₁Amsterdam₎ 1969.

51 l. 30 cm.

"Bibliografisch werkstuk in het kader van de tweede cyclus van de Bibliotheek- en Documentatieschool te Amsterdam."

JEWS IN THE UNITED STATES

American Jewish Historical Society. *Library.*
A preliminary survey of the manuscript collections found in the American Jewish Historical Society. Compiled by the Library staff under the direction of Nathan M. Kaganoff. New York, American Jewish Historical Society, 1967–

v. 22 cm.

Cover title: Manuscript collections, American Jewish Historical Society.

Cogan, Sara G
The Jews of San Francisco & the Greater Bay Area, 1849–1919; an annotated bibliography. Compiled by Sara G. Cogan. With a foreword by Moses Rischin. Berkeley, Calif., Western Jewish History Center, 1973.

xvi, 127 p. front. 25 cm. (Western Jewish Americana series, publication 2)

Cogan, Sara G
Pioneer Jews of the California Mother Lode, 1849–1880; an annotated bibliography, compiled by Sara G. Cogan. Foreword by Moses Rischin. Berkeley, Calif., Western Jewish History Center, 1968.

x, 54 p. map. 25 cm. (Western Jewish Americana series. Publication 1)

Educational Research Council of America.
The American Jewish experience. ₁Cleveland, Ohio, 1972₎

vii, 23 p. illus. 26 cm. (A Graded, annotated bibliography for grades 7–12, pt. 2)

"A collaborative project of the Educational Research Council of America of Cleveland, Ohio and the American Association for Jewish Education of New York, New York."

Glanz, Rudolf.
The German Jew in America; an annotated bibliography

including books, pamphlets, and articles of special interest. Cincinnati, Hebrew Union College Press, 1969.

xlv, 192 p. 29 cm. (Bibliographica Judaica, no. 1)

Hebrew Union College-Jewish Institute of Religion. American Jewish Archives.
Manuscript catalog of the American Jewish Archives, Cincinnati. Boston, G. K. Hall, 1971.

4 v. 37 cm.

Lifschutz, E
ביבליאגראפיע פון אמעריקאנער און קאנאדער יידישע זכרונות און אויטאביאגראפיעס אויף יידיש, העברעיש און ענגליש. צוזאמענגעשטעלט פון י. ליפשיץ. ניו-יארק, יידישער וויסנשאפט-לעכער אינסטיטוט—ייווא. 1970.

74, 2, 75-[76] p. 28 cm.

Added t. p.: Bibliography of American and Canadian Jewish memoirs and autobiographies in Yiddish, Hebrew, and English.

Marcus, Jacob Rader, 1896–
An index to scientific articles on American Jewish history. Edited by Jacob R. Marcus. Cincinnati, American Jewish Archives, 1971.

240 p. 24 cm. (Publications of the American Jewish Archives, no. 7)

Rosenfield, Geraldine.
What we know about young American Jews; an annotated bibliography. [New York, American Jewish Committee, Institute of Human Relations, 1970]

19 p. 29 cm.

Stern, Norton B
California Jewish history; a descriptive bibliography: over five hundred fifty works for the period gold rush to post-World War I. Selected and annotated by Norton B. Stern. Glendale, Calif., A. H. Clark Co., 1967.

175 p. 25 cm.

JIANGXI   see   Kiangsi

JILLSON, WILLARD ROUSE

Overstreet, Anne E
The scientific writings (geology, paleontology, mining) and cartographic work (maps, sections, sketches) of Willard Rouse Jillson: a bibliography (1913-1963) By Anne E. Overstreet. Toledo, Talmadge Press, 1963-65.

2 v. ports. 23 cm.

Vol. 2 has title "The miscellaneous writings (history, biography, bibliography, articles, addresses, narratives and poems) of Willard Rouse Jillson, a bibliography, 1907-1965" with imprint: Frankfort, Ky., Roberts Print. Co.

JINNAH, MAHOMED ALI

Husain, Syed Sajjad.
Books on the Quaid-e-Azam [by] S. Sajjad Husain. [Dacca, Society for Pakistan Studies, 1969]

11 p. 18 cm.

JIRÁSEK, ALOIS

Vacina, Ladislav.
Alois Jirásek a jeho kraj. Výběrová regionální bibliografie. Zprac. Ladislav Vacina a Hana Endlerová. Náchod, Okresní knihovna, rozmn., 1971.

47, [1] p. 29 cm. (Příspěvky k regionální bibliografii Náchodska, sv. 2)

Vorlíčková, Marie.
Soupis dokumentů a jiných úředních písemností týkajících se Aloise Jiráska a jeho rodiny ze sbírek Muzea Aloise

Jiráska a Mikoláše Alše. Autorka: Marie Vorlíčková. Praha, Muzeum A. Jiráska a M. Alše, rozmn., 1970.

26, [1] p. 20 cm. (Soupis literární pozůstalosti Aloise Jiráska, sv. 2)

Vorlíčková, Marie.
Soupis korespondence přijaté Aloisem Jiráskem od institucí, organizací a různých kolektivních odesilatelů ze sbírek Muzea Aloise Jiráska a Mikoláše Alše. Autorka: Marie Vorlíčková. Praha, Muzeum A. Jiráska a M. Alše, rozmn., 1971.

99, [1] p. 20 cm. (Soupis literární pozůstalosti Aloise Jiráska, sv. 3)

Vorlíčková, Marie.
Soupis korespondence přijaté Aloisem Jiráskem od jednotlivců. Ze sbírek Muzea Aloise Jiráska a Mikoláše Alše. Autoři: Marie Vorlíčková [a] Radim Balcar. Praha, Muzeum A. Jiráska a M. Alše, rozmn. ÚDA. 1968.

84, [2] p. 20 cm. (4 sv. soupisu literární pozůstalosti Aloise Jiráska)

JIRÁT, VOJTĚCH

Mourková, Jarmila.
Vojtěch Jirát. (1902-1945). Literární pozůstalost. Zprac. Jarmila Mourková. Praha, Památník nar. písemnictví, rozmn., 1969.

14, [1] p. 20 cm. (Edice inventářů, čís. 208)

JOAN OF ARC   see   Jeanne d'Arc, Saint

JOHANNESBURG, SOUTH AFRICA

Hughes, Blanche.
Personal reminiscences of early Johannesburg in printed books, 1884-1895, an annotated bibliography. Johannesburg, University of the Witwatersrand, Dept. of Bibliography, Librarianship and Typography, 1966.

vii l., 76 p. 33 cm.

"Compiled in part fulfilment for the Diploma in Librarianship, University of the Witwatersrand."

Winter, James Sydney.
First hand accounts of Johannesburg in English language periodicals, 1886-1895, a list compiled by James Sydney Winter. Johannesburg, University of the Witwatersrand, Department of Bibliography, Librarianship and Typography, 1967.

v, 38 p. 30 cm.

JOHN BIRCH SOCIETY

Fuerst, Martin J
Bibliography on the origins and history of the John Birch Society, by Martin J. Fuerst. 4th ed. [n. p.] 1964.

102 p. 28 cm.

Fuerst, Martin J
Bibliography on the origins and history of the John Birch Society, by Martin J. Fuerst. 5th ed. [Sacramento, Calif.] St. Didacus Co. [1965]

151 p. 28 cm.

JOHNSON, CHARLES

Gosse, Philip, 1879-1959.
A bibliography of the works of Capt. Charles Johnson. New York, B. Franklin [1970]

80 p. ports. 23 cm. (Burt Franklin bibliography and reference series 381. Selected essays in history, economics, and social science 193)

Reprint of the 1927 ed.

JOHNSON, JOHN DE MONINS

Oxford. University. Bodleian Library.
The John Johnson collection: catalogue of an exhibition. Oxford, Bodleian Library, 1971.

87 p. illus., facsims., port. 23 cm.

JOHNSON, SAMUEL

Clifford, James Lowry, 1901–
Samuel Johnson; a survey and bibliography of critical studies ₍by₎ James L. Clifford and Donald L. Greene. Minneapolis, University of Minnesota Press ₍1970₎

xvi, 333 p. 25 cm.

Based on the author's Johnsonian studies, 1887–1950, and A bibliography of Johnsonian studies, 1950–1960, with additions and corrections, 1887–1950, prepared together with D. J. Greene.

Courtney, William Prideaux, 1845–1913.
A bibliography of Samuel Johnson, by William Prideaux Courtney and David Nichol Smith. Oxford, Clarendon P., 1968.

viii, 186 p. facsims. 23 cm.

First published 1915.

Fleeman, John David.
A preliminary handlist of documents and manuscripts of Samuel Johnson, by J. D. Fleeman. Oxford, Oxford Bibliographical Society, 1967.

51 p. 25 cm. (Oxford Bibliographical Society. Occasional publications, no. 2)

Harvard University. *Library. Houghton Library.*
An exhibit of books and manuscripts from the Johnsonian collection formed by Mr. and Mrs. Donald F. Hyde at Four Oaks Farm. ₍Compiled by Sidney Ives₎ Cambridge, Houghton Library, 1966.

vi, 30 p. facsims. 23 cm.

Hyde, Donald Frizell, 1909–1966.
Catalogus bibliothecae Hydeianae: the Hyde collection of the works of Samuel Johnson, compiled by J. D. Fleeman. Cambridge, Harvard College Library, 1965.

3 v. facsims. 28 cm.

The private collection of Donald and Mary Hyde.

Mathews (Elkin) ltd., booksellers, Bishop's Stortford, Eng.
A catalogue of books by or relating to Dr. Johnson & members of his circle offered for sale by Elkin Mathews, ltd. With an introd. by John Drinkwater. ₍Folcroft, Pa.₎ Folcroft Library Editions, 1973.

vi, 110 p. front. 24 cm.

Reprint of the 1925 ed. published by E. Mathews, ltd., London.

JONCKHEERE, KAREL

Roemans, Robert, 1904–
Bibliografie van Karel Jonckheere. ₍Door₎ Rob. Roemans en Hilda van Assche. Ingeleid door Angèle Manteau en Karel Jonckheere. Met een portret getekend door Loo Nagels. Hasselt, Heideland ₍1968₎

254 p. 22 cm.

JONES, LEROI

Dace, Letitia.
LeRoi Jones (Imamu Amiri Baraka): a checklist of works by and about him, by Letitia Dace. London, Nether Press, 1971.

196 p. 22 cm. (Nether Press bibliographies; miscellaneous series, no. 101)

Hudson, Theodore R
A LeRoi Jones (Amiri Baraka) bibliography; a keyed research guide to works by LeRoi Jones and to writing about him and his works, by Theodore R. Hudson. ₍Washington, c1971₎

18 l. 28 cm.

JÖNKÖPING, SWEDEN (PROVINCE)

Jönköpings stadsbibliotek.
Förteckning över mikrofilmade landskapshandlingar, jordeböcker, mantalslängder, bouppteckningar, domböcker, generalmönsterrullor m. m. Jönköping, Stadsbiblioteket, 1972.

(2), 32 l. 30 cm.

JONSON, BEN

Ford, Herbert L
Collation of the Ben Jonson folios, 1616–31—1640 ₍by₎ H. L. Ford. New York, Haskell House Publishers ₍1973₎

30 p., 4 ports. 23 cm.

Reprint of the 1932 ed.

JORDAN

see also under Palestine (*al-Akhras; Cairo*)

Patai, Raphael, 1910–
Jordan, Lebanon, and Syria; an annotated bibliography. Westport, Conn., Greenwood Press ₍1973, c1957₎

vii, 289, ₍20₎ p. 22 cm.

Reprint of the ed. published by HRAF Press, New Haven, in series: Behavior science bibliographies.

JØRN, ASGER OLUF

Atkins, Guy.
Bibliografi over Asger Jorns skrifter til 1963. A bibliography of Asger Jorn's writings to 1963. ₍Av₎ Guy Atkins ₍og₎ Erik Schmidt. København, Permild & Rosengreen ₍1964₎

45 p. 24 cm.

Danish and English.

JOSEPH, SAINT

Nadeau, Charles, 1923–
Saint Joseph dans l'édition canadienne; bibliographie. Montréal, Oratoire Saint-Joseph du Mont-Royal, 1967.

v, 81 p. 23 cm.

Trottier, Aimé.
Essai de bibliographie sur saint Joseph. 4° éd. Montréal, Centre de recherche et de documentation, Oratoire Saint-Joseph ₍1968₎

464 p. 22 cm.

JOSEPHSON, RAGNAR

Kuylenstierna, Marianne, 1910–
Bibliografi över Ragnar Josephsons skrifter. Stockholm, Natur o. kultur, 1966.

110, ₍2₎ p. 22 cm.

JOSEPHUS, FLAVIUS

Schreckenberg, Heinz.
Bibliographie zu Flavius Josephus. Leiden, E. J. Brill, 1968 ₍1969₎

xvii, 336 p. 25 cm. (Arbeiten zur Literatur und Geschichte des hellenistischen Judentums, Bd. 1)

JOSTEN, WERNER ERIC

Werner Josten, 1885–1963; a summary of his compositions with press reviews. New York, Marchbanks Press, 1964.

79 p. port. 24 cm.

JOUBERT, LAURENT

Amoreux, Pierre Joseph, 1741–1824.

Notice historique et bibliographique sur la vie et les ouvrages de Laurent Joubert ... (Réimpr. de l'éd. de Montpellier, 1814.) Genève, Slatkine Reprints, 1971.

ii, 145 p. 22 cm.

JOUHANDEAU, MARCEL

Bibliothèque littéraire Jacques Doucet.

Catalogue de fonds spéciaux de la Bibliothèque littéraire Jacques Doucet, Paris. Fonds Jouhandeau et fonds Mauriac. Boston, G. K. Hall, 1972.

ix, 549 p. 37 cm.

Added t. p.: Catalog of special collections of the Jacques Doucet Literary Library, Paris. The Jouhandeau and Mauriac collection.

JOURNALISM

see also Periodical publications; Press

Centro di studi sul giornalismo. *Biblioteca.*

Catalogo della biblioteca. Torino, 1967–

v. 22½ cm.

Centro di studi sul giornalismo Gino Pestelli. **Biblioteca.**

Catalogo della biblioteca. Torino, 1969.

91 p. 23 cm.

Ch'êng, Chih-hsing.

(Hsin wên chu tso hsüan ts'ui)

新聞著作選粹　程之行著　〔臺北〕　臺灣商務印
書館　〔民國 60 i. e. 1971〕

2. 4. 3. 116 p. 18 cm. （人人文庫 1721-1722）

Dénešová, Klára.

Masové médiá. Súpis publikovaných prác a štúdií: 1955–1968 ... vyd. pri príležit. 15. výr. Inštitútu pre výskum masových komunikačných prostriedkov. Pripr.: Klára Dénešová. (1. časť a Otázky novinárstva: 1958–1961) a Vlasta Dočkalová (1. časť a Otázky žurnalistiky: 1962–1968.) Bratislava, vyd. Inštitút pre výskum masových komunik. prostriedkov pri VÚKVM vo vydav Obzor, rozmn. Nitrianske tlač. Nitra, 1969.

131, [3] p. [27] p. of plates. 21 cm.

Hausman, Linda Weiner.

Criticism of the press in U. S. periodicals, 1900–1939; an annotated bibliography. [Austin, Tex.] Association for Education in Journalism, 1967.

49 p. 23 cm. (Journalism monographs, no. 4)

International Federation of the Socialist and Democratic Press.

The democratic socialist press. 4th ed. Amsterdam, 1965.

100 p. 21 cm.

Ivanova, Evgeniĭa.

(Bibliografiĭa na literaturata po zhurnalisika)

Библиография на литературата по журналистика, издадена в България през периода 1944–1969 г. София, Съюз на бълг. журналисти, 1972 (деп. 1974).

246 p. 21.5 cm.

At head of title: Съюз на българските журналисти. Научно -изследователски център по журналистика.
Cover title: Българска журналистика.

József, Farkas.

A Magyar sajtótörténet irodalmának válogatott bibliográfiája (1705–1945) Összeállították: József Farkas [et al.] Szerk.: József Farkas. Budapest, Magyar Újságírók Országos Szövetsége, 1972.

427 p. 25 cm. (Sajtótörténeti könyvtár)

Table of contents also in English, German and Russian.

Price, Warren C

An annotated journalism bibliography, 1958–1968 [by] Warren C. Price and Calder M. Pickett. Minneapolis, University of Minnesota Press [1970]

x, 285 p. 25 cm.

Cover title: Journalism bibliography.

Russia (1923– U. S. S. R.). Komitet po pechati.

[Katalog knig i broshiur po voprosam zhurnalistiki.]

Каталог книг и брошюр по вопросам журналистики. 1966–1970. Москва, ["Книга,"] 1971.

31 p. 22 cm.

At head of title: Комитет по печати при Совете Министров СССР. Издательская комиссия Союза журналистов СССР.

Taft, William Howard, Oct. 24, 1915–

200 books on American journalism, an AASDJ consensus list. Compiled by William H. Taft. Columbia, University of Missouri, 1969.

30 p. 23 cm. (University of Missouri, Columbia bulletin, v. 70, no. 9. Journalism 1969 series, no. 177)

Thõmopoulos, Sõz

Ἡ περὶ τύπου καὶ δημοσιογραφίας Ἑλληνικὴ βιβλιογραφία· αὐτοτελεῖς ἐκδόσεις (1831–1967). Ἐπιμελεία: Σεζ. Θωμοπούλου. Ἀθῆναι, 1967.

31 p. 21 cm.

Pages [29]–31, advertising matter.

Thorén, Stig.

Mr Gates i arbete; en bibliografi om nyhetsurval. Stockholm, Beredskapsnämnden för psykologiskt försvar, 1971.

90 p. 30 cm. (Psykologiskt försvar, nr. 55)

JOVANOVIĆ, VOJISLAV MATE

Nikolić, Ilija.

Др [i. e. Доктор] Војислав М. Јовановић 1884–1968. ⟨Биографија. Библиографија радова⟩. Београд, ⟨Издаје аутор⟩, 1969.

68, [1] p. illus., facsims., port. 24 cm.

JOVARAS, pseud. see Krikščiunas, Jonas

JOYCE, JAMES

Deming, Robert H

A bibliography of James Joyce studies [by] Robert H. Deming. [Lawrence] University of Kansas Libraries, 1964.

180 p. 26 cm. (The University of Kansas publications. Library series, no. 18)

"List of periodicals consulted": p. 168–171.

James Joyce, 1882–1941. Werke und Deutungen. [Hamburg, Hamburger Öffentliche Bücherhallen, 1965]

30 p. 20 cm.

"Bearb. von Erika Joerden nach einer 1964 bei der Hamburger Büchereischule eingereichten Diplom-Arbeit von Barbara Voswinckel."

Slocum, John J
A bibliography of James Joyce, 1882–1941 ₍by₎ John J. Slocum and Herbert Cahoon. Westport, Conn., Greenwood Press ₍1971, c1953₎

viii, 195 p. illus. 23 cm.

Original ed. issued in series: Bibliographical series from the Yale University Library collections.

JUAN, DON

Singer, Armand Edwards, 1914–
The Don Juan theme: versions and criticism; a bibliography ₍by₎ Armand E. Singer. Morgantown, West Virginia University, 1965.

370 p. 24 cm. (West Virginia University bulletin, ser. 66, no. 6–4)

Enlargement of the earlier edition, first published in 1954 under title: A bibliography of the Don Juan theme, and the 3 supplements appearing in the West Virginia University Philological papers, 10–12, 1956–59.

JUAN DE LA CRUZ, SAINT

Ottonello, Pier Paolo.
Bibliografia di s. Juan de la Cruz. Roma, Edizioni del Teresianum, 1967.

194 p. 22 cm. (Bibliotheca Carmelitica. Series 3: Subsidia. v. 3)

Originally published in Archivum bibliographicum Carmelitanum, vol. 9–10 (1966–1967).

JUAN MANUEL, INFANTE DE CASTILE

Devoto, Daniel J
Introducción al estudio de Don Juan Manuel y en particular de el Conde Lucanor. Una bibliografía. ₍Madrid₎ Castalia, 1972.

505 p., 2 l. 22 cm.

At head of title: Daniel Devoto.

Devoto, Daniel J
Introducción al estudio de don Juan Manuel y en particular de "el Conde Lucanor," una bibliografía. Paris, Ediciones hispano-americanas, 1972.

504 p. 21 cm.

At head of title: Daniel Devoto.

JUÁREZ, BENITO PABLO

Avilés, René.
Bibliografía de Benito Juárez. México, Sociedad Mexicana de Geografía y Estadística, 1972.

845 p. illus. 24 cm.

Pasquel, Leonardo.
Bibliografía juarista veracruzana. ₍México₎ Editorial Citlaltépetl, 1972.

xiv, 54 p. illus. 19 cm. (Colección Suma veracruzana. Serie Bibliografía)

JUDAISM see Jews

JUDEO-SPANISH IMPRINTS see Ladino imprints

JUDGES

California. State Library, *Sacramento. Law Library.*
Recent material on judicial selection; a bibliography. Sacramento, 1968.

5 p. 28 cm.

Dahl, Richard C
The American judge, a bibliography, by Richard C. Dahl

₍and₎ C. E. Bolden. Vienna, Va., Coiner Publications ₍1968₎

xviii, 330 p. 27 cm.

New York (State). State Library, Albany. Legislative Reference Library.
Selection of judges; a bibliography. Albany, 1967.

15 p. 29 cm. (Convention series, no. 4)

JUGOSLAVENSKA AKADEMIJA ZNANOSTI I UMJETNOSTI

Jugoslavenska akademija znanosti i umjetnosti.
Popis izdanja Jugoslavenske akademije znanosti i umjetnosti u Zagrebu, 1945–1965. ₍Urednik Matko Rojnič. Popis izradila Iva Mihovilović₎ Zagreb, 1966.

202 p. 24 cm. (*Its* Knjižnica)

Added t. p.: Catalogus editionum Academiae Scientiarum at Artium Slavorum Meridionalium.

JUHÁSZ, GÉZA

Juhász, Izabella.
Juhász Géza (1894–1968) ₍Csontos Gábor visszaemlékezésével₎ Debrecen, Kossuth Lajos Tudományegyetem Könyvtára, 1971.

220 p. illus., port. 25 cm. (A Debreceni Kossuth Lajos Tudományegyetem tanárainak munkássága, 5)

JÜNGER, ERNST

Des Coudres, Hans Peter.
Bibliographie der Werke Ernst Jüngers. Stuttgart, E. Klett ₍1970₎

86 p. port. 25 cm.

Revision of a bibliography which first appeared in "Philobiblon" Heft 3, 1960.

JUNIOR COLLEGES
see under Dissertations, Academic

Boss, Richard D
A bibliography of the community-junior college, by Richard D. Boss and Roberta Anderson. ₍Astoria, Or., Clatsop County Community College₎ 1965.

19, 37, 4 l. 28 cm.

Burnett, Collins W   1914–
The community junior college; an annotated bibliography with introductions for school counselors. Collins W. Burnett, editor. Columbus, College of Education, Ohio State University, 1968.

122 p. 23 cm.

Padfield, William T
A bibliography of selected publications related to junior college education. Prepared by William T. Padfield. Sacramento, 1965.

iii, 75 p. 28 cm.

Cover title.
At head of title: California State Dept. of Education, Bureau of Junior College Education.

Rarig, Emory W   *ed.*
The community junior college; an annotated bibliography. Emory W. Rarig, Jr., editor. New York, Teachers College Press ₍1966₎

vii, 114 p. 22 cm. (Community college studies)

Reusch, Natalie R
The junior and community college faculty; a bibliography. Rev. ed. Compiled by Natalie R. Reusch. Washing-

ton, National Faculty Association of Community & Junior Colleges [1969]

33 p. 28 cm.

Compiled at the request of the National Faculty Association of Community and Junior Colleges at the ERIC Clearinghouse for Junior College Information.

The 1968 ed. compiled by John E. Roueche and Natalie Rumanzeff Reusch.

Roueche, John E

The junior and community college faculty: a bibliography. Compiled by John E. Roueche and Natalie Rumanzeff. Washington, National Faculty Association of Community & Junior Colleges [1968]

20 p. 28 cm.

Compiled at the request of the National Faculty Association of Community and Junior Colleges at the ERIC Clearinghouse for Junior College Information.

JURY

Flood, James Edward.

Data bank: The jury system in crisis [by] James Edward Flood [and] Philip Glennon Ryan. [Standard ed.] Brooklyn, N. Y., Policy Research Institute, 1971.

ii, 153 p. 28 cm.

JUST, CARL

Publikasjoner skrevet og/eller redigert av Carl Just 1914–1972. Oslo, 1972.

16 p. 21 cm.

JUTE

Almeida, Norma Martins de.

Juta (*Corchorus capsularis* L.); bibliografia das publicações que se encontram na biblioteca dêste Instituto. Cruz das Almas, 1968.

7 l. 33 cm. (Instituto de Pesquisas e Experimentação Agropecuárias do Leste. Lista bibliográfica no. 13)

Mia, M   M

Bibliography on jute [by] M. M. Mia [and] M. S. Rahman. Dacca, Agriculture Division, Atomic Energy Centre, 1969.

27 p. 28 cm.

JUVENILE COURTS see Children - Law

JUVENILE DELINQUENCY
see also Gangs

Cabot, Philippe Sidney de Q

Juvenile delinquency; a critical annotated bibliography. Compiled by P. S. de Q. Cabot. Westport, Conn., Greenwood Press [1971, c1946]

106 p. 24 cm.

Hawkins, Keith.

Deprivation of liberty for young offenders: a select bibliography on approved schools, attendance centres, borstals, detention centres and remand homes, 1940–1965; compiled by Keith Hawkins under the direction of Martin Wright. Cambridge, Cambridge University (Institute of Criminology) [1967].

[2], vi, 48 f. 30 cm. (Cambridge. University. Institute of Criminology. Bibliographical series, no. 1)

Hess, Albert G

The young adult offender: bibliography. Le delinquant jeune adulte; bibliographie. [Compiled by] Albert G. Hess, Franco Ferracuti [and] Julia Keh-Fang Kao Hess. Milan, Giuffrè, 1967.

vii, 198 p. 22 cm. (Scritti di criminologia e diritto criminale, 5)

English, French, German, Italian and Spanish.

Janiszewska-Talago, Elżbieta.

Die Jugendkriminalität in den Jahren 1945–1965. ⟨Übersetzung der Beilage der Zeitschrift "Przegląd penitencjarny" 1966, Nr. 2.⟩ Übers. von Gerda Schälicke. Potsdam-Babelsberg, Institut für Strafrechtspflege und Kriminalitätsbekämpfung an der Deutschen Akademie für Staats- und Rechtswissenschaft "Walter Ulbricht," 1967.

64 p. 21 cm. (Spezialbibliographien zu Fragen des Staates und des Rechts, Heft 5)

Janiszewska-Talaga, Elżbieta.

Mala bibliografia przestępczości nieletnich, 1945–1966. [Warszawa] Wydawn. Prawnicze, 1968.

84 p. 21 cm. (Prace Ośrodka Badań Przestępczości)

Seymour, John A

Family courts and councils: a select bibliography with special reference to the White Paper, "The child, the family and the young offender," 1965 (cmnd. 2742), compiled by John A. Seymour. Cambridge, University of Cambridge, Institute of Criminology, 1966.

18 l. 30 cm. (University of Cambridge. Institute of Criminology. Bibliographical series, no. 2)

Sultanbekov, A

[Bibliografiia po probleme "Trudnye podrostki i ikh perevospitanie"]

Библиография по проблеме "Трудные подростки и их перевоспитание." Сост. А. Султанбеков. Ред. Э. Костяшкин. Москва, 1971.

93 p. 20 cm.

At head of title: Институт повышения квалификации преподавателей педагогических дисциплин университетов и педвузов АПН СССР. НИИ общей педагогики АПН СССР.

U. S. *Children's Bureau.*

The prevention of juvenile delinquency; a selected, annotated bibliography. Washington, For sale by the Supt. of Docs., U. S. Govt. Print. Off. [1968]

[15 p. 26 cm.

JUVENILE LITERATURE see Children's literature